Archives, Documentation, and Institutions of Social Memory

Essays from the Sawyer Seminar

EDITED BY

Francis X. Blouin Jr. and William G. Rosenberg

THE UNIVERSITY OF MICHIGAN PRESS

Ann Arbor

First paperback edition 2007
Copyright © by the University of Michigan 2006
All rights reserved
Published in the United States of America by
The University of Michigan Press
Manufactured in the United States of America
⊗ Printed on acid-free paper

2010   2009   5   4   3

A CIP catalog record for this book is available from the British Library.

Library of Congress Cataloging-in-Publication Data

Archives, documentation, and institutions of social memory : essays
from the Sawyer Seminar / edited by Francis X. Blouin Jr. and
William G. Rosenberg.
   p.   cm.
   ISBN-13: 978-0-472-11493-1 (cloth : alk. paper)
   ISBN-10: 0-472-11493-X (cloth : alk. paper)
   1. Archives.   2. Documentation.   3. Memory—Social aspects.
I. Blouin, Francis X.   II. Rosenberg, William G.

CD931.A685   2005
027—dc22   2005017905

ISBN-13: 978-0-472-03270-9 (pbk. : alk. paper)
ISBN-10: 0-472-03270-4 (pbk. : alk. paper)

Contents

PART III. Archives and Social Memory

PART IV. Archives, Memory, and Political Culture (Canada, the Caribbean, Western Europe, Africa, and European Colonial Archives)

Preface and Acknowledgments

With the generous support of the Mellon Foundation, the Advanced Studies Center of the International Institute of the University of Michigan held a year-long Sawyer Seminar in 2000–2001 to investigate from a range of disciplinary perspectives the complicated relationships between archives, forms of documentation, and the ways societies remember their pasts. The program included nearly a hundred presentations in twenty-eight sessions. Scholars and archivists from fifteen countries participated. Our point of departure was a conception of archives not simply as historical repositories but as a complex of structures, processes, and epistemologies situated at a critical point of intersection between scholarship, cultural practices, politics, and technologies. As sites of documentary preservation rooted in various national and social contexts, archives help define for individuals, communities, and states what is both knowable and known about their pasts. As places of uncovering, archives help create and re-create social memory. By assigning the prerogatives of record keeper to the archivist, whose acquisition policies, finding aids, and various institutionalized predilections mediate between scholarship and information, archives produce knowledge, legitimize political systems, and construct identities. In the broadest sense, archives thus embody artifacts of culture that endure as signifiers of who we are and why.

This volume presents for a wider audience a substantial portion of the papers given at the seminar. We have grouped them somewhat loosely around a series of themes that emerged during the course of the discussions. In so doing, we have made an effort to integrate the contributions of archivists and others whose professional responsibilities were primarily administrative with those of scholars from the humanities and social sciences whose work focuses on specific kinds of archival research. We hope the diversity of the essays included in this volume gives readers some sense of the breadth of issues captured by the seminar, and we regret that we cannot also include the many formal commentaries offered by other participants, which proved so stimulating to our discussions. A list of all seminar contributors appears at the end of the volume.

In reading these essays we think it important to consider especially the role of archives in what seminar participants termed the production of knowledge. We propose that an archive be thought of as a site of imagination, creativity, and production, as well as of documentary preservation, a site that incorporates various sorts of assumptions about kinds of knowledge and what is knowable that are fundamental to the ways individuals and societies think about themselves, relive their pasts, and imagine their futures. This still leaves us, however, with two large questions, each deceptively simple in its formulation: what, indeed, is an archive, and what actually goes on there? Let us offer several introductory propositions about each of these complex matters in the hope that they can serve heuristically as a set of arguments against which each of the essays in this volume might be read.

First, how do we define the spatial boundaries of an archive? In the seminar we proposed that an archive be thought of as a place, whether or not it has an institutional form and whether or not it is organized and maintained by the state, public or private groups and associations, or individuals. In all cases, an archive is a place where complex processes of "remembering" occur, creating and re-creating certain kinds of social knowledge. We put quotation marks around the word *remembering* to emphasize that the processes that bring the past to life in an archive involve much more than simply access to documents. Through the processes of acquisition, classification, and preservation, archives provide those who come to inquire about the past with a mix of materials, sometimes carefully selected and orderly, sometimes quite disorganized and random, through which particular forms of individual and social understanding are structured and produced.

Archives are thus sites where past experience is variously and quite imperfectly inscribed and where the art of re-creating the past can be practiced in some way, whether skillfully or not. As sites of preservation, archives hold particular pieces of the past that are selected on the basis of particular definitions of utility and importance. They define what is knowable and known both by the documents they preserve and the materials their archivists decline to acquire or that they discard. Silences in the archive can affect understanding as much as or more than the words and pictures that create and re-create our images of the past and hence our sense of who we have become and why. Archives are thus spatially bounded as places of uncovering and re-covering, as sites of concealment and suppression as well as of the expression, projection, and revelation of individual and social pasts and futures.

What, however, do we mean by "social"? And what particular forms of social knowledge are specific to archives? Whether instituted by the state, organized by public or private entities, or assembled by individuals, archives collect the effects of pasts that are never lived in isolation. The materials in all private and personal archives link their subjects in some way to broader social processes and activities and can always be used to explore these as well as more personalized patterns of lived experience. State and national archives, of course, quite deliberately create knowledge about broader social phenomena, centering especially around the practices of the nation and the state but also around subjects that state officials have deemed of political or social importance. All documents, however, must in some way be contextualized. The materials in private archives create knowledge that is socially contextualized by the very fact of its collection. In exploring these issues, the seminar paid particular attention to the roles that different kinds of archives play in informing the larger social space of collective and individual memory. An especially difficult question in this regard is the extent to which archives deliberately or implicitly limit, shape, or otherwise structure certain kinds of social understanding. To frame the matter in a slightly different way, to what extent does the broader space of social memory converge with the more limited confines of the archives? Where are the points of conjuncture—and of difference?

A related question is whether the forms of this archives-based knowledge *always* have at least some relation to social memory, which is to say the complex and variegated ways in which societies form a sense of what they used to be like and are like now. One might argue that the parameters of this determination shift with the emergence of new social constructions (such as gender or ethnicity), an awareness of suppressed social experiences (such as discrimination or repression), and new political formulations (such as "totalitarianism" or "postcolonialism"). Still, the knowledge produced by and from archives always has "what was" as its basic reference point.

This is not to say that archives can ever open up the past in any literal way, and certainly the degree to which "what was" is related to empirical evidence, the researcher's imagination, or a mixture of the two is a matter of considerable dispute. What is not in question is that the archivally created past can only be, at best, a representation of something no longer accessible outside the processes of remembering.

As mentioned previously, by assigning the prerogatives of record keeper to the archivist, archives can also legitimize (or delegitimize) political systems, construct (or reconstruct) identities, and authenticate in particular ways the kinds of knowledge they produce. An additional concern of the seminar was thus the degree to which different kinds of archives play these roles and how they do so. To what extent, for example, do archives embody the fragments of culture whose very preservation allows them to endure as signifiers of social and national identity? How, as instituted fields of representation, do they provide the tangible evidence for memory in addition to defining memory institutionally? And if some national archives in particular are monuments in physical as well as figurative terms, to what extent does that very monumentality represent in different ways the visions societies and cultures have of themselves and of others? Through extended and quite spirited discussion, most seminar participants came to recognize that as a site of both cultural and scholarly and administrative practice, the archive in its institutional totality has to be "read" ethnographically every bit as carefully as the documents it houses and preserves.

"Reading" an archive means understanding the nature of explicit practices in addition to deciphering their implications. Here the seminar considered the multiple practices included in the concept of "archiving" itself, which include what archivists do with documents and also to and for those who want to use them. Remembering, of course, is also a process of forgetting. Appraising what is worthy of preservation in archives is thus necessarily a process as well of determining what should be excluded and forgotten. Acquisition and access are also obviously vital practices in this regard, but so is the way in which collections are organized, cataloged, and described. It is hardly too much to say, as Nancy Bartlett argues in her essay in part II of this volume, that the archive is a constant site of mediation between the materials and the archivists, as well as between the archivist and the user. Those with authority over an archive can literally determine for users what is "better forgotten."

Finally, we would suggest to readers the importance the seminar assigned to understanding archives as places of individual and social imagination, whether vibrantly so, as in archives dedicated to particular kinds of historical or literary preservation and research, or more passively, as in various administrative collections organized to preserve data or records with only limited social use. In any archive, a linkage must be made through the document to its point and context of origin. This may be accurately or falsely established, aided or confused by archival guides or, as Elizabeth Yakel writes in part II of this volume, through representations created freely or through coercion, but in any case, the linkage is necessarily an imaginary one in the sense that it can never be literal. An artful imagination, of course, is the essence of good history, just as the imaginative ordering of documents helps define a skilled archivist. An archive is thus a site of constant creativity, a place where identities may be formed, technologies of rule perfected, and pasts convincingly revisited. In sum, what goes on in an archive reflects what individuals, institutions, states, and societies imagine themselves to have been, as well as what they may imagine themselves becoming.

We are very grateful to the many sources of funding that enabled us to fully realize all the elements we thought essential to a truly wide ranging and internationally based discussion. Most important was the major grant we received from Andrew W. Mellon Foundation that allowed us to organize our exploration as a Sawyer Seminar. This generous program encourages the exploration of an issue or a set of issues from multidisciplinary perspectives. We are most appreciative to all of the people at the foundation for their encouragement and assistance.

Support for the seminar was also provided by a number of offices and departments at the University of Michigan, including the International Institute; the Office of the President; the Office of the Provost; the Horace H. Rackham School of Graduate Studies; the Office of the Vice President for Research; the College of Literature, Science, and the Arts; the School of Information; the Taubman College of Architecture and Urban Planning; the Bentley Historical Library; the Center for Russian and East European Studies; the Center for Chinese Studies; the Institute for the Humanities; the Department of English; the Institute for Social Research; the Program in Women's Studies; the Program in Comparative Literature; the Program in Medieval and Early Modern Studies; the Department of Romance Languages and Literature; and the Program in American Culture. The breadth of interest reflected in these different sources of support reflects, we think, the university community's deep commitment to interdisciplinarity as well as the vibrancy of its intellectual and scholarly life.

We want to pay special thanks to several people whose work was of enormous importance to the success of the seminar and to the completion of this volume. Nancy Bartlett, assistant to the director for academic programs at the Bentley Library, was helpful both in the conceptualization of the seminar and in working with our many international visitors. Rachel Powers, administrative assistant at the Bentley Library, was particularly helpful in the tasks relating to preparing seminar essays for publication in this volume. Michelle Austin, administrator for the Advanced Study Center at the International Institute, worked tirelessly for the entire duration of the seminar and tended with extraordinary competence to all the administrative detail that such a complex activity requires. We are also grateful to Andrea Olson of the University of Michigan Press, who gave this entire text a very careful reading. To these friends and colleagues, and to all the participants—those who lectured, those who discussed, and those who listened—we express our sincere appreciation for their many contributions to this important intellectual exploration.

FXB   WGR

The following essays in this volume though first presented at the Sawyer Seminar have been previously published and are reproduced here with permission.

Patrick Geary, "Auctor et Auctoritas dans les cartulaires du haut moyen age," in *Auctor et Auctoritas: Invention et conformisme dans l'écriture médiévale*, Actes du colloque de Saint-Quentin-en-Yvelines (*14–16 juin 1999*), ed. Michel Zimmermann, Mémoires et documents de l'Éole des Chartes 59 (Paris, 2001), 61–71.

Eric Ketelaar, "The Panoptical Archives," portions of which were published as "Archival Temples, Archival Prisons: Modes of Power and Protection," *Archival Science* 2, nos. 3–4 (2002): 221–38. Portions of this essay also appeared in "Empowering Archives: What Society Expects of Archivists," in *Past Caring: What Does Society Expect of Archivists? Proceedings of the Australian Society of Archivists Conference. Sydney 13–17 August 2002*, ed. Susan Lloyd (Canberra: Australian Society of Archivists, 2002), 11–27.

Kent Kleinman, "Archiving Architecture," *Archival Science* 1, no. 4 (2001): 321–32.

Joan M. Schwartz, "'Records of Simple Truth and Precision': Photography, Archives, and the Illusion of Control," *Archivaria* 50 (fall 2000): 1–41.

Carolyn Steedman, "The Space of Memory: In an Archive," in *History of the Human Sciences* 11, no. 4 (Sage Publications, 1998): 65–83.

Ann Laura Stoler, "Colonial Archives and the Arts of Governance," *Archival Science* 2, nos. 1–2 (2002): 87–109.

Elizabeth Yakel, "Archival Representation," *Archival Science* 3, no. 1 (2003): 1–25.

PART I

Archives and Archiving

The publication in 1995 of Jacques Derrida's *Archive Fever: A Freudian Impression*[1] was something of a curiosity in the archival community but had little resonance among historians. Derrida presented his thoughts as a lecture at a colloquium on memory and archives organized by the Freud Museum, the Courtauld Institute of Art, and the Société Internationale d'Histoire de la Psychiatrie et de la Psychanalyse. He took up, among other issues appropriate to this interesting mix of sponsors, the complex problem of "inscription": the processes through which traces of a lived past are "archived" by individuals or societies in ways that make the place of uncovering—the archive—a point of intersection between the actual and the imagined, lived experience and its remembered (or forgotten) image. The French philosopher and literary theorist was particularly concerned with how inscription, which is to say archiving, involved suppression as well as remembering. His argument linked individual and collective remembering and also institutional and psychological "repositories," the latter being, of course, the brain. As his title suggests, Derrida's focus was also on the (feverish) quest to recover what the mind or institution had buried, that is, its archived inscriptions. In his stimulating and provocative reading, archives and archiving were thus as much about the present as about the past, since the processes of uncovering were as much about the complexities of contemporary understanding as about the creation of historical narratives. "*Every* archive," he wrote with emphasis, "is at once *institutive* and *conservative*. Revolutionary and traditional."[2]

The different reactions of archivists and historians to *Archive Fever* were broadly reflected in the Michigan seminar. At our earliest sessions, Carolyn Steedman,[3] the English cultural historian, interpreted Derrida's central trope of "uncovering" as, in part, a metaphor for the complex ways in which individuals and societies process experience itself, something for which there can never really be original documents. Indeed, as she suggests in her essay in this section of the volume, in important ways experience cannot be documented at all, only transcribed from its visceral impressions into some reproducible linguistic form. For her, the virtue of Derrida's intervention is in its turn to the historical subjective, the realm of emotions, feelings, and experiences that clearly affect the ways both individual and social pasts and presents are understood but whose access lies elsewhere than in the archive. She suggests that while there is a common desire to use the archive as metaphor or analogy when memory is discussed, the problem is that an archive is not really very much like human memory and certainly not like the unconscious mind. On the contrary, Steedman maintains that unlike with memory, there is not, in fact, very much there in actual archives, though the bundles may be mountainous. And unlike human memory, which actively processes, suppresses, distorts, selectively remembers, and applies in sometimes quite different ways the memory traces of past experience, material either carefully selected for or randomly placed in an archive just sits there until it is read and used and narrativized. As Steedman put it during our discussion at the seminar, the archive is thus quite benign. The historian, the user, the social rememberer give the archive's "stuff" its meaning.

This perspective particularly engaged Verne Harris, the South African archivist and archival theorist, who countered Steedman's views in our discussions by suggesting that the notion that archives are benign reflected a "simple, stable, and uncontested" understanding of the very concept of archive itself, in which an archive is simply a repository of documents or records identified for preservation.[4] In this traditional view, one that has dominated the thinking of most archivists and archival historians since the time of Jules Michelet and Leopold von Ranke, an archive is simply the place where such records are preserved or an institution providing such places. This concept has also long been a basic principle of archivists' training, and it underpins Hilary Jenkinson's authoritative *A Manual of Archive Administration.*[5] The premise of this approach is that archival records are, in Harris's words, "the organic and innocent product of processes exterior to archivists"[6] and, despite their limitations or particular flaws, reflect historical reality.

At issue here is not simply a positivist (or "modernist") notion of fact and truth. As Jennifer Milligan shows quite neatly in her essay in this section, these were quite unstable premises in archival administration almost from the time modern archives were first organized in the nineteenth century to preserve state records and a national past. Archives were understood by definition as repositories of authentic records and hence authentic fragments of the past. The question of who was entitled to describe that past, and how those fragments might be made whole through historical reassembly, was thus linked from the start to the question of archival access and hence to the claim to authenticity itself. As European state archives developed in the emerging scientific climate of the late nineteenth century, the reliability of both documents and archivists was increasingly measured not in terms of full disclosure or the public's right to know but with regard to the state's right to control its records and thus the state's ability to narrate its past. The fact and truth of individual documents did not need to be confronted for the truthfulness of the available archival record itself as an accurate reflection of the past to come under challenge. In the process, Milligan argues, the duty of the state archivist became not to truth per se but to controlling revelation.

More than 150 years after modern national archives were first organized, these proprietary assumptions of official record keepers have hardly abated, as the essay by Robert Adler in part III and the essays of others in this volume amply testify. It follows that the archive itself is not simply a reflection or an image of an event but also shapes the event, the phenomena of its origins. To put the matter somewhat differently, all archival records are not only themselves the product of social, cultural, and especially political processes; they very much affect the workings of these processes as well, and hence they influence the kinds of realities that archival collections reflect.

The issue is how archives themselves are constituted, how they function, as well as to what ends. Kathy Marquis's analysis in this section is very much of the assumption that there is a reality capable of clear and accurate reflection in records. Based on her experience in the reference room she would challenge the idea that the event or process in its uniqueness is irrecoverable, unfindable. Marquis (along with others at the seminar) uses the term *processes* to refer to both the ordinary routines of archival administration and the broader workings of society and history. As a number of the essays in this volume explore, the ways in which records are acquired, appraised, organized, and cataloged clearly help to determine what historians and others will be able to explore about the past and how, consequently, the past can be "produced." Marquis dwells on the complexity of these processes and suggests that they do not exist as a given but rather are the product of a continuous interaction between the keeper and the user.

An important part of this interaction involves the ways in which documents and records are assembled with the archive in mind. It makes a difference whether documents are written on or off the record, so to speak; stamped with various limitations on disclosure; or assembled for institutional vaults where public access is not thought to be in question. On the other hand, diaries, memos, letters, minutes, reports, statistics—all the archival "stuff" historians take such delight in uncovering—may indeed have been shaped with this future "discovery" in mind. The very notion of an archive can thus affect not only how the past itself is shaped and represented but how it is linked to the future; how, in other words, the process of assembling archives and the process of providing access to those archives help to structure (or "write") what the future will be like. The administration of archives is integral to their essence.

The question of the document itself is obviously a central issue here, as several essays in this section demonstrate: Kent Kleinman's "Archiving/Architecture," James O'Toole's "Between Veneration and Loathing: Loving and Hating Documents," and Joan Schwartz's "'Records of Simple Truth and Precision': Photography, Archives, and the Illusion of Control." Kleinman is particularly interested in what might be called the artificial constancy of the document: the ways it "arrests temporality" and connotes a particular kind of fixity to the event, process, or authorial voice it reflects. His focus is architecture and architectural projects and the ways that all real buildings change over time so that they ultimately bear only a distant relationship to their archived drawings and plans, their documentary origins. Kleinman is personally interested in architectural reconstruction. He is consequently concerned about the ways architectural archives are used to reconstruct buildings that essentially never existed, since the buildings' real architectural lives were the consequences of processes and forces the documents cannot capture. He objects to the ways in which archived materials obscure the contingencies of actual construction and the inevitability of deterioration. The authentic written document in the archives is thus, also, an artifice.

Can the same be said for any kind of document? Does the very process of archiving documents close them off from the subjectivities of lived experience, distancing them from the contextual complexity of their origins and hence from their original meaning? Joan Schwartz suggested at the seminar that this is substantially the case for archived photographs, which usually are considered the most reliable and informative window into past realities. In important ways, photography's emergence in the last half of the nineteenth century complemented and reinforced the developing notions of "scientific" history written "from the archives" and using "authentic, original documents." The photograph seemed literally to capture a past event, permanently framing its temporal context. Unless a photograph was an outright hoax, its authenticity could not be challenged, whether or not the person who created it was known. Photographs were also apparently free from the sins of omission, since the camera, if not the photographer, left nothing out. They also allowed for a detailed exploration of elements that might not have been considered historically important at the time, such as forms of dress, hairstyles, or other fleeting elements of everyday life.

But the photograph, too, is at best a two-dimensional flattening of a multidimensional past reality, one that, like other documents, necessarily objectivizes its subject. The "science" of photography works by refracting its subjects in ways that, at best, can only suggest what they were like beyond the camera and the camera operator's vision. Moreover, like other documents, photographs can read meaning back into the past only through an interpreter, which is to say through the contextualized understandings of their user. When photographic documents are used as archival material, their content and meaning are no less contingent on those who create and

use them than is the case with other forms of documentation, their "window" on the past similarly unfixed.

As James O'Toole demonstrates, however, this two-dimensional flattening does not entirely disassociate any document from subjectivities. Veneration, loathing, and especially indifference are readily attached to various kinds of materials, often with historically profound effects. The homage accorded to "six brown and wrinkled sheets of parchment, one of them virtually illegible," as O'Toole describes the American Declaration of Independence and Constitution, constitutes a visualization of both emotive and political power, as if they were forces housed in the archive along with its documents. Similarly, the common passion at times of political upheaval to expose or destroy collections of records that are thought to embody whole systems of repression similarly attaches a social role to an archive that transcends the agency of its users. Again, in O'Toole's view, the documents do not speak for themselves but are given a ritualized life (or death) that may be fundamental, again, to the ways societies and individuals understand themselves.

Is Steedman therefore wrong to insist that the archive is benign, that it is only the user, the historian as social rememberer, who gives its "stuff" its meaning? The essays grouped in this first section of our volume should give readers a good deal to think about in these terms, as they did the seminar participants themselves, and it is our hope that they will prompt the discussion to continue.

NOTES

1. Jacques Derrida, *Mal d'Archive: Une Impression Freudienne* (Paris: Editions Galilee, 1995). Published in English as *Archive Fever: A Freudian Impression* (Chicago: University of Chicago Press, 1996).

2. Derrida, *Archive Fever*, 7. Emphasis in the original.

3. See Steedman's essay in this section of the volume: "'Something She Called a Fever': Michelet, Derrida, and Dust."

4. Harris has elaborated this argument in several publications. See esp. "Claiming Less, Delivering More: A Critique of Positive Formulations on Archives in South Africa," *Archivaria* 44 (Fall 1997) and "Postmodernism and Archival Appraisal: Seven Theses," *South African Archives Journal* 40 (1998).

5. Hilary Jenkinson, *A Manual of Archive Administration*, rev. ed. (London: Percy, Lund, Humphries, 1937).

6. Harris, "Claiming Less," 133.

"Something She Called a Fever"

Michelet, Derrida, and Dust (Or, in the Archives with Michelet and Derrida)

Carolyn Steedman

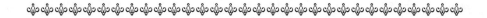

I breathed in their dust.
—Jules Michelet, *Oeuvres Complètes*, vol. 4

Archive fever, indeed? I can tell you *all about* archive fever. What (says a voice prosaic and perverse; probably a historian's voice) is an archive doing there anyway at the beginning of Jacques Derrida's *Mal d'archive*? Here, in its opening passages, Derrida shows us the *arkhe*, which he says is the place where things begin, where power originates, inextricably bound up with the authority of beginnings. In the brief account that Derrida gives us of the operation of the Greek city-state, its official documents are shown to be stored in the *arkheion*, the superior magistrate's residence. There the *archon* himself, the magistrate, exercises the power of those documents of procedure and precedent, in his right to interpret them, for the operation of a system of law.[1] The *arkhe* represents the *now* of whatever kind of power is being exercised, anywhere, in any place or time. The *arkhe* represents a principle, that in Derrida's words, is "in the order of commencement as well as in the order of commandment" (9). The fever, the sickness of the archive, is to do with its very establishment, which is the establishment of state power and authority.[2] And then there is the feverish desire—a kind of sickness unto death—that Derrida indicates, *for* the archive: the fever not so much to enter it and use it as to *have* it.

These remarks about archives open one of Derrida's most important contemplations of the topic of psychoanalysis and return to the questions he raised about it in 1967 in his essay "Freud and the Scene of Writing."[3] "Ar-chive Fever: A Freudian Impression" is further exploration of the relationship between memory and writing (or recording), a discussion of Freud's own attempts to find adequate metaphors for representing memory, particularly the very first memory that takes place, or is had, just before the thing itself, the origin, comes to be represented. This is a good reason for paying attention to Freud's own attentions to writing as an activity: in many of Freud's essays, writing is used to stand in for the psyche and all its workings.[4] Derrida sees in Freud the desire to recover moments of inception, the fractured and infinitesimal second between thing and trace, which might be the moment of truth. In "Archive Fever," desire for the archive is presented as part of that desire to find, or locate, or to possess that moment, which is the beginning of things.

But still: what is an archive doing at the beginning of a long description of another text (someone else's text, not Derrida's) that also deals with Freud? For the main part, "Archive Fever" is a sustained contemplation of Yosef Yerushalmi's *Freud's Moses: Judaism Terminable and Interminable* (1991). A historian of Sephardic Jewry with a strong interest in questions of memory, Yeru-shalmi was turned, by way of his membership in a psychoanalytic study group on anti-semitism, to the reading of Freud's *Moses and Monotheism*. In this reading, he found that Freud was also a historian or at least (in Freud's own formulation) someone who had produced a "historical novel," or a kind of historical story, in order to understand the period of baroque anti-semitism through which he was living. Yerushalmi's is a speculative account of Freud's writing of *Moses and Monotheism*, though not half as speculative as is the text itself, which is famously based on no historical evidence whatsoever. Yerushalmi on the other hand, had a fairly complete account of the process of its composition, from correspondence about it; from a hitherto unnoted draft (obtained with astonishing ease from the Freud Archive at the Library of Congress); and from the context within which Freud wrote, retrieved from newspaper files and a more general sociopolitical history of the rise of Nazism in central Europe. Yerushalmi's overall purpose in the book is to get Freud to admit (the final chapter is in the form of a monologue, addressed directly to the dead author) that psychoanalysis is a Jewish science.[5] The "impression" of Derrida's subtitle is the imprint of Judaism and "the Jewish science" on Yerushalmi and indeed on Derrida himself. But the signs and traces that Freud dealt in, and the particular sign that is circumcision, constitute the kind of archive that Derrida believes most historians would not be interested in.

The *archon* and his *arkheion* allow Derrida some commonplace speculations about the future of the archive, as the register, ledger, and letter are replaced by e-mail and the computer file. They also give rise to some pertinent discussion of the politics of various kinds of archives (anyone who had read Yerushalmi's book might have been reminded of the furor of the 1980s over notorious restrictions of access to the Freud Archive).[6] Many kinds of repositories are strapped together here in the portmanteau term *the archive* as Derrida considers their limits and limitations, their denials and secrets. It is at this point in the argument that the *arkhe* appears to lose much of its connection to the idea of a place where official documents are stored for administrative reference and becomes a metaphor capacious enough to encompass the whole of modern information technology, its storage, retrieval, and communication.

Here Derrida probably performs a move made familiar in the forty-year exercise of his philosophic technique. The binary oppositions that underpin much of Western metaphysics are made to shift by inflating a concept so that it joins up with its very opposite. This procedure can be most clearly seen at work in Derrida's long attention to the topic of writing. Common sense will always exclaim that of course speech precedes writing, in any historical or psychological description of the relationship between the two, that writing can't be (could not have been)

first. But by making "writing" include all signs, traces, mnemonic devices, inscriptions, and marks—by thus interrogating the word in order to release it from the empirical understanding that is held in place by the opposition between speech and writing—Derrida leads us to see that "writing" includes its opposite, "speech," and that the distinction (all sorts of distinctions) so long maintained by systems of Western philosophy might be thought right through to the other side. *Mal d'archive* intends to question the archive in new and productive ways by subjecting it to a rigorous scrutiny that, in its attention to the historical origins of the word *archive,* is only superficially etymological. These opening sections of "Archive Fever," where *arkhe* loses contact with the literal, everyday meaning of "archive," are the ones that have been most taken up and commented on, in the English-speaking world, since 1995.[7]

Derrida originally delivered the English-language version of *Mal d'archive* on a major occasion of what many have come to call (after him) "archivization," and this setting goes some way toward answering the question: "What is an archive doing here?" His comments about the *archon*'s home that stored the archive, "this domestication . . . this house arrest [in which] archives take place . . . ," were made in the Freud House, in Maresfield Gardens in North London. Here, in June 1994, Derrida contributed what was then called "The Concept of the Archive: A Freudian Impression" to the international conference "Memory: The Question of Archives," which was held under the auspices of the Société Internationale d'Histoire de la Psychiatrie et de la Psychoanalyse and the Freud Museum. On that occasion, in that house, Derrida looked up from the word-processed text from which he read (he makes much in "Archive Fever" of the "little portable Macintosh on which I have begun to write" [22]) and said:

> It is thus . . . that archives take place . . . This place where they dwell permanently, marks this institutional passage from the private to the public . . . It is what is happening, right here, when a house, the Freuds' last house, becomes a museum: the passage from one institution to another. (10)[8]

The immediacy of that archive—an archive in process, taking place at that moment—forces a beginning to a conference presentation and a book at the same time as it reiterates arguments that Derrida has been making for thirty years about the Western obsession with finding beginnings, starting places, and origins. The etymological aspects of its opening pages are presented with the certainty that a word (*archive, arkhe, arkheion, archon*) can never be a beginning but rather is always the mark of the empty place between the thing and its representation. The word—any word—is the mark, or at least the very best and simplest example we can have, of the impossibility of finding the beginning of anything. It is the sad knowledge that presence can never be expressed in writing—that presence can never, indeed, be expressed at all. Derrida opens "Archive Fever" with the clearest of statements that words are never a beginning, never an origin: "Let us not begin at the beginning," he said, "nor even at the archive. But rather at the word 'archive.'" What "archive" is doing there then, at all, is the work of meditating thus on starting places, on beginnings, the search for which, because it is impossible, Derrida names as a sickness, a movement toward death. Moreover, to want to make an archive in the first place is to want to *repeat*, and one of Freud's clearest lessons was that the compulsion to repeat is the drive toward death.[9]

We are often told to note the rhetorical structure of Derrida's philosophical writing as being as important as its argument, but the structure of "Archive Fever" is odd indeed. In a quite calculated way, it refuses to begin its discussion of beginnings, for all the world as if it were a primer offering lessons in the principle of deferral. We have (in the English-language version) something untitled, which is an introduction (three pages). We then have an "exergue," which occupies eight pages.[10] This *exergue* is—possibly—an object lesson in the reading practice we have learned from Derrida. He comments on it, on his own use of "a proven convention" that "plays with citation" and that gives both order and orders to what follows. "What is at issue here," he says, "starting with the exergue, is the violence of the archive itself, *as archive*, as *archival violence*" (12). In fact, there are three *exergues*, numbered and laid out as separate sections. Then there are a preamble (three pages), a foreword (twenty-six pages), theses (three of them, occupying seven pages in total), and finally a postscript (two pages). There is always trouble in getting started and finished.

The foreword carries the main argument, about Freud's Jewishness and the contribution of Jewish thought to the idea of the archive, via psychoanalysis. The archive is a record of the past at the same time as it points to the future. The grammatical tense of the archive is thus the future perfect, "when it will have been." Perhaps, says Derrida, Freud's contribution to any theory of the archive is that there isn't one: that no storehouse, especially not the psychoanalytic archive of the human psyche, holds the records of an original experience to which we may return. Psychoanalysis has been responsible for some of this trouble with archives, for it wants to *get back*: it manifests a desire for origins, to find the place where things started before the regime of repetition and representation was inaugurated.

In the French book version of "Archive Fever" there is also inserted a loose-leaf notice that is three pages long, headed "Prière d'insérer" (in my library copy it is placed behind the title page and before the explanatory note about the Freud Museum conference). This makes much clearer than can be done in English the questions of social evil with which Derrida deals. In these three pages, the sickness of the archive is also and at the same time an archive of disaster and destruction; indeed, (for the French *mal* does not mince its meaning) it is an archive of *evil*.

> Les désastres qui marquent cette fin de millénaire, ce sont aussi des *archives du mal*: dissimulées ou détruites, interdites, détournées, "refoulées." Leur traitement est à la fois massif et raffiné au cours de guerres civiles ou internationales, de manipulations privées ou secrètes.

Derrida broods here on revisionist histories that have been written out of these archives of evil (and out of archives in general), on never giving up on the hope of getting proof of the past, even though documentary evidence may be locked away and suppressed. He emphasizes again the institution of archives as the expression of state power. He appears to urge a distinction between actual archives (official places for the reception of records, with systems of storage, organization, cataloging) and what we all too frequently reduce them to: memory, the desire for origins, "la recherche du temps perdu." "Prière d'insérer" also makes plainer the relationship between psychoanalysis and archival practice that is explored in the main text. Psychoanalysis ought to revolutionize archival questions, dealing as it does with the repression *and* reading of records and the privileged place it gives to all forms of inscription. Above all, this brief insertion makes it clear that Derrida will deal not only with a feverish—sick—search for origins, not only with archives of evil, but with "le mal radical," with evil itself. The two intertwined threads of argument to follow in the main body of the text, about psychoanalysis and Yerushalmi's questioning of Freud's Jewishness, underpin a history of the twentieth century that is indeed a history of horror. To say the very least, if you read in English, without the insert and with the restricted, monovalent, archaic—and, because archaic, faintly comic—"fever" of the English translation, rather than with "mal" (trouble, misfortune, pain, hurt, sickness, wrong, sin, badness, evil . . .), you will read rather differently from a reader of the French version.

Actually, quite apart from all of this, archive fever comes on at night, long after the archive has shut for the day. Typically, the fever—more accurately, the precursor fever—starts in the early hours of the morning, in the bed of a cheap hotel, when the historian cannot get to sleep. You cannot get to sleep because you lie so narrowly in an attempt to avoid contact with anything that isn't shielded by sheets and pillowcase. The first sign, then, is an excessive attention to the bed, an irresistible anxiety about the hundreds who have slept there before you, leaving their dust and debris in the fibers of the blankets, greasing the surface of the heavy, slippery counterpane. The sheets are clean, and the historian is clean, because obsessive washing and bathing must punctuate any visit to the archives, which are the filthiest of places. But the dust of others, and of other times, fills the room, settles on the carpet, marks out the sticky passage from bed to bathroom.

This symptom—worrying about the bed—is a screen anxiety. What keeps you awake, the sizing and starch in the thin sheets dissolving as you turn again and again within their confines, is actually the archive, the myriads of the dead, who all day long have pressed their concerns upon you. You think: these people have left me *everything*—each washboard and doormat purchased; saucepans, soup tureens, mirrors, newspapers, ounces of cinnamon and dozens of lemons; each ha'penny handed to a poor child; the minute agreement about how long it shall take a servant to get to keep the greatcoat you provide him with at the hiring; clothes-pegs, fat hog meat, the exact expenditure on spirits in a year; the price of papering a room, as you turn, in the spring of 1802, from tenant farmer with limewashed walls into gentleman with gentleman's residence. Everything. Not a purchase made, not a thing acquired that is not noted and recorded. You think: I could get to hate these people; and: I can never do these people justice; and finally: I shall never *get it done.* For the fever—the feverlet, the precursor fever—usually starts at the end of the penultimate day in the record office. Either you must leave tomorrow (train times, journeys planned, a life elsewhere) or the record office will shut for the weekend. And it's expensive being in the archive, as your credit card clocks up the price of the room, the restaurant meals. Leaving

is the only way to stop spending. You know you *will not finish,* that there will be something left unread, unnoted, untranscribed. You are not anxious about the Great Unfinished, knowledge of which is the very condition of being there in the first place and of the grubby trade you set out in, years ago. You know perfectly well that despite the infinite heaps of *things* they recorded, the notes and traces that these people left behind, it is in fact, nothing at all.[11] There is the great, brown, slow-moving, strandless river of Everything, and then there is its tiny flotsam that has ended up in the record office you are at work in.[12] Your craft is to conjure a social system from a nutmeg grater, and your competence in that was established long ago. Your anxiety is more precise and more prosaic. It's about PT S2/1/1, which only arrived from the stacks that afternoon, which is enormous, and which you will never get through tomorrow.

And then, just as dawn comes and the birds start to sing, you plunge like a stone into a narrow sleep, waking two or three hours later to find yourself wringing wet with sweat, the sheets soaked, any protection they afforded quite gone. The fever—the precursor fever—has broken. But in severe cases, with archive fever proper, that is not the end at all. A gray exhausted day in the record office (you don't finish); a long journey home; a strange dislocation from all the faces, stations, connections, delays, diversions, roadwork you must endure—all these are in retrospect the mere signals of the terrible headache that will wake you at two o'clock in the morning in your own bed, the pain pressing down like a cap that fits to your skull and the back of your eyes, the extreme sensitivity to light and distortion of sound, the limbs that can only be moved by extraordinary effort, and the high temperature. Archive fever proper lasts between sixteen and twenty-four hours, sometimes longer (with an aftermath of weeks rather than days). You think, in the delirium: it was their dust that I breathed in.

The field of occupational (or industrial) disease emerged in its modern mode in Britain during the early part of the nineteenth century. The physicians and apothecaries attached to the textile-district infirmaries whose work it largely was were of professional necessity interested in the diseases arising from relatively new industrial processes and the factory system. Nevertheless, in acknowledging their seventeenth- and eighteenth-century predecessors they continued to work within a framework that had long been established of dangerous and malignant trades, especially in hide, skin, and leather processing and the papermaking industries. Moreover, attention to the environmental hazards to workers' health produced by newer industrial processes served to elaborate an eighteenth-century attention to atmospheric conditions as a cause of disease.[13]

Medical investigations of the early nineteenth century drew very marked attention to dust and to its effect on handworkers and factory workers. The largest section of Charles Thackrah's pioneering investigation of the early 1830s into "the agents which produce disease and shorten the duration of life" across the trades and professions was devoted to workers "whose employments produce a dust or vapour decidedly injurious."[14] He concentrated in particular on papermakers, who were "unable to bear the dust which arises from cutting the rags," and dressers of certain types of colored decorative leather, who needed to pare or grind the finished skins.[15] In the *Cyclopaedia of Practical Medicine* of 1833, a new category was defined, "The Diseases of Artisans." Among the many debilities suffered by handworkers discussed were those produced by "the mechanical irritation of moleculae, or fine powders," either in a reaction on the skin of the worker (the fellmonger's and tanner's carbuncle was an example of ancient provenance) or in some form of pulmonary or respiratory ailment.[16] The particular hazards of cotton dust, in the processing of fiber for spinning and weaving and in the rag trades in general (in papermaking until wood pulp largely replaced rags, in the flock and shoddy used in upholstery and bedding), continued to be investigated until well into this century, and indeed, byssinosis was not recognized in the United States as an occupational disease of cotton workers until the 1960s.[17] The maladies attendant on the skin processing and allied trades were much commented on. After woolen manufacture, leatherworking was the most important eighteenth-century industry, in terms of both the number of workers employed and its output.[18] In the United Kingdom the category of trades that were considered dangerous from the dusts they produced was widened during the course of the nineteenth century. By its end, bronzing in the printing process, flax and linen milling, cotton and clothing manufacture, brass finishing, and ivory and pearl button making were among the dusty occupations subject to regulation.[19]

Medical attention continued to be framed and categorized by the dust question. At the top of Leonard Parry's 1900 list of risks and dangers of various occupations were those "accompanied by the generation and scattering of abnormal quantities of dust."[20] Discussing occupations "from the social, hygienic and medical points of view" in 1916, Thomas Oliver urged his readers to remember "that the greatest enemy of a worker in any

trade is dust" and that "dust is something more than merely particles of an organic or inorganic nature. Usually the particles which rise with the air are surrounded by a watery envelope and clinging to this moist covering there may be micro-organisms."[21] As the defensive action of trade unions moved from questions of working hours and physically injurious labor to incorporate working conditions and health hazards, the question of dust and its inhalation remained a focus well into the twentieth century.[22]

Long before the Trade Union Congress (TUC) opened its file entitled 'Dust—Rag Flock', investigators in the yet-unnamed field of industrial medicine had categorized an occupational malaise that enjoyed only a very brief period of interest and discussion. "The diseases of literary men" sat uneasily under Forbes's 1833 heading 'Diseases of Artisans,' but nevertheless, that is where he placed them. Very briefly, for perhaps thirty years or so, between about 1820 and 1850, a range of occupational hazards was understood to be attendant on the activity of scholarship. They originated, said Forbes "from want of exercise, very frequently from breathing the same atmosphere too long, from the curved position of the body, and from too ardent exercise of the brain."[23] "Brain fever" might be the result of this mental activity, and the term was no mere figure of speech. It described the two forms of meningitis that had been pathologized by the 1830s: inflammation of the membranes of the brain (meningitis proper) and of the substance of the brain (cerebritis).[24]

Charles Thackrah divided "professional men" and the diseases of their occupations into three types: persons whose mental application was alternated with exercise in the fresh air; those who took no exercise at all; and those who lived and worked "in a bad atmosphere, maintain one position for most of the day, take little exercise and are frequently under the excitement of ambition." "Brain fever" or some form of meninginal disturbance was a hazard of this way of working.

> The brain becomes disturbed. Congestion first occurs and to this succeeds an increased or irregular action of the arteries. A highly excitable state of the nervous system is not infrequently produced. Chronic inflammation of the membranes of the brain, ramollissement of its substance, or other organic change becomes established; and the man dies, becomes epileptic or insane, or falls into that imbecility of mind, which renders him an object of pity to the world, and of deep affliction to his connections.[25]

On the face of it, the occupational hazards of bookwork once again were paid attention in the 1920s when the Association of Women Clerks focused a century of complaint about writers' cramp among clerical workers in their attempts to have it scheduled as an industrial sickness with no limit of compensation.[26] But there were arguments about the physical effect of minutely repeated movements of hand and arm; the comparison was with telegraphists (telegraphists' cramp was a scheduled industrial disease for which benefit might be claimed indefinitely) and with comptometers. It was only in the first half of the nineteenth century that scholarship and literary occupations had attached to them a specific disease of the brain.

Medical men such as Forbes and Thackrah were able to provide physiological and psychological causes for the fevers of scholarship (lack of exercise; bad air; and the "passions" of scholarship, which were excitement and ambition). By the time that a bacteriological explanation was available, "the literary man" as a victim of occupational disease had disappeared as a category. Because bacteriological understanding of the dust that had so much preoccupied these early investigators was unavailable to them, they did not consider the book, the very stuff of the scholar's life, as a potential cause of his fever. And yet the book and its components (leather binding; various glues and adhesives; paper and its edging; and, decreasingly, parchments and vellums of various types) in fact concentrated in one object many of the industrial hazards and diseases that were mapped out in the course of the century.

The hazards of leatherworking had been known and recorded in the ancient world. Right through the process, from fellmongering (the initial removal of flesh, fat, and hair from the animal skins) to the paring and finishing of the cured and tanned skins, workers were known to be liable to anthrax. In medical dictionaries and treatises of the eighteenth century, "anthrax" meant "anthracia," "anthracosis," or "carbunculus," that is, what came in the late nineteenth century to be defined as the external or crustaceous form of anthrax. Leatherworkers and medical commentators also knew that the processes of fellmongering, washing, lime rubbing, scraping, further washing, chemical curing, stretching, drying, and dressing, all gave rise to dust, which was inhaled. Descriptions of leatherworking in the bookbinding trades also show that the amount of hand paring, shaving, and scraping involved in the process (and productive of dust) remained remarkably consistent across two centuries.[27] In parchment making, skins were subjected to the same processes as leather apart from tanning, and they too were subject to remarkably little alteration between me-

dieval and modern times.[28] Indeed, the modern treatment of parchment and vellum is almost identical with very old European practices.[29] Parchment making possibly gave rise to more dust, as it involved the splitting of sheep skins (the vellum process used calfskin, which was not usually split). The many hazards of the paper trade have already been indicated. The nineteenth century saw the proliferation of a vast literature on the airborne hazards of papermaking, which declined toward the end of the century as wood pulp replaced rags as the main component.[30] Charles Thackrah commented on the disabilities that arose from letter-press printing, "the constant application of the eye to minute objects, which gradually [enfeebled] these organs," and on the headaches and stomachaches printers complained of.[31]

In mentioning "the putrid serum of sheep's blood" which bookbinders and pocketbook makers used as "a cement" he produced the most striking and potent image of the book as a locus of a whole range of industrial diseases.[32] The bacillus of anthrax was the first specific microorganism discovered. This occurred in 1850, when Pierre Rayer and Casimir Davaine observed the *petits batonnets* in the blood of sheep who had died from the disease. When Louis Pasteur published his work on lactic-acid fermentation, Davaine recognized that the little infusoria were not blood crystals but living organisms.[33] Robert Koch cultivated the bacillus, infected sheep from his cultivation, and described the life cycle of the bacillus in 1876.[34] Considerable investigative energy of the 1880s went into showing that the disease in animals and human beings was identical; that the bacillus *anthracis* was responsible for the disease in all hosts; that the skins, hairs, and wool of the animal dying of what was still, in the 1870s, sometimes called "cattle plague" or "splenetic fever" retained the infecting organism, which found access to the body of the worker in various ways.[35] Internal and external anthrax were clearly demarcated and provided with nosologies and with miserable prognoses:

> the worker may be perfectly well when he goes to business; he may in a short time become giddy, restless and exhausted; he feels very ill, goes home, becomes feverish. . . . in bad cases, in from twenty four hours to four days the patient dies unconscious.[36]

As a delegate of the National Society of Woolcombers pointed out to the TUC in 1929, "It is a disease that does not hang on very long. You get it one day and you may be dead the next."[37]

In Britain, anthrax was first scheduled as a notifiable

disease in 1892.[38] There were a rising number of cases in the following decades, despite regulation. Workers, trades unionists, and medical commentators all ascribed the increased number of cases, crustaceous and pulmonary, to the upsurge in imports of foreign hides and wools.[39] The disease remained a profound danger to workers in the woolen and allied trades and in all forms of leatherworking and skin working, until after the Second World War, though a Ministry of Labour committee of inquiry into the disease reported that all British cases of internal anthrax up to 1959 had been of the pulmonary variety.[40]

By the 1920s workers in wool, hides, and hair were quite clear that it was the anthrax spore that constituted the greatest danger. If an animal dies of anthrax and is immediately destroyed without opening the carcass, or removing the skin, there is probably no risk. However, once the bacillus comes into contact with air, it forms resistant spores.[41] Any wool, fleece, or skin touched by infected blood will contain these spores; fleeces and hides when dried are the source of dust that, containing the spores, may come into contact with skin abrasions or may be inhaled.[42] It was known by the early twentieth century that spores were "very difficult to kill."[43] A report commissioned by the leather sellers' trade association in 1911 collated existing work on anthrax, and pointed out that in many ways leatherworking provided the optimum conditions for the development of spores: that "none of the "cures" at present used to preserve hides destroy the Anthrax infection," that the temperature that might destroy the spores was utterly destructive of the hides, and that it was entirely possible that finished leather retained and conveyed the infection.[44] Certainly, the anthrax spore could come through the whole leathermaking process unscathed, though "the question as to whether finished leather can retain and convey the infection" had to remain unsettled:

> Whilst cases have occurred in men who have only handled leather, and it has been proved that the spore can pass uninjured through all the chemical solutions used in tanning, the possibility of the leather itself having become contaminated by contact with other goods can hardly ever be excluded.[45]

The key point here is that as in leather bookbinding, shoe and boot manufacture involved a disturbance (by cutting, paring, and shaving) of the finished skin that was being further processed.

In the same period as the indestructibility and fatality of the anthrax spore came to be understood, archivists and book restorers started to define a type of leather deterioration, particularly in "modern" leathers, those of the post-1880 era, when the binding and book-finishing trades began to use imported vegetable-cured leather in great quantities.[46] "Red powdering," "red decay," and "red rot" continue to be described in the literature of book conservation.[47] "Red rot" is as well known among historians as it is to archivists. A crumbling of leather in the form of an orangey red powdering, it is said to be found particularly in East India leather prepared with tannin of bark, wood, or fruits. It seems, then, that dust is more likely to arise from the disintegrating bindings of ledgers, registers, and volumes bound at the end of the last century than from older material preserved in the archives. But there is a second type of red decay known to conservationists, a hardening and embrittling (rather than powdering) of bindings, which occurs most often in leathers prepared before about 1830. This also gives rise to dust in handling.[48] It seems, from the considerable literature on this topic, that the causes of leather rot must be found in the type of tanning agent or agents used (and these have been numerous), making the finished skin more or less vulnerable to atmospheric conditions.[49] Parchment, which is essentially untanned leather, does not suffer from this kind of deterioration.

So when, in 1833 the young Jules Michelet described his very first days in the archives, those "catacombs of manuscripts" that made up the Archives Nationales in Paris in the 1820s, and wrote of restoring its "papers and parchments" to the light of day by breathing in their dust,[50] this was not the figure of speech that he intended but a literal description of a physiological process. In this quite extraordinary (and much scrutinized) passage, it is the historian's act of inhalation that gives life: "these papers and parchments, so long deserted, desired no better than to be restored to the light of day . . . as I breathed in their dust, I saw them rise up."[51] It remains completely uncertain—it *must* remain uncertain; that is its *point*—who or what rises up in this moment. It cannot be determined whether it is the manuscripts, or the dead, or both who come to life and take shape and form. But we can be clearer than Michelet could be about exactly what it was that he breathed in: the dust of the workers who made the papers and parchments; the dust of the animals who provided the skins for their leather bindings; the by-product of all the filthy trades that have, by circuitous routes, deposited their end products in the archives. And we are forced to consider whether it was not life that he breathed into "the souls who had suffered so long ago and who were smothered now in the past" but death that he took into himself with each lungful of the past.

Roland Barthes thought that a quite different process of incorporation was at work, that Michelet actually *ate* history, and that it was eating it that made him ill. The first section of *Michelet par lui-meme* (1954) was called "Michelet Mangeur d'Histoire." Barthes described Michelet's terrible headaches ("la maladie de Michelet, c'est la migraine"), the way in which everything gave him migraines, how his body became his own creation, a kind of steady-state system, a symbiosis between the historian and History, which was ingested in the manner of the Host. This ingested History was also Death: "Michelet recoit l'Histoire comme aliment, mais en retour, il lui abandonne sa vie: non seulement son travail et sa santé, mais meme: sa mort."[52] I suggest that this process did actually take place, not just by analogy with "le theme christologique"—indeed, Christian theme—that Barthes pursues here (he made much, as well, of Michelet's frequent references to drinking the black blood of the dead) but in the biological realm, as physiological process.

We must seriously consider, as Jules Michelet was not able to, the archive as a harborer of the anthrax infection. We must take note of the significant number of cases of anthrax meningitis reported between 1920 and 1950, when it became clear for the first time that the bacillus *anthricis* could cause, or result in, meningitis, though indeed its incidence was infrequent.[53] In its modern nosology, meningitis bears strict comparison with the brain fever described nearly two centuries ago, as attendant on the sedentary, airless, and fevered scholarly life, spent in close proximity to leather bound books and documents.

We may thus begin to provide the aetiology of archive fever proper; and, on a parochial and personal note, we suggest that in England, at least, the Public Record Office (PRO) is by far the most likely site for contraction of the disease. Many of the PRO classmarks consist of dust and dirt and decaying matter put into bundles in the 1780s and then into boxes 150 years later. In the County Record Offices, where, though the stacks may be hundreds of yards long, there are in fact far fewer records stored, documents have nearly always been dusted and cleaned sometime since their acquisition. But that is not strictly the point, for the red rot comes off on your hands from the spine of the ledger, the dust still rises as you open the bundle. Moreover, atmospheric conditions in the Public Record Office, being at the optimum for the preservation of paper and parchment, are rather cold for human beings. You sit all day long, read-ing in the particular manner of historians, to save time and money and in the sure knowledge that out of the thousand lines of handwriting you decipher, you will perhaps use one or two ("the constant application of the eyes to minute objects"). You scarcely move, partly to conserve body heat but mainly because *you want to finish,* and not to have to come back, because the PRO is so *far away,* so difficult to get to. That is the immediate ambition that excites you: to leave; though there exist of course the wider passions, of *finding it* (whatever it is you are searching for) and writing the article or book, writing history.[54] All of this must be taken into account, as productive of archive fever. But so must the thousands of historians be considered, who, like Jules Michelet, have breathed in lungfuls of dust and woken that night, or the next, with the unmistakable headache, "the heavy and often stupefying pain."[55] We should certainly remember that in 1947 (the last time the topic was seriously considered in the medical literature) the incidence of meningeal involvement in anthrax infection was considered to be only 5 percent.[56] But taking all of this into account, that's what my money is on. We are talking epidemiology here, not metaphor: meningitis due to or as a complication of anthrax: another kind of archive fever.

According to Benedict Anderson, Michelet went in to the archive in order to enact a particular kind of national imagining. The dead and forgotten people he exhumed "were by no means a random assemblage of forgotten, anonymous dead. They were those whose sacrifices, throughout History, made possible the rupture of 1789 and the self conscious appearance of the French nation."[57] Anderson is brilliant and brilliantly funny—on the way in which, after Michelet, "the silence of the dead was no obstacle to the exhumation of their deepest desires" and historians found themselves able to speak on behalf of the dead and to interpret the words and the acts that the dead themselves had not understood in life: "qu'ils n'ont pas compris."[58] It was not exactly Jules Michelet the historian, nor indeed the Historian, who performed this act of interpretation (though it was indeed, precisely, fixed on a day, a date, a lived time, that the young lycéen entered the portals of the National Archives and breathed in the dust of the dead). It was in fact a magistrate, also called History, who did this work of resurrection:

> Oui, chaque mort laisse un petit bien, sa mémoire, et demand qu'on la soigne. Pour celui qui n'a pas d'amis, il faut que le magistrat y supplée. Car la loi, la justice est

plus sure que toutes nos tendresses oublieuses, nos larmes si vites séchées. Cette magistrature, c'est l'histoire. Et les morts sont, pour dire comme le Doit romain, ces *miserabiles personae* dont le magistrat se préoccuper. Jamais dans ma carriere je n'ai pas perdu de vue ce devoir de l'historien.[59]

[Yes, every one who dies leaves behind a little legacy, his memory, and demands that we care for it. For those who have no friends, the magistrate must provide that care. For the law, or justice, is more certain than all our tender forgetfulness, our tears so swiftly dried. This magistracy is History. And the dead are, to use the language of Roman law, those *miserabiles personae* with whom the magistrate must preoccupy himself. Never in my career have I lost sight of that duty of the historian.]

Is this a reason for the *archon* and the *arkhe being there,* in Derrida's text? Not with a reference to the legal system of the Greek city-state at all but somehow, by some means, to Michelet's awesome yet touching image of 1872–74, of History (or the Historian, or both) charged with the care and protection of the forgotten poor and the forgotten dead? A biography of Derrida, his educational history, an account of the fate of Michelet's writing—and history writing in general—under the Vichy regime's educational "reforms," all might give us a view of his reading Michelet and a possible answer to the question of how Michelet's Magistrate got into "Archive Fever." But we would then have to dismiss this search as a tiny, pathetic example of the Western nostalgia—fever, sometimes—for origins, points of beginning, foundations.[60]

Whether we can explain the presence of the Magistrate in Derrida's text or not, we can assuredly see that he is there. Indeed we should find this particular Magistrate's presence unsurprising: we have learned from Derrida himself that texts (texts of philosophy are by far the majority of his examples) contain what *apparently* isn't there at all; that they pull against their overt meaning, in the unregarded details, in chains of metaphors, in the footnotes; on all the wilder shores of meaning that are signaled by punctuation marks, for example; by absences, spaces, lacunae, all working against their overt propositions.

Reading "Archive Fever" in this way would then be fine, if our reading produced a magistrate who apparently wasn't there. But the *archon,* his house, his justice room, his law books open "Archive Fever," and the problem is *that he is the wrong magistrate.* The *archon* operated a system of law in a slave society and had a quite different function from the kind of magistrate that Michelet figured. The *archon* dealt with slaves, the ma-

jority of local populations, only as aspects of their owners' property and personalities.[61] But the magistrate whom Michelet figures as History was, in different ways, in England and France of the modern period, specifically charged with the care and management of the poor and with the mediation of social and class relations. Michelet evoked Roman law in describing the duties and activities of his magistracy and thus might be thought to make the post-Napoleonic French justice system the groundwork of his allegory. But the same broad assumptions of the magistrate's task guided theory and practice under England's system of common law. Statute law ("law positive," in eighteenth-century language) gave the care and protection of the majority of the populace to the justices of the peace, under the poor law (this is to leave quite out of the reckoning the question of how nasty, demeaning, and actually unjust that treatment may have been in any particular case). English legal theory of the eighteenth century was quite strongly "Roman" in implication and interpretation, and the most striking legal commentator of them all, William Blackstone, understood the relationship between master and servant, between subordinates and those who ruled over them, as the first of the "great relations" of private life that the law was interested in and that on which all other forms of personal relationship subject to law (the married relation and that between parent and child) were based.[62] The local justice of the peace (and Michelet's Magistrate) were formally obliged to mediate these relationships, within social and familial hierarchies of civil society. Operating a legal system with chattel-slavery law, the *archon* did not—could not—do anything like this.

The *archon* could not do anything like the justice of the peace Philip Ward of Stoke Doyle in Northamptonshire, who sometime in April 1751 heard a complaint from a Mr. Sambrook, watchmaker of Oundle, whose apprentice had assaulted him. A servant or an apprentice who did such a thing was liable to one year's imprisonment and additional corporal punishment, but the legislation specified that two justices must sit together to pass sentence in this way.[63] Doyle had already issued a warrant (he could do that on his sole authority) when it occurred to him "upon second thoughts that I as a single justice can neither punish him upon s.21 of 5 Eliz. c.4 nor upon s.4 of 20 Geo.2 c.19." He recorded in his notebook his solution to the limits the law placed upon his actions. Calling the arrested apprentice into the justice room at Stoke Doyle House and "concealing my want of power I said the words of the Statute read over [*sic*] to him and he immediately desir'd he might be admitted [*sic*] to ask his Masters pardon upon promising never to offend more and so was forgiven."[64] The magistrate, who is *really* in Derrida's text, Michelet's Magistrate, exercises a power he doesn't always actually have, a power that always has already been inaugurated somewhere else; he files away not only official documents (though the warrant in this particular case from 1751, the hundreds of recognizances, depositions, the examinations that passed under the hands of justices of the peace and must have passed through Ward's justice room are actually lost) but also makes notations in this personal notebook (many country magistrates kept this sort of notebook) to remind himself of what he had done, as well as to remind himself of what the law said he couldn't do. And, although the nameless apprentice watchmaker of Oundle is not the best example I could produce, the stories of the poor, the *miserabiles personae,* end up in the archive too. The archive that is the real archive in "Archive Fever" is not and never has been the repository of official documents alone. And nothing starts in the archive, nothing, ever at all, though things certainly end up there.

Including, of course, dust. Though Michelet was unaware of its precise components, he breathed it in, restored the dead to the light of day, and gave them justice by bringing them before the tribunal of History. This History was what Michelet himself wrote, out of the notes and the handfuls of dust he carried away from the archive. As writing, it was also an idea, an idea of the total justice of a narrative that incorporated the past and the "when it shall have been," that is, when the dead have spoken and (the specificity of Michelet's central interest as a historian) France has been made.

Yet it is not his history of the French nation for which Michelet is remembered at the end of the twentieth century. What promotes the bright, interested question, "Was he *mad*?" when you tell people that you are reading him are all the volumes that do not seem to be works of history to the modern, professional, historical eye: work on the sea, on birds, on women and witchcraft, on mountains, insects, love . . . These were the texts, an admixture of physiology and lyricism, that entertained Roland Barthes in the early 1950s. They will probably continue to be marked as odd, though in the nineteenth-century development of the modern practice of history they were not *very* strange.

As History, as a way of thinking and as a modern academic discipline, came to be formulated, it bore much resemblance to the life sciences, where the task was also to think about the past—think pastness—about the im-

perishability of matter, through all the stages of growth and decay, to the point of recognition that "within the system of nature existing as it is, we cannot admit that an atom of any kind can ever be destroyed."[65] Nothing goes away. Physiology, in serious and popular ways, was conceived as a form of history, a connection exemplified by the chemist and physiologist John William Draper, who followed his *Human Physiology* of 1856 with *History of the Intellectual Development of Europe* in 1863. Here he sought to provide evidence of a concluding premise of his earlier work: that "the history of men and of nations is only a chapter of physiology."[66] Draper's panegyrics to the ever-moving, ever-changing sea and sky in this second work, his descriptions of the constant yielding of mountains to frost and rain, the passing of all things from form to form, suggest that Michelet's volumes on similar topics should not be read solely under the interpretive banner of romantic lyricism but as a form of history. They also make it very plain why Michelet *knew* that the unconsidered dead were to be found in the Archives Nationales and that the material presence of their dust, the atomistic remains of the toils and tribulations and of the growth and decay of the animal body, was literally what might carry them, through his inhalation and his writing of History, into a new life. He knew that they were "not capable of loss of existence."[67]

The historian's massive and overweening authority as a writer derives from two factors: the ways archives are and the conventional rhetoric of history writing, which always asserts (though the footnotes, through the casual reference to PT S2/1/1 . . .) that you *know* because you have been there. The fiction is that the authority comes from the documents themselves and the historian's obeisance to the limits they impose on any account that employs them. But really, it comes from *having been there* (the train to the distant city, the call number, the bundle opened, the dust . . .), so that then, and only then, you can present yourself as moved and dictated to by those sources, telling a story the way it has to be told. Thus the authority of the historian's seemingly modest "No; it wasn't quite like that."

There is not a way in which History (the work of historians, history writing) *could* operate differently. There is everything, or Everything, the great undifferentiated past, all of it, which is not history but just stuff.[68] The smallest fragment of its representation (nearly always in some kind of written language) ends up in various kinds of archive and record offices (and also in the vastly expanded data banks that Derrida refers to in "Archive Fever"). From that, you make history, which is never what *was* there, once upon a time. (There was only stuff, Everything, dust . . .). "There is history," says Jacques Rancière, after his long contemplation of Michelet, "because there is the past and a specific passion for the past. And there is history because there is an absence . . ."[69]

In other words, the status of history depends on the treatment of this twofold absence of the "thing itself" that is *no longer there* (that is in the past) and that never was (because it never was such as it was told.)

Contemplating Everything, the historian must *start* somewhere, but starting is a different thing from originating or even from beginning. And while there is closure in historical writing, and historians do bring their arguments and books to a conclusion, there is no—there cannot be an—End, for we are still in it, the great, slow-moving Everything. An End is quite different from an Ending, and endings are what history deals in, just as history's mode of beginning always suggests a wayward arbitrariness: "once upon a time" is the rhetorical mode, the unspoken starting point of the written history. The grammatical tense of the archive is not, then, the future perfect, not the conventional past historic of English-speaking historians, nor even the *passé historique* of the French, but is instead the syntax of the fairy-tale: "once, there was," "in the summer of 1751," "once *upon* a time."

The archive gives rise to particular practices of reading. If you are a historian, you nearly always read something that was not intended for your eyes: you are the reader impossible-to-be-imagined by Philip Ward as he kept his justice's notebook as aide-mémoire (quite different from the way that Henry Fielding, who had a good deal of horrifying fun with what went on in the justice room, *did* imagine you, a reader, with *Joseph Andrews* in your hands, reading the novel he wanted someone to read). The vestryman recording an allowance of 6d. a week in bread to a poor woman, the merchant manufacturer's wife listing the payments in kind to her serving maid (silk ribbons, a pair of stays, a hatbox!) in Howarth in 1794, had nothing like you in mind at all.[70] Productive and extraordinary as is Derrida's concept of the *carte-postale* (the idea of the relationship between language and truth that *La Carte postale* explores), of messages gone astray, not sent in the first place, or unread because you can't see them for looking at them, as in Poe's "Purloined Letter," none of it gives insight (indeed, it was not meant to) into the message that was never a message in the first place, never sent, and never sent to the historian—was just an entry in a ledger, a name on a list.[71] Moreover, historians read for what is *not there*; the silences and the absences of the documents

always speak to us. They spoke, of course, to Jules Michelet (he was actually after the silence, the whisper, the unrecorded dead: what wasn't there at all in the Archives Nationales), and they spoke to post–Second World War social and labor historians whose particular task it was to rescue and retrieve the life and experience of working-class people from the official documents that occlude them. An absence speaks; the nameless watchmaker's apprentice is important *because* he is nameless: we give his namelessness meaning, make it matter. Indeed, Rancière claims that it was Michelet who first formulated the proper subject of history: all the numberless unnoticed *miserabiles personae* who had lived and died, as mute in the grave as they had been in life. According to Rancière, Michelet's modern reputation as mere romantic—indeed, sentimental—rescuer of "the People" serves to repress both his startling originality as a historian and History's proper topic.[72]

On several occasions during the 1980s, it was very sensibly suggested by Christopher Norris that it was best for historians to have nothing to do with the manner of reading texts most closely connected with Derrida's name, best for them not to mess with deconstruction because, as a method devised for the interrogation of philosophical texts, its power lies solely in that particular terrain (and that of literature.) Norris made this point for political purposes when an extreme relativism wedded to a form of deconstruction allowed some historians to deny that certain past events had actually taken place.[73] They are presumably the historians Derrida had in mind when he raised questions about "débats autour de tous les "révisionnisms' . . . [les] séismes de l'historiographie," and which force one to ask whether it is not historians and the history they write that he has in his sights, rather than the archives that he names as the trouble in *Mal d'archive*.[74]

Considering Norris's strictures, what is clearer ten years on than it was at the time is that it was not historians who needed warning off but rather a number of cultural critics and theorists who wanted to address the question of history, or historicity, or merely to have something to say about its relationship to deconstructive practice. It was the question, or problem, of diachronicity (in the realm of synchronic analysis and thinking) that was being raised. Or the problem of pastness, *tout court*.[75] It was the urgency with which Norris needed to make his strictures against revisionist historians that perhaps prevented him from looking at what happens when the traffic goes the other way and deconstruction considers historians and the history they write. It has long been noted that alerting historians to the facts that they write in the tragic mode, or as ironists, that they plot their stories in particular ways, and that they may produce meanings that work against overt and stated arguments makes absolutely no difference at all to the historian's dogged and daily performance of positivism. The text that is usually taken to stand in for the whole deconstructive endeavor (as far as historians are concerned) when observations like these are made is Hayden White's *Metahistory*, a work now more than twenty years old. With White's work in view, it has been suggested that one of the reasons for the absence of meaning that deconstruction has for history, for the way in which deconstructive readings slither around the written history, is that deconstructive analyses do not have reference in mind. History writing, says Maurice Mandelbaum, does not refer to the Archive (or to archives), nor does it refer to the documents that archives contain. Neither is the point of reference any existing account of those documents in already existing works of history. Rather, says Mandelbaum, what is referred to are anterior entities: past structures, processes, and happenings. The writings of historians "refer to past occurrences whose existence is only known through inferences drawn from surviving documents; but it is not to those documents themselves, but to what they indicate concerning the past, that the historian's statements actually refer." Mandelbaum appears to suggest that the historian's statements thus make reference to—History.[76]

We should probably go beyond this by allowing that it is in fact the historian who makes the stuff of the past into a structure, an event, a happening, or a thing, through the activities of thought and writing: that they were never actually *there,* once, in the first place, or at least not in the same way as a nutmeg grater actually once was, for the past "never was *such as it was told.*" There is a double nothingness in the writing of history and in the analysis of history: they are about something that never did happen in the way it is represented (the happening exists in the telling or the text); and they are made out of materials that aren't there, in an archive or anywhere else. We should be entirely unsurprised that deconstruction made no difference to this kind of text, in which the historian's nostalgia for origins and original referents cannot be seen, or exposed, because there is actually *nothing there:* only absence, what once was: dust.

I wanted to write this not precisely because I was irritated by a quite unintended account of archives and archival practice given by Jacques Derrida in the various versions of "Archive Fever" that appeared between 1994

and 1996. Nor was my sole motive the fact that after a visit to the PRO I did suffer from meningitis (or what, after some reading in the history of occupational disease) I came to call—but only to myself—(real) archive fever. It was during that hallucinogenic time that the delicious idea occurred to me of behaving toward Derrida's "Archive Fever" in a manner both skittish and pedantic. In a parody (but not *quite* a parody) of empirical doggedness, I would cling to the coattails of one figure, one image, *one literal meaning* of "fever" (which wasn't even a word that was there to start with) and would find not only another kind of fever but also the magistrate who was always actually there in the text, though wrongly named. Really though (I think, really) I wanted to copy a punctuation mark, someone else's marking of the aporia between saying and writing. (To want to do that in the first place is profound acknowledgment of all that Derrida has shown us on these topics over the last thirty years.)

In 1779, Fanny Burney was taken ill when she was staying with her friend Hester Thrale, the widow of a brewing magnate. (Her *then* friend. This friendship disintegrated some years later, when Hester Thrale married an Italian—and a mere music master to boot—and became Mrs Piozzi. Many were lost at this time.) Burney was obviously a demanding invalid, or at least, Mrs Thrale found her so: "Fanny Burney has kept her Room here in my house seven Days with a Fever, or something she called a Fever," wrote her exasperated hostess, in one of the six blank quarto volumes that her husband had given her in 1776:

> I gave her every Medicine, and every Slop with my own hand; took away her dirty Cups, Spoons &c moved her Tables, in short was Doctor & Nurse & Maid—for I did not like the Servants should have additional Trouble lest they should hate her for't and now—with the Gratitude of a Wit, She tells me that the *World thinks better of me* for my Civilities to her.
> It does! does it?[77]

I am charmed by the cleverness of this entry: the move of the pen from one line to another; that exclamation mark—and the bold use of an exclamation and a question mark within one sentence; the insistence that you hear a tone of voice in words that were not, in fact, spoken aloud at all. Now Hester Thrale was, in all manner of ways, a very difficult number indeed, and she is scarcely good evidence for my case of the historian as reader of the unintended letter. She did not write for *me,* but she certainly imagined someone something like me reading her private diary, especially her academic readers, for among all its other uses, *Thraliana* was used as a source for her own philological work. She often reflected on what posterity would make of her writing:

> but say the Critics a Violin is not an Instrument for *Ladies* to manage, very likely! I remember when they said the same Thing of a Pen.
> I wonder if my Executors will burn the Thraliana![78]

and she so admired some of her apercus and turns of phrase, that she recycled them in her letters (like the Fanny Burney story). She wrote highly crafted, controlled, and managed accounts of her self, directed at future audiences. This was not the aspect of her voluminous writings that fixed my gaze. Rather, I just wanted to ask a question, like that, in some place between speech and writing: that voiced skepticism, that irony:

> "It does! does it?"—"Archive Fever, indeed? I can tell you *all about* Archive Fever!"—another way of saying, "No, not like that. . . ."

NOTES

This essay was first published in *History of the Human Sciences* 11, no. 4 (November 1998) and is reprinted with permission.

1. References in the text are to the English-language version of *Mal d'archive* published in the journal *Diacritics*: Jacques Derrida, "Archive Fever: A Freudian Impression," *Diacritics* 25, no. 2 (Summer 1995): 9–63. For the publication history of "Archive Fever," see note 6.

2. That the inauguration of national archives is intimately bound up with the development of European nation-states has long been recognized. See Jacques Le Goff, *History and Memory* (1977; New York: Columbia University Press, 1992), 87–89. Carolyn Steedman, "The Space of Memory: In an Archive," *History of the Human Sciences* 11, no. 4 (1998): 65–83, especially 67.

3. In *Writing and Difference*, trans. Alan Bass (1967; London: Routledge and Kegan Paul, 1978), 196–231.

4. Derrida has been most interested in the analogy used in "A Note upon the "Mystic Writing-Pad" (1925): *Standard Edition of the Complete Psychological Works of Sigmund Freud* (London: Hogarth Press, 1961), 19:227–32.

5. Yosef Hayim Yerushalmi, *Freud's Moses: Judaism Terminable and Interminable* (New York: Yale University Press, 1991); for the draft of *Moses and Monotheism* see 3, 16–17, and 101–103 in that volume. For surprise at ease of access to this archive, see J. M. Masson, *The Assault on Truth: Freud's Suppression of the Seduction Theory* (Harmondsworth: Penguin, 1985); and Janet Malcolm, *In the Freud Archives* (1983; London: Macmillan, 1997), especially 19–21, 27–35.

6. See note 5. Janet Malcolm gives a summary account of this affair in her book and in the postscript, which she wrote for the 1997 edition.

7. See "The Archive," special issue, *History of the Human Sciences* 11, no. 4 (1998); and "The Archive Part 2," special issue, *History of the Human Sciences* 12, no. 2 (1999).

8. Written (word-processed) in French in May 1994 (every version mentioned subsequently is most precise about the dates of composition), the English-language version (translated by Eric Prenowitz) appeared in the Summer 1995 issue of *Diacritics*), as mentioned in note 1. This then appeared in book form a year later: Jacques Derrida, *Archive Fever: A Freudian Impression* (Chicago and London: University of Chicago Press, 1996). The French version appeared in 1995: Jacques Derrida, *Mal d'archive: Une impression freudienne* (Paris: Editions Galilée, 1995).

9. This was a view expressed at many points during Freud's writing career. The clearest statement of the argument is to be found in "Beyond the Pleasure Principle" (1920): *Standard Edition of the Complete Psychological Works of Sigmund Freud* (London: Hogarth Press, 1950), 18:3–64.

10. The exergue is more common in French academic writing than in English, its literal meaning being the tiny space on a coin, below the principal device, which is used either for the engraver's initials or for the date. (I have indeed combed the dictionaries.) But its implied meaning rather than its etymological meaning comes from its scholarly use in France, where it connotes the *hors d'oeuvre*, rather than something that is integrated into the whole design, as are the initials or a date on a coin.

11. On the question of how little there is in archives, see Steedman, "The Space of Memory," 65–83. And see Thomas Osborne, "The Ordinariness of the Archive," *History of the Human Sciences* 12, no. 2 (1999): 51–64.

12. See Maurice Mandelbaum, *Philosophy, History and the Sciences: Selected Critical Essays* (Baltimore and London: Johns Hopkins University Press, 1984), 97–111, not for his criticism of deconstructive readings of history (which is discussed in the text of this essay) but for the compelling image of the stream or river in describing what it is historians work on (101, 103).

13. Jacqueline Karnell Corn, *Response to Occupational Health Hazards: A Historical Perspective* (New York: Van Nostrand Reinhold, 1992). Donald Hunter, *The Diseases of Occupations* (London: English Universities Press, 1955). A. Meiklejohn, *The Life, Work and Times of Charles Turner Thackrah, Surgeon and Apothecary of Leeds (1795–1833)* (Edinburgh and London: E & S Livingstone, 1957). The seventeenth-century authority on occupational disease most frequently referred to in the nineteenth century was Bernardino Rasmazzini. His *De morbis artificium* was first translated into English in 1705: *A Treatise of the Diseases of Tradesmen* (1703; London: Andrew Bell, 1705). See also Wilmer C. Wright, *De morbis artificium diatribe. Diseases of Workers. The Latin Text of 1713, revised, with translation and notes by Wilmer Cave Wright* (Chicago: University of Chicago Press, 1940). For eighteenth-century "environmentalist" medicine and its connection to later miasmic and contagion theories, see James C. Riley, *The Eighteenth-Century Campaign to*

Avoid Disease (New York: St. Martin's Press, 1987), 13–19 and passim.

14. C. Turner Thackrah, *The Effects of Arts, Trades and Professions, and of Civic States and Habits of Living, on Health and Longevity: With Suggestions for the Removal of the Agents which Produce Disease and Shorten the Duration of Life*, 2nd ed. (London: Longman, 1832), 63–119.

15. Thackrah, *Effects of Arts*, 66, 70.

16. John Forbes, Alexander Tweedie, and John Conolly, *The Cyclopaedia of Practical Medicine*, 3 vols. (London: Sherwood, 1833), 1:149–160, quotation at 156.

17. Leonard A. Parry, *The Risks and Dangers of Various Occupations and Their Prevention* (London: Scott, Greenwood, 1900), 34–35. George M. Kober and William C. Hanson, *Diseases of Occupation and Vocational Hygiene* (1916; London: William Heinemann, 1918), 666–69. University of Warwick, Modern Records Centre, Records of the TUC, Mss. 292/144.3/3; 144.312; D107, "Dust—Rag Flock, 1937–1947." Barbara Harrison, *Not Only the "Dangerous Trades": Women's Work and Health in Britain, 1880–1914* (London: Taylor and Francis, 1996), 58–59. Jacqueline Karnell Corn, *Response to Occupational Health Hazards: A Historical Perspective* (New York: Van Nostrand Reinhold, 1992), 147–76 for byssinosis and the recognition of industrial hazard in the United States. See also Christopher C. Sellars, *Hazards of the Job: From Industrial Disease to Environmental Health Science* (Chapel Hill and London: University of North Carolina Press, 1997); and for the truly modern hazards of work, see Catherine Casey, *Work, Self and Society: After Industrialism* (London and New York: Routledge, 1995).

18. Maxine Berg, *The Age of Manufactures, 1700–1820* (London: Fontana, 1985), 26, 28, 38–39.

19. Harrison, *Not Only the "Dangerous Trades,"* 58–59, 76. Sir Thomas Oliver, *Occupations: From the Social, Hygienic and Medical Points of View* (Cambridge: Cambridge University Press, 1916), 71–84.

20. Parry, *The Risks and Dangers of Various Occupations*, 1–42.

21. Oliver, *Occupations*, 59, 71–72.

22. Records of the TUC, Mss. 292/144.3/3; 144.312; D107, "Dust—Rag Flock, 1937–1947"; Mss. 292/144/211/6, "Anthrax, 1924–1947."

23. Forbes, Tweedie, and Conolly, *The Cyclopaedia of Practical Medicine*, 159. These works of the 1820s and 1830s nowhere mention S. A. Tissot's *De la Santé des gens des lettres* (1766), though his work was translated into English and his perceptions seem omnipresent in the 1820s and 1830s. S. A. Tissot, *De la Santé des gens des lettres* (1766; Lausanne: Francois Graiset, 1768). S. A. Tissot, *An Essay on Diseases Incidental to Literary and Sedentary Persons. With Proper Rules for Preventing their fatal Consequences and Instructions for their Care* (London: Edward and Charles Dilly, 1768). S. A. Tissot, *A Treatise on the Diseases Incident to Literary and Sedentary Persons. Transcribed from the last French Edition. With Notes, by a Physician* (London and Edinburgh: A. Donaldson, 1771). Tissot nowhere mentioned scholarship as an occupation that ran the hazard of dust or miasma; he made no reference to the headache. He attributed most of the scholar's ills to *sitting down* and not exercising.

24. Forbes, Tweedie, and Conolly, "Brain, Inflammation of," *The Cyclopaedia of Practical Medicine*, 281–312.

25. Forbes, Tweedie, and Conolly, *The Cyclopaedia of Practical Medicine*, 184–85.

26. Records of the TUC, Mss. 292 144.13/3, Association of Women Clerks, "Writers' Cramp 1925–1931."

27. David McBride, *Some Account of a New Method of Tanning* (Dublin: Boulter Grierson, 1769). The Dublin Society, *The Art of Tanning and Currying Leather; With an Account of all the Different Processes Made Use of in Europe and Asia for Dying Leather Red and Yellow* (London: J. Nourse, 1774). James Revell, *A Complete Guide to the Ornamental Leather Work* (London: James Revell, 1853). Alexander Watt, *The Art of Leather Manufacture, being a Practical Handbook* (London: Crosby Lockwood, 1885). H. C. Standage, *The Leather Worker's Manual, being a compendium of practical recipes and working formulae for curriers, bootmakers, leather dressers &c* (London: Scott, Greenwood, 1900). Society for the Encouragement of Arts, Manufactures and Commerce, *Report of the Committee on Leather for Bookbinding. With Four Appendices* (London: printed by William Trounce, 1911). Constant Ponder, *Report to the Worshipful Company of Leathersellers on the Incidence of Anthrax Amongst those engaged in Hide, Skin and Leather Industries* (London: Worshipful Company of Leathersellers, 1911).

28. R. Reed, *Ancient Skins, Parchments and Leathers* (London and New York: Seminar Press, 1972), 46–85. Ronald Reed, *The Nature and Making of Parchment* (Leeds: Elmete Press, 1975).

29. David Hunter, *Papermaking: The History and Technique of an Ancient Craft*, 2nd ed. (London: Pleiades Books, 1956).

30. Donald Hunter in *The Diseases of Occupations* (546) suggests that the change took place in the 1890s; but see Carolyn Steedman, "What a Rag Rug Means," *Journal of Material Culture* 3, no. 3 (November 1998): 259–81, especially 273–74 and references.

31. Thackrah, *Effects of Arts*, 42–43.

32. Thackrah, *Effects of Arts*, 45.

33. Jean Théorides, *Un grand médicin et biologiste: Casimir-Joseph Davaine (1812–1882)*, Analecta medico-historica 4 (Oxford: Pergamon Press, 1968), 72–123, 124–25.

34. W. F. Bynum and Roy Porter, *Companion Encyclopaedia of the History of Medicine*, 2 vols. (London: Routledge, 1993), 1:113–14. Kenneth F. Kiple, "Anthrax," in *The Cambridge World History of Human Disease* (Cambridge: Cambridge University Press, 1993), 582–84.

35. Parry, *The Risks and Dangers of Various Occupations*, 147–54.

36. Quotation from Parry, *The Risks and Dangers of Various Occupations*, 149. Also see Hunter, *The Diseases of Occupations*, 627–39.

37. Records of the TUC, Mss. 292/144/211/6, "Anthrax, 1924–1947." This is a note from Trades Union Congress, *Report* (1929), 116–18.

38. Harrison, *Not Only the "Dangerous Trades,"* 76.

39. Records of the TUC, Mss. 292/144/211/6, "Anthrax, 1924–1947." See in this file a letter dated May 20, 1925, from Ben Tillett at the Transport and General Workers' Union, with

his opinion that anthrax cases had risen since the end of the First World War because of imported hides, especially those of the Mediterranean goat, and Indian wool. He enclosed a memorandum on investigation into anthrax incidence at the International Labour Office, 1924, including the Minority Report of its Anthrax Committee. For information on this committee, see E. C. Snow (Manager of the United Tanners' Federation), *Leather, Hides, Skins and Tanning Materials*, Resources of the Empire Series (London: Ernest Benn, 1924), 71–72.

40. The Factory Department of the Home Office issued an illustrated "Precautionary Card for Workers" in 1930, which told them what symptoms of anthrax to look out for: "Take this card with you and show it to the Doctor." Records of the TUC, Mss. 292/144/211/6, "Anthrax, 1924–1947." Ministry of Labour, *Report of the Committee of Inquiry on Anthrax* (London: Her Majesty's Stationery Office, 1959).

41. Hunter, *The Diseases of Occupations*, 627–39.

42. See Philip Brachman, "Inhalation Anthrax," *Annals of the New York Academy of Science* 353 (1980): 83–93, for a history of attention to internal anthrax, by this date "primarily only of historical interest."

43. Kober and Hanson, *Diseases of Occupation and Vocational Hygiene*, 159.

44. Ponder, *Report to the Worshipful Company of Leathersellers*, 17, 44, 65.

45. Ibid., 65–66.

46. Society for the Encouragement of Arts, Manufactures and Commerce, *Report of the Committee on Leather for Bookbinding*, 12. H. J. Plender Leith, *The Preservation of Leather Bookbindings* (1946; London: Trustees of the British Museum, 1967).

47. K. J. Adcock, *Leather: From the Raw Material to the Finished Product* (London: Pitman, 1915), 107. Matthew T. Roberts and Don Etherington, *Bookbinding and the Conservation of Books* (Washington, DC: Library of Congress, 1982), 214. European Commission, Environment Leather Project, *Deterioration of Vegetable Tanned Leather*, Protection and Conservation of the European Cultural Heritage, Research Report 6 (Copenhagen, 1997). Bernard C. Middleton, *The Restoration of Leather Bindings*, 3rd ed. (New Castle, DE: Oak Knoll Press; London: British Library, 1998), 36.

48. Roberts and Etherington, *Bookbinding and the Conservation of Books*, 214.

49. Ibid.

50. "Et à mesure que je soufflais sur leur poussière, je les voyais se soulever . . ." Jules Michelet, "Preface de l'Histoire de France" (1869); and "Examen en des Remainments du texte de 1833 par Robert Casanova," in *Oeuvres Complètes* (Paris: Flammarion, 1974), 4:613–14, 727.

51. Edmund Wilson, *To the Finland Station: A Study in the Writing and Acting of History* (1940; New York: Doubleday, 1953), 8. Roland Barthes, *Michelet par lui-meme* (1954; Paris: Seuil, 1968), 89–92. Hayden White, *Metahistory: The Historical Imagination in Nineteenth-Century Europe* (Baltimore and London: Johns Hopkins University Press, 1973), 149–62. Benedict Anderson, *Imagined Communities: Reflections on the Origin and Spread of Nationalism* (1983; London: Verso, 1991). Steedman, "The Space of Memory."

52. Barthes, *Michelet par lui-meme*, 19. See Andy Stafford,

"Barthes and Michelet: Biography and History," *Nottingham French Studies* 36, no. 1 (1997): 14–23. As noted by Stafford, see Chantal Thomas on *Michelet par lui-meme* as "quelquechose come le coeur secret de son [Barthes's] oeuvre." Chantal Thomas, "Barthes et Michelet: Homologie de travail, parallèle d'affection," *La Règle du jeu* 15 (January 1995): 73–84.

53. Hunter, *The Diseases of Occupations*, 638. Robert H. Shanahan, Joseph R. Griffin, and Alfred P. von Anersburg, "Anthrax Meningitis: Report of a Case of Internal Anthrax with Recovery," *American Journal of Chemical Pathology* 17 (1947): 719–22. H. Gross and H. Plate, "Milzbrandbacillen-Meningistis" [Meningitis due to anthrax bacilli], *Klinische Wochenscrift* 19 (October 5, 1940): 1036–37. Michel Deniker, Jean Patel, and Bernard Jamain, "Meningite au Cours du Charbon" [Meningitis as a complication of anthrax], *La Presse médicale* 46 (April 13, 1938): 575–76. R. Bruynoghe and M. Ronse, "Une Infection méningée oar un bacille Anthracoide" [Meninginal infection due to anthracoid bacillus], *Comptes rendus des séances de la Sociétée de biologie* 125 (1937): 395–97. A. Hamant, P.-L. Drouet, P. Chalnot, and J. Simonin, "Un case de méningite sur aigue charbonneuse" [Hyperacute Meningitis in Anthrax], *Bulletins et mémoires de la Société medicale des hopitaux de Paris* 49 (January 13, 1933):14–15. G. R. McCowen and H. B. Parker, "Anthrax Meningitis," *Journal of the Royal Navy Medical Service* 18 (October 1932): 278–80. W. K. Dunscombe, "Meningitis due to B. anthracis," *British Medical Journal* 30 (January 1932):190. A. Aguiah, "Meningitis Caused by Anthrax in Boy of 11," *Bulletin de la Société de pédiatrie de Paris* 26 (May 1928): 285–91.

54. Tissot may not have mentioned dust, fever, or headache in *De la Santé des gens des Lettres* (see note 23), but he was eloquent on the passions of scholars: "ils sont comme les amants qui s'empotent quand on ose leur dire que l'objet de leur passion a des défauts." *De la Santé*, 122.

55. Forbes, Tweedie, and Conolly, *The Cyclopaedia of Practical Medicine*, vol. 1.

56. Shanahan, Griffin, and von Anersburg, "Anthrax Meningitis," 721.

57. Anderson, *Imagined Communities*, 198.

58. Anderson's source for his formulation is Roland Barthes's *Michelet par lui-meme*, 92.

59. Jules Michelet, "Jusqu'au 18 Brumaire" (1872–74)," in *Oeuvres Complètes* (Paris: Flammarion, 1982), 21:268.

60. For origins fever, see Jacques Derrida, *Grammatology* (1967; Baltimore and London: Johns Hopkins University Press, 1976), passim. But the attempt to find the *archon*'s origins would be fun. Working material for it may be found in Geoffrey Bennington and Jacques Derrida, *Jacques Derrida* (Paris: Seuil, 1991), 299–302. Y. C. Aouate, "Les mesures d'exclusion antijuives dans l'enseignement public en Algérie, 1940–1943," *Pardès* 8 (1988): 109–28. For the uses of history under Vichy see Robert O. Paxton, *Vichy France: Old Guard and New Order, 1940–1944* (New York: Knopf, 1972), 150–68; Jean-Michel Barreau, "Vichy, Ideologue de l'ecole," *Revue d'Histoire Moderne et Contemporaine* 38 (1991): 590–616; and Jean-Michel Barreau, "Abel Bonnard, Ministre de l'education nationale sous Vichy, ou l'education impossible," *Revue d'Histoire Moderne et Contemporaine* 43, no. 3 (1996): 464–78. See also Jean-Michel Guiraud, *La Vie intellectuelle et Artistique a*

Marseilles a l'epoque de Vichy et sous l'occupation, 1940–1944 (Marseille: Laffitte, 1988), 144–55. W. D. Hall, *The Youth of Vichy France* (Oxford: Clarendon Press, 1981), 8, 19, 40, 216–19, for the uses of history to depose the centrality of the 1789 Revolution and Republicanism in French political culture. See Nadia Margolis, "The 'Joan Phenomenon' and the French Right," in Bonnie Wheeler and Charles T. Wood, eds., *Fresh Verdicts on Joan of Arc* (New York: Garland, 1996), 265–87, for Michelet's work on Joan of Arc (originally published in 1841 as part of his unfinished history of the French people) and its use by the French Right (but not, it seems, during Vichy). See also Robert Gildea, *The Past in French History* (New Haven and London: Yale University Press, 1994), 154–65. The passage in the text concerning the Magistrate (from the uncompleted *Histoire du XIXe Siècle*) is quoted in full in Barthes's *Michelet par lui-meme* under the title "Magistrature de l'histoire."

61. Victor Ehrenberg, *The Greek State,* 2nd ed. (1960; London: Methuen, 1969), 66–74, 77–80. Orlando Patterson, *Slavery and Social Death: A Comparative Study* (Cambridge, MA: Harvard University Press, 1982), 4–5, 29, 87.

62. Sir William Blackstone, *Commentaries on the Laws of England. In Four Books,* 6th ed. (1765; Dublin: Company of Booksellers, 1775), bk. 1, 422–32. S. F. C. Milsom, "The Nature of Blackstone's Achievement," *Oxford Journal of Legal Studies* 1 (1981): 1–12. John W. Cairns, "Blackstone, an English Institutionalist: Legal Literature and the Rise of the Nation State," *Oxford Journal of Legal Studies* 4 (1984): 318–60. For the "Roman" tendencies of the lord chief justice, see James Oldham, *The Mansfield Manuscripts and the Growth of English Law in the Eighteenth Century,* 2 vols. (Chapel Hill and London: University of North Carolina Press, 1992), 1:204.

63. Blackstone, *Commentaries on the Laws of England,* 427–48. Justices of the peace were more likely to learn their law not even from one of the many editions of Richard Burns's *Justice of the Peace and Parish Office* published after 1756 but from volumes of tear-out blank warrants and summonses, such as Burns's own *Blank Precedents Relating to the Office of Justice of the Peace, Settled by Doctor Burn* (London: T. Cadell for the King's Law Printer, 1787). But in 1751, Ward probably referred to Michael Dalton, *The Country Justice. Containing the Practice, Duty and Power of the Justices of the Peace, as well as in as out of their sessions* (London: Henry Lintot, 1742), 139.

64. Lincoln's Inn Library, Misc. Manuscript 592, Manuscript Diary of Philip Ward of Stoke Doyle, Northamptonshire, 1748–51.

65. John William Draper, *Human Physiology, Statistical and Dynamical; or, the Conditions and the Course of the Life of Man* (1856; New York: Harper, 1868), 548.

66. John William Draper, *History of the Intellectual Development of Europe,* 2 vols. (London: Bell Daldy, 1864), 604. On the relationship of history to physiology, see Carolyn Steedman, *Strange Dislocations* (Cambridge, MA: Harvard University Press, 1995), 43–95.

67. Draper, *Human Physiology,* 549.

68. See P. A. Roth, "Narrative Explanation: The Case of History," *History and Theory* 27 (1988): 1–13; and Carolyn Steedman, "About Ends: On How the End Is Different from an Ending," *History of the Human Sciences* 9, no. 4 (November 1996): 99–114.

69. Jacques Rancière, *The Names of History: On the Poetics of Knowledge* (1992; Minneapolis: University of Minnesota Press, 1994), 63.

70. For the historian as a reader—always this kind of reader—of the unintended, purloined letter, see Carolyn Steedman, "A Woman Writing a Letter," in Rebecca Earle, ed., *Epistolary Selves: Letters and Letter-Writers, 1600–1945* (Aldershot: Ashgate, 1999), 111–33.

71. Jacques Derrida, *The Post Card: From Socrates to Freud and Beyond,* trans. Alan Bass (1980; Chicago: University of Chicago Press, 1987).

72. Rancière, *The Names of History,* 42–75. And see Hayden White's comments on these points in his introduction to that work (xiv–xviii).

73. Christopher Norris, *Uncritical Theory: Postmodernism, Intellectuals and the Gulf War* (London: Lawrence and Wishart, 1992); and *Deconstruction and the Interests of Theory* (London: Pinter, 1988), 16–17.

74. Derrida, "Prière d'insérer," *Mal d'archive.*

75. See for example, Derek Attridge, Geoff Bennington, and Robert Young, eds., *Post-structuralism and the Question of History* (Cambridge: Cambridge University Press, 1987).

76. Mandelbaum, *Philosophy, History and the Sciences,* 109–10.

77. Katharine C. Balderston, ed., *Thraliana: The Diary of Mrs Hester Lynch Thrale (Later Mrs Piozzi) 1776–1809,* 2 vols. (Oxford: Clarendon Press, 1951), vol.1, entry for December 1, 1779.

78. Ibid., 2:748.

The Problem of *Publicité* in the Archives of Second Empire France

Jennifer S. Milligan

In his scathing essay on the coup d'état that brought France's Second Empire to power, Karl Marx produced some of his most memorable (or at least quotable) musings on the nature of history. "Men," he wrote, "make their own history, but they do not make it just as they please; they do not make it under circumstances chosen by themselves, but under circumstances encountered, given and transmitted from the past."[1] Focused on material conditions, Marx's criticism did not extend to the Archives, where Louis Napoleon's imperial government sought to control the conditions for men to write French history. For Léon de Laborde, the director general of the Imperial Archives of France (1857–68), his institution was destined to become a critical tool in the Empire's quest for historical and political legitimacy. As the preeminent repository of French state memory, the Imperial Archives were well positioned to direct the destinies of French historical writing. "Government," Laborde opined, "has no better means to prevent the writing of bad books than to provide scholars with the means to write good ones." By opening the "arcane, impenetrable Archives," Laborde explained, the "light of history" could once again shine from its true source.[2] Creating the conditions for men to write imperial histories meant inviting scholars to the Archives to aid them in their search for historical truth, and for Laborde (among others) that truth was the voice of the official record. The centralization of historical documents under the watchful eye of trained archivists would provide what the director called "the amenable conditions of liberal *publicité*" necessary for the production of solid histories that would spread the "light of history" to the nation.[3]

Laborde's belief in the "light of history," however, blinded him to the possibility that welcoming scholars to the Archives also invited conflict over the definition of "good books." While Laborde had faith that the Archives held a single, self-evident truth, liberal *publicité* might aid and abet challenges to the Empire's interpretation of history and its political legitimacy. In spite of conscious efforts to open the institution in a bid to control the production of historical knowledge, the Empire remained unaware that the Archives also functioned on their own terms. The archival policy of *publicité* introduced the French public to its Archives and set the terms for what became a battle between state and citizen for the right to speak for national history in Second Empire France.

Publicité and the Public in the Archives of France

This battle would be fought over access to the Archives and the meaning and substance of *publicité*.[4] When Laborde referred to the "liberal *publicité*" of the Imperial Archives, he implied a complex of texts, practices, and procedures that rendered the Archives public. Archival access, albeit limited, was central to Laborde's vision of the future of French history and, by association, French politics. While the Second Empire searched history and the Archives for evidence to shore up its legitimacy (funding works on Caesar, staging historical pageants, and creating a cult of the first Napoleon), *publicité* called on the scholarly public to play a central role in this endeavor.[5] The Empire welcomed scholars to its Imperial Archives and, under Laborde's direction, produced publications and facilities that would make the institution more accessible than ever before.[6] Laborde argued that archival access not only encouraged the production of "good books," it was also good policy. As historians and governments across Europe became increasingly interested in organizing and mining state records in the name of national histories, France could hardly tout its modernity if it were perceived as unwilling to communicate historical documents. The Empire could reap the fruits of its Archives and realize its own historical destiny if it instituted proper archival policy, and *publicité* was the key to success.

Publicité meant much more than "renown," or publicity's current connotation of advertising.[7] *Publicité* implied a public-ness that both invited the public into the physical space of the Archives and bound the public interest to the contents and workings of the institution—and thus to the government that guaranteed the institution. Decrees defined the Archives as the depository of papers of public interest. Inventories were published to guide the scholars through the vast archival past. Administrative protocols governed the movement of documents. Systems of classification organized the morass of papers into discrete and accessible sections. The public reading room required space, furniture, heating, and surveillance. Archivists negotiated these texts, spaces, and procedures in order to serve the public and the government that employed them. *Publicité* could be understood as the product of these texts and practices and as such created the conditions for the revelation of historical documents held in the Archives, but it also played on a historical tension in the relationship between state and citizen. While the Empire's policy of *publicité* nominally rendered the institution "public," those same texts, practices, and procedures also worked to circumscribe (and ultimately stand in for) the potentially unbounded access guaranteed to citizens of France by the Revolutionary legislation that founded the Archives.

Archival *publicité* had a specific history in Modern France. Public access was the preeminent quality that distinguished the modern Archives, and modern French government, from its Old Regime antecedents. The archives of the Old Regime, like the workings of government, were emphatically *not* public, reserved for the lawyers, royal historiographers, and Benedictines in the service of the archives of the crown.[8] The legacy of the Revolution, in the shape of political regimes as well as in the Archives, was a requirement for a modicum of transparency in dealing with the nation/public.[9] While the degree of this transparency would be hotly debated throughout the history of France, there was no question

of returning to the Old Regime separation of the state/sovereign from the public/people. In the Archives, the right of access to government documents "to all citizens" was one of the founding rights of the institution.[10] The new Archives broke from Old Regime analogues in both content and the right to access this content, signaling the importance of transparency to understanding political authority, as well as concern with creating a new history for the new nation. The granting of citizens' access to the Archives in Revolutionary legislation suggests that possibilities for a democratic and transparent archives were at least theorized and even legislated if only to be ultimately unrealized.[11] A new relationship between the state and the nation was evident in the shape of the Archives of the Revolutionary period, and this relationship would be at issue throughout the history of both the French nation-state and its Archives.

This relationship had particular resonance in an empire obsessed with history. If *publicité* in the Archives made it possible for the imperial government to control the conditions to produce good books, the institution contained evidence of an essential lesson of limits to the Empire's power to do so. Not only did the Archives tell the story of regimes that had failed spectacularly in establishing equilibrium between state and society, it also stood as a symbol of that balance. Government, in modern France, could no longer conduct its business in a baldly authoritarian fashion, and it was impossible for a French government both to seal its Archives and to retain its legitimacy. The specificity of the Second Empire and the genius of Louis Napoleon (and eventually his downfall) was the manipulation of what appeared to be a paradox: The Empire was legitimized by referendum, but could a referendum be legitimate in a dynastic empire? The fragility of the Empire's tautological founding premise left the division of power between state and society far from clear. Controls on the press and the closing down of representative bodies, for example, proved extremely unpopular. By 1860 Louis Napoleon relaxed censorship and gave the *corps législatif* a modicum of power. Such moves recognized that the Emperor needed the nation of citizens in order to have his state and that the state and its history were powerful tools in building the nation. The Empire's efforts to produce (at least rhetorically) accessible public Archives suggest an acknowledgment that not only was the modern French state called into being in the name of the nation, but it was in the name of the nation that the old order was brought down in 1789. *Publicité* was evidence of the Empire's recognition that the institution of the Archives was just as potent a political tool as its contents—and therefore potentially dangerous.

During the Second Empire the Archives' historical role would be intensely scrutinized because of the increased attention paid to the public in shaping archival practices and policies designed to enhance national patrimony and dynastic memory. Laborde devoted his tenure to gearing the Archives of the Empire to the public, specifically the scholarly public, in the interest of historical study; for the most part the government of the Second Empire soundly supported his efforts. His tenure was marked by the publication of the first official inventories of archival holdings made available to historians,[12] the opening of an Archive's museum pitched to a less scholarly public,[13] and the fight for increased centralization of historical materials in the Archives of France—which involved a protracted battle with the Imperial Library for the right to claim preeminence in the scholarly universe.[14] There was more at stake in his light of history than simply good books, for good history was a powerful tool in the building of the French nation. If Napoleon III was known as the "schoolmaster of Europe" for his lessons to Bismarck on nationalism's power to dampen the desire for political voice, it was his own study and promotion of history that prepared him for the task of forging a nation.[15]

While the Archives of the Second Empire were not merely a farcical repeat of those of the first, the institution was nevertheless caught up in the very specific dynamics of dynastic dramas and imperial politics. The volatile mixture of interests represented in the contents and function of the Archives mirrored those that threatened to divide France under the Second Empire. The Archives contained Bonaparte family secrets, evidence of maneuverings of statesmen as public figures and private citizens, hard fact, and salacious gossip. They served the reticent imperial state, the curious public, and what Lord Acton called the "sincere quest" of scholars and historians.[16] Although the institution conserved and communicated papers in the name of the French nation, conflicts over the loyalties of the Imperial Archives made clear the difficulty of speaking for France in one voice. While Napoleon III wished to prove, as one historian put it, "one of the main theses of the Napoleonic Legend: that the Bonapartes alone were above faction and hence could govern in the general interest," the politics of the Imperial Archives revealed how difficult it was to provide evidence for such a claim.[17]

Recent scholarship on the Second Empire has stressed the vigor of democratic (or at least republican) civil society under Napoleon III's rule, and the Imperial Archives could be seen as a place where the "paradoxes of Bonapartist democracy" are amply evident.[18] These accounts, however, focus on representation or democracy as a social or political process. The Imperial Archives takes us into the cultural, raising questions about the politics of historical writing, the limits of documentary evidence, and the role of a state that not only maintained and regulated access to its Archives but required the historian-citizen to tell its story. It was around the question of the content of this story, and who should tell it, that the tension inherent in the compound "nation-state" became manifest in the Imperial Archives.

While the archival policy of publicity counted on the help of the scholars in galvanizing the moribund traditions of imperial history, imperial politics and historical scholarship had specific and often competing interests in the Archives. The Archives were the repository of the Bonaparte family's dynastic memory as well as national history. While legislation, inventories, and archivists made the Archives under director Léon de Laborde more accessible and accountable than ever in post-Revolutionary France, the limits of this project were made especially stark when it came to protecting the political and personal resonance of the Napoleonic name. The study of history, then emerging as a defined discipline, carried out political work of its own. Historical writing, developing as a distinct field, played an important role in limiting access to the Archives in the drive toward the discipline's professionalization. Increasingly, professional history insisted on the integrity of archival sources, on the state as the proper object of study, and on the objectivity (and masculinity) of its practitioners, thus closing down possibilities for other sources, methods, and bodies in history and historical study to be valued.[19] The history of historical practice, then, intersected with the history of the rise of Bonapartism in the turbulent narrative of modern France, making for an uneasy mix of interests in the Imperial Archives. To paraphrase Marx, problems presented by the public nature of the Archives required solutions that could be conceived and carried out within boundaries drawn by imperial politics, by the exigencies of historical scholarship (itself increasingly interested in archival evidence), and by competing claims for transparency and access to memory made in the name of the nation-state.[20]

The increasing focus on history and accessibility in the Archives made serving the public an essential part of the archivist's duty—the archivist was thus transformed into a nation builder. It was unclear, however, what the archivist's duty actually was, because the archivist stood at the border between citizen and state. Was he a scholar, bureaucrat, private individual, or public servant? From this shaky ground, the archivist had to negotiate between the requests (or demands) of citizens and the exigencies of government. Where was the line between what was public and what should remain in the shadow of state secrecy? These questions complicated the notion of publicity, for at its heart was the question of the proper relationship between state and citizen, a question that was far from resolved during the Second Empire.[21]

Publicity of the Archives remains an especially complex problem, for the institution stands at the nexus of state and citizen, public interest and private rights,[22] and, as some have suggested, between history and administration[23] and politics and scholarship.[24] I would like to suggest that, at least in the Second Empire, it was the tensions inherent in archival *publicité* that pitted these terms against each other. These tensions came to a head in a protracted debate over the publication of Napoleon Bonaparte's personal correspondence. Napoleon's memory was of enormous significance to national and dynastic history; no other figure could have produced a greater confluence of competing claims. Debates over the integrity of the official Napoleon crystallized around questions of archival access, forcing the Empire, and Laborde, to reckon with the limits of *publicité* in the Imperial Archives. If theorizing the relationship of power and knowledge can sometimes seem vague, this moment in the history of the Archives of the Second Empire offers a concrete case study of this founding condition for politics and scholarship in modern France.

Intimate Thoughts, Official History, and Public Archives: The Case of the *Correspondance*

The culmination of archival fervor and zeal for dynastic memory came in the project to publish the *Correspondance* of Napoleon Bonaparte.[25] This project began in 1854, charged to a commission that included the director of the Archives (then François-Armand Chabrier, replaced by Laborde in 1857) as well as a mix of political and scholarly figures, and was headed by the Maréchal Vaillant, then Minister of War.[26] The project required intimate knowledge not only of the subject matter but of the Archives as well. Napoleon had left what the commission touted as "a legacy of precious information for the future," and it was in the national interest to collect and publish correspondence, creating a portable archive

of this precious material for all.[27] The Imperial Archives, as the preeminent public depository, would be essential to this endeavor.

The preface of the first volume (1858) likened Napoleon to Caesar and his *Correspondance* to the Commentaries, anchoring the project in the genre of dynastic memory and swearing to strive for historical accuracy. The only homage worthy of the "incomparable genius" of first emperor of the French would be the restoration of the "complete, total" Napoleon to his people, and thus the Commission claimed to forbid any modification of the text of the letters. The keystone of the monument was, in the case of the *Correspondance,* the Imperial Archives, which held more than forty thousand pieces of correspondence (with twenty thousand others spread throughout various other institutions).[28] The Commission noted that such an edifice, though worthy, would be difficult to construct given the crush of available material.

Despite lofty intentions, the Commission's *Correspondance* did not live up to imperial standards. By 1863 Louis Napoleon handed the project over to his cousin, Prince Napoleon-Charles-Joseph-Paul Bonaparte.[29] This was a risky move on the emperor's part for the prince was a difficult figure in the dramas of the imperial family. Prince Napoleon had embarrassed both his cousin and the Empire at home and abroad, and his disdain for the regime was well known. However, the prince could be counted on for avuncular, if not filial, pride. His striking resemblance to the first emperor was often noted, and his feelings of animosity toward his cousin were often traced to a feeling that it was not Bonapartism, but the particular Bonaparte, that threatened to undermine the reputation of the Empire. The prince had a personal and political investment in the project, which would also introduce him to the workings of the Imperial Archives that testified to his legitimacy, in the largest sense of the word.[30]

The prince Napoleon's work on the *Correspondance,* whatever its ideological or personal motivations, was above all based on rigorous archival research. He eagerly accepted the project and declared his devotion to portraying his uncle's "most intimate thoughts," immersing himself in the Imperial Archives and vowing to take public opinion as "history's confidant."[31] The prince's experience in the Archives and the scholarly, political, and familial concerns that informed his research convinced him of the power of the institution as the locus of family and governmental secrets as well as national history. Philosophically, then, he was in absolute agreement with Laborde's pronouncements on the importance of the Archives to mediate between government and the nation.

Confusion reigned, however, over the question of the prince's place in the regime of publicity that negotiated between nation and state. It was unclear whether the prince should be considered a citizen-historian, an official on government business, or a member of the Bonaparte dynasty in search of family history (a history that just happened to coincide with that of the French nation). Initially refused entry to the Archives without the special order of the Maréchal Vaillant, the prince complained bitterly to the emperor. Access had been granted to his assistant and many others on previous occasions, so it seemed especially absurd in the case of the prince, who under the emperor's auspices had "not only the right, but the duty" to do research in the Archives.[32] In fact, Laborde had challenged the prince on the terrain of family privacy. Citing the principle of paternal privilege, the director suggested that he could not treat the emperor differently from ordinary subjects. In the case of family members seeking information on ancestors, especially information for publication, Laborde explained that it was the practice at the Archives to ask permission from the head of that family for such research to proceed.[33]

Throughout its history, access to the Archives was notoriously difficult to negotiate, and even given Laborde's regime of "liberal *publicité*" this remained the rule under the Second Empire.[34] Since the original Revolutionary legislation, public access to the central Archives had been limited by many factors, if not by law. The lack of a public reading room until 1847 might account for what is perceived of as a "lack of interest" (only seven scholarly researchers presented themselves at the Archives between 1804 and 1816).[35] "Lack of interest," however, obscured the fact that history was not yet fixated on archival research as a hallmark of professional, objective scholarship, as the Archives had not yet attained its scholarly stature.[36] Regimes preceding the Second Empire had an ambivalent, discretionary relationship to researchers, and, despite Guizot's and Michelet's investment in the Archives and history, interest in the Archives was intermittent at best. Even the opening of the public reading room was accompanied by a decree that restricted research possibilities.[37] The twinning of legal limitation and the possibility of increased accessibility stood as an acknowledgment of the potential problems posed by public access and public discourse.

The central Archives were not peculiar in their restrictions on access. Other archival depositories throughout the nation were also subject to tight regulation, and historians were variously barred from or permitted entry to the vast documentary treasures they held; for instance, the Archives of the Ministry of Foreign Affairs was considered especially ungenerous with its holdings.[38] The central Imperial Archives, however, was a public *and* state institution. Public interest, if not access, was inscribed in its identity, making the question of publicity especially problematic, especially in the face of increasing demand for and interest in historical materials that spoke to (or for) the history of the nation.[39] The Archives were placed squarely in the purview of the public under the Second Empire by virtue of legislation outlining the first official reorganization of the Archives since the legislation of 7 Messidor (tenth month of the Revolutionary calendar) (June 25, 1794), the decree of December 22, 1855, and attendant regulations of 1856. This decree specifically defined the Archives of the Empire as the institution charged with holding "documents of public interest" whose conservation was deemed "useful."[40] The regulations broached the subject of public access but did little to define its substance. The decrees of 1855 and 1856 made no specific reference to who might enjoy this general right or privilege beyond remarking that certain individuals—public functionaries, members of the Institute, established scholars and archivists—were to receive immediate attention to their archival requests and prompt explanations if a request were refused.[41] Although the state would remain custodian and gatekeeper of this depository of public interest, this legislation nonetheless positioned the Archives as an institution at the nexus of the public and the state.

The unspoken and debatable practice that obstructed the prince's research spoke to the limits of the decreed *publicité,* and other regulations seemed equally arbitrary and unevenly applied. According to article 35 of the 1856 archival regulations, requests were to be made for specific documents or series of documents. Researchers could not simply peruse the Archives' holdings at will. This galled the prince, who wondered how an employee of the Archives could possibly divine the documentary needs of every individual author. Not only was this practice counterintuitive, it was a sign of the backwardness of the Imperial Archives. In all the archives of the world, the prince claimed, none presented such an obstacle. Moreover, even the famously unwelcoming War and Foreign Affairs Archives had opened its holdings to the prince's imperial research.[42]

These initial obstacles to access were eventually cleared, and the prince came to understand the power of the Archives as the arbiter of historical truth, if only because his encounter with documents drove home the importance of this truth to the legitimacy of his family's claims to power. The Archives were a crucial institution because, as he put it simply, "History will search the Archives for its documents."[43] Rather than the historian discovering the historical truth in documents found in the Archives, history preceded and determined this truth and searched only for evidence that made sense to it, rather than of it. These were not merely abstractions for the prince: they were words he practiced as well as preached in his work on the *Correspondance*. This philosophy would also guide his dealings with the Archives and the prescriptions of *publicité* that both circumscribed and underpinned his own research and writing. History, in this case the triumph of Bonapartism, depended for its life on the workings of its Archives.

Although he began his research as a champion of access and critic of the central Archives' outmoded obstructive practices, the prince quickly came to distrust the more liberal access he seemed to support. While preparing the *Correspondance* for publication, the prince put together a plan for the reorganization of the Archives and became a scrupulous editor and gatekeeper of Napoleon's memory. If he described the public as a "confidant," this was only in documents for public consumption—his mistrust was evidenced in his choice to deliver a less than complete correspondence, and manifest in his dealings with government. The prince's change of heart was perhaps motivated by what he saw as an unprecedented explosion of "hostile works," histories critical of the Empire, based on archival documents.[44] His list included a work that reproduced papers of foreign affairs; an article on the Pope's captivity by Père Augustin Theiner (who was apparently granted access to papers in the Archives that were in an envelope marked "not to be communicated to anyone without special order");[45] the case of the Prussian scholar Sybel, who was allowed to "leaf through documents at his leisure";[46] and a work by the historian Joseph-Bernard-Othenin d'Haussonville on the Empire and the Church.[47]

L' Affaire d'Haussonville

There was indeed a surfeit of critical works from the likes of Marx and Michelet, but the Baron d'Haussonville, historian of the First Empire and eminent critic of the Second, posed a particular threat to the imperial regime.[48] If Pierre Lanfrey's polemical *Histoire de Napoleon* (1867) painted a more unflattering picture of its subject and garnered a lion's share of the public's attention, it was Haus-

sonville's more rigorous histories that worried the Empire. The first volume of Haussonville's critically acclaimed *L'Église Romaine et le Premier Empire* appeared in 1867, along with a series of articles in the *Revue des deux mondes*. In these works, Haussonville staked his own claim on Napoleon Bonaparte's memory, implicitly criticizing the prince's official version.[49] Haussonville's history included citations of letters that were conspicuously missing from the official "complete" *Correspondance*. These editorial liberties begged the question of the government's role in protecting and producing the nation's memory. They also impugned the Bonapartes' willingness, as guardians of both patrimony and present politics, to cede personal whim to public interest.

Haussonville used the Imperial Archives as a source, but more importantly as a challenge, to the illegitimate exercise of power in Louis Napoleon's France.[50] *L' affaire d'Haussonville,* as it came to be known, confronted the Empire and its Archives with limits of its control over historical information. Haussonville's publications dragged the question of publicity into the public sphere, as they threatened the Empire's historical integrity at the moment the Archives most loudly proclaimed its transparency. Archival policies and procedures were immediately reviewed with an eye toward limiting such damage in the future. Published scholarship proved particularly vexing, for histories based on rigorous archival research were difficult to attack. Censorship grew increasingly questionable because the Empire had moved toward its so-called liberal phase and Louis Napoleon was an avid patron, even producer, of historical works.[51] Well-mobilized archival evidence put many works beyond the pale of imperial intervention. The only solution, the prince insisted, was to strike before such publications could even be prepared.[52] Official action would need to be taken, quickly and quietly, within the walls of the Archives.

Work on the *Correspondance* thus gave birth to an equally important, if much less public, imperial history project. In his construction of the memory of Napoleon Bonaparte "as he would like to appear to posterity," the prince set out on an almost obsessive quest to change the administration, structure, and function of the Archives.[53] Publicity, as the cornerstone of imperial archival policy, became the focus of official critical attention. In past regimes the most sensitive documents had, according to the prince's findings, been locked up in a separate secretariat section. Centralization, and the imperial push for public access, threatened to expose these secrets. Despite the need to welcome scholars into the institution, the potential of handing over government documents to actively hostile forces was a ridiculous risk. As the prince noted, "even the best of all governments could be dragged before posterity and discredited by history if it revealed its secrets."[54] To ensure the greatest care of the written traces of government business was a matter of political necessity.

The dilemma that emerged in the context of publicity, however, was how both to protect and publicize these documents that were legally held in the name of public interest. The prince argued that a separation between archives for the public and archives for the sovereign and his family was necessary for the Bonaparte dynasty to protect its legitimacy and legacy. The Imperial Archives itself held evidence that there was ample precedent for this division. The prince noted that the governments of the First Empire, the Restoration, and the July Monarchy each understood the importance of this separation. Particularly zealous in this regard was the July Monarchy, which destroyed a number of unflattering documents including correspondence with Napoleon I, information on Bonapartist or republican conspiracies, and police papers.[55] The prince was unfazed by the consequences of this destruction of documents for the integrity of his uncle's memory. The possible denaturing of Napoleon's legacy was outweighed by the threats the papers conjured in political fantasies.

That these regimes that sequestered their secrets were (literally) history did not seem to matter to the prince, who did not explicitly connect their downfall to their archival policy. He did, however, recognize that it would be impossible to acknowledge publicly the sequestration of Napoleon's documentary memory to family, rather than national, interest and property. The link between political authority and the Archives was a clear one for the prince: the Archives were as much administrative apparatus as historical patrimony, and these functions were necessarily intertwined. The Archives' publicity was both a political necessity and a potential liability, and it was clearly in the interest of imperial politics to not only keep these Archives secret, but also to intervene in their contents. Thus, any solution taken on the potential problems posed by the institution required subtle maneuvering rather than bold usurpation. Eschewing a more radical solution that would baldly divide secret state and Bonaparte family documents from the public Archives, the prince advised instead a quiet revolution, purging the staff and reorganizing the institution "without any publicity." The genius of this solution was precisely that it did not call public attention to the internal reform, leaving the Archives in honest and devoted hands. The prince

himself planned to oversee the triage of certain "family" papers and asked the emperor to request that the entire series be sent for him to examine, in order to exercise his political prerogative—in the name of "family" honor—to intervene in the nation's history.[56]

Other critics found fault not with the structure of the Archives but with its staff. The archivist could be either a political menace or a crucial tool, destroying or maintaining the order of papers and politics in the Archives. Minister Vaillant argued that the physical and functional separation between state secret and public history in past regimes was not sufficient to guarantee the maintenance of this order; rather, the archivist was entrusted with maintaining this separation.[57] The archivists of the depository were, in previous regimes, purely administrative employees, and the bureaucratic nature of their position protected the secrets in the Archives. Vaillant explained that these men, unlike their Second Empire counterparts, were "not concerned with history or politics" and had no use for the papers in their care other than what duty required. The problems that had arisen under the Second Empire thus were seen to have less to do with contentious claims to speak for history than with unruly employees. The current Archives' staff was according to Vaillant made up of scholars who had ties to scholarly associations and who perhaps "courted publicity a little too much."[58] If this type of archivist—a scholar, interested in history or politics—was the problem, the solution would be to staff the archives with functionaries who treated their work as a purely administrative affair.

Vaillant's fantasies of pre-imperial Archives staffed by detached archivist functionaries belied the more complicated history of French archival practice. Since the Revolution, the Archives' staff was made up primarily of lawyers with a keen interest in both politics and history. Indeed, the highest positions in the archival hierarchy were considered plum political appointments. Archivists and other staff historically undermined attempts to routinize their tasks, and superiors (including Laborde) constantly complained that these employees spent more time on personal scholarship than on archival duties.[59] Vaillant's misreading of archival history, however, allowed him to ignore the deeper issues of archival politics, as he configured the problem as an easily solved personnel issue. Nevertheless, this solution required careful attention to publicity. It was clear that authoritarian maneuvers were out of the question if only because it would attract attention and might, as Vaillant put it, "elicit interpretations that it would be wise to prevent." Echoing the prince's earlier advice, an administrative move was called for. The emperor would designate someone who would be charged to sort these documents and divide them into two parts: one that could be communicated, the other that would remain secret.[60] The political philosophy behind *publicité* was perfectly mirrored in this administrative maneuver. Choosing the right archivist would quietly do the work that a brutal prohibition could not. The new regime of Imperial Archives recognized the importance of public interest and public access, so much so that it fundamentally but secretly limited this access.

This administrative solution was soon put to the test as Haussonville continued to press the integrity of the Archives' promise of serving the interests of the public. On February 28, 1868, the historian went to the Archives and requested documents for his continuing work on Napoleon's dealings with the Vatican. Haussonville had come to the Archives to follow up on articles in the *Revue des deux mondes* that revealed problems in the *Correspondance* and had recently released a second volume of his history, raising alarms behind the reading room door. The emperor was warned the next day that there was still "danger in the house of Laborde." A detailed list of the documents requested revealed his interests: some pertained to political surveillance by the police during the papal captivity (these had already been "abusively communicated," according to a report), and other documents concerning the first emperor's ecclesiastical affairs. These papers were considered particularly incendiary: the report on Haussonville suggested that there were no papers in the Archives as sensitive as the documents requested.[61]

The Archives were prepared for Haussonville's visit. Despite the potential for conflict, the historian faced a revised archival regime that seemed to accommodate his wishes. Instead of turning Haussonville away or refusing him the right to see his documents, Laborde personally accepted the request, and Haussonville received a measured official response. The slip of paper he submitted with his list of desired documents was returned to him with the simple legend: "NOT FOUND." Surely the Archives could not be blamed for sequestering documents they did not even hold or at least that could not be found.

Despite these protocols, suspicions emerged among the prince and his allies that Haussonville had secretly received his desired documents with help from within the Archives. Attention turned to possible subversive elements lurking in the Archives. Orleanist agents were imagined to have infiltrated the institution and undermined the new regulations. A report hypothesized that, once removed from the watchful eye of other archivists,

the documents had been given to Haussonville either by turncoat employees or even by Laborde himself.[62] Laborde emphatically denied these accusations, claiming that he followed the policy to the letter. Despite his avowed devotion to liberal *publicité,* Laborde explained that he had intuitively understood the regime and practices of secrecy that were only now being explicitly asked of him. According to his report, he had implemented them all along in Haussonville's case, among others. For example, when Haussonville asked for the letters and reports of the Abbé Bernier, Laborde responded that nothing was found; however, he made sure that other requests were granted in order to avoid the criticism that the Empire might be "less liberal than previous governments" in its archival access. These granted requests were first examined with great care as Laborde sorted through the requested documents, removing a number of pieces that were judged too sensitive.[63]

There were significant limits, however, to the Imperial Archives' power to limit access to historical information. While complicated procedures and official directives might prevent a historian from viewing a particular document in the Imperial Archives, the archive available to historians far exceeded the limited central depository and its jurisdiction. There were other archival locations: Haussonville himself had remarked to Laborde that papers he had seen in the Imperial Archives were of little interest compared to other archival depositories that the government maintained (against Laborde's expressed wishes) and that provided documents more freely. Haussonville's archive stretched even beyond the borders of France, for he had consulted documents at the British Museum and Records Office. In fact, Laborde argued, the centralization of all historical documents under the gaze of the imperial archivist would do much to prevent such breaches in the future.[64] Beyond these official depositories, historians could look to published histories and document collections, prepared under the auspices of previous governments whose boundaries of publicity were drawn under different ideological and political pressures. Laborde reminded the emperor that the documents communicated to Haussonville had been submitted to scholarly scrutiny in earlier regimes, especially those communicated to, and copied by, Adolphe Thiers, who used them for his work on the First Empire.[65] These archival documents thus had been moved into the public domain, perhaps hastily due to the political climate at the time, removing the Archives' responsibility for the information contained therein.

Laborde's characterization of the limited influence of

the Imperial Archives in the scholarly universe of the Second Empire seems to contradict his call to let the "light of history" shine beyond once impenetrable Archives. This could be read as a simple defensive strategy in the face of criticism, proof that Laborde's politics (or personal comfort) trumped his commitment to scholarship. This apparent reversal, however, is not inconsistent with his calls for accessible archives. Laborde's position only appears contradictory if historical scholarship is considered a domain apart from the realm of politics. At this moment in the Archives' history, the relationship between historical research and politics was being renegotiated under pressure. While hardly a revolution from below, *publicité* recognized that authority and power derived from a complex web of relations that tied government to its subjects: public access to information about government and its past, the right to publish scholarship and political criticism, and the rights of the individual to privacy that varied when the private person entered public service, be it Napoleon (and his correspondence) or an archivist at work in the Archives.

The Imperial Archives was therefore an institution fraught with ambiguity and uncertainty, but scholars and statesmen ignored or denied this instability. Scholars needed the Archives, with their official imprimatur and privileged contents, to buttress professional claims to objective histories; the Empire needed the Archives to serve as the terrain of scientific history (if only insofar as those histories jibed with imperial interests) to protect its own claims to protect national patrimony. The *fact* of this intertwining of scholarship and politics, however, threatened to undermine the Archives' claims and the work of state and scholar at the same time. Liberal scholarship and liberal politics were both predicated on the notion of an individual, objective man freely entering the space of the Archives (or the polity, or the market) to arrive independently at, and eventually disseminate, the truth about history. Any relationship to evidence (and the state) had to be seen as objective and therefore unmediated by personal or political interests, in order for scholars or government to refer to the Archives.[66] This was especially true in the context of an increasingly professionalized study of history that required both archival evidence and an objective relationship to this evidence as a new foundation for its authority.

Ironically, it was the demands of rigorous historical practice—the use of archival evidence, the citing of sources—that brought the breaches of imperial archival policy to the attention of the government. While this practice invited other scholars to consult the same documents to draw their own conclusions as to the validity of a particular argument, it nevertheless created the conditions for the impossibility of this act. By alerting the very government that had expressly hidden them (or did not in fact have knowledge of their existence), the terms of access within the Archives could be retooled to prevent further trespass. A response of "not found" suggested that a document might have been lost to history (or at least its study), but not necessarily to the state. The Empire's protocols of *publicité*, however, did not mark a reactionary departure. Although decidedly undemocratic, this response was absolutely consonant with the Archives' status as a politically central institution as well as with post-Revolutionary French archival practice.

Whatever the merits of Laborde's solution, his ideological fitness, or the truth of his statement, the *affaire d'Haussonville* spelled the end of Laborde's otherwise illustrious tenure at the Imperial Archives. Laborde was retired to the *Sénat* in May of 1868, avoiding the public scandal of dismissal. The new director general, chosen in this period of embattlement verging on paranoia, was Alfred Maury, ironically also known as the first director of the Archives Nationales of the Third Republic. Maury had collaborated with Napoleon III on his abortive *History of Julius Caesar* project; thus his historical scholarship, at least, had imperial approval.

Evidence in the Press

Installing a new director did not immediately prevent new and more incendiary revelations, as Haussonville continued to present the Empire and its Archives with new challenges. In August of 1868, the *Revue* published yet another in the series of Haussonville's studies of the Empire's dealings with the Pope. This article posed new problems as it reproduced entire missives in print, effectively entering officially sequestered material into the public Archives. An internal memo judged this new tactic as a break with a tacit understanding over the use of evidence. Haussonville, putting aside what was officially called "propriety," cited not only the text of official letters but also, and most embarrassingly, a note that had been attached to the letters in question: "this letter is not to be inserted in the correspondence of Napoleon I."[67]

The official response revealed that, despite a battery of official decrees explicitly regulating access to and use of the Imperial Archives, the relationship between the state and the historian in the institution worked according to a set of unspoken rules of conduct. Haussonville had not broken any law, but his breach of propriety of archival comportment nonetheless raised the issue of what concerned officials at first approached as a question of right [*droit*]. An investigation questioned whether an author had the right to cite state papers "that could not have been officially communicated to him;" the report asked if there could be a right to publish a treaty or secret diplomatic note, publicly claiming that the document existed, but without providing proof in print. Such abstract questions, it was decided, could only be answered in the realm of law, and that was an unbearably public arena. Thus the issue of rights was tabled.[68]

If law meant a public acknowledgment of the tacit relationship between the good historian and the state in the Archives, *publicité* required a different solution. Ingeniously, Maury shifted emphasis from the notion of authorial right, which would have involved tarrying in the courts, to the more discreet world of administration and the question of the "duty" of employees of the state. The argument followed that, if indeed Haussonville had a right to cite nonpublished, secret documents; the onus would then fall to those "employees of the state that delivered these documents to him, documents that should remain secret and whose safekeeping was confided to their honor." If the propriety of historians was beyond the ken of archival regulation, the honor of archivist was surely the Empire's business. The archivists had evidently betrayed their duty and therefore the state (and by implication the nation) that engaged them.[69] The move from rights of the author to duty of the archivist illuminated the terms of the state-citizen contract. The state could not be seen as acting against the nation: it was in the exercise of a citizen's duty to the state that rights could be restricted, but also therefore granted, to the citizens of the nation.[70] Again, the Archives could be at once public and secret, but only within the bounds of a particular politics. The status of the Archives depended on the power of the state to define the public and its interest, hence the threat posed by public discussions of the terms of access to the Archives.

Thus, the threat Haussonville posed was not that he revealed secrets from the past that undermined the legitimacy of imperial government, but that his work exposed the Empire's claims to public Archives, in the largest sense of the term, as false. This was especially evident in the very public discussion of his most damaging work, the third volume of his *L'Église Romaine et le Premier Empire,* its documentary evidence as important as its narrative content in piquing public interest. In late October 1868, the *Journal de Paris* heralded the publication, citing the appearance of several of Napoleon's letters that

had not made it into the official *Correspondance.*[71] Other newspapers picked up this story in the coming days, notably *Le Temps* and the *Journal des Débats,* spreading the news of the publication that gave lie to the prince's pretensions. Reviews reproduced passages from two reports by the prince that highlighted his editorial hubris. A quote taken from the report that announced the release of the *Correspondance* reiterated the tie between memory, history, publicity, and government: "We submit the memory of Napoleon I to the following challenge—to expose the acts of his government to the light of day, discovering the secret of his most intimate thoughts. What government has revealed itself to history with such complete frankness?"[72] This pretension to transparency particularly galled the reviewers. The *Journal des Débats* opined, "The pride that breathes in this language is" (and here is the sting of the critique) "most legitimate, provided that the facts respond to the words."[73] Legitimate pride, unlike the rhetorical, historical, and legal fictions that propped up the second Bonaparte regime, rested on the consonance of statement and fact.

The prince's words rang particularly hollow given the documents in question—up to fourteen letters regarding the papal captivity, most expressing Napoleon's frustration with the Pope's intransigence. Prévost-Paradol, the outspoken liberal editor of the *Journal des Débats,* took the prince to task in its pages: "Were these letters insignificant to history, or filled with *thoughts* so *intimate* that the public would have nothing to see here, or were they compromising to a family name?" he asked. The answer, according to Prévost-Paradol's reading of the documents, was no: the letters were "of a purely historical interest, written in the tone the emperor habitually used when he had a complaint." Not surprisingly, some found sinister motives for the documents' absence, the *Journal* imagining that the prince often "recoiled in the face of the 'intimate thoughts'" of his uncle, suggesting these omissions implied the existence of many more.[74]

Le Temps weighed in with a particularly interesting line of criticism: praising Haussonville for his work and chastising the prince for shoddy scholarship, the paper focused on the prince's curious editorial judgments. The paper acknowledged that the prince perhaps omitted these documents in his attempt to interpret Napoleon's will, that the omissions were made, "and substantial ones at that," because the publishers believed it was their duty "to reveal Napoleon to posterity as he himself would want to appear." However, the choice of letters, even if this restraint was accepted, was curious. *Le Temps* found that the documents published "reveal nothing that is not in perfect conformity with the emperor's already familiar character."[75] This was the crux of the prince's miscalculation: although he was correct about the power of history (especially the figure of Napoleon) in the nation's imagination, he had overestimated the damaging effects of the Archives' contents. This "perfect conformity" of public imagination and the content of the state's Archives (what could be a better expression of the imperial ideal of the nation?) made the prince's intervention insulting and, more importantly, illegitimate.

The prince's protection of dynastic memory against the interests of national history was publicly revealed. The anxiety that drove his censorship seemed to be unfathomable, his mistrust of his audience seen as a sign of his arrogance. Calling the absence of the documents from the *Correspondance* "inexplicable," *Le Temps* called for a new edition.[76] The *Journal des Débats* wholeheartedly agreed, remarking on the "service" that Haussonville had rendered to the public and the commission, though it imagined that the historian would be too humble to accept it.[77] The modest author had served the public, the public archive (if not the official depository) was the richer for his efforts, and the conceit of imperial history was duly exposed.

Faced with yet another public challenge to its authority and integrity, the Archives' new administration considered its options within the limits of *publicité*. Again the new director general needed to devise a solution to quell imperial discontent with the Archives' administration and to stem the flow of information from the Archives to the public. Reiterating his aversion to public scrutiny, Maury firmly stated that "the evil is done, an inquest will fix nothing," preferring to let the archivists go about their daily business of serving the administration of the state rather than treating them as suspects in a political drama. The director moved away from the earlier systemic, historical analyses of the Archives and their function and instead treated the problem as the result of a transient act of poor judgment on the part of the former director general. Laborde, according to Maury, acted imprudently but not maliciously.[78] Maury was most concerned, however, that Haussonville had given the code of the documents (publicizing their existence and thus clearing the path for public requests). To solve this archival problem, Maury turned to the archival evidence, reading the texts that Haussonville had published against the letters in the Archives to understand the extent of the damage. Comparing the documents communicated to Haussonville to passages quoted in print, Maury concluded that there was enough evidence to sug-

gest that Haussonville had indeed enjoyed access to the Archives' copies of the letters.

Access, however, did not guarantee accuracy, for there were telling discrepancies between the documents held by the Archives and Haussonville's published versions. Although Haussonville's texts were "generally exact," Maury found them to contain noticeable variations in phrasing, additions, and omissions. These differences suggested the possibility that Haussonville had either seen the originals and quickly and sloppily copied them or had instead been handed unfaithful copies. Either way, there was an archivist to blame. The passages were generally convincing, as there was enough evidence to suggest that these documents were authoritative. Despite the inaccuracies their style was consistent with Napoleon's, as indicated by the reviews. Haussonville's copies in fact shed a gentler light on Napoleon than the archival version. Maury found Haussonville's emperor "more elegant, more correct."[79]

The implications of these incongruities—for Haussonville, for the Imperial Archives, for history—went without remark in the search for a solution to the Empire's problems with archival access. However, Maury's nonchalance, like Laborde's seemingly paradoxical commitment to historical truth and embrace of government control over access to that truth, suggests that this was a formative period in the history of archival knowledge. The Archives were hardly the sole arbiters of historical truth, despite professional historians' increasing reliance on official national depositories to police its limits. The Empire, however, was obsessed with the Haussonville affair for a different reason. Haussonville's attack on Napoleon's memory was troubling, but more significantly his work threatened to reveal the fiction of the Empire's claims to speak for national history in the nation's present—what Ernst Renan would later describe as a "daily plebiscite."[80] Thus the Imperial Archives stood not just as a storehouse of national memory, but as a symbol of France's history of conflict over this memory.

Coming to a final verdict on the Haussonville affair, Maury seemed to grasp both the power of the Archives as a national symbol and possibilities of publicity that had escaped his predecessor. In his final analysis, Maury's politically expedient reading of the Archives' past ingeniously placed the Imperial Archives outside of politics and history.[81] *L'affaire d'Haussonville* could be treated as an anomalous particularity chalked up to personal motivations and mistakes rather than as a systemic ill from which broad lessons could be drawn about the power of the Archives to negotiate the relationship between state and citizen. Maury solved the problem quietly, describing his actions in a postscript to a personal letter to the emperor: "I am in the process of locking up, under special order, several sensitive documents that I have put aside."[82] An archival, administrative solution was again in place. The Archives' public face would remain the modern, accessible institution devoted to research and the interests of the nation, while its internal workings were geared to protecting this image as fiercely as it protected the secrets of government.

Conclusion

In the Third Republic, the official documentation of the *Correspondance* and *l'affaire d'Haussonville* could be accessed and read by historians in the Archives. In 1897, Léon Lecestre, an archivist in the administrative section, published a volume of letters omitted from the so-called complete correspondence. In his prefatory remarks, Lecestre explained in a footnote that the second emperor had officially suppressed some of the documents within.[83] As well as providing an important corrective in print, Lecestre invited historians of the first Empire to consult the Archives Nationales in their new "liberal regime."[84] In 1902 Eugène Welvert read the Haussonville case as the triumph of the liberal, objective historian-citizen's faith in truth and history over the state's improper exercise of particularism and family privilege.[85] The refusal of documents to Haussonville and his subsequent vindication in the press could indeed be read as a lesson in good government.

In these works, the relationship between the historian and the Imperial Archives stood for the perverse relationship between citizen and state in the Second Empire and its correction in the Third Republic. Haussonville confronted the limits imposed by an illegitimate government, expressed in restriction of access to the Archives. The state's intervention in the work of the historian, and its own attempts to produce historical work, was evidence of the Empire's unjust inversion of the relationship of politics to scholarship. When this injustice was redressed in the press, truth was eventually served. Rigorous historical practice won out as part of a vigorous civil society, and the Empire eventually fell. Moreover, Lecestre and Welvert could be seen as living and working proof of the Third Republic's liberality in archival (and by extension political) matters. Historical truth had finally found its vindication in the proper relationship of state to citizen.

Looking at the history of the Archives through the lens of publicity suggests that the workings of power within and without this institution were more complicated. One place where nascent democracy could be (and, for the Empire, had to be) squelched was within an institution historically and legally situated at the crossroads of the public and government—the Imperial Archives. Because of the special nature of the institution, however, the Empire could not simply close the Archives. Publicity limited its range of possible solutions as it offered novel ways of skirting old problems. Ironically, however, it was the very requirement of publicity that made public access an even more remote possibility. The Empire's response privileged the exercise of administrative rather than traditional political power, and it pushed the question of access and Archives further away from their revolutionary roots—as potential tools for a historically and politically informed (and thus powerful) citizenry.

Changes in archival policy came from and were constrained by the increasing cultural capital of the Archives as a seat of national history and memory and by the power of this history to define what counted as the nation. However, just as conflicting "memories" of Napoleon Bonaparte might have made for inaccurate histories (for of course both the prince and Haussonville took liberties), documents and policy could only make sense from within this fundamentally cultural and political framework. Anticipating Renan, the Imperial Archives could be seen as that place where the nation of "convergent facts" confronted the equally constitutive process of conflicting interpretation.[86]

As this essay suggests, the Archives were indeed as saturated with historical and political significance as with historical and political information. The Imperial Archives, however, did not passively contain the evidence necessary for legitimate politics or objective histories, nor did the shape of the institution merely reflect easily recognizable political interests. The lens of publicity allows us to view the Imperial Archives as an institution constituted in complex, contested histories and complicated politics—an institution that also actively helped shape the boundaries of the politically possible and the historically legible.[87]

NOTES

1. Karl Marx, *The Eighteenth Brumaire of Louis Bonaparte* (New York, 1963), 15.
2. Archives Nationales (hereafter AN) AB VI 1, "Rapport de M. le directeur général à S. Ex. le ministre d'Etat, sur le

développement excessif des archives spéciales de l'administration, et sur l'exécution du décret qui prescrit la rédaction des inventaires et leur réunion aux Archives de l'Empire," March 15, 1858.

3. AN AB VI 1, "Rapport de M. le directeur général à S. Ex. le ministre d'Etat, sur le développement excessif des archives spéciales de l'administration, et sur l'exécution du décret qui prescrit la rédaction des inventaires et leur réunion aux Archives de l'Empire,"March 15, 1858.

4. There is a dearth of histories of the French Archives. For an overview of the history of the Archives of France, see Françoise Hildesheimer, "Les Archives de France, mémoire de l'histoire," *Histoire et Archives* special issue 1 (1997), and Kryztof Pomian, "Les archives du Trésor des chartes au CARAN," in Pierre Nora, ed. *Les Lieux de mémoire*, vol. 3, book 3 (*Les Frances*) (Paris, 1992), 192–200. For a discussion of the status of archives, history, and politics at the end of the Ancien Régime, see Keith Michael Baker, *Inventing the French Revolution* (Cambridge, 1990), 31–106. For a discussion of the archives, historians, and government in the sixteenth through eighteenth centuries, see Blandine Barret-Kriegel's series *Les Historiens et la monarchie* (Paris, 1988), 4 vols.

5. See Pim Den Boer, *History as a Profession: The Study of History in France, 1818–1914,* Arnold J. Pomerans, trans. (Princeton, 1998), esp. 80–98; Stéphane Gerson, "*Pays* and Nation: The Uneasy Transformation of an Historical Patrimony in France, 1830–1870" (Ph.D. diss., University of Chicago, 1997).

6. For an analysis of Laborde's project of *publicité* and the history of the Archives of the Second Empire, see the dissertation from which this essay is culled: Jennifer Milligan, "Making a Modern Archives: The Archives Nationales of France, 1850–1887" (Ph.D. diss., Rutgers University, 2002).

7. There is an interesting shift in the definitions of *publicité* between the 1798 and 1835 versions of the *Dictionnaire de l'Académie française* that suggests the increasing inscription of this political and social concept in the law and in the nation's legal and political imaginary. The 1798 edition defines *publicité* as simply "*notoriété*," providing the following example: "*La publicité du crime le rende encore plus punissable.*" The 1835 edition adds to *notoriété* with the following definition and example: "*Il signifie plus ordinairment la qualité de ce qui est rendu public. La publicité des débats judiciaires en matière criminelle est consacrée par la charte.*"

8. See, for instance, Barret-Kriegel's series *Les Historiens et la monarchie* and Donald R. Kelley, "Jean du Tillet, Archivist and Antiquary," *Journal of Modern History* 38:4 (1966), 337–54.

9. There is a vast literature on the shifting and contested meanings of "public" and "nation" in the French Revolution and its impact on the development of the modern French polity. Although this essay does not specifically address this problem, it is informed by works such as: Keith Michael Baker, *Inventing the French Revolution: Essays on French Political Culture in the Eighteenth Century* (Cambridge, UK, 1990); Roger Chartier, *The Cultural Origins of the French Revolution*, Keith M. Baker and Steven L. Kaplan, eds. (Durham, NC, 1990); François Furet, *Interpreting the French Revolution* (Cambridge, UK, 1981); Daniel Gordon, *Citizens Without Sover-*

eignty: Equality and Sociability in French Thought 1671–1789 (Princeton, NJ, 1994); Lynn A. Hunt, *Politics, Culture and Class in the French Revolution* (Berkeley, CA, 1994); William H. Sewell, *A Rhetoric of Bourgeois Revolution: The Abbé Sieyés and What is the Third Estate* (Durham, NC, 1994).

10. For a discussion of the Revolutionary legislation, see A. Outrey, "La notion traditionnelle de titre et les origines de la législation révolutionnaire sur les archives," *Revue historique de droit français et étranger,* 5:1955, 438–63. For an analysis of the legislation in light of current archival politics, see Sonia Combe, *Archives interdites: Les peurs françaises face à l'Histoire contemporaine* (Paris, 1994), 79–102. Michel Duchein and Hildesheimer argue a different perspective: see Duchein, "L'Accès aux Archives en France de Messidor an II à Janvier 1979: Libéralisme et frilosités," *in Histoires d'Archives: Receuil d'articles offert à Lucie Favier par ses collègues et amis* (Paris, 1997), 59–69; Hildesheimer, "Échec aux Archives: La difficile affirmation d'une administration," *Bibliothèque de L'École des chartes,* 156:1998, 91–106.

11. The question of the right to access—its history, its limits, and its possibilities—haunts the history of the central Archives of France. The Revolutionary legislation on access is not seen as particularly "revolutionary" by archivists currently writing on the history of the Archives. Whether or not the archives *really were* accessible does not diminish the rhetorical and political force of the historical question of the *possibility* of access introduced at the Revolution. Combe, *Archives interdites;* cf. Duchein, "L'Accès aux Archives en France," and Hildesheimer, "Échec aux Archives."

12. Pim Den Boer, *History as a Profession: The Study of History in France, 1818–1914,* Arnold J. Pomerans, trans. (Princeton, NJ, 1998), 86; cf. Hildesheimer, "Les Archives nationales aux XIXe siècle: Établissement administratif ou scientifique," *Histoire et Archives* I (Jan–June 1997), 105–35.

13. The Musée des Archives was opened to the public in 1867. Like many of Laborde's projects, it was an expansion of a pre-existing museum—the Musée Sigilographique—with a more limited theme and public.

14. Laborde's quarrel with the Library is discussed in Hildesheimer, "Les Archives nationales aux XIXe siècle." For the official version, see Felix Ravaisson, *Rapport adressé à Son Exc. Le ministre d'Etat au nom de la commission instituée le 23 avril 1861* (Paris, 1862).

15. On the politics of Louis Napoleon and the Second Empire, see most recently Sudhir Hazareesingh, *From Subject to Citizen: The Second Empire and the Emergence of Modern French Democracy* (Princeton, NJ, 1998). See also Michael Truesdell, *Spectacular Politics: Louis-Napoleon Bonaparte and the* Fête Impériale *1849–1870* (New York, 1997); Juliet Wilson Bareau, *Manet, the Execution of Maximilian: Painting, Politics and Censorship* (Princeton, NJ, 1992); Phillip Nord, *The Republican Moment* (Princeton, NJ, 1995); David Pinkney, *Napoleon III and the Rebuilding of Paris* (Princeton, NJ, 1972); and Vincent Wright, *Le Conseil d'État sous le second Empire* (Paris, 1972).

16. Lord Acton, "Notes on Archival Researches 1864–1888," in Damian McElrath, *Lord Acton: The Decisive Decade, 1864–1874; Essays and Documents,* Bibliothèque de la Revue d'Histoire Ecclésiastique, 51 (Louvain, 1970), 131.

17. Roger L. Williams, *The World of Napoleon III: 1851–1870* (New York, 1957), 179.

18. Hazareesingh, *From Subject to Citizen*, 29. See also Phillip Nord's important work *The Republican Moment: Struggles for Democracy in Nineteenth-Century France* (Cambridge, 1995).

19. Bonnie G. Smith, *The Gender of History: Men, Women and Historical Practice* (Cambridge, 1998).

20. Works that examine the operation and meaning of "memory," looking at the way it functions as a powerful and historically specific figure, include Matt K. Matsuda, *The Memory of the Modern* (New York, 1996); Daniel J. Sherman, *The Construction of Memory in Interwar France* (Chicago, 1999); Richard Terdiman, *Present Past* (Ithaca, NY, 1993); and Yael Zerubavel, *Recovered Roots: Collective Memory and the Making of Israeli National Tradition* (Chicago, 1995). Precisely on this point is the excellent critique of the *Lieux de mémoire* project in Steve Englund, "The Ghost of Nation Past," *Journal of Modern History* 64 (June 1992): 299–320.

21. There is a vast literature on the problem of citizenship in France. A few works that inform my understanding are Etienne Balibar, *Masses, Classes, Ideas: Studies on Politics and Philosophy Before and After Marx* (New York, 1994); Rogers Brubaker, *Citizenship and Nationhood in France and Germany* (Cambridge, MA, 1992); Pierre Rosanvallon, *Le Sacré du Citoyen: Histoire du suffrage universel en France* (Paris, 1992); Joan Scott, *Only Paradoxes to Offer: French Feminists and the Rights of Man* (Cambridge, MA, 1996).

22. For a recent example, Maurice Papon was able to bring a personal defamation suit against historian Jean-Luc Einaudi for making statements, based on then classified archival evidence, about Papon's involvement in the deaths of over two hundred "French of Muslim origin" during a protest in October of 1961. See *Le Procès Papon* (Paris, 1998); Richard J. Golsan, ed., *The Papon Affair: Memory and Justice on Trial* (New York, 2000).

23. Hildesheimer, "Les Archives nationales aux XIXe siècle."

24. Cf. Léon de Laborde, *Les Archives de la France, leur vicissitudes pendant la Révolution, leur régénération sous l'Empire* (Paris, 1867); Joyce Appleby et al., *Telling the Truth about History* (New York, 1994).

25. Appeared as *Napoleon I, Empereur de France: Correspondance. Publié par ordre de l'Empereur Napoléon III*, 28 vols. (Paris, 1858–69).

26. Original commission members included Prosper Merimée and a host of political and academic figures: Baron Charles Dupin, Senator and member of the Institut; Count Boulay de la Meurthe, Senator; Senator Aupick; Members of the Conseil d'Etat Lefebvre and Chasseriau; and Perron from the Ministry of State. AN AB Va 8.

27. *Correspondance de Napoléon I*, vol. I (Paris, 1858), 1.

28. Ibid.

29. The Prince Napoleon-Charles-Joseph-Paul Bonaparte, also known as Plon-Plon (and hereafter referred to simply as the prince) played a curious part in the family and political dramas of the Second Empire. Touted as "the most brilliant failure of the century" by a commentator after his death in 1870, the prince embodied seemingly contradictory impulses: the spirit of 1848 (which pushed him even to publish a letter calling for an end to monarchies in Europe, signing the letter "citizen Bonaparte") and a wish to ascend the imperial throne that was forever out of his reach The prince's work first appeared with volume XVI of the *Correspondance*. For more on the prince, see Edgar Holt, *Plon-Plon: The Life of Prince Napoleon (1822–1891)* (London, 1973).

30. In 1861 Laborde was called to testify for the archives in a case that challenged the prince's right to claim his place in the Bonaparte dynasty. Laborde was asked to verify the authenticity of a document pronouncing the annulment of the marriage of Elizabeth Patterson to Jerome Bonaparte, the prince's father and Napoleon Bonaparte's brother. The case, brought by the Pattersons, was perhaps not surprisingly ruled in favor of the prince in imperial family court. See Milligan, "Making a Modern Archives," ch. 4.

31. AN F17 13544, report dated December 1864.

32. Letter dated July 1864. See Ernest d'Hautrive, *Napoléon III et le Prince Napoléon* (Paris, 1923).

33. AN AB Va 8, letter dated June 29, 1864.

34. Some of those turned away from the Archives' door include Michelet, Adolphe Thiers, and the Strickland sisters. On difficulties of archival access and the Strickland sisters, see Smith, *The Gender of History*, 65, 116–122; On Michelet in the Archives, see Arthur Mitzman, "Michelet et la révolution romantique," *Michelet ou la subversion du passé: Quatre leçons au Collège de France* (Paris, 1999), 128–9; On Thiers, see J. P. T. Bury and R. P. Tombs, *Thiers, 1797–1872: A Political Life* (London, 1986), 138–40.

35. Hildesheimer, "Les Archives de France, mémoire de l'histoire," 43.

36. For the state of historical studies in nineteenth century France, see Boer, *History as a Profession*; C. O. Carbonell, *Histoire et Historiens: Une mutation idéologique des historiens français, 1865–1885* (Toulouse, 1976); Kelley, *Historians and the Law in Postrevolutionary France* (Princeton, NJ, 1984); William Keylor, *Academy and Community: The Foundation of the French Historical Profession* (Cambridge, MA, 1975); Gérard Noiriel "Naissance du métier d'historien," *Genèses*, 1:1990, 58–85; Smith, *The Gender of History*, 130–56.

37. The reading room was limited to functionaries, laureates, doctors, archivists, and students of the École des Chartes.

38. For a contemporary discussion of the problems of access to the Archives of the Ministry of Foreign Affairs, see Armand Baschet, *Histoire du Dépôt des Archives des Affaires Etrangères à Paris, au Louvre en 1710, à Versailles en 1763 et de nouveau à Paris en divers endroits depuis 1786* (Paris, 1875).

39. Noiriel is especially clear on the absolute difference between historical research and writing in the early part of the century and the end of the Second Empire into the Republic, and the role of archival research in establishing "objectivity." See Noiriel, "Naissance du métier d'historien."

40. Article 2 required that "all documents of public interest whose conservation is deemed useful, and that are no longer necessary to the service of ministerial departments or their auxiliary administrations, are to be deposited in the Archives of the Empire."

41. Article 35 called for requests for documents to be submitted in writing, and that these requests be precise descriptions of the objects requested. Inaccurate or vague descriptions

would result in the dismissal of the request. The significance of detailed and public inventories is here made apparent. Article 39 allowed that "members and laureats of the *Institut*, doctors of one of the *Facultés, archivistes-palégraphes* [graduates of the École des Chartes], and students of the *École des chartes* will be given immediate attention to their requests" and would promptly receive either the requested documents or "the reason for the refusal."

42. AN AB Va 8, letter dated June 29, 1864.

43. AN F17 13544, report dated December 1864.

44. AN F17 13544, dossier "affaire d'Haussonville," letter dated September 28, 1867.

45. On the Vatican archives see Owen Chadwick, *Catholicism and History: The Opening of the Vatican Archives* (Cambridge, UK, 1978); and McElrath, *Lord Acton.*

46. For Sybel's reading of the Revolution, see Heinrich von Sybel, *History of the French Revolution,* Walter C. Perry, tr. (London, 1867).

47. AN F17 13544, letter dated September 28, 1867

48. For an excellent and exhaustive discussion of histories of Napoleon in the nineteenth and twentieth centuries, see Pieter Geyl, *Napoleon: For and Against,* Olive Renier, tr. (New Haven, CT, 1963 [1949]). For Haussonville, see 106–32. See also G. P. Gooch's classic *History and Historians in the Nineteenth Century* (London, 1919), esp. 241–64.

49. At first glance the offense seems obvious, as any work on the Roman question would be scandalous in a period when the Second Empire was treading carefully between their support for the republic and the Vatican. The prince, however, was unequivocal in his support of Garibaldi and would have had no qualms about lauding a book that embarrassed both current Empire and Papacy. For more on the Roman question, see Alexis de Tocqueville, "Speech by M. de Tocqueville on the Roman Expedition delivered in the Legislative Assembly on October Eighteenth, 1849," in *Recollections of Alexis de Tocqueville,* translated by Alexandre Teixeira de Mattos, J. P. Mayer, ed. (London, 1948), 331–45.

50. Joseph-Othenin-Bernard de Cléron d'Haussonville (1809–84) had a long and minor diplomatic and political career before retiring in 1852 and turning to historical writing and political criticism. Among his works: *Histoire de la politique éxterieur du gouvernement français, 1830–1848,* 2 vols. (Paris, 1850); *Histoire de la Reunion de la Lorraine à la France,* 4 vols. (Paris, 1854–59); *Ma Jeunesse, 1814–1830* (Paris, 1886); and the work in question, *L'Église romaine et le premier empire 1800–1814: Avec notes, correspondances diplomatiques et pièces justicatives entièrement inédites par M. le Comte d'Haussonville,* 5 vols. (Paris, 1868–69).

51. See Boer, *History as a Profession,* 78–98.

52. AN F17 13544, letter dated September 28, 1867.

53. AN, F17 13544, report dated December 1864.

54. AN F17 13544, dossier "affaire d'Haussonville," letter dated September 28, 1867.

55. Ibid.

56. Ibid.

57. AN F17 13544, letter dated October 14, 1867.

58. Ibid.

59. For a discussion of the changes in archivist's duties under Laborde's tenure, see Hildesheimer, "Les Archives aux XIXe siècle," and Milligan, "Making a Modern Archives," ch. 3.

60. AN F17 13544, letter dated October 14, 1867.

61. AN F17 13544, letter dated February 29, 1868.

62. Ibid.

63. AN F17 13544, letter dated March 9, 1868

64. AN F17 13544, dossier "affaire d'Haussonville," letter dated March 9, 1868.

65. AN F17 13544, letter dated March 9, 1868. Adolphe Thiers's *Le Consulat et L'Empire* (Paris, 1860) had already been the object of the prince's ire, for volume XVII contained a letter from Jerome Bonaparte Patterson arguing that Thiers's characterization of his parent's marriage was false. The prince Napoleon was not given an opportunity to add his own analysis. In the atmosphere of the Patterson case, this history took on a very specific political resonance, as seen earlier in this essay.

66. For an especially trenchant analysis of the positioning of the liberal subject in the professionalization of history and its relationship to nation building and politics, see Smith, *The Gender of History.*

67. AN F17 13546 letter dated October 28, 1868. The prince had put them in a special dossier (now housed in AN AB Va 8) marked 14 *"lettres inedit, lettres à garde,"* the legend followed by the prince's signature.

68. Ibid.

69. Ibid.

70. The Decree of 1855 also prohibited archivists from publishing any document, portion of a document, or work based on documents without prior authorization from the director general.

71. Paul Clère, untitled article, *Journal de Paris,* October 18, 1868.

72. Charles du Bouzet, untitled article, *Le Temps,* October 22, 1868; Prévost-Paradol, *Journal des Débats,* October 21, 1868.

73. Prévost-Paradol, untitled article, *Journal des Débats,* October 21, 1868.

74. Ibid.

75. Charles du Bouzet, untitled article, *Le Temps,* October 22, 1868.

76. Ibid.

77. Prévost-Paradol, untitled article, *Journal des Débats,* October 21, 1868.

78. AN F17 13544, dossier "affaire d'Haussonville," letter dated November 9, 1868. Emphasis in the original.

79. Ibid.

80. E. Renan, "What is a Nation?" Martin Thom, trans., in *Nation and Narration,* Homi K. Bhabha, ed. (New York, 1990), 19.

81. For a discussion of the stakes of administrative vs. judicial jurisdictions, see H. S. Jones, *The French State in Question* (Cambridge, UK, 1993), 85–111.

82. AN F17 13544, dossier "affaire d'Haussonville," letter dated November 9, 1868.

83. Léon Lecestre, *Lettres inédites de Napoléon 1er.* 2 vols. (Paris, 1897), vol. 1, n.1. An English translation was published in the United States within a year. The *New Letters of Napoleon I: Omitted from the Edition Published under the Auspices of Napoleon III,* 2 vols., Lady Mary Loyd, tr. (New

York, 1898) paraphrased the Lecestre preface, lauding the confessional qualities of the letters and passing over the reference to the Archives.

84. Lecestre, *Lettres inédites de Napoléon 1er,* vol. 1, vii.

85. E. Welvert, "La querelle du Prince Napoléon et du comte d'Haussonville," *Correspondance historique et archeologique,* August–September 1905, 225–51.

86. Renan, "What is a Nation?" 11–12.

87. The Third Republic was the zenith of the positivist movement in French historical studies. Historians such as Gabriel Monod, Ernst Lavisse, and of course Charles Seignobos and Charles Victor Langlois (also, notably, director general of the Archives Nationales from 1913 to 1929) consciously connected the republican project to the possibilities of objective scholarship. See Noiriel, *Sur la 'crise' de l'histoire* (Paris, 1996), esp. chap. 2, "La Formation d'une discipline scientifique," 47–89; Keylor, *Academy and Community,* 36–55, 75–90; Smith, *The Gender of History,* 130–56.

Not Dragon at the Gate but Research Partner

The Reference Archivist as Mediator

Kathleen Marquis

In a keynote address given to the Spring 2000 Midwest Archives Conference meeting (hereafter Sawyer Seminar), Francis Blouin set out the founding principles for this seminar as a dialogue between historians and other scholars, and the archivists who maintain documentary collections for research use. As became clear from the seminar conversations that ensued, the concept of "archive" has a broader range of definitions than those of us who are practitioners in the field might have imagined. What also became clear was that the archivist's role in the maintenance of this documentation was not at all clear.

Many of the participants, citing the derivation of the term *archives* "from the Latin *archivuum,* 'residence of the magistrate,'" appeared to conflate past and present accessibility of archival documentation. For many, the concept of archives was a purely theoretical one: "In cultural theory, 'the archive' is endowed with a capital "A," is figurative, and leads elsewhere. It may represent neither material site nor a set of documents. Rather it may serve as a strong metaphor for any corpus of selective forgettings and collections," wrote one participant. The singular lack of interest in the realities of current archival practice and theory was demonstrated by the lack of attendance by these scholars at later seminar sessions on archival topics.

Most disturbing, however, were statements such as "Foucault [in his *Archaeology of Knowledge*] provocatively warned [that] the archive is neither the sum of all texts that a culture preserves nor those institutions that allow for that record and preservation."[1] It is a useful warning to current archivists that such a perception still exists. We are only too aware that, through selection and

other factors affecting the availability of texts for collection, we house only a fraction of history's documents. Archivists also assume, perhaps naively, that our researchers have always subjected these texts to scrutiny and skepticism as to their meanings and origins.

At the same time, Blouin and others challenged archivists with the "need to become more self-aware of our role as mediators . . . between records creators and records repositories, between archives and users, between conceptions of the past and extant documentation."[2]

While I absolutely believe that the archivist has agency in the research process, I would characterize it instead as a consultancy, and myself as a partner in research.[3] I will explain this more fully later in this essay.

First, however, I have found that the fluidity of the concept of archives, among those who use archival documents but do not claim archivist as a profession, is quite disconcerting. I believe a brief digression about the purpose of keeping archives is in order. I hope to show that much of what characterizes what I consider to be an archives also highlights the contributions that I, as a reference archivist, bring to the research partnership: my knowledge of the breadth of the collections, the nature of recordkeeping, and the contextual information that gives documents their "greater than the sum of their parts" meaning.

The Repeatable Experiment

Elizabeth Yakel, in her article "Thinking Inside and Outside the Boxes: Archival Reference Services at the Close of the Twentieth Century," has put it most succinctly: "The enduring value of archives is partly that certain records can be continuing sources of knowledge."⁴ While this may no longer be the scholar's concept of archives, it is the foundation of all that the archivist works toward: the collection and description of documents to be universally available for study by anyone. The corollary most applicable to the reference archivist is that these documents should not be changed by their use but remain available for future generations to study, to use to gain new insights, and to make further comparisons.

While some very real criticisms can be leveled at the varied processes of collecting over time, there are two distinct concepts here: whether every documentary collection is necessarily incomplete, and whether anything can be an archive.

Blouin notes that "instead of directing the process of uncovering the past through available fragments, the archive is subordinated as one contested element in a variety of tangible and nontangible elements that help construct a sense, an image, a theory, or a representation of a particular past."⁵ So, are we all archivists of our own archives? That does cast a different light on the guidelines for archival use: respect original order, remove nothing from the repository, maintain an emphasis on preservation and provenance. An archival repository attempts to guarantee that all researchers' experience with a collection of documents will begin with the same available set—regardless of which collections they select or what conclusions they may draw from each collection. Other archives are, in our terms, ephemeral or inconsistent, or harder to access, or subject to interpretation by a donor still in control of the collection. All facts may be facts, all social memory useful, and all understandings valid. But, if I can't follow a set of citations and examine what was used to come to the conclusions, then there will always be just one interpretation of that fact or understanding. Archivists strive to make just the opposite possible.

Indeed, there is an implied responsibility of the archivist to guarantee, or at least be able to explain or appraise, the evidential value of documents retained by an archives. There is no question that many experiences remain undocumented. For the past several decades it has been a major aim of archivists, many educated at the same time as the new social historian, to seek out this more ephemeral documentation and enrich their collections with a broader view of society. But, once the documents were located (or even created, in the case of the growing body of oral history collections), they became

part of the archives. As such, their keepers were charged with the dual responsibilities of making them widely known and available—and guaranteeing that they remained the way they were found, unaltered and identical for each researcher.

A postmodernist approach might decree that all meanings derived from our collections are valid and useful. But the archivist still feels a responsibility to impart the original constructs—old meanings of words or contextual realities that obtained when the documents were created—for the interested researcher.

This brings us back to the concept of mediation, and the role of the reference archivist. I should clarify, first, that there are many ways in which archivists mediate between documentation and researcher. Deciding how to focus a collection, what to collect, which portions of a collection to preserve, and arranging and describing these materials for public use all inherently shape the user's perceptions of their research topic. In this essay, however, I will focus on the mediated experience of the reference interaction. Whether this happens face to face or in a digital environment, attitudes, intentions, and awareness can entirely change what the researcher discovers and whether he or she is successful in locating all the archival sources that will be useful for the project undertaken.

Dragon at the Gate?

I am very aware that archivists and researchers often play adversarial roles. Some of this comes from misconceptions about who makes access decisions and how, and a distaste for what seem like too many, or too capricious, sets of rules. Some of it also comes from a sense of ownership, not shared with the researcher, which I have observed in too many of my colleagues. When I was at the MIT Archives, the archivist told us of her predecessor, who had carefully collected the files from an institute-wide committee on academic values. But, when the faculty member who deposited those records came back to refer to them several months later, he was told, "Oh no. You can't see those now. They're in the *archives.*" Case closed. Needless to say, much of our challenge in administering the archives consisted of undoing this impression and encouraging use.

One of the most important ways in which the reference archivist can mediate the experience of a researcher in the archives is to continue what one of my colleagues calls "the conversation."⁶ This is not a particularly startling concept, but it ensures that the mutually educational process ("what are you finding?"/ "what does this say?") continues unimpeded.

The first step in mediation is to ensure that what can sometimes be an antagonistic relationship instead begins to build a research team. If the communication is bad, it often ensures that the rest of the research enterprise never even happens. Researchers come in to pick up a quick answer and then discover that it will be a long search process, and they must wait while items are retrieved, one at a time, and they can't copy things themselves, and half the collections are in offsite storage. Empowerment is actually a very helpful way to look at reference. Not wanting to look incompetent is as important a research motivator as creating research products such as getting an A on a paper or meeting a report deadline. We see it on researchers' faces as they walk in the door, we hear it in their defensive comments over the phone and e-mail.

Archival researchers often begin their interactions with "I'm new here," or "I don't know anything," or "This is going to sound stupid."[7] Clearly the first task of the archivist is not going to be defining provenance or copyright or scope and content notes. Before any other interaction can take place the archivist must make the researcher feel welcome and attended to, and that, yes, it is very possible to navigate this place and get some good and useful information for his or her project. Oh, and could you lock up all your belongings and put away your pen and we may ask you to wear gloves and come back later for your copies. It is a difficult balancing act for the reference archivist to simultaneously communicate the desirability of the researcher's presence and also the necessity of obeying rules regarding access and handling to ensure the preservation of what the researcher wants to use.

This is where archivists play an educational role. I like to stress the treasure hunt aspect of archival research with the media and with the public: it can be a tough job, but there really is treasure at the end of the hunt. And we as reference archivists are here to show you where and how to dig so that the process doesn't seem so mystifying and impossible.

This brings us back to empowerment. Archivists' pride, too, is on the line. Some of my proudest moments have been when an unhappy or disgruntled researcher feels heard and ends up having a productive time in my reading room. By assisting researchers and managing a good outcome, rather than by using our authority to point out only what they are doing incorrectly, archivists win as do the researchers. Saving face sounds like a self-

ish motivation, but it's often the reality of these interactions. The trick is to make it work for the partnership, not against it.

When I was the reference archivist at MIT, I conducted a reference interview with a visiting historian of science. He arrived asking to see what sources we had in the history of nuclear medicine. Immediately my mind began racing to the answer I thought he wanted—and coming up blank because MIT doesn't have a medical school. I felt ignorant about the nature of the topic—not an uncommon occurrence in that job—but I took a breath and said, "You know, I really don't know anything about nuclear medicine. Can you tell me a bit about it and we can see where that might lead us?" It turned out he was exploring the medical applications of research in physics, and in that field we had an abundance of collections. The researcher spent several days using personal and institute records in the archives. Braving my own sense of embarrassment to learn from him allowed me to be of much greater use in providing information about the history and organizational structure of my institution.

Reference Archivist Roles

On a typical day we play more roles than Alec Guinness in the film *Kind Hearts and Coronets*. Every day we play the roles of tour guide, teacher, consultant, salesperson, matchmaker—and certainly mediator. Each role uses different aspects of our knowledge as reference specialists and archivists to connect the wide variety of researchers interested in using our collections, the various finding aids and tools archivists construct to make the materials accessible—and the actual documents themselves.

The first step is outreach: this can be as complicated as an interactive online exhibit featuring primary source material, or as simple as making sure the archives is represented in the brochure rack at the library. The general principle is the same: archivists try never to assume that their publics understand the value of archival materials, how these materials can be useful in their professional or personal lives, or how to discover what we have and how to use it. In my position as reference archivist at an academic archives, I placed a high priority on reaching out to students and faculty, to whom I offered introductions that could be titled "What's an Archives and What'll It Get You?"[8] I also worked with administrators whose noncurrent records are held in the library. Much of this work could be summed up as the antithesis of the example I gave above: "Oh yes. Please use those records now that they're in the archives. Case opened!" We don't wait for researchers to find us. At every opportunity, we insert ourselves into the research process with reminders of the richness of our holdings and research assistance we provide.

Much of the educational work of the reference archivist does come in the form of deliberate instruction, such as orientation sessions, and online tutorials such as Yale University's.[9] Just as often, though, this education is the less formal one-on-one orientation, in-house or via e-mail, in using and interpreting primary sources. This skill is surprisingly rarely taught in any academic curriculum, so the researcher often finds him- or herself with a box of raw material and no experience in placing it within a context or evaluating its contemporary meaning. The reference archivist comes to recognize a variety of signals from a crooked finger, a tentative "excuse me?" or "hey you," all of which indicate this confusion. Our job is to help them puzzle through the item, ask the larger questions, assist in reading the ancient handwriting, explain an outdated form, help place the correspondent within the organization's hierarchy at the time of the document's creation, or suggest related reading. Often, for example, researchers don't make the connection between a faculty member as private researcher and the records they may have created in an administrative role. Helping researchers to make these connections and to think in a different way is part of the ongoing education that takes place in archival reading rooms every day. More importantly, we convey to researchers the skills to make these connections on their own the next time they encounter a puzzling bit of what Blouin calls the "available fragments of history."

Yakel also stresses the translator role of the archivist and adds that translators must understand both languages or cultures to function well.[10] Researchers approach us with questions phrased in the language of their own discipline. We rephrase the question, adding information about the nature of our records, as well as instruction in how to understand the language of our search engine, the cataloging and filing rules of the Online Computer Library Center (OCLC) database, Library of Congress (LC) descriptions, and the structure of our individual online catalogs. Indeed, LC subject headings and "neutral" descriptive language are often arcane, value laden, and hopelessly behind the times. New "natural language" keyword searches are better, as they aren't dependent on the LC authority over various iterations—but the natural language is that of the cataloguer, nonetheless. Regardless, these standardized descriptive

conventions are how our collections are to be understood. It is the reference archivist's job to translate the language and impart the skills needed to use the research tools.

Clearly, another significant role of the reference archivist is in training researchers to think like archivists.[11] This is not to say that we train them to be archivists. It means that the concept of understanding a bureaucracy in order to request the records from the appropriate office, or to think about how an individual organized their files in order to know which box to request, is a foreign one to our users. This is a perfect example of the archivist as translator; archives have a language all their own that shows no immediate signs of changing. "Scope and content note," "provenance," "EAD"—even "finding aid"—usually draws a blank ("Finding what?" I'm often asked). We not only translate the lingo of the archivist, we also convey the value of the concepts communicated by these terms: how would you express the merits of a scope and content note? And, more importantly, how would you, in just a sentence or two, sell the researcher on not skipping past this useful information to head straight for the tantalizing box list (which they do every day)?

The most traditional archival finding aid, for example, is based on a strictly hierarchical structure. Organizations exist in hierarchies, and the records of their officers are arranged that way. Even the finding aids themselves run—at least until the Encoded Archival Description (EAD) format bled the lines between physical and intellectual order—on an implacable hierarchy of series, box, folder. The series are described in the front matter, then lists of their contents follow. Series are in order but broken across boxes. Boxes are listed at the beginning but not with each folder. Once the concept is explained, it is easy to follow, but until then even the most sophisticated researcher, unfamiliar with archives, will approach us and ask us to explain how this "book" (finding aid) works. Online finding aids follow the same structure, and we are beginning to think of general instructions to orient researchers to the most effective use of these new widely available tools. Wading through this structure and translating as I go often does remind me of being a tour guide. If the past is a foreign country, then educating researchers about using archives can feel like conducting a Berlitz course.

In fact, in archival reference workshops I begin with a brainstorming session where we write down "What Every Researcher Should Know." This results in a list of what we wish researchers entering our reading rooms, or accessing us by electronic means, to understand about how archives work. In addition to the usual procedural rules, there are the assumptions that archivists make: about the hierarchical structure, about respecting original order, about the fact that most collections are organized as their creator or author intended, not rearranged for some future research use. These concepts, too, must be translated or explained—and we don't even all agree on them: witness ongoing archival discussions of the continued value of provenance!

Access restrictions also require the mediation and intervention of the archivist—to explain and to handle the process of gaining access. Consider, for example, many researchers' experiences in the Soviet Union, before and after the fall of the communist state, where bribes might be required to facilitate access, files might be withheld capriciously, and records might be sold for money to heat buildings. Blouin noted, "it is the extreme case of Soviet Russia that exposes a process that is part and parcel of all archival institutions that struggle with the challenges of bulk, historical preconceptions, and specific institutional responsibilities."[12] Most such restrictions are the result of government regulations or the wishes of individual donors on giving their private property to an archival repository. They are the conditions of the gift, not the wish of the repository.

The Society of American Archivists' Code of Ethics[13] specifies that archivists weigh equally their organizational responsibilities, or the needs of the donor, with the needs of researchers for ready access. It falls to the reference archivist to standardize the procedure of requesting access, negotiate the request in as timely a way as possible, and communicate to the researcher that this is neither a capricious nor unusual practice.

An equally intermediary role delineated by Yakel is that of the knowledge broker. The archivist often crosses boundaries in ways that other individuals in organizations or academia don't tend to: they are the true interdisciplinarians, for they not only know many areas of study, as do librarians, but they are also familiar with knowledge needs, and political realities, throughout the parent organization. Yakel argues that archivists must take their place "as an equal and active participant with users in the knowledge creation process."[14] This echoes my belief in the consultant nature of the reference archivist's work.

I originally developed my archival reference workshop with a training specialist. She informed me immediately that the job of reference in archives, as she was coming to understand it, was that of a consultant. This was news

to me. But as I considered it, I realized that consultants conduct an interview to determine a client's need and the parameters of the search, evaluate available sources, and report their analysis to the client. I had always known colleagues who used their appraisal or arrangement and description expertise to become consulting archivists. But, to me, experts were the people who entered my reading room, already steeped in the knowledge of their subject area and wondering what gems I might be hiding in my collections.

Whether I'm working with the world-famous scholar, the in-house administrator, or the undergraduate, I remind myself that, in this consulting interaction, their expertise is either in their subject or in their understanding of the product they are seeking to create (book, report, term paper). I am the resident expert in the knowledge of my collections, in my ability to educate them about how to gain access to them through catalogs, finding aids, subject guides, and so on, and in my familiarity with primary sources and the best ways to find and contextualize them.

The urge to replace this consultancy with so-called expert systems is strong. But, to get the most out of our collections, I maintain that interaction with the reference staff, not just the completion of an online questionnaire, will always be a necessary component of a successful research encounter in an archives. Researchers benefit from our knowledge of the entirety of our holdings, the strengths and weaknesses of certain collections, what's new, and information about related collections elsewhere—in other words, our expertise. Even with all the tools available, connecting particular researchers with particular sources is still a common practice. I often feel like a matchmaker when I encourage a researcher to look at a certain collection or type of collection ("No really— you'll love it!").

Recently a visiting scholar spent a week in our reading room, examining the transcripts of an early twentieth-century murder trial. The issue behind the murder was housing integration, and the question at hand was the character of the neighborhood in transition. The scholar was well versed in the uses of all the technology at our disposal and made maximum use of all the guides and catalogs I showed to him. However, in conversation, I realized that he was unfamiliar with fire insurance maps, which show the layout of residential areas such as his neighborhood. Nothing in the catalog or finding aids would have led him to this source as it wouldn't be indexed by any subject headings meaningful to him. It was our mutual research partnership—or my mediation, if you prefer—that encouraged him to search this source.

My broader knowledge of the range and nature of the sources at our disposal, and his knowledge of how to apply them to his own hypotheses, has led him to challenge widely held beliefs about the ethnicity and geography of the neighborhood in which the murder occurred.

Connecting mediation with consulting brings us to the concept of research strategy. This is the product that results from the consultancy. We can't hope to connect researchers with every document, let alone every collection that would be of use to them. But we can teach them how to use our tools, and, after listening carefully to their questions and needs, we can advise them about how best to approach our repository. We convey collection strengths, useful guides, ways to plan their time in view of offsite storage, size, and complexity of collections, and what to do about access restrictions. In addition, we understand local or institutional history or have general subject knowledge with which we can make connections they couldn't make as quickly, or perhaps at all.

Two final roles of the reference archivist are student and advocate. The student role is obvious: we learn every day from our researchers about the depth and breadth of our collections, but also about their potential uses and the types of documentation that current research demands. Especially this latter information informs a different type of mediation or "inreach" between the researcher and the rest of the archival staff: what are use trends, how are tools working, what are researchers looking for, what should we be collecting?

Unmediated Use, or Caught in the Web

I have alluded several times to mediation in the online environment. The exponential growth of e-mail research requests makes this continually more obvious. Though they often are phrased less elegantly or completely, the nature of e-mail communication allows us truly to converse about points of access, collection recommendations, or referrals in ways traditional correspondence made cumbersome. The sort of research partnership referred to earlier in this essay now often starts with an e-mail inquiry, a back and forth clarification of the request, a referral to guidelines posted on a Web page, and a better prepared researcher arriving at our door. Web sites, too, allow us to mount information that is easy to download and ponder on a researcher's own timetable. We can also include explanations, or translations, of our terminology and structure for those who choose to learn about it in this way. Think of it as self-paced Berlitz at home.

A more difficult situation concerns the use of electronic records, which never actually enter the repository but are managed by the archives via the records' office of origin. These postcustodial archives certainly will encourage unmediated use. On the other hand, making these records available will require that we produce some sort of digital mediation, or front end, to connect users with the record groups not in the archives' domain. Yakel reminds us that reference archivists often act as a filter.[15] She writes, "The archival challenge on the web becomes one of establishing a container [mechanism] that preserves or represents the evidence of the record while making explicit the thought process often involved in mediating between documents and users: *translating the user's subject-based question into a provenance-based system*" [my emphasis].[16] Certainly researchers have bypassed the reference staff for years, dismissing us with a click, declining to enter the research partnership, and navigating on their own. This may be more appealing or widespread via the Internet. The research partnership we offer is a value added aspect of archival service, not a requirement.

Conclusion

I agree with my colleagues that the concept of agency and involvement, with both the records and the researchers, is one that is rarely considered. Like all service professionals, our values tell us that good service is invisible, not obtrusive. This, however, fails to acknowledge the significant roles we play in connecting researchers and records, and especially in producing and explaining the tools we create to facilitate this process. My own observation of interactions in the reference room indicate that many of us are so frustrated with our lack of influence in the research process that we withdraw behind a wall of bureaucracy and alienation from our researchers. Thinking instead of the ways in which we already shape the archives experience—and then working to improve them—will not only enhance our researchers' work lives but remind us of our own contributions to the research partnership.

NOTES

1. These quotes are found in the seminar presentation of Ann L. Stoler, "Colonial Archives and the Arts of Governance: On the Content in the Form," in *Refiguring the Archive*, Carolyn Hamilton, ed. (Dordrecht: Kluwer), 2003. Sadly, Stoler

and others equate the contents of the archives, influenced as they always will be by the availability of documentation—and of simple societal realities such as the inability of many historical subjects to write or leave documentation behind—with the institution of the archives. She thus confuses the archives—the repository in which these records rest and are, one hopes, now made generally accessible—with the intent of the original records creators and keepers of the documents

2. "Mediation is the Message: An Archival Challenge for the 21st Century," *Archival Issues* 24:2 (1999), 111. Also, Nancy Bartlett, "Past Imperfect (*l'imparfait*): Mediating Meaning in Archives of Art," this volume.

3. Paul Conway, "Partners in Research: Improving Access to the Nation's Archive/User Studies at the National Archives and Records Administration." Pittsburgh: Archives and Museum Informatics, 1994. It was in Conway's publication that I first encountered the very apt and useful concept of this partnership.

4. Elizabeth Yakel, "Thinking Inside and Outside the Boxes: Archival Reference Services at the Close of the Twentiethth Century," *Archivaria,* no. 49 (Spring 2000), 140—60, see p. 151.

5. Blouin, unpublished opening remarks for Sawyer Seminar, Ann Arbor, Michigan, 2000.

6. Conversation with Joel Wurl, 1999.

7. In a recent e-mail query, a researcher referred to herself as "net stupid." This apology seemed as important to her as her factual request.

8. Helen Willa Samuels. I am not aware that this was a published paper, but it was the title of many articles she wrote for various newsletters encouraging potential users of the Institute Archives, Massachusetts Institute of Technology.

9. Available online at: http://www.library.yale.edu/mssa/tutorial/tutorial.htm

10. Yakel, "Thinking Inside and Outside the Boxes," 153.

11. For this wonderful turn of phrase, I am indebted to many conversations on this topic with Mary Jo Pugh, former reference archivist at the Bentley Historical Library.

12. Blouin, unpublished remarks for Sawyer Seminar..

13. Society of American Archivists, Code of Ethics, adopted 1992, also available at http://www.archivists.org/governance/handbook/app_ethics.asp

14. Yakel, "Thinking Inside and Outside the Boxes," 153.

15. Ibid., 143.

16. Ibid., 150. The earliest articulation of this concept is, of course, Pugh's "The Illusion of Omniscience: Subject Access and the Reference Archivist," *American Archivist* 45:1 (1982).

Between Veneration and Loathing

Loving and Hating Documents

James M. O'Toole

On a crisp winter afternoon in the heart of a national capital, a contingent of soldiers marches through an honor guard down the steps of a public building, bearing several large wooden cases. The servicemen—those carrying the cases are all men, while the honor guard lining the steps is made up entirely of servicewomen—load these crates onto an armored personnel carrier, and a parade steps off down the city's main street, led by the marching bands of all the military branches. After about a mile, they halt in front of another building, and their precious cargo is carried inside under the protection of four guards wielding machine guns. Two days later, the nation's president and chief justice watch as the cases are opened and their contents ceremoniously placed in a shrine of marble and brass so as to permit viewing by an awed public. Every precaution has been taken to protect the contents: with the nation at war, a conflict that threatens to expand to worldwide dimensions, the treasured objects are placed in a bombproof and scientifically controlled environment. Every night they will be lowered automatically into a secure shelter deep underground. In the great columned hall, the president delivers a patriotic address. "We are engaged here today in a symbolic act," he says, acclaiming the objects of attention and "enshrining [them] for future ages." What are those objects? The bodies of heroes from the past? The national gold reserves? No, they are six brown and wrinkled sheets of parchment, one of them virtually illegible, bearing the florid script of a previous century and a number of signatures, many of them also unreadable.[1]

Now picture a second scene, far more chaotic, but in its way no less solemn. Unruly crowds have been gather-

ing nightly in the streets of another national capital. The government, once the absolute master of its people, is crumbling but desperate to hold onto power. The tide of popular will has turned against it, however, and, with the signal that a potent foreign ally will no longer sustain the local repressors with invading tanks, the populace is stirred to new courage. Their anger comes to focus on two particular objects. The first is a massive wall of concrete and barbed wire, built to keep the city's inhabitants in and the desire for freedom out, after too many citizens had sought escape across the border; eventually the people will dance defiantly on the wall, hammer it down, and take home fragments as grisly souvenirs. The second target of hatred is an unlikely one: a drab office building in another part of the city. After a few nights of chanting outside, the crowd finally surges into the building, driving the guards away and breaking up the furniture. They make first for the banal tools of tyranny: plain metal filing cabinets, filled with paper of unassuming appearance. Impulsively, the invaders pull open the drawers, scatter the files on the floor, and stomp on them or grind them under foot, feeling the emotional satisfaction of abusing these instruments of their former abusers. Very few of the files are destroyed, however, as the leaders of the crowd move quickly to prevent the burning or shredding of these documents. Indeed, there is evidence that the government agency that had kept the files had already begun to destroy some of them, fearing that they would be turned against it if the spreading revolution were successful; the movement's leaders put an immediate stop to this, envisioning a time when the agents of oppression might be brought to justice. Even in the midst of this revolution (a relatively bloodless one), there was great concern for apparently ordinary pieces of paper.[2]

This second incident is perhaps the more recognizable, since it was carried out before the world only a little over a decade ago. It occurred in Berlin during the revolution of 1989–90, as the German Democratic Republic—such an ironic name!—was collapsing. In addition to its attack on the hated Berlin Wall, the most powerful and, in its day, effective artifact of modern tyranny, the democratic movement targeted the headquarters of the East German secret police, the Stasi, which had for years been compiling minutely detailed surveillance files on citizens and foreign visitors alike. Intended originally to gather specific evidence that could be used against individuals, the Stasi's system of record keeping became a more generalized mechanism for the enforcement of docility in the population: don't even think about opposing the regime, these files silently proclaimed, for someone is watching your every move, and you will pay dearly for the slightest misstep. The first, and more benign, incident took place in Washington, DC, in December 1952. The American Declaration of Independence and the Constitution were being transferred to the still-new National Archives building from the Library of Congress, where they had been kept and exhibited on and off for years. When President Harry Truman spoke of enshrining these parchments, bland enough in appearance but freighted with emotional power, he knew what he was talking about. Since then, millions of visitors have filed in hushed silence or respectful whispers past the display cases in the great hall of the Archives, and they have gazed feelingly at these "charters of freedom."

These two episodes have much to say to those who are interested in the larger cultural roles of artifacts, documents, and the other evidences that shape our individual and collective understanding of the past. They are instances in which documents themselves became objects of attention, valued less for their contents than for what they are as physical things. "They are not important as manuscripts," a former custodian of the Declaration and Constitution had said of them, "they are important as themselves."[3] The content of these particular records—written words on parchment or paper and, in the case of the Stasi files, records in other formats as well, including photographs and sound recordings—was subsidiary to the records as things, as objects. The words did not lose their meaning or importance, but those words had assumed a secondary position, at least temporarily. That the documents existed was the salient fact, more meaningful than the words in them.

As such, these cases offer an occasion to examine certain assumptions that we often take for granted. Living as we do in an overwhelmingly literate society, one in which the ability to read and write is considered essential, we fall unconsciously into the habit of presuming that documents mean only what the words in them mean. Records are carriers of information, and we presume that the only significant information is the words those documents speak in our mind's ears. In these two cases, however, the words of the documents are relegated to a subordinate importance. Few in the crowd in Berlin stopped to read particular files as they trampled them underfoot; what mattered instead was the emotional release of asserting popular control over those files and the covert operations that had produced them. Similarly, the ringing words of the Declaration of Independence were practically irrelevant during its enshrinement: significantly, no part of the ceremony in 1952 included an actual reading of the text. In fact, it was (and remains) virtually impossible to read the words of the Declaration from the parchment original; for that purpose, reproductions produced from long-ago engravings are more useful. Here, records as mere carriers of information have been replaced by records as artifacts, and it is that connection that I wish to explore here.

Records may be honored as objects—objects of veneration—lovingly preserved, held up for admiration, meant to stir those who behold them to feelings of nobility and devotion. The power of such documentary objects derives not from the words of their texts but from the transformation of these documents into artifacts. Records may also, by contrast, be feared and despised—objects of loathing—hated for what they were intended to accomplish and sometimes actually did. Mistreating or destroying such records springs from an emotion that goes beyond hostility toward the information they contain or the sentiments they express to a generalized revulsion at their very existence. Understanding the many layers of meaning in documents as instruments of social memory requires a consideration of these two poles and of the territory in between. Situating documents between veneration and loathing may provide us with insights that are obscured when we, relentless literates that we are, presume that texts only mean what they say. Sometimes they mean a great deal more.

Veneration

The Declaration of Independence and the Constitution are objects of widespread devotion, visited by thousands of people every year.⁴ Most simply glance at them and move on; only a few pause to read a few lines, motivated perhaps by the challenge of deciphering the unfamiliar handwriting. Almost no one takes the time to read the entire texts—they would probably be hurried along by the guards if they attempted to do so—or has an immediate practical need to check the wording. Anyone who wants to see what, for example, the Third Amendment to the Constitution actually says will more likely consult one of the thousands of printed editions, readily available. It is not the wording that attracts here, but the carrier of those words. "That's the actual Declaration of Independence," parents explain to their children, pointing to it as the "real thing" and perhaps evoking daydreams of being present when it was signed. Viewers may even come away with a false impression of it. Knowing that Thomas Jefferson was the principal drafter of its text, they may be forgiven for concluding that the handwriting is his, rather than that of the virtually forgotten Timothy Matlack, a clerk of the Continental Congress from Pennsylvania, who most likely prepared the engrossed copy that the delegates signed, a month after its adoption.⁵ The tourists have perhaps been drawn to the National Archives in the first place by their familiarity with the text, but in the document's presence they focus on its existence as much as its contents.

Foundational political documents such as these have broad emotional attraction, for citizens and others alike, and we surround them with patriotic sentiments. At least in Western democracies, written charters have become the basis for self-government, and citizens find reassurance in the mere fact that these political compacts exist. They can be referred to, even if they seldom are. Such documents now seem so culturally ingrained that we may even prize their symbolic attractions above precise authenticity. The curious history of the state constitution of Massachusetts shows this reverence for documents as objects and the apparent desire to ensure that they will have an appropriately solemn and lofty appearance. Massachusetts boasts that it has the oldest (1780) written constitution in the world that is still in effect; though amended more than a hundred times, the fundamental frame of government and the language ordaining it are still in place. At its adoption, the constitution was engrossed on nine oversize parchment sheets, each about twice the size of that of the Declaration of Independence, and these were displayed throughout the nineteenth century in the office of the secretary of the commonwealth in Boston. By the 1890s, however, the secretary noticed that "in several places the ink has faded so as to be hardly vis-

ible"—the result, no doubt, of prolonged exposure to sunlight—and he suggested that the entire document "should be copied without delay." The legislature appropriated funds so that what it called a perfect copy could be made, and every effort was made to guarantee this perfection. The copy was made on new parchment sheets of identical in size to the originals, and the text was copied by hand so that each line of the new version matched precisely the corresponding line in the old one: if a word in the original was divided over two lines, the same break was made in the copy. The copyist made no attempt to replicate late eighteenth-century orthography, using instead what would have been considered the best contemporary penmanship, but in other respects (bold headings for the various subdivisions of the document, for example) the copy matched the original precisely. The copy was checked repeatedly, both as it was being made and after it was finished, to ensure this faithfulness. The original was then retired to a specially constructed walnut case and eventually to the vaults of the state archives, rarely to be seen again.⁶

For our purposes, however, the real significance of the copy was just beginning. Two aspects of it are particularly noteworthy. First, in authorizing the making of the copy, the state legislature had specifically invested it with "the same force and effect as the original." Should there ever be a need to consult the actual document, the copy would be the text examined and its wording would be probative. Published versions or any other conceivable use of the constitution would now depend on the 1893 copy, not the 1780 original. Moreover, this new copy was so "perfect" that it was held up for veneration as if it were the original. With the original now safely set aside, the copy was put out for public viewing and, most interesting of all, was displayed without any indication that it was in fact a copy rather than the original. First in the State House itself and later in the museum of the state archives, this copy was presented to the public without explanation, and those who saw it were permitted, perhaps even encouraged, to draw an erroneous conclusion about what they were seeing. The labeling of the document spoke of the 1780 date of the text, and viewers quite naturally assumed that the object they were looking at dated from that year as well. A limited few might be able to tell that the handwriting was from a later time, and anyone who inquired further might be told that this was a copy; others went away thinking they had seen something which in fact they had not.⁷ The impulse behind both the copying and the display of that copy tells us much about how we view such documents as culturally valued objects. The desire to see and get close to the venerated documentary object is so strong that, to satisfy it, we may even be willing to bend the historical reality.

Happily, the vision of documents as beloved artifacts is not usually encumbered by such deceptions. Many institutions and organizations accord a place of honor in their headquarters to their charter, often a distinctly ordinary legal document. Like the blessed first dollar earned by a small business, framed behind the counter of the local diner, the documents that call corporate entities into being are revered, less for what they say than for the simple fact that they exist. Colleges and universities seem especially reverent of their charters, usually to no practical end. In one school I know of, each new president is handed a copy of the charter during the installation ceremony, although the real charter is an act of the state legislature, resting unacclaimed with other legislative documents in the state archives. Still, a ceremonial copy, done up in handsome leather like a diploma, is handed over from one president to the next as a symbol of the transfer of authority. Most of the published histories of universities in this country that I have sampled begin with a description of the document, whether a legislative act or an individual's will, that brought the school (or perhaps an earlier, simpler incarnation of it) into being. Often, the illustrations include a page or two of this same instrument. The standard history of the University of Michigan, for example, describes both the original and revised acts of the legislature that created the Catholepistemiad of Michigan (a word that is hard to fit into a fight song). A history of Holy Cross College in Worcester, Massachusetts, published in the 1960s, reproduces the first and last page of the 1865 "Act to Incorporate the Trustees of the College of the Holy Cross" as the facing endpapers in both the front and back of the volume. Most of the actual text is left out, since the first page of the document is given over mainly to headlines and the last page is taken up almost wholly by the signatures of the governor and legislative leaders. If this document were considered merely as what it actually is—chapter 99 of the Acts of 1865 of the Massachusetts legislature—it would hardly be accorded this place of honor. Instead, it is something more, apparently deserving of attention every time one opens the book of the school's history.[8]

Various kinds of ceremonial uses of documents further underline this reverence for them as something more than texts. A number of Christian denominations use books in processions and other rites, and the Qur'an is reverenced in Islam, but the centrality of Torah scrolls in Jewish worship is the clearest demonstration of the interaction between text and object. The scroll occupies a place of honor in the local community's worship space, and it is accorded deep respect. During sabbath liturgy, it is carried through the sanctuary, and members of the congregation may come forward to kiss it with their fingers, with prayer shawls, or (in a kind of double use of textual artifacts) with their own prayer books. Once the scriptural passage for the day has been read, the scroll is lifted up for all to see before its return to the ark. Text and object are closely connected. The procession and the acts of devotion by the congregation are preludes to the reading of a section of the text. The words obviously matter, since believers understand them to be God's words. Thus the honor of reading them aloud is great, as when a young man symbolically achieves adulthood in the bar mitzvah ceremony by reading the text of the day, an honor for which he has practiced for months. Beyond that, however, the scroll is also reverenced as an object because it is the bearer of these words, even when the words are left unspoken. The mere sight of it evokes awe and a desire to live according to its precepts. It is treated with the utmost respect: if damaged (as in a fire, for instance) it is buried as if it were a beloved member of the community—as indeed it is.[9] Thus, scrolls are neither exclusively text nor exclusively object; that they are at least partly the latter ranks them clearly among our documentary objects of veneration.

Such objects assume great importance in personal as well as institutional settings. The collection of autographs, whether by wealthy collectors who seek to amass signatures of the famous or by ordinary schoolchildren who ask classmates to sign their yearbooks, is widespread. The mere possession of the signature of another, as often as not without accompanying text, exerts a powerful attraction. Jeremy Belknap, founder of the Massachusetts Historical Society in 1791, cast a wide net in assembling materials for his cabinet, gathering "specimens of natural and artificial curiosities" as well as books and manuscripts. He was not alone, then or later. A founder of the Maryland Historical Society boasted that he had amassed a collection of the autographs of all the signers of the Declaration of Independence by 1845, barely a decade after the death of the last of them. The assembling of individual archival scraps along with larger bodies of records has been sufficiently widespread that one historian has even identified it aptly as *documania*. How many archives have collections in which the signatures of notable personages have been carefully snipped out, often by nineteenth-century editors of these letters, for trading with their fellow scholars?[10] The desire to possess an autograph is not primarily a desire to possess a text of words with meaning; the expression of best wishes is insignificant, and the too-deliberately clever boilerplate of yearbook inscriptions is not what the holders value. Rather, we prize the thing itself, the name of the person written by that person. The name may be unreadable, but still we know whose it is, and the autograph becomes in a sense both the writer's *and* ours.

Such documentary objects of desire and veneration are not unlike other kinds of artifacts that forge tangible connections with the past. In particular, they are similar to relics, which have been prized for centuries. The relics of saints were part of the Christian tradition—they are present in other religious traditions as well—from the earliest times, and their appeal lay in their power to evoke the presence of a holy man or woman from the past, now held up for veneration and emulation. Entirely mundane on their own (frequently bits of bone, hair, and other decidedly less appealing body parts), relics were invested with meaning by the community of believers because they helped bridge the gap between the earthly and the divine. They were often thought to work particular miracles, and they assumed many liturgical uses: they were embedded in altars, for example, or used for blessing. More broadly, they ensured across time the continuing presence of the saint, a person whose influence with God was understood to be especially efficacious. The desire to possess such tokens led to a flourishing relic trade in the Middle Ages and even to a brisk business in stealing them from one place and taking them to another and, further still, to counterfeiting them. Merely being able to possess them was sufficient because they guaranteed a kind of ongoing contact with their source.[11]

The borderline between relics and documents is a fluid one. In many cases, simple possession is at least nine-tenths of the motivation for our desire to acquire and keep documents as well as relics. As A. S. Byatt demonstrates in her novel *Possession*, we seem to believe that ownership of manuscripts will permit us to gain a kind of access to their writer. The narrator of Henry James's *The Aspern Papers* can eventually recognize his desire for certain letters as a form of documania, but only after his scheming to get his hands on them has led to their destruction. Yes, we care about what such documents may say, but we seem to care at least as much about simply having them. Archives may even contend with one another over the right to hold certain documentary remains. Before the translation of relics in 1952, the Library of Congress and the National Archives had argued quietly for twenty years over custody of the Declaration of Independence and the Constitution. More recently, two institutions engaged in a protracted legal battle over the papers of Martin Luther King Jr. King's papers were divided, in roughly equal proportions, between Boston University (his doctoral alma mater) and the King Center for Nonviolent Social Change in Atlanta. Failing to resolve the dispute, the two institutions finally sued one another, each claiming to be the rightful repository and demanding that the other return their holdings to the proper place. Sadly, neither repository had taken very good care of the portion of the papers it held; neither had processed their collection to any significant degree, making its use by scholars highly problematic. But having the papers was important enough to both institutions that they were willing to expend considerable time and treasure in defending those they already held and trying to get the remainder. The case ended unhappily for all concerned, with the collection still divided between the two institutions and little progress made in organizing them according to accepted professional archival standards.[12]

Possession of cherished records may also be used to support other aspirations. During his years of triumph at the start of the nineteenth century, Napoleon included archival documents in his grand plan to consolidate at Paris the cultural patrimony of Europe. The Louvre was to become the predominant center for the continent's greatest works of art, and a huge central archives was to be built for the historical records not just of the French nation but of conquered lands as well. To this end, more than 3,200 crates containing the records of the papacy, an institution that seemed destined not to survive Bonaparte, were packed and transported to Paris. Some efforts were made to reorganize and recatalog these archives of the Holy See (efforts that only introduced further disorder into an already complex archival arrangement), but improving the usability of these records was hardly the motivation for taking them. Modern notions of scholarship based on extensive use of primary sources were barely in their infancy at the time, and it was not Napoleon's intention to consolidate these and other documents so that the work of historians might be easier. No, he wanted not so much to make an archives as to make a point. The pope and other rulers were now to be consigned to the past, their records preserved as a way of highlighting the world-changing transition that the emperor had wrought. One pope (Pius VI) had died as Napoleon's prisoner; the records of all the popes were now similarly confined. Bonaparte's hopes were short lived, of course, but his actions were replicated in reverse after his downfall. Barely six weeks after his final defeat, the church documents were on their way back to Rome and to the custody of a restored papacy, though nearly a third of them were lost or destroyed in the process.[13] On both sides, the desire to possess the documents as physical things was at least equal to the desire to possess the information they contained.

More sinister examples of the desire for documents as objects are those cases in which they are stolen outright. There have been a number of recent examples in which thieves have removed manuscripts from libraries and archives, sometimes systematically and over a long period of time. One thief managed to accumulate hundreds of Revolutionary, Civil War, and other manuscripts, stolen from such august institutions as the National Archives and the Library of Congress. Though he was finally apprehended when he tried to sell some of them, his motives were not merely financial. Rather, so strongly did he desire these documents that he seems to have stolen them simply to have them.[14] The letters by George Washington and other historical worthies were now *his* and no one else's; that motivation seems to be the common one among criminals who specialize in this particular activity. That the perception of records as revered objects has spun out of control in such cases only underlines the importance of our understanding of them as such. Documents are not merely texts to be read; they are things to be prized in themselves.

Loathing

If we are sometimes attracted to documents, so we may sometimes be repelled by them. The inverse of the desire to venerate and possess documents is the desire to express our contempt for them, to abuse or punish them physically (as in the case of the Stasi files), and even to destroy them. Such hostility toward documents may begin with antagonism toward their contents and the purposes to which they may be put, but these emotions often go considerably beyond such practical concerns. During the French Revolution, for instance, crowds sometimes directed their fury against collections of records because those documents seemed to embody the systems of oppression from which they sought liberation. Since records contained the details of aristocratic privilege, they became likely targets, along with other symbols of entitlement: often, while documents were burned by mob action, coats of arms were torn from public buildings and manor houses plundered. The destruction of such records might bring immediate benefits to the

participants, of course, by removing specific evidence of debt or obligations of service. But the enthusiasm that went into the destruction of documents bespeaks a more visceral antagonism. The rural insurrections of 1789 in which documents were burned were driven by motives closely akin to those that led to the strangulation of game birds on lordly estates. There are enough other historical examples of this kind of hostility toward documents—the smashing of Confucian texts during the Cultural Revolution in China in the late 1960s, for instance, and scholars forced to watch as their manuscripts were burned in front of them by Red Guards—to suggest that this is a broadly based impulse.[15]

Often the motivation for loathing documents may be religious. If there are reasons for preserving documents as relics, so there may be a corresponding religious impulse for abusing or destroying them. Medieval relics were sometimes humiliated—taken from their monastic repositories, placed on the floor, and covered for a time with thorns or ashes—if the saint from whom the relic derived failed to perform a desired miracle or answer other prayers. Documents too may be humiliated or even destroyed. In particular, those that contain religious expressions or doctrinal formulations judged to be false or dangerous may be targets. One scholar has recently argued, for example, that it was not generalized warfare that destroyed the legendary library at Alexandria but rather the focused religious disputes among pagans, Christians, and Muslims, each group hoping to purge the texts of the others. During the Reformation, the partisan destruction of offending works of theology and service books was common to nearly all parties. In England, Catholic sacramentaries were special targets of the reformers, as were church inscriptions and gravestones that asked passersby to pray for the dead: since the reform was self-consciously doing away with the popish notion of purgatory, why continue to encourage impiety with such written exhortations? In France, Protestants who posted broadsides denouncing the Mass—the so-called Affair of the Placards of 1534—not only saw them torn down but also suffered retribution and martyrdom themselves. Later, book burning became merely one more familiar form of street theater, used by all sides as a means of party identification. The goal was not merely to silence the voices of heresy, for there were other satisfactions. Burning books and manuscripts was particularly gratifying in these religious contexts because it dramatized the consignment of ideas to the flames, just as other flames were waiting to consume the bodies and souls of the heterodox for all eternity.[16] Nor should we think of these impulses as confined to earlier historical periods; as the destruction of copies of Salman Rushdie's *Satanic Verses* in some countries attests, the desire to destroy the physical carriers of objectionable ideas is always new.

Hostility toward written records may be felt with special intensity by those whose ability to read and write themselves is limited. Because written documents are often made by, interpreted by, and primarily useful to elite groups—especially in societies just undergoing the transition to widespread literacy—records seem inherently to be objects of privilege and therefore targets of those who feel victimized by privilege. To the nonliterate, documents may even seem magical: how can such inconsequential things have so much power? Long experience of disadvantage at the hands of those who control the making and interpreting of documents can breed a lasting suspicion of them among those who lack power. Too often they find themselves in the position of the father of Tom Joad in John Steinbeck's *The Grapes of Wrath*. Just out of prison and seeking a new life for his family, Tom tells a friend how he passed his time in jail. "I learned to write nice as hell," he says, complete with all sorts of elaborate doodles and calligraphic flourishes, but this was a skill his father would never appreciate. "Pa's gonna be mad when he sees me do that. He don't like no fancy stuff like that. He don't even like word writin'. Kinda scares 'im, I guess. Ever' time Pa seen writin', somebody took somepin away from 'im." It seems natural to direct one's hatred toward an object, even a mute document, with such potential for harm. The stock melodramatic figure of the villain who cheats a widow out of her inheritance by recourse to a loophole in an obscure document is a familiar enough reminder of the role records may play in such circumstances.[17]

Hatred of documents may often stem from a more general hostility toward their source. The recent case of the prison memoir of Adolf Eichmann illustrates the transfer of hatred from the maker of a record to the record itself. While in an Israeli jail during his war crimes trial, the former Nazi officer filled 1,200 pages with reflections, screeds, self-justifications, and elaborate organizational charts that purported to demonstrate that he was far removed from the planning and execution of the Final Solution. He apparently envisioned publication of this mad apologia, going so far as to leave instructions on how the volume was to be produced—he insisted on elegant pearl-colored covers—and on how his wife was to inscribe gift copies to various old friends. At the time of Eichmann's hanging in May 1962, however, the Israeli

prime minister, David Ben Gurion, ordered the manuscript sealed and deposited in the Israeli state archives. The memoir was not destroyed, as it might have been if it had fallen into popular hands, but every effort was made to prevent its dissemination. It was, no doubt, primarily the content that Ben Gurion reviled; lest the memoir excite sympathy for Eichmann, its text had to be held back. But for more than thirty years, the manuscript itself was also kept unavailable. Only after mounting pressure from academics in the United States, Britain, and elsewhere were its contents released, with the hope (the Israeli attorney general said) that the document would in fact undercut those who were now claiming that the Holocaust had never happened. The contempt and detestation was directed principally against the content, but some measure of hostility was also directed against the bearer of that content. Newspapers produced facsimiles of some of its pages, allowing a wider public a view of the hated object.[18]

The parallel case of the bogus Hitler Diaries in the early 1980s shows a similar visceral reaction to documents, though the attitudes with which these bold hoaxes were received ran a wide gamut. When they first emerged, the diaries were treated as prized objects. The German magazine reporter who bought them from the forger was ecstatic when, after protracted negotiations over price, he actually took possession of some of them. "We are the guardians of the Holy Grail," he enthused, comparing them to the greatest—and equally fanciful—relic of all times. Once the deception began to unravel, however, after duping even so respected a historian as Hugh Trevor-Roper, worldwide popular opinion changed course. Not only were manuscripts exposed as fraudulent, but the various scholars and handwriting experts who had certified them were denounced for having been taken in a little too willingly. Similarly, *Stern* magazine, which had purchased the diaries and published excerpts, was denounced not only for abetting the fraud but also for paying so high a price for the documents in the first place; after rising briefly during the furor, its circulation fell off sharply and advertisers withdrew. In the United States, *Newsweek* was likewise criticized for hyping the diaries even when it was aware of doubts about their authenticity and for deliberately leaking portions to other news outlets in an effort to boost circulation. After the fact, Katherine Graham, owner of the magazine's parent company, admitted feebly that contributing, financially and otherwise, to the deception "bothered us."[19] Today, the Hitler diaries are viewed not so much with overt hatred as with contempt, directed both at the texts and at those who were so ready to believe them real.

Coming to loathe documents and to seek their destruction may also take a number of more benign but still meaningful forms. Even documents that have no sinister intent and derive from no evil source may become fit targets for deliberate destruction. Sometimes relief rather than anger is the motivation, but the destruction of documents may still bring genuine satisfactions. Few homeowners, for example, feel any overt hostility toward their mortgage, either as a documentary object or as a text. Almost none have ever actually read the full text, I suspect. And yet, once it has been paid off, do they not happily burn it, often gathering family and friends for this celebratory purpose? The act is purely symbolic, marking a kind of financial independence, and yet it is an act that centers around the destruction of a document. Personal correspondence may evoke similar emotions, though these may be more complex. A former student has related to me a story that still lives in his family. His father and uncles, the sons of Italian immigrants, had written home regularly during their service in the European theater during World War II. When they arrived back home at the war's end, their father, the family patriarch, ordered a sister to shred all the letters into confetti.[20] The hearts of historians and archivists sink at the scene, but perhaps we can understand the motivation nonetheless. When first received, the letters had been cherished—read and reread, passed around to remote members of the family and to neighbors for the reassurance they gave that the boys were unharmed. Once the soldiers safely returned, however, destroying their letters became a way to put the anxieties of war behind them all. What satisfaction the family felt at never again having to be reminded of those worrisome times. Consigning the letters to the bottom of a drawer or a soon-forgotten shoebox was insufficient; nothing less than their outright destruction was necessary for the emotional release it brought. This simple case attests to the powerful proportions that the loathing of records may, even temporarily, assume.

Indifference

Between veneration and loathing, of course, lies indifference. Archivists, particularly those who work in institutional settings, may need few reminders of indifference toward documents, for most of them have their own, often painful, examples of important records that were shunted aside and forgotten. The lack of interest of superiors in taking proper care of records and documentation is all too familiar. Still, a brief consideration of indifference toward records serves to highlight the poles of veneration and loathing and to demonstrate the range of reactions we have toward documents.

Documents that are now objects of veneration may once have been treated with indifference or even a kind of unthinking disdain. Here again, the Declaration of Independence has an instructive history. The relic enshrined in 1952 had suffered many indignities earlier in life. In the nineteenth century, though officially in the custody of the state department, it was often passed from hand to hand. Most of the time, the Great Expression (as it was sometimes called) resided in the building that housed the patent office. This locale was chosen because the building was thought to be fireproof—in fact, it burned to the ground only months after the document had been placed at the state department in 1877, upon its return from Philadelphia for the Centennial celebration—and because exhibit space was available for the display of various contraptions and gizmos that had been filed along with patent applications. When the Declaration was first transferred, together with the Constitution, to the Library of Congress in 1921, the librarian drove across town in a mail truck, laid the documents on some empty canvas sacks in the truck bed and returned to the library, where he rolled the parchments up and put them in the safe in his office, along with the petty cash.[21] How far this ignominious treatment was from the honor guard, the parade, and the inspiring oratory of thirty years later.

What had changed? The Declaration had always been, as the librarian had said with homey familiarity, the real McCoy, but why had it come to be treasured as an artifact as it had not been before? The mere passage of time surely played a role. The events surrounding its adoption and signing had, by the middle of the twentieth century, long since crossed over into the remote past, unremembered by anyone then alive; nor was there anyone living who could have met or heard the stories of someone who had participated in the heady events of July and August 1776. Because the document itself, like a relic, was now one of the few objects that could provide direct personal connection to those events, it had a redoubled value. Because it had survived from those historic times and so little else had, it was a tangible link between past and present. Because it had played so central a part in those formative national events—it was the document that called the nation into being, even if its expressions had to be vindicated in war—it could no longer be ignored. Beyond that, the immediate context in which the Declaration came to be venerated also played a critical role. The climate of the Korean War and the Cold War enhanced reverence for all the charters of freedom, especially as the United States saw itself increasingly in the midst of a deadly serious competition with totalitarianism and unfreedom. The tensions of the early 1950s certainly accounted for the military protection and honor guard that conveyed the Declaration and the Constitution from one repository to the other, and they also helped explain the bombproof shelter in which the documents were secured every night. Ordinary citizens were beginning to build bomb shelters in their basements and backyards; could they tolerate anything less for the sacred national relics?

The passage of time and changing contexts also explain other transitions from indifference to veneration, but they are not wholly satisfactory since we continue to ignore many documents. The paradoxes of historic building preservation are instructive here. Beginning in earnest in the early twentieth century, efforts to preserve historic structures, to restore them to the look and condition of some real or imagined original state, and to open them for admiration by tourists took hold nearly everywhere in the United States. The motives for this aspect of what David Lowenthal has called the heritage crusade are many and complex: a search for stability in the face of rapid change, the rootlessness of increasingly mobile societies, perhaps even a hostility toward modern technology. For our purposes, the noteworthy thing about the passion for preserving historic buildings and neighborhoods is that it is so often unaccompanied by a comparable passion for preserving the records of the people and institutions who occupied those buildings. Boston, for example, had an active program of historic building preservation, supported with public funds, by the time of the Second World War, but it had no formal archives program for city records until the late 1980s. Of course, archivists would argue that proper custody and organization of documentary evidence facilitates the work of restoring historic structures. But the energy directed toward certain cultural artifacts was not forthcoming for others.[22]

Indifference also seems to infect our attitude toward documents that might even now be identified as objects of possible veneration later on. It is impossible to predict future interests, of course, but certain obvious candidates for treatment as valued artifacts are ignored in the present. Just as we wonder how nineteenth century office-holders could have been indifferent to the Declaration of Independence, so may future historians and curators wonder about us. Especially as technological change transforms the materiality and (perhaps) the nature of documents and records, we may be at risk of leaving gaps in our understanding of these important shifts. Where, for example, is the first successful Xerox copy, confected in October 1938 in Queens, New York? Who has kept copies of the various incarnations of floppy disks, which in a few short years have come in eight-inch, five-inch, three-inch, and smaller sizes? Apart from the more difficult questions of whether the data on these disks is still readable or whether the hardware to accomplish the task of reading is available, not many of the objects themselves survive. Some efforts have been made to archive—usage of the word itself has become increasingly slippery—e-mail messages and Web pages, but the future may still look back on our care of these transformative things as lacking the attention they deserved. We cannot escape either our times or our own history, but we should nonetheless be on watch for our own indifferences, as well as our veneration and our loathing.[23]

Conclusion

It is now twenty years since Frank Burke first called on archivists to consider the fundamental nature of their profession, to examine the basic questions too easily shunted aside in the press of everyday activity. Why are there documentary records in the first place? Why do humans make these records that archivists collect and scholars study? What is their nature, their meaning, and how do we get at those qualities? What is the balance between practical and emotional motivation in record making, record keeping, and record using?[24] Even after two decades, we are still just beginning to explore those questions, and I hope that the foregoing, perhaps impressionistic, consideration of our reactions to documents as objects will assist that exploration.

There are ways in which records and documents come to mean more than what the words in them say. Whether as objects of veneration, of loathing, or of indifference, documents are not as sharply distinct from other kinds of cultural artifacts as those of us who work with them sometimes assume. All are carriers of information, but it is information that operates on a number of different levels at the same time, information that is both literate and nonliterate. Those who encounter such documentary artifacts—whether archivist, scholar, curator, or anyone else—ignore those different levels at their peril. Interdisciplinary conversations are of course helpful in advancing that process. But we must each also train our own self-awareness to look more deeply at these objects to which we devote our individual forms of attention. This vision will be equally beneficial to archivists who acquire, organize, and make them available, to scholars who use them to construct meanings of past or present experience, and to curators who care for them because they have the power to make connections that cannot be so well captured in words.

NOTES

1. Milton O. Gustafson, "The Empty Shrine: The Transfer of the Declaration of Independence and the Constitution to the National Archives," *American Archivist* 39 (July 1976): 271–85; Donald R. McCoy, *The National Archives: America's Ministry of Documents, 1934–1968* (Chapel Hill: University of North Carolina Press, 1978), 254–56. Though it was enshrined with the other two documents, the Bill of Rights was not part of the transfer parade because it was already in the possession of the National Archives.

2. See the accounts in the *New York Times,* December 6–8, 1989, and January 16, 1990. Earlier efforts by the keepers of these records to destroy them before the crowd broke in to save them are recounted in Timothy Garton Ash, *The File: A Personal History* (New York: Random House, 1997), 20.

3. Archibald MacLeish, former Librarian of Congress, quoted in Gustafson, "Empty Shrine," 277.

4. At this writing, it was in fact not possible to view these documents because the National Archives was renovating and redesigning the hall where they are displayed. The documents are now on view again.

5. The best recent history is Pauline Maier, *American Scripture: Making the Declaration of Independence* (New York: Knopf, 1997).

6. *Second Report of the Secretary of the Commonwealth of Massachusetts for the Year Ending December 31, 1893* (Boston, 1894), 13; *Third Annual Report of the Secretary of the Commonwealth of Massachusetts for the Year Ending December 31, 1894* (Boston, 1895), 15. On changes in orthographic styles, see Tamara Plakins Thornton, *Handwriting in America: A Cultural History* (New Haven: Yale University Press, 1996).

7. Chapter 58 of the Resolves of 1894, Original Papers, Archives of the Commonwealth of Massachusetts, Boston. I myself tacitly participated in this deception when I worked at the state archives in the middle 1970s; I like to think that I would not do so now, but I'm not entirely sure. Today, neither the original constitution nor the copy is regularly displayed in the new state archives building (opened 1985), so the deception has stopped.

8. Howard H. Peckham, *The Making of the University of Michigan, 1817–1992,* Margaret Steneck and Nicholas H. Steneck, eds. (Ann Arbor: University of Michigan Press, 1967; repr.

1994), 5–13; Walter J. Meagher and William J. Grattan, *The Spires of Fenwick: A History of the College of the Holy Cross, 1843–1963* (New York: Vantage Press, 1966), endpapers. Concern for its charter may have redoubled significance in the latter case, since Holy Cross, a Jesuit school, spent twenty years fighting with a nativist legislature to secure the legal warrant to grant degrees; ibid., 49–57, 103–7. Many other schools have similar tales about their fight for legal recognition.

9. For a description of the ceremonial uses of Torah scrolls, see Abraham E. Millgram, *Jewish Worship* (Philadelphia: Jewish Publication Society, 1971), esp. 179–81, 327–28.

10. The coinage of *documania* belongs to David D. Van Tassel, *Recording America's Past: An Interpretation of the Development of Historical Studies in America, 1607–1884* (Chicago: University of Chicago Press, 1960), 103–10. On the motives of early collectors, see Louis L. Tucker, *The Massachusetts Historical Society: A Bicentennial History, 1791–1991* (Boston: Massachusetts Historical Society, 1995), 24–28; and Richard J. Cox, "Other Atlantic States: Delaware, Florida, Georgia, Maryland, New Jersey, and South Carolina," in H. G. Jones, ed., *Historical Consciousness in the Early Republic: The Origins of State Historical Societies, Museums, and Collections, 1791–1861* (Chapel Hill: North Caroliniana Society, 1995), esp. 103–6. The first archival collection I ever processed, the papers of Charles Campbell (in the archives and special collections department of the Swem Library of the College of William and Mary, Williamsburg, VA), a mid-nineteenth century historian of Revolutionary Virginia, contained many letters from Campbell to other historians, including Jared Sparks and George Bancroft, openly offering to trade duplicate signatures that had been clipped from original letters.

11. The best contemporary treatment of the power and importance of relics is Patrick J. Geary, *Furta Sacra: Thefts of Relics in the Central Middle Ages* (Princeton, NJ: Princeton University Press, 1978).

12. I have described this whole affair in "Archives on Trial: The Strange Case of the Martin Luther King, Jr., Papers," in Richard J. Cox and David A. Wallace, eds., *Archives and the Public Good: Accountability and Records in Modern Society* (Westport, CT: Quorum, 2002), 21–35. On the general desire to possess the past, see David Lowenthal, *The Past Is a Foreign Country* (Cambridge: Cambridge University Press, 1985), esp. 13–21.

13. Owen Chadwick, *Catholicism and History: The Opening of the Vatican Archives* (Cambridge: Cambridge University Press, 1978), 14–19; see also Francis X. Blouin Jr. et al., *Vatican Archives: An Inventory and Guide to the Historical Documents of the Holy See* (New York: Oxford University Press, 1998), xx–xxii.

14. Theresa Galvin, "The Boston Case of Charles Merrill Mount: The Archivist's Arch Enemy," *American Archivist* 53 (Summer 1990): 442–50. On this subject generally, see Gregor Trinkaus-Randall, *Protecting Your Collections: A Manual of Archival Security* (Chicago: Society of American Archivists, 1995), esp. ch. 2.

15. Judith M. Panitch, "Liberty, Equality, Posterity? Some Archival Lessons from the Case of the French Revolution," *American Archivist* 59 (Winter 1996): 30–47, describes several instances of revolutionary hostility toward records; see also Carl

Lokke, "Archives and the French Revolution," *American Archivist* 31 (March 1968): 23–31. On the deliberate destruction of books, manuscripts, and other documents during the Cultural Revolution, see John King Fairbank, *The Great Chinese Revolution, 1800–1985* (New York: Harper and Row, 1986), 335–37.

16. See examples of this sort of behavior in Eamon Duffy, *The Stripping of the Altars: Traditional Religion in England, 1400–1580* (New Haven: Yale University Press, 1992), 492–93; Brad S. Gregory, *Salvation at Stake: Christian Martyrdom in Early Modern Europe* (Cambridge, MA: Harvard University Press, 1999), 90–91; and Barbara S. Diefendorf, *Beneath the Cross: Catholics and Huguenots in Sixteenth-Century Paris* (New York: Oxford University Press, 1991), 56, 65. On the destruction of the legendary library of the ancient world, see Diana Delia, "From Romance to Rhetoric: The Alexandrian Library in Classical and Islamic Traditions," *American Historical Review* 97 (December 1992): 1449–67. On the humiliation of relics, see Geary, *Furta Sacra*, 20–21.

17. John Steinbeck, *The Grapes of Wrath* (New York: Penguin Books, 1992; repr. 1992), 73–74. For a graphic image of how records may be used to take advantage of the weak, see the nineteenth-century engraving "A Flaw in the Title," reproduced in James M. O'Toole, *Understanding Archives and Manuscripts* (Chicago: Society of American Archivists, 1990), 14.

18. See, for example, Lee Hockstadter, "Israelis Release Eichmann's Memoirs," *Washington Post*, March 1, 2000; and Peter Edidin, "Eichmann's House: The Bureaucracy of Murder," *New York Times*, March 5, 2000.

19. The best general narrative of this entire episode is Charles Hamilton, *The Hitler Diaries: Fakes That Fooled the World* (Lexington: University Press of Kentucky, 1991); the

quote from the reporter, Gerd Heidemann, is on page 40. See also Robert Harris, *Selling Hitler* (New York: Pantheon, 1986); the quotation from Graham is on page 385.

20. This story is told in Stephen C. Puleo, *30,000 Miles From Home: The World War II Journey of Tony Puleo* (Boston: Privately printed, 1997), i–ii.

21. What might be called the physical history of the Declaration is recounted in detail in the *Annual Report of the Librarian of Congress for the Fiscal Year Ending June 30, 1949* (Washington, DC: Government Printing Office, 1950), 38–55. This narrative, composed just before the document's transfer to the National Archives, itself bears the odor of indifference, contained as it is, without highlight, in a long section of the report headed "Reference Services."

22. On the motivations behind historic preservation, see David Lowenthal, *The Heritage Crusade and the Spoils of History* (Cambridge: Cambridge University Press, 1998), esp. ch. 1. For an account of the origins of the historic preservation movement, see Michael Holleran, *Boston's "Changeful Times": Origins of Preservation and Planning in America* (Baltimore, MD: Johns Hopkins University Press, 1998). I am grateful to Helen W. Samuels for first calling to my attention the contrast between the preservation of buildings and the preservation of records.

23. For a sober assessment of what changes and does not change as record formats evolve, see John Seely Brown and Paul Druguid, *The Social Life of Information* (Boston: Harvard Business School Press, 2000), esp. 173–83.

24. Frank G. Burke, "The Future Course of Archival Theory in the United States," *American Archivist* 44 (Winter 1981): 40–46.

Archiving/Architecture

Kent Kleinman

Archives and Houses

It is conventional and useful for both architects and archivists to recognize that architecture exists in two distinct modes: first, the built artifact and, second, representations of that artifact. This division is useful precisely because it allows architecture in the second sense to be collected, cataloged, and protected by archival institutions without the necessity of dealing with the messy business of built work. The Le Corbusier Foundation in Paris does not collect buildings by the French master, although it is housed in one; the Mies van der Rohe archive at the Museum of Modern Art in New York contains not a single Mies building, nor is it housed in a Mies structure. A rare and instructive counterexample is the case of a lord in London who embarked on a project to "archive" several actual buildings by Mies. The pending lawsuit by the lord's future heirs, who charge that the patriarch has lost his mind (and their inheritance), suggests that the distinction between the artifact and the document is blurred at considerable risk.

However, the distinction between built work and its representations is more than a matter of convenience. For architects and for archivists, built work evidences several fundamental deficiencies, and the process of collecting and preserving its representations is a project aimed at compensating for a lack. This lack is not subtle and singular but glaring and multifaceted. Most obvious is architecture's inextricable relationship with change. Architecture of the built environment ages and weathers, is subject to quotidian appropriation, is modified by changing needs, and is part of a dynamic that resists steady state descriptors. Built works always offer more dimensions than any notion of original conception can contain. Built work is unruly in this respect, unrestrained. Further-

more, built work is hardly ever a totalized, authored product; built work has no privileged condition of finality or origin. Buildings are products of forces and persons rather than of unmediated individual inspiration and unmediated preconception, and buildings become more mediated as they leave the drafting room and enter the physical world. Built work is subject to radical reconstruction socially and iconographically without changing a single brick, and yet built work can conceivably be replicated ad infinitum through complete reconstruction using originally specified components. Almost every built work is itself a reproduction, made of reproducible and interchangeable components. In short, built work has a troubled relationship to questions of originality.

The architectural archive promises to stabilize architecture; this is the archive's task and gift. The archive confers a Benjaminian aura of originality on artifacts that are at risk of becoming mere commodities, and it allows the conceit of authorship to gain a plausible foothold. Proximity to the creative moment operates as a value in the archive but significantly less so in the built artifact; a Mies drawing, but not a Mies building, is understood as an original (thus a reconstruction of a Mies building is not seen as problematic as long as the materials used are accurate replicas, while reproducing a Mies drawing is problematic regardless of the authenticity of the materials used.) As an institution that arrests temporality, the archive effectively creates a parallel discipline to built architecture, a discipline that has as its center of gravity precisely those attributes that built work can never offer. Noble and heroic, it is the archive that offers the fundamental means of reclaiming architecture's purity. In other words, the archive is less a record of the genesis of built or projected work than it is a supplement for the qualities that the built work will inevitably lack.

The architectural archive is as much the product of desire on the part of architects as it is the result of collecting practices on the part of archivists. For it is clear that many architectural records are produced precisely to compensate for the same lack that the archive agrees to value. There is a well-established tradition in the field of architecture of producing visual material full of excess, of qualities well beyond marketing needs and the utility of construction. Architectural images—plans, sections, photographs, sketches—are almost always conceptualized in terms of the archive, as visual arguments loaded with surplus power to resist the passage of time, the burden of gravity, and the contingencies of use. Daniel Burnham's grand perspectives of Chicago, Le Corbusier's sketches of white villas, Mies's sparse collages: all were done with a degree of enthusiasm fueled by justified doubt that the executed work would attain and retain the same grandeur, the same untarnished whiteness, or the same sparseness. The archive is a home proper to these passions, which demand to be accepted on their own terms.

To claim that the archive is a memory machine distorts the relationship between architectural records and built architecture, for records are not, as it were, infant buildings. The archive is more accurately described as a machine for forgetting—forgetting that architectural projects are ontologically distinct from, and quite distant from, their representations. Buildings and documents related to buildings have utterly divergent trajectories that at best cross only at the briefest moments (e.g., during construction) and diverge relentlessly as a function of time. The function of the archive is not to *prevent* this separation but to *insist* upon it; to quarantine certain records from the contamination of age, weather, and abuse. Paradoxically, in the architecture of the built environment the same qualities of age, weathering, and usage are typically indexes of value rather than contamination. There is a discourse proper to the archive and a parallel discourse proper to the built environment, for the two domains tell different stories, offer different insights, and are mediated by different forces. There is, to be sure, cross-fertilization: studying the drawings of Louis Sullivan one learns how to see the built work of Louis Sullivan. Seeing the weathering of a work by Carlo Scarpa one learns how to read his cryptic drawings. But expecting the built and the drawn to be alike is an expectation born of ideology rather than of nature.

The division between buildings and representations of buildings outlined here is not unproblematic. In a very real sense, images of built work are themselves constructions, and built works are themselves representations. It has been argued that images of buildings constitute the true and most influential aspect of architecture, that architectural ideas are propagated through secondary media (photography in particular but drawing too of course) to the degree where the built artifact is of relatively little consequence, a mere by-product of a larger project to change the fabric of the environment.[1] In an extreme version of this model, not only is architecture extended throughout society via media channels, but the channels themselves are conceptualized as prosthetic extensions of humankind, and these prosthetic extensions *are* architecture. This was the central message and mission of "architects" such as Buckminster Fuller; John McHale; and the Archigram Group, who famously argued that the telephone, the space suit, and networks of all kinds are central to the work of the architect. The rise of schools of "environmental design" in the late 1960s signaled this expansive definition.

Additionally, it has also been argued that buildings are not just the products of conventionalized representational technologies (orthogonal projections, axonometrics, perspectives, and the like) but that buildings *are* a form of representational technology. To be sure, buildings should keep out the rain, but roofs and columns participate in an irreducible semiotic web that precludes any possibility of disinterested, unmediated apprehension. To borrow Barthes's observation on textuality, every column has already been written, every roof is a citation, built architecture is a "tissue of quotations."[2] Built work is thus a record every bit as open to, and in need of, interpretation as is a document housed in an archive.

These two formulations—the (unbuilt) document is architecture; architecture is a (built) document—are not mutually exclusive and are surely both valid conceptions of the architect's enterprise as the construction of representations. Thus the documents of the archive can claim as central a role in the definition of architecture as can the buildings themselves. The difference between the two is not one of primacy but rather one of character, and the argument being advanced here is that the two are mutually dependent, like bricks and mortar. The following picture thus emerges: two parallel and rarely intersecting conceptions of architecture exist. One, the architecture of archival records, is framed as an architecture of fixity, originality, and authorial voice. Cordoned off from the vicissitudes of external forces, this architecture is cast as a touchstone of original intent, of ideation freed from weight. The other architecture is that of the built environment. It is an architecture subject to contingent forces but nonetheless—or because of this—resplendent in its material fullness and thus not at all inferior to its archival double. Being fully present in the world, this is the architecture that moved John Ruskin to write, "how many pages of doubtful record might we not often spare, for a few stones left upon another!"[3]

These two worlds are often separate but not always. At moments, admittedly rare, an effort is launched to bring them together, to slide the architecture of the archive over the architecture of the built environment and to bring the built work into conformity with its archival double. As the worlds are typically distant from one another, the effort required to undo or reverse this distance (or to prevent distance from occurring in the case of new construction) is monumental. In particular, I am referring here to large restoration projects, although the same observations apply to modest works of historic preservation. In both cases, a state of fixity is desired that is inherently foreign to the built fabric of the world. The product of this desire can be defined as an architectural monument, wherein the gap between the archive and the building is closed and architecture becomes an archive of itself.

Such products are common features of the cultural landscape: Falling Waters by Frank Lloyd Wright, Jefferson's Monticello, the Villa Savoy by Le Corbusier, to name a few. It is important to note that such archived architectures live highly artificial lives and that decisions regarding the nature of these lives are deeply implicated in the fabrication of national, local, and discipline-specific mythologies. As suggested in the opening paragraph, archiving buildings is also a costly affair, and such projects almost always bear the imprint of economic and political power interests often operating under the umbrella of "heritage tourism." A case in point is the current effort in Buffalo, New York, to restore an early and mammoth residential complex designed by Wright in 1904, the Darwin D. Martin House. The restoration project, estimated to exceed twenty-five million dollars, involves a series of monumental "undoings," including buying back parcels of the original site that had been subdivided; fabricating pieces of furniture to replace missing originals that are now far too expensive to purchase; fabricating "new" bricks to match the original stones and cleaning the old bricks to look as they did when new; imploding a three story apartment building erected in the 1960s in the middle of the original complex; and erasing an "original" Wright window remodeling done at the insistence of Mrs. Martin, who could not see in her bedroom due to lack of adequate fenestration. Guiding this work are the extensive Martin House archives at the University of Buffalo. But the impetus for the work lies elsewhere: at an estimated two hundred dollars per day spent by the typical cultural tourist (versus ninety dollars per day spent by the leisure tourist), the Martin House Restoration Corporation anticipates bringing twenty million dollars annually to Buffalo's depressed economy.[4] "Architecture is going to be the great contribution to the civilization of the future," claimed the master (Wright), prophetically.[5]

A new architectural monument in the preceding sense was recently unveiled in the city of Prague, the restoration of a modernist villa built in 1930 by the architect Adolf Loos. Like all such projects, the work required significant use of archival records. And like all such projects, the research involved major efforts to determine and encapsulate a state of originality. But unlike with other such projects, the researchers found that the architect had, as it were, set a trap designed to prevent his work from falling prey to the monumentalizing impulse that guided the enthusiastic investigators. The second section of this essay is dedicated not so much to the story of fine archival detective work (although there was that), not so much to presenting a testament to the utility of archival records (although they were heavily used), but rather to the story of architecture's revenge on its archive.

Archiving Houses

The Villa Müller is a work of enormous complexity, the pinnacle of Adolf Loos's career as an architect, built for Frantisek Müller, the young and wealthy owner of one of Europe's largest construction firms. The villa was immediately celebrated as a masterpiece and entered architectural history as one of the canonical works of the modern period.[6] The Villa Müller survived both the war and the communistic era intact; indeed it wasn't until the advent of post–Velvet Revolution capitalism that the building's fate was endangered. In the absence of any preservation regulations that would protect the interior of the building, it appeared likely that a private owner would purchase the masterpiece and reconstruct it.

At this point the nascent Czech government, after considerable hesitation, purchased the villa and launched a high profile campaign to restore it. The Villa Müller was to become a major landmark in the city's cultural identity; the Villa Müller was to become a monument. The researchers working on the restoration project began by consulting the Loos archives at the Albertina Graphische Sammlung in Vienna. Additional valuable material was found precisely where it had been cataloged over seventy years ago, in the local building department. The villa itself became the site of forensic investigation.

As in any architectural restoration, there were many moments of doubt concerning the accuracy of the restoration project. The architect's drawings were consulted; period photographs were scrutinized; archaeological techniques were summoned. But there was doubt about the legitimacy of that supporting evidence. Were the architect's drawings in fact accurate reflections of what was built, and if not, what should govern: the architect's intentions as drawn or the building as realized under the watchful eye of the architect? Were the photographs legitimate reflections of the state of inhabitation, or were they staged? Then too, there were the typical doubts that accompany archaeological expeditions. How deeply should one dig? What if one discovers material of historic interest buried beneath material of historic interest? And, of course, there were doubts about comprehensiveness. Does it really matter what lies beneath the visible surface of things? Could one make technical improvements without sacrificing the authenticity of the work?

Every architectural restoration raises these problems. The French architect Viollet-le-Duc—who believed that his century, the nineteenth, initiated the very notion of restoration and who considered himself among the first generation of restorers—dedicated an entire chapter in his *Dictionaire raisonné* to the thorny issues involved in the restoration of buildings. He anticipated many of these problems, even those related to the then new issue of photography as evidence. "To restore a building is not to preserve it, to repair it, or rebuild it," he writes; "it is to reinstate it in a condition of completeness that could never have existed at any given time."[7] In short, to restore is always to produce a new work. Thus, in the reconstruction of the German Pavilion in Barcelona by Mies van der Rohe, the roof structure had to be redesigned in order to look original while compensating for the originally inadequate construction; drains had to be added so that the building would survive its new status as a permanent structure.[8] The story of the reconstruction of Loos's Villa Müller, no less than that of Mies's masterpiece, was full of fine detective work, dogged thoroughness, and the mental teases that required principled judgment calls.

Notwithstanding these inherent problems, after several years of monumental effort and monumental expense, the villa was brought into alignment with much of the documentary evidence that could be found. In fact, a veritable archive of documents was assembled during the process of reconstruction, and a parallel archival version emerged from the process that ipso facto certified the veracity of the restoration effort.

Or did it? Is it possible that the very proximity of the archival and built version of Villa Müller produced a fraudulent work? Is it possible that in the process of restoring the building to an original state it became less and less authentic, that this painstaking process of seamlessly superimposing the archival on the built inadvertently conflated two incompatible architectural conceptions? Could it be that architecture needs to be immunized against its archival double rather than nourished by it, that the archival impulse was a motive foreign to this architecture?

Loos himself made certain that the answers to these questions would be in the affirmative. In addition to designing buildings, the architect produced a prodigious and influential body of critical essays, texts that have influenced the field even more profoundly than his buildings. And Loos was motivated by one issue more than any other, namely, that of originality in architecture. The thread through all his written work is an assault on all those who inappropriately sought to infuse use-objects with an authorial voice. His favorite targets for critique were the members of the Wiener Werkbund: Josef Hoffmann, Henry van der Velde, and Josef Olbrich in particular. His credo was simple, or at least simply stated:

Alle . . . unzeitgemäßen arbeiten waren von künstlern und architekten geraten waren, während die arbeiten, die zeitgemäß waren, von handwerkern geschaffen wurden, denen der architekt noch keine entwürfe lieferte . . . Für mich stand der satz fest: wollt ihr ein zeitgemäßes handwerk haben, . . . so vergiftet die architekten.

[all . . . works that are inappropriate for our time were the products of craftsmen who relied on the advice of artists and architects, whereas those works that are in the spirit of the times were made by craftsmen who had not received designs from an architect . . . For me one thing was certain: if you want products appropriate for their era, . . . poison the architects.][9]

Loos was preaching what he practiced. When he stated, "Genug der originalgenies! Wiederholen wir uns unaufhörlich selbst!" (Enough original genius! Let us repeat ourselves endlessly),[10] he was describing and advocating both his architectural and his literary modus. One finds essays dedicated to the critique of originality/invention/misplaced artistry in the earliest articles Loos published for the weekly paper *Die Zeit* in 1897 and in the very last piece he penned some thirty-six years later, a veritable hymn to a simple, vernacular, wooden saltshaker, published the year of his death.[11] Loos explicitly parodies the quest for originality in his 1900 fable "Von einem armen, reichen Man" (The Poor Little Rich Man) in which a battle is staged between what might be termed the *authentic* (time-tested, utilitarian objects and environments integrated with life's dramas) and the *obsessively original*. The poor rich man is reduced to misery by an environment in which even the slippers are matched to the decor. Twenty years later, in a moving obituary to the furniture maker Joseph Viellich, he expressly advocates the culture of the well-chosen copy: "jede handwerkliche leistung ist kopie" (every work of craftsmanship is a copy) over the cult of nervous inventiveness: "nur unter narren verlangt jeder nach seiner eignen kappe" (only among dunces does everyone demand their own personalized cap).[12]

The originality that Loos so detested was not that of creative genius per se; it was that of creative genius romping in the wrong field. For Loos, architecture was the wrong field; in fact, the appropriate domain for authorial invention was limited to one domain only, namely, art, and one of Loos's lasting contributions to twentieth-century theory was to divorce architecture and art, absolutely.

As even this cursory review suggests, the name Adolf Loos and the issue of originality in works of architecture are inextricably intertwined. And this brings us back to the restored villa in Prague and, by extension, to the act of "archiving" architecture in general. For the weight of the architect's texts makes one conclusion immediately clear and inescapable: the restored Villa Müller is no longer a house. It is not even architecture, certainly not a Loos. It has undergone an ontological shift. It has instead all the trappings of an oxymoron: an original Loos.

Worse still, it has become a work of art. We know that the villa is aspiring to the status of art for the following reason: we can no longer touch it. This precondition for art is taken from Karl Kraus via Walter Benjamin. According to Benjamin, Kraus noted that

On reading the words with which Goethe censures the way the Philistine, and thus many an art connoisseur, run their fingers over engravings and reliefs, the revelation came to [Loos] that what may be touched cannot be a work of art, and that a work of art must be out of reach.[13]

Loos himself does not, to my knowledge, credit Goethe with this observation, but a kind of haptic test does ground both Loos's and Kraus's confidence in the categorical distinction between objects of use and works of art. Benjamin took up this theme of art's inherent "distance" explicitly in his 1936 essay "The Work of Art in the Age of Mechanical Reproduction." In his discussion on what brings about the decay of the aura of a work of art, Benjamin cites the public's insatiable desire for proximity. "Every day the urge grows stronger to get hold of an object at very close range by way of its likeness."[14] This desire to touch fulfills itself only when the artwork is within grasp, namely, through its reproduction, which in turn destroys the work's aura. One of the things that we appropriate in this manner is architecture, which we apprehend in a distracted manner, by habit, by use, and by touch. "Such appropriation cannot be understood in terms of the attentive concentration of a tourist before a famous building," Benjamin notes.[15] "Tactile appropriation is accomplished not so much by attention as by habit . . . The public is an examiner, but an absent-minded one."[16]

Loos embraced this distracted examiner; one might say he valorized this character well before Benjamin theorized him. The core of so many of Loos's tales swirls around the fate of those who experience the world haptically, at close range: Joseph Veillich, the chairmaker; the "poor rich man" whose fall from happiness coincides with the moment when he is forbidden to touch anything in his home without his architect's approval; the happy owner (Loos himself) of a desk whose ink stains and scratches and other signs of wear produce a sentimental reverie; and the saddlemaker, who cannot match the artistic fantasies of the design professor because he, the saddlemaker, has actually handled leather. Saddles, desks, rooms, objects of use in general are there to be touched. At the risk of being branded an essentialist—a risk that bothered Loos's generation not at all—one can say that this is a categorical essence.

To deny touch to "original" archival material is fundamental to the archive's mission. To deny touch to the villa is to transform it, not only categorically but also critically. We now pass through the halls of the villa, we gaze out onto the restored living room, we admire the extraordinary tableau, and we ask ourselves: if this work is now no longer to be appropriated in the manner Loos considered natural to architecture, just what kind of appropriation is appropriate? And because we are presented with a "building as artwork," the answer, it seems, is that we should appropriate the building in that mode long considered natural to works of art: namely, absorbed contemplation. "A man who concentrates before a work of art becomes absorbed by it,"[17] Benjamin reminds us, echoing a long history that is the root of Goethe's prohibition against touching art.

But this answer is hardly satisfying, for the simple reason that people don't respond like that to buildings, even to truly great buildings. It is difficult to imagine a visitor to the new villa frozen in suspended animation and rapt contemplation in front of a perfectly restored Loosian bathroom (unless, as is not all at difficult to imagine, the visitor is sneaking a photograph). The kind of absorption produced by artworks is not produced by architecture because this response has long been considered the product of works that are themselves self-absorbed. Absorbed contemplation, at least in many schools of thought, is an attribute of works of art, not just a description of their reception. Balance, unity, consistency, proportionality, thematic coherence: the kind of artwork capable of producing a trancelike state of total absorption is said to possess these things within the context of its own frame. This is why Loos insisted that a Beethoven symphony is different from a doorbell chiming a Beethovian riff. As conceptualized by Loos and his compatriots, artworks are distant; artworks do not, and should not, encourage the literal engagement of the beholder as does a light switch or a fireplace or a doorbell.

So we may have to revise downward our already troubling observation. No longer is Loos's house architecture. We cannot get close to it now; it is presented as a work of art. It has been rendered distant, not with a gilded frame but with equally effective velvet cords. But as art, it is of the very kind that Loos repeatedly lampooned because it cannot fully produce the contemplative state. One might disagree with Loos's conceptualization of art and architecture, of the defining essence of use objects, and of art as distant. But has the careful restoration, despite its physical accuracy, produced a work so fundamentally different than Loos's original that the *irony of that difference* threatens to occlude its appreciation? Is irony in fact Loos's final word? For Loos, as we know, always wanted to have the final word.

Loos does not, cannot, have the final word. The preceding lament suggests that if some of the energy that had gone into restoration had been spent on designing a new use, all would be better. An essential condition, the sine qua non of Loos's original architectural conception, would be restored, and thus the work would be more Loosian, more *authentic,* than in its present petrified state. But some will immediately recoil at this formulation, for it relies quite explicitly on the notion that there is a history proper to the building, and other histories that are not, and the authenticating agency for that which is proper is Adolf Loos. But one can argue against this allocation of legitimizing power just as Loos implicitly argued against the legitimizing power of the architectural archive. One can argue that it is not so much Loos

who is being represented by this project but the nascent Czech Republic, with its laudable mission to democratize access to this and many other landmark structures previously off limits, a government eager to prevent the appearance of any privileged group profiting from public expenditure, and certainly a government anxious to demonstrate that it is protecting the public's investment by encapsulating it. The story that is being constructed with this restoration can also be understood as a precise undoing, a surgical negation, of the villa's status between 1968 and 1989, when it was occupied and controlled by the Marxist-Leninist Institute of Czechoslovakia (a condition that clearly fell outside the archival conception of originality). Certainly, when the first wave of visitors tours the restored villa, the ghost of Villa Müller's immediate political past will be as present as that of its architect. In short, one can observe that works of great prominence inevitably enter into the representational machinery that turns out the building blocks of society's self-image, namely, monuments. And the final word is, of course, that the Villa Müller is no exception.

NOTES

This essay was first published in *Archival Science* 1, no. 4 (2001): 221–38, and is reprinted by permission.

1. Beatrix Colomina, "Mies Not," in *The Presence of Mies,* ed. Detlef Mertins (New York: Princeton Architectural Press, 1994), 193–222.

2. Roland Barthes, "The Death of the Author," in *Image, Music, Text* (New York: Hill and Wang, 1977), 146.

3. John Ruskin, *The Seven Lamps of Architecture* (New York: Farrar, Straus and Giroux, 1981), 169.

4. Martin House Restoration Corporation, promotional materials, Buffalo, 1999.

5. Ibid.

6. Kent Kleinman and Leslie Van Duzer, *The Villa Müller: A Work of Adolf Loos* (New York, Princeton Architectural Press, 1994). Recent articles on the restoration have appeared in the *New York Times,* January 4, 2001, F11; and *Metropolis Magazine,* February 2001, 62–65.

7. Eugène-Emmanuel Viollet-le-Duc, "Defining the Nature of Restoration," in *The Architectural Theory of Viollet-le-Duc: Readings and Commentary,* ed. M. F. Hearn (Cambridge, MA: MIT Press, 1990), 269.

8. This and other information regarding the restoration of the German Pavilion are contained in Rosa M. Subirana i Torrent, ed., *Mies van der Rohe's German Pavilion in Barcelona 1929–1986* (Barcelona: Public Foundation for the Mies Van der Rohe German Pavilion in Barcelona, 1986), 66–88.

9. Adolf Loos, "Hands Off!" in *Trotzdem* (Vienna: Georg Prachner Verlag, 1982), 132.

10. Adolf Loos, "Heimatkunst," in *Trotzdem* (Vienna: Georg Prachner Verlag, 1982), 130.

11. Adolf Loos, "Vom Nachsalzen," in *Die Potemkinsche Stadt* (Vienna: Georg Prachner Verlag, 1983), 231.

12. Adolf Loos, "Joseph Veillich," in *Trotzdem* (Vienna: Georg Prachner Verlag, 1982), 216.

13. Walter Benjamin, "Karl Kraus," in *Reflections: Essays, Aphorisms, Autobiographical Writings,* ed. Peter Demetz (New York: Schocken Books, 1986), 240–41.

14. Walter Benjamin, "The Work of Art in the Age of Mechanical Reproduction," in *Illuminations: Essays and Reflections,* ed. Hannah Arendt (New York: Schocken Books, 1968), 223.

15. Ibid., 240.

16. Ibid., 240–41.

17. Ibid., 239.

"Records of Simple Truth and Precision"

Photography, Archives, and the Illusion of Control

Joan M. Schwartz

Introduction: "Daguerreotypomania"

In December of 1839, Théodore Maurisset, a French printmaker, produced a lithograph entitled *La Daguerréotypomanie*. The scene has been described in delightful detail by Helmut and Alison Gernsheim:

> The caricature shows a crowd of people pushing into the enterprising establishment of Susse Frères, attracted by an enormous advertisement to buy daguerreotypes for New Year's gifts. Over the entrance large notices proclaim that "Non-inverted pictures can be taken in 13 minutes without sunshine." While one photographer is just aiming his camera up the skirts of a tight-rope dancer on the left, another tries to take the portrait of a child whose mother and nannie do their best to keep his struggles in check. Baron Séguier, inventor of the portable apparatus for travellers, passes by, his boxes tucked under his arm. Their contents are displayed in the right foreground, where Dr. Donné (who attempted the first portrait) holds a sitter imprisoned in a posing-chair as if he were in the stocks, calmly counting the minutes while his victim endures the torture. Above this pleasant open-air studio, daguerreotypes are etched according to Donné's system. A procession of daguerreotypomaniacs, carrying a banner with the inscription, "Down with the aquatint" passes the gallows, where a few engravers deprived of their livelihood have already hanged themselves, while other gallows are still to be let. Nearby, a group of revellers drunk with enjoyment dance to music round a mercury-box as if it were the Golden Calf. Train- and ship-loads of cameras are being exported, and daguerreotypomaniacs have good reason for holding a public meeting to worship the invention: has not competition by rival firms

(to Giroux's) already reduced the price of apparatus to 300, 250 and even 200 francs? The sun smiles benignly down on his creation. Surveying the things that had come to pass during the last few months, Maurisset adds a touch of prophecy: a photographer recording the scene from a balloon with a basket in the form of a camera—as are the railway carriages and the clock-tower surmounting the Maison Susse Frères.[1]

In this caricature, Maurisset presented a remarkably prescient view of the expectations, applications, and implications of the daguerreotype.[2] Writings by the proponents and practitioners of photography who followed elaborated upon Maurisset's themes: travel photography, portrait photography, erotic photography, aerial photography, the death of the engraver (artist), photography on paper, commercial competition, cumbersome equipment, the role of the Sun (Nature) as image-maker. Situated more broadly, the daguerreotype collaborated with the paddlewheel steamer, the steam locomotive, and the hot-air balloon to extend the powers of human observation across space and allied itself with the clock to contain and control time. *La Daguerréotypomanie* depicted, in caricature, what Charles Baudelaire later decried as "an industrial madness."[3] It also offers a visual commentary on the society which embraced not only the daguerreotype but also the *fonds* system of archival classification. In this essay, I suggest that the social origins of "daguerreotypomania" are of particular interest from an archival perspective because the defining moments in both the history of modern archives and the history of photography can be traced to the same two-year period in France, 1839–41.

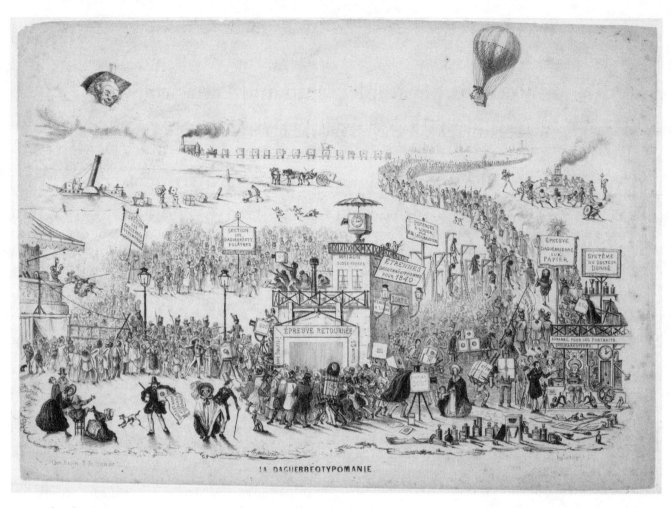

Théodore Maurisset, *La Daguerréotypomanie*, Lithograph, 1840. GEH 35071. (Courtesy of George Eastman House, Rochester, NY.)

On June 15, 1839, France's Minister of the Interior, Tanneguay Duchâtel, appeared before the Chamber of Deputies to introduce a bill that proposed to grant to Louis Jacques Mandé Daguerre (1787–1851) an "annuity for life of 6,000 francs" as compensation for his part in surrendering to the French government the details of what is arguably the first practicable photographic process. After years of collaboration and experimentation, Daguerre, a noted Paris diorama painter and theater set designer, had discovered a way to fix the image of the *camera obscura*. A drawing aid and forerunner of the photographic camera, the *camera obscura* was essentially a light-tight box with a small opening on one wall. Light passing through the opening cast an upside-down, laterally reversed but perspectively correct, image of an outside scene onto the opposite wall.[4] The optical principles of the *camera obscura* had been known for centuries; similarly, the chemical principles of the darkening of silver salts were well documented. What Daguerre managed to do was combine these prin-

ciples to produce a permanent image on light sensitive metal plates of silver-coated copper. The result was nothing short of miraculous.

The bill was passed in the lower house on July 9, 1839. The Chamber of Peers confirmed the Chamber of Deputies' decision three weeks later and, on August 19, 1839, Daguerre's process was made public before a joint gathering of the Académie des Sciences and the Académie des Beaux-Arts, Paris. As one leading historian of photography has observed, "perhaps no other invention ever captured the imagination of the public to such a degree and conquered the world with such lightning rapidity as the daguerreotype."[5] Daguerre's manual, published by order of the French government, was issued in no fewer than thirty-two editions, in eight languages, during 1839 and 1840. More experimentation followed, and, by 1841, chemical and optical improvements had resulted in increased sensitivity of daguerreotype plates, shorter exposure times, laterally corrected images, smaller cameras, and improved lenses.[6]

On August 8, 1839, Duchâtel issued a preliminary *Circulaire* that divided departmental archives into historical documents—those before 1789—and administrative documents—those after 1789. Two years later, on April 24, 1841, Duchâtel followed up with another *Circulaire* entitled, "Instructions pour la mise en ordre et le classement des archives départmentales." Nancy Bartlett traces the beginning of the modern era of archival theory and practice to this detailed framework for ordering and classifying departmental archives.[7] However, while archivists have long embraced the archival principles of *respect des fonds* and original order as a natural and objective means of preserving a truthful and accurate record of the actions and transactions of an administrative or historical past, Lara Moore has suggested that this new classification system, in fact, presented a politically charged vision of the French state after 1790 as "stable, uniform, and homogeneous," through its definition of what constituted a *fonds*.[8]

As authors as diverse as Ursula Franklin writing on the world of technology, Jonathan Crary connecting vision and modernity in the nineteenth century, and Terry Cook commenting on archival history have observed, the development of principles, practices, and technologies reflect the tenor of the times.[9] Is it, then, merely a coincidence that these seminal events in the history of photography and the history of archives took place in Paris at roughly the same time? Is it simply by chance that the announcements, of both the bill to grant the inventors of the daguerreotype process a lifetime annuity and the instructions for classification in archives, were the responsibility of the same government official, Tanneguay Duchâtel, France's Minister of the Interior? These questions point to the nineteenth-century epistemological assumptions upon which both archival practices and photographic practices rested. They also point to shared paradigmatic origins which, when revealed, contribute to our understanding of photography as a way of communicating across space and time, the place of photographs in archives, and the nature of the *fonds* as the basis for archival classification.

This essay examines early critical writing on photography in an effort to expose tacit assumptions about the nature of photography, assumptions which defined its role in society, and, by extension, the place of photographs in archives. However, the broader relevance of this research within the world of archives is predicated on the fact that the adoption of the *fonds* and the advent of photography can be traced to prevailing ideas about the nature of knowing and prevailing concerns about the pace of change. It situates the key events of 1839–41 in the empiricism of the mid-nineteenth century, a time when photographic technologies and archival classification, embraced as tools of knowing, held the promise of control over an increasingly complex world.

From Process to Praxis

In 1839, photography was a process in search of praxis. Its use was a matter of expectation and a subject of speculation. The utilitarian outlook of the nineteenth-century mind asked, *"Cui bono?"*—what is it good for? This question was a flashpoint for a spate of commentaries, lectures, and manuals of photographic manipulation on the value and uses of photography. French, British, and American practitioners, promoters, and critics of photography described the ways in which the new image-making processes had—or were expected to—become indispensable as a means of extending the powers of human observation. Enthusiastic responses ranged from sweeping generalizations to detailed predictions about its applications to art, science, and, more generally, "the business of life"—all of which were predicated on the firm belief in the reliability and authenticity of photographs as evidence. These writings shaped photography as a culturally and technologically defined practice which initially carried both artistic pretensions and scientific credentials, but which, ultimately, became a means by which people came to know the world and situate themselves in it. It is these epistemological underpinnings which are of interest to archivists for their broader relevance, by example and by analogy, to the transmission and preservation of recorded information.

In presenting "the particulars and motives" of the bill to grant Daguerre a lifetime annuity, Minister of the Interior Duchâtel called Daguerre's process "a discovery as useful as it was unexpected." Alluding to its "immense utility," he exclaimed: "It will easily be conceived what resources, what new facility it will afford to the study of science, and, as regards the fine arts, the services it is capable of rendering, are beyond calculation."[10]

To this, Joseph Louis Gay-Lussac (1778–1850), a French chemist and physicist best known for his studies on the physical properties of gases, added that the arts of industry and the natural sciences would "doubtless make numerous applications of Mr. Daguerre's process."[11]

The unprecedented ability to fix the image of the *camera obscura*, to make detailed and realistic images directly from nature, to make multiple exact copies of objects or drawings challenged the applications to which picture making had previously been put. From the beginning, there was an expectation that Daguerre had "laid the foundation of a new order of possibilities."[12] Likening the daguerreotype to the telescope and the microscope—other instruments which extended human powers of observation—French scientist and statesman François Arago (1786–1853) declared, "when observers apply a new instrument to the study of nature, what they have hoped to attain is always trifling in comparison to the succession of discovery which the instrument itself gives rise to."[13] Symbolically, Daguerre's process was announced to a joint gathering of the Académie des Sciences and the Académie des Beaux-Arts. As French photographers and critics Mayer and Pierson later pointed out, "C'est sous ce double patronage que la photographie a fait son entrée dans le monde."[14] Ideas about the photograph that emerged from these twin discourses defined, in the nineteenth-century mind, what photographs were supposed to do and how people were supposed to react to them.

Photography, Science, and Observation

Although the origins of photography have usually been traced to the aspirations of a professional diorama painter, on the one hand, and the frustrations of an amateur artist, on the other, most of the applications first envisaged for the new medium treated photography as a tool of observation, an aid to documentation, and a form of data gathering. Even at the Great Exhibition of the Works of Industry of All Nations in London in 1851, cameras and camera-made images were displayed not in the fine arts sections of the exhibition but alongside other optical instruments. Photography shared with science common roots in empiricism and positivism, an optimistic faith in unending progress, and common agendas to see and, thereby, know the world.[15]

The roots of photography can be traced to a historic meeting in Paris at the close of 1838. In December of that year, three luminaries of nineteenth-century science paid a visit to Daguerre's Paris studio. Having attempted unsuccessfully to sell his new invention by subscription, Daguerre had turned to the Paris scientific community for support in selling his process to the French government. Alexander von Humboldt (1769–1859), the great polymath, was part of a committee sent by the Académie des Sciences to assess Daguerre's new process for fixing the images of the camera obscura.[16] The significance of this encounter, between Humboldt, a "father" of modern geography, and Daguerre, a "father" of modern photog-

raphy, has largely been overlooked. Although Humboldt occupied intellectual space at the nexus of developments in the history of science and the history of photography and played a key behind-the-scenes role in the technological and cultural acceptance of Daguerre's process, he is known as only a minor figure at the dawn of photography.[17] Yet his influence on the origins, acceptance, and applications of photography as a technology of both image making and information transfer should not be underestimated. Furthermore, Humboldt's involvement in the scientific support for, and political approval of, the daguerreotype process can be taken as representative and revealing of the paradigmatic origins of photography within the discourse of science.

Humboldt's concerns shaped photographic practices; his wide-ranging mind and vast experience as an explorer, naturalist, historian, writer, and scientist directly affected assumptions about the range and effect of the camera. Daguerre's invention influenced the nineteenth-century imagination; his experience and success as a diorama painter had demonstrated the persuasiveness of realistic representation and the public fascination with visual illusions. The daguerreotype offered a way of seeing across space and time. Little wonder, then, that Humboldt, the scientific traveler, critical observer, and prolific writer, sensed the significance of this new technology.

After the initial visit of Humboldt, Daguerre showed his silvery images to a host of notable scientists, including the American inventor of the telegraph, Samuel F. B. Morse; influential British scientists Sir John F. W. Herschel and James Watt, Jr.; and the "chief architect" of the Royal Geographical Society, Sir Roderick I. Murchison. Among the names associated with the invention and initial applications of photography were many other prominent figures of Victorian science, including Thomas Henry Huxley, Sir David Brewster, Michael Faraday, James Forbes, Louis Agassiz, and Charles Darwin, as well as a number of Oxford-educated civil servants and keepers in various departments of the British Museum. This community of scientists embraced the medium of photography with curiosity and excitement; photographic evidence suggests that a great many of them, like Humboldt, were also familiar with its social and honorific functions from the experience of posing, either for fellow amateurs or for professional portrait photographers.

On the fertile ground of learned societies in London, Edinburgh, Paris, and other centers, photography was discussed as a process and shaped as a practice, both through formal papers and informal discussions. At meetings of the Royal Society, the Royal Academy, the Royal

Geographical Society, the Royal Astronomical Society, the Linnaean Society, the Botanical Society, the Ethnological Society of London, and the Académie des Sciences, photographic processes and improvements attracted the attention of highly influential people, not only as a scientific discovery in optics and chemistry but also as a method for observing, representing, and knowing the world. Many of the same leading scientists also discussed technical details and practical applications at meetings of the Photographic Exchange Club, the Photographic Society, the Amateur Photographic Association, and other photographic societies. Their experimental results and scientific advances in photography shared space with discoveries in natural history, geography, and ethnography on the pages of *Philosophical Magazine,* the *Edinburgh Philosophical Journal,* the *Literary Gazette,* and *Athenaeum,* as well as the proceedings and transactions of various societies.

Discussions about optics, chemistry, astronomy, botany, Egyptology, zoology, geology, geography, and photography were also carried on in a social context, and family ties were important in establishing domestic space as the basis of scientific pursuits. Pioneers of photography are known to have entertained the great figures of Victorian science.[18] Grace Seiberling has noted that "the clubs and societies were based initially on social contacts, but in fostering research and formalizing communication they furthered the state of knowledge in their fields and created a sense of solidarity among their members."[19] In these ways, photography entered an elite circle of gentleman scientists, instrument makers, university professors, museum keepers, military officers, and government officials whose interests and connections were nurtured through contacts and correspondence, personal as well as professional.

For this community, interest in the photograph centered on the optical-chemical transformations that produced the photograph, and on the photograph as a means of extending human powers of scientific observation. Cameras were trained on objects near and far, large and small, extending the observational powers of the microscope and the telescope in a range of disciplines. Research in archaeology was carried out through the work of Maxime du Camp, Félix Teynard, and J. B. Greene on the monuments and inscriptions of Egypt, and through the work of Auguste Salzmann on the architecture of Jerusalem. Photographs, Salzmann asserted, "are not second-hand reports; they are brutal facts."[20] Thomas Henry Huxley, John Lamprey, and Carl Dammann used photography in the comparative study of racial types.[21]

Charles Darwin included photographs in his 1872 publication on the expression of human emotions.[22] Joseph James Forrester, the Baron de Forrester, used photography in his efforts to map and improve navigation on the River Duoro through the Portuguese wine-producing districts in the hinterland of Oporto.[23] Forrester, an active member of both the Photographic Society of London and the Photographic Exchange Club, had himself learned photography from Dr. Hugh Welch Diamond, whose scientific application of photography to the study of mental disorders was presented to the Royal Society and published in the photographic journals.[24] Charles Piazzi Smyth, Astronomer Royal for Scotland, championed photography as a tool for astronomical, archaeological, and natural history purposes and asked, "What monumental research of the present age can be effectively treated without its marvellous aid?"[25]

Photography came to be part of the way in which the luminaries of Victorian science saw and explored the world. But photography was also used not so much to generate rigorous scientific data—as in Huxley's use of anthropometric photographs to study and classify the human races, or Muybridge's "electro-photographic investigation" of animal locomotion,[26] or Marey's chronophotographic analysis of the structure of movement[27]—but rather, more generally, as an enhanced form of visual note taking, a tool of observation, and an accurate and reliable means of documentation. A marvel of optics and chemistry, a "mirror" of nature, and a "window" on the world, the photograph was absorbed into engagement with physical and human reality and into the diffusion of knowledge. It was a way of communicating empirical facts—"brutal facts"—in visual, purportedly unmediated form across space and time. Photographic witnessing became a substitute for eye witnessing.[28]

Photographic Witnessing across Space

In an era when geographical movement was embraced as intellectual method, and observation was the paradigm of knowing,[29] photography made it possible to gather and disseminate all kinds of information in visual form, with unprecedented ease and accuracy; the implications were enormous. The daguerreotype—praised by John Ruskin as "the most marvellous invention of the century"—and the photograph on paper extended the authority of visual truth from the realm of actual experience to the verisimilitude of photographic realism. This changed the relationship of observer to material reality and established ways of seeing that persisted and formed the basis of an increasingly visual culture. With the advent of photography, visual processes came to predominate epistemology.

When word of Daguerre's discovery leaked to the press in early January 1839, a French newspaper predicted, "For a few hundred francs travellers may perhaps soon be able to procure M. Daguerre's apparatus, and bring back views of the finest monuments and of the most delightful scenery of the whole world."[30] Arago himself, reporting to the Académie des Sciences on his visit to Daguerre, declared that "in addition to giving the brilliant results shown, the method is also economical, easy, and capable of being used by travellers anywhere."[31]

Reciprocally and simultaneously, photography entered the nineteenth-century imagination as a way of capturing the world in precise detail and bringing it home for careful study. References to travel, geography, topography, and landscape were central to the arguments in favor of Daguerre's invention. As Duchâtel argued before the Chamber of Deputies on June 15, 1839:

> . . . to the traveller, to the archaeologist and also to the naturalist, the apparatus of M. Daguerre will become an object of continual and indispensable use. It will enable them to note what they see, without having recourse to the hand of another. Every author will in future be able to compose the geographical part of his own work: by stopping awhile before the most complicated monument, or the most extensive *coup-d'oeil*, he will immediately obtain an exact *fac simile* of them.[32]

With this statement, Duchâtel established photography as a legitimate tool of fieldwork, geographical description, and scientific data gathering. Most compelling was the argument made by Arago in introducing daguerreotype specimens for examination by the Chamber of Deputies; in it, he couched the usefulness of Daguerre's process in the glories of the great *Description de l'Égypte*:

> As you look with wonder on several pictures that will be handed to you for inspection, every one of you, Gentleman, [sic] will be aware of the prodigious advantages which might have been derived during the expedition to Egypt, from a method so quick and perfect to reproduce objects; every one of you will be struck with this reflection, that if photography had been known in 1798, we should now have correct images of a somewhat considerable number of emblematical pictures, of which the cupidity of the Arabs, or the fatal mania of certain travellers for destruction has for ever deprived the scientific world.

> To copy the millions and millions of hieroglyphics with which even the outside of all the great monuments of Thebes, Memphis, etc., are covered, scores of years, and whole legions of painters would be required. One individual, with a Daguerreotype, would effect the labour in a very short space of time. Provide the Institute of Egypt with two or three sets of apparatus, and in several of the large plates of the celebrated work the fruits of our immortal expedition, vast extents of real hieroglyphics will soon replace the fictitious ones; the drawings will every where [sic] surpass in copy and local colour the works of the most skilful painters; and the photographic pictures being submitted in their formation to the rules of geometry, will allow us, with the assistance of a very few further data, to attain the exact dimensions of the highest parts of edifices and of those most difficult of access.[33]

This emphasis placed on the use of the daguerreotype by travelers, naturalists, and scientists was, at least in part, informed by Humboldt's experiences, interests, and expectations.[34] His own extensive travels, his emphasis on empirical research, his use of scientific instruments, and his voluminous publications suggest that Humboldt's vision would have been seminal to the committee's examination of Daguerre's images, to the assessment of the process and equipment that produced them, and to the political process that made them available to the world.

Photographs were not only adopted as a convenient form of visual note taking for those who traveled; they also became a surrogate for travel. "We need no longer embark upon perilous voyages," wrote Louis de Cormenin in *La Lumière* in 1852; "heliography entrusted to a few intrepid practitioners, will make the world tour on our behalf, without our ever needing to leave our armchairs."[35] "Guided by the photograph," *The Art-Journal* declared, "we can travel over all countries of the world, without moving a yard from our own firesides."[36] George Thomas Fisher Jr., even suggested that the impression which "faithful representations of the monuments of antiquity . . . give us, even those who have never crossed the sea . . . , is but little inferior to that which the traveller receives [when contemplating] . . . the moral of a crumbling arch or a broken column, on the very spots where once they stood the glory of the age."[37] Rev. W. J. Read, addressing a meeting of the Manchester Photographic Society, even claimed that "by careful study of a series . . . [of photographs, one could] learn almost as much of a country in its general features and actual state, as by residence, and much more I think than by hasty travel."[38]

Hence, the photograph became a surrogate for travel at a time when travel was the premier avenue to knowledge of the world. This nineteenth-century emphasis on travel and the substitution of photographic witnessing for direct observation was elaborated most eloquently by Marcus Aurelius Root, who regarded "travelling, whether in foreign lands or our own, . . . as one of the most efficient means of self-culture within our knowledge." Root pointed out, "Comparatively few, however, are able to leave home and business and bear the heavy expenses thus required. But photography enables us to enjoy the pleasure and the advantages of travel without even crossing our own thresholds."[39] Echoing Read, Root goes on to suggest that the photograph was not only a substitute for firsthand experience, but that, in some instances, it was even possible to achieve a "completer and truer" understanding through photographic witnessing than by direct observation.

The concept of vicarious travel through visual representation had been mooted by Humboldt in *Cosmos,* where he suggested that such large-scale landscape paintings as panoramas and dioramas could serve, to some extent, as a substitute for traveling through different regions. Humboldt's reference to panoramas and dioramas links the function of photographic witnessing across space to the effects achieved by these visual precursors (and contemporaries) of the daguerreotype. The panorama was a 360° painting that presented to the viewer the realistic illusion of three-dimensional geographical space; the diorama was a mammoth canvas that was lit in sequence from either side using filters to present the realistic illusion of the passage of time or movement. Both employed art in "pursuit of maximum illusion." Bernard Comment has suggested that the panorama was invented in "response to a particularly strong nineteenth-century need—for absolute dominance":

It gave individuals the happy feeling that the world was organized around and by them, yet this was a world from which they were also separated and protected, for they were seeing it from a distance. A double dream come true—one of totality and of possession; encyclopaedism on the cheap.[40]

If, as Comment continues, the panorama marked the transition from representation to illusion, then photography—and, in particular, the daguerreotype invented by the creator of the diorama—can be placed in the succession of subsequent modifications which were aimed at "perfecting the illusion" and "regaining control of

sprawling collective space"[41] in the wake of the Industrial Revolution.

Root and others championed the moral use of visual images implicit in Humboldt's discussion of landscape painting. This emphasized that "the conception of the natural unity, and the feeling of the harmonious accord pervading the universe, cannot fail to increase in vividness among men, in proportion as the means are multiplied, by which the phenomena of nature may be more characteristically and visibly manifested."[42] But, as the arguments of Root and others suggest, photographs were cheaper, more truthful, more accessible, more convenient, and more egalitarian than other forms of visual imagery. Although the price of paper prints still made collecting portraits and landscape views a habit of the middle and upper classes, Root maintained that photographs offered—to "even the lowliest of the community"—opportunities for geographical education in domestic space.

By the late 1850s, the expanded use of photography on paper greatly increased the viability of the photograph as a surrogate for travel. In particular, stereoscopic views, issued in geographical series, offered the convincing impression of transporting the armchair traveler to distant destinations.[43] As a means of both education and entertainment, the stereoscopic view presented the ultimate in vicarious travel, producing an illusion of three-dimensional space which was claimed to "produce an appearance of reality which cheats the senses with its seeming truth."[44]

Photographic witnessing across space also had important societal implications. As domestic ties, social glue, and moral uplift, they were credited with contributing to the creation and maintenance of a sense of family, of continuity, and of community. But, as English essayist, translator, and art critic Lady Elizabeth Eastlake (1809–93) recognized, meaning was not an inherent or observable property:

What indeed are nine-tenths of those facial maps called photographic portraits, but accurate landmarks and measurements for loving eyes and memories to deck with beauty and animate with expression, in perfect certainty, that the ground-plan is founded upon fact?[45]

The geographical metaphor likening photographic portraits to "facial maps" and "accurate landmarks" is particularly important. The photograph, like landscape, was a factual ground plan that had to be invested with meaning through association and memory. Here, the "subjectivity" of the viewer met the perceived "objectivity" of the photograph, and yet, in the writings of Root and others, purity, goodness, and affection were presented as qualities evident in photographs themselves, and the ability to act morally upon individuals and nations was attributed to photography as a medium. These beliefs served to naturalize the content of the photograph and to veil the human choices and cultural values involved in its production and consumption. Photographs, because of their transparency and truth, were thus credited with being not only a way of seeing across space but also a way of seeing those things—qualities, characteristics, emotions, values—that, in space, had no observable manifestation.

Photographic witnessing was not only a way of studying places from afar; it was also a way of investigating peoples at a safe distance. A decade before the publication of Darwin's *On the Origin of Species,* Louis Agassiz (1807–73), Harvard scientist and the father of American natural science, commissioned Joseph T. Zealy to take a series of daguerreotypes of Southern slaves to support his theory of polygenesis. In 1862, Mayer and Pierson claimed that even a cursory glance at the lifeless plaster casts of aboriginal peoples in the anthropology galleries of museums would suffice to demonstrate the services rendered by photography to the study of racial types.[46] The use of photography in the empirical pursuit of cultural difference was clearly articulated by Rev. Read in his lecture to the Manchester Photographic Society in 1856. In his discussion of what photography "can do for the illustration and record of facts connected with Natural Science," Read explained:

> Highest in the scale of Natural Science stands Ethnography, the Natural History of the Human race, and for the furtherance of this Science great help is offered by Photography. Hitherto only the practised and skilful draughtsman has been able to collect its materials, and record the distinguishing features of the great families into which our race is distributed and divided: but now the Lens may be used instead of an eye, and the sensitive tablet instead of a hand, so that any one of us however unskilled in the use of a pencil, might well furnish the Philosopher material to be built into the Temple of Science.[47]

Apart from Read's morally loaded description of science as profane religion, this statement is interesting for the way in which it anticipates the adoption of photography to provide, in systematic, scientific, and standardized fashion, structured visual data about the body for studies of evolution and race.

Photographic Witnessing across Time

Photographic witnessing had a temporal as well as a spatial dimension. In giving immediate and direct visual access to the past, to sights/sites physically removed in time, the photograph served as an *aide-mémoire,* a device of memory, a form of time travel. As a way of fixing the look of the present, it was embraced as a medium of preservation. This had implications for shaping both individual and collective memory and identity. "Photography empowers us to preserve from the decay of time, and the fickle tenure of mortality, the true type of the features of those we love."[48] Ernest Lacan pointed out that it was thanks to the daguerreotype that viewers could contemplate "monuments which terrestial upheavals have swallowed up, like the Cathedral of San Juan de los Lagos, for example, and which no longer exist except in the print of the traveler."[49] This notion of studying photographs of buildings and monuments destroyed by the passage of time, or by natural or man-made disasters, embraced the photograph as a tool of conscious historical preservation and re-presentation.

In what might be considered architectural equivalents of the ethnographic salvage paradigm,[50] photography was employed to create for posterity a visual record of buildings and monuments fast-disappearing in the wake of progress. Writing about the Château de Polignac, Lacan expressed faith in the photograph as a medium of preservation and a belief in the essential relationship between physical form and visual appearance:

> This precious monument, like so many others, falls stone by stone; soon, it will disappear like the generations who inhabited it but, thanks to photography, it will remain such as it is still, in this design traced by light. All those venerable fragments of another age, so valuable for the archaeologist, for the historian, for the painter, for the poet, the photograph brings them together and renders them immortal. Time, revolutions, and natural upheavals may destroy them down to the last stone; henceforth they will live on in our photograph albums.[51]

In this way, photographic documentation was conflated with historical preservation in projects which served to reflect, constitute, and confirm sense of place, symbolic space, and collective memory. In photographs of "monastic piles" and "baronial halls," Fisher claimed, "every stone will tell its own tale: . . . the very spirit of the place, may now be impressed by the subtle fingers of light upon tablets of metal or sheets of paper, to speak to future ages as they speak to us."[52] Fisher's expectations for photographic witnessing across time are analogous to the goal of diplomatics as "an art by which written records from any age and of any kind are made to speak again with a full distinct voice."[53]

Cameras were pointed not only at architecture and monuments but also at public figures and public events. Fisher declared ". . . by the wondrous science, we are now enabled to preserve and hand down to future generations the *truth-telling* portraits of our statesmen, our heroes, our philosophers, our poets, and our friends,"[54] and Lacan, writing about photography of public celebrations (les fêtes publiques), exclaimed:

Photography . . . records in turn on magical tablets the memorable events of our collective life, and every day it enriches the archives of history with some precious document.[55]

Indeed, Rev. Read called photography "a handmaid to the Muse of History, in virtue of its power of putting upon record, the actual real state and appearance of persons and places as we know and see them."[56] But, despite the rhetoric of unmediated representation, the photograph was, and continues to be, the material evidence of a human decision to preserve the appearance of a person, an object, a document, a building, or an event judged to have abiding value. In the ritual act of photographic commemoration was a valorization of what in the present was thought to be worth remembering—of the surviving past and the unfolding present—in the future.[57] In this way, a subjective decision was objectified, since neither "History" nor photography, but individuals with agendas, were responsible for the process of selection.

In their advertisements, photographers urged the public to "Mark the fleeting shadow, 'ere the substance fades." For British artist, photographer, and author William Lake Price (1810–c.95), photography was a way of "fixing passing events" so that:

Posterity, by the agency of Photography, will view the faithful image of our times; the future student, in turning the page of history, may at the same time look on the very skin, into the very eyes, of those, long since mouldered to dust, whose lives and deeds he traces in the text. . . . [E]ach impressive public ceremonial will be registered and delineated; nay, even the very turmoil of the distant battle or siege and their varying aspects will be instantly fixed and transferred, with the actors, to the page of history.[58]

The same sense of historicism through photographic links to future generations is expressed in the preamble to the conditions of a prize offered by the Duc de Luynes to the Société française de photographie:

One of the most promising applications of photography is the faithful, irrefutable reproduction of historical or artistic monuments and documents, so usually destroyed by the passage of time or by revolutions. Since the immortal discoveries of Niépce, of Daguerre and of Talbot, archaeologists have been aware of the full importance of this application of photography, which is called upon to transmit precious elements to future generations.[59]

As an instrument of collective identity and memory, photography was embraced as an efficient way of copying documents considered to be historically important. In what must be considered to be a nineteenth-century technological equivalent of digitization, photography was enlisted to disseminate and promote knowledge of historical, literary, and artistic treasures by copying them and making them more widely available. Writing at length about the applications of photography to the arts, sciences, and industry, Mayer and Pierson described how photography could be employed

in the reproduction of precious documents, rare prints, historic charters, illuminated manuscripts [*vélins*], images which the Middle Ages have bequeathed to us and which remain lost to science and art which cannot rescue them from oblivion [*oubliettes*] in our archives. . . .[60]

In retrospect, what seems remarkably akin to current initiatives to increase access to archival holdings by making them available over the Internet, they proposed that

a photographic workship should operate in each of the national archives' repositories [*dépôts*], and, under the strict supervision of curators [*conservateurs*], reproduce and multiply the treasures they preserve.[61]

Linking photography, archives, and memory even further, Mayer and Pierson continued

Each province, each region [*département*], each town, each family would thus be able to have unimpeachable facsimiles of deeds which concern them and which, deposted now in the general archives or in private collections, can be neither moved nor entrusted to the public without endangering their very existence. None of our historic origins, our ancient customs, our traditions would remain unknown since this photographic paleography would have completed the work begun by [French historians] Bailly, Alexis Monteil, Augustin Thierry,

Letrone [*sic*], Michelet, Lacabanne, et al., and rendered so simple the task now so arduous for scholarly learned researchers who devote their lives to reconstructing the history of our past still so poorly known.[62]

The daguerreotype, from its invention, was known as "the mirror with a memory." Where current concern with the nature of memory, and in particular social or collective memory, has taken little account of photography (or, for that matter, archives), the relationship between memory and photography elicited comment by early critics. One writer observed:

> There is a mysterious or at least interesting resemblance between the operation of photography and the faculty of memory, as connected with that of vision. The eye is the camera-obscura whereby objects are represented on the retina, whence, in a manner to us incomprehensible, the figures are communicated to the brain. There, amidst its wonderful convolutions, are the images imprinted and retained with greater or less degree of precision and intensity conformable with the condition and quality of the recipient . . . lying concealed . . . we suppose we have forgotten, until some circumstance involuntarily recalls the impression or reproduces the visual images of twenty, or thirty, or forty years ago. What a suggestion does this convey of the eternal permanency of our thoughts and actions![63]

The technology of photography and the faculty of memory made permanent thoughts and actions, suggesting parallels with the presumed function of archival records.

These ideas, expressed by nineteenth-century writers about the photograph as a tool of observation and a surrogate for travel, as a tool of preservation and a device of memory, effectively recast the photograph as an agent of spatial and temporal collapse. The annihilation of space and time was a popular theme which linked photographs to other examples of mechanical genius which gave the illusion of greater control over one's life and surroundings. In 1858 in France, Théophile Gautier declared:

> Space and time have ceased to exist. The propeller creates its vibrating spiral, the paddle-wheel beats the waves, the locomotive pants and grinds in a whirlwind of speed; conversations take place between one shore of an ocean and the other; the electric fluid has taken to carrying the mail; the power of the thunderstorm sends letters coursing along a wire. The sun is a draughtsman who depicts landscapes, human types, monuments; the daguerreotype opens its brass-lidded eye of glass, and a view, a ruin, a group of people, is captured in an instant.[64]

At the same time that steamships, railways—the new technologies depicted in Maurisset's caricature—and the telegraph made the world physically more accessible, photographs made it visually and conceptually more accessible. They brought into view the microscopically small and telescopically far, adding cosmological scale to geographical space and temporal expanse. Photographs may not have "annihilated" space, but they radically reduced it. They made it visually possible to "be" in two (or more) places at the same time, creating the illusion of simultaneity and proximity. Photographs also may not have "annihilated" time, but they certainly altered perceptions of it. They made it visually possible to "be" in two (or more) times in the same space, creating the illusion of synchronicity and presence. The work of Thomas Richards, Edward Said, Bruno Latour, James Ryan, and others suggests that this shrinking of space and time contributed to the hegemony of Europe in the late nineteenth and early twentieth centuries and permitted the "new imperialism" to flourish. Images of empire were pervasive and were used to construct rationalizations for, and examples of, political and racial dominance over the non-white, non-Western world.[65]

The Notion of Photographic Truth

If photographic witnessing was the operative mechanism by which the photograph entered seamlessly into the relationship between observer and material reality, then photographic truth was its foundational notion. To understand the role of the photograph in the nineteenth-century imagination, it is important to appreciate this ardent belief in photographic truth, to examine the ways in which it was articulated, and to consider its consequences. A great deal of late twentieth-century theorizing about photographs seeks to demonstrate that photographs are *not* truthful records of reality; however, most mid-nineteenth-century writings about photographs claimed that they were. At a time when mimesis dominated Western thinking about the visual arts, the daguerreotype and the photograph on paper constituted "only the plain unvarnished truth; the actual is absolutely before us, and we know it."[66] They carried scientific credentials and exhibited optical precision: "The photograph, however, cannot deceive; in nothing can it extenuate; there is no power in this marvellous machine either to add or to take from: we know that what we see *must* be TRUE."[67]

However, the belief in photographic truth was not

based solely on the optical illusion of photographic realism. It was also grounded in its mechanical origins and its capacity for exact reproducibility. Photography was seen as the work of "an unreasoning machine"[68] at a time when the goal of exact reproducibility through technology held particular fascination. Whereas Daguerre's process produced a unique image, exact reproducibility was achieved through Talbot's positive-negative process and the subsequent refinements by Niépce de Saint-Victor (albumen on glass, 1847), Frederick Scott Archer (wet collodion, 1851), and Gustave Le Gray (dry waxed paper, 1851), which produced multiple prints from a single negative. Thus, the photograph on paper was part of the debates over the legitimacy of the imitative arts, the relative value of mass-produced copies, and the original work of art, which centered on electroplated, machine-stamped, and cast-iron manufactures in an age of industrialization and mechanization.[69]

Photographic truth was also a matter of mathematics. The photograph was not only thought to be visually truthful; it was believed to be scientifically correct. Duchâtel noted that in the daguerreotype "objects preserve their mathematical delineation in its most minute details, and . . . the effects of linear perspective, and the diminution of shades arising from aerial perspective, are produced with a degree of nicety quite unprecedented."[70] Arago commented that "photographic pictures . . . [submit] in their formation to the rules of geometry."[71] Gay-Lussac explained that "the perspective of the landscape of every object is retraced with mathematical preciseness," and that what was achieved was "a degree of perfection that could be attained by no other means."[72]

Above all, photographic truth was a consequence of causal genesis. Causal genesis refers to the "special relationship" between the photograph and Nature, which was the direct result of light bouncing off some portion of three-dimensional material reality to produce a visual analogue on a light-sensitive two-dimensional surface. At a time of intense interest in the properties of light,[73] the photograph commanded particular attention because the photograph was believed to be "obtained by the mere action of Light upon sensitive paper . . . formed or depicted by optical and chemical means alone, and without the aid of any one acquainted with the art of drawing."[74]

Light is that silent artist
Which without the aid of man
Designs on silver bright
Daguerre's immortal plan.[75]

In this verse, claimed to be the first poem "inspired by photography," we find the foundational rhetoric of the photograph as an unmediated representation made from nature, by "Light . . . without the aid of man."

This theme was expressed in many ways—Talbot talked about the "pencil of nature." Henry David Thoreau talked about Nature's "amanuensis."[76] "The sun is a rare truth-teller, which cannot lie to produce effect, nor err to lead astray," *The Art-Journal* declared.[77] Charles Piazzi Smyth concurred: "Whatever the sun has shone on for a second, she makes her own."[78] Whatever the terminology, the key idea projected upon photography was the same. Photography was not just a new way of seeing; it was a new way of believing. It was what Steven Shapin and Simon Schaffer have called a "technology of trust," or what record keepers today would consider a "trustworthy information system."[79]

With this ability to make photographs directly from Nature, comparisons with more overtly mediated forms of representation were inevitable. Rev. Read claimed, "The Photographer lays before us the scene itself, the Artist his own conception of it"; he went on to explain that

in examining landscapes illustrative of Topography, or National Scenery, such as those of Turner and Roberts, . . . [i]t is for the most part quite impossible to distinguish such spurious details from those which are true, and thus is diminished in no slight degree not only the pleasures, but the confidence, with which we examine it. A Photograph is quite without this defect at least. Though it be poor as a Work of Art, though it be indifferent as a Photograph, yet whatever detail we find in it is accurate, and the most trivial feature of the scene as there depicted, yields not at all to the most prominent in absolute truthfulness and reliable authenticity.[80]

Edgar Allen Poe declared the daguerreotype *"infinitely* more accurate in its representation than any painting by human hands. . . . The variations of shade, and the gradations of both linear and aerial perspective are those of truth itself in the supremeness of its perfection."[81] Where previously distant scenes were "known only from the imperfect relations of travellers,"[82] photography, one reviewer declared, "has gone abroad to verify or refute hasty, dull, or prejudiced writers—to enable us to talk with certainty of what we have hitherto not seen but only read of."[83] Even the writings and illustrations of the most respected names in science were called into question: "The Sun's opinion of Egypt . . . is better than Denon's, Champollion's, Wilkinson's, Eōthen's, or Titmarsh's."[84]

Whereas travelers' accounts and artist-made sketches were clearly humanly created and, therefore, considered suspect, camera-made images were embraced as unmediated and, therefore, unassailably truthful. In an essay entitled "Photography as an Authority," Rev. H. J. Morton expressed and reinforced a paradigmatic belief in the nature of evidence which could be extended from photographs to other archival documents:

> What we want in a witness are capacity and opportunity for accurate observation, and entire honesty. Now the camera of the Photographer has exactly these qualifications. To exquisite acuteness of vision and instantaneous comprehension of minutest details, it adds perfect freedom from all partiality and hypocrisy. It sees everything, and it represents just what it sees. It has an eye that cannot be deceived, and a fidelity that cannot be corrupted. We have abundant ocular delusions, but the camera is never under any hallucination. Behind the most accurate human there is often a very prejudiced human mind, refracting its vision; and the most skilful hand is often moved by motives which lead it to misrepresent what it professes to delineate. But the camera's eye of microscopic minuteness and exactness of vision has behind it a crystal plate that has no partiality, and the fingers of the sun that paint the pictures which that crystal surface bears, are vibrations from a great burning heart that throbs with no human passions. Hence the camera seeing with perfect accuracy and microscopic minuteness, and representing with absolute fidelity, is a witness on whose testimony the most certain conclusions may be confidently founded.[85]

This rhetoric of transparency and truth—or in archival terms, authenticity, reliability, and objectivity—that came to surround the photograph raised serious questions about the very nature of truth, particularly in relation to art. At the surface of the problem was the degree to which a mechanical device could produce a truthful picture of reality. But, as Miles Orvell has pointed out, "the real issue was of course buried in the question itself: what was a 'truthful' picture of reality? Was truth to be found in literal exactitude or in artistic generalization?"[86]

Art, Light, and Nature

However much photographs were embraced as a scientific and objective way of capturing the world, they were, first and foremost, pictures. Moreover, they were images formed by "Light," whose special, mystical quality had inspired Romantic art and literature in the late eighteenth and early nineteenth centuries. Light had moral and spiritual connections to the "infinite Creative Spirit"; the true photographer, Marcus Aurelius Root maintained,

> like the true artist in whatever sphere, should be an intermedium, through which the light of the Divine should pass unmodified and pure, producing imprints as distinctly and delicately limned, as are the images of natural objects on the surface of a crystal pool.[87]

Thus, at a time when Art served as an aesthetic conduit to Nature and the Divine, the place of photography in this discourse was not immediately clear: on the one hand, the photograph was made by light and, therefore, had divine origins; on the other hand, it was made by a machine and, therefore, was not divinely inspired.

Protracted debates ensued over the nature of photography and the ability of a mechanical device to produce art. These, in turn, were part of larger issues in literary and art criticism that struggled with the role of idealism and realism, mimesis and genius, beauty and imagination, the status of the artist and the importance of originality. A powerful metaphor with artistic, religious, and epistemological resonances, Light orchestrated an intimate and direct encounter between material object and "unthinking machine" (the camera). In this encounter, the role of the photographer, if acknowledged at all, was assumed to be less instrumental than that of the camera. Rather, the individual holding the camera and the human eye were successfully prevented from interfering with and, thereby, adulterating this wondrous moment of virtually unmediated transcription of Nature onto paper. Photography's persuasiveness, therefore, resided in its ability to pull off the ultimate media trick: it made possible seemingly unmediated transcriptions of Nature.

The contested relationship of photography and art, which centered upon the role of Light and the imagination, shaped the ways in which photographs were seen, permeated nineteenth-century thinking, and influenced the relationship between observer and material reality. Photographs, as a way of representing landscape and experiencing Nature, either were acknowledged to be a factual means of pictorial delineation and rejected as art, or were championed as art and recognized as a way to imbue landscape with meaning by exploring the essence of Nature and the handiwork of the Divine. At the heart of these debates were essential concepts of Nature and Art, the relationship between them, and their joint relationship with the Ideal. These were debated at length by such prominent nineteenth-century art critics as Charles Baudelaire in France, and John Ruskin and Lady Elizabeth Eastlake in England.

French poet, translator, and literary and art critic Charles Baudelaire (1821–67) saw photography as a "great industrial madness" that had invaded art and threatened to "ruin whatever might remain divine in the French mind."[88] He railed against the credo that "art is, and cannot be other than, the exact reproduction of Nature" and decried the "mad fools" who believed that "an industry that could give us a result identical to Nature would be the absolute of art":

A revengeful God has given ear to the prayers of this multitude. Daguerre was his Messiah. And now the faithful says to himself: "Since Photography gives us every guarantee of exactitude that we could desire (they really believe that, the mad fools!), then Photography and Art are the same thing."

Baudelaire's concept of art emphasized the exercise of imagination in the creation of beauty: a painter should paint what he dreams, not what he sees. He denigrated photography as "the refuge of every would-be painter, every painter too ill-endowed or too lazy to complete his studies." He was convinced that "the ill-applied developments of photography, like all other purely material developments of progress, have contributed much to the impoverishment of the French artistic genius," which, he added, was "already so scarce." By "invading the territories of art," photography, he declared, had become "art's most mortal enemy." This he attributed to "the stupidity of the multitude which is its natural ally."

English artist, scientist, poet, philosopher, and preeminent art critic John Ruskin (1819–1900) asserted, like Baudelaire, that art required "design or evidence of active intellect in choice and arrangement," which, he asserted, was "replaceable by no mechanism."[89] Initially Ruskin embraced the daguerreotype enthusiastically as an aid to draftsmanship, declaring it "a most blessed invention," "the most marvellous invention of the century," and "one antidote . . . amongst all the mechanical poison that this terrible nineteenth century has poured upon men."[90] Ruskin employed the camera in his study of Venetian architecture "as a means to record comprehensively and accurately . . . , virtually as an extension of the art of drawing . . . ," but as Julie Lawson points out, he "did not regard his own drawings as 'art'—he made no such claims for them. They were, in their making, aids to looking and were, subsequently, aids for mem-

ory."[91] His zeal for the daguerreotype focused on its ability to capture detail with mechanical precision and impartiality. Of some daguerreotypes he acquired on his sketching trip to Italy in 1845, Ruskin wrote:

I have been lucky enough to get from a poor Frenchm[an] here, said to be in distress, some most beautiful, though small, Daguerreotypes of the palaces I have been trying to draw—and certainly Daguerreotypes taken by this vivid sunlight are glorious things. It is very nearly the same thing as carrying off the palace itself—every chip and stone and stain is there—and of course, there is no mistake about *proportions*. I am very much delighted with these and am going to have some more made of pet bits. It is a noble invention, say what they will of it, and anyone who has worked and blundered and stammered as I have for four days, then sees the thing he has been trying to do so long in vain, *done* perfectly and faultlessly in half a minute, won't abuse it afterwards.[92]

Photography, despite its ability to render the chiaroscuro of landscape with "absolute truth and unapproachable subtilty [sic]," did not supersede the study of landscape or the use of sketching. For Ruskin, the distinction between mechanism and design constituted the essential difference between photography and art.[93]

Yet, while both Baudelaire and Ruskin clearly rejected the photograph as artistic, they recognized it as truthful. According to Baudelaire, photography's "true duty" was to be the humble servant of the sciences and arts, "like printing or shorthand, which have neither created nor supplemented literature":

Let it hasten to enrich the tourist's album and restore to his eye the precision which his memory may lack; let it adorn the naturalist's library, and enlarge microscopic animals; let it even provide information to corroborate the astronomer's hypotheses; in short, let it be the secretary and clerk of whoever needs an absolute factual exactitude in his profession—up to that point nothing could be better. Let it rescue from oblivion those trembling ruins, those books, prints and manuscripts which time is devouring, precious things whose form is dissolving and which demand a place in the archives of our memory—it will be thanked and applauded.[94]

Art, for Baudelaire, belonged in "the domain of the impalpable and the imaginary." This concern for the relative value of exactitude and imagination in photography and painting were restated succinctly and pointedly by Ruskin, who by 1874 had become disillusioned with photography as an aid to art:

Anything more beautiful than the photographs of the Valley of Chamouni, now in your print-sellers' windows, cannot be conceived. For geographical and geological purposes, they are worth anything; for art purposes, worth—a good deal less than zero.[95]

Ruskin would surely have agreed with Lady Eastlake's observation that "the success with which all accidental blurs and blotches have been overcome, and the sharp perfection of the object . . . is exactly as detrimental to art as it is complimentary to science."[96] Eastlake believed that there was an important distinction between two types of visual images. "The field of delineation, having two distinct spheres, requires two distinct labourers; but though hitherto the freewoman has done the work of the bondwoman, there is no fear that the position should be in future reversed."[97] She went on to suggest that

the whole question of success and failure resolves itself into an investigation of the capacities of the machine, and well may we be satisfied with the rich gifts it bestows, without straining it into a competition with art. For everything which Art, so-called, has hitherto been the means but not the end, photography is the allotted agent—for all that requires mere manual correctness, and mere manual slavery, without any employment of artistic feeling, she is the proper and therefore the perfect medium.

In effect, photography served to "relieve the artist of a burden rather than supplant him in an office." Its best attributes were "correctness of drawing, truth of detail, and absence of convention." Thus, having dismissed photographs as works of Art, Eastlake championed them as "records of simple truth and precision." She declared:

[Photography] is made for the present age, in which the desire for art resides in a small minority, but the craving, or rather necessity for cheap, prompt, and correct facts in the public at large. Photography is the purveyor of such knowledge to the world. She is the sworn witness of everything presented to her view. What are her unerring records in the service of mechanics, engineering, geology, and natural history, but facts of the most sterling and stubborn kind . . . facts which are neither the province of art nor of description, but of that new form of communication between man and man—neither letter, message, nor picture—which now happily fills up the space between them?

For Eastlake, the business of every photograph was "to give evidence of facts, as minutely and as impartially as,

to our shame, only an unreasoning machine can give." Clearly, photography's weakness as a mode of artistic expression constituted its strength as a purveyor of factual information.

Facts in a New Form of Communication

If there was ongoing disagreement between art critics and art photographers over the status of the photograph as art, there was general consensus on the nature of the photograph as fact, and the uses to which the new medium could profitably be put. Even critics who ranked photographs as a "Fine Art" or argued that they were not the result of a purely mechanical operation agreed that photography excelled as a vehicle for communicating facts.[98]

As "facts of the age and of the hour,"[99] photographs were ideally suited to empiricism and the nineteenth-century passion for collecting and classifying facts in pursuit of comprehensive knowledge. Prevailing ideas about collecting facts, easily transferred to the collecting of photographic facts, were an extension of the enthusiasm for collecting natural and artificial objects as a way of interrogating Nature and accumulating knowledge, which emerged in the sixteenth and seventeenth centuries in Europe, an activity based on the premise that "through the possession of objects, one physically acquired knowledge."[100] Distant pasts could be known by their remnants; distant places could be known by their artifacts. The idea of collecting as a key to understanding the world was fueled by voyages of discovery and European curiosity about distant places and peoples and was sustained by improved travel and communication. Museums and libraries were founded by family, church, and later the state as repositories of knowledge and places of scholarship for the powerful, the wealthy, and the educated. The *Wunderkammer* of the late Renaissance "attempted an articulation of universal knowledge through the possession and identification of objects."[101] In the seventeenth, eighteenth, and early nineteenth centuries, learned institutions and societies established museums to house objects for the study of geology, natural history, classical antiquity, and ethnography.[102] The valorization in the Enlightenment of empirical knowledge and scientific progress encouraged an empiricist approach to amassing not only artifacts but also facts. By the mid-nineteenth century, facts occupied a central place alongside artifacts in the Victorian project of obtaining and then controlling comprehensive knowledge.[103]

As visual facts, photographs took their place in this project as a means to know the world through possession of its images. Even the earliest expectations for the daguerreotype were very much grounded in these concerns for collecting and classifying information in the pursuit of knowledge. As early as the summer of 1839, the daguerreotype was envisaged as a quick, accurate, and enduring method of reproducing objects and "forming collections of sketches and drawings," and as a tool in "the study of species and of their organization."[104]

This idea of acquiring knowledge about the world through the accumulation of photographic images was expressly articulated in 1859 by noted American physician, man of letters, and amateur photographer Oliver Wendell Holmes (1809–94), who declared that through photography and, in particular, stereoscopic photography, "*Form is henceforth divorced from matter*. In fact, matter as a visible object is of no great use any longer," for:

> Matter in large masses must always be fixed and dear; form is cheap and transportable. . . . The consequence of this will soon be such an enormous collection of forms that they will have to be classified and arranged in vast libraries, as books are now. The time will come when a man who wishes to see any object, natural or artificial, will go to the Imperial, National, or City Stereographic Library and call for its skin or form, as he would for a book at any common library.[105]

Holmes's separation of photographic form from physical matter embodied the foundational notion, expressed by Joseph Ellis in 1847, that "The object which, photographically pictured, meets our eyes, we have indeed *seen!*"[106] As an act of representation, photography was transparent, invisible; the photograph, by extension was neutral, objective, unmediated. Seeing a photograph was effectively the experiential equivalent of observing the object directly.

This desire for unmediated representation had, in fact, been expressed some eighty years before Daguerre's announcement.[107] In the fictional work, *Giphantie*, published in 1760 in French and in English translation the following year, Charles François Tiphaigne de la Roche described a viscous substance which, through the action of light, could act upon the fugitive image produced by light reflected off objects onto a mirrored surface and fix them permanently. This substance, when coated on a piece of canvas, resulted in a painting produced by the sure and never-erring hand of Nature. Particularly interesting is de la Roche's conclusion that "de telles images valent les choses"—that is, such images are equivalent to the things themselves.[108] When, in 1839, alchemy and science fiction gave way to photography and scientific explanation, this equivalence, in which the act of mediation disappears, governed thinking about the photochemically fixed images of the *camera obscura*.

The new medium of photography offered a means of observing, describing, studying, ordering, classifying, and, thereby, knowing the world. There seems to have been little that was not susceptible to photographic delineation, and the most commonly cited subjects—among them portraits, landscapes, architecture, and public works—are indeed those that we find most frequently in collections of archival photographs. William Lake Price argued that photography "has already added, and will increasingly tend to contribute, to the knowledge and happiness of mankind" and insisted that even the "most indifferent" of photographs was "not without its value in the diffusion of knowledge. . . ."[109] This ability of the photograph to transmit, across space and across time, what were believed to be objective, whole, and self-evident facts in visual form allowed the photograph to act as a new form of communication. In this role, photography constituted a powerful new technology of information transfer that offered a more realistic, more objective, and more truthful path to knowledge through unmediated representation.

The concept of "virtual witnessing"—which I have here recast as "photographic witnessing"—has strong archival resonances. Shapin and Schaffer explain that, in writing up his scientific research, Robert Boyle sought to be "a reliable purveyor of experimental testimony" so that the readers of his reports "could take on trust that these things happened." Boyle's literary descriptions, dense with detail, were intended to produce in the reader's mind a sense of having been present at the proceedings. Intended to "mimic the immediacy and simultaneity of experience afforded by pictorial representations," Boyle's accounts served as "undistorted mirrors of complex experimental outcomes." His literary and visual mimetic devices, Shapin and Schaffer conclude, "allayed distrust and facilitated virtual witnessing."[110]

The process of "picturing"—whether in words or images—was, inevitably, a subjective one, and stress placed on the realism of the photographic image and objectivity of the photographic process effectively masked the human decision making embedded in the elements of meaning making—authorial intention, subject matter, physical format, purpose, transmission, and target audience—and veiled the communicative capacities of the photograph to reflect and inform. The facts offered by photographs were believed to be accurate, complete, and capable of producing reliable knowledge of the world. Photographs were also assumed to capture the feelings of association, the spirit of place, and the character of people, echoing prevailing enthusiasm for phrenology and other manifestations of the belief in the legibility of appearances. Repeated reference to photography as an instrument of morality and self-improvement flowed from assumptions that its ability to function in these ways derived from qualities that were intrinsic rather than assigned. In the refusal to acknowledge the selectivity, subjectivity, and situatedness of photograph production, circulation, and consumption, there was an illusion of transparency and neutrality, and collusion in naturalizing the choice of what was deemed to be correct, ideal, or historically valuable.

Shared Vocabularies of Modernity

The developments in archival classification and photographic technology in the years 1839–41 can be situated in the tradition of Enlightenment Encyclopaedists seeking to bring order and comprehensive knowledge to an understanding of the world. Emerging from late eighteenth- and early nineteenth-century zeal for inventory and taxonomy, and paralleling the natural sciences' obsession with collecting and classifying specimens, archives and photography shared a vocabulary of modernity. Their operations hinged on the meaning, applications, and implications of key words: evidence, permanence, natural order. Photographic records, like archival records, were assumed to be accurate, reliable, authentic, objective, neutral, unmediated. They also trafficked in permanence. Photography "fixed" a moment in time, "fixed" the image of the camera obscura, "fixed" the chemical development of the exposed plate or paper. Archives also "fixed" a moment in time, fixed the actions and transactions of state and church, corporate and private interests, "fixed" recorded information in its administrative, legal, and fiscal context. As well, photographs and archives shared metaphors of mirror and memory.[111] At a time when a "mirror image" signified a realistic, unmediated representation,[112] the daguerreotype was dubbed "the mirror with a memory," and the photographic image became a metaphor for memory. However, the growing literature on the nature and locus of memory has undermined single, stable notions of the past, and mirrors have also been associated with magic, illusion, and sleight of

hand. Archives and photography promised possession and control of knowledge through possession and control of recorded information.

Key to the achievement of control was classification. Beginning in the late eighteenth century and continuing well into the nineteenth, classification was embraced as tool for ordering and, thereby, knowing nature. This is evident in the work of Cuvelier in zoology, Linnaeus in botany, Berzelius in chemistry, and Lyell in geology, but "specimens" were also collected, labeled, and classified in the pursuit of historical understanding as much as in the exploration of the natural sciences. Lenoir's museum of architectural fragments and the architectural photography of the *Mission Héliographique* were conceived as vehicles for preserving and shaping collective memory and national identity in post-Revolutionary France.[113] The Obelisk of Luxor in Place de la Concorde in Paris, Cleopatra's Needle on the banks of the Thames, and the Elgin Marbles in the British Museum were part of a prevailing preservation mentality. So was the widespread collection, especially by European imperial powers, of cultural artifacts to fill the new museums of human history that were gaining popularity at the same time that national archives were beginning to flourish in the metropolitan capitals. To this intellectual toolkit for ordering the world in space and time, the *fonds* was added as yet another instrument of classification.

In his *Circulaire* of April 24, 1841, Duchâtel warned that "classification must not be subordinated [as had previously been prescribed] . . . to divisions based on political periods" and urged that "one must above all seek to arrange them in an order drawn not from the times but from the very nature of the documents and the actual sequences of affairs." Just as archives were thus considered "a natural product of the agency which created them,"[114] photography was promoted not as a tool for copying Nature but rather as a chemical and physical process by which Nature reproduced herself or a process by which, through the agency of light, objects painted themselves with "inimitable fidelity." The photographic plate was thus analogically marked with, and objectively captured, material traces of the world's concrete and "real" existence. This carries certain parallels with a Jenkinsonian view of archives in which records are natural byproducts and organic emanations, capable of speaking for themselves. Thus, the "natural" relationship between archives and administration, as well as the "natural" relationship between present and past that is preserved through archives, like the "natural" relationship between photographic image and photographic subject, was presumed to be organic and unmediated. Classification by *fonds* was the instrument by which this natural and organic relationship between document and event could be preserved.

In an age of taxonomies, inventories, and physiologies, catalogs, registers, and indexes, "photography was understood to be the agent par excellence for listing, knowing, and possessing, as it were, the things of the world."[115] If "listing, knowing, and possessing" were the intellectual means by which one came to know the world and situate oneself in space, then archival classification was a mode of "listing, knowing, and possessing" by which the French government expected to grasp its past and position the nation in time. Both photography and classification carried the promise of control over one's world—control at a time when industrialization, urbanization, and mechanization quickened the pace of life, control at a time when it seemed that the world was spinning out of control. As Janet Buerger has observed, "The nineteenth-century man, facing the increasing knowledge of his time and, more particularly, an overwhelming sense of the elusiveness of truth was fully aware that he was entrapped in a complex world of partial realities."[116] In this world, photography and archival classification seemed to offer objective means of discovering "truth that transcends time" and controlling knowledge through the accumulation and ordering of "partial realities." They were also employed by the great colonial powers to impose intellectual order on and gain administrative control over their increasingly complex empires.

Paradigm Lost: The Postmodern Destabilization of Truth

From their first appearance, photographs were assumed to be truthful representations, reliable facts, authentic evidence of some external reality. These assumptions, which came to surround the photograph, were precisely what the diplomatists and such archival pioneers as the Dutch trio and Jenkinson assumed about all archival documents. Thus, in reading the rhetoric that underpinned photographic practices in the mid-nineteenth century, important parallels can be drawn between the impartiality of photographs and archives as evidence of reality, between the invisibility of photographers and archivists as mediators in the representation of that reality, and between early photographic history and classic archival mythology. It is, therefore, not just the photographic imagination but also the archival imagination at

stake here. If, as it is now increasingly recognized, archival principles are not fixed but "reflect the spirit of their times,"[117] then little wonder that Jenkinson's emphasis on truth derived from the same fact-based empiricism which had, since the mid-nineteenth century, heartily embraced the photograph as a truthful, neutral, unmediated record.

In the 160 years since Duchâtel issued his *Circulaire* of April 24, 1841, the burgeoning volume of modern paper records, the advent of electronic records, and the increasing complexity and diversity of forms of communication, organizational structures, and records creation have resulted in an archival world "spinning out of control," wondering how to cope with the challenges of quantity, instability, and immateriality. In order to confront the problems of the postcustodial era and the information age, some archivists have returned, with renewed fervor, to the vocabularies of truth, natural order, and control. But the archival world cannot ignore the lessons of postmodern thinking about photographs—about the relationship between facts and meaning, between reality and representation—any more than it can deny similar relationships and parallel lessons in all other archival media. These lessons compel us to recognize that neither archival records nor archival practices are theory-free or value-free. Whereas the advent of electronic imaging in the world of photography has drawn attention to issues of selection and distortion, the appearance of electronic records in the realm of archives has sparked a search for ways to return to the key concepts underpinning modernity.

In the face of neo-Jenkinsonian initiatives, postmodern critics within the archival profession, notably *Archivaria* authors Brien Brothman, Richard Brown, Terry Cook, Bernadine Dodge, Verne Harris, Eric Ketelaar, Lilly Koltun, Preben Mortensen, Tom Nesmith, and Theresa Rowat, have confronted fact-based, truth-oriented notions of objectivity and neutrality and challenged positivist assumptions which, now naturalized, form the foundation of accepted archival theory and practice. To an even greater extent, historians Pierre Nora, Jacques LeGoff, Michael Kammen, David Lowenthal, Patrick Hutton, Patrick Geary, John Gillis, and John Bodnar, among others, have problematized positivist, nineteenth-century views of knowable reality, although their writings on history and memory, commemoration and the past have tended to perpetuate the invisibility of archives. In philosophy and cultural studies, external critics following in the footsteps of Michel Foucault and Jacques Derrida have discovered "the archive" as a problematic site of contested power. While the treatment of archives in current scholarly inquiry into collective memory and public commemoration has tended to be more metaphorical than institutional, this literature nevertheless offers rich opportunities for destabilizing prevailing assumptions about the nature and role of archives.[118]

Recent challenges to the interpretation and application of the principle of *respect des fonds* suggest that the principle is not, in fact, a "natural law" which all documents obey. In particular, the work of Canadian and Australian theorists has identified weaknesses or inconsistencies in the *fonds* concept.[119] In addition, American scholar Lara Moore has argued that "post-revolutionary archival and library policies are inseparable from post-revolutionary French politics." She claims that "as the political dilemmas confronting the French state changed, so too did the configuration of archives and libraries," and that "each regime tried to 'restore order' in its own way." As Moore goes on to point out, where earlier regimes "saw libraries and archives as crucial to their political legitimacy," it was only around 1840 that "the government suddenly began to focus its efforts on classification."[120] Thus, the French archival classification system of 1841 had ideological origins, origins which have since been naturalized but now need to be examined and unpacked.

This reading of responses to the first appearance and early applications of photographic technologies suggests a theoretical significance beyond the history of photography per se. More specifically, what emerges from this overview of early ideas about the nature and role of photography are interesting parallels with nineteenth- and early twentieth-century pronouncements on the essential nature and role of archives. As Sir Hilary Jenkinson repeatedly claimed, "The good Archivist is perhaps the most selfless devotee of Truth the modern world produces." His notion that archives furnished evidence that was untainted, unmediated, impartial, innocent, and authentic echoed the conviction of a host of nineteenth-century photographers and art critics who assigned to photographs a comparable role in both "the archives of our memory" and in "the business of life." But, as Terry Cook has pointed out, particularly in terms of the volume of modern records and the complexity of electronic records, "Jenkinson's views on appraisal are no longer valid for modern records or for modern society's expectations of what archives should do, nor is his perspective on the stable nature of administrations or the fixed order of record arrangement useful for modern descriptive problems."[121] Neither are assumptions about photographs rooted in a positivist paradigm, now lost.

There is another reason why the discursive origins of photography are important to a reevaluation of current archival thinking and practice. Just as the vocabularies of photography and archives were rooted in the shared epistemological assumptions of nineteenth-century empiricism, so some proponents of photography and archives have adopted common strategies of professional validation. In her account of commercial photography in Second Empire France, Anne McCauley points out that nineteenth-century manuals and histories of photography were "normally written by members of the profession who had a vested interest in glorifying their calling by likening it to scientific research."[122] The parallel with writing by some members of the archival profession is palpable. Efforts to confer upon archives the imprimatur of science are particularly revealing given the postmodern unmasking of science as a privileged mode of inquiry. Acknowledging the rhetorical appeal or special cachet of calling archival practice "scientific" rather than simply "systematic," Preben Mortensen has suggested that, "if science is thought of necessity to be independent of historical and other contexts, an archival science is not possible."[123] Or, as Candace Loewen pointed out a decade ago, neither archivists nor scientists belong to a "value-free" profession. Citing the work of feminist historian of science Ruth Hubbard, Loewen questions basic assumptions about the authority and objectivity of archival appraisal and scientific methodology:

> Having recognized some of the roots of the prevailing western world-view, we now understand more clearly how 'we view and interpret the world through cultural categories and frameworks of belief. . . . Scientists are not disembodied minds uncontaminated by ideology and unaffected by wider social interests,' nor are archivists.[124]

Recent postmodern writing on archival theory has further undermined the credibility of archival "science"—perhaps nowhere more forcefully than by Terry Cook in a new journal entitled, ironically enough, *Archival Science*.[125]

Ultimately, photographs and archives are the product of social practices which, through the containment and ordering of facts, offer the promise of knowledge and control. The way archives appraise, acquire, arrange, describe, and make accessible photographic records depends upon our understanding of the role of photographs in the business of life and, indeed, in the life of business—personal business, group business, corporate business, government business. It demands that archivists understand how and what and when photographs communicate information across space and time. This exploration of early critical writing reveals that, throughout the nineteenth century, photographs were valued as "records of simple truth and precision" and accepted as reliable and authentic evidence of some external reality. In adopting a postmodern perspective on photography as a technology of information transfer, it presents a historically grounded and theoretically informed argument which calls for serious reconsideration of lingering traces of the positivist, empiricist, totalizing paradigm that buttressed mid-nineteenth-century European views of the nature of photographic technology and photographic practice, and equally of archival "science" and archival practice. It suggests that the photographic imagination and the archival imagination are inextricably linked and can be traced to the same social origins and intellectual climate, the same desire for comprehensive knowledge and unmediated representation, which gave rise to the "daguerreotypomania" depicted by Maurisset.

This essay thus provides a perspective from which to reflect upon photographic history and archival history and to muse on their common paradigmatic origins in fact-based empiricism of the mid-nineteenth century. It proposes that the destabilization of the notion of photographic truth by postmodernist perspectives carries unsettling implications for the continued unproblematic application of the concept of the *fonds* and for attendant efforts to maintain the notion that archives are unmediated, objective, and organic. Finally, it suggests that, by parallel and by analogy, the impact of photography—as medium, document, and evidence—in the nineteenth century reflects, mirrors, and probably deeply influenced early archival theorists' views of the properties of all documents as archives.

NOTES

An earlier version of this essay appeared in *Archivaria* 50 (Fall 2000): 1–41. It was awarded the W. Kaye Lamb Prize for 2000 by the Association of Canadian Archivists.

1. Helmut and Alison Gernsheim, *L. J. M. Daguerre: The History of the Diorama and the Daguerreotype*, 2d rev. ed. (New York, 1968), 106.

2. For an analysis of this caricature, see Gary W. Ewer, "Théodore Maurisset's 'Fantaisies': *La Daguerréotypomanie*," *The Daguerreian Annual 1995* (Official Yearbook of the Daguerreian Society), 135–45.

3. Charles Baudelaire, "The Salon of 1859," reprinted in

Vicki Goldberg, ed., *Photography in Print: Writings from 1816 to the Present* (Albuquerque, NM, 1988), 124–25.

4. "*Camera obscura*" literally meant "dark room," and large, room-sized *camera obscurae* were built to provide an entertaining diversion, as well as the occasional opportunity to view an eclipse of the sun in safety.

5. Gernsheim, *L. J. M. Daguerre*, 104.

6. During the same two-year period in Britain, William Henry Fox Talbot announced his methods of "photogenic drawing" and then perfected his calotype process. In June of 1841, Talbot submitted the working details of his negative paper process to the Royal Society of Great Britain and the Académie des Sciences in Paris. At the same time, Antoine F. J. Claudet announced to these same two scientific bodies his finding that a combination of chlorine and iodine vapor greatly accelerated the daguerreotype process.

7. Nancy Bartlett, "*Respect des Fonds:* The Origins of the Modern Archival Principle of Provenance," in Lawrence J. McCrank, ed., *Bibliographical Foundations of French Historical Studies* (New York, 1991), 107–15.

8. Lara Moore, "Putting French History in Order: Archivists and Archival Classification in the 1840s," paper presented for discussion at the Sawyer Seminar of the Advanced Study Center, University of Michigan, Ann Arbor, MI, September, 20, 2000, 18. The paper was based on "Restoring Order: Archives, Libraries, and the Legacy of the Old Regime in Nineteenth-Century France" (Ph.D. diss., Stanford University, 2001).

9. Ursula Franklin, *The Real World of Technology,* rev. ed. (Toronto, 1999); Jonathan Crary, *Techniques of the Observer: On Vision and Modernity in the Nineteenth Century* (Cambridge, MA, 1992); Terry Cook, "What is Past is Prologue: A History of Archival Ideas Since 1898 and the Future Paradigm Shift," *Archivaria* 43 (Spring 1997), 17–63.

10. [Comte Tanneguay Duchâtel], "The particulars and motives of a bill tending to grant: 1st, to Mr. Daguerre, an annuity for life of 6,000 francs; 2d, to Mr. Niépce junior, an annuity for life of 4,000 fr., in return for the cession made by them of the process to fix the objects reflected in a *camera obscura,* Presented by the Minister of the Interior," Chamber of Deputies, France, June 15, 1839, reproduced in *An Historical and Descriptive Account of the Various Processes of the Daguerréotype and the Diorama, by Daguerre* (London, 1839). Souvenir reprint by the American Photographic Historical Society on the 150th Anniversary of Photography, 1989, 2.

11. [Joseph Louis] Gay-Lussac, "The Report of Mr. Gay-Lussac, in the name of a special committee charged to examine the Bill relative to the acquisition of the process invented by Mr. Daguerre to fix the images of the *camera obscura,*" Chamber of Peers, July 30, 1839, reproduced in *An Historical and Descriptive Account of the Various Processes of the Daguerréotype and the Diorama, by Daguerre,* 35.

12. Ibid., 34.

13. [François Jean Dominique] Arago, "The Report made in the name of the Committee charged to examine the Bill tending to grant: 1st, to Mr. Daguerre, an annuity for life of 6,000 francs; 2d, to Mr. Niépce junior, an annuity for life of 4,000 fr., in return for the cession made by them to fix the objects reflected in a *camera obscura,* by Mr. Arago, Deputy of the Upper Pyrénées," Chamber of Deputies, France, July 6,

1839, reproduced in *An Historical and Descriptive Account of the Various Processes of the Daguerréotype and the Diorama*, by Daguerre, 27.

14. Mayer et [Louis] Pierson, *La Photographie considérée comme art et comme industrie: Histoire de sa Découverte, ses Progrès, ses Applications—son Avenir* (Paris, 1862); repr. ed. (New York, 1979), 223.

15. For an examination of the link between photography and travel as ways of seeing and knowing the world, see Joan M. Schwartz, "*The Geography Lesson:* Photographs and the Construction of Imaginative Geographies," *Journal of Historical Geography* 22, no. 1 (1996), 16–45.

16. The other members of the committee were Humboldt's close friend, Arago, permanent secretary of the Académie des Sciences, director of the Paris Observatory, and a member of the Chamber of Deputies, and Jean-Baptiste Biot (1774–1862), a French mathematician, best known for his discovery of a fundamental law of electromagnetic theory, who collaborated with Arago on calculating the measure of the arc of the meridian and the refractive properties of gases.

17. Humboldt's connections to Daguerre and to Talbot are noted in passing in English-language histories of photography and are all but ignored in histories of science. The most extensive treatment of Humboldt's involvement in photography is Hanno Beck, "Alexander von Humboldt (1769–1859): Förderer der frühen Photographie," in Bodo von Dewitz and Reinhard Matz, *Silber und Salz: Kataloghandbuch zur Jubiläumsausstellung 150 Jahre Photographie* (Cologne, 1989), 40–59. I am grateful to Elizabeth Edwards for bringing this work to my attention, and to Geneviève Samson for the gift of the copy of *Silber und Salz* that belonged to her husband, my friend and colleague, the late Dr. Klaus B. Hendriks, to whom this essay is dedicated.

18. During the 1860s, for example, Julia Margaret Cameron's home on the Isle of Wight was a gathering place for prominent poets, writers, artists, scientists, scholars, and explorers. Among the Victorian visitors who sat for her camera were Robert Browning, Anthony Trollope, Alfred Lord Tennyson, Holman Hunt, Gustave Doré, Thomas Carlyle, Henry Wadsworth Longfellow, Sir John Herschel, Charles Darwin, Joseph Hooker, Edward John Eyre, and Richard Burton. See Helmut Gernsheim, *Julia Margaret Cameron: Her Life and Photographic Work* (Millerton, NY, 1975), esp. 15, 174, 190.

19. See Grace Seiberling, *Amateurs, Photography, and the Mid-Victorian Imagination* (Chicago, 1986), 9.

20. Quoted in Michel F. Braive, *The Photograph: A Social History*, David Britt, trans. (London, 1966), 212.

21. Elizabeth Edwards, "Photographic 'Types': The Pursuit of Method," in Joanna Cohan Scherer, ed., *Picturing Cultures: Historical Photographs in Anthropological Inquiry,* special issue of *Visual Anthropology* 3, no. 2–3 (1990), 235–58.

22. Charles Darwin, *The Expression of Emotions in Man and Animals: With Photographic and Other Illustrations* (London, 1872).

23. Larry Schaaf, "Piazzi Smyth at Teneriffe: Part 1, The Expedition and the Resulting Book," *History of Photography* 4, no. 4 (October 1980), 289–307.

24. Seiberling notes the diversity of Diamond's photographic pursuits: "He photographed antiquarian monuments for the Society of Antiquaries, mental patients at the Surrey County Lunatic Asylum, which he headed, and still lifes of game and other objects arranged like paintings for the Photographic Exchange Club." See Seiberling, *Amateurs, Photography, and the Mid-Victorian Imagination,* 21; biographical appendix, 128–29; 149, notes 12, 13.

25. Larry Schaaf, "Charles Piazzi Smyth's 1865 Conquest of the Great Pyramid," *History of Photography* 3, no. 4 (October 1979), 331–54; also his "Charles Piazzi Smyth's 1865 Photographs of the Great Pyramid," *Image* 27 (1984), 24–32.

26. Eadweard Muybridge, *Animal Locomotion: An Electro-Photographic Investigation of Consecutive Phases of Animal Movements, 1872–1885* (Philadelphia, 1887).

27. Marta Braun, *Picturing Time: The Work of Étienne-Jules Marey, 1830–1904* (Chicago, 1992).

28. Here, I put a photographic spin on the term "virtual witnessing" used by Steven Shapin and Simon Schaffer in their discussion of Robert Boyle's seventeenth-century scientific method for producing empirically based knowledge. Shapin and Schaffer, *Leviathan and the Air-Pump: Hobbes, Boyle, and the Experimental Life* (Princeton, 1985), 55–65.

29. Bernard McGrane, *Beyond Anthropology: Society and the Other* (New York, 1989), 116.

30. H. Gaucheraud, *Gazette de France* (January 6, 1839), quoted in Gernsheim, *L. J. M. Daguerre,* 85.

31. Arago to Académie des Sciences, Paris (January 7, 1839), quoted in Gernsheim, *L. J. M. Daguerre,* 84. The text of Arago's address is reproduced at length, 82–84.

32. [Duchâtel], "The particulars and motives of a bill," 2.

33. Arago, "The Report," 21–22.

34. Indeed, it is worth noting that, in Paris, Alexander von Humboldt attended the private lessons of Auguste Comte, the French founder of the philosophy of positivism.

35. Louis de Cormenin, "Egypte, Nubie, Palestine et Syrie, dessins photographiques par Maxime Du Camp," *La Lumière* 25 (June 12, 1852), quoted in Jean-Claude Lemagny and André Rouillé, eds., *A History of Photography: Social and Cultural Perspectives,* Janet Lloyd, trans. (Cambridge, 1987), 54.

36. "America in the Stereoscope," *The Art-Journal* (July 1, 1860), 221.

37. George Thomas Fisher, Jr., *Photogenic Manipulation,* 2d ed. (Philadelphia, 1845), vi.

38. Rev. W. J. Read, "On the Applications of Photography," *Photographic Notes: Journal of the Photographic Society of Scotland and of the Manchester Photographic Society* I, no. 9 (August 17, 1856), 129.

39. Marcus Aurelius Root, *The Camera and the Pencil* (Philadelphia, 1864); repr. ed. (Pawlet, VT, 1971), 413.

40. Bernard Comment, *The Painted Panorama,* Anne-Marie Glasheen, trans. (New York, 2000), 19. For an extended treatment of the panorama as "an architectural and information component of the new urban spaces and media networks" of the nineteenth century, see Stephan Oettermann, *The Panorama: History of a Mass Medium,* Deborah Lucas Schneider, trans. (New York, 1997).

41. Comment, *The Painted Panorama,* 8.

42. Humboldt went on to explain that "the knowledge of the works of creation, and an appreciation of their exalted grandeur, would be powerfully increased if, besides museums,

and thrown open like them, to the public, a number of panoramic buildings, containing alternating pictures of landscapes of different geographical latitudes and from different zones of elevation, should be erected in our large cities." Humboldt, *Cosmos: A Sketch of a Physical Description of the Universe*, Vol. II, E. C. Otté, trans. (London, 1849), 457.

43. The 1858 catalogue of the London Stereoscopic and Photographic Company already listed over one hundred thousand cards in stock. Frances Dimond and Roger Taylor, *Crown and Camera: The Royal Family and Photography, 1842–1910* (Harmondsworth, 1987), 217.

44. Oliver Wendell Holmes, "The Stereoscope and the Stereograph," *The Atlantic Monthly* 3 (June 1859); repr. in Beaumont Newhall, ed., *Photography: Essays and Images. Illustrated Readings in the History of Photography* (New York, 1980), 56.

45. [Lady Elizabeth Eastlake], "Photography," *Quarterly Review* 101 (London, April 1857); repr. in Newhall, *Photography: Essays and Images*, 94.

46. Mayer et Pierson, *La Photographie*, 164.

47. Read, "On the Applications of Photography," 184.

48. [Joseph Ellis], *Photography: A Popular Treatise* (Brighton, 1847), 41. I am grateful to my Society for American Archivists colleague, Connell B. Gallagher, director for research collections, Bailey/Howe Library, University of Vermont, Burlington, for bringing to my attention the library's holdings of early photographic literature.

49. Ernest Lacan, *Esquisses Photographiques à propos de l'Exposition Universelle et de la Guerre d'Orient* (Paris, 1856); repr. ed. (New York, 1979), 20. Author's translation.

50. For a discussion of the "salvage motif" in ethnography, see George E. Marcus and Michael M. J. Fischer, *Anthropology as Cultural Critique: An Experimental Moment in the Human Sciences* (Chicago, 1986), 24. The nature, aims, and impact of architectural salvage photography and ethnographic salvage photography can be compared using Edward Sheriff Curtis's twenty-volume photographic project, *The North American Indian*. See Christopher M. Lyman, *The Vanishing Race and Other Illusions: Photographs of Indians by Edward S. Curtis* (Washington, 1982).

51. Lacan, *Esquisses Photographiques*, 29. Author's translation.

52. Fisher, *Photogenic Manipulation*, vi.

53. Leonard Boyle, "Diplomatics," in James M. Powell, ed., *Medieval Studies: An Introduction* (Syracuse, NY, 1976), 78.

54. Fisher, *Photogenic Manipulation*, vi.

55. Lacan, *Esquisses Photographiques*, 200. Author's translation.

56. Read, "On the Applications of Photography," 130.

57. Stephen Bann argues that "modes of visual representation, from the later eighteenth century onwards, became increasingly inflected with what might reasonably be termed the vision of the past." Bann, "'Views of the Past': Reflections on the Treatment of Historical Objects and Museums of History (1750–1850)," in Gordon Fyfe and John Law, eds., *Picturing Power: Visual Depiction and Social Relations* (New York, 1988), 40.

58. [William] Lake Price, *A Manual of Photographic Manipulation*, 2d ed. (London, 1868); repr. ed. (New York, 1973), 4.

59. Victor Regnault, *La Lumière* VIII (1864), 392–96;

quoted in Philippe Foliot, "Louis Vignes and Henry Sauvaire, Photographers on the Expeditions of the Duc de Luynes," *History of Photography* 14, no. 3 (July–September 1990), 233–50, 233.

60. Mayer et Pierson, *La Photographie*, 166–67. Author's translation.

61. Ibid., 167. Author's translation.

62. Ibid., 167–68. Author's translation.

63. Ellis, *Photography: A Popular Treatise*, 47–48.

64. Théophile Gautier, in *L'Univers Illustré*, quoted in Braive, *The Photograph: A Social History*, 186.

65. Thomas Richards, *The Imperial Archive: Knowledge and the Fantasy of Empire* (London, 1993); Edward W. Said, *Culture and Imperialism* (New York, 1994); Bruno Latour, "Visualization and Cognition: Thinking with Eyes and Hands," *Knowledge and Society: Studies in the Sociology of Culture Past and Present* 6 (1986), 1–40; James R. Ryan, *Picturing Empire: Photography and the Visualization of the British Empire* (London, 1997).

66. From a review of Francis Frith's *Stereoscopic Views in the Holy Land, Egypt, Nubia, etc.*, published in *The Art-Journal* (1858), 375, quoted in Edward W. Earle, ed., *Points of View: The Stereograph in America. A Cultural History* (Rochester, 1979), 30.

67. "America in the Stereoscope," *The Art-Journal* (July 1, 1860), 221.

68. [Lady Eastlake], "Photography," in Newhall, *Photography: Essays and Images*, 94.

69. A useful technological perspective is given by Julie Wosk, *Breaking Frame: Technology and the Visual Arts in the Nineteenth Century* (New Brunswick, NJ, 1992).

70. [Duchâtel], "The particulars and motives of a bill," 1–2.

71. Arago, "The Report," 22.

72. Gay-Lussac, "The Report," 35.

73. The first photographic journal, which began publication in February 1851 in Paris as an adjunct to the Société héliographique, was aptly entitled *La Lumière*.

74. Talbot, *The Pencil of Nature*, 1–2.

75. Helmut Gernsheim claims that this was written in 1839 "by Dr. J. P. Simon, a Frenchman residing in London." Helmut Gernsheim, *The Origins of Photography* (London, 1982), 47, 267, note 15.

76. For a discussion of "the cultural semantics of photographic terminology," as well as an interpretation of Thoreau's remark, see Alan Trachtenberg, "Photography: The Emergence of a Keyword," in Martha A. Sandweiss, ed., *Photography in Nineteenth-Century America* (Fort Worth, 1991), 17–47.

77. *The Art-Journal* (1858), 375, quoted in Earle, *Points of View*, (Rochester, 1979), 30.

78. Quoted in Schaaf, "Piazzi Smyth at Teneriffe," Part 2, 32.

79. Shapin and Schaffer, *Leviathan and the Air-Pump*, esp. 55–65.

80. Read, "On the Applications of Photography," 129.

81. Edgar Allan Poe, "The Daguerreotype," *Alexander's Weekly Messenger* (January 15, 1840), 2, reprinted in Alan Trachtenberg, ed., *Classic Essays on Photography* (New Haven, CT, 1980), 38.

82. Antoine Claudet, "Photography in Its Relation to the

Fine Arts," *The Photographic Journal* VI (June 15, 1860), quoted in Helmut Gernsheim, *The Rise of Photography, 1850–1880: The Age of Collodion* (London, 1988), 66–67.

83. "Stereoscopes; or travel made easy," a review of Francis Frith's series of stereoscopic views, *Views in Egypt and Nubia*, appeared in *The Athenaeum* 31 (London, March 20, 1858), 371, quoted in Julia Van Haaften, "Francis Frith and Negretti & Zambra," *History of Photography* 4, no. 1 (January 1980), 35.

84. "Stereoscopes," quoted in Van Haaften, "Francis Frith and Negretti & Zambra," 36.

85. Rev. H. J. Morton, "Photography as an Authority," *Philadelphia Photographer* 1 (1864), 180–81.

86. Miles Orvell, "Almost Nature: The Typology of Late Nineteenth-Century American Photography," in Daniel P. Younger, ed., *Multiple Views: Logan Grant Essays on Photography, 1983–89* (Albuquerque, NM, 1991), 148.

87. Root, *The Camera and the Pencil*, xvi.

88. Baudelaire, "The Salon of 1859," in Goldberg, *Photography in Print*, 123–26.

89. John Ruskin, from his "Lectures on Art" (1870), in Goldberg, *Photography in Print*, 153.

90. Ruskin, from letters dated 1845–46, in Goldberg, *Photography in Print*, 152.

91. Julie Lawson, *The Stones of Venice: Ruskin's Venice in Photographs* (Edinburgh, 1992), 13.

92. Ruskin, letter dated October 7, 1845, quoted in Stephen Bann, *The Clothing of Clio: A Study of the Representation of History in Nineteenth-Century Britain and France* (Cambridge, 1984), 132.

93. Ruskin, "Lectures on Art," in Goldberg, *Photography in Print*, 153.

94. Baudelaire, "The Salon of 1859," ibid., 125.

95. Ruskin, "The Eagle's Nest," ibid., 153.

96. [Lady Eastlake], "Photography," in Newhall, *Photography: Essays and Images*, 92.

97. Ibid., 93–94.

98. For example, Marcus Aurelius Root began *The Camera and the Pencil* by stating his conviction that photography was "entitled to rank with the so-named Fine Arts." Root, *The Camera and the Pencil*, 19. Ernest Lacan argued, "Nous ne prétendons pas que la photographie doive être placée au rang des arts d'inspiration, comme la peinture, la sculpture, la musique; mais nous voudrions que ses oeuvres ne fussent point considerées comme les résultats d'opérations purement mécaniques." Lacan, *Esquisses Photographiques*, 78–79.

99. [Lady Eastlake], "Photography," in Newhall, *Photography: Essays and Images*, 94.

100. Paula Findlen, *Possessing Nature: Museums, Collecting, and Scientific Culture in Early Modern Italy* (Berkeley, CA, 1994), 3.

101. Kevin Walsh, *The Representation of the Past: Museums and Heritage in the Post-Modern World* (London, 1992), 20.

102. In the 1790s, for example, Alexandre Lenoir transformed the largest of the Paris depots for plundered works of art into a Museum of French Monuments where architectural fragments of pre-Revolutionary France were assembled, ordered, and displayed.

103. Thomas Richards describes the British imperial obsession with collecting in *The Imperial Archive*. The theoretical implications of accumulating information are discussed in Latour, "Visualization and Cognition."

104. [Duchâtel], "The particulars and motives of a bill," 2; Gay-Lussac, "The Report," 35.

105. Holmes, "The Stereoscope and the Stereograph," in Newhall, *Photography: Essays and Images*, 60.

106. [Ellis], *Photography: A Popular Treatise*, 45.

107. For an extended examination of the origins of photography as a history of "the desire to photograph," see Geoffrey Batchen, *Burning with Desire: The Conception of Photography* (Cambridge, MA, 1997).

108. Charles François Tiphaigne de la Roche, *Giphantie: Première Partie* (A Babylone, M.DCC.LX [1760]), 136. It was subsequently published in English translation as *Giphantie: or, a view of what has passed, what is now passing, and during the present century, what will pass in the world* (London, 1761). An excerpt from the English edition is reprinted in Newhall, *Photography: Essays and Images*, 13–14.

109. Price, *A Manual of Photographic Manipulation*, 1–2.

110. Shapin and Schaffer, *Leviathan and the Air-Pump*, 55–65.

111. The National Archives of Canada, for example, has been variously described as a "mirror of Canada past" and the "memory of the nation."

112. Sabine Melchior-Bonnet, *The Mirror: A History*, Katherine H. Jewett, trans. (London, 2001).

113. Joan M. Schwartz, "The *Mission Héliographique*: Architectural Monuments, Archival Photographs, and National Identity in Mid-Nineteenth-Century France," commentary presented at the Sawyer Seminar of the Advanced Study Center at the University of Michigan, Ann Arbor, MI, March 7, 2001. For an extended treatment of the *Mission Héliographique*, see M. Christine Boyer, "*La Mission Héliographique*: Architectural Photography, Collective Memory, and the Patrimony of France, 1851," in Joan M. Schwartz and James R. Ryan, eds., *Picturing Place: Photography and the Geographical Imagination* (London, 2003), 21–54.

114. Michel Duchein, "Theoretical Principles and Practical Problems of *Respect des fonds* in Archival Science," *Archivaria* 16 (Summer 1983), 65.

115. Abigail Solomon-Godeau, *Photography at the Dock: Essays on Photographic History, Institutions, and Practices* (Minneapolis, MN, 1991), 155.

116. Janet E. Buerger, "The Genius of Photography," in John Wood, ed., *The Daguerreotype: A Sesquicentennial Celebration* (Iowa City, IA, 1989), 53.

117. Cook, "What is Past is Prologue," 26.

118. As Cook has urged, "archivists need to explore the field of 'memory scholarship' [as well as the history of their own profession, institutions, and media] more carefully, for it puts into context many unquestioned assumptions underpinning archival theory and conceptualization, even if the authors . . . rarely explicitly address archives." Cook, "What is Past is Prologue," 50, note 3. For other references to this postmodern literature, see Richard J. Cox, "The Concept of Public Memory and Its Impact on Archival Public Programming," *Archivaria* 36 (Autumn 1993), 122–35; Joan M. Schwartz, "'We make our tools and our tools make us': Lessons from Photographs for the Practice,

Politics, and Poetics of Diplomatics," *Archivaria* 40 (Fall 1995), 73, note 122; see also Barbara L. Craig, "Selected Themes in the Literature on Memory and Their Pertinence to Archives," *American Archivist* 65, no. 2 (Fall/Winter 2002), 276–89.

119. The two most prominent Canadian critiques of the *fonds* concept are Terry Cook, "The Concept of the Archival Fonds in the Post-Custodial Era: Theory, Problems, and Solutions," *Archivaria* 35 (Spring 1993), 24–37; and Bob Krawczyk, "Cross Reference Heaven: The Abandonment of the Fonds as the Primary Level of Arrangement for Ontario Government Records," *Archivaria* 48 (Fall 1999), 131–53.

120. Moore, "Putting French History in Order," 1.

121. Cook, "What is Past is Prologue," 25.

122. Elizabeth Anne McCauley, *Industrial Madness: Commercial Photography in Paris, 1848–1871* (New Haven, CT, 1994), 13.

123. Preben Mortensen, "The Place of Theory in Archival Practice," *Archivaria* 47 (Spring 1999), 18.

124. Candace Loewen, "From Human Neglect to Planetary Survival: New Approaches to the Appraisal of Environmental Records," *Archivaria* 33 (Winter 1991–92), 97–98.

125. Terry Cook, "Archival Science and Postmodernism: New Formulations for Old Concepts," *Archival Science* 1, no. 1 (2000), 3–24.

PART II

Archives in the Production of Knowledge

Whether even the most well-intentioned and neutral scholar could ever produce an objective, scientific history has long been the subject of fractious debate among historians, as many archivists are aware. That "noble dream," as Peter Novick described this quest in an important volume some fifteen years ago, reflects for many historians a quaint legacy of romantic positivism, the failure to recognize how facts and historical truths are accessible only through creative acts of imagination.[1] The issues here are complicated. They range from whether the kinds of presuppositions historians bring to their research necessarily affect their determination of what is "factual," to an epistemological quandary about the very accessibility of the "realities" of the past, given the layered processes of mediation by which events are recorded, remembered, and retrieved.[2] Language itself is also relevant, insofar as historical narration always imposes a degree of order and meaning on what historically may actually have been experienced as chaotic and senseless.[3]

These issues are not about the integrity of historical scholarship but about its authenticity: the ways and degrees to which documents and other artifacts serve to authenticate historical "facts." Although Mary Poovey has shown convincingly that the "modern fact" has a complicated history of its own, most readers of history, if not most historians, understand facts simply as those fragments of past experience that can be verified by some reliable source.[4] History is "objective," "scientific," and "true" if it is based on authentic materials that in and of themselves constitute the links to what "really happened." As repositories of "original" materials, the notion of authenticity is thus embedded in the very meaning of *archive*.

Whatever their views about scientific history, archival historians unwittingly reinforce this idea with a stylized grammar of citation. Like the modern fact, the citation is

also a relatively modern invention, part of the move toward "scientific history" and "social science" in general.[5] In effect, the archival citation insists that the historian's descriptions are factually accurate because they are based on authentic materials and are verifiable. Even though it is often quite difficult for others to verify archival references, the citation itself connotes research as an objective process of uncovering historical truths whose very preservation in archival documents also represents them as authentic. In this common perspective, archival documents "speak for themselves."

Archival research thus reinforces many of the assumptions about objectivity and scientific history that debates among historians have, in fact (so to speak), destabilized. Absent from these debates, however, and missing in the scientific perspective, is a careful consideration of archival practices themselves: the tasks of appraisal, acquisition, classification, and description. The historians' discussion has been about how documents and archives are used, not about how they are created; how they can be accessed, not how they are selected, described, or preserved. Even less has the discussion considered how the processes of archiving might function in these ways as something more than simply the preserving of knowledge. In contrast to the ways historians have interrogated their own discipline, archives and archiving remain for most historians little more than documentary collections and the institutions that house them.

Do the professional activities of the archivist actually conform to these traditional assumptions? Is the archivist really an impartial and disinterested "keeper of the record," trained to carry out whatever tasks of acquisition and preservation the archive has been created to perform? In this perspective, the only way archivists are thought to affect the production of knowledge is through their control over access to their materials.

These were some of the most interesting and contentious questions our seminar explored. On the whole, seminar participants took quite a different position, arguing that an understanding of the past is quite actively shaped not only by how archives themselves are constituted (an issue taken up in some detail in parts IV and V of this volume) but also by both direct and indirect interventions and mediations of archivists at all levels of the archival hierarchy. Indeed, several archivists themselves took the matter even further. They argued that we are currently moving into a *very* active age of archival intervention, one that can be described as beyond *postcustodial,* in which the processes of selection, access, and even description are increasingly structured by particular cultural values, social biases, and political inclinations.

Restrictions on access to archival materials, either through systems of classification or requirements that users be credentialed in certain ways, have always been properly understood in terms of politics: as an undesirable, if inevitable, effect of power. Since archives everywhere are the creations of some institution or group, it is generally perceived that archives are always designed at some level to balance or serve particular interests: questions concerning acquisition, access, preservation, and especially classification (privacy, secrecy) are thus understandably decided in ways that privilege the objectives of those who fund and maintain the collections. In this respect, the special restrictions all state archives place on some of their materials are simply extensions—albeit sometimes egregious ones—of archival politics more generally since a de facto function of all archives has everywhere been to preserve and protect a controlling set of values and interests. At best, archivists may be able to position themselves as brokers between conflicting agendas where the politics of privacy collide with the politics of accessibility and openness.

The seminar considered these political issues at some length, concentrating especially on the implications of the idea that all archives, state and private, hold a kind of protected knowledge. As the seminar contributions grouped in this section suggest, however, it is not only the political protection of knowledge that is at issue here but its very production: the power of archives and archivists, in effect, to structure what is knowable and how it is known. And the issues at hand are not simply the obvious political problems of access or of the types of restrictions that limit "freedom of information." They have to do instead with how the archiving process works *to create* information, to produce not only social or historical understanding but the very elements of social and historical knowledge itself.

Consider the superficially simple question of acquisition. Many historians believe that the ways archives acquire material are relatively straightforward; very few understand that the overwhelming mass of materials presented to archives is either turned away as unsuitable or otherwise appraised by archivists as not sufficiently valuable to warrant the costs of preservation. The historian Atina Grossmann's discussion here of her own family papers is very suggestive in this regard. Grossmann shows that acquisition even in private archives involves a very complex set of interactions between institutions, with their own collecting priorities, and donors, who may hold different values or personal attachments to the materials and therefore have a concern about how and by whom they will be used. Grossmann is the donor in the case she describes. She writes poignantly about her fears that her father's documents and artifacts, those of a Holocaust survivor, might be misread or misused by historians if they were formally archived. She is also concerned about which archive, were she to donate the materials, would preserve their integrity and meaning as she understands it. For the moment she prefers to leave them in her closet. Frank Mecklenburg, on the other hand, is the archival administrator who assembles collections with what he believes is a clear mandate: in his case, to commemorate a lost Jewish population, to restore and reconstruct memories, and to keep a particular story from being forgotten.

As Patrick Geary suggests in his essay, archivists themselves do not generally like to emphasize their role in the rejection or destruction of documents (Geary's phrase is "destroyers of the past"). This, however, is clearly one of the archive's principal tasks in the process of accumulation, even with official state documents generated as a part of policy-making or with materials that almost any committee of professional historians would think has historical significance. Geary notes that the historian presents his or her work so as to make the archives an invisible partner. This creates the impression of direct interaction between the historian and the past. Yet all archives are compiled and grow through processes of selection, rejection, and destruction. In this compilation, Geary suggests, the archivist essentially takes on the role of an "author" of the preserved materials, acting in the service of other authors in the future.

Moreover, with paper documents, the sheer volume of materials makes retention of more than a small proportion of the total record physically impossible. The distinguished Dutch archivist and scholar Eric Ketelaar calls the acquisition process everywhere a "triage." (As much as 97 percent of U.S. government records, for example, are routinely destroyed.) Is the archivist here also an author or at least a severe editor of the past? And in either case, to what extent should this authoring or editing be more fully understood, acknowledged, and visible?

Space and physical volume are not the only problems here. One seminar participant, Richard Rockwell, showed quite convincingly the daunting problems of acquisition involved in the archiving even of digitalized social science data, a problem where space is measured in microfilm or computer rolls, not linear feet of shelving. While the widespread introduction of electronic records might well improve archival access by facilitating comprehensive finding aids and document retrieval, seminar participants suggested that many of these problems are likely to become even more complicated in the coming years, rather than easier. Different electronic languages, the ease of concealment, the ready possibility, even, of altering electronic records obviously pose new and serious issues since they further increase the power individual state agencies and officials may have over the records. The delete key is, in effect, a revolutionary paper shredder, allowing vast amounts of material to disappear in a matter of nanoseconds.

The destruction of materials obviously has a crude effect on the kinds of knowledge an archive can produce, but acquisition and appraisal practices affect the production of knowledge in more subtle ways as well. The opportunities to explore particular historical issues or to understand the possible dimensions are obviously affected by the kinds of artifacts an archive chooses to acquire. The invisibility of women and racial and ethnic minority groups within institutions that generate documents worthy of retention clearly affects the way a historian can trace the historical roles of gender systems, race relations, or ethnic identities. In the process, particular kinds of knowledge are created about each. On the other hand, the absence of archival materials relating to women may simply be because gender has only recently come to be broadly recognized as an important category of analysis. Similar arguments can be made about many other topics. The kinds of knowledge societies have about these aspects of their past will thus clearly be a product not only of what an archive has chosen to acquire but of what records were generated at all. The past may have to be written through the absence rather than the presence of documentation.

Most archivists understand this very well. Does it mean, however, that archivists should try to consider the future interests of research historians or a broader pub-

lic in appraising material for acquisition? The Danish archivist Inge Bundsgaard describes this in her seminar contribution as part of the professional archivist's duty and burden. She asks if individuals have not only the right to privacy but also the right to oblivion. This is also American historian Atina Grossmann's dilemma. Eric Ketelaar, however, following a model for appraising personal information outlined by the Canadian archivist Terry Cook, argues forcefully that the archivist should "not even try" to assess the value of the records for any future historical research. He maintains that records cannot be appraised with some imaginary future researcher in mind but must be evaluated entirely on the basis of considerations of the present.

In either case, as Stephen Nichols, Elizabeth Yakel, and especially Nancy Bartlett suggest in their essays here, archivists in all of their practices might best be thought of not as passive and impartial curators of the past, acting however professionally to preserve the existing record as well as they can, but essentially as "mediators" between the documents and their readers, between the types of knowledge created by the production and reproduction of documents themselves and the ways and forms in which that knowledge is accessible and capable of scholarly use. In Bartlett's view, even the most well-intentioned archivist can find him- or herself between the user and the material, often at the user's request. Many historians, of course, need no convincing whatsoever about the discretionary power of the mediating archivist. Western historians of Russia, for example, were required under Soviet rule to sit in isolated reading rooms and to work only on approved themes, often without the help of finding aids, and were allowed to examine only those materials the archivist thought were appropriate. As Eric Ketelaar shows, similar kinds of practices, if a good deal more subtle, have long characterized certain European archives. They are especially common in private or quasi-public repositories like the Vatican where access is still a matter of privilege. As Stephen Nichols and Elizabeth Yakel suggest, moreover, with the great advances in digitization, the archivist actually performs new kinds of transformations to the original format of materials that may affect the future of their accessibility every bit as much as traditional systems of classification.

The essays gathered here suggest that it is the archivist and the archive itself that produce knowledge and support the political, social, and cultural systems they both serve, the archivist and the archive that embody particular social, political, and cultural ideas and values. The conclusion of most seminar participants was consequently that it is also the archivist as well as the archival record whose mediating activities play a vital role in constructing what is and can be known.

NOTES

1. Peter Novick, *That Noble Dream: The "Objectivity Question" and the American Historical Profession* (New York, 1988).

2. See, among other works, Natalie Davis, *Fiction in the Archives* (Stanford, 1987); Michael Kammen, *The Past before Us* (Ithaca, NY, 1980); Bernard Bailyn, "The Challenge of Modern Historiography," *American Historical Review,* 1982, 87; Jacques Barzun, *Clio and the Doctors: Psycho-History, Quanto-History, and History* (Chicago, 1974); Hayden White, "Historical Pluralism," *Critical Inquiry,* 1986, 12; and, especially, Joyce Appleby, Lynn Hunt, and Margaret Jacob, *Telling the Truth about History* (New York, 1994). Keith Jenkins, ed., *The Postmodern History Reader* (London, 1997), contains a number of interesting articles including pieces by Lawrence Stone, Patrick Joyce, Catriona Kelly, and Gabrielle Spiegel on "History and Postmodernism" and extracts from *Past and Present* and *History and Theory.*

3. See especially Hayden White, *Metahistory* (Baltimore, 1973), and his *The Content and the Form* (Baltimore, 1987); Margaret Somers, "Narrativity, Culture and Causality: Toward a New Historical Epistemology," in *The Historic Turn in the Social Sciences,* ed. T. McDonald (Ann Arbor, 1997), and her *Narrativity, Narrative Identity, and Social Action: Rethinking English Working-Class Formation* (Ann Arbor, 1992); Philip J. M. Sturgess, *Narrativity: Theory and Practice* (Oxford, 1992); and Dominick LaCapra, "History, Language, and Reading: Waiting for Crillon," *American Historical Review* 3 (1995): 100. Among other pieces in Jenkins, *The Postmodern History Reader,* see Hans Kellner, "Language and Historical Representation." The subject has received extended discussion as well in the journals *Representations* and *Critical Inquiry.*

4. Mary Poovey, *A History of the Modern Fact: Problems of Knowledge in the Sciences of Wealth and Society* (Chicago, 1998).

5. Anthony Grafton, *The Footnote: A Curious History,* rev. ed. (Cambridge, MA, 1997).

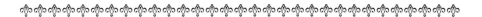

Out of the Closet and into the Archives?

German Jewish Papers

Atina Grossmann

The Institution

Frank Mecklenburg discusses the Leo Baeck Institute (LBI) Archives as an institution initially established for the preservation and generation of social memories among a group whose collective identity—as the much-mythologized German-speaking Jews of prewar central Europe—is rapidly fading, as well as a repository whose contents are increasingly relevant not only to scholarship but to the highly contested production of political culture for both Jews and Germans. The texts, photographs, and artifacts contained in the archives have long provided fodder for well-trodden academic debates about the fate of German Jewry: cultural symbiosis versus failed assimilation, proud legacy of cosmopolitan west European culture versus "dreams and delusions" in the face of eliminationist anti-Semitism. But as Mecklenburg points out, somewhat surprisingly for an institution that defined its mission as rescuing and documenting remnants of an irretrievably destroyed past, turn-of-the-millennium political culture has provided the archives with a new lease on social and political as well as scholarly life.

The unified Berlin Republic's search for identity and legitimacy and Germany's growing confrontation with multiculturalism have intensified the (both praised and ridiculed) obsession with somehow comprehending and reappropriating a missing Jewish past. This past, had, after all, been not only exterminated but also transferred in countless lifts carrying the accoutrements of German Jewish life to all corners of the globe (one could remark polemically on the curiosity that, unlike the actual Holocaust, this is often presented as a tragic loss for, rather than a crime by, the Germans, but that is another discus-

sion). At the same time, for highly divided Jewish communities in the United States, Israel, and western and eastern Europe (indeed virtually everywhere from Tokyo to Buenos Aires), the history of German Jewish struggles around secularism versus observance, acculturation versus tradition, and universalism versus particularism, and even the highly developed debates about intermarriage and reforming religious practice, have taken on (at least potentially) new resonance. Our current memory boom, fueled by panic about the loss of eyewitnesses' living memory (and perhaps our own middle-aged lapses), has led not only to a much-debated public memorial culture centered on World War II and the Holocaust but also to heightened individual fascination with genealogy, family history, and personal memoir.

Finally and more mundanely, but absolutely crucial to the maintenance of an archive, human life cycle intervenes: the refugees are dying or moving out of their family homes into old-age facilities. Their children and grandchildren need an alternative to simply chucking out the debris, the relics, and the history of this supposedly vanished but somehow constantly recycled and reinterrogated cultural group. The children and grandchildren are generally thoroughly integrated members of the (non-German) national and ethnic/religious communities in which they ended up and quite unattached—and, if at all, mostly on the level of family memoir or, in a minority of cases, in terms of scholarly work—to any notions of a German Jewish legacy. Relieved to find a safe place for papers and artifacts they dimly imagine to be important but for which they have no space and no use, they become the "donors." Ironically, many of the "users," or at least those with the greatest sense of urgency (and, one might add, funding) have been Germans determined to excavate a history that they know is theirs only in the most excruciatingly complicated ways. All of these relationships are, as Mecklenburg points out in his essay, in a particular state of flux at a moment when the LBI Archives in New York is for the first time sharing physical (and mental and psychological) space with American Jewish and east European Jewish (the background of most American Jews) archives on the one hand and on the other hand negotiating to open a separate, distinctly "German Jewish" branch in the new Jewish Museum in Berlin.

The Community

What then does all this have to do with the German Jewish papers—and multiple other artifacts—that came tumbling out of, in great piles of dust and mildew, my mother's and my aunt's closets a couple of years ago when I had to relocate both of these elderly Berlin-born ladies (much against their will) from their Manhattan apartments to nursing homes in (horrors!) the Bronx and Queens respectively? The occasion of this seminar has allowed me to start doing what so many scholars—for better and surely also for worse—have been doing recently: explicitly linking (rather than just in conversation with their friends and shrinks) personal histories and received social memories with current intellectual projects. I have permission, I imagine, to think more (probably both critically and self-indulgently) about my own overdetermined role in this story: as a historian of Germany, a child of German Jewish refugees, a past and potential donor, an occasional user, and someone who is part of a larger social and scholarly community that claims some ownership (albeit without any significant financial support) of this archive (not to mention as spouse of the research director and chief archivist).

I grew up in the 1950s and 1960s in New York City in a family of former Berlin Jews, for whom the Upper West Side of Manhattan became in some ways an inadequate ersatz extension of Weimar Berlin and in other ways a new and even better urban and urbane metropolis. My parents arrived in New York relatively late, in 1948, after a circuitous adventurous route, separately and together, through Iran, India, and Palestine; my aunt in 1949, after ten years spent working as a domestic servant in London. Their lifts (and those of other family members with other routes) contained the souvenirs not only of their upbringing in Germany but of their farflung emigration: the boxed Goethe and Schiller sets next to

Persian rugs and miniatures, the guidebooks to the Palestine desert next to ones for New York skyscrapers, the heavy down quilts of central Europe packed next to the tropical shorts and hats from India, Bauhaus pottery with ivory elephants, expressionist art books, and German chamber music programs from Tehran. They had not been in Berlin, their hometown, for over twenty years, and yet once installed in New York, they immediately became part of the quite hermetically sealed, insistently German-speaking, but also quintessentially worldly New York Yekke community that defined my childhood in the 1950s.

The LBI Archives was part of that German Jewish refugee world, along with the newspaper *Aufbau,* the Congregation Habonim, and Café Eclair, clearly more social institution than academic repository. This last circumstance was underscored by the fact that most of the employees were nonprofessionals, taking advantage of their German reparations (Wiedergutmachung) pensions to labor for little or no money in their own personal community archive. In fact, when I was a high school junior, who knew a lot of German but very little history, I worked my after-school job at the institute, cataloging what turned out to be an important collection; one of the LBI newsletters has a photo of myself and a friend, also a child of refugees, in miniskirts and lots of black eyeliner, shelving books. For years, even after I trained as a historian (German, not Jewish or German Jewish), the LBI always seemed to me to be more communal storage locker than serious archive (personal papers, not official documents—for example in the Mauthner collection).

But as the profession opened to social history; history of everyday life; women's history; gay history; history of sexuality, gender, and the family; history of madness and psychiatry, the mounds of German Jewish personal letters, diaries, and memoirs being tossed into the dumpster or carted into the institute were cast in a new and more "serious" historiographical light. At the same time it became clearer that the history of German Jewry, their life in Germany and after emigration, represented an absolutely necessary complement, and not just nostalgic coda, to German and Holocaust history. I too came to share—at least in theory—the perspective of the acquisitive archivist or searching historian whose interest generally is omnivorous, "Just hand it over, everything is interesting, will be useful to some researcher, even if you don't think so; there is virtually nothing that should not be preserved."

Only in the past couple of years since the papers literally fell out of the closets have I had to think from the combined perspective of the donor as well as of the historian user. I've dragged my feet on handing over materials that I might be thrilled to find if they were someone else's papers neatly organized in some other archive. I've engaged in all the evasive behaviors that archivists struggle with on a daily basis as they try to wrest documents away from their owners. I want to read everything myself before I give it away. But I don't have time to read it all, or even part of it, so maybe it would be better off in my attic, waiting for me to have the time. And maybe I don't really want to read it all anyway; there are plenty of things about my family I'd rather not know or have confirmed, nor am I sure that I want (or can afford) to expend the emotional energy required to confront all this material with an insider's eye. But then, why should anyone else know those things? Do I really want to let some young German graduate student who has decided to become an expert on Jews interpret my family papers—however he or she sees fit—as an example of German Jewish experience or sensibility?

And what if I want to write my own book? Perhaps if I made the leap from scattered sorting through to systematic research in my own private archive, a publisher or granting agency would give me the money that would buy me the time. But wouldn't I then have succumbed to the widespread and, to my mind, highly problematical contemporary academic propensity to write self-absorbed and narcissistic—if often quite fascinating—texts about ourselves and our own histories? Wouldn't it be better if I let go and left it to others, even callow and naive German graduate students, to forage among the debris of my mother's and my aunt's closets. And so on and so on. But, damn it, it's *my* story, my stuff. And once it's in an archive, it's no longer mine. Simply by virtue of being boxed and labeled in an archive, cataloged and categorized, and made available to others, even under whatever restrictions I choose to decree, the family remnants become public and historical. That, it seems to me, is the both the magic and the terror of archives.

Unavoidably then, and somewhat separate from my questions about whether I or someone else should work on this material, I in my dual role as donor and historian have to decide what of my inherited "stuff" should become public and historical in this manner. This raises a whole other set of questions that really do matter when we talk about archives as sites of political culture and the molding of social memory and knowledge. What does belong in an archive and what doesn't? What can in fact be legitimately thrown away or stored in the attic until it falls apart? Clearly, advanced techniques of preservation and reproduction have made it physically possible to

conserve and collect much more than ever before. But what do we really need to preserve and why? Who really needs all this stuff and why? What can the personal papers of a few more German Jews still tell us about a history that has been exhaustively researched and memorialized? At a moment when historians feel overwhelmed by the sheer mass of available data, when hardly anyone has enough time or money for long-term archival research (except commissioned studies with teams of researchers), when someone else is always already working on a similar topic, when coherent narratives constantly threaten to dissolve into microhistories or, alternatively, grand metahistories (of the twentieth century, for example), could it be that telling the highly particular idiosyncratic stories contained in personal papers is the most interesting and constructive contribution we make to historiography? How do we, the guardians of personal memory and the producers of published history, negotiate the constantly shifting borders between the "historically valuable" on the one hand and pure voyeurism or obsessive collecting on the other?

In the second half of this essay, I exemplify these questions, first by describing some of what fell out of the closets and then by beginning a historical analysis of a particular group of papers.

The Stuff

Here is a very partial and abbreviated list of some of the items I pulled out of the closets and chests in those Upper West Side apartments: discolored trousseau linens; dainty and still beautiful lace doilies; hand-painted china, both cracked and intact, from a family porcelain factory in Nuremberg; black-and-white *Feldpost* postcards sent home from the Eastern Front in World War I; garish color postcards from postwar excursions to the Alps or Redwoods; faded photographs of people whom I did not recognize but who were all "of a familiar type"; concert and theater programs from Berlin, Tehran, Bombay, and New York; scores for house chamber music quartets; menus from generations of weddings, bar mitzvahs, and transatlantic ocean voyages; elegantly tailored 1930s women's suits and matching shoes; masses of birthday cards; airplane tickets and itineraries testifying to the inextinguishable Weimar passion for tourism; rusty cameras, nail clippers, and sewing needles; piles of tattered newspaper clippings about anything remotely to do with Jews and the Holocaust; and plastic bags filled with postwar aerograms linking friends and relatives scattered all over the globe, from Tokyo to Tel Aviv, Capetown to Canberra, Buenos Aires to Boston.

From the bookshelves floated hundreds of volumes, most of them falling apart: the ubiquitous Goethe and Schiller sets but also Tucholsky, Brecht, Marx, and Emil Ludwig; the Koran and a German-Hebrew siddur; Baedeker guidebooks to virtually everywhere; 1920s sex manuals; and beautiful prints of modernist art. None of them, alas, in a condition that would attract the interest of an art or antiques dealer. But nonetheless, an extraordinary inventory of moments in life-cycle and historical time. And this list does not even include the truly embarrassing items like the manic anxious scribblings in my mother's daily calendars, the handwritten 1947 marriage contract in which my parents promised to allow each other separate vacations and "friendships," and the braid, perfectly preserved by my mother in tissue paper, that I had cut off when I was in third grade. What to keep? What to throw out? What to note as possibilities for the "object theater" planned as part of the exhibitions in the soon-to-be-opened Jewish Museum in Berlin? What belongs in an archive? In a museum? On my private shelves? In attic boxes for my own children and grandchildren to rummage in? In the garbage? Some choices are obvious—certainly no one needs any more worn copies of Goethe and Schiller and the braid has been disposed of—but most are not.

Finally, almost indistinguishably mixed in with the old newspapers and recent birthday cards and smelly prescription bottles, were the "documents": amazing, overwhelming amounts of paper recording intensely private dramas, some of them (but which part and how can one separate it from the others?) undoubtedly also of general historical interest. There was the full correspondence between my father, patiently numbering his letters from behind barbed wire while interned by the British as an enemy alien in the Himalayas, and my mother, his errant girlfriend, who had chosen to stay behind in romantic Tehran rather than follow him on what was supposed to be an escape from the Persian desert, where they, two adventuresome Berlin Jews, had met in 1935, to western civilization in New York City. She writes dreamy letters about skiing down the Iranian mountains in her bathing suit and torments him with elliptical tales of her other romances; he describes in minute detail the bizarreness of being both a European colonial and a prisoner of war, vents within the limits of censorship his anger about the clear British preference for the better-behaved Nazi Germans over the unruly antifascist German prisoners who keep insisting they should be released to join the war ef-

fort, and yearns for cold weather and female company. At the bottom of that pile there were some moving reflections by my secular father on serving as the internment camp "rabbi" and saying kaddish among the Jewish inmates in the Himalayas on VE Day for what was already then defined as the "six million" dead. These are surely powerful and intriguing texts (typed and in English thanks to the censors' demands!); however, they perhaps tell us more about British colonial rule during World War II and the life of Europeans in exotic locales than about German Jewish history as conventionally conceived (not to mention more than I ever wanted to know—or want anybody else to know—about how weird my parents really were).

There were masses of other letters: letters written by my aunts in London to the British relief agencies, begging for passage for their parents trapped in Berlin; letters that went to and fro between my maternal grandfather in Berlin and an uncle in Buenos Aires, trying to arrange last-minute passage out of Germany; letters written by my father on two risky (and still rather mysterious) journeys back to Berlin from Tehran in 1936 (he went to the Olympics) and 1938, chronicling the tightening vise, his unsuccessful efforts to get out his parents, and his stopovers in Palestine where he worked on "import/export" exchanges between Germany and Palestine via Iran; letters between a young cousin who had ended up in (what was then called) Bulawayo, Rhodesia, and her sister in London, both of them trying desperately and in vain to arrange escapes for parents left behind in Berlin; many proud, exasperated, and bemused letters from relatives and friends reporting on life in Palestine; and travelogues from a young Viennese Jewish woman who had befriended my mother in Tehran and then gone off to serve as governess to an aristocratic Arab family in Baghdad. They are postmarked from a dizzying variety of locales, but in many ways they are quite similar. The writers all veer between anxiety and despair about the situation they had left behind and seem powerless (despite enormous exertions) to change and the fascination and often exhilaration felt by young people starting life anew in strange and faraway locales. Here too, the historically relevant, the simply bizarre, and the highly individual all mix together in ways that I cannot yet fully track. I can fantasize various novels and movies, but it is not at all clear to me how these types of documents—and, as I note, this is only a very partial listing—are to be integrated into German Jewish social memory or academic history. Certainly, they are not typical of what is—as yet—to be found in the LBI. Perhaps for that very reason, they belong there.

Then there were the letters written after 1945: the painstaking efforts to reestablish communication, to discover who is alive and where, and to ascertain what had happened to the dead and the effort to digest somehow the enormity of the catastrophe that had occurred while many of the letter writers stood helplessly (and at times having a wonderful time) on the sidelines. They too come from an astonishing variety of places (some of my favorite "what if" letters are pleas from a childhood buddy of my father who had somehow ended up via Johannesburg in Tokyo trying unsuccessfully to persuade my father to give up on restarting his long-interrupted legal career in favor of joining a business exporting Japanese electronics to the United States!). There were letters from a younger brother of my father, a Catholic convert who had remained in Germany with his Catholic wife and five children until he too was taken to Auschwitz, announcing his liberation from Mauthausen. There were letters in which my father considers (and immediately rejects) offers to return to Berlin as a judge and angry exchanges about the return and sale of Aryanized property.

And then there were many more letters chronicling the rather humdrum return to bourgeois normality, whether in New York, Palo Alto, Tel Aviv, Johannesburg, London, Bern, or São Paulo: degrees completed, businesses established, children born and graduated, voyages enjoyed, and friends passed away. Here, particular questions about selection and relevance arise. Do the chatty letters sent back and forth between, say, Los Angeles and Jerusalem in 1963 (in German of course) about aches and pains, the achievements of children and grandchildren, and the latest jaunts to the Dolomites or Paris belong in an archive of German Jewish history? What about the eightieth birthday greetings mailed in 1990? Descriptions of return trips to Germany? Where does one draw the line? Does everything accumulated within the lifetime of one person identified as a German Jew count as history for a German Jewish archive? Or at least as social memory? Am I not allowed to throw out anything? Do I get to pick a date, a year, after which these papers are just family memorabilia or junk and not "history"? Is there a topic category that defines certain events as now clearly just American or British or Israeli and no longer in the purview of German Jewish history?

The History (out of the Closet)

I want to highlight two sets of German Jewish documents that clearly do qualify for the archives and there-

fore present other problems. The first bunch literally fell out of the very back of my mother's hall closet onto my head, just when I thought I had cleared out everything and was about to close up the apartment forever; the second set sits well cataloged but relatively unknown and unstudied in the Berlin Landesarchiv. Together they provoke questions about how to fit particular life stories preserved in personal papers into larger historical narratives and, more importantly perhaps for our purposes, about how the frame of the archive—where and how papers are preserved and under whose auspices—orders how they can be used and interpreted.

I am currently working on—and thinking about how best to use—the first set, documents and letters belonging to my maternal grandfather, Heinrich Busse, who survived "underground" in Berlin after his wife was deported to Auschwitz from her forced labor job during the notorious *Fabrikation* in 1943. The materials tell us very little about his life as an "illegal" and how he actually survived. A former Ullstein editor with a flair for writing, Busse clearly felt that his story had historical significance. An unsuccessful exchange of letters with Victor Gollancz and Heinz Ullstein indicates that he had hoped already in 1946 or 1947 to publish a memoir dramatically entitled *Berlin Underground*. But he never found an interested publisher, and he never seems to have written the proposed book. From the moment of going underground until just before liberation, there is—not surprisingly—no paper trail. However, the papers he did keep from the period 1945 to 1948 do, I think, tell us a good deal about postwar German history and the ever-vexed history of German-Jewish relations.

Despite the Nazi pledge to make Berlin *Judenrein* (free of Jews), Jewish life in the capital of the Third Reich had never completely stopped. It survived in precarious niches: underground among the Jewish *Uboote* hidden in factory lofts, apartments, and the shacks of Berlin's many garden plots (*Schrebergärten*); on the grounds of the Weissensee Jewish cemetery; and, both officially and secretly, in the strange ambiguous world of the Jewish Hospital (Jüdisches Krankenhaus) under the eyes of the Gestapo.[1] Indeed, the scope and variety of the Jewish presence in the vanquished former capital of a regime that had succeeded in exterminating most of European Jewry were quite extraordinary. Shortly after the war's end, some six thousand to seven thousand Jews were counted as Berlin residents. It is crucial to note here that these figures are imprecise and confusing and depend heavily on when exactly the count was taken and how *Jew* was defined. Two-thirds of those identified as Jewish survivors in Berlin shortly after the war were intermarried or the children of mixed marriages; of the five thousand to seven thousand Jews who had actually gone underground, probably no more than fourteen hundred, including my grandfather, made it to liberation. Jewish survivors in Berlin represented a high proportion of the fifteen thousand Jews who survived within the entire Reich, but of course only a fraction of the one hundred and sixty thousand who had been registered as members of Germany's largest and most vibrant Jewish community in 1932.[2]

Right after the Soviets took control of the city in May 1945, Jews received ID cards from the reconstituted Jewish community (*Gemeinde*) and "Victims of Fascism" (Opfer des Faschismus, OdF) insignia. Registrations that only days, certainly weeks, before would have meant deportation and death now had concrete benefits in terms of housing and increased rations. My grandfather's papers, kept in a brown leather folder, tell one story of these drastic shifts of identity. A March 1945 receipt under a false name from a lodging house (*Fremdenheim*) in the Berlin suburb Lehnitz still marked him as a hunted illegal. The next form dating from August 13 was a modest typed certificate (*Bescheinigung*) from the reconstituted *Jüdische Gemeinde,* Berlin, Iranische Strasse, certifying that Heinrich Busse was a full Jew and had lived hidden (*verborgen*). Then on August 28, Ausweis Nr. 2584 from the Gemeinde confirmed that he was of the Mosaic faith, had worn a star, and had lived as an "illegal"; it came with ration stamps for a pullover, socks, shirt (*Sporthemd*), and food. On August 30, Heinrich Busse was a Berliner again; he had a full Berliner ID (*Ausweis*) with photograph issued by the *Magistrat der Stadt Berlin, Hauptausschuss OdF,* certifying him, in German and Russian, as a full-fledged OdF. He was now stamped both as a Jew and a victim of fascism, an entirely helpful classification in Berlin in the summer of 1945.

On July 4, 1947, Heinrich Busse, my grandfather, reacquired his German civil identity. He was issued a real Ausweis, signed not by occupation or Gemeinde authorities but by the Berlin police chief (*Polizeipräsident*), listing his citizenship as German and omitting any mention of religion. By then, however, he also possessed a much more valuable document. Printed in French and English, a *Titre de Voyage,* or "travel document in lieu of a national passport," allowed him to enter Folkestone, England, on October 20, 1947, and rejoin two daughters who had fled to England as domestics in early 1939.

In addition to his precious official documents, Busse also saved carbon copies of all the letters he wrote from Berlin to his daughters in London and Tehran from the end of 1945 until he reached England in fall 1947; in fact he even seems to have exchanged his hard-won rations for a (surely black market) typewriter and the services of a typist. Once in London, he kept both sides of a rather stunning correspondence with some of his former rescuers. In fact, I find all of the letters quite remarkable (and problematic). I include some original German excerpts here because I am so dissatisfied with my own preliminary translations.

In the very first letter that he was able to post to his family in England on December 12, 1945, he addressed the most important question immediately, head on and unsparingly: "You will all be wondering how it is that I am saved and our dear mother was not able to escape the rabble. Well in brief, . . ." (Sie alle werden sich wohl vor allem nicht recht erklären können, dass ich gerettet bin und unsere liebe Mutti dem Gesindel nicht entgehen konnte.—Also kurz . . .) He then recounted in horrifying, riveting (and sardonic) detail that he had tried in vain to convince his wife to attempt a last-ditch flight into Switzerland and how, after his wife's deportation, he managed to outwit and outrun the three SS men who had interrupted his own preparations to finally flee, with a "now or never" (*jetzt oder nie*) leap out the window and dash for the nearby woods:

I was now preparing myself to escape alone and was prepared enough that I was planning to head out in a few hours, but then my landlady in Schlachtensee [suburb of Berlin, near the Grunewald] (a really nasty woman) called quite merrily into my room: Herr Busse, you are being taken away! And in came 3 SS soldiers and gave me a few minutes time, one was such a fresh rascal, I almost punched him in the face. I sat there, only half-dressed in housecoat and slippers and explained to him that I had to get myself ready. In one unguarded moment however, I thought to myself, now or never. And ran, just as I was, in slippers and without a hat through the backyard into the nearby woods, ran in a zigzag back and forth, finally hid myself in the bushes, and lay there, despite the cold, hungry and freezing, until the evening. As I discovered later that night from a fellow tenant, the soldier had ran after me furiously, pointing his revolver, but despite his 20 years and my 68 he couldn't get me. An achievement this surely was, a strong will and determination, also flexibility, was surely necessary but also a lot of luck. . . . Well you see I made it.

[Ich bereitete mich nun allein zur Flucht vor und war so weit fertig, dass ich in einigen Stunden losgehen wollte— da rief meine Wirtin in Schlachtensee (ein hämisches

Frauenzimmer) gamz fröhlich in das Zimmer: Herr Bussse, Sie werden abgeholt! Und herein traten 3 SS Soldaten—1 blieb zu meiner Bewachung und gab mir einige Minuten Zeit,ein ganz frecher Lümmel; beinahe hätte ich ihm eins in die Fresse gehauen. Ich sass da—erst halb angezogen, in Hausjacke und Hausschuhen—und erklärte ihm, ich würde mich fertig machen. In einem unbewachten Augenblick aber dachte ich mir: Jetzt oder nie! Und stürmte wie ich war in Pantoffeln und ohne Mützte durch den Hintergarten in den nicht weit entfernten Wald—schlug Haken rechts und links, verbarg mich schliesslich im Gestrüpp und blieb trotz der Kälte hungernd und frierend bis zum Abend liegen.—Wie ich dann in der Nacht,bei mir selbst einbrechend, von einem Mitbewohner vernahm, war der Soldat, wie ein Verrueckter tobend mit dem Revolver hinter mir hergerannt; trotz seiner 20 Jahre hat er mich schon damals 68jaehrigen aber doch nicht gekriegt . . . Leistung war es gewiss; Willenskraft und Entschlossenheit, auch Wendigkeit musste man schon aufbringen, aber auch viel Dusel habe ich immer wieder entwickelt . . . Ihr seht, ich bin durchgekommen.]

After the intervention of a nephew who had returned to Berlin in American uniform ensured a steady supply of CARE packages with food and cigarettes for black market barter, Busse quickly recovered physically and psychically. Virtually alone in Berlin, his children emigrated, his wife murdered, most of the rest of his family incinerated, his letters were full of the astonished exuberance of survival. The septuagenarian was irrepressible, full of projects and signing his letters (July 1946), "Long live life, your still full lusting for life" (es lebe das Leben! In diesem Sinne—Eurer noch immer lebenslustisger). He recorded with undiminished *Berliner Schnauze* (mouth) the strangeness of life for liberated Jews in post-Nazi Berlin. Describing a (now legendary) public Passover seder for over two thousand soldiers from the four occupying armies and including local Jews, held in April 1946 at the Schöneberger Rathaus, he noted, "there was a very good meal for free, but in exchange one had to listen [*in Kauf nehmen müssen*] for hours to an English-Hebrew service, which not a soul understood" (April 20, 1946).

But even as he delighted in the long-lost pleasures of "an English cigarette and a pitcher of coffee of the same origin," he took on the grim task of explaining the scope of the catastrophe to those who had escaped. To his son-in-law in London (whom he had never met) he sent a "devastating document" (*ein erschütterndes Dokument*), the final letter from his mother before her deportation. He added, "I can only press your hand in my thoughts and express the hope that your dear mother did not have to suffer for long. It is apparently useless to speak about any further hopes." (Ich kann Dir nur in Gedanken die Hand druecken und die Hoffnung aussprechen, dass auch Deine liebe Mutter nur kurz dem Leiden preis gegeben war. Von weitergehenede Hoffnungen zu sprechen, hat ja wohl keinen Sinn mehr.) In postwar Europe where so much survivor energy was bound up in trying to locate, or at least to find traces of, the dead and missing, people pleaded that they would be grateful for "any, even the tiniest information." They were loath to accept that, as Heinrich Busse wrote to still-hopeful relatives abroad in December 1945,

I am very much afraid that we will all have to accept the awful fact that there is no more hope. Whoever hasn't returned by now, will hardly have, as the Gemeinde tells me, the possibility of reporting or to suddenly surface with the countless refugees who are crisscrossing the country. All the search actions are only a tranquilizer, because how are we to find anyone in the midst of these millions upon millions, especially given the lack of lists and documentation.

[ich fürchte sehr, wir werden uns alle mit der furchtbaren Tatsache abfinden müssen, das jetzt keine Hoffnung mehr auf Erfolg besteht. Wer bis jetzt nicht wieder hier ist, wie mir auf der Gemeinde gesagt, wird schwerlich noch eine Möglichkeit haben, sich zumelden oder mit den zahllosen das Land durchziehenden Fluechtingen aufzutauchen. Die Suchaktionen selbst sind nur ein Berühigungsmittel, denn wie soll man praktisch jemand aus den Millionen und Abermillionen herausfinden, noch dazu managels aller Listen und Aufzeichnungen.]

Reading these letters, it became clear to me that for a very German Jew like Heinrich Busse, who at times briskly described his life in the underground as just another challenge to a hardened German gymnast for whom "there was no such thing as bad weather, just inappropriate clothing" (Es gibt kein schlechtes Wetter, es gibt nur unpassende Kleidung) (December 12, 1945), the real recognition of the irrevocable loss of his *Heimat* (homeland) and the need to find another or substitute one came only after the war had ended. He realized that despite the hopeful excitement of liberation, which had made him feel as if "newborn," there would always be—as he put it in a birthday letter to his thirty-six-year-old married daughter in London on June 18, 1946—"a sediment of mourning in the heart of your and all of our joy in life and ability to experience pleasure" (wenn auch ein Bodensatz Trauer auf immer im Kelch Deiner und unser aller Lebensfreude oder Genussfähigkeit zurueckbleiben wird).

Only in 1947, however, over two years after his liberation, when Busse had left Berlin behind forever, did he begin to articulate more fully the enormity of the German Jewish catastrophe and the persistence of anti-Semitism. He had, he acknowledged to a former business partner and rescuer,

> always, as you may know, considered myself more as a German than as a Jew, and rejected the stupid and pernicious (artificially constructed?) division between people who have lived in one land for many hundreds of years.
>
> [Ich habe mich, wie Sie vielleicht wissen, immer mehr als Deutscher denn als Jude betrachtet, die blödsinning und gesuchte Unterscheidung zwischen den seit vielen 100 Jahren im Lande lebenden abgelehnt.]

Safely arrived in London, his perspective shifted, and his letters back to Berlin expressed a rather dark view of the fraught relationship between rescued Jew and the "righteous Gentile," one characterized by banal disputes over scarce material goods and profound existential disagreements about what had actually happened in the very recent past.

> Due to the very sharp and general condemnation of Germany—not only here [in England] but everywhere abroad, I have myself become more self-critical and perhaps more clear-sighted.
>
> [Durch die sehr scharfe und allgemeine Beurteilung Deutschland—nicht nur hier sondern im gesamten Ausland—bin ich selbst etwas kritischer und vielleicht klar blickender geworden.]

Ironically (and tellingly) Busse was most bitter not about the mass of Germans whom he had long since written off but about the minority of good Germans. They had helped him survive, and he had maintained faith in them throughout the darkest days, even after his wife had been deported to her death, even after the rest of his family had either emigrated or been murdered.

During the war, the "illegals" and those living in mixed marriages or as *Mischlinge* (people of mixed blood; literally, "mongrels") had relied on the help and cooperation of Germans. Even at their most desperate, those in hiding or in touch with resistance news felt somehow vindicated in thinking that they were dealing with a "real" if minority Germany, with which they might join in reconstructing their homeland after the Nazis were defeated. After liberation, Jews were shocked and aggrieved by the sentiments revealed among even the "decent" minority. Their

rescuers complained about ungrateful Jews who received special favors from the occupiers; who were quick to emigrate, leaving their helpers behind hungry, cold, and self-pitying in a devastated city; or who (in Allied uniform) treated them insensitively in denazification procedures. Confronted with Germans preoccupied with their own misery and indifferent to, or in denial about, what had happened to their Jewish compatriots—what observers termed "the enigma of German irresponsibility"[3]—he felt the force of anti-Semitism even more painfully than when hiding in a friendly garden colony (Schrebergärten).[4]

Busse was shocked and horrified by a hectoring letter from an old business acquaintance, the furniture maker Hermann Paul, who had sheltered him, disguised as an old family retainer, in a Schrebergärten during the war's chaotic final months (at great personal risk, but not without hope of advantage after Germany's inevitable defeat). Smarting from the miserably cold winter of 1947, Paul complained that Busse, now safe in England, was ungrateful, was insufficiently generous with his care packages, and, moreover, had taken off with a radio that could have brought a small fortune on the black market. Suddenly, it seemed to Busse, he was no longer the fellow Berliner who had needed help, but just another Jewish war profiteer. He responded fiercely:

> I was speechless. [Mir blieb die Spucke weg.] . . . Even you seem to be accepting this silly as well as pernicious "Antisemitism." [Auch Sie scheinen sich ga jetzt tatsächlich zu dem ebenso albernene wie bösartigen "Antisemitismus" bekannt zu haben.] . . . I am not indifferent to what you think of me. Not in the least do I want to minimize or deny that I owe you much thanks. You behaved decently and with courage, quite unlike the overwhelming majority of Germans, toward a criminal, treacherous, and in every way deeply contemptible regime. I have expressed this to you repeatedly. But I must tell you one thing in regard to your current attitude and your outrageous version of events. As much as I value your help and your previous rejection of National Socialism—your brother Erwin had himself at the time not been shy about declaring that under the existing circumstances [late in the war] the dangers of taking me were not so great, the benefits of helping someone persecuted possibly greater. I completely understood that, and would never have thought about even mentioning this. Now however, it is necessary. Because it might at least make you—I have no such hopes anymore about your brother Erwin—more thoughtful.
>
> [Mir ist nicht gleichgültig wie Sie über mich denken. Nicht im geringsten will ich verkleinern oder bestreiten,

dass ich Ihnen viel Dank schuldig bin. Sie haben sich anständig und mutig behommen, anders als die völlig überweigende Anzahl der Deutschen gegenüber einem verbrecherischen, verlogenen und in jeder Hinsich tief verachtlichen Regime. Ich habe Ihenn dies wiederholt zum Ausdruck gebracht. Eins aber muss ich Ihnen angesichts Ihrer jetzigen Haltung und mich äussert empörenden Darstelling jetzt doch werwidern. So sehr ich Ihre Hilsbereitschaft und Ihre frühere Ablehnung des Nationalsozialismus anerkenne—ihr Bruder Erwin selbst hat sich s.Zt garnicht gescheut zu erklären, die Gefahr meiner Aufnahme halte er unter bereits vorliegenden Umständen für nicht sehr erheblich, der Nützen aus solcher Unterstützung eines Verfolgten könne sogar groesser sein. Ich habe ihm das nicht im geringsten verdacht und es hätte mir fern gelegen, diesen Umstand Ihnen gegenüber jemals zu erwaehnen. Jetzt aber ist es nötig. Weil es vielleicht wenigstens Sie (bei ihrem Bruder Erwin habe ich diese Hoffnung nicht) zu einer Nachdenklichkeit bringt.]

In another letter from London, Busse responded passionately to the laments of a young woman who had supported (and perhaps more) him during his years as an Uboot. She was, he insisted, so immersed in her own experience as a victim of war, defeat, and victor's justice that she had lost all sense of moral and historical proportion:

You have no idea how provocative it feels to those whom it affects when you now ask when will the liberators finally have satisfied their bloodthirstiness against us. When you as a German accuse them of horrendous tortures, after the entire world is still stunned with horror over the exposed and still not really admitted, somehow excused or trivialized, atrocities of the Germans, of which no one wants to be guilty or even involved. When you, despite all that has happened, literally write, "and after all, our hearts and hands are pure and with them the blood is flowing out of their collars," and other stuff like that, you refer personally to yourself and yours, but you can't possibly assume that the same would hold for the Germans as a whole and that one can expect the world simply to forget the horrors of Hitler, with which after all the broad masses generally identified.

[Du machts Dir keine Vorstellung davon, wie aufreizend es auf die unmittelbar Betroffenen wirken muss, wenn Du jetzt fragt: wann werden die Befreier endlich ihren Blutdurst an uns gestillt haben? Wenn Du als Deutsche ihnen grausame Folterungen vorwirst, nachdem die ganze Welt noch immer starr vor Entsetzen ist über die aufgedeckten und jetzt von den Deutschen noch immer nicht recht zugegeben, irgendwie entschuldigten oder verkleinerten Greultaten, an denen jetzt niemand schuldig order be-

teiligt gewesen sein will. Wenn Du trotz alledem wörtlich schreibst, "dabei sind unsere Herzen und Hände rein und ihnen läuft das Blut schon aus dem Stehkragen" und dergl. mehr, so meinst Du zwar Dich und Die Deinen persönlich, kannst doch aber unmöglich annhemen, das Gleiches für die Deutschen schlechthin gelten kann und dass von der Welt verlangt werden kann, die Untaten Hitlers, mit denen sich die breiten Massen doch weitgehend identifiziert hat, einfach zu vergessen.]

Still longing for the bracing air and beautiful lakes of his native city, he concluded that he could never again live in a city where he had to explain, even to his friends and saviors, "the not in the remotest way comparable difference between the conditions in Berlin or Germany now with those in Auschwitz, Belsen, etc." (den nicht in entferntesten zu vergleichenden Unterschied zwischen Zuständen in Berlin oder Deutschland mit jenen in Auschwitz, Belsen, usw).[5] On December 21, 1948, Heinrich Busse crossed his last border, following his middle daughter, who had recently arrived from Tehran. The U.S. Immigration and Naturalization Service admitted the seventy-four-year-old to New York City, where he became an enthusiastic resident of Morningside Heights. The last official document I found was from December 13, 1957, about a half year before he died at the age of eighty-three. It is a letter from the *Entschädigungsamt* (Department of Indemnification), Berlin, informing him of a raise in his reparations pension to DM 87 a month.

The History (in the Archive)

But there were also other ways, albeit less likely, to be a German Jew post–May 1945. The papers of Sigmund Weltlinger, a Berlin Jew who survived in Nazi Berlin and remained there after war's end, are not stored in a German Jewish archive but, as befits the *Nachlass* (literary remains) of a German government official, in the Berlin Landesarchiv.[6] Weltlinger was appointed the first Commissioner for Jewish Questions (Beauftragte für Judenfragen) with the postwar Berlin *Magistrat* and later served as a conservative Christian Democratic (CDU) deputy in the Berlin assembly (*Abgeordnetenhaus*). From February 1943, after their children had been sent to England, he and his wife lived concealed in Berlin with friends. Like many Uboots, they rarely left their hiding place, made it through several terrifying house searches, and had relatively little sense of what was going on around them. Like Busse, Weltlinger wrote postwar letters in a strongly defensive mode. He, however, was defending himself not against aggrieved Germans but against uncomprehending Jews who questioned his decision to stay in Berlin. On July 8, 1946, his niece Resilotte Lisser, now living at 750 Riverside Drive in New York, a classic Washington Heights (Fourth Reich) refugee address, wrote to her uncle and aunt in Berlin. She tried to persuade her only remaining close relatives to come to New York: "What a life we have here in freedom—it is good to live here." (Was ein Leben ist es hier in der Freiheit! . . . es lebt sich schön hier.) She assured them that everyone could find work and that they would not be a burden (*Last*). On March 3, 1947, she tried again, reflecting the thoughts of the vast majority of her fellow Yekkes living in that Viertes Reich on the problematics of what it meant to be home (*zu Hause*).

> No, for us there can be no going back, even if in my thoughts I am often back "at home." But it was all only a dream, my youth, and everything to do with it. I am at home *here* and happy!

> [Nein, für uns gibt es kein Zurück, wenngleich ich in Gedanken oft "zu Hause" bin. Es war ja alles nur ein (illegible) Traum gewesen, meine Jugend und alles Dazugehörige. Ich bin jetzt hier zu Hause und glücklich!]

She had a four-year-old American daughter with blond braids.

Weltlinger, however, did not want to leave Berlin. He had only just emerged into its daylight again, and he found the city open and fascinating. In the hard years 1946 and 1947, like so many Berliners, he and his wife went to the theater, heard Fürtwangler conduct Menuhin, and admired Gründgens, Dorsch, and many other great actors and actresses on the reopened, if unheated, stages. He was a minor big shot, privileged now as a Jew with good contacts to the Allies, enjoying the many receptions and parties with German and occupation officials.

There are silences and ruptures and inconsistencies in his stories. Of course. He reported how well they were living, better than most Berliners; his wife was greeted at receptions as Frau Stadtrat. But he also pleaded for shipments of food and clothing to be sent from New York, through the U.S. Chaplains Office, Jewish Relief Unit. On September 9, 1946, he carefully chronicled the lost and murdered, listing the names of those "unfortunately gassed" (*leider vergas*), "actually most of our old friends—one mustn't think about it" (Überhaupt die meisten unserer alten Freunde—man darf nicht daran denken). Yet he and his wife stayed on even as their children made new lives abroad. In 1951 he contended, "We have found a new and stimulating circle which makes a lot of music. We hear good operas and concerts. Berlin is right up to par." (Wir haben aber einen neuen und anregenden Kreis gefunden in dem auch viel musiziert wird. Wir hören hier auch gute Opernauffuehrungen und Konzerte. Berlin ist "ganz auf der Hoehe.") Weltlinger was not convinced by all the letters reporting on successful new lives and begging him to join the emigration. He continued to campaign for former Berlin Jews to return to a place he still considered home and mistrusted their insistence that they had created new homes. Weltlinger even made the prescient (very—about forty years) argument that a vital, ongoing Jewish community was necessary if only because Berlin was the logical destination for a future and inevitable exodus of Jews from the Soviet Union. And he wrote things about those Jews who questioned his choices that would make me cringe were I reading them as his granddaughter and not as a historian pleased to find another trove of personal letters.

History and Memory: Where?

Apparently undisturbed by such scruples, Weltlinger's son donated his papers to the Berlin Landesarchiv. Ever the Berlin patriot, Weltlinger would undoubtedly have approved. As it stands in the Landesarchiv, however, Weltlinger's Nachlass is presented primarily as an interesting example of early West Berlin communal politics. The anxious and uncomfortable debates about German Jewish identity and German Jews' relationship to postwar Germans they also contain, are entirely marginal to the social and political memory and knowledge production of the archive in which they rest. I can't help but wonder however whether these letters would read differently and be used more frequently if they were embedded in a different (and perhaps less lonely) context. Would Weltlinger's son, if given the choice now, have been willing to give the papers to the LBI archives attached to the Jewish Museum in Berlin? Would that have changed their social meaning and historiographical impact?

Alternatively, once I struggle my way through deciding when I'm ready to give Heinrich Busse's papers to the LBI, does it matter—in an age of electronic reproduction where originals have increasingly symbolic value—whether they land in New York or in Berlin? Will they be categorized in Berlin as part of the uneasy story of postwar Jewish life in the divided former capital or in New York as the long prehistory to a necessary emigration?

Will they be used to tell the story of Germans' postwar self-pity and willful incomprehension of their own responsibility or to examine the twists and turns of German Jewish identity in the shadow of the Holocaust? Or to reflect on the endlessly tortured (and still somehow fascinating) exchanges between Germans and Jews about their inextricably linked but polarized past and present, as revealed by the limits of understanding in even that most powerful (and glorified or sentimentalized) relationship of rescuer and rescued? Obviously, all those questions are relevant, but is the location likely to affect if, and to what degree, they are all addressed? What would Heinrich Busse have wanted? Would he have been pleased or horrified to be "returned" to Berlin over a half century later? Would he have preferred (my prejudice) that his memories of Berlin stay in New York? Will German scholars be more likely to read the materials productively (as Frank Mecklenburg describes) in New York, and will American and/or Jewish scholars do the same in Berlin? Will the materials have more contemporary relevance in Germany—becoming a part of debates about responsibility and memory—than in the United States, and does that matter?

Finally I return to the question of "what is history for the archives?" There are large chunks of Weltlinger's *Nachlass* that could be easily classified as entirely private, uncomfortable, and embarrassing, if a bit titillating and voyeuristic, for the researcher to read. But they are part of the package for whoever chooses to look. The same of course could be said of my grandfather's papers. Many of the letters, such as the ones from which I have quoted, are unquestionably of historical interest; with others or parts of others, the categories are much more ambiguous. They are certainly interesting were I, or anyone else, to attempt a biography of Heinrich Busse as a certain type of late nineteenth-, early twentieth-century middle-class German Jewish male; much less interesting, I would argue, if I, or anyone else, wanted to use the *Nachlass* to understand German or Jewish history from 1933 to 1955. In the meantime, the letters sit in manilla folders in my study, awaiting my interpretation, every now and then critically noted by Mecklenburg, who, of course, thinks they should be somewhere else.

NOTES

1. There is a relatively large amount of literature—histories, memoirs, diaries, and fiction (and semifiction)—on Jews who survived in Berlin. See, for example, the memoirs by Hans Rosenthal, *Zwei Leben in Deutschland* (Bergisch Gladbach:

Gustav Lübbe Verlag, 1980); Gad Beck, *Und Gad Ging zu David: Die Erinnerungen des Gad Beck 1923 bis 1945* (Berlin: Edition diá, 1995), now in English from University of Wisconsin Press; and Larry Orbach and Vivien Orbach-Smith, *Soaring Underground: A Young Fugitive's Life in Nazi Berlin* (Washington, DC: Compass Press, 1996). Also Leon Brandt, *Menschen ohne Schatten: Juden zwischen Untergang und Untergrund 1938 bis 1945* (Berlin: Oberbaum Verlag, 1984); Leonard Gross, *The Last Jews in Berlin* (New York: Simon and Schuster, 1982); Erika Fischer, *Aimée und Jaguar: Eine Liebesgeschichte, Berlin 1943* (Cologne: Kiepenheuer and Witsch, 1994); and David Wyden, *Stella: One Woman's True Tale of Evil, Betrayal, and Survival in the Holocaust* (New York: Simon and Schuster, 1992), the story of a notorious Jewish Jew catcher.

2. To the total of approximately 15,000 Jews (of a pre-1933 Jewish population of about 500,000) who survived within the Reich must be added perhaps 50,000 Jewish forced laborers who were liberated on German territory at the end of the war. See Frank Stern, "Antagonistic Memories: The Post-War Survival and Alienation of Jews and Germans," in *Memory and Totalitarianism,* ed. Luisa Passerini , vol. 1, *International Yearbook of Oral History and Life Stories* (New York, 1992), 23. The survival statistics for Berlin, as well as for Germany as a whole, are inconsistent and varied, according to who is counting whom, when and depending on how "Jewish" and "end of war" are demarcated. Andreas Nachama, "Nach der Befreiung: Jüdisches Leben in Berlin, 1945–1953," in *Jüdische Geschichte in Berlin: Essays und Studien,* ed. Reinhard Rürup (Berlin, 1995), 268–69, quotes reports similar to those used by Frank Stern, estimating that there were about 7,000 Jews in Berlin right after the war. Fifteen hundred had survived the camps, 1,250 had been "U-boats" in hiding, and approximately 4,250 had been spared deportation because they lived in mixed marriages—of these 2,250 were so-called star wearers, while the rest were privileged due to their Christian-identified children. Stern's corresponding figures are 1,155 camp survivors, 1,050 "illegals," and 2,000 mixed marriage partners and another 1,600 exempted from wearing the star. Nachama also counts the pre-Nazi Jewish population of Berlin as about 200,000, which presumably includes those not officially registered as Jews. Michael Brenner notes that "More than 2/3 of the seven thousand members of the Berlin Jewish community of 1946 were intermarried or children of mixed marriages." See Brenner, "East European and German Jews in Postwar Germany, 1945–50," in *Jews, Germans, Memory: Reconstructions of Jewish Life in Germany,* ed. Y. Michal Bodemann (Ann Arbor: University of Michigan Press, 1996), 52. Marion Kaplan, on the other hand, in her book *"Between Dignity and Despair" Jewish Life in Nazi Germany* (New York: Oxford University Press, 1988), while also noting on p. 232 the general survival figure of "approximately 15,000" surviving German Jews "within the pre-1938 borders," cites Konrad Kwiet and Helmut Eschwege in their *Selbstbehauptung und Widerstand: Selbstbehauptung und Widerstand; Deutsche Juden im Kampf um Existenz und Menschenwürde 1933–1945* (Hamburg, 1984) to state on p. 228 that "between 3,000 and 5,000 Jews came out of hiding in Germany. In Berlin, a city that once encompassed 160,000 Jewish Berliners, about 5,000 to 7,000 Jews hid, of whom only 1,400 survived." Here she counts only

those Jews who were hidden and not those (included, for example, by Nachama, Stern, and Brenner) who had survived more or less above ground in mixed marriages (or had themselves been "mixed"); on the other hand, she cites a somewhat higher number of surviving Uboots. The interesting story here may not be the precise numbers but the variations of classification and how they differ according to when and by whom the counting is done.

3. Moses Moskowitz, "The Germans and the Jews: The Postwar Report; The Enigma of German Irresponsibility," *Commentary* 2 (1946): 7–14.

4. Frank Stern in *Whitewashing the Yellow Star* posits that anti-Semitism was in many ways more visible in Germany after the war than before. For one German Jewish perspective on postwar Germans, see Hannah Arendt's much-quoted lament about Germans' "deep-rooted, stubborn, and at times vicious refusal to face and come to terms with what really happened." "The Aftermath of Nazi Rule: Report from Germany," *Commentary* 10 (1950): 342–43.

5. London, March 11, 1947.

6. Others would come back later, when the situation in Berlin had stabilized, after the division of the city and the formation of the Federal Republic. For example, Dr. Hans Hirschfeld, whose Nachlass lies in the Landesarchiv Berlin, was a veteran of World War I and the Hamburg Workers and Soldiers Council. He had fled to the United States from France in 1940 via the Pyrenees and Lisbon, but after eight unsatisfying years in the United States, working for the OSS and continuing to feel himself as exile rather than emigrant, he returned to Germany to work for Ernst Reuter's Senat. These people were the minority—absolutely—but in Berlin they loomed large. See Landesarchiv Berlin, rep. 200, NL 2014.

German Jewish Archives in Berlin and New York

Three Generations after the Fact

Frank Mecklenburg

Since 1955, the Leo Baeck Institute (LBI) is the central research institution for the history of German-speaking Jewry. The New York institute (there are affiliated Leo Baeck institutes in Jerusalem and London), with its vast archives, is in the midst of major changes. Its relationship to the public is expanding, with close association to major research and museum facilities in New York, at the Center for Jewish History (CJH), and in Berlin, at the new Jewish Museum (JMB). By becoming part of CJH, the LBI and the German Jewish legacy are recognized and integrated into the American Jewish identity, at the same time when "European Jewry" is emerging as a third force next to Israel and the United States.

The LBI became the central research archives for the history of German-speaking Jewry because at a time when no institution was interested in collecting and preserving these materials, the LBI became the only repository for the documents and personal papers of the refugees from central Europe.

Historical Background

In 1955 a group of leading representatives of German-speaking Jewry in America, Great Britain, and Israel decided to create a research center for the preservation of their own history and culture. German Jewish culture as it had been known was wiped out from continental Europe, and the expectation was that this extermination was final. Ten years after the Holocaust, the founders of the LBI agreed that in order to preserve the memory of this prolific ethnic group it was necessary to create a memorial to its vanished glorious existence. The plan was to collect as much documentation as possible to become a research archive and eventually to write a comprehensive history as the closing statement. It was to be more than merely an archive, however, but also, as the renowned historian George Mosse said, "the calling card of German Jewry." The survivors would have a safe haven for their papers, their memoirs, and their photos. The institute became—along with others such as Congregation Habonim, founded one year after Kristallnacht, or the newspaper *Aufbau*, which very quickly became the major voice for the refugees from central Europe—a social institution as well as a scholarly one.

At the time, there was no German Jewish historiography in Germany. One of the first to attempt to introduce German Jewish historiography in postwar Germany was Adolf Leschnitzer, one of the founders of the LBI in New York, who in the 1930s had built a Jewish school system for Jewish students expelled from German schools. Starting in the late 1950s, he held lectures and seminars at the Berlin Free University. The generation of senior historians in Germany, the United States, and Israel teaching and researching German Jewish history almost all went through Professor Leschnitzer's courses (these historians are about to retire).

For many years, the LBI existed as a singular entity on the Upper East Side of Manhattan, serving as a repository for the documents and a gathering point for members of the generation of refugees from Nazi Germany and widely ignored by the larger Jewish community. The LBI

Library and Archives did what other similar organizations do: acquisition, appraisal, preservation, accessioning, supporting researchers, and large historiographic projects. This took place in the 1950s, 1960s, 1970s, and early 1980s, when very few were actually interested in that history.[1] In the beginning, the LBI was run by the refugees, from the director to the archivists and librarians, the secretaries and the many volunteer helpers, who processed the incoming papers of the famous and many not famous immigrants from central Europe.

The scope of the LBI research horizon is German-speaking Jewry throughout Europe, which stretches from the eastern parts of France to the eastern parts of the former Austro-Hungarian Empire, which is usually considered Yiddish-speaking territory. However, these eastern European lands in Poland and Russia were always territories of mixed ethnicities and languages, and many important writers in Czernowitz (Chernivtzi) published in German and were speaking the language along with Russian, Polish, Ukrainian, and Yiddish. This is where LBI touches on YIVO, which is the equivalent to the LBI for the Yiddish language and which, by the way, was founded in Berlin in 1925, at a time when Berlin was one of the main places in the world for the publication of Yiddish literature along with Warsaw and New York.

During the years since 1955, the LBI has collected a vast body of information and a huge library. Since 1956, the LBI in London has published the *Leo Baeck Institute Year Book,* which has grown to more than twenty thousand pages in over 750 fifty articles on all conceivable topics in the study of German Jewish history and culture. The first forty volumes of the *Year Book* are now available on CD-ROM, searchable as a whole for research purposes and usable as a teaching tool. The CD-ROM allows you to print selected passages or articles on specific topics and assemble them in course readers or import and quote in your research. The LBI also has an academic book series, the "wissenschaftliche Schriftenreihe," published with Mohr/Siebeck in Tuebingen, Germany, which has grown to over seventy volumes. Hundreds of books in English, German, and Hebrew are published with the sponsorship of the LBI, and there are thousands of books, dissertations, and articles that are based on the archival holdings of the LBI. In the late 1980s, the catalogs of the LBI Archives were converted from cards and paper to electronic databases, and recently the LBI published its online catalogs on the World Wide Web, accessible through its Web site.

After the end of the cold war, the LBI conducted a survey of Jewish source materials in the archives of the former East Germany. After nearly ten years of work, these inventories have been published in six volumes and are growing. They too will be published electronically. The original mission of the founders to write a comprehensive history of the German Jewish people has so far resulted in the four volumes of *German-Jewish History in Modern Times, 1600–1945.* A fifth volume is in production, a history of everyday life of German-speaking Jews in central Europe between 1600 and 1945. All of these studies have been done by the LBI with an international team of senior researchers from the United States, Israel, and Germany. The founders of the LBI believed that after the publication of such a well-documented story, the LBI would have served its purpose and could close. This vision of the founders did not hold true. The LBI is moving into a new context, in the United States as well as in Germany, and the materials that no one was interested in fifty years ago are more and more in demand. Collecting and preserving the documentation of German-speaking Jews is a more active enterprise than ever before.

The primary users for this archive are German or central European academics who with increasing interest are recreating a picture of that part of the German population their grandparents' generation had killed off. They are writing about German history, trying to add its absent chapters and thus rewriting and correcting the historiography of their fathers' generation. They are not writing Jewish history but German history. Among them is a group writing specifically about the destroyed Jewish communities in central Europe. These researchers are mostly local historians and lay people, teachers, town archivists, and librarians who went first into their local archives in order to collect and recover information about the local Jewish population that went into exile or was killed. Over the past few decades, mainly since the 1980s, thousands of books have come out serving as monuments to the Jews of their communities. Until now, no survey of these literally thousands of works has been done, and I am sure it would reveal much useful information about the attitudes and aspirations of the postwar generations of Germans trying to regain information about the extinguished parts of their history.

The Jewish side in German Jewish history is mainly written in the countries of exile by the grandchildren of the generation of founders of the LBI. These historians and scholars of cultural studies are the other major user group of the archives of the LBI. The two historiographies exist side by side. There are numerous encounters of the two groups at conferences and through journals and other publications, and yet there is only limited communication, in part due to language problems. Only in recent years have young German historians started to go abroad and familiarize themselves with the historiography of the English-speaking world. The LBI has been an important destination—often the first opportunity to come into contact with "real" Jews and what is often experienced as the "Jewish" sensibility of New York. German researchers coming to New York are stepping into the territory of the exiles. They feel curious and excited, at the same time ashamed and guilty, and definitely experience something in the course of their research that they would not have experienced at home. This is particularly true with researchers coming from Austria who only recently discovered that their country played a major role in Nazi Germany and was not the "First victim" as had been declared for many years. It has always been the added appeal of the LBI that it provides access to the strange world of New York to these students from central Europe, especially the truly unique experience of an encounter with Jews who can no longer be found at home.

Now, more than fifty years after the Holocaust, Germany is debating how to memorialize the Nazi past and how the new capital Berlin is the place to do it. Berlin has ongoing and seemingly endless discussions over the need, purpose, mission, and costs of the JMB, the Holocaust Memorial, and a memorial to the Gestapo called Topographie des Terrors. But the debate does not preclude the reality that all these institutions will exist and are widely regarded as positive steps. The Leo Baeck Institute is about to open a branch of its archives as a collaborative project together with the Jewish Museum Berlin. Only five years ago, this was an unthinkable, undesirable idea, unwelcome from both sides.

The LBI Archives could also play a role in providing continuity to the new, emerging Jewish community in Berlin. Jewish communities in Germany are the fastest-growing Jewish communities in Europe. The LBI in Berlin project supplies historical background information to the new members of the Jewish community on their "predecessors" and their predecessors' traditions. Discontinuity is not a choice. The generation of recent immigrants from the former Soviet Union will either disengage from the Jewish community or relate to their own history and the German Jewish past. To connect to a Russian Jewish past is rather unlikely, though not impossible. The future will tell. However, this will lead to a situation of mixed ethnicities within central European Jewry as it existed earlier in the twentieth century. That component, the bridge and interchange between central Europe and western Europe, and eastern Europe, is ad-

dressed by a new study institute in Leipzig, the Simon Dubnow Institute for Central European and Eastern European Studies under the leadership of Professor Dan Diner. The new CJH in New York will not only provide the comprehensive European picture but also add the American side of the story by way of the American Jewish Historical Society. This will lead to the study of migration from east to west to America for which there are many traces in the archives, but due to the cold war and also the division of the Jewish world, this obvious topic was never really studied.

The German Perspective

German society is struggling with historical discontinuity. With the relocation of the capital and the change in government, the emphasis has changed. Cultural issues have moved to the forefront and are being handled by a federal minister of cultural affairs, a function that did not exist in previous governments. The missing German Jews are the symbol for the historical disruption. This reconstruction project for German history uses German Jewish history and the memory of the Nazi past manifested in the assembly of the three institutions in the center of Berlin: the JMB, the Holocaust Memorial, and the Museum of the Gestapo. As much as academic historians have come to a consensus over the meaningfulness of these institutions, it is now German journalists who have entered into the debate. The reason for them picking the JMB is that it is the only finished building at this point. This debate definitely has a new tone compared with only a few years ago. One indication of that is the recently published book *Jewrassic Park* by a cultural correspondent of the Berlin newspaper *Der Tagesspiegel*, Thomas Lackmann, who compares the new Berlin museum with a museum planned by Nazi Germany in Prague to show the vanished culture of the Jews. The analogy is, from a crude German point of view, obvious. It is meant to illustrate that this museum is a display of the disappeared Jews. The fact that the analogy indicates a fundamental insensitivity toward the Jewish minority in Germany has not occurred to Lackmann or his book editor.

The LBI is playing a major role in legitimizing the JMB as the largest museum for Jewish history in Europe. This happens at a time when there is the attempt to create the issue of European Jewry as a third force next to Israel and the United States. In *Jewrassic Park* an attempt is made to redefine German Jewish culture in Germany as an American import that has been watered down Disney style.

Germany's lingering anti-Americanism is a not-so-hidden form of anti-Semitism.

It is interesting to see how the LBI was used for this process of legitimizing the German politics of memory. The former German federal cultural minister, Michael Naumann, now publisher of the German weekly *Die Zeit,* was the major architect of building and consolidating the monuments of German memory in Berlin, taking charge of the situation when the local Berlin government left the decision-making process in chaos. The new capital is to represent memory, shame, and mourning with three major institutions and thus will provide a comprehensive symbolic order for the new capital. The JMB, designed by Daniel Libeskind, a Polish American Jew, is about to open; construction has not yet started on the Holocaust Memorial, with its design by the American architect Peter Eisenman; and the Museum of the Gestapo, designed by a Swiss architect, was stopped after initial construction. To some people, this means the whole setup in the center of Berlin is overdone, that there is too much weight given to the Nazi past, which obviously signals the discomfort that the constant reminder of the past imposes; on the other hand, the function of these symbolic and also real places of memorializing is to demonstrate that the new unified Germany does not want to let any doubts linger that three generations after the fact this history needs to be remembered for what it was.

What is peculiar about the Berlin public discourse concerning the JMB, the Holocaust Memorial, and also the Gestapo museum is that there is much criticism, a lot of reporting, and little defense. There is no exchange on matters, the criticism is carried out by minor journalistic figures, and the tone is one of discontent, complaint, and some cynicism. The refusal to recognize the continuing reality of these institutions has to be seen as a reflex of the political climate in the city of Berlin. And since the current discourse will not change the reality of these institutions, the discourse needs to be regarded as highly symbolic. The fact that LBI is "coming back" to provide the information that is necessary for a comprehensive picture of Germany is still waiting to be recognized for what it is: something deployed opportunistically but not taken seriously. The level of consciousness to do so has not been reached yet.

The peculiar journalistic case of the conservative newspaper *Die Welt* is particularly telling. This flagship paper of the Axel Springer publishing company has become a major, if not the major, voice of criticism of the JMB. For many years, especially while Axel Springer himself was still alive, there was an almost uncritical sup-

port of everything Jewish. Springer died more than a decade ago. Over the past few years, *Die Welt* has published the harshest and also the most destructive pieces that suggest it wants the museum to fail; at the very least the paper does not provide positive ideas about the future of the museum.

The LBI is the reminder that there once was a past in which Germans and Jews did live in one country, and what needs to be conveyed through the JMB in combination with the LBI is that Germany will make another attempt to integrate and tolerate minorities and strangers. At the entrance of the Reichstag, the parliament building, there is a slogan, "To the German people," which was intended to provoke the imperial powers by playing on the contrast between the undemocratic power of the kaiser versus the parliament of the people. A recently installed artwork situated in one of the courtyards of the Reichstag by the New York–based German artist Hans Haake provides a contrast to this slogan. Haake's neon sculpture "To the population" plays on the theme of the rights of the Germans versus the rights of everyone living in Germany. Are Jews in Germany accepted as an integral part of the German people? The late leader of the Council of Jews in Germany, Ignatz Bubis, was having second thoughts shortly before his death whether the once optimistic developments would in fact continue to head in the right direction. The recent rise of antiforeigner (including anti-Jewish) violence casts doubt.

A prominent issue in the debate over the LBI coming to Berlin is whether the archives will bring original documents to Berlin or microfilm copies. In fact, researchers increasingly use microfilm because in many cases the fragility of the originals makes them difficult to work with. The point is that the LBI collections will, for the first time, be available in Germany. This is often termed as a "return" to Germany, although the LBI was founded in Jerusalem and never had an institute in Germany. This is a matter of pain and ambivalence for many refugees and their heirs who specifically gave or intend to give their papers to the LBI in New York and who are already confronted with repeated pleas from the local German Jewish museums and memorial sites. If they choose the latter, the great body of German Jewish collective history will become fragmented, even if accessible. At the LBI, the integrity of this story is maintained and becomes a permanent part of the material deposited at the "archive of record."

At the same time that the German Jewish component is reintegrated into German historiography and becomes the necessary and major symbol of the memory culture, there is a current redefinition of American Jewish identity that has made space for the German Jewish heritage and that is being preserved in the newly formed CJH as part of the continuum of Jewish culture in the diaspora. Only a few years ago, the notion that the Yekkes and the Ostjuden would come to share a building, a reading room, to organize a joint project also seemed very unlikely.

NOTES

This paper was presented to the Sawyer Seminar on November 2, 2000.
An expanded German version of this essay was published in *Menora* 12 (2001).

1. Shalom Adler-Rudel, *Ostjuden in Deutschland 1880–1940: Zugleich eine Geschichte der Organisationen, die sie betreuten* (Tuebingen, Germany: Mohr, 1959); Ernst Akiba Simon, *Aufbau im Untergang: Juedische Erwachsenenbildung im nationalsozialistischen Deutschland als geistiger Widerstand*, introduction by Siegfried Moses (Tuebingen: Mohr, 1959); Selma Stern-Taeubler, *Der Preussische Staat und die Juden. A. Die Zeit des Grossen Kurfuersten und Friedrich I. Abt. 1: Darstellung, Abt. 2: Akten. B. Die Zeit Friedrich Wilhelms I. Abt. 1: Darstellung, Abt. 2: Akten. C. Die Zeit Friedrichs des Grossen. Abt. 1: Darstellung, Abt. 2: Akten. D. Gesamtregister zu den sieben Baenden*, ed. Max Kreutzberger (Tuebingen: Mohr, 1962; 1971; 1975); and Ernest Hamburger, *Juden im oeffentlichen Leben Deutschlands: Regierungsmitglieder, Beamte und Parlamentarier in der monarchischen Zeit 1848–1918* (Tuebingen: Mohr, 1968).

Medieval Archivists as Authors

Social Memory and Archival Memory

Patrick Geary

Back in the early 1970s, David Hammack, a historian of New York City, told me that the most important person in the New York City Archives was an individual whose only qualification was his membership in the Teamsters Union. The reason that this was such an important qualification, Professor Hammack explained, was that the archive was seriously underfunded and underhoused. The most daunting task the staff faced each year was to get all of the materials that they had accumulated the previous year but could not possibly preserve to the city dump in time to make room for the next year's tidal wave of paper. The teamster/truck driver/archivist was the key to this activity.

Archivists do not generally like to dwell on their role as destroyers of the past. Normally, when talking about archives, one concentrates on preservation, not on destruction. However the New York City archivist-teamster illustrates an essential component in the relationship of the present to the past: the necessity of forgetting. Friedrich Nietzsche first called attention to the importance of forgetting, at least equal to remembering, speaking of "that malleable power of a person, a people, a culture, . . . to grow in new directions, to restructure and reconstitute what is past and foreign, to heal wounds, to replace what has been lost, and to recast those molds which have been broken."[1]

Archivists are primary agents in this process, of necessity making choices about what is to be hauled to the landfill, what is to be preserved, and, perhaps as importantly, how it is to be preserved. We historians tend to prefer to ignore the fundamental role of archivists and enjoy the delusion that our clever research can bring us into some direct contact with the past. In fact, the work of historians is often constructed so as to make the archives invisible: to present the illusion of bringing the present reader into the past to which the historian, as interpreter and guide, has privileged access. In reality, historians are more likely than not providing their readers not with a tour of the past but with a tour of one or more archives, the creative work of teams or generations of archivists. It is they, through their process of selection, reorganization, and elimination, who largely determine what past can be accessed and, to a great extent, what that past might be. Archivists, one might well argue, are not preservers of their documents: they are their authors, engaged in work as creative, and as subjective, as that of those who originally penned individual texts or those modern historians who pretend to tell the past to the present.

As a medievalist, my ability to access my sources is always mitigated by archivists, most of whom are anonymous toilers in medieval monasteries and religious houses. In recent years I have come to pay more attention to them than I had in the past, asking about their role in the creation of the texts that they have transmitted to us. In this essay, I address one specific aspect of the work of medieval archivists, the compilation of cartularies or charter books, volumes that contain copies of the land records of medieval institutions, seen from the perspective not simply of preservation but of creation. I want to consider the compilers of these cartularies not as archivists but as authors.

At a very basic level, it is doubly absurd to talk about the authors of cartularies. First, we medievalists are accustomed to classifying cartularies among archival compilations rather than literary texts. They are largely copies of individual land transactions, donations, sales, exchanges, and the like, themselves the work of many scribes, or *scriptores,* writing on the order of a bishop, abbot, or other authority—over long periods of time and following specific legal or customary formulas—to record transactions normally involving the transfer of real property. We need not deny a certain creativity in the *narratio* of the charter itself, a certain literary sense of constructing reality by the scriptor, but even this mediocre level of creativity can hardly be assigned to the person who, decades or centuries later, recopied the charter into a cartulary. The cartulary, after all, exists at a secondary remove: at some point, as Wendy Davies beautifully showed in the case of the Redon cartulary, these individual charters, perhaps lying in a chest or in the pigeonholes of a monastic archive, are collected and copied into a codex.[2] As photographs, as it were, of the contents of an archive at a particular moment, it would seem absurd to assign so weighty a designation as author to the compiler of this archival material.

If speaking of the author of a cartulary seems absurd to a medievalist, speaking of any author is apparently viewed as absurd by literary scholars. The Author, as understood in traditional literary studies, is widely pronounced to be dead or, rather, never to have lived except in what Roland Barthes called *positivist capitalist ideology.* Of course, word of this death has not spread everywhere. According to Barthes, this author "still reigns in manuals of literary history, in biographies of writers, magazine interviews, and in the very consciousness of litterateurs eager to unite, by means of private journals, their person and their work; The image of literature to be found in contemporary culture is tyrannically centered on the author, his person, his history, his tastes, his passions."[3] Since Mallarmé, Barthes argued, this tyranny of the author has been replaced by language: "It is language which speaks, not the author; to write is to reach, through a preliminary impersonality which we can at no moment identify with the realistic novelists' castrating 'objectivity,' at points where not 'I' but only language functions, 'performs.'"[4]

Michel Foucault also called this modern construct of the Author into question, but at the same time he questioned the alternative offered by Barthes, that is, to grant primary status not to the author but to writing: "In granting a primordial status to writing, do we not in effect, simply reinscribe in transcendental terms the theological affirmation of its sacred origin or a critical belief in its creative nature?"[5] "This conception of écriture sustains the

privileges of the author through the safeguard of the a priori; the play of representations that formed a particular image of the author is extended within a gray neutrality. The disappearance of the author since Mallarmé, an event of our time, is held in check by the transcendental."[6]

Foucault proposed to go beyond the simple repetition of the empty slogan "the author has disappeared" and to examine the difficulties that arise in the use of an author's name. He suggested that the proper role of criticism, one might say scholarship, is not to reestablish the ties between an author and his or her work or to reconstitute an author's thought and experience through his or her works but rather that it should concern itself with the structures of a work studied for their intrinsic and internal relationships. But what, then, is a work if it is not something written by a person called an author? Moreover, is the "work" of an author everything that he or she wrote and said or only certain privileged texts?

We historians might well put aside for once our wellfounded suspicion of theoreticians and recognize that Foucault is actually raising important questions for us when we consider this peculiar type of compilation that we call *cartularies.* Foucault's call to analyze verbal clusters as discursive layers that fall outside of the familiar categories of a book, a work, or an author is particularly fitting in the discussion of cartularies, precisely because they are at once self-contained and fall outside the normal category of individual documents. These are complex and problematic volumes, well worth our consideration within the context of a discussion of archival practice in the Middle Ages.

The problems raised by Foucault, and by our cartularies, are several. These include, first, the problem of proper names. What does it mean that we can attach the name *Anamot* to the tenth-century Regensburg archivist who completed a cartulary of the charters of his monastery around 893?[7] To call this, as historians regularly do, the "cartulary of Anamot" implies more than simply labeling the cartulary itself. To assign a name to a text is, as Foucault said, more than simply indicative: it is the equivalent of a description. "The proper name and the name of an author vacillate between the poles of description and designation,"[8] in this case pointing not only to the specific quires of a certain cartulary now in the Bavarian State Archives but also to a presumed person to whom can be assigned intentional motivations, a consistent personality, a history, somehow potentially manifest in the cartulary designated by his name. Is the purpose of scholarship to reestablish the ties between Anamot as author and his oeuvre, the cartulary, and thus to reconstitute his thought and experience through his work? But if not, if we refuse to ascribe anything but the work of mechanical compilation to the monk Anamot, then we must confront the question of why the monk ensured that his name would be a part of the cartulary. Can we address the question of intentionality and personality in such a case?

In the case of Anamot, the only extent text that we can in any circumstances attribute to him is the cartulary. Otherwise, he is entirely unknown. This is not always the case with authors or compilers of cartularies. What are we to make of the case of Cozroh, the ninth-century compiler or author of the so-called cartulary of Freising?[9] Cozroh appears not only as the "author" or compiler of the cartulary but also as the scriptor of over eighty charters he then himself recopied into the cartulary. Should we see him as the "author" of the cartulary in the same sense as "author" of the charters? Are we to look for some sort of program recognizable in both productions, or in neither? Is there a person we are describing or attempting to describe in the label *Cozroh,* or is this merely a representation of a traditional charge, executed according to standard formulas on the command of a bishop?

The issue becomes even more complex when one speaks of someone like Gregory of Catena (ca. 1060–1130), the "author"of the *Regestum Farfense,* that is, cartulary of Farfa,[10] as well as of the *Liber Largitorius,*[11] which registered grants made by Farfa to others, and of the *Chronicon Farfense,*[12] which synthesized and connected much of the material in both the *Liber Largitorius* and the *Regestum.*[13] Now, in the case of a name attached not only to charters and to a cartulary but to historical and polemical works as well, when one asks if Gregory can be termed the "author" of the cartulary, one is asking not simply about the relationship between a person (Gregory) and an administrative compilation but between a number of complex texts and their possible coherence. The issue, as Foucault expressed it, is important:

> A name can group together a number of texts and thus differentiate them from others. A name also establishes different forms of relationships among texts. Neither Hermes nor Hippocrates existed in the same sense that we can say Balzac existed, but the fact that a number of texts were attached to a single name implies that relationships of homogeneity, filiation, reciprocal explanation, authentication, or of common utilization were established among them.[14]

Thus to speak of Gregory as the "author" of the cartulary of Farfa is to make claims about the putative coherence of at least three texts belonging to different genres but constituting the author's oeuvre and thus implying reciprocal explanation if not homogeneity, and thus implying an intentional agency in their composition that constructs for us a unified discourse from which we postulate an individual.

What I propose to do is very briefly to address the author question in terms of these early cartularies, all begun before 1100, and all of which are attached to personal names: Cozroh, Anamot, and Gregory. In particular I want to consider how the prefatory materials in their cartularies and the active role of their compilers in selecting and organizing their material present the twin questions of authorship and authority. My real intention is not to decide whether the term *authorship* in the sense of Roland Barthes's positivist capitalist ideology is appropriate for describing cartulary production—one can easily assume from the start that this would be wildly anachronistic—but rather to illuminate to some extent the genesis and program of cartulary production in its first centuries. In effect, I argue that the relationship between the names that appear in these prefaces diffuses issues of authority and complicates the sense of purpose and intentionality behind these documents. They are neither the mechanical compilations of archives, photographs as it were of whatever archival drudges found in their keeping, nor are they the creations of individual personalities. Rather they represent the complex intersection of various personal and communal programs that cannot be reduced to a single author, a single *auctoritas,* or indeed a single purpose.

Pascale Bourgain and Marie-Clotilde Hubert have pointed out that cartularies, prior to the twelfth century, were generally (but not, I would argue, universally) considered rhetorical constructions.[15] Their prefaces are very similar to prefaces of historical and hagiographical works and appeal to the same topoi of self-abnegation, duty, and concern for the preservation of the past that one finds in these other contemporary genres. Indeed, in so-called chronicle cartularies the very distinction of genre is entirely arbitrary: a text such as the *Gesta abbatum S. Bertini Sithiensium,* composed by Folquin, is explicitly called a "history of the abbots" of St. Bertin, although it is composed primarily of charters Folquin copied from his monastery's archives.[16] But rather than talking about these explicitly narrative cartularies, I focus on those that are indeed copies of charters not sewn together by a narrative. A number of these contain prefaces, some fairly elaborate. They present a justification and even an apology for their composition and allude to the question of authority and necessity in ways that are both significant and, perhaps, disingenuous. Let's begin at the beginning with the cartulary of Freising, one of the earliest extant cartularies, begun by the deacon Cozroh in the 830s.

According to his preface, the cartulary was compiled on the command of Bishop Hitto of Freising (811–35), who was eager to have written down in a single book "whatever he found written in individual charters and confirmed by other testimonies, both from the times of the preceding fathers as well as from his own famous rule." In a real sense, then, the *auctor* of the cartulary was not Cozroh but Hitto himself. Cozroh's own role was simply that of the instrument of Hitto's will:

And for this task, not mean but laudable, which he initiated, he sought out and found his own meanest little servant, yet still his most faithful, named Cozroh, whom he taught by his own sacred teachings, and promoted to the dignity of the priesthood. And placing upon him the weight of so great a labor, he instructed him in that way firmly to accomplish this task with care and with all circumspection: He found nothing diminished or added to, unless it was something that had been corrupted through the fault of the scribe. And he himself, conscious of his own lack of skill, as if mildly resisting, but preferring both to obey his kind instructions than to flee the weight of so great a care, with the Lord assisting, began this work.[17]

Cozroh did not explain that the choice of him as the compiler of the cartulary was most appropriate: he had been acting as a scribe, preparing charters for Freising since 820. Moreover, his duties continued after the death of Hitto until 848. However, the final compilation of the cartulary, if perhaps undertaken at the command of Hitto, was not completed for over twenty years after the disappearance of the bishop. This is evident, for example, in the treatment of one document for which Cozroh had acted as scribe and that he had later included in the cartulary. A consideration of how this document passed from original to cartulary copy suggests the complexity hidden in Cozroh's disingenuous claim that in making his cartulary he had simply followed Bishop Hitto's directions "nothing diminished or added to, unless it was something that had been corrupted through the fault of the scribe."[18]

The document records the resolution of a dispute between Bishop Erchanbert of Freising, nephew and successor of Hitto who assumed the episcopacy in 836, and the heirs of a certain Kiso in the 840s.[19] The bishop claimed that Kiso had donated a church at Strogn and

property at Berghofen to the church of Freising. Kiso's heirs, Vuichelm and Eigil, disputed the claim. However, the bishop was able to call witnesses in support of his claim, and "convicted and coerced by the laws" Vuichelm and Eigil returned the property. Some time later, however, the two appeared before the bishop and requested to be allowed to join allodial property at Berghofen that they had inherited from Kiso, to their father's gift. In return, Eigil and his mother received the properties at Strogn as life benefices.

Such a dispute and such a resolution are not at all unusual for mid-ninth-century Freising and have been analyzed in terms of Bavarian dispute resolution by Warren Brown.[20] What is peculiar is that the document that records the event is in the form not of a typical episcopal *placita* or of a formal *gueriptio* (or quitclaim) but rather of a narrative combining the story of two separate events. Moreover, although it concludes, "Ego Kozroh indignus presbiter scripsi," it seems to have been written or revised long after the date indicated: June 9, 840. By the time the document in its present form was written, Bishop Erchanbert was dead: it begins, "Quomodo quidem reverendae memoriae Erchanbertus episcopus et advocatus eius Kerhart quaesierunt unam ecclesiam at Stroagnon" (In what manner Bishop Erchanbertus of blessed memory and his advocate Kerhart claimed a church at Strognon). At a second point in the text, Erchanbert is referred to as *memoratus episcopus,* terminology that implies that he is dead at the time of the writing. The document must have received its final form sometime after Erchanbert's death in 854. Had Cozroh been present to record the events at the original placitum or at the subsequent renegotiation of the grant? One can doubt it: Cozroh used a series of formulas to designate by what authority he served as scribe. In twenty-one cases he stated that he wrote "on the order of the bishop."[21] In seventeen others, he explained that he was present and that he had written the charter after having "seen and heard" the events described.[22] In twenty-two cases, he combined the two formulas.[23] Only in ten charters did he fail to appeal either to the authority of the bishop or to his own witness but rather, as in our case, wrote simply, "Ego Cozroh indignus presbiter scripsi" (I the unworthy priest Cozroh wrote this).[24] Perhaps these formulas are without meaning, but they may suggest that Cozroh had written the final version of the notice by combining two earlier texts of which he had not been the original scriptor. The composition of this narrative, composed not only long after the death of the bishop on whose command Cozroh claimed to have begun the cartulary but over a decade after the events it describes, suggests that

Cozroh was at least adjusting and clarifying, if not perhaps writing or revising, his own earlier version of the events, if indeed such an earlier version ever had existed.

Is then Cozroh the author of his cartulary in a way that is different from his authorship of the charters that he composed, having "seen and heard" the events that they describe? His work is somewhere between compiler and creator. On what *auctoritas* did he pursue this work? According to his claims, the authority derived from Hitto, who first ordered the cartulary to be written. The mandate to Cozroh to produce the cartulary can only with difficulty be ascribed to Hitto: it was a project carried on under at least three different bishops, and one intimately related to Cozroh's role in the community. In attributing the impulse of the cartulary to a long-dead bishop, Cozroh was transferring the authority from himself to one who could not be responsible for the content of much of what he wrote. Just as the copies of the charters themselves point beyond to original charters, charters perhaps (in Cozroh's words) in danger of removal or destruction either through carelessness or by fraud, the authority of this collection points to a person long dead but whose intention to renew the written treasures of the church of Freising, its copies of sacred scripture, its liturgical texts, and the memory of its benefactors serves as transposed guarantor of the authority of this undertaking.

One sees a similar transposition of authority from the initiative of the compiler to a deceased *auctoritas* in the cartulary of Anamot, fragmentarily but tantalizingly preserved in Munich. Like Cozroh, Anamot's dedicatory preface attributes the cartulary to the initiative of his bishop Ambricho.[25] Like Cozroh, by the time the cartulary was completed, Ambricho and his successor were both dead. The authority of the compilation rests then with the departed, and the cartulary is a memorial to their memory.

Originally the cartulary, composed around 895, began with a memorial poem addressed to Ambricho and, unusually for the period, a portrait of the bishop on opposite folios, now folios 70v and 71r of the manuscript:

Behold here the beautiful form of the venerable bishop
Who often favored us with sacred kindness
Whose honor shines forth abroad through the wide
    world,

. . .

Omnipotent God, who placed the rulers of the world
Return to him full rewards for his good deeds
May he gain the special gifts of this small little book
In heaven, where true hope extends.[26]

Following the table of contents of the first book is a second dedication to the bishop:

To the most excellent lord bishop A. Anamot his humble servant.
Since I knew that your mind was always occupied with all types of study of books and with all other forms of service of the divine cult, I tried with all my effort to present this little work into the beautiful hands of your holiness. Gathering together several charters of gifts, exchanges, and sales, I brought them into the single volume of the present little collection so that, having removed error, the charters might, when necessary, be more easily located and comprehended by chapter headings.[27]

As in Cozroh's preface, the impulse for the composition of the collection is placed within a general interest on the part of the bishop in the books and texts in the service of God. It is the devotion of the bishop that brought into being the collection of charters. However, again as in Cozroh's cartulary, the bishop had died before the completion of the volume. Remarkably, in Regensburg either Anamot or a contemporary decided that this dedication need not apply only to Ambricho. Although still recognizable, the name of the bishop has been scraped out to the first letter—*A*. The editor Josef Widemann suggested that after Ambricho's death in 891 a decision was made simply to insert that of his successor, Aspert, into this space. Aspert died shortly after, in 984, and this may explain why the space was never filled in.[28] Did Anamot change his dedication to flatter a new patron? We cannot conclude this. Widemann suggested that Anamot had dedicated "his cartulary" to Ambricho but that the collection was continued to include charters from the episcopacy of Aspert and that Anamot's dedication was at first simply copied in the later copies but the name of the dedicatee was intended to be changed after the fact. It is impossible to know. The poetic dedication implies that Ambricho was already dead at the time of its composition, but there is no particular reason to assume that Anamot might not have been involved in the copying of the cartulary. It is simply impossible to ascribe either the "authority" of the cartulary to either bishop or to ascribe the authorship to an individual named Anamot. Bishops seem to have been interchangeable, and the name of the "author," Anamot, may have been but a convention representing a series of compilers of the collection.

Gregory of Catena belongs in many ways to another world from that of Anamot and Cozroh. He lived and wrote in the heat of the investiture controversy that drew

Farfa into protracted conflict with the reform papacy and the empire, and the collections that he produced are an integral part of these conflicts.²⁹ One finds nevertheless a continuity in the complex, discursive layers, on the shifting borders between narrative, polemical treatise, and administrative record—a complex of intertextual references that fall outside of the familiar categories of a book, a work, or an author.

Gregory's rich work and complex career have drawn the attention of scholars for over a century. According to his preface to the *Regestum*, Gregory, at the age of thirty-two, suggested to the abbot Bernard II and to the older monks that they authorize him to organize all of the documents relating to the monastery's rights. The result was a two-volume compendium (the *Regestum Farfense*) he entitled both *Liber Gemniagraphus*, which he explained as the "memorial of the description of the lands," and the *Claeronomalem*, or the "inheritance of the church of Farfa."³⁰ This was no simple transcription of charters. Like Cozroh and Anamot, Gregory felt free to edit documents to improve their Latin or to elucidate content that he considered no longer clear. Whether he went beyond these emendations to actually changing the content is likely if not entirely provable. Certainly his selections of documents represented the exercise of judgment and discrimination, as did his decision to copy into the register a collection of canons supporting Farfa's rights. Some have seen Gregory as the "author" or inventor of these canons, although they seem to have been drawn from an earlier collection, much in the way that the eleventh-century cartulary of St. Denis includes a canonical collection in support of that monastery's rights. The charters and the canons were intended as a whole, each implicitly referring to the other and mutually supporting monastic rights against papal or episcopal encroachment.³¹

In addition to his register, Gregory also undertook the *Liber Largitorius*, a register of grants from Farfa to others, including the period of the grant, the conditions, and the value of the property. Gregory's work was continued by his nephew Todinus around 1125, who not only added subsequent concessions but earlier ones that Gregory had omitted.

Using both the *Regestum* and the *Liber Largitorius*, Gregory then compiled the *Chronicon Farfense,* a narrative that was, even more than the *Liber Largitorius,* a collaborative effort involving Gregory, Todinus, and other, unidentified scribes bringing the history of the monastery to 1118. Finally, in 1130, he began his *Liber Floriger,* a condensed history of the monastery drawn from the *Chronicon* and the *Regestum* that also provided

a topographical index relating to charters he had copied into the other volumes.³²

All of the works were deeply interrelated: Gregory himself referred to the *Chronicon* as the "third book of charters" (*Hunc cartularum tertium librum*), and together their historical, archival, and canonical content constantly pointed to originals in the monastery's archives, in canonical collections, or in the other volumes composed by Gregory or one of his collaborators. Their authority derives from the solicited request for composition made by Gregory to Abbot Berardus and to the alleged care with which Gregory, who professed little learning (and thus, presumably, little powers of invention) copied the contents of his materials. Indeed, although Gregory composed a preface to the *Regestum,* its more formal prologue was not written by him but by Johannes Grammaticus, sometime before 1120. This prologue modifies slightly the information in the first-person preface by Gregory. Here, there is no mention of Gregory's request to be ordered to compile the volume. Instead one learns that "inspired by divine grace, it pleased lord Berardus the most reverend abbot of this church . . . to collect together all of the privileges and precepts and laws and legal charters of great age now almost entirely destroyed and having most accurately transcribed them to bequeath them to the memory of posterity." Iohannes, assuming the persona of Abbot Berardus in the third-person plural, then assured that "in copying them we have neither added, nor subtracted nor changed anything, but having corrected those corrupted parts rhetorically in respect to how they had been written, we have given them over legally through the hands of our most wise fellow brother Gregory."³³ There then follows, as in the preface to the Regensburg cartulary, a poetic dedication and a donor portrait. However, in contrast to the dedicatory verses and portrait of Regensburg at the end of the ninth century, this poem honors not Abbot Berardus but Gregory, and the portrait shows him presenting the *Regestum* to the Virgin Mary.

One can hardly make firm conclusions based on a discussion of three cartularies. But we can see that these archival compilations are very complex creations that always point to something beyond themselves. They are not the sum of anything but spill over into other texts. They are essential intertextual references. In theory, anyone who doubts the authority of the cartulary can simply consult the originals. This is the suggestion presented in the preface to the cartulary of Saint-Amand: "If anyone doubts this, let him examine the ancient charters."³⁴ Actually, as the prefaces of Cozroh and others suggest, the originals were often so badly damaged that they were illegible, if they still existed at all. This was after all one of the reasons for compiling cartularies in the first place. Moreover, cartularies never contain all of the charters of an institution, and they do not always reproduce all of the content of the originals. Moreover, as in the case of the account of the Bavarian conflict apparently composed by Cozroh, they contain documents written specifically for inclusion in the cartulary. Alone they are sometimes mere catalogs and can only be understood in their use in coordination with the originals to which they refer, but yet they purport to contain these originals. As for their compilers, even those who left their names in association with these collections were both more and less than authors. They claimed authority from without—from their abbot or bishop; authority too was vested in the referred to but invisible originals, although these might have been emended in a variety of subtle ways for present usage. Cartularies were collaborative efforts, existing at the intersection of individual expertise, command, and collaborative execution, as were all manuscripts of the Middle Ages. At the same time, if the persons whose names are associated with the collections were involved in (if not directly responsible for) their inception, they were not likely to be present at their end, if they ever did end—additions could be made and new signatures or volumes added but not necessarily in accord with an original system devised at the outset. Should Gregory be seen as the author of the *Regestum*, or perhaps Berardus, whose *auctoritas* made it possible? Or possibly Johannes Grammaticus, the "author" of its second prologue? Or perhaps it is the Presbyter Petrus, who is shown in the donor portrait offering the price of the first charter: "Presbiteri Petri sunt haec primordia libri / Solidos nanque decem pro cartis optulit ipse." The modern, romantic notion of authorship is too thin a construct to encompass the complexities hidden behind a Cozroh, an Anamot, or a Gregory. They exist at the intersection of piety, obedience, expediency, collectivity, and memory.

NOTES

This article first appeared as "Auctor et Auctoritas dans les cartulaires du haut moyen âge" in *Auctor et Auctoritas: Invention et conformisme dans l'écriture médiévale, Actes du colloque de Saint-Quentin-en-Yvelines (14–16 juin 1999)*, ed. Michel Zimmermann, Mémoires et documents de l'École des Chartes 59 (Paris, 2001), 61–71.

1. Friedrich Nietzsche, *Vom Nutzen und Nachtheil der Historie für das Leben*, vol. 2, *Nietzsches Werke, Klassiker Ausgabe* (Leipzig, 1922), 134.

2. Wendy Davies, "The Composition of the Redon Cartulary," *Francia* 17 (1990): 69–90. In his introduction to *La Cartulaire de l'abbaye Saint-Sauveur de Redon* (Rennes, 1998), 9–25, Hubert Guillotel recognized "un projet cohérent encore qu'à première vue énigmatique, don't la responsabilité doit être attribuée à l'abbé Aumond," and he spoke of a *copiste* who "had to put his work in order" (17), but he attributed no creativity to this anonymous figure.

3. Roland Barthes, *Le bruissement de la langue: essais critiques IV* (Paris, 1984), 62.

4. Barthes, *Le bruissement de la langue*, 62.

5. Michel Foucault, "Qu'est-ce qu'un auteur?" *Bulletin de la Société française de Philosophie* 63 (1969): 80.

6. Foucault, "Qu'est-ce qu'un auteur?" 79.

7. Bayerische Hauptstaatsarchiv St. Emmeram KL Lit. 5 1/3. On the manuscript see Patrick Geary, "Entre Gestion et gesta," in *Les cartulaires: Actes de la Table ronde organisée par l'École nationale des chartes et le G.D.R. 121 du C.N.R.S. (Paris, 5–7 décembre, 1991)*, ed. O. Guyotjeannin, L. Morelle, and M. Parisse, Mémoires et documents de l'École des Chartes, 39 (Paris, 1993), 13–24, esp. 23; and Patrick Geary, *Phantoms of Remembrance: Memory and Oblivion at the End of the First Millennium* (Princeton: 1994), 98–100.

8. Foucault, "Qu'est-ce qu'un auteur?" 81.

9. Bayerische Hauptstaatsarchiv Hochstift Freising Lit. 3a. See Geary, "Entre Gestion et gesta," 20–23, and *Phantoms of Remembrance*, 96–98.

10. Biblioteca Apostolica Vaticana, Vat. Lat., 8487.

11. Biblioteca Nationale Vittorio Emanuele, MS Farfa 3.

12. Biblioteca Nazionale Vittorio Emanuele, MS Farfa 1.

13. On the texts of Gregory see Ildefonso Schuster, *Abbazia di Farfa: Contributo allo studio del ducato romano nel M. Evo* (Rome: 1921; 1987), 1:21–23; Theo Kölzer, *Collectio canonum Registro Farfensi inserta*, Monumenta Iuris Canonici, série B: Corpus Collectionum, vol. 5 (Città del Vaticana: 1982), 7–9; Theo Kölzer, "Codex libertatis: Überlegungen zur Funktion des 'Regestum Farfense' und andere Kloster cartulare," in *Atti del Congresso internazionale di studi sull'alto medioevo*, Centro Italiano di Studi sull'alto medioevo (Spoleto: 1983), 2:609–53; and Mary Stroll, *The Medieval Abbey of Farfa: Target of Papal and Imperial Ambitions*, Brill's Studies in Intellectual History (Leiden: 1997), 7–15. For the context of Gregory's work within Italian historiography of the period see Walter Pohl, *Werkstätte der Erinnerung: Montecassino und die Gestaltung der langobardischen Vergangenheit* (Vienna: 2001), esp. 152–62.

14. Foucault, "Qu'est-ce qu'un auteur?" 82–83.

15. Pascale Bourgain and Marie-Clotilde Hubert, "Latin et rhétorique dans les préfaces de cartulaire," in *Les cartulaires*, 115–36.

16. B. Guérard, ed., *Cartulaire de l'abbaye de Saint-Bertin*, Documents inédits, Collection des cartulaires de France, 3 (Paris, 1840); O. Holder-Egger, ed., *Gesta abbatum s. Bertini Sithiensium*, MGH SS, XIII (Hanovre, 1881), 607–34; and Hariulf, *Chronique de l'abbaye de Saint-Riquier (Ve siècle-1104)*, ed. Ferdinand Lot, Collection de textes pour servir à l'étude et à l'enseignement de l'histoire (Paris, 1894). See Laurent Morelle, "Les chartes dans la gestion des conflits (France du nord, XIe-début du XIIe siècle)," in *Pratiques de l'écrit doc-*

umentaire au XIe siècle, ed. O. Guyotjeannin, L. Morelle, and M. Parisse, Bibliothèque de l'École des chartes, t. 155 (1997), 267–98; and "Histoire et archives vers l'an mil: Une nouvelle 'mutation'?" *Histoire et archives* 3 (1998): 130–31.

17. "Quicquid singulis cartulis exaratum certisque testimoniis confirmatum invenit, uno volumine rationabiliter includere studuit tam antecessorum patrum temporibus quam etiam sui famosi regiminis." Theodor Bitterauf, ed., *Die Traditionen des Hochstifts Freising,* Quellen und Erörterungen zur bayerischen und deutschen Geschichte, neue Folge Bd. 4 (Munich, 1905; 1967), 2 (hereafter *TF*).

18. "Hoc tamen opus non vile, sed laudabile cui commississet inquisivit invenitque tamen suum vilissimum servulum, sed tamen sui fidelissimum, nomine Cozroh, quem tamen ipse suis sacris disciplinis edocuit, et ad presbiterii dignitatem provexit. Inponensque ei pondus tanti laboris, sollicite ac omni circumspectione hoc opus peragere, eo modo firmiter praecipiens: nihil minui vel adici, nisi scribtoris vitio aliquid depravatum repperisset." Ibid.

19. *TF,* 636.

20. Warren Brown, "The Use of Norms in Disputes in Early Medieval Bavaria," *Viator* 30 (1999): 15–41. See more generally on this cartulary his *Unjust Seizure: Conflict, Interest, and Authority in an Early Medieval Society* (Ithica, 2001).

21. iussus a domno: *TF,* 462, 485, 487, 492, 499a, 501b, 515, 519, 522 (Ego Hitto . . . praecepi Cozrohe presbitero nostro et ipse sicut praecepi perfecit), 523a, 529, 533, 535, 538, 542, 549, 553, 555, 557, 571, 572, 587, 609, 611, 651, 655, 678, 686.

22. hoc videns et audiens: *TF,* 440, 554, 576a, 582, 583, 590, 601, 602, 603, 604, 626, 671, 672, 676, 679, 689, 699.

23. hoc videns et audiens conscripsi iussione: *TF,* 547c, 556, 559, 573, 580, 581b, 587, 594, 596, 598, 599, 606, 607a, 615b, 634, 660, 664, 667, 674, 680, 698, 701. In praesentia Hittonis episcopi ego Cozroh conscripsi: 588b.

24. Scripsi: *TF,* 486, 498, 531, 536, 560, 562, 600, 627, 628, 636.

25. Josef Widemann, ed., *Die Traditionen des Hochstifts Regensburg und des Klosters S. Emmeram,* Quellen und Erörterungen zur bayerischen Geschichte neue Folge Bd. 8 (Munich, 1934; 1988), vii–ix (hereafter *TR*).

26. Versus Anamodi: "Presulis hic pulchram venerandi cernite formam, / Qui nobis sacro sepe fauet merito, / Cuius honor mundo iste prefulget in amplo, / . . . Cui deus omnipotens, mundi qui regmina ponis, / Premia de factis reddito plena

bonis! / Istius et parui specalia dona libellil / In celis capiat, spes vbi vera patet." *TR,* viii.

27. EXCELLENTISSIMO DOMINO A . . . EPISCOPO ANAMOTVS HVMILLIMVS FAMVLVS. Uestram igitur mentem, quoniam in omni librorum studio ceteroque diuini cultus mancipatu semper inherere cognoueram, hoc opusculum ultronea uoluntate pulcherrimis sanctitatis uestre manibus presentare conabar. *TR,* xiii.

28. *TR,* xiii.

29. See the bibliography in n. 10 and the literature cited by Stroll, *The Medieval Abbey of Farfa,* 8–11.

30. "Porro huic libro GEMNIAGRAPHUM nomen imposuimus, idest MEMORIAM DESCRIPTIONIS TERRARUM, quia in eo huius coenobii terras a quocumque, uel ubicumque acquisitas inseruimus, et eas ad semper memorandum in uno uolumine comprehendimus. Placuit etiam nobis et CLAERONOMALEM, id est haereditalem pharphesis AECCLESIAE appellari, quoniam proprias ipsius immobiles ab initio libere demonstrat possessiones." I. Giorgi e U. Balzani, ed., *Il regesto di Farfa compilato da Gregorio di Catino* (Rome: 1879), 2:6–7; and Stroll, *The Medieval Abbey of Farfa,* 8.

31. See Kölzer, *Collectio Canonum;* and Stroll, *The Medieval Abbey of Farfa,* 9, n. 20.

32. Stroll, *The Medieval Abbey of Farfa,* 10–12.

33. "Diuina inspirante gratia, placuit domno Berardo reuerentissimo abbati huius aecclesiae pharphensis mobilissima gente progentio florentiae urbis, quatinus istius sacri coenobii uniuersa priuilegia et praecepta nec non et tomos et legales cartas nimmia uaetustate iam pene consumpta, in unum uolumen colligere eaque ad memoriam posteritatis studiosissime declarata, uaeracissime transcripta relinquere. Et hoc prudentissimo actum est consilio, ne forte, quod saepissime iam euenisse nouimus, aut custodum negligentia, aut uaetustate consumente nimia, prae dicta obliuioni traderentur praecepta, tomi, cartae, et privilegia. Quae ueraciter elucubrando nichil eis omnio addidimus, uel minuimus, nec mutauimus, sed corruptis partibus rethorice emendatis, eo respectu quo scripta erant, ea legaliter transtulimus per manus confraatris nostri magnae sagacitatis Gregorii sabinensi comitatu oriundi, in castro catinensi nobilissimis parentibus progeniti, et nostrae aecclesiae fere ab ispa infantia lacte enuriti." *Il registro,* 2:20.

34. H. Platelle, "Le premier cartulaire de l'abbaye de Saint Amand," *Le Moyen Age* 62 (1956): 318–19. See also Morelle, "Histoire et archives vers l'an mil," 131.

The Question of Access

The Right to Social Memory versus the
Right to Social Oblivion

In most modern societies public administrations process and handle huge amounts of private and personal data concerning individual citizens, thus producing great numbers of case files containing often highly sensitive information about identifiable individual persons.

It is my contention that some of this information is a vital part of the social memory of modern societies. When evaluating modern public political and administrative records, the focus is often on records containing information about political decision making and the political and administrative deliberations behind new legislative initiatives. However, the vast numbers of personal case files contain—among other things—information about how public laws and regulations and public institutions affect individual citizens in various aspects of their lives. A lot of the data contained in such files are of a trivial, repetitive, and routine character. But it is also in these kinds of public administrative files—and often only here—that we find information on the interaction of public administration and the individual citizen. These files are of value both for the individuals and for society as such. For the individual they may contain information of vital importance for the self-knowledge and self-concept of that individual. This information is also of vital importance in the formation of the self-concept of that society, particularly to the extent that these files contain information about the interaction between society as represented by public authorities and individual citizens.

Preservation of these kinds of records is threatened both by tendencies in the public debate and by practical necessities, policy, and habits of modern archival administration. The ever-more-widespread use of modern technology in public administration makes it possible both to preserve and handle a larger amount of this kind of information and to utilize the information in new and more effective ways. This might well tend to strengthen the public debate on principles concerning the creation, retention, and accessibility of such information.

When discussing questions relating to regulations concerning the retention or the disposition of official documents containing personal or sensitive information about individual and identifiable persons, the points of view tend to differ widely according to the setting/framework of the discussion. In a political setting the stress will tend to be on questions relating to the possibilities of political control of the individual. Prevailing opinions in most democratic countries will tend to favor the disposition of such data as quickly as possible, perhaps even to prohibit the creating of such data where possible. If the civil rights of individual citizens are the focus of attention, the opinions might differ. If, for instance, an individual citizen wants to complain about and to appeal the decision of a local government concerning him or her, access to all available information is of vital importance. That, of course, favors retention of all such data. On the other hand, if the focus of attention is on the right to privacy, as such, opinions will tend to favor disposition from an ethically founded point of view. That is to say a view that is respectful to the right of the individual to preserve privacy.

If we remove this discussion from the public or political sphere and place it in the world of the archives, things growing number of state and municipal electronic registers containing summary information of the same kind on an individual level. The most important of these registers have been retained and transferred to the state archives.

In the future the question of retention will be less important, in so far as these kinds of files will be created electronically and thus can be retained in their totality at no large costs—at least in so far as archival space is concerned. The Danish State Archives has already received the first electronic document systems of this kind. If this is an accurate estimate of the future, it will be only for a limited amount of time—say some fifty to seventy years—that these kinds of personal files will have been discarded in any great amount in Denmark.

Reasons behind the Danish Policy of Retention

All in all it is fair to say that the Danish State Archives in its retention policy has placed great stress on retaining at least segments of archival records containing very private and sensitive personal information concerning individual citizens. Why is that so?

According to the archival legislation, the purpose of the state archives is to make sure that those official archival records are retained that

are of historical value

serve to document circumstances and events of significant administrative or legal importance for the citizens and the official authorities

It is, of course, always possible to discuss the historical value of archival records. Personal files—of the kind that have been discussed here—will mostly tend to be a result of the practical administrative implementation of laws and regulations concerning individual citizens. As such these files are of historical value not only—and perhaps not even mostly—in relationship to the personal information they contain but far more as evidence of the way in which the administration itself actually worked. Only by studying this kind of historical evidence will it be possible to judge the relationship between legislative intent and administrative practice. It is in this administrative process that the individual citizen gets into contact with the official authorities. It has been the view of most Danish archivists that it is of crucial importance to retain a fair amount/segment of archival records that document the relationship between the state and municipal bodies and the citizens. If anything,

this can be characterized as part of the social memory of any society.

As already stated, personal files will, of course, also be regarded as archival records of significant importance for the individual citizen in so far as they concern him or herself or members of the family. It may be more difficult to judge what—if any—kinds of personal files might turn out to be of significant administrative importance for the official authorities. The tendency would presumably be to determine importance on grounds of administrative principles, that is, cases where administrative decisions have been questioned and administrative practice thereby changed.

Prospects and Questions of the Future

The possibility of retaining all important personal files in electronic form at reasonable costs, however, does not mean this will actually take place. Even given the strong administrative traditions in Denmark for registration of private and personal information as part of the public administration on both the local municipal and the local and central state levels, there are signs of a growing awareness of the ethical and political problems in connection with retaining that information.

During 1964 and 1971 fundamental laws concerning the public access to political and administrative documents at both state and municipal levels were passed. These laws are increasingly being used, not just by journalists and historians but also by members of the general public to gain access to their own personal case files before these are transferred to the archives. This, of course, has heightened the awareness of the content of these kinds of files and thereby also opens to discussion the appropriateness of the retention of such files. So far there has been no serious public debate concerning these questions, but with the growing possibilities of retaining personal files, and the growing possibilities of using these files, and combining different personal information from different electronic systems, it is a fair guess that such a discussion will come.

To my knowledge the Danish State Archives has so far had only one instance of disposition of archival records on ethical grounds. During the early 1980s a political debate arose quite incidentally concerning reports written by school psychologists on schoolchildren with various behavior disorders or other problems. The debate—and the resulting public interest—led to a revision of the regulations for retention and disposition of archival records from the public elementary schools. It was decided that these reports should be discarded after a period of ten years in order to protect these children from a possible later misuse of such information.

Other debates like this are to be expected. And the Danish State Archives has to be able to meet such challenges. How then shall the state archives respond to such a debate, which might very well put strong political pressure on the archives to carry through other mandated dispositions of various personal case files?

Social Oblivion: A Case of Limitation of Access?

One way of meeting this challenge may be to regulate and limit public access to records containing personal files holding sensitive information of identifiable individual citizens. Another similar—but in principle different—way is to regulate and limit the utilization of the information gained through access to such records.

In contrast to the United States the access to public documents/archival records produced by public authorities in Denmark is regulated by several laws, the most important of which are

> *the law on public administration,* which regulates access to citizens who are parties to a case handled and treated by public administrative authorities
>
> *the law on publicity in public administration,* which regulates the access of the public to all records in the possession of public administrative authorities
>
> *the archival law,* which regulates the access of the public to archival records transferred to the archives

The first two of these laws are administered by the public administrative bodies themselves, whether their records have been transferred to the state archives or are still in their own keeping.

The first of these laws gives individuals who are a party to a case administered by a public authority access to most documents concerning the case in question, apart from that authority's internal working notes. The second law gives the public in general a far more restricted access to all records produced by public authorities. Exempted from access are—among other things—documents containing information about

1. individual persons' private and economic circumstances
2. sensitive national security and defense interests, foreign policy interests and the like, and public economic interests

3. criminal lawsuits where the protection of the accused, witnesses, and other parties to the case is a major concern

The archival law governs access to all public archival records that have been transferred to the state archives or are more than thirty years old. The law is administered by the national archivist and, by delegation, his or her staff of local directors. As a general rule public archival records and documents are accessible by the public when they are thirty years old unless there are special reasons to protect certain kinds of information for a longer period. Normally the kind of information to be protected will be the same as mentioned in the law of publicity in public administration, that is, information about individual persons' private and economic circumstances, about sensitive national security and defense interests, foreign policy interests and the like, public economic interests, and criminal lawsuits where the protection of the accused, witnesses, and other parties to the case is a major concern.

Archival records containing this kind of information are accessible to the general public when the records are eighty years old. Apart from archival records containing information about national security, defense, and economic interest, we are talking here about records containing sensitive information about individual citizens. The archival law is meant to give the public broader access to public archival records than the two administrative laws on access. When access is given according to the general rules of the archival law, access is given to these records in their entirety and with no exemptions.

Furthermore there is the possibility for individual researchers to apply for dispensations from the general rules of access. And this possibility is being widely used. Last year the state archives got approximately three thousand such applications, of which 97 percent were granted. Half of these were applications concerning archival records containing private information about individual persons. Dispensations from the general rules are given to researchers to use specific archival records for specific purposes and on specific conditions that take into consideration the need to protect sensitive information. These principles allow the archives to grant access to the majority of applications.

I'll illustrate this with an example: A woman born in 1946 seeks access to the lawsuit dealing with the question of child support for her and her mother with the explicit purpose of getting information about her presumed father. Her mother is dead, and all the applicant knows is that she was born out of wedlock. She has never known her father. The case file is not yet eighty years old, and on closer inspection it turns out that her mother apparently had had intimate relationships with several men, three of whom the court finds can be considered equally as possible parents of the child. All three are therefore sentenced to pay child support. This is certainly a case file that should not be accessible to the general public. It contains extremely sensitive private information that should be protected out of consideration for the parties involved.

Nevertheless the application is granted because the child is considered a party to the case and therefore thought to have a legitimate right to the information. But the application is granted on the explicit conditions that the information the applicant thus gains must not be published and must not be used to make contact with the people mentioned in the file. If the same woman had applied for access to the file with the explicit purpose of finding and making contact with her presumed father, the application would have been denied. Such a purpose would not be in accordance with the legitimate need for protection of the private lives of the involved parties.

Yet another example: A historian wants to study the living conditions and patterns of social behavior among unmarried women in a specific county during World War II. For this purpose he seeks access to a selection of case files on child support for illegitimate children during this period. He states in his application that he wants to be able to quote from the files but no information will be published in such a way that individual people involved in these cases can be identified. An application like this would also be granted on the condition that no information gained through the files would be published in a way that would allow identification of individuals mentioned. And further, that quotations must not be presented in such a way that those individuals can be identified even though no names are given.

The history of the German occupation of Denmark during World War II and the following judicial purge has attracted the interest of a new generation of Danish historians. This has resulted in a growing number of applications to use archival records that are not yet generally accessible because they contain sensitive information about private individuals. Among these are the files created during the judicial purge. They contain information about the liquidation of informers carried out by members of the Danish resistance movements during the war. There are also files containing, among other things, information about economic cooperation with the Germans. Almost all such applications for access are granted

on conditions similar to the ones mentioned in the preceding. In other words when dispensing with the general rules of access, what is considered is not so much the mere access to archival records and their information but how and to what purpose information thus gained will be used.

Because the archival law grants the archives the authority to give access under specific conditions relating to the use made of the information gained through the archival records, it is possible to administer the legal regulations concerning access in a very liberal way. As long as the state archives can guarantee the protection of legitimate rights to privacy for individuals, the state archives can give liberal access both to individual citizens seeking information about themselves and their families and to the professional historian who wants to unravel recent historical events or social developments. Seen from this point of view, there is no necessary conflict between the right to social memory and the right to social oblivion, as long as this is not taken literally. And it might well be that this is part of the reason why there has not as yet been a serious public debate in Denmark concerning the retention or disposition of files containing sensitive private and personal information.

There has been a heated public debate about access to archival records in general, but this debate has focused mostly on access to records containing more general information on internal and external political questions.

The Danish archival law is due to be revised by parliament next year, and with the massive interest for public access to files and records of this kind, it is a fair guess that this revision will lead to a general twenty-five-year rule on access instead of thirty. So far there has been no indication of any wish to change the general eighty-year rule for access to records containing sensitive private and personal information. If this comes under debate, it might be in the interest of the archives to suggest that the span of years in which archival records of this kind are restricted be increased from eighty to ninety or perhaps even one hundred years. The general life expectancy has increased, and therefore there are good reasons to consider a comparable increase in the span of time these records are protected against general use.

In order to save personal case files from mandated disposition, the Danish State Archives might thus be brought into the rather paradoxical situation that it will have to accept stricter rules on access to these kinds of files while administering more liberal rules on access to all other kinds of records. As long as this is combined with the possibilities of granting access through dispensation according to the principles discussed in this essay, this will—in my opinion—be a price well worth paying.

Concluding Remarks

Social memory seems such an ambitious term to use when talking about such pragmatic things as public administrative records. Records of this kind are first and foremost historical sources to the way our public administration has interpreted its tasks and how it has implemented that interpretation.

Nevertheless archival records in the form of personal case files give us a rare opportunity to study the meeting between the public administration and the people it administers. It is, of course, important to remember that the information we find in these records is created largely in terms of the administrative bodies. Still it is here that we have an opportunity to gain the insight that will allow us to understand both the impact of official laws and regulations and the public response to these. It is also here that the historian often finds the life and color that can illustrate and personify abstract and theoretical reflections. Combined with other kinds of material, records of this kind are an important part of our social memory. During at least the last half of the twentieth century these records also have been threatened from both within and without the archives.

The sheer bulk of personal case files and other kinds of files containing personal and private information about individual persons has made them an obvious target for disposition in the attempt of the state archives to handle the huge amounts of modern administrative records. At the same time fear of political control and ethical considerations concerning the citizens' right to privacy have also threatened to pass a sentence of disposition on these records. The possibility of retaining these files in the future in the form of electronic documents makes it vital to reconsider current retention policy in archival institutions in all countries. At the same time the legitimate claims for the right to privacy make it necessary for the archives to consider how these claims can be met without disposing of valuable and vital data. Here various methods of regulating access have been brought forward as a possible solution. This essay is to be considered as a call to both researchers and archival institutions to take serious the challenges raised by the conflicting interest raised in the essay's title.

Past Imperfect (*l'imparfait*)

Mediating Meaning in Archives of Art

Nancy Ruth Bartlett

> L'imparfait est une forme du verbe qui indique les actions du passé considérées dans ce qu'elles n'ont pas encore atteint leur achèvement, qu'elles n'ont pas fini de se dérouler ou d'être en train. Il présente l'action, sans en préciser les limites temporelles. L'imparfait est généralement étranger à la notion de début ou de fin d'une action. . . . Il demeure que, souvent, les Anglophones se heurtent au problème de l'aspect: l'angle de vue, la manière de considérer le déroulement des actions du passé. En effet, en français, la forme passé composé et la forme imparfait se complètent en un système d'oppositions cohérentes là où la langue anglaise masque les distinctions en employant une seule forme de passé.
>
> —"Leçons de grammaire: L'imparfait"

An examination of mediation in archives of art is an acknowledgment of the issue of language—its definitions, its cultural and academic parameters, its multiplicities, its unexpected relationships. The French *imparfait,* while understood conventionally as a particular verb tense of the past, is an appealing example and point of departure. It is a wonderful suggestion of language "in motion," without end, of the past but moving forward in time, subject to barriers in understanding, and open to new directions and revelations. By borrowing from the French, by adding multiple meanings, we render l'imparfait no more "perfect," or "complete," but instead give it added vitality as a redefinable indicator of process, in this case a process concerning the past as much as the present.[1]

Archivists appropriate language in the act of mediating archives of art. We shape language, regulate it, box it up, measure it, mystify it, fossilize it, microfilm it, deacidify it, digitize it, download it, compress it, suppress it, encode it, and expect it to carry the weight of much of our curatorial activities and identity. Our currency is not so much pictures as text—those written words we inherit in the archival record, which is still primarily textual, and those words we create by our placing manuscripts and records under our archival responsibility, "under house arrest," to borrow a phrase from Jacques Derrida.[2]

The curatorial language of much of the past century was a progressively formalized, profession-based, modern intermediate language. It was placed between the original language of creator and other original languages—including the languages of those who helped escort the collections into the archives and those of the subsequent patrons of the archives. This is part of the "mediating" referred to in the title of this essay. Another mediation is the action taken to include or ignore, to differ and defer. The words and deeds of mediation go hand in hand.[3] They together form the "politics and poetics of archives," to quote Joan Schwartz.[4]

Politics and Poetics, Art and Archives

It is an interesting proposition for an archivist to attempt to examine the archival act of mediation as it is performed through multiple interventions in historical evidence. It is an important proposition as well since the exercise gives voice to the archivist, who in others' works is given little opportunity "to speak for him- or herself." The archivist instead is presented as an agent in and of the past, not as a contemporary peer with his or her own interests as a "scholar of record keeping."[5] In fact in some studies, the "archivist" is absent altogether, excused in the course of the fashionable, metaphorical appropriation of the term *archives* or, more prosaically, in the tacit implication that of course archives can exist without archivists.[6]

I complicate the challenge for myself all the more by considering the archives of art, particularly the historical forces at work that mediated against a place for modern art in American archives, the successful and particularly American penetrations of modern art into the archives, and, throughout this essay, the diverse languages concerning art at work in and beyond the archives. Why have I selected what might appear to be a rather specialized genre of documentation within the archives? And what exactly do I mean by *archives of modern art*? An answer to both of these questions is that a consideration of what constitutes the archives of art is itself a part of mediation. Let us for now accept a rather straightforward list of by-products of the creative artistic process. These include documents (be they visual, verbal, or aural) that reflect the actions of the artist's creative expression and his or her identity as an artist, including correspondence, diaries, records of sales, lectures, interviews, and reference photographs both of his or her art and of other inspiring images; documents concerning the personal and institutional consumptions of art, including the records of a museum's registrar, loan and gift agreements, correspondence, sales records (including auction house records), and insurance records of institutions and private individuals; documents concerning the academic and public analyses and casual views of art, including academic lectures, correspondence, and research notes as well as survey forms from museums and membership rosters for museums, galleries, and art associations; and the archive's administrative "metadata" (such as donor files, cataloging information, and call slips) relating to the archives of art in its keep. By looking at artistic creativity, patronage, and the archival enterprise, I am focusing on what seems to be a particularly interesting quartet of views and sources of actions, or "mediators." They are, as one can expect from the list of documents just mentioned, the artist, the patron, the archivist, and the academic. (Could they together inspire a new Peter Greenway film?)[7] The academic, especially the art historian, has been particularly active and imaginative lately in examining mediation and media. The archivist, on the other hand, has remained almost silent but is now, in part thanks to this series of seminars, joining the discussion. The artist of the modern era was ambivalent about archival preservation, and the expression of that ambivalence or uncertainty anticipated what is now discussed as mediation by at least a half a century; it is noteworthy that now some modern artists themselves have activated a personal interest in archives as they work to secure a legacy beyond their artwork. The patron of art has generated much documentation and is especially aware of his or her own ascending prominence in the support of artistic creation, acquisition, exhibition, and promotion of definitions of taste and value.

Let us proceed with the art historian. One in particular, Peter Schneemann, has lobbied directly for archivists' attention to the tensions inherent in negotiations for meaning and significance. In his presentation to the Society of American Archivists in 1999, he announced that "we must recognize how problematic the relationship between the power of the image and the power of the word [has] become."[8] He challenged his audience to consider the muscle of word versus the muscle of image. One can contribute to his question of intertextuality—be it visual or verbal—by looking from the perspective of the archivist at what Douglas Crimp in his book *On the Museum's Ruins* calls a "plurality of discourses."[9]

Language as Artistry

Even the Declaration of Independence, the most sanctified archival record of the United States—visited by more than a million each year in the rotunda of the National Archives—has itself only recently been reviewed for the power of its stylistic artistry by a few scholars who *read* Jefferson's text for its fine, precise literary qualities rather than *view* the fuzzy text as an image of faint traces under glass, guarded by day and entombed by night.[10] We have all, it is fair to say, come very late to the task of reviving a narrative intercourse with this document whose legibility falls far short of its iconic magnetism. Negotiating meaning here requires a deft perceptibility and appreciation, not entirely alien to the task of recognizing and appreciating the associative carriers of meaning for modern art in the archives.

Archival Provenance

Archivists in America particularize the language of archives. Let us first consider the singularly important word *provenance*. When archivists pronounce *provenance* in America, we do not feel the force of the French Revolution and Parisian ministerial nationalizing effects on disenfranchised, displaced archives located in the former ancien régime provinces. As archivists, we have only the vaguest of notions of that 1841 French ministerial decree "pour la mise en ordre et le classement des archives départementales"—which can be traced as the "ur-text" of the international, modern concept of archival provenance, a provenance that without irony, and unbeknownst to most archivists today, imposed an organizing standard on ancien régime records "under arrest" as though it were an innocent *respect des fonds*. (My investigation into the administrative archives of the archives themselves in France revealed to me that the nation-making bureaucratization of France was in fact behind the articulation and activating of a fossilizing of earlier, seized records. This was according to the principle, applied after the French Revolution and all its documentary disruptions and seizures, of *quieta non movere*—do not move that which is still).[11]

American archivists have employed this borrowed term *provenance* to signify, loosely, a respect for the original composition and context of unique, documentary information of value to the archives.[12] But the association of origin and agent is much more flexible, elastic with archives emerging out of circumstances that often evolve in a particularly American fashion. As archivists Frank Boles and Mark Greene have astutely asserted, "Because the American record environment has been among the twentieth century's most dynamic, it is not surprising that American archivists would be among the first to feel the tension between pre-existing theoretical constructs and contemporary reality."[13] In North America, provenance has recently been defined broadly to include "archiving activities. . . . The provenance of a given record or body of records consists of the social and technical processes of the record's inscription, transmis-

sion, contextualization, and interpretation which account for its existence, characteristics, and continuing history."[14] Furthermore, archivists are encouraged, in their employment of provenance among other principles, to "stop being custodians of things and start being purveyors of concepts."

An understanding of the American archivist's adaptation of "provenance" or "origin" is the key to the doors of archives of art. It is not the provenance of the ancien régime escorted into the nineteenth century by ministerial bureau bosses ordering uniform compliance in classification in such formerly independent archives as were found in the churches and intendances of Bordeaux, Marseilles, or Strasbourg. Nor is it the provenance of art history since it is not textual information intended to reflect the origin and successive ownerships of individual works of art.

Provenance as Description

Provenance as an American archival concept has meant synthetic textual information presented in "units of content"—such as archival inventories and bibliographic descriptions—and regimented physical order. It is intended to represent the original, cumulative creation of those coherent sets of records that share some sort of organic integrity and archival value. Provenance for much of the twentieth century in America was applied to archival acquisitions as a legitimizing appraisal, arrangement, and description device built upon a steel and concrete framework of enlisted coordinates such as name of creator, dates, name of repository, name of subgroup, name of series, and subject headings.[15] These coordinates themselves have been drafted from varying points on the compass and varying points in time: name of creator may stem from the Far West, and subject heading may derive from the Library of Congress in Washington, D.C., with these two identifying coordinates meeting at the name of an academic repository along the East Coast and stitched together over decades of processing and reprocessing of accumulated documents. This was the case for the creation of the Alfred Stieglitz collection at Yale University. Whereas the modern notion of archival provenance was born in the nation-making administrative offices of a French bureaucracy intent on standardizing curatorial care of seized records throughout the new *départements* in France, the notion has been fit to suit the agenda of an American archival profession in search of a common fixity. This search was conducted through the descriptive language of "tracing" in the United States, rather than the French force of law, to records in a much wider variety of public and private, newer and older repositories, including university archives, corporate archives, private church archives, state archives, federal repositories, special collections, and even art museums. With archives such as these on a much more equal footing than those on the European continent, the result was that provenance in America has not been as militaristically mandated as an astringent French ministerial decree nor as absolute as a Prussian register, which in a perhaps Calvinistic mode preordained the ultimate destiny of the record, even before its creation, to a classification system in compliance with the *Registraturprinzip* of the late-nineteenth-century Berlin.

The effort to secure and stabilize organic information of archival value—through gathering and accessioning of collections as collections, describing them in standard archival inventories (with a particularly American descriptive hierarchy straddling between the language of the creator and the bibliographic structuralism of the modern American cataloger), and transferring them into uniform units of acid-free folders and archival boxes—is the most accessible sign of a working compliance with the archival principle of provenance. Given the vast variety of repositories at work in America, the commitments to homogenize the description and packaging have truly been ambitious. Viewers from outside and from within these archives could together assess the relevance of André Malraux's observations on the organizing device of photography. Can his observations be applied to the standardizing descriptive impulses of American archives? If so, has it been more virtue or vice that American archives have in their pursuit of provenance in the modern era tried, to borrow Malraux's words, to "reduce the now even vaster heterogeneity to a single perfect similitude"?[16]

Gathering and Situating Archives

The antecedent to these descriptive activities in the archives is the gathering and situating. Here I turn to the mediating role of the artist, with three examples. First, Georgia O'Keeffe dedicated herself to a curatorial mediation in deeding many of Alfred Stieglitz's documents after his death to Yale University. O'Keeffe played a crucial role in constructing and reconstructing the salvageable evidence of her husband's life.[17] She serves our purposes as an example of artists themselves negotiating the lives of other modern artists for their fit into the archives.

Stieglitz showed little interest in memorializing the administration of his gallery, 291, writing in 1915 that "I keep no books, or records of any kind. I have done this to keep the place absolutely free." But O'Keeffe would not comply with his deliberate silence about his gallery's administration or his Kafkaesque interests in redacting his own legacy by weeding unwanted photographs from his portfolio.[18] As a secretive "dumpster diver," O'Keeffe would fish out of Stieglitz's trash his rejected photographs. In her own artistic and organizing fashion, she compiled these images into what she named her "Waste Basket Collection."

O'Keeffe claimed that she could not be an artist while attending to Stieglitz's orphaned archives.[19] And yet she was to a certain degree a creator, if not of art as she saw it then of archives, recognizing that what she was accumulating for Yale was "more archive than Art." Correspondence to and from Stieglitz was searched for and gathered by O'Keeffe and two women employed by the estate. The letters were added to his clipping files, scrapbooks, and the Waste Basket Collection at Yale. The collecting began in 1946 and continued until 1980. O'Keeffe's role in mediation between creator and archivist can be found duplicated in donor files throughout America's archives of the twentieth century. Those donor files tell a parallel story of discovery, evaluation, negotiation, and placement and are themselves an archival tale of the utmost importance, though generally closed to the public.

A second example of artist as mediator is photographer Berenice Abbott. She behaved as archivist as she mediated the archival legacy of photographer Eugene Atget and the five thousand prints and negatives he left behind in his studio. Atget himself, she implied, behaved in an archival fashion. In producing his Parisian photographs of deserted streets, he named himself "author-producer" of what Walter Benjamin labeled his "evidence" and what Atget himself described as his "documents pour artistes."[20] Abbott described Atget's work as "realism unadorned," a phrase that an archivist would have favored and could just as well have stated, however problematically.[21]

For my third example, I refer to architect Louis Sullivan. Out of circulation and out of favor at the end of his life, he would be even less directly accessible to us today had it not been for the rescue mission of his sympathetic partner, architect George Elmslie. But, unlike O'Keeffe, the rescue by Elmslie was late and, contrary to Abbott's success at rescuing Atget's photos, the surviving drawings of Sullivan—including beautiful, faint renderings of his midwestern banks and of a gorgeous nude—are pathetically few. These drawings arrived at the University of

Michigan archives as an appendage to the papers of Elmslie's brother-in-law, thereby turning from a colleague's rescue into a family gift and then an archival accession.

Loss of the Unmediated

More disappointing than the scant survival of Sullivan's artistry are the testimonies we hear from more recent artists themselves, or their close friends and family or the eventual chronicler, about the total loss of evidence of some modernists. Let's consider modern architectural design a bit more. The wife of architect Minoru Yamasaki shared with many the confusion over what to do with her husband's voluminous archives of modern buildings, from a repertoire of work that included his World Trade towers in New York. They found no archives, and now one hears the echo of her concerns in the *New York Times,* in the words of architects Frank Gehry, Richard Meier, and Robert Stern.[22]

Ambivalence of Memorializing Modernism

But let me suggest that the memory of modernism has never been all that certain, despite fellow artists as advocates, in part because of the modernist himself. Stieglitz wanted to be "free." So, too, did the illustrious group of famous architects who met in Ann Arbor, Michigan, for the first of the Ann Arbor conferences in 1940, to discuss "Coordination in Design with Regard to Education in Architecture and Allied Design." In a University of Michigan clubhouse, Walter Gropius, Laszlo Moholy-Nagy, Eliel and Eero Saarinen, Mies van der Rohe, Albert Kahn, and representatives of the Museum of Modern Art explicitly agreed that there would be no record of the meeting. Almost the only words committed to paper about the meeting were "no committees . . . no reports . . . no resolutions . . . no manifestos."[23]

Architect William Muschenheim—winner of the Peter Behrens prize in 1927 and one of the first modernist American architects to design in New York—shed all but a few of his very important color studies, and those he saved were retained on final working drawings based on high-modern Ozalid prints of low physical viability. The impermanence of such modern media gave them their "on the fly" vitality but also a swifter mortality rate.[24]

Furthermore, if a museum such as the Museum of Modern Art was ambivalent about establishing a permanent collection of art, it is understandable that it was even less certain that an archive would emerge. In fact, it was not until 1989 that the Museum of Modern Art Archives was established.

Defiance of Linearity, Archives to Art

Whereas an archivist might first think of modern artistic creativity gaining archival associations over time, there is of course the beautiful example of artist Joseph Cornell's collection, which was at its inception both art and "archive." This single artist stimulates the archivist to be on guard against a linear notion of inheritance, or a clear divide between art and archive, and engages the archivist instead in an animated dialogue with the artist who, in his case, assembled "archives of materials to turn into art."[25]

In America, especially, Cornell could entitle himself with the term *archives* since no type of repository or record has held a monopoly on the word. This warrants emphasizing. The very word *archives* has been available in the American lexicon for the artist's appropriation long before the recent transformation of the noun *archive* into the verb, *to archive,* and the generic reference to stored computer data as *archives,* and long before Shawn Smith's book *American Archives* or Jacques Derrida's *Archive Fever.*

In another wonderful variation on the archival attributes of modern art, there is the example of the Iowa Women's Archives. It was decided ten years ago to establish an archive for the history of women in the state of Iowa by arranging for the sale of one Frida Kahlo painting, entitled *Self-Portrait with Loose Hair.* Christie's sold the painting—which belonged to one of the patrons of the archival idea—for 1.5 million dollars, and the archive was founded with the proceeds of this art.[26]

But, in these very examples I exhibit my own risky inclination to search for a clear path between artistic creation and archival retention, idea and evidence, head and hand, gain and loss. Picasso helps alert me to the limitations of my understanding of visual thinking and the artistic process. According to him, "It would be very interesting to preserve photographically, not the stages, but the metamorphoses of a picture. Possibly one might then discover the path followed by the brain in materializing a dream. But there is one very odd thing—to notice that basically a picture doesn't change, that the first 'vision' remains almost intact, in spite of appearances." He continues by seeming to contradict himself, "A picture is not thought out and settled beforehand. While it is being done it changes as one's thoughts change."[27] Rudolf Arnheim

further warns me, in his book *The Genesis of a Painting:
Picasso's Guernica,* that "artists, in particular, have
learned to tread cautiously when it comes to reporting the
internal events that produce their works. They watch with
suspicion all attempts to invade the inner workshop and
to systematize its secrets."[28] One might ask if the successful invasion of workshops and systematizing of secrets
might be an alternative definition of record making and
archival shadowing at work.

Complicating Circumstances of the Origin of Origin

With Cornell and Picasso giving pause and, let's admit it,
Andy Warhol warranting some sort of claim to an identity as archivist—perhaps just as much as artist—we
might consider more carefully, and perhaps with a more
critical eye, the very origins of "origin" in the American
setting, where artist may be archivist, where Darwinian
assumptions of survival of the well-bred organic record
set collide with other forces of academic and capitalistic
appropriation and attrition at work, and where now
there is all the more recognition of what Natalie Zemon
Davis identifies, simply, in the title of her book as *Fiction
in the Archives.* In the most general of terms, the archives
of art, and their collective provenance, are a shadow, or
mirror, of American culture. Archives of art, indeed most
archives of any American genre, are themselves a product of the modern era.

The history of repositories in America began for the
most part approximately one hundred years ago. Prior to
the establishment of these archives and manuscript
repositories, Goethe's poetry applied—that in America,
as he wrote and as perhaps Americans felt, the "soul" or
"inner life" "remain untroubled by useless memory."[29]
Less romantically, Alexis de Tocqueville saw, too, the
lack of institutionalized memory-making in America,
where, he observed, "no archives are formed; and no
documents are brought together when it would be easy
to do so," or so he thought based on his pioneering work
in the archives of ancien régime records in France![30]

Three conditions inspired the modern establishment
of archives in the United States and set the stage for entrepreneurial caregivers—such as O'Keeffe and Elmslie—
and emerging institutions—especially academic and governmental archives—to define the archives of art. First,
there was the turn-of-the-century effort at professionalization among historians—with a turning away from a
seemingly provincial and impoverished classical curricu-

lum as performed in large auditoriums toward German
models of rigor and evidence in the scientific seminar set
behind "locks and keys to doors, desks, and cabinets,
[with] access restricted to a few."[31]

Second, there was the insatiable appetite of early
twentieth-century nouveaux riches throughout America's
cities, small towns, and even remote corners intent upon
what some might see, cynically, as "acquisitive individualistic hedonism."[32]

And, third, there was the crisis of the Great Depression to thank for the foundation of American archives.
The year 1934 marks the establishment of the U.S. National Archives in Washington, D.C. Until then, there
had been no official public national archives in America!

Antiquarian Sentimentality

Whereas continental archival traditions have rested on
the foundation of great medieval monasteries, cities, and
estates and a corps of *diplomatistes* well versed in documents of the Middle Ages, our much younger archival
origins belong to the leisure of gentlemen's clubs and the
Library of Congress.[33] Private repositories such as the
American Antiquarian Society or the Club of Odd Volumes were for the most part local landmarks for genteel
erudition, interior decoration, and no small measure of
self-aggrandizement, but the reach of these well-heeled
hobbyists for holdings in the "golden age for collectors"
was global.[34] I hope you won't mind the circular aphorism that the "collections made the man," by rendering
his taste manifest in his home library of rare books,
maps, and manuscripts or the academic repository of his
choosing; so, too, obviously, did "the man make the collections." As Tony Bennett points out in his book *The
Birth of the Museum,* in the early twentieth century "corporate capital moved to the forefront of the return to the
past."[35] If you consider the names of some of the premier
repositories in the United States, you can reconstruct a
pattern of wealth with the assumption that America's
cultural history was itself a marketable commodity,
available for personal consumption. This pattern of personal and private acquisition of *antiquarian text and imagery*—in the form of manuscripts, diaries, rare books,
maps of discovery, and early broadsides—is an important distinction of the American archival legacy. Hunt-
ington, Clements, John Carter Brown, Beinecke, Avery,
Newberry, Bentley, Ford—all are both names of successful capitalists and semiotic signs of a provenance of
prominence. (This name association of archives and man

continues still today, most prominently in the names of the ten U.S. presidential libraries.)[36]

Scientific Evidence and Bureaucratic Accountability

As the earlier collectors were accumulating personal holdings, a growing corps of anonymous state functionaries and academic historians were also in search of identity, and their identity in the early twentieth century in America hinged upon an alliance with what they viewed as the scientific evidence of archives made available, if not to the undistinguished general populous, then at least to the efficient bureaucrat and the instructive academic.

Documenting Art in Ordering Past and Present

In 1901 Alabama afforded the first truly public archives of a state.[37] This southern state and its neighbors also provided an indigenous landscape not only for the surveying and gathering of historical, textual records but also, later, for the functionalist, classifying vocabulary of Depression-era photographers. These photographers were hired by the U.S. Resettlement Administration to document visually the difficult lives of laborers, many displaced in southern states and in the West. Most significantly for us, the patronage of the American government and private welfare agencies at this time cracked open the door of the archives for what would eventually be appreciated as modern visual expression. (There had, of course, been earlier, isolated episodes of federal patronage of photography including the four U.S. geological and geographical surveys of the West, conducted between 1867 and 1879, soon after the photographic expeditions sponsored by the French Commission des Monuments historiques.)[38] But the greatest infusion of energy devoted to documentation destined directly for the archives, new and old, came with the greatest deprivation America had faced. The Depression saw a great proliferation of records surveys and even records creation by out-of-work artists. An economy out of order could at least be used to organize its past and impose a modern, "fundamentalist," instructive understanding upon it.[39] And as the government intervened in the welfare of the nation, it set into motion a documentary culture in which "the rational administration of the record [became] bureaucracy's favorite child."[40]

The creation and systematization of an American his-

torical construct went hand in hand. Archives were assembled, and archives were ordered. The effort to assemble was often voluntary, or feebly supported by a back-to-work paycheck from the federal government. This collecting was activated paradoxically by the Depression as much as by affluence. Collecting policies were often defined by the collectors themselves, short of any legal mandate, and many archives of the day, being born out of academic history departments or private historical societies, were modern extensions of earlier collecting habits of bibliophiles. This textuality of the archives rendered conservators especially sympathetic to the antiquarian, heroic narrative and at the same time attentive to the recruitment of more contemporary, textual, office records as "raw knowledge awaiting ordering."[41]

Modern Control over Modern Aesthetics

Given these sentimental and positivistic orientations toward the archives, there was a frailty of interest in American archives in extending this forward to modern expression. Modernism arrived at the archives as an ordering taxonomy of the past and present. Modern archives meant modern control of the past and accountability of the present, not necessarily modern aesthetics. Consider photographer Walker Evans, one of the most famous photographers hired by the Resettlement Administration. He placed distance between the attribute "documentary" and his understanding of art. He says, about his photographs, that they should be understood as "documentary style." He continues, "A document has use, whereas art is really useless. Therefore art is never a document, although it can adopt that style." Elsewhere he refers to his photographs as "pure record."[42] It seems that the more he associated them with records and documents the less he viewed them as "pure art." Evans as artist was also *documentaliste* in spirit. The one identity did not so much collide with the other as work alongside it. Consider the words of Peter Galassi, curator of the Walker Evans exhibit recently shown at the Museum of Modern Art in New York: "Evans often spoke of photography as a form of collecting." Maria Morris Hambourg, of the Metropolitan Museum of Art, observes that Evans "grasped—as few had before—that mass *production* is a basic condition of modernity, [and] his work demonstrates how *seriality*, multiplicity, and the media are implicit in every aspect of our lives" (emphases added).[43] "Powerful bits of vertical writing" constituted his lists of images, experiences, likes, and dislikes and often paralleled the photographs he preserved but otherwise reflected another version of his documentary impulses.[44] Evans was highly aware of the duality of his photography (and the duality of his image and text). He deposited selections of his work for the federal government with the holdings of the Resettlement Administration and retained other images from the very same Resettlement Administration work; the latter were ultimately accessioned as artwork at the Metropolitan Museum of Art.

Common Features of Art Penetrating the Archives

Let us now continue beyond the individual examples of the curatorial care of an O'Keeffe or Elmslie and the "documentary" role of an Evans to look more generally at how modern art penetrated into the archives.

If one were to survey at the national level the overall archival accumulation in America of records relating to the arts, one would find without a doubt that the archivist has attended to the administration of the arts, the establishment of an academic canon of art history and art education, and the consumption of the arts more than the creative production of the arts per se, especially the art of artists who vigorously defied association with established art. In addition, we now realize more than ever that governmental archives include a wealth of information on the administration of the arts in the twentieth century, including the suspicious governance of new art through censorship—witness records at the National Archives on the censorship by the U.S. Postal Services of *Esquire* magazine's illustrations during World War II—and the records of the U.S. military concerning its rescue, in 1945, of art at risk in the mines below the surface of German soil.[45]

The "ascending arts of photography and other functionally designed objects"—with their recognition by repositories starting in the 1920s as legitimate artistic expression with evidential value—are more fully represented in the archives than more purely abstract art genres.[46] One response to the disregard shown by larger repositories was the establishment of an archive dedicated solely to art—the Archives of American Art. This occurred in 1954 at the height of a modern ambition to assemble original archives centrally, in Detroit, and distribute them widely, through microfilm. The confidence of that vision, originating with the Detroit businessman Lawrence Fleischman and Detroit Institute of Arts director E. P. Richardson seems to be reflected in the title of the archives publication—*Reliable Sources: A Selection of Letters, Sketches, and Photographs from the Archives of American Art*.[47] This archive is both unique and typically American. It is unique in the breadth of its collecting for art, and it is typically American in the blending of personal papers and administrative, bureaucratic records under one roof, housing the "interiority" of artists sharing intimate correspondence, for example, and the "exteriorization" of administrative documents such as galleries' records.

Syncopations in Accessions

One can recognize a temporary displacement of the legacy of modern art that decades later can in fact establish a rhythm of recovery. Original records of the Armory Show resurfaced in 1958 and were later sold to the Hirshhorn Museum.[48] It took until 1968 for Berenice Abbott to sell her rescue of the Atget oeuvres to the Museum of Modern Art (thirty years after the rescue).[49] Archivists are just now in fact seeing another rise in pitch of much modern-era documentation reaching the archives. For the past few years, my colleagues and I at the University of Michigan have been addressing the archival legacy of architectural modernism, with drawings, photographs, correspondence, slides, posters, and oral histories now arriving from architects including seventy-five-year-old Gunnar Birkerts, who is still at work on his design of the National Library of Latvia, and William Muschenheim, that architect of the widely published Bath Houses on Long Island, built in 1930, and the original exhibit spaces for the Solomon Guggenheim Museum in New York.

In the last decades of the twentieth century, individual museums of modern art created their own, in-house archives. The Art Institute of Chicago and the Getty Center are just two examples of many.[50] The balance of mediation has shifted; archives of modern art have become a common feature of museums themselves.

Description as Mediation

But what, exactly, has become of these accumulations of archives relating to modern art, inside and outside of the museum or separate archival institution? How have they been presented? They have been presented in text, in the language of archivists and librarians rather than the language of artists or art historians, and requests for access to the archives have been required to pass through the gate of the archivist's language and syntax. There is, albeit, one charming and quaint exception. The New York Public Library began to operate a picture collection in 1926. The contents of the collection were photographs of the city, much in demand by artists and illustrators at work in the city's art industries, advertising agencies, publishing companies, and fashion houses. These artists came to the New York Public Library for inspiration for new ideas to be derived from the photographs of the city. Some of these artists had limited language ability in English and limited language ability in the ways of librarians. The librarian in charge of the collection of photographs, Romana Javitz, herself originally from Russia, devised a system to overcome language barriers. She invited the public to draw its interests as images on call slips. This is an extremely rare case of a nonverbal, artistic, negotiation on paper for pictures.[51] It is a refreshing deviation.

Archives in America are otherwise the younger cousins of libraries founded on text. The effort to organize archives, once gathered, through description was in the twentieth century mandated by new classification systems, modeled after bibliographic taxonomies, which imposed "grids of intelligibility" on a patchwork quilt of collections. These grids, though presented as objective, universal, and neutral, were highly value laden. They shouldered out explicitly creative, interpretive, individualistic attributes based on an understanding of the content of the record or a proximity to its creator, what we now recognize after the modern era as a valuable and often lost "conceptual orality."[52]

Archivists in the modern era were also prejudiced in favor of the word over the visual image. We are just now beginning to appreciate how through modern archival description the archivist used implosive devices to charge the archives. Through a stream of text ranging from calendar to index to card catalog to inventory, the archivist loaded description with the "preservation of meaning, the exercise of control, and the provision of access."[53] As archivist Luciana Duranti points out, the twentieth century saw an eventual, forceful "fragmentation" of description into these categories of preservation, control, and provision with an increasing emphasis in this "value-added description" on context and function much more than content.

Universalizing Tendencies

These "modernist universalizing tendencies" began most significantly with the Library of Congress and the Library of Congress subject headings.[54] Launched in 1901, these subject headings "codified forms of common practice" in cataloging, with the aim to render more efficient and uniform cataloging across the country.[55] If "description is revelation," as the poet Wallace Stevens suggests, then modern archival description is indeed revealing of the modernist epistemology at work in the archives.[56] The Library of Congress subject headings and the Anglo-American cataloging rules favored the English language, the Christian faith, the academic canon, and the American worldview. The problem with the establishment of a "universal" cataloging language was articulated already in 1904 by Charles Cutter, one of the early leaders in authority-controlled subject language. He writes, "some subjects have no name; they are spoken of only by a phrase or by several phrases not definite enough to be used as a heading. . . . There are thousands of possible matters of investigation, some of which are from time to time discussed, but before the catalog can profitably follow its 'specific' rule in regard to them they must attain a certain individuality as objects of inquiry, and be given some sort of name."[57]

What to do, then, with the rogue terms of modernist art and visual perception, such as Philip Johnson's term *machine art,* which he claims "just came out of the air" at four in the morning after drinking with the Museum of Modern Art's executive director Alan Blackburn?[58]

Or Alfred Barr's own ever-evolving diagram and language for cubism and abstract art?[59] Erich Mendelsohn's picture book from his trip in 1924 to America provides a provocative, alternative classification of American cities, with his inventive headings including "Typically American," "Exaggerated Civilization," "Center of the Money—Center of the World," "The Gigantic," "The Grotesque," and "The New—The Coming." But Mendelsohn's source, as published book, became sanitized and searchable through the humorless Library of Congress subject heading "Architecture—United States."

I do not mean to suggest that we should disinvite the cataloger, "the alien ego," from the task of classifying, from the admirable aim of providing access, even though in a perhaps naive heritage of universal classification the cataloger risks that in order to be useful to every kind of research and ends by serving none in particular, by mediating meaning into vacuous order.[60] The cataloger also risks severe criticism if his or her classification is perceived as too definitive, as was Barr's. The cataloger threatens to drown out other voices. Verne Harris raises this issue in his "critique of positivist formulations on archives in South Africa": "we [archivists] adopt the language of meta-narrative too easily, using our exhibitions, posters, pamphlets, and so on to tell the story of, for instance, the struggle against apartheid, or of nation building, or of transformation. The counter-narratives, even the sub-narratives, too frequently are excluded, and so we deny our audience the very space in which democracy thrives."[61]

But, to readapt the bons mots of American football, it seems that artists have handily equipped themselves with "the best offense is a good defense." Modern artists and other arbiters of new creative expression have been very clever at keeping at least one step ahead of the classifying catalogers who, despite their best efforts, can be decades behind in their pursuit of taxonomy. A case in point is that the term *postmodern* was introduced to the architectural lexicon already in 1945 by Harvard dean Joseph Hudnut in the essay "The Post-Modern House." It seems that the Library of Congress did not adopt the term *postmodernism* until 1985, when the term had gained sufficient "literary warrant" to gain admission to the Library of Congress list of authorized subject headings.

Ironically, at the same time that librarians and archivists hastened in the last couple of decades of the twentieth century to include the excluded, enhance what they called *revision flexibility,* and comprehend the confusing loss of the canon and the singular role of what they had idiomatically called *authority control,* they, too, began to risk deleting all too easily the artifact of their own scholarship, of their own applied version of modernism. Richard Brilliant, in his article "How an Art Historian Connects Art Objects and Information," recognizes the symbiotic relationship between principles of organization, content, and time when he considers the important but dated Index of Christian Art.[62] Catalogers are busily organizing their newer understandings of "natural-language processing systems," and attempting to apply what they call "enumerative vocabularies," following "post-coordinate fashions" in adapting "faceted" indexing terms such as those recently developed in the Art and Architecture Thesaurus. To clarify this in vogue vocabulary of the cataloger would require a symposium of its own; one can only hope that this vocabulary will survive as an artifact once a future alteration occurs. At the same time, Geoffrey Bowker and Susan Leigh Star's observation holds that there is a "role of invisibility in the work that classification does in ordering human interaction."[63]

Archival description prior to about fifteen years ago was a cumulative layer upon layer of text-based, paper-based description, and as Brilliant acknowledges, description could become its own apparent legacy. I remember a few years ago an astonished student brushing his hand along a page of a typewritten inventory, saying with amazement, "Wow, this is typewritten!" While I can't proclaim any wonder about the typewritten page, I do find the content and structure of that typed document fascinating, and the company of card catalog entries, bibliographies, and calendars equally so. It is perhaps due to my professional bias toward the organizing role of the archivist that I readily concur with the statement that "taxonomy, or the science of classification, is the most underrated of all disciplines."[64] Furthermore, in the current era, wherein "disintegration is . . . easier," archivists have abandoned all too readily earlier signposts of their role in mediating through description.[65]

Understanding Others' Mediation

The trouble is, for as little as we the archivists of the modern era attend to the preservation and analysis of our own profession's manuscripts—being the catalogs and inventories we have created over the past century—we lose our footing even more as we step out of the archives in search of an understanding of others' interactions with the archives.[66] Just how, for example, have art historians of the modern era verbalized an interest in archives? One might start with a fascinating example among citation studies, one that has examined the characteristics of French-, German-, and English-language fine arts monographs.[67] This study provides some useful information about the degree of precision and completeness in citations. For example, belletristic French authors apparently hold themselves far less accountable than German or English authors since the French authors offer far fewer footnotes as evidence and instead situate themselves more obviously in the center of their disputation. But studies such as this do not really advance the archivist's understanding of the *process* of the art historian in the archives. In fact, the citation study to which I just referred confesses to the inexactitude of the study itself, despite elaborate bibliometric measures taken, since there was no clear consensus of what constitutes a primary source and, even less, what constitutes a primary source warranting citation. An archivist must defer to art historians to articulate their ways of scholarly progression through the archives (just as art historians might give pause and consider probing the ways archivists articulate their own "progression" through the archives). It is up to art historians to respond to Deirdre Stam's observations that "It is only recently, perhaps as a reflection of a new self-conscious approach to the discipline, that art historians are speaking for publication about their working habits."[68] Far be it from me to claim immunity for the archivist from the criticism John-Pope Hennessey leveraged against art historians, who, according to an article of his in the *New York Times,* project their personalities into their research.[69]

I prefer instead to try to recognize the multiple personalities of the archives and hope that we *all* can discover our voices in the ongoing act of mediating modern art—as language, as image—in the archives and other realms. The past is indeed imperfect. We can assure ourselves of that by borrowing the reassuringly inconclusive observations of a fellow archivist who recognizes our collective imperfection: "Thus archive is a final resting place, but this place is actually quite restless. Not so final is the place of the final word, that is, the word of the final place. The archive as the site of raw material . . . is perhaps—in Simon Schama's wonderfully ambiguous sense—a site of dead certainties."[70]

NOTES

This essay is dedicated to the memory of a dear friend, Mary Arnheim, who gracefully balanced her knowledge of the catalog and the content of both archives and modern art. The author thanks Rudolf Arnheim, Francis Blouin, Terry Cook, Leonard Coombs, Joan Schwartz, Kathy Steiner, Zhou Xiaomu, William and Randy Wallach, and Brian Williams for their advice and support during the preparation of this essay.

The epigraph for this essay is from http://french.chass .utoronto.ca/fre180/Imparfait.html. The imperfect is a form of the verb that indicates actions of the past as though they have not yet reached their completion, as though they have not finished developing or proceeding. It represents action, without making precise temporal limits. The imperfect is generally unrelated to the notion of the beginning or end of an action. It often happens that Anglophones run into difficulty with the aspect of point of view, the manner of considering the progression of actions of the past. In effect, in French, the verb form *passé composé* (compound verb tense of the past) and the imparfait complement one another in a system of coherent oppositions, where the English language masks the distinctions by employing a single form of the past. (Translation is by the author.)

1. *Différer* is yet another close cousin of English, but as emphasized in Jacques Derrida's use in French, this infinitive carries the double meanings of "differ" and "defer." *Différer* thus evokes complex notions of mediation as well. See Robert Mugerauer, "Derrida and Beyond," in *Theorizing a New Agenda for Architecture,* ed. Kate Nesbitt (New York: Princeton Architectural Press, 1996), 184.

2. Jacques Derrida, *Archive Fever: A Freudian Impression* (Chicago: University of Chicago Press, 1996).

3. In his inspiring article entitled "'My Very Act and Deed': Some Reflections on the Role of Textual Records in the Conduct of Affairs," Hugh Taylor addresses words and deeds within the record itself. He points out that, especially with new information technologies, "the act or decision which informs the conduct of affairs grows closer in time to the document that records it. . . . Electronic communication, especially in its interactive mode, can become a continuous discourse without trace, as both act and record occur simultaneously with little or no media delay or survival." Just as documents themselves contain language and intentionality, so too does the archivist's mediation of inheritance. Taylor's article appears in *American Archivist* (fall 1988), 456–69.

4. Joan Schwartz, "'We Make Our Tools and Our Tools Make Us': Lessons from Photographs for the Practice, Politics, and Poetics of Diplomatics," *Archivaria* 40 (1995): 42.

5. Richard Cox, associate professor within the School of Information Sciences at the University of Pittsburgh, has suggested this term. Cox concedes that this proposed term is more prescriptive than established. "This means that they [archivists] need to understand what a record is, what makes a record an archival record, the history of recordkeeping systems, the organizational context of such systems, and the social, cultural, and other importance of such records." See Richard J. Cox, "Advocacy in the Graduate Archives Curriculum: A North American Perspective," *Janus* 1 (1997): 32.

6. See, for example, Shawn Michelle Smith's *American Archives: Gender, Race, and Class in Visual Culture* (Princeton, NJ: Princeton University Press, 1999).

7. This is not meant facetiously. Greenway the film artist was first a painter, then a film editor at the British government's Central Office of Information, and finally a creator of films combining art, organization, and metaphor. "Greenway started with films about organization and cataloging, replacing narrative structures with dispassionate systems of numbers and alphabets—closure is often achieved when the counting stops or the alphabet ends." See Simon Dixon, "Horizons of Artifice, Peter Greenway's Moving Metaphors," at http://www.artpapers .org/greenway/greenway.html.

8. Peter J. Schneemann, "The Artist as Art Historian: Encounters with the Papers of Artists, 1945–1960," paper presented at the Society of American Archivists Annual Conference, August 1999.

9. Douglas Crimp, *On the Museum's Ruins* (Cambridge, MA: MIT Press, 1997), 73.

10. Stephen E. Lucas, "The Stylistic Artistry of the Declaration of Independence," at http://www.nara.gov/exhall/charters/ declaration/decstyle.html. He writes, "Although many scholars have recognized those merits [as a work of political prose style], there are surprisingly few sustained studies of the stylistic artistry of the Declaration."

11. Luciana Duranti, "Origin and Development of the Concept of Archival Description," *Archivaria* 35 (spring 1993): 50.

12. Nancy Bartlett, "Respect des Fonds: The Origins of the Modern Archival Principle of Provenance," in *Bibliographical Foundations of French Historical Studies,* ed. Lawrence McCrank (New York: Haworth Press, 1992).

13. Frank Boles and Mark Greene, "Et Tu Schellenberg? Thoughts on the Dagger of American Appraisal Theory," *American Archivist* 59 (summer 1996): 299.

14. Tom Nesmith, "Still Fuzzy, but More Accurate," *Archivaria* 47 (1999): 146.

15. Umberto Eco writes of "vague chronological coordinates" for medieval documents in his consideration of "Fakes

and Forgeries," in *The Limits of Interpretation* (Bloomington: Indiana University Press, 1990), 187.

16. Crimp, *On the Museum's Ruins,* 54.

17. See finding aid for Alfred Stieglitz/Georgia O'Keeffe Archive, Beinecke Rare Book and Manuscript Library, Yale Collection of American Literature, at http://webtext.library.yale.edu/sgm12html/beinecke.sok1.sgm.html.

18. Franz Kafka is recognized as "the great modern incident" of an author requesting that all his diaries, manuscripts, and letters be destroyed. Kafka's friend and executor, Max Brod, disobeyed his wishes. See Joseph L. Sax, *Playing Darts with a Rembrandt* (Ann Arbor: University of Michigan Press, 1999), 46.

19. Jeffrey Hogrefe, *O'Keeffe: The Life of an American Legend* (New York: Bantam Books, 1992), 240.

20. See *The Encyclopedia of Photography* entry for Eugene Atget, as cited at http://masters-of-photography.com/A/atget/atget_articles1.html and http://www.kbnet.co.uk/rleggat/photo/history/atget.htm.

21. Abigail Solomon-Godeau, *Photography at the Dock* (Minneapolis: University of Minnesota Press, 1991), 33.

22. Julie V. Iovine, "America's Design Legacy . . . Going, Going, Gone," *New York Times,* February 17, 2000, B1, B18. It is ironic that Michel Foucault identified documents themselves as "monuments." See Michel Foucault, *The Archeology of Knowledge* (London, 1972), 7.

23. Nancy Bartlett, *More Than a Handsome Box: Education in Architecture at the University of Michigan, 1876–1986* (Ann Arbor: University of Michigan, College of Architecture and Urban Planning, 1995), 74.

24. Not only were the media impermanent, they were also highly varied. Starting already in the 1870s, the architectural design industry took advantage of several new, cheap, easy, and fast technologies to produce copies of unique drawings. Pencil, ink, commercial paint, colored crayon, and felt tip marker have been routinely used in several iterations of information drawn and painted upon tracing cloth, polyester film, tracing paper, and vellum paper, with adhesive tape, staples, and paper clips for collation. See Elonore Kissel and Erin Vigneau, *Architectural Photoreproductions: A Manual for Identification and Care* (New York: New York Botanical Garden and Oak Knoll Press, 1999).

25. Polly Koch, ed., *Joseph Cornell/Marcel Duchamp . . . In Resonance* (Ostfildern-Ruit, Germany: Cantz Verlag, 1998).

26. "Kahlo Painting Nets $1.5 Million for Iowa Women's Archives," *MAC Newsletter,* September 1991, 13.

27. As cited in Rudolf Arnheim, *The Genesis of a Painting: Picasso's Guernica* (Berkeley: University of California Press, 1962), 30.

28. Arnheim, *The Genesis of a Painting,* 1.

29. As cited in David Lowenthal, *The Past Is a Foreign Country* (Cambridge: Cambridge University Press, 1985), 110.

30. As cited in Ernst Posner, "What, Then, Is the American Archivist, This New Man?" *American Archivist* 20, no. 1 (January 1957), 7.

31. James Turner and Paul Bernard, "The Prussian Road to University? German Models and the University of Michigan, 1837–1895," in *Intellectual History and Academic Culture at the University of Michigan: Fresh Explorations,* ed. Margaret

A. Lourie (Ann Arbor: University of Michigan, Horace H. Rackham School of Graduate Studies, 1989): 9–39; and Bonnie G. Smith, "Gender and the Practices of Scientific History: The Seminar and Archival Research in the Nineteenth Century," *American Historical Review* (October 1995), 1157.

32. Barry M. Katz, "Technology and Design: A New Agenda," *Technology and Culture* 38, no. 2 (April 1997), as viewed at http://shot.press.jhu.edu/associations/shot/samplearts/katz.html.

33. Luke J. Gilliland-Swetland, "The Provenance of a Profession: The Permanence of the Public Archives and Historical Manuscripts Tradition in American Archival History," *American Archivist* 54 (spring 1991): 160–75.

34. See the Web site of William Clements, listed on February 25, 2000, as http://www.clements.umich.edu/Staffpages/Clements.html.

35. Tony Bennett, *The Birth of the Museum* (London: Routledge, 1995).

36. The relationship of these same men to the contemporary art market extends beyond the scope of this essay. Such a comparison should, obviously, figure into a deeper collective profile of them. Were books and works of art synonymous "visual accents" in their homes and offices? And if so, was the interest in art also antiquarian? See E. H. Gombrich, *The Uses of Images: Studies in the Social Function of Art and Visual Communication* (London: Phaidon Press, 1999).

37. See Richard Cox, "On the Value of Archival History," in his *American Archival Analysis: The Recent Development of the Archival Profession in the United States* (Metuchen, NJ: Scarecrow Press, 1990), 182–201.

38. These expeditions are the subject of Debora Rindge's paper "Photography and Geology: Scientific and Aesthetic Theories Examined in Photographs from the 'Great Surveys' of the U.S. Territories, 1867–1879," to be presented at the conference "Phototextualities: An Interdisciplinary Conference to Explore the Intersections of Photography and Narrative." See http://www.dur.ac.uk/SMEl/newsite/photo.htm.

39. See Gary Taylor, *Cultural Selection* (New York: Harper Collins, 1996), 115.

40. Posner, "What, Then, Is the American Archivist," 6.

41. Thomas Richards, *The Imperial Archive: Knowledge and the Fantasy of Empire* (London: Verso, 1993).

42. See "New York City Block, Photographer: Walker Evans," at http://memory.loc.gov/ammem/fsahtml/fachap04.html.

43. Maria Morris Hambourg, "Introduction," in *Unclassified: A Walker Evans Anthology* (New York: Metropolitan Museum of Art, 2000).

44. Sarah Boxer, "This (Click), Then This: Walker Evans, Man of Lists," *New York Times,* May 17, 2000, B3.

45. See National Archives and Records Administration Web site, including "Esquire v. Walker: The Postmaster General and 'The Magazine for Men'" by Jean Preer, at http://www.nara.gov/publications/prologue/esquire1.html.

46. Crimp, *On the Museum's Ruins,* 66.

47. See "A Bit of History," at http://www.si.edu/organiza/offices/archart/bitohist.htm.

48. Milton Brown, *Story of the Armory Show* (New York: Abbeville Press, 1988), 16.

49. Solomon-Godeau, *Photography at the Dock,* 37.

50. Brent Maddow, "Bunched Images Begetting Ideas," in *Art History through the Camera's Lens,* ed. Helene E. Roberts (Amsterdam: OPA, 1995), 350.

51. See the online exhibit "Worth beyond Words: Romana Javitz and the New York Public Library's Picture Collection," at http://www.nypl.org/research/chss/spe/art/photo/pchist/pchist2.html.

52. Theresa Rowat, "The Record and Repository as a Cultural Form of Expression," *Archivaria* 36 (autumn 1993): 198–204.

53. Duranti, "Origin and Development of the Concept of Archival Description," 52.

54. I borrow this phrase from Rowat, "The Record and Repository as a Cultural Form of Expression," 199.

55. Bella Hass Weinberg, "A Theory of Relativity for Catalogers," in *Cataloging Heresy: Challenging the Standard Bibliographic Product,* ed. Bella Hass Weinberg (Medford, NJ: Learned Information, 1992).

56. Author Norman Elliott Anderson brought Wallace Stevens's "Description without Place" to my attention. See Norman Elliott Anderson, "The Non-Neutrality of Descriptive Cataloging" in *Cataloging Heresy: Challenging the Standard Bibliographic Product,* ed. Bella Hass Weinberg (Medford, NJ: Learned Information, 1992).

57. As cited in Hope A. Olson, "Between Control and Chaos: An Ethical Perspective on Authority Control," available at http://www.oclc.org/oclc/man/authconf/holson.htm.

58. This statement appears as part of the Philip Johnson oral history available online at http://www.moma.org/research/archives/highlights/1991.html.

59. The irony is that seventy-four years after Barr presented one version of his new diagram showing the evolution of art movements, he himself has become an object of attack, as the creator of the chart that became "the religion of modern art, like the chart of the House of Windsor. . . . Whatever the reason, bucking Barr is now a museum sport. Some have tried the non-chronological approach. Others have gone for the hyper-chronological approach. . . . So far, though, the most popular way of bucking Barr is the antichronological hang." See Sarah Boxer, "Snubbing Chronology as a Guiding Force in Art: Curators and Critics, Changing the Rules, Slap the Hands of Time," *New York Times,* September 2, 2000, A19, A21. Not only has his 1936 chronology been rejected, so, too, has there been little acknowledgment of his struggle to define and re-define his understanding of modernism through multiple diagrams and through terms no longer au courant, such as *synthetism* or *orphism.*

60. Rosamund Wolff Purcell and Stephen Jay Gould write about the tradition, proclaiming "that objects of art should speak for themselves, and that commentary (particularly from someone else) can only clutter, or become an unwelcome intrusion of an alien ego." See Rosamund Wolff Purcell and Stephen Jay Gould, *Illuminations: A Bestiary* (New York: W.W. Norton, 1986), 13.

61. Verne Harris, "Claiming Less, Delivering More: A Critique of Positivist Formulations on Archives in South Africa," *Archivaria* 44 (1997): 139.

62. Richard Brilliant, "How an Art Historian Connects Art Objects and Information," *Library Trends* 37, no. 2 (fall 1988): 120–29.

63. Geoffrey C. Bowker and Susan Leigh Star, *Sorting Things Out: Classification and Its Consequences* (Cambridge, MA: MIT Press, 1999), 5.

64. Purcell and Gould, *Illuminations,* 14.

65. John Seely Brown and Paul Duguid, "The Social Life of Documents," http://www.firstmonday.dk/issues/issue1/documents /index.html.

66. If, as Nicholson Baker claims in his article "Discards," card catalog entries are the "manuscripts" of librarians themselves, then by extension the finding aid can easily be claimed as well as the archivist's "manuscripts," especially since the finding aid has been all the more unique and personally crafted. See Nicholson Baker, *The Size of Thoughts* (New York: Vintage, 1996).

67. See John M. Cullars, "Citation Characteristics of French and German Fine Arts Monographs," *Library Quarterly* 66, no. 2 (April 1996): 138–60.

68. Deirdre Stam, "Art Historians and Their Use of Illustrated Texts," in *Report of the Seminar, Scholarly Resources in Art History: Issues in Preservation,* located at http://www.clir.org/pubs/reports/cpaarth/cpaarth.html.

69. Ibid.

70. Brian Brothman, "The Limit of Limits: Derridean Deconstruction and the Archival Institution," *Archivaria* 36 (autumn 1993): 205–20.

An Artifact by Any Other Name

Digital Surrogates of Medieval Manuscripts

Stephen G. Nichols

On Artifacts

In Plato's well-known myth of Thoth from the *Phaedrus,* King Thamuz rejects Thoth's claim that his invention of writing will be a boon to humanity on the grounds that it offers an invaluable supplement to human memory. On the contrary, the king counters, it will have the opposite effect: rather than extending the human mind, it will weaken it. If people no longer have to imprint within their mind the images of things they want to remember, they will diminish their memory capacity. Writing will thereby encourage *amnesis,* forgetting.[1] Socrates takes the gloss further by arguing that writing spreads ideas indiscriminately in the world: to those with no means of understanding as well as those who might. What writing cannot do, he argues, is to provide the reader with the material presence of philosophers who can explain their words, offering glosses on each idea.

Socrates does not simply react here to untutored consumption of ideas. He also objects to eliminating the physical presence of the teacher in the learning experience. For him, the philosopher must conduct a dialogue directly with the student to guide—or, in a less neutral term, "control"—learning. On this account, the authentic pedagogical experience is the one closest to the "original" situation of the dialogue, where pupil and teacher face each other in a "live" exchange. That is where true learning occurs, he maintains, when the give-and-take of the dialogue spontaneously adapts to a living context. *Gráphein*—meaning to write or paint—can only be, Socrates says, a painting of the dialogue that cannot speak, or a written "echo" of it that repeats its words endlessly. Neither painting nor written discourse can spontaneously interact with the viewer/reader. It is not simply that painting and written discourse are a poor substitute for the original: they are, in his account, false and misleading.

Many Platonic dialogues deal with the problem of "copy" and "original." Perhaps in no other context, however, does Plato come closer to articulating a case for "the dynamic of authenticity." One might say, even, that he casts the philosopher in the role of "artifact." In any case, his arguments for "primary" as opposed to "surrogate access" make clear his scorn for the latter expediency. It also casts him as an originator of the position held by many scholars and other observers of the library world who maintain that only the primary document will do. On the issue of the one and the many, he unhesitatingly comes out on the side of the one, condemning its copies as unreliable, inadequate, or even illegible. Accessibility, preservation, and transmission concern him far less than the authenticity of the primary experience for the philosopher and his (again, the one) student.

Plato has a point. The primary experience or document has always been the touchstone for authenticity. It's hard to fault the logic of the argument. Nevertheless, we must ask ourselves if this is in fact the issue. Does it reflect reality, even that of Plato's dialogue? It seems so self-evident that only one artifact can be the original as to beg further discussion.

Yet when we come to reflect, what makes us so certain of these "truths"? How do we know Socrates' thought on this issue? He was not even present when Plato reported it. It comes down to us, of course, through a long history of transition via multiple copies in different media and in diverse languages. To refresh my memory of the myth of Thoth, and to quote the correct paragraph numbers, I consulted my French Pléiade edition of Plato's dialogues, which I had in my study, my other editions being in the office. None of these versions exactly agrees with the others, and all differ from the Greek text.

The Greek text itself has been edited from manuscripts that represent more than two millennia of transmission. We cannot begin to ascertain to what extent the manuscripts report Socrates' or Plato's actual words. And yet there is a general consensus that the "definitive" Greek editions are "authentic." Scholars agree that they represent the canonical Plato. Translations convey this tradition to a still-wider public who profits from Plato's thought, even though, as we saw, he himself condemns writing, its broad dissemination, and thus the copies of "his thought."

Clearly, we need to rethink the question of what we mean by the artifact and how it's used. The issue is not theoretical, so much as practical. It requires analyzing precisely what part of the artifact we really must consult: the physical format, or the information presented within it, or yet some other aspect of the information it conveys, or all of the above. Any kind of rethinking must also recognize that an artifact, the same artifact, presents different "faces" to different researchers, since someone from one field will seek one kind of information from the item, while others, from different disciplines will require other kinds of data, perhaps involving a wholly different way of handling the object.[2] Pragmatically, can one say that these users are even seeing the same object?[3] It has become patently evident that traditional definitions of the artifact no longer suffice. They are fine for what we have traditionally thought of as artifacts *so long as we continue to think of the artifacts in traditional ways.* The problem is that many scholars have radically changed the way they conceive of artifacts and have even broadened the category (as we'll see in a moment). It is also the case that digital media have even affected conventional approaches to collection and preservation in surprising ways.

The artifact, or unique item of historical importance, has traditionally been a unit of measure and management for determining what libraries and other repositories should collect, preserve, and make accessible. So long as there was or could be a fair degree of consensus regarding the nature of the artifact, this notion worked. Magnetic and electronic reproduction puts enormous pressure on these assumptions, however, even in the case of traditional print/paper artifacts. Traditional norms and definitions for identifying original and unique states of a document—what used to be called "the original"—

have rendered it increasingly difficult to ascertain what we mean by "an artifact."

Not surprisingly, questions about the nature of the artifact in general have caused scholars and library professionals to realize that even for the earlier part of the nineteenth century a great deal more information exists in traditional formats such as paper and image than had previously been recognized. So not only must we define the artifact in the new media but the same process now affects a considerable body of traditional information from the 1800s and before. Some of this material, such as paper, particularly newsprint, from 1850 forward, has for some time been the object of concern, owing to the brittle or acidic state of a goodly portion of it.[4] More recently, there has been a growing awareness of other kinds of artifacts from the nineteenth and early twentieth centuries that also require the attention of preservationists if they are not to disappear forever.

The growth in the bulk of materials that require preservation from the last two hundred years, and the enormous amount of information generated annually in the present, have put research libraries and other collection repositories under enormous pressure to preserve and collect on a scale not simply unprecedented but hitherto unimagined. And if the quantity of new material to be processed or the awareness of hitherto ignored nineteenth-century material were not enough, there is the boom in post–World War II output now aging on the shelves of libraries and archives and in need of preservation, much as the baby boomers of the same generation need medical care.

The nature of the artifact and the efflorescence of technologies are interesting and important subjects, but the urgent issue we face is different. The simple fact is that we have a crisis of quantity versus resources on a scale never before experienced. What is more, this compression of resources by the sheer bulk of material making claims on library budgets comes at a moment when libraries have witnessed an explosion of competing demands: for example, by the cost of acquiring and managing new technologies and systems, by the spiraling cost of acquisitions, and by the need to expand services and storage facilities.

Preservation budgets have not been increased in most libraries, and if anything, they have been reduced. In the face of the need to collect and preserve an ever-increasing variety of artifacts, while keeping abreast of information technology, preservation has been relegated to a perilous, indeed an untenable, position. While scholars demand ever-increasing attention to an ever-expanding range of candidates for preservation, library budgets simply do not support those demands. Preservation has thus become what Sarah Thomas (Cornell) terms an "unfunded mandate," the more pernicious for being often implicit. Academic institutions have learned the huge costs of penny-wise facilities management and "deferred maintenance"; it is reasonable to fear that we are now incurring similar future costs by deferred preservation. There can be no doubt, however, that at least some of what we avoid thinking about today will be lost forever by our neglect.

In sum, libraries and archives have come under pressure to develop digital information applications and the infrastructures they require as quickly as possible, on the one hand, while, on the other, they are experiencing an ever-increasing demand in the volume and variety of materials to be collected and preserved.

Important reasons hinder the ability of libraries and archives to respond adequately to these dual pressures. First, sufficient resources do not currently exist to allow these institutions to do both tasks. We do not have a way at present either to coordinate requests on the part of libraries and archives to attain the necessary funds or otherwise to assist them in making the kinds of collective decisions requisite for dealing with so vast a problem.

Second, even were sufficient resources to be made available, comprehensive criteria for identifying artifacts of the last two hundred years that must be preserved have not been established. No coordinated effort exists to bring scholars, librarians, and archivists into collaborative dialogue to identify artifacts and define their value. In short, we have not yet coordinated effort and process.

Already difficult in the case of print and visual materials of the nineteenth century, the task becomes even more complex in the case of optical and magnetic media. Such new forms of information may seem to be independent of their physical media (in that they can be copied from one storage device to another quickly and cheaply and often seem functionally identical even when very different devices are used), but no completely immaterial form of information record has yet been invented. Such resources do need to be maintained, updated, refreshed, and so on in a way sensitive to deterioration of physical media but also to maintain accessibility because hardware and software systems evolve on very short depreciation cycles. But as each new version or format is created of such information, should libraries retain the earlier versions for purposes of possible historical comparison? Should they only preserve the "information" or should they also preserve the form of presentation as

well? Will libraries not only preserve information but also manage museums of obsolete technology?

Yet the very technologies that create the problems we're facing will also permit us to coordinate effort and process in ways not hitherto possible. We should be able to track more clearly the general efforts being made by the library community as a whole to identify what must be saved and what not. We should be able to coordinate retention of the best surviving copies and avoid duplicating costly preservation efforts. We can now, at last, know with certainty what "last, best" copies of an artifact exist, and where, and therefore assign responsibility for stewardship of such items.

Pragmatic Approaches to the Artifact

One of the difficulties facing libraries and archives in this new world is the absence of consensus as to what constitutes an artifact among the various media produced by technological developments of the last two centuries.

We have few guidelines collectively devised and agreed upon by the library and scholarly communities that could help direct archivists and librarians in determining priorities for preservation and retention of the body of materials that have become available since 1800.[5] Vendors and publishers of information—both traditional and electronic—have not been incorporated in the dialogue, and indeed, the legitimate interest of vendors and publishers in protecting their property has played itself out in debates over copyright and "fair use" that have made it hard for producers, librarians, and users of information to discover and act on their very significant common interests.

We have no mechanisms for creating guidelines or for ascertaining where the responsibilities fall for making necessary decisions regarding retention, preservation, and the kinds of reformatting that might be deemed appropriate for a given artifact type. Few if any initiatives have been taken to bring the scholarly, library/archival, and vendor/publisher communities together effectively to propose preservation and collection guidelines. We urgently need to identify mechanisms for such collaboration.

First, however, let us distinguish the issues. Scholars, archivists, and librarians have always assumed a hierarchy in collections. The artifact or original document was the item initially accessioned. When it was prized for some unique aspect of its material or historical existence (e.g., status as a first edition, holograph manuscript, signed author's copy or presentation copy of a work, and so forth), the artifact was the object collected. In the absence of that uniqueness, then a lower level of care might be given and a lost or damaged copy replaced with one very different in physical manifestation (e.g., a photocopy or reprint). The value of the unique artifact could be defined variously as historically important, rare, one of a kind, associational, and so on. In each such instance, however, there was an individual, material object that someone, somewhere, defined as valuable enough to retain.

We can see how the value judgment that determined artifactual status made the traditional definitions of the artifact vulnerable. What were the grounds for deciding in favor of one object and against another? Once accessioned, artifacts then had to withstand periodic reviews, according to differing criteria, as times and tastes evolved. Most material objects decay in some way or other. And some artifacts judged worthy of collecting might already have seriously deteriorated at the moment when they were identified and proposed for an archive. Collecting, accessioning, and retaining artifacts effectively require consideration and intervention in the name of preservation. Such attention may involve no more than careful storage in ordinary library stacks, or it may involve, at the extreme, the "intensive care" of skilled conservationists laboring over a rare book one leaf at a time. But, paradoxically, collecting and retention also occasion an awareness of loss. Every artifact accessioned in a collection carries with it a reminder of objects like it that have been lost. *Loss is the rule* in the history of artifacts; retention and preservation, the exception.

Moreover, preserving an artifact involves some loss of the original state. In the case of a badly deteriorated book or newspaper, preservation will restore life to the object, rendering it once again accessible to scholars. That gain will almost certainly come at the cost of a loss of some aspect of the original state,[6] though this is a tradeoff most scholars and librarians willingly accept.

This is all by way of explaining that the artifact matters. It matters very much. Yet faced with the kind of crisis of quantity of artifacts versus scarcity of resources, the scholarly and library communities urgently need to rethink the status of the artifact in terms of its content and its material form. Without doubting that every aspect of an artifact potentially yields information that will be of use to some scholar or other, we may need to assess the relative importance of the different aspects of an artifact pragmatically. That is to say that several issues need to be confronted collectively by scholars and library professionals.[7]

First, what constitutes an artifact within the time frame of the last two hundred years? If the question is not at all obvious in the case of nineteenth-century material artifacts—for instance, baseball programs or railway timetables have not traditionally tended to be viewed as important cultural documents (although they probably would be today, and it is worth remembering that the passage of time often confers value on the ephemeral)—it becomes truly perplexing in the case of the electronic medium, where the concept of uniqueness may not even apply.

A second question concerns resources and priorities. This imperative may be spelled out as the "how, who, and when" of artifact preservation. That is to say, accepting as a reality the limitation of resources for preservation and assuming more or less consensus on the nature of artifacts: how (in what form) are they to be preserved, by whom, and when (or how often)? In other words, are all libraries or archives to be held responsible for collecting and preserving the same categories of artifacts? Put slightly differently, how much redundancy of preservation can we afford?

The issue is less to determine whether baseball programs and railway timetables from the nineteenth century, for example, are scholarly artifacts of sufficient importance to justify the expense of collecting and preserving them. It is rather one of setting priorities in the face of financial constraints that mean, practically speaking, that if one decides to collect and preserve one kind of artifact, then there will be insufficient resources in a given library or archive for other kinds.

The scholarly community has no more claim to the wisdom of the ages than does the library community. The issue is not to evaluate the artifact per se to determine what survives and what doesn't. It is rather to create a taxonomy and a method for interrogating the individual artifact that would, in a climate of finite resources, help to make a good decision on whether and how to preserve it. A "good decision" is one that occasions the least regret among the wider interested community as the years go by. Such a system would help to ensure survival of the greatest number of the most useful and valuable artifacts by intelligent analysis and classifications.

If consensus of the publisher/vendor, scholarly, and library communities could be achieved on matching preservation of specific kinds of artifacts to particular categories or kinds of repositories, it would surely be possible to rationalize on a national scale the task of artifact preservation.

Many readers will recognize that the problems we are covering here have been somewhat sensationally publicized in the last year or so by articles critiquing what is represented to be the putative "destruction" of precious archives of print materials, particularly newspapers of the last two centuries. Attempts to respond to such horror stories have simply exposed the lack of consensus within the library community regarding the problems to be faced and the means of implementing solutions. The result is that locally made decisions by responsible professionals are vulnerable to attack and mockery for no better and no worse reason than that the decisions were made by too few people with too little national and global consensus as to strategies and tactics.

Indeed both the attacks on preservation priorities and the rather defensive response by the library community have, in terms of the problems outlined in the preceding, missed the point.

The value of artifacts, however they are defined, is not the most pressing issue. It can be taken as an article of faith that artifacts must be treated with respect and preserved in so far as possible. By focusing on the *value* of artifacts for research—an issue few if any would dispute—or by singling out certain categories of artifacts, larger questions go unanswered. Worse than that, the major problems cannot be addressed because the focus is too partial, too myopic. Not the *value* of artifacts but the acquisition and allocation of preservation resources—funding and funding priorities—are the real issues at stake. *Redefining the artifact in an age of electronic and optical reproduction becomes necessary in order to assess the magnitude of the problem and begin to seek some solutions.* Stories such as we have recently witnessed about the "destruction" of print archives simply highlight, usually in a confused fashion, the indubitable theoretical incoherence of our principles and practices as regards defining and preserving artifacts. Surely, a reasonable reaction to such revelations is first to seek to address the theoretical incoherence of our practices and then to initiate and support intelligent discussion of the issues and calm planning for a more rational and transparent system.

Redefining the Artifact

For these reasons, we can see that the artifact and scholarly use of artifacts require urgent redefinition. The issue is not theoretical so much as practical. It means accepting a composite view of an object and determining precisely which parts of it one needs to study: the physical format, or the information presented within it, or yet the information it conveys under some other aspect, or all of the above. This means defining the artifact not abstractly, as a kind of ideal, but contextually, in accord with the combined concerns of scholarly and societal needs and the realities of the research libraries and archives that store primary records. The hardest part of the task is to recognize that those concerns, needs, and realities evolve over time and thus that decisions today will be reviewed with a skeptical eye repeatedly and for the indefinite future.

Artifact, primary record, and *original document* tend to be used as synonyms. Primary records and original documents are certainly artifacts, and often defined as unified objects, original documents "valued primarily as evidence or proof of the accuracy of the information they contain. Original documents are essential for many legal and scholarly purposes as proof of authenticity. The authenticity of a text, even its legal credibility, may depend on an analysis of the format."[8]

Such statements accurately define *why* artifacts are important and *how* they may be used for one purpose. But they do not delineate the different elements that constitute the focus of attention on the artifact when studied by scholars from different disciplines. Is it simple or compound? If the latter, then what are its constituents, and what kinds of information do scholars require of them? The artifact may be more complex and multiform than we've accustomed ourselves to thinking. We need an analytic account of the artifact to convey better the multiple kinds of information it makes available for different—sometimes very different—kinds of users.

Such questions prompt the following observations. Traditionally, people have viewed the artifact as a unified whole, an organic unity, rather than—as we are now beginning to think of it—as a complex object consisting of many different components, any one of which may hold intrinsic interest and be studied in and for itself. In short, one may provisionally define the artifact as a series of multiple discrete components, each potentially a focal point for scholars and others, depending on what they are studying.

Scholars and others who use artifacts may *think* of them in the aggregate as unified objects. On the other hand, when they come to interrogate the artifact for their research, they tend *to focus* on parts rather than the whole (which is not, of course, to say that the relationship of part to whole is not crucially important). From the standpoint of usage, what people normally *do* with artifacts, and this enhances their historical value, is to analyze *discrete* sets of information contained within the object. The fact that artifacts are complex, that they lend themselves to a variety of intellectual endeavors, means that we must think of them in terms of their parts, and not just as a whole. One way to think of the artifact, then, would be as a multiplicity of informational sets, *including* the material form of the object, and its contextual history, where known.[9]

Not the least aspect of the artifact's complexity is the fact that different scholars, from different fields, will perceive and use it in different ways.[10]

The preceding observations suggest the possibility of proposing a contextual definition of the artifact as follows:

> An artifact is a physical object produced at some time in the past, and attesting to a given set of practices, thinking, and ways of viewing the world, but whose importance will be defined by present and foreseeable future needs and use. The value of the artifact is strongly influenced, but not completely determined, by its unique features.

This definition rests on the following assumptions:

1. The artifact conveys historical consciousness in a number of different ways, depending on who studies it and for what purpose. Much of the information conveyed by an artifact does *not* require the presence of the physical object.
2. Surrogates of the object—photographs, Xeroxes, digital versions, and so forth—may serve to convey a large part of the information stored by the artifact. For some, perhaps many, purposes, a high-quality surrogate may convey this information better than the original. In many instances, the surrogate may make possible access and use that would be impossible if we were dependent on the original.
3. Surrogates do not obviate the need for some scholars to consult the object itself.

Not all artifacts are *artifacts* in the same way or of the same value. A brittle book is a different matter from nineteenth-century sheet music or a baseball scorecard from the 1890s. Now if artifacts consist of information that may be represented and studied in different ways, it follows that, often, a small subset of the information will be addressed by any given study. That is to say, the artifact as a whole will very often *not* be under scrutiny, but only limited elements of it. This is not to say that scholars working with subsets of the primary record should not familiarize themselves with the whole, only that their focus will be far more particular and partial.

It is also true that there is nothing *intrinsically* valuable about an artifact. Its value is culturally variable and thus subject to periodic reevaluation. Therefore, cultural forces at work in relevant communities at a given moment will determine how interested parties will view and use the artifact—the whole and its parts.

In essence, then, artifacts are complex objects: physically, materially, temporally, and perceptually. Cultural forces determine this complexity in an ongoing debate, which is continually subject to revision and never definitive. Like all cultural constructions, the status of the artifact is vulnerable. To begin with, the economic resources consumed just keeping it in a repository—even before we talk of active preservation—put artifacts at risk. There is always some skeptic who asks why we need to keep these old objects. So artifacts always compete, at least passively, to maintain their status as protected acquisitions. Artifacts are also vulnerable in having to compete for intellectual resources: for the attention of the public and of scholars who, by their attention or lack thereof, confirm the value of the holdings. In a world where more and more kinds of objects make the cultural transition to artifact status, this competition is every bit as parlous as the economic one.

Clearly, it is easier to make the case for bestowing resources on rare or semirare materials when access and rarity can balance. While public access and rarity might once have been mutually exclusive, they have now become commonplace thanks to digital surrogate versions of the artifact and its components. One may cite many advantages for surrogate reproduction. For one thing, surrogacy preserves the primary record by protecting it from suffering frequent exposure to the wear and tear that even the most careful consultation presupposes. Digital surrogacy also enhances the quality and quantity of the information that a primary record can convey. Finally, surrogacy means that one can incorporate rare and semirare materials readily into course and classroom, something not possible with the original.

Thanks to hypertext and computer enhancement of images, digital surrogacy enables a more nuanced and complete analysis of the individual elements of an artifact than would otherwise be possible. At the same time, digitization allows a more continuous and detailed comparison of the parts to the whole, or of one artifact with others. It also encourages a comparative picture of different cultural responses to the object at various historical moments. Again thanks to the power of virtual viewing, one can place, side-by-side for comparison, diverse constructions of the same artifact that would not be possible otherwise, at least not with the same ease and functionality.

By way of illustrating that the "organic whole" approach to the artifact was itself culturally conditioned by modernity, one can look at the case of the medieval manuscript. Far from offering an example of artifact as unified whole as might be expected, medieval manuscripts continually reveal their conception and execution as examples of what we have come to call *surrogacy*.

On Manuscript Artifacts

Medieval vernacular literary manuscripts, particularly the illustrated or illuminated ones, exemplify perfectly what one means when speaking of the complex constitution of artifacts. Modernity has tended to view preprint manuscripts as unique and unified "wholes." Indeed, one can argue that modernism imposed the concept of stable texts on medieval literary works. A fixed text faithfully reflecting the original work conceived and executed by the author became possible with the progressive amelioration of critical editions beginning in the eighteenth century. Yet even the authoritative texts proposed by modern editions bristle with critical apparatuses such as notes and variant readings that remind us of the mobility of vernacular literary texts in the manuscripts that preserve these artifacts of a preprint culture.

Mobile texts—texts that morph in various ways in accord with the shifting contexts of their production—were the norm rather than the exception in a manuscript culture. So much so, in fact, that we might not be far off the mark in saying that in its own time a medieval literary work could survive to the extent that it enjoyed a dynamic existence. Written down once, it would suffer the fate of cultural ephemera if it could not induce patrons to circulate it from copy to copy and continue to impress listeners who heard it read aloud and wanted copies of their own.

In the earlier part of the period, when oral performance of vernacular works dominated literary expression, textual instability would naturally have been the norm. Later on, scribes living decades or even a century or more after the death of the poets they were transcribing had ample occasion, even incentive, for producing textual flux in the form of interpolation, annotation, omission, and even rewriting. Such liberties could hardly have been seen as untoward in the absence of concepts of "intellectual property," symbolized for us today by copyright laws. Indeed, such a concept would have been impossible at the time, no matter how strongly poets identified with their creations, for society did not yet possess the means or the universal education necessary for turning literary works into mass market commodities.

So it would have been a rare scribe capable of resisting the temptation to intervene in the text he was transcribing in one way or another, especially in the absence of inhibition against the practice. We must also remember that the manuscript space was hardly the scribe's "private" domain, particularly in the case of illuminated manuscripts. Besides the scribe himself, an artist and sometimes a rubricator worked in the same space. While they did not work at the same time, each knew the other would do/had done so. So there was no sense of a proprietary manuscript space.

The artist painted his miniatures and historiated or decorated letters in spaces reserved in the columns of text. Additionally, the artist could utilize the margins and bas-de-page for more elaborate artistic flights. In either case, the rapport between text and image was immediate and so recognized, either seriously or playfully, by the artist. Now, the program of miniatures could have been determined by one of several agents: by the scribe, by the artist, or by an "editor" who directed the others. This means that at least two craftsmen assumed responsibility for the performance of each illuminated manuscript, a scribe and a painter.

It is important to recall these facts to remind ourselves of a truth sometimes easily overlooked when reading a literary text in a modern edition: the manuscript could never have been a neutral space for representing a medieval literary work. Rather, the manuscript itself must be perceived as what Ludwig Wittgenstein, in his *Philosophical Investigations,* sees not as a neutral space but more as a kind of representational imperative: "We predicate of the thing that which lies in the method of representing it."[11] In other words, the space itself belongs to representative practice. *This means that the concept of surrogacy, of copy in the stead of a fixed original, ruled the manuscript culture of the Middle Ages.*

Now I want to argue that it is in the medieval manuscript space—perceived by scribes as a performative space—that we must seek an understanding of this method of representation. By doing so, we will come to understand that textual instability in manuscripts was never simply a function of an imperfect or inefficient means of reproduction. On the contrary, it was a primary condition of manuscript representation. That is, textual mobility in manuscript culture was not accidental, not a consequence of bad technology, but *intentional.*

We have been accustomed for so long to think of the

manuscript as an imperfect technology ultimately superseded by print culture that we may have difficulty in conceiving it as anything other than a quaint artifact. Instead, let us conceptualize this dynamic space as a material artifact produced at a specific moment in a precise context of cultural history. Furthermore, let us imagine that scribes, painters, and rubricators perceived this space as one where they would inscribe a copy of another manuscript, but a copy that would intentionally differ from its model. To do this allows us to perceive the intense interest of manuscript space so that we may understand the dynamics of medieval representation. We may also come to understand how medieval manuscript culture could privilege the surrogate artifact over its original, copy over model.

Just as hypertext defines the potential of digital technology, so medieval textual mobility was a consequence of manuscript practice. Textual mobility, therefore, occurred in all kinds of manuscripts by the very nature of the technology. Only in the case of certain philosophical or theological works where accuracy of textual transmission was recognized as paramount would scribal intervention be curbed.

Taking the instability of the normal manuscript text as a given, then, I want to suggest that illuminations also encourage mobile or changing texts. Inserting a miniature painting or historiated letter in the textual column or in the margin or bas-de-page initiates a new and different kind of change in the text. This change stems directly from the intervention of the image within the discourse space. The picture may then be identified and analyzed as a form of commentary, an annotation that actively moves the text, or at least the reader's perception of it, in ways that would not happen in the absence of illumination.

In short, I want to suggest that the picture in the manuscript space is not something we must take in or perceive in addition to the verbal text. Rather, it is itself a perceiver, a gaze trained on that text as a logical result of artistic experiments empirically elaborated, according to André Grabar, by the artists of late antiquity, but conceptualized philosophically by Augustine's near-contemporary philosophical colleague Plotinus.[12]

We cannot here embark on an excursus into perception theories that helped to make possible an innovation like the illuminated manuscript. Our point is rather to note that with the insertion into the space of writing of another form of representation, one that constitutes what we would recognize as hypertext, *substitution, change,* and *surrogacy* become not only possible but normative.

To understand just how much the insertion of visual commentary unsettles fixed meaning and encourages substitutions or changes, let's imagine the following. Suppose one thinks of the manuscript miniature as a trope that offers a picture commentary or annotation on the text (including the reader's perception of it). The manuscript space of an illuminated folio thus consists of two main components that have been created by the "technology" of the manuscript, where one element—the visual—iconically represents a viewer's engagement with the juxtaposed verbal narrative. This visual record should not be construed as *the* reading of the narrative but only as one iconographic response to the text that we must contemplate simultaneously with (or as an interruption in) our reading.

It is the expectation of simultaneous (or nearly so) juxtaposed reading of one element by the other that marks the innovative nature of illumination in the manuscript matrix. More especially, the miniature offered a new venue for visual expression that adapted traditional iconography to a nontraditional setting. In the real space of a church, for example, texts and pictures were routinely juxtaposed in complex, ritualistic ways. Nevertheless, while the pictures and texts functioned in the same architectural space and derived largely from the same sources, the pictures were not usually the result of a single perceiving subject focusing on a particular text of scripture or parascripture. And even though the iconographic images surely represent the efforts of artists to come to grips intellectually with the texts they portray, the images are freestanding, independent of the biblical passages they evoke. In short, we cannot think of manuscript space as analogous to ecclesiastical space.

In other words, each space of representation exists to produce a new version of the original "artifact," be it scripture or a literary text. Rather than reproducing exactly the model that might have been provided, the manuscript—or church—offers a surrogate that alters the original. And that alteration elevates the new version to the status of a unique artifact in its own right—unique because it is different from its model, yes, but why is it different? It is different because it responds to and registers varying cultural forces that pull it in other directions.

The instability of the literary texts in manuscripts allowed them to adapt and respond to evolving cultural possibilities from one context to another. It helped them adapt to new cultural situations, and it was the cultural reality of such evolving contexts that the manuscript matrix modeled so effectively.

A Digital Surrogate of the Manuscript

As the medieval manuscript is itself a surrogate in the sense defined in this essay, we should have no qualms about incorporating it in the forms of surrogacy that our culture makes possible via information technology. Illuminated manuscripts have suffered from being rare, inaccessible, and prized by scholars as cultural and intellectual exemplars. Collectors have sought them as costly objects, often seeking to maintain their rarity by withholding them from general use. Scholars, on the other hand, have prized them as invaluable informants, testifying to cultural tastes and practices of their era. Perhaps no vernacular literary text represents this syndrome more than the thirteenth-century *Roman de la Rose* (*Romance of the Rose*), along with the work of Dante and Chaucer, the most widely disseminated literary text in the Middle Ages.

Rose manuscripts also happen to be among the earliest and most extensively illuminated vernacular literary manuscripts. Their interest for students of text and image cannot be overestimated. With over 350 known manuscripts, the *Rose* offers a challenge to art historians, literary scholars, paleographers, linguists, and cultural historians. Since the manuscripts tend to be disseminated throughout the West in widely separated repositories, it has not been possible to study and compare these manuscripts with any degree of ease.

Thanks to recent efforts by a variety of different agencies, digital surrogates of medieval manuscripts are fast becoming available. The following narrative recounts one such venture undertaken by four institutions who have pooled their resources and talents in an ambitious project involving manuscripts of the *Roman de la Rose*. Two research libraries—the Milton S. Eisenhower Library of Johns Hopkins University and the Bodleian Library of Oxford University—and two great museums—the Pierpont Morgan Library in New York and the Walters Art Gallery of Baltimore—have undertaken a project to prepare digital surrogates of some manuscripts of the *Rose*. The Web site from which this narrative has been taken may be accessed at the following URL: http://rose.mse.jhu.edu/.

The Project

The Milton S. Eisenhower Library of Johns Hopkins University and the Pierpont Morgan Library embarked upon a project to address the age-old dilemma facing research libraries: how do you increase access to materials while preserving the originals? The project *Roman de la Rose: Digital Surrogates of Three Manuscripts* originated with me as the chair of the Department of Romance Languages at Johns Hopkins University. I approached the Eisenhower library staff about digitizing medieval manuscripts to use in teaching graduate students.

Medieval manuscripts are well suited to the digital world. The fragile nature of the originals limits access to these rich documentary sources, while interest in the use of the manuscripts for research and teaching is growing. Providing access through the use of a digital surrogate is one way to allow access while preserving the fragile originals, but how to create and present that surrogate was unresolved and the focus of this project.

As library staff began to think about creating a product for use, they realized no model existed for digitizing medieval manuscripts, and in order to create a product useful for medievalists, they would need the scholars' advice. With funding from the Samuel H. Kress Foundation, the Eisenhower and Morgan libraries sponsored a colloquium in November 1998 that brought together medievalists and curators of manuscripts along with individuals specializing in the technical aspects of digitization.

The daylong colloquium produced a list of scholarly desiderata for a digitized manuscript. With funding from Ameritech Library Services, the Eisenhower Library staff spent one year creating the prototype *Roman de la Rose: Digital Surrogates of Three Manuscripts* on a Web site. The colloquium participants have tested this prototype and discussed with staff the potential for expanding the project. Hopefully other scholars will try the site and provide suggestions for improvements.

The prototype is based on three copies of *Roman de la Rose*. The *Rose* was written in two parts between 1230 and 1275 and was for the next three hundred years one of the most widely read works of the French language. The prototype is based on digital surrogates of the Walters Art Gallery's W. 143, the Pierpont Morgan Library's M. 948, and the Oxford University Bodleian Library's Ms. Douce 195.

Contained on this site are digital images of each folio of these three copies. Users can page through each manuscript and do side-by-side comparisons of folios from different texts. They can also go directly from lists of miniatures and rubrics to the folios containing these. In addition, a section of about one thousand lines dealing with the story of Pygmalion has been marked up so that the text can be searched. There are over 250 extant copies of the *Roman de la Rose* manuscript in libraries throughout the world. If the prototype site continues to enjoy the success so far obtained, the project will add other manuscripts.

Conclusion

The *Rose* manuscript project is a dramatic example not only of the cultural dependence of artifacts but also of the technical complexity posed by what was once seen as a unified object. In this case, information technology has come full circle with that of the technology of the manuscript. Digital surrogacy opens up new possibilities for studying these artifacts and of illustrating just how complex a physical object medieval scribes, artists, and rubricators conceived, planned, and executed. To return to our point of departure, the myth of the invention of writing, manuscript technology and digital surrogacy have the capacity to make works more present and more dialectical rather than less so, as Socrates feared.

NOTES

1. Plato, *Phaedrus*, 274c–77c.
2. Research disciplines train scholars to attend to the materiality of their objects of study in very different ways. It is not a criticism but a practical fact of research to note that historians, literary scholars, philosophers, art historians, historians of science, linguists, text editors, and so on are *supposed* to attend to quite different aspects of an object of study, which, in the case of artifactual objects, will certainly be complex. Sometimes there may be overlap; more often not. The needs of all serious users are legitimate, and preservation needs to serve them as effectively as possible.
3. Artifacts derive their value from how they are viewed and used in a given culture at a particular moment. As cultural variables, they will be viewed and studied differently at different periods. A holograph copy of a speech by Robespierre would certainly be viewed very differently by a royalist in Louis XVIII's government in 1816 than it would by a socialist historian in France in the 1990s.
4. See, for example, S. Branson Marley Jr., "Newspapers and the Library of Congress," *Quarterly Journal of the Library of Congress* 30 (1975): 211; Geoff Smith, "Access to Newspaper Collections and Content in a Time of Change," *IFLA Journal* 21 (1995): 282; and Richard J. Cox, "The Great Newspaper Caper: Backlash in the Digital Age," *First Monday: Peer-Reviewed Journal on the Internet* 5, no. 12 (December 2000), 20 pp., http://www.5_12/cox/index.html.
5. I use 1800 as a terminus a quo for this discussion simply because libraries and repositories routinely consider print/paper items antedating 1801 as rare. Such materials are treated as artifacts and kept in rare materials facilities. The problem of artifactual status thus arises with materials produced after 1801. It is this category that I am primarily addressing here.
6. For example, special preservation packaging, or simply removal from everyday use and access, and thus segregation from similar materials and their users.
7. So, for example, the paper, binding, and graphics of 1950s paperback books offer valuable information for the bibliographer and cultural historian of that period, but not every surviving copy of such books can or should be preserved in a way that maintains all those aspects. Sometimes such a book *should* be discarded in favor of a functionally better later printing with better binding and longer-lasting paper.
8. Barclay Ogden, *On the Preservation of Books and Documents in Original Form,* (Washington D.C.: Commission on Preservation and Access, 1989), 2.
9. Indeed, scholars do tend to approach artifacts according to what they want to use them for. A famous editor of medieval texts used to refer to illuminated manuscripts—for which he had no appreciation—as "bloody picture books." His art history colleagues, on the other hand, probably had as little regard for the literary text as he did for the miniatures. A historian of censorship in the Weimar Republic may focus on the treatment of political subjects in German film of the period in a manner very different from that of a historian of film, though each will focus on details and patterns of individual scenes and particular sequences. While each will have a good sense of the whole, they will spend pretty nearly 100 percent of their time studying and analyzing different *parts*. The whole is more frequently *inferred* than actually experienced in scholarship. Given the impossibility of encompassing the complexity of even a relatively simple artifactual object, how could it be otherwise?
10. A first edition of a novel by Charles Dickens will be used very differently by a historian of Victorian England researching the economics of the book trade, by a literary scholar concerned with different versions of the work, by an art historian interested in Victorian book illustration, by a textual historian interested in layout, by a historian of book making, and so on. Each will consult the same artifact for very different kinds of information, and each one may well not even remark on the particular information sets sought by the other researchers (or have the technical knowledge to do so).
11. Ludwig Wittgenstein, *Philosophical Investigations*, trans. G. E. M. Anscombe (New York: MacMillan Publishing, 1989): §104 (p. 46c).
12. André Grabar, "Plotin et les origines de l'esthétique médiévale," *Cahiers Archéologiques, Fin de l'Antiquité et Moyen Age* 1 (1945): 15–36. "Par les opinions qu'il a émises sur la manière don't il convient d'étudier l'oeuvre d'art, d'interroger et de jouir de toute vision et en particulier de la contemplation d'une création artistique, Plotin annonce le spectateur du moyen âge" (16).

The Panoptical Archive

Eric Ketelaar

Archeion

"There is no political power without control of the archives," Jacques Derrida writes.[1] There is no power without archives either. Since the third millennium BC, writing served recording and archiving for kings and gods, in palaces and temples. Etymology links archives to the Greek archeion, the seat of the ruling power. Although the Domesday Book was not used very frequently, as a symbol it associated archiving with royal power, like the Book of Judgment was an expression of divine power.[2] The early modern states, monarchies, and the church were information societies, their data collection and use, apart from documenting internal decision making, focusing on finance, taxation, and (mainly locally) the recording of people. The modern nation-state, however, "aspired to 'take in charge' the physical and human resources of the nation and make them more productive," as James Scott writes.[3] It therefore mobilized administrative power for surveillance and pacification and centralized the collection of data on various aspects of the population and society it had to "embrace."[4] This is demonstrated powerfully in the European states governed according to the Napoleonic model. That model is characterized by an omnipresent government, based on a uniform division of the territory and a uniformly organized administrative apparatus armed with the tools that would later identify the ideal bureaucracy.[5]

Appetite for Data

The bureaucracy of the emerging nation-state depended on *paperasserie*, the panoptical files closed with red tape, a dependency leading to an enormous growth of records production.[6] The Netherlands provides an example.[7] In 1795 the Batavian Revolution—inspired by the French Revolution—ended the federal republic of the United Netherlands. The constitution of 1798 made the new nation-state a unitary one. It was ruled according to the Napoleonic model, even before becoming legally part of the Napoleonic empire in 1811. The volume of archives created in the so-called Batavian-French period (1795–1813) in the province of Friesland is 172 running meters, which equals 50 percent of all government records created in that province during the preceding three hundred years. For the province of Gelderland the figure is 25 percent. Even in Holland (before 1795 as the most powerful of the Dutch provinces, a strenuous records creator) the archives from 1795 to 1813 measure 285 meters, equaling 17 percent of all government archives in that province since the Middle Ages.

As Clive Church remarks, "No matter that revolutionaries think of themselves as liberators they seem to end up by increasing the amount of officialdom and red tape."[8] The paperwork had to still the "growing appetite for data" of the nation-state.[9] The new government had a pressing and chronic need for information on society.[10] Everything had become property of the Dutch people and had to be deployed for the profit of the nation. National politics and power, national discipline and surveillance had to be built. These were new challenges, as new as the use of qualitative and quantitative statistical information as input for policy, legislation, and control. New also was that the data were collected and used for regional and local comparison at a national level. A new discipline was introduced (from Germany): statistics "that extensive knowledge of all the benefits which a nation really possesses or may yield," to quote Goldberg, the first Dutch minister of economic affairs, in 1800.[11]

The explosion of information necessitated new methods for storage and retrieval. New record-keeping systems were developed, based upon the pre-1795 experiences but adapted according to the new needs of the unitary state. A little later, the French introduced further and more radical changes in record keeping, as they did in all conquered countries as one of the measures of the Napoleonic model.[12] The archive became not just the interface between knowledge and the state;[13] it became the panoptical archive.

Panopticism

In the eighteenth century, Jeremy Bentham designed a panopticon, a prison where the inmates were kept under constant surveillance (*pan-optical*) by guards in a central control tower who could not be seen by the prisoners.[14] Bentham believed the power of the system to be not only that it locked up prisoners in their cells but, more so, that it instilled in the prisoners the self-consciousness of knowing that they were constantly being watched and guarded. Real panopticons have seldom been built.[15] Yet the concept of the panoptical building inspired the architecture not only of prisons but of libraries too. The best-known example is the panoptical reading room of the British Museum (1854), which expressed the power of a comprehensive and well-ordered system of knowledge resting at the heart of the then-greatest empire in the world, to be consulted under the strictest surveillance and discipline.[16]

Entire societies may be imprisoned in what Michel Foucault calls panopticism, regimes where power rests on supervision and examination that entail a knowledge concerning those who are supervised: Foucault's knowledge-power.[17] Big Brother is watching you, not by keeping his eyes continually fixed on you necessarily but primarily by making and ever checking your file. And there is not one Big Brother but a network of governmental and corporate Big Brothers. Documentary surveillance to discipline citizens is not only a tool of public government, however.[18] Every religious, economic, or social organization is dependent upon administrative power to keep track of what the organization is doing in relation to its members, workers, and clients. Consequently, each also surveys how people behave. Oscar Gandy uses the term *panoptic sort* to denote the system of disciplinary surveillance, using a number of technologies, involving collecting and sharing of information about citizens, employees, and consumers—information that is used to coordinate and control access to products and services in daily life.[19] Such "womb-to-tomb surveillance" has been called the "record-prison," as effective as the panopticon:[20] "Files of files can be generated and this process can be continued until a few men consider millions as if they were in the palms of their hands," writes Bruno Latour,[21] describing this system of surveillance and knowledge-power based on and practiced by registration, filing, and records.

Instruments of Empowerment

Records, then, may be instruments of power, but paradoxically, the same records can also become instruments of empowerment and liberation, salvation and freedom. The Nazis' obsession with recording and listing also made them receptive to the liberating effect of lists, as everyone knows who has seen *Schindler's List*. The detailed record-keeping system of the Nazis still forms an excellent source for restitution and reparation. Ongoing restitution now, a half century later, to the rightful owners or their children of works of art, diamonds, gold, and other Holocaust assets is only possible by using the records made by German institutions.[22] In the same way, the records of government institutions and church missionary societies continually supply the clues for many Aboriginal people in Australia (and elsewhere) to reunite with their families. Sometimes the logbooks of cattle or sheep stations provide references needed to link an individual to his or her parents.[23]

Records in our surveillance society reveal as much about the administering as about the administered. That is why it is so difficult to keep the right balance between, on the one hand, the requirement to destroy personal data when they have served their primary purpose, including that of serving the legal rights of the data subjects, and, on the other hand, the possibility that the files might get a new meaning and purpose in the future. Many of the files created during and after World War II that are now being used in the processes of restitution of and compensation for Holocaust assets should have been destroyed, according to both the criteria of the European Data Protection directive and most professionally accepted criteria for archival appraisal.[24] One of the lessons learned is that files created under unprecedented circumstances or in an extraordinary era—for example, during or after war, revolution, natural or man-made disasters, or political or economic crises—have to be appraised differently from those created in the course of "normal" human business.

Saving Archives

Archives can sometimes also be sanctuaries. Because the Nazi Nuremberg Laws declared everyone to be a full Jew who had four Jewish grandparents, a life could be saved if a person could prove that one of the grandparents was non-Jewish. During the German occupation of the Netherlands, several archivists were involved in forging seventeenth- and eighteenth-century registers of marriage. They faked a marriage between a Jewish forefather and a Christian, thereby saving the lives of their descendants. After the war, these faked registers were replaced by the originals, which had been kept hidden—like the proverbial needle in a haystack—in the stacks, sometimes in the company of irreplaceable Jewish archives and Torah rolls.[25]

Sometimes, quite unintentionally, archives may be safe havens. Vitaly Shentalinsky revealed how the KGB archives yielded literary treasures that had been confiscated from their authors and kept in files as evidence of the writers' alleged treason. These files also contained the original literary texts written down during the interrogations in the Lubyanka headquarters of the KGB, such as Osip Mandelstam's autograph copy of his poem about Stalin ("The Kremlin crag-dweller . . . / Fat fingers as oily as maggots . . . / And his large laughing cockroach eyes"). The poem is annotated, "Appended to the record of O. Mandelstam's interrogation, 25 May 1934," and countersigned by the interrogator.[26]

Human Rights

Records act as instruments of power. Oppressed by power, but also countervailing that power, is the basic human veneration of human rights: the right to life, liberty, and security of person and property; freedom from slavery, torture, or cruel, inhuman, or degrading treatment or punishment; and the freedom from any kind of discrimination because, as the Universal Declaration of Human Rights affirms, all people are equal before the law. Ensuring and securing these human rights has nowhere been expressed more convincingly than in societies in transition from oppression to democracy. In most of the former communist countries, the new democratic parliaments have passed laws to compensate citizens for arbitrary and unlawful nationalization in the former communist regimes. This has led to thousands and thousands of people rushing to the state archives, where they hope that the evidence they need is kept.[27] People wrongly convicted under a totalitarian regime for crimes they never committed are regularly being rehabilitated on the basis of evidence in the archives of their former oppressor.

Classic human rights enshrine these rights in terms of the citizen and the state, under the rule of law. But private business enterprises, associations, churches, universities, and others also have to adhere to them. If human rights are violated, the citizen has to be able to defend him- or herself. Here we see an essential connection between archives and human rights: the violation of these rights has been documented in the archives, and citizens who defend themselves appeal to the archives. The archives have a twofold power: being evidence of oppression and containing evidence required to gain freedom, evidence of wrongdoing and evidence for undoing the wrong.

The archival record, as John Fleckner said in his 1990 address as president of the Society of American Archivists,

> is a bastion of a just society. In a just society, individual rights are not time-bound and past injustices are reversible. . . . On a larger scale—beyond the rights of individuals—the archival record serves all citizens as a check against a tyrannical government.[28]

Archival Temples

Archives can, however, only have that power if the information has been stored some way, somewhere, such as storage in temples, as in the ancient world. Then, as in medieval times, the treasury in temples and churches contained both the treasures and the records, safely stored and hidden from the strangers' gaze.[29] Temples and churches convey by their architecture the idea of surveillance and power. The architecture and the ceremonies serve to initiate the novice: they instill submissive awe and enforce silent obedience. In our world, many archives are temples as well. Some are built as a classical temple, such as the Archivo General de la Nacion of El Salvador and the National Archives of the United States. When the cornerstone in Washington, D.C., was laid on February 20, 1933, President Herbert Hoover boasted: "This temple of history will appropriately be one of the most beautiful buildings in America, an expression of the American soul. It will be one of the most durable, an expression of the American character."[30] Modern French archival buildings have been likened to cathedrals;[31] the Public Record Office at Chancery Lane in London was one of the many archives with the appearance of a church. These represent places not only of worship but also of safekeeping records. The Australian War Memorial in Canberra combined these two functions from the very beginning. Whatever their architecture, archives serve symbolically as temples shielding an idol from the gaze of the uninitiated, guarding treasures as a monopoly for the priesthood, and exercising surveillance over those who are admitted.

Surveillance and Power in the Archives

In the preceding I refer to Jeremy Bentham's panopticon and Michel Foucault's panopticism. The power of the archive is derived from its panoptical visualization, seeing while unseen, because all records "can be superimposed, reshuffled, recombined, and summarized, and . . . totally new phenomena emerge, hidden from the other people from whom all these inscriptions have been exacted," as Bruno Latour writes.[32] The panoptical archive disciplines and controls through knowledge-power. This knowledge is embedded in the records—their content, form, structure, and context. Moreover the physical ordering of archives in the paper world and the logical ordering of digital archives express knowledge-power. Archival institutions, unlike libraries, do not publicly display their holdings to offer a panoptic view to their clients.[33] But they do display the knowledge-power of the finding aids as representations of what the public may not see openly but may expect to find behind the closed doors of the prisonlike repositories.

The search room in the archives is a panopticon as well. Researchers are called *patrons* but are subjected to a host of policing measures. They have to register and sign a statement subjecting them to the rules of the institution; they have to leave their bags and personal belongings behind before entering the search room; any papers they carry into and out of the search room are checked—sometimes by uniformed security personnel, as in the U.S. National Archives. In the search room, researchers have to keep silent, and they are under constant supervision. Some archives employ for this surveillance uniformed guards and closed-circuit television cameras (as in the National Archives of Canada and the United Kingdom's Public Record Office): the true panoptical seeing without being seen. In most search rooms, the archivist on duty is seated on an elevated platform from which he or she has a panoptic view, global and individualizing, of each and every "inmate" of the search room. Every user is enveloped in the observation by the other users and by the archives personnel. Nobody escapes this watch or the exacting ritualization of the search room.[34] The layout and furniture of the room provide a maximum of surveillance and a minimum of privacy for the researchers. They are disciplined as if they are children in a classroom; in some archives, they are even deprived of their own writing paper and pen, required to use only the paper and pencils provided by the institution.

Researchers want to consult documents: that is the sole purpose of the visit to the search room and their surrender to the power of the archives. They have a legal right to consult public archives, but that right is reconstructed inside the archives into a privilege, the granting of which has to be requested. In several countries, the researcher has to specify the reason for this request, once more allowing the archives to invade the researcher's private domain with penetrating questions. In Germany, the archives respond to the request by a formal *Benutzungsgenehmigung*: a consent to use the archives, for the given reason only. When the documents have finally arrived on the researcher's table, the user receives further instructions: documents are not to be touched with bare hands (white gloves are provided by the institution); only a limited amount of documents is allowed per retrieval or day; the making of photocopies by the researcher or the use a scanner is usually prohibited. And when the researcher is finished, he or she may approach the archivist's desk to beg, "Please, Sir, I want some more."

For a great number of documents, access is restricted to protect the privacy of individuals, or the security of the State, or the fragility of the documents. If a researcher wants to consult these documents, he or she is submitted to an even stricter disciplinary regime.[35] This involves providing more details about what the researcher wants to achieve, signing more engagements, acquiescing to more restrictions, accepting more close surveillance (sometimes involving "solitary confinement" in a special "study cell"), submitting his or her notes and drafts to the archivist for censorship, or, even further, not being allowed to take notes or to make copies of the sensitive records at all. Here, then, the archivist is indeed mediating but, as the Jedi archivist in *Star Wars: Episode II, Attack of the Clones*, as archive kingdom ruler.[36]

Professional Distrust

Any archivist will immediately object that all these measures are in the interest of the security and integrity of the archival documents, the security and integrity of the

State, and ultimately in the best interest of the researcher who otherwise would get no access at all. Many researchers would even agree—if they do not, they risk their peers' ostracism and the archivists' banishment.

I contend, though, that these noble arguments—inscribed in the archivists' code of ethics—are to a large extent rationalizations of appropriation and power.[37] There are deeply hidden reasons—very seldom talked about, let alone written about, except in the fictional world of archives.[38] The surveillance and discipline in archives are ingrained in the archivists' professional distrust of anyone other than the archivist using the archives.[39] The distrust is the psychotic shield to protect the fetish from being stained by the noninitiated.[40] The rituals, surveillance, and discipline serve to maintain the power of the archives and the archivist.

The Power of the Archivist

The panopticism of the search room corresponds to that of the files the researcher is permitted to consult. While reading in the files what public and private authorities have observed, seen, heard, and recorded, the researcher him- or herself is observed in the search room, recording and being recorded, taking notes and being noted. The archivist is the link between these different panoptical systems and fulfills a role in these different systems. As priest, as guard, as guardian? As accomplice of oppression and torture? As friend of liberation and justice? As warden of a temple sanctuary or a stark prison? As purveyor or withholder of knowledge-power? Maybe each and every one of these roles.

Is that the final verdict? No: the panoptical archive has more than one face, like the surveillance society of which the archive is both a tool and a reflection. That society "may be viewed either from the perspective of social control or from that of social participation," according to David Lyon.[41] Archives are places of surveillance, policy, and power, but the power is the citizen's power too. Surveillance, Lyon remarks, has a dual character: control and care, proscription and protection.[42] The citizen is also protected by the power of the archivist, who is able to counter fraud, violence, or just neglect with professional courage, as Theo Thomassen forcefully argues. Maintaining and strengthening professional and moral independence and staying free from interference by politics, ideology, and special interests "are vital for democracy, transparent government, public accountability and the preservation of the documentary heritage."[43]

NOTES

This essay is based upon two papers, "The Panoptical Archive" and "The Knowledgeable Archive," presented in the seminar "Archives, Documentation, and the Institutions of Social Memory," organized by the Bentley Historical Library and the International Institute of the University of Michigan, Ann Arbor, January 13 and February 14, 2001. Parts of this essay were included in my paper "Empowering Archives: What Society Expects of Archivists," in *Past Caring? What Does Society Expect of Archivists? Proceedings of the Australian Society of Archivists Conference. Sydney 13–17 August 2002,* ed. Susan Lloyd (Canberra: Australian Society of Archivists, 2002), 11–27, and in my article "Archival Temples, Archival Prisons: Modes of Power and Protection," *Archival Science* 2 (2002): 221–38.

1. Jacques Derrida, *Archive Fever: A Freudian Impression* (Chicago: University of Chicago Press, 1995), 4.

2. Michael T. Clanchy, *From Memory to Written Record: England, 1066–1307,* 2nd ed. (Oxford: Blackwell, 1993), 32–35, 150–51; and Leo Koep, *Das himmlische Buch in Antike und Christentum: Eine religionsgeschichtliche Untersuchung zur altchristlichen Bildersprache* (Theophaneia. Beiträge zur Religions- und Kirchengeschichte des Altertums) (Bonn: Hanstein, 1952).

3. James C. Scott, *Seeing Like a State: How Certain Schemes to Improve the Human Condition Have Failed* (New Haven: Yale University Press, 1998), 51.

4. Anthony Giddens, *The Nation-State and Violence,* vol. 2, *A Contemporary Critique of Historical Materialism* (Cambridge: Polity Press, 1985), 181; and John Torpey, *The Invention of the Passport: Surveillance, Citizenship and the State* (Cambridge: Cambridge University Press, 2000).

5. F. M. van der Meer and Jos C. N. Raadschelders, "Between Restoration and Consolidation: The Napoleonic Model of Administration in the Netherlands, 1795–1990," in *Les influences du 'modèle' Napoléonien d'administration sur l'organisation administrative des autres pays,* ed. Bernd Wunder (Brussels, 1995), 199–222; and Christopher Dandeker, *Surveillance, Power and Modernity: Bureaucracy and Discipline from 1700 to the Present Day* (Cambridge: Polity Press, 1990).

6. Mark Poster, *The Mode of Information: Poststructuralism and Social Context* (Chicago: University of Chicago Press, 1990), 91; and C. H. Church, *Revolution and Red Tape: The French Ministerial Bureaucracy, 1770–1850* (Oxford: Clarendon Press, 1981).

7. Frederick C. J. Ketelaar, "'Door eenheid tot orde en vastheid': Vernieuwing van de overheidsadministratie in de Bataafse tijd," *Nehalennia: Bulletin van de werkgroep Historie en archeologie van het Koninklijk Zeeuwsch Genootschap der Wetenschappen en de Zeeuwsche Vereeniging voor Dialectonderzoek* 109 (1996): 39–47.

8. Church, *Revolution and Red Tape,* vii.

9. Simon Schama, *Patriots and Liberators: Revolution in the Netherlands, 1780–1813* (London: Collins, 1977), 474.

10. Charles Jeurgens and Paul M. M. Klep, *Informatieprocessen van de Bataafs-Franse overheid 1795–1813* (The Hague: voor Nederlandse Geschiedenis, 1995), 11. Preliminary results of the Institute for Dutch History's inventorization of all infor-

mation collection processes, 1795–1810, can be consulted on www.kb.nl/infolev/ing/rgp/werkbest/batfra/intro.htm.

11. Wilhelmus M. Zappey, *De economische en politieke werkzaamheid van Johannes Goldberg (1763–1828)* (Alphen aan den Rijn: Samsom, 1967), 47; Ian Hacking, *The Taming of Chance* (Cambridge: Cambridge University Press, 1990); and Mathieu Deflem, "Surveillance and Criminal Statistics: Historical Foundations of Governmentality," in *Studies in Law, Politics and Society*, ed. Austin Sarat and Susan Silbey (Greenwich: JAI Press, 1997), 17:149–84.

12. Wolfgang H. Stein, *Französisches Verwaltungsschriftgut in Deutschland: Die Departementalverwaltungen in der Zeit der Französischen Revolution und des Empire* (Marburg: Archivschule Marburg Institut für Archivwissenschaft, 1996).

13. Thomas Richards, *The Imperial Archive: Knowledge and the Fantasy of Empire* (London, 1993), 14. On the knowledgeable archive of the nonstate sector and its interaction or even fusion with the state's knowledge, see C. A. Bayly, *Empire and Information: Intelligence Gathering and Social Communication in India, 1780–1870* (Cambridge: Cambridge University Press, 1996); Dandeker, *Surveillance, Power and Modernity*; and Oscar H. Gandy Jr., *The Panoptic Sort: A Political Economy of Personal Information* (Boulder: Westview Press, 1993).

14. Michel Foucault, *Discipline and Punish: The Birth of the Prison* (New York: Pantheon, 1975); and Poster, *The Mode of Information*, 89–91.

15. Richard F. Hamilton, *The Social Misconstruction of Reality: Validity and Verification in the Scholarly Community* (New Haven: Yale University Press, 1996), 175–81.

16. George F. Barwick, *The Reading Room of the British Museum* (London, 1929); and Philip R. Harris, *The Reading Room* (London: British Library, 1979), quoted by Jo Tollebeek, "Het Archief: de panoptische utopie van de historicus," in *Toegang: Ontwikkelingen in de ontsluiting van archieven; Jaarboek 2001 Stichting Archiefpublicaties*, ed. Theo Thomassen, Bert Looper, and Jaap Kloosterman (The Hague: Stichting Archiefpublicaties, 2001), 76–91, here 88.

17. Michel Foucault, "Truth and Juridical Forms," in *Michel Foucault: Power*, ed. James D. Faubion (London: Penguin Books, 2002), 3:58–59; Giddens, *The Nation-State and Violence*, 172–92; Anthony Giddens, *A Contemporary Critique of Historical Materialism* (Houndmills, UK: Macmillan Press, 1995), 174–76; Dandeker, *Surveillance, Power and Modernity*; David Lyon, *The Electronic Eye: The Rise of Surveillance Society* (Minneapolis: University of Minnesota Press, 1994); Frank Webster, *Theories of the Information Society* (London: Routledge, 1995), 52–73; and Matt K. Matsuda, *The Memory of the Modern* (New York: Oxford University Press, 1996).

18. Dandeker, *Surveillance, Power and Modernity*, 150–92; and Gandy, *The Panoptic Sort*, 60–122.

19. Gandy, *The Panoptic Sort*, 1, 15; and Poster, *The Mode of Information*, 91–98.

20. Arthur R. Miller, *The Assault on Privacy: Computers, Databanks, and Dossiers* (Ann Arbor: University of Michigan Press, 1971), quoted by Thomas S. McCoy, "Surveillance, Privacy and Power: Information Trumps Knowledge," *Communications* 16 (1991): 33–47, here 35.

21. Bruno Latour, "Visualization and Cognition: Thinking with Eyes and Hands," *Knowledge and Society* 6 (1986): 28. I thank Margaret Hedstrom for drawing my attention to this article.

22. Eric Ketelaar, "Understanding Archives of the People, by the People, and for the People," in *Washington Conference on Holocaust-Era Assets Proceedings*, ed. J. D. Bindenagel (Washington, DC, 1999), 749–61.

23. Rowena MacDonald, *Between Two Worlds: The Commonwealth Government and the Removal of Aboriginal Children of Part Descent in the Northern Territory* (Alice Springs: IAD Press, 1995), 72–73.

24. "Directive 95/46/EC of the European Parliament and of the Council of 24 October 1995 on the Protection of Individuals with Regard to the Processing of Personal Data and on the Free Movement of Such Data," *Official Journal of the European Communities* L 281/31, also available at www.privacy.org/pi/intl_orgs/ec/eudp.html.

25. Frederick C. J. Ketelaar, "Qui desiderat pacem," *Nederlands Archievenblad* 90 (1986): 97–102.

26. Vitaly Shentalinsky, *The KGB's Literary Archive* (London: Harvill Press, 1997), 170–75.

27. Lajos Körmendy, "Historical Challenges and Archivist's Responses, Hungary, 1945–2000," *Archivum* 45 (2000): 41–53, here 49.

28. John A. Fleckner, "'Dear Mary Jane': Some Reflections on Being an Archivist," *American Archivist* 54 (winter 1991): 8–13, reproduced in *American Archival Studies: Readings in Theory and Practice*, ed. Randall C. Jimerson (Chicago: Society of American Archivists, 2000), 21–8, here 26.

29. Ernst Posner, *Archives in the Ancient World* (Cambridge, MA: Harvard University Press, 1972; reprinted, Chicago: Society of American Archivists, 2002); and Clanchy, *From Memory to Written Record*, 154–57, 164.

30. Herman J. Viola, *The National Archives of the United States* (New York: Harry N. Abrams, 1984), 46.

31. Danièle Neirinck, "Les bâtiments d'archives," in *La pratique archivistique française*, ed. Jean Favier and Danièle Neirinck (Paris: Archives Nationales, 1993), 536.

32. Latour, "Visualization and Cognition," 29.

33. With at least one exception: the public entering the Lyndon B. Johnson Presidential Library in Austin, Texas, sees—behind a glass wall, high up in the entrance hall—rows of archival boxes with the gold-embossed presidential seal. They are—so I was told—empty, but they nevertheless give the impression that one beholds the presidential archives.

34. Arlette Farge, *Le goût de l'archive* (Paris: Editions du Seuil, 1989), 66–67.

35. Sonia Combe, "Reason and Unreason in Today's French Historical Research," *Telos* 108 (summer 1996): 149–64; and Marcel Lajeunesse and François Gravel, "L'utilisation des archives pour la défense et la promotion des droits du citoyen," *Archivum* 45 (2000): 177–78.

36. Robert A. Salvatore, *Star Wars: Episode II, Attack of the Clones*, based on the story by George Lucas and the screenplay by George Lucas and Jonathan Hales (New York: Ballantine Books), 160.

37. Michel Foucault, "Government Rationality: An Introduction" (original French version published in *Esprit* 371 [May

1968]: 850–74), in *The Foucault Effect: Studies in Governmentality,* ed. Graham Burchell, Colin Gordon, and Peter Miller (Chicago: University of Chicago Press, 1991), 60.

38. "The Fictional World of Archives, Art Galleries, and Museums" is compiled on http://www.victoria.tc.ca/~mattison /ficarch/index.htm; Arlene B. Schmuland, "The Archival Image in Fiction: An Analysis with an Annotated Bibliography," *American Archivist* 62 (1999): 24–73; Debra A. Castillo, *The Translated World: A Postmodern Tour of Libraries in Literature* (Tallahassee: Florida State University Press, 1984), 196–262; G. Stocker, *Schrift, Wissen und Gedächtnis: Das Motiv der Bibliothek als Spiegel des Medienwandels* (Würzburg, 1997); Bonnie G. Smith, *The Gender of History: Men, Women, and Historical Practice* (Cambridge: Harvard University Press, 1998), 116–29; and Cornelia Vismann, *Akten: Medientechnik und Recht* (Frankfurt: Fischer Taschenbuch Verlag, 2000), 30–66.

39. Nancy Bartlett, "The Healthy Distrust of the Archive's Inhabitant," paper of commentary remarks presented to the seminar "Archives, Documentation and the Institutions of So- cial Memory," organized by the Bentley Historical Library and the International Institute of the University of Michigan, Ann Arbor, September 13, 2000. It was in fact this paper that caused me to rethink the way archivists are using instruments of surveillance and discipline.

40. Helen Wood, "The Fetish of the Document: An Exploration of Attitudes towards Archives," in *New Directions in Archival Research,* ed. Margaret Procter and C. P. Lewis (Liverpool: University Centre for Archive Studies, 2000), 20–48.

41. Lyon, *The Electronic Eye,* 31.

42. Ibid., 219.

43. Theo Thomassen, "Archivists between Knowledge and Power: On the Independence and Autonomy of Archival Science and the Archival Profession," paper presented at the International Archival Conference "The Destruction and Reconstruction of Historical Memory: Integrity and Autonomy of Archives," Dubrovnik, 1999, in *Arhivski Vjesnik* 42 (Zagreb, 1999): 149–67, here 166. Also on: http://www.archiefschool.nl /docs/thomarch.pdf.

Archival Representation

Elizabeth Yakel

A man hath perished and his corpse has become dirt. All his kindred have crumbled to dust. But writings cause him to be remembered in the mouth of the reciter.

—Egyptian author, unknown

In *The Design of Everyday Things* Donald Norman argues for a user-centered approach to the design of the daily artifacts we take for granted.[1] While archives and archival collections are not everyday things for most people, they do document everyday things, and the archivist's representations and representational systems must characterize these everyday things for potential researchers.[2]

The term "representation" is used to refer both to the process or activity of representing and to the object(s) produced by an instance of that activity. The process of representing seeks to establish systematic correspondence between the target domain and the modeling domain and to capture or "re-present" through the medium of the modeling domain, the object, the data, or information in the target domain. To the extent that this re-presentation corresponds to, or models, the object, data, or information in the target domain the two can be thought of as representationally equivalent.[3]

This essay focuses on archival representation as a fluid, evolving, and socially constructed practice. *Representation* refers to both the processes of arrangement and description as well as the creation of access tools (guides, inventories, finding aids, bibliographic records) or systems (card catalogs, bibliographic databases, EAD databases) resulting from those activities. Throughout this essay the term *archival representation* is used for the ar-

chival function commonly and variously identified as arrangement and description, processing, and occasionally archival cataloging. I think that the term *archival representation* more precisely captures the actual work of the archivist in (re)ordering, interpreting, creating surrogates, and designing architectures for representational systems that contain those surrogates that stand in for or represent actual archival materials.

The nature of representational tools in archives also makes them everyday things for archivists. At the same time, the codification of these tools and systems has created barriers to use. Researchers must know the codes and understand the underlying classification system. Many archivists focus on the creation of representations as the ultimate function of the archivist. As a result, the inventories and finding aids have been either the much-maligned or much-venerated objects of archivists either promoting or attacking archival theory.[4] To achieve a deeper understanding of archival representation, this essay stands this argument on its head and studies archival representations and representational systems themselves in an effort to theorize about these artifacts, determine how meaning is imbued in them, and discuss the centrality of these activities to archival work. This more empirical deconstruction of archival representation owes much to the theoretical writings of Terry Cook and others who have aptly applied postmodern theories to various aspects of the archival endeavor.

Archivists actually need a deconstruction of the contexts they are trying to describe, remembering that "it is in the nature of deconstruction not just to see the wider context (those traces, or specters, stretching back into the past in an infinite regress), but also the fluidity, the flexibility, the ultimately uncontrollable nature of the context."[5]

This essay examines the representation of records by records creators, archivists, and systems. To accomplish this, it focuses on the representational practices, the artifacts of representation, and the evolutionary nature both of the primary sources that the artifacts are trying to represent and of the artifacts themselves.

An examination of the activities, systems, and products of archival representation is long overdue. The past decisions by archivists have already been scrutinized in several other archival functions, and these studies have revealed assumptions and biases in archival practice. For example, the need to reexamine old appraisal decisions has been discussed frequently since Leonard Rapport's article "No Grandfather Clause."[6] The collection assessment studies reported by Judith Endelman found that archivists' long-term perceptions of their collections were at times flawed, if not erroneous.[7] However, the archival function of archival representation has not experienced such public scrutiny even though retrospective conversion projects have uncovered discrepancies and highly misleading descriptions.[8] Despite the documented need to revisit previous collection descriptions, there have been few analyses of the nature of the original categorizations and descriptions, the revisions, or the evolution of descriptive practices. Yet descriptive practices are definitely one of the narratives, although arguably not so tacit, that Eric Ketelaar identifies in the archives.[9] The present essay explains the salient dimensions in an analysis of archival representations. Findings indicate that the function of archival representation is ongoing. In fact, one collection studied even warns users that "the content will change over time."[10] Ketelaar goes even further by arguing that the meaning will change over time as records are put to different uses. In this latter scenario, archivists should be not only revisiting poor descriptions but completing periodic redescriptions of entire archives to accommodate these changing meanings over time.[11] With this in mind, archivists should begin to think less in terms of a single, definitive, static arrangement and description process but rather in terms of continuous, relative, fluid arrangements and descriptions as ongoing representational processes. In fact, electronic records description begins at creation and continues throughout the records continuum as metadata are added to document such events as versions, access, and redaction.[12]

The idea of developing representational tools as a continuous process is evidenced by the fact that archivists increasingly replace analog representational systems—such as the card catalog or finding aids in the United States—with computer-based systems—such as machine-readable cataloging (MARC) or encoded archival description (EAD). This is also important because the artifacts of archival representation are more than access tools. For better or worse, they have also been collection management tools for archivists. As such, archival representations and the technologies that archivists rely on to create, view, and communicate information about primary sources are occasions for structuring. Structuring is the ongoing processes of actions, interactions, decision making, behavior, and cognition that form the basis of organizational life.[13] In this case, archival representational practices are structuring elements. The creation of each inventory or guide reinforces, extends, or transcends previous artifacts. Thus, each new representational artifact contributes to the knowledge base of the repository at the same time it changes it.[14] These processes are iterative, dynamic, and interrelated.

Let's extend this line of inquiry to the classification and representational systems in archives. Archival representations can present a creator's, an archivist's, and potentially even a user's view of the collection as well as how the archivist frames the underlying papers or records for the world. Hanne Albrechtsen and Elin K. Jacob argue that these schemes need not communicate solely internally but are links between collections and users.

> The notion of the classification scheme as a transitional element or "boundary object" offers alternative to the more traditional approach that views classification as an organizational structure imposed upon a body of knowledge to facilitate access within a universal and frequently static framework. Recognition of the underlying relationship between user access and the collective knowledge structures that are the basis for knowledge production indicates the dynamic role of classification in supporting coherence and articulation across heterogeneous contexts.[15]

Archivists are not yet at this dynamic point where archival categorizations for access and collection management are transparent, flexible, and effective tools for both users and archivists. Furthermore, archivists must transcend boundaries at each end of the archival spectrum, not only between users and primary sources but also between creators and creating organisms and the archives. The discussion in Australia has primarily focused on the archival boundary through which records may pass when moving from office of origin to the archives. In a successful transition, the boundary object or records must maintain coherence in both communities (office and archives).[16] Therefore, a discussion of representational coherence across this boundary between the creator and the archives follows.

Representations by Creators

The representation or organization of knowledge has been a concern for creators of that knowledge as well as archivists and librarians since the Middle Ages. Rosalind McKittrick identifies a functional arrangement of manuscripts and codices in Carolingian monasteries.[17] Peter Burke argues that larger cultural ideas about the order of the universe were reified in the organization of libraries during the Renaissance.[18] McKittrick's and Burke's findings support Eviatar Zerubavel's contention that categorization is not an individual cognitive process but rather the result of a complex dynamic of cultural and social forces. At the same time, the categorization process seeks to divide and isolate by "drawing fine lines" among meaning and representations "as if they were discrete, totally detached from their surroundings."[19]

Representational systems are manifestations of both a culture as well as the infrastructure to support that culture. These representations structure later descriptive processes by creating acceptable boundaries of thought and discourse around the practice of archival representation. At the same time, successful representational schemes must support a degree of ambiguity. As Geoffrey Bowker and Susan Leigh Star note, categorizations also need to allow for change, permeability, and different levels of adherence by separate entities in the culture.[20] These variables of culture, identity (variously bringing together and pulling apart), and adaptability to change are seen in the representations of creators that follow.

Colin Mackenzie served as a cartographer and surveyor for the East India Company in colonial India in the late eighteenth and early nineteenth centuries. During the course of his thirty-eight-year career in India, he amassed a collection of historical records and artifacts through the employ of other British officials as well as native Indian assistants. Mackenzie's collection of accounts, records, and artifacts is as much a reflection of his own culture as it is a history of the Indian subcontinent he sought to document. Mackenzie's "arrangement of the collection" was passive, although even this affected the records.

> The collection of information meant the appropriation of knowledge in more than just a revenue-related sense. When local documents were collected, authority and authorship were transferred from local to colonial contexts. The different voices, agencies, and modes of authorization that were implicated in the production of the archive got lost once they inhabited the archive.[21]

Later organizers of the collection, and there have been several, have further obscured the culture and identity, authority and authorship. Transfer of coherence of the records from the local to the colonial and later to a more historical context resulted in a loss of meaning for the original local creators of the records. Ironically, while the records have been reorganized for repurposing, historians have been trying to reconstruct their original context since Mackenzie's time.

Yet representations can also reflect recoveries of identity. After Vatican II, all religious orders were ordered to revise their constitutions and rules. This process required that religious communities examine their "charism," or the original spirit or vision of the group. As a result, communities rushed to the archives for information, often finding their records in chaos.[22] This connection is explicitly stated in the policies and procedures manual for the Salem Heights Archives.

> Importance: Archives have become particularly important in the post–Vatican II period of history as a source for the process of renewal, enabling Sisters to keep in touch with their roots—historically and spiritually—and ensuring renewal and adaptation within the context of the spirit and history of the Congregation.[23]

In order to recover their roots, order was needed in the archives. Although presented as following provenance, a common schema promoted by early instructors of religious archives workshops is more accurately identified as functional in nature. Furthermore, these functions supported the redrafting of religious constitutions and rules. While there are local adaptations in the names of the divisions, the overall structure of the schema mirrors the Dewey decimal system and features nine "record groups" classifications: (1) Founder(s) and Foundation, (2) Chapters, (3) General Superiors, (4) Administration, (5) Treasury/Finance, (6) Provinces, (7) Houses/Missions/Parishes, (8) Formation/Spirituality, and (9) Publications. This is one example of the assertion by James M.

O'Toole that religious archives are different in that external, nonarchival beliefs influence the archives.[24] I would go further than O'Toole, who noted that religious archives are different because they are based on denominational identities. In the case of women religious, the archives both helped form or reform a particular religious identity and were then, in turn, reformed by that new identity. One might theorize also that the development and implementation of this schema, which is pervasive in the archives of religious communities, formed a way for religious communities to be in the archival world (avowing to adhere to provenance) but not quite be of that world (developing a peculiar definition of provenance).

Creators evolve representational systems for more mundane reasons also. The Henry Ford Office records and the Edsel Ford Office records from the Ford Motor Company Archives, 1914–52 (now housed at The Henry Ford in Dearborn, Michigan) have been organized in several ways over the years. Initially (ca. 1914–21), in the in-house system, every folder reflected a personal or corporate name or a subject heading. In 1919, general folders labeled *A, B, C,* and so on began to appear. These files contain both subjects and personal and corporate names. This early system was apparently derived from Winthrop Sears (of the Sears library cataloging fame). From July 1921 through 1929, the Library Bureau automatic index system was imposed on the files. This was a numerical filing system based on the names of individual correspondents and companies. This was expanded in July 1923, as a result of an expanding amount of incoming mail, by adding more precise subdivisions of personal and corporate names. As the Ford Motor Company records became more complex, yet another expansion of the system occurred in January 1927. Documents were alphabetized according to person or company, although the exact part of the name of a company used for filing is often inconsistent. In this latter system, each alphabetized item is assigned a code: the first part of the code comes from the first letter of the last name of an individual or the first letter of the principal word of the company; the second part of the code comes from the first letter of the first name of the individual or the first letter of the secondary word of the company name. In 1930 the filing system again changed to the Amberg Numerical System. This again created a more complex yet detailed approach to the organization of office records. The Amberg system had greater depth than the Library Bureau system. For example, in the Library Bureau system the letter *A* had five subdivisions, while in the Amberg the letter *A* had forty-three. In the Amberg system, the names of the correspondent, company, or subject were alphabetized using the initial letters, assigned a code number, and filed in the folder of the same number. Thus, relatively unskilled clerks were able to identify the correct files and work swiftly. To foster greater efficiency, the Amberg Company even sold either prelabeled folders or adhesive labels for file folders. With all its detail, though, even the Amberg system was abandoned in 1950 for another in-house system based primarily on the names of correspondents and businesses with limited subject access.[25]

In studies of creators of records (historians and office workers respectively), Barbara Kwansik and Tom Malone have examined the representations and categorizations of these individuals.[26] The articles by Kwansik and Malone demonstrate that functionality as well as contextuality (such as an approaching deadline) and spatial orientation (the function of reminding) are key factors in personal representational models of records management. Translating these into archives, where functionality may not be readily apparent and the context is long alienated from records, can pose an impossible obstacle to both identifying and maintaining provenance and representing an original order.

To a certain extent, original order assumes an underlying, coherent filing system. Translating the models of original order, identified by Malone and Kwansik, into the archives where temporality does not lend itself to organizations is difficult. Any transfer into boxes automatically includes a loss of context and provides a substantial obstacle to maintaining provenance and re(presenting) an original order.

As Brothman has noted, when records cross the boundary from office to archives, complexities are muted and an idealized version of original order is often adopted. At times, archivists impose socially constructed schemas on records to provide intellectual coherence.[27] Whether these schemas are the record groups cited by Brothman, subject based, functional, or temporal approaches, they often reflect an imposed information organization that would be alien to the creators and is in no way organic to the originator. With that, let us change our perspective and examine some of these representations by archivists.

Representations of Archivists

Within the broad dictum of archival principles and practices, there appears to be substantial variation in the organizational and classification schemes. Furthermore, the social, cultural, political, and economic factors influencing the development of these schemes are very diverse. Recent efforts to define and design more collective representational schemes, such as MARC and EAD in the United States, have tried to both establish minimal standards and accommodate some differences. Geoffrey Bowker and Susan Leigh Star refer to this process as convergence. Convergence is the double process by which information artifacts and social worlds are fitted to each other and come together.[28] Understanding this convergence, both in terms of overall archival organizational schemes and in terms of the information artifacts (e.g., MARC records and EAD finding aids) represented within these schemata, is essential for the creation of surrogates that have meaning in other social systems and transcend time and space.[29] Mediating between original artifacts and archival representations can be difficult, particularly over time.

In the United States, the theory and practice of representation focused initially on what were considered historical manuscripts. Historical manuscripts covered both personal papers and organizational records since the organizational records under consideration had been alienated from their originating body. One early attempt to standardize the representation was by J. C. Fitzpatrick at the Library of Congress. His *Notes on the Care, Cataloging, Calendaring and Arranging of Manuscripts* was first published in 1913. By the third edition in 1928, he had developed representational guidelines and assumptions. One implicit assumption is that rearrangement is usually necessary to counter not only the "derangement" of documents but also the repurposing (or changing functionality) of records as they move from administrative to historical use.

> Official papers under the control of the archivist come to him usually with an arrangement and indexing born of administrative necessity, and in no wise competent to answer the needs of the historical investigator. Useless and faulty as such an arrangement may be for students of history and economics, it is well to allow it to stand until such time as the rearrangement scheme has been thoroughly worked out.[30]

A tension in Fitzpatrick's treatise is the inability to reconcile the representation of the broader arrangement scheme with the very detailed description of items. Fitzpatrick argues for the use of an itemized listing (calendar) or card catalog to describe the contents, whereas the overall arrangement that is seen by the researcher as he

or she peers into the box is meant to explicate context and establish the relationships among the materials. However, it appears that the necessities of arrangement and future location of the papers were paramount.

The impetus for expediency in the creation of early representational systems can be illustrated through the manuscript collections in the Houghton Library at Harvard. Collections are categorized by "shelf marks" primarily according to language or country, but also by subject, collectors, or library department. This classification scheme is further elaborated for convenience:

> Manuscripts are classed as *MS,* generally a manuscript that stands independently on the shelf as a codex; *fMS,* a MS taller than 12 inches; *pfMS,* an oversized MS; or *bMS,* boxed manuscripts generally loose papers in folders. For example, bMS AM 1704 (945) no. 6 is a letter from James Walker to John Gorham Palfrey, the sixth chronologically of twenty grouped as the 945th item or group in American boxed manuscripts 1704th American manuscript or collection of manuscripts to have been catalogued in this series [italics original].[31]

Also of note here is the construction of the shelf marks. While these serve the researcher by creating unique, identifiable call numbers to use when requesting a collection, they also contain essential information for the archivist to use in managing and locating the collection. In one case the categorization has persisted long after the original reason for the designation has ended:

> Earlier in this century it was the practice of Harvard's manuscript cataloguers to reserve the shelf numbers MS 800.1 etc., for small collections kept in manuscript boxes of a certain size. Many of these "800" numbers still survive, although the reason for them disappeared when the collection was rehoused in boxes of uniform size.[32]

Archival codes are ubiquitous. In addition to the manuscript numbers at Harvard, there are several other designations that serve as location devices as well as provide collection management information. Accession numbers record the yearly growth of an entire archives or manuscript collection. Storage numbers connote incompletely processed collections. Call numbers reflect an attempt to incorporate the materials in a larger library classification scheme. And finally, some collections are simply called by their names.[33]

As demonstrated in the preceding, archival representational systems do evolve. When, if, and how that evolution is presented has always created a problem for archivists. The maintenance of older inventories can also be seen as a form of archival pentimento, the (re)discovery of a representation underlying a newer one. Archival accountability and the ability to reverse the archivist's judgment and arrangement are perhaps behind Fitzpatrick's directive to maintain older representational tools.

> The official indexes and finding-list catalogues of such collections should always be preserved no matter how useless they may seem after the rearrangement of the papers. If these indexes are bulky and space consuming, they may be condensed by a group classification or outline record, for archival consultation, before being sent to the storage basement. It is the part of wisdom to leave their destruction to the next generation.[34]

While Fitzpatrick urges the archivist to keep copies of older representational tools for his or her own consultation, some archives openly provide these to researchers. The finding aid to the Roy Dikeman Chapin Papers at the Bentley Historical Library on the University of Michigan campus is a typical example of an evolutionary finding aid. There is no pentimento here. Multiple narratives are allowed to coexist, although their order gives some preference over others. Roy Dikeman Chapin was president of the Hudson Motor Car Company and briefly served as U.S. secretary of commerce, 1932–33. His papers arrived at the Bentley in several accessions. The earliest and largest acquisition occurred in 1940. Throughout the past sixty years, the Chapin papers have been represented by a variety of representational tools: two version of cards in the card catalog, two versions of the finding aid, and three versions of MARC records.

The earliest finding aid for the Roy Dikeman Chapin Papers is a twenty-seven-page document that begins with a half-page narrative description of the contents. The remainder of the finding aid is an inventory/calendar of selected letters, reports, and so forth. The selection criteria used to select these items is not stated. The selections are eclectic, and not all of the documents from any subject are fully identified. The descriptions of items are fairly terse, although the archivist did tarry long enough to judge a few as "interesting." The narrative itself also suggests the most fruitful research topics in the collection.[35]

This initial finding aid appears to be the source of the first set of catalog cards. On these catalog cards, the selection of materials on the finding aid was further pared down, and individual cards were typed with summary information for each item, organized by correspondent.

These cards, though, also contain other information, largely coded. The catalog cards contain the location information and the donor number(s). I say *coded* because although the call numbers are placed in the location on the card associated with call numbers, their format is unique. The other codes refer to donor numbers, which were not indicated on the first finding aid.

The current finding aid follows a modern form with which most archivists will be familiar. It is six pages, half of which contain contextual, authority, and descriptive data. The finding aid provides more detailed acquisitions information. Also, it provides a higher-order contextualization or summary of the materials, identifying and describing the overarching series schema. The remaining three pages provide brief descriptions on the box level noting the series and then the chronological period contained in each box. Neither finding aid has a specific authorial attribution, although the later finding aid notes that the collection was processed by the "Michigan Historical Collections staff." Other changes in the finding aid demonstrate dynamism in the collection: the inclusive dates have been changed and, accordingly, the physical extent or amount has increased.[36]

This modern finding aid is also the basis for other current representations of the collection: an EAD finding aid and MARC records in two separate bibliographic networks—the Online Computer Library Center (OCLC) and the Research Libraries Information Network (RLIN). The MARC records are similar, containing identical content, but the order of information elements varies. Ironically, one of the salient features of the scope note, the higher-level summarization of the papers into series, is missing from the networked bibliographic descriptions. The collection summary focuses on genre terms and the identities of correspondents. Contextual information is also absent: the detailed biography in the finding aid is replaced by a two-line synopsis of Chapin's crowning achievements. This creation of MARC records has also led to the re-creation of the new catalog cards. The original catalog cards were photocopied and inserted in the back of the finding aid. The new cards, though, lack the distinctiveness of the old cards. While correspondents are listed individually, each card is the same, with only the subject or correspondent's name changed at the top of the card.

The EAD finding aid also mirrors the paper or analog one but makes some small, but significant, modifications.[37] The series identification is partially separated from the scope and contents note, and this note begins with a global summary for the first time followed by the series descriptions. The series descriptions are repeated within the actual contents list. Copyright information is also included in this representation.

The guides to the Chapin collection do form a coherent whole. Each contributes some piece toward a better understanding of the Chapin papers. But, the representations also present different perspectives. Taken together one has the feeling of viewing something through different lenses: some providing broad aerial views, others small slices of information. What do researchers make of all this information about the Roy Dikeman Chapin collection? Do researchers appreciate the technologies and processes that resulted in those new cards in the catalog, the finding aid at the front of the binder, or the online EAD finding aid? Do they know they are looking at over half a century of archival technology, waiting there for them to discover/recover? Are all the representations valuable? Do they realize the representations refer to the same, albeit evolving, artifact?

Another form of archival pentimento asserts itself when collections are rearranged in an attempt to re-present the creator's original order. One example of this is the Alexander Winchell Papers at the Bentley Historical Library. Winchell, a professor of geology and paleontology at the University of Michigan and later chancellor of Syracuse University, meticulously arranged his records into 284 volumes that were numbered. The meticulousness with which he arranged and categorized things is apparent today in a volume documenting his library.[38] Winchell's order of his records, though, has long since vanished. An archivist originally reorganized the Winchell papers in the 1930s using size more than content or original order as a guide.[39] In 1940, abstracts of selected letters were completed.[40] In 1992, the collection was reorganized, and most of the original order was restored. Still, the collection is organized as much by form or material or genre as it is by Winchell's order. Ironically, or perhaps in a continued attempt to assert itself, many volumes continue to bear Winchell's numerical identification. Additionally, the 1992 finding aid features a concordance between the current box numbers and the 1930s imposed volume and folder numbers. As a result, the collection is encoded in both by the creator and then recoded or decoded by successive archivists.[41]

Rearrangement and representation by the archivist may also be a technological imperative. Archbishop of Cincinnati John B. Purcell's letters were apparently stored in an antique pigeon-holed case and arranged alphabetically. The name of the correspondent and the date were clearly marked on the back of each letter.[42] In

the process of archivalization this original order was represented to fit into the standard, sterile, technology of the archives—the document box. While representing the records in archival boxes is of course an administrative necessity and archivists eschew becoming curators of technology museums (either of past or future digital technological systems), this is a reminder of how archivists can alter representational systems and at the same time maintain the original order (in this case alphabetical). Representational and record-keeping systems are fragile and extend beyond order and organization and into the context of the creator, the creator's culture, and the technologies that bind them together.

Representational Systems

Representational artifacts (such as finding aids, inventories, and index cards) form larger representational schemata that are implemented in archives using a variety of technologies or tools. In the evolution of these technologies, archivists have moved through a number of different genres in attempting to discover (recover) the most appropriate representational systems for archival and manuscript collections. Archivists have employed card catalogs, calendars, shelf lists, finding aids, subgenres of finding aids encoded in Hypertext Markup Language (HTML) and Standardized General Markup Language (SGML)/extensible Markup Language (XML)/EAD, and finally derivatives of finding aids: MARC records to manage and to provide access to collections. Each of these represents a different technology and a different philosophical approach to privileging information, emphasizing information, and the level of granularity of the information. Steven L. Hensen discusses these forms and their inherent differences.[43] In spite of all of these genres of access tools, over the past twenty years the finding aid has emerged as the "canonical form" of archival representation in the United States. I explore two genres that have become increasingly interrelated: card catalogs and finding aids (and briefly touch on their associated subgenres and manifestations). These two genres of archival representational tools are both discussed because of their interconnections and, in some historical cases, dependency upon one another.[44]

Card Catalogs

Nicholson Baker laments the demise of card catalogs in libraries.[45] The aura of and intense feelings about these card catalogs appear to have permeated the culture. In 1990, artist David Bunn took possession of the two million cards in the Los Angeles Central Library's catalog. Last year, Bunn used the catalog cards to create installations of poems formed by juxtaposing the cards in different ways. In the words of one reviewer:

> He has paid loving attention to them ever since, embracing their physicality, age, and obsolescence. He spins poems from the titles running across the tops of the cards, honors the catalog's systemic order and succinct formality, and credits the catalog with personality, history, ideology, and even an unconscious.[46]

Richard J. Cox, Jane Greenberg, and Cynthia Porter, however, provide a broader perspective and examine card catalogs as an essential part of library history, particularly the history of the applications of technology in libraries.[47] Unlike libraries, many card catalogs in archival and manuscript repositories are still in use, although some have been totally replaced by and subsumed by cards generated through new technologies, as in the case of the Chapin papers. Studies are needed to examine the nature of card catalogs for manuscript repositories and archives and the social systems in which they were created.

The continuing relevance of using card catalogs in archives is apparent throughout the Houghton Library's handlist. Researchers are constantly directed to various card catalogs as a first step in gaining access to collections. For example, a note concerning the James Family Papers indicates that "all available aids must be used: catalogue cards, pink slips, and both new and old indexes."[48] Yet even this card catalog has changed over the years. As with most manuscript catalogs, cards originally represented individual items. Beginning in 1984, collection-level descriptions began to be prepared for large collections. At the same time, the practice of not assigning subject headings persisted. Cards were made for all correspondents and addressees as well as for selected genres of records (e.g., diaries). Interestingly these practices appear to have continued into the online public access catalog (OPAC) and its successor the integrated library system (ILS).

Richard C. Berner examined the relationship between card catalogs and finding aids in an attempt to identify archives with integrated descriptive systems. In a 1971 survey, he found little integration, only four out of forty-four respondents consciously used the card catalogs as an entry point (index) into the finding aids—although an additional sixteen respondents noted that the card catalog could be used that way. In conclusion, Berner notes "that function [an integrated index to the finding aids] of the catalog, however, seemed to have been discovered rather than preconceived." Apparently archivists' lack interest in reflecting on their representational artifacts and systems is not new.[49]

Finding Aids

Finding aids are the canonical form for current archival access for researchers. At the same time, they act as collection management tools for archivists.[50] They have achieved the status of a canonical form because they are the basis for other representations, such as MARC records and other various forms of networked information exchange (online finding aids).[51] In other words, finding aids are representations of archival records and papers that are in turn used as a basis for the creation of other, second-order representations. It is significant to note that even in the digital environment (such as in EAD), archivists treat the finding aid as a document genre rather than as a set of discrete data elements. One consequence of this focus on the finding aid as document genre has been the slow development of uniquely digital representations for archival representations. The concentration on finding aid as document rather than as one of many potential representations of discrete data elements has also led to problems of reusing archival data across the archival continuum and problems in the development of true collection management systems for archives.[52]

In the United States, finding aids have evolved throughout the twentieth century. In the past twenty years, the pace of this evolution has quickened. In this evolution, the information elements within finding aids that facilitate access (historical or biographical information, scope and contents notes, series descriptions, subject analysis) as well as those that support collection management (accession information, processing attribution, call numbers) have emerged and are now somewhat standardized. Still, the creation of finding aids, and with it the promise or potential of access, is inherently a political act. In order to better understand the underlying social systems behind finding aids, four aspects are explored: creation, construction, components, and consequences.

Creation of Finding Aids
There are several aspects of creation that appear to be most salient. The first is authorship and with it authority. The second is that just as the finding aid as a genre is evolving, individual finding aids themselves evolve, and

this can be traced through their fluid authorship. Finding aids are dynamic documents. A third point is the relationship between creation and access.

The relationship between authorship and authority of finding aids is critical for both archivists and researchers. Many finding aids lack overt attribution. However, this cannot be taken to be an indication that they lack authority. Since they act as both collection management and access tools, finding aids embody several different types of authority. For archivists, the finding aid contains authority control data. For example, the biographical or organizational history note is the authoritative source for quick summary information on institutional entities and individuals. For researchers, the presence and placement of the finding aid in the archives is an implicit sign of authority. Additionally, for researchers, the finding aid is the most (although not necessarily a good) authoritative source of knowledge about a collection. Are finding aids worthy of this vesting of authority? Exactly what is the nature of this authority?

The most immediate source of this authority is the author. Authorial influence and attribution of finding aids deserve greater attention. Richard J. Cox, among others, has argued that appraisal decisions should be attributed.[53] His arguments also apply to finding aids. Attribution and perhaps even the addition of the authors' biographies is essential contextual information for researchers in evaluating the authority and perspective of the finding aid. The dynamism of finding aids (and the underlying collections that they represent) can also be traced through the authors. For example, the Rensis Likert finding aid at the Bentley Historical Library indicates its authors over time: "Thomas Powers, 1975; Avra Michelson, 1982; Brian Williams, 1990; and Mike Brostoff, May 1995."[54] In this case, the authors should not be viewed as a group of disparate individuals simply adding descriptions of materials to an existing finding aid but as an intellectual tradition.

The distributed networked environment has resulted in distributed authorship. Now two separate archivists can claim authorship: one for the original analog representation of the finding aid and another for the second-order representation, the EAD finding aid. Interestingly, the second-order author may be more visible. In the case of the Trotsky Collection at the Hoover Institution on War, Revolution and Peace at Stanford University, the finding aid notes that the collection was generically "Processed by: Hoover Institution Staff" but "Encoded by: Hernán Cortés."[55] Encoding finding aids is not always a routine matter. Information is moved around, as-

sumptions are made about administrative as well as descriptive information, and other liberties are taken with the original text and structure of the finding aid.[56]

Another confounding element concerning the creation of finding aids is that although archivists like to think that they are the sole creators of finding aids, they are not. For example, the Trotsky Collection, compiled by the Socialist Workers Party and now housed at the Hoover Institution, contains a guide to the letters by Leon Trotsky in the Exile Papers section of the Leon Trotsky papers at Harvard University.[57] Interestingly, there is more information concerning this correspondence available through the Hoover Institution than through Harvard University. A number of alternative indexes to records in the Vatican Archives have also been published. Some of these have met with the blessing of the archives staff, while others have not.[58] What drives the creation of these competing metanarratives or finding aids? Is it a desire for more detailed information? Is it the desire to liberate information?

Construction of Finding Aids

Finding aids did not always look the way they do today. Thirty years ago, now familiar information, such as scope and contents notes and biographical and historical data, was absent. Finding aids were extended inventory lists that detailed folders, and often items. The representational goal was the explication of the arrangement. Currently, entirely different information elements are emphasized. Proportionally, biographical and historical sketches and contents notes can take up more space than the folder listing. This addition of the historical and biographical notes signals the emerging emphasis on representing context. Both the access and the collection management data now represented in finding aids support this change. Likewise, the inclusion of scope and contents notes and series descriptions demonstrates two trends. One trend is the rise of more global or collection-level synthesis of collection contents. The second trend is characterized by the decreasing granularity of the contents descriptions. Instead of item-by-item lists, the contents are represented by an inventory of boxes or folders, with a genre designation and broad dates of materials in the folder. One could argue that the granularity and specificity have moved from the contents list to the front matter (e.g., biography, donor information, and restrictions), where one may find details of the provenance of the records.

The origins of the trend toward more front matter and less granularity are unknown. I posit several interconnected hypothesis. First, the trend reflects a closer adherence to provenance and with this the requirement of understanding that the evidential context of the records is essential for establishing authority of the source. This may be the result of the increased professionalization of the archival community in terms of identifying a theoretical base and more organized educational opportunities. Second, archivists have had the realization that to manage a greater volume of records, item-level description was no longer feasible. Finally, the historical trend of examining the "underclass," or those not often individually documented in records, may have also played a role in more collection-level rather than individual descriptions and more functional and provenancial representations of records.

Components of Finding Aids

The dynamism of finding aids is also visible in their components. Users can see changes in understanding of the collections, new interpretations of the records, and new information on papers emerging out of the finding aids. A few examples from the Bentley Historical Library include everything from a reevaluation of provenance to the addition of both physical details and information about the records to an existing finding aid. For instance, the Udvandrerarkivet, Aalborg, Denmark, became the Aalborg universitetscenter, Danske Udvandrerarkiv. In the Russell Barnes finding aid, a death date was added, the volume increased, and a second accession required the addition of a "+Mrs." to the donors' area. These later accessions are literally penned or written in within the existing contents listing of the finding aid and appear to be "interleaved" with the earlier like materials. The William Lawrence Clements Papers contains penciled-in notes that there are "Photographs in Box 3," and at the end of the collection an additional pointer leads to further papers of Clements in the Clements Library. The Paul Lincoln Adams Collection originally noted that the collection was restricted. This has been crossed out, and a note "Restrictions lifted on 11-26-90" is penned below. In one case, a space for the final date of the papers to be donated has purposefully been left blank for the John D. Stevens Papers. Thus, the archivist anticipated changes and almost expected to amend the finding aid. While these examples may seem inelegant in our age of word processing and obsessive formatting, enabling the researcher to view these changes is important. Having version control of finding aids helps archivists to visualize the growing understanding of their collections and to see the convergences among and within collections. As we move more aggressively into the digital domain, examining means of making this evolution trans-

parent is important. Otherwise, these notes will be simply overwritten when changes are made and the evolution of the records and their surrogates will be obliterated.

Consequences of Finding Aids

As noted in this essay, finding aids are the basis for second-order representations of archival collections: MARC records and HTML- and SGML/EAD-encoded finding aids. The development of EAD and its relationship to finding aids is the most critical event in the evolution of finding aids to date. There are two related aspects of this convergence between the technology of the finding aid and the technologies of networked information exchange that I find disturbing. First, I fear that the evolution of finding aids will slow as the costs are weighed of changing the networked archival information. Second, finding aids have now become technologically bound (or perhaps technologically unleashed?), but their form relies on an older, and some would argue obsolete, analog document genre. This inhibits creative use of networked information and the emergence of new digital representational forms for the representation of primary sources. In the second case it is not only evolution that is impeded but innovations in access and in the structuring of archival work. If the encoding process is seen as an add-on at the end of the descriptive process it will not lead to reenvisioning archival representation in light of new technologies. Third, the implementation of initiatives such as EAD and MARC entails the adoption of standards and best practices. While standards can promote increased consistency and create platforms for increased information exchange and easier retrieval, there are downsides to these initiatives. Formalized standards are very difficult to change, and as these standards become ingrained in the education of new generations of archivists, it will become increasingly difficult for archivists to envision new ways of practice.

> The information that gets stored is at best what can be stored using the currently available technology: the encyclopedia came to mirror the affordances of its technological base. In this process, people naturalize the historically contingent structuring of information; they often begin to see it as inevitable.[59]

Finding aids also represent the convergence of collections management and access systems. The increasing number of components that support managerial functions in the finding aid over time indicates that, on some level, archivists are thinking about collections management when creating finding aids. The breaking out of an "administrative information" section in EAD finding aids supports this claim. Archival access tools have always won out over collections management tools, and as a result, archivists have tried to recover managerial functions within these access tools. The fit has not been good, and the structures created for access are not always hospitable to administrative functions. But until a technology that represents collections management information is created, descriptive representational systems will serve these two (sometimes contradictory) purposes.

Conclusions

The structuring of representation practices by creators, archivists, and systems enables or inhibits the meanings of representations as they cross boundaries of space (creator to archives), time, and use. In terms of creators, representational artifacts contain a substantial amount of information concerning the institutional, professional, and cultural structures in which they were created. When they are taken out of their original milieu, however, context is lost. Transferring or translating context into the archival realm is also problematic because archivists embed records into additional macrostructures (perhaps more precisely identified as the information architectures) of overarching classification schemes as well as into the microstructures of card catalogs and finding aids. In turn, the maintenance and creation of these structures form the basis of ongoing routines, interactions, behaviors, and knowledge that comprise archival organizational memory and practice. The archival representations, then, demonstrate not only the evolving physical collections and intellectual understandings of collections but also changing perspectives on collection arrangement, description, and management. Each successive representation and representational system builds on its predecessors, recovering what was judged valuable in a given temporal and cultural context, incorporating or discarding what was deemed essential or not, respectively. More recent representational systems have been built around digital technologies, such as MARC and EAD. These have hastened the process of stabilizing the forms and standardizing the data elements in archival access tools. The great benefit of these technologies has been the exchange of archival information among other archives as well as researchers. Yet, the full costs and benefits of the structural effects of these evolutionary developments are not yet known.

Archival representation processes are neither objective nor transparent. As such, archivists need to be more conscious of the activities that structure the creation of representations, their social construction, as well as their appropriate uses. Archival representations speak not only about the collections for which they act as surrogates but also about archival practice and archivists. The Egyptian invocation at the beginning of this essay, which one archivist deemed appropriate to include in a finding aid, may have been as much a reflection on the archival content being described as on a particular representation being constructed. Because of their ubiquity, it is these representations that may be the most enduring evidence of the archivist and by these "writings cause him to be remembered in the mouth of the reciter."

NOTES

This essay was first published in *Archival Science* 3, no. 1 (2003): 1–25, and is reprinted with permission.

The epigraph for this essay is the invocation at the beginning of the Kelsey Museum of Ancient and Mediaeval Archaeology Archives finding aid, University of Michigan.

1. Donald Norman, *The Design of Everyday Things* (New York: Doubleday, 1990).

2. I refer to the archival function most commonly known as *arrangement and description* as *archival representation*. I think this better characterizes the actual outcome of the archivist's work and also signifies how the output should be viewed.

3. Elin K. Jacob and Debora Shaw, "Sociocognitive Perspectives on Representation," *ARIST* 33 (1998): 146.

4. John Roberts, "Archival Theory: Much Ado about Shelving," *American Archivist* 50, no. 1 (winter 1987): 66–74.

5. Terry Cook, "Fashionable Nonsense or Professional Rebirth: Postmodernism and the Practice of Archives," *Archivaria* 51 (spring 2001): 32. Cook is quoting Stuart Sim's *Derrida and the End of History* in this passage. Other authors who have questioned archival narratives and texts, although not particularly in the area of archival representation, are Brien Brothman, "The Pasts That Archives Keep: Memory, History, and the Preservation of Archival Records," *Archivaria* 51 (spring 2001): 48–80; and Eric Ketelaar, "Archivalisation and Archiving," *Archives and Manuscripts* 2, no. 2 (May 1999): 54–61.

6. Leonard Rapport, "No Grandfather Clause: Reappraising Accessioned Records," *American Archivist* 44, no. 2 (spring 1981): 143–50.

7. Judith Endelman, "Looking Backward to Plan for the Future: Collection Analysis for Manuscript Repositories," *American Archivist* 50, no. 3 (summer 1987): 340–55.

8. Dennis Meissner, "First Things First: Reengineering Finding Aids for Implementation of EAD," *American Archivist* 60, no. 4 (fall 1997): 372–87. See also Patricia Cloud, "RLIN, AMC, and Retrospective Conversion: A Case Study," *Midwestern Archivist* 11 (1986): 125–34.

9. Eric Ketelaar, "Tacit Narratives: The Meaning of Archives," *Archival Science* 1 (2001): 131–41.

10. Henry James Collection, Houghton Library, Harvard University, http://hcl.harvard.edu/houghton/ (accessed January 2001). This reference is no longer online.

11. Ketelaar, "Tacit Narratives," 139.

12. See Margaret Hedstrom, "Descriptive Practices for Electronic Records: Deciding What Is Essential and Imaging What Is Possible," *Archivaria* 36 (autumn 1993): 53–63; and Wendy Duff, "Will Metadata Replace Archival Description? A Commentary," *Archivaria* 39 (spring 1995): 33–38.

13. This idea is derived from Stephen R. Barley, "Technology as an Occasion for Structuring: Evidence from Observations of CT Scanners and the Social Order of Radiology Departments," *Administrative Science Quarterly* 31 (1986): 78–108.

14. Anthony Giddens, "The Constitution of Society: Outline of the Theory of Structuration," Berkeley, University of California, 1984. The idea of structuring, or structuration, originated with Giddens. The idea is that community members (in this case archivists) create processes and artifacts that contain embedded meanings for that community. Change in these processes and artifacts can be deliberate or inadvertent as members work to maintain the processes as well as the community surrounding these activities.

15. Hanne Albrechtsen and Elin K. Jacob, "The Dynamics of Classification Systems as Boundary Objects for Cooperation in the Electronic Library," *Library Trends* 47, no. 2 (fall 1998): 293.

16. Chris Hurley, "The Making and the Keeping of Records: (1) What Are Finding Aids For?" *Archives and Manuscripts* 26, no. 1 (May 1998): 71–72.

17. Rosalind McKittrick, *Carolingians and the Written Word* (New York: Cambridge University Press, 1989).

18. Peter Burke, *The Social History of Knowledge: From Gutenberg to Diderot* (Malden, MA: Polity Press, 2000), 81–115.

19. Eviatar Zerubavel, *The Fine Line: Making Distinctions in Everyday Life* (Chicago: University of Chicago Press, 1991), 5.

20. Geoffrey Bowker and Susan Leigh Star, *Sorting Things Out: Classification and Its Consequences* (Cambridge, MA: MIT Press, 1999), 266

21. Nicholas B. Dirks, "Colonial Histories and Native Informants: Biography of an Archive," in *Orientalism and the Postcolonial Predicament: Perspectives on South Asia*, ed. Carol A. Breckenridge and Peter van der Veer (Philadelphia: University of Pennsylvania Press, 1993).

22. The *Catholic Archives Newsletter* ran stories in January and July 1982 documenting the use of archives in the redrafting of constitutions.

23. Sr. Mary Clarita Hudson, CPPS, and Sr. Mary Linus Bax, CPPS, (Salem Heights Archives) *Archival Policies and Procedures* (Dayton, OH: Sisters of the Precious Blood, 1992), pages unnumbered.

24. James M. O'Toole, "What's Different about Religious Archives?" *Midwestern Archivist* 9, no. 2 (1984): 94–95.

25. Finding aid for the Ford Motor Company Archives, n.d., Henry Ford Museum and Greenfield Village Research Center, Dearborn, Michigan.

26. Barbara Kwansik and Tom Malone, "How Do People Organize Their Desks: Implications for the Design of Office Information Systems," *ACM Transactions on Office Information Systems* 1, no. 1 (January 1983): 99–112.

27. Brien Brothman, "Orders of Value: Probing the Theoretical Terms of Archival Practice," *Archivaria* 32 (summer 1991): 84.

28. Bowker and Star, *Sorting Things Out,* 82.

29. The difficulty of transcending time and space in reference mediations is also treated in Elizabeth Yakel, "Thinking inside and outside the Boxes: Archival Reference Services at the Millennium," *Archivaria* 49 (2000). Brothman, "Memory, History, and the Preservation of Records," 79, also makes this point when he discusses the difference between simple access and access over time and the need for archivists to transcend both physical and intellectual barriers to accomplish this.

30. J. C. Fitzpatrick, *Notes on the Care, Cataloging, Calendaring and Arranging of Manuscripts,* 3rd ed. (Washington, DC: Government Printing Office, 1928), 4.

31. Houghton Library, *Manuscripts and Drawings: A Handlist of Finding Aids with a List of Published Guides* (Cambridge, MA: Harvard University, 1985), 5. Hereafter cited as *Handlist*. Also available online, http://hcl.harvard.edu/houghton /departments/msdept/handlist.html#list.

32. Houghton Library, *Handlist,* 5.

33. Houghton Library, *Handlist,* 5.

34. Fitzpatrick, *Notes on the Care, Cataloging, Calendaring and Arranging of Manuscripts,* 4.

35. Roy Dikeman Chapin finding aid, n.d., Bentley Historical Library, University of Michigan.

36. Michigan Historical Collections Staff, Roy Dikeman Chapin finding aid, n.d., Bentley Historical Library, University of Michigan.

37. Roy Dikeman Chapin finding aid (EAD version), Bentley Historical Library, University of Michigan, http://www .hti.umich.edu/cgi/f/findaid/findaid-idx?type=simple&c=bhl &view=text&subview=outline&id=umich-bhl-851435 (last checked March 12, 2002).

38. Library Catalogue, 1852, box 15 (formerly v. 233), Alexander Winchell Papers, 1833–91, Bentley Historical Library, University of Michigan.

39. Leonard A. Coombs, Alexander Winchell finding aid, June 1992, Bentley Historical Library, University of Michigan, i.

40. Alexander Winchell Collection, twenty-seven sample entries, March 22, 1940, Bentley Historical Library, University of Michigan.

41. Leonard A. Coombs, Alexander Winchell finding aid, June 1992, Bentley Historical Library, University of Michigan. The EAD version of the finding aid is available at http://www.hti.umich.edu/cgi/f/findaid/findaid-idx?type= simple&c=bhl&view=text&subview=outline&id=umich -bhl-86321 (last checked March 12, 2002).

42. Don H. Buske, "The Historical Archives of the Chancery of the Archdiocese of Cincinnati," *Ohio Archivist* (spring 1997): 3.

43. Steven L. Hensen, "The Evolution of Archival Description," *American Archivist* 60, no. 3 (summer 1997): 284–96.

44. Richard C. Berner, "Manuscript Catalogs and Other

Finding Aids: What Are Their Relationships?" *American Archivist* 34, no. 4 (October 1971): 367–72.

45. Nicholson Baker, "Discards," *New Yorker,* April 4, 1994, 64–86.

46. Leah Ollman, "Relics of the Material Age," *Art in America* 88, no. 11 (November 2000): 134–39.

47. Richard J. Cox, Jane Greenberg, and Cynthia Porter, "Access Denied: The Discarding of Library History," *American Libraries* (April 1998): 57–61.

48. Houghton Library, *Handlist,* 18.

49. Berner, "Manuscript Catalogs and Other Finding Aids."

50. The hypothesis that archival finding aids are both access and collection management tools is not discussed in detail here.

51. Steve Hensen, *Archives, Personal Papers, and Manuscripts,* 2nd ed. (Chicago: SAA, 1992).

52. I differentiate between the Australian records continuum and the archival continuum. By *archival continuum* I mean to focus on the archival administrative activities and functions vis-à-vis records. This does not mean only activities that occur once the records are transferred into the physical archives or even into a distributed custody arrangement.

53. Richard J. Cox, "Archival Anchorites: Building Public Memory in the Era of the Culture Wars," *Multicultural Review,* June 1998, 59.

54. Thomas Powers, Avra Michelson, Brian Williams, and Mike Brostoff, Rensis Likert finding aid, 1975–95, Bentley Historical Library, University of Michigan.

55. Hoover Institution, Register of the Trotsky Collection, 1917–80, http://www.oac.cdlib.org:80/dynaweb/ead/hoover/reg_190/@Generic__BookView;cs=default;ts=default (last checked March 12, 2002).

56. Meissner, "First Things First." Meissner discusses the need to reengineer finding aids because encoders were spending time synthesizing and looking for information. Encoders for the Historic Pittsburgh Project at the University of Pittsburgh also did a substantial amount of data manipulation and in some cases made very far-reaching assumptions about the intent of the author of the finding aid.

57. Hoover Institution, Register of the Trotsky Collection, 1917–80, http://www.oac.cdlib.org:80/dynaweb/ead/hoover/reg_190/@Generic__BookView;cs=default;ts=default.

58. One example is P. Pecchiai, "Le carte de fondo 'Corsica' nell'Archivio vaticano," *Archivio storico di Corsica* 9, no. 4 (1933): 3–7.

59. Bowker and Star, *Sorting Things Out,* 107–8.

PART III

Archives and Social Memory

The diverse essays included in this section take up complicated questions about the role of archives in conditioning social memory and creating certain kinds of cultural understandings. The complex relationship between social memories and elements of social culture is itself a growing area of concern in the fields of history, literature, anthropology, and social psychology. Not surprisingly, the relationship between archives and social memory provoked lively discussion among scholars in all of these fields at our interdisciplinary seminar. At its core, the question involves a set of issues that bear directly on understandings of what is a record, what is record keeping, and ultimately what is an archive.

Consider perhaps the most basic issue here: the significance of written records themselves. To what extent does the value of these records, as they are acquired, preserved, and administered by archival institutions, rest on cultural assumptions and conditions? To what extent, in other words, does archiving reflect particular social structures and cultural conventions that assign meaning to knowledge itself and the ways it is accessed? In his essay "The Historical a Priori and the Archive," Michel Foucault has famously argued that even the positivist implications of language give a particular kind of authenticity to archived documents. From this perspective, the written word itself is coveted as a direct link to past reality, whether it is "discovered" by the scholar in some archive folder or viewed like the U.S. Declaration of Independence and Constitution in hermetically sealed display cases. Yet as Foucault also maintains, the kind of authenticity embedded in written documents not only reflects particular (and most would say, very sensible) cultural conventions but also tends to obscure the possibility—Foucault would say likelihood—that the documents were created and retained in most "unscientific" ways. Can we therefore agree that in either case, the "written-

ness" of most archival documents affects what is and can be remembered, and how?[1]

The notion that archives may play a critical role in the formation of social or collective memories is neither familiar to many archivists nor well understood by many historians. As a construct, memory is much broader than history. This is not simply because archivists decide through the processes of appraisal "what is remembered and what is forgotten, who in society is visible and who remains invisible," as Canadian archivist Terry Cook suggests in his essay in this volume, but also because the notion that social memories can be shaped so directly undermines established notions of historical "truth": the cultural assumptions about what counts as knowledge. As we will see in part IV of this volume, these assumptions, or archival "truth claims," as Ann Stoler calls them, have had a particularly strong effect on colonial archives of various sorts but concern all archives in every social or cultural context. For example, one point raised early in the seminar was that the archival profession itself in North America and Western Europe has had a significant investment in maintaining the notion that archival documentation embodies particular kinds of truth: ones that can be referenced and hence "verified," ones that are at least partly, in other words, created by the real and symbolic capital of archival institutions themselves.[2] At stake here are not only the epistemological issues discussed in part II but also the ways in which the monumentality of many state and national archival buildings registers cultural assumptions of their meaning. The impressive classical colonnade of the U.S. National Archives links what is housed there to the foundations of Western learning. The imposing marble facade of the Soviet Party Archives once bespoke the power of an ideology and a state system whose authority was not to be questioned. This is not to suggest that the documents in either place are necessarily fabricated or otherwise "false" (although they certainly could be) but instead to argue that they reflect broad cultural assumptions about where one needs to go to find the "truth" of the past and how it should be presented.

Scholars will not ordinarily complain to archivists about having only some fraction of the documents they need to tell their stories when they think the materials have not survived; they also usually accept restrictions based on generally recognized principles of national security or individual privacy. Yet social and cultural conventions clearly compromise claims to access the past as it "really was." As we know, archivists routinely exercise great power over what documents are preserved. Cook argues that when the "true past" is understood as contingent on the archivist, the objectivity game is exposed as fundamentally flawed. Whether or not this has created the "willful blindness" about how social memories are constructed that Cook thinks affects both historians and archivists, there can be little doubt that modern memory is, to some significant degree, archivally dependent and formed. To what degree, however?

Pierre Nora thinks modern memory is "above all, archival," as Cook indicates.[3] Similar assumptions underlay the admirable Canadian effort to create "total archives," as Laura Millar describes. The "total archive" was conceived as bearing responsibility not only for government records of recognized historical value but also "for the collection of historical material of all kinds and from any source which can help in a significant way to reveal the truth about every aspect of Canadian life."[4] Here, social memory was seen as a essential element of national identity, whose multiethnic or multicultural elements must therefore be reflected in archival collections. Former International Council on Archives president and national archivist of Canada Jean-Pierre Wallot has called archives "houses of memory" whose keys access a continuously rerooting past.[5] Even if one accepts these premises, the question remains of what should and should not be included in the archived "totality." The physical bulk, the weight of processing, the enormity of cataloging, even the uncertain line between "artifact" and "ephemera" make the "total archive" concept, however noble, difficult to really conceive, let alone implement.

David Lowenthal clearly dislikes the idea of "total archives." He dismisses what Cook, Verne Harris, and other archival theorists called at the seminar (and elsewhere) this postmodern approach to the archives/social memory question. Lowenthal calls it a distortion of the archives' "canonical" role. By invoking the notion of "canon,"

Lowenthal distinguishes what he regards as essential to collective memory and national identity from what he regards as the substantively uncertain elements of heritage. He wants a more formal collective remembering based on a historical science devoted, at least in principle, to commonly acceptable truths. He argued at the seminar that the result of current changes in archival holdings, access, and repute is, among other consequences, the attrition of historical awareness. He argues that while some observers may laud today's flood especially of electronic data as heterogeneous and multivocal (as well as accessible, reproducible, and disposable), "these benefits, if such they be, come at a heavy cost: the loss of an enduring social framework grounded in an abundance of shared cultural references."

Readers skeptical of this view will want to pay close attention to Patrick Wright's, Joan van Albada's, and Alessandro Portelli's essays in this section. While selecting and placing artifacts and documents in glass cases is a deliberate effort to frame social memory, a more powerful process can also take place in quite different and even random ways, as Wright shows in his lively discussion of Britain's "traditional" red telephone booths. The "petrified spirit of the welfare state itself" hiding "against rough weather" in the "old red box" clearly evoked a spirit, a set of cultural values, and even the mentality of public good and public service that even the most competent historians might have difficulty teasing from archival documents.

Are memories formed in this way less legitimate—which is to say, less historically accurate—than those cultivated by archives? The president of the International Council on Archives, van Albada, also regards the archive as a cultural phenomenon that goes beyond textual associations inherent in fundamental archival terminology. He emphasizes, however, archival terminology and the ways its different meanings and purposes are themselves culturally bound. Van Albada argues that archivists must reach beyond the accepted definitions, which form boundaries that are inherently Western and confining. He calls for a broadening of definitions of archival terminology to encompass archival needs of nonscript societies. Millar, too, worries that huge quantities of historically valuable materials, especially those of groups such as Canada's indigenous First Nations, will be excluded from social memory and historical understanding because of text-based archival terminology and definitions.

Wright and Millar also point implicitly to another important issue in the links among archives, memory, and popular culture: the fact that memories are and should be contested media in which historical pasts are both made and remade in constant interaction with all sorts of new facts and stimulations. Documents and artifacts may give meaning to memories, framing them in historical contexts and giving them narrative form, but it is important to think about how memories shaped in this way relate to lived experience and what sort of arguments are being brought to bear to tame the chaos of remembered experience into the order of historical understanding. One might argue, in other words, that archives do and should serve a socially healthy purpose precisely in stimulating rather than flattening this contestation, since contest itself is a vital element of any search for truth. Here in slightly different form is another argument not only for the centrality of archives in the formation of memory but also for the importance to this effort of what Millar describes as "multivocality."

Not surprisingly, multivocality is one of the qualities of oral archives that so intrigue Portelli, a distinguished Italian scholar. Like others at the seminar, Portelli takes a broad view of the "memory problem," recognizing its connections to sources outside the traditional purview of archives. While this can be seen as reinforcing the need for specialized repositories like the Holocaust Museum in Washington, D.C., or the German-Jewish archives in Berlin and New York Frank Mecklenburg discusses elsewhere in this volume, it also points to the need to recognize the centrality of the nontraditional in archival acquisition more generally as well as in accessing and examining social memory.

Portelli is therefore also concerned with absences in traditional archives and the ways they affect a society's capacity to remember. For him, what is most important about the tape recorder is that it gives voice to those whom archives tend to silence. It thus disrupts the categories and hierarchies that engender silence. In this way, oral historians not only access the meaning of certain kinds of memory, facilitating in the process the formation of both individual and social identities, but also contribute with their sources to the creation of documents. Rather than demean oral testimony as a form of documentation, however, as one sometimes hears in arguments against including oral materials in traditional archives, direct interactions with a source give historians at least the opportunity to probe for clarity even in memory's most murky waters. Indeed, the obvious methodological traps in oral history tend to make its practitioners far more alert to the problems of their work than is often the case with traditional archival historians.

Such self-consciousness is in particularly short supply, moreover, when it comes to the memory of famous historical actors. Here the reliance on specially archived materials often induces researchers to reflect particular kinds of social myths and hence to give social memories particular kinds of cultural meaning. The final essays in this section, by Robert Adler, William Joyce, and Judith Endelman, take up these issues as they relate to U.S. presidential libraries and especially to the memory of John F. Kennedy. Joyce explores the work of the Assassination Records Review Board; Adler details the controversy between the Kennedy Library and a private collector of Kennedy memorabilia; and Endelman, a principal curator at The Henry Ford, looks closely at the social and cultural meaning of the Kennedy limousine.

What is particularly interesting in Joyce's discussion of the Assassination Records Review Board in this regard is that the board was established on the political assumption that the release of restricted documents would finally end the controversy about the Kennedy assassination. Yet the tens of thousands of released pages did not—indeed, could not—make the record "complete." Many agencies continued to withhold materials, including the President's Foreign Intelligence Advisory Board, whose existence the review board discovered only late in its work, and the Kennedy Presidential Library, which refused access to the presumably important papers of the president's brother, Robert F. Kennedy, including those from his tenure as attorney general. The board itself proved less open to scrutiny, however justified the reason, by sealing the records of its closed meetings until 2017. Not surprisingly, the board concluded its work without finding any documentation that would definitively answer the questions that constituted its original charge, giving rise in some minds not to the reasonable assumption that there were none but to the counternotion that had brought the board into being: that the truth about the assassination remained concealed in the records.

Adler, a prominent Washington attorney, based his essay on his work with a private collector of Kennedy memorabilia. Adler describes an extensive pattern of maneuvering by the Kennedy Presidential Library to control his client's use of Kennedy artifacts. Adler argues that the pattern of concealment resulted as much or more from the Kennedy family's desire to create and preserve a particular way of remembering the president and his brother as from a desire to conceal particular kinds of information. The fascinating story Adler describes of the presidential library's challenges to materials held in private hands seems to have had little to do with the actual historical value of documents and artifacts the collector possessed, which the library had ignored for years, but instead to have emanated from the collector's desire to do with them what he wished. Controlling JFK's mementos and records was a way of controlling what uses could be made of "his" past, how the former president was and could be remembered.

This is not a problem unique to the American presidential library system. As Paule René-Bazin shows in part IV, major figures in the French political establishment have also shown a reluctance to submit records to the control of the archives. These complex issues of control of the papers of public officials are not just a matter of politics—though politics are important—but also a matter of shaping memory and defining legacy. In her essay on the Kennedy car and the Lincoln chair, Endelman asks whether "all objects tell the truth" and are therefore "essential to the study of history." Her sensible answer, which she shares with Gaynor Kavanagh,[6] is that material objects, along with some kinds of documents, "trigger" emotions and memories—that is, culture-bound forms of accessing familiar stories about the past—whether or not they are grounded in "true" histories of the subject.

The variety of approaches taken by seminar participants to the roles archives may play in evoking or otherwise conditioning social memories are well reflected in the essays that follow. They are certain to stimulate further discussion.

NOTES

1. Michel Foucault, *The Archaeology of Knowledge* (New York, 1972), esp. pt. 3, chap. 5, "The Historical a Priori and the Archive."

2. See the discussion of these questions by seminar participant Elizabeth Kaplan, "We Are What We Collect, We Collect What We Are: Archives and the Construction of Identity," *American Archivist* 63 (2000): 126–51.

3. As cited in John R. Gillis, ed., *Commemorations: The Politics of National Identity* (Princeton, 1994), 15.

4. Laura Millar, this volume, citing W. I. Smith, *Archives: Mirror of Canada Past* (Toronto, 1972), 9–10.

5. Jean-Pierre Wallot, "Building a Living Memory for the History of Our Present: Perspectives on Archival Appraisal," *Journal of the Canadian Historical Association* 2 (1991): 282, as cited by Terry Cook, this volume.

6. Gaynor Kavanagh, "Objects as Evidence, or Not?" in *Museum Studies in Material Culture*, ed. Susan M. Pearce (London, 1989).

Remembering the Future

Appraisal of Records and the Role of Archives in Constructing Social Memory

Terry Cook

Appraisal occurs primarily today on the records of yesterday to create a past for tomorrow. What kind of past should the future have? This essay represents in part a narrative about archival appraisal, that function that selects for long-term preservation as society's memory roughly 1–5 percent of the total documentation of major institutions and considerably less from private citizens. In keeping with the internationalism of these seminars, which featured voices from many countries, this essay is perhaps more a postmodern story from Canada than an exposition of appraisal strategy and criteria or a detailed critique of various other narratives (schools of thought?) about appraisal.

Appraisal imposes a heavy social responsibility on archivists. As they appraise records, they are doing nothing less than shaping the future of our documentary heritage. They are determining what the future will know about its past, which is often our present. As a profession, we archivists need to realize continually the gravity of this task. We are literally creating archives. We are deciding what is remembered and what is forgotten, who in society is visible and who remains invisible, who has a voice and who does not. In this act of creation, we must remain extraordinarily sensitive to the political and philosophical nature of documents individually, of archives collectively, of archival functions, of archivists' personal biases, and especially of archival appraisal. That process defines the creators, functions, and activities to be included in archives by selecting which documents become archives and thus enjoy all subsequent archival processes (description, conservation, exhibition, reference, and so

on) and, just as starkly and with finality, which documents are destroyed, excluded from archives, forgotten from memory.

Appraisal is thus central to the archival endeavor—indeed, it is the *only* archival endeavor, a continuing activity without end, the heart of archives. And it is controversial. Pioneering archivists and some writers still believe that appraisal is unarchival, wrenching records from their original context of creation. For the majority of archivists, who recognize the necessity of selecting some part from an unmanageable whole, differences abound on the principles or concepts (or theories) that should animate appraisal or that define the "value" or "significance" or "importance" of records—all terms used in archival legislation and by archivists, usually without definition or reflection. "What makes the good?" the Greeks long ago asked. What makes something have value, be worth preserving and remembering? Not surprisingly, without clear first principles, the resulting strategies and methodologies have achieved no consensus.

Both parts of this essay's title, "Remembering the Future: Appraisal of Records and the Role of Archives in Constructing Social Memory," might alarm, even frighten, many archivists and indeed historians and other users of archives. Both halves are contrary to archival orthodoxy. Both clash with the stereotype of the archivist's widely accepted role in society. Archivists remember the past, not the future. They deal with history, not current or future events. They do not construct social memory—that is the role of historians and other users of the archive who, through their works, create the stories and narratives, the myths and memories, that underpin our collective identities. Archivists are rather a kind of invisible bridge, or honest broker, between creators and users of records. Archivists are guardians of the past, not its interpreters. Archivists are in the preservation business, not the memory one.

Indeed, until the 1980s, archivists, at least in Canada, often described themselves—proudly—as "the handmaidens of historians." In retrospect, that phrase is astonishing for its servility and its gender connotations. Until recently, women remained largely invisible in social and historical memory, relegated as the silent and usually unrecognized supporters of male accomplishment; so too, archivists have remained invisible in the construction of social memory, their role also poorly articulated and rarely appreciated. I might go further and say that just as patriarchy required women to be the subservient, invisible handmaidens to male power, historians and other users of archives require archivists to be neutral, invisible, silent handmaidens of historical research.[1] I will return to this point later in the essay.

My message is simple. Archivist are active agents in constructing social and historical memory. In so doing, they have an obligation to remember or consider the needs and expectations of the future as much as to conserve or remember the past. Furthermore, in so doing, archivists must reflect society's "values" rather than those of prominent sponsors or traditional users and must leave a transparent account of the reasons why keep/destroy decisions were made. And historians and other users of archives need to engage in this archival process rather than deny it, as has heretofore largely been the case.

My approach here (and to appraisal) is consciously postmodern. My colleague at the University of Manitoba, Tom Nesmith, has written that especially for those of us inheriting the British empirical tradition,

> one of the key things that Western philosophy has sought to marginalize or "efface" is the "sign" or means of communication. . . . [T]his indicates a desire for "pure presence without representation" or a clear understanding of reality without much consideration of the effects of communication processes on what we know. . . . This effacement of the sign has made archives a "ghost" or all but invisible in the knowledge creation process, and thus society.[2]

Along this same line, Patrick Geary, a historian of medieval European memory and a previous participant in these seminars, labels as "Phantoms of Remembrance"

those scribes and clerics who helped to shape the medieval record through their little-noticed archival activities, ensuring thereby "memory and oblivion" for the events and figures of their times.[3] Concerning such translucent "ghosts" of archives, Jacques Derrida counsels that we must recognize and learn how to live "with the ghost . . . how to talk with him, with her, how to let them speak or how to give them back speech." To make the invisible visible once more, to make the inarticulate articulate, "we must speak," Derrida says, "to the ghost."[4] So, especially in archival appraisal, we take a journey with these archival memory phantoms.

Let me expand a little (in I hope a not irrelevant aside) my assertion that archivists remain shadowy ghosts to most historians and other users. Scholars are just lately beginning to see that notions of the objective or "invisible" archive were reinforced by nineteenth-century historians undertaking what they assumed (hoped?) was objective, scientific history in the von Rankean mode. By definition, that required in turn a neutral, impartial, objective, "natural" archives. Yet this blindness toward the ghosts of archives (or their invisibility) continues well past the often-shared origins of the two professions in the 1800s.

In the past decade or so, a tremendous outpouring of historical writing has concerned memory, how societies chose to commemorate the past, the institutions and symbols that individuals and groups create to reinforce their identity, power, and status in the present. These works range from analyses of historic sites to war memorials, from plaques and markers to public commemorations and holidays, from theater, music, and films to cemeteries, antiques, preserved ruins, even Disneylands and similar pieces of organized nostalgia and heritage tourism. And with rare exceptions, these authors all have one thing in common: they are silent about the role of archives as memory institutions or the function of archives and archiving in society—despite the fact that national, state, and local archives were being created and then defined and shaped at the same time as many of the institutions and movements and celebrations about which such historians write. (The shining exception to this rule are the medievalists, including Michael Clanchy, Patrick Geary, and Jacques Le Goff.) We have a growing shelf of books by historians that analyze the founding, evolution, and animating values of nineteenth- and twentieth-century museums, art galleries, and libraries, even zoos—all institutions engaged in and reflecting the social constructions of cultural memory. Yet as of the turn of this century, no books did the same for archives. Invisible ghosts indeed. In the wake of Derrida's landmark volume (published in English in 1996), this has finally begun to change—as these Sawyer Seminars witness—at the level of journal literature and conference papers. Why?

There is more to this invisibility, this ghostly archive, surely, than mere oversight or historians' kindly trust that archivists go about their business in a responsible way. My former National Archives colleague, Brien Brothman, asserts that historians are collectively—if maybe subconsciously—afraid to venture into this area. This exclusion of archives from historians' consciousness—archives as process and as institution and as records—is, Brothman believes, "a peculiar form of disciplinary repression or blindness."

Symptomatic of this blindness is historians' relegation of discussion of archival sources to the margins—to introductions, prefaces, postscripts, or footnotes or endnotes—rather than the integration of them into the text, as is the convention in almost every other social science discipline. Brothman wonders if this may in fact be a "blindness of insight," an unconscious recognition by historians that "the distancing, the spacing, between archives and history" is essential to the "empowering" traditional discourses of both professions. Without this distance, he continues, "the differentiation between the archival object (the record or document, the artefact) and the historical object (the book, the article, knowledge [of the past]) begins to break down; archives and history begin to transgress each other, pollute each other." He notes that Canadian historian Susan Mann has mused, in reviewing A. S Byatt's *Possession,* that "the traditional distinctions between fact and fiction, literature and history had become 'decidedly blurred.'" She might have added, between archives and history and myth and reality. This blurring frightens both professions as they have traditionally been defined—history working on the edges of archives, archives working on the edges of history, each threatened, if moving too closely together, in Brothman's phrase, by canceling "out the purity of each other's intentions, each other's object[ivity]." That assumes the traditional view for both professions that objectivity is possible.[5]

Brothman's insights seem to be borne out inadvertently by the major scholar on that question, Peter Novick. In his influential book, *That Noble Dream: The "Objectivity Question" and the American Historical Profession,* Novick manages, over 629 pages of text, not to mention the role or impact of archives or of the archival choosing and subsequent (re)arrangement and description of histo-

rians' source material as having any influence whatsoever on the question of objectivity.[6] Perhaps if for historians the archive needs to be natural, objective, neutral, invisible, in terms of its holdings, then the whole question of how the stuff actually gets in the archive must surely be beyond the pale. A leading Canadian historian, Joy Parr, graphically illustrates this point. In a reflective essay in the *Canadian Historical Review,* she cautions historians that historical interpretation begins not when they write their texts but long before, when they open boxes in archival reading rooms.[7] In those archival boxes, historians choose to read only certain files, to scan only certain images or posters or maps, to focus only on certain authors or groups or regions, to take notes regarding or to photocopy only certain documents. Historians then impose on these chosen, privileged documents a further limitation of a particular narrative and interpretative framework. Actually, the picture is considerably more stark than Parr paints. The major act of historical interpretation occurs not when historians open boxes but when archivists fill the boxes, by implication destroying the 98 percent of records that do not make it into those or any other archival boxes. This is the great silence between archivists and historians. It is called archival appraisal.

In terms of archives and the future—the "remembering the future" part of my title—let me cite the well-known words of Canadian National Archivist Sir Arthur Doughty, who said in 1924, in a phrase that appears on posters and mugs found in many Canadian archivists' offices as well as on the base of the only statue ever raised officially in Ottawa to honor a civil servant, "Of all national assets, archives are the most precious. They are the gift of one generation to another, and the extent of our care of them marks the extent of our civilization."[8] I focus less on Doughty's archival "assets"—the actual records that form the foundation of American or Canadian studies in a multitude of disciplines—than on Doughty's notion of "care" and his concept of archives as a "gift" to the future. What do archivists do to records—how do they "care" for them, and, perhaps most importantly, how do they choose which archives to place under such "care"? How do they fill Parr's boxes that historians encounter in the reading rooms of a nation's archives? What knowledge and skills are required to do this? What is the collective nature of this "gift" of memory communicated across generations with various technologies? How does the present choose the past by which the future will "know itself"? And in so doing, has Canada developed approaches that are distinctive and perhaps informative to those who practice archiving elsewhere?

Another Canadian national archivist and past president of the International Council of Archives, Jean-Pierre Wallot, has set the inspiring goal for archivists of "building a living memory for the history of our present." The resulting "houses of memory," in his words, will contain the "keys to the collective memory" that the world's citizens can use to open doors to the personal and societal well-being that comes from experiencing continuity with the past, from a sense of roots, of belonging, of forming various identities.[9] In the rootlessness of the wired global community, in the mobility that undermines extended families and oral traditions, where the speed of life makes yesterday recede quickly into the distant past and tomorrow approaches with so much uncertainty, French historian Pierre Nora responds by asserting that "modern memory is, above all, archival. It relies entirely on the materiality of the trace, the immediacy of the recording, the visibility of the image."[10]

Here there are clear resonances with Marshall McLuhan's and especially Harold Innis's pioneering Canadian work on the history and theory of communications technology from the late 1940s to the late 1960s—long before the postmodern revolution arrived in the English-speaking world. In a long series of historical works, Innis demonstrated the importance of recording media and the technologies of communication in forming and maintaining empires, all of them based on monopolies of knowledge, that allowed for the exercise of power over space and time. All such media have built-in biases in their communication, Innis asserted, leading to his famous student Marshall McLuhan's aphorism that the "medium is the message."[11] Archives are the material traces of just such media, the concrete fragments that form our memories, the way we conquer time across generations, as Doughty said, the way our society legitimizes and memorializes itself, the way we influence the future by shaping the past. What then, in Innis's phrase, are the "biases" of archives as a collective communication medium between the past and the future?

To address if not definitively answer these questions, I will explore the Canadian archival voice, especially in appraisal, and its broader ramifications for international archiving, but I first will discuss archivists' traditional thinking about archives—probably the views held by most users of archives if they were to think consciously about the institutions in which they do their research. I will then look at radically new formulations about archives—what might be called the "postmodern archive"—and suggest

why Canada has taken a lead in its articulation, especially in appraisal. I will then briefly conclude by suggesting that Canadian distinctiveness in this area has global significance in our new century of networked communications, where the realization of McLuhan's "global village" threatens to homogenize all distinctiveness into a universal blandness.

Traditional archival theory and professional practice was first articulated in nineteenth-century Europe, after centuries of informal development, and then was exported around the world, including to the United States, Canada, Australia, and South Africa.[12] This development paralleled the emergence of history as a university-based discipline and profession. Most of the early professional archivists were trained as historians at such universities.

Just as much of the early professional history focused on the political, legal, and economic character of the nation-state, so too were the first articulations of archival principles strongly biased in favor of the state. Almost all the classic tomes about archival methodology were written by staff members of national archives. Not surprisingly, most focused on government, public, or corporate records and their orderly transfer to archival repositories to preserve their original order and classification, and most relegated private and personal archives to the purview of libraries and librarians. Indeed, to this day, archives in Europe generally look after only the official records of their sponsoring governments, while national or regional or university libraries take custody of personal manuscripts. That tradition remains strong in most other English-speaking countries, although not in Canada.

Moreover, these early archival writers lived in an era of document scarcity, where their experience was based on dealing with limited numbers of medieval documents susceptible to careful diplomatic analysis of each page or with records found in well-organized departmental registry systems of the emerging modern nation-state, existing within stable, centralized administrations exhibiting classic Weberian hierarchical structures. Most completely ignored the appraisal and selection of modern archives as these terms are now understood; indeed, such activity by archivists was strongly discouraged as "unarchival." Clearly influenced by Darwinian thinking and metaphors, the pre-1930 archival pioneer thinkers asserted that records coming to archives from state departments were a kind of natural, organic residue left over from administrative processes. Archivists then kept this residue in pristine order in the archival building. Indeed, archivists in Britain were called "keepers," reflecting that earlier mind-set.

State officials rather than archivists would therefore decide which records would survive by a process of natural winnowing the wheat from the chaff according to administrative and political needs. The records themselves were viewed as value-free vessels reflecting the acts and facts that caused them to be created. Archivists kept the records, in the words of one early theorist, "without prejudice or afterthought" and were thus viewed—indeed, extolled—as impartial, neutral, objective custodians. A pioneering writer with enormous influence even asserted that the archivist is "the most selfless devotee of Truth the modern world produces." And notice it is *Truth* with a capital *T*.[13]

Such traditional approaches sanctioned archives' and archivists' already strong predilection, as state institutions and employees, to support mainstream culture and powerful records creators. Such approaches privilege the official narratives of the state over the documented stories of individuals and groups in society or, indeed, their interaction with and influence on the state. The rules for evidence and authenticity so adopted favor the textual documents from which such rules were derived at the expense of other media for experiencing the present and thus of viewing the past. The positivist and "scientific" values permeating such thinking prevented archivists then and since from adopting and then documenting multiple ways of seeing and knowing. Archivists seek or reimpose an original order rather than allowing for several orders or even disorders to exist among records and thus in their descriptions. Researchers are instead presented with a well-organized, rationalized, monolithic view of a record collection that may never have existed that way in operational reality. And this traditional view seriously hobbles archivists trying to cope with the new technology of electronic records, where archivists' active intervention up front in the processes of record creation rather than passive receipt of records long thereafter is the only hope that today's computer-based history can be written tomorrow. Moreover, the volumes of modern paper records and the electronic record require the archivist to appraise records to choose the typically 1 or 2 percent that will be designated as archival; this active construction of select fragments of the past into social memory is of course completely at odds with the earlier notion of archivists as passive keepers of an entire body or residue of records handed over by their creator. An even greater absence of order or system is apparent in the record-keeping habits of private individuals and organizations.

In addition to these alterations in recording technologies, a marked change has occurred over recent decades in the reasons why archival institutions exist—or at least public and publicly funded archives (self-funded private business archives do not share fully in these developments). A collective shift has taken place during the past century from a juridical-administrative justification for archives grounded in concepts of the state to a sociocultural justification for archives grounded in wider public policy and public use. Simply stated, it is no longer acceptable to limit the definition of society's memory solely to the documentary residue left over (or chosen) by powerful record creators, whether Richard Nixon or Oliver North, Soviet commissars or state police in apartheid South Africa, Canadian military officers in Somalia or doctors working with tainted blood products for Health Canada, Queensland politicians or Tokyo Olympic Games organizers. Public and historical accountability demands more of archives and of archivists.[14]

As a result, Canadian archivists working in publicly funded institutions have begun to think in terms of documenting the process of governance, not just of governments governing.[15] "Governance" includes cognizance of the dialogue and interaction of citizens and groups with the state, the impact of the state on society, and the functions or activities of society itself as much as the inner workings of government structures. The archivist in appraisal and all subsequent actions should focus, this argument goes, on the records of governance, not just on records of government, when dealing with institutional records. This perspective also better complements the work of archivists dealing with personal papers or private "manuscript" archives. I will return to this point.

These various changes make archivists active mediators in shaping the collective memory through archives. Because of the need to research and understand the nature of the functional and structural context in which records are created and in which the record-keeping and media-generating processes take place and because of the need to interpret records' relative importance as the basis for modern archival appraisal and description as well as for making choices for preservation, exhibitions, and Web site construction, the traditional notion of the impartial archivist is no longer acceptable—if it ever was. Archivists inevitably will inject their personal values into all such activities and thus will need to examine very consciously their choices in the archive-creating and memory-formation processes, and they will need to leave very clear records explaining their choices to posterity. The ghosts must become flesh and blood.[16]

In this rethinking of the traditional state-centered and positivist framework for archives, and substituting a distinctively postmodern alternative in the ways I have suggested, Canadian archivists have led the way internationally. I would estimate that at least 75 percent of the world's English-language publications on the postmodern archive have been written by Canadians.[17] Perhaps it is fair to say that the fiercest opposition to the postmodern archive also comes from Canada. This is not surprising because postmodern archivists have repeatedly challenged five central principles of the traditional archival profession.

1. Archivists are neutral, impartial custodians of "Truth," managing records according to universal, value-free theories.
2. Archives as documents and as institutions are disinterested by-products of actions and administrations.
3. The origin or provenance of records must be found in or assigned to a single office rather than situated in the complex processes and multiple discourses of creation.
4. The order and language imposed on records through archival arrangement and description are value-free re-creations of some prior reality.
5. Archives are (or should be) the passively inherited, natural or organic metanarrative of the state.

Some of these generalizations about postmodern archives are supported by a growing literature on the history of archives as well as the wave of philosophical writing appearing in journals since the late 1990s—as noted earlier, since the publication of Derrida's *Archive Fever*—all showing archives to be extremely problematic as loci for memory. Historians are at last discovering the historicity of the archive. Maybe more archivists will soon follow. The tone of this work is well set by historian Jacques Le Goff, who notes that "the document is not objective, innocent raw material but expresses past society's power over memory and over the future: the document is what remains." What is true of each document is true of archives collectively. By no coincidence, the first archives were the royal ones of Mesopotamia, Egypt, China, and pre-Columbian America. The capital city in these and later civilizations becomes, in Le Goff's words, "the center of a politics of memory" where "the king himself deploys, on the whole terrain over which he holds sway, a program of remembering of which he is the center." First the creation and then the control of memory leads to the control of history and thus mythology and ultimately power. Feminist scholar Gerda Lerner also convincingly demonstrates that such power lay be-

hind the first documents, the first archives, and the subsequent formation of societal memory and that it was remorselessly and intentionally patriarchal: women were delegitimized by the archival process in the ancient world, a process that continued well into the twentieth century. During the first major event of the French Revolution, the storming of the Bastille and its rural counterparts in 1789, the Parisian mob was not trying—motivated by ideals of liberty, equality, and fraternity—primarily to free prisoners but rather was intent on destroying the king's tax and feudal land records housed in the old fortress to eliminate evidence of outstanding public debt and servitude. Many other examples are now coming to light (more than a few in papers presented at the Sawyer Seminars) of archives collected—and later weeded, reconstructed, even destroyed—not to keep the best juridical evidence of legal and business transactions, as traditionally supposed in archival mythology, but to serve historical and sacral/symbolic purposes for those figures and events judged worthy of celebrating or memorializing within the context of their time.[18] But who is worthy? And who determines worthiness? According to what values? Historical research, in summary, suggests that there is nothing neutral, objective, or "natural" about the process of remembering and forgetting.

Why have Canadian archivists taken this distinctive lead in reconceptualizing the archive? I think the influence of McLuhan and Innis cannot be discounted; their concerns with nonprint media, communications technologies, and the biases they carried in shaping past civilizations as well as our own are insights that were consciously transported to the world of archives and how records and media shape the past. Hugh Taylor, a disciple of McLuhan and a leading Canadian archivist of the 1970s and 1980s, fundamentally influenced a whole generation of young archivists.[19] I think too that the same generation of now senior archivists trained as historians that is doing this writing in Canada saw, through the study of the history of records, the central French and English dualism of Canada, and its multicultural and First Nations (or aboriginal) layers what the United Nations has declared to be the most ethnically diverse country in the world; thus, these archivists perceived early on the existence of different stories, mixed narratives about and multiple interpretations of similar past events and even the same past texts, that generated doubts about "Truth" and objectivity in recorded memory. Not just history but the recording of it was filled with diversity and ambiguity.

A second contributing factor, complementing the first

and in some ways its workplace manifestation, is the "total archive" approach. Canada alone of First World nations has developed at the national level the total archives approach, where almost all public archives in the country—national, provincial, territorial, municipal, university, and regional—acquire as part of their mandate, within one archival institution, a total archive of roughly equal extents of both public, government, or sponsoring institution records and related private-sector records and to take into their archives the total record in every recording medium (including film, television, paintings, and sound recordings, which in many countries are divided among several other repositories). In effect, the separated European and American and Australian public archives and historical manuscript traditions are combined inside one institution. Although there are many reasons why total archives evolved in Canada since the nineteenth century, this integration of the public and private reflects the same wider vision of archives I've just mentioned, one sanctioned in and reflective of society at large, of the total historical human experience, rather than limited to a view of archivists solely as the custodians of official state records.[20] If Canadian philosopher and novelist John Ralston Saul is right that during the 1840s Canada invented the first postmodern nation, respecting diversity, complexity, and a culture of minorities rather than a monolithic national myth, then perhaps it is only natural that Canada has also invented the postmodern archive.[21]

This Canadian approach to archives has manifestations in working reality beyond just the total archives orientation; it is more than an academic exercise in theoretical or postmodern redefinition. And nowhere is this more evident than in new approaches to archival appraisal.

In the early 1990s, the National Archives of Canada developed the concept, strategy, and practice of "macroappraisal" to select the 1 or 2 percent of government records that have enduring value as archives from among all the documentation created in thousands of information systems in tens of thousands of offices. The National Archives did so within the total archives policy umbrella and postmodern cultural ethos.

Macroappraisal finds sanction for archival "value" of determining what to keep and what to destroy not in the dictates of the state, as is traditional, or in following the latest trends of historical research, as has been more recent practice, but in trying to reflect society's values through a functional analysis of the citizen's interaction with the state. But macroappraisal is about more than just functional analysis, which is what some other coun-

tries have mainly drawn from the Canadian model. Macroappraisal focuses on the functions of governance rather than the structures or activities of government per se, emphasizes the interactive functioning of citizen and group as much as that of the state, encompasses all media rather than privileging text, searches for multiple narratives and hot spots of contested discourse rather than accepting the party line, and deliberately seeks to give voice to the marginalized, to the "other," to losers as well as winners, by looking anew at case files especially and electronic data. Then, based on such research analysis, macroappraisal chooses the most succinct record in the best medium for documenting these phenomena. Macroappraisal is especially helpful—essential—for appraising electronic records.

All societies (including the archivists residing in them) assign greater or lesser value to different dimensions of the three-way interplay of social structures, societal functions, and citizens and groups. This interplay is how society functions. And what is important is the process of interplaying rather than the three separate entities per se. And in turn, such value assignment to particular socialfunctional phenomena will determine, when this insight is transformed into an appraisal model, which related records are declared to be archival or which are not. Macroappraisal theory posits that archivists may determine such societal values by specifying the generic functional attributes and points of special intersection, conflict, or interplay among the creators of records (that is, structures, agencies, actors); sociohistorical trends and patterns (that is, revealed through functions, programs, activities); and clients, customers, citizens, or groups on whom both function and structure impinge and who in turn influence both, directly or indirectly, explicitly or implicitly. Macroappraisal theory explores the nature of these agents and acts and the interconnections or interrelationships between them and assigns greater importance, or "value," to certain functional-structural factors than to others. This is why it is known as "functional appraisal." Because the functional context of creation and contemporary use determines value, macroappraisal is a provenance-based approach. Because it looks first at functions rather than records, it has been called a "topdown" approach. The fact that appraisal has traditionally focused on the value of records has led this approach, which focuses first on the value of functions, to be called "macroappraisal." To get people thinking—or just to stir up trouble—I have often said of this approach to appraisal value determination that although archivists have traditionally appraised records for eventual use by researchers, archivists should neither appraise records nor try to anticipate their use.[22]

Macroappraisal gives strategic priority to functions and work processes at the top, not to recorded products or records emerging at the bottom from those functions and processes. I hasten to add that "top-down" relates to a functional decomposition methodology, not to administrative hierarchy or to an assumption that records at the top created by the elite inherently carry more value. Corporate and governmental practices have long used such functional strategic thinking (as opposed to theoretical concepts), and it is evident today in business system analysis and system design in the world of computers, in current interest in business process reengineering and government restructuring, as well as increasingly in records management file classification and indexing and financial and human resource planning and measurement systems. And so, I thought back in 1989, why not also consider its applicability in archival appraisal? Macroappraisal, then, represents a congruence of theory and strategy.

The macroappraisal strategic approach has its greatest value precisely on this point. The reasoning behind the macroappraisal approach is simple enough to state. Institutions have certain formal or internally developed functions assigned or sanctioned by democratic societies; in this way, institutions are a filter for societal trends, activities, needs, and wishes, for the things and concepts that society values. For these assigned functions, the institutions articulate various subfunctions and sub-subfunctions, which are allocated to different administrative structures or offices, each with a mandate to perform or implement such a function, part of a function, or perhaps parts of several functions. These offices in turn create various programs and activities to meet their functional mandates, some continuing, some short term and temporary, which in turn lead to specific actions and individual transactions between the functional office and the citizen, organization, or group in society. For the efficient operation or delivery of these transactional interactions, information systems are built. Citizens, clients, groups, companies, and associations interact with these functions and structures, programs and activities, and, depending on the latitude and flexibility allowed for this interaction, in turn shape, challenge, and modify these programs to varying degrees. Of all these steps and processes, the record itself is the final evidence within those information systems of all these acts and transactions and of citizen/societal interactions. This means that the contextual milieu in which records are created—what I have called their conceptual rather than their physical provenance—

is determined by all these factors: functions, subfunctions, sub-subfunctions, structures, programs, activities, actions, transactions, and client interactions as well as records-creating processes, systems, and technologies. By focusing archival research on analyzing—that is, "appraising"—the importance of manageable numbers of these functions, programs, and activities rather than on appraising billions of records or tens of thousands of systems, series, and collections, the archivist can see the whole forest rather than just a few trees. Seeing the whole context ultimately means that poorer and duplicate records are more easily identified and eliminated and that the most succinct, precise, primary record in the best medium for a particular function is more readily targeted (or "appraised") for archival preservation. In short, macroappraisal strategy shifts the initial and major focus of appraisal from the record to the functional context in which the record is created.

Using such knowledge gained by an institutional functional analysis, the main appraisal questions for the archivist are not what has been written (or drawn, photographed, filmed, or automated), where it is, and what research value does it has. Rather, based on this kind of functional-structural decomposition or analysis, the key appraisal questions are (1) what functions and activities of the creator should be documented (rather than what documentation should be kept?) and (2) who, in articulating and implementing the key functions, programs, and transactions of the institution, would have had cause to create a document, what type of document would it be, and with whom would that corporate person cooperate or interact in either its creation or its later use? These questions beg a third—really the most important—appraisal question: which records creators or "functions" (rather than which records) have the most importance? Conversely, and just as important from the total archives perspective, which functions are poorly documented in institutional records and must be complemented or supplemented by private manuscripts, other archival media, oral history projects, and nonarchival documentation (publications, "gray literature," buildings, inscriptions, monuments, museum and gallery artifacts, and so on), none of which are necessarily collected by archivists—or at least by institutional or corporate archivists. Only after these questions are answered can archivists target realistically the records or series of records likely to have greatest potential archival value.

After the macroappraisal is completed and the series or classes or systems or collections of records are before archivists for appraisal, traditional appraisal criteria can be applied where greater granularity is necessary or desirable. Such criteria are used to refine further the value of individual records or small groupings or series of records within the theoretical-strategic functional-structural matrix. Political, technical, legal, and preservation issues are also considered at this point. Known research uses may also be considered—at this final stage only, not driving the process. If the strategy is called macroappraisal, these record-related criteria constitute microappraisal. Such microappraisal criteria involve assessing such factors as age; uniqueness; aesthetic, intrinsic, or symbolic value; time span; authenticity; completeness; extent; manipulability; fragility; duplication; monetary value; and usefulness. Such appraisal criteria are certainly used now in the daily work of archivists and are well articulated in our literature; thus, no more need be said about them here.

Macroappraisal in Canada occurs at three levels: first, between all the various institutions or records creators or functions falling under the collection jurisdiction, mandate, or acquisition policy of an archives; second, between the various functional programs of a single institution or records creator; and, finally, between the various functions and activities of a single program or function within that creator—all using various criteria for assessing the importance of functions to institutions' mandates. For a macroappraisal strategy to work based on functional weighting, we found that a whole new relationship between the archives and government agencies was needed to implement what we termed a planned approach to records disposition. This established that records disposition must proceed in a logical manner, that records-creating agencies must be ranked and then approached in priority order, that formal negotiated disposition plans using project management methodology must be in place, and that each appraisal project must proceed comprehensively across a function, not in small administrative fragments, not medium by medium, not (at least at first) by looking at a few isolated examples of records in a few subregistries, and not (as is usual) in response to the latest space crisis in some part of the creating department. We also asked some hard questions about basic past assumptions regarding assigning or approving retention periods for nonarchival records and about focusing on passive records-destruction approvals rather than active archival targeting.[23]

Macroappraisal requires a firm commitment by the archives to research by its archivists and transparency to the future concerning its decision making. Choosing the best records requires extensive research by archivists—several months' worth for a large functional appraisal project. I will conclude by focusing on these two corollaries of macroappraisal—research and transparency—since the complexity of research by archivists is sometimes not well understood, thus making it easier to dismiss its importance when defining educational standards or employment competencies and since, given the "blindnesses" referred to previously, more transparency and accountability is evidently required so that we can see what we are doing and so that others can see and hold us to account. More germane to this volume, getting inside such research (even if by generalizations rather than concrete examples) reveals the degree to which archivists subjectively construct the past through appraisal.

To identify the small archival portion from the immense larger records universe, archivists undertake original research to discover the historical and contemporary functions and structures and key individuals that may be considered either representative of the whole or, conversely, special or outstanding in some way. Within governments, corporations, or the larger society, these functions, structures, and individuals are always changing and evolving over time and space, and archivists need through their research to identify and evaluate these changing trends. Archivists do this research in advance of general published historical knowledge because to produce such knowledge, historians depend in part on archivists' prior work. After appraisal and acquisition targets are developed based on this research, additional research into the history of the targeted individuals, groups, associations, communities, and institutions is required to determine which records in the most appropriate medium will best document that individual or institution's activities, including interaction with other individuals, groups, and institutions. Research into communication patterns and the nature and characteristics of recording media is required, as is research into organizational culture and information systems. New insights from organizational theory suggest that the functional-structural-transactional framework that underpins macroappraisal will need to be expanded to include new insights into how radically changing networked organizations work, including how formal memory products such as documents and records and filing and record-keeping systems interact with or exist sometimes entirely separate from informal but effective organizational memory strategies and learning systems and how these in turn are affected by different managerial styles, collaborative workplace discourses, and social networks that increasingly are recognized as animating organizational behavior.

This complex array of contextual factors of both traditional and new organizational theory will naturally influence the nature of the records being created and thus become factors that the archivist must research carefully to determine the significance or value of the records of a particular organization or creator or function or activity or citizen interaction.

The macroappraisal approach spends very little time researching and assessing historical themes or the latest trends in historiography and trying to match these to the kinds of records chosen (or appraised) as archival. That was the approach developed by archivists in the United States in the 1940s and copied pretty much worldwide when archivists perceived that the old Darwinian approach of taking custody passively of natural residues designated by administrators was untenable in an age of bureaucratic expansion and voluminous paper records. This was a major step forward from the older passive approach, attempting to perceive the trends and values important to society, if through the filter of academic historians, as the animating force in appraisal rather than leaving the selection of records to the processes and whims of their creator. But setting appraisal or memory values based on past, present, or anticipated historical research use patterns is fraught with conceptual and practical problems. This does not mean that macroappraisal should not be pragmatic or should result in records chosen not being useful. It does mean that archival appraisal, for all its subjectivity, requires a defendable intellectual framework rather than following the shifts of the academic marketplace "moved by the changing winds of historiography."[24]

As a second corollary of macroappraisal, in addition to this extensive research into the records' context, these research results must be made transparent to the future. We archivists must remember the future. We must allow ourselves to be held accountable by revealing the research-based and personal suppositions on which keep/destroy decisions have been made. We must agree that we will be wrong in some appraisal decisions, that posterity needs to know why we left them the memory legacy that we did.

Perhaps our ghostly invisibility as archivists exists in part because our clients do not know what we do in terms of authorizing the widespread destruction of sources of possible use to them. Might archivists generally have been very lucky, except for our colleagues at the U.S. National Archives and Records Administration, in escaping close public and legal scrutiny of our appraisal decisions? Might that be because the transparency and accountability for which our profession increasingly calls among record creators is not something that we practice very well ourselves—in terms, for example, of making very widely known our appraisal choices, the reasons for them, and the research documentation supporting those choices? Do we even have well-articulated reasons for those choices? Why do we think researchers, especially in this postmodern environment, are interested only in descriptions of the records already in our archives—our well-researched illuminations of the scope, content, and creator context of "our" records—but not in the reasons why we have those particular records and not others?

For government and institutional records, I propose that we place negative entries in our record group inventories, providing researchers with a description of all the series and collections in all media that we did *not* acquire from a particular record creator alongside the ones we did acquire and the appraisal reasons why decisions were made both to acquire and to not acquire. I think we should link all our series in descriptive inventories to the extensive, research-based appraisal reports, recognizing that some long-standing open-ended series may be acquired over several decades based on different appraisal decisions or reasoning by different archivists. More stark yet, I propose that appraising archivists should be documented with a vita on file, complemented by biographical and autobiographical details of their values used in appraisal. For private-sector or thematic archives, I think we should provide the equivalent evidence of our choices—perhaps lists of all the possible individuals, groups, and associations falling within the collecting mandate of our institution, as researched and considered by the archivists, contrasted with the much smaller list of those collections or fonds appraised as archival and acquired—and explanations of why those choices were made, using what criteria, based on what concepts of value or significance, employing what methodologies, by which archivists, reflecting what personal and professional values.

Because we do not generally make such information on our thought processes available, assuming that we even have articulated them to our own satisfaction, researchers see only a predefined universe—predefined by the archivist, among others. What they see is what they get. They do not see what we saw as archivists before the appraisal decisions were made to give them what they get. This perhaps explains why archives, unlike galleries and museums, have generally escaped the culture wars and why our construction of societal memory via appraisal—and subsequent archival actions—so far remains unchallenged, even (as I suggested earlier) ignored. Is what we archivists do so unimportant? Or is it invisible, unknown, inarticulate? Do we shun the challenge of public scrutiny? And if so, why? The ghosts of archives apparently still haunt us. There needs, in short, to be a better integration of the archivist (the subject) with the records (the object) in memory narratives.

Can this Canadian archival distinctiveness contribute internationally in the twenty-first century? Is there a future for the postmodern archive? I believe the quick answer is yes, and on several levels. If there are benefits of the Canadian way of diversity, ambiguity, tolerance, and multiple identities in John Ralston Saul's postmodern state, then the Canadian parallel way of remembering via macroappraisal, of approaching the creation and preservation of memory in archives, might well speak strongly to the world's citizens concerned in this new century about the homogenizing and globalizing bias of the new media and record-creating technologies. Those desiring to construct archival memory based on celebrating difference rather than monoliths, multiple rather than mainstream narratives, the personal and local as much as the corporate and official, may find in Canada's distinctive approach to appraising archives some useful perspectives and tools for their task.

Steven Lubar, a specialist in the culture of information technology for the Smithsonian National Museum of American History, reminds us that "we must think of archives as active, not passive, as sites of power, not as recorders of power. Archives don't simply record the work of culture; they do the work of culture."[25] Words such as *culture* and *power* are not neutral, but then, neither are Doughty's descriptions of archives as "precious assets" or the greatest gift across generations of our "civilization." What kind of gift to "civilization" or "culture" does this generation of archivists wish to make? How do archivists want the future to remember them as they construct a past for that future? The answers rest with how we conceive of, set strategies for, develop criteria concerning, implement in practice, and then document our decisions in archival appraisal.

NOTES

The heart of this essay was a paper presented at the Sawyer Seminars. Portions of the text have appeared elsewhere; other portions appear here for the first time.

1. On the invisible or marginalized role of women in the historical enterprise and implicitly in the archival one, see Bonnie Smith, *The Gender of History: Men, Women, and Historical Practice* (Cambridge and London, 1998). See also Gerda Lerner, *The Creation of Feminist Consciousness: From the Middle Ages to Eighteen-Seventy* (New York and Oxford, 1993), esp. chap. 11, "The Search for Women's History"; Anke Voss-Hubbard, "'No Documents—No History': Mary Ritter Beard and the Early History of Women's Archives," *American Archivist* 58 (winter 1995): 16–30.

2. Tom Nesmith, "Still Fuzzy, but More Accurate: Some Thoughts on the 'Ghosts' of Archival Theory," *Archivaria* 47 (spring 1999): 150 n. 18.

3. Patrick J. Geary, *Phantoms of Remembrance: Memory and Oblivion at the End of the First Millennium* (Princeton, 1994). Michael Kammen refers to the *Mystic Chords of Memory* as the main title of his book on the creation of American tradition, memory, and a usable past (New York, 1991).

4. Nesmith, "Still Fuzzy," 149.

5. Brien Brothman, "The Limits of Limits: Derridean Deconstruction and the Archival Institution," *Archivaria* 36 (autumn 1993): 205–20.

6. Peter Novick, *That Noble Dream: The "Objectivity Question" and the American Historical Profession* (Cambridge, U.K., 1988).

7. Joy Parr, "Gender, History and Historical Practice," *Canadian Historical Review* 76 (September 1995): 354–76.

8. Arthur Doughty, *The Canadian Archives and Its Activities* (Ottawa, 1924), 5.

9. Jean-Pierre Wallot, "Building a Living Memory for the History of Our Present: Perspectives on Archival Appraisal," *Journal of the Canadian Historical Association* 2 (1991): 282.

10. Pierre Nora, as cited in John R. Gillis, introduction to *Commemorations: The Politics of National Identity*, ed. Gillis (Princeton, 1994), 15.

11. See Harold A. Innis, *The Bias of Communication* (Toronto, 1951); Harold A. Innis, *Empire and Communications* (Oxford, 1950). For interesting commentaries about McLuhan in terms of memory and communications, see Patrick H. Hutton, *History as an Art of Memory* (Hanover, Vt., 1993), 13–17; Paul Levinson, *Digital McLuhan: A Guide to the Information Millennium* (London, 1999). For a new assessment of Innis in light of postmodern sensibilities, see Charles R. Acland and William J. Buxton, eds., *Harold Innis in the New Century: Reflections and Refractions* (Montreal and Kingston, 2000).

12. See Terry Cook, "What Is Past Is Prologue: A History of Archival Ideas since 1898, and the Future Paradigm Shift" *Archivaria* 43 (spring 1997): 17–63. At the risk of facing charges of self-promotion, I believe this may be the best place to start for nonarchivists wishing to explore the history and evolution of archival thinking generally in the English-speaking world and in particular for Canada, and the assertions of the following paragraphs are documented in this article as well.

13. Sir Hilary Jenkinson flourished in Britain's Public Record Office during the first half of the twentieth century and wrote the first major English-language text of archival theory and practice, *A Manual of Archive Administration* (London, 1922; rev. 2d ed. 1937; reprint 1968). For a discussion and citations, see Cook, "What Is Past," 23–26.

14. This paragraph reflects my central argument in "What Is Past." See also Eric Ketelaar, "Archives of the People, by the People, for the People," *South Africa Archives Journal* 34 (1992): 15–26, reprinted in Eric Ketelaar, *The Archival Image: Collected Essays* (Hilversum, 1997). For a new volume of case studies of the critical role of records and archives in underpinning public accountability in democracies, see Richard J. Cox and David A. Wallace, *Archives and the Public Good: Accountability and Records in Modern Society* (Westport, Conn., and London, 2002).

15. See Ian E. Wilson, "Reflections on *Archival Strategies*," *American Archivist* 58 (fall 1995): 414–28. For archivists merely (and meekly) to do what they think their government sponsors want regarding institutional records or what archivists think will please these sponsors and thus show that archivists are good corporate players worthy of continued funding is, as Shirley Spragge says, too easy (and too irresponsible) an abdication of archivists' cultural mission and societal responsibilities. See her "The Abdication Crisis: Are Archivists Giving up Their Cultural Responsibility?" *Archivaria* 40 (fall 1995): 173–81.

16. For more detail on the postmodern turn within archives and the archival profession, see, in addition to Cook, "What Is Past," two complementary articles, Terry Cook, "Archival Science and Postmodernism: New Formulations for Old Concepts," *Archival Science: International Journal on Recorded Information* 1.1 (2001): 3–24; Terry Cook, "Fashionable Nonsense or Professional Rebirth: Postmodernism and the Practice of Archives," *Archivaria* 51 (spring 2001): 14–35, which provides more detailed support for the generalizations that follow.

17. For an extensive list of relevant Canadian and other citations, current to the summer of 2001, see Cook, "Fashionable Nonsense," 20 n. 14. A very important (and non-Canadian) addition is Carolyn Hamilton, Verne Harris, et al., *Refiguring the Archive* (Cape Town, 2002).

18. See Jacques Le Goff, *History and Memory,* trans. Steven Rendall and Elizabeth Claman (New York, 1992), esp. xvi–xvii, 59–60. Feminist scholars are keenly aware of the ways that systems of language, writing, and information recording and the preserving of such information once recorded are social and power based, not neutral, both now and across past millennia. See, for example, Gerda Lerner, *The Creation of Patriarchy* (New York and Oxford, 1986), esp. 6–7, 57, 151, 200; Riane Eisler, *The Chalice and The Blade* (San Francisco, 1987), 71–73, 91–93. Lerner's more recent study, *Creation of Feminist Consciousness*, details the systemic exclusion of women from history and archives and women's attempts starting in the late nineteenth century to correct this by creating women's archives; see esp. chap. 11, "The Search for Women's History." On the Paris mobs, see Janice Panitch, "Liberty, Equality, Posterity? Some Archival Lessons from the Case of the French Revolution," *American Archivist* 59 (winter 1996): 30–47. For other examples and citations, see Cook, "What Is Past," 18, 50. We have the sad case in our own time of the deliberate records destruction in Kosovo and Bosnia to efface memory and marginalize peoples or to hide illegal or embarrassing behavior, as in Watergate and the Enron scandal, among others. See again many of the studies in Cox and Wallace, *Archives and the Public Good.*

19. Taylor was a three-time provincial archivist and influential director in the 1970s at the National Archives of Canada. For but five examples of his important articles bringing McLuhan and contemporary social and cultural theory to bear on archival perspectives, see Hugh Taylor, "The Media of the Record: Archives in the Wake of McLuhan," *Georgia Archive* 6 (spring 1978): 1–10; Hugh Taylor, "Information Ecology and the Archives of the 1980s," *Archivaria* 18 (summer 1984): 25–37; Hugh Taylor, "Transformation in the Archives: Technological Adjustment or Paradigm Shift?" *Archivaria* 25 (winter 1987–88): 12–28; Hugh Taylor, "My Very Act and Deed: Some Reflections on the Role of Textual Records in the Conduct of Affairs," *American Archivist* 41 (fall 1988): 456–69; Hugh Taylor, "Opening Address," in *Documents That Move and Speak: Audiovisual Archives in the New Information Age: Proceedings of a Symposium Organized for the International Council of Archives by the National Archives of Canada* (Munich, 1992). For aspects of Taylor's major impact, see Tom Nesmith, "Hugh Taylor's Contextual Idea for Archives and the Foundation of Graduate Education in Archival Studies," in *The Archival Imagination: Essays in Honour of Hugh A. Taylor,* ed. Barbara Craig (Ottawa, 1992), as well as many of the essays by Taylor's disciples and admirers in this Festschrift in his honor. The volume also contains a bibliography of his work to that date. An annotated collection of his best archival essays is forthcoming: see Terry Cook and Gordon Dodds, eds., *Imagining Archives: Essays and Reflections by Hugh A. Taylor* (Lanham, MD, 2003).

20. For detailed analysis of its historical evolution and future prospects, see Laura Millar, "Discharging Our Debt: The Evolution of the Total Archives Concept in English Canada," *Archivaria* 46 (fall 1998): 103–46; Laura Millar, "The Spirit of Total Archives: Seeking a Sustainable Archival System," *Archivaria* 47 (spring 1999): 46–65. For a critical overview, see Terry Cook, "The Tyranny of the Medium: A Comment on Total Archives," *Archivaria* 9 (winter 1979–80): 141–49; Terry Cook, "Media Myopia," *Archivaria* 12 (summer 1981): 146–57.

21. John Ralston Saul, "The Inclusive Shape of Complexity," keynote address presented at the International Conference on Canadian Studies, "The Canadian Distinctiveness into the Twenty-first Century," University of Ottawa, 18 May 2000, published in *The Canadian Distinctiveness into the XXIst Century,* ed. Chad Gaffield and Karen L. Gould (Ottawa, 2003), 13–27. See also John Ralston Saul, *The Unconscious Civilization* (Concord, Ont., 1995).

22. The initial texts on macroappraisal are Terry Cook, *The Archival Appraisal of Records Containing Personal Information: A RAMP Study with Guidelines* (Paris, 1991); Terry Cook, "'Many Are Called but Few Are Chosen': Appraisal Guidelines for Sampling and Selecting Case Files," *Archivaria* 32 (summer 1991): 25–50; Terry Cook, "Mind over Matter: Towards a New Theory of Archival Appraisal," in *Archival Imagination,* ed. Craig. Other important conceptual analyses are Richard Brown, "Macro-Appraisal Theory and the Context of the Public Records Creator," *Archivaria* 40 (fall 1995): 121–72; Richard Brown, "Records Acquisition Strategy and Its Theoretical Foundation: The Case for a Concept of Archival Hermeneutics," *Archivaria* 33 (winter 1991–92): 34–56; Richard Brown,

"The Value of 'Narrativity' in the Appraisal of Historical Documents: Foundation for a Theory of Archival Hermeneutics," *Archivaria* 32 (summer 1991): 152–56; Terry Cook, "Macroappraisal and Functional Analysis: Appraisal Theory, Strategy, and Methodology for Archivists," in *L'evaluation des archives: Des necessites de la gestion aux exigences du temoignage,* Groupe Interdisciplinaire de Recherche en Archivistique, 3d symposium (Montreal, 1998). For its historical context, see Cook, "What Is Past." Both Cook and Brown drew inspiration from Hans Booms, "Society and the Formation of a Documentary Heritage: Issues in the Appraisal of Archival Sources," trans. Hermina Joldersma and Richard Klumpenhouwer, *Archivaria* 24 (summer 1987): 69–107; originally published 1972; and from the structuration theory of British sociologist Anthony Giddens. Several published case studies of implementing macroappraisal are Jim Suderman, "Appraising Records of the Expenditure Management Function: An Exercise in Functional Analysis," *Archivaria* 43 (spring 1997): 129–42; Catherine Bailey, "From the Top Down: The Practice of Macro-Appraisal," *Archivaria* 43 (spring 1997): 89–128; Candace Loewen, "From Human Neglect to Planetary Survival: New Approaches to the Appraisal of Environmental Records," *Archivaria* 33 (winter 1991–92): 87–103; Jean-Stephen Piche and Sheila Powell, "Counting Archives In: The Appraisal of the 1991 Census of Canada," *Archivaria* 45 (spring 1998): 27–43; Jean-Stephen Piche,"Macro-Appraisal and Duplication of Information: Federal Real Property Management Records," *Archivaria* 39 (spring 1995): 39–50; Ellen Scheinberg, "Case File Theory: Does It Work in Practice?," *Archivaria* 38 (fall 1994): 45–60.

23. For the strategic "disposition" as opposed to the appraisal side of the macroappraisal approach, see, in addition to the sources in n. 22, Eldon Frost, "A Weak Link in the Chain: Records Scheduling as a Source of Archival Acquisition," *Archivaria* 33 (winter 1991–92): 78–86; Bruce Wilson, "Systematic Appraisal of the Records of the Government of Canada at the National Archives of Canada," *Archivaria* 38 (fall 1994): 218–31.

24. F. Gerald Ham, "The Archival Edge," in *A Modern Archives Reader: Basic Readings on Archival Theory and Practice,* ed. Maygene F. Daniels and Timothy Walch (Washington, D.C., 1984), 328–29. Appraisal by use is most closely identified with American appraisal theory as pioneered principally by T. R. Schellenberg and his colleagues from the 1940s onward. Schellenberg's fullest statement of his oft-cited principles appears in "The Appraisal of Modern Public Records," *National Archives Bulletin* 8 (1956), an extract of which is more readily available in Daniels and Walch, *Modern Archives Reader,* 57–70. The Society of American Archivists also sanctioned this approach: see Maynard J. Brichford, *Archives and Manuscripts: Appraisal and Accessioning* (Chicago, 1977). Schellenberg's influence remains strong; a recent textbook chapter asserted that his secondary values relating to "research uses" remain "the principal concern of archivists" in appraising records (Maygene F. Daniels, "Records Appraisal and Disposition," in *Managing Archives and Archival Institutions,* ed. James Gregory Bradsher [Chicago, 1988], 60).

25. Steven Lubar, "Information Culture and the Archival Record," *American Archivist* 62 (spring 1999): 15.

Creating a National Information System in a Federal Environment

Some Thoughts on the Canadian Archival Information Network

Laura Millar

The Promise of CAIN

In late 2001, the Canadian Council on Archives, a publicly funded agency that oversees archival development in Canada, launched the Canadian Archival Information Network (CAIN), an online network of Web sites and databases designed to bring together intellectually the spectrum of activity taking place in archival repositories across the country. The network aims to provide electronic access to information about archives through searchable fonds-level archival descriptions, along with news and facts about archival programs. The developers of CAIN ultimately see the network as a tool for "communication, consultation, coordination, and cooperation" between archival stakeholders and the archival community. Its goal is to transform the archival landscape for both researchers and archivists, to "tear down the walls of archives' readings rooms and open every archives across Canada to all Canadians."[1]

The Origins of CAIN

In Canada, the search for a coordinated electronic archival network has emerged out of the country's distinctive archival history. This history began with the premise of public responsibility for culture, the idea that government must play a central role in creating an identity for a large and diverse country. This sense of public obligation has evolved into a belief in the importance of continuing public support for society within a framework of public-private partnerships. In archives, this focus on public responsibility was formalized in what became known as the concept of "total archives," the view that national and provincial archival institutions were responsible

> not only for the reception of government records which have historical value but also for the collection of historical material of all kinds and from any source which can help in a significant way to reveal the truth about every aspect of Canadian life.[2]

Inherent in the total archives philosophy were the following concepts:

1. the government had a central role to play in the culture of the country;
2. the government also had a responsibility to help Canadians foster a sense of their identity, given the country's small population and expansive terrain and its proximity to its southern neighbor, the United States;
3. the acquisition of private-sector records and the preservation of copies of historical material from other sources were valid archival activities for publicly funded institutions because such records bolstered Canadian identity; and
4. public institutions had a responsibility to preserve in one central, publicly accessible location archival materials in all media, from print to audiovisual materials to cartographic documents.

Total archives was all records from all sources in a centralized, publicly funded archival repository. Leaving the care of history strictly to private agencies, corporations, or local groups without any government intervention was not an acceptable option in Canada.[3]

From the late 1800s to the 1970s, a handful of publicly funded institutions acquired and preserved both public and private records as part of the total archives concept.[4] In the 1980s and 1990s, the total archives concept was overtaken by a belief in an "archival system." The term signaled a redefinition of total archives in the face of three realities: the decentralization of public functions, a growing sense of regional identity and regionalism, and diminished public funding for cultural programs.

The essence of the archival system was that responsibility for society's documentary heritage must now be shared among the federal, provincial, and territorial governments. Further, the private sector must become more involved in the care of the nation's written record. In this vision of an archival system, a disparate group of public and private archival repositories would work together to acquire and preserve aspects of Canada's documentary past. Through collaboration and cooperation, these institutions would preserve a balanced record of Canadian society.

One of the first priorities for this emerging archival system was the development of the Rules for Archival Description (RAD), Canada's archival descriptive standard. In 1986, the Bureau of Canadian Archivists published a study of a Canadian working group established to assess the potential for and scope of archival descriptive standards. In 1987 the bureau published *A Call to Action,* which initiated the creation of RAD. The finished RAD began to appear in French and English in 1990.[5]

At the heart of RAD was the philosophy that "the organization of all descriptive work proceed from the more general to the more specific level of description."[6] The first, most general level of description was the *fonds,* which was defined as the whole of the records, regardless of form or medium, automatically and organically created and/or accumulated and used by a particular individual, family, or corporate body in the course of that creator's activities or functions.[7] As will be seen later, much archival development in Canada hinges on the acceptance of the centrality of the fonds.

In 1991, as RAD was being developed, work began on the construction of online union lists of archival descriptions. The Archives Association of British Columbia led the way with the establishment of the British Columbia Archival Union List (BCAUL), a tool for information sharing and interinstitutional cooperation. As of 2001, BCAUL included more than nine thousand fonds-level descriptions from 163 institutions.[8]

In 1995, Alberta established a task force to plan a network policy following on a successful pilot project to develop an electronic communications network. In 1997, the Archives Society of Alberta established the Archives Network of Alberta (ANA). In 1998 the Alberta and BC databases were linked together in an interprovincial union list, and Alberta added more than six thousand fonds-level descriptions to the BC database. At the same time, the Yukon Territory and the Northwest Territories started to develop their own union lists, and in 1999–2000 their databases were linked to the BC Archives Network Web page, forming part of what was called the Canadian Northwest Archival Network (CanWAN). Other provinces began to develop union lists, and now the plan is to blend all these lists into the CAIN database, which was officially launched on 20 October 2001.[9]

The Fonds and CAIN

The heart of the success of the CAIN—particularly the union list component—will be the commonality of practice among institutions, particularly in description. To achieve homogeneity, RAD has been declared the descriptive standard. According to the CAIN planning committee, RAD compliance and the creation of fonds-level descriptions are key goals: "projects that would detract from or delay achieving the goal or top priority of having all archival holdings in a province/territory described at the fonds level according to RAD . . . will be given a lower priority."[10]

Inherent in RAD, of course, is the acceptance of the fonds—of whole bodies of records as opposed to single items—as the primary unit of arrangement and description. In principle, the CAIN system will not include items or artificial collections. The organizers of provincial and territorial networks have already established policies that focus on the description of fonds rather than items or collections. According to the planners of the BCAUL system (which as the first online union list became the de facto model for other databases), "single items are considered as fonds only if they meet the following criteria: whether the item is all that remains of the fonds, whether the item covers a span of years, whether there is evidence of an accumulation."[11] CAIN has followed this lead and focused its efforts on the fonds.

On the surface, this decision makes eminent sense. Why catalog individual photographs when a backlog of ten meters of textual records threatens to knock down the door of the storage vault? In Canada, many well-intentioned archival practitioners used to take collections of records apart physically and organize materials by subject or medium, destroying provenance in the process. A focus on the fonds has raised awareness of the integrity of records, the idea of original order, and the priority of a general control of all holdings. The Canadian Council of Archives has done admirable service by requiring, through its funding mechanisms, that attention be paid first to general administrative, physical, and descriptive control of holdings before any more detailed work is done.[12] The focus on the fonds has helped many institutions clarify their priorities, manage their workloads, and gain overall control of the materials in their care. Excluding discrete items from an online descriptive tool seems logical.

What about collections, though? The BCAUL project team recognized that the inclusion of collections in the database was important; team members knew that "a significant amount of important material would be omitted if [collections] were excluded." In this case, the definition of a "collection," taken from the RAD rules, referred to

> an artificial accumulation of documents of any provenance brought together on the basis of some common characteristic, e.g., way of acquisition, subject, language, medium, type of document, name of collector, to be treated for description purposes as a descriptive unit under a common title.[13]

So, if a donor brought in a collection of archival materials—such as a collection of photographs or of original documents on a particular topic—the archivist could describe these records as that donor's collection and include that information in the database, probably with the donor as "creator." However, if the archival institution itself created a collection from disparate items received in the repository, this "artificial" collection was not to be included in an online description. It was simply a conglomeration of items, and items were not to be added. If a fonds could not be identified, the material would not be described in the database.[14]

The question is, if an electronic network focuses on the fonds and consequently excludes items and artificial collections, does it truly reflect the holdings of archival repositories? Can it ever? Should it?

The Fonds and the Canadian Experience

While the idea of the fonds was first clearly articulated in Europe in the nineteenth century, only in the past fifteen years or so, with the publication of RAD and the decision to require RAD compliance for certain publicly funded archival work, has the Canadian archival community really accepted the idea. Instead, Canadian archivists focused on the concept of total archives and the importance of preserving historical materials regardless of their origins.

Underlying the total archives concept was the well-ingrained belief, outlined earlier, that publicly funded archival institutions ought to be the preeminent repositories for historical records. The archival repository existed to house and make available not just public records but also private materials, no matter the source or the medium: government records, private manuscripts, maps and plans, photographs, sound recordings, visual art, even artifacts, trophies, medals, and coins. There was no focus on the fonds. Faced with a mass of materials in all media, accepted with minimal documentation from diverse sources, the archivist usually chose to take in whatever arrived and try to make sense of it later. A business ledger acquired long after the rest of the company's records would simply be inserted in the collection, with a note in the accession log recording its receipt. Two photographs from the same donor, given years apart, would be accessioned and processed separately, perhaps with donor information included in the description, perhaps not. Anonymous photographs would just be added to the hundreds or thousands of other miscellaneous images in the repository's photographic "collection."

Without the fonds to guide them, some total archives became as chock-a-block full as Fibber McGee's closet. Each followed its own unique archival practices, including acquiring and accessioning materials as items, not fonds or groups. This practice was especially common in smaller, community-based archival repositories. For example, in one community archival institution, the archivist faces a long legacy of item-oriented management. She has described a large number of fonds that can be included in the CAIN database, but she also has in her repository more than five hundred discrete "items." Some of these materials are separate accessions from the same creator, brought in bit by bit over time but accessioned separately, not as part of one fonds. Others are complete diaries and journals, photograph albums, or registers of small corporations.

While the institution has perfectly adequate finding

aids for these records, none of the "items" has been described electronically. The archivist claims she has neither the time nor the resources to reconstruct the bits and pieces in hand to try to find a fonds. And if she cannot include the five hundred or more items in an online database as an artificial collection, with keywords to highlight subjects and names, she will leave the records as they are and not incorporate them into new systems. Reorganizing and redescribing them are not her priorities.

One could argue that it is simply the archivist's responsibility to make redescription a priority, but such work is not always possible or logical. Online descriptions inevitably will remain incomplete pictures of a repository's holdings. If only fonds are included in databases such as CAIN, and if archives hold vast quantities of records that are not fonds, online union lists will not accurately reflect what archives hold.

Archival Coordinators: Gatekeepers or Stewards?

The reality of databases is that they work only if they are rigorously structured. Through its funding programs, the Canadian archival community has developed a mechanism to ensure consistency and rigor by requiring a strict adherence to RAD. To help institutions conform to these descriptive requirements, a group of archival advisers has emerged across the country, funded by the public purse. The CCA program provides funds for provincial and territorial councils to hire archives advisers as well as educators and network coordinators to serve the community's educational and informational needs. These advisers have often become the "help line" for archival institutions in the individual jurisdictions, traveling around provinces or territories, organizing workshops and training sessions, coordinating regional meetings, and helping institutions share resources and expertise. Many of these advisers have been the sole incumbents in these positions from the time public funds for the archival system were first made available in the 1980s and 1990s. Their knowledge of their community is immense; they are walking finding aids.

What burden of responsibility has been placed on their shoulders? How much influence do they have over the state of archives in their region? Is that influence fair to them, to the archival community, or to the users of archives? It is possible that these coordinators are becoming, in effect, gatekeepers. Such a role implies a level of responsibility that is perhaps not what the archival system intended or what the archival community needs. Should these coordinators guide the development of the

archival system? Or should they simply oversee but not control networks?

Consider the processes for adding fonds-level descriptions to the electronic union lists such as CAIN. Archival institutions create descriptions using RAD and then send the descriptions to the host server to be added to the database. Someone—the archival adviser, a network coordinator, or someone else acting on behalf of the national system or provincial or territorial council—vets the descriptions before they go onto the system. This person looks for errors and inconsistencies, ensures that information is coded correctly so that it can be uploaded onto Web servers, and reviews the descriptions to ensure that the materials conform to the criteria established (such as including only fonds or collections).

These responsibilities make the coordinators gatekeepers. In the process of doing their job, they are determining what goes into the system and what is left out. It is true that most regions have formalized guidelines and criteria, but most of the coordinators have indicated that the review process is ultimately governed by their knowledge of the system and their patterns of decision making. And their decisions are based on the realities of their provinces or territories, the kinds of institutions that exist there, and the kinds of records found in their communities.

In some provinces, for example, strict lines have been drawn excluding all items or artificial collections from online databases. In these instances, if an archivist has created an artificial collection out of several thousand discrete photographs, that information will not go into the database. In other regions, the exclusion of collections or items is an official policy, but coordinators or advisers have unofficially chosen to break the rule in certain situations. In one province, the system operates on the premise of inclusivity: if the records are in an institution, they are to be described on the database. Consequently, some of the records described are not true fonds, and some records described remain unprocessed and unavailable. Advisers have been lenient about the level of RAD compliance required in descriptions as a means of getting institutions to participate in the network. The advisers suggest that they will tighten the criteria later, when everyone is on board.

Some coordinators have expressed concern that a large percentage of nonfonds holdings in repositories might not be included in online descriptions. In some regions, the coordinators have helped institutions construct artificial collections from the various items in their repository so that information about disparate materials can be brought together in one RAD-compliant record. In other regions, the coordinators are encouraging institutions to create separate "historical resources" databases, briefly describing all the different holdings of the archival repository, so that users can at least know in a general way what kinds of materials might be available and where.

The very real challenges of establishing and adhering to criteria were well expressed by one archivist. "I am finding myself wanting to make some exceptions to my own rules," this person said, adding that "really great photo collections would be nice to include . . . but I have had to make these 'rules' so that I do not have to include every collection of royal family memorabilia or genealogical notes, etc. I am often torn between serving the users, who don't care as much about fonds versus collection, and keeping up our standards of fonds only."

The challenge coordinators face is compounded by reality. Canada is simply so large and diverse that standardization of practice seems an unachievable goal. What is important in one part of the country may be irrelevant in another. Canada functions in two official languages, French and English, but in parts of the northern territories official communications take place in nine or ten languages. In British Columbia, more people speak Chinese than French. In the North, cold is so pervasive that there are about thirty different Inuit terms for *snow*. Most Vancouver residents have not seen a snow shovel in years. The prairies are farming country; Newfoundland is a fishing center. In British Columbia, logging and mining are major industries, but there are few records of logging in the urban centers of southern Ontario. The history and therefore the records of each part of the country are sufficiently distinct in their content that coordination of descriptions—with the need for authority files, keyword lists, and indexes—seems impossible. How can the archival community represent the records of a diverse federation in one database?

CAIN may never be comprehensive. Perhaps it never should be. Still, it seems that at least some percentage of the materials sitting in archival repositories, particularly discrete items and artificial collections created by institutions themselves, may never be described on electronic information networks. At the moment, the decision about what goes in and what is left out is not uniform. Institutions and coordinators are making decisions based on their realities. Of course, one could argue it has always been thus and so it shall ever be. From the early days of card catalogs to today's wild kingdom of the World Wide Web, practices can conform only to a certain extent. Exceptions have to be made, and rules have to be broken. The question is, does it matter?

It matters if the Canadian archival community is to ensure that CAIN is the first stop on the research path, not the only stop. It matters if archivists want users to know that a negative search result is not necessarily an answer but perhaps just an absence of information. But it matters less that the information in networks is comprehensive or selective than that archivists explain how their decisions were made.

The Tongues of Men and of Angels

The general public is probably unaware that subjective decisions are made about what information is included in a network. Indeed, the average citizen appears unaware that decisions are ever made about the acquisition and preservation of historical materials. Users of archival tools, such as online databases, believe that the system is comprehensive and coordinated. They search for a topic, and if they get a negative answer, they might naturally assume that no information is available. Or they could face a myriad of answers, which may mean that they weren't asking the right question. To make electronic systems really useful, archivists need to understand who uses archives, how, and for what. In Canada, this leads back to the issue of the evolution of the Canadian archival community from total archives to archival system to archival network.

Total archives encouraged one-stop shopping for archival information. An archival researcher could go to one institution and, in theory, find almost anything he or she wanted. As long as the records related to the jurisdiction in question and had been preserved, they would be found somewhere in the storage room of the total archives.

Because the archivists in these institutions were dealing with all manner of material in all media—everything from one item to fifty boxes—and because they did not always respect the integrity of the fonds, they developed a range of descriptive systems. Inventories described whole fonds and collections; photograph catalogs allowed item-by-item searches; map indexes followed cartographic rules; oral history transcriptions offered line-by-line access. A kaleidoscope of systems accommodated the spectrum of researchers and resources.

To explain the diversity of systems, the archivist became a walking finding aid, physically leading the user through the different tools and ultimately, one hopes, to the desired resources. A dialogue could take place to help the user get the information he or she wanted or at least to realize that it couldn't be found. The eccentricity of the total archives system encouraged the development of contorted information tools. They may not have been uniform or logical, but someone was always standing behind them to explain and interpret them for the user.[15]

Today, this quaint total archives universe is being replaced by a coordinated network. Structured databases provide logical and uniform descriptions of holdings. But the databases are clearly not always logical. And the information in them is not always consistent. Much that is in repositories is not included in the networks. This material has been excluded because it does not conform to the rules established. But now there is no one standing next to the user at the computer, explaining the search results. Is the archival community beginning to speak in tongues, creating a babel unintelligible to users?

Giving What They Want, or What They Need?

Communication involves dialogue. The Canadian archival community has not actively sought input from users in the development of online tools. And online networks do not have regular mechanisms to ask users if they have found what they want, how they found it, and how the systems could be improved. When people come in the door of the repository and ask questions—relevant, silly, or otherwise—individual archivists can interpret for them and, at the same time, reassess institutional practices. But the tools to allow this reassessment do not yet exist in the electronic environment.

CAIN developers have encouraged the archival community to "engage its users in an open dialogue regarding the nature of information to be included on the network to ensure that CAIN is a useful and productive research tool." They also suggest that archival institutions should undertake user studies "to ensure that the content of the network remains relevant."[16] Many of the existing online databases have incorporated contact links on their sites, allowing users to e-mail questions or comments to the coordinator. Many of the queries received concern how to use the database or why a certain search was not successful. In effect, the coordinators and advisers are becoming the reference archivists for their regions, which is not part of the job description.

Beyond this ad hoc process, none of the existing union list projects has incorporated a formal user analysis or environmental scan. Users did not participate in the work of steering committees or task forces developing archival networks. This absence of widespread user

input goes back to RAD, which was developed without formal input from the user community.[17]

If archivists have not consulted with the public, how will the developers of online union lists know that the tools serve the public adequately? How do archivists know what the public wants? Talking to users means listening to them, which can be a daunting prospect. Users may offer comments archivists do not want to hear. In particular, users may not understand the concept of the fonds and the idea of the selective inclusion of information on databases. As Paul Maxner, an archivist from Nova Scotia, argued, "I think we should talk about *fonds* and the public reaction to it and come up with something that works. The word *fonds* has flopped."[18]

In response to Maxner's comments, Wendy Duff, an archival studies professor at the University of Toronto and a key participant in the development of RAD, noted that

> my research on users has certainly convinced me that English users do not understand the word and having it in the title places a barrier between them and their use of our descriptions. . . . [I]f we are to communicate with someone we must do it in a language that he or she understands.[19]

If people don't like the word *fonds,* archivists need to address that reality, which of course makes the Canadian archival community nervous, given the amount of energy and resources it has put into developing descriptive systems.

People may not care what a fonds is, but archivists can use tools such as CAIN to explain the concept and engage in a dialogue with users about its validity. At the very least, online networks should include information explaining the context within which the databases have been created. On union list or institutional home pages, archivists could explain what is included in a database, what is not included, and why. And if archivists do not know what the users understand and what they want and do not want, archivists should simply ask. As Duff proposed, "we need to know more about what our users would want."[20] Then archivists need to clarify their systems and terminology or find new words with which to communicate.

All Fonds Are Not Created Equal

But archivists also need to be sure that the words they use actually mean what the archivists say they mean and do what the archivists really want them to do. Archivists talk about the concept of the fonds and argue that it represents the record-keeping function. But what is the relationship between how an organization or an individual creates records and how he, she, or they come to see those records as valuable enough to go to an archival repository? Descriptions are only representations of records, but they have the power to become their own reality. If descriptions homogenize archives as fonds, do they reflect the reality of records creation and record keeping?

Eric Ketelaar has examined the impetus for "archivalisation." He suggests that records have to be created and kept—they have to be valued—by their creators before they can be acquired and preserved by an archives and used by the larger society. Archivists need to acknowledge the disconnect between the reality of records in the hands of their creators and those same records in an archival institution. The concept of the fonds tries, in part, to replicate the first reality by focusing on the archival vision of provenance and original order. In so doing, perhaps the concept negates the validity of the second reality: that records can follow a confused and chaotic path from creation to archives.[21]

The term *provenance* is fraught with complications. Consider its different use in the museum world. Today, work is under way around the world to clarify the transfer of ownership of works of art acquired by galleries after the Second World War. To this end, information is needed about provenance—what archivists would call the custodial history. While curators have often documented the life of an artifact or a piece of art, not just its creation, archivists have given more weight to the idea of original order than to custodial history. Archivists need to ask whether the custodial history is equally important, whether it too is part of the story of the records.[22]

The reality of records is that even though they may have at one time formed part of a fonds, they rarely come to archival institutions as fonds. In community archives, for example, many donors bring materials to the archives one or two items at a time. They bring more and more as they build a relationship with the archivist and come to trust the institution. Over time, sometimes over years of patient negotiations, a community archivist may piece together a fonds from the various accessions brought in by a family or group. And if the archivist cannot put together a fonds, the institution usually retains alternate systems—from artificial collections of photographs to vertical or clippings files—to accommodate the oddities that perhaps will never warrant full archival

treatment but are nevertheless worth preserving. How does this pattern of donation, which is part of the social order of that particular type of archival institution, relate to the concept of the fonds?

And what about the archival institution's importance to the donor? Some people want to see their records in an archives because it means a little piece of them survives after they are gone. They want to see "their" item available in a public place. As Sue McKemmish has suggested, people's records become "evidence of me." To manage records and serve the creators and users of those records, archivists need to understand people's reasons for preserving their documentary memory.[23]

This understanding reaches beyond description. Urging an acceptance of "social inclusion" in archival management, Ian Johnston has argued that the records of black and Asian Britons are underrepresented in archival repositories in the United Kingdom. Because "their" records are not in archives, members of these ethnic groups are not regular visitors to archival repositories. As a result, they may not appreciate the role of archives in their lives. So they don't donate records. The circle is broken only when someone identifies the void and takes action. Whose job is it?[24]

By focusing on the fonds without acknowledging the personal and cultural influences on the creation of records, archivists may by default exclude the records of those people who do not create or use records in such a way that the materials come to archival repositories as fonds. Native groups rely on oral traditions as much as written records. Are these fonds? How do Asian Britons create records, and does that affect their acquisition as fonds? How do Asian Canadians, senior citizens, women, children, or the disabled create and use records? How do archivists relate those different record-keeping processes to the arrangement and description of fonds?

The fonds is an artificial idea; it is a concept created by archivists for their own use. The fonds is a way to impose a hierarchical order on the documentary environment to understand and perhaps control it. Think, in comparison, of the taxonomic ordering of the natural world. The rhinoceros has no idea that it forms part of the order *perissodactyla*. A rabbit doesn't know that it is part of one family in the order *lagomorpha*. Records have no idea that they are fonds. If archival databases rigidly reflect an imposed hierarchy, archivists are in danger of including only information about those archival materials that fits the norm. Perhaps archivists omit information about artificial collections or items not because they are not fonds but because these materials have not yet been assigned a place in the archival hierarchy.²⁵

If RAD is the premise for archival description and if RAD focuses on the fonds, what happens to those records that do not conform to the norm? Ultimately, archivists may find that the extraordinary becomes the ordinary and the ordinary disappears from view. An inherent danger is not just that materials will not be described but that because they cannot be described according to established rules, they may not be perceived as fonds. Then they may not be deemed worthy of preservation. RAD may become not just a standard for description but a standard for appraisal. The Vegas Valley leopard frog didn't know it was classified as an amphibian. But it doesn't matter now, because the Vegas Valley leopard frog is extinct. Will certain types of archival materials become extinct in a structured archival environment?

Reality Check: The Search for Funds and the Implications for Sustainability

By now, some archivists are asking, "Who has time for all this theoretical speculation? I have records to process, and fonds to describe, and a limited amount of time and money to do it." Therein lies another significant question about the future of CAIN: its sustainability over time.

In Canada, total archives, the archival system, and the fledgling archival network have always depended on public funding. And grant-funded efforts are, by definition, project oriented. Project-based management, while it can result in significant short-term achievements, does not lay the groundwork for long-term sustainability. Signs already indicate that the Canadian network may not be sustainable without strong management and oversight. Look at the history of funding for RAD-compliant descriptions.

In one province, CCA funds were used to send project staff to visit archivists and help institutions prepare descriptions for the database and to raise awareness of RAD and the concept of the fonds. Once this initial work was completed, CCA funds were shifted to new priorities on the assumption that archives would have achieved a new level of management and would maintain their descriptive practices. Have they? It is possible that institutions will not maintain their descriptions and that the network will consequently suffer. Conversely, centralized control of the system could violate the democratic idea that regions or institutions can choose whether to participate in networked systems.

In another province, the number of institutions belonging to the provincial archival council increased as funds appeared to create RAD-compliant descriptions. In this case, membership was a requirement for the receipt of funds. After the descriptive work was finished, some institutions let their memberships lapse. They decided they had no more records to describe and thus did not need more money. No need for money, no need to belong to the provincial council. But the archival council had established links in its electronic network to these institutions' Web sites. Does the council now have an obligation to maintain the links? Does the institution? Should the descriptive records from these institutions be removed from the database to avoid setting up blind leads for users? Or should the institution be required to maintain its own links and remain part of the system? What if the institution receives more archival materials and wishes to add them to the database? Does it need to rejoin the council? And will it quit again later?

In another example, one institution's fonds-level descriptions were prepared with the help of advisers from the provincial council, but for various reasons the archives themselves were never processed. A complete fonds-level description exists on the electronic union list, but the records themselves sit in boxes on the floor of a basement storage room, awaiting conservation treatment and processing at some undetermined point in the future. The archivist in charge is scrambling to find whatever grants are available just to keep the institution operating. He does not know how he will find the resources to bring these materials under even minimal control in the near future. In this case, the picture of coordination and control presented by the electronic fonds-level description is not matched by the reality of the storage vault.

In 1998, Duff surveyed Canadian archives to determine their implementation of RAD. While she found significant evidence that RAD was used by institutions across the country, particularly in smaller communities, she noted that "the actual degree of compliance with the detailed requirements of RAD should be studied," and she argued that while "most archives said they used RAD . . . what was meant by 'use of RAD' was not defined." She also noted that many archivists suggested that a lack of "time and money" hindered the use of RAD.²⁶

Studies such as Duff's need to be conducted regularly and rigorously if the archival community is to assess the sustainability and validity of its work. But this again raises the question of gatekeeping versus stewardship. Should the online environment be inclusive or simply representative, a tasty appetizer or a full meal deal?

Achieving the Potential of CAIN

To make CAIN all it can be, the Canadian archival community needs to reassess its priorities. Archivists need to focus not on how to make information fit descriptive systems but rather on how to use descriptive tools to fulfill the ultimate goal: to acquire, preserve, and make available society's documentary heritage. As Gary Mitchell, the provincial archivist of British Columbia, has said, descriptive standards in the hands of gatekeepers set up a barrier, but descriptive standards in the hands of stewards can serve the essence of the archival role: heightened access.[27]

A key archival priority is sharing information. CAIN can be a remarkable tool for communications and networking. Instead of focusing on pristine fonds, CAIN could accept the chaotic nature of archives and become more of an information center, a bulletin board about the state of archives. CAIN could, for example, include information not only about materials already in archival institutions but also about records that have not yet been acquired. Archivists could set up databases holding snippets of leads, partial descriptions, and even just questions and queries. Such information might help archivists and users know what records are out there, whether fonds or not. Archivists could also use CAIN as a vehicle for sharing researcher requests and acquisition tips and leads. CAIN could include electronic chat rooms for archivists interested in different professional issues, for historians seeking information, and for geneologists or schoolteachers wishing to access relevant resources or share information. CAIN's full potential lies in its ability to bring archivists and users together, to help share information between professionals and the public.[28]

Archivists also have to remember funders' priorities. All Canadian archival endeavors—RAD, electronic networks, the control of holdings—have been financed with public money. Perhaps it does not represent a lot of money compared with defense spending or digitization of government services or the construction of transportation infrastructure, but it does nonetheless constitute an expense. Archivists need to build positively on the work done to date and to frame future projects in ways that are not only archivally relevant but also fiscally responsible and, ultimately, sustainable. Archivists also need to draw the private sector into the process, something Canadians have done poorly so far, perhaps because of the Canadian belief in the sanctity of the public purse.

The Canadian archival community can achieve the best out of CAIN only if archivists retain their ultimate focus as a profession: to help preserve society's documentary memory. As Brian Speirs, the provincial archivist of Nova Scotia and a strong supporter of the CAIN system, has acknowledged, "we sometimes lose sight of the fundamental premise that CAIN is for the Canadian public and only secondarily for archivists." One of the ways to keep this focus is to keep going back to users and colleagues to share experiences and seek input and advice. Only by listening to the public will archivists know if the systems and structures established are giving them what they want as well as what archivists believe they need.[29]

The descriptive systems archivists have created are not perfect. But the records described in those systems are also not perfect. The marvelous reality of archives is that they do not conform. As archivists build on existing networks to develop the CAIN system, they have an opportunity to assess critically and realistically the strengths and weaknesses discovered to date. Nothing is ever perfect; a German proverb reminds us, "Could everything be done twice, everything would be done better." With the development of CAIN on the shoulders of existing networks, Canada has a unique opportunity: a second chance to improve on its successes. The archival community should take full advantage of it.

NOTES

The author is very grateful to the University of Michigan for funding received through the Advanced Study Center of the International Institute, which greatly facilitated the ability to conduct research into this topic.

In researching this essay, the author accessed the wide range of publications and Web-based sources cited herein and communicated with many of the people involved in coordinating union list or network initiatives in their provinces and territories. Their answers to questions and their interest in the research are very much appreciated. The input of the following people is gratefully acknowledged: from British Columbia, Ann Carroll, Heather Gordon, and Bill Purver from the Archives Association of British Columbia and Gary Mitchell from the British Columbia Archives and Records Service; from Alberta, Michael Gourlie, Susan Kooyman, and Janet McMaster of the Archives Society of Alberta; from Saskatchewan, Tim Hutchinson of the University of Saskatchewan Archives, about the Saskatchewan and Manitoba Information Networks (SAIN/MAIN); from Ontario, Loren Fantin from the Archives Association of Ontario, about ARCHEION; from Nova Scotia, Meghan Hallett of the Council of Nova Scotia Archives about ArchWay; from the Northwest Territories, Richard Valpy of the Northwest Territories Archives about the NWT databases and union list; and from the Yukon Territory, Diane Chisholm and Lesley Buchan of the Yukon Archives about the Yukon Archives database. Contact was also made with the CAIN coordinator, Kristina Aston.

Much of the information in this essay is drawn from these

communications as well as from visits to selected institutions and discussions with members of the archival community, particularly but not exclusively in British Columbia. Given the anecdotal nature of the information, any personal comments or opinions offered in conversations have been rendered anonymous. The purpose here is not to highlight individual examples but rather to study the larger issues.

The author is also grateful to Heather MacNeil of the University of British Columbia for her valuable insights and support in our many conversations.

1. Canadian Council of Archives (hereafter CCA), Information Highway Task Force, *Raising CAIN: Building Canada's Archival Information Network,* draft report, 15 November 1997, 4, available electronically at http://www.cdncouncilarchives.ca /rai_cain.html.

2. W. I. Smith, "Introduction," *Archives: Mirror of Canada Past* (Toronto: University of Toronto Press, 1972), 9–10.

3. For an analysis of the concept and history of total archives, see Laura Millar, "Discharging Our Debt: The Evolution of the Total Archives Concept in English Canada," *Archivaria* 46 (fall 1998): 103–46; Laura Millar, "The Spirit of Total Archives: Seeking a Sustainable Archival System," *Archivaria* 47 (spring 1999): 46–65.

4. This growth is traced in detail in Laura Millar, "The End of 'Total Archives'? An Analysis of Changing Acquisition Practices in Canadian Archival Repositories" (Ph.D. diss., University College London, 1996).

5. Bureau of Canadian Archivists (hereafter BCA), *Toward Descriptive Standards: Report and Recommendations of the Canadian Working Group on Archival Descriptive Standards* (Ottawa, 1986); Jean E. Dryden and Kent M. Haworth, *Developing Descriptive Standards: A Call to Action* (Ottawa, 1987); BCA, *Rules for Archival Description* (Ottawa, 1993). In 2001, a Canada-U.S. Task Force on Archival Description was established to consider the reconciliation of American and Canadian descriptive practices; for more information on this group, called CUSTARD, go to the CCA website at http:// www.cdncouncilarchives.ca/archdesreport.html.

6. BCA, *Toward Descriptive Standards,* 59.

7. BCA, *Rules for Archival Description,* D-3.

8. Archives Association of British Columbia, *British Columbia Archival Union List—Background Report* (rev. May 1999), available at http://aabc.bc.ca/aabc/bcaulbac.html. See also Christopher Hives and Blair Taylor, "Using Descriptive Standards as a Basis for Cooperation: The British Columbia Archival Union List," *Archivaria* 35 (spring 1993): 85; also available at http://www.cdncouncilarchives.ca/cain4.html. See also Bill Purver, "British Columbia Archival Network, parts 1 and 2," *AABC Newsletter* 10.1 (winter 2000); 10.2 (spring 2000), available at http://aabc.bc.ca/aabc/newsletter/10_1/ bcanret1.htm and http://aabc.bc.ca/aabc/newsletter/10_2/ british_columbia_archival_network.htm. Information was also provided by the network coordinator, Bill Purver.

9. Information about Alberta's activities was provided in conversation with Susan Kooyman of the Glenbow Archives of Alberta and from Janet McMaster's report to the Archives Society of Alberta on the CAIN implementation study, 31 March 1999 (copy provided to the author in January 2001). To see the CanWAN system, go to the BC Archival Network Web page and follow the links, or go to http://aabc.bc.ca/aabc/canwan .html. To see the NWT site, go to http://www.pwnhc.learnnet .nt.ca/nwtac/nwtac.html. The Yukon Archives Union List is available at http://www.whitehorse.microage.ca/yca/sections/ yaul/yaul.html. To see the Saskatchewan Archival Information Network and the Manitoba Archival Information Network (SAIN/MAIN), go to http://www.usask.ca/archives/sain-main. See also the data entry guidelines at http://www.usask.ca/ archives/sain-demo/dataentry.html. Information was also provided by Tim Hutchinson in Saskatchewan. In Ontario, the ARCHEION Web site is at http://archeion-aao.fis.utoronto.ca. The four Atlantic provinces are all in the early stages of network development. Nova Scotia's online database is called ArchWay, and Prince Edward Island and Newfoundland are developing networked systems. New Brunswick is embarking on a bilingual system, since it is an officially bilingual province. Quebec is developing its own French-language system. Nunavut also plans to participate in CAIN. For Nova Scotia, see http://fox.nstn.ca/~cnsa/archway/introtodescription.htm and http://fox.nstn.ca/~cnsa/archway/format.htm. Specific information was also provided by Meghan Hallett in Nova Scotia. For information on Newfoundland's provincial archives, see http://www.gov.nf.ca/panl/. For the Prince Edward Island provincial archives, see http://www2.gov.pe.ca/educ/archives /archives_index.asp. For information on New Brunswick's provincial archives, go to http://gov.nb.ca/archives/. Information about the Nunavut government is available at http://www.gov .nu.ca/eng. The National Archives of Canada has developed an online union list called ArchiviaNet, which provides electronic access to the public and private holdings of the largest and oldest archival institution in the country. For access to ArchiviaNet, go to www.archives.ca and follow the links. Finally, for CAIN itself, go to http://www.cain-rcia.ca/.

10. CCA, "Blueprint for the Canadian Archival Information Network," 10, available at http://www.cdncouncilarchives .ca/cain_ip.html.

11. Hives and Taylor, "Using Descriptive Standards," 74.

12. The CCA website, particularly http://www.cdncouncil archives.ca/index_e.html, outlines the CCA's different funding programs and their criteria for approval.

13. BCA, *Rules for Archival Description,* D-3.

14. Hives and Taylor, "Using Descriptive Standards," 75.

15. In some instances, such as at the Public Archives of Canada in Ottawa, the media element of the total archives orientation became a source of conflict among professionals, as debates raged over the relative value of provenance versus pertinence and medium versus content. See, for example, Terry Cook, "The Tyranny of the Medium: A Comment on 'Total Archives,'" *Archivaria* 9 (winter 1979–80): 141–49; A. Birrell, "The Tyranny of Tradition," *Archivaria* 10 (spring 1980): 248–52; Terry Cook, "Media Myopia," *Archivaria* 12 (summer 1981): 146–57.

16. CCA, Information Highway Task Force, *Raising CAIN,* 13.

17. This is not to say that individual institutions have not gathered information about their users' reactions to descriptive tools. In 1992, Carolyn Heald addressed the issue of reference services in archives, and in 1994 Susan Kooyman examined researchers' reactions to the still new RAD. However, the archival

community as a whole needs to find a way to jump the gap between anecdotal impressions and institution-based findings. They need to examine user reactions across institutions and in different regions. See Carolyn Heald, "Reference Service in Archives: Whither a Professional Ethos?" *Canadian Library Journal* 49 (October 1992): 353–59; Susan Kooyman, "*RAD* and the Researcher," *Archivaria* 37 (spring 1994): 104–10.

18. Message posted on the ARCAN-L listserve, ARCAN-L@majordomo.srv.ualberta.ca, from Paul Maxner, 4 January 2001.

19. Message posted on the ARCAN-L listserve, ARCAN-L@majordomo.srv.ualberta.ca, from Wendy Duff, 8 January 2001.

20. Ibid.

21. See Eric Ketelaar, "Archivalisation and Archiving," *Archives and Manuscripts* 27 (1999): 54–61.

22. There are diverse sources on the issue of provenance in museums and the art world. A small sampling of journal and art magazine sources, particularly with regard to recent research into artistic provenance, includes the following: Michael Daley, "The Back Is Where It's At," *Art Review* 52 (June 2000): 44–45; Robert Read, "Probing Provenance," *Art Newspaper* 83 (July–August 1998): 25; Raphael Rubenstein, "Museums and Holocaust Heirs: An Update," *Art in America* 88.4 (April 2000): 33, 35; Martin Bailey, "British Provenance Probes," *Art Newspaper* 102 (April 2000): 14; Doris Athineos, "Phony Provenances Shake the Art World," *Forbes,* 12 August 1996, 168–71; Antony Griffiths, "Scribbles on the Backs of Prints," *Print Quarterly* 12 (March 1995): 75–78; Peter Barberie, "Thoughts on Exhibiting a Pende Mask," *Record of the Art Museum* 58.1–2 (1999): 62–69; Hubertus Czernin, "Law of Return?" *Art News* 97.10 (November 1998): 80; P. Budd, R. Hatterty, A. M. Pollard, B. Scaife, and R. G. Thomas, "Rethinking the Quest for Provenance," *Antiquity* 70 (1996): 168–74.

23. Sue McKemmish, "Evidence of Me . . ." *Archives and Manuscripts* 24.1 (May 1996): 28–45.

24. See Ian Johnston, "Whose History Is It Anyway? The Need for U.K. Archives to Undertake Pro-Active Acquisition" (master's thesis, University College London, 2000). The author is grateful to Johnston for providing access to his thesis and for offering valuable insights and ideas.

25. Finding aids such as fonds-level descriptions are narratives and so are created with inherent biases and orientations relating to their form and structure. There is scope for investigation of the concept of narrative theory and the study of reference materials as a genre. The author is grateful to Diana Wegner of Douglas College's Department of Communications for insights in this area and recommended areas of investigation, many of which remain to be pursued.

26. Wendy Duff, "The Acceptance and Implementation of Rules for Archival Description by Canadian Archives: A Survey," *Archivaria* 47 (spring 1999): 41.

27. Personal communication with Gary Mitchell, 5 January 2001.

28. Consider the model established at Simon Fraser University in British Columbia. The Canadian Publishers' Records Database (CPRD) was created in the early 1990s as an online guide to archival records relating to English-language book publishing in Canada. As the initial research progressed, organizers realized that a great quantity of publishing records had not yet made their way into archives. To include in the database only those materials already in archival repositories was to exclude a vast portion of Canada's publishing history. And ignoring records still in publishers' offices left the records at risk of loss or neglect, further diminishing the resource base for information about publishing in Canada. The project organizers decided that the database would document not only records found in archives and libraries but also records still in publishers' offices. The CPRD database now serves not only as a finding aid but also as a networking tool. Researchers can find information on publishers' archives, archivists can find out if other institutions have acquired complementary records, and publishers can identify archival institutions that might be interested in their records. More information on the CPRD database is available at www.sfu.ca under the Canadian Centre for Studies in Publishing.

29. Brian Speirs, "Canadian Archival Information Network Update," *Council of Nova Scotia Archives Newsletter,* June 2000, available at http://fox.nstn.ca/~cnsa/news/confiss2/confcain.html. Such consultations involve not only the public user but also representatives of allied institutions, including librarians and museum curators. Librarians have been consulted at various stages throughout the development of RAD; archivists should maintain those links so that both professions can continue to learn from each other. It would be particularly interesting for archivists to know more about the experiences of the Canadian museum community, which developed the Canadian Heritage Information Network (CHIN) in 1972 and is now referred to by CHIN managers as "the electronic gateway to the museum community in Canada and beyond." Information on the CHIN network includes a guide to Canadian museums and galleries, records of artifacts, research and reference information, a heritage forum, virtual exhibitions, educational information and online training, and topical information. Some people have criticized CHIN as inadequate or poorly designed, but that is all the more reason to compare experiences and learn from the museum community's mistakes, if mistakes there are. For more on CHIN, go to http://www.chin.gc.ca/.

Archives, Heritage, and History

David Lowenthal

Diverse archival aims mirror diverse uses of the past in general. At one extreme are disinterested efforts to learn and understand what has actually happened; at the other, partisan zeal to fabricate a past that suits present needs—to forge an identity, to secure a legacy, to validate a conquest or a claim, to prove a preeminence. The role of archives in these contrary goals is symptomatic, indeed, crucial. The conflict is exemplified today in a widening gulf between established archival repute and emerging archival reality.

Texts, like artifacts, have long been treasured in Western culture, both as historical data and as heritage icons. Because the holy books of Jews and Christians embodied God's actual words, their preservation was divinely ordained. Princes and prelates venerated relics and amassed manuscripts, inscriptions, and works of art and antiquity. Conserving records and relics became a public duty and a private aspiration, whether in the face of erosion, pollution, avaricious pillage, or iconoclastic spoliation.

Many other cultures long dwelt more on orally transmitted memories and ritual processes than on tangible and archival heritage. But collectors the world over now emulate Western obsessive concern with material evidence of the past. UNESCO spearheads campaigns to return antiquities taken from former colonial and other lands. The repatriation of lost heritage is deemed integral to the identity and self-respect of nations and of minorities. Archived evidence of cultural continuity can be crucial as tribal bona fides or to sustain local tradition against global pressures.

During the nineteenth and twentieth centuries, archival records came to be valued as reliable repositories of truth, seedbeds of unabridged and veracious history. Open to inspection by all and preserved for all time, archives promised an authentic, untampered-with past. If archivists were

no longer, as for ancient Sumerians, "supervisors of the universe," they were at least the trustworthy stewards of its annals.[1] "The good Archivist," in Sir Hilary Jenkinson's canonical statement of 1947, "is perhaps the most selfless devotee of Truth the modern world produces." That credo—today "at best outdated, at worst inherently dangerous," in one professional's verdict—was until recently too comforting to challenge. "Archivists have been slow to question our profession's long held view of archives and archival records as sites of historical truth."[2]

But this austere, holier-than-thou ideal is now much tarnished. Under growing assault, archives are no longer held to be immortal but now are seen as transient, no longer unabridged and unedited but partial and bowdlerized. They are witnesses not to unadorned truth but to invented contrivance. Just as a "presidential library" today seems a contradiction in terms,[3] so the word *archive* now conjures up confusion, conspiracy, exclusivity. As in José Saramago's cautionary novel, archival repositories are shown to be realms of abuse, irregularity, forgery, and fraud.[4] Once epitomes of the fixed and unblemished record of history, archives now betoken the partisan dubieties of heritage. They are no longer open to all but only to some, often to none in their entirety. Access is ever more curtailed; the very existence of an archive is often known only to a select few. Their prevalent image is like the ad for "Glenlivet Archive" whiskey: a special bottling not generally available to the public.[5]

This fall from virtue distresses those who once lauded archives as paragons of trustworthy permanence. Some react by spurning archives—doubting their commitment to stewardship, pillorying their curators, denying them funds, acquiescing in their dissolution. Natalie Zemon Davis's *Fiction in the Archives*[6] might perhaps better be retitled *Friction in the Archives*. No longer the august arbiter of unquestioned fact, the archive is now a prime locus of doubt and discord.

How and why has this come about? What does it bode for the future?

Misreading Archival History

Mistaken assumptions of previous archival perfection underlie much current dismay. The great libraries of the ancient world were hailed as sanctuaries of the supposed totality of recorded history.[7] The spread of printing lent archives further acclaim as repositories of uncorrupted and unabridged primary sources. Yet actual usage mocked claims of archival plenitude, probity, integrity, and openness. Indeed, written texts long served more to shackle than to liberate inquiry. The sacredness of Holy Scripture made the written word crucial to centralized authority in Jewish, Muslim, and Christian society. Empowered by Emperor Constantine's fourth-century edicts, the Church told Christians what to think and how to act. Missals guided every arena of life in minutest detail, down to which fingers to use for particular gestures. Written texts entrenched theocratic tyranny over vast reaches of monotheistic time and space.

Most archives originated as instruments of landowners' and lawgivers' control. They were the private property of seigneurs and statesmen, conceived and preserved to entrench power and privilege. Archives confirmed and certified rights to land, labor, rents, and produce. Entry to archives was confined to princely, priestly, and scribal elites. "Let the wise instruct the wise," as Mesopotamian tablet texts early enjoined, "for the ignorant should not see them."[8] Not surprisingly, the ignorant who were kept out trashed and burned archives whenever they got hold of them, like Wat Tyler's companions in the Peasants' Revolt of 1381.

Access prohibition was not limited to the ignorant; perusal by the learned might be yet more subversive. In Venice not even the doge could be left unaccompanied in the archives, whose keeper himself was supposed to be illiterate lest he be tempted to read the papers in his care. Secrecy inhered in the very definition of archival holdings, commonly termed "secrets of state." To this day, the Vatican archival collection is formally designated *segreto*. In this regard, archives mirror the agencies they serve. All governments walk a fine line between needs to make information public—proclaiming laws and decrees to be obeyed, for instance—and incentives to keep it private, even at the risk of inflaming rumor and sedition.[9]

Long subjugation under ancient charters and property deeds made archives a key target of French Revolutionary iconoclasm. Many holdings escaped the flames only by being rededicated as essential to national memory; there was never enough time to sort out which papers should be purged as infamous reminders of unjust privilege, "servitude et fanatisme," and which should be saved as historic public legacies. But although the national archives were widely touted as the property of all French citizens, habits of archival exclusion remained ingrained; custodians continued to restrict access, to enforce draconian codes of entry, to confine use to the decorous few.[10]

Elitist embargo was by no means solely French. Open "the heritage neither to Barbarians nor to the Philistines, nor yet to the Populace," declaimed Matthew Arnold in 1869; as late as 1931, Aldous Huxley would confine access within "the great Culture Family," distancing "wretched outsiders."[11] Class-conscious hauteur remains the English custodial norm; asked why they had rejected visitors' requests for published data on housing and school facilities, local council officers in the 1970s replied, "Well, those people were a bit scruffy; they didn't seem properly entitled to see it."[12]

Gentility is no guarantee of archival security, however. Indeed, the gentrified may be especially apt to conceal, even to destroy, evidence of demeaning antecedents. In Tasmania, largely settled by early-nineteenth-century convicts transported from Britain, archival annals are replete with tales of vandalism by Establishment worthies anxious to preserve the fiction of a felon-free family history. Sheets torn out of convict records attest the need to disclaim any taint of criminal ancestry—a need exemplified by an eminent jurist who fainted when he espied a miscreant forebear in the Hobart registry. "Come quick!" exclaimed the archivist: "His Honour has collapsed among the Arthur Papers."[13]

If less blatantly secretive than the English, many U.S. agencies move heaven and earth to hide records from public scrutiny. Aghast at the flood of requests launched under the U.S. Freedom of Information Act (FOIA) (given teeth in 1975 in the outraged wake of Nixon's erased Watergate tapes), the FBI urged the National Archives to destroy copies of its field-office notes on what proved to be a false assurance that the originals survived in FBI headquarters.[14] Deletions from and ever-longer delays in publishing the annual volumes of *The Foreign Relations of the United States* more and more distort the public record, marking a "drastic decline" in Americans' access to their recent history.[15] Retreat from the relative openness and transparency of the late 1970s has been aggravated by post-9/11 security fears. White House executive orders and justice department fiats from an administration termed "the most secretive in recent decades"[16] have closed access to manifold previously available National Archives and other records and blocked the declassification of many more.[17]

Federal agencies react to FOIA requests, now over four million a year, by *curtailing* access; in 2003 the government spent over a hundred times as much keeping things secret as making them available. "We overclassify information," admitted a defense department official in August 2004, not "to hide anything but to err on the side of caution." Caution breeds not just overclassification but pseudoclassification, with an enormous volume of "sensitive but unclassified" (SBU) documents closed to FOIA requests. Executive gag orders quash legislative oversight to such an extent that, said a congressional aide, "we don't even know what we can't talk about."[18]

Concealment in Britain follows suit in every respect. A British Freedom of Information Act became law in January 2005, promising public access to a vast range of information. But the act specifies so many exemptions and is so costly to invoke that many fear "the endemic culture of secrecy will become yet more entrenched." To evade disclosure, "officials will simply avoid putting things in writing." In many cases—such as court records, information supplied in confidence or whose disclosure "would prejudice the effective conduct of public affairs"—officials have little to fear, for "a public authority does not even have to tell you whether it holds the information requested, let alone provide it."[19] Indeed, the word *archive* in Britain gains new meaning. A recent inquiry about 1970s farmwork elicited a Department of Environment, Food and Rural Affairs response that the file had been archived. "When I asked where the archive was kept, I was told that 'archived' meant 'destroyed.'"[20]

The Chaos of Accumulation

Uncontrollable accretion is a second cause of archival degeneration. To be sure, excessive hoarding is common among most types of tangible legacy. Heritage accumulates by its very nature: stockpiling is the raison d'être of stewardship. We amass out of habit and then contend that keeping stuff is good for us and for posterity. Parsimony sanctioned the storage bags labeled "Pieces of string too short to use" and the auto-icon of Jeremy Bentham left in perpetuity to University College London.

Anal-retentive obsession motivated the hoarder of countless jars of his own excrement, the Kansas museum curator gloating over thousands of coils of barbed wire, and Sir Vauncey Harpur-Crewe, who stuffed shells and shards and rocks and swords onto every shelf of every room in Calke Abbey, now an English National Trust shrine to his lust for acquisition.[21] Such hoards can be so burdensome as to be lethally toxic. Like Mark Twain's *Connecticut Yankee,* mortally marooned among the rotting corpses of his electrocuted enemy knights, some custodians would sooner perish amid putrescence than cull their collections.[22]

Archival buildup poses still graver problems because it seems inherently commendable. Judeo-Christian teaching sanctifies the written word, endorses its accumulation, even forbids its destruction. Holy books are repositories of God's actual utterances. To Orthodox Jews, all writing is potentially sacred; lest it contain God's name, not even a grocery list may be jettisoned. This injunction famously preserved inviolate the Geniza cache of medieval documents, which had been walled up and forgotten for six centuries in a Cairo synagogue.[23]

Once the prime province of tax collectors, archives now mushroom in every venture; as Pierre Nora notes, the keeping of records expands from government and academe to bakeries and beauticians, from heraldry experts to roots-seeking hoi polloi.

> No epoch has deliberately produced as many archives as ours, owing to technical advances in reproduction and conservation and to our superstitious respect for these traces. As traditional memory fades, we feel obliged religiously to accumulate the testimonies, documents, images, and visible signs of what was, as if this ever-proliferating dossier should be called on as evidence in some tribunal of history. Hence the inhibition against destroying, the retention of everything. . . . In former times, only great families, the Church, and the state kept records; today memories are recorded and memoirs written not only by minor actors in history but by their spouses and doctors.[24]

The pace of accretion is exponential: the archives of each U.S. president are said to outnumber those of all his predecessors combined. Every day adds twenty thousand new items to the Library of Congress, even though it retains fewer than 2 percent of government records.[25] Storage space, personnel, conservation, and indexing lag ever further behind accessioning.

Archivists are besieged by hopelessly contrary diktats—adjured on the one hand to collect only what "they can afford to responsibly arrange, describe, preserve, and provide access to," compelled on the other to keep everything dumped on them.[26] Accessions so deluge state and local archives that acquisitions are often kept secret lest the public demand to peruse data there are no funds to conserve, let alone to organize. Elephantiasis afflicts artifactual archives as well. Responsible archaeologists take pride in not digging but instead in surveying, trusting that future generations may excavate with less loss of information. Yet new finds still mount up too fast to record, to process, even to store. Totally out of warehouse space, the Museum of London in 1998 faced "absolute disaster."[27]

Laments of information glut go back to Seneca, but two later innovations—fifteenth-century printing and twentieth-century electronic reproduction—have gravely aggravated the problem. The proliferation of printed material between 1550 and 1750 led Robert Burton to feel oppressed by "a vast chaos and confusion of books" and Denis Diderot to fear "a time will come when it will be almost as difficult to learn anything from books as from the direct study of the whole universe, . . . almost as convenient to search for some truth concealed in nature as . . . to find it hidden away in an immense multitude of bound volumes."[28] So pervasive was early-modern concern about the explosion of books, the flood of facts, the innumerable new species of things and ideas, and the multiplication of authorities that one wonders "how and why a phenomenon so patently old can periodically and convincingly be re-experienced as a fundamental symptom of the new."[29]

Print made writing cheap and easy to disseminate; electronics diffuses texts everywhere instantaneously. With both advances, unselective proliferation brought unhappy side effects. To supply a broader but less learned public, publishers printed more and more rubbish. But informed judgment still enabled gatekeepers of the printed word—editors, archivists, librarians—to sift classic wheat from common chaff. The computer and the Internet allow no such informed scrutiny. The more easily data are produced, the harder they are to filter.[30] Overload progressively inhibits retrieval: in 1997, one-third of the World Wide Web's 320 million pages were indexed; in 1999, of 800 million pages only one-sixth were indexed. By 2002 the amount of data produced had more than doubled, with 800 megabytes for every person on the planet; the e-mails sent would have filled the British Library half a million times.[31]

Far from promoting knowledge, this avalanche of raw data imperils it. It forces us to spend more and more time attending to "information as garbage, information divorced from purpose and even meaning"—not just with "more statements about the world than we have ever had," in Neil Postman's phrase, but, because the Internet cannot distinguish between true and false, with "more *erroneous* statements than we have ever had."[32] Bereft of cataloging and other aids, Internet users cannot evaluate the glut they face and, worse still, have no idea what may be missing. More and more unable to see the forest for the trees, historians of recent centuries envy scholars of ancient and medieval times for having so little raw material at their disposal.[33]

We moderns wander along the endless corridors of Borges's Babylonian library, surrounded by all possible books in the universe but unable to locate what we seek among the infinite clutter of useless gibberish. The dream of unlimited access becomes an anarchic nightmare. Borges compared his own lot as a blind librarian to that of Midas, dying of hunger and thirst in the midst of food and drink. *Twilight Zone*'s sole survivor of a nuclear cataclysm relives the Midas/Borges fix: heartened at least to find that all the world's books are still available to him, he suffers the final catastrophe of breaking his indispensable eyeglasses.[34] Our Internet world becomes that of Stanislaw Lem's robot, who greedily devours data on "the sizes of bedroom slippers available on the continent of Cob, . . . and six ways to cook cream of wheat . . . and the names of all citizens of Foofaraw Junction beginning with the letter M." At last he cries "enough," but "Information had so swathed and swaddled him in its three hundred thousand tangled paper miles, that he couldn't move and had to read on, about . . . the courtship of the carrion fly and why we don't capitalize paris in plaster of paris."[35] We have gone, as Simmel predicted almost a century ago, from the blissful poverty of the Franciscans' *nihil habientes, omni possidentes* (having nothing, possessing everything) to *omni habientes, nihil possidentes* (having everything, possessing nothing).[36]

Glut incites iconoclasm even among stewards of the word. Librarians delight in dumping books—"our own slum clearance program"[37]—and shredding newspapers. They demonize old paper and dismember shabby tomes because "they hate the stuff and want to get rid of it at all costs."[38] Destructive purification "seems to excite people." They fling out card catalogs "because *they hate them*. They feel cleaner, lighter, healthier, more unpolysaturated, when all that thick, butter-colored paper is gone."[39] These are not just bogeymen dreamed up by the gadfly Nicholson Baker. Federal agencies commend archivists who radically cull, reward those who ruthlessly deaccession. Federal grants encouraged universities to put "greater emphasis on the *discarding* of books rather than their storage," wrote a gratified Yale librarian.⁴⁰ "Not since the monk-harassments of 16th century England," concludes Baker, "has a government tolerated, indeed stimulated, the methodical eradication of so much primary-source material."⁴¹

Throttled by congestion, unable to budge among their "mass of interlocked things, the great squared-up block of objects, of totems, of purchases made and accreted . . . packed as tightly as the stones at Machu Picchu," T. C. Boyle's fictional addicts of acquisition end by begging exterminators to scrape them of everything they own.⁴² No wonder actual archivists and librarians are sometimes tempted to excise the cancer of accumulation by a root-and-branch clean sweep, to scrap their cluttered holdings in exchange for sparse and spacious purity.

The Perils of Innovation

Dearth rather than excess remains our most abiding fear, however. Archival extinction seems more terrifying than indecipherable surfeit.⁴³ Habituated to rely on the written record, we are utterly vulnerable to its threatened loss. We lack the memory skills of our preliterate forebears. In memory's stead, the accrued annals of myriad precursors situate us in the far lengthier stream of historical time. Bridging vicariously experienced remote pasts with recent familiar times, the written record alerts us to the intricate interplay of continuity and change. But the priceless benefit of this literate palimpsest demands the assured perpetuity of archival stocks. Dread lest they disappear has haunted humanity since the dawn of the written record.

Yet our power to reproduce that record has augmented exponentially, from manuscript to print, print to photocopy, copier to computer. Why does each innovation that multiplies the written word at the same time aggravate anxiety about its very survival? Some shun any new technology as a rupture with sacred tradition; much as book lovers blame the attrition of serious reading on computers, so the sixteenth-century Benedictine monk Trithemius mourned the print-induced demise of manuscript copying, a vocation that infused monastic life with moral meaning.⁴⁴ Others worry lest the documentary babe perish with the change of bathwater: "time and again we are hoodwinked by new technology 'guaranteed' to save us space, time, labour or money . . . and then discover that it is twice as expensive and half as efficient as what we had before."⁴⁵

In truth, conservers of the written word have good cause to worry. Inherent in each reproductive novelty lurks some fearsome new agent of decay. The vellum of medieval manuscripts lasted a thousand years or more, rag paper usually much less, paper from wood pulp less still. Indeed, the imminent crumbling to dust of late-nineteenth- and twentieth-century books—though grossly exaggerated by those eager to rid library shelves of them—became the chief rationale for their replacement by microfiche, microfilm, and computer disks. Film and electronic reproduction and storage are, however, notoriously imperfect: "the history of photographic facsimiles is littered with disasters, pages missed, volumes skipped and passages rendered illegible."⁴⁶ And the pace of loss in ink and print is glacial compared with electronic attrition. NASA computer data from the 1960s have dissolved into a series of 1s and 0s, unreadable since the destruction or obsolescence of the hardware and software that created them.⁴⁷ As with cellulose-nitrate movie film and audio and video tapes, technical advances hasten the demise of electronic data; the brief life expectancy of Web pages lowers every year, and few traces remain of extinct Web sites.⁴⁸ We are in the digital Dark Age of "dead media, most of them with the working life span of a pack of Twinkies," concludes Bruce Sterling. Interred with past computers (Altair, Amiga, Amstrad . . .), adds Stewart Brand, "are whole clans of programming languages, operating systems, storage formats, and countless rotting applications. . . . Everything written on them was written on the wind, leaving not a trace."⁴⁹

Manuscripts that remain undiscovered, hence undisturbed, can well survive for centuries; printed books normally endure for generations even if not actively conserved. Electronic texts thus neglected yield nothing at all a mere decade on. Yet the ubiquity of their obsolescence goes unheeded; "those at the cutting edge of machine-readable records," observes a government archivist, "are often the very ones who seriously believe that technological progress will halt tomorrow so that what's readable today will be for centuries."⁵⁰ We are unlikely to find crucial obsolete equipment in Ye Olde Antique Computer Shoppe.⁵¹ That demons of decay accompany angels of proliferation also reflects devaluation of what is easily copied. Data made superabundant depreciate in worth. Hence less effort is made to preserve them; indeed, surfeit makes their endurance a nuisance. Like biblical moth and rust, decay and obsolescence are welcomed for clearing the decks of outdated rubbish.

No less corrosive than the new technologies are the

habits they engender. A former Librarian of Congress terms the Internet "inherently destructive of memory. You think you're getting lots more information, [but] you've made a bargain with the devil. You've slowly mutated and become an extension of the machine."[52] Historians no longer do much research that requires reading old newspapers "because their libraries don't keep the old papers to read, and microfilm is a brain-poaching, gorge-lifting trial to browse."[53] Surfing the Web shortens attention spans, mangles literary structure, skews study toward the very recent past, and privileges action over reflection.

Indeed, reflection becomes a dispensable luxury. "TV people are an entirely different breed," explains Tina Brown. "Print people like to think they are more thoughtful, but that's only because they can afford to think slowly. Editors and writers can doodle around for weeks without doing much."[54] Impatience with sustained inquiry impoverishes language; "difficult" classics are inaccessible unless abridged and streamlined. Books are advertised and read as decontextualized adjuncts to films. The audiovisual age is postcritical: credible information is only what's seen on the screen. Indeed, it is thought credible because it is on the screen, for which, unlike texts, there are no rules or routes of verification.

New Trends Jeopardize Archival Accessibility

The open archive of the past was a goal never fully achieved. Nonetheless, advances toward literacy and social inclusion won access for ever more users. Much today newly imperils that openness. As noted, glut and disarray diminish facilities for archival use. The dizzying pace of information technology confines the latest modes of retrieval to experts while consigning familiar time-tested means of access to the dustbin. High-tech apparatus and costly databases restrict archival use to the well equipped and the well-off, and "market forces continually compound these pressures," notes James O'Donnell: "Today, libraries can buy an encyclopedia and put it on the shelves for anyone to use. Tomorrow, they may have to pay a large fee to get the encyclopedia, then be charged an additional fee for every use of the resource, be forbidden to let anyone not a member of a particular university community have any access to it at all, and be required to give it back if they stop paying an annual fee."[55]

With ever less data on open shelves, the general public is more and more excluded. From a public service, the archive becomes a privatized commodity. The omnium-

gatherum gives way to the specialized data bank—the word itself suggests moneyed sequestering. Market forces render archival contents increasingly ephemeral. Up-to-the-minute utility to corporate consumers not only dominates data retrieval but determines data survival; material of less immediate "relevance" or of mere "antiquarian" interest gets ditched. Just as journals once open to all become accessible online only to the few, once-public archives drift into pay-for-use services. Data thus withdrawn from ready scrutiny ceases to be veridical for or veracious to society at large. Rather than repositories for reaching consensually agreed truths, archives become propaganda dossiers for special interests.

The enfranchisement envisioned by Internet pioneers has proved abortive and short-lived. At the start many dreamed that the expert would "no longer stand between people and their pasts," because "the Net would empower individuals. The little guy could disseminate his views without a publisher or distributor. The humble activist could download reams of free data." Instead, governments use the Net to snoop, entrepreneurs convert it into a shopping mall, and global business preempts its cables.[56] "The democratic and anarchical dreams of the early Web pioneers are not just threatened by the commercialization of the Internet, but by [corporate] firewalled protective networks."[57] In theory, Web-based publications can be accessed from any of the world's 100 million terminals; in practice, they are less accessible than the rarest library books. "In a world of encryption, commercially sensitive information, pay-as-you-view websites, [and] copy protection technology, the transmission and distribution of recorded knowledge . . . is becoming severely restricted."[58] The Internet archive has "put the future of the past—traditionally seen as a public patrimony—in private hands," concludes a historian. Adobe eBook subscribers are warned that the books they download may not even be read aloud.[59]

Pressures on corporate history writing further subvert archival integrity. What should be done, a seminar group was asked, if a researcher on contract to write a business history found archival material embarrassing to the firm? The answer: to destroy the evidence would be unethical; instead, reshelve it under lock and key to minimize the chance it is ever seen again.[60] This is no mere perverse fancy; as I will show, it is common archival practice in heritage affairs.

Paradoxically, well-meant efforts to extend archival participation to once excluded minorities may further imperil open access. Like regal and papal potentates of yore, tribal and other indigenes often consider archival knowledge sacred and exclusive to their own elites, defiled or polluted if seen by outsiders. Mainstream promotion of universal ideals can backfire when minorities prescribe or proscribe what is acquired and who may view it. After encouraging Maori-curated exhibits, New Zealand museums were saddled with Maori diktats that put these exhibits off-limits to non-Maoris and to Maori women. Similar policies of exclusion apply to Maori-owned archives.[61]

Museums and archives bend to minority sensibilities even when demands are not expressly voiced. Political correctness may oblige repositories to eliminate or sequester matter offensive to anyone. To counter widespread looting and faking, more and more museums turn down antiquities of dubious pedigree and on occasion yield up those they already have. To display unprovenanced items is rebuked as an incitement to theft. Because a 1994 London Royal Academy classical exhibition lacked adequate context on the origins of these treasures, it was assailed for tacitly endorsing pillage and illicit trade—"antiquity laundering."[62] Some would ban research use or even mention of artifacts with a dubious pedigree. Smithsonian archaeologists are enjoined not to cite certain artifacts returned to tribal claimants. To get permission to use Apache blood samples, geneticists studying disease resistance had to agree to refrain from any research "that might contradict traditional views of the tribe's history."[63]

More menacing than the old Papal Index's detailed explicit prohibitions, modern rules for exclusion are vague and variable, the Orwellian inspectorate protean and anonymous. Hypersensitive, we police ourselves against exposure to the sinister, the sexist, even the satirical. Data from written and oral sources thought tainted are disallowed. To be sure, clandestine wiretaps, coerced confessions, and induced false memories offer valid precedents for barring some types of evidence. The growing porosity of communication raises cogent concerns about privacy; even your kid sister may turn Big Brother. Our self-archived lives are more and more open to all. But legal controls against such evils can be so sweeping as to preclude legitimate freedom of inquiry.

Consider, for example, the chilling effect on oral history of federal institutional review board (IRB) scrutiny in the United States. IRBs were first set up to ensure that "human subjects" in medical experiments had given their informed consent and were treated ethically. But oral history is now lumped together with medical research. Like physicians, historians must supply detailed questionnaires before conducting interviews, avoid "sensitive" topics, alert informants to likely risks and discomforts, guarantee anonymity, and promise to destroy (or to stash privately at home) interview tapes after research has been published. While such constraints are the norm in biomedical research, they are anathema to historians, whose interviews are typically open-ended and whose data must be open to public scrutiny. For nuts-and-bolts programmatic surveys, it makes sense that data once used be destroyed or privatized. But for historians, this precludes contingent inquiry, comparative criticism, and future verification or revision by others.

The threat is not confined to research that uses oral interviews; federal review boards extend concern for informant privacy back to historical events in the public record. "Some IRBs have questioned [historians'] use of sources in the public record, including newspapers and manuscripts collections, simply because they deal with the activities of human beings." In the end, federal oversight conveys a warning that "controversial, difficult, or challenging topics cannot be addressed in historical research." The dilemma faced by oral historians was no bizarre exception; it highlights quandaries confronted by numerous archival suppliers and users. As government-funded projects multiply, academic officials find it convenient to oversee all campus research under university IRBs. Hence constraints initially intended for work supported by federal grants—seldom the case with historians—come at length to apply to any university-based research. Administrative fiat thus encumbers all inquiry and all source materials with curbs devised for applied research of immediate utility. The mere notion that information might have a value beyond the narrow purpose for which it was first gathered is viewed askance as suspicious, elitist, even seditious.[64]

Why Heritage Subverts Archives

Nothing begins life in an archive, and few things remain there forever. Most holdings alternate between archival and nonarchival locales and functions. Documents originate for personal or social aims—to set a plan, state a view, justify an act, assert a claim, argue or judge a dispute. When archived, family and state papers are initially confidential, heritage withheld from public view. Only after thirty or fifty or seventy years or more does general access outweigh concern for privacy; archival records then become public history. At length, if rare or sacred like Dead Sea Scrolls or Shakespeare first folios, documents may be showcased as collective heritage; their talismanic worth as tangible witnesses to some pivotal event or personality now surpasses their value as historical evidence.[65] According primacy to "the fetish of the document," the archive is revamped from information center to reliquary shrine.[66] Seemingly embarrassed to be "seen for what it is: a treasure trove of records available to any citizen interested in examining them," the U.S. National Archives aims "to reshape its image from that of a fusty repository for the nation's documents to that of a modern, interactive museum, exhibition space and education center."[67] (To one recent visitor, the National Archives' vast Maryland repository rather "radiates a sense of intrigue.")[68]

In an era steeped in nostalgia for the recent past, yesteryear's relics may perilously encroach on the active present. An Oakland museum was on the verge of acquiring California's disused gas chamber when the state reinstated the death penalty; the "obsolete" engine of execution almost had to be clawed back from exhibit hall to death row. Concurrently, exclusive private rights to heritage reassert legal force over augmented realms of creativity ever farther back in time. Newly extended copyright restrictions presage grievous inroads on an ever-shrinking public domain; given current trends, soon "we won't be able to quote Chaucer without the say-so of some pompous descendant."[69]

Because heritage issues are often heatedly contentious, managing heritage records is an especially arduous task. Adversarial polemics set the tone and comprise the bulk of relevant data. Issued from a daunting congeries of sources—government circulars, accounts of rallies, partisan broadsides, legal threats, minutes of disputes over ownership, control, access, conservation—heritage materials are ephemeral, fragmentary, discontinuous, hard to classify. And repositories habitually cordon off such data by realm, by discipline, and by national or ethnic context. The protean nature of heritage defies comprehensive coverage. To collect and classify more than a tiny fraction of its vital records is beyond the capacity of any library or archive. Yet archival breadth is essential to keep us aware of the intricate complexity of what Pierre Nora terms *lieux de mémoire*, Raphael Samuel "theatres of memory," Michael Kammen "mystic chords of memory."[70]

Curating such materials is a political as well as a scholarly minefield. As the amalgam of all our pasts, heritage ought ideally be shared among all humanity. But this global precept gets little more than lip service, if that, from national and local stewards. Instead, heritage usually features as the unique and jealously guarded property of some particular group. It is amassed, hoarded, pre-

served, and construed on behalf of national and tribal partisans. Quests to magnify one's own heritage and to engross or suppress that of rivals are legion and unending. Romans strove to expunge Carthaginian memory, Nazis to eradicate that of Jews.[71] From ancient Alexandria to modern Sarajevo, museums and libraries have been prime targets of enemy assault, with more lost to willful than to accidental incineration.[72] In Siegfried Lenz's archetypal novel, *The Heritage,* a Masurian folk museum's artifacts suffer recurrent perversion at the hands of chauvinist invaders, first Russian, then German, then Polish. In the end, the despairing director sets fire to his whole collection, so as to "bring the collected witnesses to the past into a final and irrevocable safety from which they could never again be exploited for this cause or that."[73] Fact follows fiction: to expunge the odium of prior museum display, ancestral bones and artifacts repatriated to tribal groups are nowadays apt to be consigned to purifying flames.

Fire is not the only mode of purging a defiled legacy; burial and excision are common alternatives. William Fee, the missionary founder of Berea College, Kentucky, so loathed slavery that he literally knifed out every scriptural reference to servitude; displayed in Berea's library, Fee's butchered Bible attests his faith that evil can be undone by excision. (Per contra, scriptural references to freedom and revolt led apprehensive slaveholders to prohibit slaves from reading the Bible—indeed, from reading at all.)

That the archival "record must reflect full diversity and complexity, not an edited compendium that celebrates a specific world view or a single group," is a professional credo widely endorsed.[74] But it is largely disregarded by heritage stewards. As a Pequot Indian spokesman recently insisted, the tribal archives are their own; in them "the tribe can document its history in its own words and images, not those of others."[75] This possessive take is not uniquely Pequot; as already noted, it is Maori, Masurian, American. "The archival record doesn't just happen; it is created by individuals and organizations, and used . . . to support their values and missions," writes Elisabeth Kaplan. "Archivists are major players in the business of identity politics. Archives appraise, collect, and preserve the props with which notions of identity are built," and archival holdings confirm and justify the authority of those views.[76]

The ongoing Elgin Marbles affray exemplifies the fractious role of archives in heritage issues. Claims of peerless stewardship long buttressed British retention against Greek repatriation demands; the British Museum professed to secure the frieze, removed from the Parthenon two centuries ago, against Athenian air pollution and instability. But the British custodial image was badly dented in 1998, when a new edition of William St Clair's definitive history divulged the dreadful damage done in the late 1930s. The art collector Lord Duveen had given the museum a new room in which to display the Elgin Marbles; at his behest (Duveen wanted them to be white, as he mistakenly thought classical sculpture should be), they underwent drastic "cleaning" with chisels and Carborundum.

When the damage was discovered, museum officials sought to conceal the actual mutilation and then to slur over the harm done. The first shocked reactions—"mutilation," "crime," "destruction"—gave way to "great damage," then just "damage"; "technically damaged" at length eased into "unauthorized methods of cleaning" and "inappropriate restoration treatment."[77] The press was deceived, Parliament hoodwinked, even curators kept in the dark. Among those complicit, as museum trustees, were the prime minister and the archbishop of Canterbury, anxious to avoid offending Greece as a wartime ally. Yet stonewalling continued even after St Clair's exposé—to minimize the extent of loss, to shrug off blame, to sustain the repute of museum and nation as caretakers.[78]

Only the disclosure of zealously hidden archival papers brought the saga to light. Published records were deeply deceptive; indeed, disguise was their intent. It took unpublished sources—photographs, minutes of meetings, interviews with workmen, confidential reports, and personal letters—to reveal the facts. Piercing the carapace of self-protective secrecy required uncommon expertise and persistence. The contortions of museum concealment all but defy credence: 1930s files normally open after thirty years were withheld from scrutiny as "current" data well into the 1990s by being bound with ongoing documents. The bloated "file" was so unwieldy it could not be properly shelved.[79]

Denying that unwanted data even exist is typical in heritage affairs. In the 1980s New York's American Museum of Natural History (AMNH) secretly schemed to absorb the holdings of the Museum of the American Indian (MAI), all the while publicly promising joint custody in new custom-built premises. When the deal collapsed, the ensuing lawsuit forced the AMNH to disclose internal memos and letters showing that its offer had been a sham, cloaking the takeover aim. The AMNH had doctored its own architects' reports, fed the MAI misleading data, juggled and misdated letters, and hidden the damning discrepant evidence in its files.[80]

Archival concealment similarly gained Connecticut's Pequot Indians tribal bona fides as well as land crucial for their hugely lucrative Foxwoods Casino. On the pretence of racial injustice woefully protracted, tribal lawyers persuaded Congress to waive normal Bureau of Indian Affairs scrutiny, obscured the flagrant lack of Pequot tribal continuity, and mapped as "tribal"—hence beyond Connecticut jurisdiction—lands that had never been Pequot. In ensuing brawls with private property owners and the state, Pequot claimants invoked sagas of ancient wrongs demanding redress, paraded federal imprimaturs (won from complaisant congressmen ignorant of local affairs), and kept mum about the concoction of the grossly inflated "definitive" tribal lands map, for years withheld from public scrutiny.[81]

These episodes are unusual only in having come to light by ferreting out normally concealed data. Blatant misuse of archival holdings is not the exception but the rule in heritage matters. Precisely because such quarrels are never just about the past but deeply affect ongoing rivalries and present reputations, heritage research is sure to be frustrated by hidden, lost, and doctored archival material. Such perversions are bound to persist as long as heritage stewards cleave to Sir Henry Taylor's classic dictum that "a secret may be sometimes best kept by keeping the secret of its being a secret."[82]

Even the most canny historians sometimes fail to bear in mind the pitfalls posed by such impediments, as Jonathan Steinberg ruefully reported of his own dealings with the Deutsche Bank. He had agreed to help survey the bank's World War II archives for a let-the-chips-fall-where-they-may report on Nazi complicity. Only too late did Steinberg become aware that subordinate aides—not he and his fellow historians—would initially sift the impossibly voluminous data. Nor had he realized that the records to be scrutinized excluded a substantial cache of Deutsche Bank directors' so-called "family" archives.[83]

Erosion of Familiar Terms of Discourse

Current changes in archival practice profoundly affect how we use and what we think of the past. Perhaps the most somber effect of the new "post-custodial" archive[84] is the attrition of historical awareness. Some laud today's flood of electronic data as heterogeneous, multivocal, instantly accessible, infinitely reproducible, and readily disposable. But these benefits, if such they be, come at a heavy cost: the loss of an enduring social framework grounded in an abundance of shared cultural references.[85]

The fading away of familiar terms of discourse is a complaint recurrently voiced by every passing generation.[86] But today's media and schooling lend this lament new cogency. Once-memorable people, events, and common idioms ebb into oblivion ever more swiftly. Media dispersion that makes fame and infamy global also makes them fleeting; for those devoid of history, temporal depth conveys no meaning. A confrontation in Paris left the writer Alethea Hayter fearful that historical consciousness would soon "be not merely eclipsed but extinguished." An anglophone visitor at Sainte Chapelle asked Hayter what the place was all about.

> "Well," I began, "it was built by Saint Louis . . ." "Saint Louis?" was her puzzled reply ... "Yes, it was built by a king of France who went on a crusade . . ." "Crusade?" she asked, bewildered. Despairingly I persevered. "Yes, he went on a journey to the Mediterranean, and brought back a sacred relic, the Crown of Thorns . . ." "Crown of Thorns?" she queried, still more at sea. At that point I gave up; I felt unable to insert any idea of the significance of the Sainte Chapelle into a mind which had been given no context of European history or Christian belief at all.[87]

The erosion of canonical names and dates maroons many today in the narrowest of presents, precluding fellowship with any past. The 1930 historical spoof *1066 and All That: A Memorable History of England, Comprising All the Parts You Can Remember, Including 103 Good Things, Five Bad Kings and Two Genuine Dates* no longer amuses readers because few but the most elderly have even heard of the persons and events it ridicules.[88] Archival change may be more a symptom than a cause of such temporal attrition. Yet "our entire collective subjective history . . . is encoded in print," notes Sven Birkerts. Hence, the shift from print to visually oriented electronic culture "has rendered a vast part of our cultural heritage utterly alien."[89] The lack of any frame of reference leaves today's children bereft of a crucial "arc of connectedness," in Harry Belafonte's words: "Mandela might just as well be Abe Lincoln and Dr. King, Jesus Christ."[90]

To be sure, some communal references persist; mass-media consumers share extensive repertoires in sports, music, fashion, and popular culture. But that store of data is trivial, inchoate, and ephemeral; it nourishes no discourse beyond its own short-lived icons; it links its devotees with only a very recent past; its substance is too thin to support a meaningful social fabric.[91] Google's reservoir of six billion documents seems "the shallowest ocean on earth, overloaded with sex, sports, conspiracy theories and pop stars" and short on all but the most recent history, largely to do with film costume drama: not the Mother of God but Madonna, not Milton but Milton Keynes, not the Hundred Years War but Star Wars.[92] Pop culture does not compensate for "the loss of the historical frame of reference, the amputation of the time dimension from our culture." To be "in the swim," noted an eminent art historian, is not equivalent to "being in the culture."[93]

Some contend that the ease and speed of modern information retrieval makes such cultural memory redundant—why store in the mind names and dates readily found in databases? But to have references at our fingertips, so to speak, is by no means the same as having them in our head. To converse, to compare, to contrast, even to consult an encyclopedia requires a stock of common knowledge that is not merely on tap but ingrained, part of general communal awareness. That is why great classics remain canonical: their enduringly resonant words and allusions bridge barriers of time and culture. "It is the destiny of those grave, restrained and classic writers, with whom we make enforced and often painful acquaintanceship at school," wrote Robert Louis Stevenson a century ago, "to pass into the blood and become native in the memory."[94]

Stevenson's precept is integral to informed reliance on our archived legacy. Textual sources open to inspection and reexamination still underpin our way of finding and confirming truth. But archives seem ever more alien to modern modes of perception. They are underfunded and neglected (compared with our art and architectural heritage) because "archives are more difficult to experience," in a British estimate. "Archives are essentially textual; they have to be interpreted through an intellectual effort. . . . They are cerebral, and cerebral is not what captures the public imagination."[95]

Indeed, archives are commonly stigmatized not only as tediously cerebral but dirty, disease-ridden, death-inducing. Derrida's *mal d'archive* is not a new ailment; eighteenth- and nineteenth-century essayists repeatedly reviled archives as dusty, moldy, and rotting, their users richly deserving the ailments they engendered.[96] This was no mere figure of speech; archives literally bred disease, just as the working of leather for parchment and bookbinding gave rise to anthrax. At the Archives Nationales in Paris in the 1820s the historian Jules Michelet restored papers and parchments "to the light of day as I breathed in their dust"; Michelet actually ate history, observed Roland Barthes, and eating it made him ill.[97] The demise of two archival aides, employed by H. C. Lea in 1870 to copy records for his *History of the Inquisition,* ominously echoed that fearsome agency; Signori Bugazzi and Uccelli perished in swift succession "re infecta" (the business being unfinished) in the Florentine archives.[98]

That archival hazards mirror human frailty is the burden of the Nobel laureate Saramago's *All the Names.* Saramago's central registry shelves particulars of everyone living and dead, but finding a file in the unlit labyrinthine corridors is a perilous task. Lost in the dark disarray of these catacombs, one researcher emerges only after a week, starving, thirsty, delirious, having survived only by ingesting quantities of old documents. Above all, custodial negligence and corruption frustrate attempts to segregate records of the living from those of the dead. Mortality would doom this effort in any case; for archives, like humans, are fated to be fragmentary, partisan, and transient.[99] And changes in the one vitally affect the other. "What is no longer archived in the same way," observes Derrida, "is no longer lived in the same way."[100]

NOTES

1. Sumerian inscription quoted in *Naissance de l'écriture: Cunéiformes et hiéroglyphes,* ed. Béatrice André-Leicknam and Christiane Ziegler (Paris: Éditions de la Réunion des musées nationaux, 1982), 326.

2. Elisabeth Kaplan, "We Are What We Collect, We Collect What We Are: Archives and the Construction of Identity," *American Archivist* 63 (2000): 144, 147.

3. Richard Cohen, "Buy Patriotic Socks at the Library," *International Herald Tribune,* 15 February 2001. Sarah Bird's *Alamo House: Women without Men, Men without Brains* (New York: Norton, 1986), mocks Lyndon B. Johnson's presidential library as the repository not of secret letters from Ho Chi Minh and "blueprints of the Great Society" but of copies of brownie recipes and public responses to the time LBJ lifted his dog by her ears (Arlene Schmuland, "The Archival Image in Fiction: An Analysis and Annotated Bibliography," *American Archivist* 62 [1999]: 50).

4. José Saramago, *All the Names* (London: Harvill, 1999).

5. Cited in William J. Miller, "Archives, Archivists, and Society," *American Archivist* 61 (1998): 259.

6. Natalie Zemon Davis, *Fiction in the Archives: Pardon Tales and Their Tellers in Sixteenth-Century France* (Cambridge: Polity, 1987).

7. Donald R. Kelley, *Faces of History: Historical Inquiry from Herodotus to Herder* (New Haven: Yale University Press, 1998), 207–8.

8. Quoted in *Naissance de l'écriture,* 336.

9. Peter Burke, *A Social History of Knowledge* (London: Polity, 2000), 139–46. Vatican refusal in 2001 to allow full archival access led a historians' commission to suspend its study of the Church's role in the Holocaust.

10. Krzysztof Pomian, "Les Archives: Du Trésor des chartes au Caran," in Pierre Nora, *Les lieux de mémoire* (Paris: Gallimard, 1984–92), III: *Les France,* 3: *De l'archive à l'emblème,* 181–90; Michel Duchein, "The History of European Archives and the Development of the Archival Profession in France," *American Archivist* 55:1 (winter 1992): 14–25; Simone Balayé, *La Bibliothèque Nationale des origines à 1800* (Geneva: Droz, 1988); Alberto Manguel, *A History of Reading* (New York: Penguin, 1996), 239–40.

11. Matthew Arnold, *Culture and Anarchy* (1869; Cambridge: University Press, 1960), 210; Aldous Huxley, "On the Charms of History and the Future of the Past," in his *Music at Night and Other Essays* (1931; Harmondsworth: Penguin, 1950), 190.

12. David Vincent, *The Culture of Secrecy: Britain, 1832–1998* (New York: Oxford University Press, 1998), details the crumbling of public trust as growing erosion of privacy accompanies persisting secrecy in government.

13. Geoffrey Stilwell, quoted in Christopher Koch, "Archival Days—An Afterword," in *Tasmanian Insights: Essays in Honour of Geoffrey Thomas Stilwell,* ed. Gillian Winter (Hobart: State Library of Tasmania, 1992), 230. Only lately have Tasmanian gentry begun to treasure rather than trash archival evidence of lowly origins. Enthralled by records of low-life forebears, one well-born young man told his father, who turned pale. "Yes, my boy, that's all very well; but you must never let the aunts know" (Geoffrey Stilwell, personal communication, 1977).

14. Athan G. Theoharis, "Introduction," 12, and "The Freedom of Information Act versus the FBI," 30, in *A Culture of Secrecy: The Government versus the Public's Right to Know,* ed. Athan G. Theoharis (Lawrence: University Press of Kansas, 1998).

15. Page Putnam Miller, "Why We Can't Read Our Own Mail: Access to the Records of the Department of State," in *Culture of Secrecy,* ed. Theoharis, 207–8.

16. Philip Aftergood, Federation of American Scientists, quoted in Elisabeth Bumiller, "Bush Orders a 3-Year Delay in Opening Secret Documents," *New York Times,* 28 March 2003.

17. Celestine Bohlen, "Whose History Is It, Anyway? The Public's or the Officials'?" *New York Times,* 24 February 2002; Bruce Craig, "Records Withdrawn from Public Access," *American Historical Association Perspectives* 40:5 (May 2002): 16; Bruce Craig, "State Secrets, Advisory Committees, and the CIA," *American Historical Association Perspectives* 42:2 (February 2004): 14–16; Bruce Craig, "Combating Government Secrecy—An Update," *American Historical Association Perspectives* 42:7 (October 2004): 15–16. On Canadian culture-of-secrecy issues, see Jay Gilbert, "Access Denied in *The Access to Information Act* and Its Effects on Public Records Creators," *Archivaria* 49 (spring 2000): 84–123.

18. Quotes in Eric Lichtblau, "Material Given to Congress in 2002 Is Now Classified," *New York Times,* 20 May 2004, A18; "Emerging Threats: Overclassification and Pseudo-Classification," congressional subcommittee hearing, 2 March 2005, reported in National Coalition for History, Washington Update 11:9, 4 March 2005. For an overview, see Geoffrey R. Stone, *Perilous Times: Free Speech in Wartime from the Alien*

and Sedition Acts of 1798 to the War on Terrorism (New York: Norton, 2004).

19. Anthony Burton and Keith Mathieson, quoted in Alex Wade, "Everything You Want To Know . . . ," *The Times* (London), 24 August 2004, T2: 23.

20. Geoffrey Humble, "Out of Harm's Way," letter, *The Times* (London), 29 July 2004.

21. Philipp Blom, *To Have and to Hold: An Intimate History of Collectors and Collecting* (London: Allen Lane, 2002); Martin Drury, "The Restoration of Calke Abbey," *Journal of the Royal Society of Arts* 136 (1988): 497.

22. Mark Twain, *A Connecticut Yankee in King Arthur's Court* (New York, 1889); David Lowenthal, *The Past Is a Foreign Country* (Cambridge: Cambridge University Press, 1985), 63–66.

23. Ernst R. Curtius, *European Literature and the Latin Middle Ages* (1948; London: Routledge and Kegan Paul, 1953), 310–19; Paul E. Kahle, *The Cairo Geniza* (Oxford: Blackwell, 1959), 4. Such documents were not intended for archival perpetuity but for burial in consecrated ground.

24. Pierre Nora, "Entre mémoire et histoire," in *Lieux de mémoire*, I: *La République* (1984), xxv–xxviii.

25. Daniel Boorstin, "The Enlarged Contemporary" (Reith Lectures, 1975), *The Listener*, 11 December 1975, 788; John Carlin, "Records Everywhere, but How Are They Going to Survive?" *The Record* 5:1 (September 1998): 1–3.

26. Diane Vogt-O'Connor, "Archives—A Primer for the 21st Century," *Cultural Resource Management*, 22:2 (1999): 7; "Clogging the Archives," *International Herald Tribune*, 1 April 1998. See also Abby Smith, *The Future of the Past: Preservation in American Research Libraries* (Washington, D.C.: Council on Library and Information Resources, 1999).

27. Museum of London director Simon Thurley, quoted in Nigel Hawkes, "Archives Are Bursting as Past Catches up with Present," *The Times* (London), 20 March 1998, 11. See also Simon Tait, "Too Much Stuff? Disposal from Museums," *The Times* (London), 17 November 2003.

28. Robert Burton, "Anatomy of Melancholy" (1621), quoted in Douwe Draaisma, *Metaphors of Memory: A History of Ideas about the Mind* (Cambridge: Cambridge University Press, 2000), 36–37; Denis Diderot, "Encyclopaedie" (1751–52), quoted in Daniel Rosenberg, "Early Modern Information Overload," *Journal of the History of Ideas* 64 (2003): 1.

29. Rosenberg, "Early Modern Information Overload," 9.

30. Elizabeth L. Eisenstein, *The Printing Press as an Agent of Change: Communications and Cultural Transformations in Early-Modern Europe* (Cambridge: Cambridge University Press, 1979); James J. O'Donnell, *Avatars of the Word from Papyrus to Cyberspace* (Cambridge: Harvard University Press, 1998), 70, 90.

31. Kurt Kleiner, "Search Engines Can't Keep Up," *New Scientist*, 19 July 1999, 11; "Brain Drain" and "No Stopping the Megabytes," *The Times* (London), November 1, 2003.

32. Neil Postman, *Building a Bridge to the 18th Century: How the Past Can Improve Our Future* (New York: Viking, 1999), 89–92.

33. Geoffrey J. Giles, "Archivists and Historians: An Introduction," in *Archivists and Historians: The Crucial Partnership*, ed. Geoffrey J. Giles (Washington, D.C.: German Historical Institute, 1996).

34. Jorge Luis Borges, "The Library of Babel" (1941), in his *Collected Fictions* (New York: Penguin, 1998), 112–18; Manguel, *History of Reading*, 292.

35. Stanislaw Lem, *The Cyberiad* (1967; New York: Harcourt Brace Jovanovich, 1985).

36. Georg Simmel, "The Concept and Tragedy of Culture," in *Simmel on Culture: Selected Writings*, ed. David Frisby and Mike Featherstone (London: Sage, 1997), 73; originally published in *Logos* 2 (1911–12).

37. Xerox ad in *Microform Review*, July 1976, quoted in Nicholson Baker, *Double Fold: Libraries and the Assault on Paper* (New York: Random House, 2001), 31.

38. Robert Darnton, "The Great Book Massacre," *New York Review of Books*, 26 April 2001, 16.

39. Baker, *Double Fold*, 54; Nicholson Baker, "Discards," in *The Size of Thoughts: Essays and Other Lumber* (London: Chatto and Windus, 1996), 157.

40. John H. Ottemiller, "The Selective Book Retirement Program at Yale," *Yale University Library Gazette* 34:2 (October 1959), quoted in Baker, *Double Fold*, 88–89. A more recent and benign glimpse of book conservation at Yale is given by Jonathan Spence ("Save That Book!" *American Historical Association Perspectives* 42:8 [November 2004]: 3–5).

41. Baker, *Double Fold*, 16.

42. T. Coraghessan Boyle, "Filthy with Things," *New Yorker*, 15 February 1993, 76–87.

43. Not all share this view. Which imagined scenario promises a wiser future: one where every document created is kept and can be promptly retrieved, or one where a neutron bomb has destroyed (only) all record repositories? No one has polled responses to the query posed by Leonard Rapport twenty years ago ("No Grandfather Clause: Reappraising Accessioned Records," *American Archivist* 44 [1981]: 150; but see the demurral by Karen Benedict, "Invitation to a Bonfire," *American Archivist* 47 [1984]: 43–49).

44. Johannes Trithemius, *De laude scriptorum* (1492), cited in O'Donnell, *Avatars of the Word*, 81.

45. Richard Morrison, [untitled], *The Times* (London), 10 May 2001, 7.

46. H. R. Woudhuysen, "Vandals of Colindale," *Times Literary Supplement*, 18 August 2000, 14.

47. O'Donnell, *Avatars of the Word*, 48. A 1986 laser disc version of the Domesday Book is already unfathomable because the computers made specially to read it have become obsolete (*ArtWatch UK Newsletter* 15 [Spring 2002]: 21). For a summary review, see Susan S. Lazinger, *Digital Preservation and Metadata: History, Theory, Practice* (Englewood, Colo.: Libraries Unlimited/Greenwood, 2001), 5–16.

48. Brewster Kahle, "Setting the Stage," in *Time and Bits: Managing Digital Continuity*, ed. Margaret MacLean and Ben H. Davis (Santa Monica, Calif.: J. Paul Getty Trust, 1998), 39; Diane Vogt-O'Connor, "Is the Record of the 20th Century at Risk?" *Cultural Resource Management* 22:2 (1999): 21; Paul Andrews, "The Virtual Dead Live on in Museum of Web Failures," *International Herald Tribune*, 25 May 2001, 13; Jim McCue, "Can You Archive the Net?" *The Times* (London), 29 April 2002; Shannon Henry, "Dot-Com Era's Froth to Be Kept for Posterity," *International Herald Tribune*, 29 June 2002; Roy Rosenzweig, "Scarcity or Abundance? Preserving the Past in a Digital Era," *American Historical Review* 108 (2003): 735–62.

49. Bruce Sterling and Stewart Brand, quoted in Stewart Brand, *The Clock of the Long Now: Time and Responsibility* (London: Weidenfeld and Nicolson, 1999), 84.

50. Gerhard L. Weinberg, "The National Archives and Records Administration: Goals for the Future," in *Historians and Archivists: Essays in Modern German History and Archival Policy,* ed. George O. Kent (Fairfax, Va.: George Mason University Press, 1991), 319.

51. Katie Hafner, "A Preservation Jam for the Digital Age," *International Herald Tribune,* 11 November 2004, 18.

52. James Billington, quoted in Joel Achenbach, "Is the Information Age Making Us Any Wiser?" *International Herald Tribune,* 16 March 1999.

53. Baker, *Double Fold,* 39.

54. Tina Brown, "Even with the Washington Marine Corps Band, Star Power Is Lacking in the Bush Administration," *The Times* (London), 1 May 2003, T2:3.

55. O'Donnell, *Avatars of the Word,* 95.

56. Sebastian Mallaby, "Libertarians No Longer Rule the Net," *International Herald Tribune,* 4 September 2000. A 2000 federal ruling made it illegal to browse certain electronic documents, depriving digital information users of rights open to users of printed data in reference libraries (*Federal Register,* 27 October 2000, cited in *American Historical Association Perspectives* 39:1 [January 2001]: 19–20).

57. Mike Featherstone, "Archiving Cultures," *British Journal of Sociology* 51 (2000): 178.

58. McCue, "Can You Archive the Net?"

59. Rosenzweig, "Scarcity or Abundance?" 737, 744.

60. Darlene Roth, "The Mechanics of a History Business," *Public Historian* 1:3 (spring 1979): 36; Peter Novick, *That Noble Dream: The "Objectivity Question" and the American Historical Profession* (Cambridge: Cambridge University Press, 1988), 515. On business destruction of potentially sensitive corporate information, see Gord Rabchuk, "Life after the 'Big Bang': Business Archives in an Era of Disorder," *American Archivist* 60 (1997): 40.

61. Stephen O'Regan, "Maori Control of the Maori Heritage," and David J. Butts, "'Nga tukemata: Nga taonga o Ngati Kahungunu' (The Awakening: The Treasures of Ngati Kahungunu)," in *The Politics of the Past,* ed. Peter Gathercole and David Lowenthal (London: Unwin Hyman, 1990), 95–106, 107–17; Evelyn Wareham, "'Our Own Identity, Our Own Taonga, Our Own Coming Back': Indigenous Voices in New Zealand Record-Keeping," *Archivaria,* 52 (fall 2001): 41–42.

62. Stephen Farrell, "Collectors Blamed for Looted Antiquities," *The Times* (London), 13 March 1997; Colin Renfrew, *Loot, Legitimacy, and Ownership: The Ethical Crisis in Archaeology* (London: Duckworth, 2000), 30–31, 78.

63. Phil Cohen, "Totems and Taboos," *New Scientist,* 29 August 1998, 5.

64. Linda Shopes, "Institutional Review Boards Have a Chilling Effect on Oral History," *American Historical Association Perspectives* 38:6 (September 2000): 54–57. In September 2003, the U.S. Office for Human Research Protection excluded most oral history research funded by the Department of Health and Human Services from IRB review requirements; other federal agencies were expected to follow suit; Yet many university IRBs continue to scrutinize and vet oral history research (*American Historical Association Perspectives* 41:9 [December 2003]: 13, 22; 42:6 [September 2004]: 9; and 42:9 [December 2004]: 11–12).

65. Pomian, "Les Archives: Du Trésor des chartes au Caran," 171–75, 222.

66. Frank G. Burke, "The Future Course of Archival Theory in the United States," *American Archivist* 44 (1981): 40–46; Helen Wood, "The Fetish of the Document: An Exploration of Attitudes towards Archives," in *New Directions in Archival Research,* ed. Margaret Proctor and C. P. Lewis (Liverpool: University of Liverpool Centre for Archival Studies, 2000), 20–48.

67. Sarah Shoenfeld, "An American Treasure, the Way It Was," *New York Times,* 23 September 2003.

68. Bret Schulte, "How They Keep History Alive," *Washington Post,* 6 July 2002.

69. Richard Morrison, [untitled], *The Times* (London), 29 June 1999. Posthumous copyright under French law and European Court of Justice rulings has added thirty or more years of putative life to the estates of artists and writers, such as Charles Péguy and Alain-Fournier, who died untimely (Julian Barnes, "Letter from Paris," *Times Literary Supplement,* 21 December 2001, 13). On the almost limitless bloating of copyright, see Lawrence Lessig, *The Future of Ideas: The Fate of the Commons in a Connected World* (New York: Random House, 2001).

70. Nora, *Lieux de mémoire;* Raphael Samuel, *Theatres of Memory,* vol. 1, *Past and Present in Contemporary Culture* (London: Verso, 1994); Michael Kammen, *Mystic Chords of Memory: The Transformation of Tradition in American Culture* (New York: Knopf, 1991). See also David Lowenthal, "Distorted Mirrors," *History Today* 44:2 (February 1994): 8–11; David Lowenthal, "History and Memory," *Public Historian* 19 (1997): 31–39.

71. The politics of archival access, exclusion, sequestration, and destruction feature in two special issues of *History of the Human Sciences,* 11:4 (November 1998) and 12:2 (May 1999), notably Richard Harvey Brown and Beth Davis-Brown, "The Making of Memory: The Politics of Archives, Libraries and Museums in the Construction of National Identity," 11:4 (1998): 17–32; Wolfgang Ernst, "Archival Action: The Archive as ROM and Its Political Instrumentalization under National Socialism," 12:2 (1999): 13–34; and Michael Lynch, "Archives in Formation: Privileged Spaces, Popular Archives and Paper Trails," 12:2 (1999): 65–87.

72. Matthew Battles, *Library: An Unquiet History* (New York: Norton, 2003), 156–91; James Raven, *Lost Libraries: The Destruction of Great Book Collections since Antiquity* (London: Palgrave, 2004).

73. Siegfried Lenz, *The Heritage* (New York: Hill and Wang, 1981), 458.

74. Vogt-O'Connor, "Is the Record of the 20th Century at Risk?"

75. Donna Longo DiMichele, "The Archives and Special Collections of the Mashantucket Pequot Tribal Nation," *Cultural Resource Management* 22:2 (1999): 15–17.

76. Kaplan, "We Are What We Collect," 126, 147.

77. William St Clair, *Lord Elgin and the Marbles,* 3d rev. ed. (Oxford: Oxford University Press, 1998), 281–313; William St Clair, "The Elgin Marbles: Questions of Stewardship and Accountability," *International Journal of Cultural Property* 8 (1999): 391–521.

78. St Clair, "The Elgin Marbles," 453–54.

79. St Clair, *Lord Elgin and the Marbles,* 307–8; St Clair, "The Elgin Marbles," 449.

80. Roland W. Force, *Politics and the Museum of the American Indian: The Heye & the Mighty* (Honolulu: Mechas, 1999), 120, 239–43.

81. Jeff Benedict, *Without Reservation: The Making of America's Most Powerful Indian Tribe and Foxwoods, the World's Largest Casino* (New York: HarperCollins, 2000), 99, 113–16, 118–23, 126–37, 251–53.

82. Henry Taylor, *The Statesmen* (1836; Cambridge: Heffer, 1957), 65.

83. Jonathan Steinberg, "Gold, the Holocaust, and the Deutsche Bank," paper presented at the twelfth conference of the Australian Association for European History, Perth, Western Australia, 6 July 1999. See also Jonathan Steinberg, *The Deutsche Bank and Its Gold Transactions during the Second World War* (Munich: Beck, 1999); Michael Pinto-Duschinsky, "Giants Who Lie in the Shadow of the Swastika," *The Times* (London), 5 September 2000; Richard J. Evans, "History, Memory, and the Law: The Historian as Expert Witness," *History and Theory* 41 (2002): 327.

84. F. Gerald Ham, "Archival Strategies for the Post-Custodial Era," *American Archivist* 44 (1981): 207–16.

85. This issue is elaborated in David Lowenthal, "Dilemmas and Delights of Learning History," in *Knowing, Teaching, and Learning History: National and International Perspectives,* ed. Peter Stearns, Peter Seixas, and Sam Wineburg (New York: New York University Press, 2000), 64–82.

86. In 1947 Dorothy L. Sayers felt impelled to translate *The Divine Comedy* to make Dante intelligible to a "public which knows no History, no Classics, no Theology and has almost forgotten its Bible" (letter to the dean of Chichester, quoted in the *Times Literary Supplement,* 17 December 1999, 12–13).

87. Alethea Hayter, "The Rise and Fall of Clio" (review of Carl Schorske, *Thinking with History*), *Spectator,* 18 July 1998, 38.

88. W. C. Sellar and R. J. Yeatman, *1066 and All That* (London: Methuen, 1930); Raphael Samuel, "One in the Eye: *1066 and All That*" (1990), in his *Island Stories: Unravelling Britain* (London, 1998), 209–12.

89. Sven Birkerts, *The Gutenberg Elegies: The Fate of Reading in an Electronic Age* (New York: Ballantine, 1994), 19–20.

90. Harry Belafonte interview by Mary Willis, *Modern Maturity* 45:3 (May–June 2000): 87.

91. To the dismay of souvenir merchandisers, once-famed pop icons (Frank Sinatra, Janis Joplin, Bob Marley) remain in popular memory only briefly. Even Marilyn Monroe and James Dean are hardly known by today's young, who take no interest in legendary old-time celebrities (Jeffrey Zaslow, "Yesterday's Icon; Today's Nobody," *Wall Street Journal,* 2 May 2002).

92. David Hochman, "In Searching We Trust," *New York Times,* 14 March 2004, Sunday Styles, 1–2.

93. Ernst Gombrich, *The Tradition of General Knowledge: Oration at the London School of Economics and Political Science* (London: LSE, 1962), 11, 21. Gombrich blamed this loss on academic overspecialization and dread of "smattering."

94. Robert Louis Stevenson, *The Ebb-Tide* (1894; London: Heinemann, 1912), 3.

95. Stella Rimington, "A Hidden National Asset: Archives Can Speak to Us across the Centuries," *The Times* (London), 2 December 2002, 7.

96. Schmuland, "Archival Image," 42–45; Jacques Derrida, *Archive Fever: A Freudian Impression* (Chicago: University of Chicago Press, 1995), 87–91.

97. Carolyn Steedman, "Something She Called a Fever: Michelet, Derrida, and Dust," *American Historical Review* 106 (2001): 1168–72; Carolyn Steedman, *Dust* (Manchester: Manchester University Press, 2001).

98. George Perkins Marsh to Henry Charles Lea, 22 June and 1 August 1870, University of Pennsylvania Library Special Collections, Philadelphia; David Lowenthal, *George Perkins Marsh, Prophet of Conservation* (Seattle: University of Washington Press, 2000), 331.

99. Saramago, *All the Names,* 7–9.

100. Derrida, *Archive Fever,* 180.

How Privatization Turned Britain's Red Telephone Kiosk into an Archive of the Welfare State

Patrick Wright

One day in July 1988, I stood on the concourse at London's Waterloo Station thinking of the hopes once entertained by late politician Anthony Crosland. As a leading Labour Party intellectual in the mid-1950s, Crosland had dreamed of a less austere socialism where the uniformity of the reforming state would weigh less heavily on the life of the nation. As he wrote in *The Future of Socialism,* it was a time for a "reaction against the Fabian tradition" with its reliance on state-led initiative. The mixed economy could be expected to deliver higher exports and old-age pensions, but only a "change in cultural attitude" would make Britain "a more colourful and civilized country to live in." The country should have more nightlife and open-air cafés, pleasure gardens, repertory theaters, and statues to brighten up the new housing estates. Better design was needed not just for furniture and women's clothes but also for streetlights and telephone kiosks.[1] The reference to telephone kiosks brought Crosland to mind.

Thirty years later, and in a land now governed by Margaret Thatcher's Conservative Party, the Royal Corps of Transport Band was warming up the crowd for the launch of Mercury Communication's new pay phone system: a banner mounted over the head of its ceremoniously besworded conductor showed a victorious cavalry charge at the Battle of Waterloo and promised "The Greatest Advance since 1815." Here was British Telecom's private rival, much grown since it was first licensed in 1982, opening its latest assault on a public domain where the franchise certainly was being extended. Waterloo Station may have previously had the grimy and uni-

form look characteristic of so much nationalized space, but in the age of privatization and niche marketing, it had come to resemble a shopping mall: diversified, colorful, and superficially more civilized, too.

After the band had ripped through "Ghostbusters" and "In the Mood," the managing director of Mercury Communications stood up in his appointed place between Casey Jones's hamburgers and the Knicker Box and declared a "first for Britain." We were standing in a newly "competitive arena," and Gordon Owen was proud to be cutting into British Telecom's monopoly for the first time. Unfettered by a public-service obligation of the kind that had prevented British Telecom from confining its phone boxes to the most profitable sites, Mercury would be concentrating its "state-of-the-art" pay phones at airports, railway terminals, and new shopping malls—all the while, of course, loudly denying charges of skimming the cream. The new phones would be especially convenient for people wanting to make international calls. They would accept credit cards, but coins were a thing of the past. A special Mercury card had been introduced, but Owen also looked forward to the day when Mercury's growing list of private subscribers, most of which are businesses, would be able to use the company's pay phones with the equivalent of a PIN number, logging the charge back onto their account.

Owen promised a facility distinguished by "reliability, cleanliness, and value for money," and although Mercury obviously had no intention of mounting a universal public service for the convenience of every welfare bum in the land, he stressed that everything possible would be done to accommodate genuinely disabled consumers. Wheelchair access had been built into the designs wherever possible, and volume adjustment would be provided to help the hard of hearing. The Mercurycard was notched on one side to help people with sight problems, and phones would even squeak obligingly to tell blind or partially sighted users when their cards were running out.

Next up was Lord Young, secretary of state for trade and industry, who would unveil the new kiosks. Diversity is an essential part of enterprise culture, and Mercury certainly wasn't going to make the mistake of coming up with a uniform design for all its locations. There were three models to unveil, each designed to fit into "different parts of the society." Fitch and Company had come up with a "totem concept" pay phone booth that, as the press release put it, took "Mercury's key requirements" and "embodied them in a powerful, physical form." The result had already been dubbed the Art Deco kiosk, but to me it looked less like a totem pole than an extruded 1950s-style gas pump. The model provided by Machin Designs was named the Ogee Pylon. The designers claimed that in this version of Mercury's kiosk, "classical aesthetic values are executed in a sophisticated system of structural components," but I was inclined to agree with architecture critic Gavin Stamp, who at that moment was telling a radio reporter that it looked more like a conservatory of the kind you might expect to find in Islington, a gentrified area in north London, than a proper public telephone kiosk.

However, the neoclassical pay phone designed by John Simpson and Partners had the greatest impact. The astonished guffaws were out before the covers had properly hit the ground, and the next morning's papers showed Lord Young in this kiosk, making the inaugural call to Sir Erik Sharp, the chairman of Cable and Wireless (of which Mercury was a subsidiary). Both Mercury and the Department of Trade and Industry had already issued press releases insisting that Young spent the call congratulating Sharp on the speed with which his company had carried through its assault on British Telecom's heartland. However, hindsight now suggests that the old boys may actually have been sorting out the tactical details of a different exchange, the one that would elevate Sir Eric into the House of Lords as Lord Sharp of Grimsdyke, thus making way for Lord Young of Graffham to slide into position as the magnificently paid executive chairman of Cable and Wireless only two years thereafter.

John Simpson may have been ambitious, but he was no such smooth operator. Looking frankly disconcerted by the derisive hoots that greeted his cast-aluminum clas-

sical kiosk, he found a moment to talk me through some its many distinguishing features. He pointed to the ornate finial on top of the roof, a decorative touch that also provided ventilation and that could, if need be, house an antenna. Then there were the winged sphinxes flanking and, indeed, struggling to dignify the monstrous Mercury logo. Per Mercury's requirements, the gap at the bottom of the side panels was intended to discourage tramps and dossers from using this new service as a public convenience of a different kind. The fluted Doric columns at the corner were certainly ornamental, but they also had the practical advantage of providing a curved edge that would be less easy to vandalize.

Flagship on the Rocks

How, I wondered briefly, might one explain all this to Anthony Crosland? At the end of November 1987, John Butcher, a junior industry minister, had announced the government's decision to break up British Telecom's phone booth monopoly. "The idea," as he said at the time, "is to see a much greater number of different types of call-boxes installed and available to the public, and to provide British Telecom with competition in what has hitherto been a restricted market."[2] Launched as the "flagship" of Thatcher's privatization program in November 1984, British Telecom PLC had seemed to work fine for a while. Chairman Sir George Jefferson and Chief Executive Iain Vallance made all the right noises as they sailed off into the new world. They promised to shake off the grim legacies of nationalization and turn their overmanned, badly managed, and ill-equipped organization into a properly tight ship that would be both profitable and better for its customers.

British Telecom was declaring huge profits by 1997, yet it was also coming under fire from all sides. In three short years, the flagship of privatization had been renamed the "most loathed institution in Britain." Consumer surveys declared British Telecom the worst public service in the land. There was evidence of overcharging (with some subscribers, including the Bank of England, eventually receiving a refund). The long-promised technological improvements, which included the introduction of digital exchanges and a new labor-saving switching technology known as System X, had caused havoc, striking central London and City exchanges hardest of all.[3] As the service declined and complaints soared, British Telecom set about squandering large fortunes on advertising campaigns designed to manipulate public opinion. The company's leaders evidently considered it easier to establish a new corporate image than to improve the service.

British Telecom tried to counter the rising tide of criticism. It blamed its own engineers, who had been on strike earlier in 1987. It blamed the fact that it had once been a nationalized industry and was therefore full of sullen and morose employees who couldn't all be retrained in a day. It blamed vandalism for the problems with its call boxes—some 25 percent of which were found to be out of action in a damning survey conducted by the regulatory body, Oftel. Indeed, BT even sent an exhibition of ingeniously vandalized pay phones to tour British schools to show what the company was up against.[4] In the end, however, BT caved in. Jefferson may previously have distinguished himself at the head of the privatized British Airways, but British Telecom's shareholders wanted blood, and he resigned ignominiously at the September 1987 annual general meeting. There was to be no place in the House of Lords for him.

Newspapers were quick to interpret the story. For the conservative *Daily Telegraph*, British Telecom chaos didn't raise doubts about the wisdom of privatization but provided yet more support for the dogmas of liberal theory: privatize a nationalized industry without breaking it up into competing units, and all you get is a private monopoly. The liberal *Guardian* drew broadly comparable conclusions, declaring that British Telecom was displaying the "classic symptoms of a monopoly: defending itself from competition, refusing to publish the criteria according to which it measured performance, failing to innovate, and overcharging."[5] Nobody bothered to recall that in the days when the system was run by the General Post Office, a strong and generally accepted case had existed for the essential uniformity of a public service such as the telephone system. Not a single journalist chose to mention 1912, when the British telephone system had been nationalized in an attempt to overcome the failure that had marked the earlier years of multiple and partly private ownership, or exploited the irony of the fact that, in those days, when Britain had what was widely known as the worst telephone system in the civilized world, it had seemed obvious that the telephone network should be run by a single statutory body.[6]

A Matter of Style

Such was the general background to the Mercury pay phones, but how, as Crosland himself might have won-

dered, to account for the style of the most eye-catching model? Why should the new kiosk look like a crudely engineered collision between the Acropolis and a wedding cake? What could possibly have motivated John Simpson's absurd classical design?

At the beginning of 1985, Vallance, who at that time was managing director of BT's Local Communications Service, had announced that his newly privatized organization would be taking a "radical approach to the problems inherent in today's outdated payphone service." Those old, coin-operated red telephone boxes would soon be things of the past, replaced by yellow, anodized aluminum kiosks and card-operated phones. Privatization hadn't freed BT of its public service obligation, but there was a need for more efficient and vandal-proof facilities. The new designs would be more accessible to wheelchair users (for whom the old red phone boxes were a nightmare) and less inclined to scalp anyone over six feet tall. They would also be more open than the old red telephone boxes. Litter and unpleasant smells would blow away, and the homeless would feel less tempted to move in on cold winter nights. Just as Mercury was to do a few years later, BT stressed the needs of the disabled, who knew the impracticalities of the old red telephone box in close detail. Behind all the smooth talk, however, many suspected a hidden motivation. The newly privatized BT was concerned with earning a profit, and a redesign would not merely help to create that much desired new corporate image: it would surely also provide the perfect cover under which to carry out a secret but thoroughgoing reorganization of the service. Confronted with these suspicions, BT admitted that hundreds of boxes had indeed been moved in the changeover but regretted that (conveniently enough, as critics recognized) it had no method of classifying these changes and was therefore simply unable to say whether the redesigned service had also been concentrated at more lucrative sites.

The man who launched the redesign would soon replace Jefferson as British Telecom's chair. Questioned at the 1988 annual meeting by angry BT shareholders devoted to the old red phone boxes, the fast-moving Vallance insisted, "There is no accounting for taste." In fact, his newly privatized industry had already found a very good way of accounting for taste. If the old phone boxes had their admirers—not least in the United States, where many of these uprooted British icons were finding their way into service as cocktail cabinets and shower stalls—so much the better. They could be auctioned off, and long may demand outstrip supply.

A voluntary association, an architectural conservation

group called the Thirties Society, initiated the defense of the old red phone box. Denouncing the auctions as a squalid asset stripping of the public sector, society members wasted no time extending the traditions of cultural connoisseurship to street furniture, declaring the hitherto taken-for-granted old red telephone box a vital part of the national heritage. Writing in the early 1940s, George Orwell, in his study of wartime patriotism, *The Lion and the Unicorn,* had cited suet puddings, misty skies, and red pillar boxes as essential emblems of Britishness; by the 1980s, the old red telephone box had also "entered into" the nation's soul.[7] While the philistine Vallance saw only outdated pay phones, these campaigners recognized the kiosks with which architect Sir Giles Gilbert Scott had set out to civilize a rampant technology as significant works of architecture that were "wholly classical in spirit."[8] The K2 was Scott's original kiosk. Dating from 1927, it had been brought into service mostly in London. The smaller and more familiar K6 was designed in the mid-1930s and was still being installed until 1968. Thanks to a scheme announced in April 1935, the K6 had been set up in remote villages all around the country as "a special concession" designed to commemorate George V's jubilee. The organizers of the jubilee scheme recognized that money could have been saved by fitting phones into existing rural post offices, but freestanding kiosks were chosen because they afforded extra privacy, visibility, and accessibility. Because the scheme was an extension of a vital public service, people accepted that it should be paid for out of "general funds" and not "left dependent on the ability of some small community to contribute to the cost."[9]

Quickly dubbed the Jubilee Kiosk, the K6 went on to become, as BT itself admitted, an "established British institution." Nevertheless, the kiosk's introduction was fiercely contested during the 1930s, especially in rural areas. From Oxfordshire to the Lake District, local branches of the Council for the Preservation of Rural England denounced the new kiosks as eyesores, complaining especially about the insidious "intervention of red" into their villages.[10] But the Post Office resisted the group's arguments in favor of green or stone-gray camouflage, rallying such forces as the Royal Fine Arts Commission and Sir Edwin Lutyens in support of the chosen red.[11] Light gray would show up every "ribald scrawl" and be stained by dogs and rain. Green wouldn't stand out to the eye of the wayfarer who might need to make an emergency call. And as John Gloag, a designer who at that time was also on the Central Executive Committee of the Council for the Preservation of Rural England, pointed out, if the principle of camouflage were accepted for every modern amenity in rural areas, we would end up "thatching everything, including motor coaches."[12] A dark "battleship gray" was eventually permitted in areas of outstanding natural beauty (as long as the window bars remained red), but the Jubilee Kiosk went on to become an otherwise uniform feature of the national landscape.[13]

Those who rallied to the defense of the old red phone box in the 1980s might easily have extended their appreciation of this endangered national icon to include the interior fittings chosen in the 1930s by a special interdepartmental Post Office committee. The members of this committee went out of their way to come up with an interior fit for well-mannered British ladies and gentlemen. They resolved that the backboard should be made of polished Bakelite rather than plywood. They decided to include a cigarette holder, an umbrella rack, and a beveled mirror for "feminist users" despite the Traffic Section's concern that callers with urgent business would "occasionally be kept waiting" while ladies adjusted their makeup. The committee wanted to install hard-backed telephone directories and was reluctant to accept that they would have to be chained to the kiosk. The committee opposed all but the most limited publicity; there was to be no external advertisement, and the limited space allowed for internal notices (which were to be properly framed and mounted on the backboard) was reserved for information about the operation of the phone itself. While it would have been desirable, even in those days, to include a "Monogram . . . like that used by the Public Relations Department," there was no space left after the functional notices had been accommodated, and the idea was abandoned.[14]

Scott's Jubilee Kiosk was distinguished not just by its design but also by the uniformity of its presence. The new pay phones introduced by Vallance in the 1980s were of a mediocre design borrowed from the United States, but they too had a broader significance. Under the new British Telecom system, a single type of kiosk would no longer be used in all places. Paving the way for Mercury's later and more exclusive collection, BT's new range was designed so that different models could, in Owen's well-chosen words, be "put in different parts of the society." The postprivatization kiosks would stand as BT's humble contribution to growing social polarization. Nobody could be entirely certain any longer of getting a door, but, according, to the new Vallance equation, the better your area, the more kiosk you could expect to find on your street corner. Users in respectable neighborhoods and well-policed thoroughfares would still be offered a roof, at least some walling, and a choice between card- and coin-operated phones. The new and growing underclass, meanwhile, would have to settle for a sawn-off metal stump with an armored card-operated phone bolted onto it.

By the 1980s, the red Scott kiosk had itself become emblematic of the traditional nation that fifty years earlier it had been thought to despoil. Indeed, the Jubilee Kiosk was to be defended as the endangered archive of social and public aspirations now threatened by Thatcher's economic reforms. In August 1986, a K2 kiosk in the London Zoo's Parrot House became the first telephone box ever to receive listed-building status. An old public service that had become indefensible as a "private monopoly" could at least be saved as part of the nation's architectural heritage. Meanwhile, the "quality" newspapers—themselves torn between their old ways and frenzied modernization—had been printing rousing letters in defense of the old red phone box, some of them coming from expatriates who were apparently still shocked by the passing of windmills, steam engines, and the farthing. The *Guardian* mustered a wistful article by Richard Boston, who scorned the new designs ("all the vandal's work has been done already—except peeing on the floor") and eulogized the disappearing works of Sir Giles Gilbert Scott. Newspapers all over the world (including, most eloquently, the *Frankfurter Rundschau*) contributed their own elegies for this icon of old England. BT's auctions went ahead but were quite overtaken by this embarrassing cult of the old red phone box. Many papers printed evocative photos of Britain's heritage going under the hammer, but the *Independent* caught the most poignant episode of all. On 14 September 1988, it showed one of Scott's kiosks being hoisted out of native land near Swindon in preparation for a journey to the Falkland Islands, recently won back after General Galtieri's invasion, where it would be installed "for members of the armed forces to use for phoning home."

A Symbol of National Embarrassment

Thatcher's policies of deregulation and economic liberalism had ripped many gaping holes in Britain's national fabric, yet the threat to the red phone box rather than those to schools, hospitals, coal mining, or manufacturing industries finally triggered revolt from the Right, a revolt in which the red phone box was suddenly reborn as the acceptable face of state-imposed uniformity. Writing in *The Times*, (29 January 1985, p. 10) Conservative philosopher and gadfly Roger Scruton regretted the "tyr-

annical pursuit of novelty" and the inevitable but "horrifying advance of science." He saw the Scott kiosk as one of the last creations of a "disciplined tradition of design whose products included the Gothic factory, the Palladian clubhouse, the Pullman railway carriage and the Bombay shirt." He didn't care what a phone box looked like in a place such as Birmingham (an industrial city "where modern architects have already done their work"), but the Scott kiosk should continue to grace real England: every village green, every moor, every hillside should have one as an emblem of stability. Scruton liked the plinth, the classical outline, and the embossed crown that, far from just serving as a ventilator, stood over the nation's communications as a "symbol of national identity, and promise of enduring government." He was so impressed by the color that he renamed it, turning what had been known as Post Office red since the Royal Fine Arts Commission chose it in the 1930s into the more ideologically correct imperial red. A vehement antimodernist, Scruton looked at the K6 and even managed to approve an "interesting suggestion of Bauhaus naughtiness in its fenestration."

Charles Moore, editor of the *Spectator*, took up the subject in the *Daily Telegraph*. For him, the Scott kiosk spoke most evocatively of enduring national values at the point where they were being broken up by BT's brutish workforce. More ambitious for the nation than Scruton, Moore argued that the Scott kiosk could actually exert a civilizing influence in those urban areas that had been ruined by modernism and the welfare state. Even in the most dismal postwar housing estate, the old red telephone box sent out signals of hope—its classical lines and proportions offering an image of the traditional hierarchies to which society could return. Had Moore been more thoroughly acquainted with the inner city, he would have found incontrovertible support for his theory of architecture as a creator of social behavior. In many urban areas, drug dealers had felt at home with the pay phone system only since Vallance removed the Scott kiosks (in which the police could trap suspects simply by putting a foot against the door) and replaced them with open booths that provided the vigilant hoodlum with far greater visibility and a quick escape. Even without this supporting evidence, however, Moore denounced BT's decision to replace these kiosks as a classic example of the British ability to spit on our luck: "we think that we have achieved something by smashing up the old, leaving its shards in the street and replacing it with a featureless affair of plastic and low-grade metal."[15] Pressed by an unfriendly critic, he was happy to go further: "British Telecom had 77,000 little equivalents of Big Ben before they started their destruction, 77,000 objects which commanded the affection of their customers, and now they have squandered that affection."[16]

As chairman of the Thirties Society, Gavin Stamp had wandered the land photographing well-placed Scott kiosks wherever he found them. Stamp now advanced his own intriguingly volatile version of the argument from his other position as the *Spectator*'s architecture critic. Finding himself increasingly disturbed by the government's "blinkered refusal to recognize the valuable and essential role" of the public sector, he valued the Scott kiosk not just as a work of architecture that may well have been inspired by no less a figure than eighteenth century classicist Sir John Soane but also as a sympathetic and serviceable piece of street furniture.

At last the argument seemed to be getting somewhere. Would Stamp place the blame where it obviously belonged—on privatization itself? Would he conclude that the only way of defending the Scott kiosk and the standards of public service it symbolized was to immediately renationalize British Telecom? Having suffered considerable inconvenience on his own line in King's Cross, a part of London that had become something of a red-light district since he had moved in, Stamp had recently written to Jefferson protesting that "British Telecom could be no worse if it were nationalized and that in fact it was better when it was."[17] BT must have feared the direction in which his thoughts were moving, for at that moment Stamp's phone seems to have gone permanently out of order, forcing him to conduct his business through "new, squalid kiosks" that had already been "conspicuously disfigured by a rash of prostitutes' sticky advertisements on the windows."[18] Overwhelmed with frustration at the "monstrous private monopoly" that was BT, Stamp fumed and fulminated and failed to follow his argument through to its logical conclusion.[19]

More generally, the *Spectator* struggled to hold concurrently at least three partly contradictory positions on British Telecom. It remained unwavering in its advocacy of privatization. It was anxious to see the old red telephone box saved. It wanted to see improvement and indeed technological innovation in Britain's telephone service. By May 1987, it was evident that this intriguing acrobatic performance was going to end in a painfully contorted heap on the floor. Just as the *Spectator* was celebrating the final demise of nationalization as a reputable political concept, its phones joined the other victims of BT's new switching technology. A gleeful Des Wilson, at that time still a respected social campaigner with a distinguished record of work for the homeless, wrote in to

point out the confusion of that week's editorial page: on the top half a leading article headed "Nationalization doesn't work" and at the bottom of the same page a note apologizing for the inconvenience caused by the collapse of the *Spectator*'s telephones ("A large part of our telephone system has been broken by British Telecom and has still not been mended after ten days. The company is unable to tell us what is wrong or when the full service will be restored."). As Wilson asked, "Perhaps you could explain the inconsistency between the claims you make for privatization and the reality?"[20]

With embarrassed fury, the *Spectator* pursued its complaints through the labyrinth of BT management, eventually laying them at the door of the doomed Chairman Jefferson only a week or so before his unexpected resignation. Lively discussion and correspondence filled the magazine throughout the summer of 1987. The letters page was used to foment an insurrection among the privatized company's new shareholders led by J. R. Lucas, an Oxford don who, having expressed his determination that the privatized industry's new shareholders should recognize their responsibilities and get British Telecom to "pull up its socks," went to BT's annual meeting and chastised the new management for its "blithering incompetence and invincible complacency."[21] As a right-wing ideologue who had been a tireless advocate of privatization, Digby Anderson also communicated his embarrassment on the letters page: he admitted that BT had turned out to be an "uninspiring advertisement for the cause."[22] Another correspondent borrowed a spare conspiracy theory from the wilder reaches of the *Sunday Telegraph*. According to A. Green, who wouldn't give an address for fear of suddenly finding his phone service out of order, BT's socialist employees were targeting advocates of privatization for special treatment. Meanwhile journalist Bernard Levin, an enthusiastic admirer of Thatcher, wrote in to whine about the "thieving bastards" whose new-style pay phone had claimed his money without even so much as connecting his call.[23]

But no one could be entirely convinced. The *Spectator*'s whole outlook was founded on the conviction that nationalization had disfigured the face of the nation, but, whichever way you looked at it, the story of the old red telephone box pointed accusingly in the opposite direction: here was privatization completing the mission of the destructive state bureaucracy it was meant to have vanquished. A "Telecom Horror Contest" was launched in a bid to divert attention from the embarrassing implications of this story. The *Spectator* announced with much trumpeting that a surplus Jubilee Kiosk bought at a BT auction in early 1987 would be awarded as a prize to the provider of the worst disaster story. By this time, however, the *Sunday Times* had already counted up the bizarre uses to which people were putting old red telephone boxes, and it was apparent that the *Spectator*'s was just one more variation on the theme of the telephonic henhouse.[24] It was fitting that the eventual winner of the Telecom Horror Competition came from Ohio: at least there was a chance that he would accept his prize and then the whole guilty, squawking, and by that time, rather filthy package could be bundled up and shipped conveniently over the horizon.

A sense of guilt as well as aggravated patriotic pride established the Scott kiosk as such an evocative symbol in the camp of the privateers. Far from standing as an image of transcendent authority, as Scruton had jokingly imagined, the embossed crown on the Scott kiosk was actually the mark of the old Post Office. As the privatization program rolled on, the old red telephone box became the evocative symbol of endangered ideals of public service, of a socially conceived provision that should, as the emblematic kiosk now suggested, be reliable, uniform, and equally available to all. Seizing this interpretation as early as 1983, the British Telecom trade unions had adopted the Scott kiosk as a symbol of their opposition to management's privatizing measures. Similarly, when Stamp tried to awaken BT to this traditional shrine's value to public communication, he used an emphasis reminiscent of George Orwell's essay "England Your England," describing the Scott kiosk as "decent," "solid," "sympathetic," and "serviceable." Here again was the vocabulary of public service taking refuge under a contemporary architectural gloss. Far from having been finished off, as the advocates of privatization kept claiming, that old idea of the common good had escaped into heritage country. Hiding against rough weather in the old red telephone box was the petrified spirit of the welfare state itself.

In the real world, meanwhile, or at least at Waterloo Station, Mercury was offering increased polarization in the pay phone system and a range of conspicuously ill-mannered phone booths that shrieked design at citizens now distinguished only by the credit cards in their wallets. The classical kiosk, however, had a special meaning of its own. John Simpson, its designer, was a young architect with a growing reputation as a classical revivalist. He subscribed to the conventional revivalist belief that "art and culture reached a pinnacle in the years around 1800, and that the architecture of this period is a better, indeed more appropriate, basis for development than the 'modern' architecture of recent years."[25] In the style

wars of that period, Simpson stood in the anti-Enlightenment camp alongside architects like Robert Adam and Quinlan Terry, and his espousal of classicism was accompanied by the usual polemical denunciations of modernism as the style of postwar egalitarianism and state-led social reform.

As a self-declared "real architect," Simpson greatly admired the old red telephone box. Indeed, as we stood together in Waterloo Station, he told me that his classical kiosk was intended to sit firmly in the sadly uprooted tradition of Sir Giles Gilbert Scott. Mercury's gaudy logo was a poor substitute for the embossed crown on the Scott kiosk but at least, as Simpson claimed in his publicity handout, his model was a proper building rather than just a nondescript piece of disposable street furniture. Unlike BT's new pay phones, it had been designed to form "part of the traditional urban townscape." Indeed, it should be sited "in the manner of statues or fountains to enhance the quality of public space." Simpson would have liked to see his cast-aluminum classical kiosk issued in red or maroon, but Mercury evidently balked at erecting such an obvious memorial to its rival's better days. Ostensibly a tribute to the old red telephone box, Simpson's crudely realized classical kiosk was not to be mistaken for just another piece of trivial postmodern pastiche. Columnist Simon Jenkins may have greeted it as "a phone box on which . . . an artist had been at work," but it deserved to be remembered not for its aesthetic pretensions but as the monstrous contrivance that finally finished off the idea of universal public service by reducing it entirely to a matter of style.

In this respect, it may have been the true telephone box of its time. Yet Simpson's kiosk would not be adopted. Sensing that it had wandered into a symbolic minefield, Mercury preferred to install a more neutral model for its service, which, in any event, managed to withstand the rising tide of mobile phone technology for only a few years. British Telecom now actively restores the remaining red telephone boxes. If these reinstated kiosks now seem strangely mannered, it is not only because many of them have been preserved in situ even after the demolition of the buildings and housing estates they were once thought to redeem. They stand there now not so much as public amenities but as symbolic archives of the idea of public amenity. The old red telephone kiosk is now the place to go if you want to remind yourself of the old ideals of the reforming postwar Labour governments: an oddly positioned and undeniably tight little space dedicated to those defeated ideas of state-led uniformity and universal social provision.

NOTES

1. C. A. R. Crosland, *The Future of Socialism* (London: Cape, 1956), 521–22.

2. *The Independent* (London), 26 November 1987.

3. The *Sunday Times* (London) described System X as the "£5 billion blunder" (9 August 1987).

4. The traveling exhibition, which included kiosks that had been filled with flour, set in concrete, and incinerated with a butane lighter, was described in "Troubles by the Boxful for BT," *Evening Standard* (London), 28 September 1987. British Telecom liked to treat vandalism as if it were an entirely recent problem, but literary evidence reveals that telephone kiosks were suffering rough treatment even in the 1940s, when, according to BT's theory of postwar degeneration, British manners should still have been intact. The hero of John Lodwick's novel, *Peal of Ordnance* (1947), enters a telephone box to find the usual disordered scene: "The booth smelt of urine and spittle gouts. He opened the directory; obsolete, tatty and well-thumbed . . . signatures in the bargain (Jack H. Rossback; USN Yonkers, NY), and here and there addresses underlined with words of advice: 'Call her up any time. She'll be there.'" By the 1960s, a Canadian poet accustomed to visiting London wrote a poem about a character named Roderick who enters a telephone box and then finds that the door has disappeared: trapped, he spends his time calling friends for help and, when his money runs out, chatting up the girl at directory information. In the end, the booth fills up with beard and excrement, and it becomes impossible to tell from outside whether Roderick is living or dead. See Lionel Kearns, "Telephone," in *By the Light of the Silvery McLune* (Vancouver: Daylight Press, 1969).

5. *The Guardian* (London and Manchester) 24 September 1987.

6. Charles R. Perry, "The British Experience, 1876–1912: The Impact of the Telephone during the Years of Delay," in *The Social Impact of the Telephone,* ed. Ithiel de Sola Pool (Cambridge: MIT Press, 1977), 68–96.

7. George Orwell, *The Lion and the Unicorn: Socialism and the English Genius* (London: Secker and Warburg, 1941).

8. See Clive Aslet and Alan Powers, *The British Telephone Box . . . Take It as Red* (London: Thirties Society, 1987).

9. Quoted from papers held at the Historical Information Centre, British Telecom Archives, London.

10. The BT Archives include a number of patiently argued letters written by the post office's G. E. G. Forbes to council members. In a final sentence of a 24 June 1936 letter concerning the Lake District, he was reduced to wondering "whether the exclusion of these minute patches of red from the District is so important as all that."

11. This battle against red interventions in rural England would continue to rage in distant villages for several decades. Even in the early 1990s, visitors to the Dorset village of Litton Cheney would find a Jubilee Kiosk that was green rather than red thanks to the nocturnal and evidently rather hasty activity of local vigilantes.

12. "Colour of 'Jubilee Design' Kiosks," memo 2687/36, British Telecom Archives, London.

13. The decision to allow battleship gray to be used in "very exceptional cases" was made on the recommendation of the Royal Fine Arts Commission, but not until 1948.

14. See F. T. Judd, *Post Office Engineers Journal* 29 (October 1936): 175–80.

15. Charles Moore, "Better Red than Dead," *Daily Telegraph,* 29 December 1986.

16. Charles Moore, *Spectator,* 22 August 1987.

17. Gavin Stamp, letter to the editor, *Spectator,* 6 June 1987.

18. Gavin Stamp, letter to the editor, *Spectator,* 15 August 1987.

19. Gavin Stamp, letter to the editor, *Spectator,* 30 May, 1987.

21. *Spectator,* 25 July 1987.

22. *Spectator,* 27 June 1987.

23. *Spectator,* 29 August 1987.

24. Tim Rayment, "A Phone Box Needs Love When Its Number Is Up," *Sunday Times* (London), 17 May 1987.

25. Quoted in Alan Powers, *Real Architecture: An Exhibition of Classical Building by the New Generation of Architects* (London: Building Centre Trust, 1987), 58.

Archives

Particles of Memory or More?

Joan van Albada

As a nonnative speaker of English, I am not subtle in the use of the language. English came to me as a foreign language through Kipling and Shakespeare, with words such as *swans, Thames, prince, murder* and *dagger* and *poison.* Archival English came to me in the 1980s thanks to committee work for the International Council on Archives (ICA). So I was struck when Verne Harris claimed in his paper, "Law, Evidence, and Electronic Records: A Strategic Perspective from the Global Periphery," presented at the Seville Congress on Archives, that his work belongs to those who are in the global periphery of our profession as opposed to those who are in the hub. I responded in an e-mail to him that real periphery now belongs to those who have a different mother tongue from English, the current international language of choice in ICA. Lack of intimate knowledge of the language—by which I mean really understanding concepts in their overtones and undertones—can be alienating. Language as carrier conveys concepts created over time by professional practice and theory and formed and biased by their surrounding administrative traditions and overall organizational and national culture and subcultures. I am not complaining about English or about having a different mother tongue; I am merely stating as a matter of fact that concepts go with language just as wines go with dishes in France.

Native speakers may function as onlookers in their own culture by choice or character; nonnative speakers, however, too often function by necessity as onlookers for lack of active command of appropriate vocabulary or for lack of understanding of the hidden or implicit meaning of words exchanged by native speakers. Nonnative speakers have no choice but to use words without know-

ing their exact contextual or emotional meanings. Nonnative speakers are innocent of using words in an insulting way—at least in most cases—and are unwillingly guilty of abusing words, since their underlying values may allow for other uses in other languages.

An example: for the Beijing Congress on Archives (1996), our Chinese colleagues organized a number of exhibitions. Returning from the magnificent tour of the Great Wall, our bus stopped at some municipal archives to see an exhibition of the repository's most interesting items. The documents created by government agencies included a picture of Great Leader Mao swimming across a river, a printed poem by him carrying his signature, a calligraphy by a recently retired staff member, and a soccer trophy—a huge one. Each item had been put in a nice shrine, with an explanatory text in English attached to the outside of the display. All items were called archives. A colleague from England muttered aloud several times, his tremolos and pitch going up immensely in particular at the trophy and the calligraphy. He explained that he was disturbed by the exhibit's inclusion of "nonarchival" material and by the abuse of English and of official ICA terminology in many of the explanatory notes. More taken by the exhibits than by the explanations, I asked him to demonstrate a few examples of abuse. It took me some time to explain to him that as a municipal archivist, I was never concerned when a prize diploma and pictures and videos of an official ceremony had to be accompanied by the trophy or by any other object or if the files of a shipyard arrived with models of the boats constructed there. Keeping good relations with important players in a municipality is Lesson No. 1 of any municipal archivist. I am not rigid on such professional issues and could therefore easily have mounted a similar exhibition with many objects and terms not mentioned in ICA's *Dictionary of Archival Terminology*. In the end, we agreed it was not the exhibits themselves but the descriptions that caused his problem. Reflecting on my experiences when he had calmed down, we concluded that the word *archives* might have a different connotation in Chinese, something like "important object reflecting an event in the past." On later visits to China, I learned that the Chinese definition is indeed more permissive than the English one. In international exchanges, however, one sticks to the use of the received ICA terminology.

Another example: four archivists, all nonnative speakers, enjoying lunch somewhere in Uzbekistan and discussing access to archives. I became rather puzzled by what was being said and therefore asked my three companions to define the meaning of the word *access*. To no surprise of mine, all three had been using different definitions. To Archivist No. 1, access to archives meant the existence of a legal framework allowing research in archives; No. 2 was referring to finding aids; No. 3 was thinking of having a desk and electricity. Definitions 1 and 2 fit within the definition of the ICA dictionary; 3 seemed a nondefinition. To this third colleague, however, legal framework and finding aids were sheer luxury, as in the end the director of the archives decides who will be allowed to see what finding aids and what documents and to take what notes.

A third example: in quite a number of countries, archival legislation is on par with legislation in the most advanced countries. However, in others the archives receive no accessions because the government is a closed organization controlled by a political party, a family, or the like, unwilling to hand over any files to organizations connected to an ICA that underline such terms as *access, democratic control, accountability,* and so on.

Why these examples? We tend to read or listen and understand from our own set of codes. When discussing priorities in institutional policy, in preservation, in access, in appraisal, in introducing standards, one should first compare those codes. Codes in metropolitan countries tend to differ from codes in commonwealth countries; codes in no two commonwealth countries are alike. So far, little has been done to compare those codes and to analyze the origins of their differences, possibly because the ICA's values have for a very long time been set by these metropolitan countries, which also dominate the ICA's two working languages, English and French. To paraphrase, "What is good for England (or France) is good for the rest of the ICA." This expression is over-

done, but there is some truth to it. You will not be surprised to learn that I would like to introduce into all archival programs a course such as Comparative Analysis of International Archivology. It would be even better to allow for deviations within a country: the course could be called Comparative Analysis of Archivology in a Multicultural Setting.

When contemplating the title of this essay, I looked up the words *archives, particles,* and *memory* in Funk and Wagnalls Standard Dictionary, International Edition of 1970. It's not the most recent edition, but I added it to my library when I first started taking classes at the Netherlands' Archives School, at that time directed by Eric Ketelaar. I was taken in particular by the definition of *memory,* which allows for multiple meanings for the essay title:

1. The mental process or faculty of representing in consciousness an act, experience, or impression, with recognition that it belongs to time past.
2. The experiences of the mind taken in the aggregate and considered as influencing present and future behavior.
3. The accuracy and ease with which a person can retain and recall past experiences.
4. That which is remembered, as an act, event, person, or thing.
5. The period of time covered by the faculty of remembrance: beyond the *memory* of man.
6. The state of being remembered, posthumous reputation: The *memory* of Washington will endure.
7. That which reminds; a memorial; a memento.

Further reading reveals *memory*'s synonyms: *recollection, remembrance, reminiscence, retrospect, retrospection.* The dictionary continues:

Memory is the faculty by which knowledge is retained or recalled; *memory* is a retention of knowledge within the grasp of the mind, while *remembrance* is having what is known consciously before the mind. Either may be voluntary or involuntary. *Recollection* involves volition, the mind making a distinct effort to recall something or fixing the attention actively upon it when recalled. *Reminiscence* is a half-dreamy *memory* of scenes or events long past; *retrospection is* a distinct turning of the mind back upon the past, bringing long periods under survey.

The antonyms of *memory: forgetfulness, oblivion, oversight, unconsciousness.*

At a first glance, one might decide to limit the meaning of memory when referring to archives to simply "that which reminds; a memorial; a memento." However, to my way of thinking, archives are not so static. Archives to me represent a kind of living organism, growing, breathing, suffering, enjoying, an organism with which one can communicate, an organism that can be belittled, burned, falsified, nurtured, exploited, used, and abused. However, this organism is not an organism in its own right; the organism reflects us—the archivist, the administrator, the records manager, the family, the politician, the owner, and the thief, the corrupted ones and those who will be corrupted. Therefore I have come to the conclusion that the memory in this essay title refers to all seven explanations and to the synonyms and antonyms together.

A side step. In 1990 I attended a committee meeting in Weimar, German Democratic Republic. As at most ICA meetings, we visited the local museum. I was particularly taken by a painting of the Virgin and child by Cranach the Elder, not because of any religious emotion but because of her smile. Her tenderness was not stereotypical, as on icons, but real; she was enjoying her child, and a masterful hand brought alive her enjoyment in this painting. The hand also offered in the background a glimpse of the local countryside before it had suffered the devastations of the modern brown-coal industry. The meeting was held a few days before the unification of East and West Germany. Weimar had been invaded by salesmen from Western Europe who tried to bedazzle the locals and to sell them overpriced cheap Western products, most likely made in Taiwan or in China, in return for the few West German marks the soon-to-be former East Germans had saved for the uncertain future.

Neither smile and enjoyment and scenery nor my anger at those salesmen and buyers will be preserved in an archive. At best, some charters relating to property of the farms shown in Cranach's paintings and a few licenses to sell goods on the street have entered or will enter an archive.

Some months ago, I had a chance to meet with the national archivist of a country in northeastern Africa. I learned that she believed her government archive should have a single priority: the preservation of the pictures of some sixty-five thousand people who had died for that country as martyrs in recent liberation wars. We discussed how the ICA could assist in assessing and acquiring the most appropriate techniques for doing so. Given her archive's annual budget, all income for the foreseeable future—if not in perpetuity—would be needed to finance this undertaking. In this case, all smiles will be kept, but nothing else.

A few years ago, while I was serving as the director of the municipal archives of Dordrecht, a town south of Rotterdam, I received a visit from an inspector of our provincial state archives. He came to claim the records of a state high school that for some reason had been transferred to the municipal archives instead of to the state archives. Because they were not high priority, the files had not yet been processed. Law was on his side; the boxes were moved to the state repository. State appraisal criteria were applied, almost all files relevant to the local community were disposed of, and a few files on the relationship between school and ministry were selected for permanent retention. A few years later, the law was changed: records of state high schools should be transferred to municipal archives. The remaining boxes were returned to our repository, their content now meaningless to us since all files relating to the school and its local staff had been removed. I considered disposing of the remainder but decided against it because doing so might have created misunderstanding at all levels. Should one define archives as the reflection of the context of the archivist?

At a UNESCO-organized meeting on cultural diversity held in Stockholm in 1998, I was present at a discussion between a historian from a West African country and someone from Europe. The subject was the preservation of intangibles as archives of a culture. The Westerner had some difficulties in allowing the African to have opinions of his own: she wanted to force him into Western definitions. He cried, "Madam, visit my country, and I will show you the forest of my ancestors. But while I will be communicating with my forefathers, you would not hear them whispering. You would see at best trees." Most people present did not understand what he meant. I had the chance to drink a beer with this very kind man later on, and we discussed the problem of definitions and standards derived from cultures based on registration of property and related issues as opposed to those concentrating on memorizing transcendental relations.

In 1991, at the Maastricht symposium Archives without Boundaries, the late Joshua Enwere, former national archivist of Nigeria, characterized African culture as being found in dance, music, painting, and sculpture. Consequently, the museums and libraries that chronicle these art forms are the institutions that receive the greatest resources. He reported that many developing countries do not feel it appropriate to support archives that contain mainly colonial records; they would rather develop strong oral history programs.

These Maastricht and Stockholm episodes are among my dearest experiences because they have burned into my memory the necessity for archivists to probe beyond what cannot be heard or read. I hope to convince the

ICA to allow for a wider definition of key terms, allowing the integration of other notions regarding "archiveness" from non- or less-script cultures and thereby allowing archives to become more comprehensive, to allow in smiles and whisperings, and to have similar value in all cultures.

So far I have been referring to memory and archives created by preceding generations, archives that we receive *ex post*. I will now address some issues concerning prospective archives creation and memory—archives *ex ante*.

While doing a little background research for my intuitive approach to this subject, I read about Richard Wagner and his quest to create operas as *Gesammtkunstwerk*—that is, including all necessary ingredients from opera house to music, from text to mise-en-scene, from casting to engineering. I tried to work memory out as *Gesammtkunstwerk*: archives feeding in like other mementos, created and preserved in and by context, surviving human and natural disasters. As an archivist, I favor considering archives as the music, the carrier of the drama, and allowing other professions to add to this whole, to this construct. I am not inclined to compare myself with Wagner, but I would like to think of archives as a construct, as a *Gesammtkunstwerk,* a work to be created in one's mind and by one's hands.

Because I like to plan to save myself from wasting energy, I have never understood why our profession prefers to be working *ex post* instead of *ex ante*. In other words, should the archivist as well as the records manager influence records creation? This question has been answered in the affirmative with regard to electronic archives. Several archivists are heavily involved in discussing and designing the prerequisites for electronic records—their design, creation, and preservation. Here, however, I will restrict myself to discussing traditional archives today and to some aspects of archiving *ex ante*, of documenting present time and near future.

Dordrecht was a leading city in the early ages of the Dutch Republic. It even enjoyed a golden century in painting prior to the rest of the province of Holland. Curators and art historians preparing exhibitions are among the frequent visitors to the Dordrecht archives' reading room, looking for information on late-sixteenth- and early-seventeenth-century painters and painting and on life in that era in general. To little avail. Yes, they located important information about housing, birth and death certificates, and so on, but they found little on context, about the paintings—no correspondence between painters and their clientele or between painters and manufacturers of materials. To prevent such an oblivion with regard to

living painters and to facilitate research in centuries to come, I invited curators of the Dordrecht Museum to provide me with names of artists who should be considered potential subjects of future research. They were reluctant to provide me with information, ending in a blunt refusal to share any responsibility in such an appraisal and thereby depriving the archives of information needed to set up a comprehensive acquisition scheme for the construction of the beaux arts part of this *Gesammtkunstwerk* called archives.

Dordrecht is famous for its bell tower. Most local art museums have a painting or watercolor of the tower, the church, and the rest of the riverside. About five years ago, I hired a photographer to take a 360-degree panoramic picture from the tower at noon on the first Mondays of winter, spring, summer, and autumn, whatever the weather—fog, sunshine, hailstones, rain, or snow. Colleagues from other cities have undertaken similar initiatives. Such initiatives regarding audiovisual documentation are quite acceptable in the Dutch profession, though they do not involve archives proper.

How different was the response to my proposal to strive for a comprehensive documentation of current society by identifying functions, organizations, and individuals to be documented and to be assisted in their record keeping. The introduction of proactive acquisition techniques and engaging the archives in the creation of a *Gesammtkunstwerk* seemed to be an indecent proposal. The prevailing view holds that archivists should sit at the end of the sewer of society, taking in refuse, taking in archives of the bankrupt private sector or from estates, without risking dirtying their hands by applying interventionist techniques, by adding particles to memory, by creating archives, by making themselves responsible and thus vulnerable in doing so.

The context of archivists and of records managers is essential for understanding their doings, writings, and jargon. It might be interesting to study changes in archivists' professional behavior on the basis of their professional careers—a subject to be added to the ethnography of the profession.

"Archives: Particles of Memory or More" may be a suggestive title; "Archivists, Doorkeepers of Memory and Oblivion" might have been better after all. I would be grateful if this essay would assist in drawing attention to the need to introduce "comparative analysis of archivology in a multicultural setting" in archival degree programs and if the professional global hub would start really listening to the periphery and allow for the introduction of notions strange to metropolitan countries.

Lookin' for a Home

Independent Oral History Archives in Italy

Alessandro Portelli

In 1970, Italian activist historian and cultural organizer Gianni Bosio wrote, in his description of the work of the Istituto Ernesto de Martino, Italy's first and most important sound archive and research center for people's cultures,

> Just as the advent of the printing press marked the passage from the city-states to the Signoria, from a mainly oral shared culture to the use of means of communication as an expression of the ruling class, the advent of the tape recorder once again provides the culture that relies on oral communication with the means to emerge, to become aware of itself, and thus to unravel all those forms of expression that can be placed against, not alongside, the forms and genres of the ruling culture.

The analogy with the advent of the press was crucial. As writers from Eric Havelock to Jack Goody have shown, the advent of writing accompanied and accelerated the development of Western rationality by making language available for analysis and study and therefore for self-awareness.[1] The tape recorder, Bosio points out, does the same for the voice: speech finds a stable and reproducible support that allows it to be objectified and analyzed. The voice, a universal means of communication, can thus achieve the same degree of self-reflexivity and self-awareness that was earlier reserved for a more restricted medium such as writing. Bosio was less interested in the fact that the tape recorder allowed scholars a closer study of nonhegemonic cultures than in the fact that it enabled the working classes to study themselves, their culture, and their history. The working class might use the tape recorder not just to speak *for* but also *about* itself and most importantly to *listen* to itself.

The tape recorder, then, would not merely provide another source for historians and anthropologists but would indeed disrupt the categories, hierarchies, divisions of labor in history and ethnology in the academy, in the labor movement, and in the Left. When the working class speaks for itself and hears itself, leaders and scholars are less necessary. "There are many in the Left," Bosio went on, "who think the tape recorder is an irrelevant, useless, or diabolical instrument. . . . When the working class movement generates leaders and officers who attempt to exorcise the tape recorder, it is time for the movement to grow up and exorcise its own leaders."[2]

The idea that the tape recorder allowed the working class to speak for itself also blurred the distinctions between disciplines and sources. Named after Ernesto de Martino, the great Italian ethnologist who first recognized the historical and political significance of southern Italian rural culture as well the role of what he described as "progressive folklore" in the north, the institute identified all forms of oral culture and tradition as sites of working-class memory. For example, the rediscovery of the extraordinary tradition of anarchist song created a heightened awareness of the importance of this half-forgotten movement and provided radical movements and leftist dissenters with a songbook that remains very effective today.

As Bosio put it, the hegemonic and academic division of "folkloric man" from "historical man" had to be overcome by placing folklore in history and using it as a historical source as well as by recognizing its bearers as historical agents—"citizens of our own country" in de Martino's phrase. This generated one of the most peculiar traits of the Istituto Ernesto de Martino and of its related institutions: the unification of music, oral history, and other forms of expression. This is a consequence of the global approach to research: the same field encounter may yield both music and stories.[3] The tapes in the de Martino archive, then, hardly ever fall neatly into the categories of ethnomusicology, folklore, oral history; it was necessary to develop a brand-new method for cataloging them, since established systems were inadequate.

Conversely, this meant that the history of the working class, through its own forms of expression, would replace the history of the party and of the union. While leftist history took into account only experiences that could be represented as leading to the formation of the Communist Party, Bosio and his colleagues resurrected the memory of "heretical" groups (from anarchists to nonorthodox Marxists and religious utopists) and studied such aspects of working-class life as religion, ritual, and social life.

Inevitably, the Istituto de Ernesto Martino remained somewhat suspect both for academic scholarship and for the bureaucracy of the Left, for its stubborn and nonsectarian independence that refused to identify with any group or party and thus both included and antagonized them all. This did not keep it from amassing the most important oral archive in Italy and perhaps in Western Europe, including folk music, oral history, and events of political significance (demonstrations, rallies, meetings); the collection now holds more than six thousand tapes and sixteen thousand recorded hours.

The institute generated a network of organizations and projects that included a record label, Dischi del Sole; a publishing outfit, Edizioni Bella Ciao; and a cluster of folk and political singers, Il Nuovo Canzoniere Italiano. These groups were instrumental in creating the independent and antibureaucratic spirit among students and workers and the urge to speak for themselves that led to the 1968–69 uprisings.

But as Woody Guthrie once said, "Folk song is big if labor is big," and to some extent the same applies to oral history. The growing sectarianism of the New Left in the 1970s, the rise of terrorism, the Communist Party's increasing drift toward the center of the political spectrum, and the decline in political activism brought the Istituto de Martino to the verge of disappearance. It was kept together by the stubborn passion and underpaid work of few people, foremost among them Franco Coggiola. In the 1990s, it received a new lease on life when a grant and an offer of space from the city of Sesto Fiorentino, a suburb of Florence that has had a leftist movement since the 1880s. The institute has become one of the rallying points for much of what remains of the Left and has been helped by a slight revival of interest in folk music.

The Circolo Gianni Bosio was established in Rome as an independent local branch of the Istituto de Martino.[4] While it adopted the same basic approach as the parent organization, the Circolo's work differed in important ways. First, we had a local and regional rather than a national perspective (which did not prevent it from carrying out projects in other regions of Italy, such as Umbria or Calabria, and even abroad, from the United States to China; conversely, the Circolo can hardly be labeled "local" when it is situated in Italy's capital and largest city). As a consequence, we were involved to a greater extent with the question of the forms of expression of the urban working class and urban folklore. Rome was an ideal environment for this approach. Its nearness to the rural south and the ongoing massive migration of southern rural people enabled us to follow the changes in rural folklore in the urban context; for example, songs of religious pilgrimage were reinterpreted or remade into songs of struggle. The pilot project, conducted even before the group was formally established, resulted in the documentary recording *Roma, la borgata e la lotta per la casa* (The Slums of Rome and the Squatters' Movement), which included interviews with migrant workers, songs, street rallies, and encounters with the police. While we continued to research music, other forms became more important; the Circolo Gianni Bosio developed many of the more original current approaches to oral history in Italy and internationally.

However, the Circolo struggled with problems of money and, most importantly, of space. Like most alternative cultural groups in Rome in the 1970s, the Circolo was literally underground, housed in a roughly refurbished cellar that was almost adequate for concerts, seminars, and music classes but certainly was no place to store precious tapes. Thus, while the creation of an archive constituted our foremost aim, it remained unfulfilled.

The lack of an archive and the project-oriented approach to fieldwork converged in shaping our interviews. Rather than all-purpose oral histories and life histories, we collected interviews that focused on specific themes—war and resistance, work, education, and so on. Indeed, one peculiarity of oral history is that historians contribute to the creation of their documents, which gives all oral history documents a personal signature. Because oral historians are not only the users but also the creators of their archives, they retain a peculiarly intense relationship with their material—indeed, they are often reluctant to part from their tapes, which thus remain scattered in smaller or private archives (a matter to which I will return shortly), as if fit only for use by their collectors.

No matter how project oriented, however, oral history materials lend themselves to multiple uses and users. Rather than carrying out single-issue interviews, in fact, we always saw the theme of the project as an angle through which the interviewee's experience took narrative form. On the one hand, we believe that the historian's agenda must be placed in the broad context of the narrator's life experience and in the history of the place and the community; on the other hand, in a dialogic interview, the historian's agenda must make space for the narrator's, thus broadening the scope of the dialogue. Narrowly focused projects widen as fieldwork proceeds: a history of post–World War II labor struggles in Terni became a full-fledged oral history of the town from the 1830s to the 1980s; a study of the Fosse Ardeatine massacre (Rome, 1944) became the fulcrum for an oral history of the city of Rome from 1870 to the 1990s. To this should be added the fecund polysemy of oral discourse and narrative discourse: there is always more in an oral narrative performance than either the interviewer or the interviewee intends or is even aware of. A third party is likely to look at the material from another angle and find unforeseen information and insights.

Thus, project-oriented material becomes archive-worthy material: a great deal of material on the tapes does not refer exclusively to the original topic and may be useful to scholars, activists, and citizens looking for something else. The Terni tapes will become the core of an oral archive in Terni, while the Fosse Ardeatine tapes have been used in a number of projects on the history of twentieth-century Rome.

In fact, our ambition is to use this material, together with other tapes amounting to more than five hundred recorded hours, as the core of a Central Archive for the Oral History of Resistance and War in Rome and eventually for a general Central Archive for Oral History. Our idea is that just as scholars automatically use more traditional archives for their research, they may also have one place where they can go (and therefore *must* go) to check out oral history material. After this material is gathered in one place and made available, there is no longer any justification for overlooking it: oral history and its voices gain a place in the broader field of historiography.[5]

However, what do we mean exactly when we speak of "oral sources?" We have assumed that the source is the person, the narrator her/himself (which is why oral historians can go back any number of times to the same source and dig out more information and insights). The

tape and the eventual transcript are representations, created jointly by the source and by the historian, of the dialogic performance of the field encounter. Any third party using this material in an archive, then, finds documentary sources originated in oral fieldwork rather than oral sources proper. Whether these documents are in the shape of "envelopes of sound"[6] or whether they come in written form as transcripts, they present themselves as texts as opposed to the dialogic performance of the interview. The users of oral history archives cannot perform the essential act of the oral historian in the field: they cannot ask questions and get new answers. (Of course, they interrogate these texts metaphorically, as any reader does with any text. But here I am talking about the actual conversation, the interview, the mutual exchange of gazes and words between two or more actual persons.)

These, then, are not oral documents but rather documentary texts originating in orality, a definition that can actually be applied to any number of documentary sources, such as trial records, minutes, parliamentary records, police interrogations, public speeches, and so forth. I think historians would do well to remember that so much of what they take for granted as written document is indeed a transcript—we do not know how accurate—of oral speech acts. The main difference, of course, is that the act of writing these words down often has a performative quality: words spoken in court, in Congress, in a meeting do not become effective until they are included in the record—as opposed to the recording. To make them more impersonal, they are often weeded out of whatever trace of dialogic orality they originally had: the language becomes standardized and official, the structure is monologic. The meaning of oral history documents, conversely, lies precisely in their oral dialogic means of production, and users of these documents should always be aware of the dialogic and oral origin of the material they are using, no matter how many times removed they are from the original source.

This is not to demean the function of orally generated archival documents; indeed, it is a way of making oral history a part of the tool kit of every historian—not just oral historians—and thus to inject, albeit indirectly, the "infection" and the "inflection" of the voice into written historiography and to force the writings of institutions and authorities to confront at least the echo of popular speech and the points of view it represents.

However, the original oral source is the person, and most researchers and scholars therefore tend to create their own interviews and ask their own questions. This, I believe, is an attitude to be encouraged, at least because some firsthand experience of interviewing is essential to a proper understanding of interviews found in archives. Also, from an activist perspective, the interview itself is a transformative experience for both sides involved. Of course, the misconception that all it takes to conduct an interview is two persons and a tape recorder may generate a naive, superficial approach to interviewing, yet a bad interview is better than no interview at all, and even an incompetent interview can work wonders in the hands of a competent user.

But the real problem arising from this state of things is the extreme dispersion of oral sources. The bulk of the existing tapes are stowed away in forgotten drawers in private homes, in union or political offices, in cultural clubs and such, or on back shelves in other archives. I keep coming across small treasure troves of memory that, like the boll weevil in the ballad, are literally lookin' for a home. Bringing them together under one roof, transcribing and cataloging, making them available is in itself an important task of re-membering, putting scattered memories together, making them part of a whole through which they can speak to us. The project—or, perhaps more realistically, the dream—of the Central Archive of Oral History was born with this vision in mind.

The special relations that exist among the historian, the source, and the archive means that the creation of the tape and of the archive are part of a broader project involving activities both up- and downhill from the interview and the tape. In *Mumbo Jumbo,* Ishmael Reed writes of museums as "art detention centers"; in the Italian experience, archives have long been document detention centers: libraries, archives, and museums have often hesitated to let their collections be used, and only recently have they developed a degree of interactivity and openness.[7]

In the case of the Istituto de Martino and the Circolo Gianni Bosio, music was a vehicle that helped generate public use of the collection through records and concerts. The archive is not a separate institution where tapes are held in custody but rather a wheel within wheels of cultural, artistic, and political creation and organization ranging from concerts to record production to scholarly research to grassroots organizing. For example, the most innovative and influential group in the Italian folk revival, the Canzoniere del Lazio, developed its initial repertoire entirely from the collection of the Circolo Bosio. The musicians connected with our movement always rooted their performances in the historical vision founded on their relationship to the archive and sought not only to entertain their audiences and raise their con-

sciousness but also to renew their historical memory. We have often brought our "oral sources" back to speak or played excerpts from the archive in seminars and classes; the research on resistance has generated a successful and effective one-man theater show as well as countless seminars and meetings with students in schools all over the city (and an award-winning book).

Another problem, however, is intrinsic to the sound shape of the archive. Using a sound archive is such a time-consuming and cumbersome affair that researchers are often discouraged and just go through the transcripts, thus missing the essence of the documents. To facilitate access to the actual documents, then, a painstaking process of indexing and referencing is needed so that users can have quicker access to the topics they seek. Such indexing ought not merely list topics but also give some hint as to sound quality and narrative quality. This confirms that all operations concerning the tape are already critical and interpretive—from the myriad decisions confronting the transcriber to the judgments that must be made in indexing.

Cataloging tapes is much more time-consuming than cataloging books or documents. Tapes do not come with the paratextual material—titles, names of authors, place and date of origin, index of contents, index of names—that help librarians or readers figure out what books or documents are about. Instead, all of this material must be created by historians and archivists, which means that creating a catalog card for a tape requires listening to the whole thing, possibly more than once. Two or three hours of listening ultimately may yield one catalog card.

This is not a matter only of time but also of money. The state archive system gives grants for the cataloging of private or independent collections but has a set rate for each catalog card based on the time and work required for a paper document. The idea that archival documents may be based on supports other than paper is now rapidly making headway in the public system and affecting legislation. We are now negotiating one such grant, trying to convince the funders that what is already low pay for books and papers is widely off the mark when it comes to oral history tapes. Conversely, a number of our operators are volunteers, or—alas—unemployed, so that even that pittance may ultimately be better than nothing.

The other problem is that tapes are very delicate objects. There are minimal requirements for storage, maintenance, regular replay. Furthermore, each tape is a rare tape, a unique document, and must be treated as such. This means that one cannot offer for frequent public consultation of original tapes. The cost of making copies and burning CDs for public use is very high in terms of both equipment and time, especially for a self-funded operation like ours. One partial solution we have found is to include copying and indexing costs in research grants: this was the case with our projects on the history of marginal youth in Rome sponsored by the Salesian fathers and the Jewish community or the history of water in Rome sponsored by the public water and power agency. On other occasions, when we have agreed to deposit copies of our tapes in other archives, we have stipulated that the pact include transcribing and/or indexing and extra copies for our own archive. This is part of my agreement with the University of Kentucky and of the one negotiated with the city of Terni.

Finally, the real problem: space. The Circolo Bosio suspended its activity in 1988 because of lack of funds (we couldn't even pay the rent on that damp cellar) and a crisis in political activism. It was reactivated in 2000 with both the old group and newer, younger members. We felt that, on the one hand, the older generation had reached a time in its life cycle when again we had time for volunteer activist work, and whatever we had lost in energy and leisure was made up by the fact that we had more experience and pull (those of us who had been students in the 1970s were now professors, lawyers, architects, and so forth, and those who had been obscure underground musicians were now nationally known artists). We also felt that the crisis in the Left, the demise of a number of organizations and groups, the systematic demolition of the culture of the labor movement and antifascism created a space and a need that we could fill. Bosio's warning about how cultural work is intrinsically political because it must create the political freedom it needs for its own existence is more stringent than ever. Indeed, the rebirth of the Circolo Bosio met with more success than we expected: in a year not too long ago we gained more members and generated more events than we ever did when the Left was supposed to be on the rise, perhaps because there isn't much else to turn to.

From the beginning, the archive was the most important item on our agenda. We decided to name it after Franco Coggiola, the soul of the Istituto de Martino and its archive, who died in 1996. We put together a list of our prospective holdings and on this basis received a certification as an archive "of national historical interest." We approached the city government for a space and received many generous promises but no concrete action. A collective that had been granted the use of a building by the city agreed to let us use a room, but just as we

were getting ready to put the archive together, we discovered that the building had no electricity. In September 2000, we decided to appeal to the solidarity of the national and international activist and scholarly community. Through public meetings and e-mail, we floated the following petition:

> The Franco Coggiola Archive and Library, established in Rome by the Circolo Gianni Bosio, has lost its space. This archive is the result of more than thirty years of fieldwork in oral history, folk music, and popular culture in Rome, in central Italy, and in parts of the United States and other countries. It has been declared an "archive of relevant historic interest" by the regional authorities. It includes more than three thousand hours of recordings as well as books, records, and videotapes and has served as the basis for important scholarly work (the Franco Coggiola Archive is the source for all the oral history documents published in a recent collection sponsored by the local administration on the resistance in Rome) as well as for the revival, study, and teaching of oral traditions and folk music.
>
> The archive had to give up its historic space (a cellar in the San Lorenzo neighborhood) because the dampness was destroying the tapes and books. The goodwill shown in countless meetings with city officials has not resulted in a concrete alternative. The archive was recently forced to remove its collections from the temporary space offered by a cultural association (Ex Rialto Occupato) because, during maintenance work, the power cables were cut off and six months of meetings and discussions with city officials and the electric company have not sufficed to restore it.
>
> A democratic society and its culture thrive on independent, accessible, highly qualified structures such as the Franco Coggiola Archive and the Circolo Gianni Bosio. The civic spirit of those who keep them going, the knowledge preserved and made available, the activities (stages, seminars, music) that make it a living space, and the resources offered to scholars make them especially important as a democratic cultural resource for the city of Rome and beyond.
>
> We therefore invite all local institutions as well as cultural and political organizations to work toward making this important resource again available to citizens, cultural workers, artists, and scholars.
>
> In a spirit of public service, the Circolo makes the materials of the archive available by arrangement. For information, and for the catalog, e-mail bosiocircolo @hotmail.com.

In the space of less than a month, we received 397 signatures from twenty-two countries.[8] The signatories included historians, folklorists, anthropologists, musicians, archivists, journalists, and ordinary citizens from all over the world. Barbara Dane, a great blues singer, record producer, and political activist, wrote,

> It is absolutely essential that the Franco Coggiola Archives which was established by the Circolo Gianni Bosio not only survive but that it be properly housed in order to be available to future generations of scholars and other interested people. This collection is irreplaceable, and without it there will be a very serious lack of information about an entire era of popular culture and life, especially as expressed by those people who lived it.
>
> The fact that this Archive has been made through the efforts of a handful of dedicated and foresighted scholars is some kind of modern miracle in the first place. If it would be lost to the future, it would be a crime.
>
> The world looks to Rome and Italy as fundamental sources of human history, where the highest respect is paid to the past in order to build a better future. Do not fail in your responsibility to preserve and maintain this significant reservoir of information about our collective past, for whatever happens in Italy affects the world.

During Rome's 2001 mayoral election campaign, I ran into Walter Veltroni, the Left's candidate. No sooner had I said hello than he asked, "What's the news on your archive?" "I'm waiting to hear from you," I replied. Our petition has clearly made a number of prominent persons and institutions aware of our quandary yet has yielded no concrete results. Veltroni's campaign was successful, and we were hoping it would help to put our archive on sounder footing. In fact, the new administration appointed me as the mayor's representative for the promotion and protection of historical memory in Rome, an important recognition of the meaning of oral history and of our work. But we have received no assurances about space. We took over an abandoned public school in the center of Rome, cleaned it up, managed to get a gift of furniture and some money for equipment, and started the archive, only to find out that the city plans to reopen the school and evict us (although given the slow pace of action by public institutions, we have some time before anything will happen). It makes a great deal of sense that we of the Circolo Gianni Bosio, who started out with the squatters' movement in the 1960s, should seek a rebirth by becoming squatters ourselves. After thirty years, the voices, the oral history, and the music of the people of Rome are still lookin' for a home.

NOTES

1. Eric C. Havelock, *The Muse Learns to Write: Reflections on Orality and Literacy from Antiquity to the Present* (New Haven: Yale University Press, 1986); Jack Goody, *The Domestication of the Savage Mind* (Cambridge: Cambridge University Press, 1977).

2. Gianni Bosio, "Elogio del magnetofono" (1970) in *L'intellettuale rovesciato* (Milan: Bella Ciao, 1975), 170–71.

3. Consequently, the Istituto Ernesto de Martino had to develop its own techniques for cataloging and describing tapes.

4. See Alessandro Portelli, "Memory and Resistance: A History (and Celebration) of the Circolo Gianni Bosio," in *The Battle of Valle Giulia: Oral History and the Art of Dialogue* (Madison: University of Wisconsin Press, 1997), 40–54.

5. For a brilliant use of secondhand oral history sources by a non–oral historian, see Claudio Pavone, *Una guerra civile: Saggio sulla moralità nella Resistenza* (Turin: Bollati Boringhieri, 1991). In his overall analysis of the Italian Resistance, Pavone uses my published interviews with partisans in Terni in ways that are both original and correct.

6. Ronald J. Grele, *Envelopes of Sound* (1975; Chicago: Precedent, 1985).

7. See *Archivi sonori*, proceedings of three seminars organized by the State Archives in 1993–95 (State Archives Office: Rome, 1999): *Atti des seminari di Vercelli (22 gennaio 1993), Bologna (22–23 settembre 1994), Milano (7 marzo 1994)* (Rome: Ministero per I Beni e le Attività Culturali, Ufficio Centrale per I Beni Archivistici, 1999).

8. The signatories included 165 from Italy, 120 from the United States, 47 from Britain, 25 from Mexico, and smaller numbers from Argentina, Austria, Australia, Belgium, Brazil, Canada, Cuba, France, Germany, Israel, Norway, New Zealand, Portugal, Spain, Sweden, Switzerland.

The Public Controversy over the Kennedy Memorabilia Project

Robert M. Adler

"Whatever I do or say," President Kennedy said . . . "Mrs. Lincoln will be sweet and unsurprised. If I had said just now, 'Mrs. Lincoln, I have cut off Jackie's head, would you please send over a box?' she still would have replied, 'That's wonderful, Mr. President, I'll send it right away. . . . Did you get your nap?'"[1]

The Troublesome Issues Raised by the JFK Memorabilia Controversy

Evelyn Lincoln served as John F. Kennedy's personal secretary in the White House. She is credited with saving from extinction various notes, drafts, doodles, and miscellaneous Kennedy memorabilia that otherwise would not have been preserved.[2] Following JFK's death, the Kennedy Library, Senator Ted Kennedy, and John F. Kennedy Jr. directly asked Lincoln to donate her collected memorabilia to the library.[3] She responded by donating some of her collection. At her death in 1995, she bequeathed other memorabilia to another collector, Robert L. White. Three years later, White attempted to auction some of his Kennedy memorabilia received from Lincoln as well as other items he had collected over the past thirty or so years.[4] The Kennedys, the Kennedy Library, and the National Archives for the first time vigorously challenged Lincoln's ownership of her memorabilia collection, publicly asserting that she had breached the public trust by taking an overwhelming number of items for herself.[5] A lead editorial in the *New York Times* on 16 March 1998 delineated the conflicting interests of the public's right to preserve these historic materials and White's claim of private ownership:

These are not things personal to the Kennedys. They are personal to the nation. Today, by law, such doodlings by Bill Clinton would be defined as Presidential records, government property. But the Kennedy papers, along with his briefcase and writing desk—face the auction block, and an afterlife in someone's den. The National Archives is now hot to get them. The Archives has no money to buy such things. Perhaps it should. But instead, on Friday, it threatened to sue, on the basis of the ambiguous deed of gifts.

Robert White has already given up some things. Perhaps, after a weekend's thought, he and his wife will give up more of the nation's heritage.

The actions by the Kennedy Library, the Kennedy Library Foundation, and the Kennedy family (including the interactions among the three) raise the perplexing issue of the extent of a conflict between the legitimate goals of a presidential library and the effective control of that library by the former president's family on issues of importance to it.[6]

The conflict between the apparent interests of the former president's family and the presidential library itself became evident in the events surrounding the controversy over Lincoln's JFK memorabilia collection. The Kennedy Library, backed by the National Archives and its lawyers, essentially claimed that Lincoln had stolen the JFK memorabilia she claimed as her own. Yet after the controversy subsided in 1998, documents obtained from the library as the result of Freedom of Information Act (FOIA) requests revealed that: (1) library officials and the Kennedy family knew and accepted that Lincoln legitimately owned the collection; (2) rather than challenging Lincoln's ownership during her lifetime, library officials and the Kennedy family concentrated on attempting to convince her to donate her collection to the library; and (3) any conceivable claim against the collection was tenuous as a result of the ambiguities in the initial deed of gift and of the anecdotal and speculative nature of the evidence against Lincoln.[7]

After Lincoln's death in 1995, library officials quickly realized that she had not left the library the "treasures" they had anticipated. Nonetheless, the library took no action to assert a claim against her remaining memorabilia collection, even though the institution's officials were fully aware that she had possessed documents of exceptional historical importance as well as unique items of memorabilia (such as the briefcase that JFK carried on his last trip to Dallas as well as some of its contents).

Not until the November 1997 public announcement of the Guernsey's auction did the library threaten legal action. If the Kennedy Library and the National Archives really believed in the strength of their claims, why wait thirty-five years before asserting them? Because of pressure asserted by the Kennedy family as a result of the fact that White, a stranger to whom they had no connections, had their family's possessions and was prepared to sell them for personal gain?[8] Because the Kennedys and the library were content, although not entirely comfortable, with White having the memorabilia collection but not with his attempt to sell some of it? The answer is not clear; however, in the settlements with White, the National Archives and the Kennedy family permitted the majority of his consigned lots to be sold at auction. Given the National Archives' and the Kennedy family's extensive resources for pursuing litigation, the fact that they chose to settle for a small number of the consigned lots speaks to the weakness of their claims. Conversely, White was retired. His wife was a secretary. Other than a modest home, their only real asset was the collection. A Goliath national archive and presidential library and David-like private collector were struggling over the right to records and artifacts of unquestioned historic importance. There was also the matter of Evelyn Lincoln's good name.[9]

Background

In 1952, Evelyn Lincoln was working on Capitol Hill as part of Georgia Congressman E. L. Forrester's secretarial staff. She also had a nighttime job in the office of the Democratic clerk of the House of Representatives. JFK was then thirty-five years old and serving his third term in the House. Unhappy with her jobs, Lincoln volunteered for JFK's Senate campaign.[10] After JFK won the election, he offered her a position in his Senate office, and when he was elected president, she became his personal secretary.[11] She worked for him for almost twelve years, from 3 January 1953 until 22 November 1963, when he was killed. Thereafter, she remained a trusted friend of the Kennedy family.

After his death, all of JFK's White House memorabilia was immediately moved to the Old Executive Office Building, where it was stored in three rooms. Lincoln was placed in charge of inventorying this material, remaining in that position until May 1967. During this period, Jackie Kennedy sent Lincoln a number of handwritten notes that expressed strong continuing confidence in her. In October 1964, Jackie Kennedy invited Lincoln to come to New York City to attend Caroline Kennedy's First Communion.[12] Lincoln accepted, and Jackie Kennedy subsequently wrote to Lincoln,

> I was so touched at your coming all the way up here for Caroline's First Communion. . . . [T]here was nothing pleasant in it for you—just being sweet to a little girl who loves you so much—and whose life you made so happy. . . . I remember those early days when the major part of your morning you spent pasting together those Indian headbands for her out of the labels in your desk and letting her do a great deal of typing—with the President dashing in and out of your office with slightly more urgent things for you to do—
>
> Both my children spent so many hours in your office—it was the best way they could see their father—and if you hadn't been so sweet to them and made them feel that they were more loved and wanted there than any important visitor—they would have missed so much of their closeness with him—and they would have so many less memories of him—Those memories—which are so vivid to them—are the greatest treasure they have—They both know how much their father loved them and that means more to them than anything I could do to help them now—And you made so much of that possible—I love you for all that you were to him and them and me. . . . Their happiness is all that matters now—and you contributed so much to it by coming here—at such effort and discomfort for you—

I wish you could come back sometime and stay with us—and let us take care of you—you must sleep late and have [a] fattening breakfast in bed. . . . I think it would be so good for you to have a little reprieve from always living & working where you are surrounded by memories.

With all my love dearest Mrs. Lincoln and my thanks for all that you did for Caroline on Saturday. It would have touched Jack so much—[13]

Significantly, as reported in a memorandum appearing in the Kennedy Library files, Lincoln spoke with Jackie Kennedy on 7 March 1964.

Mrs. L is worried . . . that we might take all of her things away from her, that everything she . . . has will become govt. property, that very personal papers and objects which she thinks should belong to Mrs. K will become govt property. Mrs. K. suggests that I drop a word now & then to reassure her on this score.[14]

This document clearly recognized Lincoln's legitimate ownership of her Kennedy memorabilia. It is very difficult to reconcile these statements with the 1998 assertions by the National Archives and Kennedy family members that Lincoln betrayed her trust by keeping items that rightfully belonged to the Kennedy family or the library.

During 1964–66, according to a number of documents in the Kennedy Library files, various individuals were concerned about Lincoln's performance in organizing JFK's memorabilia. Some memos expressed irritation at the slow pace of her work.[15] Arthur Schlesinger Jr. and Jackie Kennedy expressed concerns about the amount of time Lincoln was taking.[16] Robert Kennedy apparently served as a watchdog for Lincoln and was concerned that she was not spending enough time working on "the doodles" because she was writing a book.[17] He directly confronted Lincoln about these concerns, and in an apparent effort to defend herself, she wrote to him on 24 September 1965, explaining that from the beginning, Jackie Kennedy's uncle, Wilarth (Lefty) Lewis, had urged her to work on JFK's handwritten notes that she had saved over the years. According to Lincoln, because of her unique ability to decipher JFK's handwriting and her status as the only person who knew the notes' historical context, she was asked to forget about organizing the files and instead to concentrate on the notes. She added, "So this is what I have tried to do. It is tedious and sometimes I will spend as much as 3 or 4 hours on one page. But I am ever mindful of the greatness of the man for whom I worked and no task is too difficult to perform for him." Nonetheless, in November 1965, all of the pa-

pers and objects that had been in Lincoln's charge (with the exception of the doodles, photographs, and certain negatives) were removed from her custody.[18]

Nevertheless, Lincoln still apparently had Jackie Kennedy's trust. In a handwritten 29 June 1966 note, Jackie Kennedy discussed the disposition of the family furniture that remained under Lincoln's care, and on 7 November, Jackie Kennedy asked Lincoln to help in giving Christmas presents to JFK's children, brothers, and sisters.

Jackie Kennedy, Robert Kennedy, and Edward M. Kennedy donated JFK's papers, documents, and other memorabilia to the National Archives through a 25 February 1965 deed.[19] However, the critical conveyancing portion of the deed was hopelessly ambiguous on its face. It lacked an inventory or other identification of the property to be gifted. Instead, the only specification of donated property was the general statement that it had belonged to and related to the life and work of JFK and that "he [had] intended [that it] should be so deposited."[20] Excluded from the gift was any memorabilia that JFK had not intended to be deposited in the presidential archive or that the donors determined "to be of special or private interest to the personal family of John Fitzgerald Kennedy, his wife and children, parents, brothers and sisters." The deed further provided that the donors reserved the right to regain title to and possession of any items irrespective of the fact that such items had previously been delivered to the archives.[21] (Kennedy Library documents reflect that Jackie Kennedy liberally exercised that right.) The deed did not begin to suggest whether the items held by Lincoln were to be included in the devise.

The legal foundation for any possible National Archives claim to title to Lincoln's memorabilia would necessarily be the conveyance to the archives under the deed.[22] However, its inherent ambiguity and, even more significantly, the Kennedy family's explicit right to regain ownership of memorabilia previously "donated" to the archives (thus never placing the property out of the family's reach) creates substantial doubt regarding the deed's enforceability.

There is a very strong argument that the deed failed to convey title to memorabilia held by third parties, including Lincoln and White. This conclusion is supported by an abundance of case law.[23] All of this raises the question of whether the National Archives, although aware of the weakness in its legal position, nonetheless aggressively asserted a title claim in deprivation of Mr. White's rights.[24]

After 1967

Despite the termination of her services, Evelyn Lincoln remained in continuing contact with Kennedy Library officials and members of the Kennedy family for the rest of her life. Lincoln also continued to transcribe JFK's handwriting and to provide descriptions of each document in its proper context. She also stayed in regular contact with Kennedy Library officials, who continued to extend various courtesies to her.[25] Lincoln was named as one of the library's seventeen initial board members. As one of a select few "who had a special relationship with or played a significant role in the public life of John F. Kennedy," Paul J. Kirk Jr., a Kennedy confidante, asked her to suggest invitees to the Kennedy Library's opening, and she was invited to the library's groundbreaking ceremony.[26]

Although during the 1998 controversy, Kennedy Library officials as well as Kennedy family members publicly stated that they had not previously been aware that Lincoln possessed a significant JFK collection, documents show that library officials knew as early as 1977 that Lincoln had important memorabilia. On 27 April 1977, Senator Edward Kennedy wrote to Lincoln, stating his purpose in doing so as obtaining additional materials for the Kennedy Library from her collection as well as others. According to Senator Kennedy, most of what had been collected did not "reflect the facets of President Kennedy that you and I remember best, and from which visitors would learn the most. It is for that reason that I am asking your assistance." The letter continued, "Because of your close association with the President, it may be that you have such material, and that you might be willing to consider making it available to the Library, either as a gift or as a loan." Eight months later, the library's director, Dan H. Fenn Jr., wrote to Lincoln, again requesting the donation of her papers. In closing, Fenn wrote, "We are making this special effort on acquisitions now. . . . If you have any questions about the disposition of your papers . . . please write or call."[27]

Fifteen years later, the late John F. Kennedy Jr. wrote to Lincoln,

Because of your long and special relationship with President Kennedy, based on the fact that you were his personal secretary from the day he entered the Senate until the end of his life, you are in a unique position . . . to help future generations know my father as a politician, a leader, and a man and to understand the events and personalities of his times.

. . . Any files which you have relating to your writings, as well as any other papers you may have collected and kept over the years would be most welcome additions to the rich holdings of the Kennedy Library's archives. They would also be a wonderful tribute to the memory of President Kennedy, whom you served so well over so many years, and a fitting monument to your personal and professional relationship with him. . . .

I hope you will agree with me that this is the perfect time to reconsider the question of the donation of your papers to the Library. From the Library's perspective, it clearly is. . . .

Please give this request very careful consideration and let me know what you decide to do with your papers. . . . The director and staff of the Library are anxious to help you in any way they can with the details of your donation.

Shortly thereafter, Lincoln telephoned William Johnson, the library's chief archivist, to inform him that she had decided immediately to donate two file cabinets of material.[28] After the library received this material, it raised no questions regarding Lincoln's legal title to her Kennedy memorabilia. The internal documents produced by the library in response to FOIA requests do not raise this issue. Moreover, available documentary evidence offers no indication that the rather sizable nature of this donation prompted library officials to inquire about whether Lincoln held other JFK memorabilia.

Robert White's Relationship with Evelyn Lincoln

Robert White was a salesman of industrial cleaning supplies who lived with his family in the Baltimore, Maryland, area. He had started collecting as a teenager and first corresponded with Evelyn Lincoln in 1963, shortly before JFK's death.[29] They sporadically exchanged correspondence for a number of years thereafter.[30] White first met Evelyn Lincoln in 1975, when she and her husband invited him to lunch. On that occasion, they discussed White's Kennedy collection and their mutual love and respect for the Kennedys. Sometime in 1985–86, Lincoln telephoned White and again invited him for lunch. During that visit, she told him that she would like to share with him the private Kennedy items she had collected over the years, and she mentioned that she had retrieved Kennedy's doodles from the trash. White had previously been unaware that Lincoln had a Kennedy memorabilia collection. Lincoln never showed White the entire collection; instead, at intervals, she invited White to her home and showed him a preselected group of items.[31] Lincoln gave White these items, together with an oral history surrounding them. In many cases, Lincoln also provided White with typed explanations of how Kennedy had used the documents or items of memorabilia.[32]

On 5 April 1989, Lincoln explained how she had collected her JFK memorabilia.

> I have been a collector of memorabilia most of my life and due to my relationship with important people I have been fortunate to collect many interesting items to add to my growing collection. Most of the items I have collected have either been given to me or have been discarded.
>
> The collection which I have made available to you is the John F. Kennedy collection, which I started in the early 1950's. Many of these personal items have been saved from extinction by me. Many items were given to me by John F. Kennedy, others were discarded items, even from the waste basket. . . .
>
> I have over the years given you, when necessary, letters of authenticity to accompany each item I have made available to you. I am sending this letter to you to be added to your collection for future generations.[33]

Evelyn Lincoln's Death and the Devise of JFK Memorabilia to the Kennedy Library and Robert White

Evelyn Lincoln died on 11 May 1995. Her husband died forty days later. Their wills contained identical dispositive provisions for the JFK memorabilia. As the survivor, only Harold Lincoln's will was required to be probated under Maryland law. Under that will, two filing cabinets, labeled "BS" and "NY," were devised to the Kennedy Library. The presidential and U.S. flags that had stood behind JFK's desk in the Oval Office were given to John Knox, a friend of Evelyn Lincoln's, for the Irish Room at the University of Pittsburgh. Three filing cabinets of documents were left to a niece, Lisa Dale Norton. White received one filing cabinet labeled "ES" as well as "Kennedy memorabilia, such as briefcase, signing table, rocker and stereo."[34]

At the Kennedy Library's request, it received a copy of Harold Lincoln's will. The library did not question or challenge Evelyn Lincoln's ownership of the JFK memorabilia; indeed, according to an affidavit from the estate's executor, he made library officials aware that the material devised to White included memorabilia from the JFK administration, and "no one from the Kennedy Library ever expressed any surprise that Mrs. Lincoln had this memorabilia." Moreover, according to the executor, the

Kennedy Library did not suggest or assert that during her lifetime Lincoln had inappropriately collected and retained a substantial quantity of Kennedy memorabilia. Neither the library nor the Kennedy family questioned or challenged the will's devise of Kennedy memorabilia to White.[35] Instead, according to the executor,

> The only inquiry that I received from any Kennedy family member with respect to Mrs. Lincoln's JFK memorabilia was during a telephone call I made to Melody Miller, an assistant to Senator Edward Kennedy. (This communication occurred while I served as the Executor.) During this call, Ms. Miller asked me to keep an eye open for anything in Mrs. Lincoln's collection which might reflect poorly on the Kennedy family. I said that I would.

The two filing cabinets given to the Kennedy Library arrived in Boston in February 1996. In a 13 February e-mail, Johnson, the chief archivist, wrote, "at first glance we did not see any priceless treasures."[36] The Kennedy Library confirmed its disappointment at the low quality of the memorabilia in Lincoln's filing cabinets. On 29 February, Johnson acknowledged that although the acquisition included "some very worthwhile material," during a very cursory examination

> we did not encounter many more of the "treasures" which Mrs. Lincoln was believed to have kept through the years—some of which were in earlier papers she placed in the Library during her lifetime and the balance of which she implied, or perhaps I inappropriately inferred, would eventually end up here in her papers. It may be that we now have everything that exists and will find more in the papers when we really get into them, but I wanted to make you aware of what I have been able to determine thus far. Please advise whether in your view we do in fact now have everything that is out there.[37]

During 1996, White and his JFK memorabilia collection attracted significant media attention. He appeared on television programs in the Baltimore-Washington area, *Today,* and *Dateline NBC;* major articles appeared in the *Washington Post,* the *Washington Times,* the *New York Times,* the *Boston Globe,* and the *Baltimore Sun.*[38] These stories detailed the significant JFK-related items White owned, such as the briefcase and JFK's passport from his Senate days. These reports disclosed that White had "vast" Kennedy memorabilia acclaimed as the world's largest private JFK collection. Despite all this public attention, the Kennedy Library made no protests and asserted no claims to White's items.[39] Instead, Frank Rigg, the library's curator, publicly downplayed the quality of White's collection, stating in a 24 May 1996 *New York Times* article, "The White collection pales in comparison with that of the JFK Library and Museum in Boston, a branch of the National Archives, which has 32 million documents, 300,000 photographs and 17,000 artifacts." According to the same article, Rigg stated that he would not comment on the White collection without seeing it.

The Announcement of the Guernsey's Auction: The Kennedys and the National Archives Spring into Action

The Guernsey's auction was publicly announced during November 1997. For the first time in thirty-five years, the Kennedy Library (and those close to JFK) publicly claimed that Evelyn Lincoln had engaged in foul play. Various major publications reported statements by library officials and the Kennedy family challenging Lincoln's ownership of the memorabilia. As the 18 March 1998 auction approached, these allegations grew in intensity. On 1 January 1998, under the headline "Kennedy Loyalists Question Ownership of Items Set for Auction," the *Washington Post* reported that "Paul Kirk, chairman of the family-controlled Kennedy Library Foundation, suggested that the secretary, the late Evelyn F. Lincoln, might not have been the rightful owner of many of the items she amassed during her 12 years as Kennedy's secretary in Congress and the White House." Kirk threatened litigation: "You can be sure that serious questions will be raised in appropriate venues by appropriate parties and authorities regarding the provenance of these items." Former Kennedy speechwriter Ted Sorensen was quoted as saying, "It's outrageous. . . . She has no legal entitlement. . . . I don't think that *I'll* be bidding on it."[40] On 11 January, the *Boston Globe* reported that although the Kennedys had long been "aware that Lincoln . . . had accumulated many of the president's personal belongings after his death, some with the approval of Mrs. Kennedy and Robert F. Kennedy," unnamed sources "close to the Kennedys" claimed that questions remained unanswered regarding Lincoln's title to the memorabilia:

> Kennedy allies said the key legal question is whether Lincoln was permitted to keep the material as a permanent owner or merely a custodian.

Asked why the Kennedys waited so long to try to regain the property, a source close to the family said, "Events transpired, and nobody wanted to go through that day again," referring to the assassination. "Then Bobby was gone," the source said, referring to Robert F. Kennedy's assassination in 1968.

The Assassination Review Board's Deposition of Robert White

Almost immediately after the public announcement of the Guernsey's auction, the Kennedy Library and the National Archives began to prepare for litigation. Their first formal step was the Assassination Records Review Board's 16 January 1998 subpoena of White for highly questionable reasons. The subpoena required White to appear to be deposed and to produce a number of documents.[41] At first blush, the document requests had some superficial validity in that they appeared to represent legitimate efforts to assist the board in its effort to gather documents relating to Kennedy's assassination. However, it quickly became clear during the deposition several weeks later that this effort actually had an ulterior motive—to compel sworn testimony from White regarding his understanding of Evelyn Lincoln's claim of legitimate title to her JFK memorabilia collection. Such issues fell totally outside of the review board's statutory mandate.[42] Only the smallest fraction of that collection had any relation whatsoever to the assassination, a fact well understood by the review board. Nonetheless, despite the strenuous objections of White's counsel, the review board insisted on eliciting testimony from White regarding his understanding of the provenance of such items as the rocking chair given by JFK to Lincoln. After this line of questioning persisted, White's counsel instructed him not to respond to further questions along those lines.[43]

From documents later produced by the Kennedy Library in response to FOIA requests, it became even more apparent that these discovery efforts had been improperly coordinated with the National Archives in its effort to seek evidence with which to challenge White's title to the Kennedy memorabilia.[44] This represented a flagrant abuse of the Assassination Review Board and its delegated powers. The review board's statutory mandate did not extend to investigating title issues relating to Kennedy memorabilia, particularly when the items had no conceivable bearing on JFK's assassination. The National Archives had no legal mechanism by which to review White's memorabilia collection or to take his statement under oath relating to the title issues. Clearly understanding this predicament, the National Archives and the review board combined forces for those purposes.

The Legal Claims against Robert White and His Collection

As the Guernsey's auction approached, media coverage grew. Most of it focused on the outcry from the Kennedy Library and those close to JFK. The Kennedy family publicly criticized Evelyn Lincoln and the auction.[45] The family and the National Archives began to assert formal claims. On 6 February 1998, counsel for Caroline B. Kennedy and John F. Kennedy Jr. sent a letter to White's counsel demanding that White refrain from selling or consigning for sale any items he received from either of the Lincolns except for any item for which credible contemporaneous evidence (presumably from JFK or Jackie Kennedy) demonstrated an attempt to convey ownership of the item to the Lincolns. Otherwise, all other items were to be returned to their rightful owners, Caroline and John Kennedy. On 13 February, counsel for the executors of the last will and testament of Jacqueline K. Onassis made a similar demand. And on 10 March, the National Archives made the same demand to Guernsey's, asserting that the archives had reason to believe that many of the documents intended for auction "belonged to the United States." The letter requested that National Archives representatives be allowed to examine the items scheduled for auction as well as be provided with Guernsey's information on their provenance. The National Archives threatened to sue Guernsey's if it either sold or attempted to sell items properly belonging to the United States.[46] The Kennedy Library's Public Affairs Office leaked to the media information regarding the National Archives' demand to Guernsey's.

White's lawyers, Justice Department lawyers, National Archives officials and attorneys, Kennedy Library representatives, and White immediately began negotiations regarding the matter. The discussions were cordial and to the point. A settlement agreement was reached within several days. Under it, the National Archives was permitted to take possession of items described in seven identified lots in the auction catalog, including a number of documents and a table (the "signing table") frequently used by JFK in the Oval Office.[47] In return, the National Archives (including the Kennedy Library) agreed to release White from all claims relating to the balance of the items consigned by White in the Guernsey's auction.[48]

Despite substantial progress between White's representatives and the National Archives in reaching a settlement, Caroline Kennedy and John Kennedy Jr. as well as Kirk issued strongly worded press releases on 16 March 1998. The Kennedys attacked Evelyn Lincoln, alleging that she had taken "advantage of her position as our father's secretary, and later as the custodian of objects intended for the Library, by taking home with her countless documents and objects that had belonged to our father and to the United States Government" and identifying four types of materials they sought from White.[49] Kirk's press release, issued on behalf of the Kennedy Library Foundation, also asserted that Lincoln had breached the trust of the Kennedy family and the United States.

After reaching a settlement with the National Archives, White's counsel began settlement negotiations with counsel for Caroline and John F. Kennedy Jr. After a number of telephone discussions, an agreement was reached late on the evening of 17 March. Caroline Kennedy approved the agreement, but it remained subject to John F. Kennedy Jr.'s approval. But time was running out: the auction was scheduled to begin at 2:00 P.M. the following day.

Although the National Archives' claims had been settled and an agreement with the Kennedy family was at hand, Sorensen appeared on *Today* on the morning of 18 March and made the strongest accusations to date:

> I am outraged that some of [President Kennedy's] own personal material and proper belongings of the government are being auctioned off for someone's own personal profit.
>
> I feel sorry for Mrs. Lincoln, who was a devoted secretary of the President's. I don't think she knew what she was doing when she took property that belonged to the family, belonged to the estate and belonged to the government. [The property] was misappropriated, it was taken by someone [Evelyn Lincoln] who had no right to it.
>
> With all due respect, its too bad for Mr. White that he's let his greed outrun his devotion to the Kennedys, because those who do not have good title cannot pass on good title. Mrs. Lincoln did not have good title, and Mr. White I think knew that when he, I think, purchased or induced her to give or bequeath these items to him.

Two hours later, John F. Kennedy Jr. approved the settlement terms reached the prior evening.[50]

The auction proceeded.[51] As the media correctly reported, White received approximately $1.3 million in proceeds from the sale, which included approximately 10 percent of his JFK memorabilia. From November 1999 until

August 2003, the significant remaining items in White's collection were on permanent display at the Florida International Museum in St. Petersburg. While these exhibits did not lead to a legal challenge, the Kennedy Library's adversarial posture continued. On 15 May 2000, Kennedy Library Foundation officials wrote to the secretary of the Smithsonian Institution, criticizing its establishment of an "affiliate" relationship with the Florida museum. After recounting the dispute between the library and White, the writer stated, "I am deeply disappointed that the Smithsonian Institution, this country's leading museum, would get itself involved in this exhibition. Given the public record of our dispute with Mr. White, I find it especially disappointing that the Smithsonian would do so without consulting with the Kennedy family or the Kennedy Library or Foundation." The Smithsonian was undeterred. On 9 June 2000, the secretary responded, "We were aware of the dispute several years ago involving the Library, the Kennedy family and Robert White concerning whether Mr. White had legal ownership of his Kennedy memorabilia and particularly of the Evelyn Lincoln collection of Kennedy material. During our discussions with the Florida International Museum, we researched the issues of Mr. White's ownership of this collection and found nothing out of order. We then proceeded in earnest with an affiliation and the loan of Smithsonian collections for the Museum's exhibition."[52]

Conclusion

The Kennedy Library has, at public expense, improperly assailed a collector, Robert White, by publicly denouncing title to his collection, the legitimacy of which it earlier recognized, by targeting him by misusing the discovery powers of the Assassination Review Board, by using its influence on other museums in an effort to have them shun the collection so that it would not be made generally available to public exhibition, and by using its declassification powers to prevent the private property of Mr. White from being restored to him.

The library's course of conduct suggests that it subordinated its own prescribed role of preserving the memory of JFK to one of becoming a politically motivated entity bent on following its own agenda for ill-defined and unregulated purposes in contravention of the rights and protections afforded a citizen. The occasional public criticism of the Kennedy Library on similar issues had no discernible effect. The Kennedy Library, like other presidential libraries, is an institution charged with the public

trust. The record of its approach to Mr. White and his Kennedy memorabilia collection suggests that it has followed the dictates of the president's family, and those close to it, rather than fulfilling the responsibilities it has assumed in operating so as to further the interests of the public at large.

Postscript

Following Mr. White's death in 2003, discussions started with Gary M. Stern, the general counsel of the National Archives, in an effort to reach a settlement of all possible claims against the Robert White JFK memorabilia collection. As of this date [March 14, 2001], settlement has not been concluded, although it appears likely. Mr. Stern brought a much more balanced and conciliatory perspective to the complicated issues involved. If a settlement is reached, he deserves substantial credit.

NOTES

The author is a partner in the Washington, D.C., law firm of O'Connor & Hannan, L.L.P. He has served as Robert L. White's counsel since 1997, when White conducted his controversial auction of Kennedy memorabilia in New York City. The author has also represented White in connection with claims against him and his JFK memorabilia collection by the National Archives, the estate of Jacqueline Onassis, and Caroline Kennedy and John F. Kennedy Jr. The author has also represented the owner of a Cuban Missile Crisis map whom the National Archives sued for its recovery. The map was originally owned by Evelyn Lincoln (see n. 22). Mr. White passed away on October 11, 2003. Prior to his death he made many contributions to this paper. The author currently represents Mr. White's estate in issues relating to the Kennedy memorabilia collection. The views set forth herein are the author's alone.

1. Theodore C. Sorensen, *Kennedy* (New York, 1965), 55–56.

2. As early as 1965, the *Saturday Evening Post* reported that Lincoln had saved these doodles.

3. Until 1978, papers and other historic materials prepared or created during a presidency were the property of the individual president, not of the United States; see, e.g., Opinion of the Attorney General of the United States, *Title to Presidential Papers—Subpoenas,* 43 Op. Atty. Gen. 11, 1974 U.S. AG LEXIS 1 (6 September 1974). However, the Watergate scandal led to the enactment of the Presidential Records Act of 1978 (44 U.S. secs. 2201 et seq.), which provided that any presidential record was the property of the United States rather than of the individual president. It was not made retroactive to JFK's presidency.

4. The market value of memorabilia, even JFK memorabilia, did not appreciably rise until the 1980s, and only the

1996 Jackie Onassis auction elevated the level of public attention to Kennedy memorabilia and the high prices it could obtain. The auction garnered some $35 million. Important historic items were sold, including the table used by JFK for the signing of the Nuclear Test Ban Treaty in 1963.

5. There is evidence that immediately after JFK's death, Jackie Kennedy disposed of a number of the president's personal items. (Evelyn Lincoln to Robert White, 29 July 1994 ["When Jackie was moving out of the White House in December 1963 she was moving to the Harriman home in Georgetown. So she set up a room in that house with several long tables. On these tables she placed their discarded clothing. She also had baskets for smaller items. She then invited friends to come over to this room and choose any item or items they desired."]). See also Caroline Latham and Jeannie Sakol, *The Kennedy Encyclopedia* (New York, 1989) ("After the President's assassination, Jacqueline Kennedy gave [George] Thomas [Kennedy's] rocking chair from the Oval Office as a memento of the man he had served so faithfully for so many years [as a valet]."). Dave Powers, a former White House aide to JFK and later the curator for the Kennedy library, sold at a Sotheby's auction (November 1997) JFK manuscript notecards and other handwritten notes of the president. In Mary Gallagher's 1969 book, *My Life with Jacqueline Kennedy* (New York, 1969), she wrote: "On the fifth day [after Kennedy's assassination], I worked with her [Jackie Kennedy] on distribution of gifts to JFK's closest aides and others. His ties went to "the Irish Mafia." . . . Golf shirt to Carol Rosenbloom. Cigar case to Pierre Salinger. At one point, Jackie said to me, 'Oh, Mary, I'll see to it that you get something of Jack's, too. But first I want to take care of the people in the White House before we leave' (338). Mary Gallagher served as Jackie Kennedy's personal secretary.

6. In the case of the Kennedy Library, the family's controlling position may well explain why the library has taken various measures to restrict public access to a number of materials. The library has been very slow to declassify documents, and many important documents remain unavailable to the public. For example, the Robert F. Kennedy Personal Papers, which are documents he acquired during JFK's administration, remain closed. Researchers seeking access to the Papers of Joseph P. Kennedy must first obtain the consent of a committee, presently headed by Arthur Schlesinger Jr. Researchers may copy only three to four pages at a time of the journals handwritten by JFK in 1951 during his Senate years. (White provided these journals to the Kennedy family in March 1998 as part of the settlement agreement.)

7. Much of the documentation referenced in this essay was obtained from the Kennedy Library through FOIA requests by White's counsel. While many documents were produced, the archives asserted various statutory exceptions to the production of more than seventy-five documents. The extent to which the Kennedy Library sought to protect from disclosure a large number of documents that most observers would consider to involve only mundane issues relating to a collector and his collection reveals the library's contentious approach to White.

8. White publicly stated at the time of the auction that his primary purpose in doing so was to build a museum to display his remaining Kennedy memorabilia collection.

9. The National Archives' and the Kennedys' attack on White caused quite a stir in the collecting community. White was well known and highly respected in that world and at one time had been named Fox Network Collector of the Year. The collector community rallied to his defense and expressed alarm about the precedent set by the federal government's challenge to what most observers considered a very clear-cut case that Lincoln legitimately owned the memorabilia.

10. Evelyn Lincoln, interview by Barry M. Goldman, January 1990 (White collection, copy in the author's possession).

11. According to Sorensen, *Kennedy,* 263, Lincoln even controlled some of the access to the president. She also handled all of his incoming and outgoing telephone calls (Evelyn Lincoln to William Noble, 23 February 1994, White collection, copy in the author's possession).

12. Jackie Kennedy to Evelyn Lincoln, 20 October 1964 (White collection, copy in the author's possession).

13. Undated letter from Jackie Kennedy to Evelyn Lincoln (White collection, copy in the author's possession).

14. Undated memorandum from "Bert" entitled "Notes on Conversation with Bert" (White collection, copy in the author's possession).

15. In defense of Lincoln, the problem does not appear to have been one of her own making. She was probably assigned to the task as a result of her familiarity with JFK and his memorabilia. However, neither she nor anyone assisting her had any archival training or background. She also was serving several masters (including Jackie Kennedy) who were giving her conflicting and unclear instructions.

Evelyn Lincoln wrote to Jackie Kennedy on 21 April 1964, explaining why so much time was required. For example, she still needed to write a description of each article "*i.e.,* when he got it and where he got it" (White collection, copy in the author's possession). That oral history was viewed at the time as quite important and as information that Evelyn Lincoln perhaps was uniquely qualified to provide (Robert H. Bahmer to Mrs. John F. Kennedy, draft, 19 June 1964 ["We hope to be able to get from Evelyn additional information that she has about President Kennedy's relationship to or use of many of these objects, which will eventually make possible a fuller, richer and more interesting description"]) (White collection, copy in the author's possession).

16. Arthur Schlesinger Jr. to Robert F. Kennedy, 14 July 1964, and memorandum, 20 July 1964, recording a telephone call of that date from Jackie Kennedy (White collection, copy in the author's possession).

17. Interview of Burke Marshall, n.d., 64. In an undated handwritten note to a Dr. Grover (chief archivist for the National Archives), Jackie Kennedy also expressed her surprise that Lincoln was writing a book. See also Lefty Lewis to Wayne C. Grover, 29 January 1965 ("Last night at dinner Jackie Kennedy said that you are having renewed Evelyn trouble and wouldn't I help?"). Nonetheless, during the same period, Jackie Kennedy continued to write personal notes to Lincoln (see Jackie Kennedy to Evelyn Lincoln, January 1965). (All sources cited in this note are from the White collection, copy in the author's possession).

18. Herman Kahn to Robert F. Kennedy and Mrs. John F. Kennedy, 22 November 1965 (White collection, copy in the author's possession).

19. This was the date of acceptance by the National Archives. The deed was made effective 22 November 1963.

20. There is no other known document in which JFK or the donors more specifically expressed their intentions regarding which items were donated.

21. Paragraph 3 (ii) of the deed provided, "The Donors shall have and specifically reserve the right to retain title and possession and to regain possession of any items that the Donors in their sole discretion may determine in accordance with this paragraph the Third are excluded from the purview of this gift, irrespective of the fact that such items may have been theretofore delivered to the Donee." As a matter of law, the retained right to regain title and possession should mean that the deed of gift was invalid on its face.

22. In April 2002, the National Archives for the first time filed a lawsuit seeking to recover a limited number of documents originally held by Evelyn Lincoln. See *United States v. Gary J. Zimet et al.,* case no. 02 Civ. 3027, filed in the U.S. District Court for the Southern District of New York. The action sought to recover a map (containing JFK's handwritten notes made during the Cuban Missile Crisis indicating the location of Soviet missile silos) and documents containing notes written by JFK relating to the 1962 enrollment of James Meredith at the University of Mississippi. The government's stated basis for its legal claim was the deed. A motion to dismiss the complaint was filed, generally relying on the arguments and case law described in n. 23. The motion primarily relied on the argument that the deed was legally defective in the donors' right to regain the donated property. However, the court denied the motion on the ground that the donors' right only extended to regaining their personal property—not to the entirety of the donated JFK memorabilia. However, documents produced by the Kennedy library revealed that Jackie Kennedy sent to the library lists of items she either wanted returned or sent to named third parties. Many of the them were clearly JFK memorabilia and not simply "personal items."

23. Under the laws of most jurisdictions, the essential elements of an inter vivos gift are donative intent, delivery, and acceptance. See *Ross v. Fierro,* 659 A.2d 234 (D.C. App. 1995); *In re Estate of Gilgore,* 389 N.Y. Supp.2d 634 (N.Y. App. Div. 1976). To support donative intent, it must be shown that the donor clearly and unmistakably intended to permanently relinquish all interest and control over the specific property that is the subject of the purported gift (see *Ross v. Fierro*). In the case of the deed, no such specification existed. In factually similar cases, where the donors failed to specifically identify the gifted property, courts have held that general expressions of donative intent do not establish a gift. See *First National Bank v. Howard,* 302 S.W.2d 516 (Tenn. App. 1957); *Kennedy et al. v. Milligan,* 915 S.W. 2d 784 (Mo. App. 1996). Further, to establish a valid inter vivos gift, most jurisdictions require an actual transfer of *all* right and dominion over the res by the donor—the delivery must place the gifted property beyond the dominion and control of the donor. See *Duggan v. Keto,* 554 A.2d 1126 (D.C. App. 1989). That certainly did not occur with the deed wherein the Kennedy family specifically retained the right to regain title to and possession of even items previously transferred to the library. Courts have uniformly held that for a gift to be valid, it must be put beyond recall. See *Silverman v. A.*

and L. Heel Corp., 228 N.E.2d 720 (1967); *Jackson v. Twenty-third St. Ry. Co.,* 88 N.Y. 520, 526 (N.Y. 1882); *Commissioner of Corps. & Taxn. v. Ayer,* 83 N.E.2d 260, 262.

24. In one document obtained by a FOIA request, the National Archives appears to have recognized the federal government's lack of a claim. See Brad Gerratt (director of the Kennedy Library), memorandum, 23 May 1996. (White collection, copy in the author's possession).

25. See Dan H. Fenn Jr. (director of the Kennedy Library) to Evelyn Lincoln, 5 August 1974; Dave Powers (museum curator of the Kennedy Library) to Evelyn Lincoln, 21 July 1975, 15 June 1976, 16 August 1978, 15 January 1980. See also Lincoln to Fenn, 16 May 1972, 12 June 1972; and letter contract, 21 July 1972, between the John F. Kennedy Library and Evelyn Lincoln. (All sources cited in this note are from the White collection; copies are in the author's possession).

26. "Officers and Trustees of the John F. Kennedy Library," 23 November 1965, Robert F. Kennedy Papers, Senate Correspondence, Personal File 1964–68, Kennedy Library; Paul G. Kirk Jr. to Evelyn Lincoln, 7 May 1979; Steven E. Smith (president, Kennedy Library) to Evelyn Lincoln, 6 May 1977 (All sources cited in this note are from the White collection; copies are in the author's possession).

27. Edward M. Kennedy to Evelyn Lincoln, 27 April 1977; Dan H. Fenn Jr. to Evelyn Lincoln, 27 December 1977 (White collection, copies in the author's possession).

28. John F. Kennedy Jr. to Evelyn Lincoln, 9 August 1992; William Johnson to Evelyn Lincoln, 27 August 1992; Charles U. Daly (director of the Kennedy Library) to Evelyn Lincoln, 4 November 1992. (White collection, copies in the author's possession).

29. While most of White's JFK memorabilia collection originated with Lincoln, many other important items did not. For example, White made personal contact with Earl Ruby, Jack Ruby's brother, and at Earl Ruby's invitation drove to his Michigan home to go through old files belonging to Jack Ruby. White found a number of documents of historical importance, including a diary prepared by Ruby while he was incarcerated. White purchased these documents from Earl Ruby, and they became part of White's memorabilia collection.

30. Following Kennedy's death, it was not until 1976 that there was any contact between Robert White and Mrs. Lincoln. On 2 December 1976, Lincoln wrote to White, answering a number of his questions. She enclosed a picture, taken in her apartment, of White sitting on "one of the President's chairs, which was given to me, and which stood in my office in the White House" (White collection, copy in the author's possession).

31. White and his wife, Jackie, became close friends of the Lincolns, celebrating birthdays and anniversaries together.

32. See, e.g., Evelyn Lincoln to Robert White, 14 February 1986, 19 May 1986, 22 April 1991. (White collection, copies in the author's possession).

33. Evelyn Lincoln to Robert White, 5 April 1989 (White collection, copy in the author's possession).

34. The briefcase was a particularly significant item in that President Kennedy carried it with him during most of his political career and had it with him on his November 1963 trip to Dallas.

35. The Maryland statute under which the will was probated included a procedure for such a challenge, which was required to be filed within six months after the date of death or within two months of the mailing of notice to interested parties. See Md. Code Ann., Est. & Trusts, sec. 8–103.

36. William Johnson to Brad Gerratt and Allen Goodrich (e-mail), 13 February 1996 (White collection, copy in the author's possession). The library would have properly been surprised by not receiving all of Lincoln's memorabilia since she had previously clearly intended to donate her entire collection to the library (Evelyn Lincoln to Robert F. Kennedy, n.d., White collection, copy in the author's possession). An earlier will made such provision. While it is not entirely clear why she changed her mind, she told White several years before she died that the Kennedys had forgotten about her. She also confided in him that she was "hurt" at not being invited to Caroline Kennedy's wedding.

37. William Johnson to Stephen Blakeslee, 29 February 1996 (White collection, copy in the author's possession). It is unclear whether this letter was sent or was merely drafted. In a 29 March 1996 letter (or draft), Johnson did not mention that the library had failed to encounter more of the "treasures." The library never asked for any disclosure of the contents of the filing cabinets left to White or Norton. Similarly, the library never asked to review or copy any of the documents in the filing cabinets so that it could become aware of their significance or content.

38. See "JFK Trove Available for Love, Not Money," *New York Times,* 24 May 1996; "These JFK Relics Aren't for Sale," *Boston Globe,* 2 June 1996; "All the President's Stuff: Maryland Collector Robert White Has a Museum's Worth of JFK Memorabilia," *Washington Post,* 20 August 1996; "The Remains from Camelot," *Baltimore Sun,* 16 June 1997.

39. Importantly, a significant amount of quality JFK memorabilia is held by private individuals who have collected Kennedy because he was a martyred president. Much of this material was originally acquired by JFK's White House staff, his Secret Service detail, and others close to him. Abundant evidence shows that this phenomenon occurred largely as a result of Jackie Kennedy's generosity. For example, while White was the main consignor, only 40–45 percent of the lots in the auction originated with him. The remaining lots were offered by numerous other individuals.

40. Astoundingly, Kennedy Library officials even gave a code name to their crusade against White: Operation Bobwhite. See Will Johnson to Dorothy Sloan (e-mail), 29 [*sic*] February 1998 ("the only player in 'Operation bobwhite'"); see also William Johnson to Brad Gerratt, Charles Daly, Megan Desnoyers, and Frank Rigg (e-mail), 4 September 1997 ("Subject: The bobwhite flies again"). (Sources cited in this note are from the White collection; copies are in the author's possession).

41. A number of the document requests were directed toward records obtained by White from Evelyn and Harold Lincoln (subpoena attachment B, para. 5). White was also required to produce all correspondence with other individuals regarding the terms of the Lincolns' wills (subpoena attachment B, para. 7).

42. The review board's function was to facilitate the gathering of JFK assassination records in conjunction with the statute's stated objects: (1) to provide for the creation of the President John F. Kennedy Assassination Collection at the National Archives; and (2) to require the expeditious public transmission of such records to the national archivist and their public disclosure. See 44 U.S.C. sec. 2107 (b)(1)–(2).

43. See excerpts from White's deposition taken by the Assassination Records Review Board, 3 March 1998, 1, 2, 38, 39, 40, 41, 89, 90, 91, 92, 93, 103, 104, 105, 106.

44. On 30 January 1998, Brad Gerratt wrote to William Johnson, Frank Rigg, and Megan Desnoyers via e-mail, "Chris Runkel [acting general counsel of the National Archives] spoke to DOJ [the Department of Justice] to attorney who represents [the review board] at DOJ. The subpoenas they have out for White will likely cover the material referenced in the phone call. Chris will talk to [T] Jeremy [Gunn, executive director and general counsel] next week and then get back to us regarding any action that should be taken from there." See also Kevin Jessar (assistant general counsel, National Archives) to Brad Gerratt, 24 February 1998 (transmitted with a letter from White's counsel to a review board attorney that contained an itemized list of the items of memorabilia White received from Evelyn Lincoln or from the Harold Lincoln estate).

45. See "Going, Going . . . ," *New Yorker,* 19 January 1998; "600 Scraps in Camelot's Attic for Kennedy Dreamers' Bids," *New York Times,* 11 March 1998; "Whose JFK Memorabilia?" *New York Times,* 13 March 1998; "Kennedys Assail JFK's Late Secretary," *Washington Post,* 17 March 1998; "Kennedy Children Oppose an Auction of Memorabilia," *New York Times,* 17 March 1998.

46. Guernsey's responded by letter on 11 March 1998, expressing its interest in cooperating with the investigation and asking for further specification of the claims ("it seems only fair and appropriate that you supply us with a complete list of the items in question so that this matter can be promptly resolved.") White's counsel also responded by letter on 11 March 1998. National Archives' representatives were permitted immediately to inspect the items in the auction. A number were identified as possibly containing classified information. Guernsey's and White immediately consented to remove these documents from public display and to turn them over to government representatives.

At no time prior to the public announcement of the Guernsey's auction did any federal agency ever seek to review Lincoln's documents to determine whether they contained classified information. Although the Kennedy Library had specific notice that Lincoln had custody of an abundance of documents from the Kennedy administration, federal agencies made no known requests during her lifetime to review these documents for national security purposes. No such requests occurred until 1999. The FBI sought permission, which was freely given, to review White's collection to determine whether any of the documents might be classified. The examination took place in August 1999 in St. Petersburg, Florida, where the collection was stored in a secure vault of the Holocaust Museum. The two FBI agents (who had previously been identified) arrived with a member of the Kennedy Library staff. (There had been no prior indication—or even a hint—that a library representative would be present.) The FBI identified twenty documents, numbering no more than a hundred pages, that might contain classified information. White voluntarily turned the documents over at the time for the limited purposes of allowing the federal government to conduct a thorough classification review. The review was to be conducted by classification experts at the Kennedy Library. After the passage of more than three years, the review was finally completed. In response to verbal and written protests from White's counsel over the course of two years, the FBI supervisory agent continually relayed his frustration at not receiving the cooperation of the Kennedy Library.

47. As a result of his back problems, President Kennedy signed documents at this table because it was lower than his desk. Lincoln had kept this table in a walk-in closet in her apartment, storing household items and personal effects on it.

48. The settlement with the National Archives was originally confirmed by a letter agreement dated 16 March 1998, two days before the auction. The agreement was formalized in a settlement agreement dated 19 March 1998.

49. The press release was out of sync with what was actually transpiring at the time. The National Archives' claims were settled within a very short period. At no point did the settlement discussions break down. Settlement was reached on 16 March 1998, the same day that these press releases were issued. Moreover, no breakdown in communication occurred between counsel for the Kennedys and White's counsel. Instead, everyone's attention was initially devoted to the National Archives settlement. As soon as that was concluded (16 March), settlement discussions began in earnest with respect to the Kennedy family claims. Like the National Archives' settlement, the negotiations between counsel for the Kennedys and White's counsel were amicable and quickly reached a successful conclusion after their counsel's demand letter was received. This being the case, the real motive behind these press releases is unclear.

50. Because the auction was only hours away, insufficient time existed to draft a formal settlement agreement. Rather, the settlement documents consisted of a term sheet and a "joint statement." The term sheet listed the items to be returned to the John F. Kennedy Library: (1) the two 1951 JFK journals, and (2) the Oval Office clock. Additional items were to be transferred to Caroline and John Kennedy Jr.: the St. Christopher medal money clip; (2) any Kennedy family prescriptions in White's possession or control; (3) one wallet used by JFK in the 1960s, possibly with him in Dallas; and (4) a two-page letter from Jacqueline B. Kennedy to Evelyn Lincoln erroneously dated September 1963. In exchange, Caroline and John Kennedy Jr. relinquished all claims of ownership to the remaining items that White had received from Evelyn Lincoln or the Harold Lincoln estate and had consigned to the Guernsey's auction. The joint statement distributed to the press acknowledged the agreement reached by Caroline and John Kennedy Jr. with White. Significantly, it stated, "As part of this agreement Caroline and John Kennedy have relinquished any claim of ownership to the Lincoln items consigned by Mr. White to Guernsey's, apart from the items that Mr. White has agreed to transfer to the John F. Kennedy Library [and to the Kennedy family] as part of this agreement."

51. The presidential and American flags bequeathed under Harold Lincoln's will to James Knox for the Irish Room at the University of Pittsburgh were consigned to the auction. However, on the eve of the auction, the Kennedy Library (or the foundation) contacted the University of Pittsburgh and made legal threats if the flags were auctioned. The university decided to withdraw the flags from the auction. See Jerome Cochran (assistant chancellor, University of Pittsburgh) to Arlan Ettinger, 17 March 1998 (White collection, copy in the author's possession). Although the university later demanded the return of these flags, Guernsey's declined, claiming that it was nonetheless owed commissions. Despite the Kennedy Library's claims of ownership of these important flags, it took no immediate action to recover them. Instead, the flags remained with Guernsey's. After several years passed, the flags were privately sold by Guernsey's.

52. Part of White's JFK collection was exhibited at highly publicized events in Nashville, Atlantic City, and Dallas (Texas State Fair). Thousands attended. Some 200,000 people viewed the collection at the Texas State Fair in the fall of 2002. The National Archives (and the Kennedy family) raised no objections. According to a Dallas news report, the Sixth Floor Museum at Dealey Plaza (which has a large exhibit related mostly to JFK's assassination) intentionally did not play a role in the exhibit because "We're being respectful of the family's feelings." At the same time, according to the article, a spokesperson for the National Archives stated that it was "keeping a close watch on [White's] collection." See "Fair Shows Rare Side of JFK," *Dallas Morning News,* 11 October 2002.

Classified Federal Records and the End of the Cold War

The Experience of the Assassination Records Review Board

William L. Joyce

In the fall of 1992, Congress passed the President John F. Kennedy Assassination Records Collection Act (PL-102-526, codified as 44 U.S.C. 2107) (ARCA) in an attempt to address the suspicion that the federal government had been involved in a cover-up of the November 1963 assassination of President John F. Kennedy. Soon after taking office and eager to reassure the public, President Lyndon B. Johnson appointed a commission to investigate the slaying of the president, the President's Commission to Investigate the Assassination of President Kennedy, more commonly known as the Warren Commission. The commission concluded that Lee Harvey Oswald, acting alone, was responsible for the president's murder. Government officials sowed suspicion of this conclusion by withholding information from the Warren Commission, a fact that gradually became known to the American public over the following decades. Within a few years of the release of the commission's findings, 65 percent of Americans disagreed with its findings. By the 1980s, this number had grown to more than 80 percent. In 1991, Oliver Stone claimed in his movie *JFK* that a conspiracy of the "military-industrial complex," together with unnamed government officials and elements of organized crime, were responsible for Kennedy's death. At the conclusion of the film, Stone noted that many government records concerning the assassination were closed and that a good many were scheduled to remain unavailable for examination until as late as 2029. These facts, together with the suspicion directed at the Warren Commission report, motivated Congress to pass ARCA.

In this essay, I will discuss the act's provisions and the work of its creation, the Assassination Records Review Board (ARRB), some problems that the board encountered, and the principal results of its efforts. Finally, I will provide some recommendations for addressing the problem of excessive secrecy in government. The efforts of the board led to the declassification of thousands of documents and the opening of more than 4 million pages of material now located in the President John F. Kennedy Assassination Records Collection at the National Archives. However, the board's greatest accomplishment arguably lies in demonstrating the effectiveness of a federal body independent of those who classify documents.

As suspicions grew about the Warren Commission's conclusions, several other official efforts sought both to review the commission's work and to progress beyond it. The most notable effort was the investigation undertaken by the House Select Committee on Assassinations (HSCA) in the mid-1970s. In addition, the Senate Select Committee to Study Government Operations with Respect to Intelligence Activities (the Church Committee), the Rockefeller Commission (formally the President's Commission on CIA Activities within the United States), and the House Select Committee on Intelligence (which produced the Pike Report) to varying degrees included the assassination of the president among their mandates. These investigations did little more than document that government agencies had been less than fully forthcoming to the Warren Commission about events surrounding the assassination. Indeed, the HSCA's report suggested that there was reason to believe that a conspiracy had in fact existed, but the committee ran out of funds—and possibly political will—before its work could be carried to its conclusion.

The fact that so many people saw the government as participating in a conspiracy only heightened suspicions about the closed records concerning the event. A public policy problem inhered in the facts surrounding the assassination and its aftermath: the assassination and the government's response to it introduced issues of secrecy in government; accountability; the importance of a knowledgeable, informed citizenry; and the urgent need for a new, more generous declassification policy by which to regulate government secrecy and to do so with a greater degree of openness in government. Continuing secrecy regarding the assassination of JFK seemed, especially after the passage of more than thirty-five years, less justifiable in a period of relaxed international tensions following the collapse of the Soviet Union and the disintegration of the Soviet bloc. Indeed, one wonders whether the act could have been passed at all without the extraordinary events that unfolded in the late 1980s in the Soviet Union and Eastern Europe and the accompanying unprecedented relaxation of international tensions.

The collapse of Soviet dominion over Central and Eastern Europe also loosed a veritable flood of information from Soviet archives and from former officials that has deepened understanding of the Cold War and the extent of Soviet espionage among the Western allies. In addition, the release of decoded Soviet cables from the VENONA project also helped document Soviet penetration of the Western governments. Contentious issues, the Rosenberg spy case and that of Alger Hiss, for example, are now better understood, if not resolved, as a result of the new information.[1] It has also become clear that the Red Scare of the 1950s (McCarthyism) represented an indiscriminate and ineffectual effort by the Right to discover Soviet spies, mostly recruited from the Left (particularly the Communist Party), in the U.S. government. But if the movement did not affect the course of Soviet espionage or the American response to it, the witch hunt contained witches—lots of them.[2]

President Kennedy's assassination was enmeshed in the complicated matrix of activity that was the Cold War. From the conflict in the Congo to the erection of the Berlin Wall, the Bay of Pigs fiasco, the Cuban Missile Crisis, the burgeoning conflict in Southeast Asia, and more, the global mayhem and diplomatic tensions of the Cold War made the early 1960s a deeply unsettled time. Conflict among the superpowers made them secretive,

and this excessive secrecy complicated understanding of the assassination even if it didn't mask a conspiracy. When the Cold War eased after the collapse of the Soviet Union, pressure on the government to open its files concerning the event and its aftermath became far stronger.

ARCA's charge to the ARRB was not to investigate the assassination but rather to release as many of these restricted documents as possible. Lawmakers commented, in the words of one of the legislative reports, that the review board's efforts

> will stand as a symbol and barometer of public confidence in the review and release of the government's records related to the assassination of President Kennedy. . . . Several provisions [of the act] are intended to provide as much independence and accountability as is possible within our Constitutional framework.[3]

In many respects, the act in fact accomplished its purpose of conferring independence and accountability on the board. ARCA's provisions were as remarkable in their breadth as in their sweeping character. The act provided that the board could

1. issue subpoenas;
2. grant immunity to witnesses at hearings or through depositions; and
3. order federal officials to comply with the provisions of the act, including transferring assassination records to the board's custody.

The legislation also provided a considerable degree of guidance for how the board should undertake its work. This guidance constituted a far more sweeping and compelling mandate to open restricted records than that provided, for example, by the Freedom of Information Act. ARCA

1. stated unequivocally that the standard to be followed by the board was a "presumption to disclosure" for classified assassination records;
2. provided detailed guidance concerning instances in which disclosure would be limited if not altogether eliminated;
3. provided that in the event of a postponement, any redacted information should be summarized through the provision of substitute language;
4. designated the president as the sole entity to whom government agencies could appeal and provided that this was a "nondelegable" authority;
5. allowed Congress to overturn a board determination concerning congressional records only by passing a resolution specifically doing so;

6. required all government offices to identify and transfer all assassination records to the National Archives and charged the board with reviewing all records that agencies believed should remain classified; and
7. assigned the Senate Committee on Governmental Affairs and the House Committee on Government Operations oversight responsibility for the board.

Despite the act's passage in October 1992, the ARRB was not confirmed by the U.S. Senate until February 1994 and was not sworn in until April of that year. Soon thereafter, the board began meeting to find office space, hired a staff, and arranged high-level security clearances (a very slow process), as well as initiated the policies and procedures that would guide its work. The calendar envisioned by the act turned out to be unrealistic as a result of the project's complexity and sensitivity.[4]

Among its first tasks, the board determined in large measure its own jurisdiction by drafting a definition of an assassination record that was eventually published in the *Federal Register*:

> An assassination record includes, but is not limited to, all records, public and private, regardless of how labeled or identified, that document, describe, report, analyze or interpret activities, persons, or events reasonably related to the assassination of President John F. Kennedy and investigations or inquiries into the assassination.[5]

Board priorities included the FBI's "core and related" files pertaining to the assassination, HSCA subject files, and the CIA's 201 (personality) file on Lee Harvey Oswald. The challenge that the board faced in framing its definition was to make it broad enough to include records that might contain information relevant to the full range of theories about how and why the president had been shot without making it so broad that no amount of time would suffice to permit the board to conclude its work.

The board also defined "additional records and information" as including "all documents used by government offices and agencies during their declassification review of assassination records as well as other documents, indices, and other material (including but not limited to those that disclose cryptonyms, code names, or other identifiers that appear in assassination records), that the Review Board had a reasonable basis to believe constituted an assassination record or would assist in the identification, evaluation or interpretation of an assassination record."[6] Records failing either definition were designated not believed relevant (NBR) but might contain other redacted information.

The same chapter of the *Federal Register* identified sources of assassination records, including entities of the federal government as well as state and local governments, records repositories and archives, individuals, and foreign governments. While the board pursued federal records as priorities, it also sought state, local, and private records, and it deposed individuals seeking to clarify records-related issues.[7] In the course of its work, the ARRB conducted half a dozen hearings around the country, soliciting advice about where additional assassination records might be found.

The vast majority of records was, of course, stored in federal agencies. Restricted assassination records were identified by more than thirty government agencies and offices, including the FBI and the CIA, each of which had roughly three hundred thousand pages of redacted documents, as well as the Defense Department, the National Security Council, the Secret Service, and the Department of State.

The ARRB's review process and voting procedures concerning federal records evolved very slowly, in part because the board was tilling new soil and in part because the board was independent and had little assistance in orienting itself to federal procedures.[8] When eventually hired, the board's roughly twenty-five staffers were organized into teams (basically, for the FBI, the CIA, and "military" records). Records of other government agencies and those of private individuals were covered by staff assignment as appropriate. Staff members prepared record information forms, identified the redactions, and classified them according to categories enumerated in the legislation and fine-tuned by previous board discussions/determinations. All restricted records were tracked carefully, redaction by redaction. Security for housing such documents was, of course, carefully monitored and regulated. Board offices had to be approved by the CIA, and secure communication lines were installed, including a special fax line. (In fact, the CIA eventually established a security classified information facility within ARRB offices to expedite review of the agency's records.)

Policies evolved to assist the board and staff in weighing clear and convincing evidence of demonstrable harm as a standard for postponement against the act's standard of "presumption of disclosure." The board soon developed policies for a variety of recurring issues, such as

1. Social Security numbers;
2. CIA station issues, crypts, digraphs, cover, and other information;

3. identification of FBI and CIA agents and informants;
4. confidential relationships with cooperating foreign governments.[9]

The context for board discussions/determinations was set by the legislation, which specified "grounds for postponement of public disclosure of records" (section 6). Information in records might be "postponed from disclosure" if clear and convincing evidence showed that the threat to U.S. military defense, intelligence operations, or conduct of foreign relations was such that disclosure outweighed the public interest because disclosure would reveal

1. an intelligence agent whose identity requires protection;
2. an intelligence source or method which is currently utilized or reasonably expected to be utilized;
3. any other matter currently relating to the military defense, intelligence operations, or conduct of foreign relations:
   a. the public disclosure of the assassination record would reveal the name or identity of a living person who provided confidential information to the U.S. and would pose substantial risk of harm to that person;
   b. the public disclosure of the assassination record could reasonably be expected to constitute an unwarranted invasion of personal privacy that would substantially outweigh the public interest;
   c. the public disclosure would compromise the existence of an understanding of confidentiality currently requiring protection between a government agent and a cooperating individual or foreign government where disclosure would outweigh the public interest; and
   d. public disclosure would reveal a security or protective procedure currently utilized by the Secret Service or other government agency responsible for protecting government officials and where disclosure would outweigh the public interest.

Board meetings were conducted every three or four weeks from April 1994 until 30 September 1998.[10] The staff facilitated the review of materials by flagging redactions as green, yellow, or red issues, depending on the difficulty of interpreting the redaction in the context of earlier board decisions. As time went on, the frequency and volume of board determinations made the process easier to administer because staff members had clearer guidance on what recommendations to make. By the same token, the board's earliest meetings were excruciating for their extensive discussions of fine points and comparatively

modest conclusions as well as occasionally contradictory decisions. But the board gradually developed a consensus approach to a great many issues, and a version of review board "common law" created a body of precedent that permitted growing understanding of the issues and efficiency in the review of records. Growing numbers of green issues enabled the board to vote thousands of records opened (including more than five thousand at one meeting) by following, for example, policies that postponed the disclosure of Social Security numbers and portions of agent crypts.[11]

In fact, the ARRB-approved releases contained very few redactions. Those that were taken used substitute language to explain what had been omitted. Furthermore, the board worked hard to limit redactions only to the directly relevant language. No documents or even pages within documents were withheld in toto.

The board voted on about twenty-seven thousand documents, while another thirty-three thousand were opened by "consent release," whereby agencies recognized board policy and initiated release of the documents on their own authority. This development was a welcome recognition that the board's policies had a persuasive impact on agency perceptions of the information they manage and that, given inducements, agencies could participate meaningfully in the release of heretofore classified government records.

The ARRB also undertook a great many separate initiatives concerning potential assassination records in private hands and ultimately acquired, among others, the papers of Lee Rankin, general counsel of the Warren Commission; records created by New Orleans district attorney Jim Garrison, who undertook, unsuccessfully, the only legal action tried as a consequence of the assassination, the trial of Louisiana businessman Clay Shaw for conspiracy to murder President Kennedy; the papers of Edward Wegman, Shaw's chief defense attorney; FBI agent James Hosty, who had been assigned to Oswald in Dallas when he returned from the Soviet Union; Warren Commission staff member Wesley Liebeler; and attorney Frank Ragano, whose clients included New Orleans organized crime boss Carlos Marcello. In addition, the board acquired Louisiana grand jury records concerning Garrison's prosecution of Shaw.[12]

Perhaps the board's most controversial action occurred in early 1997 when it voted to "take" the privately owned original eight-millimeter movie film of the assassination taken by Dallas businessman Abraham Zapruder. For safekeeping, the film had been held on deposit since 1978 at the National Archives, although it appeared to be too fragile to be run through a projector because it had shrunk about 0.5 percent and the sprocket holes were damaged. The board also engaged the Eastman Kodak Company to study the original film and the three surviving first-generation copies, looking for additional evidence to explain anomalies between the film and the operating properties of the Bell and Howell home movie camera used by Zapruder, whether the "edge print" of the original contained any additional evidence, and issues concerning the chain of custody of the film.

In the spring of 1997, the ARRB conducted a public hearing on this matter, televised on C-SPAN, at which a number of experts provided testimony on issues relevant to the "taking." In the end, the board concluded that it had to preserve for public access the only original visual record of the assassination, horrifying though it may be, and arguably the most famous home movie ever taken. However, the board's action created a situation in which the Justice Department and the Zapruder family had to agree on a purchase price. When the experts completed their examination and filed their reports, the sides remained $29 million apart. Government appraisers put the value of the film at $1 million, while the Zapruder family's experts compared the film favorably to Vincent Van Gogh's *Sunflowers,* sold at auction in 1987 for $40 million, and Michelangelo's *Leicester Codex,* which Bill Gates purchased in 1994 for $30.8 million. The family agreed to a cap of $30 million, and three federal arbitrators split the difference, awarding Zapruder's heirs $16 million plus retention of the film's copyright.[13]

The authorizing legislation initially gave the board two years in which to do its work, with the board having the option to request support for a third year. The board exercised that option and then requested a final fourth year, promising the Republican Congress that an extension for fiscal year 1998 would be the final request. With that additional time, the board argued that it would complete review of the CIA's "sequestered collection" (records requested but not reviewed by the HSCA), the most relevant of the FBI's assassination records remaining to be reviewed (some 200,000 pages worth), pursue some other leads, and otherwise bring its effort to a point that would permit closure for its work. The board also argued that the additional time might offset to some extent the dissatisfaction surrounding the respective incomplete efforts of the HSCA and the Senate Select Committee on Intelligence. For a variety of reasons, including the fact that the review board exemplified a federal agency that could be shut down, Congress readily approved the ARRB's request.

In contemplating its limited existence and the sunset provision built into the original legislation, the board established a compliance program with all government agencies and offices with which it had contact. Through this program, the board elicited statements from all government offices with assassination records that they had reviewed their files conscientiously and that they could warrant—under penalty of perjury—that they had indeed identified and reviewed all records bearing on the assassination. The board ultimately completed the compliance process, though the FBI and the CIA did not complete their review of assassination records before the board was obliged to conclude its work.

The board's slow start was further complicated by a number of housekeeping concerns that no one could have foreseen (for example, finding that funds had not been appropriated when the board was created, having to find office space, and even procuring identification cards). Moreover, the legislation prohibited the ARRB from hiring staffers with previous government experience or who had pursued prior research on the assassination. Because all staff members needed the highest security clearance to pursue their work, those provisions resulted in slow, costly security checks on all those hired. In addition, and despite the congressional charge that agencies cooperate with the board, the major classifying agencies worked unevenly with the board. Specifically, some agencies sent public relations staff to the initial meetings to argue that the board should simply "trust" the agencies' best and seasoned judgment. Throughout the course of the board's existence, most agencies remained reluctant to alter an extremely cautious approach to declassification. In addition, some agencies adopted very labor-intensive declassification procedures, refusing to declassify any information before it had been reviewed line-by-line by several reviewers, regardless of the age of the documents or their subject matter. The fact that the statute now required the identification of specific instances of harm to justify continuing postponements came as something of a shock to all of the agencies.[14]

The ARRB failed to gain access to the papers of Robert F. Kennedy. These files (including much of Kennedy's records as attorney general in his brother's administration) are located at the Kennedy Library in Boston, though access is maintained through a committee of family members. The work of the board was slowed and then completely derailed by the untimely death of Michael Kennedy, chairman of the access committee and the family member most interested in the disposition of his father's papers.

Late in its work, the ARRB also discovered the President's Foreign Intelligence Advisory Board, which agreed to a settlement with the ARRB but then appealed to the White House that it should not be subject to ARCA because it had a "personal relationship" with the president. President Clinton ultimately denied, shortly before leaving office, both the PFIAB appeal and that of the Secret Service concerning the ARRB release of the names of individuals identified by the Secret Service prior to the assassination as threats to the President.[15]

The board's productivity, particularly during the last two years or so of its existence, is all the more remarkable in light of those early obstacles. In addition, the legislation's sunset provision caused board staff members to depart for better job opportunities. In its last months, the board was shorthanded in its struggle to meet its statutory responsibilities.

Passage of Executive Order 12958 in 1995, the first executive order on the declassification of federal records after the end of the Cold War, gave new impetus to the declassification of federal records, mandating that all federal records more than twenty-five years old be declassified within five years. The order also shifted the cost burden to the agencies by imposing costs to maintain classified records rather than imposing costs on declassification efforts. In the late 1990s nearly 800 million pages of classified federal records had been declassified, an extraordinary achievement; in its most recent report to the president, the Information Security Oversight Office (ISOO) of the National Archives indicates that over 980 million pages of classified information have now been declassified.[16]

The rapid expansion of electronic records and legislation mandating page-by-page review of records containing classified information on nuclear weapons, however, led to a slowing down of the volume of declassification. At the same time, there were increases in derivative classification (records with classified information from one agency appearing in the documents of another agency) and in the number of those empowered to classify records in the first place. The goal of declassifying all federal records more than twenty-five years old within five years had to be pushed back to December 31, 2006. ISOO keeps careful watch over the process and recently calculated that some 260 million pages of classified information over twenty-five years old remains to be declassified by the December 2006 deadline. ISOO projects that most agencies will meet the deadline but that a number, including the Treasury (and the FBI), Commerce, and Energy will not. Additional time (to 2009) has been

granted for the declassification of derivative information, and special media (including motion pictures and audiotapes) have until 2011 to be declassified.

At the same time, there have been disquieting developments concerning secrecy in government. Late in the year 2000, Congress very nearly passed a bill that would have required prison time for those divulging classified information. This sweeping legislation was ultimately stricken from an intelligence agencies authorization bill, but the danger was apparent. The federal government came close to passing an official secrets act. The outcome, in light of Senator Daniel Patrick Moynihan's initial effort to undertake meaningful reform of the government's classification practices, provided disappointing evidence of the inertia and resistance that characterize the culture of government offices that classify federal records.[17] Beyond that, passage of the PATRIOT Act shortly after 9/11, the removal of large quantities of government information from government documents and Web sites, and the emergence of a new, extralegal category of government information—sensitive security information—demonstrate that the government has in fact become less open, less accountable, and less susceptible to rational deliberation as a vehicle for change. In addition, the reliability of information developed by government intelligence agencies has also come under fire, raising additional questions about the very purposes of secrecy in government. The need for persistent vigilance in protecting the public's right to know and the importance of holding government officials accountable have never been more urgent.

Several aspects of the work of the ARRB appear to warrant consideration in contemplating future declassification efforts, particularly in addressing sensitive government records relating to controversial topics (such as, for example, the assassination of Abraham Lincoln, the blowing up of the battleship *Maine,* U.S. entry into World War II, the war in Vietnam, and the assassination of Dr. Martin Luther King Jr.).

1. A legislative mandate from Congress is essential, and that legislation must contain provisions enforceable by sanctions.
2. Any reviewing body must be independent of the classifiers and the custodians of classified information.
3. A legislative standard of a "presumption to disclosure" is an essential tool.
4. Government agencies should be obliged to present "clear and convincing" evidence according to specified "grounds for postponement" to continue to restrict access to records. Substitute language should be mandated to explain all postponements.

5. The number of those permitted to classify documents must be further reduced.

6. Those classifying documents should be instructed to determine the length of time of restricted access and should be charged with specifying when and how often the restrictions should be reviewed. Each time a restriction is verified, the generating agency should be "taxed" for the separate maintenance of the information.

7. The problem of referrals for "third-party equities" (classified information of one agency appearing in a document of another) must be addressed in future declassification activities either by designating a lead agency to coordinate releases or by convening representatives of all agencies with interests in selected groups of important documents and referring information to one another all at once. A second, complementary approach would establish uniform substitute language as a means of dealing with certain categories of recurring sensitive equities.

8. Future declassification efforts, particularly those entailing a search for records, should incorporate a compliance program as an effective means of eliciting full cooperation in the search for records.

9. Both the Freedom of Information Act and Executive Order 12958 should be strengthened, the former to narrow the categories of information automatically excluded from disclosure, the latter to add independent oversight to the process of review when agency heads decide that records in their units should be excluded from release.

The board's experience led to the release of a great deal of information on the assassination of President John F. Kennedy and threw fresh light on the activities and record of the Kennedy administration. However, no documents were discovered that might be characterized as "smoking guns," nor did any documents provide direct evidence of the existence of a conspiracy to murder President Kennedy. To be sure, some groups had means and motive, especially given the unsettled period of the early 1960s, but, more than forty years after the event, there is simply no evidence.

Beyond that, and arguably of still greater importance, the ARRB's experience can guide future policy concerning the declassification of federal records, particularly those that are both sensitive and controversial. A federal body with powers similar to those conferred on the board could well make such records accessible to the American people and at the same time promote accountability of federal officials. That would be no small accomplishment.

NOTES

Permit me to declare my participation in the work of the board, so that there is no misunderstanding about my views on this topic. I served as a member of the board, having been nominated by President Clinton in September 1993 and confirmed by the Senate in February 1994. We were sworn in and commenced our work in April 1994. Other board members were John R. Tunheim, chairman; Henry F. Graff; Kermit L. Hall; and Anna K. Nelson. The board went out of business via a "sunset" provision in the authorizing legislation on September 30, 1998.

1. Several recent books have taken advantage of the availability of new information about espionage during the Cold War, including Allen Weinstein and Alexander Vassiliev, *The Haunted Wood: Soviet Espionage in America—The Stalin Era* (New York: Random House, 1999); John Earl Haynes and Harvey Klehr, *VENONA: Decoding Soviet Espionage in America* (New Haven: Yale University Press, 1999); for the 1960s and 1970s in particular, Christopher Andrew and Vasili Mitrokhin, *The Sword and the Shield: The Mitrokhin Archive and the Secret History of the KGB* (New York: Basic Books, 1999). Thomas Powers has written a shrewd and insightful review essay on this broad subject; see "The Plot Thickens," *New York Review of Books*, 11 May 2000. A valuable reassessment of our understanding of the Cold War in light of recent developments is John Lewis Gaddis, *We Now Know . . . : Rethinking Cold War History* (New York: Oxford University Press, 1997).

2. See Powers, "Plot Thickens."

3. See the Senate Committee on Government Affairs. *President John F. Kennedy Assassination Records Collection Act of 1992*, STREP 102-328, 102d Cong., 2d sess. (1992), 30.

4. The act called for the board to begin reviewing assassination records within 180 days of enactment of the legislation; it took more than eighteen months, however, for board appointees to be nominated, investigated, and confirmed, much less to initiate operations.

5. 36 C.F.R., chap. 14, pt. 1400 (1 July 1995). See also John R. Tunheim, "Government Secrecy and the Kennedy Assassination Records," paper presented at the Government Secrecy in a New Administration and a New Century Symposium, 5 December 2000. Cited with permission.

6. 36 C.F.R., chap. 14, pt. 1400 (1 July 1995).

7. To reduce confusion and contention, the board expended no small effort to depose individuals involved in the treatment of the president at Dallas's Parkland Memorial Hospital and in the autopsy. In addition, much work was also done on the autopsy photographs to try to develop additional information. See *Final Report of the Assassination Records Review Board* (Washington, D.C.: U.S. Government Printing Office, 1998), 121–24.

8. In April 1995, the ARRB became the first group of private citizens in American history to vote to declassify federal records.

9. For a full discussion of the evolution of the board's policies concerning redactions in classified records, see *Final Report*, 41–74.

10. In the course of its existence, the ARRB conducted twenty-two public meetings, seven public hearings around the

country seeking advice concerning evidence on the assassination and where to find it, and fifty-four closed meetings at which classified documents were reviewed. The closed meetings were all taped, and those tapes will be released in 2017.

11. A 27 May 1999 news release from the National Archives and Records Administration provides a useful statement of the types of records reviewed and released by the ARRB:

—itineraries of the presidential campaign of then Senator John F. Kennedy in 1959 and 1960;
—copies of public statements and press conferences of Senator Kennedy; documents showing the dates, starting points, destinations, and mileage of the flights taken by the campaign plane during 1960, with the exception of July 1960; and related documents concerning the campaign. 311 pages.
—the Russell Holmes Papers. 50,000 pages of CIA documents maintained by Holmes in his role as the custodian of the Oswald 201 file as well as the segregated collection of CIA records compiled for the investigation of the House Select Committee on Assassinations (HSCA). Holmes was the CIA liaison for all inquiries on the assassination after the end of the HSCA investigation until his retirement.
—documents from the Department of Defense, Department of Justice, General Services Administration, and other sources relating to the disposition of the casket used to transport the body of President Kennedy from Dallas to Bethesda Naval Hospital. 43 pages.
—FBI records consisting of three series: 50,000 pages of "House Select Committee on Assassinations (HSCA) Administrative Folders," including 9,000 pages of "HSCA Ticklers," some 13,000 pages of "JFK Act Administrative

Files," and around 9,000 pages of CIA miscellaneous files including the files of the director of central intelligence (DCI), CIA history files, Office of Security files, and other record series. The subjects covered include a wide range of issues related to the assassination: DCI meeting notes, Cuba, and other matters.

12. New Orleans District Attorney Harry Connick Sr. unsuccessfully appealed this transaction all the way to the U.S. Supreme Court before the records were transferred to the National Archives.

13. *Final Report of the ARRB,* 124–26. See also Ellen Joan Pollock, "Reel Value: Is It a Home Movie or National Treasure? The Government Plans to Buy Zapruders' Famous Film, but Not for $30 Million," *Wall Street Journal,* 20 May 1999, A1; Ellen Joan Pollock, "Film of JFK's Assassination Gets a Price Tag of $16 Million," *Wall Street Journal,* 4 August 1999, B1. The purchase price of the film was roughly twice the total four-year congressional appropriation for the board.

14. Agency staff repeatedly reminded board members that no government employee had ever been fired for classifying information.

15. These were the only two outstanding appeals of AARB decisions that were unresolved when the board dissolved, and both were ultimately denied by President Clinton. The FBI withdrew all of its appeals; the CIA never appealed a board determination.

16. For the most recent ISOO report go to http://www .archives.gov/isoo/reports/2004_declassification_report.html.

17. See Daniel Patrick Moynihan, *Secrecy . . . the American Experience* (New Haven: Yale University Press, 1998).

"Just a Car"

The Kennedy Car, the Lincoln Chair, and the Study of Objects

Judith E. Endelman

By looking at the things that people used and the way they
lived, a better and truer impression can be gained in an hour
than could be had from a month of reading.[1]

Do all objects tell the truth? Are artifacts essential to the study of history? Can we understand the past by looking and examining the things people used and made, as Henry Ford believed? The study of material culture, which grew out of anthropology and the study of preliterate cultures, has had only a minor influence in the historical profession. Texts and, to a lesser degree, visual evidence have been the primary sources for the reconstruction of the historic past. What can the study of material culture offer the study of history?

Although academic historians generally ignore objects as sources of evidence, museum curators often give primacy to the object and its interpretation. A museum curator might look at a steam traction engine and tell you what it "says." However, what the steam engine "says" is filtered through the curator's deep knowledge of the topic. While material culturists might argue that "only artifacts preserve the authentic voice of the inarticulate,"[2] in truth, when the museum curator observes the steam traction engine, he or she sees it in the context of the history of steam power, agricultural history, the history of power sources, and all the other steam traction engines he or she has examined and studied.

Members of the public from museumgoers to murder mystery readers are quite comfortable with the concept of artifacts as evidence. Physical evidence—an object found at the scene of a crime that solves the mystery—is a familiar plot twist in murder mysteries and gives rise to the phrase *smoking gun*. Similarly, a 1998 study of Americans and their connection to the past revealed that museumgoers believed that displayed objects, unmediated and without any interpretation, were a source of truthful information about the past.[3]

Before the Civil War, most museums were "cabinets of curiosities" and Barnumesque freak shows. They displayed objects, such as two-headed snakes, for their shock value rather than for their educational significance. In the late eighteenth century, however, Charles Willson Peale established what is considered the first true museum in the United States, the American Museum in Philadelphia. Peale believed in the primacy of objects, and his museum took an unusual approach for its time, displaying natural history specimens according to the Linnaean method. Peale's museum, with its orderly rows of plant and animal specimens, was designed to instruct rather than titillate its visitors. The object without context was the text. (Unfortunately, however, the American Museum did not survive into the second half of the nineteenth century.)[4]

After the Civil War, museums revived the Peale model and strived to present an intelligent, orderly world. They replaced the collections of the bizarre and the freakish with rational, systematic displays. These exhibits reflected the assumption that objects could tell stories and that objects as much as text were sources of knowledge and meaning. Museum curators laid out rows of objects in glass cases in a precise relationship intended to convey a narrative history. These museums sought to teach visitors about the natural world through a close observation of ordered specimens. As William Wilson, founder and director of Philadelphia's Commercial Museum, wrote to Edward Everett Ayer of Chicago's Field Museum, "All museum material should speak for itself upon sight. It should be an open book which tells a better story than any description will do."[5] The thing itself, unexplained, unmediated, and uninterpreted, was seen as the source of knowledge and understanding.

Not just casual visitors but also scholars and scientists could learn their discipline from a close examination of objects rather than through the lens of existing scholarship. Louis Agassiz, a Harvard natural scientist, would introduce a new student to the study of zoology by presenting him with a fish in a specimen pan and instructing him to "Look at the fish! Look at the fish!" From direct observation and examination, Agassiz maintained, the student could begin to acquire knowledge of the field.[6]

Henry Ford believed that the past lives of ordinary people could be understood not by reading about them but by examining the objects they made and used. Ford believed that artifacts, not documents or books, could tell the "real" American history. In setting about creating a collection and a museum to tell the story of American invention and ingenuity, Ford eschewed books and documents in favor of steam engines, spinning wheels, and chairs.[7] Only one book drew Ford's favor —the *McGuffey Reader*, a nostalgic nod to the one-room schoolhouse of his childhood.

Ford believed that "the real history of people was not expressed in wars, but in the way they lived and worked."[8] Not only was this a radical view for its time, it is a surprising one for an industrialist and would have found sympathy from such thinkers as Karl Marx and Marxist historian E. P. Thompson, whose book *The Making of the English Working Class* (London, 1965) helped to launch the social history revolution.

Ford claimed that his most famous quote, "History is bunk," was a misunderstanding. The history taught in schools—political and military history—was bunk. What mattered was the history of everyday people.[9] He attempted to tell that history at the Henry Ford Museum and in Greenfield Village. Just as Agassiz carefully ar-

ranged his specimens at Harvard's Museum of Comparative Zoology, Ford arranged his engines, farm equipment, and spinning wheels in orderly rows to illustrate the principle of technological progress. Ford oversaw these arrangements himself, as his museum was to have "no curators and no experts."[10] Most of Ford's acquisitions were artifacts that had once belonged to ordinary working people, many of whom sent him their children's outgrown infant clothes or their old scythes and threshers. When a small item appeared in the press in 1940 about Ford's interest in collecting shoes, donors from across the country sent in more than twenty-five pairs.[11] Written documentation of everyday life is generally sparse, and rarely do people write about their use or manufacture of material goods. Thus, these objects formed the primary "text" for study, to be interpreted just as an anthropologist might study the material culture of a preliterate society.

Much can be learned from studying objects. By visually examining the earliest automobiles, for example, one can clearly see their roots in the bicycle and carriage industries. And who has not examined a whalebone corset and connected that restrictive garment to the role of women in late-nineteenth-century America? In both of these examples, the objects reinforce and make evident what we have learned from other sources. They offer tangible proof of what we may have only read. Moreover, by closely studying automobiles or corsets, the astute observer can begin to see technological refinements and adaptations as these two industries evolved over time and learn something not available from other sources.

Henry Ford delighted in this kind of study, learning about the past by "looking at the things that people used"[12] rather than from written or even visual sources. Although Ford claimed to be interested only in the history of ordinary people, he also "delighted in [objects] that had some association with great American historical figures" and historic events. (Antique dealer Israel Sack acquired many of these items for Ford.)[13] What can we learn from association objects that we cannot learn from other sources? What is the value of artifacts associated with famous historic events?

Two of the best-known and most popular artifacts in the collections of The Henry Ford are associated with presidential assassinations. One was acquired in Henry Ford's time; one was not. One had a strong connection to the event; the other did not have the same popular association. Does an examination of either of these objects reveal more to us about the event than is already known from written accounts or eyewitness statements?

The catalog record for accession 29.1451.1 describes an "upholstered seat rocking chair with walnut carving, foliage motif, upholstered back, slip seat, arms of silk damask, and a klismos[14] base in a rococo revival style." It features an innovative rocking mechanism. The headrest is stained. The upholstery is frayed. The chair is quite ordinary. As an addition to a museum's furniture collection, better examples of this rather common chair are readily available. Without other sources of evidence, the chair yields few clues to its origins. However, when coupled with eyewitness accounts, reports, and documents, it corroborates certain recorded accounts and supplies a visceral and emotional connection to the tragic events of April 1865.

On 14 April 1865, the management of Ford's Theatre learned that Abraham Lincoln planned to attend that evening's performance of *Our American Cousin*. They immediately set to work furnishing the president's box, fetching an upholstered rocking chair that was always brought out for the president. (When the president was not in attendance, this chair was a favorite of the ushers.) That evening, John Wilkes Booth shot Lincoln while he was sitting in that chair and watching the play. According to eyewitness accounts, Lincoln's blood stained the chair as well as the dress of actress Laura Keene, who rushed to his side in the presidential box. In the ensuing confusion, someone also brought Lincoln a glass of water, which may have spilled on the chair.[15]

A week after the assassination, the War Department seized and removed the "death chair," and it remained in the private office of Secretary of War Edwin Stanton for two years. It was transferred to the Department of the Interior in 1867 and became the property of the Smithsonian Institution, where it was stored in a basement for many years. It was not displayed because of the Smithsonian's policy of not exhibiting objects associated with presidential assassinations. An 1873 photograph of the chair was not printed because of a concern that "it would again stir up publick feeling which could do no good and might do a great deal of harm."[16]

In 1929, Blanche Chapman Ford, the surviving heir of the chair's owner, applied for and won possession of the chair, which was returned to her. She immediately wrote to Henry Ford, offering to sell him the chair. He declined to buy it because it was "too gruesome a piece of furniture to put in his museum."[17] Nevertheless, in December 1929, the chair was sold at an American Art Association Anderson Galleries auction and purchased by Sack, acting as agent for Henry Ford. Blanche Ford believed that the chair would make her rich, but it brought only

Fig. 1. The iconography of Lincoln's assassination often focused on the flags and buntings surrounding the presidential box and the escape of John Wilkes Booth. The chair in which Lincoln sat is barely visible in this illustration from the cover of Frank Leslie's *Illustrated Newspaper*, 6 May 1865. (From the Collections of The Henry Ford [G3629].)

twenty-four hundred dollars. The auction-buying public of the late 1920s was far more interested in letters written by Abraham Lincoln and Edgar Allan Poe, which sold for far more money. (A Lincoln letter in the same auction sold for seventy-eight hundred dollars).[18]

Why did the sale of the Lincoln chair fail to ignite the public's interest? Perhaps because there was never a strong association between President Lincoln and this particular chair. Lincoln was never photographed in the chair before his death. Only the Ford's Theatre staff knew that this was the chair in which Lincoln liked to sit when he attended the theater. The chair was not an object of particular public interest at the time of the assassination.

It was seized, removed from the theater, never cleaned or repaired, and stored out of the public eye for more than sixty years. By that time, the number of Americans who were even alive at the time of the assassination was small.

What can we learn about the events of the fateful evening of 14 April 1865 from examining this chair? The chair does corroborate some of the eyewitness accounts, although the evidence is confusing. The stains on the headrest appear to be hair oil. The stains on the chair back and seat appear to be blood but could be water. Over the years, there has been much speculation about these stains. In 2000, the museum conservators had the stains tested to confirm their composition. The stains on the headrest are indeed hair oil, probably from the ushers' frequent use of the chair. There are water stains and bloodstains, although it is not known whose blood it is. There are also plaster stains, probably from plaster that fell on the chair while it was stored in the basement of the Smithsonian.

The use of traditional historical narrative sources, forensic science, and a material culture analysis of the chair complete the story of the events surrounding and following Lincoln's assassination. Henry Ford purchased a mundane object—a chair— and then displayed it to the public within the contextual framework of the assassination of Lincoln. The chair became a relic, imbued with the sense of the tragedy of Lincoln's death at the end of the Civil War. To heighten the emotional content of the chair, it contained blood—presumably the blood of the martyred president. The chair acquired value, meaning, and an association with a historic event that was not recognized at the time. In essence, by displaying the chair and declaring it to be of value, Ford created an additional meaning for the chair far beyond its value to the curator, who might view it as an ordinary nineteenth-century rocker.

The crowds peering into the interior of the 1961 Lincoln presidential limousine X-100 at Henry Ford Museum are looking at what might be the most famous artifact in the museum's collection. This is the famous "Kennedy car," the car in which John F. Kennedy was assassinated in Dallas in November 1963. Unlike the Lincoln chair, this car bears little resemblance to the car pictured in the parade on that fateful day. There are no bullet holes, no stains, no blood.

In January 1961, Hess and Eisenhardt, custom coachbuilders, took delivery of a 1961 Lincoln Continental convertible for conversion to a presidential parade car for the newly inaugurated President Kennedy. Although Hess and Eisenhardt added bulletproofing, platforms for

Fig. 2. Does looking at Lincoln's blood on the chair bring us closer to his spirit? Actor Raymond Massey, who played Lincoln in the 1940 film *Lincoln in Illinois*, stares at the stains on the encased chair on display at Greenfield Village, ca. 1946. (From the Collections of The Henry Ford [P.O.8024].)

Secret Service agents, and other features, they could not detract from the car's sleek, stylish elegance—adjectives that could also easily be used to describe the young president and first lady.

The parade car came with a collapsible black vinyl roof for additional privacy, but it was typically used as an open car, symbolizing the openness, accessibility, and confidence of the Kennedy administration. Kennedy's favorite feature was said to be the powered rear seat, which raised him ten inches to give the public a better view of him and his companions.[19]

The Lincoln Continental had a strong association with Kennedy before his death as well as with the events surrounding his death. The parade car carried the Kennedys down the main streets of many American and European cities, leaving a rich visual record of the "Kennedy car." The image of John and Jacqueline Kennedy in the back seat of the car, she in the now famous pink suit

Fig. 3. After Kennedy's assassination, the presidential limousine was rebuilt and repainted, leading some Henry Ford Museum visitors to question whether the car on display is actually the "Kennedy car." (From the Collections of The Henry Ford [B.90245].)

and pillbox hat, filmed most notoriously by Abraham Zapruder, is our strongest visual memory of the Kennedy assassination.[20]

After the assassination, the Kennedy car, like the Lincoln chair, was seized. The Warren Commission scrupulously examined the car for evidence that might shed light on a conspiracy. Finding none, the commission returned the car to the White House, which shipped it to Hess and Eisenhardt to be rebuilt and reinforced to provide better presidential protection. Unlike the Lincoln chair, the Kennedy car was reupholstered, and all traces of blood were removed. The "quick fix," as it was called enclosed "the passenger area in a rolling bunker of steel, titanium, and bulletproof glass, strengthen[ed] the powertrain to handle the added weight, and retrim[med] the passenger compartment to efface any damage from the assassination."[21]

When the rebuilt, fortified, bunkerlike car appeared at the White House in 1964, it was said that a superstitious Lyndon Johnson hesitated to ride in it until a coat of black paint was added over the original midnight blue. Thus, the Kennedy car, like the Lincoln chair, was hidden—not in a basement but in plain sight, under layers of steel, titanium, glass, and paint. The disguised car went on to serve Presidents Johnson, Nixon, Ford, and Carter.

Its third life, as a museum object and assassination relic now known as the Kennedy car, began in 1977. In that year, the White House retired the X-100 and returned it to the Ford Motor Company, which subsequently donated the car to The Henry Ford. Echoing the Smithsonian's policy of not exhibiting artifacts associated with presidential assassinations as well as Henry Ford's designation of the Lincoln chair as "too gruesome," the museum decided not to exhibit the car until Caroline and John Kennedy Jr. "reached maturity." The car went on public display in 1983.[22]

Memories of people and their familiar objects can trigger powerful emotions. Rudolf Arnheim notes that in the Bible, Joseph's coat of many colors, a gift of his father, "stands for Jacob's partiality, and the blood stains depict the assault upon the favorite. [The blood on the coat] is a powerfully visual abstraction of the family drama."[23]

Observers have commented that the rebuilt, fortified "quick fix" car symbolized the president's increasing isolation and retreat from the people in an era of antiwar protests and other forms of street theater. Perhaps, however, there is something deeper, more emotional, and less calculating at play. Like Joseph's beautiful coat now stained with blood, the sleek, elegant Lincoln Continental, now similarly "stained," would forever remind a

Fig. 4. Kennedy favored the open Lincoln Continental because it allowed him to be visibly prominent, as seen in this Chicago street scene, March 1963. (Courtesy of Walter P. Reuther Library, Wayne State University.)

grieving public of the loss of its beloved, handsome young leader. So that the limousine could continue to provide transportation for the president without continuing to carry this bitter memory, the evidence—the visual association—had to be eradicated.

The 1961 Lincoln presidential limousine X-100 is a complicated artifact. It is a mass-produced, manufactured object. It was customized for President Kennedy and then almost completely rebuilt. A close examination of this object can certainly teach about manufacturing, car customization, materials, and processes. Comparing the car's style and design in 1963 and after the quick fix in 1964 might lead to some conclusions about American society and its relationship with its presidency—from the open accessibility of a convertible to the armored fortress of a tank. For the full story and history of this car, its use, and its role in particular events, the student of material culture must reach beyond the object and draw on the resources and tools of other historical specialties.

Understanding an event as complex as the Kennedy assassination requires the use of many different types of evidence. Few museum curators today would suggest a sole reliance on objects to understand historical narrative. Like the Lincoln chair, the Kennedy car is a powerful relic, a physical object that witnessed a cataclysmic event. It serves, as objects often do, as a "trigger to emotion or memory, . . . a visual shorthand."[24]

Stuart Davies has argued that the range of source material for twentieth- and twenty-first-century history is such that "the object has no value as evidence" and that the main value of history collections is that they "materially assist in the presentation of the past to the public."[25] The Lincoln chair, the Kennedy car, and similar artifacts do provide an emotional hook that connects the museum public to an historical event. And one hopes that the power of relics such as these will stimulate museum visitors to want to learn more.

In the mid-1990s, historians Roy Rosenzweig and

David Thelen asked fifteen hundred Americans about their connection to the past and how it influenced their daily lives and hopes for the future. The study revealed that people cared deeply about history that touched them personally (thus, the strong interest in the Kennedy car by baby boomers and their parents). Rosenzweig and Thelen found that Americans, bored by history learned in school and distrustful of any history produced for an ulterior motive, whether commercial or ideological, "put more trust in history museums and historic sites than in any other sources for exploring the past."[26] People trusted history museums because they believed that museums had no particular agenda, that objects don't lie, and artifacts in museums could be approached on their own terms, unmediated, and without interpretation. A forty-four-year-old painter from Wisconsin, for example, said he trusted museums because by displaying objects "for everybody to see, the museum isn't trying to present you with any points of view. . . . You need to draw your own conclusions."[27] Many respondents believed that by being face to face with artifacts from the past, they were reexperiencing moments without mediation. In an echo of Louis Agassiz and his admonition to "Look at the fish!" a visitor to the Dinosaur Museum said he knew he was seeing the real thing when he looked at fossil remains because the "bones are right there. The bones don't lie."[28]

Do all objects tell the truth? Are artifacts essential to the study of history? The study of objects can teach us a great deal about how people lived and worked, what they used and how, and what they valued. Study a tobacco cutter or a housewife's apron and you will learn something about the culture and the period in which these items were used. Then place that examination within the context of all that you have learned from reading newspapers, books, and magazines and from studying photographs and other visual documentation about the region and the time period of their use, and you will learn even more from those humble objects. Objects can tell the truth, but they can speak most eloquently when they are studied within the context of other forms of evidence.

NOTES

I am indebted to Bill Pretzer of The Henry Ford and John Dean of the University of Versailles for their helpful comments.

1. Henry Ford, quoted in Eunice Fuller Barnard, "Ford Builds a Unique Museum," *New York Times Magazine,* 5 April 1931, 1.

2. Cary Carson, "Material Culture History: The Scholarship Nobody Knows," in *American Material Culture: The Shape of the Field,* ed. Ann Smart Martin and J. Ritchie Garrison (Winterthur, Del., 1997), 402.

3. Roy Rosenzweig and David Thelen, *The Presence of the Past: Popular Uses of History in American Life* (New York, 1998), 105–6.

4. For a history of the American Museum, see Charles Coleman Sellers, *Mr. Peale's Museum: Charles Willson Peale and the First Popular Museum of Natural Science and Art* (New York, 1980).

5. William Wilson to Edward Everett Ayer, 16 July 1894, Field Museum Archives, quoted in Steven Conn, *Museums and American Intellectual Life: 1876–1926* (Chicago, 1998), 4.

6. Martin Marshall, professor of marketing at the Harvard Business School, related the Agassiz story to me in 1992.

7. Henry Mercer, the founder of the Mercer Museum, followed a similar approach in developing his collection. In 1923 Ford visited Mercer's museum in Doylestown, Pennsylvania, and found the model on which to base his museum (Conn, *Museums,* 159–60).

8. Ibid., 156.

9. Henry Ford always maintained that his most famous quotation was actually a misquotation. As reported in the *Chicago Tribune* in 1916, Ford said, "History is more or less bunk. We don't want tradition. We want to live in the present, and the only history that is worth a tinker's dam is the history we make today" (quoted in Robert Lacey, *Ford: The Men and the Machine* [New York, 1986], 252).

10. Barnard, "Ford Builds," 2.

11. Edwin Cox's syndicated column "Private Lives" appeared in newspapers on 5 June 1940 with the following item: "Collector's pieces—Breaking the tycoon tradition, Henry Ford has never acquired Old Masters, rare books, or objets d'art, but he gets a whale of a kick out of collecting a sample of *every type of shoe ever made in the U.S.!*" (Henry Ford Office and General Clip Books, 1940, vol. 153, acc. 7, Benson Ford Research Center, The Henry Ford, Dearborn, Michigan.

12. Quoted in Barnard, "Ford Builds," 1.

13. Kenneth N. Metcalf, "Biography of a Chair," *Lincoln Herald* 63, no. 4 (winter 1961): 201–2.

14. A chair style popular in the mid–nineteenth century.

15. Metcalf, "Biography," 196–202.

16. Thomas W. Smillie to Mr. Cox, 10 March 1896, Smithsonian Institution files, copy in accession file for 29.1.1451.1, Registrar's Office, The Henry Ford, Dearborn, Michigan.

17. Blanche Chapman Ford to Henry Ford, 1 May 1934, accession file 29.1.1451.1.

18. Newspaper clipping, [December 1929?], accession file 29.1.1451.1.

19. John Christie, "Parade Car," unpublished paper, 1996, in research files for 78.4.1, Benson Ford Research Center.

20. In the late 1990s, Paul's Model Art, a German company, produced a collectible die-cast 1:43 model of the Kennedy car, with miniature versions of John and Jackie Kennedy (in the pink suit and hat) in the back seat and John and Nellie Connally seated in front.

21. Christie, "Parade Car," 13, and other materials in research files for 78.4.1, Benson Ford Research Center.

22. Research files for 78.4.1, Benson Ford Research Center.

23. Rudolf Arnheim, *Visual Thinking* (Berkeley, 1969), 170.

24. Gaynor Kavanagh, "Objects as Evidence, or Not?" in *Museum Studies in Material Culture,* ed. Susan M. Pearce (London, 1989), 130.

25. Stuart Davies, "Collecting and Recalling the Twentieth Century," *Museums Journal* 85 (1985): 27–29, quoted in Kavanagh, "Objects as Evidence," 134–35.

26. Rosenzweig and Thelen, *Presence,* 105. The "trustworthiness of sources" scale in descending order was museums; personal accounts from grandparents or other relatives; conversation with someone who was there; college history professors; high school teachers; nonfiction books; movies and television programs (91).

27. Ibid., 106.

28. Ibid.

PART IV

Archives, Memory, and Political Culture

(Canada, the Caribbean, Western Europe, Africa, and European Colonial Archives)

In setting as one of the seminar's principal goals the exploration of the roles that archives play in the production of knowledge, it was clear to us from the start that we could not confine our discussions within one specific national framework. The relationship between archives and the constructs of a national past is a very close one. State archives are almost always dependent on governments for their existence. They are sustained to serve the state, however its interests may be defined. Like the interests of society more broadly, these are in constant evolution, as are those of individual citizens and their local communities. Since the nature of that evolution affects the structure of national archival practices, it also defines what states expect from their archives and archival administrations. In essence, archives often become a function of a particular kind of state politics—a politics of conformity as well as, sometimes, a politics of opposition.

The seminar consequently placed a strong emphasis on the contrast between different national systems in exploring how archives function culturally, socially, and politically. The participants came from Asia, Europe, and Africa as well as North America and engaged the complex question of national particularity with energy. By necessity, the seminar could only explore these matters by means of select examples. Still, our range was broad enough for us to reach some interesting conclusions, as we think the essays here and in part V will show.

Our discussions focused almost exclusively in this regard on state-based archives. In this section, we group presentations about colonial archives and the postcolonial archival model (Cooper, Stoler, and Williams/

Wallach); archives in states transformed by revolutionary events in the Yucatan and the Caribbean (Scott/Martinez/Zeuske, Dubois, and Eiss); and archives in evolving stable states (Wilson, Burguera, René-Bazin, Graf, and Kansteiner). In each of these cases, the archives have become part of a larger set of issues, especially the often contested question of state definition.

The essay by the distinguished American historian Frederick Cooper is based on his experience with the archives of French West Africa. Cooper discusses the real challenge of recovering a social memory unmediated by the effects of colonial institutions and constructs. He sees the basic contrast as that between the genuineness of the oral tradition and "the Eurocentrism of the written record"—or as he says, "popular memory set against elite documents." But it is not so simple to reconfigure the archives to conform to some sort of elusive "authentic past." Documents of the colonial age are on the one hand a vestige but also are a record of a particular time. Memories may contradict or limit the primacy of these documents as an authentic source, yet memory is also multifaceted and in the final analysis deeply personal and "mediated across a more recent experience." What, then, is the archive's relationship to the African colonial past?

The anthropologist Ann Laura Stoler offers an intriguing set of answers. In her view, the role of archives in producing elements of social and national culture is particularly clear in the colonial case, whether colonial archives are located in the metropole or the elsewhere within an imperial system. The perceived need of these systems to classify populations according to specific racial or ethnic categories embeds distinctions in documents and archives that may have little or no relationship to the kinds of differences drawn within societies themselves and hence to local understandings and memories of the past. Race can be quite literally read into these pasts—"constructed," in the current social science terminology—along a full panoply of specified racial attributes, in the very process of building an archival collection around racialized subjects. Documentation then serves to create and authenticate the entity being cataloged through the very significance of the archival institution itself and the presumptive attributes of its cataloging and classificatory systems.

Like Cooper, the important question for Stoler is therefore not only about the archive's relationship to colonial pasts but also about the "authenticity" of that past and whether archival documentation creates or reveals it. Part of this issue involves archival "truth claims," as Stoler suggests, as well as the cultural assumptions about what counts as knowledge, as we have discussed in the introduction to part III. These questions also animate Rebecca Scott and her colleagues, who explore the Cienfuegos provincial archive in Cuba as a "place of memory" and ask what oral and written sources can tell us about how "a country came to be what it is imagined to be." The absence of obvious references to race identity in the Cienfuegos materials suggests a kind of archival complicity in forming certain kinds of national narrative. As this important essay suggests, new questions about the particularities of "national" pasts as well as a concurrent need for affirming individual and community experiences diminished or suppressed by broader national purposes have led here and elsewhere to a renewed examination of the archive and its roles.

As historians have shifted in their interests from institutions to a broader exploration of social and cultural systems, in which individuals and local communities must find a place, the relevance of archives has also changed. Documentation on matters like race and race identities is difficult to uncover in a culture where the official view is that they are nonexistent. Cultural and social understandings do not easily or necessarily connect these kinds of question with documentation. As with other colonial and postcolonial archives, the processes of archival mediation in the provincial archives of Cienfuegos were both more subtle in their silences and more aggressive in their celebration of the past than in other kinds of archives. The Cuban archive consequently proved a fertile area for exploring carefully the relationship between documentation and social memory for archivists and scholars who had moved beyond established categories and could explore the significance of archival holdings in the light of new questions and issues.

Laurent Dubois and Paul Eiss also confront the "possibilities and the limits of the archives left by slavery and emancipation" in the Caribbean, as Dubois puts it. In their search for sources, both are forced to confront the "absences and silences" in the archives. Here Dubois and Eiss address concerns discussed in the previous section by Portelli and Wright. No matter the evolution of categories or the redefinition of documentation, if the documents were destroyed or never created, there can only be silence. As Dubois suggests, this is all too often the case with the records of subordinate cultures, prompting scholars like himself to turn to other kinds of materials, such as novels, to "uncover the voices and actions of slaves and ex-slaves . . . to understand their struggles." Although the evidence here may be more problematic (as indeed is the subjective relationship the historian develops with his sources), Dubois suggests that novels in this instance be thought of as a different sort of archive, one apart from the "social and political forces" that have shaped the institutional archives of the French Caribbean.

Paul Eiss, on the other hand, shows rather dramatically how the Yucatan "emancipation" after the 1914 liberation decree was framed in official documents as a series of liberating and redemptive events, imparting to the archive a meaning about the nature of change that was quite different from popular experience and recollection. As a consequence, the Mexican "archive of redemption," as Eiss neatly labels it, was "not just a physical site for the storage of documents" but a calculated instrument for remembering Mexico's future, as Terry Cook might put it. The Yucatan's archive of redemption structured an official cultural narrative as enduring as it was feigned.

For Brian Williams and William Wallach, two distinguished archivists at the University of Michigan working with the archives of the African National Congress (ANC) at the University of Fort Hare in South Africa, the issue is not one of ANC redemption but one of the transition in national South African identity and the reconstruction of a national past. Theirs is a fascinating example of how archives can function within a transforming society and nation. Records once elevated become diminished, while those once diminished become the core sources of a new national identity. In the Fort Hare case, material once suppressed as subversive has now become a symbolic cultural prize in demand even beyond South Africa's national boundaries. Here again the question of what, exactly, is a "national" archive comes under close scrutiny.

It is also in this regard that the case of Canada is so interesting and important. The Canadian colonial connection to France and Britain evolved much more gradually than did colonial relationships elsewhere, which partly explains the emergence of a particularly Canadian understanding of national culture and its importance to national life. Language differences and strong local community identifications have contributed to a much stronger sense of the problem of sustaining a unified history and a common understanding of a single national past. As Ian Wilson, the national archivist of Canada, implies, Canadians have become notoriously suspicious of anything that tries to pass as a hegemonic national narrative.

One consequence of this, Wilson notes, is the general avoidance of history in public discourse. Instead, history has become more a "matter of division and dispute rather than a force for unity." Wilson traces the evolution of the rhetoric in Canada as it relates to defining the function and purpose of archives as a state service. He shows how early notions of the role of archives in sustaining and informing a unified sense of the national past have yielded in Canada to a more conscious effort to make archives a place of memory, a place where the documents of a contested past are collected and preserved through the multiple efforts of more than six hundred separate archival institutions. What, then, might we properly consider the "national" archive here? Although the seminar, by design, did not focus extensively on the American case in this regard, the question is particularly relevant in the American context as well, since U.S. archival activity is also spaced over a variety of important state and local institutions and jurisdictions. Indeed, most Americans might be surprised to know that the U.S. National Archives was not created until 1934.

As the essays in this section illustrate so well, colonial and postcolonial archives illustrate neatly the complex intersections between "official" archives, constructs of state power, and national definition. Both the composition of documents as well as the ways they are appraised and acquired at a certain point in time reinforce the role of state archives as collaborators in an "official" process of history making and memory formation, whether this collaboration is by design or, less deliberately, as an institutional effect. It could also be argued that the great archival systems of Western Europe were born of a certainty in the clarity of national purpose and the importance of history

as a source of validation for national self-definition and that to achieve this end archives here were designed not only to collect and make available certain kinds of nationally "relevant" material but also to function within a specific rhetorical framework.

In the United States, this framework is famously reflected in the familiar aphorism "what is past is prologue"—a kind of utilitarian ideal that underscores the functionality of archives in the security of the national ideal. Ian Wilson notes a similar phrase often repeated in Canada: that archives are "a gift from one generation to the next," a kind of celebration of the importance of archives for national unity. Paule René-Bazin of the Archives of the Department of Defense in France recalls the circular of the Direction des Archives de France that celebrated in a comparable way the importance of memory as "a powerful cement for each society, as it carries its history and transmits values from one generation to another." Especially in Western Europe, these rhetorical turns give a particular kind of legitimacy to state archives and "official" memory. (Not incidentally, they also define the strategies for budget hearings from year to year.) Even in the face of sophisticated scholarly challenge, rhetoric of this familiar sort combines with the structure and presence of archives buildings to define a "monumental" understanding of national pasts.

As a number of seminar participants insisted, there are serious practical as well as analytical contradictions in this process of definition. René-Bazin points out in his contribution, for example, that high political figures often do not willingly transfer papers to the archives, however much they espouse the archive's value to national purpose. The assembling of archives is also perpetually intertwined with particularities of the law. In France, the Mitterand, Balladour, and Mauroy papers all were problematic accessions despite, or perhaps because of, the national importance of the individuals involved. These cases raise broader questions about the actual processes by which state archives are assembled as well as about the goals and loyalties of the authorities who control them. And as Mónica Burguera implies in her impressive essay here, the roles of archives in these circumstances stand in some contrast to other, much less constrained or "administered" sources of memory and identity: as she shows for Spain, "cultural, linguistic, and ethnic ties have come to represent potential alternative nationalities," ones "capable of questioning the legitimacy of the Spanish state from within."

An additional problem in this regard is raised by Christoph Graf, director general of the Swiss Federal

Archives (SFA). In the years following World War II the Swiss archives quietly conformed to the general perception that Switzerland was a neutral bystander to the events of those years. This rhetoric was based on a kind of national consensus that gave form to the archives and its contents. Graf presents for discussion several "politico-historical events" that deeply affected the SFA and Switzerland as a whole. One of these pertains to the charges that Switzerland, although formally neutral, facilitated many financial transactions with the Nazi regime and held dormant many accounts of its victims. Graf suggests that these accusations opened an enormous wound in Swiss self-identity. Swiss archives then assumed the role of active "historical information center," having to uncover, redefine, and present large amounts of documentation that were formerly silenced and suppressed by the particularities of Swiss national self-perception. Wulf Kansteiner describes a comparable process in his fascinating study of German television archives and their role in the making of German collective memory.

Here again the seminar confronted questions about the role of archives when an individual memory challenges prevailing collective ones, when local memories contest the "great story," when history becomes histories and the past becomes pasts. Clearly in the Swiss case, the divergent memories created contested meanings for state documents and the language of statecraft. As Graf puts it

rather quaintly, the singular institution of the SFA in this circumstance "became somewhat politicized," although he also emphasizes the constructive mediating role of the SFA in matching curiosity with available documentation.

All of the essays in this section illustrate in different ways the significant broadening in recent years across scholarly disciplines in the understanding of what constitutes a "national" framework of social, cultural, or even geographical unity, as well as a continuing debate about the realms and forces that properly constitute the "political." State archives engage both of these issues in complex ways. As formal institutions of social memory, their acquisition and collection procedures tend naturally to privilege established perspectives as monuments to specific traditions. They often tend as well to constrain new political and national understandings and hence the diversity and richness of social memory itself.

The particular national systems represented in the essays that follow in the next two sections reflect a range of practices and structures. They engage directly the impact of archival acquisition on historical understanding and identity formation. They also raise ongoing questions about the cultural conditions and preconditions for national archival systems and explore how these preconditions may shape the historical record in different cultural and political contexts. Like the seminar discussions themselves, the essays constitute absorbing ground for additional reflection and research.

Memories of Colonization

Commemoration, Preservation, and Erasure
in an African Archive

Frederick Cooper

In June 1995 the National Archives of Senegal orga-nized the "Colloquium Commemorating the Cente-nary of French West Africa" in Dakar. On the face of it, this was a peculiar event: a proudly independent African nation celebrating the anniversary of its own coloniza-tion. The event itself was unlike any other colloquium most of its academic participants had ever attended: we were guarded by men with automatic rifles, driven be-tween sessions and social events in a caravan of buses and Mercedes, and escorted by policemen on motor-cycles. We were addressed by the president of Senegal and the minister of cooperation of France, by the first lady of Mali and the ambassador of France, as well as by a former governor-general of French West Africa (AOF). History was being invoked and marked in public speech and ceremony, even as the contents of that history—questions of colonialism, regional integration, and social history—were being discussed by scholars. The conjunc-ture of topic and style made this public colloquium into a strange and disturbing moment in the uneasy relation-ship of Africa to its colonial history.

This essay is a reflection on that event, partly from the perspective of a participant and eyewitness, partly from the perspective of a historian who has worked in colonial archives, including those of Senegal.[1] The peculiarity of the commemoration highlights an issue that is basic to the preservation of historical information in former colonies. The past of the new African nation is recorded in the old colonial archive. The difficulty this poses is not so much that these archives reflect a "colonial point of view"—that is obvious—but that the categories and units of

analysis that shape the colonial archive also shape other forms of historical preservation and memory. African his-torians, since the 1960s, have trumpeted that oral tradi-tion is the antidote to the Eurocentrism of the written record—popular memory set against elite documents.

But the transmission process by which historical mem-ory arrives at the ear of the researcher is not innocent of the effects of colonization. The "community" that au-thenticates individual recollection and that provides a lin-guistic and social basis for collective self-identification may itself have been preserved because colonial authori-ties recognized it, reinforced the power of the "chiefs" who became its spokesmen, recognized or created courts and councils where elders discussed among themselves what constituted tradition, and sometimes wrote down histories whose texts filtered back into orally transmitted memory. When historians from different African coun-tries wrote in the 1960s and 1970s histories of "the Luo" or "the Yoruba," they were taking as givens ethnic units whose singularity was the product of the units of territo-rial administration in colonies as well as the product of longer-term processes of linguistic and cultural differenti-ation and amalgamation. These units of understanding cannot of course be reduced to colonial inventions, but the most thoroughgoing efforts to see beyond colonial categories require a close examination of the categoriza-tion process. Even some of the tensions within African communities for which careful oral research—when ask-ing more sensitive questions than what "the Kikuyu" think of "their" history—reflect a jockeying for position vis-à-vis colonial institutions.[2] And the history of the

IV: ARCHIVES, MEMORY, AND POLITICAL CULTURE

IV: ARCHIVES, MEMORY, AND POLITICAL CULTURE

colonial era, far from being divided into "official transcripts" and "hidden transcripts" (in the misleading phraseology of James Scott), reflects multidimensional engagements, as different political actors tried to use whatever connections and resources were available to them.[3]

As Ranajit Guha and others have recognized, the colonial lexicon can itself be analyzed, its categories specified, and its blind spots noted.[4] This does not mean that one can decode a colonial document and arrive at a "true" picture of a certain event or of the social structure of an indigenous community at a certain time; rather, such historically attuned readings of colonial documents are themselves necessary to decode other kinds of lexicons, to specify other kinds of categories, to note other kinds of blind spots. Fortunately, colonial officials in, say, 1930 did not know what was to befall their successors in 1960. They had no reason to hide their racism or their cultural chauvinism and had every reason—as bureaucracies inevitably carried out debates and jockeyed for position within themselves—to make themselves understood within terms that were persuasive within the colonial power structure at any given time. As Luise White has observed, archives record struggles over the vocabulary through which power was to be exercised, and hence colonial officials were never able to describe their practices in entirely imperialist terms.[5] Colonial archives are no more independent of "the colonized" than oral traditions are independent of "the colonizer."

In their final years, officials may have become more conscious of how much they had to conceal, but they still had to function, and retrospective destruction—and plenty of documents were burned—ran up against the untidiness of administrative structures. Carbon paper is the great friend of anyone trying to unravel what went on in a twentieth-century bureaucracy. The language of colonial documents was never transparent but was always revealing. Archives help us see not only a singular past corresponding to a French or British view of the proper colony or a singular past corresponding to a budding "nation." They are unwieldy institutions whose contents provide more clues about the past than their architects intended to give. Archives will themselves be the subject of fruitful investigation, and interpretations of their contents will continue to provoke varying interpretations and vigorous debate. What is less sure is how well they will be preserved, whether new dossiers from independent governments will be placed in them, and whether scholars will have access.

Back to Dakar in June 1995. Some 150 scholars and archivists from Africa, Europe, and North America—most of them specialists on different aspects of twentieth-century African history—came to Dakar for the weeklong event. Senegal's president, Abdou Diouf, told the opening session of the colloquium, held in Senegal's National Assembly, that our responsibility was "to make of memory illumination for the future." Mme Adam Konaré, first lady of Mali, expressed her hope that "knowledge and power be reconciled at last on this African territory."

What knowledge and whose power? Whose memories and what future? Here was a moment that most academics would dream of, when scholars ranging from young graduate students to distinguished archivists and professors—from all over francophone West Africa, Europe, and North America—could share in the sense that their work had entered a world of power. But for many people present, young historians from Africa as much as this middle-aged American professor, the event accomplished precisely the opposite. All the trappings of power in which the discussion of historical memory took place served to tell us that Africa's future was too important and too fragile to allow the ambiguities of its past to get in the way. An examination of *how* history is effaced through public ceremony—and how historians find themselves trapped in the process—reveals much about the difference between invoking history and examining its contents. The troubling element of the colloquium was not simply that it commemorated what many historians would rather condemn but that the question that mattered the most politically could only be approached obliquely: how the forms of power specific to a colonial situation shaped the way power could and could not be exercised after independence.

From the moment I had received the invitation to the colloquium, it had seemed both bizarre and irresistibly interesting. The end of AOF might have seemed a better moment than the beginning of it for the National Archives of Senegal to honor, but, ironically, the international colloquium celebrating thirty years of African independence had been held a few years previously in *France*.[6] The event of 1895 being commemorated in Africa had occurred when the French military was still embroiled in its bloody conquest of West Africa and the government decided that it should group the domains it was carving out—cut into by territory that Great Britain, Germany, and Portugal were taking for themselves—into a single federation, the better to coordinate the domination and exploitation of this vast space and diverse population.

The letter of invitation to the colloquium suggested that its theme would be African integration—the possibility that the small states into which French-speaking West Africa had been broken after the end of colonial rule and the collapse of the French-run federation could work together in a better way to facilitate common progress. It seemed to me to contain even a touch of irony, a hint that the colonial regime's ability to develop integrated structures across West Africa—for however selfish and oppressive a purpose—cast a critical light on the inability of independent African regimes to act in the common good. In any case, the invitation implied that a serious discussion of what the experience of sixty-five years of colonial rule had meant and still means for West Africa was the center of the agenda.[7]

Stimulating discussions did take place in Dakar. But the event was a commemoration, complete with a logo printed on every paper—"Creation AOF 100 year Dakar 1895–1995"—as well as a postage stamp issued by the Senegalese government for the occasion, commemorative T-shirts, a commemorative briefcase given to each participant, posters with maps of AOF put up all over Dakar, parades, and public ceremonies. The detailed discussions of scholarly papers were sandwiched between elaborate ceremonies. The former took place in the kinds of conference rooms where scholarly meetings usually take place, while the latter were in the kind of official spaces scholars rarely see, including the presidential palace and the garden of the French embassy. The opening and closing speeches were covered by Senegalese television and newspapers—and even got a brief if condescending mention in *Le Monde*. But most important, the historians and archivists who presented their ongoing work on colonial history—crammed into sessions of up to ten papers each—witnessed the public events, lent them by their numbers legitimacy and importance, and took away whatever lessons the event had to offer.

The academic sessions and the published two volumes of the proceedings—consisting of ninety-six papers taking up over twelve hundred pages of text—served a salutary purpose. The organizers and editors went to pains to give this part of the project intellectual integrity. But neither oral nor printed version produced an extended reflection on the most basic issues: they are too long and too disparate. The editors' introduction warns against "celebration" and "nostalgia." They note the period's importance to African history and argue that—whatever the motivations of the colonizers—France's attempt at solving problems on a large scale is relevant to the future, to the "realization of the panafricanist dream." But at the project's end they are no more able to draw conclusions about the significance of this history than they

were at the beginning. They, like the participants, have been overwhelmed.[8]

The conference and the volumes revealed how alive research on colonial Africa is. Despite concerns about the collapse of institutional support for research and university education in Africa and despite recent laments about the state of francophone scholarship,[9] African scholars, French scholars, and others are doing prodigious research on a wide variety of topics.

Several of the papers demolished thoroughly the myth that AOF represented a model for integration of African territories over a large area. AOF, we learned, had failed as a unit of planning, as a structure over which rational transportation structures could be built. Transport had been designed to drain the country; banking supported a narrow structure of import-export rather than a broad and diverse pattern of investment in different resources, regions, and people. The French language did provide a medium for communication across linguistic diversity, but the stark separation of anglophone and francophone West Africa made regional coordination difficult. The monetary unit that France continued to support after decolonization—the CFA franc—presented certain advantages, but the 50 percent devaluation of the franc a year and a half before the conference, at the will of the French government, showed where the power really lay. All this and more was said, and none of it mattered. The participants I talked to were well aware that their ideas were being marginalized as they themselves were being feted.

A building played a role in the 1995 colloquium. The archives of Senegal are an invaluable institution to anyone concerned with the colonial past. Of all the federations through which France administered its African dominions, only AOF retained its own archives; the others were taken to France. Senegal took over these records, and its archives—under the direction of Saliou Mbaye—have been a model of archival professionalism and scholarly openness and integrity. Under Senegalese direction, previously inaccessible collections—including those of the first years of Senegal's independence—have been cataloged and opened. All this has been done under material conditions that would drive archivists in more privileged surroundings to despair. Located in the corner and basement of the Building Administratif—the monument to bureaucratic power and bad taste left by the departing colonial regime—the archives cannot store their invaluable collections in secure conditions or provide adequate space for archivists and researchers to do their work.

A new building is much needed, but in these days of structural adjustment an expensive project to save the past is not an obvious priority. Hence the importance of soliciting French help, in this as in many other domains. The minister of cooperation insisted in his speech to the Dakar colloquium that a special relationship between France and Africa would remain in place, and the next month President Jacques Chirac made his first state visit to Africa to show that his administration would not "disengage" from the continent.[10] But the special relationship is the consequence of a history.

The centenary of AOF offered a once-in-a-lifetime opportunity to showcase the international importance of the National Archives. Scholars from outside Senegal were, in this sense, being put on display, but this was a kind of exploitation that historians would happily accept. In this regard, the key moment of the week came within the first hour, when President Diouf announced that a new building would be constructed for the archives. The loudest applause to be heard that week greeted his statement. As witnesses, we had done our job.

But whatever the history that may be one day uncovered in the archives, the ceremonies and the witnessing were saying how that history could be talked about in public. The framing speeches were the key: that of the president and of the French minister of cooperation at the opening session and of the former governor-general of AOF at the closing session. Younger African scholars were hearing how the linkage of power and history should be fashioned; extensive press coverage announced how colonialism was to be talked about beyond small academic circles.

The opening speeches were presented in the National Assembly of Senegal—the seat of democratic legitimacy. As we entered the hall, we walked along a red carpet between two rows of presidential guards, dressed in red uniforms and caps, each holding a sword pointed upward in front of his face, starkly at attention, staring straight ahead, somehow ignoring the heat. By the side was a group of men beating drums—the tam-tam that accompanied most political appearances and marked the cultural authenticity of a political event. We were ushered by armed guards into the seats normally used by parliamentary deputies. In the galleries above the National Assembly floor, there was an audience—the populace seemed to be present. But a Senegalese colleague sitting next to me explained that the crowd was led by an "animateur," a supporter of the ruling party co-opted or paid to bring out the spontaneous support of the "crowd" for the president.

After opening formalities, the first words went to Jacques Godfrain, minister of cooperation of France. He told us he was making his first trip in this capacity outside of France; the government of Jacques Chirac had just been designated. He spoke in the languages of relationships: "The relations between Senegal and France are deep."[11] He told the historians about the key dates in the history of AOF: its founding in 1895, the opening of the leading school in 1912, the founding of medical research institutes and other such structures during the early decades of the century, the election of an African to the French legislature in 1914, the founding of an African political party in 1946, the transfer of a large measure of political autonomy to individual colonies in 1956, and the granting of independence in 1960—the one line that received applause. In the last century, after the creation of AOF, "history accelerated for better and sometimes for worse." The relationship between France and Senegal had been "at times difficult." The Senegalese were thanked for helping to restore French liberties during World War II. In the future—and here he spoke in the measured tones of a cabinet officer making a policy statement—Africa would continue to receive "very particular attention" in French foreign policy.

And so the conquest of African territory, the exercise of power by an alien government, the invidious distinction between French "citizens" and "subjects," and the institutions that became the focus of anger and mobilization—forced labor and the "indigénat" as well as African political mobilization—were assimilated into "relationships" with their inevitable "difficulties."

President Diouf then spoke in similar tones: France and Senegal shared a "common" history. He quoted in the course of his remarks the noted French historian Fernand Braudel (to the effect that a complex, undecided history had to be projected into the present) but not the distinguished Senegalese historian Cheikh Anta Diop or the Senegalese poet—and his predecessor as president—Léopold Sédar Senghor (discussed later). Diouf, like Godfrain, acknowledged difficulties in the relationship. While AOF was a

work of colonization, following a logic and pursuing objectives inscribed in the colonial perspective, it is still the case that what this means for us, today, in our future projects, goes beyond that historical significance. It is thus up to us, who are engaged in the effort to lead our continent in good conditions toward the challenges of the next millennium, to make memory the illumination of the future.

The elision of the colonial past and the African future thus occurred within a single sentence, with no expression of what actually happened during colonial rule, with no suggestions of how colonial institutions left future rulers with both openings and constraints. The breakup of AOF received a more meaningful examination: the "joy of independence" existed alongside the "sadness of balkanization." How French actions led to that balkanization was not mentioned, nor was the fact that certain African elites acquired a vested interest in territorial institutions and helped to bring about the failure of federal ones.[12]

With the speeches made and the promise of a new archives witnessed, the assembled guests walked again the gauntlet of sword-bearing guards, proceeded to the museum next door to attend opening ceremonies of an exhibit of copies of colonial documents taken from the archives, and then went (some of us on foot, others in Mercedes) to the presidential palace for a reception in the massive and majestic hall overlooking the ocean—in a palace originally built for the French governor-general.

The African president and the French minister were presenting the soft version of memories of colonialism: a "relationship," sometimes troubled as are all relationships. The hard version was the closing bracket that framed the working sessions in the middle. Indeed, the last word was given to the federation's last governor-general, Pierre Messmer. Messmer, a leading Gaullist and at one point de Gaulle's prime minister, exuded authority in his bearing and his voice. The governor-general had returned. Saliou Mbaye introduced Messmer by pointing out that it was his decision to leave the archives of AOF in Dakar rather than take them to Paris. Messmer unabashedly accepted the credit. There was still enough of the naive researcher left in me to hope that he might tell us something about his own role in the crucial years when AOF broke up into a series of independent countries—a subject of my own research. But no. He chose instead to narrate his version of colonial history—saying that historians and sociologists had got it wrong. The core of his conception was that after two centuries of "African war" France had brought peace and security. With peace came railroads, schools, and hospitals; cadres were trained to administer Africa.[13] Here was the old line through which France had embraced colonization in its most "republican" moments in the nineteenth century and had defended it for much of the twentieth and that was now transformed into the notion of "cooperation": universal progress would be brought from its source to Africa. Messmer delivered all this to an audience that, as he knew perfectly well, knew better but that—out of politeness and deference to our Senegalese hosts—would do nothing but listen.

I walked out of the final session with some of the younger historians from Africa with whom I had been talking extensively over the course of the week. They were upset and bitter. "That was not AOF he was talking about," said a scholar from Benin. Another perspective came from a young white man who was working in a junior management position at the hotel where the conference was being held and who had listened to part of Messmer's talk: he was excited by what he had heard; "I wish I'd been here in Senegal fifty years ago," he told me.

In between the soft and hard versions of the colonial past, the colloquium was more like a typical academic event, except that so many people had been invited to give papers that the presentations went by in a blur with little time for discussion. We had come to Dakar to display by our presence how wide the web of learning was that had spun outward from the Senegalese archive, but it mattered less what we had to say.

Other elements of the mise-en-scène stand out: the caravans of buses and Mercedes to vast receptions at the end of each day and the attentive presence of young women designated as "hostesses," in specially designed yellow dresses the first day, in blue dresses the next, and in evening gowns for the gala at the national theater. In the middle of the conference, we took Sunday off to go to Saint Louis, the original French settlement in Senegal and its first capital. A parade of four buses escorted by three motorcycle policemen made the four-hour journey there and back in a single day. True to the colonial traditions of hierarchy, a set of especially distinguished visitors made the journey by chartered airplane—similarly select participants had been assigned a Mercedes with a driver for their use throughout the conference. At Saint Louis, we sat in a reviewing stand to hear a tam-tam, a military band, and a few speeches of welcome. Then we were driven around Saint Louis in buses for a few minutes and carted off by bus and canoe to a spit of land where we feasted on roasted sheep. Then we went back to Saint Louis and the reviewing stand, where we watched different neighborhood associations, mostly women, parade before us in their finery or present short dances to the accompaniment of more drummers. Perhaps I was being hopeful again in thinking that some of the dancers were gently mocking the whole iconography of colonial power and African resistance—a woman on a horse carrying a plastic submachine gun. After a quick museum tour, there was another reception with speeches by the governor of the district and the mayor of the town, ending with a ride in air-conditioned comfort with police escort back to Dakar.

There were numerous notes of ambiguity and discomfort—continual criticism from younger scholars in the corridors and at dinners and receptions of the idea of commemorating colonization, of the public speeches, and of the organization of the colloquium. There had been, I learned, considerable disagreement about the format in the Senegalese "scientific committee" that had been consulted about planning the event. In the plenary session the day after the opening ceremonies, one talk by a Senegalese historian who was then minister of the environment represented the clearest effort to get some discussion beyond relationships into the public part of the event. Abdoulaye Bathily is an able and highly regarded professor of history at the Université Cheikh Anta Diop in Dakar. For years, he was the leader of a leftist opposition party—in a country that is officially multiparty but where the entire patronage apparatus was controlled by the president's Socialist Party. Bathily's party had joined a coalition government, and Bathily became a minister. Bathily spoke after the French ambassador to Senegal and other dignitaries had given another round of the by then familiar fluff about the "depth of ties" between France and Africa. Bathily made the simple point that this colloquium was "extraordinary" in that it celebrated a "defeat." But commemorating a defeat offered another possibility at forging collective identification. Bathily had two more points that went beyond anything said before. First, AOF did not represent the only unifying experience in African history; the empires of Ghana, Mali, and Gao had also united large and diverse groups of West Africans under a single political structure. Second, AOF itself could not be equated to integration but had to be understood in terms of the French effort to exploit its colonies. He warned against any "nostalgia" for AOF. His talk was refreshing, the first words spoken in public that corresponded to the history scholars knew something about. Yet if one knew the work of Bathily the historian, one realized how much more cautious Bathily the minister was being. His writing on the early empires emphasizes the divisions of power and class within them.[14] The comparison with AOF offers the possibility of exploring distinct ways in which state power encounters geographic and cultural diversity. But that was an opportunity Bathily chose not to take. And it was a sign of how slippery the ground was on which the colloquium was taking place that his warning to a predominantly African audience against colonial nostalgia was appropriate and necessary.

This talk and a series of plenary addresses that followed were held in the sumptuous conference hall built for Senegal by Arab oil interests: we were treated to luxurious decor, comfortable seats, simultaneous translations, and an excellent lunch at midday. But it was a complicated relationship between form and content. Another historian cum politician seemed to be working within the critical space his colleague had opened up. Iba der Thiam had also been an opposition leader, serving at one time as minister of education, and remains a member of the university's history department. For Thiam, colonial history was one "long battle." From the efforts of Blaise Diagne to show that a black could represent the citizens of Senegal in the French legislature to independence itself, every success was followed by efforts to take it away and opened up new struggles. His argument is a valid one, but it is in some ways the mirror image of the colonial apologies we had heard too much of earlier: to say that everything is a struggle is as much an exercise in mythologizing as saying that everything is progress.[15] Indeed, it is ironic how easily Thiam's intervention fit into the colloquium's tone and how little people there commented on it, yet Bathily's more profound challenge created a stir among the scholars I talked to. The French could have their "mission civilisatrice," and the Senegalese could have their "independence struggle." Both sides can agree that the nation-state represents the apotheosis of their effort, even if one claims that colonial tutalage deserves credit for Africans' ability to run their own governments and the latter claims that nationalist movements deserve that credit.

A similar ambiguity was found in the plenary address of Samir Amin—the noted economist of Egyptian origin who has lived and worked in Senegal for many years. He frankly characterized Africa's present situation as catastrophic and denounced neocolonial economic forces as its root cause. But this talk, like much of Amin's large corpus of writing, left much unexamined: insisting that the only relevant scale for analyzing economies is the global one, Amin has condemned himself to recasting endlessly his global model without being able to probe its component parts individually. The seriousness of the call in his Dakar speech for fundamental reforms in the world economy is contradicted by his own analysis of how much the status quo benefits capitalist powers, while his hopes of building a partially autonomous African economy is weakened by his caution in examining internal power relations in Africa. Amin's critique of global capitalism becomes assimilable to the claims made by African states against the West, while his less developed critique of structures within Africa is ignored.[16]

What thus was happening at the plenary sessions was

an opening up of certain arguments that went beyond the "relationship" of the initial speeches but avoided the kind of specific rereading of colonial history that would actually challenge the master narrative of state building, whether the centrality of the state was a consequence of colonial tutelage or nationalist mobilization. The overseas speakers were understandably cautious. They steered away from the thorny history of decolonization. They explained that it is not only Africans who have had difficulty consolidating small units into big ones and that much of the integration that has taken place elsewhere in the world has been coercive.

The final plenary address, by Boubacar Barry, a Guinean historian long resident in Dakar, gently questioned the basic premises of the colloquium, noting in particular that the very presumption that AOF should be a model for future integration missed one of the crucial divisions created by colonization—between francophone and anglophone Africa—and that any serious conversation about integration should not begin with AOF but with an analysis of the lines of affiliation and communication as they actually exist and as they actually define regions with meaning to people's lives. Barry began his talk with a reference to two French historians, Jean Suret-Canale and Catherine Coquery-Vidrovitch, both of whom were present, and acknowledged their role in developing a historiography critical of colonial rule and in encouraging African students to pursue such inquiries. His remark made clear that there were alternative ways of talking about a French-African connection, which neither split the world into colonizers and colonized nor homogenized everybody into a Franco-African relationship. Barry had no need to make explicit that his evocation of anticolonial French scholars implied that others had made different choices. If anyone didn't realize this, former governor-general Messmer would remind them.

But all that was said—carefully—to question the premise of a commemoration shrinks before a startling silence in both the dignitaries' addresses and the plenary session. Other than a passing mention, no one said anything about Léopold Sédar Senghor, a figure around whom an entire colloquium focusing on African engagement with colonialism, on the significance of the past for independent Africa, and on the question of "territorialization" versus "integration" could have been organized. The word *balkanization* appeared repeatedly in planning documents and opening speeches, but it was Senghor who in the late 1950s built a campaign against balkanization, battling—vigorously if briefly—to prevent the splintering. Why should Senghor have been so

noticeably absent? The only reason I can think of is that his name would invoke precisely the ambiguity that the colloquium was structured to avoid: because he spoke against the specific pattern by which colonial rule gave way to independence, he renders problematic the smooth assimilation of the colonial state and the independent state into the bland category of "relationship." The most profound question facing Senegal today—as it has been for the last forty years—is what to make of its independence. Senghor tried first to save something of the West Africa–wide nature of AOF—creating a unit large enough for effective economic and political coordination—and then to preserve a portion of it in the form of a short-lived union of Senegal and its inland neighbor Mali. That federation failed as its leaders, Modibo Keita and Senghor himself, became increasingly anxious that the relatively solid political machines out of which each had risen in his respective territory would be compromised by efforts by the other to recruit the disaffected in the other's bailiwick.

The rapid demise of the Mali Federation was an emblematic instance of the failure of efforts at transforming colonial forms of integration into Pan-African ones. Colonial borders—arbitrary as they were—have proved the most durable product of colonialism. Senghor's name thus invokes a history in which the heroes of African independence—reluctantly and knowingly in Senghor's case but less so in other instances—became entrenched in a postcolonial status quo built around reinforcing their own power. Here were memories of colonization and decolonization too ambiguous for public debate outside of the most scholarly of the scholarly sessions.[17]

What colonialist arguments like Messmer's and nationalist interpretations like Thiam's both ignore is how the struggles actually took place, how deeply both colonial governments and the political parties that contested and took over the institutions of the state interpenetrated and affected each other. Neither colonialist nor nationalist memories of colonization put the focus on how individuals, families, and other social groups confronted the range of factors affecting their lives, on how people drew resources from kinship networks and colonial schools, finding constraints and opportunities in both. They do not dwell on all the selfish or ill-considered compromises that were made or show how people preserved their integrity in the face of conflicting pressures.[18]

The labor unions that Thiam cited, for example, focused on the racism of colonial practices in organizing work in the 1940s and 1950s and insisted that any claim that Africa was French meant that African workers should be paid the same as metropolitan workers. They were turning imperial rhetoric into a powerful claim-making device. Political and social movements shook the colonial regimes precisely because they saw the vulnerability behind colonial officials' hopes that Africans could be made into more productive, orderly people in the interests of empire. By the mid-1950s French rulers were beginning to realize that such demands—posed by associations they had to recognize and in language they could not ignore and backed by implicit or explicit threats of the extension of Algerian- or Vietnamese-type revolutions to sub-Saharan Africa—threatened formidable costs in wages, social services, and investment without the corresponding transformation of Africa into either the image of France or its obedient and productive subordinate.

It was at that time that colonialism and nationalism found a ground for an entente. Nationalists' resolute insistence on Africa as the focus for affiliation and aspiration offered an alternative to a limitless escalation of demands—even at the expense of a genuine devolution of power. France moved away from the universalizing and centralizing tendency within its own imperial ideology. The price of independence for each territorial unit, from Senegal to Niger, would be that it would have to live off its own resources. A federal solution risked implying that the poorest territories should be subsidized by the richest, which came dangerously close to implying that France should make up the difference. Some African leaders, most notably Senghor, realized that they were being asked to make a Faustian bargain, to accept power in small, diverse states and to give up the possibilities of integration as well as to surrender a common platform from which to make demands. But the power that was being offered was real enough, the alternative too abstract. The independence that French-speaking Africans accepted in 1960 was that of the individual territory, based on colonial borders, without regard to cultural affinities and differences and with vastly unequal resource bases.

The 1950s in West Africa was a time of engagement and struggle but not a clash of a monolithic colonialism and a pure nationalism or an authentic anticolonialism. That is why the political, economic, and moral choices made by numerous farmers, trade unionists, market women, and schoolteachers—when to make a deal, when to refuse, when to argue in terms that a European administrator understood, when to reject the colonial framework—were painful at the time and evoke difficult memories afterward.

Colonialism has left no single set of memories but rather a complex array as people try in their own ways to come to grips with what the experiences of external power, of struggle, and of sovereignty mean to themselves, to past and future generations, and to the different collectivities to which they feel attached. Even if one gives up the illusion of finding an "authentic" past, one can find bits and pieces of illuminating recollection. Let me cite a small example from interviews done in 1994 as part of a project on oral history in the post-1945 period, which I organized along with Dr. Babacar Fall of the Ecole Normale Supérieure of the Université Cheikh Anta Diop and Dr. Robert Korstad of Duke University.

At an interview with a leading trade unionist of the 1950s, Alioune Cissé, I listened to a Senegalese graduate student ask Mr. Cissé about the "glorious days" of Senegalese trade unionism. The young student and the old trade unionist understood each other perfectly—they were talking about the 1950s. The trope of the "golden age" is a standard one in oral history. That the golden age should be located in a time of struggle rather than of victory points to the ambiguous relationship of memories of colonialism and memories of political independence. Cissé put the blame squarely on the French: their strategy of territorialization in 1956 cut off efforts to strive for a wider unity and a broader basis for setting standards for wages and working conditions that the union movement had sought. Cissé, as he described his life, had both enjoyed the fruits of independence and fought battles for what he believed in—he had become an important ambassador for Senegal but at one point was detained in prison by the Senghor regime for leading an "illegal" strike. Other activists of the 1950s to whom the groups of students spoke were more bitter, referring to the corruption of the postcolonial regime, to the riches acquired by politicians, to the unions losing their autonomy and becoming the "auxiliaries" of the political leadership. At our workshop, students commented on how modestly some of the people they regarded as heroes and heroines of anticolonial politics now lived and wondered aloud whether those with the most political integrity had prospered the least.

All this suggests how difficult it is to come to grips with memories of colonialism: people who grew up under colonial rule and spent many years fighting it were not telling us a story that was a simple inversion of the French minister's "relationship" or the governor-general's "civilizing mission." Their stories were necessarily mediated across a more recent experience that contains both unabashed victories—the end of a demeaning regime—and ambiguities, the inability of almost all African states to deliver the common prosperity the nationalist movements promised, the oppressiveness of some postcolonial regimes, the contrast in almost all of them between a political elite that has used institutions of the former regime to enrich itself while co-opting and repressing alternative structures. But colonial regimes were themselves ambiguous in their effects, creating a reality of openings and closures that Africans could not ignore, forcing moral choices far more complex than "resistance" or "collaboration," with effects not easily predicted at the time.

I wish neither to argue that the iniquities of postcolonial states lessen the iniquities of colonial states nor to join in a blanket condemnation of "the state." But recognizing the importance of state structures in today's world makes it all the more essential to question exactly what those structures are, the choices that were made in establishing them, and the ways those choices opened and closed possibilities for individuals and groups to make their histories.

The colloquium of 1995 was as much a commemoration of a particular mode of decolonization as it was of the creation of a colonial structure in 1895, of a decolonization that cemented African subordination even as it redefined the terms, of a decolonization that put in power a particular elite—and negotiated the exclusion of too radical alternatives to Franco-Senegalese cooperation. The colloquium commemorated the Senegalese state as it commemorated France's colonization. Thirty-five years after Senegal became independent, its position in the world economy was so vulnerable, its need for French help to build the institutions necessary to define its sovereignty and to perform the functions of a government so great, that it had to commemorate its colonial past in a very peculiar way.[19]

The scholarly workshops within the centenary make clear that interesting and important work can be done in Senegal and that it can be talked about openly. The colloquium was disturbing because its form and the contents of its public components set forth a particular way of talking about the connection of Africa and its colonial past, a language that corresponds to Africa's current penary and acute dependence on outsiders for assistance. Within such a language, memories of colonization—not just the bitterness of domination but the intensity and complexity of Africans' engagement with European power and culture—are not so much ignored as publicly effaced, publicly diluted, publicly banalized. Invocation of a historic relationship of France and Africa substitutes for analysis of just what that relationship was.

Scholars attending the conference—quite well aware that what was being commemorated was a defeat, that

the idea of a Franco-African "relationship" was problematic if not offensive—were put in a position where they had to sit quietly and commemorate something they did not want to celebrate, to listen to speeches that elided or denied what they knew to be the most central questions. All of us—Senegalese, other Africans, Westerners—did precisely this. We did it out of politeness and out of hope that the ritual we were participating in would indeed bring concrete benefits to the Senegalese archives.

Was the dual form of the conference telling us that we could have our scholarly debates, but when things really mattered, when resources must be obtained, then we had better talk about the colonial nature of Franco-African history in carefully measured tones? Was the colloquium helping to spell out a way of talking about history that was simultaneously nationalist and neocolonial, giving the colonized credit for resisting what the colonizers were given credit for accomplishing? Was the history of a "relationship" the past that a future of French "cooperation" demanded?[20]

Many years after the centenary, it looks as if the new archive and library building will soon be built, although it remains temporarily stalled in the uncertainties surrounding the election of a new president, Abdoulaye Wade, who in 2000 defeated Abdou Diouf. So perhaps the commemoration will have concrete results. But the event remains a curious episode in Africa's relationship to its history. The politics of memory are about forgetting as much as remembering, and the politics of scholarship are about excluding information as much as expanding knowledge. Parts of the commemorative conference were inclusive, engaged, critical. But the whole event was choreographed so that such parts remained what they usually are—academic presentations—while others made history into something vastly more public, explicitly linked to present-day concerns. The academic sessions, by their very nature, did their share of excluding and forgetting. Meanwhile, scholars were being taught something much more unusual, and a wider public was sharing in the lesson. They were being taught what kind of past the present of an African state required: a colonization that could be celebrated.

NOTES

I would like to thank Jane Burbank, Mamadou Diouf, Achille Mbembe, and Luise White for encouraging me to proceed with this essay and for offering their comments. The author bears sole responsibility for what is said.

1. The proceedings of this conference have been published

in two enormous volumes, 1,273 pages long. Another volume, published by the Archives du Sénégal with the support of the Ministère de la Coopération of France, contains—neatly segregated from the scholarly papers—the speeches of the president and other dignitaries, plus diplomatic-sounding resolutions and a general report. Charles Becker, Saliou Mbaye, Ibrahima Thioub (sous la direction de), *AOF: réalités et héritages: sociétés ouest-africaines et ordre colonial, 1895–1960* (Dakar: Direction des Archives du Sénégal, 1997), 2 vols.; *Commemoration du Centenaire de la Création de l'Afrique Occidentale Française (AOF), Dakar 16–23 Juin 1995* (Dakar: Direction des Archives du Sénégal, 1997).

2. The methodological and reflective literature on oral history is large, from the foundational text of Jan Vansina, *Oral Tradition: A Study in Historical Methodology,* trans. H. M. Wright (Chicago: Aldine, 1965), to the proceedings of a recent conference, David William Cohen, Luise White, and Stephan Miescher, eds., *Words and Voices: Critical Practices in the Oral History of Africa* (Bloomington: Indiana University Press, 2001).

3. James C. Scott, *Domination and the Arts of Resistance: Hidden Transcripts* (New Haven: Yale University Press, 1990). For a critical perspective on such approaches, see Frederick Cooper, "Conflict and Connection: Rethinking Colonial African History," *American Historical Review* 99 (1994): 1516–45.

4. Ranajit Guha, "The Prose of Counterinsurgency," in *Selected Subaltern Studies,* ed. Ranajit Guha and Gayatri Spivak (New York: Oxford University Press, 1988), 45–86; Ann Stoler, "'In Cold Blood': Hierarchies of Credibility and the Politics of Colonial Narratives," *Representations* 37 (1992): 140–89.

5. Luise White, *Speaking with Vampires: Rumor and History in Colonial Africa* (Berkeley: University of California Press, 2000), 210, 241.

6. The proceedings of this commemoration/colloquium were published as Charles-Robert Ageron and Marc Michel (sous la direction de), *L'Afrique noire française: l'heure des Indépendances* (Paris: CNRS Editions, 1992).

7. These goals are brought out in the introduction to Becker, Mbaye, and Thioub, *AOF: réalités et héritages,* 1:5–8.

8. Ibid., 1:7.

9. See the series of articles in *Politique Africaine,* 1996–98, including interventions by Charles Didier Gondola, Catherine Coquery-Vidrovitch, and Jean Copans.

10. "Le Président de la République fait sa première visite officielle en Afrique," *Le Monde,* July 20, 1995.

11. For Godfrain's text, see *Commemoration,* 11–13. The relationship argument was long ago dissected by Aimé Césaire, *Discours sur le colonialisme* (Paris: Présence Africaine, 1955).

12. Diouf's speech was reported verbatim in *Le Soleil,* June 17–18, 1995, and is reprinted in *Commemoration,* 7–10.

13. *Commemoration,* 54–58.

14. Bathily's speech is in *Commemoration,* 23–29. See also Abdoulaye Bathily, *Portes d'or: le royaume de Galam (Sénégal) de l'ère musulmane au temps des négriers (VIIIe–XVIIIe siècle)* (Paris: L'Harmattan, 1989).

15. Iba der Thiam, "Le combat des populations africaines pour la démocratie, l'égalité et la justice: l'exemple du Sénégal, 1895–1945," in Becker, Mbaye, and Thioub, *AOF: réalités et héritages,* 1:250–63. Thiam is the author of a nine-volume doc-

torat d'état, "L'évolution politique et syndicale du Sénégal Colonial de 1890 à 1936," Thèse pour le doctorat d'Etat, Université de Paris I, 1983.

16. Among Samir Amin's many works, see *L'accumulation à l'échelle mondiale* (Paris: Anthropolos, 1970), and *Itinéraire Intellectuel* (Paris: L'Harmattan, 1993).

17. One of the workshops heard a paper from Janet Vaillant, which focused on Senghor, "The Problem of Culture in French West Africa: 1937. 'Assimiler, pas être assimilé'," in Becker, Mbaye, and Thioub, *AOF: réalités et héritages,* 2:682–96. See also her *Black, French, and African: A Life of Léopold Sédar Senghor* (Cambridge: Harvard University Press, 1990). For a narrative of the split up of French West Africa, see Joseph-Roger de Benoist, *La balkanisation de l'Afrique Occidentale Française* (Dakar: Nouvelle Afrique, 1979); on more recent politics, see Momar Coumba Diop and Mamadou Diouf, *Le Sénégal sous Abdou Diouf* (Paris: Karthala, 1990).

18. I have set out my own views on these and related questions elsewhere: "Conflict and Connection," and *Decolonization and African Society: The Labor Question in French and British Africa* (Cambridge: Cambridge University Press, 1996). See also Frederick Cooper and Ann Laura Stoler, eds., *Tensions of Empire: Colonial Cultures in a Bourgeois World* (Berkeley: University of California Press, 1997).

19. This was not the only conference held in Dakar in the summer of 1995. Another commemorated the life of Cheikh Anta Diop—along with Senghor one of the two striking absences from the AOF commemoration. Diop is in his own way a problematic figure, his view of a unified and unifying African past being in many ways a contrast to the efforts of a younger generation of Senegalese and other African scholars to bring out the differentiated and contestatory nature of history. But his political activism in the 1950s and his influential scholarly writing represent a real challenge to relationship history, suggesting that any discussion of regional integration in Africa must begin with connections across the African continent itself. Still another conference was organized in late June by the Council for the Development of Social Science Research in Africa (CODESRIA). This is one of the most encouraging lights among African institutions increasingly dimmed by financial stringency and the reluctance of governments and outside donors to believe that basic questions are worth thinking about. CODESRIA is publishing a series of papers and books that analyze critically both the structure of the global political economy and the structure of African states.

20. The French foreign policy establishment indeed rethinks from time to time what the word *cooperation* is supposed to mean, and a collection of explorations published before the commemoration was notable for its technocratic approach—stressing tighter control of projects—its language of blame and didacticism directed at African governments, and the contradiction between its call for a "dialogue" with Africa and the absence from the volume of any African voices. Serge Michailof, ed., *La France et l'Afrique: Vade-mecum pour un nouveau voyage* (Paris: Karthala, 1993). Reading this volume after the colloquium, I could not help but wonder if the colloquium was not doing for history what Michailof's team was doing for politics.

Colonial Archives and the Arts of Governance

On the Content in the Form

Ann Laura Stoler

> Genealogy is gray, meticulous and patiently documentary.
> It operates on a field of entangled and confused parchments,
> on documents that have been scratched over and recopied
> many times.
>
> —Foucault, *The Archaelogy of Knowledge and the Discourse on Language*

This essay is about the colonial order of things as seen through its archival productions. It asks what insights about the colonial might be gained from attending not only to colonialism's archival content but to its particular and sometimes peculiar form. Its focus is on archiving as a process rather than archives as things. It looks to archives as epistemological experiments rather than as sources—to colonial archives as cross-sections of contested knowledge. Most important, I want to suggest that colonial archives were both transparencies on which power relations were inscribed and intricate technologies of rule in themselves. The essay's concerns are two: to situate new approaches to colonial archives within the broader "historic turn" of the last two decades and to suggest what critical histories of the colonial have to gain by turning further toward a politics of knowledge that reckons with archival genres, cultures of documentation, fictions of access, and archival conventions.

Archives, Epistemological Skepticism, and the Historic Turn

Some four decades after the British social anthropologist Evans-Pritchard's unheeded warning that anthropology would have to choose between being history or being nothing and Lévi-Strauss's counterclaim that accorded history neither "special value" nor privileged analytic space, students of culture have taken up a transformative venture, celebrating with unprecedented relish what has come to be called "the historic turn."[1] Some might argue that anthropology's engagement with history over the last two decades, unlike that recent turn in other disciplines, has not been a turn at all but rather a return to its founding principles, inquiry into cumulative processes of cultural production but without the typological aspirations and evolutionary assumptions once embraced. Others might counter that the feverish turn to history represents a significant departure from an earlier venture, a more explicit rupture with anthropology's long-standing complicity in colonial politics.[2] As such, one could argue that the historic turn signals not a turn to history per se but a different reflection on the politics of knowledge—a further rejection of the categories and cultural distinctions on which imperial rule was once invested and on which postcolonial state practices have continued to be based.

Engagement with the uses and abuses of the past pervades the disciplines but nowhere more than in this burgeoning area of colonial ethnography. Over the last decade students of the colonial have challenged the categories, conceptual frame, and practices of colonial authorities and their taxonomic states.[3] Questioning the making of colonial knowledge and the privileged social categories it produced has revamped what students of the colonial take to be sources of knowledge and what to expect of them. Attention to the intimate domains in which colonial states intervened has prompted reconsideration of what we hold to be the foundations of European authority and its key technologies.[4] In treating colonialism as a history of the present rather than as a metaphor of it, a new generation of scholars are taking up Michel De Certeau's invitation to "prowl" new terrain as they reimagine what sorts of situated knowledge have produced both colonial sources *and* their own respective locations in the "historiographic operation."[5] Some students of colonialism are rereading those archives against popular memory;[6] others are attending to how colonial documents have been requisitioned and recycled to confirm old entitlements or to make new political demands. As part of a wider impulse, we are no longer studying things but rather the making of them. Students of colonialisms inside and outside of anthropology are spending as much time rethinking what constitutes the colonial archive as they are reconsidering how written documents collide and converge with colonial memories in the postcolonial field.

But if Evans-Pritchard's warning some thirty-five years ago that "anthropologists have tended to be uncritical in their use of documentary sources" had little resonance at the time, it has more today. For however deep and full the archival turn has been in postcolonial scholarship of the 1990s, what is more surprising is how thin and tentative it can still remain.[7] Anthropologists may no longer look at archives as the stuff of another discipline. Nor are these archives treated as inert sites of storage and conservation.[8] But archival labor tends to remain more an extractive enterprise than an ethnographic one. Documents are still invoked piecemeal and selectively to confirm the colonial invention of traditional practices or to underscore cultural claims.

Anthropology has never committed itself to "exhaust" the sources, as Bernard Cohn once chided the historical profession for doing with such moral fervor. But the extractive metaphor remains relevant to both.[9] Students of the colonial "mine" the *content* of government commissions and reports but rarely attend to their peculiar form. We look at exemplary documents rather than at the genealogies of their redundance. We warily quote examples of colonial excesses—if uneasy with the pathos and voyeurism that such citations entail. We may readily mock fetishisms of the historian's craft, but there remains the shared conviction that access to what is classified and confidential are the coveted findings of our sound and shrewd intellectual labors.[10] The ability to procure them measures scholarly worth. Not least is the shared conviction that such guarded treasures are the sites where the secrets of the colonial state are really stored.

There are a number of ways to frame the sort of challenge I have in mind, but at least one seems obvious: steeped as students of culture have been in treating ethnographies as texts, we are just now critically reflecting on the making of documents and how we choose to use them, on archives not as sites of knowledge retrieval but as sites of knowledge production, on archives as monuments of states as well as sites of state ethnography. This is not a rejection of colonial archives as sources of the past. Rather, it signals a more sustained engagement with those archives as cultural artifacts of fact production, of taxonomies in the making, and of disparate notions of what made up colonial authority.

As both Ranajit Guha and Greg Dening long have warned, "sources" are not "springs of real meaning," "fonts" of colonial truths in themselves.[11] Whether documents are trustworthy, authentic, and reliable remain pressing questions, but a turn to the social and political conditions that produced those documents, what Carlo Ginzburg has called their "evidentiary paradigms," has altered the sense of what trust and reliability might signal and politically entail. The task is less to distinguish fiction from fact than to track the production and consumption of those facticities themselves. With this move, colonial studies is steering in a different direction, toward inquiry into the grids of intelligibility that produced those "evidential paradigms" at a particular time, for a particular contingent, and in a particular way.[12]

Students of the colonial have come to see appropriations of colonial history as infused with political agendas, making some stories eligible for historical rehearsal and others not.[13] Troubling questions about how personal memories are shaped and effaced by states too have placed analytic emphasis on how past practices are winnowed for future uses and future projects.[14] Such queries invite a turn back to documentation itself, to the "teaching" task that the Latin root *docere* implies, to what and who was being educated in the bureaucratic shuffle of rote formulas, generic plots, and prescriptive asides that make up the bulk of a colonial archive. The issue of official bias gives way to a different challenge: to identify the conditions of possibility that shaped what could be written, what warranted repetition, what competencies were rewarded in archival writing, what stories could not be told, and what could not be said. Andrew Ashforth may have overstated the case in his study of South Africa's Native Affairs Commission, when he noted that "the real seat of power" in modern states is "the bureau, the locus of writing," but he may not have been far off the mark.[15] That every document comes layered with the received account of earlier events and the cultural semantics of a political moment makes one point clear. What constitutes the archive, what form it takes, and what systems of classification signal at specific times are the very substance of colonial politics.

From Extraction to Ethnography in the Colonial Archives

> The transformation of archival activity is the point of departure and the condition of a new history.
> —De Certeau, "The Historiographic Operation"

If one could say that archives were once treated as a means to an end by students of history, this is no longer the case today. The pleasures of "a well-stocked manuscript room with its ease of access and aura of quiet detachment" are a thing of the past.[16] Over the last decade, epistemological skepticism has taken cultural and historical studies by storm. A focus on history as narrative and on history writing as a charged political act has made the thinking about archives no longer the pedestrian preoccupation of "spade-work" historians, of flat-footed archivists, or the entry requirements of fledgling initiates compelled to show mastery of the tools of their trade. The "archive" has been elevated to new theoretical status, with enough cachet to warrant distinct billing, worthy of scrutiny on its own. Jacques Derrida's *Archive Fever* compellingly captured that impulse by giving it a name and by providing an explicit and evocative vocabulary for its legitimation in critical theory.[17] But Natalie Davis's *Fiction in the Archives,* Roberto Gonzalez Echevarria's *Myth and Archive,* Richard Thomas's *Imperial Archive,* and Sonia Coombe's *Archives Interdites,* to name but a few, suggest that Derrida's splash came only after the archival turn had already been made.[18]

This move from archive as source to archive as subject gains its contemporary currency from a range of different analytic shifts, practical concerns, and political projects. For some, as in the nuanced archival forays of Greg

Dening, it represents a turn back to the meticulous "poetics of detail."[19] To others—such as Michel-Rolph Trouillot in his treatment of the archival silences of the Haitian Revolution and David William Cohen in his "combings of history"—it signals a new grappling with the production of history: what accounts get authorized, what procedures were required, and what about the past is possible to know.[20] For Bonnie Smith, archival research along with "the seminar" were the nineteenth-century sites where science was marked with gendered credentials.[21] Archivists obviously have been thinking about the nature and history of archives for some time.[22] What marks this moment is the profusion of fora in which historians are joining archivists in new conversations about documentary evidence, record keeping, and archival theory.[23] Both are worrying about the politics of storage, about what information matters, and about what should be retained of an archive as paper collections give way to digital forms.[24]

In cultural theory, "the archive" is endowed with a capital A, is figurative, and leads elsewhere. It may represent neither material site nor a set of documents. Rather, it may serve as a strong *metaphor* for any corpus of selective forgettings and collections—and, as important, for the seductions and longings that such quests for, and accumulations of, the primary, originary, and untouched entail.[25] For those inspired more directly by Foucault's *Archaeology of Knowledge,* the archive is not an institution but "the law of what can be said," not a library of events but "that system that establishes statements as events and things, that "system of their enunciabilities."[26]

From whichever vantage point (and there are more than these), the archival turn registers a rethinking of the materiality and imaginary of collections and of what kinds of truth claims lie in documentation.[27] Such a turn converges with a profusion of new work in the history of science that is neither figuratively or literally about archives at all. I think here of Ian Hacking's studies of the political history of probability theory and state investments in the "taming of chance"; Steven Shapin's analysis of the social history of scientific truths, where he traces the power to predict as one enjoyed by, and reserved for, cultured and reliable men; Mary Poovey's work on how the notion of the "modern fact" was historically produced; Alain Desrosieres's study (among many others) on statistics as a science of the state and Silvana Patriarca's study on statistics as a modern mode of representation; and Lorraine Daston's analysis of the development of classical probability theory as a means of measuring the incertitudes of a modernizing world.[28] One could also add Anthony Grafton's essays on footnotes as the lines that lead into moral communities and their claims to truth.[29]

What these all have in common is a concern with the legitimating social coordinates of epistemologies: how people imagine they know what they know and what institutions validate that knowledge. None treat the conventions and categories of analysis (statistics, facts, truths, probability, and footnotes) as innocuous or benign. All converge on questions about rules of reliability and trust, criteria of credence, and what moral projects and political predictabilites are served. All ask a similar set of historical questions about accredited knowledge and power—what political forces, social cues, and moral virtues produce qualified knowledges that in turn disqualify others. To my mind, there is no area of scholarship more relevant to how we view archival conventions and their archiving states.

But the archival turn can be traced through other venues as well, suggesting that something resembling ethnography in an archival mode has been around for some time. Carlo Ginzburg's microhistory of a sixteenth-century miller, like Natalie Davis's use of pardon tales in *Fiction in the Archives,* drew on "hostile" documents to reveal "the gap between the image underlying the interrogations of judges and the actual testimony of the accused."[30] Neither was intended as an ethnography *of* the archive, but both gesture in that direction. In Davis's explicit attention to "how people told stories, what they thought a good story was, how they accounted for motive," these sixteenth-century letters of remission are shown to recount more than their peasant authors' sober tales. Pardon tales registered the "constraints of the law," the monopoly on public justice of royal power, and the mercy that the monarchy increasingly claimed.[31] Davis's "fiction in the archives" demonstrated fashioned stories that spoke to moral truths, drew on shared metaphors and high literary culture, and depended on the power of the state and the archived inscriptions of its authority.

While recent participants in the archival turn have been taken with Derrida's contention that "there is no political power without control of the archive," this insistence on the link between what counts as knowledge and who has power has long been a founding principle of colonial ethnography.[32] Trouillot's insistence in his study of the Haitian Revolution that "historical narratives are premised on previous understandings, which are themselves premised on the distribution of archival power," allowed him to track the effacement of archival traces and the imposed silences that people have moved around and beyond.[33] Nicholas Dirks's observation that early colonial historiographies in British India were dependent on native informants who were later written out of those histories drew attention to the relationship between archiving, experts, and knowledge production.[34] Christopher Bayly's more recent focus on the ways in which the British intelligence service in colonial India worked through native channels places the state's access to "information" as a nodal point in the art of governance and as a highly contested terrain.[35] My own examination of those "hierarchies of credibility" that shaped colonial narratives in the Netherlands Indies attended to the "storyed" distributions of the state's paper production. Not least, I sought to trace how rumors spread by a beleaguered native population disrupted the criteria of what made up a reasonable, reliable, and readable plot.[36]

As Foucault provocatively warned, the archive is neither the sum of all texts that a culture preserves nor those institutions that allow for that record and preservation. The archive is, rather, that "system of statements," those "rules of practice" that shape the specific regularities of what can and cannot be said.[37] Students of colonialism have wrestled with this formulation to capture what renders colonial archives both as documents of exclusions and as monuments to particular configurations of power.

Both Gonzalez Echevarria and Thomas follow Foucault in treating the imperial archive as "the fantastic representation of an epistemological master pattern."[38] For Thomas that archive is material and figurative, a metaphor of an unfulfilled but shared British imperial imagination. The imperial archive was both the supreme technology of the late nineteenth-century imperial state *and* the telling prototype of a postmodern one, predicated on global domination of information and the circuits through which facticities move. Gonzalez Echevarria locates the archive as both relic and ruin, a repository of codified beliefs, genres for bearing witness, clustered connections between secrecy, power, and the law.[39] It was the legitimating discourses of the Spanish colonial archives, he argues, that provided the Latin American novel with its specific content and thematic form. For both Thomas and Gonzalez Echevarria, the archive is a template that decodes something else. Both push us to think differently about archival fictions but reserve their fine-grained analysis for literature, not the colonial archives themselves.[40]

Whether the "archive" should be treated as a set of discursive rules, a utopian project, a depot of documents, a corpus of statements, or all of the above is not really the question. Colonial archives were both sites of the imaginary and institutions that fashioned histories as they concealed, revealed, and reproduced the power of the state.[41] Power and control, as many scholars have pointed out, are fundamental to the etymology of the term *archive*.[42] From the Latin *archivuum*, "residence of the magistrate," and from the Greek *arkhe*, "to command," colonial archives ordered (in both the imperative and taxonomic sense) the criteria of evidence, proof, testimony, and witnessing to construct their moral narrations. "Factual storytelling," moralizing stories, and multiple versions—features that Hayden White ascribes to what counts as history—make sense of which specific plots "worked" in the colonial archives as well.[43] It was in factual stories that the colonial state affirmed its fictions to itself, in moralizing stories that it mapped the scope of its philanthropic missions, and in multiple and contested versions that cultural accounts were discredited or restored.

Viewed in this perspective, it is clear that the nineteenth- and early twentieth-century archives of the Dutch administration in the Indies were not to be read in any which way. Issues were rendered important by how they were classed and discursively framed. Official exchanges between the governor-general and his subordinates, between the governor-general and the minister of colonies, and between the minister and the king were reference guides to administrative thinking, abbreviated cheat sheets of what counted as precedent, what was deemed relevant, and what were to be considered "concerns of state." Appended with expert testimonies and commissioned reports, dossiers traced who cribbed from whom in the chain of command. Attention to moments of distrust and dispersion, reversals of power, and ruptures in contract have been the trademarks of critical political and social history for some time. What has changed is how effectively these moments identify, how what Richard Thomas has called these "paper empires" filed and classified as a part of their technologies of rule.[44]

If it is obvious that colonial archives are products of state machines, it is less obvious that they are, in their own right, technologies that reproduced those states themselves.[45] Systems of written accountability were the products of institutions, but paper trails (such as weekly reports to superiors, summaries of reports of reports, and recommendations based on reports) called for an elaborate coding system by which they could be tracked. Colonial statecraft was built on the foundations of statistics and surveys that demanded an administrative apparatus to produce and process that information. Multiple circuits of communication—shipping lines, courier services,

and telegraphs—were funded by state coffers, and systems of taxation were amplified to keep them flush. Colonial publishing houses made sure that documents were selectively disseminated, duplicated, or destroyed. Colonial office buildings were constructed to make sure they were properly cataloged and stored. And not unlike the broader racialized regime in which archives were produced, the "mixed-blood," "Indo" youths, barred from rising in the civil service ranks, were the scribes that made the system run. Employed as clerks and copyists in the colonial bureaucracy, they were commonly referred to as "copy machines" and then disdained for their lack of initiative, their poor command of Dutch, their skill at imitation, and their easy adaptation to such degraded roles.

Attention to the epistemic and textual scaffolding of the colonial state renders an ethnographic reading of the archives very different from what studies of colonialism looked like several decades ago, as what constitutes "ethnography" has radically changed in the same time. An ethnography "of" and "in" the colonial archives invites more attention to the social relations and material conditions in which archives were produced, to their editing or dissenting voices, to how commonsense was crafted, and to which categories were privileged and resilient and which were demoted or ignored.

Along the Archival Grain

If one were to characterize what has informed a critical approach to the colonial archives over the last fifteen years, it would be a commitment to the notion of reading colonial archives "against their grain." Students of colonialism inspired by political economy were schooled to write popular histories "from the bottom up," histories of resistance that might locate human agency in small gestures of refusal and silence among the colonized.[46] As such, engagement with the colonial archives was devoted to a reading of "upper class sources upside down" that would reveal the language of rule and the biases inherent in statist perceptions.[47]

The political project was to write "un-State-d" histories that might demonstrate the warped reality of official knowledge and the enduring consequences of such political distortions. In Ranajit Guha's formulation, colonial documents were rhetorical slights of hand that erased the facts of subjugation, reclassified petty crime as political subversion, or simply effaced the colonized. The political stakes were put on the analytic tactics of inversion and recuperation: an effort to resituate those who appeared as objects of colonial discipline as subaltern subjects and agents of practice who made—albeit constrained—choices of their own. Within this frame, archival documents were counterweights to ethnography, not the site of it.[48]

But colonial authority and the practices that sustained it permeated more diverse sites than those pursuing this "romance of resistance" once imagined. If Marx's insistence that "people make their own history, but not exactly as they please," informed these early efforts to write histories of popular agency, they also underscored that colonial rule rested on more than the calculated inequities of specific relations of production and exchange. In looking more to the carefully honed cultural representations of power, students of the colonial have turned their attention to the practices that privileged certain social categories and made them "easy to think." Not least, we have become more cognizant of how colonial vocabularies can slip surreptitiously from their historical moorings and reappear as explanatory concepts of historical practice rather than as folk categories that need to be explained.[49]

A focus in colonial studies on those tensions of empire that were at once intimate and broad has placed sex and sentiment not as metaphors of empire but as its constitutive elements.[50] Appreciating how much the personal was political has revamped the scope of our archival frames: housekeeping manuals, child-rearing handbooks, and medical guides share space with classified state papers, court proceedings, and commissions as defining texts in colonialism's cultures of documentation. Raymond Williams's treatment of culture as a site of contested not shared meaning has prompted students of the colonial to do the same. In turning from race as a thing to race as a porous and protean set of relations, colonial histories increasingly dwell on the seams of archived and nonarchived ascriptions to redefine colonial subsumptions on a broader terrain.[51] However we frame it, the issue turns on readings of the archives based on what we take to be evidence and what we expect to find. How can students of colonialisms so quickly and confidently turn to readings "against the grain" without moving along their grain first? How can we brush against them without a prior sense of archival texture and its granularity? How can we compare colonialisms without knowing the circuits of knowledge production in which they operated and the racial commensurabilities on which they relied? If a notion of colonial ethnography starts from the premise that archival production is itself both a process and a powerful technology of rule, then we need not only to brush

against the archive's received categories. We need to read for its regularities, for its logic of recall, for its densities and distributions, for its consistencies of misinformation, omission, and mistake—*along* the archival grain.

Assuming we know those scripts, I would argue, diminishes our analytic possibilities. It rests too comfortably on predictable stories with familiar plots. It diverts attention from how much colonial history writing has been shaped by nationalist historiographies and nation-bound projects. It leaves unquestioned the notion that colonial states were first and foremost information-hungry machines in which power accrued from the accumulation of more knowledge rather than the quality and redistribution of it. Moreover, it takes as a given that colonial statecraft was motivated and fueled by a reductive equation of knowledge to power and that colonial states sought more of both. Not least, it makes irrelevant failed proposals, utopian visions, and improbable projects because they never "happened" and thus were "nonevents."[52] Reading only against the grain of the colonial archive bypasses the power in the production of the archive itself.

Civilities and Credibilities in Archival Production

If colonial documents reflected the supremacy of reason, they also recorded an emotional economy manifest in disparate understandings of what was imagined, what was feared, what was witnessed, and what was overheard. Such a reading turns us to the structures of sentiment to which colonial bureaucrats subscribed, to the formulaic by which they abided, to the mix of dispassionate reason, impassioned plea, cultural script, and personal experience that made up what they chose to write to their superiors and in the folds of official view. Dutch colonial documents register this emotional economy in several ways: in the measured affect of official texts, in the biting critique reserved for marginalia, and in footnotes to official reports where assessments of cultural practice were often relegated and local knowledge was stored. Steven Shapin's set of compelling questions in his social history of truth could be that of colonial historians as well. What, he asks, counted as credible, what was granted epistemological virtue and by what social criteria? What sentiments and civilities made for "expert" colonial knowledge that endowed some persons with the credentials to generate trustworthy truth claims that were not conferred on others?

Colonial archives were, as Echevarria notes, legal

repositories of knowledge and official repositories of policy. But they were also repositories of good taste and bad faith. Scribes were charged with making fine-penned copies. But reports on the colonial order of things to the governor-general in Batavia and to the minister of colonies in the Hague often were composed by men of letters whose status in the colonial hierarchy was founded as much on their display of European learning as on their studied ignorance of local knowledge, on their skill at configuring events into familiar plots, on their cultivation of the fine arts of deference, dissemblance, and persuasion. All rested on subtle use of their cultural know-how and cultural wares. As Fanny Colonna once noted for French Algeria, the colonial politics of knowledge penalized those with too much local knowledge and those with not enough.[53] In the Indies, civil servants with too much knowledge of things Javanese were condemned for not appreciating the virtues of limited and selective familiarity.

Christopher Bayly, in a thoughtful study of the development of an intelligence system by the British in India, argues that the mastery of "affective knowledge" was an early concern of the British colonial state, which diminished throughout the nineteenth century as that state became more hierarchical and as governing became a matter of routine.[54] But I would argue the opposite: that affective knowledge was at the core of political rationality in its late colonial form. Colonial modernity hinged on a disciplining of one's agents, on a policing of the family, on Orwellian visions of intervention in the cultivation of compassion, contempt, and disdain.

The accumulation of affective knowledge was not then a *stage* out of which colonial states were eventually to pass. Key terms of the debates on poor whites and child-rearing practices from as late as the 1930s, just before the overthrow of Dutch rule, make that point again and again. When classified colonial documents argued against the support of abandoned mixed-blood children—and that "mothercare" (*moederzorg*) should *not* be replaced by "care of the state" (*staatszorg*)—they were putting affective responsibility at the heart of their political projects. When these same high officials wrote back and forth about how best to secure "strong attachments" to the Netherlands among a disaffected, estranged, and growing European population, *feeling* is the word that pervades their correspondence. Dutch authorities may never have agreed on how to cultivate European sensibilities in their young and on just how early in a child's development they imagined they needed to do so. But at stake in these deliberations over "upbringing"

and "rearing" were disquieted reflections on what it took to make someone "moved" by one set of sensory regimes and estranged from others. Colonial states and their authorities, not unlike metropolitan ones, had strong motivation for their abiding interest in the distribution of affect and a strong sense of why it mattered to colonial politics.

Cultural Logics and Archival Conventions

> The archive does not have the weight of tradition; and it does not constitute the library of libraries, outside time and place—it reveals the rules of practice. . . . its threshold of existence is established by the discontinuity that separates us from what we can no longer say.
> —Foucault, *The Archaelogy of Knowledge and the Discourse on Language*

One way to refigure our uses of the colonial archive is to pause at, rather than bypass, its conventions, those practices that make up its unspoken order of rubric and reference. Archival conventions might designate who were reliable "sources," what constituted "enough" evidence, and what could be inserted in the absence of information. Conventions suggest consensus, but it is not clear what colonial practitioners actually shared. Archival conventions were built upon a changing collection of colonial truths about what were secrets and what mattered to state security, what sorts of actions could be dismissed as prompted by personal revenge or crimes of passion or could be accredited as political subversions against the state.[55] Such conventions exposed the social taxonomies of race and rule but also how skillfully, awkwardly, and unevenly seasoned bureaucrats and fledgling practitioners knew the rules of the game.

Attention to these conventions may lead in two directions: to the consensual logics they inscribed but much more directly to their arbitrary rules and multiple points of dissension. Political conflicts show up in the changing viability of categories and disagreements about their use. But as Paul Starr suggests, "information out of place"—the failure of some kinds of practices, perceptions, and populations to fit into a state's ready system of classification—may tell more.[56] Detailed commentaries on European nurseries in the colonies might be expected to turn up in reports on education, but the very fact that they consistently showed up elsewhere—in reports on European pauperism and white poor relief and in recommendations to quell Creole discontent—suggests that what was "out of place" was often sensitive and that it was children cued to the wrong cultural sensibilities that were dangerously out of place.

Colonial Commissions as Stories That States Tell Themselves

As Ian Hacking says of social categories, archives produced as much as they recorded the realities they ostensibly only described. They told moral stories, they created precedent in the pursuit of evidence, and not least they create carefully tended histories. Nowhere is this history-making work more evident than in the form of the commission of inquiry or state commission. By definition, commissions organized knowledge, rearranged its categories, and prescribed what state officials were charged to know. As the anthropologist Frans Husken notes of Dutch commissions in colonial Java, "'when nothing else works and no decision can be reached, appoint a commission' was a favorite response of colonial authorities."[57] But commissions were not just hesitant pauses in policy and tactics of delay. Like statistics, they helped "determine . . . the character of social facts" and produced new truths as they produced new social realities.[58] They were responses to crisis that generated increased anxiety, substantiating the reality of that crisis itself.[59] By the time most commissions had run their course (or spawned their follow-up generation), they could be credited with having defined "turning points," justifications for intervention, and, not least, expert knowledge.

The various commissions produced on the problem of poor whites in the Indies between the 1870s and early 1900s and those carried out in South Africa between the early 1900s and the late 1920s are exemplary of what I have in mind. There are certain general features that they share.[60] Both produced published and publicized volumes: *Pauperism among the Europeans* (published between 1901 and 1902) and *The Problem of Poor Whites in South Africa* (published between 1929 and 1932).[61] Both commissions were about indigent Europeans and their inappropriate dispositions toward work, racial distance, sexual propriety, and colonial morality. Each requisitioned administrative energy and expertise and entailed several years of labor, thousands of pages of text, scores of interviewers, and hundreds of interviewees. Prominent civil and government figures graced their mastheads with authority. Both were redemptive texts offering plausible stories of state exoneration and targeted blame.

In the case of the Indies, the commission's starting point—that concubinage was the source of the poor white problem—prompted probing questionnaires on who bedded with whom, on bastard children, and on intimacies of the home that incurred the wrath of hundreds of irate colonial Europeans who refused to answer and condemned the Indies government as an "inquisitionary state." Both commissions were repositories of colonial anxieties, unsettling testimonies to the insecurity of white privilege, to the ambiguities of membership in the privileged category of "European," and to the making of a public welfare policy solidly based on race. Both worried less about the increasing numbers of impoverished whites because they worried over something else more. As stated in the Carnegie Commission, the "propinquity of . . . [poor white] dwellings" to "non-Europeans" tended to bring native and white into contact, to "counteract miscegenation," to weaken the color line, and to promote "social equality."[62] The worry was over an ease of meeting and conversation.

These commissions could and should be read for their extraordinary ethnographic content but also for the content in their form. First, like other colonial commissions, they marked off clusters of people who warranted state interest and state expense. Second, they were redemptive texts, structured to offer predictions based on causal accounts of exoneration and blame. Third, both commissions were documents to state historiography in the making and monuments to why history writing mattered to consolidating states. To prescribe the future, they rewrote the past in dramatic and compassionate narrative. In defining poverty in the present, they also dictated who later would count as white—and therefore whose children of what hue would be eligible for state aid.

In doing all of these things, they wrote, revised, and overwrote genealogies of race. Neither of these commissions were the first of their kind. On the contrary, they were made credible by how they mapped the past onto prescriptions for the present and predictions of the future. They also showed something more—how practices were historically congealed into events and made into things: how an increase of unemployment and impoverishment among European colonials became a "problem" called "poor whiteism," with attributes of its own. "Poor whiteism" defined physiologically and psychologically distinct sorts of persons, with aggregated ways of "being in the world," with specific dispositions and states of mind. Like other colonial commissions, these commissions were consummate producers of social kinds.

Commissions and statistics were features of statecraft in similar ways. Both were eighteenth-century inventions consolidated by the nineteenth-century liberal state.[63] Both instantiated the state's public accountability and its right to judge what was in society's collective and moral good. But commissions commanded more moral authority as they purported to scrutinize state practice, to reveal bureaucratic mistakes, and to produce new truths about the workings of the state itself. Moreover, these poor white commissions were quintessential products of "biopolitical" technologies. Not only did they link the relationship between parent and child, nursemaid and infant, to the security of the state. They sought ethnographic, eyewitness testimonies from participant-observers that what individuals did in their homes—whether they went barefoot, spoke only halting Dutch, lounged on their porches, or did not make their children say morning prayers—were practices linked directly to the state's audit of its own viability.

Both commissions and statistics were part of the "moral science" of the nineteenth century that coded and counted society's pathologies. While statistics used deviations from the mean to identify deviations from the norm, commissions joined those numbers with stories culled from individual "cases" to measures gradations of morality.[64] Commissions in turn affirmed the state's authority to make judgments about what was in society's collective and moral good. Both were prescriptive and probabilistic tools whose power was partially in their capacities to predict and divert politically dangerous possibilities.

Like statistics, the commission demonstrated the state's right to power through its will to truth. In the Indies, the Pauperism Commission conferred on the state moral authority by demonstrating its moral conscience and disinterested restraint, its willingness and commitment to critically reflect on its own mishaps, to seek the truth "at whatever cost." But its power rested in more than its calculation of the moral pulse of the present and its implications for the future. The Indies Commission justified its license to expend funds, time, and personnel in part by rehearsing the past and remembering and reminding its readership of its enduring weight. Historical narratives shape these texts with stories that deflected the causes of deprivations and inequities away from the present as they rehearsed the enduring burden of earlier policies of former administrations.

Finally, these commissions were quintessential quasistate technologies, both part of the state and not, at once a product of state agents but constituted invariably by members outside it. If modern states gain force in part by creating and maintaining an elusive boundary between themselves and civil society, as Tim Mitchell has argued,

such commissions exemplified that process.[65] Their specific subjects were state generated but often researched and written by those not in their salary. Both the Indies and Carnegie Commissions delegated bodies of experts equipped to assess morality (religious experts), deviance (lawyers, educators), and disease (doctors) and on whom the state conferred short-term and subject-specific voice and public authority. They instantiated the ways in which the state exercised its will to power by calling on outside expert authorities to verify the state's ability to stand in for public interest and its commitment to the public good.

Archival Seductions and State Secrets

As archivists are the first to note, to understand an archive one needs to understand the institutions that it served. Such information as what subjects are cross-referenced, what parts are rewritten, and what quotes are cited not only tell us about how decisions are rendered but how colonial histories are written and remade. Information out of place underscores what categories matter, which ones become commonsense and then fall out of favor. Not least, they provide road maps to anxieties that evade more articulate form.

The commission is one sort of archival convention, while "state secrets" are another. States traffic in the production of secrets and the selective dissemination of them. In this regard, the Dutch colonial state was gifted at its task.[66] As Weber once noted, the "official secret" was a specific invention of bureaucracy that was "fanatically defended" by it. The designations "secret," "very secret," and "confidential" registered more than fictions of denied entry and public access. Nor did they mostly signal the pressing political concerns of the colonial state. More important, such codes of concealment were the fetishized features of the state itself. State secrets named and produced privileged knowledge, designated privileged readers, while reminding the latter what knowledge should be coveted and what was important to know. The secreted report, like the commission, created categories it purported to do no more than describe. In the Indies, the classified document commanded a political weight that called for secret police, paid informants, and experts.

Secrets imply limited access, but what is more striking in the Dutch colonial archives is how rarely those items classified as "confidential" (*vertrouwelijk, zeer vertrouwelijk, geheim,* and *zeer geheim*) were secrets at all. Some surely dealt with clandestine police and military tactics (such as preparations for troop movements to protect planters against an attack), but far more of these documents were about prosaic, public parts of Indies life.[67] If one could argue that the disquieting presence of European beggars and homeless Dutchmen in the streets of Batavia were "secrets" to those in the Netherlands, they certainly were not to the majority of Europeans who lived in the colony's urban centers.

What was classified about these reports was not their subject matter—in this case, indigent "full-blooded" Europeans and their mixed-blood descendants—but rather the conflict among officials about how to act on the problem, their disparate assessments of what was the cause and how many there were. Some reports were classified because officials could not agree on whether there were twenty-nine mixed-bloods in straitened circumstances or tens of thousands.[68] In short, documents were classified as "sensitive" and "secret" sometimes because of the magnitude of a problem—other times because officials could not agree on what the problems were. But perhaps what is more surprising is the range of confidentialities that students of colonialism expect them to divulge. State secrets are not necessarily secreted truths about the state but rather promises of confidences shared. If state secrets are more attention-getting annotations than conventions of concealment, then how state secrets were produced, what was a secret at one time and later not, may index the changing terms of what was considered commonsense, as well as changes in political rationality. As Marc Ventresca argues in a study of why and when states count, statistical information in the eighteenth century was considered a source of state power and therefore not published. Public access to state statistics was a nineteenth-century phenomenon.[69] State secrets made up a basic feature of the colonial archive, a telling element in the production of fictions of access displayed by their content as well as form.

Colonial Archives as "Systems of Expectation"

To take up Jean and John Comaroff's invitation to "create new colonial archives of our own" may entail not only, as they rightly urge, attention to new kinds of sources but different ways of approaching those we already have, different ways of reading than we have done.[70] In turning from an extractive to a more ethnographic project, our readings need to move in new ways through archives both along their fault lines as much as

against their grain. De Certeau once defined the science of history as a redistribution in space, the act of changing something into something else. He warned that historical labors in the archives must do more than "simply adopt former classifications"; they must break away from the constraints of "series H in the National Archives" and be replaced with new "codes of recognition" and "systems of expectation" of our own.[71] But such a strategy really depends on what we think we already know. For students of colonialisms, such codes of recognition and systems of expectation are at the very heart of what we still need to learn about colonial polities. The breadth of global reference and span of lateral vision that colonial regimes unevenly embraced suggest that ethnographies of the archives rather than extractions from them may be more appropriate for identifying how nations, empires, and racialized regimes were fashioned—not in ways that display confident knowledge and know-how but in paper trails and traces that bear the imprint of disquieted and expectant modes.

NOTES

This essay first appeared in *Archival Science* 2, nos. 1–2 (2002): 87–109, and is reprinted by permission. It represents a condensed version of chapter 1 from my book in progress, *Along the Archival Grain* (Princeton: Princeton University Press, forthcoming). Parts of it are based on the 1996 Lewis Henry Morgan Lectures delivered at the University of Rochester, entitled "Ethnography in the Archives: Movements on the Historic Turn."

1. E. E. Evans-Pritchard, "Social Anthropology: Past and Present, The Marett Lecture, 1950," in his *Social Anthropology and Other Essays* (New York: Free Press, 1951), 152; Claude Lévi-Strauss, *The Savage Mind* (Chicago: Chicago University Press, 1966), 256.

2. For some sense of the range of different agendas of the current "historic turn," see Nicholas Dirks, Geoff Eley, and Sherry Ortner, eds., *Culture, Power, History* (Princeton: Princeton University Press, 1994); Terrence J. MacDonald, ed., *The Historic Turn in the Human Sciences* (Ann Arbor: University of Michigan Press, 1996); specifically on history in the anthropological imagination, see Gerald Sider and Gavin Smith, eds., *Between History and Histories: The Making of Silences and Commemorations* (Toronto: University of Toronto Press, 1997). Also see Richard Fox, "For a Nearly New Culture History," in *Recapturing Anthropology: Working in the Present*, ed. Richard G. Fox (Santa Fe: School of American Research Press, 1991), 93–114, and James Faubion, "History in Anthropology," *Annual Review of Anthropology* 22 (1993): 35–54.

3. See, for example, the introductions and essays in Nicholas Dirks, ed., *Colonialism and Culture* (Ann Arbor: University of Michigan Press, 1992), and in Frederick Cooper and Ann Laura Stoler, eds., *Tensions of Empire: Colonial Cultures*

in a Bourgeois World (Berkeley: University of California Press, 1997).

4. See my "Genealogies of the Intimate," in *Carnal Knowledge and Imperial Power: Race and the Intimate in Colonial Rule* (Berkeley: University of California Press, 2002).

5. See Michel de Certeau, "The Historiographic Operation" (1974), in his *The Writing of History* (New York: Columbia University Press, 1988).

6. See, for example, Michel-Rolph Trouillot, *Silencing the Past: Power and the Production of History* (Boston: Beacon, 1995); David William Cohen, *The Combing of History* (Chicago: University of Chicago Press, 1994); and Ann Laura Stoler and Karen Strassler, "Castings for the Colonial: Memory Work in 'New Order' Java," *Comparative Studies in Society and History* 42, no. 1 (2000): 4–48 and the references therein.

7. E. E. Evans-Pritchard, *Anthropology and History* (Manchester: Manchester University Press, 1961), 5.

8. See Carlo Ginzburg, *Clues, Myths, and the Historical Method* (Baltimore: Johns Hopkins University Press, 1989).

9. Bernard Cohn, "History and Anthropology: The State of Play," *Comparative Studies in Society and History* 22, no. 2 (1980): 198–221.

10. On the trips to archives as "feats of [male] prowess" in nineteenth-century middle-class culture, see Bonnie G. Smith, "Gender and the Practices of Scientific History: The Seminar and Archival Research in the Nineteenth-Century," *American Historical Review* 100, no. 4–5 (1995): 1150–76.

11. Ranajit Guha, "The Proses of Counter-insurgency" (1983), in *Culture, Power, History,* ed. Dirks, Eley, and Ortner, 336–71; Greg Dening, *The Death of William Gooch: A History's Anthropology* (Honolulu: University of Hawaii Press, 1995), 54.

12. Carlo Ginzburg, "Clues: Roots of an Evidential Paradigm," in his *Clues, Myths, and the Historical Method,* 96–125.

13. David William Cohen, *Burying SM: The Politics of Knowledge and the Sociology of Power in Africa* (Portsmouth, NH: Heineman, 1992).

14. Joanne Rappaport, *Cumbe Reborn: An Andean Ethnography of History* (Chicago: University of Chicago Press, 1994). Also see the contributions to Sarah Nuttall and Carli Coetzee, eds., *Negotiating the Past: The Making of Memory in South Africa* (Capetown: Oxford University Press, 1998).

15. See Andrew Ashforth, *The Politics of Official Discourse in Twentieth-Century South Africa* (Oxford: Clarendon Press, 1990), 5.

16. This phrase was used by Jane Sherron De Hart to underscore the "problematics of evidence" in contemporary historical reconstruction. See "Oral Sources and Contemporary History: Dispelling Old Assumptions," *Journal of American History* 80 (September 1993): 582.

17. Jacques Derrida, *Archive Fever: A Freudian Impression* (Chicago: University of Chicago Press, 1995).

18. Natalie Davis, *Fiction in the Archives: Pardon Tales and Their Tellers in Sixteenth-Century France* (Stanford: Stanford University Press, 1987); Thomas Richards, *The Imperial Archive: Knowledge and the Fantasy of Empire* (London: Verso, 1993); Roberto Gonzalez Echevarria, *Myth and Archive: A Theory of Latin American Narrative* (Cambridge: Cambridge

University Press, 1990); Sonia Combe, *Archives Interdites: Les peur francaises face a l'Histoire contemporaine* (Paris: Albin Michel, 1994). See Dominick LaCapra, "History, Language, and Reading," *American Historical Review* (June 1995): 807, where he also notes that the "problem of reading in the archives has increasingly become a concern of those doing archival research."

19. See, for example, Dening's *The Death of William Gooch: A History's Anthropology* (Honolulu: University of Hawaii Press, 1995).

20. Trouillot, *Silencing the Past*; Cohen, *Combing of History.*

21. Smith, "Gender and the Practices of Scientific History."

22. On the history of archives and how archivists have thought about it, see Ernst Posner's classic essay, "Some Aspects of Archival Development since the French Revolution" (1940), in *A Modern Archives Reader,* ed. Maygene Daniels and Timothy Walch (Washington, DC: National Archives and Record Service, 1984), 3–21; and Michel Duchein, "The History of European Archives and the Development of the Archival Profession in Europe," *American Archivist* 55 (winter 1992): 14–25.

23. See, for example, Richard Berner, *Archival Theory and Practice in the United States: An Historical Analysis* (Seattle: University of Washington Press, 1983); Kenneth E. Foote, "To Remember and Forget: Archives, Memory, and Culture," *American Archivist* 53, no. 3 (1990): 378–93; Terry Cook, "Mind over Matter: Towards a New Theory of Archival Appraisal," in *The Archival Imagination: Essays in Honour of Hugh A. Taylor,* ed. Barbara L. Craig (Ontario: Association of Canadian Archivists, 1992), 38–69; and James M. O'Toole, "On the Idea of Uniqueness," *American Archivist* 57, no. 4 (1994): 632–59. For some sense of the changes in how archivists themselves have framed their work over the last fifteen years, see articles in *The American Archivist.*

24. Terry Cook, "Electronic Records, Paper Minds: The Revolution in Information Management and Archives in the Post-Custodial and Post-Modernist Era," *Archives and Manuscripts* 22, no. 2 (1994): 300–329.

25. This metaphoric move is most evident in contributions to the two special issues of *History of the Human Sciences* devoted to "the archive" (1, no. 4 [November 1998] and 12, no. 2 [May 1999]). Derrida's valorization of "the archive" as imaginary and metaphor predominates both. On the archive as metaphor, see also Allan Sekula, "The Body and the Archive," *October* 39 (winter 1986): 3–64

26. Michel Foucault, *The Archaeology of Knowledge and the Discourse on Language* (New York: Pantheon, 1972), esp. Part III, "The Statement and the Archive," 79–134.

27. See, for example, Patrick Geary's *Phantoms of Remembrance: Memory and Oblivion at the End of the First Millennium* (Princeton: Princeton University Press, 1994), esp. "Archival Memory and the Destruction of the Past," 81–114.

28. Ian Hacking, *The Taming of Chance* (New York: Cambridge University Press, 1990); Steven Shapin, *A Social History of Truth: Civility and Science in Seventeenth-Century England* (Chicago: University of Chicago Press, 1994); Mary Poovey, *A History of the Modern Fact: Problem of Knowledge in the Sciences of Wealth and Society* (Chicago: University of Chicago Press, 1998); Alain Desrosieres, *The Politics of Large Numbers:*

A History of Statistical Reasoning (Cambridge: Harvard University Press, 1998); Silvana Patriarca, *Numbers and Nationhood: Writing Statistics in Nineteenth-Century Italy* (Cambridge: Cambridge University Press, 1996). On the power of "suasive utterance" in the making of scientific truth claims, see Christopher Norris, "Truth, Science, and the Growth of Knowledge," *New Left Review* 210 (1995): 105–23; Lorraine Daston, *Classical Probability in the Enlightenment* (Princeton: Princeton University Press, 1988).

29. Anthony Grafton, *The Footnote: A Curious History* (Cambridge: Harvard University Press, 1997).

30. Carlo Ginzburg, *The Cheese and the Worms: The Cosmos of a Sixteenth-Century Miller* (London: Penguin, 1982), xvii, xviii.

31. Davis, *Fiction in the Archives*, 4.

32. Derrida, *Archive Fever*, 4.

33. Trouillot, *Silencing the Past*, 55.

34. Nicholas Dirks, "Colonial Histories and Native Informants: Biography of an Archive," *Orientalism and the Postcolonial Predicament: Perspectives on South Asia*, ed. Carol A. Breckenridge and Peter van der Veer (Philadelphia: University of Pennsylvania Press, 1993), 279–213.

35. Christopher Bayly, *Empire and Information: Intelligence Gathering and Social Communication in India, 1780–1870* (Cambridge: Cambridge University Press, 1996).

36. Ann Laura Stoler, "In Cold Blood: Hierarchies of Credibility and the Politics of Colonial Narratives," *Representations* 37 (1992): 151–89.

37. See Foucault, *Archaelogy of Knowledge,* esp. Part III, "The Statement and the Archive," 79–134.

38. Richards, *Imperial Archive*, 11.

39. Echevarria, *Myth and Archive*, 30.

40. Thus for Richards, Hilton's *Lost Horizon* and Kipling's *Kim* are entries in a Victorian archive that was the "prototype for a global system of domination through circulation, an apparatus for controlling territory by producing, distributing and consuming information about it." Richards, *Imperial Archive,* 17.

41. This link between state power and what counts as history was long ago made by Hegel in *The Philosophy of History,* as Hayden White (*The Content of the Form: Narrative Discourse and Historical Representation* [Baltimore: Johns Hopkins University Press, 1987]), points out:

> It is only the state which first presents subject-matter that is not only adapted to the prose of History, but involves the production of such history in the very progress of its own being. (12)

42. See Echevarria, *Myth and Archive,* 31, for a detailed etymology of the term.

43. See White, *Content of the Form,* esp. 26–57.

44. On this point, see Trouillot, *Silencing the Past.* On the relationship between state formation and archival production, see Duchein, "History of European Archives."

45. See my "Racial Histories and Their Regimes of Truth," *Political Power and Social Theory* 11 (1997): 183–255.

46. For a more detailed account of these changes in research agenda, see the new preface to my *Capitalism and Confrontation in Sumatra's Plantation, 1870–1979* (Ann Arbor: University of Michigan Press, 1995).

47. I discuss some of these issues in "Perceptions of Protest: Defining the Dangerous in Colonial Sumatra," *American Ethnologist* 12, no. 4 (1985): 642–58.

48. For a recent and sophisticated version of this culling project, see Shahid Amin, *Event, Metaphor, Memory: 1922–1992* (Berkeley: University of California Press, 1995).

49. See my "Genealogies of the Intimate."

50. See my "Sexual Affronts and Racial Frontiers," *Comparative Studies in Society and History* 34, no. 3 (1992): 514–51.

51. See J. Chandler, A. Davidson, and H. Harootunian, eds., *Questions of Evidence: Proof, Practice, and Persuasion across the Disciplines* (Chicago: University of Chicago Press, 1994).

52. These points are further developed in my "Developing Historical Negatives: Race and the Disquieting Visions of a Colonial State," in *Historical Anthropology and Its Vicissitudes,* ed. Brian Axel (Durham, NC: Duke University Press, forthcoming).

53. See Fanny Colonna, "Educating Conformity in French Colonial Algeria," in *Tensions of Empire,* ed. Cooper and Stoler, 346–70.

54. Bayly, *Empire and Information.*

55. On the administrative distinctions between the "political" versus the "private" and the "criminal" versus the "subversive," see my "Perceptions of Protest," and my "Labor in the Revolution," *Journal of Asian Studies* 47, no. 2 (1988): 227–47.

56. Paul Starr, "Social Categories and Claims in the Liberal State," in *How Classification Works: Nelson Goodman among the Social Sciences,* ed. Mary Douglas and David Hull (Edinburgh: Edinburgh University Press, 1992), 154–79.

57. Frans Husken, "Declining Welfare in Java: Government and Private Inquiries, 1903–1914," in *The Late Colonial State in Indonesia,* ed. Robert Cribb (Leiden: KITLV, 1994), 213.

58. Ian Hacking, "How Should We Do the History of Statistics?" in *The Foucault Effect: Studies in Governmentality,* ed. Graham Burchell, Colin Gordon, and Peter Miller (Chicago: University of Chicago Press, 1991), 181.

59. This is a good example of what Ian Hacking calls "dynamic nominalism" or "the looping effect" in categorization.

60. I discuss the politics of colonial comparisons elsewhere and therefore will not do so here. I have used the 1902 Indies Pauperism Commission, commentaries around it, and inquiries that preceded it in much of my writing over the last fifteen years on the construction of colonial racial categories. The South African Carnegie Commission and the inquiries that preceded it are compared in a chapter in my forthcoming book *Along the Archival Grain.* A more general discussion of the politics of comparison can be found in my paper "Tense and Tender Ties: American History Meets Postcolonial Studies," delivered at the Organization of American Historians in April 2000, and in my paper "Beyond Comparison: Colonial Statecraft and the Racial Politics of Commensurability," delivered as a keynote address at the Australian Historical Association in Adelaide, July 2000.

61. Students of colonialism could come up with a host of others. For an unusual example of someone who deals with the commission as a particular form of official knowledge, in this case of the South African Native Affairs Commission, see Ashforth, *Politics of Official Discourse.* Also see Frans Husken's

discussion of the Declining Welfare Commission in Java, in "Declining Welfare in Java."

62. *The Poor White Problem in South Africa,* Report of the Carnegie Commission (Stellenbosch: Pro Ecclesia Drukkerij, 1932), xx.

63. Royal commissions have a longer history still. See, for example, David Loades, "The Royal Commissions," in his *Power in Tudor England* (New York: St. Martin's Press, 1997), 70–82. On statistics and state building, see Alain Desrosieres, "Statistics and the State," in his *Politics of Large Numbers,* 178–209. For the twentieth century, see William J. Breen, "Foundations, Statistics, and State-Building," *Business History Review* 68 (1994): 451–82.

64. See Arjun Appardurai's discussion of numerical representation in colonial India as a "key to normalizing the pathology of difference," in "Number in the Colonial Imagination," in *Modernity at Large: Cultural Dimensions of Globalization* (Minneapolis: University of Minnesota Press, 1996), 114–38.

65. See Gramsci's discussion of "state and civil society" in *Selections from the Prison Notebooks,* ed. Quintin Hoare and Geoffrey Smith (London: Lawrence and Wishart, 1971), esp.

257–64; and Timothy Mitchell, "The Limits of the State," *American Political Science Review* 85 (1991): 77–96.

66. George Simmel (*The Sociology of George Simmel,* ed. Kurt Wolff [London: Free Press, 1950]) once wrote:

the historical development of society is in many respects characterized by the fact that what at an earlier time was manifest enters the protection of secrecy; and that, conversely, what once was a secret, no longer needs such protection but reveals itself. (331)

67. Algemeen Rijksarchief, Geheim No. 1144/2284. From the Department of Justice to the Governor-General, Batavia, 29 April 1873.

68. Algemeen Rijksarchief, Verbaal No. 47. From the Department of Justice to the Governor-General, 28 March 1874.

69. Marc Ventresca, "When States Count: Institutional and Political Dynamics in Modern Census Establishment, 1800–1993." Ph.D. diss., Stanford University, 1995, 50.

70. Jean and John Comaroff, *Ethnography and the Historical Imagination* (Boulder: Westview Press, 1992).

71. De Certeau "Historiographical Operation," 74–75.

The Provincial Archive as a Place of Memory

The Role of Former Slaves in the Cuban War of Independence (1895–98)

Rebecca J. Scott

Few questions of historical interpretation are more passionately debated than those that have become intertwined with a national narrative and with the definition of how a country came to be what it is imagined to be. For the island nation of Cuba, political independence was forged in a lengthy series of wars against Spanish colonial rule, ending in a direct encounter with U.S. expansionism. Those wars began in 1868 and concluded in 1898 with the departure of Spanish troops, followed by a military occupation of the island by U.S. forces. In 1902 the first Cuban republic emerged, but it was bound by the infamous Platt Amendment, which guaranteed to the United States a right of renewed intervention. The wars themselves were thus both a triumph and a defeat, a touchstone for national pride, and—in the outcome—a source of nationalist disappointment.

Each political generation in Cuba interpreted the wars of independence anew, trying to incorporate the heroes and the dynamic of those wars into a story that legitimated—or, in the hands of critics, challenged—the subsequent order of things. After the victory of the Cuban revolution in 1958–59, the new leadership undertook a process of socialist construction that was also a refusal of U.S. hegemony, and the active recollection of past struggles became a key element in the legitimation of current ones. By the 1970s the sweep of Cuban history came to be officially described as *cien años de lucha,* "one hundred years of struggle." The 1895–98 war and selected members of its pantheon of heroes—particularly José Martí and Antonio Maceo—had been folded into a con-tinuous battle against external imperial enemies and domestic antipatriots, and the 1959 triumph construed as the apotheosis of the formation of the Cuban nation.[1]

Such an interpretation required that one of the most delicate questions in Cuban history—that of race and slavery—be handled in a somewhat gingerly way. Some of the heroes of the first war for independence (1868–78) had been slaveholders. In the postrevolutionary context it became important to emphasize the moment at which they liberated their slaves rather than the long years during which they had profited from slave labor or the constraints they had imposed on those they nominally freed.[2] Other officers and soldiers in the wars of independence had been former slaves or the descendants of slaves. In the climate of revolutionary enthusiasm after 1959, these earlier black and mulatto rebels came to be seen as the embodiment of a struggle for social justice as well as for national independence, their efforts to break the chains of colonialism a continuation of prior struggles to escape or break the chains of slavery. But it was important that they be seen to have struggled primarily as *Cubans,* striving toward a transracial national liberation and not as black rebels locked into an inconclusive conflict with a hesitant white nationalist leadership. In the postrevolutionary view, black and white rebels by 1895–98 shared ideals of racial "confraternity" that were later betrayed by the compromised twentieth-century republics but then vindicated by the more recent revolutionary process.[3]

In describing the national narrative in this way, I do not

mean to suggest that it was merely a convenient invention or a conscious distortion. The story of the achievement of Cuban national independence *is* a stirring one, and the transracial ideal of Cuban nationality that held sway at the turn of the nineteenth into the twentieth century was an ideological and social achievement of remarkable dimensions to be impressed by Cuba's accomplishment, one has only to contrast it with the Anglo-Saxonism that had developed in the United States by midcentury or the systematic disfranchisement of African Americans allowed to stand by the U.S. Supreme Court in a key decision in 1903.[4] The 1901 Cuban constitution, though often scorned for its incorporation of the Platt Amendment, was equally notable for its categorical guarantee of universal manhood suffrage, despite pressures from the U.S. occupiers to institute more restrictive measures.[5] Cuban society, just fifteen years after slave emancipation, endorsed a formal definition of citizenship that mirrored the famous statement attributed to Antonio Maceo—that in Cuba there were neither whites nor blacks but only Cubans. This forthright assertion was grounded both in Maceo's principled antiracism and in the unity that he sought to build in the wars of independence.[6] When the wars were over, one of the strongest guarantors of such equality was the presence of black veterans, whose sense of entitlement as citizens was unmistakable.

For historians, however, a coherent and in many ways admirable national narrative can be both an inspiration to research and a significant obstacle to understanding. By 1994–95, when the collective project I will describe shortly was taking shape, the currents of challenge to this aspect of the Cuban national narrative were unmistakable. In 1995 Aline Helg published an innovative work entitled *Our Rightful Share: The Afro-Cuban Struggle for Equality, 1886–1912,* in which she criticized many of Cuba's national heroes and denounced what she saw as a "myth of racial equality" that "undermined the formation of a black collective consciousness." A key element of this myth, in her view, was a false portrait of the 1895–98 war: "the myth inculcated the idea that racial equality had been achieved in the Cuban military forces that fought against Spain."[7] At the same time, Ada Ferrer was completing a doctoral dissertation on race and nationality in the period of the Cuban wars of independence, subsequently published as *Insurgent Cuba: Race, Nation, and Revolution, 1868–1898.* Ferrer demonstrated the continued coexistence within Cuban national ideology of both racism and antiracism. In contrast to Helg, Ferrer emphasized that nationalist ideas and the experience of shared military struggle served

both as a weapon against discrimination and as a cover for discrimination.[8]

Within Cuba, young scholars had begun to pose questions about the remembering of national heroes and the representation of the *mambí,* the Cuban separatist soldier.[9] The distinguished Cuban philosopher Fernando Martínez Heredia pointed more and more insistently to the role of racism in Cuban history—not racism as a "legacy" of slavery alone but racism as an active ideology integrally connected to Cuban nationalism.[10] The historian Jorge Ibarra directly engaged Helg's portrait of the founding figures of Cuban independence, conceding portions of her argument while vigorously refusing her effort to locate the origins of the "myth of racial democracy" in the leadership of the Cuban revolutionary army of 1895–98. Ibarra situated such mythmaking and opportunism as there was in the twentieth-century republic itself, not the independence struggle.[11]

In this context, the study of black and *mulato* soldiers in the wars of independence, their experiences and aspirations, and the opportunities and exclusions that they faced became a matter for urgent examination—and immediate contention. The presence of former slaves among the rebels, and of black officers within the insurgent ranks, was invoked on every side of the debate—yet even so basic a datum as their approximate numbers could not be estimated. Much of the polemic involved rereadings of familiar texts and attributions and reattributions of motives. Ferrer broke new ground by looking carefully at recruitment and surrenders, as reflected in Cuban and Spanish archives, and by giving a close reading to rebel correspondence and to the memoir literature, including the rarely cited autobiography of a black soldier, Ricardo Batrell Oviedo. But because Ferrer's focus was the entire island over the thirty years of anticolonial warfare, and because most lists of rebels included no racial labels, even she found it difficult to describe the social composition of the Ejército Libertador with precision.

A logical next step was to narrow the focus enough to get closer to the ground in a particular zone, to plunge into local and regional archives to see if there was some way to circumvent the silence on race imposed first by the record keepers and later by protective nationalists. In the mid-1990s, as politicians and scholars began to prepare for the centennial of the end of the 1895–98 war, several historians were converging on a single region on the south coast of the island, Cienfuegos. During the second half of the nineteenth century, the river valleys of Cienfuegos had been ideal for the growing, processing, and transporting of sugar, and the region had developed into a major plantation zone. Cienfuegos was, moreover, a dramatic theater of war in the final independence struggle. With thousands of former slaves and a large rebel brigade, its history could provide an ideal case study.

More important, however, was the quality of its local archive. The Provincial Historical Archive, located on Twenty-seventh Street, just off the Plaza Martí, occupies the first floor of a converted house, next to a preschool playground and directly opposite a fire station. Researches and deliberations there are thus invariably accompanied, through the open windows, by sirens and diesel engines in times of fire or fire drill and, more often, by the young firemen's baseball practice, catcalls, and conscientious washing of the trucks with the fire hoses when there are no fires. The permeability of the reading room to sound is matched by the vulnerability of the whole building to weather: tropical storms blow holes in the roof, sending water pouring down. The decision of the upstairs neighbors to raise pigs on their terrace did not improve matters.

But the richness of the holdings and the vitality of the intellectual life in and around the archive compensate for these *inconvenientes*. Cienfuegos is a city known not only for its sugar-exporting port but also for its music, its architecture, and its revolutionary traditions. The archive's director at the time, Orlando García Martínez, born in a working-class neighborhood of the town and trained as a historian at the University of Las Villas during the 1970s, had been tenacious in pulling documents of all kinds into the archive, while serving also as president of the provincial Union of Artists and Writers of Cuba (UNEAC). He has succeeded in preserving the municipality's voluminous notarial records, judicial records, and minutes of the town council, reflecting both the history of the town and the history of its agricultural hinterland. García, moreover, had developed a reputation for being willing to retrieve that which other state agencies plan to throw away, lining up trucks to bring the bundles to the archive instead of the paper recycling facility. Thus the Cienfuegos archive now holds some of the judicial records of the larger provincial capital of Santa Clara; the municipal records of the key sugar town of Santa Isabel de las Lajas; the original drafts of the 1961 cadastral survey of property in the entire region; and the before, during, and after writing samples of every person from Cienfuegos taught to read and write during the revolutionary Literacy Campaign of the early 1960s.[12]

García knows most of these collections of documents well and has long been writing the history of the region, including a close examination of its wartime experiences.

The archive's emergence as a locus for the study of race and revolution, however, dates to the arrival there in 1994 of a visiting researcher, Michael Zeuske. Born in Halle, East Germany, Zeuske was trained by the distinguished historian Manfred Kossok of the University of Leipzig, wrote his doctoral dissertation on an early nationalist movement in Venezuela, and prepared a second doctorate on Latin American independence struggles in comparative perspective. His scholarly formation inclined him to look at the big picture and to seek parallels between Latin American and European revolutions. But with the emergence of a movement of popular contestation on his home ground of Leipzig during 1989, and the fall of the Berlin wall later that year, followed by the dramatic transformation of the East German academic climate, Zeuske chose to shift his research focus. He moved away from the macrostructural analysis of revolution and sought to understand a social movement from the inside. He decided, moreover, to undertake sustained research in Cuba, where he had lived as a boy in 1963–65, when his father, Max Zeuske, had been a visiting East German specialist on assignment with the new revolutionary Cuban government, charged with assisting in the formation of the first worker-peasant university in Havana.

Michael Zeuske brought to the documentary riches of the Cienfuegos archives a new and inherently volatile question: what *was* the actual pattern of political incorporation of former slaves in rural Cuba after the abolition of slavery in 1886? Did they indeed join the anticolonial movement in large numbers in 1895, or were they perhaps drawn into the webs of political clientelism that expanded as the Spanish colonial state lowered property requirements for voting and made room for a legitimated Cuban "autonomism" in the 1880s and 1890s? Zeuske began work in the archives of Santa Clara and Cienfuegos, compiling lists of rebel soldiers and scrutinizing them assiduously.

Painstaking scrutiny was necessary because racial labels almost never appear on lists of this kind. The strength of the transracial, or race-blind, ideal of nationality was such that Cuban separatists generally declined to record racial attributions when drawing up recruitment lists, and the victorious Cuban nationalists also refrained from including them when they compiled nominal records of rebel veterans. In effect, the written record was intentionally designed to ratify José Martí and Antonio Maceo's principle of race blindness. It thus erased evidence of racial distinctions. Even if such attributions had been consequential in social interactions and frequently uttered as explicit labels, they would not appear in the written record. The challenge for Zeuske was to find some way of identifying the social—and perhaps racial—categories that were behind the lists he had found but that the lists themselves never employed.

This same problem had plagued my own comparative work on postemancipation societies. In both Cuba and Brazil—in sharp contrast to the United States—former slaves were usually not identified as such in most written records, and thus from the point of view of the documents they vanished into a vast rural population, however unlikely it might be that their status as former slaves had disappeared in social practice.[13] I was trying to work around this archival obstacle by identifying individual slaves who had lived on particular plantations and following them into freedom through plantation records for the 1880s and 1890s. Particularly detailed documents existed for two adjacent plantations—Soledad and Santa Rosalía—located a few miles from the town of Cienfuegos. I decided to restrict my focus to that region in hopes that I might learn enough through the history of identifiable individuals to be able to trace more generally the situation of former slaves and their descendants. So in 1996, I too ended up smelling the diesel of the fire trucks from the reading room of the Provincial Historical Archive of Cienfuegos.

The point here is not to marvel at the coincidences that brought three strangers together—one from central Cuba, one from Saxony, and one from Michigan—and turned them into friends and collaborators. After all, life is full of such coincidences. What is more interesting is the way in which working in a specific regional archive nourished three different methodological approaches to these questions and opened up possibilities for expansion of the research itself, particularly through the avenue of oral history. The oral histories in turn "electrified," to use Michael Zeuske's phrase, the whole enterprise. I shall briefly sketch the three methodologies and the preliminary findings and then turn to the oral history—at which point the archive appears, as in my title, as a place of active remembering rather than simply a place of documents.

First, Zeuske's approach. Concentrating on the lists of recruits that he had compiled and on the Cienfuegos sugar zones of Santa Isabel de las Lajas and Cruces, he set out to estimate the proportion of those in the rebel ranks who were actually former slaves, based on what he described as a "structural/name-based" technique. After identifying what he believed to be the major "slave surnames" for Lajas and Cruces, those adopted by slaves from the largest plantations as they achieved their freedom, he combed the enlistment records to find them. To

our collective surprise he came up with very low estimates of the numbers of former slaves among the rebels. He even noted that the names of former slaves from Lajas and Cruces were more likely to be found on the lists of those who voted in the colonial elections in favor of the mild-mannered Autonomists than in the ranks of the Cuban rebels. When he began to present these results, several of us critiqued his methods and thought that his estimates had to be wrong.[14] In all of our minds, the independence war has long been linked to the fight against slavery, and it seemed somehow logical that former slaves would naturally gravitate to the rebel ranks. What did it mean if they did not?

Based in the archive itself, with very few material resources but a great deal of determination, Orlando García decided in 1997 to tackle the issue of the social composition of the Liberation Army head-on, undertaking the compilation of a relational database that would include every soldier who served in the Cienfuegos Brigade of the rebel army between 1895 and 1898. Using pension records, manuscript recruitment lists, notarial archives, and published lists of veterans, he began to develop not a mere sample but a complete portrait of one brigade. By the brute-force method of reading every available record, he would try to create a minibiography for each soldier. In the process, he came across racial labels for individuals in collateral records, particularly the baptismal records sometimes included with pension requests, even though such labels are absent from the military records. He was by this means able to develop something of a statistical profile of the composition of the force—though, of course, the racial labels, like any contingent and relational social construction, shift and turn from document to document.

The risks and the benefits of this strategy are equally clear. It takes the patience of a saint to assemble and complete over a thousand such personal dossiers, rigorously maintaining the source references necessary to follow up on any detail as necessary. Moreover, computers are notoriously unhappy in a humid tropical environment beset by power outages. But García succeeded. At an international conference held at the Cienfuegos archive in March 1998 he shared the first results, jolting one of Cuba's most distinguished historians, Jorge Ibarra, into a vigorous counterattack.

García argued that there were, in effect, two successive rebel armies in Cienfuegos. The first dated to 1895–96 and was predominately composed of men from the countryside, many of them black and *mulato*. The early recruitment of rebels seems to have mirrored the composition of the rural working population of the Cienfuegos hinterland and thus was nearly equally divided between those who traced their ancestry primarily to Spain or the Canary Islands and those who traced it to Africa. Casualties in the early encounters with the Spanish forces were high. After a dramatic and disastrous set of rebel reverses in 1897, which brought large numbers of surrenders, the war settled into a harrowing stalemate. Net recruitment to the insurgent ranks fell below zero. Following the explosion of the U.S. battleship *Maine* in early 1898, however, it began to appear likely that the United States itself would enter the war and that Spain might actually lose. In 1898 new Cuban recruits to the rebellion appeared—but this time they were disproportionately white and urban, of some schooling, often professionals. By rebel policy, even if they did not have military training or experience, their degrees gave them immediate access to officer status, thereby privileging them over longer-serving and more experienced black and *mulato* soldiers.[15]

When the war ended in late 1898, many of the officers of this "second army" stepped forward to inherit the nationalist mantle—but many of the earlier black and *mulato* officers and soldiers had been killed in battle or by disease or were consciously sidelined.[16] The chronology sketched by García for the Cienfuegos Brigade makes it easier to understand how very disparate images of race and the war experience might coexist, encompassing both a memory of black leadership and cross-racial collaboration, from 1895 through 1897, and a sense of displacement of black officers and soldiers by white ones, particularly as the war came to a close in 1898.

García's findings also helped to explain why the war might raise very high expectations among Cubans of African descent, expectations that when disappointed would leave a legacy of bitterness. It is at this juncture that his findings intersected with the question of the defining of freedom in a postemancipation society. I had for some years been reading the correspondence of the administrators of the Santa Rosalía sugar plantation, papers that had come to rest—after the expropriation in the early 1960s of major sugar properties—in the National Library in Havana. I had also been gathering information on the adjacent Soledad plantation, owned after 1884 by Edwin Atkins of Belmont, Massachusetts. These estates together held several hundred slaves and were situated at the edge of and in the midst of the fighting during the 1868–78, 1879–80, and 1895–98 wars. Unlike Zeuske and García, I had begun not with lists of insurgents but with lists of slaves and workers, and then I worked forward, trying to figure out who had joined the

insurgency and why and what had become of those who did not join. The administrators' correspondence made it clear that men with the surnames Sarría and Quesada, former slaves on these two estates, were important figures in the rebellion. The administrators insulted and disparaged them as bandits but could not ignore them. Moreover, since I was tracing individuals, I was able to follow the paths of men and women who were involved with the insurgency in various ways, including those men who later left the rebel ranks.[17]

As I reconstruct the process of collective discovery—and I may be making it more linear and logical than it seemed at the time—we were able to break through the apparent contradictions of our various findings thanks to a series of fortuitous documentary discoveries and to the emergence of the Cienfuegos Provincial Historical Archive in the spring of 1998 as a place of shared memory as well as scholarly inquiry. The very openness of the space of the archive to the world of Cienfuegos beyond it, such a risk for the documents that reside there, became a new source of life for the history they recorded.

Early in my research I had stumbled on a receipt for a mule claimed by a former slave, Ciriaco Quesada, after a showdown with the administrator of the Santa Rosalía plantation in August 1899. The more closely I examined this incident, the more I became convinced that it reflected a widespread contest over rights to property and citizenship in the immediate aftermath of the war, one in which black and *mulato* veterans played an important role.[18] I began to wonder whether anyone named Quesada, descended from those families from Santa Rosalía, might still live in Cienfuegos. An ideal place to pose that question, it turned out, was the Provincial Archive itself. Schoolteachers and retired lawyers and schoolchildren and poets and anyone needing a copy of a notarized document eventually end up at one of the tables in the reading room. When I mentioned my interest in locating individuals named Quesada to Félix Tellería, who is a *babalao* (santería priest), a geographer, and a colleague of Orlando García in the Cienfuegos branch of UNEAC, he recalled that one of his neighbors was a former schoolteacher named Araceli Quesada y Quesada. He thought her family might indeed have come from Soledad or Santa Rosalía. He would talk with her.

When I arrived at the archive a few days later, Araceli Quesada y Quesada was waiting for me, a flower in her hair and a sheaf of papers in her hands. She explained that she was only in her sixties and therefore did not have memories going back terribly far—but that her aunt, Caridad Quesada, now blind and in her late seventies, knew a great deal. When Araceli Quesada heard from Félix Tellería that I was doing research on Santa Rosalía, she took the initiative of asking her aunt some questions and compiled about ten pages of notes on their conversation. Would I be interested in talking them over?

Caridad Quesada's memory, it turned out, was filled with stories, detailed genealogies, and songs, including epic political ballads sung by her uncle Cayetano Quesada. She also had been carefully taught the names of her cousins, near and far, so that she wouldn't marry one by accident—and she was able to trace out the relations among dozens of the descendants of former slaves of Santa Rosalía. By the time we finished going over these notes with Araceli Quesada, Orlando García and I quickly decided that at the conference we were organizing for March 1998 we would invite members of the Quesada and Tellería families to participate in a roundtable on memories of the postslavery period.

That roundtable, during which Caridad Quesada burst into song, was a turning point. The quest for evidence now seemed to belong to the Quesadas and Tellerías as well as the historians. Moreover, one member of the audience invited us to meet his grandfather, Tomás Pérez y Pérez, age ninety-six, who had worked all his life on Soledad. Tomás Pérez, it turned out, had known Ciriaco Quesada, the protagonist in the 1899 battle over the mule. "He was a tall man, quite thin." The microhistory of Santa Rosalía began to take on weight and volume.

The methodology that emerged was a pragmatic and improvised one. Because our research was based in a local archive whose director knew half the town—and the other half knew him—personal recollections and documentary evidence tumbled over each other every day. Caridad Quesada spoke to us about her uncle Cayetano Quesada, born to a slave mother on Santa Rosalía. His veteran's pension record was there in the archive, and we could double-check birth dates and the service record, verify residence, and have the material for new questions. We followed these clues out into the countryside, walking the trail that Ciriaco Quesada had ridden the day of the showdown over the mule—and finding the house where Cayetano Quesada's daughter, Ramona Quesada de Castillo, still lived. She, in turn, talked about her father. We learned that Cayetano and Ciriaco Quesada had lived side by side on a plot of land in the hamlet of San Antón. Her brother Humberto Quesada, who still cultivates that *sitio*, showed us the avocado tree that their grandfather Alejandro had apparently planted after the family achieved full legal freedom

from slavery and moved to settle a few miles away from the Santa Rosalía plantation.

Oral history, of course, has some awkwardness that archival research does not. One morning when I reached the archive, Félix Tellería's father, Fermín, was waiting. He had some family papers in his shirt pocket, and he had come to speak with me about his father, Trino Tellería, also a veteran of the 1895–98 war. We had already located Trino Tellería's pension record in the archive, so I read it aloud to Fermín—and faced the embarrassing moment when I realized that the pension request had been filed in 1937 by Fermín's sister, Nazaria, who in the course of her petition had sworn that she had no brothers or sisters. Fermín Tellería looked more or less bemused by this implied denial of his existence and I learned a quick lesson about the misleading formalisms that sometimes undergird seemingly rigorous written documentation.[19]

In sum, the rough-and-ready technique of sharing written records orally and of recording oral testimony in writing made possible a dialogue between types of sources that seemed to accelerate the research process exponentially. But what of our early questions about Afro-Cuban participation in the 1895–98 war? On the one hand, it seemed to be everywhere—we had found an abundance of grandparents, parents, and uncles who had been veterans. On the other hand, its linkage to slavery now appeared to have a twist. Often the black veterans who had survived in memory were not precisely former slaves. As we traced the genealogies and linked names to slave lists, we found that a common pattern was for the soldier to be the freeborn son of a slave mother or of parents held under the *patronato*, the notional "apprenticeship" that was imposed on most slaves at the time of formal abolition in 1880. In other words, the process of gradual emancipation in Cuba had—by freeing children beginning with those born in 1868 but retaining working-age adults in bondage into the 1880s—created a very particular category of young man: one whose own legal status was that of nominal freedom but who had grown up largely within the world of slavery to which his mother, and often his father, still belonged.

Here was part of the answer to the puzzle posed by Michael Zeuske's early findings. It may well be that former slaves from the largest sugar plantations in Cienfuegos—those whom he identified through their possession of classic "slave surnames" like Zulueta, Terry, and Moré— were in fact relatively rare among the recruits to the rebel army. The most productive plantations, owned by the wealthiest entrepreneurs, were fortified to prevent both rebel incursions and rebel recruitment. Moreover, the great majority of their former slaves were by 1895 well over the age of thirty, with many over forty or over fifty. But at the edges and in the interstices of the sugar zones, and in the mid-sized plantations like Santa Rosalía, much less well fortified, there were former slaves in their thirties, like Ciriaco Quesada, who joined forces with coworkers to form the rebel bands that emerged early in the war. There were also *muchachones,* young men in their teens or early twenties, born free, who were responsive to appeals to join the rebellion in the summer and fall of 1895.[20]

Caridad Quesada's uncle Cayetano Quesada was just such a *muchachón,* born free to a slave mother, and he joined up at the age of seventeen. With Cayetano Quesada's trajectory in mind, Michael Zeuske went back to a sample of thirty-seven well-documented requests for back pay filed by the surviving families of black and *mulato* rebel soldiers killed during the war. Sure enough, the free sons of slave mothers emerged as an important group among these soldiers, recruited alongside a smaller number of men who were themselves born into slavery and another group born to long-free families of color.[21]

In conjunction with Zeuske's and García's statistical data, the life histories built up through this encounter of documents and memories suggest a new way of thinking about the question of black and *mulato* participation in the war. Rather than envisioning a diffuse and continuous set of "struggles" for freedom—in which the fight for personal freedom leads naturally to participation in the fight for national freedom—we can try to locate the recruits themselves in the precise social fields in which they operated. We can situate them within families and gain some sense of the accounts they might have wished to settle with the state that had sanctioned slavery and in some cases with the individuals who had held their parents in bondage. We can explore whether their relative youth and physical mobility brought them in contact with revolutionary activists and whether plantation work groups served as nuclei for rebel bands.

Tracing the process of recruitment this way provides no magic key to motivation—a target that always seems elusive, no matter how carefully one refines one's methodology. But assembling such life histories and situating them within the history of these plantations can provide a sense of the social composition and work experience of the small groups who came together before and during the war. These "bands," often operating under highly personalized leadership, took to the woods around the Soledad plantation in 1895, stealing horses, torching cane, and settling grudges—and furthering the cause of Cuban independence, indirectly or directly. Later they would be constituted as formal companies of the Cienfuegos Brigade.

These groups seem to have emerged from the war as clusters of individuals bound by mutual loyalties and shared antagonisms—and undoubtedly divided by some rivalries. Armed, mounted, and quite sure of their own strength, they were quick to contest attempts to place limits on their freedom and citizenship. They could join forces, for example, to help one of their number keep a horse acquired during the war by testifying on his behalf at the property registry to the legitimacy of his claim, enabling him to acquire title under procedures set up by the U.S. occupation government. And in the case of Ciriaco Quesada, they could back up his claim to recover a mule once the war was over—a mule that the administrator at Santa Rosalía certainly did not want to turn over to the Quesada family.[22]

By looking closely at these small groups and their members one can see the storied "cross-racial" alliances as very concrete things, while at the same time glimpsing some of the fracture lines within them, lines that could widen with time. The same comrades who might stand together at the property register in Arimao could be wedged apart by the scheme of racial privilege that governed employment on the Soledad plantation.[23] They could then be united again in the electoral alliances, particularly of the Liberal Party, that were made possible by the 1901 constitution and its guarantee of universal manhood suffrage.

Tracing individuals one by one, we also learn some of the subtle markers of color and status, coded references that at first appeared mere formalities. Revolutionary record keepers had emphasized the equality of Cuban citizenship by refusing to add the old colonial color labels—*pardo, mulato, moreno, negro*—to the names of recruits as they drew up enlistment registers. Moreover, they often avoided further invidious distinctions by eschewing the use of doubled surnames, the classic Iberian signal of legitimate descent.[24] But this formal egalitarianism could be undercut elsewhere by the conventions of notaries who drew attention to—or even imposed—distinctions in naming patterns that encoded status and perhaps color. Thus in Nazaria Tellería's pension request she was listed as Nazaria Tellería SOA—*sin otro apellido,* "without another surname." Ordinarily using a single surname signaled illegitimacy, as the child born outside marriage could claim the mother's surname but not a paternal surname.[25] For Nazaria Tellería, however, this was clearly not the case—she had been recognized by her father and she used his name. The gratuitous placing of the three-letter initial SOA after her name may well have been linked to a detail that was mentioned explicitly elsewhere in the document: that she and her father were categorized as *mestizo*, the common Cuban term implying mixed African and European ancestry, often used as a genteel label for those who had earlier been denominated *pardo* or *mulato*. The republican notaries had quietly adapted a label from the late colonial era, using it to call attention to the status of those who now appeared before them as Cuban citizens.[26]

Conclusion

Studying the racial fault lines of a society that has tended to deny them is often a thankless task. Moreover, and ironically, one runs the risk of overinsisting on the salience of color, precisely because the history of denial is so strong. By focusing on a single locality, the three of us have pieced together one strategy for working on and around this problem. For the relatively small number of individuals whose genealogy or social circumstances we can trace in detail, we are able to examine directly the situation of descendants of slaves in central Cuba, without relying on intervening markers of slave ancestry that may or may not appear in a given body of documentation. Independent of whether Cayetano Quesada is referred to by a color label in a particular written record, we know that his parents were slaves on the Ingenio Santa Rosalía. His recruitment to the Liberation Army during its first months thus stands as a direct instance of a young man born free into the world of slavery who chose the path of insurgency. His life history, in conjunction with those of his neighbors Ciriaco Quesada, Claudio Sarría, Rafael Iznaga, and others, may help illuminate the process by which such men made similar choices.[27] At the same time, the life history of his neighbor Ramos Quesada, who remained on the Santa Rosalía plantation during the war to guard the cattle against rebel incursions, may illustrate another sort of choice.[28]

Continuing the story beyond 1898, through the U.S. occupation and into the first years of the republic, it becomes possible to make progress in examining the multiple legacies of the rebellion. We seldom know for certain the thoughts and motivations of soldiers, yet traces have been left in the way in which Cuban veterans established claims to property and citizenship after the war. Their assertions of entitlement as patriots, alongside their often complex negotiations within the entangling webs of an emerging system of clientelism, begin to speak for them.[29]

In this particular provincial archives, as in other local archives in Cuba, the key records are located not in careful seclusion but in a building whose door opens, both literally and figuratively, onto the street. The Quesada, Pérez, and Tellería kin did not hesitate to bring additional documents and photographs to the project, taking various initiatives, commenting on our preliminary findings, and suggesting interpretations, almost from the beginning. Questions of race in Cuba and elsewhere are delicate, but we have found that they need not be unspeakable. The "social construction of race" is an ongoing process that people can and do talk about, not just a now fashionable analytic label. Tomás Pérez y Pérez, son of an ex-slave mother and a Spanish immigrant father, knew very well that the racial labels attributed to him varied according to context, and he was willing to reflect aloud on the ways this affected his employment and the social situation of his family. Ramona Quesada had also thought about the "blackness" of her father and herself as descendants of the slaves on Santa Rosalía—as well as the "whiteness" of her husband, Evelio, as a descendant of Canary Islanders. The "social construction of race" is an often brutal process, and these life histories help to illuminate its unfolding in a notionally race-blind republic.[30]

Here lies the unanticipated benefit: precisely because we have been able to trace slave ancestry with relative precision, we need not assume and impute a fixed meaning to that ancestry. And because we need to explain our findings along the way to those who knew many of the people we are writing about, we are particularly open to challenge and clarification. By anchoring our hypotheses in an ever widening and ramifying set of life histories, we can, if appropriate, let go of the revisionist zeal to insist on the primacy of racial discrimination at the same time as we relinquish the heroic picture of revolutionary unity. The resulting stories become more complex, taking shape both within the historiography as it is now emerging and within the community of Cienfuegos itself.

But what of the national narrative? Did we, like good fin de siècle students of the subaltern, overturn the national narrative?

I suppose not quite. Instead, we expanded our sense of the elements that have to be accounted for in any such narrative. The construction and interpretation of these life histories and collective biographies might be seen as an attempt to fulfill the goal set out by Arlette Farge in her work on the historian in the archive. In her text, Farge implicitly recalls the romantic conviction expressed by Jules Michelet that the historian can exhume and re-store life to the dead through work in the dust of the ar-chive.[31] Gently rebuking such a presumption, Farge sug-gests a more open-ended, and ultimately collaborative, picture.

> On ne ressuscite pas les vies échouées en archive. Ce n'est pas une raison pour les faire mourir une deuxième fois. L'espace est étroit pour élaborer un récit qui ne les annule ni ne les dissolve, qui les garde disponibles à ce qu'un jour, et ailleurs, une autre narration soit faite de leur énigmatique présence.

> (One does not bring back to life those whom we find cast up in the archive. But that is no reason to make them suf-fer a second death. And the space is narrow within which to develop a story that will neither cancel out nor dis-solve these lives, that will leave them available so that one day, and elsewhere, another narrative may be built from their enigmatic presence.)[32]

NOTES

With the collaboration of Orlando García Martínez (Unión Nacional de Artistas y Escritores de Cuba—Cienfuegos) and Michael Zeuske (Universität zu Köln), this essay was presented at the Boston-area workshop on Latin American history held at the David Rockefeller Center for Latin American Studies. Scott, García, and Zeuske would like to thank the participants in both the Michigan and the Harvard seminars, particularly Francis Blouin, Monica Burguera, Alf Luedtke, William Rosen-berg, John Coatsworth, and Barbara Corbett. Scott also thanks George Reid Andrews, Sueann Caulfield, Alejandro de la Fuente, Ada Ferrer, Aims McGuinness, Peter Railton, Anne Scott, John Scott-Railton, and Thomas Scott-Railton for help-ful suggestions on the text. The essay has been published in the *New West Indian Guide/Nieuwe West-Indische Gids* 76 (2002) and in *History Workshop Journal* 58 (2004).

1. For an early and careful examination of the ideology of one hundred years of struggle, see Louis A. Pérez Jr., "In the Service of the Revolution: Two Decades of Cuban Historiogra-phy, 1959–79" (1980), reprinted in Louis A. Pérez Jr., *Essays on Cuban History: Historiography and Research* (Gainesville: University Press of Florida, 1995).

2. Already in 1961 the Afro-Cuban Marxist philosopher and activist Walterio Carbonell saw this as a misguided strat-egy and called on the revolutionary leadership to cease seeking validation through the canonization of slaveholding founding fathers. Carbonell later ended up ostracized, his position ap-parently characterized as racially divisive. See the impassioned plea, dedicated to "Fidel and the new generation of writers," in Walterio Carbonell, *Crítica: Cómo surgió la cultura nacional* (Havana: Ediciones Yaka, 1961). On Carbonell's subsequent fate, see Hugh Thomas, *Cuba: The Pursuit of Freedom* (New York: Harper and Row, 1971), 1433.

3. A subtle and enduring expression of this national narra-tive is Miguel Barnet, *Biografía de un Cimarrón* (Havana: Insti-tuto de Etnología y Folklore, 1966). The classic enunciation by a historian is in the eloquent *Ideología mambisa* by Jorge Ibarra (Havana: Instituto Cubano del Libro, 1972): "Al proclamar la confraternidad étnica, la igualdad jurídica y la libertad política, la vanguardia revolucionaria del 68 [1868] sentaba las bases definitivas para la formación de la nación cubana" (21). For an interesting critical view from the prerevolutionary period, see Raúl Cepero Bonilla, *Azúcar y abolición* (Havana: Editorial Cénit, 1948).

4. On the national, as opposed to simply Southern, dimen-sions of the endorsement of black disfranchisement in the United States, see Richard H. Pildes, "Democracy, Anti-Democracy and the Canon," *Constitutional Commentary* 17 (2000): 295–319.

5. The pioneering work on the debate concerning suffrage is that of Alejandro de la Fuente, first published in "Myths of Racial Democracy: Cuba, 1900–1912," *Latin American Re-search Review* 34 (1999): 39–73, and elaborated in *A Nation for All: Race, Inequality, and Politics in Nineteenth-Century Cuba* (Chapel Hill: University of North Carolina Press, 2001).

6. Ibarra, *Ideología,* 51, gives the phrase as "Joven, aquí no hay blanquitos, ni negritos, sino cubanos." Ibarra dates it to 1870 but unfortunately gives no primary source citation. The meaning of the phrase itself, if these are indeed the words Maceo uttered, is ambiguous, for he uses not the terms *blanco* and *negro,* which could be construed as racial descriptors, but *blanquitos y negritos,* diminutive terms that could be seen as derogatory. It is thus not entirely clear whether Maceo was re-jecting racial categories as such or their derogatory variants.

7. Aline Helg, *Our Rightful Share: The Afro-Cuban Strug-gle for Equality, 1886–1912* (Chapel Hill: University of North Carolina Press, 1995), 16.

8. Ada Ferrer, *Insurgent Cuba: Race, Nation, and Revolu-tion, 1868–1898* (Chapel Hill: University of North Carolina Press, 1999). See also de la Fuente, *A Nation for All,* for a dis-tinction between racial democracy as a project and racial democracy as a fait accompli.

9. One such study subsequently appeared as a book: Blan-camar León Rosabal, *La voz del Mambí: Imagen y mito* (Ha-vana: Editorial de Ciencias Sociales, 1997).

10. See Fernando Martínez Heredia, "El Problemático Na-cionalismo de la Primera República," *Temas* (Havana), 24–25 (January–June 2001): 35–44. An expanded version, translated by Lara Putnam, appears in English in *Cuban Studies* 33 (2002): 95–123, with the title "Nationalism, Races, and Classes in the Revolution of 1895 and the Cuban First Republic."

11. See the essay by Jorge Ibarra, "Comentarios acerca de 'Mitos de democracia racial: Cuba, 1900–1912,'" in Fernando Martínez Heredia, Rebecca J. Scott, and Orlando García Martínez, eds., *Espacios, silencios, y los sentidos de la libertad. Cuba, 1878–1912* (Havana: Editorial Unión, 2001; reprint, Havana: Editorial de Ciencias Sociales, 2002), 332–45. As with the work of Martínez Heredia, Ibarra's criticisms circulated orally and in typescript for some time before reaching print.

12. For a guide to the holdings of this and other provincial, municipal, and local archives, see Louis A. Pérez Jr. and Re-becca J. Scott, eds., *The Archives of Cuba/Los archivos de Cuba* (Pittsburgh: University of Pittsburgh Press, 2002).

13. See the afterward to Rebecca J. Scott, *Slave Emancipation in Cuba: The Transition to Free Labor, 1860–1899,* 2d ed. (Pittsburgh: University of Pittsburgh Press, 2000), and the introduction to Scott et al., *The Abolition of Slavery and the Aftermath of Emancipation in Brazil* (Durham, NC: Duke University Press, 1988).

14. See Michael Zeuske, "'Los negros hicimos la independencia': Aspectos de la Movilización Afrocubana en un Hinterland Cubano. Cienfuegos entre Colonia y República," paper presented at a conference in the Cienfuegos Provincial Historical Archive, March 1998, and published in Martínez, Scott, and García, eds., *Espacios, silencios,* 193–234.

15. See Orlando García Martínez, "La Brigada de Cienfuegos: Un Análisis Social de su Formación," in Martínez, Scott, and García, eds., *Espacios, silencios,* 163–92. It was on this last point that Ibarra disagreed, arguing that the privileging of training and education was simply necessary to provide professionals such as doctors for the army. García countered with the statistics showing that the number of doctors and lawyers was very small and argued that officer status functioned as a class and racial privilege rather than a pragmatic measure.

16. The best study of the dynamics of the process of sidelining is the essay by Ada Ferrer on the court martial of Quintín Bandera, "Rustic Men, Civilized Nation: Race, Culture, and Contention on the Eve of Cuban Independence," *Hispanic American Historical Review* 78 (November 1998): 663–86.

17. This research has now been incorporated into Rebecca J. Scott, *Degrees of Freedom: Louisiana and Cuba after Slavery* (Cambridge, MA: Harvard University Press, forthcoming).

18. An early version of this inquiry was presented at the 1998 conference in Cienfuegos and was published as Rebecca J. Scott, "Reclamando la Mula de Gregoria Quesada: El Significado de la Libertad en los Valles del Arimao y del Caunao, Cienfuegos, Cuba (1880–1899)," *Illes i Imperis* (Barcelona) 2 (spring 1999): 89–107, and then in Martínez, Scott, García, eds., *Espacios, silencios,* 23–52. A revised version appeared as "Reclaiming Gregoria's Mule: The Meanings of Freedom in the Arimao and Caunao Valleys, Cienfuegos, Cuba, 1880–1899," *Past and Present* (February 2001): 181–216.

19. Pensión interesada por Nazaria Tellería, como hija del veterano Sr. Trino Tellería Santana, Año de 1937, in Fondo Juzgado de Primera Instancia de Cienfuegos, AHPC. Trino Tellería had in 1929 formally recognized his paternity of Nazaria Tellería, born in 1901. She first asserted in her 1937 pension request that her father had never been married and hence had left no other legitimate or recognized children. Later in the document she swore that he had left no other natural or legitimate children. This was misleading, since the children of even an unrecognized union were *hijos naturales* if the parents had been in a condition to marry at the time of the birth—that is, if the union was not adulterous, bigamous, or otherwise prohibited. (Fermín Tellería's birth—to the same father and mother—had probably been recorded in the town of Camarones rather than in Cienfuegos).

20. The general dynamic of recruitment in the region is discussed in Scott, "Reclaiming Gregoria's Mule"; and García Martínez, "La Brigada de Cienfuegos."

21. See Michael Zeuske, "Lux Veritatis, Vita Memoriae, Magistra Vitae—116 Vidas y la Historia de Cuba," in *Historia y memoria: Sociedad, cultura y vida cotidiana en Cuba, 1878–1917* (Havana: Centro de Investigación y Desarrollo de la Cultura Cubana Juan Marinello, 2003), 55–81.

22. On the right to register horses and the claim for the mule, see Scott, "Reclaiming Gregoria's Mule."

23. The question of racial privilege on the Soledad estate has become clearer as the correspondence of the owner and administrator has come to light. See the correspondence of Edwin F. Atkins in the Atkins Family Papers, Massachusetts Historical Society, and an initial discussion in Rebecca J. Scott, "Race, Labor, and Citizenship in Cuba: A View from the Sugar District of Cienfuegos, 1886–1909," *Hispanic American Historical Review* 78 (November 1998): 701.

24. See, for example, the enlistment register for the third company of the first battalion of the Regimiento de Infantería "Cienfuegos," in Expediente 60, Inventario 1, Documentos relativos a la inspección general del Ejército. . . 27 de Noviembre de 1896, Colección de documentos del Ejército Libertador, Archivo Histórico Provincial de Villa Clara, Santa Clara, Cuba (photocopies in the possession of Michael Zeuske). In this list the ex-slave soldier Ciriaco Quesada is listed with a single surname, as are all the other soldiers and officers in the company.

25. On the rules governing the use of surnames, see Rafael Pérez Lobo, compiler, *Código Civil y Constitución* (Havana: Cultural, 1944), articles 119–41 of the 1889 Civil Code. The stigma associated with the single surname is suggested by the 1927 ruling that gave even "natural children" the right to use a double surname: "En la inscripción de hijos naturales se hará constar a los efectos del caso primero de este art., el apellido completo paterno y materno de la persona que lo reconozca, a fin de que, siendo en esta forma usado por dichos hijos, no revelen obstensiblemente la ilegitimidad de su origen" (Resol. Secr. Justicia 15 July 1927, 47).

26. The question of "race marking" in late colonial and republican Cuba is a complex one, and these observations on the use of the initials SOA are quite preliminary. See Michael Zeuske, "Hidden Markers, Open Secrets: On Naming, Race-Marking and Race-Making in Cuba," *New West Indian Guide/Nieuwe West-Indische Gids* 76 (2002): 211–42.

27. See Rebecca J. Scott, "Tres Vidas, una Guerra. Rafael Iznaga, Bárbara Pérez y Gregoria Quesada entre la Emancipación y la Ciudadanía," in *Historia y memoria.*

28. On Ramos Quesada, see the correspondence to and from Santa Rosalía that is held in the Fondo Manuscrito Julio Lobo, Biblioteca Nacional "José Martí," Havana; and David Sartorius, "Conucos y Subsistencia: El Caso del Ingenio Santa Rosalía," in Martínez Hereolia , Scott, and García Martínez, eds., *Espacios, silencios,* 108–27. The doctoral dissertation by Sartorius ("Limits of Loyalty: Race and the Public Sphere in Cienfuegos, Cuba, 1845–1898," Ph.D. diss., University of North Carolina, 2003) examines the phenomenon of loyalty to the Spanish state on the part of some Cubans of color.

29. On this point, see Rebecca Scott and Michael Zeuske, "Property in Writing, Property on the Ground: Pigs, Horses, Land, and Citizenship in the Aftermath of Slavery, Cuba, 1880–1909," *Comparative Studies in Society and History,* 44 (2002): 669–99.

30. For a vivid picture of an equally complex process on the

shifting terrain of the border states and upper south in the United States, see Pauli Murray, *Proud Shoes: The Story of an American Family* (New York: Harper and Brothers, 1956).

31. Jules Michelet wrote: "J'ai donné à beaucoup de morts trop oubliés l'assistance dont moi-même j'aurai besoin. Je les ai exhumés pour une seconde vie," Jules Michelet, *Histoire du xixᵉ siècle,* vol. 2, *Jusqu'au 18 Brumaire* (1872), preface, in Michelet, *Oeuvres Complètes* (Paris, 1982), 21, 268. The ref-

erence to his own future need for exhumation becomes clearer in the light of an earlier draft, cited in the editors' note 4: "Je mourrai bientôt et moi-même, avec mes longs travaux, je serai un souvenir, un fait du 19ᵉ siècle dont j'écris l'histoire." See also Carolyn Steedman, "The Space of Memory: In an Archive," *History of the Human Sciences* 11 (1998): 65–83.

32. Arlette Farge, *Le goût de l'archive* (Paris: Editions du Seuil, 1989), 145; translation mine.

Maroons in the Archives

The Uses of the Past in the French Caribbean

Laurent Dubois

yo palé mwen dè libèté, dè égalité	they talk to me of liberty, equality
yo menm di mwen fraternité	they even say fraternity
men ès tout sa sé vwé	but is all that true?
sé sa yo di, men és tout sa sé vwé	that's what they say, but is it all true?
libété pa vini tou sèl	liberty didn't come by itself
fô yo té goumé	they had to fight
nèg mawon pa atann papyé	the maroons didn't wait for papers
pou yo té chapé	to escape from them

—Voukoum, "Kolon-la"

In the heart of Basse-Terre, the administrative capital of the island of Guadeloupe, sits a prison. It is notorious for its overcrowding and antiquated facilities and also because over the years a number of local activists who have fought for independence from France have been imprisoned there. The concrete walls of the prison, topped by barbed wire, run along one of the main boulevards of the town. Underneath the barbed wire is a mural, painted in the 1980s with the support of local cultural officials. It represents the slave trade: a line of slaves in chains and the famous Maison des Esclaves, of the slave port of Gorée, from where slaves were embarked on ships for the Middle Passage. And it presents symbols of bondage and resistance in the Caribbean: a maroon in a spiked iron collar, a machete and a stalk of sugar cane, a drum, and a conch shell—the latter of which was used on plantations to call slaves to work and by maroons as a call to attack. Nearby, in 2001, was a small poster sporting a representation of a "document"—a piece of yellow parchment, curved at the ends. On it was an excerpt from a historical document, a list of maroons "held in the prison of Basse-Terre." The list—which was reproduced from an eighteenth-century newspaper and included names, descriptions, and "country marks"—is similar to many others available in the archives of Guadeloupe and in archives throughout the Americas. Within the archives, then, it is a fairly unremarkable document. Its placement next to the prison, however, transforms it into something very different.

Members of the independence movement in both Guadeloupe and Martinique have often referred to the history of the maroons in presenting their political and cultural agenda, associating their contemporary struggle with that of these ancestors. The maroons are seen as precursors for those who resist in the present, as heroes who refused the colonial order, struck out violently against it, and created their own communities in the heights of the island. In slavery times, it is often recalled, they were hunted down by a police force—the *maréchaussée* (many of whose soldiers, as is less often recalled, were actually slaves or free coloreds)—and when caught, according to the stipulations of the French *Code Noir* that governed slavery, were stamped with a fleur-de-lis on their first offense, had their hamstrings cut on their second, and punished with death for further attempts at flight.[1] Aimé

Césaire called on the history of the maroons in his *Note-book of a Return to My Native Land* when he wrote, "I accept . . . the spiked iron-collar / and the hamstringing of my runaway audacity / and the *fleur-de-lys* flowing from the red iron into the fat of my shoulder."[2] More recently, in the song quoted in the epigraph that begins this essay, the group Voukoum has evoked the maroons as a way of countering the way they see the history of Guadeloupe too often told—as a story of its white colonists and of the generous actions of the French state in freeing the slaves in 1848 and making the island a department in 1946.[3] The literary and cultural presence of the maroons is vibrant in the contemporary French Caribbean—through novels, plays, songs, and carnival costumes called *nèg-mawon*—and the placement of an archival document pertaining to them in front of Basse-Terre's prison is a powerful gesture of criticism made through a potent and well-understood analogy.

The document was placed there as part of a townwide project of the public presentation of historical documents, led by the director of cultural affairs in Basse-Terre, the historian Josette Faloppe.[4] In the main park of Basse-Terre, the Champ d'Arbaud, for instance, were posters of the famous declaration written by Louis Delgrès, a free-colored officer, as he battled the French troops who reestablished slavery on the island in 1802. Among these documents, however, it is the one placed in front of the prison that most directly speaks to and reflects the political situation on the island. The prison is overseen by the centralized police force of the French state, whose members are often mostly from metropolitan France, on short tours of duty in Guadeloupe. The local government of the town, however, is in the hands of local Guadeloupean administrators and politicians, who for most of the past decades have been firmly on the Left. Within the ranks of the local administration are several who share many of the sentiments and hopes of those who have agitated for independence of the island. Although they work within the French administrative system, they argue for the need for more local autonomy in social and economic decisions and have propelled an impressive array of cultural initiatives (such as the placement of historical documents in Basse-Terre) aimed at valorizing the particularities of the Guadeloupe and the French Caribbean.

Through both the mural and the list of the maroons, the archive of slavery is made present in the streets of Basse-Terre and is called upon as part of a present-day cultural and political struggle. This is one of many ways in which the past of slavery, slave resistance, and eman-

cipation is brought to bear upon contemporary debates about the political status and economic future of Guadeloupe. As in Haiti, where the evocation of the Haitian Revolution takes place within a web of silencing explored by Michel-Rolph Trouillot,[5] the ambiguities and complexities of the past, and of the documents it has left, are often overlooked in the production of contemporary narratives. At the same time, the French Caribbean has seen a rich discussion about both the possibilities and the limits of the archives left by slavery and emancipation, most notably through several novels that take on the problem of history and incorporate the archival document as a literary form. These novels interestingly confront a broader problem faced by all those who seek to write the history of slavery and, more particularly, the stories of the slaves themselves—the absences and silences in the archives. In a sense, their aim is similar to that of historians of the Caribbean who seek to uncover the voices and actions of slaves and ex-slaves and to understand their struggles. Yet they also have a very different relationship to the question of evidence and a different sense of how to imagine the relationship between present needs and the facts of the past.

There has not been much productive discussion between historians and novelists in the French Caribbean, to a large extent because many see their approaches as fundamentally different and incommensurable. Some novelists have argued that traditional historical work, because of its dependence on archives written by white masters and colonial officials, can never tell the true story of the people of the Caribbean, while historians have sometimes criticized the ahistorical and mythological approaches of novelists. Yet, as I hope to suggest, the relationship between history and fiction can in fact highlight important issues about the constitution of the archive of slavery and emancipation in Guadeloupe. In this essay, I begin by describing the material archives of the history of Guadeloupe and some of the ways they have been constituted through the history of the island, as well as the social and political forces that shape both the structure and the use of these archives. I then move on to a discussion of the ways in which novelists have made archives of a different sort part of their literary work in the quest for the production of histories for the present of Guadeloupe. Finally, I draw on some of my own research to suggest the ways in which the silences of the material archives have in some ways been overdrawn by such novelists. In general terms, the kinds of points I make here about the archives of Guadeloupe could, of course, be made about almost any archive and any historical problem, but I hope that the specifics of this case can help illuminate the broader problem of interpreting archives as "agencies of cultural difference," as well as suggest the possibilities for a more sustained discussion between the various groups who take it upon themselves to narrate the past in the French Caribbean.

Archives on the Margins

What makes up the archives of Guadeloupe? Their material existence is, of course, intimately tied up in the complicated relationship between the Caribbean island and the French metropole. As is the case in many colonial contexts, a large percentage of the documents relating to Guadeloupe are in fact not on the island but in metropolitan France, either in Paris in the National Archives or else in collections of documents that were moved to the "Section Outre-Mer" (Overseas Section) of the National Archives in Aix-en-Provence in the 1980s. It was only in 1946, after Guadeloupe became a department of France, that it received its own archival institution, into which official documents were to be deposited rather than sent to metropolitan France. In principle, then, all documents pertaining to the history of the island before 1946 are in metropolitan France. Those who wish to research these documents in Guadeloupe can do so through microfilms, which exist thanks to the Mormons, who deposited copies of those they made for their own archives. There are, however, important exceptions to this division of the archives. Anything pertaining to Guadeloupe that has been discovered or deposited in the archives since 1946 is located in the local archives. This includes a vast archive of judicial documents from the second half of the nineteenth century, which are now being cataloged. It also includes a large group of notary archives from the eighteenth century, which were deposited by the descendants of these notaries in the late 1960s and whose richness is in fact hidden by official inventories in the metropole—which makes it seem that the local archives do not contain anything that is not in the metropolitan archives, when in fact the local ones are richer and more complete.

When they were created in 1946 the Departmental Archives of Guadeloupe were installed in an administrative building in Basse-Terre. They remained there until the 1980s, when—in part because, like many other local archives in France, they experienced increasing use by genealogical researchers—they were moved to a larger building. A new building was built for the archives, out-side of Basse-Terre near a somewhat isolated hilltop village several kilometers away. In a curious architectural gesture, the new building was built partly surrounded by a moat and a wall, so that it looks not a little like a fortress. The director of the archives lives on-site, and there is a guard who lives near a locked gate at the entrance to the drive that goes to the director's house. All the social tensions of Guadeloupean society are powerfully visible in the functioning of the archives themselves. The various directors of the archives, who are appointed by a central administration from the relatively small group of candidates with the appropriate degrees and training, have consistently been from metropolitan France, along with the assistant to the director. The employees, meanwhile, who staff the desks and create inventories, are almost all from Guadeloupe. Having worked in the archives for much of their lives in many cases, they have little hope of vertical movement within its administrative structure. The archive is a zone of subterranean resentments and frustrations on both sides, a fact that significantly slows down the work of creating inventories and therefore influences the shape and accessibility of the collections there.

What actually makes up these archives? Much of the material available in metropolitan France consists of administrative correspondence, military reports, maps, and other traces left by the official business of governing the colony of Guadeloupe. They chronicle the complaints and struggles of planters, the economic history of the island, and sometimes acts of resistance by slaves. They are written from a variety of perspectives—local planters versus metropolitan administrators, military versus civilian officials, and so forth—and so reflect debates about colonial governance in a variety of ways. Of course, like most such material, they contain virtually no documents emanating from the majority slave population of the island or even from the educated *gens de couleur* (free coloreds), although in times of political transformation and crisis this is less true. In both the metropole and the local archives of Guadeloupe, however, documents that provide the foundation for work on the social history of the island are also present—such as notary registers, *état civil*, and some juridical documents. Quantitatively, most of these documents relate to the property, marriages, births, and business arrangements of the whites of the island, although there are some documents drawn up by free coloreds and some plantation inventories that include lists of slaves, as well as some documents pertaining to the sale or emancipation of slaves. Through these documents, then, a picture of the social world of Guadeloupe can be drawn, though this depends often enough on piecing together fragments and confronting many gaps.

The form of the archives and the possibilities for the writing of history they represent also shift according to the political and legal conflicts of the period. One salient example of this can be seen in archives relating to periods of emancipation, which in Guadeloupe occurred between 1794 and 1802 (when slavery was reestablished by troops sent by Napoleon Bonaparte) and after 1848. The movement from slavery to freedom, and the contested and contradictory movement from slavery to a limited citizenship, depended upon another fundamental transformation—the transformation of legal objects into legal subjects. After 1794 and 1848, ex-slaves rushed to solidify their hold on property and to legitimize familial relationships they had maintained in slavery. They did so by having notarial records and *état civil* documents drawn up, which required them to present (and, often enough, to select or invent) family names.[6] A process of social change and struggle was therefore also a documentary process that shaped the form of the archives in various ways. The right to write up a document was a way of securing rights that had previously been denied; a way of solidifying the economic stakes of familial relationships, such as inheritance; as well as a way of securing a hold over land and property in the countryside and the cities.[7]

At the same time, periods of emancipation were also periods of increased social control, as colonial administrations sought ways to limit the mobility of ex-slaves and to maintain plantation labor. In 1796 and 1797, for instance, administrators produced censuses of unprecedented detail in Guadeloupe in order to make it possible to enforce policies that required ex-slaves who were not in the army to remain on their plantations. The censuses listed everyone on the island and categorized them according to age, profession, and race—and for this purpose a new racial category, that of "red" (for free coloreds), was invented. Emancipation, then, also led to the creation of new groups of documents that, precisely because of their coercive intent, are extremely valuable for contemporary researchers. These documents, interestingly, drew on the previous form of plantation inventories in the sense that they allowed for "comments" about individuals; this column was used almost exclusively in describing ex-slaves as, for instance, *"divaguant"* (ramblers), a new term for the old practice of running away from the plantations. At the same time, the official censuses were more systematic and were aimed at the production of statistics about the island as well.[8]

As in many other contexts, the relationship between state coercion and documentation—the production of what has been called (in a very different context) the "archives of the repression"[9]—has been crucial in the formation of the archives of slave societies. What is known about the maroons, for instance, is primarily the result of their capture and imprisonment; the document reproduced on the poster that now sits near the prison of Basse-Terre was the result of successful repression of the maroons and a mechanism for having them return to their plantations. The same is true with regard to the history of slave conspiracies, such as those explored in detail by David Barry Gaspar and Winthrop Jordan. In these cases, it is precisely because a certain revolt *did not* happen that the archives available to historians are so rich. It was because of the success of coercion that archives were produced, because officials urgently sought testimonies as a mechanism for defusing a revolt and capturing its organizers. These testimonies provide extremely rich information about the process of organization that preceded revolt, because it is precisely this process that interrogators wished to know about. At the same time, of course, the very conditions under which slave testimonies were taken in the context of Antigua, for instance, have allowed critics to claim that there is a good chance that the conspiracy painted in such detail was in fact an invention, a tale told under duress that later historians have found themselves taken in by. The importance of "archives of repression" in the documentation of slave rebellion also means that in many ways we know more about the organization of failed revolts than we do about the organization of successful ones. The process through which the 1791 insurrection in St. Domingue, for instance, was actually organized can only be understood through fragmentary information and occasional interrogations gathered after the fact. Indeed, the event that is often presented as the foundational moment in the Haitian Revolution—the Vodou ceremony that is supposed to have taken place at Bois-Caïman, in St. Domingue, in August 1791—is essentially absent from the archives, and its very existence has been the subject of intense debate.[10]

If the intent of the local administration in drawing up censuses to control ex-slaves or in gathering testimony on slave revolts is relatively easy to identify, the exact intent that ex-slaves had when they drew up documents is sometimes less clear. This is the case, for instance, for a variety of documents in which ex-slaves from various plantations came together to inscribe new arrivals from Africa—who had been captured by French corsairs and brought to Guadeloupe—in the *état civil* registers. The ex-slaves gave these new arrivals new, French names and placed them in the register of births. The meaning of this act—and whether it was the result of encouragement by local officials or an entirely self-motivated action—is difficult to pin down. The form these documents take, in comparison to the registers drawn up by the local government years later when these same individuals were sold as slaves—and which included descriptions of their bodies, their "country marks," and their abilities as laborers—is a striking illustration of the ways different regimes produced radically different forms of documentation. In other contexts, it is easier to see the ways in which ex-slaves themselves constituted their own archives through the use of notaries. In 1799–1801, for instance, a number of ex-slaves who had been freed by their masters, rather than by the general decree of emancipation of 1794, deposited and registered various papers and statements affirming their freedom in preparation for a potential return of the system of slavery. The struggles for rights on the part of ex-slaves then, and the attempts of the local administration to respond to and contain these struggles, influenced both the form and the content of the archives.

What stories can be told with these archives? Quantitatively speaking, the vast majority of those who use these archives (often tourists from metropolitan France) are doing genealogical research with the aim of crafting family histories or are Guadeloupeans who are doing research into their families for pleasure or for legal reasons involving inheritance or landownership. Genealogy is, of course, an arena in which the past of slavery is ever present in both the content and the form of the archives. For most Antilleans of African descent, it is only possible to trace their family tree—with the exception of ancestors who were whites or free coloreds—back to 1848, when the registers of ex-slaves that are the starting point for much genealogical research were produced. The white residents of the island (referred to by most Afro-Antilleans and increasingly by themselves with the term *béké*) usually have a much more extensive and broader set of resources on which they can draw in exploring their family histories. I once watched a conversation between one such *béké* genealogist and an Antillean of African descent. The *béké* asked—probably already knowing the answer—how far back the latter could trace his ancestry. In response to his calling up of the date 1848, the *béké* proudly announced that he had been able to trace his ancestry back to the first decades of the colony in the mid-sixteenth century. Perhaps an unconscious oversight or perhaps a very conscious affirmation of a claim to the is-

land, the gesture powerfully highlighted the ways in which the constitution of the archives themselves could be used to legitimate a certain kind of narrative of precedence. Such a narrative is also present in the conference room of the archives, which is surrounded by portraits of the governors of Guadeloupe from the eighteenth and nineteenth centuries—all of whom were white and many of whom came to the island on tours of duty from the metropole. The linking of archival inequalities to social inequalities can be extremely potent in contemporary Guadeloupe, and it is one of the reasons why a series of novelists have suggested through their work that it is in fact impossible for the material archives to tell the true story of Guadeloupe and particularly of the majority of its population, who are descended from slaves.

Archives in the Fiction

Perhaps more than in any other region, poets and novelists of the Caribbean, and particularly the French Caribbean, have taken up the task of writing history and writing about history and have used the archive itself as a literary form in their work. One of the earliest works that highlighted the issue of what was missing from the archives was the 1972 novel *La Mulâtresse Solitude*. It was written by André Schwartz-Bart, a Polish Jew who had survived the death camps and written about his experience in his 1959 *Le dernier des justes* and who came to Guadeloupe with his wife, the novelist Simone Schwartz-Bart. As he read up on the history of Guadeloupe, Schwartz-Bart came across a passage in Auguste Lacour's nineteenth-century *Histoire de la Guadeloupe* that refers to a "mulatresse Solitude" who fought with Delgrès; she was pregnant when she was captured and gave birth to her child before being executed by the French army. In Lacour's version, Solitude's "hate and rage was explosive." She taunted and tortured white prisoners, acting as the "wicked genius" of the rebels, "exciting them to the most extreme crimes." This passage, which describes Solitude's actions during the fighting between French troops and Guadeloupean insurgents in 1802 and presents her as a violent and vicious person, represents the only existing historical information about her. Using this as his starting point, however, Schwartz-Bart wove a story about her life that placed this moment in a larger context, telling the history of her sufferings in slavery and her resistance against it. Nearly the entire story, including many of the details of her role in 1802, was necessarily an invention, an extended improvisation based on a fleeting mention in one historical work. But his novel incited a process of the popularization of her story, and today there is a street named after her and a statue of her in Guadeloupe. The success of his novel, of course, depended to an important degree on the fact that it was seen as the story of an actual slave. The influence of the novel on discussions of slavery in Guadeloupe can be seen in the fact that in 1985 the historian Arlette Gautier entitled her study, one of the first devoted to the history of enslaved women in the French Caribbean, "Les soeurs de Solitude."[11]

Almost a decade later, Daniel Maximin wrote a novel, *L'Isolé Soleil* (translated as *Lone Sun*), that more openly explored the problem of writing a history of Guadeloupe and of recovering stories left in silence by the archives. Maximin also used the available works on Guadeloupean history, notably Lacour, in his work. The way he did so, however, highlighted the ways in which the archives themselves were insufficient for writing a total history of the island and of its slaves and their descendants. Maximin, a Guadeloupean from the town of Saint-Claude, moved to metropolitan France with his family as an adolescent and eventually went to university in Paris. It was, in fact, work on a doctoral dissertation that led him to write fiction. He had worked on his subject—the way European colonialism had constructed visions of the "other"—for some time before concluding that he also had to provide another side to this story. He decided to write about history from the perspective of Guadeloupe, and his advisor encouraged him to do so, telling him to write this in whatever way he wished or felt comfortable with. What emerged was part history, part novel. Maximin confronted the problem he sought to answer in his dissertation through the main character of *L'Isolé Soleil,* Marie-Gabriel. The novel chronicles her attempt to write the history of her island. She uses the "journal of Jonathan," a diary left behind by one of her ancestors, as her antidote to the silences of history. The journal—not unlike the book kept by the main character of Michael Ondaatje's *The English Patient*—is a scrapbook collected from various sources. In one scene, for instance, Maximin shows Jonathan reading in his master's library and then tearing out a page from a book to place in his journal. It is a scene that echoes a moment in C. L. R. James's *The Black Jacobins,* where Toussaint Louverture is presented reading and rereading a famous passage from the Abbé Raynal's work, which warned that the only thing missing for the slaves of the Americas to rise up and slaughter their oppressors was a great leader, a "Black Spartacus."[12] In both cases,

slaves are shown reading European texts and drawing on them for their own struggles for freedom.

The "journal of Jonathan" is, then, an archive of a particular sort. In Maximin's work, it is in fact made up of existing historical documents that he collected from secondary sources or through his research. Its significance in the novel, however, is that it has been constituted by the slave Jonathan and left as a kind of family inheritance for Marie-Gabriel. Just as important as what has come to be in the journal is the way in which these documents were gathered and placed there. The constitution of the journal as part of a struggle for freedom becomes part of the novel's story and teaches Marie-Gabriel as much about the history as what is actually in the documents. If the "journal of Jonathan" is an archive, then, it is one whose history contrasts sharply with the history of state archives, which may include some of the same documents but whose constitution is the result of a different set of historical processes. Maximin's novel presents us with a powerful image—that of an archive of slavery constituted not by the system that administrated and protected slavery but by a slave himself and handed down from generation to generation as a powerful inheritance. For Marie-Gabriel, the notebook symbolizes a direct connection with the past and therefore opens up new possibilities for her to assert ownership over a stolen history.

L'Isolé Soleil presents the various aspects of this written and oral archive as being part of a continuing discussion about how to imagine the history of the island. The characters in this novel, for instance, debate the legacy of Louis Delgrès, who like Solitude fought the French troops sent to reestablish slavery on the island in 1802. Rather than surrender, Delgrès blew himself and his followers up on a plantation in Guadeloupe, something some of the characters in the novel see as a dramatic but ultimately self-centered gesture whose evocation obscures the other, quieter forms of resistance practiced by his contemporaries. Indeed, the novel, the story of Delgrès, and the other tales of resistance kept in the "journal of Jonathan" coexist with other forms of memory, particularly songs and stories transmitted between several generations of women. These orally transmitted histories highlight the forgotten stories of women's resistance, and through them these stories—as well as the actions of maroons, of African gods, and nature itself—are written into history as unacknowledged sources of historical change. The terrain of cultural memory emerges as a complex arena through which the myths of the past must always be reworked in relation to present demands.[13]

Maximin's novel takes up the task of telling the history of the island, particularly of one of its most dramatic episodes, and of transmitting actual historical documents, even as it highlights the multiplicity of other forms of memory. He also plays with the relationship between past and present and the relationship between the struggles of Guadeloupeans and those of other peoples of African descent in the Americas—for instance, by naming his eighteenth-century characters Georges and Jonathan, after the Jackson brothers, whose dramatic role in the controversies surrounding the Black Panther party in the 1960s Maximin followed from France. An incident in which Angela Davis visited Guadeloupe and was protected from arrest by the French police by local radicals makes its way into the novel. So too does a dramatic plane crash that occurred above the island's volcano, which in the novel results in the death of Marie-Gabriel's father and the destruction of a journal he had been keeping from her. The explosion of the plane echoes the constant threat of the explosion of the volcano, itself layered with the echoes of the explosion Delgrès set off as his last resounding gesture. So Maximin's work both draws on the existing archive to tell a necessary story and invents what he sees as a necessary archive of song, music, and written text that tells the true story of his people. At once playful and epic in scope, his novel is a rich exploration of the possibilities of written history.

Maximin's work was an inspiration to a better-known novel, Patrick Chamoiseau's *Texaco*. The winner of the prestigious Prix Goncourt, *Texaco* takes as its subject the history of a community on the outskirts of Fort-de-France, Martinique, whose name comes from the fact that it was built on the abandoned site of an old oil refinery. As the story opens, the community is under the threat of being razed and replaced by government projects, a threat exemplified by the visit of a local official whose short walk through the community ends abruptly when he gets hit in the head by a rock thrown by an unknown assailant. Marie-Sophie Laborieux, the main character and leader of the community, realizes that to save her community she must tell this official its whole story, so that he will understand the history that resides there. What then emerges is a long and complex tale about the world that followed the end of slavery in Martinique. The text is interrupted periodically by excerpts from a notebook, which in the novel is presented as an archival document from the Bibliothèque Schoelcher—Martinique's major historical library. As in Maximin's work, this archival document is invented and yet presented as a real historical document. It grants a certain historical tone to the narrative, so that in addition to Chamoiseau's voice there

is a "primary source" that speaks from the various moments depicted in the novel.[14]

These novels—themselves part of a much larger tradition of fictional writings about history that includes the work of Edouard Glissant, Maryse Condé, and Simone Schwartz-Bart—present fascinating engagements with the problem of the "archive" of the islands of the French Caribbean. Their success and importance derive in part from the fact that they beautifully tell the dramatic history of the French Caribbean. *Texaco* (along with another one of Chamoiseau's novels, *Chronique des Sept Misères*), for instance, raises many of the issues that historians of slave emancipation and its aftermath explore—the struggle to consolidate rights over land and political rights; the movement from plantations to the towns; and the changing racial, social, and economic relationships in the colony. Maximin's work effectively and dramatically describes the struggles of Louis Delgrès, as well as his ex-slaves followers, in the late eighteenth century. The stories they tell and the documents Maximin excerpts in *L'Isolé Soleil* have therefore reached a wide circulation beyond the circles of those who have read the historical work about the island. These novels depend on this body of historical work, but they also distinguish themselves from it by starkly stating their concern with speaking a history for the present and in a sense narrating a "true" past that the documents do not contain. Maximin said in an interview: "The present always invents a past for itself out of its own desire." And in the opening pages of *L'Isolé Soleil,* Maximin commands Marie-Gabriel to make "truth serve the imagination and not the opposite." The message that pervades both these novels is that the present needs a past that in many ways it cannot grasp through traditional history. They are histories, dialogues about the meaning of history, and denials of the value of empirical history all at once. They highlight what their authors see as the absences in the archives and surpass them by telling history nonetheless. And they have become crucial texts for the French Caribbean public's vision of the history of their islands.

A Prayer for the Archives

In the struggle to produce significant pasts, however, such novels have also overemphasized the silences in the archives. All too often it is assumed in contemporary Guadeloupe that the archives will not speak stories of resistant slaves, when in fact many stories have not been fully researched. Such is the case, for instance, with a

1793 slave revolt that took place in Trois-Rivières. This revolt—the largest in the history of the island—has traditionally occupied a very small place in the historiography, to a large extent because many historians have followed the lead of the nineteenth-century Auguste Lacour in seeing it less as a slave revolt than as an episode in which various white political groups used slaves as troops. Most recently, for instance, the historian Lucien Réné Abenon has argued that the slaves involved in the revolt were essentially "slaves under the command of political forces they did not understand."[15]

In researching the history of the revolt, I brought together a few new pieces of information garnered from the notary registers in Guadeloupe, as well as an account of the event that was not previously analyzed in detail, in order to present a different reading of the revolt at Trois-Rivières. I uncovered details about the revolt's leader, Jean-Baptiste, that had either consciously or unconsciously been elided from Lacour's account and those that followed it. This allowed me to reread the other existing accounts of the event; I presented Jean-Baptiste's actions as an effective and carefully crafted political intervention and showed how the insurgents effectively presented themselves as citizens who acted in the service of a besieged republic. I used this particular event as a window into the broader process through which slave insurgents mobilized and transformed the language of rights during the 1790s, arguing that the events of this period lay the political foundations for the final abolition of slavery in 1848, which was propelled by the abolitionist Victor Schoelcher. A recent review of the work summarized this broader argument by somewhat inaccurately transforming Jean-Baptiste into a "famous pre-Schoelcherian abolitionist." But in Trois-Rivières, Jean-Baptiste is barely remembered, despite the efforts of the activist, teacher, and historian Carlomann Bassette—who spent several years in the Basse-Terre prison in the early 1980s. In 1993 Bassette built a monument to the revolt of 1793, mounting a large stone and inscribing it with a plaque that reads, "1793–1993: Chaque événement, tragique, épique, héroïque, est sève de la mémoire" (Each event, tragic, epic, or heroic, is the sap of memory). But he has not yet fulfilled his goal of surrounding the monument with the list of the names of both the victims and the insurgents—only a few of the latter of which are known at all.[16]

The historian Michèle Duchet has recently highlighted the importance of the "black hero" who appeared in eighteenth-century texts such as that of the Abbé Raynal; certainly, from C. L. R. James to Michel-Rolph Trouillot, the figure of a slave turned rebel leader has captivated audiences and been central to the creation of historical narratives.[17] This is certainly true in Guadeloupe, where the island's best-known hero, Louis Delgrès, continues to occupy an important place in the debates about the past and future of the island. The one piece of writing attributed to him—his 1802 proclamation—is widely circulated and printed on a metal plaque in the fort that now carries his name in Basse-Terre. This proclamation cannot be found in any archive; its text is known through the work of Auguste Lacour—who in fact suggested that it was written not by Delgrès but by a sympathetic white creole who joined the insurgents and was later executed. Its historical meaning is complex, and the document has in many ways found itself saddled with a significance it probably did not have at the time it was written. It is not entirely clear whether Delgrès's political allegiance was primarily to the integrated army he was a part of or to the people of Guadeloupe as a whole, and there is little evidence that Delgrès had in mind the creation of an independent state.

Yet today Delgrès is seen as a hero who fought the French in order to preserve the people of Guadeloupe from slavery, and for independence activists he is often called upon as a precursor who understood the need for independence from France. In 1995 the group Voukoum organized a procession in honor of Delgrès's last combat. Preceded and announced (as it always is) with a series of whips cracked against the road, the group marched from Fort St. Charles, through the town of Basse-Terre, and up the slopes of the Soufrière volcano to Matouba. Along the way, poems and historical accounts were read, and music accompanied the march. Voukoum's evocation of Delgrès interestingly sought to reverse the usual understanding of the course of emancipation in Guadeloupe. The 1848 abolition happened in late April and early May, during the same period of the year that the 1802 reestablishment of slavery occurred; so during the time set aside to celebrate the abolition decreed from France, Voukoum marched in memory of 1802 and its historical martyrs. This event was carried out with the support of Daniel Maximin, who in 1998 also drove another act of commemoration for Delgrès, this time by the French state itself. In April of that year, on the date of the abolition of slavery in 1848, an inscription to Delgrès, along with one to Toussaint Louverture, was added to the Pantheon (France's "Temple of Heroes") in Paris in the hall that leads to the crypt that includes the tomb of Victor Schoelcher. Like Voukoum's work, the placement of these plaques also makes it so that visitors have to pass by Delgrès and Louverture to get to Schoelcher.

Both acts represent a public presentation of a historical argument that attempts to resituate the history of Guadeloupe in relation to France and to highlight the complex contributions of the island's slaves to the history of the move from property to freedom and ultimately to republican citizenship. A series of celebrations during May 2002 once again included Voukoum in celebrations of Delgrès's struggle in 1802.[18]

The evocation of the past in the contemporary French Caribbean, then, takes place through the intertwined production of historical narratives, fiction, and public events and monuments. Even as the archives are critiqued and supplemented by invention in various novels, they also supply the foundation for new stories that can help reconfigure the historical narratives of the island. Still, the process through which historical narratives are to be diffused and incorporated into life on the island depends to a large extent on the work of cultural groups and writers who see themselves in some sense as the guardians of the island's history. And, indeed, their work is central to the production of future histories. In researching and writing about Guadeloupe, I was influenced in my research by the ways in which works of fiction, particularly that of Maximin, dramatized the history of the island and presented the need for a telling of its multiple and sometimes subterranean histories. Fiction widened the scope of my historical imagination, enabling me to make connections I had not thought of before between particular stories I encountered in the archives and the broader narrative I eventually developed. This was particularly true for my reading of notarial records, which in turn enabled me to see the ways in which ex-slaves themselves (in a way not entirely unlike what Maximin's hero Jonathan did in creating his journal) had constituted their own archives in the pursuit of freedom. Maximin's interest in the history I was writing, in turn, was an important part of enabling me to publish this work in French and making it available in Guadeloupe. Some examples from the work have since been used by Maximin and other Antilleans working in the Socialist Party and by the government in presenting arguments about the need for, and possibility of, accepting *both* Guadeloupe's long history of connection and dialogue with the French republic and its cultural and historical particularities, notably in a 1999 report arguing for various reforms in cultural, educational, and economic policies relating to the Départements d'Outre-Mer. The archive of slavery, then—brought into the present through the intertwined work of novelists, historians, cultural administrators, and musical groups—continues to be used as a tool, and sometimes a weapon, in the de-

bates and confrontations over the future of the French Caribbean.

NOTES

My title echoes that used by Michael Zeuske, "The *Cimarron* in the Archives: A Re-Reading of Miguel Barnet's Biography of Estaban Montejo," *New West India Guide* 71, no. 3–4 (1997): 265–79, in an essay that presents an interesting Cuban counterpoint to the questions taken up here. I would like to thank Frederick Cooper, David Pedersen, and Rebecca Scott for their helpful comments.

1. See Louis Sala-Moulins, *Le Code Noir ou le calvaire de Canaan* (Paris: Presses Universitaires de France, 1988). Unlike the maroons of Jamaica or Suriname, the maroons in Guadeloupe never signed treaties assuring their freedom in return for sending back new slave runaways, and so they are not saddled with the stigma that sometimes accompanies them in the former contexts.

2. Aimé Césaire, *Aimé Césaire: The Collected Poetry,* trans. Clayton Eshleman (Berkeley: University of California Press, 1983), 73.

3. Voukoum describes itself as a *mouvman kiltirel* (cultural movement) and has a workshop where traditional drum making and costume making are taught and practiced; they have also done oral history projects, interviewing older Guadeloupeans about lost carnival traditions, in part with the aim of reintegrating the practices of political critique and subversion into a contemporary carnival that has lost many of these elements. The album with the song "Kolon-la" is called *On Larèl, On Lèspri* and was released in 1996.

4. See Josette Fallope, *Esclaves et Citoyens: Les noirs a la Guadeloupe au XIXe siècle* (Basse-Terre: Société d'Histoire de la Guadeloupe, 1992).

5. Michel-Rolph Trouillot, *Silencing the Past: Power and the Production of History* (Boston: Beacon Press, 1995).

6. On the process of naming in 1848, see Priska Dégras, "Figures de nom: du déni à l'acceptation," in Marcel Dorigny, ed., *Esclavage, résistances, et abolitions* (Paris: Editions du CTHS, 1999), 469–80.

7. This larger process of transformation in Guadeloupe during this period had much in common with what would occur later in other postemancipation contexts; see Thomas Holt, *The Problem of Freedom* (Baltimore: Johns Hopkins Universith Press, 1992), and the essays in Frederick Cooper, Thomas Holt, and Rebecca Scott, *Beyond Slavery* (Chapel Hill: University of North Carolina Press, 2000).

8. I discuss these censuses in "'The Price of Liberty': Victor Hugues and the Administration of Freedom in Guadeloupe, 1794–1802," *William and Mary Quarterly,* 3d series, 56, no. 2 (April 1999): 363–92.

9. See Dominique Julia, "Histoire Religieuse," in Jacques Le Goff and Pierre Nora, eds., *Faire de l'histoire* (Paris: Gallimard, 1974), 137–67, quoted in Carlo Ginzburg, *The Cheese and the Worms* (Baltimore: Johns Hopkins University Press, 1980), xxi.

10. See David Barry Gaspar, *Bondsmen and Rebels: A Study of Master-Slave Relations in Antigua* (Durham: Duke

University Press, 1993), and the different readings in John Thornton, "War, the State, and Religious Norms in Coromantee' Thought: The Ideology of an African-American Nation," in Robert Blaire St. George, ed., *Possible Pasts: Becoming Colonial in Early America* (Ithaca: Cornell University Press, 2000), 181–200; Winthrop Jordan, *Tumult and Silence at Second Creek* (Baton Rouge: Louisiana State University Press, 1996); and Douglas Egerton, *Gabriel's Rebellion* (Chapel Hill: University of North Carolina Press, 1993). I explore the issue of the Bois-Caïman ceremony in more detail in "The Citizen's Trance: The Haitian Revolution and the Motor of History," in Birgit Meyer and Peter Pels, eds., *Magic and Modernity: Interfaces of Revelation and Concealment* (Stanford: Stanford University Press, 2003); see also David Geggus, "La cérémonie du Bois-Caïman," in Laënnec Hurbon, ed., *L'insurrection des esclaves de Saint-Domingue* (Paris: Karthala, 2000), 149–67, and Léon-Francois Hoffman, "Un mythe national: la cérémonie du Bois-Caïman," in Gérard Barthélemy and Christian Girault, eds., *La République Haïtienne: Etat des Lieux et Perspectives* (Paris: Editions Kharthala, 1993), 434–48.

11. André Schwartz-Bart, *La Mulatresse Solitude* (Paris: Seuil, 1972); Arlette Gautier, *Les soeurs de Solitude: la condition féminine dans l'esclavage aux Antilles du XVII au XIX siècles* (Paris: Editions Caribéennes, 1985); the work Schwartz-Bart drew on is Auguste Lacour, *Histoire de la Guadeloupe* (Basse-Terre: Impr. du Gouvernement, 1858).

12. C. L. R. James, *The Black Jacobins* (New York: Vintage, 1963). The Abbé Raynal oversaw the writing of the *Histoire philosophique et politique des établissements et du commerce des Européens dans les deux Indes,* a multivocal text that went through many different editions in the eighteenth century, issued both defenses of slavery and this powerful warning, and highlighted the ways Europe had been transformed by colonial expansion; Michael Ondaatje, *The English Patient* (New York: Knopf, 1992).

13. Daniel Maximin, *Lone Sun,* trans. and with an introduction by Clarisse Zimra (Charlottesville: University of Virginia Press, 1989).

14. Patrick Chamoiseau, *Texaco* (Paris: Gallimard, 1992), was translated as *Texaco* (New York: Vintage, 1997).

15. Lucien Réné Abenon, "Les révoltes serviles à la Guadeloupe au début de la Révolution," in Dorigny, ed., *Esclavage,* 209–15.

16. *Les Esclaves de la République* (Paris: Calmann-Lévy, 1998); Blaise Ndjéhoya, "Esclaves et colonisés dans les idéaux de la République," *Continental: Afrique en March* (August–September 2000).

17. Michèle Duchet, "Esclavage et marronnage: le héros noir," in Dorigny, ed., *Esclavage,* 91–98; James, *Black Jacobins;* Trouillot, *Silencing the Past.*

18. For more on this, see my "Haunting Delgrès," *Radical History Review* 78 (fall 2000): 166–77.

Redemption's Archive

Remembering the Future in a Revolutionary Past

Paul K. Eiss

> It's a poor sort of memory that only works backwards.
> —the White Queen, *Through the Looking Glass*

While Alice brushed the White Queen's tousled hair, the monarch offered her employ as a lady's maid for a salary of two pence a week, along with a regular ration of jam. As Lewis Carroll relates in *Through the Looking Glass,* Alice was disinclined to accept in any case. Nonetheless, she grew disturbed when the White Queen informed her that the offered jam was only to be given "every other day"—that is, only "yesterday" and "tomorrow" but never "today." Alice immediately realized that she would never receive jam on the series of "todays" that she worked but rather could only enjoy the expectation of receiving it in the future or perhaps the memory of having received it previously. In response to Alice's questions about the proposed arrangement, the White Queen attributed her confusion to the "effect of living backwards," a prospect that "always makes one a little giddy at first." The White Queen explained that Alice lived "forwards" and was thus condemned to remember only "backwards." The White Queen, on the other hand, lived "backwards" and could remember "both ways," informed by a previous experience both of the future and of the past. The monarch was so confident of her faculties that she had the King's Messenger sent to prison for punishment in advance of his trial and sentencing. "Of course," the White Queen explained, "the crime comes last of all."[1]

Despite the strangeness of Carroll's tale, the White Queen's prophetic memory finds many parallels outside Wonderland. In modernizing regimes, notably in times of revolutionary political and social change, the invocation of the future becomes a preeminent theme of political discourse. The claims of governing parties and figures to the power to remember both ways transform the politics of collective memory, redefining the recollection of the past and its events and traditions in relation to an imagined future. Even the present may be understood as a moment of rupture, an intelligible transition between a superseded past and an emergent future, guided by political leaders who claim the privilege of knowing the shape that future will take. Whether under socialist or capitalist auspices, the historical experiences of schemes of authoritarian modernization evoke other elements of Carroll's tale as well. Claims to privileged knowledge of the future and, effectively, to the ability to remember both ways provide alibis for the failure to realize utopian ideals in the present and justifications for the deferral of their fulfillment to an indefinite future.[2]

Such claims and alibis were common currency among revolutionary leaders in Yucatán in the early years of the Mexican Revolution (1910–17). In the mid-nineteenth century a massive indigenous rebellion led to the destruction of most commercial agriculture in Yucatán, particularly the sugar plantation economy of the southeast. Decades of conflict and population loss throughout the state left regional elites in a fragile position, unable to consolidate political control over the peninsula or to reestablish a stable source of income and state revenues.[3] From the 1870s, however, Yucatecan elites seemed to have found their salvation in henequen, a spiny plant whose fiber was used in the production of rope and cordage. With westward expansion in the United States, the demand for fiber increased along with its price, and the invention of decorticating machinery facilitated large-scale production. The future of the peninsula, and the conclusive victory of Hispanic "civilization" over indigenous "barbarism," seemed to depend on the fortunes of the emerging henequen hacienda economy.[4]

During the reign of Mexican president Porfirio Díaz (1876–1911), henequen monoculture expanded throughout northwestern Yucatán, producing a bonanza of profits for planters and the state. Confronted by the difficulties of satisfying the labor demands of the burgeoning regional henequen economy, local elites and the state government set in place a legally sanctioned system of debt servitude to force Maya-speaking populations to work on the haciendas. Though a thoroughly contemporary institution, the system of indigenous debt servitude was infamous in Mexico and abroad as an antiquated form of "Indian slavery" that marked Yucatán as a "feudal" backwater of the nation.[5] Even after the fall of Díaz in 1911, and amid the onset of civil war throughout Mexico and several insurgencies in the Yucatán peninsula, Yucatecan elites were able to preserve indigenous debt servitude and to continue the production and exportation of henequen fiber.[6] In 1914, however, Venustiano Carranza, the national leader of the Constitutionalist revolutionary movement, ordered the issuance of a decree ending debt servitude. No longer seen as representative of Mexico's archaic past, Yucatán seemed to stand for the possibilities of its future. As war raged elsewhere in the country, under the Constitutionalist governments of Colonel Eleuterio Avila and General Salvador Alvarado Yucatán came to be known as a relatively peaceful social "laboratory" where novel revolutionary social reforms could be attempted years in advance of their implementation at the national level. Yucatán became a place where the future of the revolution, and therefore of Mexico, might be encountered.[7]

Recent studies have illuminated local, regional, and national processes of state formation in the Mexican revolutionary period and have dedicated particular attention to the struggles of diverse social and political actors to establish or contest the terms of the emerging cultural and political hegemony of the postrevolutionary state.[8] As this essay demonstrates, such struggles were inseparable from struggles over the significance of historical events and their commitment to historical memory, whether "official" or "popular." Beyond simply enforcing a set of provisions relating to labor, Yucatán's revolutionaries set out to realize an epochal rupture that would abolish archaic Mexico and inaugurate a radically different society of the future in its place. Like Carroll's White Queen, state-level revolutionary leaders claimed privileged understanding of the nature of the event of liberation in advance of its occurrence. In attempting to realize their visions, they met the distinct and sometimes contradictory interpretations of indigenous workers, who adopted a similar rhetoric of temporal break but understood the event of liberation in ways that sometimes diverged sharply from the event envisioned by government officials.

Numerous archival and ethnographic studies have demonstrated how the exigencies and interests of the present can transform the past, as memories and historical narratives are constructed in the wake of events.[9] This study of the memory of the future in Yucatán during the Mexican Constitutionalist Revolution explores the ways "event making" might take place in advance of the event itself, shaping its commitment to memory *before* and *during* its occurrence as much as in its aftermath. Determined to end indigenous debt servitude, officials of the revolutionary governments of Eleuterio Avila (1914–15) and Salvador Alvarado (1915–18) set out to instigate a radical transformation of hacienda society by overthrowing a previous "epoch of slavery" and inaugurating a future "epoch of liberty." Alongside their efforts to transform the politics of labor on the haciendas, government officials dedicated themselves to imagining, enacting, and documenting the liberation, which they committed to official memory as a moment in which indigenous laborers were redeemed by the revolutionary state.

Nonetheless, after several years of direct interventions to "redeem" workers by identifying and exorcising surviving elements of slavery, government officials began to join forces with *hacendados*, preserving henequen revenues by enforcing labor discipline and countering the challenges posed by workers. In so doing, government officials consigned liberation to the past as an achieved event. In the eyes of indigenous workers, however, slavery seemed to survive in many guises. For them, much of liberation's potential remained unrealized in the present, though perhaps possible in the future. Although indigenous workers' claims on liberation—like Alice's jam—would be consigned to the past and deferred to the future, their experiences during the revolution helped to shape a distinctive framework for historical memory that has endured to the present.

Liberation's Alibi

In 1911 Mexican president Porfirio Díaz was overthrown and the revolutionary leader Francisco Madero acceded to the presidency. Subsequently, Yucatán experienced years of conflict, as feuding planter factions incited local insurgencies in support of their political favorites for state office, sometimes promising liberation or even land to workers who left the haciendas to join the struggle. While political organizers may have held forth the promise of liberation to hacienda workers, the leaders of the contending movements—who vociferously demanded the "regeneration" and even "redemption" of indigenous workers—shared an unwillingness to challenge indigenous debt servitude directly. Along with reformist Yucatecan institutions like the Social Action League (Liga de Acción Social, a group of progressive hacendados) and the newspaper *Revista de Yucatán* of editor Carlos R. Menéndez, they eschewed a "sudden" and "imprudent" act of emancipation that might endanger the haciendas and the production of henequen. Rather, Yucatán's reformers advocated "methodical" and "gradual" labor and educational reforms to benefit indigenous workers not considered sufficiently educated, responsible, or "civilized" to exercise the prerogatives and responsibilities of freedom. After General Victoriano Huerta overthrew Francisco Madero and reestablished dictatorial rule at the national level, Yucatecan planters put aside their differences to preserve the continued production of henequen fiber, and insurgent forces were demobilized throughout most of the peninsula.[10]

The definitive abolition of debt servitude would come only in 1914, with the overthrow of Huerta's dictatorship by a coalition of rebel groups determined to restore constitutional rule. Shortly after occupying Mexico City in August, Constitutionalist leader Venustiano Carranza appointed the Yucatecan colonel Eleuterio Avila as provisional governor of Yucatán and ordered him to issue a decree liberating indebted workers on the peninsula's henequen haciendas. Carranza intended the measure as a way of advancing cautiously toward a limited reform platform that could help to build a wider base of popular support for the Constitutionalist cause while preventing a costly civil war from spreading to Yucatán, where it might have threatened henequen revenues that financed the Constitutionalist army.[11]

On 11 September 1914, shortly after his arrival in Mérida to assume office and shortly before the promulgation of the liberation decree later that day, Governor Eleuterio Avila addressed troops assembled in the city's central plaza. He heralded the imminent end of the "old regime" and the disappearance of the debt system; the arrival of this "promised redemption" would transform indigenous "pariahs" into "citizens."[12] Indeed, the liberation decree, issued later that day, seemed to break with the notion of gradual emancipation in favor of an immediate transition to free labor, an event that would reshape radically the terms of labor on Yucatán's henequen haciendas. Avila's decree annulled the debts of hacienda laborers, whether held by hacendados, *encargados,* or labor contractors, and forbade the payment of such debts in labor or personal services. Hacienda workers no longer were to be bound to the haciendas. They were to be free to move about at will, and in exercising their right they might choose to remain on the haciendas or to leave them. Owners, encargados, and local political authorities and police would no longer pressure laborers to work on any estate, whether such labor was remunerated or not, and would no longer apprehend workers for nonpayment of debts. Physical violence, corporal punishment, and arbitrary imprisonment—routine elements of the hacienda labor regime—were expressly forbidden. Finally, to monitor enforcement of the decree and to resolve any conflicts that might emerge between hacendados and workers, an Immigration and Labor Department would be established.

The editors of *La Revista de Yucatán* welcomed what they termed Avila's "decree of salvation" (*decreto salvador*), declaring their intention to second his initiative by commissioning a translation of the decree into Yucatec Maya, the lingua franca of Yucatán's indigenous rural working populations. Over the course of three centuries of language contact, Yucatec Maya had changed radically, with the disappearance of much of the vocabulary found in the oldest colonial lexicons and the incorporation of Spanish terms into spoken and written Maya. Such changes were especially marked in the henequen zone, where the level of incorporation of Spanish words led some to refer to the language of daily communication as "modern" or "mixed" Maya. A translation was indeed published in *La Revista de Yucatán* on 20 September 1914; in the spirit of common usage, it incorporated Spanish terms, surrounded by quotation marks and sometimes modified by Maya suffixes, into the surrounding Maya text.[13] However, Avila's government soon published its own, official Maya translation of the decree, which was drafted by the Yucatecan scholar of Maya Santiago Pacheco Cruz and published by a press called "The Future."

Pacheco Cruz had spent his childhood on a henequen hacienda and two years before the liberation had published a well-known dictionary and language-instruction manual in contemporary Maya.[14] Despite his own fluency in contemporary Maya, however, Pacheco Cruz endeavored to translate the liberation decree into an "authentic" or "pure" Maya text, with results both archaic and neologistic. In distinction from the earlier Maya version published in *La Revista de Yucatán*, Pacheco Cruz rejected the use of Spanish terms in favor of obsolete terms drawn from colonial-era dictionaries.[15] In some cases he even minted novel Maya equivalents for the contemporary Spanish political terminology of Avila's decree. Pacheco Cruz openly acknowledged the potential incomprehensibility of his Maya version; in a text accompanying the decree, he instructed those reading it to hacienda workers that, if their audience did not understand the decree, they were to explain it to them in "modern, or mixed Maya, which they understand best." He may have felt it appropriate to fashion a legalistic language for the translation of the decree, imagining that its purity lent authority to a revolutionary government that claimed to act on behalf of indigenous populations. Perhaps Pacheco Cruz used "pure" Maya terms in an attempt to alter the meaning of the original decree, tempering its potentially dangerous language of rights and class. By Pacheco Cruz's pen the Spanish term for right (which in *La Revista*'s translation had been left as the Spanish *derecho*) became "idea" or "thought" in Maya, and the Spanish phrase "sacred and inalienable civil rights that are born and grow with man in well-constituted democracies" was transformed into the cryptic Maya phrase "very sacred ideas that are born and grow with man in enlightened thoughts."

Notwithstanding the differences between the Spanish text of the 1914 decree and Pacheco Cruz's Maya translation, both versions shared an identical series of provisions that would have substantially altered the conditions of life and work on the haciendas if enforced. Moreover, in the text of the decree these provisions were embedded within an encompassing vision of the scope and nature of the liberation as an event yet to come. Both versions strongly characterized "dictatorship" and "liberty" as sociopolitical conditions corresponding to distinct historical periods. As points of reference for the possibilities of political and social change, both versions of the decree evoked a distant previous epoch of social

justice and legitimate rule, as well as a period of corruption and misrule in the more recent past. The Spanish language version made oblique reference to a prior and legitimate political regime, the Liberal Republic founded by the constitution of 1857. The Maya version did not evoke a legitimate political republic located in the past but rather a bygone "state of well-being" or "goodness" of the "great pueblo" when it was ruled by good and moral men. According to both versions of the decree, the legitimate polities of the distant past had been subverted by corruption and dictatorial rule in the more recent past. In the Spanish version, the institutions and achievements of the Liberal Republic were fundamentally subverted both by debt servitude and by the rule of dictators like Porfirio Díaz and Victoriano Huerta. The Maya version related that the previous "state of well-being" had been "broken by the bad thoughts of an evildoer (or bad man) against the goodness of the great pueblo."

In both versions of the decree liberation was portrayed as a redemptive event of the future that would restore an idealized past. By abolishing servitude and corruption, the Constitutionalist revolutionary government would break with the corruption of the Díaz regime and restore a legitimate social and political order that would be founded on the rights and well-being of citizens. According to Avila's Spanish decree, through the liberation the Constitutionalist movement would reactivate the "sacred and inalienable rights" of the citizen under the republic, and encourage "social evolution" by bringing its "noble and exalted ideals of redemption and justice to the most remote corner of the Nation." Part of that evolution would be the "moral, intellectual and material betterment of the proletarian class." According to the Maya version of the decree, the Constitutionalist rebellion also would restore the past, through the "return of a state of well-being" and the achievement of the "well-being of the very poor." In the imminent event of liberation, Constitutionalist leaders would "improve the state of things" by realizing "the very good and lofty ideas of the great life, and rectitude." Despite abolishing an old regime and inaugurating a new social and political order, the authors of the decree held the preservation of the hacienda system and henequen wealth as sacrosanct. As one official in the Avila government later recalled, on the eve of the liberation Avila and other members of the government felt "general horror" at the thought of the economic collapse that might result if fiber production were interrupted. The decree's authors envisioned the liberation as a dramatic political and social transformation enacted against a backdrop of general stability and labor tranquility.[16]

In the language and provisions of the 1914 liberation decree, revolutionary authorities thus envisioned the liberation before it occurred as a significant large-scale and collective event, enacted on and experienced by Yucatecan society as a whole. In the immediate aftermath of promulgation and before the decree had been publicized widely, several proposals swiftly appeared, calling for the commitment of the liberation to public memory in monumental form. In the pages of *La Revista de Yucatán* Carlos Menéndez suggested that the text of the decree be "engraved in gold, on a marble tablet, to serve as an example for future generations." Hacendado José Canto seconded the proposal, calling for the collection of funds to finance the construction of a monument to the "emancipation of the indigenous race." To "perpetuate the memory" of the liberation, Canto called for the erection of a monument or plaque with an "inscription alluding to an event of such great importance for the history of our fatherland" (*historia patria*).[17] Notwithstanding such proposals, the drive to commit the imminent event to memory was focused less on the construction of monuments than on the monumental quality of the decree's enunciation and inscription in personal experience and testimonial form. In the days following the decree's promulgation Carlos Menéndez declared the importance of "publicity, publicity, and more publicity" for its realization and called for the designation of Maya-speaking government agents to disseminate the decree throughout the countryside. Only through such means could the liberation be realized as an event; once publicized the decree would be indelibly "inscribed in the conscience of the people, in the soul of yesterday's pariahs, now raised to the status of citizens and free men."[18]

Such concerns were reflected in the decree and circulars relating to its enforcement, which elaborated a framework through which localized experiences of liberation were to take place as memorable and historic moments of personal and group redemption. A government circular issued less than two weeks after the decree's promulgation called for government commissioners to visit haciendas across the state to read the new decree to workers. In Pacheco Cruz's Maya version, the Spanish term *comisionado* was translated with a Maya term that literally means "informers" or "translators" of the "word," a term used in the past to refer to Christian missionaries. According to the religiously charged language of the Maya decree, through its reading workers would "hear" the "vision of the lord Great True Man" (that is, Governor Avila) and would come to understand the decree's "spirit" or "soul" through the ex-planations of the new missionaries. Each of these local renderings of the decree would be performed and recorded in the archive as individual acts of redemption—partaking in and making manifest the event of collective redemption anticipated by the authors of the decree.

Other provisions of the decree suggested that the governmental presence on the haciendas could itself become a legible marker of temporal break signaling the realization of the liberation. The regulations relating to the establishment and activities of the new Immigration and Labor Office manifest a vision of the realization of a postliberation future of labor relations institutionalized and mediated by the state. To borrow the language of Circular Number Three, the office would secure "peace and concordance" between workers and employers by reconciling laborers' rights with "public and private interests" in the continued production of fiber. Beyond providing a model for the state as the enforcer of liberty on the fincas, the decree and the circulars thus necessitated the visible performance and documentation of such memorable acts of intervention to produce a state of social concord consistent with the successful and controlled realization of the liberation. As the provisions relating to dissemination and enforcement make clear, the authors of the decree went beyond situating the present moment in relation to the memories of a superseded and corrupt past of servitude and dictatorship and of a future of liberty and virtue. Through these provisions the authors of the decree addressed the *credibility* of liberation as an event. They established the terms under which the occurrence and nature of the liberation could be verified and specified, how documentation about its consequences might be produced, and how a conclusive archive of the liberation might be assembled.

Accounts of the liberation as a local event appeared in *La Revista de Yucatán* within days of promulgation. They consisted of descriptions of encargados reading the decree to assembled workers, who subsequently declared their gratitude to the governor and the hacendados, their satisfaction with conditions on the fincas, and their determination to continue working and residing on the fincas. On Hacienda San José Tzal workers reportedly listened "religiously" to encargado José Leal Acosta, who read the decree with the assistance of a Maya translator. Leal then took advantage of the assembly to read a government decree penalty for robbery and other crimes against "public order." He showed the workers photographs of executions that had been published in *La Revista*, a technique described in the article as "graphic—right at the Indian's level of comprehension."[19] Similarly, the beginnings of a government archive of the event of liberation are found in the documentation produced by officials of the Avila government in the weeks and months following promulgation. Acts of propagation by hacendados, commissioners, and other government officials were committed to documentary memory in the context of investigations of compliance with or violation of the decree and were collected in the state archives.[20] Moreover, the eventual creation and staffing of the Immigration and Labor Department implied the production of documentation within the context of the insertion of government representatives into a mediating role in conflicts between laborers and hacendados over wages and the price of goods sold to workers in hacienda stores. Indeed, the extant documentation from the department gives the appearance of a liberation decree propagated and enforced on individual haciendas, of wages increased and prices lowered.[21]

Through such measures the archive and the reading public were prepared for the production of an officially sanctioned memory of the liberation as an actually occurring event, both as a concatenation of memorable local experiences of redemption and as a collective happening. It remained only to consign the event to history as an achieved past, confirming and consolidating the previous vision of it as an anticipated future and the reports in *La Revista de Yucatán* that had suggested that the liberation was taking place exactly as anticipated.[22] Thus, on 28 September, just two weeks after promulgation, the governor called for district military commanders to report back to him on the "moral effects" of the liberation decree in the rural districts. Their reports show remarkable similarity in substance, tone, style, and even the words chosen to describe the effects of the decree. In almost all cases, the news was good—liberty was compatible with the continued production of fiber. With the promulgation of the decree, the commanders reported, a certain "restiveness" was evident among the "servants." Many of them had left the fincas, determined to "taste" or "feel" liberty. After the visits and instruction of the commissioners, however, this disquiet had passed. Although a few workers had chosen to leave fincas where wages and treatment were not acceptable, most had returned "tranquilly" after a few days and now dedicated themselves to their work with increased vigor. Though work slowed at first, the pace of production soon returned to normal or even improved. The hacendados readily increased wages and granted other benefits to their workers, and all now fulfilled the letter and spirit of the liberation decree. On the haciendas and in the pueb-

los, as the military commanders reported, hacendados and workers alike "rejoiced" and welcomed the coming of the liberation.[23] Thus Avila's government and the press, through legislation and then actual intervention on the fincas and documentary practices, had committed the future to memory in stages: first as an imminent event; then as an ongoing process; and finally as an achieved past in official memory. This, to borrow the terminology of the Maya decree, was the "state of well-being" that liberation brought and the memory of the future—now past—that the event offered to its archive.

The remarkable narrative uniformity of these renderings of the liberation did not stem solely from the archival strategies developed to document and memorialize the event of liberation. It was also a product of struggle on the ground. From the moment of promulgation, articles in *La Revista de Yucatán* compared liberated workers to impulsive children and to blind men suddenly restored to vision and dazzled by sunlight, and they repeatedly emphasized the need to issue a series of regulations aimed at controlling their actions. Only thus could the government ensure that the decree was not "misunderstood" by workers who might otherwise indulge themselves in laziness, drunkenness, and "libertinage." Alongside reporting of the felicitous results of the decree, *La Revista* published a few reports warning of "antipatriotic and malevolent interpretations" of the decree. Through threats and enticements some individuals were reported to be persuading indigenous workers to abandon the haciendas for the "life of savages, in the forest."[24] As early as 19 September, in Circular Number One, Eleuterio Avila also mentioned the danger posed by "agitators" who deliberately "misinterpreted" the decree and committed the crime of "incitement" (*cohecho*) by telling "servants" to abandon the haciendas or face punishment by the government. The identity of these offenders, though mysterious in the circular, is suggested by a communication authored by Governor Avila. He ordered a military commander facing the exodus of large numbers of workers from the haciendas to be "diplomatic" in ensuring that "Capital—which is the tributary of public revenues and without which there would be no Government—not be dissolved" as a result of the departures. Avila elliptically suggested that the commander, without "restricting or detracting from liberty," use his own "sound judgement" to prevent the depopulation of the fincas through the activities of so-called *cohechadores*.[25]

The meaning of *cohecho* is not immediately evident. The term may be translated as "seduction," "incitement," or "enticement." Hence it is not so much a criminal act committed in the past as the act of influencing others in such a way that they might become liable to violate the law in the future. Surviving archival records of cohecho investigations suggest that hacendados and local officials were using Circular Number One within days of its issuance as a means to identify and root out troublemakers. The majority of the surviving cohecho cases provide evidence of the prosecution and punishment of workers for actions or even words that were considered likely to inspire fellow laborers to challenge the terms of work and remuneration on the fincas in the name of liberty. For example, on a hacienda in the district of Ticul three workers were jailed by soldiers and the hacienda administrator, "one of them for having said, and the other for having heard, that the two-week period of notice referred to in Circular Number 1 had already ended, and that they should be given their liberty." In November, the encargado of Hacienda San Antonio in Tixkokob requested that the worker Esteban Kantún be prosecuted because he encouraged other workers to demand higher wages. According to the encargado Kantún insisted in his "work of destruction, going several times—concealed under the shadows of night—to continue his work as an agitator among the other hands." In the case of Kantún and all the other cohecho cases involving allegations of labor incitation, without exception, the accused were sentenced by Governor Avila to imprisonment as *cohechadores*. One military commander complained that the cohecho allegations were a "contemptible" strategy to oblige workers to return to the haciendas, thus "making a mockery of the humanitarian law that has come to raise the Indians up to the category of citizens." Most government officials and military commanders, however, appear to have suffered no such attacks of conscience, judging from the evidence of their active pursuit of "offenders" in the few surviving cohecho records.[26]

In making their own claims on the significance and consequences of the liberation decree, workers seem to have envisioned the possibilities of a future liberation that diverged from the official script in ways informed by their own long-standing struggles over life, labor, and liberty on and off the haciendas. These visions, however, would be included neither within the authorized event of liberation nor in its enactment and commitment to official memory. Rather, they were expunged from the general story of liberation recorded in archives and newspapers, to be relocated in fragments to the penal records of crime, corruption, and disorder. Though liberation was the signal public event of the Avila government, the co-

hecho investigations played in counterpoint to it and were used to police its boundaries, as a form of systematic repression concealed behind the official liberation. Despite the cohecho prosecutions, the official memory of the liberation—that is, that most workers happily remained on the haciendas—was inscribed in the archives and press reports in conformity with the postliberation future that had been anticipated by the decree's authors. Little note was taken of the experiences of people like Manuel Cimé, who, according to an inquiry into the cause of his death by hanging, "decided to end his life, due to the upset caused by the prospect of being forced to return to the finca he had left." Such episodes were left sparsely documented, in fragments lying outside the organized and authorized recollection of Avila's liberation. In line with the official story, *La Revista*, which had provided abundant and celebratory coverage of the liberation and its consequences, remained silent on the matter of the cohecho investigations.[27]

But while Avila's government and the Yucatecan press worked at producing an official memory of liberation enacted and fulfilled, political shifts soon overturned his government and its attempt at event making. In January 1915, as a result of increasing evidence of his alliance with Yucatecan planters against Carranza's policies, Avila was recalled from the peninsula and replaced by General Toribio de los Santos, who immediately set about imposing forced loans on Yucatecan hacendados. A coup was not long in coming, led by Abel Ortíz Argumedo, a Yucatecan military officer widely supported by the hacendados in his bid to take control of the state government. In March Carranza sent General Salvador Alvarado with an army to retake the peninsula, and the general quickly established himself as the new governor of Yucatán.

Alvarado, unlike Avila, explicitly referred to the system of indigenous servitude in Yucatán as "slavery." Years later he would write that when he arrived in the peninsula he found Yucatecan workers still mired in "abject servitude" despite the promulgation of Avila's decree; they were subject to the irons of a "bitter slavery, in which they had learned, from fathers to sons, that they could dream of no other happiness than alcohol, and could hope for no other liberation than death." Alvarado immediately presented his own plans for sweeping social reforms as an attack on "slavery" on various fronts, a far-reaching program for the liberation that Avila, in his view, had never even attempted to realize. Thus, from 1915 on, the prestige and modus operandi of the new revolutionary government depended on the *denial* of the previous "event" of liberation in 1914 rather than on its confirmation in official memory.[28]

Under the Alvarado government, which secured the freedom of workers to depart the henequen fincas at will, the prosecution of workers under the circulars against cohecho ceased. Furthermore, the new government often took action to provide "retroactive" justice to workers for previous abuses against them that may have been legal in the times they were committed, such as beatings or nonpayment of wages. However, Alvarado studiously ignored the more recent violations of individual liberties that had taken place through the cohecho prosecutions, abuses in which some officials who later joined his government were implicated. Thus the worker José Isabel Flores, who was charged with cohecho for discussing the liberation decree with other laborers and was then imprisoned and threatened with execution, complained fruitlessly to Alvarado about the events of 1914. His pleas were dismissed.[29]

Eleuterio Avila and his government had claimed to "remember" the future in 1914, and law, archive, and even the press were dedicated to making reality conform to that memory. Where the official version of the event was challenged by workers, the crime of cohecho had been invented as a repressive alibi, preserving the integrity of liberation's official memory and consigning other visions and memories of the time to the penal archives, in fragments. While liberation was to be remembered as official redemption, cohecho was to be forgotten as criminal perdition. Ironically, however, Avila's liberation would remain an event of the future only—envisioned, anticipated, performed, and recorded before the fact but ultimately denied its place in the historical past. Avila's prospective and fragmentary archive of liberation and the records of repression under the cohecho law eventually shared the same fate. They represent not so much pasts silenced by exclusion from the archives as fleeting memories of futures relocated, contained, and ultimately forgotten, their narrative in fragments, their archive inchoate, their monument unbuilt.

The Agony of the Past, the Violence of the Future

Sir: is it true that the Revolution has triumphed there? Is it true that the Past agonizes there, under the heavy, inescapable and violent blows of the Future? That Tradition, Custom and Habits acquired for many years in our pueblo—with the approval of the Powerful, and the men of former governments—today face new horizons? If that is true, then my ideal is there! Continue on that road. The masses have yearned for their redemption for years and years.

—Adolfo Cardeña, Mexican consul, to Salvador Alvarado. Douglas, Arizona, July 1915

To observers like Cardeña throughout Mexico and abroad, Yucatán under Alvarado's rule seemed to dramatize both the promise and the peril of the revolution's violent break with the past and its bold encounter with the future.[30] While Avila's measures had referred to earlier times of corruption, it was only under Alvarado that the state government unequivocally identified the prerevolutionary past—up to and even including the period of Avila's rule—as a period of "slavery." Thus, the epochal contrast between past and future in the concept of redemption was no longer figured as the restoration of the legitimacy of a distant past or as an easily achieved transition between successive epochs. Rather, Alvarado's government anticipated an extended battle of starkly opposed social orders and political regimes—one a past of slavery and the other a future of unprecedented liberty. In place of the liberation as a discrete event, Alvarado foresaw a violent conflict between times of liberty and times of slavery, in a hotly contended present.

For Alvarado, to realize the liberation of Yucatán, much more was needed than the end of debt servitude. Rather, the officials of Alvarado's government acted on many fronts simultaneously, publicly identifying and exorcising elements of a corrupt and archaic "epoch of slavery" (época de esclavitud) and inaugurating an "epoch of liberty" (época de libertad) in its place. The broad scope of these interventions led Alvarado to become a relentless legislator during his time in Yucatán, from 1915 to 1918. The centerpiece of his legislation was a collection of five laws issued in 1915 (labor, land, and cadastral reform as well as laws relating to the state treasury and municipal government), which Alvarado and others referred to as the "five sisters." Often compared by his contemporaries to the five books of Moses, the "five sisters" did not simply comprise a series of regulations. They were meant to galvanize a people and indicate a path to the promised land—hence the title of the publication in which the laws are published together: *Where We Are Headed* (*A donde vamos*). Alvarado's aspirations to the status of a Mosaic redeemer were evident in frequent references to Yucatán under his governance as a "promised land." One high government official, Florencio Avila y Castillo, even called the state a "Sinai" where the "tablets of Constitutionalist law speak the truth to the pueblo."[31]

The redemptive paradigm that Alvarado placed at the center of his policies was in some respects a novel framework. It far surpassed previous invocations of redemption in political rhetoric and predated by decades the redemptive paradigm adopted by Mexican president Lázaro Cárdenas as a framework for national social reforms in the late 1930s.[32] Nonetheless, the concept would have been somewhat familiar to rural populations in Yucatán, through popular Catholicism and local cults of saints and of the Virgin.[33] Moreover, during the insurgencies of 1911–13 pueblo and hacienda dwellers in some areas of the state had already begun to challenge the regime of "slavery" in the name of "liberty" and in connection with wider regional movements that called for the "redemption" of indigenous workers. It is then unsurprising to find a fully elaborated appeal for a redemptive liberation in a lengthy petition presented to Salvador Alvarado just a few weeks after his arrival in Yucatán. In it, several hundred residents of the pueblo of Hunucmá requested the return of common lands alienated over the previous decades. Throughout their appeal, the people of Hunucmá repeatedly evoked the temporal rupture between times of slavery and times of liberty and drew upon the concept of redemption to structure their description of exploitation past and present and of the future that might break with those oppressive legacies. According to the petitioners, their "liberty" had been "lost and submerged for centuries in the hands of the powerful landowners," a situation they described as characteristic of an era of "slavery." With the 1914 liberation decree, they related, many of the poorest workers escaped the "hands of the opulent landowner" and sought refuge with the residents of Hunucmá. However, due to the lack of lands for building houses or cultivating subsistence plots, many workers and their families were forced to return to the fincas they had left, and the oppressive power of the hacendados—and, with it, slavery—was left largely intact. With the arrival of Alvarado, who proposed to issue radical labor and land reform measures, these "grave evils" might finally be remedied. They hoped that what they referred to as the general's "great work of redemption" would free them from their "opprobrium and misery" in the imminent future, through access to land and "honorable work."[34]

Through his sweeping vision of redemption Alvarado attempted to arrive at a populist vision of redemption capable of incorporating such languages of popular grievance with his own utopian claims to knowledge of the future and the power to realize it in the present. Soon after his arrival in the state the general institutionalized redemption as a model for revolutionary governance through the creation of the Office of Information and Propaganda, which was charged with disseminating the new decrees and laws of the revolutionary government and reporting back to the general on conditions on the haciendas. Under the direction of Florencio Avila y Castillo, the office employed a corps of fifteen propaganda agents who, as Yucatecans and Maya speakers, were charged with enacting revolutionary reforms and with making the revolution comprehensible to rural populations. The new agents were instructed to realize the liberation that had been forestalled in 1914. They were to do so, as Florencio Avila y Castillo put it, by "engraving the Revolution's principles and reforms in the soul of the pueblo."[35]

In Alvarado's vision of the liberation, the full realization of that future event would rest upon an educative relationship between the state and the people, in which revolutionary laws and principles would be inculcated as "teachings" (*enseñanza*), as Alvarado specified in his *Cartilla*, or primer, for the agents. Those teachings would go beyond the enunciation, dissemination, or translation of the law to intervene in the memory of the past and of the future in the minds of indigenous workers. Thus, to "redeem the Indian" the agents would combat the legacies of "slavery" and the "whips" of the old masters. First, they would investigate the origins of their suffering—and all of the "tears or voids of their personality" in the abuses of the past. Then, through the revolution's teachings they would "restore to them the consciousness of their dignity, which has been crushed." As Alvarado's *Cartilla* makes clear, the propaganda agents, even more than the officials commissioned to disseminate the 1914 liberation decree, were intended to be something like missionaries of liberty and ground-level architects of official memory. The "redemption" they were ordered to enact in pueblos and on haciendas involved direct intervention into workers' memories of the abuses of slavery and its effects and into their perception of the time of liberation as an imminent future in which the revolution would transform their lives.[36]

More than just the end of debt servitude, this was a matter of the transmutation of souls, and its realization required the systematic documentation of the coming redemption. Outside of communicating with, "teaching," and "redeeming" rural workers, the agents were to report in detail on their efforts directly to the general. In a draft of the *Cartilla*, Alvarado had ordered, "let history be written." In the final version agents were enjoined to keep a daily narrative account of their labors and experiences, as well as to complete questionnaires with information on the haciendas and pueblos they visited. Central to their duties was the production of accounts that narrated the liberation as an experience of profound personal redemption in the places they visited and corroborated the emergence of a future epoch of liberty among the ruins of slavery. The archive that collected such tales of the future, and the newspapers that disseminated them, presumably would confirm a memory of the revolution as a redemptive cause that delivered indigenous workers from bondage and punished the iniquity of the hacendados. The liberation would be committed to memory as an event that exorcised the past and heralded the onset of a radically different future of social and political relations.

Indeed, within weeks of Alvarado's arrival in the peninsula, military officials and propaganda agents began traveling the hacienda zone, visiting henequen fincas and pueblos on tours of inspection and forming a documentary record of their doings and experiences.[37] In many cases officials of Alvarado's revolutionary government discovered and denounced the "despotism" or tyranny of encargados and hacienda administrators. While in the documentation produced by officials of the Avila government hacendados had appeared to cooperate in and welcome the advent of the new times, in the records of the Alvarado government many hacendados were reported to be treating workers as if they still lived in the "times of the dictatorship" or the "times of slavery," preventing them from enjoying their new rights as citizens and workers. As evidence mounted of systematic violations of the provisions of the liberation decree relating to freedom of movement, government officials ordered one military commander to remedy the "unspeakable abuses that are committed daily, despite the laws passed to ensure the liberty of the peons." He was instructed to impose "exemplary punishments" to correct hacendados who still preserved "depraved customs and odious practices from the times of the dictatorship."[38]

For Alvarado's government, then, prior epochs of dictatorship and slavery were still very much in evidence on many of Yucatán's henequen haciendas in the form of restrictions on mobility, physical punishment, unacceptably low wages, and other abuses. When confronted by evidence of such abuses, government officials denounced hacendados and administrators as "slavers" and endeavored to realize the frustrated reforms on the haciendas they visited. Typically they apprised workers of their

rights under the new laws and encouraged them to find work on other haciendas if they were unsatisfied with working conditions or remuneration. In other cases, agents and military officials dismissed hated encargados or administrators or intervened to raise wages or lower food prices in hacienda stores.[39] In documenting such actions, the propaganda agents framed them as memorable moments in which reforms were realized locally as liberatory and redemptive events. After giving brief descriptions of the haciendas visited and the reactions of working populations to their visits, government agents generally testified to the satisfaction of laborers with settlements achieved through the intervention of the agents in disputes with employers. On one hacienda, for instance, agents found that through deception the encargado had acted "with great detriment to the future that the sacred Constitutionalist revolution has prepared for the workers."[40] Another agent related that, because of a speech he delivered on a hacienda, workers there "saw with surprise and delight that the times of slavery had ended, that their rights are now respected and that their labor will be justly compensated." On visiting a finca near Hunucmá to settle a conflict between laborers and the owner, the agent Abelardo de la Guerra explicitly highlighted his visit as a moment of redemption, reporting that while speaking to the workers in Maya about the revolution they listened to him "religiously." By his own account, his words "poured over their hearts like a salutary stream watering a plant. When I finished my speech, from all the mouths of my listeners came a thunderous and spontaneous hurrah for the Revolution, which had brought them undreamed of benefits."[41]

The accounts produced by the propaganda agents, like those of their predecessors under Avila, tended to construct and confirm the ruler's vision of liberation as a memorable event of the future. In distinction from the agents of 1914, however, they represented the liberation not just as a series of acts of dissemination but as a concatenation of redemptive events that clearly demarcated the past and documented the transition from the slavery of the past to the liberty of the future. Through such documentation, which is much more plentiful than the Avila government's surviving records, Alvarado's revolutionary government produced something like the "archive of redemption" that Avila had envisioned but never realized. To all appearances, Alvarado's agents not only had ended practices typical of "slavery" but had convinced indigenous workers and pueblo residents that a profound rupture had occurred. A past of slavery had been sundered from the realized future of liberation, now present in their lives and in their memories, transforming them from oppressed "Indians" into liberated Mexican workers and citizens.

This archive of redemption was not just a physical site for the storage of documents, but it also involved a network of correspondence and communication that linked workers and agents with government officials and the media. Some propaganda reports passed from the general's hands directly to the archive (marked "*archivo*"), while others were forwarded to officials in other departments. After closing the offices of other peninsular newspapers and confiscating the printing presses of the Church and the conservative newspaper *La Revista de Mérida*, Alvarado established a newspaper called *The Voice of the Revolution* (*La Voz de la Revolución*) as the state's daily paper and the government's newspaper of record. Reports were selected by the general and the director of the Information and Propaganda Office, to be published in *La Voz* as evidence of the revolution's wondrous deeds. Following a description of a propaganda meeting in one pueblo, for instance, the author of one newspaper report declared:

> Thus we see that the revolution's work is not a beautiful mirage that fades as men near power, and disappears completely when they achieve it. On the contrary: in its governmental form the Revolution turns its eyes toward the pueblo, hears its cries, and sees its needs. What the pueblo previously thought impossible, as this transcribed communication clearly demonstrates, appears before its surprised and grateful eyes, transformed into beautiful, palpable reality.[42]

A newspaper account of events in another pueblo declared in the second year of Alvarado's government:

> Here, all the sentiments of the pueblo have been united as one. The people have been permitted to feel the effects of the beneficent Revolution that has come to redeem the pariahs and rescue them from their misery. The Revolution, triumphant, has rescued them from their helotism. Now they are no longer slaves—they are free citizens and the government, desiring to better their condition, is distributing lands to them.[43]

Reports from the propaganda agents and other officials who visited the haciendas frequented the pages of *La Voz de la Revolución* in 1915 and 1916. Thus, the reading public in Yucatán and Mexico was provided with daily exposure to tales of redemption under governmental auspices—memorable accounts of abuses reme-

died, joyous workers apprised of their rights, wages raised, justice fulfilled.[44]

Government officials avidly collected, circulated, and published such stories of redemption and wove them into accounts of the realization of the future as an achieved past in Alvarado's Yucatán. Information and Propaganda Office director Florencio Avila y Castillo's *Diario revolucionario* was the first such account, one that recorded the first year of the revolution as a chronologically and calendrically organized rendering of Alvarado's laudable actions and decrees and the pueblo's enthusiastic reception of them. One entry in the *Diario* comments on the departure of indigenous workers from a finca in search of higher wages elsewhere: "This event, which seems so common, is of great importance if one considers that in epochs that are not so distant, the servant could not leave the finca freely. He was not treated like a citizen, free in his person and his actions, but rather like a Helot or a slave entirely subject to the will of the master."[45] For government officials, as for many pueblo residents, the freedom of movement seemed the consummate expression of the desire of the free worker and functioned as a memorable marker of temporal break. It distinguished the realized future time of the revolution from the times of the slavery that had preceded it and provided the basis for the representation of liberation— Alvarado's liberation—as a quotidian and mundane process, as well as a historic event.

Despite Avila y Castillo's triumphant evocation of a future realized in the *Diario,* however, evidence of the survival of times of slavery continued to surface even into the second year of Alvarado's revolution, suggesting that the violent struggle between past and future would be an ongoing feature of the revolution in Yucatán. Almost one year after Alvarado's arrival in Yucatán a boiler exploded on a large hacienda. When one of the owners visited to inspect the damage, it was reported, his servants lined up to kiss his hand, to the master's great pleasure. Alvarado was deeply shocked that this servile practice, which he had outlawed in a circular the previous year, continued on the fincas. He immediately declared that the government would energetically search out and punish those who violated the circular.[46] In a circular of 9 March 1916 Alvarado declared the practice of *besamanos* to be evidence of the resilience and endurance of the rejected past, a manifestation of "moral slavery" in which hacendados "obliged their servants to continue rendering the homage of former times." *Besamanos* was an "open wound" that exuded the "foul, odorous fumes" of slavery past. Once again the general called on propaganda agents to encourage workers to remember the future in the present. They were to "remind" the workers "incessantly" that they were "free men now; that it is shameful to humiliate themselves before the old 'masters' by kissing their hands; that now they should stand before them with head held high; . . . and that they should insist on being treated like free and independent men, not like pathetic pariahs and beggars." Through their work of "purification," the agents would bring a "redemptive wave" to the haciendas that finally would ingrain the memory of liberty in the hearts and minds of indigenous workers and realize its consequences in their working lives. According to the authors of news reports on *besamanos* in *La Voz de la Revolución*, the past could grow again in the spirits of the workers like a weed unless the memory of liberty was repeatedly incited in the minds of workers and hacendados: "The revolution cannot triumph until a revivifying wind fills and dignifies every spirit, until its sacred fire burns in every heart and shines forth from every gaze, until democracy and liberty penetrate every brain. It is urgent to uproot this weed that is growing again, choking the generous seed that the Revolution has sown in the heart of the pueblo."[47]

More than one year after Alvarado's arrival in the peninsula, allegations and "discoveries" of the persistence of "despotism" and traces of the "old system of previous epochs" or the times of slavery on the fincas were frequent. An investigation into abuses by encargados on Hacienda Yaxché de Peón, for instance, revealed that unfair wages and prices, as well as the sexual seduction or harassment of the wives of workers, showed "all the features and aspects of the dictatorial epochs." When workers on Hacienda Citincabchén were found to be bitterly opposed to their encargado due to "matters from the past," including the encargado's previous "vigorous mistreatment" of a now deceased worker, he was suspended from his post. Encargados who threatened to evict workers without observing the provisions of the labor law were admonished, like the encargado of Hacienda Dzib, to "forget their antiquated stratagems" or face censure and punishment by the state government and local authorities.[48] One of the most dramatic of such "discoveries" was made in July 1916, when propaganda agents visited Hacienda Copó in the Mérida district. Workers there had complained that a Spanish administrator, Joaquín Dueñas, preserved "slavery" on the place and paid them unacceptably low wages. Once on the finca the agents spoke to the assembled workers of the virtues of the "Revolution transformed into Government." Upon asking the workers to clarify their previous complaints, they noted a "murmur" and "hesitant words" that seemed to indicate anger that they didn't dare to express openly. When nobody responded to their questions, the agents urged them to speak freely, reminding them of the rupture between the times of slavery and liberty and endeavoring to

make them see that the times in which the "master" with his great riches and powerful social influence did whatever he wanted, and ruled lives and consciences, were over. We made them understand that the Revolution had ended that awful state of things; that the Revolution had destroyed that archaic social edifice; that now, everyone was equal before the Law's August majesty. We repeated to them that they should behave like free men, no longer subject to the dominion of a master.

Two workers, apparently emboldened by such oratory, finally came forward to complain about low wages (.60 pesos per day) and about the "despotism" of Dueñas. One reported that, when he had told the administrator of his intention to go to the governor to make him aware of the workers' misery, Dueñas had insulted him, declaring that "he ruled on the finca, and that they had to obey him." However, it was only when the administrator claimed that he paid the workers a daily wage of one peso and showed documents to that effect to the agents that a "tumult" and "imprecations" erupted among the workers. They declared that the records were falsified and that Dueñas, like the other administrators, was trying to "deceive [the agents], as they have always deceived the authorities in the past." Agent Pérez declared in his report on the incident that he believed the workers and described the finca as one of the last redoubts of slavery in the peninsula: "Hacienda Copó is a den of the reaction, where the master rules and the slaves obey; where the master has destroyed [*cegado*, "blinded"] every sentiment of liberty and dignity; where the worker is treated like a beast of burden; where plots are hatched against the Government; where rumors and stories that harm the Government are invented."[49]

The sanguine rhetoric of some government agents, however, obscured fundamental shifts in government policy that augured a very different role for the revolutionary government in the henequen zone. Venustiano Carranza's interest in maximizing profits and revenues in the henequen sector led him to oppose and eventually repeal many of Alvarado's costly reform efforts, and federal resistance had a dampening effect on the new revolutionary policies. If throughout 1915 officials were dispatched to the fincas with a broad mandate to incite an as yet unrealized transition from slavery to liberty, by late 1916 such a transition was assumed to have already occurred on most haciendas under the stewardship of government officials. After the promulgation of a new labor law at the end of 1915, the propaganda agents were charged with explaining the new law on the haciendas in such a way as to secure—in terms that recall the language of the 1914 decree—the "concordance" of capital and labor in a modern free labor system. They would inform employers of the "necessity of treating their workers well, since they are the ones who have helped to develop and preserve their capital," but would also impress on the workers "the importance of harmonizing their demands with the interests of their employer, whom they should not see as an enemy, but rather as a collaborator in life's struggles." Gone was the overriding revolutionary interest in discovering evidence of surviving elements of slavery and the emphasis on instilling a sharp sense of the distinctions between slavery and liberty in the memory and perceptions of indigenous workers.[50]

With the establishment of a new Labor Department and the issuance and dissemination of detailed regulations aimed at closely supervising and disciplining hacienda workers' every action on or near the henequen fields, the emphasis of labor policy continued to shift.[51] Government involvement on the fincas was now aimed largely at the defense of "custom" and "order" rather than at instigating a radical break between an oppressive past and a liberated future. Hacendados who had resisted the incursion of revolutionary authorities a few years earlier now asked the government for assistance in enforcing labor discipline in the face of increasingly organized challenges by workers. When accused by workers of mistreatment or disrespect, encargados and administrators often deflected the scrutiny of the government onto the workers themselves by accusing them of committing infractions against the new labor codes and dismissed their disgruntlement as an irrational response to justifiable attempts to correct their behavior.[52]

Labor Department officials continued to find in the workers' favor when encargados or administrators violated the terms of the law, typically by denying them the pay or benefits that legally were their due. However, such was not the case for most complaints over remuneration. In many cases, Labor Department agents and other government officials seem to have been unsympathetic to worker demands for higher wages and loathe to exorcise the past and inaugurate the future by intervening on the fincas, as they had in 1915.[53] In the face of the resistance

of administrators and hacendados to improving the terms of remuneration, the agents generally gave a formulaic recitation of the labor law to discontented workers. They declined to support their right to strike and informed them that they were free to leave the haciendas if they were unsatisfied with the conditions of their employ. The prior epoch of slavery and the event of liberation both had been consigned to the past, and the "free" labor system had been fully realized in the present; hence, the state's interventions into the battle between past and future gave way to a faith in the justice that officials imagined to reside in the unrestricted operations of a presumably free labor market.

As their interest in the abuses of the past on the haciendas waned, government officials also showed increasing interest in learning which workers were leading challenges to wages or working conditions on the fincas. Using language and practices reminiscent of the cohecho investigations of 1914, revolutionary officials and hacendados labeled such workers "promoters of disorder" or "ringleaders" who induced other, diligent workers to make unreasonable claims, to desert the fincas, or to attack "public wealth" by damaging henequen plants and thereby the interests of the haciendas and of the government.[54] Hacienda workers were increasingly "reminded," like the workers of Hacienda San Antonio Tuc, that "now we are in the Constitutional epoch, and so if they insist on damaging the owners' interests they will be punished according to the law."[55]

Amid this shift, Alvarado declared the conclusive triumph of the revolution on Yucatán's henequen fincas. After two years of his rule, Alvarado claimed that the government had "protected all workers' movements . . . unfailingly, securing in every case salary increases." Strikes, according to a letter Alvarado sent to President Carranza in November 1916, were settled not through "unjust means" or force but by "studying and resolving labor issues justly." Through such measures, the continued production of wealth through the export of fiber was assured but was based on free, rather than forced, labor and on a harmonious balance between the rights of the worker and the rule of law.[56] Perhaps the most remarkable representation of the situation in Yucatán came in the form not of an official report but of a "strange and interesting dream" that Alvarado reported having over the course of several nights in 1917. Published that year as *Mi sueño* (*My Dream*) and widely read and republished thereafter, his recollection of that dream served as a manifesto at a moment in which the general sought to renew his rule of the state in upcoming gubernatorial elections.

In *Mi sueño,* a text strongly reminiscent of Edward Bellamy's *Looking Backward,* Alvarado described himself voyaging to the future and bearing witness to the land of progress and modernity that Yucatán would become if his revolution prevailed. Imagining a look backward from the future toward the present, Alvarado's narrative is driven by the strange power of the revolutionary future viewed as an achieved past. Alvarado described arriving at the formerly sleepy Yucatecan port town of Progreso (Progress), now filled with hotels, offices, cafés, restaurants, movie theaters, and markets. Along the coast, the marshy coastal savanna—previously unmarked by industrial or agricultural activity—was covered by oil towers, tanks, and pipelines. Turning his gaze inland, Alvarado found that the landscape of Yucatán's rural interior had been transformed as dramatically as its port city, as if a "powerful, vital spirit was passing over the land, transforming Yucatán and filling it with marvels." Yucatán was no longer a state of enormous disparities in wealth. It had become a land where "the wealth of the country, produced by everyone, now flowed for the benefit of everyone." As a result of such bounty, roads and railways had been built to unite country and city. Farms and work colonies spread over formerly desolate areas, now populated by immigrants who had come from other parts of Mexico and from abroad to work them. "As if by enchantment," the general recalled, Mérida had expanded to the size of New Orleans and Havana and had become the financial, commercial, industrial, and scientific center of the Caribbean.[57]

Yucatán's future inhabitants were transformed as radically as its landscape. In his dream, Alvarado saw that due to a wide variety of policies that he had instituted—including the liberation, labor, and land reforms and the municipal government and fiscal reforms—the traces of a feudalistic past of ethnic and class domination had been completely eradicated. The hacendado of the future, no longer a feudal lord, had become a modern capitalist employer who treated workers as equals. Indigenous workers had undergone a metamorphosis even more dramatic. With the liberation, it is true, workers had abandoned their labors and resisted working any more than the minimum to survive. Nonetheless, as a result of being justly remunerated for their labors, indigenous workers gradually discovered that "there was more to life than just eating tortillas, drinking corn gruel and sleeping in a torn hammock." As indigenous workers learned the pleasures of "civilization," they began to desire "previously unknown commodities" and thus labored diligently in order to earn money to purchase

them. Finally, they gave up their antiquated clothing, "erasing forever" the "depressing stigma of caste." As his dream concluded, Alvarado encountered a strange being called the "Spirit of the Race," who charged him with creating the Yucatán of his dreams—a mission the general accepted, just before awakening.

In less dramatic fashion, officials of the government (particularly of the Labor Department) also played a role in authoring a roseate vision of the situation in the countryside for the reading public in Yucatán and elsewhere in Mexico. In the area of the pueblo of Tixkokob, hacienda workers reportedly were "equitably remunerated and well treated by the encargados who, in the past, were their executioners." Writing of the dramatic transformation of working conditions in the vicinity of Hunucmá, a Labor Department inspector declared that, unlike in "other times" when the "capitalists used subterfuge to avoid paying workers just wages," by 1917 workers were enjoying the "immense benefits that the Glorious Constitutionalist Revolution has brought them, thanks to the indomitable efforts of their leaders." "Today," the report concluded, "the workers of the countryside are no longer the way they were in other times. Today, they are aware of their actions, and even if the reactionary elements so desired, the state of abandonment and slavery in which they lived will never return."[58] Inspired by such reports, newspaper accounts of the situation of the fincas were equally sanguine, heralding the dawn of a new age on the fincas. The advent of just conditions of work and remuneration had modernized the henequen industry, and government attempts to instruct workers in the memorable distinction between slavery and liberty had transformed the presumably apathetic Indian peon into the presumably industrious Mexican worker and citizen. This was the future redemption that Alvarado had envisioned in 1915 and had realized in his time as governor.[59] An article that appeared in *La Voz de la Revolución,* entitled "How the Worker-Citizen Is Trained in Yucatán," exemplifies the trend. It included a description of life on Hacienda Teya near Mérida, where workers enjoyed "splendid" treatment by hacendado Alfredo Medina and the protection of Alvarado's labor law. The workers there had been redeemed by their experience of free labor.

> They love the finca with true faith, because they have found happiness and well-being there. . . . They dress well and bathe every day, and their bodies and customs have become truly hygienic. . . . The workers are supported morally and materially, and are being educated as

citizens. They are conscious of their rights and of their responsibilities, and receive the affectionate and paternal encouragement of their employers. The worker is no longer a pariah, nor an animal, nor a slave. He is independent, free and strong.[60]

While Alvarado and officials in the revolutionary government became increasingly implicated in the defense of the henequen labor regime and worked at consigning the time of liberation and its struggles to the past in official memory,[61] workers showed their determination to reject the narrowing limits of Alvarado's redemption. Although no longer appealing to the revolutionary government to "redeem" them, workers—like the residents of Hacienda San Antonio Cholul, who alleged that overseers beat and exploited them "as if we were slaves"—continued to evoke the idea of contending times of "slavery" and "liberty." A Labor Department agent rejected the demand of workers on Hacienda Sodzil that an encargado and an administrator be expelled from the finca. While the workers opposed the two "because in the old days they used to beat them and to this day they are angry," the government official responded that "their complaint was unjustified, and that such things happened to everybody before, but what was important was that now they were not mistreated." While government officials showed diminishing interest in searching out and punishing the abuses of prior epochs, workers continued to place the condemnation of the old customs of previous epochs of slavery and the demand for liberty at the center of their complaints.[62]

As officials in the revolutionary government seemed to abandon their earlier zeal for uncovering slavery and inaugurating liberty, workers and pueblo residents grew increasingly frustrated. On 7 December 1917 a group of workers of Hacienda Tecoh addressed a letter to the governor denouncing the actions of their encargado and the policies of the Labor Department. After workers there challenged wage levels and maize allotments on the finca, the encargado had a group of them arrested by municipal police. According to the workers, the encargado had behaved "as if we were in slavery," with the knowledge and support of the director of the Labor Department. The workers directed a provocative question to Governor Alvarado: "Will it be just if 'Slavery' returns, Señor Governor? If that is the way things will be, then we will go to the Cemetery to bury ourselves alive rather than become slaves again." Several days later, the director of the Labor Department sent a letter to the commissary of the finca—presumably the encargado's appointee—with orders to expel several of the workers

from the finca within one week and to send him further information on the "obstructionist labor of the agitators." On Hacienda Xcanatún a similar incident occurred just two months later, as Alvarado's time as state governor came to an end. Authorities of the finca threatened workers with imprisonment if they cut the leaves badly. When one man asked for a raise, an encargado even threatened to shoot him and harangued other workers. "Calm down," he told them. "Soon the old laws will return . . . and Slavery will return as before."[63]

In 1917, remembering his year as director of the Labor Department in Yucatán, Carlos Loveira recalled with bitterness the attitude of many workers who visited his office in Mérida. Despite his efforts and the efforts of the government on their behalf, they seemed profoundly ungrateful. "Often they entered my office," he wrote, "to give their speeches, but then soon left—with a liberty previously unknown to them—saying that we were all bourgeois, that we were becoming a sequel to Porfirio Díaz, and that we were turncoats." These spokesmen, according to Loveira, considered the department bourgeois because it refused to satisfy their sense of "revolutionary justice," which was in his view actually thinly veiled "personal interest." The disgruntled ex-director consoled himself in his memoirs, noting that "At the very moment I write these lines, men of the caliber of Gorki and Kropotkin are also being called bourgeois by not a few irresponsible fanatics of the Russian Revolution."[64]

For workers on Tecoh and Xcanatún and in Carlos Loveira's office, years of avowedly radical governmental and legal challenges to the organization of labor on the henequen haciendas had resulted in a situation that differed strikingly from the future they might have imagined in 1915. By 1917 some workers were beginning to refer to the period of revolutionary rule as a time of continued slavery or as a time when the return of slavery might lie in the near future. In so doing, they showed that they were no longer convinced by the paradigm of redemption, at least not the version propounded by the Alvarado government. Rather, they took up the temporal categories of slavery and liberation and drew on them to formulate a critique of the government that claimed to be the guarantor of the end of slavery and to make their own claims on what liberty might mean. While in 1915 Alvarado had offered the new legislation relating to labor as the clearest evidence of the definitive end of the times of slavery and the advent of the times of liberty, years later many indigenous workers still awaited the liberation and struggled to give it substance.

Conclusion

As I began my research in Yucatán in 1995, I took the Maya version of the 1914 decree to ex-haciendas and pueblos in the Yucatecan countryside. Upon hearing me pronounce the words of that document, I imagined, people who had lived through the liberation as children or their descendants might share with me their interpretations of the decree or memories of its momentous passage. Perhaps their recollections might contrast with those of government officials and the "official story" of the state-sponsored historiography. When I did read the decree in Maya, however, I met incomprehension and curious eyes. The simultaneously archaic and neologistic Maya language of Santiago Pacheco Cruz's translation of the decree was not the language of my interlocutors or even of their immediate ancestors. Moreover, no one seemed to remember the passage or even to have heard of the existence of the decree that had, in theory, ended their bondage or that of their parents or grandparents. The year 1914 was for them undistinguished.

While the liberation was not remembered as a discrete event, enacted, disseminated, and enforced by decree, I soon found that slavery and liberation were anything but forgotten.[65] When I posed questions not about the decree but rather about the "epoch of slavery" and the "epoch of liberty"—terms I heard used frequently when discussing the past in the pueblos and haciendas of the henequen zone—I encountered a very different kind of memory, deeply ambivalent in nature. Hacienda and pueblo residents, both the elderly and their descendants, seemed to locate stories about situations of exploitation and confinement, political abuses, and corruption in the "times of slavery" whether they had been committed during the *porfiriato* or under revolutionary rule—perhaps even as far in the past as the mid-nineteenth-century Caste War.[66] Some even viewed slavery nostalgically, crediting the free provision of food, clothing, and medicine to the system of servitude. Many associated times of liberty not only with the advent of greater personal freedoms but also with eras of political upheaval, violence, and dislocation—whether before, during, or after the revolution. Even more striking was the use of both terms to refer to aspects of contemporary life. In the 1990s political corruption, labor exploitation, economic crisis, and poverty led residents to compare some aspects of their lives to slavery. Hence, with regard to economic crisis and currency devaluation, pueblo residents sometimes declared: "Now we are slaves again—slaves to the *peso*" or "slaves to our stomachs." The migration and gang violence of the same years, however, seemed to some to be evidence of opportunities and perils typical of an epoch of liberty. Slavery and liberty were seen not as definitive states or periods but rather as alternating conditions that have happened before and will happen again and may even overlap.

The remarkable ability of my interlocutors to "remember the future and anticipate the past"[67] has deep roots, some of them in the early revolutionary period. Officials in the revolutionary governments of Eleuterio Avila and Salvador Alvarado promised the fruits of liberation to workers in return for their loyalties from 1914 onward. Like the White Queen, however, they withheld some of those fruits, first deferring them to the future and then consigning them to the past. Envisioned, realized, and committed to memory, the future was their alibi. By 1917, in the perceptions of many government officials, the bygone times of slavery were clearly distinguishable from the present times of liberty. The event of liberation could become a subject of history, and the abuses of slavery could be forgotten or remembered as proper to a earlier age. Alternative memories of the liberation as an event of the future could be dismissed as excessive or irrational, when they seemed to violate the already realized liberty of Yucatán's free labor system. By separating epochs that for a time seemed to intermingle, government officials sought to begin and end a period of radical challenges on their own terms. After enjoying the White Queen's two-way memory, they now seemed, like Alice, to remember only one way and were determined to convince workers that they now lived in different times.

For indigenous workers, however, it had become apparent that free labor would incorporate many aspects of the previous slavery. They no longer faced beatings or confinement and had the right to leave the haciendas where they worked. If they chose to remain on the fincas, now it would be under the compulsion of hunger and poverty rather than legal and physical coercion. After several years of revolutionary government it had become clear to many workers that slavery and liberty—at least the "official" liberty—were both founded upon their exploitation. By 1917 they were living both ways, sometimes seeming to travel from times of slavery to times of liberty and at others facing what seemed to be slavery's return. Slavery and liberty, they will remember, may sometimes share the same time and place.

NOTES

For their comments and suggestions I would like to thank David Akin and the anonymous reviewers for *Comparative Studies in Society and History,* as well as Fernando Coronil, Geoff Eley, Michal Friedman, Patrick Geary, Paul Kramer, Kali Israel, Rick

Maddox, Aims McGuinness, Sonya Rose, Bill Rosenberg, Rebecca Scott, Paul Sullivan, Jay Winter, and the participants in the University of Michigan Advanced Studies Seminar entitled "Archives, Documentation, and the Institutions of Social Memory."

An earlier version of this essay was published in *Comparative Studies in Society and History* 44, no. 1 (January 2002): 106–36. Reprinted by permission.

1. See Lewis Carroll, *Alice in Wonderland* (New York: Norton, 1971), 150–51.

2. For discussions of the relations between modernism, authoritarianism, and the memory of the future, see Paul Connerton, *How Societies Remember* (Cambridge: Cambridge University Press, 1989); Rubie S. Watson, ed., *Memory, History, and Opposition under State Socialism* (Sante Fe, NM: School of American Research Press, 1994); Ann Laura Stoler, "Developing Historical Negatives: Race and the (Modernist) Visions of a Colonial State," in Brian Keith Axel, ed., *From the Margins: Historical Anthropology and Its Futures* (Durham, NC: Duke University Press, 2002); Matt Matsuda, *The Memory of the Modern* (Oxford: Oxford University Press, 1996); James Scott, *Seeing Like a State: How Certain Schemes to Improve the Human Condition Have Failed* (New Haven: Yale University Press, 1998); and Fernando Coronil's critique of Scott, "Smelling like a Market," *American Historical Review* 106, no. 1 (February 2001).

3. On Yucatecan society up to and including the Caste War, see Nelson Reed, *The Caste War of Yucatán* (Stanford: Stanford University Press, 2001); Moisés González Navarro, *Raza y tierra: la guerra de castas y el henequén* (Mexico City: El Colegio de México, 1979); Terry Rugeley, *Yucatán's Maya Peasantry and the Origins of the Caste War* (Austin: University of Texas Press, 1996); and Don Dumond, *The Machete and the Cross: Campesino Rebellion in Yucatán* (Lincoln, NE.: University of Nebraska Press, 1997).

4. For detailed analysis of the expansion of henequen monoculture, the consolidation of local elites, and the "informal empire" of U.S. companies, see Gilbert M. Joseph, *Revolution from Without: Yucatán, Mexico, and the United States, 1880–1924* (Durham, NC: Duke University Press, 1982); Allen Wells, *Yucatán's Gilded Age: Haciendas, Henequen, and International Harvester, 1860–1915* (Albuquerque, NM: University of New Mexico Press, 1985); and Steven C. Topik and Allen Wells, *The Second Conquest of Latin America: Coffee, Henequen, and Oil during the Export Boom, 1850–1930* (Austin: University of Texas Press, 1998). For a survey of these topics and others in the historiography of modern Yucatán, see Gilbert M. Joseph, *Rediscovering the Past: Essays on the Modern History of Yucatán* (Tuscaloosa: University of Alabama Press, 1986).

5. While the system of forced indebted labor in Yucatán was not chattel slave labor, the term *slavery* was widely used to refer to debt peonage and related practices of exploitation and abuse. Hence I will use the term *slavery* in conformity with local usage throughout this essay, though without thereby equating debt servitude with chattel slavery. On the workings of the haciendas in the late nineteenth and early twentieth centuries, see Wells, *Gilded Age;* Piedad Peniche Rivero, "Gender, Bridewealth, and Marriage: Social Reproduction on Henequen Haciendas in Yucatán (1870–1901)," in Heather Fowler-Salamini and Mary Kay Vaughn, eds., *Women of the Mexican*

Countryside, 1850–1990: Creating Spaces, Shaping Transitions (Tucson: University of Arizona Press, 1994); and Christopher Gill, "The Intimate Life of the Family: Patriarchy and the Liberal Project in Yucatán Mexico, 1860–1915," Ph.D. diss., Yale University, 2001.

6. Allen Wells and Gilbert M. Joseph, *Summer of Discontent, Seasons of Upheaval: Elite Politics and Rural Insurgency in Yucatan, 1876–1915* (Stanford: Stanford University Press, 1996).

7. On the political elaboration and limits of a project to transform henequen agriculture and the state under Constitutionalist and Socialist rule, see Joseph, *Revolution from Without;* and Paul K. Eiss, "Redemption's Archive: Revolutionary Figures and Indian Work in Yucatán, Mexico," Ph.D. diss., University of Michigan, 2000. For an overview of the historiography of the revolutionary period, see Joseph, *Rediscovering the Past.*

8. See especially Gilbert Joseph and Daniel Nugent, eds., *Everyday Forms of State Formation: Revolution and the Negotiation of Rule in Modern Mexico* (Durham, NC: Duke University Press, 1994). Also see Daniel Nugent, *Spent Cartridges of Revolution: An Anthropological History of Namiquipa, Chihuahua* (Chicago: University of Chicago Press, 1993); Ana Alonso, *Thread of Blood: Colonialism, Revolution, and Gender on Mexico's Northern Frontier* (Tucson: University of Arizona Press, 1995); William H. Beezley, Cheryl English Martin, and William E. French, eds., *Public Celebrations and Popular Culture in Mexico* (Wilmington: Scholarly Resources, 1994); Mary Kay Vaughn, "Cultural Approaches to Peasant Politics in the Mexican Revolution," *Hispanic American Historical Review* 79, no. 2 (1999): 269–305; Mary Kay Vaughn, *Cultural Politics in Revolution: Teachers, Peasants and Schools in Mexico, 1930–1940* (Tucson: University of Arizona Press, 1997); Marjorie Becker, *Setting the Virgin on Fire: Lázaro Cárdenas, Michoacán Peasants, and the Redemption of the Mexican Revolution* (Berkeley: University of California Press, 1995); and Adrian A. Bantjes, *As If Jesus Walked on Earth: Cardenismo, Sonora and the Mexican Revolution* (Wilmington, DE: Scholarly Resources, 1998).

9. See, for instance, Joanne Rappaport, *Cumbe Reborn: An Andean Ethnography of History* (Chicago: University of Chicago Press, 1994); Patrick Geary, *Phantoms of Remembrance: Memory and Oblivion at the End of the First Millennium* (Princeton: Princeton University Press, 1994); Shahid Amin, *Event, Metaphor, Memory: Chauri Chaura, 1922–1992* (Berkeley: University of California Press, 1995); Michel-Rolph Trouillot, *Silencing the Past: Power and the Production of History* (Boston: Beacon Press, 1997); and Richard Price, *The Convict and the Colonel: A Story of Colonialism and Resistance in the Caribbean* (Boston: Beacon Press, 1998).

10. Wells and Joseph, *Summer of Discontent.* For various manifestos of the gubernatorial candidates and declarations of the Liga see *Diario Yucateco,* 15 and 25 June, 7 July, 17 Aug., and 15 Sept. 1911; and *Revista de Mérida,* 11 Dec. 1913. See also Liga de Acción Social, *Trabajos de la 'Liga de Acción Social' para el establecimiento de las escuelas rurales de Yucatán* (Mérida: Imprenta Empresa Editora, 1913). On the press in prerevolutionary and revolutionary Yucatán, see Ben Fallaw, "Tinta Roja," *Unicornio* 10, 1 Oct. 2000.

11. Decrees abolishing debt servitude were enacted at

roughly the same time by Eulalio Gutiérrez in San Luis Potosí, Joaquín Mucel in Campeche, Luis Felipe Domínguez in Tabasco, and Pablo González in Puebla and Tlaxcala. Berta Ulloa, *Historia de la revolución mexicana: 1914–1917. La constitución de 1917* (México, DF: El Colegio de México, 1983), 272, 347. For a concise analysis of the Carranza years, see Héctor Aguilar Camín and Lorenzo Meyer, *In the Shadow of the Mexican Revolution: Contemporary Mexican History, 1910–1989* (Austin: University of Texas Press, 1993).

12. *Revista de Yucatán,* 19 and 23 Aug.; and 12 Sept. 1914.

13. See the translation by Nicanor Vázquez in *Revista de Yucatán,* 15 and 20 Sept. 1914. The Spanish decree and Vázquez's Maya translation also were published in *El Agricultor* 93 (Sept. 1914).

14. On Pacheco Cruz's involvement in the Avila government, see Santiago Pacheco Cruz, *Recuerdos de la propaganda constitucionalista en Yucatán* (Mérida, 1953). The liberation decree and circulars one through four of the Avila government are included in Spanish and Maya versions in *Recuerdos,* 37–48. The Maya version was published originally as Santiago Pacheco Cruz, *Traducción literal al idioma yucateco del decreto expedido a favor de los jornaleros de campo y de las circulares que se relacionan con estos* (Mérida: Imprenta "El Porvenir," 1914).

15. In some cases Pacheco Cruz drew upon terms of authority used in the indigenous republics of the colonial period, when pueblos in most of the state were governed by *cabildos* and authorities who communicated and produced documentation in Maya. In others, as in the translations of the terms for secretary and military commanders, Pacheco Cruz invented new conglomerate Maya titles composed of words that seemed to him to convey the meaning of the Spanish political titles. For a discussion of the terminology of political office in indigenous pueblos, or *cahob,* of the colonial period, see Matthew Restall, *The Maya World: Yucatec Culture and Society, 1550–1850* (Stanford: Stanford University Press, 1997), 64–71.

16. Albino Acereto, "Historia política desde el descubrimiento europeo hasta 1920," in *Enciclopedia yucatanense,* vol. 3 (México, DF: Gobierno de Yucatán, 1946), 367–68.

17. *La Revista de Yucatán,* 13 and 25 Sept. 1914.

18. *La Revista de Yucatán,* 12 and 15 Sept. 1914.

19. *La Revista de Yucatán,* 17 and 18 Sept. 1914.

20. See, for instance, E. Murillo Comandante militar (CM) Maxcanú to Gobernador, 26 Sept. 1914, Archivo General del Estado de Yucatán (AGEY), Poder Ejecutivo (PE), Gobernación (GOB), Box 441; and L. C. Meléndez, CM Izamal, to Gobernador Provisional, 23 and 26 Sept. 1914, AGEY, PE, Justicia, Box 453.

21. For a few among many examples, see E. Avila to F. Guillermo, CM Tixkokob, 30 Sept. 1914, AGEY, PE, GOB, Box 493; R. Sánchez, CM Peto, to Gobernador, 6 Oct. 1914, AGEY, PE, GOB, Box 493; L. C. Mélendez, CM Izamal, to Gobernador Provisional, 23 Sept. 1914, AGEY, PE, Justicia, Box 453; F. Guillermo, CM Tixkokob, to Sec. Genl. Del Gobierno, 5 Nov. 1914, AGEY, PE, Milicia, Box 453; and "Diligencias practicadas contra Juan Polanco como agitador, para remitir al Superior Gobierno del Estado," AGEY, PE, Milicia, Box 453.

22. See reports on the rural districts published in *La Revista de Yucatán,* 17 Sept.–8 Oct. 1914.

23. For examples of the responses, see R. Sánchez, CM Peto, to Gobernador, 6 Oct. 1914, AGEY, PE, GOB, Box 493; and F. E. Guillermo, CM Tixkokob, to Gobernador, 8 Oct. 1914, AGEY, PE, GOB, Box 493.

24. *La Revista de Yucatán* 13, 15, 19, 20, 21, and 24 Sept. 1914.

25. E. Avila, Gobernador, to F. Guillermo, CM Tixkokob, 30 Sept. 1914, AGEY, PE, GOB, Box 493. For a military commander's inquiry into whether he should honor the requests of the local hacendados to force servants to return to their fincas, see A. Duarte, CM Tekax, to G. Valencia, Gobernador, 25 Sept. 1914, AGEY, PE, GOB, Box 493.

26. See Jefe Sección de Inmigración y Trabajo to M. González Brito, CM Ticul, 28 Oct. 1914, AGEY, PE, GOB, Box 493; F. Guillermo, CM Tixkokob, to Sec. Genl. del Gobierno, 5 Nov. 1914, AGEY, PE, Milicia, Box 453; and M. Narváez Pérez, CM Espita, to Gobernador, 26 Dec. 1914, AGEY, PE, GOB, Box 493.

27. "Diligencias en averiguación de la causa de la muerte de Manuel Cimé vecino que fué de la finca Dzemul. Juzgado primera instancia Motul," AGEY, Justicia (1914), Box 942.

28. Salvador Alvarado, *Mi actuación revolucionaria en Yucatán* (México, DF: Impresa Franco-Mexicana, 1920), 8.

29. J. I. Flores to S. Alvarado, Gobernador, 17 Apr. 1915, AGEY, PE, GOB, Box 495; and M. Pantoja Solís to Gobernador, 21 Apr. 1915, AGEY, PE, GOB, Box 495. For Mena Brito's allegations regarding the previous involvement of officials who later joined the Alvarado government in preventing the enforcement of the 1914 liberation decree, see Bernardino Mena Brito, *Reestructuración histórica de Yucatán* (México, DF: Editores Mexicanos Unidos, 1969), 103, 125–26.

30. Adolfo Cardeña, Consul del Gobierno Constitucionalista de México, to General Salvador Alvarado, 19 July 1915, AGEY, PE, GOB, Box 490.

31. See Salvador Alvarado, *A donde vamos,* reprinted in Salvador Alvarado, *Obra* (México, DF: Liga de economistas revolucionarios de la República Mexicana, 1979); and Florencio Avila y Castillo, *Diario revolucionario* (Mérida: Imprenta y linotipia La Voz de la Revolución, 1915).

32. See Becker, *Setting the Virgin on Fire;* and Bantjes, *As If Jesus Walked on Earth.*

33. On popular religion in nineteenth-century Yucatán, see Terry Rugeley, *Of Wonders and Wise Men: Religion and Popular Cultures in Southeast Mexico, 1800–1876* (Austin: University of Texas Press, 2001).

34. José Pío Chuc et al. to Exmo. Señor Gobernador, 2 May 1915, AGEY, PE, GOB, Box 479. For another example of workers using the paradigm of redemption in making petitionary claims, see "Expediente relativo a la apelación interpuesta por Lorenzo Manzanilla contra una resolución del comandante militar de Temax en la Queja de Nicolás Ruz," AGEY, PE, Justicia, Box 512.

35. See 1915 district assignments of propaganda agents, 9 Oct. 1915, AGEY, PE, GOB, Box 472; and the 1916 assignments in S. Alvarado, Feb. 1916, AGEY, PE, GOB, Box 551.

36. Avila y Castillo, *Diario,* 83; S. Alvarado, "Circular a los Agentes de Propaganda del Estado," 17 July 1915, AGEY, PE, GOB, Box 490; Salvador Alvarado, *Cartilla revolucionaria para los agentes de propaganda,* 3 Sept. 1915, AGEY, PE, GOB, Box 473.

37. For instance, for reported raises in Temax, see Gerardo Espadas, AP Temax, 25 Sept. 1915, AGEY, PE, GOB, Box 475; in Motul, see Gobierno to CM Motul, 3 Nov. 1915, AGEY, PE, GOB, Box 490; in Tixkokob, see questionnaire of Abelardo de la Guerra, AP Tixkokob, 5 Sept. 1915, AGEY, PE, GOB; in Acanceh, see questionnaire of Francisco J. Balam, AP Acanceh, 5 Sept. 1915, AGEY, PE, GOB. For other press reports on such arrangements see "Ya el indio antes desvalido encuentra apoyo en la autoridad," 24 Apr. 1915, *La Voz de la Revolución* (*VdR*), and "Otra vez obtienen justicia de la Revolución los Indios. Se les atendió en una queja y se destituyó a un encargado de finca," 29 July 1915, *VdR*.

38. Of. May. Int., to R. Aguirres, CM Mérida, 2 Aug. 1915, AGEY, PE, GOB, Box 497.

39. For a few examples of the multitude of incidents of this kind, see Tomás J. Velasco, CM Ticul, to Gobernador, 3 June 1915, AGEY, PE, GOB, Box 503; and "Notas del despacho de la Oficina de Información y Propaganda Revolucionarias" (OIPR) 20 Aug. 1915 and 7 Sept. 1915, AGEY, PE, Gob, Box 475.

40. See Antonio Pérez H. to Florencio Avila Lopes [sic], Jefe de la OIPR, 30 Aug. 1915, AGEY, PE, GOB, Box 475; and Ceferino Gamboa, AP, and José I. Tec, AP, to Florencio Avila y Castillo, Jefe de la OIPR, 30 Aug. 1915, AGEY, PE, GOB, Box 475.

41. "A los sirvientes de otra finca llegan los beneficios de la Revolución." 26 Apr. 1915, *VdR*; Abelardo de la Guerra, AP Hunucmá, to Jefe OIPR, 13 Jan. 1916, AGEY, PE, GOB, Box 487; Francisco Javier Balam, AP Acanceh, to Florencio Avila y Castillo, Jefe de la OIPR, 5, 6, 8, and 10 Sept. 1915, AGEY, PE, GOB, Box 475; Pablo Ramírez, AP Abalá, 2 May 1916, AGEY, PE, GOB, Box 475; José I. Tec, AP Motul, to Florencio Avila y Castillo, Jefe de la OIPR, 21 Sept. 1915, AGEY, PE, GOB, Box 490.

42. See R. García Nuñez, Ing. Dir. Comisión Agraria y de Trabajos Públicos (CATP), to governor, citing correspondence of Rafael Gasque C., Ing. Ayud. Tixkokob, 29 Apr. 1915, AGEY, PE, GOB, Box 479; and "La obra revolucionaria no es un hermoso miraje que se esfuma conforme los hombres se acercan al poder." 4 May 1915, *VdR*.

43. Report from Halachó. 1 Oct. 1916, *VdR*.

44. For articles on abuses committed by encargados or hacendados and their remedy, see, among the many other examples in *La Voz*, "Otra vez la revolución acude en auxilio de los jornaleros de campo," 6 June 1915; "Un mayordomo esclavista estropeó vilmente a un sirviente y lo mandó encerrar," 7 July 1915; "El encargado de Catmis apalea a un jornalero," 10 July 1915; and "Otra vez obtienen justicia de la Revolución los Indios. Se les atendió en una queja y se destituyó a un encargado de finca," 29 July 1915.

45. Florencio Avila y Castillo, *Diario revolucionario*, 98. This departure is also mentioned in the documents of the OIPR. See "Notas del despacho," of the OIPR, 20 Aug. 1915, AGEY, PE, GOB, Box 475.

46. See "La horrible catástrofe del sábado en la hacienda S. Ignacio," 6 Mar. 1916, *VdR*; "Los besamanos en las fincas de campo, son obra de reacción: el viento de libertad que sopla por toda la República sacudida por la mayor de sus revoluciones, debe barrer todos los rancios servillismos," 9 Mar.

1916, *VdR;* and "Los besamanos," 25 Mar. 1916, *VdR*. For Alvarado's original circular against *besamanos,* see S. Alvarado, Governor, to military commanders, 6 Aug. 1915, AGEY, PE, GOB, Box 490.

47. Salvador Alvarado, Circular against *besamanos,* 9 Mar. 1916, AGEY, PE, GOB, Box 516. Responses to the circular from local military commanders accompany the circular. See also "Combatiendo el servillismo en las fincas del campo: el comandante militar de Izamal castiga a un Administrador que aun consiente el besamano," 18 Mar. 1916, *VdR;* and Cuauhtémoc, "Besamanos," 25 Mar. 1916, *VdR*.

48. A. Villanueva R., CM Hunucmá, to Gobernador, 15 Feb. 1916, AGEY, PE, GOB, Box 538; Juan Joachim, Inspec. Admin. Ticul, to Srio. Gral., 20 July 1917, AGEY, PE, GOB, Box 558.

49. See Antonio Pérez H., AP Mérida, to Eladio Domínguez, Jefe del Departamento de Trabajo (DT), 11 July 1916; Mercedes Cisneros Cámara et al., to Gobernador, 2 Aug. 1916; and Eladio Domínguez, to Gobernador, 4 Aug. 1916, all in AGEY, PE, GOB, Box 538.

50. "Instrucciones a los propagandistas," undated 1916, AGEY, PE, GOB, Box 475; Jefe Depto. de Agri. y Trabajo, to Gobernador, 22 Dec. 1915, AGEY, PE, Gob., Box 557.

51. Salvador Alvarado, *Código del trabajo del estado de Yucatán (México), Decreto num. 722* (Mérida: Talleres "Pluma y Lápiz," 1917). For regulations posted on specific haciendas, see AGEY, PE, GOB, Boxes 598 and 601.

52. See, for instance, for Hda. Acú in Maxcanú, Gonzalo Fuentes Sánchez, Pres. Mun. Halachó, to Jefe DT, 8 Feb. 1918, AGEY, PE, GOB, Box 656; and for Hda. Ruinas de Aké in Tixkokob, Felipe Solís, to Jefe DT, 15 Feb. 1918, AGEY, PE, GOB, Box 656. For analyses of the federal moves against Alvarado's policies, see Joseph, *Revolution from Without;* and Eiss, "Redemption's Archive."

53. See, for instance, for Hda. Yaxché near Hunucmá, Virgilio Arce Méndez, Agente DT, to Gobernador, 11 July 1917, AGEY, PE, GOB, Box 558. See also Isidro Poot, Pres. Liga Hunucmá, to Pres. Liga Ctrl., 12 Aug. 1917, AGEY, PE, GOB, Box 564; and Felipe Carrillo Puerto, Pres. Liga Ctrl., to Jefe DT, 7 Aug. 1917, AGEY, PE, GOB, Box 558.

54. There is extensive evidence of Labor Department tracking and identification of "problem" workers and their expulsion from fincas throughout the henequen zone. See, for example, Andrés Cardós, to Jefe del DT, 16 Nov. 1916, AGEY, PE, GOB, Box 516B; and Felipe López, Inspec. Gral., to Jefe DT, 17 Dec. 1917, AGEY, PE, GOB, Box 579.

55. Tomás Gamboa R., to Jefe DT, 4 Feb. 1918, AGEY, PE, GOB, Box 656.

56. See Salvador Alvarado, Gobernador, to Venustiano Carranza, 31 Nov. 1916, AGEY, PE, GOB, Box 556; and undated document AGEY, PE, GOB, Box 471.

57. See Salvador Alvarado, *Mi sueño* (Mérida: Maldonado Editores, 1988), 57, 62–68, 76, 83. For a comparison with the "magical state" and petroleum revenues in Venezuela see Fernando Coronil, *The Magical State: Nature, Money and Modernity in Venezuela* (Chicago: University of Chicago Press, 1997).

58. Alonso López, CM Tixkokob, to Gobernador, 9 Oct. 1916, AGEY, PE, GOB, Box 557; Enrique López R., Inspec. Admin. Hunucmá, to Gobernador, 8 June 1917, AGEY, PE,

GOB, Box 597; "Notas del dia de los asuntos resueltos en el transcurso del mes enero de 1918," DT, AGEY, PE; GOB, Box 638; "Copias de las notas de los asuntos resueltos en este Departamento del Trabajo durante el transcurso del mes de febrero del presente año, remitidos a la Voz de la Revolución y Peninsular," DT, 28 Feb. 1918, AGEY, PE, GOB, Box 638.

59. See, for instance, Agrófilo, "La cuestión palpitante en Yucatán," *El Henequén,* 1 May 1917.

60. "Como se forma el obrero ciudadano en Yucatán," 8 Oct. 1917, *VdR.* This article was reprinted from the newspaper *Los Sucesos* of the nearby southern state of Tabasco.

61. Alvarado confirmed such accounts in his memoirs of the years in Yucatán (first published in a series of articles in the Mexico City newspaper *El Universal* beginning in 1918). Alvarado, who accused hacendados of wanting to return Yucatán to the old times of slavery, evoked popular memory of his actions in the state as the most convincing evidence his redemptive work. To the skeptical reader he declared that "SIXTY THOUSAND SERFS, transformed into free and aware citizens by the WORK OF REVOLUTION, can speak of what I did in Yucatán based on their own experience." Salvador Alvarado, *Mi actuación revolucionaria en Yucatán* (México, DF: Impresa Franco-Mexicana, 1920), 9, 45.

62. For a few examples, see Evelio Narváez, Pres. Mun. Abalá, to Jefe DT, 31 Jan. 1918, AGEY, PE, GOB, Box 656; and Fernando Cáceres, Inspec. Admin., to Jefe DT, 2 July 1918, AGEY, PE, GOB, Box 620.

63. See Abelardo Ramírez, to Jefe DT, 19 Nov. 1917, AGEY, PE, GOB, Box 579; Gonzalo Batún et al., to Gobernador, 7 Dec. 1917, AGEY, PE, GOB, Box 579; Jefe DT, to Com. Mun. Hda. Tecoh, 10 Dec. 1917, AGEY, PE, GOB, Box 595; and José Santos Pech, to Jefe DT, 6 Feb. 1918, AGEY, PE, GOB, Box 656 (emphasis in original).

64. Carlos Loveira, *De los 26 a los 35 (lecciones de la experiencia en la lucha obrera)* (Washington, DC: Law Reporter Printing, 1917), 159.

65. These observations are based on fieldwork in the vicinity of Tetiz, Yucatán, Jan. 1995–Aug. 1996; May–Aug. 1997; June–Aug. 2000; and June–Aug. 2001.

66. Contemporary populations of eastern Yucatán (that is, outside the henequen zone) use the term *epoch of slavery* to refer to the situation of indigenous populations before the midnineteenth-century Caste War. See Paul Sullivan, *Unfinished Conversations: Mayas and Foreigners between Two Wars* (Berkeley: University of California Press, 1989), 161–73; and Victoria Bricker, *The Indian Christ, the Indian King: The Historical Substrate of Maya Myth and Ritual* (Austin: University of Texas Press, 1981), 224–53. Given the absence of similar language in the documentation of the Caste War period, the usage of the term *slavery* in this way seems to be a more recent development, likely dating from the revolutionary period.

67. I borrow this phrase from Nancy Farriss's study of dual conceptions of time (that is, cyclical and linear) among the pre-Hispanic and colonial-era Maya, "Remembering the Future, Anticipating the Past: History, Time and Cosmology among the Maya of Yucatan," *Contemporary Studies in Society and History* 25 (1987): 566–93. The temporal perspective of indigenous populations in the revolutionary period and thereafter thus has considerably older cultural precedents. See also Bricker, *The Indian Christ;* and Miguel León-Portilla, *Time and Reality in the Thought of the Maya* (1973; reprint, Norman: University of Oklahoma Press, 1988).

Documenting South Africa's
Liberation Movements

Engaging the Archives at the University of Fort Hare

Brian Williams and William K. Wallach

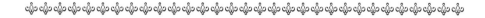

> The purpose of studying history is not to deride human action, nor to weep over it or to hate it, but to understand it—and then to learn from it as we contemplate our future.
>
> —Nelson Mandela

As the machinery of apartheid was being dismantled, agreements were signed in 1992 designating the University of Fort Hare as the custodian of the "Liberation Archives." The Liberation Archives was conceived as a symbolic union of the archival records from several of the political organizations that had helped bring about the overthrow of apartheid. Organizations agreeing to deposit records and artifacts at Fort Hare included the African National Congress (ANC), the Pan Africanist Congress (PAC), the Azanian People's Organization (AZAPO), the Black Consciousness Movement of Azania, and the New Unity Movement. The process of locating and gathering archival material from the liberation organizations had begun in the wake of the national government's historic announcement in 1990 to lift the official bans on the ANC and PAC along with restrictions on nearly three dozen other organizations.

The ANC and PAC archives are by far the largest record groups at the University of Fort Hare and are the main focus of this essay. The records of these organizations were also central to the archival initiatives undertaken jointly by the University of Michigan (U-M) and the University of Fort Hare between 1997 and 2000.[1] In addition to discussing the specific projects undertaken by the U-M, the authors address the context of the University of Fort Hare and the impact of apartheid

policies on the documentary record in relation to the ANC and PAC, as well as the political, organizational, and archival issues influencing the archives and its relationship to social memory.

The authors of this essay, both archivists at the U-M's Bentley Historical Library, participated in the U-M/Fort Hare joint initiatives. Their roles included developing an archival processing plan for records housed at Fort Hare's Centre for Cultural Studies,[2] consulting on archival issues with the center's administrators and staff, and overseeing the processing and preparation of paper-based and electronic finding aids for the Liberation Archives and other record groups at the center and at the University of Fort Hare Library, along with performing other administrative and archival tasks.

Politics of Placement

Without an appreciation of the University of Fort Hare's history, the placement of the archives at this relatively remote location would seem unusual. A researcher seeking to locate the archives of the liberation organizations might at first look to one of the larger urban areas such as Johannesburg, Cape Town, and Pretoria; in established research universities in South Africa; or in national research centers or museums, for example, the former Robben Island prison (now a national museum), an institution synonymous with Mandela and other imprisoned freedom fighters. Instead, the archival records reside in one of the oldest historically black universities in Southern and Eastern Africa, the University of Fort Hare, found within a remote, rural, and disadvantaged area of the Eastern Cape. The place where the records of liberation are located attests to the bitter legacy of apartheid—an Afrikaans term meaning "apartness"—and becomes, to a certain degree, part of the archival context.

The agreements to place the archives of the liberation movements at the University of Fort Hare were recognition of the important role the university played as the primary institution of higher education for black South Africans and as the alma mater of many of the leading liberation figures. To a lesser extent, the decision was a repudiation of the South African State Archives Service for its complicity in legitimizing apartheid.[3] Speaking at the opening of the ANC archives, then deputy president Thabo Mbeki argued that Fort Hare was "incontestably . . . the natural home" for the archives.[4] In a message, Mandela spoke of the "immense importance" of the ANC archives.

> These archives are the single most complete record of the ANC, especially in the period after its banning in 1960. They are instrumental in documenting the untold history of South Africa. . . . The organization further recognises that the archival material contains the seeds of our new democratic order. A study of the [ANC] comprises an intrinsic part of our understanding of our society, the transition we have recently experienced and what the future may hold. The ANC archives provide a window into this significant period of our country and fill the vacuum in historical continuity.[5]

The decisions by Mandela and other leaders to place the archives of their liberation movements at the University of Fort Hare were politically and historically motivated. They recognized the central role that the university played in nurturing black African leaders and rewarded Fort Hare with what could be viewed as part of the founding papers of the new South Africa in the post-apartheid period. Certainly their decision to locate the archives at Fort Hare in a research center focusing on the study of cultural heritage of black South Africans was also an attempt to memorialize the liberation struggle and to create a monument to those who participated in the conflict. As the director of the University of Fort Hare's Centre for Cultural Studies wrote, "The historical anti-apartheid role

of Fort Hare's student body, which included President Mandela, Robert Sobukwe, and other leaders of the National Struggle for Liberation justify locating this important Archive on the Alice campus."[6] The archives become not only a place to document South Africa's "untold history" but also a center to support a more inclusive writing of the nation's history as it moves from a society that privileged one group over another to a "non-racial, non-sexist democracy" envisioned by Mandela.[7]

The University of Fort Hare

The campus of the University of Fort Hare is situated in the town of Alice, along the Tyume River in the rural area of South Africa's Eastern Cape. The University of Fort Hare, established as the South African Native College during World War I, is a microcosm of the history and turmoil of South Africa.[8] Its "chequered history," noted Oliver Tambo, the leader of the ANC-in-exile, is "a mirror of the struggles of the oppressed people" in South Africa.[9] The roots of its founding by Scottish missionaries and black educationalists reflected the competing objectives of colonialism and self-determination. An incubator of African nationalism, Fort Hare educated an unparalleled number of black leaders and played a key role in the liberation struggle. The university suffered a fate similar to most African institutions during apartheid when the government extended "Bantu Education" policies to higher education. These policies were meant to take away local autonomy from historically black colleges and universities in favor of state control. The policies transformed Fort Hare from alumnus Nelson Mandela's description as "a beacon for African scholars from all over Southern Central and Eastern Africa" to secondary status as a regional tribal college.[10] Under Bantu administration, admission was restricted primarily to Xhosa-speaking students from the homelands of Transkei and Ciskei.[11] From 1960 until the end of apartheid, Fort Hare endured a steady descent from historic institution to historically disadvantaged institution.

The university has sought to encourage the use of the liberation organizations' archives for research and to promote the role of Fort Hare in developing the leadership and ideas of the anti-apartheid movement. These archives have restorative potential and are a source of empowerment for the university as it struggles to overcome the inequities created by apartheid. In recent years, instabilities stemming from declining enrollment and charges of fiscal mismanagement have made the post-apartheid transition even more difficult. Critical self-assessments and a new administration have launched a strategic plan seeking to restore Fort Hare to prominence.[12] The archives are an important part of this strategic plan.

Politics of Remembering and Forgetting

The conflict of cultures ultimately leading to the system of apartheid was exacerbated by the discovery of gold and diamonds in the latter half of the nineteenth century and the crude economics predicated on the need for inexpensive and controllable labor for the extractive mining operations. Unlike the colonial plundering of the Congo in the nineteenth century popularly recounted by Adam Hochschild in *King Leopold's Ghost,* the native population of South Africa did not endure a physical holocaust. Instead of large-scale extermination, as in the Congo, the South African native population was systematically marginalized and disenfranchised by colonial authorities through official and unofficial segregation and other racist actions. The politics of remembering and forgetting in South Africa are, however, similar to those involved in Belgian rule over the Congo. For example, state records documenting Leopold's reign of depredation in the Congo were reportedly burned over eight days in Brussels.[13] As the beginning of a new political order in South Africa was becoming evident, the records of the old regime were subject to massive "unauthorized destruction." The *Sunday Times* reported a security officer as stating:

> It was wholesale destruction. At John Vorster square alone something like 35,000 files were dumped. We lost count of how many shredders burnt out in the process, but the beer was flowing and the fires were burning high at the South Africa Police rugby ground at Arthur Bloch Park.[14]

In South Africa, the state archives helped legitimize and sustain apartheid rule through "silences" and "systematic forgetting." Opposition to apartheid, the "simmering memory of resistance and struggle," in the words of the South African archivist Verne Harris, "was forced into informal spaces and the deeper reaches of the underground."[15] The liberation movements lived a shadowy existence as they fought to emerge from colonial domination. State control of memory dramatically influenced what was documented. The battle has now moved to the informal spaces of collective memory in the struggle of remembering against forgetting.

The axiom "who controls power, controls history" holds true in South Africa. In the aftermath of apartheid, an African nationalist historiography has reemerged, which, as the historian Leonard Thompson cautions, "may lead to partisan works resembling a mirror-image of Afrikaner nationalist writings."[16] Archives figure prominently in these historical debates and become disputed sites in new battles of intellectual nationalism.

In discussing the significant role played by archivists in "moulding the future of our documentary heritage," the Canadian archivist Terry Cook reminds archivists of the seriousness of that task. He writes, "we are literally . . . deciding what is remembered and what is forgotten, who in society is visible and who remains invisible, who has a voice and who does not."[17] Wanting to make visible what was invisible and hear what was not heard during the era of apartheid, Mandela saw a need to document "the untold history of South Africa," in essence calling for a rewriting of the nation's history. He understood the power of archives as a tool of subterfuge.

> The majority of South Africans have . . . been deliberately misrepresented in the official history of South Africa. Archival resources that have previously been preserved in our national repositories have condemned this country's African inhabitants to historical obscurity. The records that do exist serve only to perpetuate the myths and obscure the horrors of apartheid.[18]

Mandela's views are quite apparent—those in power can use or misuse records for their own purposes. Archives can be a tool to conceal or a weapon to reveal. He viewed the availability of the ANC archives as a means to reverse the myths and distortions promulgated in the previous regime—and to aid in the process of remembering, recalling, and rethinking the past in a way that bears more likeness to his own sense of reality.

Politics Influencing Creation

Before turning to the physical archives of the liberation movement, it seems appropriate to address some of the conditions influencing the creation of documentation. The literal "apartness" of apartheid emanated from the legislation that enforced separation between white and black South Africans in rural areas and regulated the presence of blacks in urban areas.[19] Additions to these core statutes of apartheid further eroded the basic rights of black South Africans. The ANC, and its predecessor, the South African Native National Congress, had been largely ineffective in opposing the various segregation measures and numbered about five thousand members by the time the Afrikaner Nationalist Party came to power in 1948.

The creation of archives was never a central focus of the liberation organizations—nor of most any organization.[20] The liberation movements were largely grassroots organizations, and the business of keeping the organizations vital and mobilized made secondary any serious thought to documenting history. The ANC of the late 1940s, Mandela noted, "did not have a single full-time employee, and was generally poorly organized, operating in a haphazard way," hardly a structure conducive to good record keeping.[21] Other reasons may also affect the creation of records. An archivist at the University of Fort Hare and a Canadian historian commented in a 1998 joint article, "Given the necessarily clandestine nature of some of the ANC's activities as a revolutionary organization, conventional correspondence and records may have sometimes represented a security risk."[22] The PAC, established in 1959 by Robert Sobukwe following a rift within the ANC over cooperation with non-Africans, was struggling to develop its own administrative structure along with a constituency. Viability of these organizations, not to mention the capacity to document themselves, was imperiled by the increasingly restrictive legislation imposed by the state aimed at curtailing opposing organizations and points of view.

The Nationalist monopoly on power took control of the past, developing a "political mythology" that "distorted the past for nationalist purposes."[23] Control of the present was ensured by a stranglehold on media and the implementation of increasingly repressive security and censorship legislation. These policies profoundly altered and shaped the nature of the documentary record. Debate within South Africa was stifled, and the liberation leaders were effectively silenced, leaving a one-sided discourse.

The central piece of legislation was the Suppression of Communism Act instituted in 1950, which allowed the government wide latitude in defining "communism." Provisions of the act enabled the state to disband organizations, to enforce prohibitions on publications, to seize documents, and to ban or deport individuals. The act can be understood in the broader cold war context that gave rise to McCarthyism and "Red squads" in the United States, but the South African equivalent continued unabated for several decades and grew increasingly suppressive.[24] Additional legislation made it a punishable offense to even possess banned publications and documents. Be-

yond influencing what was created, these policies also raise questions about what was *not* recorded.

The Impact of Censorship

In light of government restrictions on writings by banned persons, the creation of archives achieved a symbolic status manifested in a rejection of colonialism and a step toward controlling history. The threat of prison sentences and deportation for possessing banned material served as an obvious deterrent to the creation of archives, but it also ascribed an immeasurable value to documentation as a tangible sign of resistance.

The Congress of the People held in 1955 represented a high point for the internal liberation movement and also illustrated the lengths to which the state resorted in order to silence opposition. The congress preceded adoption of the Freedom Charter, a document equivalent to the U.S. Bill of Rights or the Declaration of Independence as a defining national document. Before discussion of the Freedom Charter concluded, the congress was broken up by state security forces citing treason. Subject to a banning order and unable to participate in the convention, Mandela watched from the periphery and described the event: "The police began pushing people off the platform and confiscating documents and photographs," even taking the catering signs.[25]

The infamous Treason Trial that followed passage of the Freedom Charter was preceded by large-scale seizure of documentation when police raided 460 offices and homes in their search for evidence of treason and sedition, coming away with books and pamphlets.[26] In all, 156 individuals were arrested. Mandela, among those arrested, recounted how the first month of the trial was devoted to the submission of evidence by the state: "One by one, every paper, pamphlet, document, book, notebook, letter, magazine, and clipping that the police had accumulated in the last three years of searches was produced and numbered; twelve thousand in all."[27] In one sense, in its efforts to seize documents, the state had inadvertently created an archive consisting of some twelve thousand documents and artifacts. Seventy-five boxes of trial-related records are held by the University of Witwatersrand,[28] but much of the original documentation seized by the state was destroyed between 1990 and 1994 as part of a state campaign of "collective amnesia."[29]

The most trying days for the ANC and PAC followed the 1960 mass-action anti-pass law protest sponsored by the PAC in an effort to upstage the ANC. The peaceful protest turned violent when police fired on protesters at Sharpeville. The unrest sparked by the "Sharpeville Massacre" led to the declaration of a state of emergency and the outlawing of the ANC and PAC.[30] For the PAC, less than a year old, banning was a crippling blow, as the administrative structure had not sufficiently developed to support movement underground and the establishment of foreign missions.[31]

The ANC had developed preliminary plans for underground and external operations and had dispatched Oliver Tambo out of South Africa before the banning. The ANC internal plans were dealt a severe blow when police raided the underground headquarters in Rivonia in 1963 and confiscated hundreds of additional documents and papers. Like the Treason Trial, the Rivonia Trial saw thousands of documents and photographs presented as evidence. Three decades later, the national archivist admitted that documents used as evidence in the trial were missing: "The official records of the Rivonia Treason Trial transferred to the National Archives Repository by the Supreme Court are missing. The investigation embraces a search for the missing volumes and endeavors to secure copies from other sources."[32]

For the exiled ANC and PAC, the 1960s would be devoted to consolidating their external structures, fundraising, promoting international awareness, and coordinating guerrilla and sabotage operations. When the movements turned to armed struggle, the clandestine nature of the guerrilla armies eschewed the generation of documentation. The organizations lacked the luxury enjoyed during the "Great Crusade" of World War II, when historians like S. L. A. Marshall followed men into battle and conducted post-combat briefings and interviews in the immediate aftermath of battle, creating a form of intentional and instantaneous history.[33] The PAC records at Fort Hare, however, include a fascinating collection of individual dossiers on soldiers in the armed wing, Azanian People's Liberation Army. While few detailed accounts of guerrilla and sabotage operations exist, additional information about these operations has come to light through the hearings of the Truth and Reconciliation Commission.

The Impact of Organizational Structure

An important adjunct for archives is an understanding of the organizational structure and processes that lead to the creation of documentation.[34] The location of missions had a large influence on the nature of the documentation.

Before the ban on the ANC was lifted in 1990, it operated thirty-three missions and bases. Overseas missions functioned generally as lobbyists and fund-raisers generating position statements and propaganda, while missions within the African continent detail the development of networks, coalitions, and training sites. The early years illustrate the challenges of organizing and building coalitions and of arousing international support. The turn to armed struggle and the major influx of exiled Africans after the 1976 Soweto uprisings added training and resettlement to the tasks of the missions. Indeed, the Solomon Mahlangu Freedom College (SOMAFCO) in Tanzania is a prime example of a community and educational institution created for the generation exiled after the Soweto township revolts. SOMAFCO has a profound meaning for many South Africans, and the records, artifacts, and teaching tools of SOMAFCO were among the first to arrive at Fort Hare.[35]

Publications produced by the external missions reflect the differing faces of the mission. Those aimed at cultivating international awareness indicate a stronger self-consciousness in their creation. Other publications served as internal organs and are couched in revolutionary rhetoric. The liberation organizations also frequently reprinted key documents to both educate prospective members as well as to combat censorship and banning orders by virtue of sheer quantity. Revitalizing and reusing prior themes and images was also common within the publications. Sam Nzima's famous 1976 photograph from Soweto of a student carrying fatally wounded Hector Peterson was a politicizing image that was used on hundreds of publications, posters, and buttons in the decades that followed.

Archival Landscape at Fort Hare

At the University of Fort Hare, the archives of the liberation organizations are recognized as an important asset, and control of the archives has been nearly as tempestuous as the question of who controls the history. The agreements designating Fort Hare as the repository for the Liberation Archives assigned custody of the archives to the university's Centre for Cultural Studies. First begun as the Centre for Xhosa Literature, the center's mandate broadened sufficiently to encompass a more widely based cultural studies center with jurisdiction over the art gallery and the museum collection of ethnographic artifacts.[36] Shortly after the historical materials began arriving piecemeal from their exiled locations, tensions flared.

326

IV: ARCHIVES, MEMORY, AND POLITICAL CULTURE

What the center's director referenced as a "raging archives dispute" in his annual report resulted in demands by the ANC that its archives be placed elsewhere on campus.[37] Lingering political rivalries between the ANC and PAC may have played a part in the removal, but the end result was the relocation of the ANC archives to the University of Fort Hare Library. The political implications of the relocation notwithstanding, the decision strained already limited capacities as two separate facilities and staffs were now required to administer the archives. The removal of the ANC archives also signaled an end to the formal use of the title "Liberation Archives" when representatives of the ANC archives committee reportedly found the title untenable in their desire for complete disassociation.

For the University of Fort Hare Library, the ANC archives were a tremendous burden on already constrained resources, but they also served to fill in a significant gap in resources about the liberation struggle. Apartheid policies had barred libraries from acquiring holdings contrary to the state position, particularly those that failed to earn approval from state censors. The result at the Fort Hare Library was a massive void in holdings on the history of South Africa, particularly the growth of African nationalism and the fight for liberation. Given this situation, the archival records assume greater importance as a vital resource for studying and understanding the history of the liberation movement and the broader history of South Africa.

Building Relationships between the University of Fort Hare and the University of Michigan

Beginnings

In 1991, during the end years of apartheid in South Africa, a delegation from the U-M, led by Charles Moody, vice provost for minority affairs, visited the University of Fort Hare to begin a multiyear effort to explore cooperative ventures between the two universities.[38]

By 1996 the U-M had secured United States Information Agency (USIA) funding for a three-year project in support of several objectives, including these focused on archival activities.

- To establish technology-based collections management at the DeBeers Centenary Art Gallery and the Centre for Cultural Studies at the University of Fort Hare.
- To assist in the development of archives management

procedures relevant to the archival holdings of the Centre for Cultural Studies, including preservation and conservation techniques and the application of digital technology to increase access to records.
- To support observation and consultation related to the development of an archival education curriculum, and to facilitate the exchange of archival information, literature and materials.[39]

Professor Margaret Hedstrom, of the U-M School of Information (SI), assumed responsibility for planning the archival (and other) parts of the grant. The U-M's Bentley Historical Library was brought in as a partner because of its expertise in the administration of modern archival records.[40] In the summer of 1997 Hedstrom conducted a needs assessment of Fort Hare's archival programs and proposed a series of next steps. From the beginning, U-M's approach was to build upon and improve an existing archival capacity at the University of Fort Hare. The goal of this effort was to establish a professional staff educated in archives and records management, knowledgeable about current standards and best practices, and adept in the use and application of appropriate archival tools. Additionally, major segments of Fort Hare's liberation archival holdings would be arranged and described and a digital infrastructure established to support work within the archives. The goal of the USIA grant was not just the completion of several short-term projects within the archives but the building of an ongoing, professionally run archival program at the University of Fort Hare.

A vision is more easily imagined than realized. Politics, personalities, and unrealistic expectations presented serious obstacles to bringing about all the desired end results. While significant accomplishments were achieved during the three-year period of grant activity, the ultimate objective of building archival capacity at the University of Fort Hare still awaits final completion.

Resignations within the archival ranks at the center made it more difficult to sustain programmatic growth and made more clear that retention of key staff would be essential to the evolution of the archives. The situation at the University of Fort Hare Library, which holds the ANC records, was quite different. Several staff members had archival education or training and significant experience working with archives and manuscript collections. For example, the acting director of the University of Fort Hare Library received her graduate education at the U-M's SI, where she took archival courses and was exposed to the work of the university's various archives and manuscript collections. Similarly, the archivist at the University of Fort Hare Library assigned to process the ANC archives had obtained a master's degree in archival studies from the Loughborough University in the United Kingdom and had undertaken advanced archival courses at the University of Witwatersrand. Other staff members also had archival training and experience. The library staff's base level of archival knowledge and skills was promising in terms of further development of a strong archival program.

U-M's Planning for the Fort Hare Project

Even before Hedstrom's 1997 needs assessment study, the U-M and the University of Fort Hare implemented some parts of the collaborative project, most importantly providing educational opportunities for Fort Hare Library and Centre for Cultural Studies staff. Advanced education and training for select staff members were key elements of the overall plan to build archival capacity at Fort Hare. Hedstrom also envisioned the involvement of SI graduate students, who could apply their knowledge and skills to real archival situations at Fort Hare.[41]

Hedstrom, Francis Blouin (director of the Bentley Historical Library and SI faculty member), and Bentley Library archivists met in the fall of 1997 to discuss preliminary plans regarding the archival initiatives at Fort Hare and the selection process for the SI students who would participate in the work there. Brian Williams and William Wallach, both experienced in project and program planning, traveled to South Africa in early spring 1998 to develop and refine a work plan for the processing of the liberation movement archives housed in Fort Hare's Centre for Cultural Studies.[42] After this preprocessing planning by the U-M archivists, SI students spent six weeks in Fort Hare and began to implement Wallach and Williams's processing plan.

Status of the Archival Records at Fort Hare Prior to the U-M Project

The liberation movement archives that arrived at Fort Hare did not arrive complete. They were the end product of liberation, the residue of revolution, the records of offices abruptly closed after the startling end of apartheid. The materials came in sporadic shipments from the exiled outposts where the liberation movements had once operated in their effort to raise international awareness and to coordinate the internal struggle from abroad. Banning and censorship had driven the organi-

zations underground and abroad to sympathetic nations. Records from the ANC arrived after preliminary processing at Luthuli House, the ANC headquarters in Johannesburg. The records included administrative files, financial records, correspondence, topical files, publications, photographs, audio-visual material, and artifacts ranging from buttons and T-shirts to posters and artwork. On the whole, there is little documentation generated from within South Africa before the lifting of apartheid, and the bulk of the documentation is from the 1980s and early 1990s with limited material from the 1960s and 1970s.[43]

Following the 1992 agreement to deposit the PAC archives at Fort Hare's Centre for Cultural Studies, M. Gqobose, a member of the PAC's National Executive Committee for the Eastern Cape region, sent a memorandum to all PAC offices and missions around the world seeking information about the quality and nature of the records and asking them to ship the records to Fort Hare. After listing the types of archival and museum items of interest, he wrote, "[W]e entreat you to avoid destroying any of the above mentioned materials in your office. We . . . implore you not to allow anybody to destroy, or release to any other person or institution" the archival and museum materials.[44] His appeal worked, and in the spring of 1995 the center began receiving PAC records and artifacts. Eleven large metal trunks were shipped from Tanzania, each of which contained disordered and unfoldered piles of administrative records; sixty-two cartons arrived from the New York PAC office/UN mission, which also were in no apparent order; and twenty-two boxes were transferred from the London PAC office. The boxes and trunks contained administrative records and publications, much like those received from the ANC. Other PAC offices and missions in Zimbabwe and elsewhere also transferred documentation to Fort Hare. Exiled officers who had retained records sent them on to the new liberation movement archives.[45]

The return from exile added another dimension to the archives. These records became a history recovered. It is a theme with other implications—the physical exile of both records and people provokes a debate that exists as an undercurrent. A seldom described tension exists between those who remained within South Africa and those who chose to leave or were forced into exile. Inferences exist that those not in exile were not part of the struggle. The politicizing power of such inferences is broad, and such tensions are part of the social fabric at Fort Hare.

Devising and Implementing the Processing Plan

Working with an assistant archivist trainee at Fort Hare's Centre for Cultural Studies, the U-M archivists surveyed the liberation archives (primarily the PAC archives), identified its organizational structures, devised a processing plan, identified individual record subgroups and possible series within these subgroups, defined appraisal criteria to apply in determining which records to retain and which were of no archival value, developed a finding aid model, and agreed on final products, including cataloging records and encoded finding aids to enhance intellectual access to information about the archives. Brian Williams returned to Fort Hare and in May–June 1998 helped coordinate the processing work of the eight SI students based on the plan he and Wallach had developed.[46] The SI students intensively processed PAC records during this first summer's visit to the University of Fort Hare. After their return to Michigan, several students continued working on the project. They completed catalog records and finding aids for the PAC missions processed during the summer and created encoded versions of the finding aids, which were then mounted on the Centre for Cultural Studies's Web site, which other U-M students continued to develop for the center.

With funding from USIA and the Kellogg Foundation, U-M faculty and students made two additional trips to Fort Hare in the summers of 1999 and 2000 to continue their work. During these trips archival projects focused on processing and improving access to the ANC records at the Fort Hare Library. Project staff also developed a unified Web site for Fort Hare's renamed center (the National Heritage and Cultural Studies Centre) and the library, a major breakthrough given the tensions between the two units. The Web site, titled "The University of Fort Hare Collections," offers one portal through which researchers can link to information about the liberation movement and other holdings at Fort Hare's Library and the center. The lack of cooperation between the library and the center does not bode well for the research community in the long run. There is no doubt that access to information about the liberation archives has been greatly enhanced not only through the processing of the records but also through the establishment of Web sites about the collections. Disputes between the two Fort Hare units eventually led to intervention by top university administrators. In Strategic Plan 2000, designed to restructure Fort Hare, the university's vice chancellor announced plans to settle the archives dispute and "establish unified, centralised and efficient management of Uni-

versity-held archives."[47] Implementation of Strategic Plan 2000 is under way at Fort Hare, but it is too early to tell if the goals set for unifying and centralizing archival collections at the university will be successful.

Meaning of the Archives

In his speech at the opening of the ANC archives at the University of Fort Hare on March 17, 1996, Thabo Mbeki spoke to the "living reality of the archives" and to the archives as a "school both for the philosophers and the historians as well as the agitators and the activists."[48] As mentioned previously, Nelson Mandela identified the archives as the "single most complete record of the ANC" and a vital link in "documenting the untold history of South Africa."[49] The archives are both more and less than that. The archives assume an almost ethereal quality as a monument to triumph over supreme adversity, yet they fall to earth mired in the minutia of polemics, propaganda, and the mundane tasks of administration. It is difficult to separate the rhetoric of freedom from actual content. The archives are part and parcel of the mirroring of the "humaneness of the actors in the process of making history."[50] Mandela and other liberation movement figures have become veiled in romance, and the archives at once reinforce these notions while also stripping away the shroud of myth to reveal an underlying humanity. Maamoe and Stapleton, who wrote about the ANC records at the University of Fort Hare, sound a more realistic tone, noting that "it is unlikely that the archives will meet the lofty goals of stimulating the complete revision of South African history" as indicated at the ceremony opening the archives.[51]

Foreign and Domestic Engagement in Fort Hare's Archives

Perhaps because of the cachet of Fort Hare's famous alumni and its historical significance, or because of the desire to redress the past, several players, both foreign and domestic, have rushed in to support the University of Fort Hare. Hosts of universities, primarily American, have cultivated exchange programs and joint projects. In the past, many of these initiatives have gone uncoordinated, negotiated without the benefit of centralized input. There has been no shortage of players willing to help with the Liberation Archives and matters of cultural heritage. Good intentions notwithstanding, to some it might be construed as a more benign form of imperialism, the last vestiges of colonialism. At least four U.S. institutions advanced various plans and programs aimed at developing the cultural heritage resources at Fort Hare.[52]

In addition to the U-M's cooperative arrangement with Fort Hare, there is an important partnership involving the University of Connecticut and the ANC, dating from March 1999. The agreement links the ANC, the University of Connecticut, and the University of Fort Hare in a variety of projects including archival cooperation, oral history programs, conferences, exchanges, and training. The most notable aspect of the agreement designates the University of Connecticut as the official repository for ANC materials in North America. Under terms of the agreement, University of Connecticut archivists will direct the copying of ANC records for "safekeeping" and will organize and catalog the materials, sharing some of the materials on the Web.[53] Publicity for the University of Connecticut project is abundant and alludes to the creation of a North American mirror site, although the means used to copy the archives have not been specified. While the Connecticut agreement opens the ANC archives to a wider audience and enables additional scholarship, the agreement is interpreted less positively by some at the University of Fort Hare.

ANC archival records arrive at Fort Hare after review and preliminary processing at the ANC's Johannesburg headquarters. The flow of records from Johannesburg to the Fort Hare Library has ceased, perhaps since the 1996 dedication of the ANC archives at Fort Hare, fueling speculation about when or if remaining archival records will be sent and whether the University of Connecticut agreement has impacted transfers to Fort Hare. The entry of another institution—the University of Connecticut—taking on the responsibility of guardian of the ANC historical records has caused some concern at Fort Hare, even if the records at the University of Connecticut are copies. No matter how beneficial the relationship and how good the intentions might be for the ANC and the University of Connecticut, some at Fort Hare view the new partnership as a diminution of the university's role as the designated archival repository for the ANC, the "incontestably . . . natural home" for the ANC archives, as Mbeki wrote.[54] They also ask whether the significance of the archives can be fully appreciated outside of the context of Fort Hare and the surrounding area. The agreement and further written documents from the University of Connecticut raise questions about the extent of archival expertise at Fort Hare, which standards and descriptive practices will be used, and whether changes made at

one institution require changes at all institutions. When the archives are seen in the light of a documentary heritage once prohibited and painfully recaptured and now made accessible by the professional archival staff at the Fort Hare Library, the act of sending copies outside of South Africa takes on greater meaning. Does sending copies of the ANC archives to the United States raise questions of cultural imperialism, even if clothed in the most benign of intentions? Control of history and control of historical documentation are important issues and take center stage in South Africa's transition to a new democracy.

The Larger South African Archival Scene

The changeover to a democratic society has opened a new dialogue of memory of which the archives are a vital part. Just as the Truth and Reconciliation Commission provided a forum for both victims and perpetrators to contest memory and to understand their experiences, so have archives become more than silos of memory as they document both the oppressed and the oppressor. The archives at the University of Fort Hare are part of the larger South African archival heritage. As Eric Ketelaar reminds us, "Archives are neither red nor brown, black nor white. Archives document, black *on* white, the diversity of activities and actions—right or wrong—on all sides."[55]

It is important to note that the archives of liberation movements at Fort Hare are not the sole source of information about South Africa's struggle for democracy. Several other institutions house archival record groups and personal papers documenting both the anti-apartheid movement and those organizations in favor of the policy of apartheid. The archives of South Africa's liberation struggle cannot be found in any one archives or library but rather are held throughout the nation and world in fragmentary pieces. For example, the University of Witwatersrand's Historical Papers Department has a wide variety of materials, serves as the official repository for organizations such as the South African Institute of Race Relations, and holds political and trial material dating from the 1950s to the 1990s.[56] Also housed at Witwatersrand is the South African History Archive (SAHA), which deposited their materials at the university in 1994. SAHA was established in 1988 by the United Democratic Front and the Congress of South African Trade Unions to document the history of opposition to apartheid.[57] A national collaborative program called Digital Imaging South Africa (DISA) has taken on a project, located at the

University of Natal, titled "South Africa's Struggle for Democracy: Anti-Apartheid Periodicals, 1960–1990," covering a period of three key decades in the growth of opposition to apartheid rule.[58] Additionally, supporters and scholars of the liberation movement throughout the world have collected primary source materials and have issued them in printed volumes and microfilm. Among the foremost of these is the projected seven-volume *From Protest to Challenge: A Documentary History of African Politics in South Africa, 1882–1990.* This work includes a compilation of primary sources plus explanatory text placing the documents into historical context. The documents, interviews, and biographical materials used to produce volumes 1–3 were microfilmed and published in 1977 as *South African Political Materials: A Catalogue of the Carter-Karis Collection,* which is available worldwide.[59] These collections and projects add to the universe of documentation on the struggle for liberation. The concern of those at the University of Fort Hare is whether the archives of the liberation movements held at the university will be marginalized by other resources at better-funded institutions. As an institution that is isolated, poorly funded, and beset by internal conflicts that diminish what resources are available there, the opportunity to play a prominent role as a repository of the nation's memory is at risk.

The new democratic government in South Africa affirmed the importance of archives by making the National Archives of South Africa Act the first major piece of cultural legislation enacted. The act acknowledged the role of archives and archivists as shapers of social memory, while stressing transparency of motives and accountability. It also highlighted past imbalances, noting "the need to document aspects of the nation's experience neglected by archives repositories in the past."[60] The archives act was developed amid what public archivists in South Africa describe as a "transformative discourse" that has replaced outdated practices and epistemologies rooted in the 1950s.[61]

The transformation has acknowledged the public archives role as "willing lackey" of the apartheid government and has identified a set of exclusionary obstacles beyond the realm of collecting policies.[62] The reservation of archival jobs for whites not only prevented blacks from becoming archivists but also produced generations of archivists trained under apartheid models. The language of apartheid left much of the archival literature and description written in the Afrikaans language and thus inaccessible to the majority of the population. Change has led to some bilingual guides in English and Afrikaans, but it still

excludes the population for whom these are not their native languages. Outreach and inclusion are further hindered by the high illiteracy rates and the distant location of state archives from the rural areas. Appraisal in the public archives is being reshaped, adopting macroappraisal models advocated by the Canadian archivist Terry Cook and, in the words of the South African national archivist Marie Olivier, ensuring that "the heritage of all the country's people can be nurtured and conserved without prejudice."[63] For the University of Fort Hare, the archives of the liberation struggle remain a defense against previous policies that "condemned" South Africa's "African inhabitants to historical obscurity."[64]

NOTES

The authors thank fellow seminarians Nancy Bartlett and Verne Harris for their critical reading of this essay and Seán Morrow and Robin Trehaeven, both from the University of Fort Hare, for their important insights. A longer version of the essay was published in *Comma: International Journal on Archives,* no. 1–2 (2000): 45–67.

The quote given in the epigraph to this essay is from Jennifer Crwys-Williams, ed., *In the Words of Nelson Mandela* (Parktown, South Africa: Penguin Books, 1997), 35.

1. These archival initiatives were part of a larger effort by the University of Michigan, Michigan State University, and the University of Fort Hare to assess and assist in improving the cultural heritage programs at Fort Hare, including its holdings of archives, art, and historical artifacts. For the purpose of this essay, the authors will focus only on the archival components of the project. The University of Michigan received funding from the United States Information Agency and from the Kellogg Foundation to support its work with the University of Fort Hare.

2. The Centre for Cultural Studies is now known as the National Heritage and Cultural Studies Centre, a name change that occurred at the dedication of its new building in September 1998.

3. Ethel Kriger, "Redressing Apartheid-Engendered Social Ills: A Core Archival Function? Transformation and the Public Archivist in a Post-Apartheid South Africa," *Archivum* 45 (2000): 140.

4. Speech of Deputy President Thabo Mbeki at the opening of the ANC archives, University of Fort Hare, March 17, 1996. Available at http://www.ufh.ac.za/collections/Library/ANC_Materials/Mbeki-speech.htm (accessed October 2002).

5. "Message from President Mandela" in brochure "Inside the ANC Archives" (Johannesburg: African National Congress, ca. 1996).

6. Available at http://www.ufh.ac.za/collections. Among the other significant leaders educated at Fort Hare are Oliver Tambo and Govan Mbeki of the ANC; Mangosuthu Buthelezi of the Inkatha Freedom Party; Eluid Mathu, the first African member of the Kenya Legislative Council; the former president

of Zimbabwe, Robert Mugabe; the former prime minister of Lesotho, Ntsu Mokhehle; and the former prime minister of Zambia, Fwanyanga Mulikita.

7. "Message from President Mandela."

8. The South African Native College was affiliated with the University of South Africa until 1951, when it was designated as the University College of Fort Hare and affiliated with Rhodes University. In 1960 administration resided with the Ministry of Bantu Education. In 1970 it gained nominal autonomy as the University of Fort Hare under Ciskei's status as a separate administrative territory.

Ciskei was granted internal self-government on 1 August 1972 and achieved full "independence" from South Africa on 4 December 1981. Seán Morrow and Khayalethu Gxabalashe, "The Records of the University of Fort Hare," *History in Africa* 27 (2000): 482.

9. "A Message from O. R. Tambo: Chancellor of the University of Fort Hare." Original at the University of Fort Hare. Available at http://www.si.umich.edu/fort-hare/tambo.htm.

10. Nelson Mandela, *Long Walk to Freedom* (Boston: Little, Brown, 1994), 43.

11. J. F. Ade Ajayi, Lameck K. H. Goma, and G. Ampah Johnson, *The African Experience with Higher Education* (Athens: Ohio University Press, 1996), 36.

12. Fort Hare's Strategic Plan 2000 is available online at http://www.ufh.ac.za/sp2000.asp and at http://www.si.umich.edu/fort-hare/UFHStrategicPlan2000.pdf.

13. Adam Hochschild, *King Leopold's Ghost* (New York: Houghton Mifflin, 1998), 294.

14. Razia Saleh, "A National Archival Policy for a Democratic South Africa," master's thesis, University of London, 1993, 20, as quoted by Lekoko S. Kenosi, "Accountability, Ideology and Documentary Heritage: An Overview of South Africa's Archival Landscape," *Escarbica Journal* 19 (2000): 7.

15. Verne Harris, "The Archive and Secrecy in South Africa: A Personal Perspective," *Janus*, no. 1 (1999): 7.

16. Leonard Thompson, *A History of South Africa*, rev. ed. (New Haven: Yale University Press, 1995), xii–xiii.

17. Terry Cook, "From the Record to Its Context: The Theory and Practice of Archival Appraisal since Jenkinson," *South African Archives Journal* 37 (1995): 33, as quoted by Kenosi, "Accountability, Ideology," 4.

18. "Message from President Mandela."

19. The 1913 Native's Land Act enforced separation in the rural areas, while the 1923 Urban Areas Act dealt with the urban areas.

20. Records are usually a by-product of activities and transactions. After the transaction is over, the organization may or may not have a business need to keep a record of that transaction. When a record is kept long-term, then it may become a part of the archives because it has continuing administrative or other value. Other organizational and personal records may migrate into an archival environment through luck or serendipity or as an afterthought.

21. Mandela, *Long Walk to Freedom*, 107.

22. T. J. Stapleton and M. Maamoe, "An Overview of the African National Congress Archives at the University of Fort Hare," *History in Africa* 25 (1998): 421.

23. Thompson, *History of South Africa*, 198.

24. Other key acts include the Riotous Assemblies Act of 1956; the Unlawful Organizations Act of 1960; the Sabotage Act of 1962; the Terrorism Act of 1967; and the Internal Security Act of 1976. These acts are generally described in Thompson, *History of South Africa*, 198–99, and more specifically throughout Christopher Merrett, *A Culture of Censorship: Secrecy and Intellectual Repression in South Africa* (Macon, GA: Mercer University Press, 1995).

25. Mandela, *Long Walk to Freedom*, 173.

26. Merrett, *Culture of Censorship*, 28.

27. Mandela, *Long Walk to Freedom*, 209.

28. Information available at http://www.wits.ac.za/histp/collections.htm.

29. Harris, "Archive and Secrecy," 8–9.

30. Merrett, *Culture of Censorship*, 58.

31. For a detailed look at Sobukwe and the PAC, see Benjamin Pogrund, *How Can Man Die Better: Sobukwe and Apartheid* (London: Halban, 1990).

32. *Annual Reports of the National Archivist and State Herald,* Department of Arts, Culture, Science, and Technology, Pretoria, South Africa 1995–97, 21.

33. Marshall served as chief historian for the European Theater of Operations. For a prime example of the postcombat interviews, see S. L. A. Marshall, *Night Drop: The American Airborne Invasion of Normandy* (Boston: Little, Brown, 1962).

34. For detailed histories, including commentary on organizational structures and the work of missions, see Tom Lodge, *Black Politics in South Africa since 1945* (New York: Longman, 1983), and Thomas Scott, *The Diplomacy of Liberation: The Foreign Relations of the ANC since 1960* (London: Taurus Academic Studies, 1996).

35. Seán Morrow, in one of the first published studies to utilize the archival holding at Fort Hare, offers a study of SOMAFCO and ANC activities in exile in his article "Dakawa Development Centre: An African National Congress Settlement in Tanzania, 1982–1992," *African Affairs* 97, no. 389 (October 1998): 497–521.

36. For a fascinating history of the building of a collection of African artifacts at Fort Hare, see Seán Morrow, "'The Things They Have Made Will Live Forever': The Estelle Hamilton-Welsh Collection in the F. S. Malan Museum, University of Fort Hare," *Journal of South African Studies* 22, no. 2 (1996): 271–85.

37. Centre for Cultural Studies, "1995–1996 Report," University of Fort Hare, 1, 14–15.

38. The visit to South Africa had many purposes and included, perhaps most importantly, the presentation to Mandela of an honorary degree conferred on him in absentia by the University of Michigan in 1987.

39. "Rebuilding for the Future: South African Academic Exchange between the University of Fort Hare and the University of Michigan," grant proposal from the University of Michigan to USIA, 1996.

40. The Bentley Historical Library, established in 1935, serves both as the University of Michigan Archives and as a collecting archives, with a focus on the history of the state of Michigan, its people, and nongovernmental institutions and organizations.

41. Hedstrom et al., "Preservation, Management, and Use

of Archives and Museum Collections at the University of Fort Hare," unpublished consultants' report, September 18, 1997, 21–22.

42. Archival processing involves several steps: the appraisal or identification of records that should be preserved long-term because of their administrative, historical, financial, or other value; the ordering of these records into a useful scheme to promote physical retrievability; the reboxing or refoldering of the records to promote their preservation; and the description of the archival records according to agreed upon conventions and best practices to promote intellectual access.

43. Stapleton and Maamoe, "Overview of the African National Congress Archives," 414, 421.

44. M. Gqobose to Chief Representative, PAC Offices, March 1, 1994. Gqobose wrote that he and the center director were interested in a variety of archival and museum material, including printed documents such as birth, death, and marriage records; political statements, speeches, and conference/solidarity body records; nonprinted audiotapes and videotapes, photographs, and oral recordings of political deliberations; promotional items, including posters, stickers, buttons, paintings, and calendars; museum items such as sculptures, flags, guerilla uniforms, and woven items; and publications, including official organs and journals.

45. Centre for Cultural Studies, "1995–1996 Report," 12–13.

46. Others, including U-M faculty members Hedstrom and David Wallace and doctoral candidate Denise Anthony, shared coordinating responsibilities over the students' six-week period in South Africa.

47. Strategic Plan 2000.

48. Speech of Deputy President Thabo Mbeki.

49. "Message from President Mandela."

50. Tambo, "Message from O. R. Tambo."

51. Stapleton and Maamoe, "Overview of the African National Congress Archives," 422.

52. Institutions with programs include the University of Michigan, available at http://wwwsi.umich.edu/fort-hare/; Michigan State University, available at http://www.isp.msu.edu/africanstudies/research.php; the University of Connecticut, available at http://www.sp.uconn.edu/~wwwanc/index.html; and Howard University, available at http://www.howard.edu/newsevents/capstone/2001/april/news2.htm.

53. "African National Congress—Partners with UConn,"

NEA Newsletter, July 1999, 15. Also see http://www.advance.uconn.edu/1999/990308/03089901.htm.

54. See http://www.ufh.ac.za/collections/Library/ANC_Materials/Mbeki-speech.htm.

55. Eric Ketelaar, The Archival Image: Collected Essays (Hilversum: Verloren, 1997), 15.

56. See http://www.wits.ac.za/histp/index.htm.

57. See http://www.wits.ac.za/saha/. See also Razia Saleh, "The South African History Archive," Innovation, no. 4 (June 1992).

58. See http://disa.nu.ac.za. Staff from Cornell University have played a role in consulting on digital imagining technology for this project.

59. Thomas Karis and Gwendolen M. Carter, eds., From Protest to Challenge: A Documentary History of African Politics in South Africa, 1882–1964, vols. 1–4 (Stanford: Hoover Institution Press, 1972–). Volume 5 in this series is edited by Thomas Karis and Gail M. Gerhart. Also see Susan G. Wynne, comp., South African Political Materials : A Catalogue of the Carter-Karis Collection (Bloomington, IN: Southern African Research Archives Project, 1977). This is a guide to the collection microfilmed by the Cooperative Africana Microform Project from the material deposited in the Melville J. Herskovits Africana collection of Northwestern University Library.

60. Section 3(d), referenced in Verne Harris, Exploring Archives: An Introduction to Archival Ideas and Practice in South Africa (Pretoria: National Archives of South Africa, 1997), 61.

61. Verne Harris, "Redefining Archives in South Africa: Public Archives and Society in Transition, 1990–1996," Archivaria, no. 42 (fall 1996): 6. See also Verne Harris, "Transforming Discourse and Legislation: A Perspective on South Africa's New National Archives Act," Archives News 39, no. 2 (December 1996).

62. Kriger, "Redressing Apartheid-Engendered Social Ills," 140.

63. Marie Olivier, "New Societal and Technological Realities: Challenges for the National Archives of South Africa," in Place, Interface, and Cyberspace: Archives at the Edge. Proceedings of the Australian Society of Archivists Conference Fremantle, 6–8 August 1998 (Canberra: Australian Society of Archivists Incorporated, 1999), 101.

64. "Message from President Mandela."

"The Gift of One Generation to Another"

The Real Thing for the Pepsi Generation

Ian E. Wilson

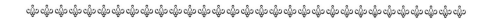

Several months ago and before I was appointed the national archivist of Canada, I was invited to speak at a symposium to honor Terry Cook and to reflect on his career as an archivist at the National Archives. I used the occasion to place before members of our profession the key dividing point that has distinguished my approach to the archival endeavor over the past twenty-five years from that of Terry; it is a fundamental distinction, and its influence can be discerned in our various articles. Analysis of the full intellectual impact of our two perspectives should be left, I think, to a future graduate student; however, let it be known that while Terry is passionate about Coca Cola, I far and away prefer Pepsi, and these are the battle lines for my discussion of our respective positions.

While I was preparing my comments for the Cook symposium, the Canadian federal government announced that it was embarking on a study of the future of the National Archives and the National Library.[1] I was tempted to change the focus of this essay into a study of the appointment of dominion, or national, archivists since 1872, when the National Archives was established.[2] While I decided not to change my approach, I felt that the historical theme would be a useful point of departure.

From 1872 until 1999, only six men had served as Canada's national archivist, and the appointment of each provides useful insight into the conditions of the time. Douglas Brymner, dominion archivist from 1872 to 1902, was a Presbyterian journalist and certainly had aptitude for this new position, but I suspect, more importantly, that he had solid Conservative ties. He received the appointment, but after an initial burst of activity the fledgling archives went into obscurity during

the Liberal years of Prime Minister Alexander Mackenzie and had to be reactivated when Sir John A. Macdonald was again in power in 1878—a cautionary tale, reenacted over the years in other governmental archives when an archive, which must serve as the neutral repository for all political perspectives, becomes too closely identified with partisan leanings.

On Brymner's death in 1902, interest in the federal appointment was lively. One enterprising journalist, H. F. Gardiner, Liberal editor of the Hamilton *Times*, published a pamphlet supporting his own candidacy, quoting one endorsement: "He already carries in his cranium a tremendous store of knowledge of the beginnings of Canadian history" such that he would be an excellent archivist.[3] The successful candidate, Arthur Doughty, had the good fortune to be in Quebec assigned to investigate the location of the Battle of the Plains of Abraham. This brought him to the attention of the governor-general, Lord Minto. Doughty's enthusiasm and evident ability commended him to His Excellency and through him to the government of the day. For those who are interested in the educational requirements for the job and who have labored long and hard for a graduate degree, Doughty's career path is instructive. Every biographical dictionary published in his lifetime carried the same phrasing: he was "educated at Oxford University; MA, Dickinson College, Carlisle." On investigation I found that the only record available at Oxford suggests that Doughty spent two months there in 1884. He did not graduate. As for his MA, in 1889 he wrote to Dickinson College in Carlisle, Pennsylvania, and asked for an honorary degree. He was refused. The following year he wrote again, claiming to be acquainted with President

Grover Cleveland; this time he met with success and received his degree in the mail. Despite his lack of formal credentials he was among the most active and successful of our national archivists.

From the time Doughty turned seventy in 1930, there was intense speculation regarding his successor. He retired to become dominion archivist emeritus in March 1935 and died in December 1936. The prime minister, R. B. Bennett, had an extensive file regarding the succession. The two internal candidates were Gustave Lanctot and James F. Kenney, with Professor A. L. Burt, a noted Canadian historian teaching at the University of Alberta and subsequently at the University of Minnesota, as the most likely external candidate. The bulk of the correspondence on the issue had little to do with the needs or future of the institution but largely concerned a debate on whether the next deputy minister in Ottawa should be a French Canadian Catholic or an Irish Catholic. Every bishop and archbishop in the country, it seems, had an opinion and expressed it to the prime minister. Bennett clearly gave up on trying to make the appointment and left it to his successor, Mackenzie King, who in turn refused to make a decision as long as Doughty was alive. Lanctot was finally appointed, almost a year after the death of Sir Arthur.[4]

Even though the topic is of current interest, at least with an archival audience, I will leave the more recent successions and a full analysis of the factors at play to a paper after I retire. It is, however, a topic well worth pursuing as the circumstances of each appointment provide insight into the preoccupations of the governments who come to grips with the decision. The appointment lies at the intersection of partisan politics, the concerns of the academic community and of cultural policy objectives, and, increasingly, the imperatives of modern administration. In recent decades, the appointment has also provided a tangible indicator of the degree of convergence between the archivists' increasing sense of profession and the views held by decision makers of the archival role in society. The choice of an archivist is a multilayered political decision, and the role accorded archivists in the process inevitably reflects the government's perception of whether the profession articulates narrow self-interest or the broader public interest concerning the archival function within Canadian society. The credibility accorded the profession by the government directly reflects how archivists and their institutions present themselves to the public and to the public's elected representatives. And this brings me around to my announced subject— "the gift of one generation to another": the real thing for the Pepsi generation.

The title of this essay mixes three advertising slogans, each intended to convey images and more or less value-laden meaning to its audience. The latter two slogans are clear for anyone attuned to modern mass media; the first is recognizable to a few select archivists as a phrase from Arthur Doughty's oft-quoted promotional description of the value of archives. More about that anon.

"The real thing" refers, of course, to that which Terry Cook has devoted his professional career: Coca Cola and, of course, the integrity of the archival record. In a media age where *Star Wars* may be past or future, dinosaurs and space warriors have equal digital reality, the moon landings may have taken place on a Hollywood backlot, historical fiction represented by Forrest Gump blends seamlessly with history, and conspiracy theories abound, society requires an institution dedicated to information, selected on defined criteria and preserved in the full context of its creation as evidence of action, decision, and transaction—information in all documentary media, from both public and private sources. This is the evidence, flawed as it sometimes may be—this is the social memory that each generation inherits, uses, adds to, and passes along to the future. This is the fundamental archival role, one that grows more important as we explore the wonders of the information age.

In this essay I want to focus on public awareness and use of the archival record. But first I want to make absolutely clear an essential precondition of effective archival service. Unless our archives are committed to the integrity of the record and to maintaining its attributes as record, and unless these archives are staffed by archivists and other professionals knowledgeable about that record, its creation, its conservation, its continuity, and its peculiarities, whatever I may say about the public potential of archive will be so much hollow theory. My remarks assume that expert staff, coming from many disciplines but united in their dedication to the vitality and current relevance of the archival functions, and I will build on that solid base.

"The Pepsi Generation," which now I believe is "Generation Next," is one of the more successful advertising slogans, suggesting modernity and future orientation. This provides effective contrast with Coca Cola, whose faithful appear to have difficulty with change. A few years ago when Coca Cola decided that change was necessary, some of the more rabidly faithful launched a campaign against change and demanded stability. I believe Terry was the local president of the rabidly faithful. Fortunately, as an archivist he has shown himself more open to change, recognizing the fundamental necessity of reinterpreting and refining essential archival principles to adapt to the demands of rapidly evolving administrative practice and technology. The challenge, as it always has been for archivists in a North American context, is to champion and represent the value of the record in a society focused very largely on the future. This has been the challenge faced by the successive dominion archivists, no less than by us.

Douglas Brymner, through his many years of relative solitude and benign neglect, had time to consider the role of the archivist.

The functions of the archivist are not the same as those of the librarian; neither can he be called an historian. He collects the document from which history is to be written, and must, therefore, have a sufficient knowledge of the works that exist treating not only of the subjects with which he has to deal, but also of other which have, at first sight, a very slight and indirect bearing on them. As an archivist he has to collect the rough material to be formed into structures of exquisite beauty in the hands of the skilful workman, or to be raised by the dishonest and incompetent into unsubstantial constructions, which crumble into ruins before the first rude blast of adverse criticism. . . . He must not forget that he is only the pioneer, whose duty is to clear away obstructions; the cultivated fields will follow.[5]

Reflecting the origins of his office in response to a petition from "literary inquirers" rather than as a public record office, Brymner thus saw his role as being in support of historical research. In 1888, in one of his more public statements, he envisioned the archives as "a great storehouse of the history of the Colonies and Colonists in their political, ecclesiastical, industrial, domestic and in a word in every aspect of their lives as communities."

The years separating us from Brymner melt away, and we recognize that the journalist had indeed become an archivist with this statement that he added to his vision.

It may be a dream but it is a noble dream! It has often spurred me to renewed effort, when the daily drudgery—for it is drudgery—was telling on mind and body.[6]

Doughty built on this vision, both in words and action, transforming the National Archives from its rooms in the basement of the Langevin Block to its visible site on Sussex, enlarged in 1926; expanding the collection; and focusing his most quoted statement on values rather than specific content:

Of all national assets, archives are the most precious. They are the gift of one generation to another and the extent of our care of them marks the extent of our civilization.

Given the number of times this statement has been cited in articles and speeches, inscribed on the pedestal of a statue, on a mug, a poster, and in a variety of reports and pamphlets, it has proved the most enduring Canadian archival representation of this century. It is worth spending a few minutes considering its origins.

In the form I have just cited, this quotation appeared in an eighty-eight-page booklet published by the Public Archives in 1924: *The Canadian Archives and Its Activities* by Arthur Doughty. This booklet appeared at the apex of Doughty's tenure as dominion archivist. Through most of the 1920s, the archives' collections were being discovered by a dynamic new group of Canadian historians, mainly war veterans, exploring, often for the first time, the sources gathered in the archives. It was a lively time: Adam Shortt and his assistant, Arthur Lower, were working on a series of documentary volumes; the Queen's University summer school provided a graduate program in history; newly appointed historians in universities across the country[7] were spending their summers in Ottawa, researching and discussing their findings; and the tennis court on the front lawn of the archives offered a clublike atmosphere. As A. L. Burt wrote to his wife: "It is very interesting to see the actual renaissance of Canadian history in the course of preparation."[8]

Doughty had spent most of 1923 overseas, seeking out the records of Canada's colonial past in the parlors and drawing rooms of the descendants of the old British and French administrators. Canada's war effort had earned gratitude and respect, and giving archival material to the archives of the new nation proved to be an accepted tribute to the memory of that sacrifice. One of Doughty's wartime contacts, Sir Campbell Stuart, assisted the process through the establishment of the Canadian History Society in Britain and the Société d'histoire du Canada in France. The inaugural dinners for these societies at Claridges in London and at Versailles in France were effusive outpourings of praise for the dominion, for its illustrious history, and for its archives. The booklet *Canadian Archives and Its Activities* provides the record of these dinners, including these remarks by the duke of Devonshire.

I can only offer one word of advice to all of you who may have documents and papers of interest to Canada, and that is, the sooner you produce them the better. You will have to do so in due course, and to save you both time and temper you had better do it with the greatest possible alacrity.[9]

The last part of the Durham papers, together with the Murray, Monckton, and Townshend papers; the extraordinary Northcliffe Collection; the Elgin-Grey correspondence; and a host of other family records and artifacts, found their way to the archives.[10] Doughty's collecting abilities had already earned royal commendation earlier in 1923 when, on being presented to Queen Mary, she remarked that "she had been warned not to leave any loose things about."[11]

Doughty's bold assertion regarding the value of archives embodies that confident postwar era, but it had its origins earlier, in less certain times. Doughty's first version of this quotation was written in August 1916, when the full extent of the war effort was becoming painfully obvious and the outcome was still unpredictable. Doughty had gone overseas in April 1916 to assist with the work of Max Aitken's Canadian War Records Office. In an article entitled "Canada's Record of the War," Doughty shifted from his more habitual justification of archives on cultural grounds to argue for the proper handling of modern administrative records as a duty of the state.

> The archives are, of all our national assets, the most precious—they are the bequest of one generation to another, and the extent of our care of them marks the extent of our civilization.

He continued:

> Archives fulfil so many and exalted missions. Each day that passes is a triumph for an archive, for each day some mere scrap of paper permits justice to prevail.

He commented on the commercial uses of archives and their value in determining rights to land, resources, and administrative decisions. In conclusion, he argued,

> Thus the fiat has gone forth that records must be preserved. And so what the literary inquirer asked for merely as a favour, the man of commerce now demands as a right—namely, the proper care and reasonable access to records.[12]

Doughty's phrasing and terminology blend the business concept of asset with the emotionally laden attempt to maintain civilization during a war that threatened European confidence in that very idea. The reference to the power of a "mere scrap of paper" evokes the enemy's dismissal of the treaty protecting the borders of Belgium, the rationale for Britain's entry into the war.

The direct correlation made by Doughty of archives as a measure of civilization may have been inspired by a comment that was published in the American Historical Association (AHA) *Annual Report* for 1913 but only appeared in print in 1915. Dr. Charles M. Andrews of Yale University, in presenting the first draft of a textbook for use by archivists, observed that

> It has been well said that "the care which a nation devotes to the preservation of the monuments of its past may serve as a true measure of the degree of civilization to which it has attained."

He expanded on this theme in a way that undoubtedly appealed to Doughty.

> Among such monuments, and holding first place in value and importance, are public archives, national and local. For a nation to ignore them or so to neglect them as to place them in jeopardy is a disregard of obligations so serious as to warrant the charge of indifference due to inferior intelligence and in this respect a ranking among the backward nations of the earth. Such a position no first-class State can long endure. For no higher reason than the maintenance of its dignity and self-respect, such a State should reverse its policy, and, recognizing the sacredness of its archives, place their preservation, care and publication among the leading objects of its activity.[13]

Interestingly enough, Andrews does not give the source for his vague statement "It has been well said." T. R. Schellenberg cited this statement by Andrews in an article that appeared in 1966 but gave as a source the 1910 International Congress of Archivists and Librarians, held in Brussels. Schellenberg provided no basis for this attribution, nor have I been able to locate this in any of the published material from that influential congress.

Whatever its source, Doughty was carefully following the discussions about archives in the AHA; it was about the same time as he first drafted his famous statement that he also clearly espoused the *principe de provenance* as the basis for archival arrangement. This principle had been presented at Brussels as the consensus among European archives, and the congress passed a resolution adopting the principle for "the arrangement and inventorying of archives." The concept was first described in the AHA *Annual Report* for 1910 (but not published until 1912).[14] Doughty's memorandum to Sir George Foster in March 1917, proposing the War Records Survey, is his first clear statement on the importance of provenance. Launched by order in council the following month, the survey attempted to document the duties and functions of each agency involved in the Canadian war effort. "Only by this system," Doughty advised, "can the relationships of one document to another, and the workings and relationships of the bodies which produced them, be indicated, and the presence of any gaps in the records be detected."[15] Doughty had adopted the principle of provenance and had adapted the first version of his noted quotation directly from the AHA reports on the Brussels congress.

Doughty's quotation was a proud, confident assertion of the value of archives. It was written in the midst of uncertainty as the veneer of civilization seemed perceptibly to erode as the battle raged on the Somme that horrific summer and fall of 1916. It was published at the height of the archives' success under Doughty as research use and acquisitions blossomed, confirming Doughty's promise to Prime Minister Sir Wilfrid Laurier,[16] at the beginning of his archival career, that the archives would be "an important factor in our national life."[17] While Doughty had many ways to explain, justify, and promote archives, this one has survived and retains its currency. It went beyond Doughty's earlier presentations of archives as the objective basis for a scientific, national, unifying unbiased historiography, the cultural equivalent of the economic policies known as the "National Policy." It was more than a statement of the functions and role of archives. It was a value statement, linking the archives with fundamental social values: of assets for the business community and to civilization itself, expressive of archives' broader cultural purposes. And, as advertising specialists tell us, there is no more powerful statement than one that is rooted in and resonates with the fundamental values of a society.

During his long career, Doughty worked his famous statement into various other speeches, trying different versions. In the 1930s he used it as follows:

> It seems to me that of all our national assets archives are the most precious. They are the gift of one generation to another, revealing the achievements of those who have passed on. They belong to no individual, they are the property of the people and many of their civil rights are bound up in them.[18]

On the evening Doughty died, the prime minister, Mackenzie King, issued a press statement in which he quoted the 1924 published version of Doughty's quotation. And, in his diary, King wrote that Doughty had been "one of the closest and truest friends I have ever had. I know of no man who seemed to be more a true knight in pursuit of the ideal."[19]

King immediately accorded Doughty two distinct honors, both unique for a civil servant: he directed that the flag on the National Archives be flown at half-mast and the institution be closed for the day of the funeral, and on

the day after Doughty's death he secured his cabinet's approval for an official statue honoring his departed friend.[20]

In the decades following Doughty, Canadian archivists, assured of the support of their colleagues, the historians, turned their attention to the challenges of modern records management and to establishing their role within government, shifting their emphasis in their presentations. The terminology moved away from concepts of civilization, becoming the terminology of a public record office serving government and scholars. In addressing the Massey Commission on the needs of the archives, Dr. W. Kaye Lamb, dominion archivist from 1948 to 1968, dwelled on modern records management. In his presidential addresses to both the Canadian Historical Association and the Society of American Archivists, he took justifiable pride in the recent opening of the first federal records center and in the proactive role archivists were playing in the appraisal and selection of official records. His only comments on the public service role of the National Archives recalled Brymner, not Doughty, in referring to the archivists as

> the miners who laboriously dig out the ore from which historians will smelt their fine gold. . . . We expect historians to look to us for information and guidance, and we are glad to furnish both to the best of our ability.[21]

In more recent years, Canadian archivists have revisited Doughty's proud declaration, expanding on the idea of continuity implicit in the "gift of one generation to another" and of civilization and developing increasingly the vocabulary of social memory. Dr. Wilfred I. Smith, our fifth dominion archivist, marked the centenary of the archives in 1972 with this description of archives:

> It is a mirror of past experience, a collective national memory, the basis of a cultural heritage, the source of history, the record of victories and defeats, achievements and failures, the product of individual and collective endeavours in all aspects of life in a community.[22]

In one of my own more optimistic moments, in concluding the 1980 Social Sciences and Humanities Research Council of Canada (SSHRCC) report, *Canadian Archives,* I urged that, if the recommendations of the report were followed,

> Archives collections can indeed become the recorded social memory, comprehensive in scope, growing systematically and accessible to all who want to draw upon it.[23]

These expressions of memory have been followed through the 1980s and 1990s by more strident versions. The National Archives' *Annual Report, 1986–1987* linked archives to a quotation by Elie Wiesel, a recent winner of the Nobel Peace Prize:

> Memory is probably the most important asset that the human being can have. Without memory, we wouldn't be what we are. Without memory, there would be no future.[24]

In the preface to *Treasures of the National Archives of Canada,* Dr. Michael Swift, the assistant national archivist, commented:

> As this country's collective memory, archives provide the continuity of culture and the building blocks of nationhood.[25]

Now, reading almost any report penned by archivists for general use, the concept of archives as a place of memory is firmly enshrined. The mission statement of the National Archives is most explicit, beginning with these ambitious words:

> To preserve the collective memory of the nation and of the Government of Canada and to contribute to the protection of rights and the enhancement of a sense of national identity.[26]

Dr. Smith's description placed emphasis on the object: the collection, as a mirror, as a record, as a source, or as a product. The SSHRCC report again focused on the collections, accessible but with the memory understood as the record. The current mission of the National Archives, though, takes the ambition much further, not by addressing the holdings as the end in themselves but by speaking to the results or social impact of using these collections. The phrases "collective memory of the nation" and "the enhancement of a sense of national identity" imply use, purpose, understanding, and the development of knowledge. The archival holdings in this sense are not inert. The mind of the user needs to interact with the holdings, seeking and providing pattern, context, significance, value, and, ultimately, public interpretation. Only through this dynamic interaction do the holdings fulfill their potential, being transformed from information to meaningful memory. The role of the archives becomes to reunite the public with the evidence of their past, making the archives a vital link in creating the social memory. By emphasizing memory rather than just collection or asset, the archives assumes a more active function in its society.

It would be reassuring and comforting to end this essay here. As a profession we have revived the public role of archives as the social memory from some of the obscurity of the post-Doughty decades. We have convinced ourselves of the public importance of our enterprise, and we confidently quote Sir Arthur Doughty whenever we need a lofty value statement. But for me, a doubt remains. Does anyone else share our perception of this fundamental role? Do we even share it?

Does the user recognize the archives as a repository of the social memory, much less as the "gift of one generation to another" in the way we so boldly assert? Thus far, I have not been able to find any such suggestion. Dr. T. H. B. Symons, in his influential 1975 report on Canadian studies, devoted a full chapter to the importance of archives. Such attention from an informed user had been long in coming. "It is not too much to say," he observed, "that Canadian archives are the foundation of Canadian studies."[27] His focus was on Canadian studies at the universities, and he approached the archival system from the perspective of university research, not the public at large. The Applebaum-Hébert report of 1982 was even more prosaic, referring to the National Archives as "a vital heritage custodial institution."[28] It did quote a sentence from the National Archives' brief outlining the importance of the archival record in ensuring that history is not forgotten, but the commission itself did not explore these aspects of the archival endeavour. Dr. David Cameron, in his 1996 review of the impact of the Symons report, accorded some justice to the archival claim of being the "collective memory" but noted that libraries and museums had some share in this claim.[29]

No less disturbing is the disappearance of the National Archives from studies dealing with Canadian historiography or Canadian identity. In recent years, a series of studies have explored aspects of memory and World War I. In these the archives' very active role receives scant attention. Maria Tippett, in her excellent study *Art at the Service of War: Canada, Art, and the Great War,* and, more recently, Jonathan Vance, in his book *Death So Noble: Memory, Meaning, and the First World War,* both touch on Doughty's relationship with Aitken but entirely miss the archives' valiant effort to become Canada's place of memory for the war.[30] The grand conception of Aitken, Doughty, and their contemporaries—their holistic approach to evidence as archives, war records, war trophies, war art, and war memorials—is dismantled into art, monument, and prose without ever recognizing the multidimensional perspective they were trying to realize. Gathering and preserving records, archival film, and photographs as forms of commemoration are entirely ignored. Similarly, the historian of Canadian historiography, Carl Berger, assumes the existence of the archives and the infrastructure it provided for the emerging historical profession, never noticing that in part the evolution of the profession reflected a deliberate federal policy.[31] This is odd.

Even those who commissioned and designed the monuments to Canadian statesmen pointed directly to the archival record. The heroes of Canada are not portrayed many times larger than life or enshrined in Greek temples. They are not on horseback with drawn sword or placed on columns high above the crowd. The statues I am familiar with are essentially life-size: John A. Macdonald, George-Etienne Cartier, Oliver Mowat, Joseph Howe,[32] and others, holding simply pen and paper, the tools with which they built a country. Their legacy, these monuments suggest, is to be found in archives. Those who spend many hours in our reading rooms seem to take this for granted, seldom considering why these institutions came to be or why society continues to support them or what their role may be in Canadian society beyond supporting an immediate research project.

Is it possible that our increasingly strident insistence on the importance of archives to memory reflects a fear that the record itself is no longer valued as it once was? The glowing phrases of Arthur Doughty ring hollow in a more cynical age. The "lessons of the past" prized by previous generations become relative and reflect opinion as much as lasting verity. Our political leaders seldom cite history; in fact, they avoid it, for it is too often seen as a matter of division and dispute rather than a force for unity. And the technological future looms, seemingly disconnected from our past experience. As our museum colleagues have found, heritage is useful as a tourism attraction; but is it the basis for self-knowledge? As a recent test of basic Canadian historical facts in a Quebec junior college and an Ontario high school demonstrated, our graduating students lack even the most fundamental outline of the structure of our collective past. It is in this context that we must now frame the mission of our archives.

In his 1996 study, David Cameron was blunt in his conclusions.

Archives have a relatively poor—or faint—public image and are viewed by many as being recherché in the worst sense; namely, being the exclusive purview of scholars and academics with an interest in the obscure and inconsequential. The expansive view that archivists have of their role and of the holdings for which they are responsible is far from being shared by the public at large.[33]

Some years ago, Bernard Amtmann, a noted Montreal antiquarian bookdealer, condemned our profession. Amtmann, a new Canadian with all the passion of an immigrant for his adopted country, referred to Canadian archivists as "the undertakers of Canadian history."[34] Like Doughty, he loved the romance of our past and prized each document as a direct, at times emotional, link with that past. For him, as for many of our users, the original document provided an unmediated, imaginative connection with those who went before. And while his business depended on selling such documents, he mourned their passing.

In our hands, the material is alive. It becomes a treasured reality, not simply another number on an all but inaccessible shelf. And we sell it, imparting in some measure the fascination of our discovery and the beauty of our adventure. It is not yet dead, but it loses its life in the institutional embrace. But we remember the fragrance we have traded away.[35]

The imperative to conserve, to protect, the fragile reminders of our past is at the heart of our profession and our mission. Yet this separates the people from their heritage. They have entrusted our profession with these treasures. Increasingly, we are the only ones who now can approach the originals. The "gift of one generation to another" seems to be the gift to an obscure profession. As we seek to cope with increasing volumes of information and as we shift media to preserve or provide access, we lose sight of the imaginative or even the symbolic power of the original. Our challenge as an ancient and respected profession on the eve of the millennium is to realize the potential and the opportunity inherent in our ambition to provide "the collective memory of the nation," to let the documents speak, to enable people to transform our records into their stories.

There are several dimensions to the challenge we face. I highlight a few here. First, we need to recognize the breadth and diversity of our clientele. We do not serve just those who enter our doors or who contact the archives. Our fundamental professional responsibility is to apply clear and defensible appraisal criteria to the official record, ensuring the protection of citizens' rights whether or not they ever think of contacting the archives. We preserve the integrity of the record—the authoritative information in its context of origin as evidence—and provide it, when that is all that is needed with our professional warranty as to its degree of authenticity. Terry has urged that we provide all archival users with a full course in the archival process and all the metadata we hold regarding the record. This would be the archival equivalent of the "Full Monty," and for many, probably most, it is far more than they want to know.[36] They do need our professional warranty as to the context of the information, without knowing the mysteries behind that warranty.

Second, we urgently need to communicate with all our clientele and to raise awareness of the role of archives and the availability of the record should it be required. As a profession, we have spent the last twenty-five years developing the infrastructure of a profession: we formed two associations and the bureau;[37] established *Archives* and *Archivaria* as leading journals; developed graduate courses in universities across Canada; established a basis for joint action as an archival system—the Canadian Council of Archives (CCA); developed descriptive standards for all archival media; and hosted a successful international congress. Terry and I, and many others, had a role in this and spent long hours working for it. Why? We are excellent at talking among ourselves, quoting Doughty and convincing ourselves of the importance of our task. The challenge for the next few decades is to maintain the basis of the profession, certainly, but at the same time it is to take our message outside to a broader public—confident and able as a profession with an important role in society.

Our third challenge, especially for those of us in the larger institutions, is to remember that the Canadian archival heritage is not just within a few walls. It is housed in at least six hundred archives across the country. We have long had distributed archival custody in Canada, and the Canadian Archival Information Network (CAIN) project,[38] coupled with descriptive standards, suggests that we may finally be able to provide more centralized access.

Fourth, we need to understand why some societies support archives and others do not. For example, there are wide disparities in the levels of support afforded archives in Canada. The province of Ontario contributes a mere $0.58 per capita, whereas the provinces of Quebec and Nova Scotia support archives to the sum of $2.50 per capita.

Finally, while we address the professional challenges of electronic records, voluminous government files, and Web access to archives, we cannot permit ourselves to lose sight of the imaginative power of the treasures in our keeping. Our holdings constitute meaningful communications over time, linking the minds of generations. These can be intensely personal. Perhaps the group we

traditionally think of as our users are blasé about the materials they see, but those of you who have worked with less experienced users know firsthand their undiluted emotion as they encounter the archival record for the first time:

- the schoolchild reading a diary from her hometown, with familiar surroundings and landscape, but written 150 years ago;
- the "eureka" from behind the microfilm reader as a genealogist finds another ancestor;
- the tears, as someone who never thought they would use an archives finds the record of the abuse they suffered in a provincial institution many decades ago;
- the indignity of aboriginal researchers approaching the records written largely by others about them.

All these anecdotes and countless others that can be added speak eloquently of the power and force of the "real thing," the archival record.

Sir Arthur Doughty succeeded in his struggle to build the National Archives of Canada for several reasons:

- he demonstrated the passion and devotion that is a requirement for all archivists: this we share;
- he made the link to core political concerns—knowledge of Canadian past, regional histories, new immigrants: this we recognize as a continuing commitment; and
- he formed a coalition with researchers, journalists, and others who shared his concerns; this we need to rebuild.

Our challenge for the twenty-first century is not, therefore, to build a profession. We already are a profession, with the infrastructure and the confidence that goes with that. No, our challenge is no less than to reconnect the Canadian people with the evidence of their heritage, their social memory. For the National Archives of Canada, the major challenge now is to design the public access center for the Canadian archival heritage, the place of the Canadian memory, the public face of the National Archives, and indeed the archival system. It must be a place of imagination, where all documentary media and technology come together to engage the public in a dialogue with their past. Archives staff—archivists and other professionals—need to reaffirm their commitment to the integrity of the record and to public service alike—attitudes not just for management but for the full archival team. We need to devote significant effort and resources to awareness, for there is a growing public interest in our history and a sense that the educational system is no longer providing this fundamental framework. Sales of books on Canadian history, television programs and channels, and the growth of genealogy and local history as hobbies all point to this interest. And the 15 million hits on the National Archives of Canada Web site suggest people are looking. The public awaits. Done properly, the National Archives and with it the Canadian archival system can truly become "the gift of one generation to another" or the "real thing" for the "Pepsi generation."

Oh, by the way, can anyone tell me why one formulation of cola is significantly different than another?

NOTES

This essay was originally presented at the National Archives Staff Symposium on April 6, 1998, honoring Dr. Terry Cook on his retirement. Dr. Cook has earned an international reputation for his writing on archival theory. Within the National Archives, he ensured that archival practice was solidly rooted in theory while, conversely, intensely practical experience informed his work on theory. Most especially he continues to encourage and teach a new generation of archivists to think and explore the intellectual foundations of the profession. This essay is based on my presentation to Dr. Cook. Accordingly, it retains the style and flavor of the day, including the humor he and I have enjoyed over the years.

1. On March 12, 1998, the Honourable Sheila Copps, minister of Canadian heritage, announced the launch of consultations on the "future role and structure of the National Archives of Canada and the National Library of Canada." The final report to the minister, by Dr. John English, entitled *The Role of the National Archives of Canada and the National Library of Canada,* was released in the summer of 1999.

2. The position of national archivist was vacant for more than two years, from the retirement of Dr. Jean-Pierre Wallot on June 6, 1997, to the announcement of my appointment on July 5, 1999.

3. Pamphlet, "Press Opinions on the Appointment of H. F. Gardiner to the Office of Dominion Archivist," nd, ca. 1902–3, np.

4. National Archives of Canada (NA), Mackenzie King Papers, MG 26, series J13, Diary, December 1, 1936. Lanctot was appointed by order in council, PC 2871, dated November 26, 1937.

5. Douglas Brymner, "Canadian Archives," *American Historical Review* 3, no. 2 (December 1888): 151.

6. Brymner, "Canadian Archives," 162–63.

7. For example, Frank Underhill, W. L. Morton, Lester B. Pearson, J. B. Brebner, William Mackintosh, A. L. Burt, Donald Creighton, and Harold Innis.

8. A. L. Burt to his wife, July 9 and 13, 1926. Quoted in Lewis H. Thomas, *The Renaissance of Canadian History: A Biography of A.L. Burt* (Toronto: University of Toronto Press, 1975), 90, 92.

9. Arthur Doughty, *Canadian Archives and Its Activities* (Ottawa, 1924), 37.

10. John George Lambton (1st Earl of Durham), James Bruce (8th Earl of Elgin), Charles Grey (2d Earl Grey), James Murray, Robert Monckton, and George Townshend were prominent military officers and colonial administrators. The Northcliffe Collection consists of rare and printed material regarding the careers of Monckton, Townshend, and other individuals involved in the Seven Years' War.

11. NA, Doughty Papers, MG 30, series D26, vol. 8, Diary, March 16, 1923.

12. Arthur Doughty, "Canada's Record of the War," typescript in NA, Records of the National Archives, RG 37, vol. 155. Published in *University Magazine* 15 (December 1916): 471–72.

13. AHA, *Annual Report,* vol. 1, 1913 (Washington, DC, 1915), 264.

14. AHA, *Annual Report,* 1910 (Washington, DC, 1912), 285.

15. NA, RG 37, vol. 352, Memorandum, Doughty to Foster, March 22, 1917.

16. Sir Wilfrid Laurier was prime minister of Canada from 1896 to 1911.

17. NA, Sir Wilfrid Laurier Papers, MG 26, series G, vol. 422, 112650–60, Doughty to Laurier, August 4, 1906.

18. NA, Norman Fee Papers, MG 30, series D143, vol. 2, Doughty, manuscript speech, 1.

19. NA, King Diary, December 1, 1936.

20. NA, King Diary, December 2, 1936, and King Papers, C114701. The estimates for 1937–38 included sixteen thousand dollars for the statue. The contract was given to R. Tait McKenzie. He died before any significant progress had been made, and the task then fell to Emanuel Hahn of Toronto to finish the work, but as he had never seen Doughty in life and as few photos of Doughty in later life were available, the statue lacks authenticity. It had been intended to cast the statue in Belgium, but due to the outbreak of war this was done in Montreal (see undated press clipping in Doughty Papers, vol. 2).

21. W. Kaye Lamb, "Presidential Address," in Canadian Historical Association, *Report of the Annual Meeting, 1958,* 1–12 (quote at p. 4). Also available at the Canadian Historical Association Web site, www.cha-shc.ca/bilingue/addresses/index.htm.

22. Wilfred I. Smith, "Introduction," in *ARCHIVES: Mirror of Canada Past/Miroir du passé du Canada* (Toronto: University of Toronto Press, 1972), 2.

23. *Canadian Archives: Report to the Social Sciences and Humanities Research Council of Canada by the Consultative Group on Canadian Archives* (Ottawa: Social Sciences and Humanities Research Council, 1980), 106.

24. National Archives of Canada, *Annual Report, 1986–1987* (Ottawa, 1987), 6.

25. *Treasures of the National Archives of Canada* (Toronto: University of Toronto Press, 1992), 7. This book was published on the occasion of the 125th anniversary of the National Archives.

26. National Archives of Canada, *Strategic Approaches, 1994–1998* (Ottawa, 1994), 5.

27. T. H. B. Symons, *To Know Ourselves: The Report of the Commission on Canadian Studies* (Ottawa: Association of Universities and Colleges of Canada, 1975–84), 2:69.

28. *Report of the Federal Cultural Policy Review Committee* (Ottawa, 1982), 130. This committee, co-chaired by Louis Applebaum and Jacques Hébert, was appointed by the federal government in August 1980 to review Canadian cultural institutions and cultural policy.

29. David Cameron, *Taking Stock: Canadian Studies in the Nineties* (Montreal: Association for Canadian Studies, 1996), 169.

30. Maria Tippett, *Art at the Service of War: Canada, Art, and the Great War* (Toronto: University of Toronto Press, 1984); Jonathan Vance, *Death So Noble: Memory, Meaning, and the First World War* (Vancouver: University of British Columbia Press, 1997). This oversight has since been corrected in an article by Robert McIntosh, "The Great War, Archives, and Modern Memory," *Archivaria* 46 (fall 1998): 1–31.

31. Carl Berger, *The Writing of Canadian History: Aspects of English-Canadian Historical Writing, 1900–1970* (Toronto: University of Toronto Press, 1976).

32. John A. Macdonald, George-Etienne Cartier, Oliver Mowat, and Joseph Howe were leading Canadian politicians who figured prominently in the debates over the confederation of the British North American provinces.

33. Cameron, *Taking Stock*, 181.

34. Personal conversation.

35. Bernard Amtmann, "An Open Letter to Canadian Archivists," *Canadian Archivist* 2, no. 4 (1973): 47.

36. For Terry's views on this, see his article, "Viewing the World Upside Down: Reflections on the Theoretical Underpinnings of Archival Public Programming," *Archivaria* 31 (winter 1990–91): 123–34, esp. 130–31.

37. The Association of Canadian Archivists (ACA) was established 1975, l'Association des archivistes du Québec (AAQ) in 1967, and the Bureau of Canadian Archivists/le Bureau canadien des archivistes (BCA) in 1976.

38. CAIN was developed to provide fonds-level descriptions for all Canadian archival resources and, in turn, the essential descriptive context for digitization projects. After this essay was delivered, CAIN was renamed Archives Canada. Further information is available at the network's Web site, www.archivescanada.ca.

Social History, Public Sphere, and National Narratives

The Social Origins of Valencian Regional Imaginary in Nineteenth-Century Spain

Mónica Burguera

During the past twenty years, the approaches and perspectives associated with both poststructuralism and feminism have prompted historians to question the centrality of some of social history's most basic assumptions, opening the door to what Patrick Joyce has called a "self-reflexive and historicized understanding" of social history and its epistemological legacy.[1] In particular, many scholars now agree that race, gender, class, and national identities do not, as was previously thought, derive exclusively from a network of social referents external to language but rather arise from a system of representations in which language and its referents undergo a continual process of mediation. This focus has renewed historians' interest in some forms of knowledge production and/or memory construction, such as the process of literary creation, that have historically been marginalized within a Western, male, and white modernity. It has also helped bring about a more critical approach to operative master narratives, as historians have become increasingly aware of the epistemological instability at the heart of all historical writing and have learned to recognize the political and emotional dimensions of these narrative texts. These theoretical and methodological developments, which call attention to the interconnectedness of fluid and changing identities, on the one hand, and to the instability of historical narratives, on the other, have drawn many historians' attention to the multiple channels of power, resistance, and cultural exchange that pulse at the heart of identities once perceived as fixed.[2]

As a further result of this process, many historians have also made it their goal to decenter and destabilize national narratives,[3] as the old twofold historical myth of origins and national continuity has given way to a view of the nation as an "imagined community," to use Benedict Anderson's celebrated term.[4] According to this view, both material and ideological processes, themselves shaped by a series of hierarchical power relations, stand behind the process of nation formation. It is within this context that I wish to situate this essay, focusing on how historical narratives work to create and perpetuate fictitious representations of those naturalized communities. Specifically, I would like to incorporate some of the contributions mentioned previously to show how the nationalist literature of a particular place and time—Spain in the 1960s and 1970s—both evoked and perpetuated a fictitious historical narrative constructed in an attempt to understand Valencia's supposed "failure" to articulate a cohesive national identity during the 1800s. The paradoxes resulting from this particular use of the past, I suggest, can only be exposed if we dismantle and thoroughly examine the symbolic structures upon which Valencian identity was grounded during the late 1800s. To this end, I examine two texts (published in 1859 and 1889) that can be seen as paradigmatic of the kind of broad regional narrative in which a whole host of class, gender, ethnic, and linguistic differences were assumed, evoked, and projected onto Valencian rural society by distinguished members of the city's urban middle classes. In short, my goal here is to explore the process through which modern identities get fixed within the narrative structures of political discourse.

Writing the Nation as an Absence

Spanish approaches to the history of national identity began to take shape during the last decade of the Franco regime and in the early years of the country's transition to democracy. Initially, this impulse came from the so-called peripheral nationalities, especially the Catalans and the Basques. Influenced by European historiographical trends then current in Europe, such as those proposed by the French Annales school and by a broader Marxism, this postwar Spanish literature emphasized the class structures underlying Castile's cultural domination within the Spanish state. In this context, invoking the rise of the peripheral nations was equated with recapturing the cultural essence of the popular classes. This vision of Spain as a territory made up of numerous internal "nations" also reinforced previous assumptions about the intrinsic weakness of the Spanish state. Within this framework of a presumably failed nationalization, historians attributed different rates of modernization or nationalization to the various territories within nineteenth-century Spain. Thus, while they saw Catalonia and the Basque Country as having been rapidly industrialized by a relatively strong bourgeoisie, they categorized other culturally differentiated territories such as Galicia and Valencia as weak, peripheral preexisting identities that had ultimately proved incapable of overcoming the oppression of the modern Spanish state.[5]

The Valencian case is particularly interesting because of the sizeable body of historical literature generated during the 1960s and 1970s, in which scholars tried to historically reconstruct Valencia's identity as a potential nation. In the early 1960s Joan Fuster, one of the most productive Valencian intellectuals of the time, reflected in his celebrated book *Nosaltres els valencians* (We, the Valencians), "What are we, the Valencian people? Compelled, as always, to close the gap between 'what we are' and 'what we should be.'"[6]

This was an enormously influential articulation of Valencian identity and its peculiarities (or rather its anomaly), the founding question in what would later become a strong nationalist tradition among Valencians scholarship and members of the political left. It was also a resurrection of the past, reviving a historical narrative of regional specificity that had been fabricated during the 1800s and placing it for the first time within the context of the new scientific history.

Fuster approached the history of the Valencian nation as the history of an absence. The history he described was that of a people who should have become a nation but had not (yet) done so. At the time, this was an appealing view; the pessimistic atmosphere created by almost twenty-five years under Franco's dictatorship made it easy to add "the nation" to a long list of historical failures. In recasting the longings of the Valencian people—redefining its ethnic, linguistic, and cultural boundaries and ultimately inventing its unfulfilled destiny as a nation—Fuster was reacting against a centralized and repressive regime that had long imposed the Spanish-Castilian culture onto the Valencian people while simultaneously suppressing cultural plurality within the Spanish state. It was in light of this repression that he launched his criticism of the nineteenth-century elite, attributing the Valencian nation's failure to emerge to these "insurgent" leaders' inability to articulate a modern political nationalism within a region marked by a profound backwardness.[7]

Several theoretical assumptions, all of them marked by the conceptual opposition "backwardness/modernity," shape Fuster's basic argument. Here he argued for the existence of an "authentic" Valencian identity dating back to at least the thirteenth century. This identity, he posited, derived from a "popular" cultural community that spoke a unifying language (Valencian) and that—by virtue of that same linguistic difference—was ethnically differentiated from all the other groups historically occupying the same territory. The Valencian nation's failure to emerge during the last quarter of the nineteenth century was due to the absence of an industrial bourgeoisie in that region and, by extension, to the Valencian elite's inability both to modernize the city's social structures and to nationalize the popular classes. In essence, Valencia's failure to develop into a nation represented a failure, on the part of the Valencian elite, to come together as a cohesive political unity.

Significantly for our purposes, Fuster's thesis turned on a cultural view of Valencian identity that slides into a political project of nationalism and independentism. It was an equation that worked well within the presumed climate of economic, social, and ideological backwardness that characterized Spain in the 1960s, in which becoming (culturally) national was understood as becoming (economically, socially, and, more explicitly in his texts, politically) modern—and, by extension, democratic and anti-Francoist. In this context, Fuster's political advocacy of an ethnic community that needed to become a nation emerged, rather ingeniously, as a project of modernization.

For Fuster, the Valencian nation's failure to materialize during the nineteenth century was due to the city's inability to create an alternative and specific project of modernization, one capable of challenging the inherent traditionalism of the Spanish state, with its ingratiating focus on Castile.[8] While Valencia's nineteenth-century cultural renaissance, headed by the literary movement known as the *Renaixença,* could and should, have prompted the development of a modern national consciousness, this was not what happened. Instead, Renaixença conservative leaders silenced the movement's more progressive voices while simultaneously promoting a folklorist re-creation or idealization of the countryside that was devoid of any underlying political meaning.[9] Misguided by the weakness of the agrarian bourgeoisie, Valencia's rural peasantry's protean national consciousness was aborted before it had time to fully develop.[10] In the 1960s, this dormant national consciousness needed to be awakened.

> The countryside is everything in the *País Valenciá* [Valencian Country]. Ours is fundamentally an agrarian economy, one that largely determines the generic character and behavior of our society. . . . The peasants . . . [and] their political evolution have always been dependent upon their capacity to recognize themselves as a class and as members of their own country.[11]

Fuster's contentions still hold sway over scholarly interpretations of the Valencian past, as evidenced by the vast number of studies in which the same theoretical contradictions and assumed internal coherence continue to give rise to the same or similar conclusions. Although some economic and political readings of Valencian history have recently questioned his underlying structural dichotomy between backwardness and modernity, suggesting a less linear process of change, the essentialist notion of an as yet unformed national Valencia identity still prevails in literary and cultural histories of this region.

Innovative as these developments were in their day, the time has come for historians to reconsider the process of (non-)identity formation in light of the current academic debates regarding the nature of identity in general and, more specifically, the nature of cultural and national identities. I have argued that Fuster invented a fictitious historical Valencian ethnic specificity, one that had not yet articulated itself as a (modern) nation or—to use Anderson's term—as a (modern) political community, during the time of his writing. Yet in my opinion, understanding *why* Valencian identity failed to become a national community is less important (if, indeed, it is important at all) than is recognizing the *historical contingency* of that pre-

sumed identity, as well as the community or communities (both real and imagined) that played a role in its articulation.[12] When read from this angle, Fuster's imaginative approach to that fictitious national history becomes a platform from which to problematize the rise of modern nations as new forms of political imagination and consciousness, based on preexisting and homogeneous cultural unities.

Exploring these issues requires unraveling the ideological and symbolic systems that produced the daily lived illusion of a Valencian cultural and political homogeneity, something I have tried to do by pointing out how that illusion got institutionalized in the 1870s around various fixed images that were seen by the urban elite as evocative of a broader regional mode of being. As Ferran Archilés and Manuel Martí have shown, this regional illusion was constructed in close dialogue with the broader Spanish national imageries of the time, so that it fit neatly inside the limits of the emerging Spanish state.[13] And, as I will suggest in the following pages, it was organized around multiple class, gender, ethnic, and language differences.

Fuster's work and the studies it inspired sought to highlight the tension between national and popular consciousness in nineteenth-century Valencia; thus, they focused largely on Valencian popular identity and on the latter's exclusion from a legitimate national political project, arguing that the city's elite had depoliticized the people's (Valencian) identity during the nineteenth century and excluded it from its modernization process. But what if we unstabilize that notion of a Valencian identity as a fixed category—an underlying essence—that failed to become a modern nation? In fact, a look at some of the Valencian literature published during the second half of the nineteenth century suggests that the regional imaginary noted earlier actually crystallized within the context of a *public debate,* in an atmosphere characterized by permanent social unrest and popular public contestation. During this confrontation between urban elite and rural peasantry, Valencia's public sphere became the space where middle-class intellectual and discursive productions of identity met head-on with popular processes of identification and/or contestation.[14] Instead of assigning the Valencian people a fixed and dormant ethnic identity, one exclusively predefined in terms of linguistic difference, my reading seeks to expose some of the nineteenth-century local identities "in the making" generated during the moment of violent social conflict, in which class, gender, linguistic, and communal meanings overlapped.

Imagining the Valencian Region in the Nineteenth Century

> An illustrious and grandiose city set in the midst of a vast garden: that is everyone's idea of Valencia.[15]

Thus did Teodoro Llorente, father of the conservative Valencian Renaixença, introduce his literary journey into Valencia's hinterland in the last decade of the nineteenth century. Throughout the 1800s, developments within the city of Valencia had sharpened the contrast between the *urbis* and the surrounding countryside. The period between 1850 and 1900 witnessed a sizable increase in the Valencian population, from around sixty-seven thousand inhabitants in 1842 to two hundred thousand in 1900. Significant economic growth, a consequence of the commercialization and intensification of agricultural production, also began in the middle decades of the century, as a limited but rapid mechanization of Valencian industry—dependent in part on agrarian dynamism—significantly reshaped the landscape of both the city and its surrounding countryside, the so-called Valencian *Huerta*, or "Orchard."[16] Also during this period, the Valencian middle classes started to express anxieties about the social costs of "modernity," and in the 1860s the "social question" was publicly promoted as much by the press as by other bourgeois institutions.

Since the early modern period, representations of the Valencian landscape had tended to celebrate the abundance and beauty of the Huerta, but this focus began to change during the 1850s and 1860s. At that time, representations of the Huerta became both increasingly homogenous and ironically increasingly central to the historical depiction of the Valencian peasantry. The dichotomy between city and countryside they represented captured an essential aspect of the contemporary cultural imagination in the city of Valencia, transformed as it was by the aftermath of the liberal revolution, the spread of capitalism, and, in this particular case, the rise of a Valencian regional imaginary.[17] The city/country dichotomy itself was the product of an increasingly powerful urban public sphere where, in the midst of the sociopolitical shifts mentioned earlier, Valencian identity was imagined, formulated, and finally reified, in texts shot through with landscape, gender, class, and language dichotomies. Significantly, it was precisely when the inhabitants of the Huerta became visibly resistant and publicly violent toward the municipal authorities and the social order in general that they were "fixed" by the region's elites into an authentic essence of an idealized Valencian mode of being.[18]

As part of a general European vogue for literature on customs and manners, the book *Los valencianos pintados por sí mismos,* (Valencian Self-Portraits) was published in Valencia in 1859.[19] This was a collection of articles written during the mid-1800s and (in some cases) previously published in different journals that had been brought together in an album of "sketches" on everyday life. With its diverse array of writers representing a variety of liberal political affiliations, the book became one of Valencian Romanticism's most representative literary works. Its authors, drawn from the literary scene taking place in the capitol, supported and contributed to regional versions of European Romanticism's nationalist contributions, infusing with nostalgic sentiment many of the cultural materials that would later be taken up by the Renaixença literary movement. Each of the brief essays featured in the book was presented as a picture capturing one aspect of the Valencian people, freezing the latter in a visual attempt to "fix a runaway image." On the whole, the book intends to give the effect of having captured the gestures of a society in motion, simultaneously fixing these and projecting them as "types that might soon disappear." A desire to capture the realities of contemporary regional life was, in fact, the essential purpose of the book, which stated its wish to "portray types using a relatively skillful, delicate touch, but one that is always true, always real, alive and original."[20]

It is this putting into print of what was seen as a timeless regional reality that makes *Los valencianos pintados por sí mismos* one of the most interesting literary sources available for the period. In its projected illusion of an atemporal reality, one finds multiple depictions of a society caught between a stable and harmonious countryside and the dynamic, conflict-ridden urban space that was the city of Valencia itself. The first and last essays of the collection, for example, were devoted to "the Valencian man" (*valenciano*) and "the Valencian woman" (*valenciana*), respectively. Both essays were written by the same author and were meant to demonstrate the kind of stability that the idiosyncratic and idyllic Valencian rural world should ideally generate, with the peasant family at its center. We can see this didactic focus, first, in the author's reference to a unique Valencian identity that he viewed as grounded in its particular past, represented here in terms of provincial difference.

> None of the native people from the provinces governed by the Spanish Monarchy deserves such profound and philosophical study as the Valencian does. Whether its originality is due to [the region's] privileged climate, or

to the memory of a Moorish domination whose legacy still persists in the province, the truth is that the Valencian differs noticeably from the peoples of other provinces in his customs, his manners, his character, his modes of being, and even in his daily language.[21]

The author's uneasy projection of an idealized middle-class lifestyle onto the Huerta peasantry's everyday world is also revealing. In effect, he attributed opposed but complementary roles to men and women, evoking a family-based structure grounded in the ideology of "separate spheres" or the "discourse of domesticity." In keeping with this ideological frame, the female peasant's role was represented as intrinsically dependent on her life cycle.

Once the Valencian woman becomes a wife, she becomes keeper and owner of a farmhouse and of some small plots of land, and so has the right to be heard in the family assemblies. Here, a new life begins for her. While her husband works in the fields, she arranges and cleans the vegetables in order to take them to the city's open market.[22]

Overall, the essay reveals a tension between the acceptance of change—framed as the problematic acceptance of women's presence in a public, working, and ultimately political world—and the desire to perpetuate a series of universal gender definitions sustained by the most deeply rooted of collective illusions: that different social and emotional practices and functions should be attributed to men and women.

Nevertheless, his portrayal failed to capture the reality of peasant life in the Huerta. For despite the patriarchal structure of that society, a pressing need to maintain economic stability within the peasant household meant that women's work was deeply valued by the Huerta's peasant community. Power relations within the peasant family economy, for example, were never based on clearcut assumptions or on the rigid norms corresponding to a bourgeois social order. On the contrary, during the second half of the nineteenth century traditional women's tasks (such as the sale of vegetables and garden produce in the Valencian city market) became progressively central to the economic stability of peasant households in the Huerta.

The conflicts engendering the "Question of the Orchard" a few decades later confirm the unfitness of middle-class depictions to accurately describe the peasant world surrounding the provincial capital, with its climate of ongoing resistance.[23] Throughout the nineteenth century, the Huerta peasantry's forms of resistance, based on a particular "moral economy," usually involved different spaces of negotiation between country dwellers and the urban residents. This ongoing confrontation between Valencia's rural residents and their urban counterparts developed into a public debate regarding the "violence of the Huerta" in the late 1870s, when peasants refused to pay rents to urban landowners or to take their usual produce to the Valencian market. In this instance, it was the Huerta's peasant women who made explicit the discontent of the community as a whole, through their active political presence in the strike. The conflict soon came to be seen as a problem of "public order" and was described repeatedly by both conservative and liberal presses as the "unanimity of terror" or the "coalition of silence." The political dimension of these events, which implied a questioning of the Valencian municipal authorities' ability to maintain "public order" in the face of civil unrest, affirmed the presence of the Huerta's peasantry in debates that would otherwise have been confined within the urban public sphere. From that moment on, representing the Huerta became an ideological exercise in social and political negotiation between Valencia's political urban elites and the Huerta peasantry, with their strategies of collective resistance. The Huerta's ambivalence in the eyes of the Valencian elite, its ability to slide between harmony and violent contention, was part and parcel of what James Scott has called a "public transcript" or a contradictory encounter between two different political cultures with different social interests in mind.[24]

During the period between 1875 and 1880, while these conflicts were unfolding, the Valencian literary renaissance sought to capture and preserve what it perceived as the essence of the Valencian identity and language. From the very beginning, the Renaixença fell under the control of its most conservative participants, who, nevertheless, kept publishing their literary works in Valencian and celebrating annual festivals (*Jochs Florals*) in honor of *la terra* (the land, in the feminine).[25] The celebrated "queen" of the Jochs Florals epitomized the feminization of the discourse on the Valencian identity as it was being systematized by its promoters—a feminization that was part of a broader idealization process that always looked at the idyllic landscape of the countryside for inspiration.

In the late 1880s, right after the "Huerta Question" had reached its zenith, the leader of the renaissance movement, named Teodoro Llorente, published a book to Valencia as part of a collection on the Spanish provinces.[26] *Valencia* is emblematic of the complex ways in which the Huerta's inhabitants had by that time entered into the cultural imagination of the Valencian urban elite, showing a reified bucolic idealization of a paternalistic and patriarchal world, crystallized in the peasantry of the Huerta. The gendered basis upon which this provincial illusion rested is evidenced by the different working tasks and natures Llorente assigned to the men and women of the Valencian countryside. As he put it, the peasants of the Huerta

> certainly are a rural race, being very attached to their land. . . . The man (husband and father) is always in the fields, from sunrise to sunset. . . . The woman doesn't work on the fields, as women do in other counties; here she is more respected, and is also a hard worker. She takes care of all the domestic tasks, and transports the vegetables into the city. . . . The sons collect manure everywhere. And the daughters work in the factories and become temporary cigar-makers, spinners, or weavers.[27]

On the other hand, Llorente's reference to the distinctive language spoken inside the Huerta betrays some of the contradictions inherent in his created figure, "the Valencian." In the nineteenth century, language increasingly functioned as a sign of class distinction; thus, while the urban middle classes spoke Spanish (Castilian), the popular classes from both city and countryside communicated in Valencian. The greatest paradox of Llorente's book, a product of middle-class education and literacy, was that it upheld the authenticity of the Valencian language in a text written in Spanish. However, such paradoxes aside, it is worth questioning whether the use of a different language was, indeed, tantamount to a symbolic expression of ethnic specificity.[28]

Apparently, linguistic difference did constitute an important form of resistance among the peasants of the Huerta. Language—Valencian in this case—was a defining feature of the peasantry's social and political identities as a community, serving as a symbol of rural identity and an important class marker. We see both of these functions at work during the first wave of strikes opening the "question of the Huerta," when the mayor of the city issued a municipal order preventing the so-called *fematers* from leaving their horses in the streets (the fematers were mostly boys from the countryside who emptied the city of its waste for the purpose of fertilizing their families' fields). The order implied that *two* boys rather than *one* needed to accompany each horse, a decision that soon sparked a reaction among the fematers and the Huerta peasantry as a whole. During the ensuing strike, the country people popularized this song:

L'alcalde de Valensia	(The mayor of Valencia
diu ca ordenao	has ordered
que cada fematero	each fematero
lleve criao	to bring a servant.
Pobre marqués,	Poor marquis
Pobre marqués,	poor marquis
Pobre marqués,	poor marquis
El dia que lo pilleu	if the femater
Els femater	ever catch him!)

The burlesque resonance of the song pointed to two contrasting notions of respectability, indicating the social distance that the fematers and the peasantry as a whole felt between themselves and the urban middle classes. Thus, the word *fematero,* a Castilian version of the Valencian *femater* and one that had been spontaneously coined by the peasants, rhymed with the two other Castilian words in the song: *criao* (servant) and *marqués* (marquis). All three Castilian words symbolized the opulence and pompousness of that language and, by extension, of the mayor's order itself. By means of this cunning play on words, the peasants' song sought to emphasize the useless pretentiousness of an order issued in Castilian against the needs and wishes of the humble hardworking dwellers of the Huerta, represented in the figure of the femater.

My point here is that equating language with ethnic difference, or even with a cohesive cultural identity, is probably too reductive. At least in the situation cited previously, the relationship between language and class difference is much more flexible and fluid than that. If anything, the use of Valencian becomes in this context a symbol of popular subalternity, class conflict, and peasant respectability, as defined by the Huerta community itself.

To be sure, the idealization of the Huerta as an essential image of Valencian identity aimed to obscure a darker reality: namely, the conflictive nature of Valencia's relationship with its countryside. The implicit result of this regional discourse, which emerged during the middle decades of the nineteenth century and was reified and institutionalized from the mid-1870s onward, was the depoliticization of a long-resistant peasant community. As we can infer from Llorente's comment in 1889:

> The annals of Valencia do not register peasant conflicts, even though there used to be some kind of organization among them. Our parents, speaking of our grandparents, remember the "snail" [caragol in Valencian in the original] of the Huerta, something that is almost forgotten today. That snail was the horn that used to call all peasants to arms. It was largely legendary; but it definitely sounded sinister to the French. The Valencian peasant

did not hesitate to join in that national task of exterminating the invader. . . . The fatidic snail has been silent ever since, depriving the Valencian countryside of that element of gloomy poetry.[29]

Here, Llorente was remembering the Huerta's peasantry engagement in the war against Napoleon—the so-called war of independence in Spain. Through a very selective depiction of the Huerta's violence, one that erased any shadow of barbarism from the faces of the Huerta's peasantry, he created an image of the peasant as the epitome of the loyal Valencian. In this fictitious image, the peasants of the Huerta showed their courage on only one occasion and only in allegiance to their nation: the Spanish one.

The political significance of these Valencian middle-class images of the Huerta cannot be underestimated, for they idealized and institutionalized a series of symbolic structures that would provide a basis for later conceptions of what it meant to be "Valencian." As part of this process, Llorente and others of his class produced the illusion of a harmonious and stable countryside, making it out to be the basis of a timeless regional mode of being. The series of conceptual dichotomies (urban versus rural, political versus cultural, male versus female, and even regional versus national) around which they built this idealized world carried out a specific political function, moreover, serving to obfuscate the frictions of a changing social context.

Historical Imagination and an Open-Minded Past

It was in this contradictory depiction of the Valencian identity and its peasantry that Fuster found the cultural materials with which to reinvent a nation almost a century later. In this way, the regional imaginary to which we have been referring not only shaped later regionalisms but also served as the foundation for the revisionist nationalist histories stimulated from the 1960s onward. In spite of the critical and pathbreaking nature of the latter in the context of Franco's Spain, these histories clung to nineteenth-century conceptions and ideologies in at least two important ways.

First, the nineteenth-century urban middle classes assigned to the Valencian people as a whole a defined and delimited ethnic historical specificity. Thus far, I have tried to show how they gave imaginary shape to their region using images drawn from the rural idyll that they imagined the Huerta to be. In the cultural imagination of

these classes, the society of the Huerta was organized around a series of gender, class, language, and landscape difference and was evoked partly in response to the social and political shifts that had begun to threaten their world during the 1850s and 1860s. This same presupposition of an ethnic specificity has shaped nationalist histories inspired by Fuster's work. However, those histories did define and delineate Valencian ethnic specificity differently, placing language at the heart of Valencian cultural identity's authenticity. Yet none of them ever pointed to the ways in which this presumably immobile ethnolinguistic identity may have also overlapped historically with, for instance, its gender, class, or communal identities.

Second, a depoliticization of the popular consciousness is at work both in the folkloric texts of the nineteenth century on the Huerta peasantry and in later contexts in which the Valencian (agrarian) people appear as a naive, apolitical essence of the national soul. Here, the blurred frontier between culture and politics is an important referent. For as I have tried to show, Valencian literary production between circa 1850 and 1900 cannot be understood as intrinsically apolitical but should rather be seen as the precursors of a regional specificity that became reified and institutionalized within a context of social and political contestation. To be sure, in the peasantry's resistance, one finds a social and political consciousness—one, however, that can be categorized as neither "national" nor "regional" but that rather revolved around the self-definitional interests, principles, and images of the Huerta community. In a way, the nineteenth-century middle classes' maneuvers to silence this social and political popular unrest have implicitly remained within later interpretations of popular consciousness formation. For the interpretative illusion of a dormant Valencian cultural essence, to be revived during the 1960s, could only be sustained— paradoxically—by excluding the Valencian people from their own process of political awakening, that is, by drawing a clear-cut distinction between their cultural and political identity, instead of analyzing the ways in which they are intrinsically intertwined.

When, in 1962, Fuster answered his own question regarding the nature of Valencian identity, he offered a lasting national narrative of what "should have been but never came to be"—a narrative that, having been legitimated by the political context of dictatorship and cultural centralism, would come to exercise a profound influence on Catalan- and Valencian-speaking scholarship regarding Valencian culture and literature. Forty years later, I want to answer that question in another way, suggesting that Valencian identity was never fixed and that, on the contrary, it has historically always been open to contingent social, political, and cultural processes of differentiation, in which subaltern groups, and peasantry among them, were crucial agents. In my opinion, like all historical identities, the instability of Valencian identity can no longer be understood exclusively in ethnic and linguistic terms.

By the nineteenth century, the basic conceptual dichotomies around which the middle classes articulated their fictitious image of Valencia (political versus cultural, urban versus rural, public versus private, and male versus female) already formed part of a Spanish national imagery. From the time of its conception, this image has contributed to a broader Spanish national modernity whose exclusions and contradictions remain, even today, largely unquestioned. That lasting influence makes it especially necessary for us to see the liberal revolution and the nineteenth-century construction of the nation-state in terms of a close dialogue between local and national levels of political power. At the beginning of the twenty-first century, as a newly democratic Spain continues to struggle for plurality, it is crucially important for scholars to recognize the various exclusions behind the historical construction of the nation—exclusions based on ethnicity and language, to be sure, but also on gender, race, class, and many other categories of difference that have historically perpetuated an uneven power structure.

Until now, debates within Spanish historiography have essentially focused on making sense of Spain's recent incorporation into European democracy, as historians continue to discuss what has been called "the Spanish normalcy."[30] This sense of Spain's historical particularity within Europe has also shaped Spanish scholarship's focus on the broader political issues currently surrounding European construction efforts. But in the present political context, as in many other areas of Europe, the Spanish nation-state faces two challenges. On the one hand, cultural, linguistic, and ethnic ties have come to represent potential alternative nationalities, ones capable of questioning the legitimacy of the Spanish state from within. Fuster's work and legacy are some of the most influential examples of the intellectual and cultural thinking from which these alternative political traditions have sprung during the 1960s and 1970s.[31] On the other hand, the effects of regular immigration have raised political concerns over how class, gender, and race identities square with current notions of nationality, territoriality, and citizenship—political concerns that have only recently reached public opinion. With these challenges in mind, it is critical to begin exposing Spanish historiography to renewed sensitivities and alternative narratives, ones that will allow scholars to recognize the instability at the heart of all historical writing and permit them to make room for new interdisciplinary forms of knowledge production and memory construction. It is our political responsibility to revise our past, to analyze the politics behind its memories, and to affirm the plural and hybrid nature of identity in what is becoming an increasingly globalized society. After all, isn't it by pushing our historical imaginations a little further that we are able to restore multiple historical narratives with an open-ended future?

NOTES

I want to thank Ferran Archilés for his comments and suggestions. Special thanks also to Kathy Camp, Laura Cunniff, and Sam Temple, who read earlier versions of this essay.

1. "The End of Social History?" *Social History* 20, no. 1 (January 1995): 73–91.

2. Representative feminist contributions include, for instance, Joan W. Scott, "The Evidence of Experience," in T. J. McDonald, ed., *The Historical Turn in Human Sciences* (Ann Arbor: University of Michigan Press, 1994), 379–406; Judith Butler, "Contingent Foundations: Feminism and the Question of 'Postmodernism,'" in Seyla Benhabib et al., eds., *Feminist Contentions: A Philosophical Exchange* (New York and London: Routledge, 1995), 35–57; and Kathleen Canning, "Feminist History after the Linguistic Turn: Historicizing Discourse and Experience," *Signs* 19, no. 21 (1994): 368–404. On the reception of poststructuralist debates among social historians, see Geoff Eley and Keith Nield, "Farewell to the Working Class?" and "Reply: Class and the Politics of History," both in *International Labor and Working-Class History* 57 (spring 2000): 1–30 and 76–87, respectively. Influential texts from the so-called black British cultural studies include, for example, Stuart Hall, "Ethnicity: Identity and Difference," in Geoff Eley and Ronald Suny, eds., *Becoming National: A Reader* (New York and Oxford: Oxford University Press, 1996), 339–49; and Paul Gilroy, *The Black Atlantic: Modernity and Double Consciousness* (Cambridge: Harvard University Press, 1993).

3. In this sense, the impact of postcolonial studies on British imperial history and nationalism has been pathbreaking. See Catherine Hall, "Introduction: Thinking the Postcolonial, Thinking the Empire," in Catherine Hall, ed., *Cultures of Empire: A Reader. Colonizers in Britain and the Empire in the Nineteenth and Twentieth Centuries* (New York: Routledge, 2000), 1–33; and Antoinette Burton, "Who Needs the Nation? Interrogating 'British' History," *Journal of Historical Sociology* 10, no. 3 (1997): 227–48. The current dialogue between feminist and postcolonial approaches is clear, for instance, in Ann Laura Stoler, *Race and the Education of Desire: Foucault's History of Sexuality and the Colonial Order of Things* (Durham, NC: Duke University Press, 1995); and Anne McClintock, *Im-*

perial Leather: Race, Gender, and Sexuality in the Colonial Contest (New York: Routledge, 1995).

4. Benedict Anderson, *Imagined Communities: Reflections on the Origin and Spread of Nationalism* (London: Verso, 1983).

5. The thesis that a weak territorial nationalization in nineteenth-century Spain provided the basis for the rise of alternative national identities has shaped current debates on Spanish nationalism. Seminal works on this issue range from Borja de Riquer's pathbreaking essay, "La débil nacionalización española en el siglo XIX," *Historia Social,* no. 20 (autumn 1994): 97–114, to José Álvarez Junco's recent study, *Mater Dolorosa. La idea de España en el siglo XIX* (Madrid: Taurus, 2001). These perspectives have been problematized in Ferran Archilés, "Quien necesita la nacion debil? La débil nacionalización española y los historiadores," in Juan José Carreras Ares et al., eds., *Usos Públicos de la historia: Ponencias del VI Congreso de la Asociación de Historia Contemporánea,* Zaragoza (Madrid: Marcial Pons, 2004), 302–22. For debates on nationalism in Spanish historiography, see Claire Mar-Molinero and Angel Smith, eds., *Nationalism and the Nation in the Iberian Peninsula: Competing and Conflicting Identities* (Oxford and Washington, DC: Berg, 1996); Xoxé Manuel Núñez, *Historical Approaches to Spanish Nationalism* (Baden: Nomos, 1996); and Xoxé Manuel Núñez, "The Region as Essence of the Fatherland: Regionalist Variants of Spanish Nationalism (1840–1936)," *European History Quarterly* 31, no. 4 (2001): 483–518.

6. Joan Fuster, *Nosaltres els Valencians* (Barcelona: Edicions 62, [1962] 1992), 15. See Pedro Ruiz, "Consideraciones críticas sobre la nueva historiografía valenciana de los anos 60 y 70," in Azagra et al., ed., *De la sociedad tradicional a la economía moderna* (Alicante: Instituto de cultura "Juan Gil-Albert," Diputación Provincial de Alicante, 1996); and "Nacionalismo y ciencia histórica en la representación del pasado valenciano," in Paul Preston and Ismael Saz, eds., *De la revolución liberal a la democracia parlamentaria. Valencia (1808–1975)* (Valencia: Biblioteca Nueva-Universidad de Valencia, 2001), 19–48. On Joan Fuster's legacy and continued influence among Spanish historians, see the two monographs on this subject: *Homanatje a Joan Fuster* (Generalitat Valenciana: Conselleria de Cultura, 1994); and *L'Espill,* Segona Època no. 10 (spring 2002). For a critical reconsideration of Fuster's notion of Valencian national identity, see Ferran Archilés, "Ni carn ni peix? Joan Fuster i la identitat nacional dels valencians," *El Contemporani,* no.2 (2002).

7. This interpretation shaped, for instance, Alfons Cucó's argument in his book, *El valencianisme politic. 1874–1936* (Valencia: Garbí, 1971).

8. It is important to note the centrality of the Catalan case to Fuster's argument. The rise of Catalan nationalism was taken by him to represent a normative process of nationalization, against which the Valencian case appeared to be an anomaly. Fuster's intellectual dialogue with Jaume Vicens Vives is significant; in particular, see his *Noticia de Cataluña* (Barcelona: Ed. Destino, 1954). On Catalan nationalism, see Albert Balcells, *Catalan Nationalism* (London: Macmillan, 1996); Daniele Conversi, *The Basques, the Catalans, and Spain: Alternative Routes to Nationalist Mobilization* (London: Hurst, 1997); and Mon-serrat Guiberneau, *Nations without State* (London: Polity, 1999).

9. A reconsideration of the conservative contributions to the construction of a Valencian identity is Rafael Roca Ricart, "Estudi preliminar," in Rafael Roca Ricart, ed., *Teodoro Llorente. Escrits politics (1866–1908)* (Valencia: Alfons El Magnanim-Diputacio de Valencia, 2001). The most recent interpretation of the Valencian Renaixença is in Ferran Archilés and Manuel Martí, "Satisfaccions gens innocents. Una reconsideració de la Renaixença Valenciana," *Afers,* no. 38 (2001): 157–78.

10. Recent studies on the Valencian bourgeoisie have nuanced earlier interpretations by stressing its dynamism as a social group. See Anaclet Pons and Justo Serna, *La ciudad extensa. La burguesía comercial-financiera en la Valencia de mediados del XIX* (Valencia: Diputación de Valencia, 1992).

11. Fuster, *Nosaltres els Valencian,* 187, 192.

12. See Prasenjit Duara's critical approach to modernization theories, *Rescuing History from the Nation: Questioning Narratives of Modern China* (Chicago: University of Chicago Press, 1995); and "Historicizing National Identity, or Who Imagines What and When," in Geoff Eley and Ronald Suny, eds., *Becoming National: A Reader* (New York and Oxford: Oxford University Press, 1996), 151–77.

13. Ferran Archilés and Manuel Martí, "Ethnicity, Region and Nation: Valencian Identity and the Spanish Nation-State," *Ethnic and Racial Studies* 24, no. 5 (September 2001: 779–97).

14. I am referring to the debates opened by Habermas's conceptualization of the public nineteenth-century sphere in his *The Structural Transformation of the Public Sphere,* trans. Thomas Burger (Cambridge, MA: MIT Press, [1962] 1989). See Mary Ryan, "Gender and Public Access: Women's Politics in Nineteenth-Century America," and Geoff Eley, "Nations, Publics, and Political Cultures: Placing Habermas in the Nineteenth Century," both in Craig Calhoun, ed., *Habermas and the Public Sphere* (Cambridge, MA: MIT Press, 1992), 259–88 and 289–339, respectively; and Geoff Eley, "Edward Thompson: Social History and Political Culture: The Making of a Working Class Public, 1780–1850," in Harvey J. Kaye and Keith McLelland, eds., *E. P. Thompson: Critical Perspectives* (Cambridge: Polity Press, 1990), 12–49. More recent accounts of historians' uses of the public sphere appear in Anna Clark, "Contested Space: The Public and Private Spheres in Nineteenth-Century Britain," *Journal of British Studies* 35 (1996): 269–76; John L. Brooke, "Reason and Passion in the Public Sphere: Habermas and the Cultural Historians," *Journal of Interdisciplinary History* 29 (1998): 43–67; and Harold Mah, "Phantasies of the Public Sphere: Rethinking the Habermas of Historians," *Journal of Modern History* 71 (March 2000): 153–82.

15. Teodoro Llorente, *Valencia* (Barcelona: Daniel Cortezo y Cía. 1887): 2:435.

16. On the social and political transformations taking place in nineteenth-century Valencia, see Jesús Millán, "La revolución liberal y la remodelación de la sociedad valenciana," in Paul Preston and Ismael Saz, eds., *De la revolución liberal a la democracia parlamentaria. Valencia (1808–1975)* (Valencia: Biblioteca Nueva-Universidad de Valencia, 2001), 49–74.

17. On the interpretation of landscape as a cultural construction of variable meaning, see Raymond Williams, *The Country*

and the City (New York: Oxford University Press, 1973); see also Simon Pugh, ed., *Reading Landscape: Country-City-Capital* (Manchester: Manchester University Press, 1990), especially Nicholas Green, "Rustic Retreats: Visions of the Countryside in Mid-Nineteenth-Century France," 161–76; and W. J. T. Mitchell, "Introduction," in his *Landscape and Power* (Chicago: University of Chicago Press, 1994), 1–5. See also the recent overview by Leonard Guelke, "The Relations between Geography and History Reconsidered," in *History and Theory: Studies in the Philosophy of History* 36, no. 2 (May 1997): 216–34.

18. On the Huerta peasantry's political culture and the public debates and representations of urban conflicts taking place in Valencian during the second half of the nineteenth century, see Mónica Burguera, "Gendered Scenes of the Countryside: Public Sphere and Peasant Family Resistance in the Nineteenth Century Spanish Town," *Social History* 29, no. 3 (August 2004): 320–41.

19. *Los valencianos pintados por sí mismos* (Valencia: Imprenta de La Regeneración Tipográfica, 1859).

20. "Introducción," in *Los valencianos pintados por si mismos*.

21. "El valenciano," in *Los valencianos pintados por si mismos*, 9.

22. "La valenciana," in *Los valencianos pintados por si mismos*, 393.

23. The conflicts may be followed through the press from February 1878 to September 1882.

24. James Scott, *Domination and the Arts of Resistance: Hidden Transcripts* (New Haven and London: Yale University Press, 1990).

25. The alternatives were viewed as potentially more democratic and progressive (and therefore nationalizing) options, which were vetoed by the conservative and oligarchical Valencian Restoration leaders.

26. Teodoro Llorente, *Valencia*, vol. 2 (Barcelona: Daniel Cortezo y Cía, 1887).

27. Llorente, *Valencia*, 439–40.

28. See Peter Stallybrass and Allon White, *The Politics and Poetics of Transgression* (Ithaca, NY: Cornell University Press, 1986).

29. Llorente, *Valencia*, 455–56.

30. For debates on "Spanish normalcy" and its consequences for interpretations on nineteenth-century Spanish liberalism, see Isabel Burdiel, "Myths of Failure, Myths of Success: New Perspectives on Nineteenth-Century Spanish Liberalism," *Journal of Modern History* 70 (December 1998): 892–912.

31. These traditions strongly influenced the Spanish "state of autonomies" that followed the constitution of 1978. In the case of Valencia the process of "linguistic normalization" was at the heart of its autonomy statute signed in 1982 clearly following Fuster's thesis. For nationalisms in Spain after Franco's dictatorship, see Xoxé-Manuel Núñez, "What Is Spanish Nationalism Today? From Legitimacy Crisis to Unfulfilled Renovation (1975–2000)," *Ethnic and Racial Studies* 24, no. 5 (September 2001): 719–52.

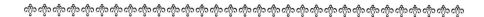

The Influence of Politics on the Shaping of the Memory of States in Western Europe (France)

Paule René-Bazin

Let me begin this essay by noting the contradictory attitudes of two French politicians with regard to the presidents of the republic whom they had served closely. I quote from two highly successful books that they have published in recent years. The first quote is from Alain Peyrefitte, a future minister but at the time a young aide to General de Gaulle. The story takes place at the Elysee in April 1965.

The General hurls at me It's scandalous! He shows me a small book on his desk which has just been published. A minister takes part in a negotiation on behalf of the Government, in the name of France, and two or three years later, he makes public state secrets about a mission he had been entrusted with!
What a lack of judgement. That's shameful. . . .
—A.P. At Foreign Office, we must keep the secrets to which we are privy for thirty years.
—G. de G. Thirty years, I don't ask for so much. History accelerates but ten years, that is the least.

The point of view of Peyrefitte is different from that of General de Gaulle. This quote reflects a time twenty years later.

Ten years: I forced myself to treble this period. De Gaulle didn't think like François Mitterrand, who felt that "Nowadays, there are no more state secrets" but like Louis the Fourteenth who in 1661 had coined a medal on the secret of King's council representing Harpocrate, God of silence, who puts his finger on the mouth. Comes consiliorum, Latin legend says: silence is Councils' companion.[1]

Jacques Attali was a member of François Mitterrand's team. When he published his book *Verbatim* of his talks with the president, seemingly with his agreement, Mitterrand indicated a very different view of secrecy.

What has happened here has gone on the shelves of History more quickly than expected. . . . At that time, at that place, I was a witness and an actor of virtually all foreign policy and an important part of France's domestic policy.
In these times of great hopes, in this country which gave me much, my passion of justice did not go well with prevailing inaction but action was equally difficult to reconcile with the ephemeral and secret.[2]

Attali's book achieved great success in bookshops, though certainly many were scandalized by his candor and revelations. The archivists, in particular, entrusted by law with keeping state secrets, felt exposed and diminished.

These stories show two councillors of heads of state under the Fifth Republic; though of two different generations, they came from what we call the highest part of French administration. Their radically different attitudes seem very indicative of the evolutions and contradictions in France toward power, recent history, and memory of the events transmitted by those who lived them.

In France, the memory of state is privileged with regard to any other form of memory, for it perhaps more than elsewhere coincides with the collective memory of the French. In fact, unlike a lot of other countries where national feeling preceded the building of a state, France, especially since the fourteenth century under the reign of

Philippe le Bel, was built around the state. This construction, undertaken under the ancien régime, was completed by the republic after the 1789 revolution. Historically, a strong, close, passionate, exacting relation with the state was thus built up.

In spite of the efforts undertaken to break that centralization, which was judged excessive, this relation still underpins French political life, as the minister of civil service, Michel Sapin, described in a paper published in the daily *Le Monde,* entitled "Un État plus transparent et plus efficace" (A More Transparent and More Efficient State). Archives, as instruments and products of government and power, are intimately linked to that relation. Maybe more than anywhere else, the actors of politics therefore influence the constitution of archival *fonds* and concern themselves with the use that is or will be made of them.

In this essay, I shall try to account for these evolutions or revolutions, mentalities, and practices, which have a profound impact on the constitution of the archival fonds and their use. Owing to the positions I have been holding for many years, I shall turn my attention to the contemporary world, referring to the works of Perrine Canavaggio and Chantal Bonazzi.[3] I shall largely rely on examples drawn from the specific experience of French national archives. International comparisons will naturally follow.

Archivists and Politicians: Methods of Action and Respective Responsibilities for the Constitution of Contemporary Memory

The Archivist, Formerly a Passive Receiver Becomes an Interventionist Actor

Representation of the past, individual and collective, is inseparable from the documentary artifact. The archivist knows better than anybody that the record of the past is always threatened with disappearance. Marked by a still positivist training, the archivist wants to be as objective as possible, taking his references from the law. He sometimes forgets that he is also an active part of a society in which certain traces are removed and destroyed; others are provisionally suppressed or definitely forgotten, depending on the concerns of society at large. The archivist is more and more "the person who knows how to destroy." He tries to reflect the collective unconscious and local necessities. Philosopher Paul Ricoeur's book, in just a few days, became an indispensable element in the heated discussions among the different disciplines in universities as well as in the political and judicial worlds for many years, focusing on the challenge of faithfulness and the requirement of historic truth.[4]

The archivist, by working to add archival fonds, struggles to find his place within these discussions when he keeps the documentary traces that will make up historians' raw material and that will allow the state and every citizen to establish their connection with the past.

Politicians' Intervention Has Changed Too

Since the French law on archives of 3 January 1979 was adopted, archivists and jurists have tried, with some difficulty, to demarcate the scope of public and private archives respectively, which are two theoretically distinct fields of archival intervention. In fact, the subject of reflection moves, according to the time, nature, and conditions of political practice.

The boundaries between public and private life that determine the nature of the archives and the way and means of their administration have become more and more blurred. They remain determined by the nature of the political regime, whether monarchic or republican, authoritative or democratic, centralizing or based on decentralized institutions. For instance, it is easy to find common factors to characterize the archives of monarchies apparently as different as Great Britain, Spain, or Morocco.

The definition of what one means by the term *politician* has become problematic. In 1985 the society of French archivists called on the French historian René Rémond, also a renowned political scientist, who had attempted to give a definition to the term *politician:* "anyone who detained, if only for a while, a piece of political power." He made also an inventory or a typology of the politicians:

—Presidents of the Republic
—Members of the government
—Their collaborators; cabinet ministers, high-ranking officials, very often associated with or even at the origin of political decisions
—Members of Parliament, about three hundred senators and six hundred representatives under the fourth Republic, very different from each other on account of the length of their political life, its importance and the diversity of the levels of responsibilities they held; (example of Paul Reynaud)
—Leaders of political parties who often own unique archival fonds of the parties themselves and of the documents linked with the functions they carry out both inside and outside of the institutions; (example of PSU's archives)

—Union leaders and notably workers; (numerous examples in the Maîtron dictionary)
—Grass-root members including those exercising responsibilities; (example of UNEF or Vietnam committees)
—Supranational politicians, notably, the European ones; (Jean Monnet, *Commissaire au Plan* in France but above all one of the "Fathers of Europe"; example also of Pierre Uri)
—Some journalists; (examples of Pierre Viansson-Ponté and Hubert Beuve Mery).[5]

Definitions of the establishment such as this one are closely linked to their authors' political life in that each of these groups produces records; they pose to the archivist some problems, notably with respect to their legal nature, their way of collection, their period of confidentiality, and the procedures of their communication. The constitution of the memory and then of the history of our countries will depend on the ways in which these problems will be solved.

A report presented to the French government by state councillor Guy Braibant in 1995 directly broaches the question in its first chapter, dedicated to the archives of political authorities. Its proposals are the starting point of several articles of the law on archives that is under preparation in France. The unanimity among the archivists and the historians can be taken for granted.

> The status of the political archives must be strengthened and reformed The archives produced by the political authorities (President of the Republic, members of the Government or local executives) or by their cabinets in the discharge of their public duties have a public nature for the same reason as those applying to the archives of the executives of the administration, the army and the diplomatic service.[6]

However, their position is often in contrast to that of many actors of political life who are worrying about the demands and means of coercion from archives administration to obtain and control the deposit of their papers.

In the Constitution of the Archival Fonds There Is the Need to Choose between the Person or the Function

In France the contemporary French politician maintains a close link with his papers. He usually wishes to keep them near him, to use them a long time after his term of

office to fulfill the functions to which they correspond; he wants to be able to destroy them to protect himself or his former collaborators or partners; he wants in any case to decide on the place and the way and the means of their keeping and their use. Very often he bequeaths his papers to his family, who considers, sometimes for generations, that the records thus constituted are a part of their inheritance and feels invested with the duty of preserving the memory of their ancestor.

Perrine Canavaggio analyzed the historical and legal arguments that characterize this attitude, the practice of which is very traditional, finding its roots in the ancien régime. Her study clearly shows that royal power was unable to ensure respect of "the notion of public interest and State interest, State and King being in fact inseparable."[7] The laws of the French Revolution, like those of the empire, avoided the question. In 1970 Robert-Henri Bautier, in the archive administration handbook published by French Archives Services, suggested that "French Public Records did not contain any papers of the XVIIIth century Great State Secretaries." The definition of what constituted a public record was vague.

The law of 3 January 1979, still in force, marked great legal and practical progress and has given archivists an authority on which to base a claim that public records are those that "derive from the activity of State."[8] The unanimity on this point can amply be taken for granted within the community of archivists, but not elsewhere, especially among the political leaders and the civil servants who hold high responsibilities very close to political life.

A draft law that is now elaborated promises important progress, but it is still at its very beginning in spite of five years of draft work.

Many examples illustrate the questions raised, which are most often solved in a pragmatic manner by the archivists who do the utmost to overcome the contradictions between the legal constraints and what they perceive as a necessity for future historians, as well as the wills of the holders of political archives.

Privilege the Person: Paul Reynaud's Example (1878–1966)

This French politician's career began with his election as regional councillor of the department of Basses-Alpes in 1913 and concluded with his resignation from his mandate as representative of the National Assembly in 1962, when he opposed national elections for the president. As regional councillor, provincial deputy then Parisian, repeated minister during the Fourth and Fifth Republics, prime minister in 1940 at the origin of the appeal to General de Gaulle, and framer with others of the constitution of the Fifth Republic, Reynaud was one of the main actors in contemporary French history. One finds some records concerning his scattered action in the institutions where he was associated. But most of his archival legacy can be found in a fonds in his name, deposited at the National Archives in 1971 by his family at the instigation of the Association of Friends of Paul Reynaud.[9] This fonds, now fully processed, comprises a hundred small boxes, corresponding to fifteen linear meters. Some files deal with Paul Reynaud's professional life before political work began. However, files of his numerous collaborators are not in the archives.

Privilege the Function: Pierre Mauroy's Example (1928–)

This politician, a militant socialist, held many posts, including mayor of Lille (one of the main cities of France), member of Parliament, first secretary of the Socialist Party, prime minister in President Mitterrand's first three cabinets from 1980 to 1984, president of the international federation of town partnerships, and other positions. He gathered most of his private archives in his town of Lille and entrusted them to an archivist of his choice. Pierre Mauroy, as prime minister, delivered to the National Archives all of the documents from the period he spent at Matignon as prime minister. He also ordered all of his associates to do the same. This collection of records amounts to more than three hundred big boxes, or about one hundred linear meters. It is especially composed of the prime minister's correspondance, his collaborators' notes, and their complementary working files, complementary from the political point of view of those files provided by the civil servants of the general secretariat of the government. It is a coherent and first-class body of records for understanding the political changes of the Fifth Republic.

A Solution for the Future: Respect the Principle of Functional Origin while Also Enhancing the Importance of the Man—The Example of Edouard Balladur (1919–)

This high-ranking civil servant, who succeeded Pierre Mauroy as prime minister from 1993 to 1995, had previously held very different responsibilities as councillor to Georges Pompidou, who was prime minister and then president of the republic after General de Gaulle; minister of finance; and then various electoral mandates. Edouard Balladur's archives happened to be scattered notably among those of Pompidou's collaborators within the presidential archives, among the records of the Ministry of Finance, and among the records of other prime ministers and those of his own cabinet members. Geographically, the first files were kept in Paris. Subsequent records were kept in the suburbs of Paris at the archives service of the Ministry of Finance and the latest ones at the National Archives, but at their center at Fontainebleau, fifty kilometers away from Paris. To begin with, Edouard Balladur had expressed his wish to gather in a single archives repository a special holding in his name consisting of all the documents that were related to his career. Yielding to the archivist's arguments regarding the risk that such a move would destroy the organic structure of the existing archival series by taking specific documents out of their context, the former prime minister finally agreed to give up his plan. He then decided to insert into the existing series the select documents that he had kept in his possession. At the same time, the National Archives committed itself to publish a personalized book in the name of Edouard Balladur, reconstituting all his papers drawn from sections in various finding aids.

From Pragmatism to Law

After World War II and without hesitation, archivists first of all concerned themselves with the collection of those archives that they thought to be essential for understanding their own time. The legal status of these fonds and the nature of the commitments made on that occasion seemed to them to be of secondary importance. Within the same perspective, many institutions, universities, libraries, and associations then undertook to constitute collections of documents, sometimes in competition with the public archival institutions. This is how, for instance, Institut d'études politiques de Paris solicited the donation or the deposit of archives of many of their former students who had embarked on a political career, such as Michel Debré, former prime minister of the General de Gaulle; and Vincent Auriol, president of the republic after World War II. The agreements and conventions regarding acquisition of the archives have significantly evolved during the last half century, from the contract of deposit to the deposit under a delivery protocol.[10]

- The contract of deposit treated the archives as if they were private and respected all clauses put forward by their owners.
- The delivery protocol eluded the question of the legal status of the documents taken into custody. It was understood that the documents were public records originating from the activity of the state but that their authors would be considered as their owners, given the very personalized nature of their interventions and the necessity for them to retain access throughout their life.
- The idea of deposit is now planned to be included in new draft legislation, but it is still controversial. In any case it would appear as a protocol of legalized delivery.

The last available example is that of President François Mitterrand's archives. The main part of them was delivered to the National Archives, but the text signed does not mention anywhere their public nature. The twelve thousand boxes corresponding to the archives of the president and of his associates were not to be combined with the private archives corresponding to Mitterrand's political life prior to becoming president. These private archives were to be held by a private foundation.

Should the Conservation Be Centralized? The Role of the State

The Sites of Conservation: Bunker or Labyrinth?

In a country as centralized as France, it is still very often difficult to find one's way through the archives of the politicians. In this regard, consultation of the *Guide to the Papers of Ministers and Secretaries of State from 1871 till 1974*, which lists hundreds of places of archives, is most telling.[11]

The National Archives, whose function is to keep the archives of the central government, is a prestigious and attractive place. It is very impressive due to its size (several hundred linear kilometers) and its organization (five centers disseminated on the national territory, the historic center being in the heart of Paris, articulated in sections, of which two at least are entrusted with actively participating in the process of constituting the contemporary memory).

The regional archival repositories, and sometimes even the municipal ones, emerge as the natural recipients for the archives of the local politicians and political institutions. Particularly attached to their native regions, some of the elected politicians do not hesitate to transfer all their archives to local repositories, knowing that their memory will be better honored there than in Paris. For example, one of Mitterrand's advisors, Michel Charasse, did not hesitate to take all his archives from the presidential archives and deposit them in the regional archives of the district where he had been elected. The researchers, sometimes taken aback by the distance and the expenses involved in traveling to these local archives, are very often rewarded for their efforts by the customized welcome they receive in the smaller institutions that wish to see their treasures used. This is how it is possible to find the archives of Max Lejeune in the regional archives of the Somme region, those of Michelet in Corrèze, those of Ramadier and Queuille in Aveyron, or those of Robert Schuman in Moselle.

Next to the official archives structures, and sometimes in competition with them, a throng of other bodies have recently emerged to collect the archives and sometimes even objects around the theme of a person or an institution. There are several reasons for the emergence of these activities:

- the shortcomings of the state's services, whose financial means do not always enable the full attention to the fond;
- the lasting economic crisis in France since the 1970s, which has very much contributed to the will to safeguard the heritage of a greater number and variety within the population; years ago there was not so much interest in this breadth;
- the development of contemporary history research and the will to get access to the necessary sources, which are protected by law; and
- the will to exalt the memory of the great actors of the contemporary political life.

Foundations were created to collect the archives, based on the American model but without the same financial resources. In 1971 the National Foundation for Political Sciences, whose present chairman is René Rémond, thus created the Center for the History and Studies of the Twentieth Century, which is in a good position to collect the archives belonging to the many former "political science" students, who account for the majority of the present generation of politicians in France. The archives of the president of the republic, Vincent Auriol; those of the prime minister, Michel Debré; and those of Edouard Daladier have thus transited through this center, where they have been ordered, cataloged, and analyzed before going to the National Archives.

General de Gaulle bequeathed his archives directly to the National Archives, but the Fondation de Gaulle, whose purpose it is to promote his memory, has received many documents of various natures from many Gaullist personalities, and in particular from the Rassemblement Populaire Français (RPF) fond. This movement has been created by Gaullists who had been very active on the French political scene after World War II.

More recently, President François Mitterrand transferred the majority of the archives of his two seven-year terms to the National Archives but also decided to entrust a foundation named after him to deal with all the documents pertaining to his private life and to the rest of his political career.

Much smaller foundations each year receive help from the state in terms of funding and human resources; a certain number of centers have recently been created by the trade unions and by the political parties. The archives of these institutions are privately owned by nature. Their conservation was rarely done in decent conditions, and the losses are irrecoverable. These centers, often related to the management of the Archives de France and at first working with volunteer research workers, undertook to provide the appropriate training or to hire professionals.

The Archives de France is keenly aware of its principal function by law as the repository for the records of the nation. At the same time, because of the emergence of such a variety of archival activities, the Archives de France aims at presenting itself as a competent interlocutor and provider of legal and technical advice pertaining to archival science, which is being developed in French universities. As early as 1971 the Archives de France had created a commission for contemporary private archives. Once a year, it would gather people responsible for the main political archives conservation institutes. It is now very much assisted in its tasks by the Association of French Archivists.

The Archives: Sources for History or Objects for Commemoration?

Political archives are like a treasure. The politician who created them is at first the sole owner. He keeps his papers for himself for a while or entrusts them to one of his close assistants. Then he may decide to entrust his papers to a repository of some kind. He very often is the first of the material's users, writing his memoirs in order to justify or enlighten his actions. Later he becomes a "memorialist." The case of Michel Debré, prime minister under General de Gaulle in 1958, is the latest example of this behavior.[12]

There are different and often contradictory approaches to the fate of political collections.

1. Posterity—the family or the spiritual heirs—often feel invested with a duty to commemorate. They may release hagiographic publications that do not have the least scholarly or scientific pretense. Some documents will even be displayed like museum exhibits (such as beautiful documents, pictures, famous signatures, and drafts of speeches).

2. The researchers, be they academics or journalists, get special access to otherwise restricted collections but are often shown only some documents selected for them by third parties. A colloquium organized in January 1999 called "To Change Life: François Mitterrand, 1981–1984"[13] illustrated both the interest and the limits of this guided use of an archives kept in more than twelve thousand boxes at the National Archives, along with many copies or additional documents gathered by various assistants and often dispersed with them.[14] The fascination this privileged access to personal papers has on the historians who have been selected is sometimes so strong that they forget to use the essential complementary fond represented by the archives of the prime minister or of the main government services.

3. A judge, on the other hand, enjoys unrestricted access to the archives he deems necessary to consult. By means of commissions of inquest, he gets access to the files, wherever they may be kept and whatever may be their legal status. This practice, long limited to the criminals of World War II, has recently been generalized. Upon presentation by a judge of a rogatory commission, the archivists must hand over to the justice all the documents they may have been entrusted with, even those restricted by the depositor or his representative. The "contaminated blood" scandal is probably the first example of this new use of archives in the service of justice. Later followed the "Elysées eavesdropping" scandal and then many other ones. The use of archives has thus been opened by certain legal precedents. This openness has probably led to the destruction of documents and a reluctance to officially hand over documents to the National Archives.

In the last few years, the so-called legal historiography became more fashionable, especially during the trial of former prefect Maurice Papon, charged with war crimes and sentenced to ten years of imprisonment. Even if at the time of the verdict the judge and the historian disagree, both professions follow the same investigating approach. Indeed, the historian does not have to judge. "History has been assigned the task of judging the past, of teaching the modern world in order to serve the future generations: our attempt does not pretend to such lofty assignments."[15]

The witness has now become an essential actor of the contemporary history that is being elaborated. He is invited to participate to research colloquiums and seminars, where his intervention is often at the origin of conflicts. His testimony is, more often and in a most systematic way, collected by historians according to the theme of their research or by archivists who want to add to their incomplete written sources or who try to render the background in which their creation needs to be understood.

The polemics, actors, witnesses, or historians often make use of the archives in order to justify their ideological positions on the twentieth century. Thanks to the archives that have been partially opened in Moscow, violent disputes in France have recently torn teams of historians apart, most of them former militants. Usually these disputes have been about communism in France or in the socialist countries or about the reality of the "résistance" in France during World War II, at a time when historical science still does not make it possible to make sweeping assertions.

Finally, due to the pressure of various groups, the state is ever more often trying to meet the French people's desire to protect the memory of contemporary history, that is, the one they have actually lived. A recent parliamentary report dealing with this theme says:

> Memory is a powerful cement for each society, as it carries its history and transmits values from one generation to the other. . . . This duty of memory is essential, as it keeps and reinforces the feeling of belonging to the Nation. Today, the need to remember, to analyse, to recognise aims at showing to the youth that democracy, freedom and human rights are fragile values which, in a few years time, almost got swept away by an economic crisis and by a vicious ideology.[16]

The state thus attempts to celebrate and commemorate its historic heritage. The state conducts cultural and educational activities to keep traditions alive. It is also entrusted with making the people aware of what the places of memory are and of remembering the events it considers to be essential. The increasing pressure put on the state by various groups organized by the community may worry the many people who remain attached to the tradition of laïcity. Paul Ricoeur expresses this preoccupation in the foreword to his book.

> Public preoccupation: I remain troubled by the worrying spectacle given by the excess of memory here, the lack of it there, not to say anything of the influence of commemorations and the abuses of memory—and of its lapses.

The idea of a policy of the right memory is, in this regard, one of my confessed civil themes.[17]

More modestly, the archivist asks himself questions about the consequences of the need for him to keep all the recorded traces of individual life paths. Those involved in these experiences, or later their heirs, might want to consult the record. If nothing is there then it would be the archivist who would be blamed.

In-depth archival processing is affected by these constraints. In a political culture based on republican equality there is an assumption of transparency toward everyone. Recently, this has been reinforced in the deontological rule that the existence of every archives fonds must be reported, even if its access is still limited or even forbidden. Current research instruments and finding aids are now written with this in mind. They should reflect the exact content of the documents without revealing its detail. This, for example, is how the researcher will know that the files of the intelligence service or the collaborators' trials instructed after World War II have been kept. He will be guided by landmarks (numeric index), but the access to the nominative list will be restricted to the archivist.

Evolving information technologies make it possible to create those multilayered indexes that are now largely used. At the same time, the minutes of interdepartmental meetings or the correspondence of the prime ministers will be minutely analyzed in a database, whose access will be restricted, and a general presentation will be established in an index that will be more widely distributed.[18] It is on the basis of the latter that the applications for access could be formulated. In the same spirit, many guides have been published: guides by archives departments since the 1950s (for example, guides by local archives services);[19] guides to archives fonds to facilitate the access to dispersed archives of various origins (for example, guides to the judiciary and penitentiary archives);[20] and guides to sources by research theme (for example, music, horses, or the history of the working class).[21]

As a conclusion to these somewhat scattered statements and reflections on the sometimes disconcerting evolutions of memory in Western Europe, I shall simply remind you of the method for the classical approach to sources, whatever their date or their support, whose value remains permanent and which one should always keep in mind.

- An archives item isolated from its context will lead to a wrong interpretation.

- An archives fonds, as opposed to what many people believe, isn't neutral. It always reflects the intervention of an institutional authority, of a political, economic, or social power. Only the critical analysis of the item, coupled with a good knowledge of the period, makes it possible to extract the "objective" signification of the documents. It would therefore be very naive to take the voluntary confessions of the accused of the great trials in the socialist countries at their face value. The sources they constitute should be used in the same way as the letters of remission before the French Revolution, which used the arguments of the defendant to attenuate his sin and to obtain his pardon.

This essay has been voluntarily limited to the French experience. One should, however, already start thinking of the future evolutions in European terms. The authority of the state over all the archives and more generally over a majority of institutions involved in the constitution of materials that form the documented memory of our times is very strong in France. This is not so in all the other member states of the European Union. In order to take these particular histories into account, will it be necessary in the future to reduce the role of the state sovereignty over archives and to distinguish other levels of responsibility for documentation, in application of the principle of subsidiarity as proclaimed in the Maastricht Treaty? Time will tell, but it is clear that the memory of the states involved in the construction of Europe will certainly come from the realities associated with this evolving political process.

NOTES

1. Alain Peyrefitte, *C'était de Gaulle* (Paris, 1994), 17.

2. Jacques Attali, *Verbatim,* vol. 1: 1981–1986 (Paris, 1993).

3. Perrine Canavaggio, "Les archives des cabinets ministériels et leur collecte: Problémes et propositions," *La Gazette des archives,* no. 119 (1982): 266–83; Perrine Canavaggio and Chantal de Tourtier-Bonazzi, "Les archives des hommes et des partis politiques en France depuis la Seconde Guerre mondiale," *Archives et bibliothéques de Belgique* (1989): 41–58.

4. Paul Ricoeur, *La mémoire, l'histoire, l'oubli* (Paris, 2000), 676.

5. René Rémond, "Qu'est-ce-qu'un homme politique?" *La Gazette des archives,* no. 133 (1986): 115–21.

6. Guy Braibant, *Les archives de France,* rapport au 1er ministre (Paris, 1995).

7. Perrine Canavaggio, "Les archives dupouvoir exécutif en France et à l'étranger," *Revue administrative,* no. 259 (1991): 65–73; no. 260 (1991): 163–71.

8. The law on archives dated 3 January 1979, title 2, article 3.

9. Archives privées (AP) de Paul Reynaud, 74 AP.

10. In French archival terms, *depot* is used for private archives, while *versernent* is used for public archives.

11. Chantal de Tourtier-Bonazzi and François Pourcelet, *Guide des papiers des ministres et secrétaires d'Etat de 1871 à 1874,* 2d ed. (Paris, 1984).

12. Cf. the memoirs of Michel Debré.

13. P. Milza, S. Berstein, and J. L. Bianco, eds., *François Mitterrand: les années du changement, 1981–1984* (Paris, 2001); Actes du colloque organisé par l'Institut François Mitterrand et le Centre d'histoire de l'Europe du Xxe siècle, Paris, 1999.

14. See Robert Belleret, "François Mitterrand, la mémoire au secret," *Le monde,* May 10, 2000. Mysterious in both life and death, the former president had a genius for blurring the tracks. His archives, be they public or private, are locked, whereas the parallel archives are dispersed here and there.

15. Marc Bloch, *Apologie pour l'histoire ou métier d'historien* (Paris, 1949), quoted by Antoine Prost, "L'historien, le juge, le témoin et l'accusé," in *Le génocide des Juifs: Entre procès et histoire 1943–2000,* Berlin symposium, ed. Florent Brayard (Brussels: Complexe, 2000), 289–300.

16. *Le défi de la mémoire,* rapport parlementaire, 1998.

17. Ricoeur, *La mémoire,* 1.

18. Paule René-Bazin, "Vers une informatique archivistique," *La Gazette des archives,* no. 129 (1985): 114–22. Jean Luquet, "La base de données Varenne," *La Gazette des archives,* no. 176 (1997): 87–95.

19. Circular AD 69-2, issued by the administration of the Archives of France 8 April 1969.

20. Jean-Claude Farcy, *Guide des archives judiciaires et pénitentiaires en France (1800–1958)* (Paris, 1992).

21. Michel Dreyfus, *Les sources de l'histoire ouvrièr, sociale et industrielle en France* (Paris, 1987).

The Role of the Swiss Federal Archives during Recent Politico-Historical Events and Crises

Christoph Graf

In the last ten years, the Swiss Federal Archives (SFA) has been involved in three politico-historical events. First, as might be known in the United States, for the past four years Switzerland has found itself at the center of a struggle for justice and truth for the victims of the Holocaust. Second, Switzerland is scrutinizing the history of its relations to the Republic of South Africa after 1945. Third is the discovery of the secret card indices of the Office of the Federal Public Prosecutor (Bundesanwaltschschaft), containing private data about hundreds of thousands of Swiss citizens and foreigners, that caused a nationwide scandal in Switzerland in 1989. I will discuss these sensitive political issues and elaborate on the archival, political, and historical strategies of the SFA to overcome the politico-historical crises. I will then look at the new Federal Archival Law that came into effect in 1999.[1] The SFA had to change and adjust its practice in the middle of a rush on its documents related to World War II and other issues. Historical information can be heavily politicized! I conclude this essay by showing that archives have to adjust to that fact and have to develop strategies for open archives for the good of the future of our societies.

Switzerland in World War II

Before I discuss the SFA's strategy to handle the crisis on World War II–related issues in historical and archival terms, it's necessary to outline the historical context of Switzerland's role in World War II in order to understand the position of my country and of the SFA in that crisis. I do this with just a few remarks, as I do not have the time to elaborate on the historical facts themselves. Switzerland, a tiny country in the heart of Europe, was not occupied by Nazi Germany and kept its crucial role as a neutral country in terms of international law throughout the war.[2] Switzerland tried to keep that neutrality in the political and economic sphere too. This made it an important place for economic and financial transactions for both the Allies and the Axis.[3] At the end of World War II the Allies tried to secure the assets of firms and individuals of Nazi Germany in Swiss financial institutions for German reparation to the victims of the Holocaust and of the war, as well as to the Allies.[4] At the outbreak of the cold war, pressure ceased, which prevented Switzerland from scrutinizing its recent past. This scrutiny only happened after the end of the cold war, when the victims of the Holocaust started their struggle for justice and reparation.[5] The struggle became public in Switzerland, the United States, and Israel when Jewish organizations in 1996 accused Swiss banks of holding back heirless accounts of Holocaust victims. Pressure increased when the president of the United States Senate Banking Committee, Alphonse D'Amato, accused Switzerland of having collaborated economically and financially with Nazi Germany. The Federal Council, Switzerland's federal government, asked the SFA and the Department of Foreign Affairs to handle the crisis for the federal administration.

The major problem at that time was to get an overview of the historical facts for the various heavily debated issues within very short time limits. Therefore the

SFA asked a renowned Swiss historian to identify pertinent records in a preliminary overview.[6] This inventory helped the SFA to estimate time and financial resources necessary to undertake the profound studies, and it was an important instrument for a parliamentary commission to establish and to mandate a historical commission.

The Independent Commission of Experts, Switzerland—Second World War was established by federal law on December 13, 1996.[7] This law granted full access to public as well as private Swiss archives, a worldwide premiere for a historical investigation. The nine internationally renowned experts started their work at the beginning of 1997.[8] Their mandate has been to investigate the volume and fate of assets moved to Switzerland before, during, and immediately after World War II, as well as other World War II–related issues, from a historical and legal point of view and to present a final report by the end of 2001 at the latest.[9] A preliminary report entitled *Gold Transactions in the Second World War: Statistical Review with Commentary* was published in December 1997;[10] an interim report entitled *Switzerland and Gold Transactions in the Second World War* was published in May 1998;[11] and the report *Switzerland and Refugees in the Nazi Era* was published in December 1999.[12]

As the political pressure on Switzerland did not cease, the federal administration undertook preliminary short studies and overviews in order to handle the accusations in various fields, such as refugee policy, gold transactions, and dormant accounts. While the SFA functioned as a historical research and information center for the federal administration, a task force in the Federal Department of Foreign Affairs focused mainly on the coordination of the various government agencies involved and on international information and communication.[13] It is important to say a few words about the three main issues of refugee policy, gold transactions, and dormant accounts before coming back to the role of the SFA.

Refugee Policy

Switzerland represented a refuge in the heart of Europe for many victims of Nazi persecution and war. However, up until a period well into the war, the authorities adhered to the principle that Switzerland was not a country of asylum but rather one of transit. But those political and social forces who wanted to maintain the Swiss humanitarian tradition applied pressure in order to enable children, families with small children, and the elderly to obtain authorization to enter the country. From 1938 to 1945 Switzerland accepted 65,000 civilian refugees, 104,000 military refugees, and another 66,000 refugees in the peripheral regions. The exact number of persons turned away is unknown; however, historical research proves that it would exceed 30,000 individuals, among whom were a considerable number of Jews.

The SFA identified important record groups related to refugee issues, published inventories and studies, reconstructed statistics about refugees admitted and turned back, and generally helped scholars and researchers to reconstruct the Swiss refugee policy as well as other World War II–related issues.[14] This archival and historical work brought the SFA into difficult and sometimes heavy debates about Switzerland's handling of World War II–related issues. It soon became very clear that historical information is political information—in certain situations at least—and therefore the SFA became somewhat politicized. It had to fulfill its task as a memory of the nation in clearing up the past.

Gold Transactions

During World War II, the prime objective of the Swiss National Bank (SNB) was to maintain public confidence in the Swiss franc. The measures the SNB undertook to achieve this were twofold: it did all it could to bind the currency firmly to gold and to maintain its free convertibility. When the assets of continental European countries deposited in the United States were frozen in June 1941, the Swiss franc, which was freely convertible, was used increasingly in international payments. The SNB responded to the demand for Swiss francs by purchasing gold. It bought a total of 279 tons of gold valued at nearly 1.4 billion Swiss francs from the Axis powers. Purchases from Germany (249 tons) began in 1940 and continued until the end of the war. The SNB acquired a total of 363 tons of gold for the sum of 1.8 billion Swiss francs from the United States, Great Britain, and Canada. The gold was deposited in accounts in London, New York, and Ottawa, where it was blocked until the end of the war.

The Reichsbank and the central banks of the European countries had opened gold accounts at the SNB to facilitate payments between their countries. These payments were carried out at the SNB headquarters in Berne but at the initiative of the countries concerned. In 1939 the Reichsbank repatriated 17 tons of gold from Berne, of which 12.5 tons had originated from the Bank of Czechoslovakia. Between 1940 and 1945, the Reichsbank delivered 336 tons of gold to the SNB headquarters in Berne. Of this, the SNB purchased 249 tons; the other major buyers—on a much lower level—were Portugal (44 tons), Sweden (18 tons), the Bank for International Settlements (12 tons), and Romania (10 tons). In addition, the Reichsbank delivered gold directly to Swiss commercial banks. There are uncertainties about the amount of these deliveries, but it is sure that they took place mainly between 1940 and 1942.[15]

The SFA helped the SNB and the historical commissions to identify their pertinent record groups, as well as facts and figures, in order to reconstruct the flow of gold and currency in their various forms.

Dormant Accounts

The Independent Committee of Eminent Persons (ICEP), as the cornerstone of the process of financial compensation for owners of dormant accounts or their heirs, was founded through a memorandum of understanding between the Swiss Banks Association (SBA) on the one hand and the World Jewish Restitution Organization (WJRO) and the World Jewish Congress (WJC) on the other hand. It was chaired by Paul Volcker, the former chairman of the U.S. Federal Reserve Bank, and consisted of six members, of whom three were appointed by the SBA and three were appointed by the WJRO and WJC. The ICEP identified fifty-four thousand dormant assets deposited in Swiss banks, of which twenty-five thousand might have a relation to the Holocaust. The Swiss Banking Commission says that only twelve hundred assets clearly belong to Nazi victims. The ICEP report, published in December 1999, stated that accounts in general have not been closed, inadvertently or deliberately, against legal regulations or auditing obligations.[16]

The SFA supported audit firms mandated by the ICEP to identify pertinent records and to establish huge databases related to their mandate.[17] It was necessary to study complicated decision-making processes and structures as a precondition.

The Role of the SFA in World War II–Related Issues in General

The three World War II–related issues previously discussed show that archives have an important role in working on a country's past. This task is manifold. Clearly, archives first of all help to identify their own pertinent records and to prepare the field for historians to

work on them. But the activities of the SFA in this case went far beyond that.

The SFA supported various commissions in their work. It helped identify pertinent records in Swiss and non-Swiss public archives with the assistance of archival networks and established contacts to archives and other historical commissions. It published finding aids as well as archival and historical articles and books, and it organized various conferences and roundtables on these issues.[18]

The SFA also had an important role within the federal administration. It helped to establish the historical commission, prepared statements of the Federal Council, and supported the Federal Department of Foreign Affairs and others agencies. When the SFA realized that not all government offices had transferred all of their World War II records to the SFA, it organized a wide-range project to secure all pertinent records before 1970 for the historical commission and other future research.

The SFA used the international archival network for an intensive exchange of information with the National Archives and Records Administration in Washington, D.C., and other national archives. It transferred hundreds of thousands of copies, microfilms, and databases of large pertinent record groups to research centers and museums, such as Yad Vashem in Jerusalem and the United States Holocaust Memorial Museum in Washington, D.C. To the last two institutions it transferred microfilms of the files of twenty-two thousand Jewish refugees from 1936 to 1945,[19] in total 1.4 million frames (images) and the corresponding database it had established.

The SFA was involved in court actions too. Following the settlement agreement between Swiss banks and class actions, the U.S. District Court for the Eastern District of New York had to handle the allocation and distribution of the settlement fund. To establish the corresponding plan, the court had to get information about potential claimants of the five classes. For the administration of the so-called refugee class, the SFA established and transferred to the court a list with the names of fifty-one thousand civilian refugees admitted in Switzerland and a list with the names of sixty-five hundred refugees turned back at the Swiss border. For the administration of the so-called slave labor classes, the SFA established a list with German corporate identities that had their revenues transferred to Switzerland before 1945 and a list of Swiss firms that used forced labor in their German branches.[20]

These activities of the SFA in World War II–related issues continued until 2001. Before I summarize the archival and historical strategies of the SFA to overcome this politico-historical crisis, I will discuss the other two publicly debated historical and political issues in which the SFA was strongly involved. The first is Switzerland's relations to the apartheid state of South Africa; the second is the discovery of secret card indices and files of the Office of the Federal Public Prosecutor.

Switzerland's Relations to South Africa

The Federal Council, on account of several parliamentary inquiries, in March 1999 decided to establish a governmental commission that would study various aspects of the relations between Switzerland and the Republic of South Africa during the time of apartheid. The commission presented its report in July 1999.[21] The SFA was a member of this commission and established an inventory as an analytic finding aid (*kommentierte Bestandesanalyse*) to pertinent record groups for this and future studies. The inventory contains reference to records in various research fields.[22] The SFA identified at least thirty-six hundred files that reflect different aspects of these economic, financial, political, and cultural relations.

The parliamentary inquiries are the result of the political pressure of former antiapartheid movements in and outside Switzerland. They followed the example of the World War II–related issues, demanding research on Swiss, German, and American capital transfers to the Republic of South Africa during apartheid. Swiss banks and other firms maintained an involvement in South Africa because neutral Switzerland had not imposed sanctions. The Swiss Federal Parliament thought it best to study Swiss relations to South Africa within existing structures and programs of scientific institutions instead of establishing a special legislation and structure as it had done for the World War II–related issues. The Federal Council therefore decided on May 3, 2000, to prolong National Research Program 42, entitled "Foundations and Prospects of Swiss Foreign Policy." This program of the Swiss National Science Foundation has the following aims: (1) providing decision-making assistance for government departments in the face of the increasing complexity and interdependence of international relations; (2) educating the electorate, that is, raising its level of knowledge and awareness of problems; and (3) monitoring and improving the coherence and effectiveness of Swiss foreign policy.[23] It is very interesting to analyze decision-making structures and processes in the case of Switzerland's relations to South Africa. These relations posed a wide range of new questions in conceptualizing and living neutrality toward the apartheid regime.

The SFA played a significant part within the scientific community and the national research management to conceptualize this "South Africa module" of the National Research Program 42. It was represented in the board of the program and monitored the module very closely, because it was very crucial for researchers to have access to pertinent records. The new Federal Archival Law imposes a normal closure period of thirty years. Access to documents within that period is possible under certain conditions. The competent federal authority then had to give permission on a written demand. For the Swiss–South Africa research program, the Federal Council therefore asked the federal administration to handle demands as liberally as possible and asked the SFA to coordinate this process. The debate about Switzerland's relations to South Africa and the question of access to pertinent records were and are two other acid tests of the crucial role the SFA has to play in creating transparency and in facilitating historical research on politically highly sensitive issues.

The Discovery of Secret Card Indices and Files of the Office of the Federal Public Prosecutor

When the iron curtain was falling in Europe in 1989, Switzerland experienced an unexpected national crisis— parliamentary investigations revealed the existence of secret card indices to information in files about the political attitude and activities of hundreds of thousands of Swiss citizens and foreigners gathered by cantonal and federal police units.[24] Federal law established the right of persons concerned to be informed about their card index and file on demand. The Federal Council and one part of the Federal Parliament then wanted to destroy the original cards and files, arguing that the information gathered violated law on the secrecy and privacy of private persons. Nobody objected to that. Nevertheless, historians began to think on these records as an important source for future studies on Switzerland during the cold war. The SFA was the spearhead of that movement and asked in parliamentary hearings to transfer the records to the SFA, where they would be kept safe *from* further use by federal authorities and ready *for* further scientific or other use by third parties after a period of fifty years. After a difficult, long process of decision making, the Federal Parliament decided that the records were not to be destroyed but rather transferred to the SFA. The respective law imposed expired in 2001. After that, these records will fall under the new Federal Archival Law.

This gives me the opportunity to introduce this law before I close with remarks on the SFA's strategies to handle difficult politico-historical events.

The Federal Archival Law

The new Federal Archival Law of June 26, 1998, was enforced in October 1999.[25] The SFA therefore had to change and adjust its practice in the middle of a wide public debate and crisis on historical issues and during a rush on its documents related to these issues. Due to this coincidence, the archival legislation process was an extensive public debate and became heavily politicized. I would like to give some background information on the new law and mention the consequences of implementing it in archival practice.

Archives fulfill a key function for the continuity and transparency of the constitutional state. The aims of the new law are, first, to guarantee the evidence and transparency of the activity of the federal state; second, to enable efficient records management in the administration; and, third, to provide the records for historical, social, and cultural studies.

The law clearly regulates the area of applicability of the archival regulations.[26] In general, all federal authorities and agencies, as well as third-party institutions that execute federal tasks, fall under the new Federal Archival Law—two among a few exceptions are the Federal Court and the Federal Insurance Court, which have their own archives due to separation of powers. However, the archival regulations of these institutions must be compatible with the Federal Archival Law.

All offices and agencies falling under the new law are obliged to offer their records to the SFA. The SFA appraises the records before transferring them physically. This is a change of system. Previously the SFA took records from the offices without having the capacity to check their value systematically. The appraisal of records by the SFA is an important tool for ensuring that all very important documents will be kept safe for future generations. The new law is part of a complex of regulations that ensures to manage and keep records in a systematically integrated process.[27] The new Federal Archival Law, therefore, is the basis for a modern, efficient information management of the government and the administration.

The Federal Archival Law stipulates new regulations for using the records. For the first time in Switzerland, the right of free access after a closure period of thirty years is written law and therefore guaranteed beyond any doubt. For that reason the Federal Archival Law is part of the constitutional right to information. The period of thirty years is de facto an international standard. The closure period for access to individual files with sensitive personal data as well as to a limited number of clearly defined record groups is prolonged to fifty years. It can be shortened under certain conditions.

The new Federal Archival Law guarantees a modern archival policy in Switzerland in the time to come. It stipulates transparency, a principle that will guide the future administration. It enables citizens to control the government and its administration democratically and forms an important basis for historical and social studies. It is, of course, narrowly coordinated with the legislation on privacy and freedom of information.

Summary

The three recent politico-historical events discussed here show that archives have an important role in working on a country's past. This task is manifold. Clearly, archives first of all help to identify pertinent records and to prepare the field for historians to work on them. But modern archival strategies and activities go far beyond that.

Archives help scholars, researchers, and commissions not only to identify pertinent records but to support them by establishing contacts to other institutions with the help of archival networks. They encourage and facilitate research by publishing finding aids and analytic inventories, and they participate in the evaluation of their sources. Archives should open their gates to and become a partner of the scientific community. Archives play an important role in the government and the administration. They support and regulate efficient records management, secure relevant records, and provide archival and historical know-how. They can help to manage national research programs and projects in historical contexts.

The handling of the recent politico-historical crises was an acid test for the SFA's double strategy as an archive and a historical research and information center. It became evident that securing records, making them accessible, and mediating them to the researchers are three different parts of one assignment. Archives open the gate to the past. They are an important part of the collective memory of a society and help to reconstruct the past as a condition for the present and future social identity of a nation. The SFA learned that openness and transparency are two eminent preconditions for fulfilling the social and political functions that archives and historical information centers have toward their country, citizens, and government.

NOTES

1. *Bundesgesetz über die Archivierung (BGA)* of June 26, 1998, and *Verordnung zum Bundesgesetz über die Archivierung (VBGA)* of September 8, 1999.

2. See Bonjour, Edgar, *Geschichte der schweizerischen Neutralität, Vier Jahrhunderte Eidgenössischer Aussenpolitik,* vol. 4, 1939–45 (Basel, 1970), 2.

3. See Daniel Bourgois, *Business helvétique et Troisième Reich: milieux d'affaires, politique étrangère, antisémitisme* (Lausanne, 1998).

4. See Stuart E. Eizenstat, *U.S. and Allied Efforts to Recover and Restore Gold and Other Assets Stolen or Hidden by Germany during World War II,* Preliminary Study (Washington, DC, 1997); Linus von Castelmur, *Schweizerisch-alliierte Finanzbeziehungen im Übergang vom Zweiten Weltkrieg zum Kalten Krieg, Die deutschen Guthaben in der Schweiz zwischen Zwangsliquidierung und Freigabe (1945–1952)* (Zurich, 1997).

5. For an excellent Swiss Web site on that issue, with a chronology of events, updates, links to important other sites, and so on, see http://www.giussani.com/holocaust-assets/; see also the Web site of the United States Holocaust Memorial Museum, which has an international list of current activities regarding Holocaust-era assets, http://www.ushmm.org/assets/.

6. Peter Hug, *Analyse der Quellenlage für mögliche Nachforschungen im Zusammenhang mit dem Bundesbeschluss betr. die historische und rechtliche Untersuchung des Schicksals der infolge der nationalsozialistischen Herrschaft in die Schweiz gelangten Vermögenswerte* (Berne, 1996).

7. Bundesbeschluss vom 13. Dezember 1996 betreffend die historische und rechtliche Untersuchung des Schicksals der infolge der nationalsozialistischen Herrschaft in die Schweiz gelangten Vermögenswerte.

8. The members of the commission were Prof. Jean-François Bergier, chairman, Dr. Sybil Milton, vice chairwoman, Dr. Wladyslaw Bartoszewski, Prof. Saul Friedländer, Prof. Harold James, Prof. Georg Kreis, Dr. Jacques Picard, Prof. Jakob Tanner, and Prof. Daniel Thürer; the Web site of the commission is http://www.uek.ch/.

9. A decree of the Federal Council of December 19, 1999, describes the mandate of the commission. The commission describes it as follows: "The Commission's mandate covers the gold trading and foreign currency transactions conducted by the Swiss National Bank and by private commercial banks. The objects of the investigation are all assets moved to Switzerland including insurable values and cultural assets, both of the victims of the Nazi regime as well as of its perpetrators and collaborators. The relations of Swiss industrial and commercial companies with the National-Socialist economy—especially regarding their involvement in 'aryanization measures' and the exploitation of forced labourers—are also examined. Another key topic is Swiss refuge policy in connection with Switzerland's economic and financial relations with the Axis powers

and the Allies. The study also includes the post-war period including government measures for the return of unlawfully acquired assets (*Washington Accord 1946,* Resolution the reporting of dormant accounts 1962)."

10. Independent Commission of Experts Switzerland—Second World War, *Gold Transactions in the Second World War: Statistical Review with Commentary,* a contribution to the Conference on Nazi Gold, London, December 2–4, 1997 (Berne, 1997).

11. Independent Commission of Experts Switzerland—Second World War, *Switzerland and Gold Transactions in the Second World War,* Interim Report (Berne, May 1998).

12. Independent Commission of Experts Switzerland—Second World War, *Switzerland and Refugees in the Nazi Era,* Report (Berne, December 1999).

13. Task force "Switzerland—Second World War" of the Federal Department of Foreign Affairs, see http://www.taskforce.ch/.

14. See, for example, "Die Schweiz und die Flüchtlinge," *Studien und Quellen,* Zeitschrift des Schweizerischen Bundesarchivs, no. 22 (1996); Guido Koller and Heinz Roschewski, "Flüchtlingsakten 1930–1950, Thematische Übersicht zu Beständen im Schweizerischen Bundesarchiv," *Inventare* (1999).

15. See http://www.snb.ch/e/publikationen/.

16. Independent Committee of Eminent Persons, *Report on Dormant Accounts of Victims of Nazi Persecution in Swiss Banks,* Geneva, December 1999; see http://www.icep-iaep.org.

17. The SFA helped to establish a database of the 1945 freeze of German assets in Switzerland.

18. Peter Hug and Marc Perrenoud, *In der Schweiz liegende Vermögenswerte von Nazi-Opfern und Entschädigungabkommen mit Oststaaten / Les avoirs déposés en Suisse par des victimes du nazisme et les accords d'indemnisation conclus avec les pays de l'Est,* Bundesarchiv *Dossier 4,* Berne, 1997; *Flight Funds, Looted Property and Dormant Assets. Status of Research and Its Perspectives. Publication according to the Information Day at the Swiss Federal Archives, 25th February 1997,* Bundesarchiv *Dossier 6,* Berne, 1997.

19. SFA, E 4264 (-) 1985/196 and 1985/197, N-series.

20. See the official Web site of the Holocaust Victim Assets Litigation against Swiss Banks and other Swiss Entities, at http://www.swissbankclaims.com/.

21. Interdepartementale Arbeitsgruppe "Schweiz—Südafrika," *Die Beziehungen zwischen der Schweiz und Südafrika,* Berne, 1999; the report is available in French, German, and Italian.

22. Schweizerisches Bundesarchiv, Eidg. Departement für auswärtige Angelegenheiten (Hg.), "Schweiz—Südafrika 1948–1994, Archivbestände und parlamentarische Vorstösse," *Inventare* (2000).

23. For further information, see the Web site of the Swiss National Science Foundation, http://www.snf.ch/en/rep/nat/nat_nrp_42.asp, and the Web site of National Research Program 42, http://www.snf.ch/NFP42/.

24. I refrain from detailed footnotes and give some references for further information only. See, first of all, the final report of the parliamentary commission: *Bericht der Parlamentarischen Untersuchungskommission (PUK) vom 22. November 1989: Vorkommnisse im EJPD [Eidg. Justiz- und Polizeidepartement],* Berne, 1989; *Ergaenzungsbericht der Parlamentarischen Untersuchungskommission (PUK) vom 29. Mai 1990,*

Vorkommnisse im EJPD, Berne, 1990; see also Georg Kreis, *Staatsschutz in der Schweiz, Die Entwicklung von 1935–1990, Eine multidisziplinäre Untersuchung im Auftrage des Schweizerischen Bundesrates,* Berne, 1993; Markus Büschi, "Fichiert und archiviert, Die Staatsschutz-Akten des Bundes 1960–1990," *Studien und Quellen* 24 (1998).

25. *Bundesgesetz über die Archivierung (BGA)* of June 26, 1998, and *Verordnung zum Bundesgesetz über die Archivierung (VBGA)* of September 8, 1999; see http://www.bar.admin.ch.

26. The new Federal Archival Law enacts archival regulations for the federal state. The twenty-six cantons (states) in Switzerland have their own regulations.

27. The following regulations belong to this complex: *Bundesgesetz über den Datenschutz* of June 19, 1992, and the *Regierungs- und Verwaltungsorganisationsgesetz* of March 21, 1997, both with their respective decrees, and the directives of the Federal Department of Home Affairs about records management in the federal administration of July 13, 1999.

Television Archives and the Making of Collective Memory

Nazism and World War II in Three Television Blockbusters of German Public Television

Wulf Kansteiner

Television archives play a vital role in the day-to-day business of the television industry. They help television makers identify footage and ideas for the programs of tomorrow. Consequently, the archives are organized to support the production process, and any other function is secondary to that objective. At the same time, by default not design, television archives contain the cultural legacy of the twentieth century and play a key role in the infrastructure of modern memory. On the one hand, they house the blockbuster television events and hit series that are recycled so frequently that they seem to be permanently established in the public sphere. Reruns of *Law and Order,* the best Hitler footage, or coverage of the life and death of Princess Di are omnipresent on our cable systems and hardly get a day's rest between broadcasts. On the other hand, television archives contain hidden treasures that have rarely or never been seen by the public eye: programs not deemed fit for prime time audiences that were broadcast in the wee hours of the morning or that for legal or political reasons have never been aired at all. Since cultural preservation and research are not the primary functions of television archives, some of these marginal holdings are regularly destroyed and our cultural memory diminished in the process.[1]

In principle, selective use is characteristic for the holdings of any archive or library. However, as a result of limited access and great potential reach, the selective use of television archives has far-reaching social and cultural consequences. The images and stories stored as tapes and digital files might shape the perceptions of millions of viewers, or their existence—and possible impending destruction—might only be known to a few archivists. The difference between fame and obscurity is determined by a small group of television administrators who decide on the station's lineup. They try to get the most mileage out of the network's treasured possession of broadcasting rights without alienating audiences, political supervisors, and business partners. They determine how the contents of the archive, which reflect all current licenses and contracts, are deployed to attract the largest number of viewers at minimal expense.

Since television is our most important medium of historical reflection, the popular and obscure visions of the past contained in the archives illustrate beautifully the difference between actual and potential collective memories. As an Egyptologist, Jan Assmann was probably not thinking of television when he first made this differentiation. He argues that cultural memories occur in the mode of potentiality when representations of the past are stored in archives, libraries, and museums and occur in the mode of actuality when these representations are adopted in new social and historical contexts. Assmann also points out that in the transition from potential to actual cultural memories (and vice versa), representations change their intensity, social depth, and meaning.[2] His remarks capture the dynamics of the making and unmaking of collective memory in the age of electronic media, although with television, unlike in the case of more traditional media, the transition from potential to actual collective memories can literally take place overnight.

The following case study analyzes cultural memories of the Nazi period produced by West German television during the era of the public television monopoly. From 1954 to the late 1980s German audiences had to make do first with one and then, since 1963, with two national public television networks. Commercial competitors were licensed in 1984, but it took several years before they reached a substantial audience and before the public service monopoly had been effectively transformed into a dual television system. The administrators and producers of the public service networks ARD and ZDF, closely supervised by the Federal Republic's political elite, pursued very active politics of memory. In patriarchal fashion they distributed politically correct interpretations of the Nazi period for the benefit of a population that was considered in need of reeducation by its own political leadership as well as its foreign partners. Between 1963 and 1993 the ZDF alone aired over twelve hundred programs about the Nazi past, totaling over eight thousand minutes of airtime.[3]

Rather than taking on that overwhelming number of programs, we will have a closer look at a select few shows that the television makers of the ZDF considered particularly suitable for general consumption and scheduled repeatedly in prime time. Even in the era of the public television monopoly it was not unusual to see expensive television plays and documentaries rescheduled at least once after their initial release. But this recycling generally only took place in off prime-time hours during the afternoon and late night because the viewers, restricted to two channels, tended to reject repeat performances during their favorite television hours. Therefore, the programs discussed here belong to a select group of productions that television makers considered so compelling, important, or popular that they presented them several times in prime time despite intense internal competition for these programming slots.

In the course of the analysis we will find out that television archives contain much more than the audiovisual records of past television fare. Their holdings also provide valuable insights into the communication processes surrounding the production and the reception of the programs in question. Without this information we could not even begin to assess the political, cultural, and social relevance of the visions of the Nazi past that have survived in the archives of German public television.

On July 20, 1965, the ZDF broadcast the docuplay *Bernhard Lichtenberg,* which commemorated the resistance activities of a high-ranking Catholic cleric in Berlin in the Third Reich. Lichtenberg—in the official position as *Domprobst* of St. Hedwig, the third highest representative of the Catholic Church in Berlin—had sharply criticized the violence in the concentration camps in 1936, had prayed for the German Jews from the pulpit since the pogroms of November 1938, and had written a letter of protest against the Nazis' euthanasia campaign in August 1941. As a result of his public demonstrations and a denunciation, Lichtenberg was finally arrested in October 1941 and sentenced to two years' imprisonment for "political malice" and "abuse of the pulpit" in May 1942. Lichtenberg, sixty-seven years old and suffering from a heart condition, survived the two years of imprisonment but died on November 5, 1943, during his transfer from Berlin to Dachau, where he was supposed to be incarcerated indefinitely.[4]

The program on Lichtenberg would turn out to be the ZDF's most frequently aired show about the history of Nazism. It was broadcast four times in prime time and six times altogether, most recently in 1996, when Lichtenberg was beatified by the pope.[5] *Bernhard Lichtenberg* is a prime example of the controversial genre of docuplay that the ZDF television makers found particularly suitable for the coverage of contemporary history. Based on careful reviews of the historical record, the docuplays presented important historical personalities and events through fictitious dialogues and play scenes. In this fashion, the programs presented a seamless, invented narrative universe that was simultaneously presented as fact. Not surprisingly, many reviewers criticized the misleading combination of fact and fiction and the inappropriate claims of authenticity, but viewers generally appreciated the appealing, consistent historical visions.[6]

The ambivalent epistemological status of the ZDF docuplays gave rise to a number of lawsuits. The most prominent case occurred in 1973, when the Federal Republic's constitutional court prevented the broadcast of a docuplay about the 1969 murder of four West German soldiers because the play violated the private sphere of one of the lesser perpetrators.[7] In the case of *Bernhard Lichtenberg* the successful team of Maria Matray and Answald Krüger, who had already written a number of docuplays for the ZDF, based their script on the Gestapo files and the records of the criminal proceedings. But their diligence did not save the station from legal troubles. The first two broadcasts in 1965 and 1966 included the actual names of Lichtenberg's denunciators, who successfully sued the station for slander and forced the omission of their names and deeds from any future broadcast.[8]

Bernhard Lichtenberg was presented to an audience

that was already familiar with the Catholic Church's ambivalent record in the 1930s and 1940s, because the premiere of Rolf Hochhuth's *The Deputy* in Berlin in February 1963 had caused a heated and persistent debate about the Vatican's policies during the Holocaust.[9] A number of reviewers therefore welcomed the television play as an attempt to set the record straight and to document the courageous resistance and suffering of many German clerics in the Third Reich.[10] The play was neither the first nor the last ZDF program about the topic that painted such a favorable image of the clergy. From 1963, the ZDF's first year on the air, through the mid-1970s, a fair number of productions highlighted the deeds of religiously motivated detractors of euthanasia and racial laws.[11] But *Bernhard Lichtenberg* emerged as the most compelling contribution because the priest had displayed such exceptional moral integrity in his lifetime and the actor Paul Verhoeven had managed to project that disposition particularly convincingly. Because of his acting skills, the traditional aesthetic framework of the docuplay—play scenes in stark, understated settings interrupted by contemporary quotes from Nazi leaders—enhanced the effect of authenticity and did not seem forced or artificial. Even reviewers who were generally skeptical about the genre applauded Verhoeven's accomplishment.[12]

The acting and the upbeat message about human persistence in times of extreme oppression might also explain the favorable audience reaction. All six broadcasts of *Lichtenberg* outperformed the competing ARD programs in the ratings.[13] In the course of three decades over 50 million viewers have seen the docuplay, a number that far exceeds the benchmark of 20 million Germans who watched the blockbuster *Holocaust* in 1979.[14] Apparently, the viewers were not just willing to watch *Lichtenberg* but actually appreciated the specific perspective on the history of the Third Reich. The ZDF received seventy-nine letters after the first broadcast in 1965. All but one of the letter writers praised the show, and many specifically welcomed the timely defense of the beleaguered clergy. In addition, there were a surprisingly large number of requests for additional screenings, which the ZDF administrators gladly honored.[15]

In principle, these reactions are not representative for the general audience, but they do match the findings of a detailed, representative study that the polling company Infratest conducted for the ZDF. Between 1963 and 1974 Infratest regularly supplied ARD and ZDF with qualitative research data about the viewers' assessment of their television fare. The report about *Lichtenberg* indicates that the show reached the grade of 5 on a scale between −10 and +10, which was considered surprisingly positive given the subject matter. In fact, even viewers who admitted their dislike for inquiries into the burden of the past grudgingly admitted the high quality of Verhoeven's performance.[16] The experts at Infratest also delivered an explanation for the success of the program, which is as difficult to prove as it seems compelling.

> The personality and actions of the minister from Berlin might represent a general ideal, possibly even unconsciously desired ideal, which is fueled by a pervasive guilt complex. Bernhard Lichtenberg was what many today wish they could have been: A courageous fighter who, knowing about the consequences, nevertheless followed his conscience and did not avoid danger. Viewed from this perspective the figure of Lichtenberg is embraced by the audience in an act of "projective exoneration."[17]

In 1968 the mood among the audience had already shifted. There are no detailed reports about the reactions of the viewers after the rerun of *Bernhard Lichtenberg*, but a number of letters have survived in the archives. As in the past, most members of the audience who bothered to write supported the ZDF's optimistic politics of memory, but there were a lot more critical voices than before. Some correspondents criticized the play and used the opportunity to vent their anger about the activists of the student movement and to denounce an alleged global socialist conspiracy that, in its most extreme version, reached from Vietnam over East Berlin to Bonn and included the television makers of the ZDF.[18] But two viewers in particular engaged in a pointed, critical exchange of letters with the ZDF staff and, independently of each other, revealed the dubious rationale that informed programs like *Bernhard Lichtenberg*. They rejected the attempt to use the deeds of a few upright clergy members to rehabilitate an institution that, taken as a whole, had failed to mount any meaningful resistance against the segregation and extermination of the Jews of Europe. Consequently, in their opinion, the ZDF's historical coverage could only be considered objective if it acknowledged that failure to the same extent that it had already documented the integrity of the few upright church officials like Lichtenberg.[19] The same conclusion had already been reached by Walter Jens, a professor of rhetoric at the University of Tübingen, who was the only among forty reviewers in 1965 who unequivocally stated that "the film of Maria Matray and Answald Krüger follows the known facts yet only reveals half of the truth. Not the hatred of the regime but the silence of his superiors turned the Domprobst of St. Hedwig into an outcast."[20]

The shift of opinion in the audience between 1965 and 1968 is a small grassroots marker of the fundamental transformation of the Federal Republic's historical culture, which, during the second half of the 1960s, turned from a culture of consensus into a divisive, volatile arena of political reckoning. Even in the late 1950s and early 1960s there had been a number of high profile anti-Semitic scandals and Nazi trials that caused much concern among West Germany's cultural and political elites and their foreign friends.[21] But only the provocations of the student movement, covered in detail on television, made many citizens join in the fray and express their own political opinion and memory of the Nazi past. Letters to the ZDF were one of the venues open to that general public, and as a result a docuplay like *Bernhard Lichtenberg*—which had been designed to foster an already existing selective, consensical, and optimistic vision of the past—became the subject of controversy between the program makers and some members of their audience.

The German churches were not the only institutions that needed a moral face-lift after 1945. The same applied to the military, which had reinvented itself as Bundeswehr and a NATO partner but which occasionally still collided with its dubious record in the Third Reich. Again, the ZDF was happy to oblige, especially since viewers loved military history in general and World War II history in particular, as long as the crimes of the Wehrmacht remained invisible. The combination of audience interest and cold war propaganda needs resulted in a whole string of productions that celebrated the military resistance against Hitler. The programs were instrumental in transforming the assassins of July 20, 1944, from traitors into proto-democratic heroes and in providing the new military with anti-fascist role models.[22]

The creation of such selective coverage, which pleased viewers and political superiors, created no problems for the ZDF television makers, but they encountered serious challenges when they dealt with foreign films whose producers did not share the benign perception of the German military. The editorial staff of the ZDF was particularly concerned about feature films from the Soviet bloc and from Hollywood since they tended to present the former enemies as fascist ideologues and/or mindless brutes.[23] Despite these reservations many World War II films from foreign countries, especially from the United States, found their way into German living rooms since they were fairly inexpensive and the audience appreciated them. But the ZDF personnel screened the produc-

tions carefully and occasionally eliminated scenes that might have been particularly offensive to German viewers. That fate befell the famous Hollywood movie *The Longest Day*, an all-star reconstruction of the Allied invasion of Normandy on June 6, 1944.[24] Technically brilliant and featuring an unprecedented deployment of extras and weaponry, the three-hour film presents a conventional war epic that is neither historically accurate nor particularly emotionally compelling. The German participants of the battle appear somewhat wooden and confused but generally likeable.

Feature films have had a strange career on German television. Initially, all media experts and television executives assumed that movie aesthetics would never work on the small screen. But when ARD and ZDF broadcast feature films, primarily for lack of German-language television productions, the audience reacted very favorably, and the public networks created separate departments to handle the purchase of distribution rights.[25] In the 1950s and 1960s films were still traded in small packages, which gave television makers a lot of flexibility to pick and choose for their audience. Already in the 1970s, however, the German market was effectively controlled by the media mogul Leo Kirch, who had amassed a huge inventory of foreign and domestic films, including many U.S. titles.[26] As a result, the television stations were forced to purchase large packages of films that contained a few highlights as well as many second-rate productions. In addition, part of the negotiations had to be undertaken "blind," that is, without any concrete knowledge of the films in question. This frustrating situation invariably resulted in legal bickerings as television executives tried to exchange as many films as possible after the fact.

The Longest Day was part of a large deal with Kirch's company Beta that was concluded in March 1968. According to the terms of the agreement, the ZDF was to choose 270 feature films from a list of 1,000 movies at a price of approximately ninety thousand deutsche marks per film.[27] The film was not available for inspection in 1968 but was provisionally included in the deal anyway. In July 1970 one member of the ZDF editorial staff had a first opportunity to watch the film and objected to its misrepresentation of the German officer corps and its glorification of war and Allied sacrifices.[28] But all attempts to exchange the movie for another production failed. Even a personal meeting between Kirch and representatives of the ZDF could not resolve the issue, and the station was stuck with a production that nobody in the station deemed particularly suitable for broadcasting.[29] In fact, resistance against the movie increased as more members of the staff saw it personally. There were two major concerns. First, in the eyes of many employees *The Longest Day* misrepresented the history of World War II. In addition to the negative representation of the German side, they were especially critical of the famous scene with Curd Jürgens (representing General Blumentritt), in which he complains about his superiors' lack of courage to wake up Hitler and demand necessary tank reserves. This scene, the ZDF staff concluded, might give rise to another stab-in-the-back myth and convince viewers that without Hitler the German military could have prevented the invasion and won the war. Second, they objected to the movie's aesthetization of warfare through humor, U.S. heroism, and gratuitous violence. Especially the younger members of the staff took *The Longest Day* as an opportunity to voice their critique of U.S. militarism and imperialism in general and the war in Vietnam in particular. The head of the ZDF's division for feature films, Klaus Brüne, expressed this concern very delicately when he recommended refraining from showing the film in light of the "current political psychological disposition of the viewers in the Federal Republic."[30] The staff member who had initially been asked to see the film through the complex technical and editorial screening process was less circumspect. In his mind, *The Longest Day* was "a hypocritical, imperialistic, miserable piece of work which expresses disdain for human beings from other [i.e., non-U.S.] backgrounds" and therefore violated the charter of the ZDF, which specifically required all members of the ZDF to further peace and international reconciliation.[31] To express his principled, conscientious objection, he refused his signature on a routine document and asked to be released from all editorial responsibility for the film.[32]

The reservations of the ZDF staff were neither unusual nor unprecedented. *The Longest Day* had already received negative reviews in most German newspapers upon its release in Germany in October 1962. The critics had dismissed the film as "pro NATO military kitsch" blown up to gigantic proportions,[33] and there was no need to amend that judgment when it became known that the U.S. Defense Department had generously supported the production with money and materiel.[34] In the end this impressive consensus did not make any difference. Commerce won over conscience since in times of very tight budgets even public television could not justify shelving an expensive film that Kirch, strengthened by his monopoly position, simply refused to take back.

The Longest Day aired on June 4, 1974, as the ZDF's contribution to the fortieth anniversary of the Normandy invasion. In order to correct at least the worst alleged offenses, the ZDF broadcast a shortened version. Some of the more humorous scenes were omitted since they detracted from the serious topic of warfare, and the viewers were also spared the opening scene, which shows the pursuit and execution of a resistance fighter by a German military officer.[35] The few critics who bothered to review the television screening unknowingly repeated all the points of criticism that had already been raised within the ZDF, including the distasteful distribution of U.S. military propaganda against the background of the war in Vietnam.[36] But the audience reacted very differently. Despite the fact that the screening was interrupted for an hour of news, 18 million viewers representing almost half of West Germany's television households watched until 11:10 p.m. on a Tuesday night.[37] Under these conditions *The Longest Day* was not just one of the longest but also one of the more successful broadcasts of 1974.[38] The interest of the audience explains why the ZDF renewed the broadcasting rights twice and aired the movie three more times, once even in prime time.[39] Over the years a total of 35 million German viewers have seen the U.S. reenactment of the Normandy invasion.[40]

Very few letters from viewers have survived in the archives, but we still have access to the ledgers of the ZDF's public relations department, whose staff records all phone calls to the station. Most of the callers, eighty-one to be precise, appreciated the film but complained vehemently about the one-hour interruption. A minority of twenty-five viewers were outraged by the negative representation of German soldiers and "screamed and cried on the phone."[41] Similar reactions were recorded during the second prime-time screening in 1984, when some callers rejected what they perceived as the "humiliation, defamation, and stultification of the German nation."[42] Such emotional outbursts were not unusual; they are part and parcel of the process of coming to terms with the past in Germany. But the response of the public indicates that different layers of interpretation existed side by side. Apparently, all German viewers of *The Longest Day,* from the television executive to the couch potato, disliked the representation of German soldiers as inferior strategists. Perhaps they were even all "sick and tired of the fact that the Americans always win the war," as one viewer put it very succinctly.[43] But from the administrators and intellectuals of the early 1970s, the film elicited strong negative reactions consisting of an overdetermined mixture of principled pacifism, belated anti-fascist resistance, and unacknowledged injured national pride. Their critical attitude toward U.S. policies and propaganda combined outrage about inhumane policies in Vietnam with the desire to resist such policies, just as their parents should have resisted Nazism, and the satisfaction to have a legitimate reason for criticizing the United States. These reactions were neither consistent nor rational. For instance, the editorial staff of the ZDF insisted on the evil nature of the Nazi regime and its war of aggression but would still censure "one-sided," negative depictions of German soldiers. Consequently, they removed the opening scene of *The Longest Day,* as if the Nazi military had not been gratuitously violent and criminal. In contrast, the reactions of at least some members of the public were less self-reflexive but also more honest and more consistent. They simply rejected representations of World War II that made German soldiers look bad or that blamed Germans for crimes against humanity. Their anti-Americanism, if we want to call it that, was still linked to World War II and not to Vietnam.

Considering the few data available, it is difficult to come to any precise conclusions about the popular memory of the Nazi period in West Germany. However, many factors, including the data given previously, indicate a bifurcation of German memory discourse between elite discourse, on the one hand, and a popular discourse, on the other, which developed at different speeds. For many intellectuals in the aftermath of the student movement who followed the theoretical debates about fascism, the beginning of the New German cinema, and a new wave of autobiographical literature, the 1970s already marked a phase of active reflection about the burden of the past. In contrast, the general population did not yet engage in such reflections, in part because popular media like television did not yet feature any compelling, entertaining programs that could help create and sustain a self-critical interest in history. That happened only in the early 1980s after the broadcast of *Holocaust.*

On May 1 and 3, 1975, the ZDF aired a television play that epitomized all that was wrong and great about the public television monopoly. On the one hand, ARD and ZDF clearly limited their viewers' choices and presented them with programs that they had not asked for and often did not appreciate. Nowhere was that more apparent than in the field of contemporary history. On the other hand, without competition and generously funded through viewer fees, the stations could afford to produce superb prime-time fiction and pursue politics of memory that challenged public opinion. *Tadellöser & Wolff,* the program in question, illustrates these contradictions like few other programs.[44] The television play was based on

an autobiographical novel by Walter Kempowski, which had been published in 1971 to general acclaim by the critics and the reading public.[45] In a microstudy of Nazi society Kempowski describes the family life of a bourgeois merchant family in the seaport of Rostock between 1938 and 1945. With a great eye for detail he captures the everyday woes and rites of passage of the family's three adolescent children and the apolitical, deeply conservative attitudes of their parents. The literary tableau does not focus on the political events of the Third Reich but shows how fascism impinges on the characters' lives and how they adapt to the new realities. Like many members of the elite they disdain the Nazis' crude methods but nevertheless tolerate and even identify with their domestic and foreign policy agenda.

Already in 1971 the ZDF commissioned two reports about Kempowski's book to determine if *Tadellöser & Wolff* was suitable for television. The first reviewer firmly denied that question. In his opinion, the novel contained many perceptive insights about everyday life in the Third Reich but the loosely connected scenes lacked a clear narrative focus and could not easily be transposed to the screen. In addition and more important, the idyllic bourgeois microcosm reconstructed by Kempowski failed to reflect any of the horror and brutality of the times and thus misrepresented the Nazi era.[46] The second reader acknowledged both problems but came to very different conclusions. Considering that the viewers were familiar with the political history of the Third Reich and might have had similar experiences as the characters in the novel, they should be able to absorb Kempowski's precise aphorisms even without further historical contextualization. Also, in his reading, the book represented a powerful indictment of the German middle class because it illustrated how the bourgeoisie permitted itself to be co-opted for the fascist cause. Consequently, he recommended that the necessary cuts, which would transform the book into a manageable film script, should retain the book's balance in the representation of seemingly apolitical everyday life and historical political events. Only this balance would capture and express what he perceived as Kempowski's primary message: that the private is political, especially in times of a dictatorship. In conclusion, he assessed *Tadellöser & Wolff* as a high-risk project worth the effort.[47]

The ZDF staff clearly followed the advice of the second reader and retained the service of the filmmaker Eberhard Fechner. Fechner had directed a number of programs for the ARD, including three well-received historical documentaries that chronicle twentieth-century German history through the lens of individual lives in specific social settings.[48] In these and subsequent films he focused increasingly on the causes and the memory of the Third Reich and the Holocaust.[49] With an obsession for detail that matched Kempowski's and the eye of a documentary filmmaker he managed to transform Kempowski's precise literary observations into similarly precise visual language. Fechner wanted to construct a mise-en-scène that recalled the 1940s in all possible respects. Therefore, he carefully selected the props and locations and even simulated the lighting and camera angles of the Nazi cinema. Ideally, from the film's appearance, the average viewer should not be able to tell the difference between *Tadellöser & Wolff* and films produced in the Third Reich. This aesthetic strategy reflected Fechner's didactic objective of recreating the perspective of the contemporaries of the Third Reich without judgment and the arrogance of hindsight. The audience should become familiar with the dilemmas and distractions of the citizens of Nazi Germany before they tried to explain their moral and political failures. Consequently, Fechner made the unusual decision to shoot the whole film in black and white. Concerned about the film's reduced audience appeal, the ZDF executives initially questioned that decision but ultimately relented. Apparently, they were convinced by Fechner's concept and were also happy to save money on the less expensive, black-and-white production.[50]

Judging by the reviews Fechner succeeded beautifully in recreating the atmosphere of the 1940s. The critics began to rave about *Tadelöser & Wolff* before it was even aired, and the praise intensified after the broadcast. The reviewers thought that the film represented the past perfectly[51] and found the bourgeois microcosm of the Kempowski family so compelling and attractive that they even mimicked the family's private language in their own texts.[52] However, the unusual agreement between journalists of different political color, who often found themselves on different sides in the battles of memory politics, is itself cause for suspicion. Fechner might have captured the sadistic trappings of an authoritarian school system; the mixture of adventure and brutality in the Hitler Youth; the misogynist, rebellious tone of the youth subculture; the air of defeat among the emotionally crippled veterans of World War I and the Great Depression; and the fatalistic persistence of their wives, who kept up bourgeois pretenses under any circumstances, including total military and moral collapse. But he also, perhaps more successfully, captured the postwar wishful thinking and projections of a bourgeois elite that had always been reluctant to admit responsibility and was certainly not compelled to change tack by an aesthetically brilliant but politically flawed program like *Tadellöser & Wolff*. Fechner provided an opportunity for pleasurable nostalgia by reproducing the surface of everyday life in the Third Reich without recreating its less visible but equally important underpinnings, that is, the fear and unease caused by the precise knowledge about camps and deportations and the less precise knowledge about military defeat and large-scale crimes in the east.[53] In this sense, *Tadellöser & Wolff* accurately reflected the memory of the Nazi era, but not its history.

There is no indication that the general public appreciated *Tadellöser & Wolff* as much as the professional critics did. The two parts of the television play have been broadcast at least five times by the ZDF, twice in prime time.[54] Over the years at least 15 million viewers have watched *Tadellöser & Wolff*, but the film never attained audience majorities; its ratings were similar to or even lower than the ratings of the competing programs of the ARD.[55] These results reflect the vagaries of the television schedule and the persistent reservations about the topic of Nazism, but they also indicate that the idiosyncratic aesthetics of Fechner's relatively slow-moving, black-and-white production had limited appeal for some segments of the audience. In fact, the feedback from viewers suggests an interesting divide. On the one hand, the station received a number of extremely positive letters from viewers who echoed the critics' praise and emphasized how much the program reflected their own personal memories of the Nazi years.[56] These fans even picked up pen and paper to express their appreciation of the reruns of *Tadellöser & Wolff* in subsequent years.[57] On the other hand, the viewers who decided to call the station during or after the broadcasts expressed their "unanimous disapproval."[58] They rejected further coverage of the Nazi past, regretted that their fees were spent on such projects, and claimed that the program included numerous historical mistakes, for instance, regarding the "insipid" dialogues.[59] It seems that viewers who preferred and felt comfortable to convey their opinions in writing accepted the programs as "their own" history, whereas viewers from other backgrounds, perhaps less educated, did not recognize themselves in the events on the screen. These impressions suggest that *Tadellöser & Wolff* was a socially divisive media event that captured bourgeois history for bourgeois audiences but had limited impact outside that target group.

Tadellöser & Wolff is a great and early example of the wave of programs on everyday history that thoroughly transformed the image of the Third Reich in the Federal Republic starting in the late 1970s. The mass media of the Federal Republic, just like its historians, had initially focused on the political history of the Third Reich and neglected to explore the social fabric of Nazi Germany and the popularity of the regime. In the early 1970s novelists, filmmakers, and historians, who had themselves experienced Nazism as children or adolescents or who were born after the war, began to fill the gap through autobiographical works and projects on everyday history during fascism.[60] Many of these literary, historical, and visual texts produced in the aftermath of the student movement highlighted the failures of the bystanders of the regime and documented the crimes that their passivity had made possible. However, as everyday history made its way into the mainstream as a compelling, entertaining new paradigm of historical representation, it lost some of its self-critical edge and the texts simply stressed the normality of everyday life. The crimes of the regime and the involvement of thousands of perpetrators were often covered under an appealing layer of everyday minutiae that made the time of the 1930s and 1940s look very much like everyday life before and after fascism. In this process of transformation a paradigm of historical analysis, which had been crafted as a tool for self-critical historical exploration, became a venue for collective amnesia.

The three programs discussed here gained prominence for different reasons. At the time of the initial broadcast, *Bernhard Lichtenberg* represented a belated moment of consensus in the arena of German memory politics. The program makers and their political supervisors, as well as the audience and the critics, agreed that the docuplay was a particularly suitable reflection of Nazi history. That consensus unraveled during the political upheavals of the 1960s, but the initial agreement provided enough momentum to carry the production through several reruns in the course of three decades. Thus the long television career of *Bernhard Lichtenberg* illustrates how the construction and deconstruction of collective memories became a complex, multilayered process through political debate and generational strife. Apologetic, defensive interpretations of Nazism, which originated in the political culture of the 1950s, have existed side by side with much more self-critical representations of more recent origin.

The Longest Day was aired against the vehement opposition of the ZDF's editorial staff in charge of movie acquisitions. The protests were dismissed by an executive leadership that felt that it lacked the financial and political flexibility to keep the movie off the air. But the feature film only became one of the classics of popular military history as a result of the favorable response of the German audience. In addition, the debates inside the station show that the radicalization of German memory politics after 1968 was not necessarily the primary objective of many political activists in the public limelight or behind the scenes. Even with hindsight it is difficult to determine to what extent the insistence on the proper acknowledgment of German guilt was simply a convenient tool to dislodge a political generation from power that had determined German politics since 1945. Reinterpretations of German history, however important for contemporaries and subsequent generations, were often merely the side effects of political struggles with much more presentist concerns. Finally, the reception history of *The Longest Day* demonstrates that German memory politics were always an international arena. Even the consumers at home—and not just the political elite—had to come to terms with foreign representations of German history that did not mesh with their own memory and understanding of that past. Such contradictions were accepted because the past was not just the cause for some pain but also the source of fabulous entertainment. In fact, only the exceptional use value of historical representations of Nazism as distraction and leverage explains the popularity of the German pursuit of memory politics.

Tadellöser & Wolff certainly confirms the entertainment potential of the history of the Third Reich, although this media event catered to a very specific audience that shared an appreciation of cinema history and a similar horizon of experience. Fechner's television play was carried from broadcast to broadcast by the television makers themselves, their colleagues in the print media, and viewers of similar social background with similar aesthetic interests. For them, *Tadellöser & Wolff* was the best television imaginable, but for viewers with less sophisticated tastes and exclusive childhoods, the program offered neither authenticity nor entertainment. More important, the television play encouraged none of the viewers to question their selective, self-serving memories or interpretations of Nazism. The opportunity to make prime-time television for your peers, which public television executives occasionally indulged in, no longer exists. In the dual television system, productions of such exceptional intellectual and cinematic quality as *Tadellöser & Wolff* are not funded and, if they were produced by some small economic miracle, would probably not surface in prime time in one of the major networks.

The combination of inappropriate self-adulation, militaristic glorification, and aesthetic simulation, which our analysis of the historical blockbusters of the ZDF reveals, supports the assessment of an insightful critic of

Tadellöser & Wolff, who concluded in 1975 "that we guilty Germans are still not able to present anything but half-truths about the Nazi era."[61] In all fairness one must emphasize that the historical coverage of German public television was much better than the small sample in this essay indicates. Especially in the 1980s the ZDF produced or purchased some remarkably self-critical programs about the Nazi past, including productions that focused on the disturbing legacy of the "Final Solution" and, more specifically, on the perpetrators of the Holocaust.[62] But these programs were rarely repeated and certainly never in prime time. As a result, a documentary like *Dr. W: Ein SS-Arzt in Auschwitz,* an excellent, nuanced exploration of the mind-set of the SS camp personnel, aired at 10:00 p.m. in front of 2.7 million viewers.[63]

Despite the interesting data on television reception, which television archives contain and which we could use for the analysis here, it is impossible to determine the precise impact of television programs on the historical consciousness of their viewers. However, as Jan Assman reminds us, any text about the past can only become a reference point for actual collective memories if it is taken out of the archives and brought into circulation. Consequently, the blockbusters of the ZDF historical programming are much more likely to have shaped the collective memory of the nation than the station's marginal historical reflections directed at minority audiences.

NOTES

1. The impressive variety as well as the restrictive access policy of television archives are documented in Wolfgang Klaue, ed., *World Directory of Moving Images and Sound Archives* (München: Saur, 1993). For an excellent survey of the history and administration of German television archives, see Susanne Pollert, *Film- und Fernseharchive: Bewahrung und Erschliessung audiovisueller Quellen in der Bundesrepublik Deutschland* (Potsdam: Verlag für Berlin-Brandenburg, 1996).

2. See Jan Assmann, "Collective Memory and Cultural Identity," *New German Critique* 65 (1995): 125–33. For a survey and assessment of the field of collective memory studies, see Kerwin Lee Klein, "On the Emergence of *Memory* in Historical Discourse," *Representations* 69 (2000): 127–50, and Wulf Kansteiner, "Finding Meaning in Memory: A Methodological Critique of Collective Memory Studies," *History and Theory* 41 (2002): 179–97.

3. Wulf Kansteiner, "Nazis, Viewers, and Statistics: Television History, Television Audience Research, and Collective Memory in West Germany," *Journal of Contemporary History* 39 (2004): 575–98.

4. Bernward Dörner, "Hintergründe einer Seligsprechung," *Süddeutsche Zeitung,* June 17, 1996.

5. *Berhard Lichtenberg,* ZDF, July 20, 1965; November 13,

1966; November 17, 1968; March 30, 1973; November 5, 1978; and June 16, 1996.

6. For a critical survey of the development of the genre, see Knut Hickethier, "Fiktion und Fakt: Das Dokumentarspiel und seine Entwicklung bei ZDF und ARD," in Helmut Kreuzer and Karl Prümm, eds., *Fernsehsendungen und ihre Formen* (Stuttgart: Reclam, 1979), 53–70.

7. Ernst Fuhr, "Persönlichkeitsrecht und Informationsfreiheit," *ZDF-Jahrbuch 1973,* 89–97.

8. Internal memo of the ZDF's head legal council, Ernst Fuhr, to the station's director for programming, Joseph Viehöver, February 21, 1968.

9. Anat Feinberg, *Wiedergutmachung im Programm: Jüdisches Schicksal im deutschen Nachkriegsdrama* (Köln: Prometh, 1988), 33–46; and Fritz Raddatz, ed., *Summa inuria oder Durfte der Papst schweigen? Hochhuths* Stellvertreter *in der öffentlichen Kritik* (Reinbek: Rowohlt, 1963). Lichtenberg's name is actually mentioned on the first page of Hochhuth's *Der Stellvertreter* (Rowohlt: Reinbek, 1963).

10. "Dokument des Widerstands," *Allgemeine Zeitung Mainz,* July 22, 1965; Hilde Bold, "Der 20. Juli im Fernsehen," *Ruhr-Nachrichten,* July 22, 1965; and "Das meinen wir," *Kieler Nachrichten,* July 22, 1965.

11. See, for example, the television plays *Zwei Tage von vielen,* ZDF, March 11, 1964; *Geheimbund Nächstenliebe,* ZDF, March 14, 1964; and *Nicht Lob, noch Furcht,* ZDF, September 16, 1972; and the television documentary miniseries *Kirche, Staat und Katholiken,* ZDF, November 1 and 5, 1967; and *Priester auf dem Schafott,* ZDF, April 21, May 5, May 19, and June 16, 1972.

12. "Bernhard Lichtenberg," *Badische Neuste Nachrichten,* July 24, 1965; Günther Hahn, "2. Programm," *Recklinghäuser Zeitung,* July 22, 1965; and "Bernhard Lichtenberg," *Suttgarter Zeitung,* July 23, 1965.

13. *Infratest-Index* 28 (1965): 17; *Infratest-Wochenübersicht,* November 13, 1966; *ZDF-Jahrbuch 1968,* 164; *Infratest-Wochenübersicht,* March 30, 1973; *telejour,* November 5, 1978; *GFK-Fernsehforschung,* June 16, 1996.

14. The number of 50 million viewers is a very conservative estimate based on the ratings mentioned previously and the size of the German television audience published in the respective editions of the *ZDF Jahrbuch.* The audience of *Holocaust* has been very carefully studied; see, for instance, Uwe Magnus, "*Holocaust* in der Bundesrepublik: Zentrale Ergebnisse der Begleituntersuchung aus der Sicht der Rundfunkanstalten," *Rundfunk und Fernsehen* 28 (1980): 534–42, 535.

15. The ZDF's division for public opinion compiled an internal report about the reception of *Bernhard Lichtenberg* dated August 12, 1965, which supplied a statistical analysis of viewer correspondence together with selective quotes.

16. *Infratest-Index* 28 (1965): 17–20.

17. *Infratest-Index* 28 (1965): 17.

18. That is, for instance, the essence of a well-written anti-Semitic, anti-socialist pamphlet of twelve pages, dated November 23, 1968, which a viewer from Göttingen sent to the ZDF. The same viewer had initially only sent a postcard dated November 17 on which he protested the alleged similarities between the ZDF and the East German television network DFF but, encouraged by the ZDF's staff's response, he mailed his

impressive handwritten diatribe. A similar, equally well-written yet more laudatory anti-socialist letter reached the ZDF from a viewer in Düsseldorf, dated November 18, 1968.

19. The two viewers were a law student from Munich, who sent two letters dated November 17 and November 26, 1968, and a teacher from Mainz, who also intervened twice, on November 17 and December 30, 1968.

20. Momos (Walter Jens), "Ein UFA-Propst," *Die Zeit*, July 30, 1965.

21. Werner Bergmann, *Antisemitismus in öffentlichen Konflikten: Kollektives Lernen in der politischen Kultur der Bundesrepublik 1949–1989* (Frankfurt: Campus, 1997).

22. See the broadcasts of the German movies *Es geschah am 20. Juli*, ZDF, July 20, 1963; *Canaris*, ZDF, January 9, 1966; *Der 20. Juli*, ZDF, July 22, 1966; the television documentaries *20. Juli–20 Jahre danach*, ZDF, July 20, 1964; *Deutsche gegen Hitler*, ZDF, July 20, 1969; as well as the docuplays *Claus Graf Stauffenberg*, ZDF, July 17, 1970; and *General Oster*, ZDF, August 28, 1970.

23. The ZDF even produced a feature about these stereotypes; see *Deutsche im polnischen Nachkriegsfilm*, ZDF, October 24, 1966.

24. *The Longest Day*, directed by Ken Annakin, Bernhard Wicki, Andrew Marton, and Gerd Oswald, produced by Darryl Zanuck (Twentieth Century Fox, 1961).

25. Irmela Schneider, "Ein Weg zur Alltäglichkeit: Spielfilme im Fernsehprogramm," in Helmut Schanze and Bernhard Zimmermann, eds., *Das Fernsehen und die Künste* (München: Fink, 1994), 227–301.

26. Kirch's media empire continued to grow through the 1980s and 1990s, but he failed in his endeavor to establish pay television in Germany. The subsequent collapse of his companies in spring 2002 caused the biggest bankruptcy in German media history; for a summary of the history and collapse of the Kirch empire, see the online version of the *Süddeutsche Zeitung*, at http://www.sueddeutsche.de/wirtschaft/branchenpolitik/44419/index.php (accessed June 18, 2002).

27. The general parameters of the contract, called "Beta V," are included in the minutes of a meeting between Kirch and representatives of the ZDF that took place in the office of Dieter Stolte on July 19, 1972. The minutes were written from memory by Dieter Krusche, dated July 21, 1972.

28. *Endabnahmeprotokoll* (minutes of the final internal review), dated July 16, 1970. This routine procedure occurs before any production is cleared for broadcast and covers both content and technical quality of the program in question. Normally that process would only take place once, but the archives contain the impressive number of six "final" internal reviews for *The Longest Day*. All but the last of the reviews (dated March 18, 1974) severely criticize the movie.

29. See note 27.

30. Internal memo of Klaus Brüne, dated August 30, 1973, summarizing the discussion after a screening the day before in the presence of several staff members.

31. Quote from an internal memo addressed to Klaus Brüne, dated August 8, 1973. The staff member in question also compiled a detailed timeline of the review process within the ZDF and the communications with Beta addressed to Brüne, dated June 20, 1973.

32. Minutes of the meeting of the editorial staff in the division for feature films, September 7, 1973.

33. Heinz Ungureit, "Bumsdi-Heroismus," *Frankfurter Rundschau*, October, 29, 1962; see also Alexander von Cube, "It's a Long Day: Alliierte Invansion in der Normandie als Kostümfilm," *Vorwärts*, November 7, 1962; and Friedrich Wagner, "Monsterschau von der Invasion," *Frankfurter Allgemeine Zeitung*, October 24, 1962.

34. "Pentagon: Hilfe von Goldfinger," *Der Spiegel*, April 19, 1971.

35. The cuts amounted to 15 minutes and reduced the film from 172 to 157 minutes. Made in 1973 and maintained through every one of the subsequent three broadcasts, the cuts are documented in the Deutsche Institut für Filmkunde in Frankfurt and acknowledged in letters to viewers; see, for example, the letter by Jürgen Labenski, member of the ZDF's division for feature films, which he sent to a viewer in Schönbrunn-Haag on December 7, 1992.

36. Henk Ohnesorge, "Langer Tag an langem Abend," *Die Welt*, June 6, 1974; Michael Stone, "Alles oder nichts," *Tagesspiegel*, June 6, 1974; and, especially, "Alptraum in Bildern," *Badische Zeitung*, June 6, 1974.

37. *Infratest Wochenübersicht*, June 4, 1974.

38. At least ten feature films achieved higher ratings in 1974, but they concluded before the end of prime time. For a list of the most successful programs of 1974, see *ZDF-Jahrbuch 1974*, 137–41.

39. *The Longest Day*, ZDF, June 4, 1984; November 28, 1992; October 21, 1993; the 1984 screening was in prime time and attracted 15 million viewers.

40. *ZDF Presse Aktuell*, June 8, 1984; *GFK—Fernsehforschung*, November 28, 1992; *GFK—Fernsehforschung*, October 21, 1993.

41. Minutes of the ZDF telephone service (Ergebisprotokoll des Telefondienstes), June 4, 1974.

42. Minutes of the ZDF telephone service, June 4, 1984.

43. Minutes of the ZDF telephone service, June 4, 1974.

44. The term "Tadellöser & Wolff" is an idiomatic expression used by the characters of the television play meaning "just perfect" or "great."

45. Walter Kempowski, *Tadellöser & Wolff: Ein bürgerlicher Roman* (München: Hanser, 1971).

46. One-page typed report by W. R., Munich, September 8, 1971.

47. Four-page typed report by H. H., July 18, 1972.

48. *Nachrede auf Klara Heydebreck*, NDR, November 29, 1969; *Klassenphoto: Erinnerungen deutscher Bürger*, ARD, January 17 and 19, 1971; and *Unter Denkmalschutz: Erinnerungen aus einem Frankfurter Bürgerhaus*, ARD, February 4, 1975. Fechner's work is discussed at length in Egon Netenjakob, *Eberhard Fechner: Lebensläufe dieses Jahrhunderts im Film* (Weinheim: Quadriga, 1989).

49. See especially *Der Prozess*, NDR, November 21, 23, and 25, 1984, which covers the criminal trial of the staff of the death camp Majdanek conducted in Düsseldorf between 1975 and 1981.

50. Memo of Helmut Rasp, member of the subdivision I for television plays, to his superior Stefan Barcava, head of the main division for television play and film, June 20, 1974. The

production cost approximately 2 million deutsche marks, a sum that surpassed the agreed upon budget by 25 percent; see letter by Frithjof Zeidler, with the production company Polyphon, to the ZDF division of budget and finance, February 18, 1975.

51. Representative of the many enthusiastic reviews are Kurt Lothar Tank, "Sepiabraune Vergangenheit," *Deutsches Allgemeine Sonntagsblatt,* May 11, 1975; "Beispielhaft," *Frankfurter Rundschau,* May 5, 1975; "Tadellöser & Wolff," *Hamburger Abendblatt,* May 5, 1975; "Als wir schlitterten," *Stuttgarter Zeitung,* May 5, 1975; "Aus dem Familienalbum," *Westdeutsche Allgemeine Zeitung,* May 5, 1975; Effi Horn, "Bilder aus dem deutschen Familienleben," *Münchner Merkur,* May 3, 1975; and "Tadellöser & Wolff," *Bild-Zeitung,* May 3, 1975.

52. See, for example, Birgit Lahmann, "Wie isses nu möglich," *Deutsche Zeitung Christ und Welt,* May 9, 1975; and Cordula Zytur, "'Gutmannsdürfer'," *FUNK-Korrespondenz,* May 7, 1975.

53. A minority among the reviewers criticized the misleading, harmless, and idyllic rendering of Nazi society; see "Ein angenehmes Mosaik," *epd: Kirche und Rundfunk,* May 8, 1975; "Krieg aus der Froschperspektive," *Augsburger Allgemeine,* May 5, 1975; and especially Momos (Walter Jens), "Von Folter und Verbrennung keine Rede," *Die Zeit,* May 9, 1975.

54. *Tadellöser & Wolff,* ZDF, May 1 and 3, 1975; December 17 and 18, 1979; May 5 and 6, 1985; February 9 and 10, 1989; and August 16, 1992.

55. *Telejour,* December 17 and 18, 1979; *GFK-Fernseh-forschung,* May 5 and 6, 1985; *GFK-Fernsehforschung,* February 9 and 10, 1989; *GFK-Fernsehforschung,* August 16, 1992. The ratings for the first broadcast of *Tadellöser & Wolff* in 1975 have never been released since the company teleskopie had serious problems calibrating their hardware and collecting their data during the first six months of its contract with ARD and ZDF. However, unofficial ratings were shared with the production company Polyphon; see the letter of Annemarie Schriever, a secretary for the division 1 for television plays, addressed to Frithjof Zeidler, July 25, 1975.

56. See, for instance, the letter sent to the ZDF by Ilselore and Günter K. from Düsseldorf, dated May 5, 1975.

57. Letter by Sigrun F. from Bremen, dated January 4, 1978.

58. Minutes of the ZDF telephone service, December 17, 1979.

59. Minutes of the ZDF telephone service, May 1, 1975.

60. Winfried Schulze, ed., *Sozialgeschichte, Alltagsgeschichte, Mikro-Historie* (Göttingen: Vandenhoeck & Ruprecht, 1994).

61. "Ein angenehmes Mosaik," *epd: Kirche und Rundfunk,* 8 May, 1975.

62. Wulf Kansteiner, "Entertaining Catastrophe: The Reinvention of the Holocaust in the Television of the Federal Republic of Germany," *New German Critique,* 90 (fall 2003): 135–62.

63. *Dr W.: Ein SS-Arzt in Auschwitz,* ZDF, September 12, 1976; see also the *telejour* report for the same day. The program was repeated once on September 16, 1977, at 4:10 p.m. in front of an even smaller audience.

PART V

Archives and Social Understanding in States Undergoing Rapid Transition

(China, Postwar Japan, Postwar Greece, Russia, Ukraine, and the Balkans)

As the essays grouped in this final section indicate, an important aspect of the Michigan seminar was its attention to the particular circumstances of archives in China, Russia, Ukraine, and the Balkans. Our concern here was not only to engage archivists and archival historians from these regions in the broader discussion with colleagues from other regions, but to extend the points of comparison between archives in stable or relatively stable states to those in states in the process of rapid and even radical transition. With China, Russia, Ukraine, and the Balkans, these discussions naturally centered even more directly on the question of archival politics.

The relationship between state archives and governments necessarily involves politics in any society, as we have noted. So, indeed, does the relationship between nonstate archives and the organizations or collectives that sponsor them. Implicit in the organization of any repository is the idea that its collections will serve the state or society in ways its sponsors intend. The knowledge produced by and through the archive is assumed to serve rather explicit goals and needs, whether they are those of the state, the public, or individuals. As the essays by Atina Grossman and Robert Adler elsewhere in this volume testify, individuals as different as American presidents and the children of Holocaust survivors can be extremely reluctant to deposit their private papers in an archive that serves broader interests, fearing their own archived story might not be properly researched and told.

Politics also affects archives in other ways, however, and again in all societies and all archives. Questions of acquisition, appraisal, preservation, and especially access are fundamentally political ones in the sense that they involve the application of quite considerable power in the name of quite particular values and goals. What distinguishes an archive from a collection of memorabilia is, in part, the application of a specific set of criteria about what should and should not be acquired and preserved, and for whom. Even in the most democratic of societies and the most accessible of archives, decisions about all of these matters reflect certain political values and interests, whether these are reflected formally, in charters or legislation (such as the U.S. Federal Records Act), or informally and more crudely, as in the former Soviet Union. In either case, the archival scholar is always engaged with the politics of protected knowledge and the interests that created it. As Penelope Papailias writes in her fascinating analysis of the ways refugee memory and the Ottoman past were archived in postwar Athens, the archive is always in some way a process whereby texts of a particular sort are "written."

That these texts can serve profound individual and social needs, or crude, single-minded political purpose, is clear from the essays by Leslie Pincus and Robert Donia. Pincus explores what she calls a "revolution in the archives of memory" that occurred with the founding of the National Diet Library in occupied Japan after 1945. She movingly shows how this struggle was driven in large part by the need to give voice to the trauma of war, to find meaning to attach to almost indescribable loss. The struggle to create a National Diet Library after the Hiroshima and Nagasaki bombings was very much a struggle over how and why the past could be remembered, how, as Pincus describes it, collective memory could be produced "in different registers and with different ideological valences." The library was imagined as "a vast repository for the accumulated past of humankind, as a memory machine for emergent forms of collective organization, and as a site for new, democratic forms of deliberative practice." Donia's contribution on libraries and archives in postsocialist Bosnia and Herzegovina, on the other hand, is about precisely the opposite impulse: the deliberate strategy on the part of the Serbs to obliterate meaning by burning libraries and turning their artillery on specific archives and museums. Donia calls this "memoricide." In this case, the texts "written" by these archives and libraries were about unacceptable pasts and hence inadmissible futures. Their destruction was part of a deliberate attempt to destroy the possibilities of collective memory by obliterating its physical and documentary referents.

Participants in the seminar may have assumed that deliberate strategies of this sort underlay archival practices in Communist China and Soviet Russia, since the politicalization of historical analysis and state control over information are obviously among the key elements of authoritarian regimes. Here, however, the seminar produced a number of very interesting surprises. The papers by the American Sinologist Beatrice Bartlett and the Chinese archivist Du Mei demonstrate both an extraordinary range of record keeping in China historically and what seems to be a relatively high level of recent access and use. Bartlett characterizes an eclectic "archival impulse" in late imperial China, disposed to saving everything. The Qing archives are thus rich in social history material, although there is little indication that documenting social or sociopolitical relations was the intention of the archivists. Bartlett shows rather deftly how these materials can be used to construct broader elements of social memory that attached different meanings to events than those imposed officially. Although there are many cases of what Bartlett describes as "deliberate forgetting," in which important documentation is now missing from the record, and while access to such materials as rebel confessions has been restricted as a way of protecting official versions of the past, an abundant amount of material is still available.

As Du Mei indicates, moreover, restricted access to archives does not mean that archives were relatively underused by scholars in China. Especially during the 1980s, interest in the archives seems to have increased exponentially, reaching more than 5 million annual users by 1987. As many as 23 million files may have been accessed be-

tween 1983 and 1987, and substantially more since. William Kirby's very interesting contribution shows that while huge numbers of files on the People's Republic of China (PRC) itself contain material still regarded as "unsuitable for foreigners," the PRC archives also contain an immense quantity of accessible papers on a wide range of Republican-era institutions, especially those of the pre-revolutionary business community. If Qing and Republican government materials have been neglected since 1949, and if officials continue to show no interest in promoting archival scholarship about the Communist regime itself, the period since the early 1980s has still witnessed in Kirby's view a revolution in the professional organization of Chinese archives, as well as in public access to archival materials for the period before 1949.

The participation of Du Mei herself in our seminar and a fruitful series of collaborative workshops between Michigan and Chinese archivists in Ann Arbor and Beijing affirm Kirby's observation. If archival history for most PRC archives ends with the Communists coming to power, there is still reason to anticipate more rather than less openness in the future. If that happens, scholars researching the history of the Communist regime are likely to find archival materials structured very much in the way that Vladimir Lapin shows they were in Soviet Russia: organized and cataloged according to a fixed hierarchy of ideologically determined categories. As Lapin shows in detail, particular kinds of knowledge were created in Soviet archives not only through restricted access, but through the very nature of archival practices themselves. These privileged certain kinds of subjects and organized material in ways that both formed and re-created basic premises of a class-conflict understanding of the historical process. Indirectly, this forced many researchers to frame their scholarship in comparable ways, since the categorization of archival material largely determined what researchers were able to access and write about.

What is interesting about Lapin's presentation is not simply the peculiarities of the Soviet experience but the way they reflect tendencies common to *all* historical archives, even if to an exaggerated degree. As the essays by Ann Stoler, Fred Cooper, Rebecca Scott, and others in part IV of this volume suggest, categorical classifications have proven to be a key process in the creation of certain kinds of colonial "knowledge" and "understanding"; and even in the most open of societies, archival "knowledge" is necessarily grouped by categories that implicitly guide the researcher toward a recognition of their importance and acquires particular meaning in this way. The quotation marks here signify that knowledge and understanding constructed in these ways is essentially imposed on the materials by the categories of the archivist, rather than those that the researcher might deem historically important. The scholar's need to "read" the archive itself along with its documents is no less pressing in open societies than in those under authoritarian rule.

A similar argument can be made about what fabricated documents along with silences in the archives reveal about political culture. The fascinating essays by Ziva Galili and Abby Smith both deal with archival revelations, albeit in very different ways. Galili suggests how silences in the Soviet archives worked effectively to distort historical understanding about the revolution of 1917; Smith treats us to an inside look at how even very well intended archivists found themselves unable to escape the political uses to which post-Soviet revelations were being put. Here fabrication occurred not in the sense of falsification, but in the ways documents were selected and displayed to produce a certain effect. The essays by Jeffrey Burds, Serhy Yekelchyk, and Boris Ananich, on the other hand, all indicate how the opening of the Soviet archives has verified that many archived materials are literal fabrications of one sort or another: false reports submitted by officials to their superiors, inaccurate descriptive materials designed to satisfy the expectation of the recipient rather than to provide accurate information, and especially the fabrication of confessions and other investigative materials relating to purges and show trials. Each of

these contributions shows how even corrupted documents can be used in surprisingly informative ways: by a reading of silences, by interpreting the role of certain kinds of language, by discerning different levels of power and authority, even by understanding the fabrications themselves as authentic testimony about the political process as a whole. Boris Ananich shows quite persuasively, for example, that the pattern of fabrication in the Stalinist show trials had significant antecedents in tsarist Russia, especially in the famous investigation of the Decembrist uprising in 1825. He also shows that a close reading of the fabricated documents themselves can reveal a great deal about the actual nature of the investigative process and even the mentality of the investigators. The "reliability" of documents in Soviet archives is thus more than a function of their veracity, although the tasks of interpretation in these circumstances place a high burden on the skills and probity of the researcher.

In all, the contributions in this section suggest that the most interesting problems of historical and social documentation embedded in archival practices transcend national and geographic distinctions, especially those that engage archives and documentation with issues of social memory and political culture. Comparative analysis not only reveals commonalities in the ways knowledge is constructed under very different political, social, and cultural regimes, but also helps clarify what familiarity, tradition, and "common practice" often tend to conceal.

Revolution in the Archives of Memory

The Founding of the National Diet Library
in Occupied Japan

Leslie Pincus

At the welcome dinner held in Tokyo in December 1948 for the distinguished visitors from the U.S. Library Mission, Hani Gorô, recently elected Diet member and chair of a newly established National Diet Library Steering Committee, raised his glass in greeting: "To guarantee that our National Diet Library will serve as the foundation for the establishment of democracy in Japan," he vowed, "I only ask that I be allowed to have my bones buried beneath its foundation stones."[1] Charles H. Brown, head librarian at the University of Illinois and president of the National Library Association, responded in kind: "Mr. Hani, allow me to say just this: Please make room for me, because I also wish to lay my body beneath the cornerstone of the National Diet Library."[2]

While these pledges may have been purely metaphorical, they convey the shared passion of representatives of former enemy countries for the project at hand. But metaphors aside, the truth may be that someone's bones are, in fact, buried beneath the cornerstone of the original National Diet Library (NDL). They would belong to another passionate founder of the NDL, Nakai Masakazu, the library's first deputy director and guiding light during its inaugural four years. At least this is what Hani suggests in the closing lines of a profoundly moving eulogy to Nakai in 1952. It is not unheard of in Japan to bury a portion of a person's remains at a sacred site, and perhaps even to expect that the spirit of the deceased will linger a while to watch over the living.

Producing Memory in Post-Defeat Japan

Just three years before his appointment to the National Diet Library, Nakai had greeted Japan's defeat in the Pacific war as the head of a small town library in eastern Hiroshima prefecture; that unremarkable site would soon become the general headquarters for a local culture movement with radical democratic aspirations. Within a year of the defeat, the movement had succeeded in bringing together intellectuals, farmers, and laborers, both men and women, in multiple locations throughout eastern Hiroshima prefecture, in an unprecedented social experiment to understand their histories and restructure their consciousness along with their social existence. In the summer of 1946, as part of this movement, Nakai helped to organize a people's university with classes held in at least twenty towns and villages across the prefecture. Nakai used the English term *escalator system* to describe the logistics in a still war-torn Japan that enabled over forty lecturers (drawn both from the local Workers Culture Association and from the major metropolitan universities), accompanied by local youth, to tramp from village to village, their rucksacks filled with rice; their lectures and seminars dealt with anything from Marxism and rural economic crisis to mass culture and avant-garde art.

In the summer of 1947, Hani Gorô took advantage of an invitation to lecture at this *Khaki daigaku* (summer-term university) to persuade his colleague to come to Tokyo and serve as the first director of a new National Diet Library. Nakai accepted Hani's request and spent the four years that remained to him before an untimely death in a struggle to build a mass-democratic, cultural institution. The connection between the Hiroshima Culture Movement and the new Diet Library is most obviously suggested by the trajectory of a single individual whose work linked these as well as other enterprises: during the volatile decades of Japan's mid-twentieth century, Nakai's diverse aptitudes and passions took him from academic philosophy to experimental filmmaking, from Popular Front activism to political imprisonment, and from local organizing to a new cultural bureaucracy. But here I would like to reach beyond the commonsense connections so easily made among the varied engagements of a single individual by recourse to the unity of a human life. In the spirit of this volume on the institutions of social memory, let me suggest an affinity between the immediate postsurrender Hiroshima Culture Movement and the establishment of the National Diet Library by way of collective memory, both its production and its erasure. This connection will only become explicit at the end of a somewhat tortuous itinerary leading through the complexities of Occupation policy and the struggles of early postwar politics. Ultimately, however, I hope to demonstrate that both enterprises partook in a more encompassing project in early postwar Japan to produce collective memory in different registers and with different ideological valences.

Japan's defeat in the Second World War gave rise to multiple exigencies to recall the recent past for various and, sometimes conflicting, reasons: to express the trauma of war; to give meaning to loss (more often sustained than inflicted); to reveal (or obscure) the locus of guilt and responsibility for the war, or for Japan's defeat; to seek redemption; and perhaps most significantly, to produce a prehistory for a reimagined postwar future. In the discussion that follows I explore the beginnings and unfolding of some of these compulsions to invoke memory, to shape it, and to place it in intimate relation to documentary evidence of the past.

In the *kôza* (seminars) that formed the core of the Hiroshima Culture Movement, Nakai enjoined local residents of devastated towns and villages of eastern Hiroshima prefecture to "remember" wartime experience; he encouraged them to redecipher that experience in light of a much longer history, still present in consciousness as atavistic "structures of feeling." Taking the form of self-interrogation, such memory work was often the first step in a broadly liberal and leftist endeavor to create a social subject capable of producing and sustaining democratic political culture in the present. Those who

aspired to this social self-transformation, to a "revolution of consciousness," had to first engage in a critical operation directed at their own existing subjectivity for complicity with what some referred to as "emperor-system fascism." Whether it was the call for a "community of contrition" among self-critical intellectuals, or the conviction among revisionist leftist writers that they must first root out their own "internal 'emperor systems'" before turning a critical eye to society, the principal charge leveled against oneself, and by extension, against the entire nation, was a failure to attain modern subjectivity.[3] In his early talks to local Hiroshima audiences of farmers and workers, Nakai sought to convey in the most concrete and vivid terms how their subjectivity was structurally implicated in the violence of the wartime state and how the specificity of their everyday lives had found its grim expression in battlefield atrocities in Asia.[4] In graphic demonstration of these elusive relations, Nakai reinvoked the war, drawing for his purposes on the archives of local lore, war stories, literary legacies, and folk wisdom. Ultimately he hoped that the cultivation of self-aware individuals would lend itself to the creation of a new social space—a public sphere of sorts where free exchange of ideas and thoughtful mediation of differences would lead to new social solidarities.

While Hiroshima farmers and laborers confronted war memory in a project of self-critique and self-determination, the Occupation administration (often referred to as SCAP, Supreme Command for the Allied Powers) was producing its own public performances of memory and history through a different set of apparatuses. In December 1945, SCAP initiated a number of war-guilt campaigns through the media, primarily the press and radio, to reveal through "direct presentation to the Japanese people . . . the true history of the war, with precise and convincing indictment of the individuals and groups responsible for the war and the defeat."[5] In radio programming for war guilt, the Civil Information and Education (CIE) Section set itself a threefold task: to present a history of the Pacific war, to disclose war atrocities, and to cover war crimes trials. Arguably, the centerpiece of this educational campaign was a radio program called *Now It Can Be Told*, CIE's version of war history presented in the melodramatic style of the American *March of Time* series[6] and touted as the "first radio version of the true account of Japan's aggression, atrocities and defeat to be heard in Japan."[7]

The series premiere was timed to coincide with both the anniversary of the attack on Pearl Harbor and the naming of class A war criminals, a small number of whom would be tried in the prolonged "showcase" Tokyo Tribunal. The tribunal, too, was mobilized for war-guilt education, its voluminous transcripts selectively condensed for daily fifteen-minute radio programs on BCJ (Broadcasting Company of Japan). SCAP officials may have disagreed behind the scenes on specific issues of war responsibility and historical causality, but the explicit message of CIE programming was unambiguous: guilt lay primarily with a small clique of military men (and their civilian supporters) who "engaged in a common plan or conspiracy" to secure domination of Asia and, to this end, waged "wars of aggression."[8] Ordinary Japanese people—however tainted with responsibility for the war by virtue of culture and race—were largely represented as victims of a massive campaign of deception by the wartime regime. Such a view was convenient for a number of different constituencies, including wartime elites who had managed to evade the purges and trials, for Emperor Hirohito, in the midst of a transfiguration as popular savior and apostle of peace, and for SCAP and the U.S. government, who required the services of existing political and economic Japanese elites for successive postwar tasks of pacification, reform, reconstruction, and rearmament. SCAP's particular rendering of war guilt, which prevailed through much of Japan's long postwar era, ultimately undermined the early efforts of Nakai and others to conduct a collective interrogation of Japan's modern history and to understand why the wartime regime had been able to capture the hearts and minds of the Japanese people.

If SCAP officials strove to establish both specific guilts and the comprehensive culpability of the Japanese past, they also labored intensively to confiscate textual traces of that past in a large-scale program of media guidance, surveillance, and censorship. The story of how, in the first weeks and months of the Occupation, plans for relatively lenient control of information yielded to a program of maximum surveillance has been told elsewhere.[9] For our purposes, let us note that an elaborate censorship apparatus located in General Douglas MacArthur's General Headquarters (GHQ) operated from September 1945 to September 1949 (and beyond in modified form) as the concrete implementation of what one scholar describes as an "obsession with the reorientation of the Japanese mentality."[10] The censorship operation entailed an elaborate list of forbidden topics, subject to revision; but the one that remained constant, John Dower tells us, was a prohibition of any public acknowledgment that censorship (very undemocratic in itself) existed.[11] Ironically, the beginnings of this veiled regime coincided uncomfortably

with MacArthur's "civil liberties directive" abrogating Japan's repressive Peace Preservation Law and restoring freedoms of assembly and speech. In this "censored democracy," occupiers as well as occupied were no doubt aware of the contradictions between the aims of democratic reform and the requirements of surveillance. As just one example of SCAP's circumspection, nearly the entire Kabuki repertoire, judged offensive for its "feudalistic" content, became one of the more high profile casualties of censorship. In the words of one representative from the Press, Pictorial, and Broadcasting Division, "'nearly any selection' of a Kabuki play contains elements that make the minds of the audience 'receptive to the ideals of the old order.'"[12] Yet it was the cultural legacy of the "old order" preserved in this same repertoire that provided Nakai with his texts for a critical study of "the past in the present" in Hiroshima's "people's university." Without the documentary and imaginative sources of that past at hand, how could people reinterpret their own histories, personal as well as collective? How were they to reimagine the relation between past and present?

In March 1946, SCAP issued its first orders for withdrawal of prewar and wartime publications deemed nationalistic and militaristic from bookdealers, warehouses, and bookshops.[13] Though the evidence is hard to come by, the existence of indexes of confiscated books and directives implemented through the Ministry of Education attests to the existence of a fairly systematic policy.[14] Anecdotal evidence still circulates in eastern Hiroshima prefecture of book seizures from the local library by the Australian military units sent to Hiroshima in lieu of Americans.[15] SCAP's rigorous censorship regime persisted through 1949 and thus overlapped with the planning for, and inception of, the National Diet Library. I cannot help but wonder whether confiscation lists might have helped to shape initial Diet Library collections and catalogs—this despite the founders' comprehensively inclusive vision of the National Diet Library. Moving into less evidentiary territory, perhaps we need to ask, if only rhetorically, whether collective memory (or its script) is housed in archives and libraries. As we shall see, Nakai Masakazu would creatively engage this question once he embarked on what he called "the way of the library."

The Political Origins of the National Diet Library

The possibility of a new National Diet Library seems to have first emerged in the context of political reform during the early Occupation period. Both presurrender planning and postsurrender directives included strongly worded recommendations to strengthen the position of the national representative assembly. In February 1946, SCAP—disturbed by the absence of reformist intent in the modest constitutional revision proposed by Japanese statesmen—gave its Government Section a mandate to draft (in little more than a week) a constitution that would, among other things, replace an "inviolate and sacred" emperor with a "symbolic" one and place sovereignty in the hands of the people. Over the objections of Japan's sitting government, an American-authored Constitution promulgated in March 1946 substituted the supremacy of a popularly elected Diet for imperial sovereignty in an article that read, "[T]he Diet shall be the highest organ of state power and shall be the sole lawmaking organ of the State."[16]

Despite a new postwar Constitution and Japan's first general election under universal suffrage in April 1946, in the view of SCAP officials, the Diet still appeared to be unable or unwilling to assert its democratic mandate against a "feudalistic bureaucracy which dominates the national government."[17] As part of a concentrated effort to create a more independent and powerful Diet—one not beholden to this "feudalistic bureaucracy" (left largely intact, it should be noted, by the Occupation)[18]—Justin Williams, chief of the Government Section Legislative Branch, submitted a series of recommendations in September 1946 including, among other things, the establishment of a Diet Library and legislative reference services.[19]

This suggestion was taken up almost immediately by newly established National Diet Library Standing Committees in the two houses of the Diet, the members of which clearly took their job extremely seriously.[20] Interestingly, it was the head of NDL Committee in the House of Councilors (the successor of the reactionary House of Peers), newly elected to the Diet, who proved to be the most progressive legislative advocate of the Diet and the most committed to its "revolutionary" role in a democratizing Japan. This was Hani Gorô, a Marxist historian who had welcomed Japan's defeat and surrender little more than a year earlier from behind prison walls, convicted, like Nakai, of "thought crimes." Over the next year or more, he worked continuously on plans for the National Diet Library, devoting his time and energy to discussions, negotiations, and political machinations with Diet members, with Justin Williams and others from SCAP's Government Section, and with the representatives of a Library Mission sent from the United States—all the while entertaining aspirations that seem,

in retrospect, both utopian and disappointingly modest. For Hani, the National Diet Library would serve as the instrument by which "the tyranny over knowledge, on which all tyranny is based," is wrested from the hands of the bureaucracy and monopoly capital. It was to be both a "citadel of popular sovereignty" and the means of realizing a "peaceful revolution."[21]

In the *Report of the United States Library Mission to Advise on the Establishment of the National Diet Library of Japan,* submitted to General MacArthur in February 1948, the authors professed that their own role in the establishment of the NDL had "been merely catalytic—[the Mission] has only assisted in the formulation of ideas and purposes which existed before its arrival in Japan. That it could perform its task with satisfaction and rapidity was due in the first place to the enthusiasm and energy of the Library Committees; to the effective sympathy of the principal officers of the Diet; to the support of many unofficial bodies and persons. But above all, the successful conclusion of the Mission's work was due to the excellent teamwork between the Diet Committees and the officials of the Japanese Government and of GHQ, SCAP."[22] While the Occupation had a proven record of masking its own authoritative (and authoritarian) interventions by overstating Japanese initiative, the testimony of some of the Japanese participants in the founding of the National Diet Library would seem to corroborate the truth of the *Report,* at least in what concerns their own "enthusiasm and energy" during the planning stages. On the other hand, early deliberations on the National Diet Library were not nearly as harmonious as the U.S. library ambassadors purported; nor was the role of the Library Mission merely a supportive one.

In their report, the chairman of the U.S. Library Mission, Verner W. Clapp (associate director of the Library of Congress), and his colleague, Charles H. Brown (director of the University of Illinois Libraries and president of the American Library Association), listed their priorities regarding those whom the NDL should serve: "[T]he Library Mission has considered, first, the needs of the Diet members themselves; next, the needs of the National Government in all its branches; and, throughout, the service of the nation as a whole." On the question of the political significance of this new public institution, the ambassadors were in general agreement with the most passionate advocates among their Japanese colleagues: a Diet library at the head of a new national library system, they wrote, is "not only an essential instrument for efficient employment of national informational resources, but also a potent engine of democracy. Its effect is to make available to all what would otherwise be reserved to the few; to put the possessions of the nation genuinely at the service of all its citizens."[23]

The authors began the *Report* with a brief statement on the inadequacy of existing institutions serving the research needs of the Diet: "Both Houses of the National Diet of Japan have had their separate libraries since 1890. But because the Diet, prior to 1946, had no final responsibilities, its requirements for exact and extensive information were correspondingly small. . . . The Diet libraries never developed either the collections or the services which might have made them vital adjuncts of genuinely responsible legislative activity."[24] Though Japanese supporters of the new National Diet Library were in full agreement with the report on the inadequacy of existing library facilities, they were apt to reverse cause and effect in their own historical assessment: it was precisely because the executive branch controlled access to crucial documentary information that the legislature was rendered powerless. With this assessment, progressives on the Japanese side underscored the conflict and contention that marked the prewar political process as well as the mechanisms by which informed deliberation and dissent had been purposefully restricted and ultimately suppressed. As Hani explained it, until Japan's defeat, the "emperor-system bureaucracy," as the executive branch of government, had seized monopoly control over all political documents on a principle of "executive secrecy that relied on infinitely expanding interpretations of what constituted classified information."[25] Deprived of access to information, the people and the elected representatives of the pre-1945 Diet had become increasingly disempowered. "The true revolutionary significance of the NDL," Hani explained, lay in the fact that the Diet "as the legislative organ of popular sovereignty would now exert control over any and all political documents relevant to the legislative function."[26] Hani and other like-minded legislators argued for a library collection that would include not simply books, but all official materials, published and unpublished ("even memos written in pencil"), to enable Diet members to fulfill their legislative mission thoroughly and responsibly.[27] They were particularly emphatic about including an unprecedented provision in the National Diet Library Law that would bring reference sections and libraries in every ministry and administrative unit of the government under the full authority of the National Diet Library as "branch libraries."[28]

In practiced Occupation style, Verner Clapp drafted the new National Diet Library Law (February 1948) largely on his own. In the spirit of adding their own stamp to the American-authored document, Japanese legislators argued for a preamble to the new law, composed by Hani Gorô. In the 1920s, as a visiting scholar in Freiburg, Hani had been deeply impressed by the words (originally from the book of John in the New Testament) he had seen engraved on the lintel of a university building: "Wahrheit wird Man frei machen."[29] These same words would appear in both English and Japanese versions of the preamble: "The National Diet Library is hereby established as a result of the firm conviction that truth makes us free and with the object of contributing to international peace and the democratization of Japan as promised in our Constitution."[30] Recent history had persuaded Hani that truth could be discovered and preserved in print; but, as Hani's son hastened to add in a 1995 interview, it was a firmly held conviction on the part of both his father and Nakai that "books did not exist in their own domain removed from life in the real world; rather, they had the power to profoundly move people and lead them to momentous crossroads."[31]

Though minor differences of opinion or perspective may have separated Japanese legislators on the NDL Standing Committees from the U.S. library ambassadors, the most bitter point of contention in plans for the NDL predated the arrival of the Library Mission. It concerned the choice of inaugural director—a choice deeply embroiled in contemporary politics, in interpretations of the recent past, and in imagined political futures. The disagreement, at first glance simply a partisan battle between newly elected progressives and incumbent conservatives, proved to be considerably more complex. Hani's multipartisan committee (with former aristocrats and conservatives among its membership) in the House of Councilors decided unanimously in favor of Nakai Masakazu, an individual they deemed sufficiently energetic, talented, and visionary to create this new political-intellectual institution.[32] Their counterpart committee in the newly empowered and presumably more democratic House of Representatives responded to Nakai's nomination with a resounding vote of "no confidence." Their reasoning: "During the war, Nakai Masakazu was arrested under the provisions of the Peace Preservation Law, indicted, and thrown in prison, just like the communists." Their conclusion: "We are absolutely against appointing that kind of person as NDL Director."[33] If Hani's memory of the wording of the opposing opinion is to be trusted, the committee sabotaged the nominee with the logic of analogy and the assurance that their American occupiers would concur with their antileftist stance.

What proved to be an irresolvable deadlock over the

question of the directorship seems to have initiated the Government Section's invitation of an American Library Mission in the first place. Grateful for Occupation intervention against entrenched conservatism, Hani was convinced that the expert advisors from the Library Mission, Clapp and Brown, would weigh in Nakai's favor. As it turned out, however, SCAP and the Library Mission counseled compromise, ending in an arrangement in which a senior politician and experienced bureaucrat, Kanamori Tokujirô, would occupy the director's position and Nakai would be named deputy director. When the lower house Steering Committee members argued against Nakai by demanding that an individual of "high character . . . without intellectual bias" occupy the position, they betrayed deep-seated animosities against the left in the guise of a liberal humanist appeal to ethical cultivation and impartiality. The Library Mission, wittingly or not, reinforced this bias in the new National Diet Library Law. Under the "Administration" section, the qualifications for chief librarian included "freedom from political bias" along with "integrity and high intelligence," "administrative ability and a great capacity for leadership." The director was explicitly enjoined to "abstain completely from all partisan activities."[34]

The resemblance between the translated language in the National Library Law and the words of conservative legislators is perhaps only slightly more than coincidental. But the final accord between the occupiers and Japan's established political elite was far from fortuitous, since anticommunism was something close to an obsession on both sides of the Pacific.[35] Japan's antileftist campaigns, beginning with the appearance of the first socialists at the turn of the century, became the overriding task of the "Special Higher Police" during the interwar period. As John Dower has so effectively demonstrated, fears of Communist infiltration from without, from below, and even from above became the stuff of official nightmares during wartime.[36] On the American side, despite SCAP's early rehabilitation of political prisoners of Japan's wartime state, ample evidence suggests that anticommunism pervaded GHQ long before an explicit shift in Occupation policy in 1949 marking the inception of a cold war world—a shift commonly referred to as the "Reverse Course."[37] There is no little irony in the fact that Japan's defeat and an occupation in the name of democracy failed to redeem those few individuals who had dared to oppose the Japanese wartime state. Official political memory in Japan, it seems, has been largely impervious to the ideological reversals and critical reassessments of the past that began with Japan's surrender.

An Apparatus for Collective Memory

According to Hani Gorô, once the NDL actually opened its doors in June 1948, Kanamori receded into the background of an "honorary" directorship while Nakai assumed the substantive tasks of institution building. Close observers of Nakai's career maintain that he condensed a lifetime's worth of work in the brief four years of his tenure at the Diet Library—planning and implementing legislative research and evaluation sections; establishing a branch library system; assembling journal article indexes and a national bibliography of books and journals; producing extensive newspaper clipping collections and a printed catalog card system. In her 1995 interview with Hani's son, Ishii Noriko (who made her own career in one of Japan's largest bibliographic services) pointed out the prescience of Nakai's conception of the library: "Nakai laid the foundation for our own contemporary information systems with a rapid-fire assembly of the elements of a 'library domain' in the form of an extensive information network."[38]

But perhaps most intriguing of all is a series of essays Nakai published during this final stage of his peripatetic career. Here social memory and history reemerge, but in a different discursive register from the Hiroshima Culture Movement, now combining a mass-based humanism with high technological modernism. The essays project a vision of the library as a vast repository for the accumulated past of humankind, as a memory machine for emergent forms of collective organization, and as a site for new, democratic forms of deliberative practice.

In a 1948 essay on the new National Diet Library, Nakai begins with a statement of faith: "Even amidst these hollowed out ruins of war, culture has never once ceased in it development"—a faith in human progress that prevailed despite the war and its depredations.[39] The sheer accumulation of books in the enclosed space of the library testified eloquently to "the discovery of language"—of speech and writing—that made books imaginable and to the power of words to "substitute language for blood, discursive resolution for violence."[40] If the enclosed space of the library housed a documentary record of human history, it also offered the means for the redemption of past wrongs. Nakai's angel of history may have soared exultantly on the winds of progress, but even an angel could have its lapses and history could go awry: "If in our 5,000 years of history, transgressions have been committed; if the history of our own twentieth century has fallen into error, it is only the culture of the book, with its powerful demonstration of thousands of years of human will and aspiration, that offers the key to healing the wounds of that history."[41] Nakai envisioned the library not only as a repository for a richly varied cultural legacy, but also as a space in which to assuage the pain of history's iniquities and to resolve the historical problems inherited from the past. The redemption of history, once practiced at the local level in relation to the specific histories of farmers and laborers, assumed universal proportions in the National Diet Library.

Nakai may have imagined the library as a cloistered world of print separated from an ethically ambiguous field of history; but he also projected a near future in which the walls of the library would be dismantled: "The concept of 'a library without a reading room' is not a paradox; simply by establishing a system of indexing, catalog cards, and a communication network, we will have a library of vastly different proportions that will offer new kinds of accessibility and service. Even now as speak, the library is undergoing a metamorphosis into its future form—from a repository of books to an immense organization redefined as an information center."[42] New forms of media, whether photographic or electronic, were transforming the meaning of the library: "As print publications are absorbed into microfilm, microfiche, and telephone networks, the concept of the library as a distinct space is being destroyed."[43] From "sacred repository" to "department store" to "information network"—the historical transformation of the library had powerful social implications. Clearly Nakai's own appreciation of recent developments in information media had everything to do with his conviction that the redefinition of the library from *bashô*/place to *hataraki*/function promised universal access to knowledge as well as the dissemination of intellectual culture to the masses (*taishû*).[44]

In the midst of this historical transformation, the concept of "library as memory" was not just metaphorical: In the early 1930s, in the wake of a second industrial revolution, Nakai had detected a shift in cultural formations—a shift in which individual time and private memory were yielding to collective history and documentation, where mechanized technologies were replacing human perception. Now, in the late 1940s, Japan, he claimed, was swept up in the tide of a world history moving from the individualist culture of an early capitalist formation to new collective forms of organization generated by advanced capitalism: "The individual memory function is in the process of transforming into the library index and classification functions. Just as in former times the bard recited from memory, now the library is expected to fulfill an analogous function; in other words, the library must perform an extensive, accurate, and powerful memory operation on a national scale." Replacing the mental faculties of a single individual, the library—reimagined as "precision machinery, glistening with machine oil and highly polished, functioning in smooth and total silence"—was to serve as an immense memory apparatus. Within this apparatus, the subject who remembers is no longer the individual, but "the masses" (*taishû*) or "the collective" (*shûdan*).[45]

Ultimately, Nakai envisioned the library as a site for the development of new kinds of collective practice. If the organ of collective memory is a system of "signs indexing a comprehensive assemblage of documents" in the form of a library catalog, then the organ of collective praxis is the committee, a group that acts through deliberation and representation. Judging only from Nakai's postwar essays on the National Diet Library, it is all too easy to picture this "committee" as one unit in a bureaucratic apparatus, its members part of an expert elite commissioned by the state and underwritten by the nation; and, to a certain degree, such an impression would not be unwarranted. To be sure, during his tenure at the Diet Library, with organizational rationality as a priority, Nakai played a central role in building the foundation of the intellectual-administrative bureaucracy that the National Diet Library was to become. In the essays from those years, he not infrequently conflated the "group"—a term he had used in both the prewar years and post-defeat Hiroshima to refer to a concrete and specifically located social constituency—with the nation. Did he perhaps envision his own role as the guardian of Japan's "national memory"?[46]

Even as we acknowledge this shift in language and social subject in Nakai's last years at the National Diet Library, it is nevertheless instructive to speculate on the meaning of the "committee" in light of earlier writings. In 1936, Nakai published a two-part essay in *Sekai bunka* (World Culture)—a journal he and like-minded colleagues created to introduce European Popular Front culture and politics to a regional, and largely intellectual, audience—titled "Iinkai no ronri" (The Logic of Committee). Confronted in the 1930s with the precipitous rise of both finance capitalism and an intensifying police state, Nakai attempted to represent the conditions, both historical and contemporary, for the emergence of a participatory social democracy. Cleaving closely to both the movement of Western civilization and a Marxist methodology, "The Logic of Committee" outlines a dialectical history of the *logos,* tracing the interwoven development of social formations and epistemology. Each successive epistemology is embedded in a material regime of representation: First the "spoken logic" of classical rhetoric, followed by the "written logic" of the medieval *vita contemplativa,* and more recently, the "printed logic" of a modern world moved by literate publics and centered on *technê.* Finally, the logic of *technê,* with its conceptual power to bend nature in the direction of human purpose, reaches completion as it becomes incorporated into the "logic of production."[47] In good dialectical fashion, Nakai explains how "in the crisis that announces the collapse of a given formation, each of these logics becomes itself a moment of mediation, transforming into something other and yet preserving something of itself."[48] Now, in Nakai's own 1930s, all of these historically generated representational modes of logic—debate, contemplation, *technê,* practice, production—have become moments in the construction of a new social-epistemological mode: *the logic of committee.*

In this present stage, however, the movement of the dialectic itself has deflected the logic of committee: As the "production formation" rises to dominance, the logic of *technê* is distorted, becoming alienated from its original human purpose. Within this distorted formation, an intensifying movement toward division of labor and commodification effectively destroys the distinctive character of the committee as a *critical* and *cooperative* entity. Human beings (i.e., the masses) become estranged from their own sense of purpose, and, ultimately, from themselves as human beings. Nevertheless, despite this bleak view of his own historical moment and even within the highly repressive milieu of the mid-1930s in Japan, Nakai maintained a profound faith in the power of the human faculty of self-expression. Heir to a dialectical history of logic, the masses are endowed with the capacity to represent themselves and change the course of history. Moved by an overwhelming sense of alienation, they discover their own power as they seek to represent the very lack that impoverishes their lives. Inaugurated by this negative mediation, the committee becomes the possession of the masses as they restore its original social logic, initiating a process that itself becomes the "propeller of history": beginning with the proposal, the committee moves to debate and resolution; from resolution, to plans and their execution; then to the crucial phase of critique; and finally to renewed debate and a second-order resolution. In the reiteration of this process through a third, fourth, and even fifth order, the logic of committee works to transform both subject and object in a back-and-forth movement between proposal (trial) and error—a movement that gradually brings logic closer to conditions on

the "ground" of history. In this way, the committee serves as the organ of praxis for the masses, its logic is the mechanism by which a progressive history is given shape.[49] Though Nakai only invoked the committee in passing in the essays written during his tenure at the Diet Library, his densely elaborated "Logic of Committee" essay—however cursory my own summary here—invests this emergent social-epistemological formation with a complex history and utopian possibility as a mechanism for deliberation and representation in a mass democracy. It is worth recalling, too, that it was this 1936 essay that originally inspired Hani Gorô to nominate Nakai as founding director of the National Diet Library.

Judging from early Diet Library records as well as Nakai's own essays, the notion of the library as site for *mass collective deliberation* remained largely undeveloped, in practice as well as in theory. Nevertheless, the record does show that in the first four years of the National Diet Library Nakai both initiated and chaired numerous committees that addressed organizational as well as substantive issues—committees for general Diet Library planning and relations with an expanding nationwide network of libraries, for example, and others for the improvement of reader services and exhibitions of documents relating to the new Constitution and human rights. In profound agreement with Hani's inaugural vision for the National Diet Library, Nakai also devoted a great deal of energy to developing an infrastructure for independent legislative research.[50] If, however, there was popular participation in early Diet Library deliberations, or if, in fact, people's committees did operate under the auspices or with the support of the Diet Library, I have not yet been able to uncover any historical tracks.

During his tenure at the National Diet Library, Nakai was clearly working against powerful forces of opposition—opposition that began with his nomination and extended beyond an early death into what might be called his historical legacy. Even the compromise decision to name Nakai as deputy director was greeted with a demand from the National Diet Library Standing Committee in the lower house that his wartime record be brought forward. The public prosecutor's office in Kyoto, where Nakai had originally been arrested and interrogated as an offender of the Peace Preservation Law in the late 1930s, was asked to provide documents pertaining to "Nakai's actions and ideological tendencies . . . among other things" to the Standing Committee.[51] In other words, the legislative organ of Japan's new postwar democracy availed itself of evidence produced by the wartime "thought police" with the objective of sabotaging Nakai's appointment. One irony among many in Japan's postwar polity, the archives of a publicly discredited organ of Japan's wartime state remained very much a part of collective memory as well as the official record. In 1947, SCAP's Government Section still possessed the reformist will to counter this strategy, but antagonism to Nakai's presence at the Diet Library persisted. Demands from legislators and bureaucrats for his resignation multiplied; flyers reading "Get the 'red' out of the Diet Library" were regularly tacked up on walls in and around the Diet Library building; this along with more subtle forms of intimidation dogged Nakai's every step and restricted his powers.[52] During these early postwar years, perhaps even more than in the mid-1930s, Nakai relied upon metaphor and abstraction to convey his views in published writings. In fact, the crowning irony of the early postwar for Nakai and others with similar intellectual genealogies may be that they actually enjoyed more freedom of expression before the war than after. Ultimately, the same powerful undercurrents of repression that made self-restraint prudent are very likely responsible for the dearth of Diet Library documents attesting to Nakai's activities during his tenure as deputy director.[53]

Did Nakai succeed in nurturing new forms of democratic collective practice during his four years at the Diet Library? Was he able to begin his self-appointed task of creating a library that would serve as a vast memory apparatus for an independent citizenry? At least for the moment, such questions must go unanswered, subject as they are to the political constraints of both the historical past and that past as it has been documented and remembered. Clearly there are widely recognized cases where the Diet Library provided documents that aided both popular and legislative opposition to authoritarian politics. Perhaps the most notable instance was the defeat of conservative prime minister Yoshida Shigeru's notorious proposal for a "prevention of destructive activities law" designed to repress opposition movements and activists.[54] Since then, countless citizens have no doubt culled documentary evidence from the Diet Library in support of a wide range of public issues and interests. If, however, the library does serve as a collective memory apparatus as Nakai once imagined (or as a repository of documentary traces, as I would be more apt to put it), it is largely an inert one that needs to be activated by the agency of collective will and action. In Japan's postwar society—dominated by a paternalistic, if not always authoritarian, bureaucracy in close cooperation with a powerful economic sector, where the reach of social power extends deep into everyday life and popular memory—the formation of an independent, collective agency has proven to be a daunting task. In 1947, still in Hiroshima, Nakai could not but acknowledge that reemerging forces of reaction from both inside and outside the ranks of the local culture movement were proving to be an insurmountable obstacle to social transformation in the countryside. Encouraged by the invitation from Hani Gorô, he resolved to take his struggle from the hinterlands of Hiroshima to the center of power in Tokyo: "Cultural enlightenment by itself cannot solve the problem," he wrote. "Politics, power itself, must become an agent of enlightenment. We have to be prepared for a long struggle—ten, even twenty years of sustained confrontation with the central institutions of power, the Diet and the bureaucracy—if we are to institute and organize this vast project of Enlightenment."[55] Ultimately, that struggle was curtailed, if not crushed, by the very bureaucratic apparatus that Nakai himself helped to build.

NOTES

I owe a debt of gratitude to the participants in the Sawyer Seminar "Archives, Documentation, and the Institutions of Social Memory" for creating an intellectual space in which this essay could come into being. Unless otherwise indicated, the translations are mine.

1. Hani Gorô, *Toshokan no ronri* (Tokyo: Isetan Shoten, 1981), 79.

2. Nakai Masakazu, "Kokuritsu toshokan ni tsuite," *Tôkyô shimbun* (September 24, 1948).

3. J. Victor Koschmann, *Revolution and Subjectivity in Postwar Japan* (Chicago: University of Chicago Press, 1996), 64–66.

4. See my essay "'Salon for the Soul': Nakai Masakazu and the Hiroshima Culture Movement," in *positions: east asia cultures critique* 10 (spring 2002): 173–94, for a detailed discussion of Nakai's postdefeat lectures.

5. Bradford Smith, information director of SCAP's Civil Information and Education (CIE) Section, quoted in Marlene J. Mayo, "The War of Words Continues: American Radio Guidance in Occupied Japan," in *The Occupation of Japan: Arts and Culture*, ed. Thomas W. Burkman, (Norfolk, Va.: General Douglas MacArthur Foundation, 1988), 57–58.

6. Mayo, "The War of Words Continues," 58.

7. Marlene J. Mayo, "Civil Censorship and Media Control in Early Occupied Japan," in *Americans as Proconsuls: United States Military Government in Germany and Japan, 1944–1952*, ed. Robert Wolfe (Carbondale: Southern Illinois University Press, 1984), 307.

8. This was the language of the indictment brought against the defendants at the Tokyo Trial. Quoted in John Dower, *Embracing Defeat: Japan in the Wake of World War II* (New York: W. W. Norton, 1999), 456.

9. Mayo, "Civil Censorship and Media Control," 282. Mayo describes information control policies under the Occupation as "an integrated and comprehensive program aimed at

making changes in Japanese ideologies and attitudes of mind. The occupiers were to see to it that Japan's feudal mentality and chauvinism, its belief in divine mission and its 'extensive racial consciousness' were transformed into wholesome, democratic and peace-loving attitudes" (282).

10. Ibid., 288; see also Dower, *Embracing Defeat*, 406–7.

11. Dower, *Embracing Defeat*, 407.

12. Quoted in Mayo, "Civil Censorship and Media Control," 310–11.

13. Ibid., 310.

14. This information emerged from initial conversations with the Asia librarian at the University of Chicago, Okuizumi Eizaburô, who has documented indexes with titles such as *Senryô-gun kara boshû o mezerareta tosho* and *Senryô-gun sesshu tosho mokuroku*. See his "A Chronological Account of the U.S. Censorship and Information Policy to Japan During the Allied Occupation, 1945–1952," *Meisei daigaku sengô kyôiku-shi kenkyû kiyô* 14 (June 30, 2000): 129–72.

15. One local scholar in Onomichi alludes to the existence of a list of several hundreds of book titles that Nakai presumably "sequestered" sometime in 1946 from the Onomichi City Library and relocated for safekeeping.

16. Quoted in Hans H. Baerwald, "Early SCAP Policy and the Rehabilitation of the Diet," in *Democratising Japan*, ed. Robert Ward and Sakamoto Yoshikazu (Honolulu: University of Hawaii Press, 1987), 137.

17. Baerwald ("Early SCAP Policy," 138) quotes this phrase from a memorandum Justin Williams of SCAP's Government Section sent to his superiors, General Whitney and Colonel Kades.

18. Under guidance from Washington planners, SCAP had preserved most of Japan's prewar and wartime bureaucracy as a consequence of the immediate postsurrender decision to conduct an "indirect occupation" in Japan through existing government structures.

19. Baerwald, "Early SCAP Policy," 139.

20. These new standing committees were intended to overcome the pre-1945 subordinate status of Diet committees that had been bound in relationship of one-to-one correspondence with the various ministries. Designed to cover all major fields of legislative activity, the new committee structure was part of a larger reform of the Diet in September 1947 that emulated the 1946 U.S. Legislative Reorganization Act. Ibid., 142.

21. Hani Gorô, *Toshokan no ronri*, 162–63; quoted in "'Shinri ga warera o jiyû ni suru'—Sengo toshokan no rinen to Hani Gorô-Nakai Masakazu—Hani Susumu-shi to kataru," Ishii Noriko and Hirakawa Chihiro, interviewers, in *Toshokan zasshi* 89, no. 8 (August 1995), 580.

22. Kokuritsu kokkai toshokan, ed., *Kokuritsu kokkai toshokan jûnen-shi, shiryô-hen* (Tokyo: Kokuritsu Toshokan, 1980), 200–201. (The original English-language report is included in this compilation of documents on the founding of the National Diet Library.)

23. Ibid., 201–2.

24. Ibid., 198.

25. Hani, *Toshokan no ronri*, 163.

26. Ibid., 160–61.

27. Ishii and Hirakawa, "Sengo toshokan no rinen," 577.

28. Hani, *Toshokan no ronri*, 167. Hani tells a fascinating story about the document collection in the Tokyo Research Division of the semigovernmental South Manchurian Railroad Company (Mantetsu). Despite (or because of) its vanguard status in Japan's colonial enterprise in north China during the 1930s and early 1940s, Mantetsu became a clearinghouse for the most advanced research on political economy in China and elsewhere. When Justin Williams brought it to Hani's attention that the Ministry of the Treasury was on the verge of procuring the entire collection (probably sometime soon after the promulgation of the National Diet Library Law in 1948), Hani proceeded to call the minister before a joint panel of the two NDL Standing Committees, at which he was "persuaded" that the NDL should house the Mantetsu Research Division collection (170).

29. Ibid., 38.

30. *Kokuritsu kokkai toshokan jûnen-shi*, 227. The phrase was later carved in stone in front of the current National Diet Library building.

31. Ishii and Hirakawa, "Sengo toshokan no rinen," 577.

32. Apparently, one of Hani's most brilliant colleagues, Miki Kiyoshi (who died in prison at the end of the war), had deemed Nakai worthy of succeeding to his own position on the Philosophy Faculty at Kyoto Imperial University in the early 1930s, declaring that Nakai would someday surpass him intellectually. Moreover, Hani himself had read Nakai's 1936 essay, "The Logic of Committee," with great interest and concluded that "Nakai had no equal in his mastery of modern systems of collective deliberation" (*Toshokan no ronri*, 78).

33. Quoted in Hani, *Toshokan no ronri*, 32.

34. *Kokuritsu kokkai toshokan jûnen-shi*, 208.

35. Hani recalls that toward the end of the struggle over Nakai's nomination, Justin Williams summoned him and proceeded to reason as follows: "We fully support what you are trying to do; but the problem is there's so much obstruction going on. Obviously, there's quite a bit of suspicion that you're a secret member of the Communist Party, and that's really got us blocked in. If you would just consider publishing a denunciation of the Communist Party, just this once . . . ." Hani responded to this ploy with shrewd irony: "Well, I'd be glad to write what you suggest; but you know, there's no justice in criticizing a party that's not in power. So how about this: Why not try letting us hand power over to the Communist Party? Once that happens, on the very next day, I promise you, I'll criticize the Communist Party left and right." After that, Hani adds, Williams never mentioned the idea again (Hani, *Toshokan no ronri*, 40–41).

36. These fears of Communist-inspired insurrection "from within" became more pronounced as the war situation worsened. In February 1945, Konoe Fumimaro, early champion of Japan's war of invasion in China and a "New Order" at home, advised the emperor to bring a speedy end, however compromising, to the war in hopes of staving off an imminent Communist revolution initiated from within the upper ranks of the military. See Dower, *Embracing Defeat*, 480–81.

37. During the Reverse Course, the Occupation administration drew closer to persisting concentrations of conservative power in Japan, abandoning the spirit of democratic social and political reform that characterized the early Occupation in favor of economic reconstruction and remilitarization.

38. Ishii and Hirakawa, "Sengo toshokan no rinen," 580–81.

39. Nakai Masakazu, "Kokuritsu kokkai toshokan ni tsuite," in *Nakai Masakazu zenshû* (hereafter *NMz*) (Tokyo: Bijutsu shuppan-sha, 1981), 4:209.

40. Nakai Masakazu, "Nijû seiki no itadaki ni okeru toshokan no imi," in *NMz*, 4:268–69.

41. Ibid.

42. Nakai ("Toshokan no mirai-zô," in *NMz*, 4:295).

43. Ibid.

44. Nakai, "Kikô e no chosen—'bashô' kara 'hataraki' e," in *NMz*, 4:274–77; for discussion of the social implications of the new "functional" library, see "Rekishi no nagare no naka no toshokan: kojin-teki na mono kara shûdan-teki na mono e," in *NMz*, 4:282–89.

45. Nakai, "Rekishi no nagare no naka no toshokan," 284–85.

46. At the same time, it is worth noting that Nakai was pre-scient in his equation of the nation (*kokumin*) with a "national public"—a concept that he wrested from the ruins of the "imperial subject" in the wake of Japan's defeat in the Pacific war.

47. Nakai, "Iinkai no ronri," in *NMz*, 1:46–108; see especially chapters 9, 10, and 11.

48. Ibid., 68.

49. Ibid., 103–8.

50. Inaba Masanari, "Nakai Masakazu no bunka kikô-ron: Kokuritsu kokkai toshokan," *Shisô no kagaku*, special issue, no. 9 (November 1974): 18–21.

51. Ibid., 11.

52. Ibid., 11–14.

53. Ibid., 17–18. Inaba quotes Sumitani Takeyoshi, who claims that even the official records of the Standing Committee for NDL Planning have largely disappeared, under the ministrations, he suggests, of the "opposition within the NDL."

54. Ishii and Hirakawa, "Sengo toshokan no rinen," 582.

55. Nakai, "Chihô bunka no mondai," in *NMz*, 4:184–85.

The New Masters of Memory

Libraries, Archives, and Museums in Postcommunist Bosnia-Herzegovina

Robert J. Donia

Institutions of social memory in Bosnia-Herzegovina have undergone dramatic changes in status, ownership, and management during the 1990s. Several institutions were physically damaged or destroyed during the siege of Sarajevo (1992–95) and required reconstitution and rebuilding on a large scale. But even before the war began, the triumph of nationalist political forces and the end of socialist rule had initiated far-reaching changes in the country's major institutions. Nationalist leaders reconstructed some long-standing institutions, allowed others to atrophy, and established new ones in support of their political and cultural objectives. Furthermore, in the aftermath of the Bosnian war, international influences increasingly affected the structure and role of collective memory in the country.

This essay focuses on five institutions of social memory in Bosnia and Herzegovina to illuminate the far-reaching changes that have taken place since the late 1980s. Of these, three institutions existed for several decades before 1990: the National and University Library, the Archive of Bosnia-Herzegovina, and the Regional Museum. One institution, the Bosniak Institute, was created in Zurich, Switzerland, but moved to Sarajevo only in 2000. The fifth institution, the International Criminal Tribunal for the Former Yugoslavia, is located in The Hague, the Netherlands, and was mandated in 1993. The changing role and ownership of cultural memory in Bosnia-Herzegovina is evident in the history of each of these five institutions.

An Overview

The oldest institutions of social memory in Bosnia-Herzegovina were founded by religious associations. These include several archives of the Franciscan Order, which has operated continuously in Bosnia since the 1340s; the holdings of several Serbian Orthodox monasteries; and the collections of the Gazi Husrefbeg Library in Sarajevo, an institution that dates from 1537. In the nineteenth century, national revivals in Croatia, Serbia, and Slovenia fostered the growth of new institutions, secular yet sectarian, devoted to recording the history of a single national group.[1] In Bosnia-Herzegovina, national consciousness developed later than elsewhere, and national cultural societies (Prosvjeta for Serbs; Napredak for Croats; Benevolencija for Jews; and Preporod and Gajret for Bosnian Muslims) were not founded until early in the twentieth century. These national societies in Bosnia-Herzegovina never attained the influence of their pioneering counterparts in neighboring South Slav lands. Still, their collections grew rapidly, and they became major repositories for books and manuscripts pertaining to their particular groups.

The first public institution of social memory in Bosnia was the Regional Museum (Landesmuseum or Zemaljski muzej), founded in 1888 under the sponsorship of the Habsburg administrators in Sarajevo who then governed Bosnia-Herzegovina.[2] In addition to artifacts, the museum housed a library and the records of the pre-1878

Ottoman regional government, so for some years it served as an archival repository and library as well as a museum. In 1913, the museum collections were moved about a mile west into a complex of four specially built neoclassic structures that were loosely modeled on museums elsewhere in the Habsburg monarchy. Behind this generous expenditure lay a political motive: the Habsburg occupiers wanted to highlight Bosnia's indigenous cultural heritage in its campaign to negate Serbian and Croatian nationalist influences from neighboring lands.

No other major public secular institutions of memory were established in Bosnia-Herzegovina until after World War II. In 1914, Habsburg officials approved the establishment of a regional archive to house its millions of documents, but the institution had not yet been established when war broke out and most such activities stopped.[3] The government of Royal Yugoslavia (1918–41) encouraged and supported institutions of collective memory in the primary cities of its three major nationalities (Ljubljana for the Slovenes, Zagreb for the Croats, and Belgrade for the Serbs) but founded no major public institution of social memory in Bosnia-Herzegovina.

The relative paucity of institutions was remedied in the first decade of socialist rule, which began in 1945. Guided by the belief that each of the six republics of Yugoslavia should have its own cultural and educational institutions, socialist leaders in their first years of rule established the University of Sarajevo, the National and University Library, the State Archive of Bosnia-Herzegovina, and the Museum of Liberation. They also supported the Regional Museum and strengthened its scientific programs. At the same time, most archival holdings of the Regional Museum were transferred to the State Archive, and the records of the Ottoman regional government were turned over to the newly established Oriental Institute.

In most respects, the Communists were devoted and able custodians of collective memory. Government-sponsored public institutions were well financed, generously staffed, and given favorable quarters and facilities for their work. However, certain policies of these institutions were influenced by the regime's ideological disposition, particularly in the early years of Communist rule. Communist-led institutions often blocked users from investigating opposition political parties, dissidents, partisan atrocities during World War II, the Yugoslav secret police and intelligence agencies, and other politically sensitive topics.

In the first decades of Communist governance, projects on the workers' movement prospered at the expense of

other inquiries. Archivists prodigiously collected and published documents on the origins of the workers' movement and the Communist Party. By the 1970s, however, scholars had found ways to justify all manner of studies as related in some way to the working class, and the scope of permissible topics broadened along with the political decentralization and liberalization of the Tito regime. Institutions of social memory acquired broad mandates to collect materials, and their holdings were used extensively by researchers and the public. With decentralization, individual institutions acquired greater latitude to determine their own acquisition and usage policies.

The rise of nationalist parties in 1990 and 1991 presented a number of dangers to this rich legacy of pampered public institutions. The general economic crisis of the time made it more difficult for governments to provide financial support for the large staffs and elaborate facilities enjoyed by public institutions of memory under Communism. Public cultural institutions were also threatened by the prospect that the newly emerging nationalist parties would seek to divide their holdings along ethno-national lines. Most ominously, when war broke out in March and April 1992, these institutions faced the imminent threat of physical annihilation from artillery bombardment and resulting fires.

In the first several months of the war, Serbian forces besieging Sarajevo purposefully destroyed or damaged several carefully chosen institutions of collective memory. The Olympic Museum, filled with artifacts and documents from the 1984 Winter Olympics, was gutted in May 1992 by Serbian artillery. The Oriental Institute, together with its Ottoman-era manuscripts and provincial government records, was completely destroyed. In August 1992 an artillery assault set the National and University Library ablaze, and the vast majority of its holdings were annihilated along with the interior of the turn-of-the-century building.

International public opinion was outraged by these barbaric assaults on Bosnia's cultural heritage. There was a global outpouring of emotional support, but very little financial assistance, for the reconstitution of these collections. But the offensiveness of these assaults on Bosnia's collective memory should not obscure the fundamental changes in the management and ownership of social memory that were already underway. In addition to destroying document collections, the assaults marked the beginning of major changes in Bosnia's visual environment that began during the war and continued in peacetime.

The region's nationalists assign great significance to

visual representatives of collective social memory. In both the Serbian- and Croatian-controlled sections of Bosnia there has been wholesale destruction of the reminders of Ottoman rule and the Islamic faith. Virtually every city and town in the Republika Srpska contains an empty lot near its city center where the town's mosque had been located prior to being dynamited and bulldozed by local Serbian authorities. And since the war's end, Bosnian Serb leaders have resisted efforts to rebuild destroyed historical monuments such as the Ferhadija Mosque in Banja Luka.

Many mosques in the Croat-controlled territory of the Bosnian Federation have also been damaged or destroyed. The spirit of vengeance and vindictiveness was embodied in the former artists' colony of Počitelj, just a few miles from the Adriatic coast. Built on a hillside during the Ottoman period, the town was restored with great care and became a thriving artists' colony in the 1980s. Most of its buildings were destroyed or damaged in the first two years of the war. Croatian nationalists erected crosses on the ruins of significant monuments, most conspicuously on the ruins of the modest but architecturally magnificent mosque in the center of the hillside.[4] Five years after peace came to Bosnia, the crosses announced that the vengeful spirit of the Crusades is alive, fostered by vindictive Croatian nationalists.

Restoration and new construction in the various national areas follow a pattern of glorifying the religious heritage of the dominant group. Throughout the Republika Srpska, Serbian Orthodox churches have been restored, repaired, and maintained in immaculate condition. In the town of Srebrenica, center of the area where more than seven thousand Bosniaks were slaughtered in 1995 by nationalist Serb forces, the local Serbian Orthodox church sits atop a small hill overlooking the square where the bulldozed mosque used to be. It is easily the best-maintained building in town.

In Bosniak-controlled areas, large new mosques are being built with funds from Saudi Arabia and other Islamic countries. Millions of dollars are being spent on these structures, most of which are being built in a lavish, monumental contemporary style that clashes architecturally with that of more refined Ottoman-era mosques. In an effort to allay the inevitable criticism that these funds could be better spent on jump-starting the economy, leaders of the Bosnian Islamic community characterize these facilities as "cultural centers" in addition to mosques. With rare exceptions, Bosniaks spared the religious monuments of others during wartime. But in the postwar building campaign, the Bosniak desire to

dominate the visual landscape emanates from each of these mosques that tower over surrounding structures and the countryside.

The National and University Library

The National and University Library was established in 1945 as the People's Library (Narodna biblioteka). Its holdings were seeded by collections confiscated from the national cultural societies (which were dissolved by the Communist regime) and some other confessional, national, and personal libraries in Bosnia, but most of the 2 million volumes in its collections as of 1990 had been acquired during the Communist era. The library held an irreplaceable collection of Bosnia's periodical press dating to the mid-nineteenth century. In 1955 the library was moved to an architecturally distinctive pseudo-Moorish triangular building that was built in Austro-Hungarian days to be Sarajevo's city hall.

Shortly after the 1990 multiparty elections, representatives of the three victorious nationalist parties discussed dividing some of the library's holdings among them. Claims to the library's materials were couched in the language of "restitution," namely that certain holdings had been wrested by the Communist government from the major national cultural societies after 1945 and should rightfully be returned. These talks followed the principles of an agreement reached among the nationalist parties immediately after the election, wherein the three victorious nationalist parties agreed in principle to divide offices, civil service appointments, and many governmental functions among themselves. But these talks ended without results because the parties could not reach a specific agreement, and the library's holdings were still intact when the war began.

The Serbian nationalist assault on the library had all the earmarks of a carefully planned attack. On August 25, 1992, the Serbian forces cut off the water supply to the city (something that happened periodically) and commenced bombarding the building, reportedly with a total of forty shells fired from four different artillery positions in the hills above the city. They also dropped mortar shells on the narrow streets surrounding the building to prevent access for firefighting vehicles. The fire burned all day, and ashes of burned books fell from the darkened summer skies. As described by one of the librarians who began that day in the building, "What had been a great Library was a black and gloomy ruin."[5] Over a million volumes were burned that day, as well as a rich collection of nineteenth-century periodical press, the card catalog, computers, microfilm, and photographic equipment. The burning of Sarajevo's library has become a global emblem of the "memoricide" practiced by the nationalist extremists who waged war against Bosnia-Herzegovina and its civilian population.[6]

After the library's destruction, the staff and few surviving holdings were temporarily accommodated in a three-story modern building on the south bank of the Miljacka River. Stacks of surviving materials and new acquisitions piled up in the damp basement. The library's director, Dr. Enes Kujundžić, an Arabic specialist who studied both in the Middle East and at the University of Chicago, made various trips abroad seeking support for rebuilding the facility and reconstituting its collections.[7] UNESCO's president, Federico Mayor, urged U.N. member countries to pledge $100 million for a new building. Coming at a time when most major libraries worldwide had already adopted electronic catalogs and were becoming institutions for information management, the library's destruction seemed to offer an opportunity to create a more contemporary institution on the heels of its catastrophic losses.

Instead, the library leadership and most of its staff have seen their mission as reconstituting that which was lost. They have reestablished many of the now archaic procedures of the prewar years and concentrated on the replacement or acquisition of traditional printed materials. In an effort to follow the institution's progress, I visited the library on several occasions between 1994 and 1999. On my last visit in early 1999, I watched the staff process a new acquisition. In the beautiful archaic cursive writing seen in archival documents from a century ago, the receiving clerk entered a new volume's essential information in a huge ledger and assigned it an "inventory number." The book was then passed to another librarian, who manually prepared a small slip of paper for the library's physical card catalog. After the acquisition had been processed manually, the entire process was repeated electronically, using electronic cataloging software donated by Slovenia. On each of my visits, the director made a point of telling me how many librarians were employed. It seemed a throwback to the Communist era, when success was measured primarily in number of employees rather than the adoption of modern methods that reduced the need for staff.

But archaic practices are not the only obstacle to reconstituting this once distinguished institution. The General Framework Agreement for Peace in Bosnia and Herzegovina of November 1995, commonly called the Dayton Agreement, stipulated that Sarajevo be demilitarized.

When the Army of Bosnia-Herzegovina left the Tito Barracks in Sarajevo, numerous dreams and schemes were proposed to transform the barracks into a university and educational center. The National and University Library moved into the first floor of a two-story former barracks building. (The second floor is occupied by the Oriental Institute, another institution that lost its holdings owing to Serbian bombardment.) With its archaic card catalog and small, overheated reading room, the National and University Library is still a far cry from its prewar incarnation.

But the staff's retrogressive approach is not the main obstacle to reconstituting the library and its holdings. The Dayton Agreement also diminished the institution's importance within Bosnia-Herzegovina and inherently limited the resources available to it. According to the constitution that was imbedded in the treaty, responsibility for cultural and educational institutions such as the library was assigned to local governmental units. Nationalist Serbs and Croats have established separate libraries in their respective areas of control to rival the one in Sarajevo. In Croat-controlled West Mostar, nationalists used funds from the European Community to reconstruct the city's library, renaming it the National Library.[8] The title leaves unspecified the "nation" to which the library belongs, but the display of Croatian nationalism during the library's festive opening in July 1995 left little doubt that it was a Croatian cultural institution.[9] Serbian nationalists in the Republika Srpska renamed the Communist-era National and University Library Petar Kočić as the National Library of the Republika Srpska and promoted it as a counterpart to the Sarajevo institution, which they characterized as a Bosniak or Bosnian Muslim library. The political trifurcation of Bosnia-Herzegovina has thus been accompanied by a proliferation of institutions of social memory in areas controlled by each of the three nationalist parties.

The Regional Museum

In Sarajevo, the targeted destruction of the institutions of memory occurred principally during the first five months of war. Some facilities and structures—such as the mausoleum in the Jewish cemetery—were more likely casualties of intense front-line hostilities than a calculated strategy of destruction. The buildings of the Regional Museum suffered substantial damage during fighting in 1992, but its collections were preserved in basement quarters or evacuated to safer locations early in the war.

The museum houses Bosnia's most celebrated manuscript, the fourteenth-century Jewish family Bible known as the Sarajevo Haggadah. The manuscript has a storied background, including various unconfirmed stories about being spirited into the nearby hills during Nazi occupation and being buried under a tree.[10] On a day of Serb bombardment in 1992, Dr. Enver Imamović—then a university history professor who later served as director of the museum—enlisted the assistance of two police officers, secured the Haggadah in a box, paused with the police officers on the steps of the Regional Museum to pose for a picture (in which they all appear remarkably composed), and set off across town to a secret location. He subsequently told visitors that this was accomplished amidst heavy shelling of the city center.

The Haggadah's secret destination turned out to be the vault of the National Bank of Bosnia-Hercegovina, a massive structure in the city center with a secure basement area. But Jewish activists remained deeply concerned for the safety of this unique treasure and lobbied for an international "rescue" to retrieve the manuscript and deliver it to Israel.[11] Bosnian president Alija Izetbegović rejected this initiative, contending that the Haggadah was not only an artifact of Jewish culture but also a vital part of Bosnia-Herzegovina's cultural legacy. After false rumors circulated that the Bosnians had traded the Haggadah for a planeload of arms, the Bosnian government permitted the Haggadah to be moved to the Jewish synagogue for a Passover seder on April 15, 1995. Although he did not remain for the seder, Izetbegović addressed a small gathering of Muslims, Croats, Serbs, and Jews, making sure that foreign reporters could also confirm that the Haggadah was being well cared for.[12] The manuscript was then returned to the bank vault, and after the war it was given back to the museum.

The Regional Museum's holdings survived the war largely intact, but the building was seriously damaged. Parts of the roof were blown off by artillery shells, and almost no windows were left unbroken. But it was one of the first buildings in Sarajevo to be fully restored. Chosen by international mediators as the site of the first meetings of the three-person presidency, the building was largely repaired in 1996–97. With few funds and little outside interest, the museum had not yet reopened to the general public as of summer 2000.

The Archive of Bosnia-Herzegovina

Habsburg administrators generated over 23 million records and reports while governing Bosnia-Herzegovina from 1878 to 1918. These documents constitute a rich source of information about all aspects of life in the country around the turn of the last century. Most documents from this forty-year rule were forwarded from Sarajevo to appropriate ministries in Vienna, where they remained until the end of World War I. Then, pursuant to treaties among the Habsburg successor states, the Austro-Hungarian reports on Bosnia-Herzegovina were transported to Belgrade, where they were housed in Yugoslavia's archives for the next twenty-two years.[13] After German troops conquered Belgrade in 1941, the Nazis sent the documents back to Vienna, where they remained through the war. During their second stay in Vienna during World War II, many documents received a Nazi stamp.

At the end of World War II, the Austro-Hungarian documents were returned to Yugoslavia. In accord with the policy of giving each republic responsibility for its own cultural and educational institutions, the Communist-led Yugoslav government in 1947 created the State Archive of Bosnia-Herzegovina in Sarajevo to house these well-traveled documents. The archive is located in the Presidency Building, a thick-walled boxlike structure built in the 1880s by Austro-Hungarian administrators to house their executive offices. The Habsburg-era documents have returned home to the very building in which many of them were originally prepared in the nineteenth century. The archive also contains governmental records from the interwar Royal Yugoslav period (1918–41), World War II (1941–45), and the forty-five years of Communist governance (1945–90).

In the 1970s, I had the pleasure of using the Archive of Bosnia-Herzegovina while doing research for my Ph.D. dissertation on the political life of the Bosnian Muslims during Habsburg rule. Access was limited to certified scholars with well-defined projects, and initially archival staff members were stingy with materials, restricting me to five documents per day. I admit to being helped in this regard by the arrival of a fellow American graduate student, a vivacious young woman who lingered for hours each morning over coffee with the archive director in his spacious corner office. After many coffees and a lot of charm, she convinced him to liberalize our access. Thereafter both she and I were allowed to see all the documents we wanted.

The collection was almost wholly intact, and huge index volumes compiled by Austro-Hungarian clerks were immensely helpful in identifying appropriate documents. A few key reports related to the assassination of Archduke Francis Ferdinand in 1914 were missing, reportedly because a user had taken them to his home at the time Belgrade was bombed by the Germans in April 1941. Still, I concluded that Communist Yugoslavia was a generally responsible custodian of the records of previous regimes.

During the recent Bosnian war (1992–95), the Presidency Building's thick walls and vaultlike construction proved ideal safeguards for the document collections. Mortars and rockets fell all around the building during the four-year siege of Sarajevo, but these and sniper bullets did little more than chip away at the decorative exterior facades. In 1993 the building became considerably more cramped. Many government officials relocated to the building after being driven by repeated Serbian shelling from their offices in the newer high-rise Parliament building. Some documents were crammed into basement quarters and exposed to greater moisture and insect damage, but most of those problems proved transitory. The archive was closed during the war, but most of the staff returned to work after the Dayton Agreement and enabled the institution to reopen.

I returned as a user in 1998 to find that the document collection had reached war's end with no major losses. The former reading room, sparsely appointed but spacious enough to accommodate a dozen users, had been converted to a director's office. The corner office, where my female colleague had schmoozed her way to academic greatness in 1974, was vacant for the moment, and as a visiting scholar I was accorded singular use of this huge room. Other users were crowded around a lunchroom-sized table in a small interior space that had previously been the archives' photographic darkroom. As the sole occupant of a room the size of President Izetbegović's office a floor above, I suffered attacks of guilt, knowing that my scholarly colleagues were crammed into a closet-like interior enclosure. But subsequent developments relieved me of the agony. When I revisited in 1999, the newly designated "Director of the Archives of the Federation of Bosnia-Herzegovina" had taken up residence in my corner office. Thereafter, I rubbed elbows with my colleagues in the former darkroom amidst the fading smell of chemicals that once developed my microfilms.

Having survived the war virtually unscathed, the archive came under a complex administrative structure dictated by the peace agreements. The Washington Agreements, concluded in March 1994 under American auspices, created a Federation of Bosnia-Herzegovina consisting of territories controlled by the Bosnian Croat and Bosniak belligerents. The agreement ended their armed conflict, but power in the federation has been more divided than shared between the two groups. The

federation Constitution specifies that each governmental unit be headed by a minister of one nationality and a deputy minister of the other. The two chiefs swap places regularly. Consequently each minister and deputy minister has developed a distinct coterie of loyalists of his own nationality. Thus the federation and certain of its "cantons" are served by two bureaucracies working separately but in parallel. For the archive, this means that two offices were needed to accommodate federation officials: one for the director, and one for the deputy director.

The Dayton Agreement (November 1995) further complicated the archive's administration. The treaty designated the federation as one of two "entities" making up Bosnia-Herzegovina. The other entity, the Republika Srpska, occupies 49 percent of Bosnia's territory but in all other respects is an equal counterpart to the federation. Bosnia-Herzegovina, the central state, has limited powers and functions, and maintaining a central archive is one of these. The director of the Archive of Bosnia-Herzegovina requires an office, just as do the director of the Archive of the Federation of Bosnia-Herzegovina, and the deputy director of the Archive of the Federation of Bosnia-Herzegovina.[14] The reading room was forced into the Presidency Building's cramped interior, it turned out, by the need to provide prime office space for each of the three directors.

The postwar archive also has two separate administrative staffs. Reflecting the relative allocation of resources to the various levels of government, the Archive of Bosnia-Herzegovina, the central institution, has three employees, while the Archive of the Federation of Bosnia-Herzegovina has nineteen, as of summer 2000. Owing to the deadlock among nationalist political forces in the Assembly, the Archive of Bosnia-Herzegovina has not been funded, and only in summer 2000 was a new law drafted to organize and regulate the archive's activities.[15] The Archive of Bosnia-Herzegovina, despite having a staff of only three persons, managed to procure some capital equipment, but these machines are not available for use by employees of the federation archive. Large copying machines stand idle while the many members of the staff of the federation archive bemoan the shortage of duplicating equipment.

And what of the Serbian entity? In Banja Luka, the capital of the Republika Srpska, an Archive of the Republika Srpska has been established. It seeks to match the federation archive in prestige and resources.

Inevitably, there have been proposals to divide the extraordinary archival holdings, either between the two entities or among the three contending nationalities. So far these have gone nowhere, but their success or failure rests largely with the future electoral fortunes of the major nationalist parties. It is likely that future development and acquisition policies of all three archival institutions will reflect the priorities of nationalist politicians and their protégés in the archival leadership positions. The archive in the year 2000 is an institution with three directors, two distinct staffs, one corpus of holdings, and no likelihood of adopting modern methodologies any time soon.

The Bosniak Institute

Behind the Catholic cathedral in Sarajevo, a modestly proportioned two-domed Turkish bath building, known as the Hamam, stands as a reminder of Sarajevo's sixteenth-century Golden Age. In 1999, a huge construction project was begun on three sides of the Hamam. A streetside sign announced intentions to build a "Bosniak Institute" on the site, following a design that preserved the centuries-old domes and adopted their curvature in the three-story contemporary addition.

The Bosniak Institute is a project of Adil Zulfikarpašić, a former partisan from a wealthy Bosnian Muslim landowning family who moved to Switzerland after World War II.[16] In Zurich, he went into the construction business and multiplied the family fortune many times over. As the only Bosnian Muslim in emigration with significant wealth, Zulfikarpašić founded an émigré journal, *Pregled,* that he used to advocate "Bosniak" rather than "Bosnian Muslim" as a designation for his people. He established the Bosniak Institute in a four-story building in Zurich. With generous support from its founder, the institute has assembled a substantial collection of books, periodicals, documents, and artifacts from the Bosniak past. It also includes Zulfikarpašić's valuable art collection.

By virtue of his wealth and the influence of his journal, Zulfikarpašić became a significant figure among Bosnian Muslim nationalists in the 1980s. Alija Izetbegović, imprisoned by the Communists for Bosnian Muslim nationalist activities in 1983, beat a path to Zulfikarpašić's door in Zurich immediately upon his release from jail in 1989. Some observers contend that the Party for Democratic Action (SDA), the principal Bosnian Muslim nationalist party to compete in the 1990 elections, was founded at Zulfikarpašić's Zurich residence. Zulfikarpašić returned to Bosnia in triumph in 1990 and, as vice president of the SDA, campaigned vigorously for the party. But he failed to win the support of the party's religious conservatives and angered them with his efforts to reach an agreement with Serbian nationalists. Frustrated and under intense criticism, he resigned before the elections and founded his own party, the Muslim Bosniak Organization.

After his party failed to garner significant votes in the November 1990 elections, Zulfikarpašić returned to Zurich and spent the wartime years lavishing his money and attention on the Bosniak Institute. Following the signing of the Dayton Agreement and the end of war, Zulfikarpašić again became a frequent visitor to Sarajevo. In the tradition of wealthy Ottoman officials centuries ago, he donated generously to help complete a large new mosque in a Sarajevo suburb. Also in the Ottoman tradition, a mosque was named after him. The Adil-beg Mosque is a monumental structure that dominates the nearby countryside, following the trend of mosques built with the assistance (and influence) of Islamic countries.

After the war, Zulfikarpašić established a Sarajevo office of the Bosniak Institute and used it to gather more books and manuscripts. In 1998 he struck an agreement with the city to purchase the old Turkish bath and relocate the holdings of the Bosniak Institute to Sarajevo. The new plans required demolition of an older structure that housed the extensive holdings of the Archive of the City of Sarajevo. The staff and holdings of this public institution were dispersed to four different locations around the city, creating major disruptions. The archive's new quarters are substantially less accommodative to staff and to users than its former facilities.

Zulfikarpašić has indicated that his valuable art collection will remain in Zurich, presumably safe from the vicissitudes of Balkan political changes, but all other materials have been moved to the new Sarajevo facility. Zulfikarpašić's institute, with virtually unlimited financial resources, is in a much better position to build its collections than are public institutions such as the National and University Library and the Archive of Bosnia-Herzegovina.

When completed in early 2001, the institute fulfilled a Bosniak national dream as a national monument. With its alabaster walls and graceful curves invoking the Ottoman past, the new buildings will tower over the nineteenth-century Catholic cathedral across the street. The new Bosniak Institute constitutes a triumph of privately financed Bosniak nationalism over both religious rivals and nonnationalist public and secular institutions. It promises to be the premier institution of written social memory in Bosnia and Herzegovina, and it will be under the exclusive control of a founding father of twentieth-century Bosniak nationalism or his heirs.

The International Criminal Tribunal
for the Former Yugoslavia

As these changes in institutional ownership have oc-curred, another international body has begun to have a major impact on the region's sense of the past. The International Criminal Tribunal for the Former Yugoslavia (ICTY), created by U.N. Security Council resolution in 1993, has emerged as both a major investigative agency and an enormous repository of documents. The ICTY was slow in getting started. Some of its most wanted suspects remain at large, and only a few trials have been concluded. Nevertheless, both prosecutors and defense attorneys have shown a voracious appetite for documentary evidence in support of their cases. The ICTY maintains an office in Sarajevo, with no sign on the door and no insignia on its vehicles, and its investigators regularly visit document repositories and interview witnesses throughout the region. Bosniak officials have cooperated extensively with the ICTY's investigators. Many indictments and cases have relied heavily upon documentation gathered and supplied by officers of the (former) Bosnian government and preserved in Bosniak-controlled repositories.

Croatia and Serbia, in contrast, have until very recently resisted cooperation with the tribunal. Stipe Mesić, elected president of Croatia after Franjo Tudjman's death in December 1999, reversed the previous regime's truculent opposition and offered full cooperation. Before his election, Mesić had appeared as a prosecution witness in the case against Croatian general Tihomir Blaškić, and his testimony apparently enhanced his stature with much of the Croatian electorate. Once in office he proposed a resolution, subsequently passed by the Croatian Parliament, promising full and open cooperation with the ICTY, and he opened the state's archives to full review by tribunal investigators. In less than a year, the tribunal's prosecutors have already used the Croatian records to their benefit in cases against several war crimes defendants, and the document collection has been immensely enriched by records from Croatia.

Serbia has remained largely uncooperative with the tribunal even after Yugoslav president Milošević was turned over for trial in June 2001. Some cooperation has been forthcoming from the government of Montenegro and from the anti-Milošević leadership of Bosnia's Republika Srpska, but neither of these polities has yet disgorged anything near the massive documentation that Bosniak authorities and the Croatian government have made available.

Other organizations possessing relevant information have also balked at providing access. Among the most informative reports were prepared by observers of the European Commission Monitoring Mission (ECMM), most of whom compiled daily reports on political, economic, and military developments in their zones of responsibility. At first the ECMM offered relatively unrestricted access to prosecution investigators, but they have rebuffed many inquiries from defense attorneys. More recently they closed access to all reports except for specified "need to know" inquiries from prosecutors. ECMM officers threw me out of their Sarajevo headquarters in 1999 just after they had inadvertently shown me some revealing reports about wartime military conflict in the city.

The ECMM is not alone in its reluctance to open its documents for ICTY inspection. Cooperation from Western governments has often been halfhearted as well. Pentagon intelligence officers concerned about disclosing intelligence sources and methods have regularly opposed American disclosure of some information. The Bosniak Agency for Information and Documentation (AID) has been more forthcoming with information than any of the Western agencies or governments that demand greater "transparency" in Bosnian affairs.

Despite the widespread reluctance of many governments and institutions to cooperate fully, the ICTY's activities have generally accelerated access to information about the recent war in the region. The ICTY has already become an institution of great importance for social memory in the region. Tribunal investigators have interviewed thousands of witnesses and survivors and assessed their accounts in light of relevant documentation from various sources. There are restrictions on the use of almost all of this documentation, but in the course of trials much of it has come to light and added substantially to the information available about the war in the former Yugoslavia.

The ICTY's growing corpus of information presents the international community with an unprecedented challenge to use new technology and innovative finding aids to assure access and usability to future generations.

Conclusion

The recent history of these five institutions reveals a powerful transformation in progress. Social memory in Bosnia-Herzegovina is gradually moving from the public, state-controlled sector to ownership by individuals and political formations with distinct national outlooks and agendas. The new elites are either creating or reviving distinctive contours in the visual landscape and introducing new policies into archives, museums, and libraries under their control. These transitions-in-progress have been strongly influenced by the international community's policies and resource allocations. Preferring to negotiate with nationalist leaders in hopes of reducing mutual hostility, international representatives have left the old state-sponsored unified institutions largely to their own devices.

Since the war's end, leaders of the old state-sponsored institutions have been engaged in a campaign of anachronistic retrofitting. Focused principally on restoring their institutions' prewar state, they are slowly rebuilding anachronistic institutions designed to function in a world that no longer exists. Unwilling to update their agendas and embrace new methodologies, these multiethnic state-sponsored bodies have fallen prey to the voracious appetites of the new nationalist elites for more narrowly focused, nationally defined institutions of social memory.

It remains to be seen how these new elites will manage the institutions that they carved from the former public-sphere socialist establishments. The first wave of atavistic national destruction swept through the land early in the war, most viciously in the Serbian activities that accompanied and followed their ethnic cleansing campaigns. But the era of overt destructive memoricide has apparently passed. Each nationalist elite must now define the specific policies of collection, maintenance, and access as they assume the leadership of institutions that have come under their control.

NOTES

1. Peter Pavel Klasinc, "Slovenia," and Drago Roksandić, "Croatia," in *Austrian History Yearbook: A Guide to East-Central European Archives* 29 (1998), pt. 2.

2. *Spomenica stogodišnjice rada zemaljskog muzeja Bosne i Hercegovine 1888–1988* [Commemoration of a hundred years of work of the Regional Museum of Bosnia-Herzegovina, 1888–1988) (Sarajevo: Zemaljski muzej Bosne i Hercegovine, 1988). The terms Landesmuseum (German) and Zemaljski muzej (Bosnian) may be rendered in English as "Regional," "Provincial," "State," or "National" Museum. "Regional Museum" is employed in this essay.

3. Kemal Bakaršić, "Bosnia and Hercegovina," in *Austrian History Yearbook: A Guide to East-Central European Archives* 29 (1998), pt. 2, 1–10.

4. I visited Počitelj in May 1999, and I confirmed that the crosses were still there in May 2000, but it is possible that they have been removed since then.

5. Tatjana Praštalo, "Death of a Library," *Logos* 8, no. 2 (1997), 97.

6. Tatjana Lorkovic, "National Library in Sarajevo Destroyed; Collections, Archives Go Up in Flames," *American Libraries,* October 1992, 736 and 816; see also the editorial "Erasing Bosnia's Memory," *Washington Post,* October 16, 1992, A24.

7. Burton Bollag, "Rebuilding Bosnia's Library," *Chronicle of Higher Education,* January 13, 1995, A35.

8. After U.S. officials negotiated peace between Croat and Bosniak leaders in the Washington Agreement of March 1994, the European Union was given the task of administering the city of Mostar. In accord with its policy of rebuilding structures wherever they had been located before the war began, the European Union provided funds to reconstruct the library. Croatian nationalists used this international aid to reconstruct the preexisting facility and transform it into a Croatian institutional rival of the Sarajevo library.

9. Robert J. Donia, "A Test Case for the Muslim-Croat Federation," *Transition,* November 3, 1995, 26.

10. Kemal Bakaršić, "Rare Books: The Story of the Sarajevo Haggada," *Judaica Librarianship* 9, no. 1–2 (spring 1994–winter 1995), 135. This article summarizes the various accounts of the Haggadah's travels in World War II and in 1992.

11. Marian Wenzel, "The Zemaljski Muzej, Sarajevo, in March 1995," *Museum Management and Curatorship* 14, no. 2 (1995): 203–5.

12. Roger Cohen, "Bosnia Jews Glimpse Book and Hope," *New York Times,* April 16, 1995, 7.

13. Bozo Madžar et al., *Arhiv Bosne i Hercegovine 1947– 1977. Povodom tridesetogodišnjice osnivanja Arhiva i početka rada arhivske službe u Bosni i Hercegovini* [Archive of Bosnia-Herzegovina, 1947–1977. On Occasion of the Thirtieth Anniversary of the Founding of the Archive and Beginning of the Work of Archival Service in Bosnia-Herzegovina] (Sarajevo: Svjetlost, 1977).

14. The director of the Archive of Bosnia-Herzegovina as of 2000 was also its prewar director. Matko Kovačević has energetically tackled many of the archive's challenges and worked to build good relations with the archive's diverse constituencies.

15. Angelina Albijanić, "Historija pred Nestankom," *Dani,* August 4, 2000, 48–49.

16. Adil Zulfikarpašić, *The Bosniak* (London: Hurst, 1998). His family history and background are elucidated in a dialogue with Milovan Djilas and Nadežda Gaće.

Writing Home in the Archive

"Refugee Memory" and the Ethnography
of Documentation

Penelope Papailias

The archive appears to have taken the place of historical narrative as a key locus for critical historical reflection. This shift from historiography to the archive has a number of implications. For one, it draws attention from the closed authoritative historiography to the multiplicity of texts involved in documenting the past and to their open potential for generating future histories.[1] Besides the historian-author, many other actors—archivists, informants, donors, and researchers of various kinds—are revealed to animate the archive. This sociality contrasts sharply with the stereotype of the archive as solitary and lifeless. The archive is also characterized by a diverse range of practices, including reading, classifying, reclassifying, documenting, donating, destroying, hiding, hoarding, collecting, and exposing. The relative invisibility of these activities, in contrast to the "heroism" of writing, is not coincidental but dependent on and confirming of gender, class, and ethnic hierarchies of scholarship. Thinking of the archive as a "process whereby texts are written" rather than as a mere "accumulation" (Echevarría 1998, 24) of documents provides a framework for a textual anthropology of the archive that focuses on the social interactions, layered temporalities, and rhetorical forms generated by and generating archival categories and documents.[2]

The archive also introduces a materiality sorely lacking in treatments of history as narrative, thus bringing into focus the political economy of archival production. While classic works of historiography can be reproduced and circulated without particular regard for their status as artifact, archives are defined by their connection to the authenticity of the original. The epistemology of archives is not static or universal, of course, but shaped by culturally and historically contingent technologies, genres, and habits of documentation. Although for Derrida, the archive occupies a "privileged *topology*" (1996, 3) close to power, it might be more useful to think of archives (and counterarchives) as located simply in some kind of relation to power. The monumentality of archives (or their conspicuous lack of monumentality) symbolizes the relative coherence of the collectivities that have created them, whether families, nation-states, political parties, or transnational communities. The archive according to Derrida must have an exterior ("*No archive without outside*" [1996, 11]) in order to have an interior that can be concealed. Everyday practices of governing can be read from the lineaments of archives while "fictions of access" represent a powerful tool of political legitimation (Stoler, this volume). The archive is always a fantasy of the political.

Given new relevance by the pragmatic concerns of archival construction in the age of digitization, the current interest in the cultural history of archives and archiving has been concerned primarily with powerful states, usually former colonial powers (for instance, Richards 1993; Combe 1994; Stoler, this volume). The present essay, which concerns a minor Greek archive, approaches the subject of the archive from a deliberately ex-centric location. I ask what might be learned from looking to the margins of Europe, to personal rather than state archives and to the archiving practices of those who are not professional historians or archivists. How might this perspective contribute to understanding relations of power between and within societies, as well as the intersection of people's lives with contested processes of public recollection?

Anatolia in Athens: Private Archives, National Contexts

Indeed, Greece would seem a most unpromising place to study archival culture. If the monumental architecture of the state archives of major European countries imposingly proclaim their colonial pasts and contemporary authority, the fact that the Greek state archives were settled in a permanent building almost a century after their establishment in 1914 speaks eloquently to Greece's position in global hierarchies.[3] In any case, much of the material needed to write a history of modern Greece is housed in foreign archives, such as the British Foreign Office, the American State Department, and the Ottoman archives, testifying to various regimes of direct and indirect domination and rule. Perhaps the only truly "successful" archiving project in modern Greek history was that undertaken by the security police. Thus, for many Greeks, the words *file* (*fakelos*) and *archives* (*archeia*) bring to mind political surveillance long before historical scholarship.[4] In this context, though, it is perhaps understandable why private and independent archives abound in Greek society, some aiming to supplement, others to subvert, the order and content of state archives.[5]

The subject of this essay is just such an archive, set up to collect the testimonies of Greek Orthodox refugees from Turkey. These refugees settled in Greece in the wake of the 1922 Asia Minor Catastrophe, as it is usually called by Greeks.[6] At this time, Kemalist forces routed the invading Greek army, sparking the mass exodus of the Greek Orthodox community. In the ensuing population exchange, the first compulsory one in modern history, at least one and a half million Greek Orthodox and 400,000 Muslims were exchanged between Greece and Turkey.[7] This event marked the birth of the modern Turkish state, as well as the end of centuries-long Greek presence in Anatolia. In 1930, just seven years after the population exchange was agreed upon in Lausanne, a cosmopolitan Greek aristocrat, Melpo Logotheti-Merlier (1890–1979), established the Center for Asia Minor Studies with the aim of "salvaging" the history and culture of Asia Minor Hellenism. Refugees were called on to describe the physical and built landscape, social life, ethnic relations, and religious practices of their native homelands, as well as to narrate stories of their "exodus" (the biblical connota-

tions of this term being very much intended). In the end, the center collected and archived over 145,000 manuscript pages of historical and cultural data from over 5,000 refugees, who were interviewed from the early 1930s to the early 1970s (though most were contacted between 1955 and 1965).

On one level, this essay considers the role this particular archive has played and continues to play in forming and reforming Greek cultural memory about Anatolia and the refugee experience. The catastrophe, with its clear before and after, graphically symbolized by Izmir (Greek Smyrna) in flames, is arguably the quintessential event of modern Greek history. The influx of refugees was such an important catalyst for the country's economic, as well as social and cultural development, that scholars typically consider 1922, not 1832, the real date on which the modern Greek nation was founded. Over time, the catastrophe, with its seemingly unambiguous morality of Greek victimhood and Turkish barbarity, would prove an easier story to narrate than other more divisive and fragmentary stories of loss, such as those of the Greek civil war (1946–49) or of transatlantic labor migrations. Similar to the way that the Holocaust has defined testimony and memory on a global scale, discourses on the Asia Minor Catastrophe were the first to conceptualize the ordinary Greek as witness to and victim of history.[8]

The representation of the catastrophe in Greek public discourse has, as might be expected, undergone numerous transformations over the course of the twentieth century. At the time it occurred, the influx of refugees increased the population by almost a quarter, causing tremendous social problems and political antagonisms that polarized natives and refugees. The distinct cultural and linguistic features of the refugees made them easy targets for nativist ire. Their Greekness was often challenged, as reflected in the derogatory epithets commonly directed at them, like "Turkish seed" (*tourkospori*) or "baptized in yogurt" (*yiaourtovaftismeni*) (Mavrogordatos 1983, 194). During the war years of the 1940s, this cleavage would be overshadowed by the conflict between the political right and left that culminated in civil war.[9] A public discourse on "lost homelands" (*hamenes patrides*) of Anatolia would not develop until the 1960s (Liakos 1998). The catastrophe was then recast as an archetypal story of *national* loss, which opposed Greek victims (now stripped of undesirable signs of cultural and linguistic difference) to Turkish subjugators. This narrative would be powerfully reinforced by the new refugee crisis in Cyprus in 1974 and the worsening of Greek-Turkish relations.

Since 1989, in the context of a new upsurge of nationalism, as well as a climate of ethnic self-discovery, an extensive memory industry continues to proliferate around the commemoration of Greek Anatolia.

When Merlier began her project in 1930, however, Greek society would just as soon have forgotten Asia Minor Hellenism together with the debacle of the Greek campaign.[10] Indeed, as she often complained, no national institution took on the task of researching and documenting the Greek Anatolian past. Enabled by the fact that Merlier's husband, Octave, was the director of the French Institute of Athens for many years, the center ended up occupying an extranational space and being supported financially by the French state until 1963. As a private institution, the archive also played a special role within the Greek political landscape: most of its researchers were leftists who had been barred from working in the civil service during the politically repressive post–civil war years.

Reform of cultural memory usually cannot proceed without reform of memory work itself. In addition to disputing national narratives of Greek history, the center also critiqued the methods of Greek academic history and folklore. Given the politically conservative state of the Greek university at this time, true scholarship, Merlier might have argued, could *only* thrive outside of the academy; thus, she aimed not so much to achieve as to supersede its standards. By bringing French scholarship and archival culture to Athens, Merlier would make Greeks into producers rather than subjects of Orientalist knowledge. Drawing on Greek literary modernism, Merlier also hoped to bring dry historical scholarship to life by infusing it with narratives of personal experience.

As a high modernist project, the center's archive happens to be highly reflexive about the conditions of its production. It preserves an array of documents describing ongoing debates about how to do research, as well as about the particular conditions in which data was collected. In these reports about the everyday business of memory work the contexts, as well as the tensions, involved in the process of eliciting memories have been encoded. This essay is constructed around three different genres of texts produced in the course of creating the archive: Merlier's work letters; the field notes of the researchers; and informant reports, brief biographies written by researchers about their refugee informants. Each of these texts defines different subjects in the archive: Merlier, the master archivist and first reader; the researchers, in their dual role of listener and scribe; and, finally, the refugee informants as both eyewitnesses and living proof of the former Greek presence in Anatolia.

In this essay, I consider how conceptions of national identity, citizenship, and class in 1950s and 1960s Greek society were actively reworked in the process of mapping Anatolia and transcribing refugee biographies, as well as in documenting the research itself. Through experimentation with my own narrative style, I have also attempted to convey something of the dynamism with which textual forms, temporalities, and social worlds intersect in the making of an archive.

Reading in the Archive Today

In Melpo Merlier's day, the center was located in Kolonaki in the heart of Athens's highbrow cultural and intellectual life. Perpetually understaffed and underfinanced in relation to its goals, the center was a hub of activity as researchers shuttled between deskwork and fieldwork, as well as for many their regular jobs at the French Institute. The messianic goal of documenting the culture and history of Greek Orthodox populations of Asia Minor before the deaths of the last informants added a sense of urgency to the center's daily operations. Today, on the other hand, the center with its tiny staff is housed in a large historical building in the Plaka, Athens's old town and principal tourist zone. With its more modest research objectives and equally shaky finances, the center is a peaceful place cut off from the public life of the city if not from contemporary developments in Greek and international historiography. Just as finding a way into the archive requires but also enhances an understanding of the political climate and epistemological frameworks within which it took shape, reflection on how people are using the archive today sheds light on the current historical moment and contemporary conceptions of historical knowledge and practice.

The center's small reading room is located on the top floor of the building, up a flight of handsome wooden stairs. The metal cabinets flanking the back wall of the reading room "contain" the province of Cappadocia in row upon row of bulging manila envelopes with small, neatly folded pages. Black-and-white photographs enlarged into posters hang on the walls of the cavernous building. Many depict students in Greek schools in Asia Minor shortly before the tragic events of 1922. Like photographs of Jewish life before the Holocaust, these images elicit a sentimental reaction from the viewer, who knows that shortly after the pictures were taken the young people depicted in them all became refugees (Hirsch 1997, 20). Downstairs from the reading room,

Merlier's and her husband's heavy wooden desks, assorted memorabilia, and vast personal archives slumber, enshrined in silence. Photographs of prominent political figures, such as Charles de Gaulle and the Greek prime minister Eleftherios Venizelos, as well as of famous Greek writers, attest to the Merliers' membership in an elite circle of cosmopolitan liberals.

Like most first-time visitors to the center, I was introduced to its collections through *The Last Hellenism of Asia Minor*, the catalog for the center's major 1974 exhibition and a kind of résumé of the contents of its archive (Merlier 1974). The outside cover, with its striking photograph of a minaret standing beside an Orthodox church, announces the center's embrace of religious diversity and focus on interethnic relations. Inside, one cannot help but be struck by the *numbers*. Progress was accounted for in manuscript pages: material collected on each Greek settlement is totaled and tabulated down to the very last fraction: 2,163 Greek settlements, 1,375 studied, 5,000 informants, 145,000 pages of data. Although many days I would be the only person working at the center, over time, I saw a varied cast of figures move through this space: people of Asia Minor ancestry working on histories of their region or city of origin; local historians from other parts of Greece looking for information about refugees who settled in their towns; other graduate students and academics, working on projects about nationalism and ethnicity in the Ottoman empire or on the cultural life of Greeks in Asia Minor. Once I even met a man who was trying to find the testimonies his grandparents had given to center researchers. While some people worked with materials from the oral archive, many others used the center's other resources: its extensive library of historical books, European travelogues, registers from former Greek communities of Asia Minor, books written in Karamanli (Turkish language printed in Greek characters), and photograph and folk song archives.

On one of my first visits to the center, I met Ioanna Petropoulou, a center researcher and archivist, as well as an expert on Cappadocia, whose writings have helped dispel the aura that had long shielded "Merlier's Center" from critical scrutiny. Petropoulou quickly became the interlocutor to whom I presented my early impressions of the personalities and politics of the different people—researchers, key informants, and Merlier herself—whom I encountered as I read in the archive. Today, as evident by Petropoulou's own recent writings about the center, the legacy of the oral archive is being reconsidered and its collections being read in new ways.

For one, the Yugoslav wars of the 1990s and the heightened nationalisms that emerged throughout the Balkans during that period have led to a renewed interest in the history of the Ottoman empire both prior to and during its traumatic dismantling. While popular rhetoric on Greek lost homelands in Anatolia has tended to stoke nationalist and especially anti-Turkish sentiment, for many would-be cultural reformers the Anatolian past represents a fertile site to locate an indigenous ethic of multiculturalism.[11] Merlier herself had perceived the center's research as a means to further the cause of Greco-Turkish reconciliation and had pushed researchers to find signs of harmonious interethnic relations in the refugees' narratives. Researchers today are often surprised to find that their desires for the past are reciprocated by those of an earlier generation of memory workers.

The center's archive also has attracted new interest of late from students of the refugee experience. Although the center was set up for the purpose of studying Greek Orthodox life in Asia Minor, material recorded primarily for bureaucratic purposes is now being read against the grain by scholars seeking information about the settlement of the refugees in Greece.[12] Petropoulou (1997), for instance, realized that she could use a fragmented collection of refugee settlement reports to argue against some of the dominant mythologies of "lost homelands" discourse (i.e., the ethnic and linguistic homogeneity of the refugees, as well as their undying "memory" of their homelands). In the process, she also revealed the cultural heterogeneity of "native" Greeks.

Finally, as Greek academics have become interested in oral history, the current staff at the center increasingly finds itself being called on to speak about Greece's "oldest and largest collection of oral history" (Kitromilides 1987, 22; Yiannacopoulos 1993). While this oral archive might have been something of an embarrassment a short time ago, today it is hailed as the center's distinctive contribution to Greek historical scholarship. The use of the term "oral *history*" to speak about the center's research is, of course, anachronistic. Merlier herself always used the term "oral *tradition*" (*proforiki paradosi*), reflecting the fact that she came to history from orality, not vice versa. Merlier's initial interest in the "voice of the people" can be traced back to a common agenda of bourgeois elites, who championed the demotic, vernacular language in Greece's highly politicized language debates, as well as to a well-established tradition of folk song collecting. On the other hand, Merlier's approach to voice could be said to have posed a radical break with earlier conceptions of orality. Merlier had been trained in ethnomusicology in Paris, and the center's project actually grew out of a major song collecting project she undertook in 1930 using the most advanced sound recording technology of the day.[13]

It was the refugees' unprecedented dislocation and resettlement that pushed them from the static eternity of the folk into time and pushed Merlier herself to the study of folklore and history. Seeking a "culture concept" for her project, Merlier initially turned to the Greek folklore establishment, adapting its questionnaires and archival practices. If, as Derrida suggests, "archivization produces as much as it records the event" (1996, 17), technologies and genres of documentation are critical in shaping the content of what is ultimately re-collected. It is not insignificant, then, that the researchers would use a philological model of documentation based on the methods of the Greek folklore discipline (i.e., pen and paper transcription rather than sound recording; interviews and questionnaires rather than participant observation), instead of the ethnomusicology Merlier had studied in Paris or the new trends in French history and ethnology she was following.[14]

Even though Merlier saw the center's research as evolving alongside European intellectual trends, in reality, a variety of methodologies, culled from nineteenth-century folklore scholarship, ethnomusicology, pre-Braudelian geographical history and literary modernism, coexisted and quite often clashed under the vague rubric of oral testimony. In introducing the story, personal experience, and memory into a project of ethnological and geographical fact gathering, Merlier established a chronic tension at the heart of the archive between the authority of refugees' voice and the exigencies of "objective" documentation. This unorthodox state of affairs seems to reflect the fact that the center was located not only on the intellectual margin of Europe, but also on its geographic one. The fact that the center made systematic use of oral sources, however, is rather remarkable considering that the first officially recognized oral history project began in New York in 1948 (Perks and Thomson 1998, 1). The center's unorthodox theoretical bricolage that resulted in this early use of oral sources might best be understood less as a failure of scholarship than as an artifact of the struggle to find a language with which to speak about what was then a new global phenomenon: the refugee.[15]

Diaspora, Maps, Letters: Making a Home in Hellenism

When I first started looking into the history of the center, it was often pointed out to me that Merlier never brought

to a satisfying conclusion this grand project that lasted over forty years. With the exception of an unremarkable article on Cappadocia, she never actually wrote anything about Asia Minor. Part of her unfinished dissertation on Greek folk songs lies filed among her personal diaries and diplomas from piano study, accompanied by a sad little note in French: "Cast a glance July 20, 1952. What melancholy. So much work without being able to finish it." Yet, despite this apparent failure to write, her prolific letter writing, notes, and multiple introductions to the work of the center have spread their calligraphic trails throughout the archive. Indeed, if one seeks a voice in the center today, it is certainly much easier to get a sense of hers than that of the refugees. Rather than a mere byproduct of research, her writings about the center's research, like her many "work letters" (grammata ergasias), are constructions in their own right that attempt to compose gaps and contradictions between amateur and professional scholarships, imaginative and empirical observation, and her personal life and modern Greek history.

Consider this letter. It is September 1956, and Merlier sits in a café in Geneva, studying a map of Pontos, a region located along the Black Sea. Merlier usually spent at least half the year and sometimes longer in Geneva or, in later years, in Aix-en-Provence, where her husband Octave taught modern Greek at the university. This map had been sent to her by the center's two cartographers, whom she refers to proudly, if rather grandiosely, as a "department." With the maps spread before her, she writes:

> My dear, missed researchers of the Cartographic Department,
> I am in Bel D'Or, opposite my hotel, where I came to take two coffees one after the other to settle my spirits, which are not first rate. I took with me a lot of work, because I came at 8:30, just after I ate.
> I am here a little like I am at home. On the couch where I sit, right and left, I spread out my papers in stacks on stacks: letters from Aglaia [Ayioutanti, the assistant director]; my letters for the "centerites" [i.e., the researchers]; map drafts. On the table, pencils, pencil sharpeners, paper clips. My neighbors here, both near and far, are scandalized, looking at all these implements. Their curiosity, however, reached its zenith when, having unfolded the sketch of Yesil Irmak on my table, I studied the memo from the Cartographic Department and followed it on the sketch. I was quite lost in my thoughts about southern Pontos. When I raised my head, ten eyes from three tables, were looking at me with sympathy and sweetness. I smiled at them gratefully and continued.
> You might ask—Is this a beginning for a work letter

to be typed? I also thought of this. But I think it is. Is it right for one always to separate work from life? Then, how would you know my dear Cartography department the sympathy that your maps call forth?[16]

The scene Merlier paints here, like those in which she describes "buffet tables laden with papers," suggests the genteel form her academic research takes, as well as the thin line that separates a "work letter" from a personal one.

It is not surprising that Merlier was most at home with herself as a writer when she wrote letters. Aside from their association with elite women's schooling and communication, letters in their circulation create diasporic networks. The letter offers Merlier the possibility of bringing together disparate temporalities and territories, allowing her to be many people at once: Swiss café lounger, director of an archive in Athens, and even a Pontic time-traveler; in short, a certain kind of cosmopolitan Greek. As Andrew Hassam (1990) has argued about the travel diary, the almost formulaic invocation of the scene "as I write" creates a space in which a narrator can move and speak. In creating a scene of writing, the letter—and the time and space needed to write it—delineates a concrete "here" where Merlier can feel "a little like she is at home." Svetlana Boym (1998) has coined the term *diasporic intimacy* to describe the "fragile coziness of a foreign home." This notion of diaspora as a site of intimacy and furtive pleasure, rather than melancholy, is useful for reading Merlier's letter. Her encampment in the café with reports, papers, letters, paper clips, and pencils constitutes a fragile home. A certain pleasure lies in erecting it in such an anomalous space.

Merlier's fascination with the refugees' situation might have had something to do with the fact that she herself was a kind of a refugee. Born in Xanthi (Thrace) in 1890, she graduated from the elite Zappeion Academy in Istanbul and studied music in Dresden, Geneva, Vienna, and Paris, where between 1920 and 1925 she taught modern Greek at the Sorbonne. Merlier belonged to a cosmopolitan Greek world, in which Alexandria, Izmir, and Istanbul were more important centers than Athens and being Greek was not coeval with citizenship in the narrow confines of the Greek state. The events of 1922, however, shattered this world of diasporic Hellenism. Like Anatolian artists and writers, Merlier sought a new way to define "home" and her Greek identity. The map of Asia Minor described in her letter opens up a chronotope of a lost homeland that in moments of historical reflection and reverie can join her adoptive

home in Western Europe to her parochial one in Greece. In this vision, Athens would constitute a central, though not exclusive, point of reference.

In locating the center in Athens, though, Merlier made a bold gesture. So long an *object* of study by the West, Greece would now take on a large-scale Orientalist project of its own. If Merlier was bringing Greece to France, proposing a vision of Hellenism that Europeans could look at with "sympathy and sweetness," she clearly also perceived herself as bringing France to Greece, overleaping the local academic establishment by introducing new theories, technologies, and, as often as she could, experts from metropolitan Europe. There is a distinctly colonial feel to the focus on mapping, as well as the martial terms used to describe the collecting trips ("missions," "campaigns," "voyages"). The center's aim was to "resurrect" the homelands of the refugees, and Merlier would often remind her researchers that they were the "builders" of the settlements, transplanting them on to Greek ground with the raw material of the informants' narratives. Materials were categorized according to Greek place name, and the basic cartographic units were the seventeen ancient Roman provinces rather than Ottoman administrative or Orthodox ecclesiastical ones. Founding the archive in Greece, thus, appears as an attempt to incorporate a greater Hellenism—the failed, but now re-collected, Greek irredentist dream—within the Greek national narrative, a "recuperation" of the failed military plan on an ideological level (Petropoulou 1996, 416).

Merlier's projection of an imagined "there" into the space of Asia Minor can also be understood if we situate her project alongside Greek literary and cultural modernism, whose defining context was also the shrinking of Hellenism after the events of 1922. As Vangelis Calotychos explains, in imagining a Hellenism broader than the narrow physical territory of the Greek state, Greek literary modernists looked to the Aegean to discover an aboriginal nature and a Greek East (though one devoid of Turkish elements). Asia Minor, thus, became the "*topos* of Greek loss, and not a Turkish present" (1992, 60). In this context, it is not surprising that the center began its research with refugees from Cappadocia (and later Pontos) rather than with the more familiar and more clearly "Greek" communities of northwestern and western Asia Minor.[17] The research journeys entailed in making the center's archive, thus, can be seen as physical enactments of new geopolitical relationships. The surprise expressed in discovering the exotic East from and in Athens reflects a new nation-based vision of Hellenism that, following the catastrophe, would replace the multiple, decentered relationships of the historic Greek world. While the imagined topos that would be reconstructed by the center was Asia Minor, in practice, it could only be approached through specific movements within the space of the nation and its capital city. The making of the archive, as a result, can be seen as a reflection of the growing concentration of the country's economic, political, and cultural life in Athens during postwar reconstruction.

Yet, if scholarship precedes and follows conquest, what can we make of the recording of the Greek presence in Asia Minor *after* Greek irredentist ambitions had been forever thwarted in the region (Kitromilides 1987, 29)? The archive's resemblance to an Orientalist knowledge project is not only belied by the timing of its construction, but also by the fact that it was set up on the basis of personal initiative and without the support of the Greek state. Rather than a nexus of power/knowledge, the order of the archive often seems more like a reflection of Merlier's personal fastidiousness and sense of etiquette, reflected in her fussiness about penmanship, her ban on the use of ballpoint pens, her tradition of sending Christmas cards to the refugees, and her penciled-in grammatical corrections to the researchers' field notes. Merlier seemed to treat the archive much like a home that needed to be kept impeccably neat. "I will be so happy to see our Archives put in order; they will already be unrecognizable after the first housekeeping (*nikokirema*) which you will have done to them," she writes from Aix-en-Provence in 1967.

For Merlier, the conjunction of "work" and "letter," like that of "personal" and "archive," allows her to transcend narrow definitions of both identity and scholarship. As material circuits and imaginative spaces, work letters enable Merlier to weave her personal history back into Hellenism through the mediating figures of a resurrected Anatolia and a modernizing Athens. Letter writing can be seen as the modus vivendi of any diaspora intellectual, in Merlier's case, emerging out of her self-appointed role as purveyor of cosmopolitan knowledge (in Greece) and of exotic fieldwork goods (in France). As opposed to the field notes of the researchers, the letter is not a strictly empirical genre. It creates a space for fantasy and speculation in which Merlier can assume her role as dreamer of the archive.

Merlier's reliance on the highly feminized genre of the letter, however, also exposes the gendering of history. The determination to call her letters *work,* as well as to do work in spaces of leisure, seems to have reflected her own difficulties in defining what she was doing in the absence of institutional structures. As Merlier seemed aware, the "personal" nature of this archive made it vulnerable to critique as the amateur project of a "lady of leisure." Her commitment could be decried as the selfish satisfaction of a whim, her turn to narrative as an extension of women's pleasure reading, her diplomacy as resort hopping, and her center a classroom she built so she could play professor. Yet, as Bonnie Smith cautions, only the "interlacing" of men's and women's historical writing reveals the extent to which professionals have "constructed their standards of excellence by differentiating themselves from a low, unworthy, and trivial 'other'" (1998, 9), so often embodied in the woman historian as obsessive amateur and vain scribbler.

Although letters connect worlds, they also mark distance and signal absence. Rather than part of a dialogue, they can form a solipsistic reverie. Reflecting the tendency to read intellectual history from the top down, or as Nicholas Dirks has noted, to seek in the archive the "originary voice of an author or the guiding presence of a master orientalist" (1993, 308), the center's research has only been appraised through reading Merlier's writings about it even though she herself never did fieldwork. The field reports of the researchers have never been systematically examined.

City, Buses, Notes: Memory Work in Post–Civil War Athens

While the personal histories of Merlier and the refugees have been carefully documented, the center's archives contain little information about the researchers. The few biographies of the original researchers that have been recorded focus exclusively on their academic credentials and accomplishments. Yet, one of the first bits of local folklore I learned at the center was that it had been a haven for Communists and liberals. Even though many researchers had university degrees in philology, they could not work in public schools because of their family's or their own political records. Several researchers had been jailed or exiled before or after working at the center. The close relatives of others had been murdered during the Nazi Occupation or the civil war.

In this section, I situate the center's research within local political contexts and, at the same time, consider how this research was very much about suppressing those contexts. I focus on the "fieldwork reports" (*deltia metavasis*) that researchers were required to submit with their data and that have been permanently filed alongside them. Reflecting Merlier's attempt to reform historical scholarship with modernist writing, these fieldwork tales were clearly addressed to Merlier as the archive's first reader. As a disciplined routine of scholarship and a formulaic scene of writing, the field notes served an instrumental purpose in the construction of the social identities of the researchers.

For many researchers, the refugee quarters are depicted as gateways into a mysterious Eastern world. Often it is through entrance to a backstage area, a courtyard or the interior of a home, that the researchers feel they have come into contact with the real Asia Minor. One researcher reports:

Skouze street, where Baloglou lives is a pretty street with old aristocratic Piraeus houses. The number 28, however, of the same street, is above a very old door, which leads to a big courtyard and around which in a row, door-to-door, are squalid residences. . . . The image that opens before me, as I wait for Penelope Baloglou, is reminiscent of scenes from the Neo-realist Cinema. Clothes spread out on lines, dirty, weak children who run around and hit each other, and one or two men, who prepare the cutting of the onions for the famous *souvlaki,* which will be sold from carts on the streets. Such squalidness! But so it is; in a few minutes Mrs. Penelope Baloglou comes and takes me to her room. Poor, small, semi-basement, but well-kept and cute.[18]

In this passage, we see that Asia Minor is just behind a door on a "respectable" street. The researcher temporarily occupies the position of cinematographer as she waits for Baloglou to come; the scene presents itself to her only as a simulation of itself. It is almost *too* real to be real. Its difference corresponds to her expectation; it looks like the kind of place from which the *souvlaki* carts with their tasty Eastern foods might come. The predictable shock occasioned by this scene, the disconcerting juxtaposition of the "old aristocratic houses" and the "squalid" courtyard, might lead to disgust if another door did not lead to a dignified and neat interior.

The myriad little journeys by bus, tram, metro, and foot that the researchers etched through the streets of the city created field zones in the refugee quarters that were simultaneously different time zones, connected but distinct from the modern center of the city. Although peasants from remote Cappadocia had been transformed into members of the urban proletariat living in shanties a few kilometers from downtown Athens, memory work would restore them to their Anatolian villages and their traditional occupations. At the same time, the field reports of the researchers denied the political character of the refugee neighborhoods, many of which had become known during the war less as "little Cappadocias" than as "little Moscows," by depicting them primarily as spaces of cultural difference and precapitalist social life.

While researchers and informants often turned out to share common political histories and views, memory work seems to have brought class identities sharply to the fore. Refugee homes were sites of intense household production, and researchers would often come upon informants at the most inconvenient moments to ask them to remember for them. While researchers idealized the legendary hospitality of the Anatolian Greeks, turning a conversation about the past into historical research more often than not interrupted traditional practices by which a stranger would be welcomed into a house. It seems that many informants were uncomfortable when researchers, after they had drunk their coffee and eaten a sweet, wanted to start formal questioning. As one researcher complained:

Practically one hour had passed and with the back-and-forth about various family matters, which Mrs. Anastasia tells me, the work still hadn't begun and my watch showed 6:05. But how can you stop her when she narrates a life full of pain, toil and struggle, and she thinks that you are a hope maybe to help her. On her own, though, at some point she tells me to take out my paper and we begin work . . . But Mrs. Anastasia gets up for various tasks around the house and in the meantime she loses her thought and has to start again.[19]

In a similar incident, a researcher reports an informant's hesitation.

I can't, I can't today, she said with effort, but nevertheless she said it. She is a very polite person and it was an effort to refuse. "I'm tired, I'm sick, I have a headache," she added more softly. She opened her drawer and took a pill for her headache. "Ok, since you can't work; we won't work today." I closed my notebook and started to talk with her again, about the work, but without writing. I asked her about her village, Rision. She told me all she knew. "Now that I would like to write," I said, "We have to be able to make other people understand what Rision is." "Ah, now my headache is gone, write it."[20]

While one can only conjecture how these women spoke about their past during the course of everyday life, the frame for conversation imposed by the researchers' documenting practices often seems to have been off-putting and perhaps reminiscent of refugees' dealings with Greek bureaucracy during the course of their resettlement. As these informants were clearly aware, writing was the only way that "idle talk" could be transformed into memory work. In writing down the refugees' testimonies, researchers would not only transcribe speech into writing, but also translate foreign languages and dialects into demotic Greek. Even though Merlier wanted to hear stories from the mouths of the informants, she actually discouraged researchers from taking down whole texts in dialect, instead suggesting that they note a few characteristic words and phrases in quotation marks.

As artifacts of professional discipline, the researchers' field notes attest to the transformation of a space of dialogue into a site of historical labor. In these reports, the white-collar labor of listening and scribing was defined in contrast to the manual labor of the working-class refugees, as well as to Merlier's elite reading and writing practices. Failed encounters seem to have been recorded so frequently in field notes because these reports doubled as time cards with which researchers accounted for their yield of data. Silences also provided the researchers opportunities to paint touching scenes that demonstrated their sympathy for the refugees' pitiable condition: a condition so often "beyond words." The refugees' silences and refusals, though, might also be interpreted as commentaries on the peculiar violence of memory work itself. As suggested by Michel-Rolph Trouillot, such silences are not external or incidental to the production of history but "inherent in the process, both as part of production itself and as part of its result" (1997, 38).

Memory, Voice, Biography: Identifying the Refugee

Triandafillidi, Evmorfili. Evmorfili Triandafillidi was born in Tripolis [Pontos]. As she told me, she is 82 years old. She is illiterate and speaks only the Pontic dialect. She lived mainly in Tripolis. Around 1909 she went to Russia, from where she left in 1919 for Greece. Most of her relatives from Tripolis were lost. She is a willing, but not at all good informant. She doesn't have memory and it is difficult to communicate with her. She lives with her son-in-law. Two of her sons were killed in the *Dekemvriana*. She lives in a tent opposite no. 192 on Kallirois St., in the Sfageia district (Ano Petralona). Tram Kallithea, Karayianni stop.[21]

This spare summary of a shattered life was documented by a researcher in 1957. Resonant with allusions to the city's intimate memories and places, it dashes a brushstroke across a city still emerging from the devastation of

the war years. It also shines a light on one of its most marginal residents. Its keywords open up tragic themes in modern Greek history: *Petralona,* one of the many refugee communities that sprouted up on the edges of the city. The *Pontic* Greeks, an ethnic group that suffered an especially tragic fate, marked by multiple dislocations, purges, and forced movements, both prior to and after the catastrophe. The *Dekemvriana,* or "December days," the bitter street fighting in Athens in December 1944—the opening moves of the civil war.

Filed as an informant report, this document and the failure it records reveal in miniature the way that the center's project attempted to transform the biological individual into a historical subject and specifically a "refugee." The informants were expected to possess a unique life story and memories that could be expressed and transmitted despite the physical and emotional suffering caused by this ordeal, as well as by a second and, for some, even more painful one. In many ways, the making of these reports resembles countless other bureaucratic procedures through which refugees had already passed in the process of becoming Greek citizens. In documenting the refugees' biographies and weaving them into the fabric of the archive, the center both authenticated the data it had collected and inserted the refugees' personal stories into a national narrative that now included Asia Minor Hellenism and the catastrophe. At the same time, these biographies illuminate central, unquestioned assumptions, underlying the center's research: a bourgeois notion of the individual and of identity (*taftotita*), as well as the idea that identity is naturally defined in relation to a national history.

In many ways, the center's approach to its informants mimics state practices of identification. In his study of the distinctive way that institutions and practices of memory shaped French modernity, Matt Matsuda (1996) describes how the creation of personal files for vagabonds and criminals, including photographs, measurements, and descriptions, offset challenges to national identity posed by these dislocated and wandering peoples. Like the vagabond, the refugee is also a problematic citizen, whose cultural difference and disconnection from community and family appear to threaten social order. Following the catastrophe, many refugees moved around the country for a period of five years trying to decide the best place to live (Yiannacopoulos 1992, 32). During the course of their resettlement, refugees were then gradually registered by state and local authorities. The informant reports, thus, can be seen as yet another tool of location that "makes sense" of Evmorfili by connecting her story to modern Greek history and filing her personal information within a bureaucratic apparatus.

Characteristic products of the center's methodological bricolage, the informant reports developed out of Merlier's early folk song research. In a 1935 essay, Merlier explains that it would be ridiculous to claim that a Pontian singer is from Attica if she has only lived in Greece since 1922 or 1924. Displacement demands explanation: a story of movements. Merlier, thus, decided that every singer should be photographed and have their biography noted. Along with this information, Merlier says that a few remarks should be made to give a sense of the "personality of the subject." As an example, she reproduces a photograph of Eleni Spirou, seventy-nine years old, with the following comment: "She lives in Piraeus (Neos Kosmos), exchanged 1922, photographed 1930, she sang two songs, her husband is a sailor. The woman is charming (*haritomeni*) with lots of life and spirit. She only speaks her dialect" (1935, 18–20). It might not be an exaggeration to say that the difficulty of doing these "simple" biographical sketches drove Merlier to launch a systematic investigation of the culture and history of Greek Anatolia, using the refugee as a key source. In the everyday work of the center, these informant reports would become an integral part of the research routine. Although now permanently archived with the data, while research was still going on the reports were kept in a working file in the center's office and updated periodically. That is why Evmorfili's "address" and directions to her tent are recorded. Since research was seen as a replicable experiment, researchers were supposed to check through existing informant reports to get names and addresses of informants, especially of "reliable" or "juicy" ones.

As a *bad* informant, though, Evmorfili's case raises several questions about these routine acts of identification. For one, is she even a "Pontian"? Is her "Anatolian past" alive in her memory after her ten-year sojourn in Russia and her many years in Greece? In order to distinguish themselves from autochthonous Greeks, refugees and their offspring would often refer to themselves as refugees (*prosfiges*) when they wanted to claim a history of displacement and suffering, but as Mikrasiates (people from Asia Minor) to stress a distinct (often superior) cultural heritage (Hirschon 1989). On the one hand, reaching out to Evmorfili as a *Pontian* would valorize an identity that had made her a victim of racism and discrimination in the past. On the other hand, much must have conspired to make Evmorfili think of herself primarily as a *refugee*. Ongoing problems with refugee compensation and housing plagued many families for

decades after their arrival in Greece.[22] It is 1957, thirty-five years after the "catastrophe," and Evmorfili is still living in a tent. If the researcher had asked her about her experiences of trying to get compensation for lost property or deal with her current housing situation, might she have had more to say?

But what if neither the label of refugee or of Mikrasiatis fits? After the deaths of her sons in the war, how could Evmorfili remember Pontos? When she returned to Greece from France in 1948, Merlier herself wondered whether it would be possible to write about Asia Minor after World War II and the Holocaust. She realizes that she must weigh the tragedy of the population exchange against so much new suffering.

> When the Asia Minor disaster (*halasmos*) took place it was, even on a global scale, an unprecedented event. Since World War II, population movements, enslavement, genocide, and the annihilation of millions of people from the earth have thrown into oblivion the Asia Minor tragedy. With one difference though. Asia Minor in the history of the world and not only of Greece occupies a privileged place. Everything about its geography, history, modern folk culture in the broadest sense interests and moves first, of course, Hellenism but also world thought. (1948, 24–25)

This passage reveals the characteristic ambivalence of the center's project. Is it the *tragedy* of the refugee crisis that defines the research or the Orientalist *glories* to be discovered in the Greek Anatolian past? In Evmorfili's case, it is hard to ignore the fact that she is a recent victim of war. Other informant reports provide similar glimpses of devastating wartime losses: "During the Occupation he lost one child. The youngest of his three daughters, an angel of twelve, who died in the winter of 1942 from hunger."[23] One might also ask whether political orientation had come to overshadow refugee background as a determinant of identity. Urban refugees and their children were highly represented in the ranks of the Communist Party. The reference to the Dekemvriana in Evmorfili's brief biography leads one to assume that her sons had been active in the wartime resistance.

Evmorfili's silence brings up a final question: Can she even turn her memories into narratives? While she is *willing* to help, she is not *able* to remember ("She has no memory"; she is "not at all a good informant"). Is her past—any past—narratable? In expecting historical testimony to be as spontaneous and spirited as an oft-repeated folktale or folk song, the researchers implicitly assumed that their informants had a way of talking about themselves as historical actors. Evmorfili is not alone in her speechlessness. Many reports describe inadequate informants.

> Sofia Karfoulou is an old informant of our Center. She doesn't seem to know many things, or probably she has forgotten, as she says.[24]

> Maria Palitsoglou. As an informant she doesn't say much. It is difficult to make her speak. I don't know anything, the others told you about it, she tells me constantly.[25]

> Prodromos Mezoglou. Because he lived days of horror, as his family says, he is not quite right in the head. When you think he is well, the same moment he gives signs of unbalance. No one therefore can depend on his information.[26]

Ann Stoler and Karen Strassler (1999) have argued that the belief that people, particularly people living on the margins of society, can compose their lives into narratives remains widespread in the current fascination with the study of memory in colonial studies. They challenge a hydraulic model of memory in which it is assumed that memories are "housed as discrete stories awaiting an audience," available to be "tapped" by researchers. In addition, they question whether such fully formed alternative narratives necessarily circulate among subalterns, who are often lacking scripts; audiences; and, above all, the authority to craft them.

Unlike oral historians, though, Merlier and her researchers were not looking for a counterhistory or for subaltern knowledge; for them, oral testimony should complement, not challenge, written texts produced by educated refugees. Even though Merlier did not want educated refugees to give oral testimony in their stiff and formal Greek, in practice it turned out that researchers spent much of their time speaking to educated refugees. While someone like Evmorfili would have been visited one time, some educated male refugees were consulted over and over and ended up serving as gatekeepers of local memory. One researcher established semiregular meetings with a priest from Cappadocia. The children off at school, they would work at a desk while his wife sat patiently in the corner, only now and then adding an appropriate comment: "I found him waiting for me in the little garden and we started work immediately. His wife sat near us and listened to us while crocheting."[27] In addition to speaking the language of scholarship, these refugees also spoke an idiom of Greek the researchers understood. At least one of the reasons that researchers found it "difficult to communicate" with Evmorfili was that she only spoke Pontic dialect.

While refugees mostly ascribe their silence to a lack of memory, on a few occasions, refugees seem to question the value of historical research. On a hot day in 1956, a researcher finds her informant sitting in the shade across from his barbershop.

> As we talk we hear next to us a slow song [for circle dancing]. The old man who had been reading the paper was also Pontic from Kerasounda and accompanied our talk, participating also, with a Turkish song from his homeland. Except for the song however he was not willing to say even one word. Neither would he say his name—nor let the others say his name—nor did he want to talk.[28]

Seen as a performative utterance rather than a denotative statement, the man's singing troubles the presumption that refugees' oral discourse could always be transformed into an artifact of historical knowledge relating to a distinctly Greek past.[29] First, by singing: while Merlier's research began with music, her training led her to view songs as "tokens" of Anatolia that the refugees had brought along with them as they did icons, community registers, and front-door keys. By contrast, *singing*, as transformable social performance and renewable mode of remembrance, cannot be so easily reified and concretized, rooted to distinct national spaces and languages, and reduced to a logic of "before" and "after." Second, through language: despite the center's interest in linguistic diversity and oral discourse, the ultimate goal of research was to record refugee memories in demotic Greek as well as in writing. The old man's Turkish song, by contrast, hangs in the air as a refusal to render an alien world into an understandable idiom of cultural difference or to "settle" his memories in Greece. Last, by name: he will not give his name or leave a trace, nor will he identify himself within the maps and histories of Hellenism the center is constructing. Were there others like him whose stories would not be inscribed because they could not commit to "Greece"?

Although considered a purely practical matter by the researchers, locating the refugees within the physical space of the nation and on imagined memory maps of Anatolia demonstrated how history, like bureaucracy, clamps down on people's shifting and overlapping "residences" in diverse languages, communities, and experiences of suffering. Through the tiny window opened by these refusals and silences, however, we glimpse, if only in a fragmented way, traces of truly lost lives, which could not be divided, packed up, and borne across the Aegean for redemption.

Archival Reflexiveness

There is a danger that current research on the cultural history of archives will be limited to studies by archivists and historians of "their" archives, especially if these archives happen to be located in "privileged topologies." This essay has focused on an idiosyncratic private archive as a way of broadening the definition of archives and the scope of possible research. In addition to illuminating the contests over cultural memory within a particular cultural and political context, a minor archive, such as the one examined in this essay, also reveals aspects of the relationship of dominant archival cultures to peripheral ones.

Private archives are not outside of or irrelevant to discussions of state archives; they are important sites in which social actors actively construct their relationship to the state, assimilating its categories of identification or challenging them. In the wake of the radical shrinking of Hellenism caused by the Asia Minor Catastrophe, Merlier used her archive to construct a new notion of Greekness that involved both the imaginative reconstruction of Anatolia and the recentering of the Greek world in Athens. Merlier set up this personal archive with the aim of combating the national forgetting of Greek Anatolia and used oral testimony of ordinary people to challenge historical orthodoxies. By creating a virtual census of Anatolian Greeks and "relocating" them in their original homelands, the center's research could be seen as insisting on the noncoincidence of Greek citizenship and Greek nationality. Yet, asking the refugees to speak if not Greek, always *as Greeks,* ultimately reflected a shocking and glaring blindness in the center's research: the failure to take into account the fact that people whose lives had been irrevocably shattered and destroyed by the divisive politics of nationalism and the violence of campaigns of ethnic supremacy (whether Greek or Turkish), people whose present existence in their "Greek homeland" had been painfully marked by racism and ghettoization, would identify naturally, proudly, and unproblematically through the discourse of the nation.

Over time, the Anatolian past and the catastrophe have come to define memory and testimony within Greek public historical culture. The center's research can be said to have established a prototype for a depoliticized discourse on Greek ethnic difference and for concepts of historical practice and knowledge that would later become hegemonic: the refugee quarter as an ethnic enclave and space of memory work; the refugee as a one-person unit of collective memory; and Greek Anatolia as a category of the national imagination. By translating and transforming the refugees' stories, often told in "strange" dialects of Greek or even Turkish, into documents written in demotic Greek and filed in the country's symbolic center, the center could be seen as incorporating alien Greeks into the nation's self-conception, as well as into a bourgeois worldview. In treating their informants as forever-refugees, the researchers in the 1950s and 1960s repressed (both because of the center's goals and the prevailing political situation) the wartime experiences of their informants, as well as their own. Remembering Anatolia had the effect of causing the willful forgetting of other stories, thus transforming social spaces of recent and ongoing political and class conflict into worlds of exotic cultural difference. In retrospect the silencing of the civil war and its legacy entailed in the execution of this memory project is stunning.

Archival categories and documents take shape in dialectical relationship with particular genres and technologies of documentation. The difficulties encountered in extracting "refugee memory" exposed the particular ways that the center's archival practices created memory as a material artifact. In transforming the social space formed by hospitality and dialogue into one of structured memory work, this research erased other modes, idioms, and practices of remembering. In using the literary testimony as a template for the normative genre of remembrance, the researchers effectively individualized memory and assumed its *essential* historicity. Their archiving practices, thus, normalized the idea that personal history is an integral unit of collective history, as well as the very idea that personal identity should be conceived in terms of national history.

While looking at archives in ethnographic ways provides insight into the political circumstances and epistemological frameworks in which they were constructed, thinking about how people "read in the archive today" illuminates the contemporary historical moment and new conceptions of historical knowledge and practice. While archives tend to be associated with the mundane operations of a passionless bureaucracy, it is just as important to consider desires and fantasies, fulfilled or not, that both propel the original making of archives and drive their ongoing physical and conceptual reordering. Today, against the backdrop of the post–Cold War upsurge in Balkan nationalisms and escalating global refugee crises, as well as in the context of academic paradigm shifts that have brought attention to memory politics and historical culture, the center's archive has become newly relevant and open to novel kinds of readings. Interestingly, both today and in the past, the center's oral archive, which aimed to recover, not conceal, signs of cultural hybridity in the Greek Anatolian past, has been conceived by its archivists and many of its users as a potential counterpoint to mainstream Greek nationalism. Indeed, one of the things that is most striking about the center's oral archive is how it institutionalized the Anatolian past as a key topos of Greek cultural memory, as well as of its reform.

In this essay, I used textual ethnography both as a way of researching an archive and as a way of writing about it. As opposed to a text/context model of the role of language in society, textual ethnography examines the co-construction of rhetorical forms and social relations. In the case of the center, producing and archiving documents enacted a complex mobilization of social actors and chronotopes. Behind-the-scenes texts, like letters, field notes, and informant reports, with their depictions of intimate scenes of writing, turned out to be critical devices of legitimation that strategically introduced personal histories into dominant narratives of citizenship, at the same time that they questioned them. The itineraries traced by the letters Merlier sent from France and Switzerland to the researchers in Athens, as well as by the field reports researchers sent her about their collecting journeys from the center of Athens to working-class neighborhoods where the refugees lived, mapped routes, contact zones, and symbolic topographies that, in turn, defined the shifting contours of national, class, and political identities. The center's archive also created a place of its own: an alternative intellectual and social sphere, a kind of "home," for various people dislocated by a repressive postwar Greek society, including cosmopolitan aristocrats, middle-class educated people stigmatized with left-wing histories, and disenfranchised refugees.

A final issue involves the relation of the center's archive to archives in general. While the Center for Asia Minor Studies might play a significant role in the Greek landscape of cultural memory and historical production, one might ask what significance this little archive, located at the edge of Europe and created on the basis of a single individual's vision and determination, could hold when placed in a discussion about the state archives of a major Western power. The epistemological uncertainty and bricolage that characterized the center's research appears to be a characteristic sign of intellectual "underdevelopment." Yet, the center's unusual use of oral testimony might make us pause to consider how political conditions in the Balkans had created the circumstances for an active, if underconceptualized, engagement with refugee and postcolonial issues before such phenomena and the language to speak of them had emerged in Western Eu-

rope. This ethnography of the making of an archive on the margin of Europe might be taken as a challenge to a top-down understanding of shifts in theoretical paradigms that ignore the particular cultural and historical contexts in which social knowledge is produced.

NOTES

1. Indeed, for Hayden White modern historiography is defined by its closure in contrast, for instance, to annals or chronicles, which present the world as a "mere sequence without beginning or end or as sequences of beginnings that only terminate and never conclude" (1987, 24). He notes: "The demand for closure in the historical story is a demand, I suggest, for moral meaning, a demand that sequences of real events be assessed as to their significance as elements of a moral drama" (21).

2. On the "ethnography" and "biography" of archives, see Stoler 1992; Dirks 1993. As loci of research practice, historians' *archive* and anthropologists' *field* can be compared "as textual, interpretive activities, as disciplinary conventions, and as strategic spatializations of overdetermined empirical data" (Clifford 1990, 54–55).

3. The permanent building for the state archives long seemed to be under permanent *construction*, with documents, the great bulk uncataloged, stored in various rented spaces around Athens, as well as in basements of public buildings. See "Archives without Beginning or End," *To Vima*, May 5, 1996. The new building of the Greek General State Archives, built on land donated by a private benefactor in 1972, finally opened in November 2003.

4. The files of the Security Police, some dating as far back as the interwar years and others continuing through the civil war (1946–49) and the military dictatorship (1967–74), were burned on August 30, 1989, after the formation of the first post–civil war coalition government. While destroying the files was seen as a way to eradicate a painful past and decades of social stigma, the possibility of writing about the state's persecution of the Left through a history of its practices of archiving and surveillance—as is possible, for instance, in the case of the former East Germany with Stasi archives—has been significantly compromised.

5. For more on the culture of personal archives in Greece, see Papailias 2005.

6. Turks, on the other hand, refer to this event simply as *mübadele* (the exchange) and to the people who came to Greece from Turkey as *muhacir* (one who migrated).

7. Religion was the criteria for the exchange. The 1923 Convention Concerning the Exchange of Greek and Turkish Populations arranged for "a compulsory exchange of Turkish nationals of the Greek Orthodox religion established in Turkish territory, and of Greek nationals of the Moslem religion established in Greek territory." The exchanged peoples automatically became citizens of the state in which they were resettled. The Greek Orthodox population of Istanbul and the Muslim population of Thrace were excepted from the exchange.

8. Although it might be argued that a popular sense of the self as a historical subject emerges in the context of leftist ide-

ology and mass participation in World War II Resistance, discourses on the catastrophe are the first to conceptualize the ordinary person, and especially the victim, as a giver of testimony. A dominant theme of Greek literature both before and after World War II, the catastrophe also proved a galvanizing point for the development of the narrative technique of first-person testimony in Greek literature (Doulis 1977).

9. A common view is that "refugees" simply became "Communists." In reality, the refugee vote, which in the interwar period had been firmly behind liberal prime minister Venizelos, split along rural-urban lines. Urban refugees were heavily represented in the ranks of the Communist Party, and rural refugees tended to support the political right (Mavrogordatos 1983).

10. Although the 1923 Lausanne Convention had specified that refugees would be compensated for immovable property left behind, the 1930 Ankara Convention signed by Venizelos and Ataturk withdrew these obligations. The Refugee Settlement Commission (RSC), an autonomous organization that had overseen resettlement, was also disbanded in 1930. Even though the problems of the refugees were far from solved, the state clearly signaled its desire to close this chapter of Greek history.

11. Far from making bridges to Turkey, "lost homelands" rhetoric is usually concerned with recalling Turkish persecution. Anatolian Greeks tend to portray themselves not just as Greek but as more Greek than (and superior to) mainland Greeks, as well as to emphasize the commercial success of Europeanized Greeks in Asia Minor. By contrast, the center deliberately focused its research on remote and ethnically Turkish regions, such as Cappadocia, rather than affluent commercial centers like Izmir (Greek Smyrna). Researchers were instructed to seek out refugees who had lived humble lives in Asia Minor and were now marginalized in Greek society.

12. The center's publication *Refugee Greece* (Yiannacopoulos 1992) is composed primarily of this kind of material, particularly photographs of refugee settlements.

13. Although Merlier originally planned to collect and archive songs from all over Greece, she soon decided to focus her efforts on the songs of refugees from Thrace and Asia Minor, whose cultural traditions after the catastrophe were especially vulnerable to loss and transformation.

14. On Merlier's intellectual background, see Petropoulou 1998.

15. The "refugee" as a modern "object of social-scientific" knowledge and a "legal problem of global dimensions" did not emerge until after World War II (Malkki 1995). In the 1920s, though, with the violent uprooting of populations during the Balkan wars and Russian Revolution, displaced peoples were already starting to become a subject of international management. Attesting to the protean nature of the category "refugee" at the time of the population exchange, the proposal for the Convention Concerning the Exchange of Greek and Turkish Populations was introduced under the heading of "repatriation of prisoners" and the exchanged populations were referred to as "involuntary emigrants."

16. Work Letters (9/22/56), 59.

17. Cappodocia, in particular, symbolized a Greekness both the most tenuous (most Orthodox populations were Turkish-speaking and shared the culture of the local Muslims) and the most authentic (there were surviving islands of medieval Greek

speakers). Izmir (Greek Smyrna) might have been the center of the Greek (and European) presence in Asia Minor, but its horrific burning would always bring to mind Turkish violence and a scene of closure; in addition, as an urban center, Izmir represented Western capitalist modernity. Cappadocia, on the other hand, in addition to preserving traces of an age-old Hellenism, could stand as a symbol for a harmonious world of precapitalist and prenationalist social relations.

18. Archive of Oral Tradition, Fieldwork Report: Cappadocia, Nigdi (12/4/57). Researcher: Eleni Gazi; informant: Penelope Baloglou.

19. Archive of Oral Tradition, Fieldwork Report: Cappadocia, Nigdi-Kayiavasi (5/10/57). Researcher: Eleni Gazi.

20. Archive of Oral Tradition, Fieldwork Report: Pontos, Trapezounda [Trabzon] (9/25/57). Researcher: Hara Lioudaki; informant: Vasiliki Papadopoulou.

21. Archive of Oral Tradition, Informant Report: Pontos, Tripolis (5/13/57). Researcher: Eleni Karatza.

22. Most observers agree that given the great numbers of refugees and the political and economic instability of the Greek state, the settlement of the refugees (which was accomplished with the help of numerous international organizations) was a significant achievement. However, the mishandling of refugee compensations and the liquidation of properties in Turkey led to decades of frustration and economic hardship for many refugees. For the most part, rural refugees fared better than urban ones. In 1952, there were 14,241 families living in shanties, who were entitled to urban settlement; in 1978, 3,000 urban families were still waiting for settlement (Mavrogordatos 1983, 186–91).

23. Archive of Oral Tradition, Informant Report: Cappadocia, Kaisareia [Kayseri]. Researcher: Ermolaos Andreadis; informant: Mihalis Avramidis.

24. Archive of Oral Tradition, Informant Report: Cappadocia, Farasa (4/29/55). Researcher: Aglaia Loukopoulou.

25. Archive of Oral Tradition, Informant Report: Cappadocia, Farasa (1/24/54). Researcher: Aglaia Loukopoulou.

26. Archive of Oral Tradition, Informant Report: Cappadocia, Farasa (4/22/55). Researcher: Aglaia Loukopoulou.

27. Archive of Oral Tradition, Fieldwork Report: Cappadocia, Farasa (8/25/53). Researcher: Aglaia Loukopoulou; informant: Papathodoros.

28. Archive of Oral Tradition, Fieldwork Report: Pontos, Trapezounda [Trabzon] (7/5/60). Researcher: Eleni Gazi.

29. In his study of Bedouin historical practices, Andrew Shryock has argued persuasively against the lures of ethnohistory and historical ethnography that while incorporating oral sources translate them into yet another kind of document, thus, erasing the *practices* of oral history and the *structures* in which it circulates. While seeming to question hegemonic Western models of historiography, these strategies, he suggests, simply extend them (1997, 11–37).

REFERENCES

Boym, Svetlana. 1998. "On Diasporic Intimacy: Ilya Kabakov's Installations and Immigrant Homes." *Critical Inquiry* 24 (2): 498–524.

Calotychos, Vangelis. 1992. "Westernizing the Exotic: Incorporation and a Green Line around a Non-Space." *Journal of the Hellenic Diaspora* 18 (2): 35–67.

Clifford, James. 1990. "Notes on (Field)notes." In *Fieldnotes: The Makings of Anthropology,* ed. Roger Sanjek, 47–70. Ithaca: Cornell University Press.

Combe, Sonia. 1994. *Archives interdites: Les peurs françaises face à l'histoire contemporaine.* Paris: Albin Michel.

Derrida, Jacques. 1996. *Archive Fever: A Freudian Impression.* Trans. Eric Prenowitz. Chicago: University of Chicago Press.

Dirks, Nicholas. 1993. "Colonial Histories and Native Informants: Biography of an Archive." In *Orientalism and the Postcolonial Predicament: Perspectives on South Asia,* ed. Carol Breckenridge and Peter van der Veer. Philadelphia: University of Pennsylvania Press.

Doulis, Thomas. 1977. *Disaster and Fiction: Modern Greek Fiction and the Impact of the Asia Minor Disaster of 1922.* Berkeley: University of California Press.

Echevarría, Roberto González. 1998. *Myth and Archive: A Theory of Latin American Narrative.* 2d ed. Durham, N.C.: Duke University Press.

Hassam, Andrew. 1990. "'As I Write': Narrative Occasions and the Quest for Self-Presence in the Travel Diary." *Ariel* 21 (4): 33–47.

Hirsch, Marianne. 1997. *Family Frames: Photography, Narrative and Postmemory.* Cambridge: Harvard University Press.

Hirschon, Renée. 1989. *Heirs of the Greek Catastrophe: The Social Life of Asia Minor Refugees in Piraeus.* Oxford: Clarendon Press.

Kitromilides, Paschalis. 1987. "The Intellectual Foundations of Asia Minor Studies: The R.W. Dawkins–Melpo Merlier Correspondence." *Bulletin of the Center for Asia Minor Studies* 6:9–30.

Liakos, Andonis. 1998. "The Ideology of 'Lost Homelands.'" *To Vima,* September 13 (in Greek).

Malkki, Liisa. 1995. "Refugees and Exile: From 'Refugee Studies' to the National Order of Things." *Annual Review of Anthropology* 24:495–523.

Matsuda, Matt. 1996. *The Memory of the Modern.* New York: Oxford University Press.

Mavrogordatos, George. 1983. *Stillborn Republic: Social Coalitions and Party Strategies in Greece, 1922–1936.* Berkeley: University of California Press.

Merlier, Melpo. 1935. *Essai d'un tableau du folklore musical grec: Le syllogue pour l'enregistrement des chansons populaires.* Athens: Société pour la Propagation des Livres Utiles.

———. 1948. *The Archive of Asia Minor Folklore: How It was Founded—How It Worked.* Athens: Collection de l'Institut Français d'Athènes (in Greek).

Merlier, Octave. 1974. *The Last Hellenism of Asia Minor: Exhibition of the Work of the Center for Asia Minor Studies.* Athens: Kentro Mikrasiatikon Spoudon (in Greek).

Papailias, Penelope. 2005. *Genres of Recollection: Archival Poetics and Modern Greece.* New York: Palgrave Macmillan.

Perks, Robert, and Alistair Thomson. 1998. *The Oral History Reader.* London: Routledge.

Petropoulou, Ioanna. 1996. "L'image de L'Orient." *Deltio Kentrou Mikrasiatikon Spoudon* 9:415–20.

———. 1997. "Artifacts of the Refugees." In *The Uprooting and the Other Homeland: Refugee Cities in Greece.* Etaireia Spoudon Neollenikou Politismou kai Genikis Paideias. Athens: Moraitis School (in Greek).

———. 1998. "The Ideological Trajectory of Melpo Merlier: The Center for Asia Minor Studies and the Formation of the Archive of Oral Tradition." In *Testimonies in Auditory and Cinematic Records as Historical Source.* University of Athens, Department of History and Archaeology. Athens: Katarchi (in Greek).

Richards, Thomas. 1993. *Imperial Archive: Knowledge and Fantasy of Empire.* London: Verso.

Shryock, Andrew. 1997. *Nationalism and the Genealogical Imagination: Oral History and Textual Authority in Tribal Jordan.* Berkeley: University of California Press.

Smith, Bonnie G. 1998. *The Gender of History: Men, Women, and Historical Practice.* Cambridge, Mass.: Harvard University Press.

Stoler, Ann L. 1992. "'In Cold Blood': Hierarchies of Credibility and the Politics of Colonial Narratives." *Representations* 37:151–89.

Stoler, Ann L., and Karen Strassler. 2000. "Castings for the Colonial: Memory Work in 'New Order' Java." *Comparative Studies in Society and History* 42 (1): 4–48.

Trouillot, Michel-Rolph. 1997. "Silencing the Past: Layers of Meaning in the Haitian Revolution." In *Between History and Histories: The Making of Silences and Commemorations,* ed. Gerald Sider and Gavin Smith, 31–61. Toronto: University of Toronto Press.

White, Hayden. 1987. *The Content of the Form: Narrative Discourse and Historical Representation.* Baltimore: Johns Hopkins University Press.

Yiannacopoulos, Yiorgos A. 1993. "The Reconstruction of a Destroyed Picture: The Oral History Archive of the Center for Asia Minor Studies." *Mediterranean Historical Review* 8 (2): 201–17.

———, ed. 1992. *Refugee Greece: Photographs from the Archive of the Center for Asia Minor Studies.* Athens: Center for Asia Minor Studies.

Qing Statesmen, Archivists, and Historians and the Question of Memory

Beatrice S. Bartlett

The great government book-collecting project of eighteenth-century China, the "Complete Library in Four Branches of Literature,"[1] offered the Qing government (1644–1912) an opportunity to proscribe and even destroy works it found offensive, particularly those that expressed antigovernment or anti-Qing sentiments. An imperial edict deputed high officials to supervise the burning of the works on the government's Index Expurgatorius at a site outside the capital city, Peking. After that, except for a remnant surviving in Japan or Europe, the presumption was that all copies of these works were permanently lost, just as the court had intended.

But the story has a happy ending: when the Qing archives were opened after the fall of the dynasty in 1912, the forbidden and supposedly destroyed books were found safely secreted inside the Grand Council archival vaults in the imperial palace. These works had survived because an unknown eighteenth-century hero—probably a high official with archive-supervisory responsibilities—defied the court's directive. He could not bear to destroy books. Apparently he was more concerned with memory than with obedience.[2]

A second story illustrates a similar archival impulse. In some Qing reports to the throne, the three characters for the name of Sun Yat-sen, the rebel leader who eventually rose to be extolled as the founding father of modern China, were disparaged by being written with a dog signific to the left of each character—a common form of derision (in our parlance, probably similar to calling someone "a dirty dog"). The repository, a Republic of China government organization, felt it had to prohibit such sacrilege—mocking the founder of the nation could not be allowed. I am told that the reports in question

have been removed from the open collection and are now hidden away in the Taibei Palace Museum, available only by special permission.[3] Again, the evidence was not destroyed but secreted.

These stories allow us to see one of the driving principles behind Qing archival preservation—save everything. As demonstrated by the preservation of the forbidden books and the documents with the derogatory dog symbols, this imperative included saving items not necessarily in the government's interest. This has been fortunate for the cause of preserving social memory. Although the Qing government made very little effort to reach out into the society and collect what might be regarded as items of social memory, and although these did not survive well when left beyond the government's protection, if such items did reach the archives, there was little risk of discard or loss. Fortunately, the concept of pre-archivage—weeding out documents deemed of minimal interest before turning them over for storage—was not known to the archivists of Qing times.[4]

Yet another feature of the Qing archives illustrated by these stories was that many Chinese government archival installations—and there are very few private holdings—are pleasingly eclectic, with contents going far beyond the category of government documents. As in the tale of the eighteenth-century books saved from burning, Chinese archives may even preserve printed books.[5] In addition, artifacts (not just drawings of the artifacts, which are also preserved, but in some cases the artifacts themselves) were saved, as well as song-sheets, court circulars, and even a few private papers. Newspapers and other items we might not consider appropriately archival frequently turn up. A Chinese archive is likely to be a repository of a vast assortment of items. Anything may be held in its vaults.

A Chinese Definition of Social Memory?

In writing this essay, I have not found a clear definition of Chinese or even Qing "social memory" that might find favor with the archival profession. Because the discussion of memory has been a debate conducted primarily among historians in the West, their definitions do not precisely fit the Chinese case. Maurice Halbwachs, one of the earliest Western historians to grapple with the problem, drew his main distinction between "individual memory" on the one hand and "collective" or "social memory" on the other.[6] Some analysts have found the two principal kinds of memory to be "private" and "public."[7] Two comparative historians discussing memories of twentieth-century wars in Japan, Germany, and the United States equate memory of the wars with the official versions that dominate news stories and textbooks and suggest that social memory is unofficial memory.[8] For the Chinese case, however, my own findings are quite different.[9]

From my study of archival practice in Qing times, I observe that Qing officials did not frame their discussions of archival practice in terms of individual and collective memories, nor did they employ any of the other Western dichotomies outlined above. Instead, they divided their holdings into two large groups of archived materials, one in the outer court (*waichao* 外朝), and one in the inner court (*neiting* 內庭). The first consisted of what the government wanted known, a form of memory that might be described as "managed," "authorized," or "official." Documents in this category expressed the state's version of events and were allowed to circulate in the vast, open, outer-court bureaucracy; eventually most of these came to be housed in the vaults of the Grand Secretariat Great Treasury (Neige daku 內閣大庫). The second, for want of a better term, may be said to have consisted of "everything else"—official secrets, personnel evaluations, heterodox rebel confessions, unofficial materials, documents too cumbersome to circulate, miscellany, and the like.[10] These were held in the inner-court archives, chiefly in the Office of Military Archives (Fanglueguan 方略館).[11] In this scheme, both outer- and inner-court materials could be official, but in addition, documents of social or unofficial memory might be deposited in both kinds of archival holdings.[12] In a broad sense, unofficial memory embraced all

kinds of background information helpful in understanding both the official and the alternative or unofficial views. Much of that information would have been collected by Qing government personnel acting in their official capacities. Because of Qing archivists' laudable willingness to save almost everything, I tell my graduate students that they should not ignore the official archives even when collecting materials for studying the unofficial side of history, as well as local archives if those are appropriate.[13]

But what about nongovernment and nonofficial sources of information that were not held in government archives? Would these be fruitful sources of social memory? The answer is that they surely would be—but only if we can locate them, a dubious prospect indeed. During the Qing, little effort was made to preserve the unofficial or the private. Much has been lost. The reader may well ask why present-day archivists and historians in search of Qing social memory do not zealously scour the country for privately held collections of personal papers.[14] But aside from printed book collections, Qing policy discouraged families from holding on to such papers.

One eighteenth-century example of the court's accusation against an individual will suffice to demonstrate the dangers that might lurk in a private hoard. In the Yongzheng reign (1723–35), a government examination commissioner chose one of the topics from an ancient classical text—what we would call an essay question—with the subject, "Where the people rest" (*weimin suozhi* 維民所止). The Yongzheng emperor, or someone in his entourage, looked at this quotation and observed that its first and last characters resembled those of the emperor's reign title (Yongzheng 雍正) but with a significant difference: in the quotation the tops of the characters resembling the reign-title characters "Yong" and "Zheng" were removed. By a tortured process of reasoning, the selected quotation was then viewed as recommending that the emperor have his own top—or head—lopped off. Indeed, in the eighteenth century this was assumed to be the motive behind the official's choice of examination question.

As a result, the hapless official was forthwith cast into prison, where he died. His male family members were also imprisoned and his widow consigned to internal exile.[15] The story of this official's fall became well known at the time and warned others against harboring anti-Qing sentiments—or at least against committing them to paper. Ridding one's home of anything that might some day be the object of a twisted interpretation and taken to be incriminating evidence of antigovernment views was a necessity in the face of an imperial paranoia so strong it could wreck an entire family. Although in China periods of official paranoia have alternated with occasional mild relaxations, in general it may be said that private papers and letters did not survive well. Few private and unpublished family or business papers from Qing times are today available for consultation.[16]

So for social memory from Qing times, the Chinese official archives must be our chief recourse. There, memories rising from the society take many forms. Although much evidence that we would eagerly read today never found its way into official archival storage, nevertheless, even a haphazard search of government archives may retrieve valuable materials. One of the most obvious examples of social memory in the Qing archives is rebel confessions—these often describe the heterodox beliefs that inspired rebellions and identify the master-disciple networks that transmitted those beliefs throughout the countryside. Another example lies in the records of criminal cases preserved in the archives, which might also contain antigovernment anguish. Many officials sent in the information basic to social memory or essential for illuminating context when fulfilling reporting requirements on prices, weather, harvests, and earthquakes. I once came across an official provincial document that described a plague of grasshoppers, complete with an enclosed drawing of the nasty creatures' nests.[17] Such a report served an official purpose in the Qing and yet today can help us understand the unofficial.

It is probable that in the end, neither official nor unofficial memories can be preserved in all their fullness of detail—they are ideal types that cannot be fully assembled and grasped in all their diversity. In many instances it is more difficult to dredge up social memories than to become informed on the well-publicized and widely circulated official statements of government-managed memory. The retrieval and preservation of social or unofficial memory may be eased for archivists who assemble materials on the twentieth century, for which we have much more documentation in the form of newspapers, letters to newspaper and journal editors, historical movies, television programs, textbooks, personal reminiscences, oral histories, and interviews, almost none of which survive for the Qing.

A Manual of Qing Archival Policy

Let us imagine that the Qing statesmen, archivists, and historians in charge of supervising the archives were to compose a rule book of prescribed archival practice, par-

ticularly in relation to social memory. What prescriptions would such books contain? The Qing's high official supervisors were committed to upholding the approved views—in some situations they might even have determined what these should be. In what follows I have used both the archival supervisors' arrangements and storage methods as well as their occasional explanations of policy to pull together some of the advice and regulations they might have written had they composed an office training manual for instructing the next generation of archivists.[18]

In the imaginary guide, the primary aim of archival preservation would have been, of course, to protect the regime and allow no antigovernment views to circulate widely, even if inscribed in government documents. Next would have been the aim of preserving the imperial face. The emperor had to be portrayed in the best possible light: losses of the imperial temper or evidence of imperial incompetence or even of indecision had to be treated as national secrets. A tertiary consideration would have been to preserve the face of officials, provided that such did not conflict with the first or second aim. When the Yongzheng emperor, for instance, scathingly wrote to a local official, "You are just one of those mediocre provincial officials appointed on a trial basis because I could not find anyone better," although this put the official in an unfavorable light, the document was allowed to circulate and even appear in print.[19] Supervising officials may have decided that the emperor's withering insight was more worthy of publication than any secret handling that might have been sensitive to the official's need for face. Or the official may not have possessed enough clout at court to prevent publicizing this stroke of imperial wit.

The archival supervisors' aims, if carried out, guaranteed a view of the government as all-powerful, effective, and orderly. The government was to be portrayed as offering thoroughgoing control from the center and organized to discourage challenges. Such an outlook offered little hope to those who championed alternative views—and of course that was precisely what was intended. On rare occasions an archivist might save some prohibited books or documents, but for the most part the archives were designed to preserve the government's story.

The chief curatorial method was to create a structure that accomplished the same thing as our classification systems—top secret, secret, and so forth. The Qing government achieved this with its two parallel but separate communication systems, one—the old open, outer-court (*waichao*), nonsecret system inherited from the previous dynasty (the Ming)—and the secret one created in the early Qing that operated in the inner court (*neiting*). The two systems possessed separate document streams, separate methods for processing the documents on their arrival at the capital, separate storage systems for archiving the documents, and separate systems for using documents to write official historical works.[20] This strict division had the advantage of compartmentalizing not only the documents but also the personnel allowed to see them.

The two systems were not exactly alike. By mid-Qing times (the eighteenth century), the old outer-court system was a structure operated by a vast bureaucracy through which documents could circulate easily. This structure included methods for making selected documents available to the officials and in cases of certain public announcements to the population of the country at large. The best-known of the vehicles fulfilling this purpose was the *Peking Gazette* (*Tangbao* 塘報), a court circular that was regularly dispatched to government offices in the provinces to make selected documents widely available in a timely fashion. Many official historical works were also compiled from documents that circulated in the outer court.

The inner court possessed almost the same structure, but one in which access to its secret documents and facilities was limited to a small coterie of Grand Council high officials, clerks, errand runners, and other staff—possibly little more than two hundred men.[21] Accordingly, the inner court had its own document stream (the palace memorials),[22] its own processing offices (the Chancery of Memorials [Zoushichu 奏事處] and the Grand Council), its own archive (the Office of Military Archives [Fanglueguan], which actually contained much more than just military reports), and its own publications (chiefly the campaign histories [*fanglue* 方略]).

But it was not a case of the left hand not knowing what the right hand was doing. The separation between the two systems was not rigid—there were crossovers. These were achieved not by bureaucratic regulations or traditional routines but personally, through the high supervising officials. By means of personal directives—sometimes emanating from a source as high as the emperor himself—documents could flow between the two courts, although the main direction was from the secrecy of inner-court storage to the openness of the outer court. As just about everything that came to hand was saved, the primary issue was not what to save but what to disseminate.

Having provided the background necessary to understand how the system might have been manipulated, I shall take up four principal methods of restricting or allowing circulation of documents as these developed over the course of the middle Qing (eighteenth and early nineteenth centuries): first, reducing opportunities for publication; second, direct action to arrange circulation; third, a secret enclosure system; and fourth, in some cases arranging that a report conveyed information needed to protect the government. The training manual that I have envisioned might well have described several more ruses for ensuring that the archives told the government's story rather than raising specters of social memory—but my four examples will suffice.

The earliest method that the imaginary rule-book might have treated was the reduction of opportunities for publishing archival documents. Toward the end of the Yongzheng period (1723–35), at a point when nearly all palace memorials, and indeed the entire system, were kept secret, the court decided to celebrate the accomplishments of the reign by publishing considerable numbers of edicts and reports to the throne.[23] The centerpiece of this publication effort was a printed edition of thousands of the emperor's own handwritten responses (vermilion rescripts) on the provincial palace memorials (*Yongzheng Zhupi yuzhi* 雍正 硃批諭旨), an enormous compilation that publicized the emperor's painstaking concern for government affairs.[24] In permitting such publications, high officials, archivists, and editors ruled out state secrets, concealed imperial weakness, and allowed certain officials to enjoy a high reputation because of their inclusion in a work sponsored by the throne.

In particular, the printing of the Yongzheng palace memorials offered an opportunity to use selected documents to display an active, effective government, headed by an emperor whose lengthy vermilion rescripts showed him to be devoted to duty. In the Yongzheng-period inner court, documents were packed for archival storage in three separate groups: "published" (*yilu* 已錄), "yet to be published [in a new edition that in the end was never undertaken]" (*weilu* 未錄), and "not to be published" (*bulu* 不錄). The final prohibited category concealed not only national secrets but also the emperor's and the officials' weaknesses—these also a kind of national secret. This final category is also a good place to look for evidence of unofficial memory.

For example, a report early in the reign from one of the Six Boards at the capital described the lamentable results of an examination to identify translators well versed in both Manchu and Chinese. When the results were graded, only 9 men of the 414 who originally took the test were deemed truly capable of accomplishing the desired translation work, while 116 individuals were rated only "ordinary" (*pingchang* 平常). A large bottom group consisted of 289 men who did not qualify at all—

47 of these had turned in totally blank test papers.²⁵ Such a dire state of translation proficiency would not have reflected well on the government. It was reasonable to suppress such a report.

Other secrets eliminated in the publication of the Yongzheng palace memorials suggest how desirable it may be to go through the list of prohibited items.²⁶ A proscribed report of YZ7 (1729) listed the "nourish-honesty" (*yanglian* 養廉) stipends then being paid to Gansu provincial officials.²⁷ Also prohibited were many staff memoranda written to suggest a recommendation or path of action for the emperor's consideration. Frequently Yongzheng would simply copy these with scarcely a change into his vermilion rescripts on the memorials, which would then be returned to the author so he would learn the imperial views. Such staff recommendations had to be concealed, lest the emperor appear incapable of framing the policies regularly attributed to him alone.²⁸ Often these memoranda dealt with the thorny details of government finance and are well worth examining today. In fact, I developed a habit of identifying the prohibited memorials in the files and scrutinizing them with especial care.²⁹

Another midreign communication on military encampments was probably denied outer-court circulation because it revealed that at the highest levels in the inner court, the government had connived to deceive the outer court about the existence of the then-secret palace memorial system. The imperial calligraphy on this report begins with a recital of current regulations (doubtless known only in the inner court) for sending important information to the outer court without revealing the existence of the palace memorials: "What ought to be reported in a routine memorial [i.e., a report in the outer-court stream], accordingly report. It is not permitted because of [something in] a palace memorial not to send in a routine version." But in the final section, after this lecture on regulations, the emperor suddenly reversed himself and concluded: "In this case, that temporarily need not be done."³⁰ This confusing rescript may have been withheld because it showed the government in a thoroughly bad light, not only because of the conniving that produced duplicate reports—one for each communication system—but also because of the revelation of imperial indecision, qualities deemed unsuitable for publication.

An example of how officials' face was taken care of appears in a report from the end of the reign. Here, the emperor kept up his sarcastic needling on the subject of official inadequacies: "This memorial has much gloss-

ing," he wrote, "You [surely] did not read it over."³¹ What had probably happened was that the provincial governor-general had simply forwarded the local financial official's report without checking. The memorial was withheld from circulation, possibly because this official was highly regarded and as a result was given protection against unfavorable publicity. In fact, many candid personnel reports from the Yongzheng period were secreted lest the emperor's and the reporting official's comments should become widely known. In one exposition, a provincial memorialist described a subordinate as only ordinary, beside which the emperor exclaimed: "Yes" (*shi* 是). Later the emperor castigated another official with the statement, "I fear his sense of integrity needs looking into," and agreed with the memorialist's frank assessment of a third as "scatterbrained" (*qingtiao* 輕佻).³² Revelation of such candid comments could have been extremely damaging to morale throughout the bureaucracy.

Another kind of tinkering with the archival record appears in documents purportedly published from archival originals. The published Yongzheng-period memorials exhibit curious differences between the archival originals and their published forms. When I compared about two hundred reports with their published versions, I found only five instances in which the published versions did *not* display differences. Some of the changes were utterly insignificant; nevertheless, researchers would like to be assured of verisimilitude. The eighteenth-century editors frequently condensed a provincial author's verbiage and even rewrote the emperor's comments. Apparently the editors sought to give the imperial writing an elevated tone. For instance, one published rescript had the emperor quoting the classical philosopher Mencius, but the archival original yields no imperial reference to the sage or his works.³³ This editorial strategy was intended to reinforce the image of deep classical learning as part of the public imperial persona.

Later in the eighteenth century, the system came to be manipulated in another way—which our imaginary guidebook of prescriptions might have described—when the palace memorials had become both more numerous and less secret. This was accomplished by having high supervising officials, or sometimes the emperor himself, determine which palace memorials would be released to the outer court. Release was a serious matter, because it not only made the memorial content available to the many potential readers in the large outer-court bureaucracy, but also allowed the document contents to be included in the court circular (*Peking Gazette*) as well as more formal official publications. Reports thus fated would be ordered "turned over" (*jiao* 交) to the outer court.[34] Occasional imperial rescripts also prescribed release of memorial enclosures to the outer court with the formula "Also send the enclosure" (*dan bingfa* 單並發). In this way, large numbers of once secret palace memorials reached the outer-court bureaucracy. Our hypothetical manual would show that inaction easily preserved archival secrets—a special determination was needed to forward each individual memorial, and another to send on an enclosure.

A third kind of manipulation that may be observed in the middle to late eighteenth century was the practice of writing covering palace memorials that summarized situations but left the details—often significant details—to enclosures. The covering document—but not its enclosure—would then be released to the outer court. We know this practice had become prevalent by the end of the eighteenth century because it excited the imperial alarm, causing the Jiaqing emperor (r. 1796–1820) to caution officials against excessive use of what he called the "secret enclosure" (*jiapian* 夾片) system.[35]

How did the secret enclosure system work? Enclosure content was filled with what officials in the field had decided should be treated as unofficial memory. Frequently enclosures were written to convey details that might otherwise have clogged the narratives in the covering memorials—long lists of local crop and harvest conditions, for instance, food grain price levels, rain and weather facts, earthquake and flood reports, and maps. Another candidate for enclosure treatment was the confessions of captured rebels. Confession enclosures usually contained seditious information that had to be secretly stored in the inner-court archives and kept out of general circulation. Hundreds of such confessions, usually submitted as enclosures, today survive in one or two copies only from the late eighteenth and nineteenth centuries. They detail the organizations, beliefs, and hopes behind dozens of rebel groups all over China. Twenty-five years ago, a Yale graduate student, Susan Naquin (now teaching at Princeton), was the first to make substantial use of such documents, studying a set from an 1813 attack on the palace. Rebels were rounded up in and around Peking and extensively debriefed under Grand Council auspices, possibly with the use of torture. Naquin was able to tease out an entire book that for the first time in English or Chinese published a narrative and analysis of the nature of a Chinese sectarian rebellion.[36] Of course, the evidence of such sedition could not be permitted to circulate to the outer court, appear in the *Peking Gazette,* or be inscribed in the official historical works. Accordingly,

today most confessions are still to be found in the secret inner-court archival holdings.

Archival materials can only be as good as the quality of information collected. A fourth kind of limitation that might have been prescribed in our imaginary manual involved restricting the kind of information collected in the first place. This practice met the larger goal of managing information so that it told the government's, rather than any other, story. For example, as it was thought desirable to protect officials, a report on a local uprising had to be composed to clear those involved of any and all dereliction of duty. The aim was to ensure that nothing damaging about the officials would be on file even in the top secret archives, and with high inner-court grandees supervising the taking of depositions, this was not difficult to arrange.

An example of this occurs in the Zhong Renjie case of 1841, when the captured leader was asked in the course of his interrogation if his uprising had been long in the planning. Of course, no rebel leader would be recorded as having answered such a question in the affirmative, lest the officials on the spot be accused of failing to uncover a rebellion in its planning stages. Zhong Renjie's confession complied very clearly with this requirement: "We were terrified and seized the town because we had killed an official, definitely not because we had plotted the rebellion beforehand." With this statement firmly incorporated in Zhong's deposition, the local officials (who may very well have been carrying out the initial interrogations) ensured that they would be off the hook. As a result, we shall never know if Zhong's small uprising really did erupt spontaneously, as the confessions piously attest, or was long-planned and carried out right under the noses of unobservant and lazy local officials.[37] In similar fashion, managed confessions might control other aspects of the reporting on an uprising. Much information we might like to have is forever lost, and the information that survives in the archives has to be interpreted in the light of the suspicion that some of it may have been noted to clear officials of blame rather than to determine facts.

Deliberate Forgetting

With the Qing archives so well managed and so much memory preserved, if not necessarily circulated, mention must be made of some of the few examples of deliberate official discard of documents. In these cases it apparently was not enough to bury an incriminating document in a secret holding—the document had to be destroyed. One instance concerns a missing archival record of an important imperial decision. In 1748, the grand councillor, Noqin, was sent to the southwest front to lead the Qing armies against the Jinchuan rebels. Unfortunately, Noqin was soon forced to admit defeat. When his reports of defeat reached the Qianlong emperor, Noqin was scheduled—without the formality of a trial—to be beheaded. To make matters worse, the sword of his brave grandfather, a hero of the Manchu conquest years, was hastily dispatched to the southwest to be employed in carrying out the execution, which was ordered to take place in full view of the assembled Qing armies.[38]

The archival record of this tale would surely make interesting reading, but one of the key pieces of evidence for the entire year of Noqin's demise, the "Record Book of [Grand Councillors'] Deliberations," a compilation of probably several hundred pages, is missing.[39] What is more, the file was not lost *after* the fall of the Qing, when so many other palace relics were stolen by eunuchs—it has been missing at least since the first Grand Council archives inventory was compiled in the late eighteenth century.[40] This early disappearance of a potentially embarrassing record in contrast with very few other losses of Grand Council documents strongly suggests the use of that special archival oubliette—an archivist's purposeful destruction of a set of documents. In this case the proscribed topic was probably the terrible evidence and consequences of keen imperial frustration, disappointment, and even loss of temper.[41] For the Qing archivists, protecting the imperial face was the all-important goal.

Another deliberate example of archival forgetting that plagues our research today is the Grand Council archivists' failure to preserve the alternate position papers composed in response to the imperial order for a high-level deliberation.[42] In each instance, the final agreed-on position paper was copied for various files and preserved, but the alternatives appear to have been destroyed. This may have happened because of an unwritten "unanimity rule" to the effect that if the deliberating officials presented *one* unanimous position paper, the emperor was all but bound to accept it and did so in nearly every case. On the other hand, if the officials presented more than one position, the emperor was free to decide for himself. Bureaucratic solidarity could thus trump imperial will; bureaucratic disunity—and any surviving evidence of it—handed the decision-making power to the monarch.[43] Accordingly, to preserve an official dissent that had been registered along the way to final unanimity was to risk destroying the officials' op-

portunity to decide. There was no question but that records pertaining to dissent had to be destroyed.[44]

Conclusion

In relation to the Qing archives, social memory may be defined as a document-based remembrance different from or even in opposition to the official version of events. The government's authorized tales were the ones that circulated most freely. Nevertheless, with some crucial limitations, Qing government archivists also preserved many alternative views and accounts. This is a boon to present-day researchers because private papers do not survive well in China.

When using these materials, researchers must be aware of the nature of the limitations on Qing data collection—the poor survival rate of private papers, the management of reporting at the source, the special aims of archival collection and preservation, and the restrictions on circulation and publication. There were many such limitations—I have been able to describe only a few of the most notorious.

NOTES

In the notes below, the abbreviation TPM signifies documents in the Qing archive holdings of the Taibei Palace Museum. At the museum, a report to the throne may be retrieved by its assigned number; a document that has been published may usually be retrieved in the printed edition by its date. In the following notes, I supply this information, plus the name of each document's author.

I am grateful for the assistance of the late Chao Chung-fu of the Taiwan Academia Sinica, Chuang Chi-fa of the Taibei Palace Museum, Ju Deyuan of Beijing's Number One Historical Archives, and Wei Qingyuan of the People's University Archives Department in Beijing. I also happily acknowledge the suggestions of two Yale graduate students, Edward Melillo and Shou-chih Yen. I thank Professor Keith Wrightson for arranging for me to present an earlier version of this essay at a Yale History Department lunch. Chinese terms and names in this essay are romanized according to the pinyin system, with modern personal names rendered according to the personal preference—Wade-Giles or pinyin—of the individuals named.

1. Chinese: Siku quanshu (四庫全書).

2. In the 1980s, an enterprising Taiwan publishing house printed the forbidden works.

3. I know this only as a story and do not claim to have inspected the reports themselves.

4. Had certain Grand Council documents been weeded, I might never have come across lists of tables of food ordered each day for the council, which I employed to estimate the number of staff members on duty there each day. See my *Monarchs*

and Ministers: The Grand Council in Mid-Ch'ing China, 1723–1820 (Berkeley: University of California Press, 1991), 172. The Grand Council archives also yielded other kinds of information that in different archival situations might have been discarded. On pre-archivage, see Guy Dubosq, *The Records Center: Idea and Instrument* (Washington: VIII International Congress on Archives, 1976). In contrast to weeding, occasional deliberate destruction of certain materials did take place, a subject I discuss later in this essay.

5. After the fall of the Qing dynasty (1912), many printed books, some from as early as the Song dynasty (960–1279), were also discovered in the Grand Secretariat archives.

6. Maurice Halbwachs, *The Collective Memory,* trans. Francis J. Ditter and Vida Yazdi Ditter (French edition, 1950; New York: Harper & Row, 1980), passim; see also Paul Connerton, *How Societies Remember* (French edition, 1950; New York: Cambridge University Press, 1989), 1 and passim.

7. For example, Charles S. Maier, *The Unmasterable Past: History, Holocaust, and German National Identity* (Cambridge, Mass.: Harvard University Press, 1988), 149.

8. Laura Hein and Mark Selden, "The Lessons of War, Global Power, and Social Change," in Laura Hein and Mark Selden, eds., *Censoring History: Citizenship and Memory in Japan, Germany, and the United States* (Armonk, N.Y.: M. E. Sharpe, 2000), 3–50. Western historians of China have not dealt much with questions of memory, but when they do, the focus is usually on twentieth-century events such as the Nanjing Massacre and the Cultural Revolution. See, for example, Vera Schwarcz, "How to Make Time Real: From Intellectual History to Embodied Memory," in Gail Hershatter et al., eds., *Remapping China: Fissures in Historical Terrain* (Stanford: Stanford University Press, 1996), 13–24, and Schwarcz's "The Burden of Memory: The Cultural Revolution and the Holocaust," *China Information* 11, no. 1 (summer 1996): 1–12.

9. My focus on the Qing rather than archival policy through all of China's dynastic history is largely due to the fact that few original documents survive for dynasties before the Qing. For instance, about five thousand archival items survive for the Ming period (1368–1643), whereas the figure commonly given for Qing holdings is approximately 10 million items (*Qingzhu Zhongguo diyi lishi dang'anguan chengli liushi zhounian, 1925–1985* [Felicitations to the Number One Historical Archives of China on the sixtieth anniversary of its founding, 1925–1985] [Beijing, 1985], 9). Note that the latter is only a very general figure: it enumerates materials only at the Number One and does not differentiate between a single "item" of three lines and a six-hundred-page record book, also rated a single "item." Yet the six-hundred-page album might contain as many as five hundred separate documents.

10. One kind of formal and not very descriptive personnel evaluation (the *kaoyudan* 考語單) was stored in the outer court.

11. Before the Qing inner-court system was developed, there was a way of holding secret documents in the outer-court vaults known as the Grand Secretariat Great Treasury (Neige daku). Such documents were specially labeled "secret" in the Great Treasury logbook, the "Record of Silken [i.e., imperial] Words" (*Silunbu* 絲綸簿). Once the inner-court system was developed, however, the designation "secret" only rarely appeared in these outer-court logbooks.

12. I described the Qing outer and inner courts in *Monarchs and Ministers,* chap. 1 and passim. After the Kangxi reign (1661–1722), the inner-court repositories were generally used for documents that may be described as consisting of unofficial memory.

13. Unfortunately, as a result of the civil wars that have beset China in recent centuries, local archives have survived much less well than those of the central government. Frequently a local archive's holdings date not from the beginning of the dynasty but only near the end, and even then contain only a few documents from before the twentieth century. For a highly useful bibliography of descriptions of the local archives of China, see Ye Wa and Joseph W. Esherick, comps., *Chinese Archives: An Introductory Guide* (Berkeley: University of California Institute for East Asian Studies, 1995).

14. In fact, in recent years Chinese archivists and historians have investigated old libraries and other holdings and have located a few lesser-known works.

15. L. Carrington Goodrich, "Cha Ssu-t'ing" (Ja Siting), in *Eminent Chinese of the Ch'ing Period* (Washington, D.C.: U.S. Government Printing Office, 1944), 22. The quotation comes from the Chinese classic, *The Great Learning* (chap. 3, 1). There is nothing in the original text to suggest sedition. See *The Chinese Classics,* trans. James Legge (reprint, Tabei: Wenxing Shudian, 1966), 1:362.

16. Even when government officials' private papers have been published, they rarely reveal confidential information of any kind. An example from my own research on the founding of the Qing Grand Council (the equivalent of a central government high privy council) is the autobiography of Zhang Tingyu, a Qing statesman closely involved in the council's founding and early growth. His autobiography reports hardly a word about the great event, and in some respects may be viewed as deliberately misleading, yet this key official certainly must have been well informed on the subject. See *Chenghuaiyuan zhuren ziding nianpu* [Chronological autobiography of [Zhang Tingyu]], 6 juan, preface dated 1749 (reprint, 2 vols., Taibei: Wenhai, 1970).

17. TPM, Palace Memorial YZ 016212 and enclosure, YZ2/8/7 (Sept. 23, 1724), Chen Shiguan. I am indebted to Professor Frederick W. Mote of Princeton University for identifying the depicted bugs as grasshoppers when I showed a slide of the document in the course of speaking at Princeton in 1979. Professor Mote assured me that plagues of grasshoppers as well as locusts do occur. The covering memorial has been published in *Gongzhongdang Yongzhengchao Zouzhe* [Palace memorials of the Yongzheng reign] (Taibei: Palace Museum, 1977), 3:24–26, but without its very interesting enclosure.

18. In fact, such booklets explaining some of the Qing government's archival practices are held in the Beijing Number One Historical Archives. Unfortunately, however, these guides are silent on many of the subjects of interest in this essay. Additional explanations most often appear in memoranda (*zoupian* 奏片) addressed to the emperor and composed by high statesmen, archivists, and historians. By the early nineteenth century one such manual of prescriptions for Grand Council practice had been printed: *Shuyuan jilue* [Materials on Grand Council history], comp. Liang Zhangju (reprint, 2 vols., Taibei: Wenhai, 1967). The archives also contain earlier, unpublished rule books: see for example the record book held in the Beijing

Number One Historical Archives, "Junjichu guizhu jizai" [Notations of Grand Council regulations] and TPM, "Junjichu wenyi dang" [Record book of Grand Council lateral communications [dispatched from the council's archives office]].

19. TPM, handwritten imperial rescript (excerpt) on the yellow summary (*tiehuang* 帖黄) for Palace Memorial YZ 018965, YZ 7/10/28 (Dec. 18, 1729), Futai. The document was first circulated in the *Yongzheng Zhupi yuzhi* [Vermilion rescripts [and palace memorials] of the Yongzheng [emperor]], first appearing in an experimental edition printed in 1732.

20. For a table explaining these structures, see *Monarchs and Ministers*, 18–19.

21. Calculation from *Monarchs and Ministers*, 172.

22. "Memorial" is a nineteenth-century translation of the Chinese term for "report to the throne."

23. Edicts first appeared in collections such as the "Yongzheng Shangyu Neige" [[Open] edicts to the Grand Secretariat] and "Baqi Shangyu" [Edicts to the Eight Banners].

24. On this work see my "The Secret Memorials of the Yung-cheng Period (1723–1735): Archival and Published Versions," [Taibei] *National Palace Museum Bulletin* 9, no. 4 (Sept.–Oct. 1974).

25. TPM, Palace Memorial YZ 021955, YZ1/2/16 (Mar. 22, 1723), Board of Civil Office report. In fact, nearly all memorials from officials posted at the capital were put in the prohibited category. This memorial has recently been published in *Gongzhongdang Yongzhengchao Zouzhe* [Palace memorials of the Yongzheng reign] (Taibei: Palace Museum, 1977), 1:90. The emperor's Manchu rescript, omitted from this edition (this was the museum's editorial policy for all Manchu rescripts), stated that the 116 second-class candidates should be sent for a further year of training to see if they might qualify.

26. When I made a close study of the Yongzheng government, I paid particular attention to the reports in the "prohibited" category. This can best be accomplished in the Taibei Palace Museum, whose card catalog provides this information as well as records of provenance for Yongzheng palace memorials. Long ago the Beijing Number One Historical Archives refiled its palace memorials according to eighteen large subject categories, a labor that also destroyed the documents' provenance.

27. TPM, Palace Memorial YZ 011817, undated, Xu Rong. The memorial can be dated approximately by examining the surrounding memorials in Xu Rong's archival packet, which bear the dates YC7/R7/9 (Sept.1, 1729) and YZ8/1/26 (Mar. 14, 1730).

28. See for example TPM, Palace Memorial YZ 019792, undated, Yinxiang and others, printed in *Gongzhongdang Yongzhengchao Zouzhe* 26:259. The imperial rescript that largely incorporated the high officials' recommendations appears in YZ 008880, YZ7/4/[no day] (1729), Yang Kun, and was published in the Palace Museum's Yongzheng palace memorials (13:102). The Taibei Palace Museum has many such pairs from the Yongzheng period. A different system for providing the emperor with advice was developed under the Qianlong emperor (r. 1736–95).

29. The Taibei Palace Museum's excellent memorial card files for the Yongzheng palace memorials include information on the publication status of each memorial—that is, their *yilu, weilu,* and *bulu* categorizations.

30. TPM, handwritten vermilion comment on Palace Memorial YZ 011573, YZ7/9/17 (Nov. 7, 1729), Maizhu. There are several such Yongzheng rescripts suggesting an imperial willingness to operate beyond regulations.

31. TPM, imperial marginalia on Palace Memorial YZ 011676, YZ13/7/15 (Sept. 1, 1735), Maizhu.

32. TPM, imperial marginalia on Palace Memorial YZ 011822, undated slip lacking author identification. It is reassuring to know that Yongzheng sometimes waxed enthusiastic about subordinates, as when he wrote in this same document of a circuit intendant: ". . . I can completely vouch for him. You must not be hard on him, he is someone who will work hard. Tell him what I have said."

33. TPM, Palace Memorial YZ 008020, YZ13/2/9 (Mar. 3, 1735). Publication of the circulated memorial cited here was in the *Yongzheng Zhupi yuzhi* (see n. 19).

34. A notation to this effect would have been inscribed in the inner-court logbook, picturesquely known as "Register for Keeping Up with Matters as They Come to Hand" [*Suishou dengji* 隨手登記]. On this record book, see my "Ch'ing Documents in the National Palace Museum Archives: Document Registers: The Sui-shou teng-chi," [Taibei] *National Palace Museum Bulletin* 10, no. 4 (Sept.–Oct. 1975).

35. *Jiaqing Shilu* 24/19a–20a, JQ2/11/24 (Jan. 10, 1798). Although only the word *jiapien* was employed, the rest of the passage shows that the enclosures of imperial concern contained secret information. There are other uses of the term *jiapian.*

36. See Susan Naquin, *Millenarian Rebellion in China: The Eight Trigrams Uprising of 1813* (New Haven: Yale University Press, 1976). See also Naquin's "True Confessions: Criminal Interrogations as Sources for Ch'ing History," [Taibei] *National Palace Museum Bulletin* 11, no. 1 (Mar.–Apr. 1976): 1–14 plus frontispiece. Confessions were not always handled uniformly. Some of this type of information arrived in the memorials themselves (*zhengben* 正本), some in enclosures.

37. See Philip A. Kuhn and John K. Fairbank, with the assistance of Beatrice S. Bartlett and Chiang Yung-chen, *Reading Documents: The Rebellion of Chung Jen-chieh,* 2 vols. (Cambridge, Mass.: Harvard University John King Fairbank Center for East Asian Research, 1986; rev. ed., 1993), 17. I thank Professor Kuhn for this insight, which I first encountered when, as a postdoctoral fellow, I participated in his Qing documents class at Harvard in 1981–83.

38. Alfred Kühn, "Chang Kuang-ssu" (Zhang Guangsi), in *Eminent Chinese of the Ch'ing Period* (Washington, D.C.: U.S. Government Printing Office, 1944), 43–45.

39. This would be the *Yifu dang* (議覆檔) for QL14 (1749).

40. See the Grand Council archival inventory (Beijing Number One Historical Archives #2258), "Han Junji dang'an zongce," passim. The last item inventoried is dated QL55 (1790), which suggests an inventory done in QL56 (1791), but the record also breaks in the middle with a last middle item of QL42 (1777), suggesting an inventory carried out in QL43 (1778).

41. Noqin was a distant imperial connection and had been a trusted member of the Grand Council, so the emperor may all the more keenly have despaired at the news of the military defeat.

42. These were known as "Memorials of Deliberation in Response [to the imperial order]" (*yifu zouzhe* 議覆奏摺). Such

discussions were usually carried out by grand councillors, but were sometimes done in conjunction with a board or other group.

43. There were some exceptions to this pattern, but the fact of the many imperial requests for *more* than one position certify that in the Yongzheng and for most of the Qianlong reign the unanimity rule prevailed. See an instance of the Yongzheng emperor's desperate attempt to divide his officials so that he might decide a case: "If [the deliberating officials] are unable to come to a unanimous position, there is no objection to [their producing] two recommendations, or three recommendations—all are permissible." TPM, Palace Memorial YZ 020204, YZ2/6/8 (July 27, 1724), imperial rescript on the envelope of a Gao Chengling memorial. The issue here was the particularly vexing one of condemning men to death.

44. We know of other kinds of purposeful destruction of materials by Qing archivists. Sometimes when the storage vaults became too crowded, documents regarded as nonessential might be burned to make space for newcomers. This happened more in the Grand Secretariat than in the Grand Council archives. For an early example see *Gongzhongdang Kangxichao zouzhe* [Palace memorials of the Kangxi reign] (Taibei: Palace Museum, 1976), vol. 8, *Manwen yuzhi* [Manchu documents], 14–17, document of KX16/3/10 (April 21, 1677).

The Role of Archives in Chinese Society

An Examination from the Perspective of Access

Du Mei

The contemporary Chinese archival system is based on those agency archives offices (*dangan shi*) that were established in the early 1950s, right after the founding of the People's Republic of China in October 1949. The system is structured and developed according to the principle of a unified leadership and administration at different levels. It consists of three types of archival institutions, each of them having clearly defined, state-mandated functions and responsibilities. These three types include archives administration departments (*dangan ju*), archives offices within agencies (*dangan shi*), and archives (*dangan guan*). The first type includes national and local (including provincial, municipal, and county) archives administration departments, which are government agencies responsible for all archival endeavors within their respective administrative jurisdictions. These include formulating and implementing archival laws, regulations, policies and standards. Archives of this type are involved in making overall plans, exercising supervision, and providing guidance to archival programs of the state and party agencies, social and mass organizations, enterprises, scientific and cultural institutions, and other organizations under their jurisdiction. A second type we can call archives offices within agencies, organizations, enterprises, and institutions are responsible for the custody of their own archival records and for the transfer of those with long-term value to relevant archives (*dangan guan*). The third type consists of archives at all levels (national, provincial, municipal, and county) and of various kinds (comprehensive,

special, departmental, business, institutional)[1] that are cultural and scientific institutions, responsible for receiving, collecting, arranging and keeping archival records of state and social interests within their respective jurisdiction and making them available to users.

This network or system has the potential of broadly documenting and archiving the Chinese social memory since it structurally and institutionally covers almost every organization and nearly all activities of society. They include rural village councils, urban residential committees, social organizations, professional associations, business enterprises, scientific and cultural institutions, and governments at all levels. However, this potential for comprehensiveness needs to be examined more closely within the Chinese archival context of the past half century.

A South African archivist once stated that archivists determine which elements of social life are imparted to future generations.[2] It should be reasonable to say that they also determine which elements of past social life are imparted to current generations. With a focus on comprehensive state archives, which have the legal responsibility to provide public access to records, this essay reviews how archives are used and how they function in recalling and reproducing the past in China. By doing so, it attempts to identify problems that need to be given conscientious consideration and reflection by the Chinese archival community.

A Retrospective

From their inception in the 1950s, current archival institutions would remain closed to the general public and

The views expressed in this essay are those of the author. They do not represent the authority of the State Archives Administration of China.

individual researchers for more than thirty years. They were not legally open to the public until 1987. In that time, the typical archive was an administrative and politically oriented service, located within a complex or courtyard of party or government buildings. Its invisibility to society bespoke a confidential purpose. It was closed but very "active" under some special circumstances. Ironically, this period during which the archives were not legally open to the general public was also an era when archives twice experienced nationwide massive interaction with related agencies and organizations.

The process of establishing archives in the 1950s coincided with a series of political and economic movements, including the suppression of counterrevolutionaries, the anti-Rightists campaign, and the Great Leap Forward. That first generation of contemporary Chinese archivists were actively involved in these movements with a goal of "serving the political fight." Huge quantities of archival records, especially political files created by the old regime (Guomindang government), were used for the purpose of targeting "anti-Party evidences." During the Great Leap Forward campaign in 1958, a policy was developed to call for archivists to "make full and active use of archival materials in socialist construction, and to serve the socialist revolution in the fields of economy, politics, and ideology." The policy led to a fever of "massively collecting, compiling and using archival records" in archival institutions all over the country. According to one report, 20,852 files of records in the county of Hebei were consulted in order to compile supporting materials for the ongoing movement from January 1 to July 31, 1958. The Commercial Department of Henan province mounted more than thirty thousand big-character wall posters, half of them based on archival materials.[3]

Another important role archives played in this time period was to provide information for industrial, agricultural, and construction projects. Such projects were a major function of the state, especially under the planned economy. For instance, the official reports to the imperial throne during the Qing dynasty include data about the flow of discharge of the Yellow River. These data are preserved in archives, which were used in the process of designing the Sanmenxia Reservoir.

This flourishing level of archival activity came to an end in March 1965, when a central circular criticized loose control over the past usage of archives, pointing out that the various uses of archives had caused political problems for the party and state and should be stopped. Many archives ceased operation during the Cultural Revolution of the following decade. Those surviving archival institutions were clearly defined as confidential agencies, and any cultural attribute associated with them was criticized as "revisionist." Archival doors were closed for more than a dozen years until 1979, when China started its policy of reform and opening up to the outside world. Throughout the 1980s, "history" became an overwhelming theme of interest and activity. All over China there were attempts to address the task of rewriting history, or in other words, "history experienced a process of reconstruction." As the Central Party made a decision to resolve "historical questions left over from an earlier period," archives all over the country were consulted. According to use statistics from the State Archives Administration, archives at all levels and of various kinds experienced an increase in the number of users from 2,117,715 in 1983 to 5,361,777 in 1987. The total number of files provided to users increased from 6,626,575 to 23,380,328 over this five-year period. One of the main purposes for consultations was to redress grievances and mishandled cases in past political campaigns. Another purpose of these visits to the archives derived from several projects focused on the compilation of historical materials and annals of local histories. It is a long-standing Chinese tradition called "compiling historical materials and local annals in a flourishing age." Such research occupied 66.6 percent of total consultations to archives in 1987, while at the same time, academic research made up only 1.2 percent of such visits.[4]

As China rapidly developed economically, there was increasing interest in scientific and technical records housed in archives. For example, archives proved very important in the decision-making process of the Three Gorges Dam project. In this project, archival institutions provided over 1,500 files of hydrological archives and tens of thousands of maps and drawings.

It is easy to discover some similarities between the access peaks that occurred in the 1950s and those of the 1980s. The increase in both periods was connected with special political and historical climates. Many users were functionaries from within the related agencies and institutions (including archival institutions themselves). "Serving the Party and State's central task," as the guiding ideology of archival work, was formed and developed in the process. This statement of ideology and goals was articulated in the 1950s and has been evoked ever since.

The recurrence of this statement in the 1980s was associated with a different political, economical, cultural, and social context from that of the 1950s. This more recent context allowed a variety of possibilities and great freedom for the archival profession to develop in a more healthy manner. Primary examples are the successful endeavors leading to the statutory openness of archives to the public.

In 1980, the Central Party Committee approved the establishment of the State Archives Bureau[5] to open the historical archives, which include archives of old regimes and archives of the Communist Party–led revolution before 1949, preserved in the state archives at national and provincial levels. Their contents are made available for examination by historical research institutions and related agencies. A regulation titled "The Method of Opening Archives," issued by the State Archives Bureau in September 1985, opens to the public all records dating thirty years or earlier in archives at all levels and of various kinds. Two years later the Archives Law of the People's Republic of China[6] was issued. This law legally authorized the right of public access to archives and the responsibility of archives to make their records available.

The 1990s witnessed a drastic change in every aspect of Chinese society. As the transition of the political and economic system deepened, commercialization accelerated rapidly. Encountering suddenly such a sharp shift in policies, the whole society experienced a kind of psychological change. Restlessness and an appetite for quick success and instant benefits became almost a universal fever. Archivists, generally at a low social and economic status, felt frustration and pressures both from inside and outside. The traditional constraint still existed, while new pressures emerged. Archivists were affected by the temptation of "a relatively comfortable life" (*xiaokang shenghuo*), while society seemed less interested in archives. Although more and more archival holdings were open and research conditions improved, the number of visits dropped sharply. Compared with 1987, the number of visitors dropped by 62.2 percent in 1995. Archivists were pushed to find a solution to this problem. Pressure, in some way, could be a motivational force for creating new ideas. A good illustration might be the most popular topics discussed within the archival community, both at meetings and in some seventy archival journals during the 1990s. They included archival work and the market economy, the commodity value of archival records and charges for services, the development of scientific and technical archival information, the social effect and economic benefit of archival records, the reexamination of appraisal practices, and the social functions of archives. Obviously, an awareness of and influence by the market economy accompanied archivists' awareness of serving society. At the same time, the approach of archivists to their work underwent a change. Obscurity, once a virtue

of archivists, was no longer valued. Archivists longed for social recognition and consciously started to publicize their work and themselves both to leading bodies and to the public. A new strategic goal was established: "to fully activate the social effects and economic benefits of archival information around the Party and State's central task." Ideologically, this goal did not break out of the frame of a traditional conception of archival service; however, it did introduce flexible and multiple forms of service toward society.

In this new approach, the social effects of archives were associated with serving the national goal of "the construction of a socialist spiritual civilization" (also translatable as "socialist ethical and cultural progress"). In practice, this involved three types of actions. The first was organizing archival exhibitions or other publicity events on the occasion of national and local commemorative activities. It was in this way that archives for the first time entered directly into the field of vision of the public and were expected to play a role for reinforcing ceremonial decorum, for recalling memories of laudatory acts and heroic deeds, for glorifying economic achievements and scientific and technological advancements, and for demonstrating great benefits brought about by access to archives. The second type of action has been the compiling and providing of archival materials around a particular task in a given period so as to meet the specific demands of important departments. The third type of action has been the developing of archival information, the compiling and publishing of archival records on special subjects, which may bring public attention to the archives and added benefits to society at large.

Attaching importance to economic benefits of archives is more or less associated with serving the national goal of "the construction of socialist material civilization" (also translatable as "material progress"). With the high degree of importance attached to economic development, and with the rapid advancement of scientific and technological research, scientific and technological consultation in archives went up significantly, making up 23 percent of the total use of comprehensive archives in 1995. At the same time, business archival programs were thriving and prospering, and proud of their achievements. In an effort to measure the benefits, the State Archives Administration in 1994 issued guidelines titled "Regulation to Calculate the Economic Benefits Gained by the Use of Archives." This publication described a process by which archivists could calculate these economic benefits.

Cooperating with the media has been a new trend over the last couple of years. Increasingly, any significant success of an archival institution is measured by its being "seen on TV, heard on the radio and read in the newspaper." However, while eagerly embracing the media, the archives have lacked a cool-headed and conscientious study of the proper ways of promoting the archives, especially through displays and other media. An ongoing focus is the so-called leisure society. At an academic symposium on the role of archives in the leisure society held in Beijing last year, participants optimistically suggested that "archival work should tap its own market share in the leisure industry. In addition to exhibitions and publications, we should develop new markets to meet various demands of society."[7] The idea was obviously stimulated by the Fourteenth International Congress on Archives held in Seville in September 2000 but tailored to suit the Chinese context by Chinese assumptions and imagination.

Since the 1980s, archives in China have generally experienced a transformation from closure or partial closure to greater access. Regretfully, in the process, for historical reasons and given the sociopolitical context of decision making, the "central task" and "benefit," not the public, usually have come first on the archives' list of priorities. A political way of thinking, as an ideological heritage, has deeply embedded itself and greatly influenced the construction of archival reality and culture. Archivists seem to have difficulty in developing a normal and professional approach and in breaking out of this frame to reflect and represent the multiple social and historical phenomena and various demands upon social memory.

In terms of the current reality, this political and pragmatic approach has had its positive side and has achieved a great deal. By focusing on the central task—major state activities—archival work usually can gain attention from leaders and a variety of other groups, and therefore gain financial support. For instance, the total footage of archival repositories increased 52.4 percent from 1983 to 1990. Also, the funds allocated centrally for the preservation of archives at risk increased from 4 million Chinese yuan in 1994 to 12 million in 2001. Since much retrospective work has been achieved, this is quite significant. Some backlogs can be diminished and some weak points can be improved. For instance, in 1956, to address the pressures of political struggle, all the political records of the old regime were arranged and described. During the Great Leap Forward campaign, archival institutions fulfilled the arrangement and description of records accumulated and created

since 1949. This was also the case in the 1990s. In order to provide an active service, or even more strategic, proactive service to leading bodies, archives began to pay more attention to acquisition and enrichment of their holdings and the development of finding aids. The image of archives is becoming visible in society. This may attract potential users.

I would like especially to mention archival development in rural areas. In order to carry out the policies and strategies of improving agricultural and rural work developed by the Third Plenary Session of the Fifteenth Congress of the Central Party Committee, a national conference on archival work about agriculture and rural areas was organized by the State Archives Administration in 1999. It called for a strengthening of archival programs in this field, which include archive and records programs of township agencies, and agricultural productivity and business activities. The aim is to better serve agricultural development and entrepreneurial peasants. Now many local archives have begun to provide a deposit service for the peasants' land contract deeds. The local archives also have started to collect records relating to family planning in rural areas, the transparency of village public affairs, grassroots democratic elections, "a relatively comfortable life" families, charges and prices of electricity, home ownership, cooperative deposit funds, and so forth.

In this current transitional era, we should also be aware that the central-task approach might be the best, most efficient, and ideal strategic choice for a period of time, but in the long run may yield some negative consequences, especially related professional issues and issues of social memory. When highlighting some elements of historical memory, the current practice of archives in China might overlook elements much more valuable to the public and the memory of society as a whole. Actually, over the past two decades, there has been, on the one hand, an increasingly strong awareness of archival participation in social affairs and increased archival publicity and educational programs for the public. On the other hand, we still have to face the reality of very little research and public access to archives, and a persistent isolation from humanistic research circles and the public. In fact, the archival community has been slow to provide the necessary nourishment to current historical writings and in a broader sense to the collective memory of the nation. This phenomenon is complicated. I would now like to turn to some of the relevant issues that should be given more concern, reflection, and reexamination by our Chinese archivists.

The Quality of Archivists and Institutional Culture

It is well known that the professional quality of the archives plays a very important role in defining the quality of archival institutions. This means establishing proper professional behavior and conduct, a healthy cultural atmosphere, an efficient way of working, and a value system, all of which further affect the social functioning of archives. The situation in China is evolving toward the establishment of such an environment, despite major problems and challenges. According to the 1999 Annual General Statistic Data of the Nation's Archival Endeavor, there are a total of 23,530 professional archival staff working in 3,046 comprehensive state archives throughout China. Since archival work has long been regarded as secret, political, and rote, archivists used to be characterized by traits such as "modest and unassuming" and "sedate and obeying." In recent years, personnel employment criteria and methods have changed, giving priority to educational background and capability. However, there are still ongoing serious problems. The overall educational level of Chinese archivists is low. Currently about 45 percent of archivists have college certificates, 16 percent have a bachelor's degree, and only 4 percent have a higher degree. This has been one of the major obstacles for the fundamental reform of archives over the past two decades.

Legislatively, state archives at all levels are cultural institutions. However, in practice, most of them merge together with the archives administration departments at the same level under the same leading board. Therefore, they function more as departments of government agencies than as independent public and cultural institutions. This model has its advantage in ensuring the institutional status and budget of archives. However it also introduces into individual archives a hierarchical system that makes it more difficult to institute an archival ethos and an archival value system. Archives, as cultural institutions, are more bureaucratic than their counterparts, such as libraries and museums. The bureaucratic environment molds a majority of professional officials, who act cautiously and lack a sense of social and historical responsibility. Public opinion supports this view. A survey conducted by Changshu Municipal Archives last May showed that 51 percent believe the city archives is a government agency not a cultural institution, and 2 percent think it is a Communist Party organ.

This situation brings some problems and difficulties. First, professional practice is controlled and limited by common practice and rules of political and administrative concerns. Archivists are situated in a system and institutional culture that does not quite encourage questioning and independent action. Departing from this norm of behavior is difficult. Faced with enticements of promotion and benefits, archivists are not apt to question established and possibly outmoded practices or to act independently to overcome the conservative inertia often found in archival institutions. The archival community also lacks active and effective communication and cooperation with academic and historical circles or with other related professions.

Under these circumstances, the role of archives in documenting and recalling social memory, to a certain degree, is dependent on the moral spirit of archivists and on an independent system of professional values or related responsibilities. Such a system would allow archivists to see beyond the more mundane techniques and specific administrative processes involved in "keeping archives" to the ultimate societal values of "using archives" for the benefit of the wider community. The newly drafted "rules of job-related responsibility of archivists" by the State Archives Administration attempts to develop a system of responsibility, but still focuses on the technical and management side, failing to give necessary attention to professional ethics and values. A clear characteristic of the Chinese archival community has been to stress the omnipotence of technology. But to magnify technology beyond its utility as a tool and to hold it as a key to all archival challenges will squeeze out wisdom and create barriers to more productive and useful paths.

Availability and Publication of Archives

Although making archives available to the public has been stressed over the past decade, the first priority and main concern of both archival studies and practice is still the safe custody and preservation of records. The proportion of archives thirty years or older that are available for public access remains at a low level. Access varies from archive to archive. This situation can be explained by several realities.

First, there are neither efficient external checks nor pressures on archives. The stereotypical, long accepted distinction between records (as party and state documents) and archives (as personal files) makes archives seem irrelevant to common people. Those who happen to visit an archive for a private purpose, for instance, to look for some evidential documents helpful for their application for welfare benefits, do not receive good service, as should be their right. When service is refused, they seldom complain. Worse, even historical and academic circles haven't formed an external counterbalance to challenge the restrictions on access or to follow any administrative proceeding whereby they can argue for access to archival material.

Second, archivists lose nothing by not providing access, but they take some risks by doing so. Twenty kinds of archives are listed in *The Explanation of Measures for the Implementation of the Archives Law*[8] as unsuitable for opening to the public when they become thirty years old. These restrictions are based on the laws and acts of state security, copyright, protection of intellectual property, rights relating to inventions, patent rights, and so on. These measures are complicated and require archivists to have both the necessary knowledge to interpret them as well as a sense of public service to put them into practice. In addition, there are also some other uncertain personnel and political factors that make the consequences of opening archives difficult to predict. Afraid of getting in trouble, many state archivists usually choose to play it safe and prefer to restrict access. A typical attitude toward challenging responsibility is to take no risk, rather than to work a problem through to a proper conclusion. Nonetheless, some leaders of archives are well educated and open-minded, and they can deal well with the demands of greater access. But, when leaders of archives are timid and lack a sense of social responsibility, the situation is not satisfactory. What makes this attitude a serious problem is that, nowadays, state archives are enjoying much more freedom to provide access to the whole society. But there are still many archivists who ardently believe that "to safeguard and close to public use" is the most important service and role for the archivist.

Another reality is that what we can provide for the public is not satisfying. Having placed emphasis on the administration of archives for service to the state and government, archive repositories are full of party and government documents, administrative records, and official documents of scientific and technological projects, which usually are irrelevant to common people. Fortunately, archivists have become aware of the problem, and therefore, are giving priority to acquisition and expansion of holdings relevant to all sectors of society.

The condition of archival records also constitutes a widespread problem that impedes their availability. Large quantities of records that should be made available have not been properly arranged and described, or they are in poor physical condition. Chinese archives follow a very strict and painstaking filing and arrangement system. Anyone who visits a Chinese archives repository will be impressed by the neatly bound files arrayed on shelves or cabinets in good order. Within each file (on average two centimeters thick), there is a list of titles of all items[9] and a note sheet providing some information relating to the filing process. Each page within a file is numbered. On the cover of each file, the archivist creates a synthetic title for the file (also consisting of the three parts described in note 9), the span of dates, and an archival code consisting of the fonds number, the catalog number, and the file number. It is a really time- and labor-consuming process that has long been criticized and is now undergoing slow reform. It is hoped that a new method as well as a variety of reproduction technologies and the Internet will speed up the process of describing and providing access to archives.

As mentioned above, the privileged clients of archives are leading governmental bodies and those involved in work of the central task. A great deal of money and labor could be involved in focusing on significant social events, serving the central task, "giving full scope of the central theme of our times," and creating a sensation. However, you will rarely find brochures or pamphlets available for the convenience of researchers. Regular user-oriented service has not improved. An article in *Archives Science Study* well represents this value orientation. Discussing the current popular approach of "proactive service," the author writes:

> The clients who could be the targets of our proactive service are those who will not directly send a request to the archives; however the archives can know their access demands through certain channels. Therefore, there is no possibility that these clients will be ordinary units and individuals, since they don't have such an influence and archives don't have ways to learn their needs either. Proactive service has no way to serve these users. So, the clients of proactive service can only be certain powerful Party and government agencies . . . and actually those leaders who are responsible for commanding a central task. . . . Compared with passive service (referring to the old ways of providing access), proactive service could create many more effects and returns with just a small amount of work which will therefore be more worthwhile.

How to provide proactive service? The author continues: "Since the leaders are busy with various state affairs and have no time to consult archival resources, we should compile for them high quality reference materials, which are brief and to the point and cover a wide range of subjects that are helpful for promoting the central task."[10] Archival journals have carried many articles sharing the successful experience of finding out and understanding intentions of leading bodies and providing "proactive reference service," which shows that the idea is accepted widely in the Chinese archival community.

The motive of seeking "benefits" and following a formalist working style may also cripple some significant programs. For instance, as a result of great efforts by archivists over the past years, many state archives have been nominated by local governments as "patriotic bases for the young generation." This program provides archives with a good opportunity to let young people learn the past of their city, their district, the lives of their ancestors, and to arouse their interest in archives and become future users. Regrettably, although some archives would mount exhibitions, most of the archives stop doing anything after the successful and energetic ceremony of "hanging an inscribed board" on the main entrances of the archives, usually attended by local leaders and media. Since these ceremonies always carry a sort of publicity and educational mission and an air of authority and doctrinal approach, I am afraid that our young generation will take an attitude of disinterest in "revolutionary history," and at the same time their interest in exploring the past will diminish.

At present, in addition to being wary of archives of power, we should also be on the alert concerning the power of archivists. When enjoying our legal privilege, archivists commonly lack the necessary awareness of how this privilege can be abused and become autocratic. The process of using archives to do research usually involves publishing archival records or quoting part of original records in publications. The Archives Law entrusts archival institutions with the authority to make public records of state archives. With respect to collectively owned or individually owned archives, owners have the right to make them public but should abide by the relevant state regulations and may not endanger the security and interests of the state or encroach upon the lawful rights and interests of others. "The Measures for the Implementation of the Archives Law" (1999) specify and clarify the concept and forms of the publication of archives as follows:

> Publication of archives refers to making public, for the first time, the original archives or their contents, in their entirety or in parts, through the following means:

1. Publishing through newspapers, magazines, books, or audiovisual and electronic publications;
2. Broadcasting by radio and on TV;
3. Disseminating through the Internet;
4. Reading or publicizing in public occasions;
5. Publicizing compilations of historical archives or materials in full text or abstract; and
6. Exhibiting or displaying original archives or their duplicates in public places.

Accordingly, researchers have the right to have access to archives, but they do not have the right to publish them first. The researchers are dependent on the archivists, who by law are responsible for publishing archives. In this way, archivists deeply participate in historical writing and the construction of memory.

Editing and publishing archival collections, which is a major means to make archives public, is a long tradition in China and has contributed heavily to the decision-making process, scientific research, and historical writing over the past several decades. The products usually fall into these categories:

1. Selected collections of important official documents and statistics
2. Materials directly in the service of economic development
3. Materials in the service of political work and central tasks
4. Annals, documentary histories, and archival collections of special subjects
5. Guides to archives

Archivists now have both the legal responsibility and legal authority to do this work.

The Archives Law also calls for placing research archivists at archival institutions to strengthen research and compilation of archival and historical materials, which is regarded as "an important tool to provide efficient use of archives, and could meet various demands of the society to a maximum and widest scope." However, this assumption overlooks some serious issues. First, the compilation and publication of archival records will never catch up and meet the various needs of the whole society. The huge quantity of and variety of modern records are incredibly hard to deal with.

Second, the subjects and options of archival publication are decided upon by the perspectives, positions, viewpoints, and qualities of the persons who do the compiling. Indeed, in order to avoid mistakes in "political and general knowledge," archivists might naturally present a montage of records, cutting and tailoring them like film directors, according to the standards permitted or prohibited by the mainstream ideology. Up until now, archivists have not consciously examined how and to what degree they should mediate the original records. They are not even aware it constitutes an issue or problem.

Third, since there are no strict rules or procedures relating to compiling archives for publication, it is hard to prevent archivists from monopolizing records in order to achieve personal advancement, better economic effects, and social benefits. This behavior has been seriously harming the accessibility of archival records by the public and other researchers. At present, there is no efficient social force or rule to monitor archivists abusing their power. The harm this presents to historical research is obvious.

Conclusion

It seems to me that, whether consciously or unconsciously, the Chinese archival community has never been able to divorce itself from "big event worship." Long-formed ideas and behavior contribute to an inertia within archival institutions, which strongly affects how we view the past and the present. Our perception of society tends to focus on what is positive and visible and neglect that which is negative and invisible. Our choices in identifying and preserving the past and helping society to understand its past tend to follow the politics of the present order. That is, we do our job within the priorities and directions of the dominant forces of society. Increasing commercial motivations have made the situation more complicated. Although the approach and practice have historical causes that reflect the dilemmas of reality, archivists can easily choose to forget their obligation to the past and neglect their social roles as keepers and providers of collective memory. Facing drastic political, cultural, and economic transitions, which are resulting in fundamental changes at the basic structure of Chinese society, presents archivists with an important task. We must find new ideological resources to efficiently promote archival thinking and practice, to reconstruct our perception of issues, and especially to reflect on our work as archivists and on the role of archival institutions.

I want to conclude with introducing you to an exhibit, which, I hope, indicates a new trend. On the occasion of the fiftieth anniversary of the founding of the People's Republic of China and the twentieth anniversary of the "reform and opening-up," the Beijing Municipal Archives sponsored an exhibit titled Let Yesterday Tell Today: Retrospective on Beijing Commodity Tickets. The exhibit demonstrated the creation and disappearance of the system of commodity tickets, once occupying an essential place in the everyday life of ordinary Chinese families, between 1953 and 1993. The exhibit traces the economic and political evolution of Beijing. It was a hit. By focusing on the ordinary life of Chinese citizens and by displaying living conditions of common people in a specific period of time, it recalled, to a certain degree, a sort of collective memory instead of an official memory.

The new approach is different from the traditional approach in at least two ways. First, it starts to take the popular perspective and take notice of the common life, rather than just highlighting big events. The subject and content of archival publicity give a certain proportion to the life conditions of people in addition to "nationwide" campaigns. Second, municipal archives have begun to give more emphasis to local concerns. In fact, many local archives are increasingly paying attention to documenting "microhistory" and collecting records and relevant materials with local characteristics. Through these measures the archival community can establish "grassroots archival holdings," which have been so far neglected. This new trend is at an early stage. It is hoped it will have a bright future and bring in substantial reform of the social function of archives and archivists.

NOTES

I express my heartfelt thanks to Nancy Bartlett and William Wallach for their generous help in my preparation of this presentation. Both of them sacrificed a great deal of spare and weekend time to read the draft and offer suggestions and corrections. Unless otherwise indicated, translations are mine.

1. For instance, Shanxi Provincial Archives is a comprehensive state archive at the provincial level; Beijing Urban Constructive Archives is a special state archive at the municipal level; the Archives of the Ministry of Foreign Affairs Office is a departmental archive at the national level; and the Archives of Renmin University and the Archives of the Chinese Academy of Science are institutional archives.

2. Quoted by Terry Cook in his presentation at the Sawyer Seminar: "The Role of Archives in Constructing Social Memory."

3. All the data and examples are from Fu Hua, "Expansion of Providing Access to Archives," *China Archives* 5 (1999).

4. Fu Hua, "Expansion of Providing Access."

5. The State Archives Bureau is translated as the State Archives Administration after 1993, when it and the Central Archives merged.

6. The Archives Law of the People's Republic of China was adopted at the Twenty-second Meeting of the Standing Committee of the Sixth National People's Congress on September 5,

1987, and revised in accordance with the Decision on the Revision of the Archives Law of the People's Republic of China adopted at the Twentieth Meeting of the Standing Committee of the Eighth National People's Congress on July 5, 1996.

7. Lin Chi, "A Summary of the Symposium on the Role of Archives in the Leisure Society," *Archives Science Study* 3 (2000).

8. Ed. Guo Shuyin (China Law Publishing House, 2000).

9. In China, each document has a rubric that consists of three basic parts: author, subject, and type of document. The type of document expresses the function and hierarchical relation between author(s) and addressee(s).

10. Lin Chi, "A Summary."

Archives and Histories in Twentieth-Century China

William C. Kirby

Although the existence of state archives has been traced back to the fourth and fifth centuries BC in the West and perhaps all the way back to the Shang dynasty in China,[1] the establishment of permanent, public, national archival institutions dates only from the French Revolution, with the creation of the Archives nationales in 1790. The immediate reasons for founding such institutions, such as the British Public Record Office (established 1838), the National Archives of the United States (1934), the Academia Historica (Guoshiguan) of the Republic of China (1947) or the Central Archives (Zhongyang dang'anguan) of the People's Republic of China (1959) have varied, but in their broader purposes they appear to have had several aims in common: to increase bureaucratic efficiency, by centralizing the storage of government records; to assist and protect the government by providing an ongoing record of its own activities and commitments; to preserve the cultural/political heritage of the nation, as defined by the state; and—finally—to preserve the records of the past for present and future historians.[2] (Arguably, only this last was a main aim of the original Guoshiguan, the State Historiographer's Office under the Qing, with the aim above all to manage the dynastic story for posterity.)[3]

Although designed primarily to serve the authorities, modern archives have been best loved by historians. Not long after the founding of the Public Record Office, a report complained: "Our Public Records excite no interest, even in the functionaries whose acts they record, the departments whose proceedings they register; or the proprietors to whose property rights they furnish the most authentic, perhaps the only title-deeds."[4] At the same time, amateur and professional historians in Europe

were developing an obsession for unlocking the presumed secrets of archival collections. Thus Ranke wrote passionately of his desire (*Lust*) for the data in archival manuscripts, which he imagined as "so many princesses, possibly beautiful, all under a curse and needing to be saved."[5]

The tension between the purposes of the state, some of which are meant to be kept secret, and the insatiable *Forschungslust* of the modern historical profession, has of course never been resolved. But the very existence of public archives has changed the way historians work. Historians have come to take it for granted that access to archives storing the "primary" materials of history, what Marc Bloch called "the evidence of witnesses in spite of themselves,"[6] is essential to their craft. This is not because primary materials are always superior to narrative sources of earlier generations; nor it is because they are necessarily true—indeed they may be full of lies and distortions. But, as Bloch reminds us, theirs is the "kind of distortion [that] has not been especially designed to deceive posterity."[7]

From the point of view of historians, many of the great advances in archival access in the twentieth century have come when governments have lost their ability to deceive posterity, notably by collapsing in war and revolution. After the First World War, European governments competed with each other in the selective publication of documents designed to show how each was innocent of "war guilt"; but it was only after Germany's defeat in the Second World War, when its archives were seized and microfilmed by the Allies (an event that in turn prompted a fuller opening of Allied archives), that a comprehensive archival investigation of the origins of the first war was possible. The more recent, sudden demise of the Soviet Union and its Eastern European allies—the archives of which had been largely off limits to scholars—is already having a far-reaching effect on historical research and seems likely to promote greater openness in other archives.[8] Although many governments have adopted policies of unveiling archival materials after regular intervals (commonly thirty or fifty years), the historian's best friend remains the government that ceases to govern.

This, after all, is one reason why research in Qing archives has faced fewer political obstacles than has scholarly work on either Nationalist or Communist China. But as the case of the Qing archives demonstrates, the support of governments is essential to the archival endeavor, for the defeat or disappearance of a regime does not by itself open its archive. Early Republican governments were positively lethargic in their approach to records, including their own. The Lishi Bowuguan (Historical Museum) founded in the late Qing to house imperial archives was ill-funded and ill-managed under the Qing, and then starved under the Republic. The Republican government cared so little about the source materials of its predecessor that tens of thousands of pounds of documents were allowed to be sold for pulp, and more would have been sold had it not been for the determined intervention of private scholars. Matters improved somewhat with the establishment in 1928 of the Institute of History and Philology of the Academia Sinica, but as Lo Hui-min has pointed out, the fact that archival material continued to be measured by weight as late as the Sino-Japanese war was a sign of the "infant state of Chinese archival development."[9] The intervention of the war and civil war meant that it was not until the 1950s that professional archival work would be supported by governments in a manner that ultimately would make the First Historical Archives in Beijing and the National Palace Museum archives in Taipei the world-class institutions that they are today.

Republican archives, too, were neglected in the first half of the century. The Guoshiyuan proposed by Sun Yatsen, renamed Guoshiguan (Academia Historica) under Yuan Shikai (seeking no doubt the legitimacy of continuity with the Qing institution), underwent several early incarnations and many false starts before being constituted as the central government archive under the Nationalists. But that did not happen, finally, until January 1947. (It says something about the locus of power in Nationalist China that the Party Archives Commission of the Guomindang [Dangshihui] was established much earlier, in 1930,[10] perhaps because Party archives were

deemed most important to the actual working of government.) Even in the 1950s, government ministries in Taiwan were rumored to have sold documentary materials for pulp; it took the passage of legislation to force them to give the Academia Historica the right of first refusal to their papers. Still, government bodies were free to deposit their archives elsewhere (as the Ministry of Economic Affairs did with the Institute of Modern History of the Academia Sinica)[11] or to hold on to them themselves, as has been the case with the post-1927 materials of the Republic of China's Ministry of Foreign Affairs.

Delay in the opening of Republican- and especially Nationalist-era historical archives continued after 1949. The lag in systematizing Republican archives on Taiwan reflected the familiar reluctance of governments to release materials about their own recent past, in this case complicated by the continuing state of civil war. Thus the first *Nationalist-era* documents on Taiwan to be opened extensively to scholars were captured materials of the *Communist* movement, housed in the Bureau of Investigation of the Ministry of Justice.[12] Despite prodigious publication projects on Republican history, particularly by the Guomindang Party Archives, the Academia Historica, and the Institute of Modern History, direct access to archival materials was significantly limited until the 1980s.

For its part, the new People's Republic of China (PRC) government on the mainland showed no interest in promoting scholarship (as distinct from political study) in Chinese Communist Party (CCP) historical materials. But under the official assumption that the era of the Republic of China (ROC) had definitively ended and that its dynastic history could be written, the PRC government devoted its attention to organizing the archives of its Nationalist enemies. The Nanjing Organization Office of the Third Historical Institute of the Academy of Sciences—known later as the Second Historical Archives—was founded in February 1951 to catalogue materials inherited from the Guomindang Party Archives, Academia Historica, and innumerable other collections of Republican archives. Although some materials from these collections would be used in published collections of documents in the 1950s, the enormous scale of the archival work (which centralized Republican records as they had never been under the Republic), the early PRC's official culture of secrecy (which contradicted the very concept of a public archive), and the political disruptions of the years 1958–78 (above all the Cultural Revolution) all meant that it was not until 1980 that the collections of the Second Historical Archives could be formally opened to scholarly inquiry.[13]

Since the early 1980s, there has been a revolution in

the professional organization and public access of Republican archival materials on both sides of the Taiwan Strait. The Second Archives and several major provincial and municipal archives in the PRC, as well as the Academia Historica and the Institute of Modern History of the Academia Sinica on Taiwan, now have state-of-the-art storage facilities, preservation programs, cataloguing systems, and retrieval capacities.[14]

PRC archives—in particular the Second Archives and the Shanghai Archives, but also many others—have redefined the nature of a state archive, with holdings that extend well beyond those of formal government bodies. If revolutions are a historian's best friend, a Communist revolution must be the best friend of the business historian. The early PRC completed the nationalization of all Chinese and foreign companies, whose assets, including their archives, therefore belonged to the state. As a result, PRC archives are responsible for the papers of nongovernmental, Republican-era institutions such as private industrial companies, banks, and educational institutions that came under government (*guoying*) management either in the later stages of Guomindang rule or in the first years of Communist authority. The Shanghai Municipal Archives, for example, holds records of private organizations and firms ranging from chambers of commerce to tobacco companies,[15] and in 1993 it received the archives of nine major commercial banks of the Republican era whose papers had been housed with the People's Bank of China. The Business History Archive of the Economics Institute of the Shanghai Academy of Social Sciences, established in 1992, also has major holdings of pre-1949 commercial firms and has quickly become a major resource for historians of Chinese business. These are but a few of the "private" treasures of PRC archives.

The impact on international scholarship of this newfound archival openness and diversity has been extensive, as old fields were revisited and new ones initiated. In the study of Shanghai alone Elizabeth Perry reopened the field of labor history, which had lain dormant in the West since the work of Jean Chesneaux;[16] Frederic Wakeman brought to light the dark, underworld struggles of the police and their adversaries;[17] Emily Honig investigated migrant culture, Jeffrey Wasserstrom student culture, and Wen-hsin Yeh and Linsun Cheng the world of modern banking—all assisted by archival sources that were not open to research until the mid-1980s.[18] If fifteen years ago international scholars despaired of gaining any substantial access to Republican archives, the danger today may be of a surfeit of materials, even if full, public access to archives, including their catalogues and finding aids, is

still by no means the rule. Certainly few serious research proposals in Republican Chinese history can now omit mention of the multiple archival collections in China and Taiwan that might bear on a topic.[19]

This new situation serves to remind us of how far the practice of archival opening has come in a very short period, and, at the same time, how incomplete it remains. It is striking to recall that the major works that defined the field of "Republican China" in the West until a decade or so ago were based on little or no Chinese archival evidence. For example, influential studies of the Nationalist regime by Qian Duansheng (Tuan-sheng Ch'ien), Lloyd Eastman, and Tien Hung-mao[20] had to be based primarily on published material of the period. Seminal works on social and economic history relied mainly on materials available outside China, for example the investigations of the north China plain conducted by the Research Bureau of the South Manchurian Railway Company.[21] Indeed, a distinguishing trait of the entire body of Western historiography of Republican China has been its heavy debt to *non*-Chinese archival material. Compared, for example, with modern U.S., British, French, or German history, the use of foreign archives in this field has played an unusually important role.

This historical "archive gap" has been perhaps most clearly evident in the study of China's international relations after 1927. Until very recently the history of Sino-American diplomatic relations during the Nationalist period was based almost exclusively on American documentation, which was extensive and available in both published and archival form. In a similar fashion the study of Sino-American business and economic relations in the Nationalist period had largely to be limited to those topics for which foreign primary material seemed ample; the same was true for studies of Sino-American intellectual and technological cooperation.[22] In the broader field of Chinese business history of the Republican era, it was no accident that the most highly regarded scholarship focused on firms with foreign partners or competitors with extensive documentation outside China.[23]

The "archive gap" is now closing for historians of Republican China in both its mainland and Taiwan eras: so much is clear from the wealth of materials simply in the fields of business and economic history.[24] For the materials of post-1950 Taiwan, although the ROC has still not passed, in final form, its much debated Archive Law (now with a Freedom of Information Act attached to it), both the Academia Historica, which has inherited the Chiang Kaishek papers, and the Guomindang Party Archives are following the lead of the Institute of Modern

History in making available archival materials of the 1950s, 1960s, and 1970s.

Indeed, a repoliticization of archives and history has done much to transform historical research in Taiwan during the past decade. In Taiwan, the rigid control of the Guomindang government over its history and historical materials gave way to political expediency when, in the early 1990s, it became imperative to address the memory of "2-28," that is, of the uprising against Nationalist rule that began on February 28, 1947, and its subsequent, bloody suppression. For the Guomindang to survive the increasingly provincialized politics of Taiwan after the democratic reforms of the late 1980s and early 1990s, the open discussion of this once-taboo topic became a necessity. Once this decision was reached, research on 2-28 exploded. An official commission under the Executive Yuan gathered documents from public and private archives, employing the news media to search island-wide for materials. Subsequently, archives and scholars on both sides of the Taiwan Strait (and indeed on both sides of the Pacific) rushed to print volumes of documents as well as new scholarly interpretations. In the process, 2-28 has been largely excised as a potentially fatal historical burden for an increasingly Taiwanized Guomindang.[25]

The 2-28 inquiries gave a public face, and for the first time serious public money, to what has now become a leading trend among academic and public historians in Taiwan: the writing of a distinctly Taiwanese, as distinct from Chinese, history of the island. The establishment of the new Taiwan Historical Institute (Taiwan shi yan-jiusuo) at Academia Sinica is only the most visible manifestation of the rise of local histories; even the "national" archive, the Academia Historica, is now gathering the former provincial archives. Meanwhile, the advent to state power of the former Taiwanese opposition, the Democratic Progressive Party, has meant that the archives of the former Guomindang government are being open (still selectively to be sure) at a much faster pace than before.

Unfortunately, the same degree of opening cannot yet be said to exist in institutes and archives in the People's Republic. The enormous *Zhonghua minguo shi* [History of the Republic of China] project, published in multiple volumes over two decades, has given employment to hundreds of historians, as one would expect of the official dynastic history of the PRC's predecessor. Yet it falls well short of the *zheng shi* (standard histories) of its imperial predecessors in clarity of form or voice—indeed over the course of its volumes one can witness a great confusion of interpretive categories, with Marxian

analyses in general retreat.[26] Were it a project designed to stimulate further research, its scholarly apparatus (notes and citations) would be found woefully inadequate. It is perhaps not surprising that its historical judgments have been made more difficult by the fact that the Republic of China still exists on Taiwan: for the sake of a future reunification, certain personalities and events of the latter years of Guomindang rule on the mainland are described less critically than they are in most Western accounts. The same concern, to have the history of the Republic somehow serve the cause of national reunification, has led the Second Historical Archives to restrict access to the papers of Guomindang leaders. So if PRC historians seek to do serious work on Chiang Kaishek these days, they go to the Academia Historica in Taiwan.

One should note that the one area of absolute archival openness serves, in a very emotional way, the contemporary Chinese state's promotion of nationalist sentiment. For over twenty years, historical materials on Japanese atrocities in China, particularly the massacre at Nanjing, have been a mainstay of archival compilations and exhibitions.[27]

Yet of massacres of Chinese, by Chinese, during the history of Chinese Communism and of the People's Republic, the archives as yet reveal little. And in general, a large and continuing archive gap exists for those who wish to write the history of the CCP and of the PRC. Early Western works that disagreed on the nature of the pre-1949 Communist movement[28] were united in their inability to use the main collections of Party historical materials in the CCP/PRC Central Archives or Central Military Commission Archives (Zhongyang junwei dang'-anguan). This is still the case. While the archives of the CCP's founder and early mentor, the Comintern, are open and, increasingly, published,[29] there is no independent, archive-based scholarship even of the Comintern emanating from China itself. Even the most publicized works of contemporary history of recent years show the enduring restrictions of the Party-state.

Take the case of the "memoirs" of Bo Yibo. Bo Yibo, a CCP elder, was among the least ideological of PRC leaders in the 1950s. As finance minister in 1953, his moderate tax policies for private capitalists aroused the ire of Mao Zedong, and led to Bo's temporary dismissal. Bo was among the leading planners who dragged their feet in setting goals at the outset of Mao's Great Leap Forward in 1958. In the wake of the Leap's disastrous failure, he was among the architects of China's economic recovery program. Thus it is appropriate that a "memoir" in his name would attempt the first effort by the

Communist leadership to interpret the economic history of the 1950s. This publication was only possible, however, in the context of Deng Xiaoping's push for further economic reform in the early 1990s. Although published under Bo's name, it may be more appropriately viewed as a central committee collective (and selective) memoir, stressing the most positive aspects of a putative (pre-Leap) "golden age," and the overall wisdom of the Party, even in its darkest hours. There is no evidence that Bo or anyone else had independent access to archival material; at most, archivists worked with the secretaries of leaders and the central committee to select for this project the materials that could be used in it. In his afterword, Bo makes it clear that this was a volume that could be published only with the direct support of the central leadership, which in turn made possible the assistance of the Central Archives, the Central Party School, the Party History Office, and so on. Yet for all this archival assistance, there is not a footnote in sight.[30]

Despite the enormous amount of officially sanctioned publication in China on the early People's Republic, this remains more an outgrowth of the sanctioned study of "Party history" (*dang shi*), in the hands of party archivists, than it is the subject matter for professional historians in China. Although excellent work has begun on the foreign relations of the PRC in the writing of its "state history" (*guo shi*),[31] the domestic story remains tightly controlled, and in any realm the unofficial history of the PRC cannot yet be written.

It may be that with the publication of the *Tiananmen Papers* we have the first nonsanctioned reproduction of documentary materials on state leaders since the Cultural Revolution. However, a historian must be cautious about a compilation that bears many structural similarities to official compilations, such as the multivolume *Jianguo yilai Mao Zedong wengao* [Documents of Mao Zedong since the founding of the state]: documents are reproduced with minimal information on provenance or document type; documents lack any identifying codes or numbers; the compilations are selective; and the editors are unnamed.[32]

The PRC has promulgated a high-sounding, and indeed well-meaning, Archive Law. By law, all archival material can be made available for research after thirty years. Yet there are big exemptions: matters of state, public security, national defense, and foreign relations, not to mention, in the case of foreign scholars, matters unsuitable for foreigners. So the archives in fact remain closed to all save official historiographers. Although we can now begin to rethink the Communist Revolution on the basis of serious archival work on the precommunist period, we cannot do the same for the history of the People's Republic.[33] The reason for this may be quite simple, given what we now know of the several millions killed in the "anticounterrevolutionary" campaigns of the early 1950s and the 30–40 million who perished under the Leap: no government whose legitimacy still rests on the revolution of 1949 and the consolidation of Communist power in the 1950s could open these archives and survive.

History did not end in 1949. Indeed, on certain topics it is possible to do serious work on the CCP and the early PRC in selected provincial and local archives.[34] Yet for most PRC archives, history still ends with "liberation." The relationship between archives and the writing of modern Chinese history seems, then, to be repeating itself: just when the opening of Chinese Republican archives had begun to redress the international imbalance of historical materials, an even greater imbalance has emerged for the years after 1949.[35] British Foreign Office documents written on (and in) China are declassified through the late 1960s. Those of the German Democratic Republic and its party leadership are catalogued and open through the year 1989 (another happy result of a fallen government); those of the pre-1991 Soviet Union are opening more gradually, but opening nonetheless, led by the former Baltic republics. Now even Taiwan's archives are largely open through the 1970s. We know from published guides that the large majority of extant Chinese archival material on the mainland deals with the years after 1949. But while the archives of the imperialists as well as of the socialist brothers now welcome historians, those of the People's Republic remain exclusively—true enough to the original purpose of archives—in the service of the state.

NOTES

1. See Ernst Posner, *Archives in the Ancient World* (Cambridge, Mass.: Harvard University Press, 1972); *Zhongguo dang'an shiyeh gaikuang* [The Archival Endeavor of China] (Beijing: Zhongguo guojia dang'anju, n.d.).

2. See T. R. Schellenberg, *Modern Archives: Principles and Techniques* (Chicago: University of Chicago Press, 1956), 3–10.

3. See Beatrice Bartlett, "Archival Management in the Late Imperial Era," paper presented to the Conference on Modern Chinese Historical Archives at the University of California, Berkeley, 1994.

4. House of Commons Select Committee, "On the Perilous State and Neglect of the Public Records" (1848), quoted in Schellenberg, *Modern Archives*, 7.

5. Leonard Krieger, *Ranke and the Meaning of History* (Chicago: University of Chicago Press, 1977), 105.

6. Marc Bloch, *The Historian's Craft* (New York: Vintage, 1953), 61.

7. Ibid., 62.

8. See, for example, Mark Kramer, "Archival Research in Moscow," and Kathryn Weathersby, "New Findings on the Korean War," both in *The Cold War International History Project Bulletin,* no. 3 (fall 1993); Mark Bradley and Robert Brigham, "Vietnamese Archives and Scholarship on the Cold War Period: Two Reports," Working Paper No. 7 of the Cold War International History Project, Woodrow Wilson Center (September 1993); Shuguang Zhang and Jian Chen, *Chinese Communist Foreign Policy and the Cold War in Asia: New Documentary Evidence, 1944–1950* (Chicago: Imprint Publications, 1994); and, most recently, on Sino-Soviet relations, "The Cold War in Asia," *The Cold War International History Project Bulletin,* no. 6–7 (winter 1995–96), and "Leadership Transition in a Fractured Bloc," *The Cold War International History Project Bulletin,* no. 10 (March 1998).

9. Cyrus Peake, "Documents Available for Research on the Modern History of China," *American Historical Review* 38 (October 1932): 61ff; Lo Hui-min, "Some Notes on Archives on Modern China," in D. Leslie et al., eds, *Essays on the Sources for Chinese History* (Columbia: University of South Carolina Press, 1973), 205.

10. *Guoshiguan gaikuang* (Taibei, 1984), 1–3; on the Qing State Historiographer's Office see K. Biggerstaff, "Some Notes on the *Tung-hua lu* and the *Shi-lu*," *Harvard Journal of Asian Studies* 4, no. 2 (July 1939): 101–15.

11. See *Jingji dang'an hanmu huibian* [Catalogue of economic documents] (Taibei: Zhongyang yanjiuyuan jindaishi yanjiuso, 1987–).

12. See Peter Donovan et al., *Chinese Communist Materials at the Bureau of Investigation Archives, Taiwan* (Ann Arbor: Center for Chinese Studies of the University of Michigan, 1976).

13. On the early history of the Second Archives see *Zhongguo di'er lishi dang'anguan jianming zhinan* (Beijing: Dang'an chubanshe, 1987), 1–2.

14. See, among other publications: *Dangdai Zhongguo de dang'an shiyeh* (Beijing: Zhongguo shehui kexue chubanshe, 1988); *Zhongguo dang'an fenlei fa* (Beijing: Dang'an chubanshe, 1987); *Zhongguo dang'an nianjian* (Beijing: Dang'an chubanshe, 1992–); Lu Shou-chang, *Xiandai shiyong dang'an guanli xue* (Taibei, 1983); *Guoshiguan gaikuang* (Taibei: Guoshiguan, 1984). Professional and scholarly periodicals reviewing the state of archival work include: *Dang'an gongzuo* (Beijing); *Dang'an yanjiu* (Beijing); *Dang'an qingbao* (Beijing); *Dang'anxue tongxun* (Beijing); *Shanghai dang'an gongzuo* (Shanghai); and *Jindai Zhongguo yanjiu tongxun* (Taibei).

15. *Shanghaishi dang'anguan jianming zhinan* (Beijing: Dang'an chubanshe, 1991); Parks M. Coble, "Business History Research in Shanghai," *Chinese Business History* 1, no. 2 (April 1991): 5–7.

16. Elizabeth J. Perry, *Shanghai on Strike* (Stanford: Stanford University Press, 1993); Jean Chesneaux, *The Chinese Labor Movement, 1919–1927* (Stanford: Stanford University Press, 1968).

17. Frederic Wakeman, Jr., *Policing Shanghai* (Berkeley: University of California Press, 1995).

18. Emily Honig, "Migrant Culture in Shanghai: In Search of a Subei Identity," and Jeffrey Wasserstrom, "The Evolution of Shanghai Student Protest Repertoire," both in Frederic Wakeman, Jr., and Wen-hsin Yeh, eds., *Shanghai Sojourners* (Berkeley: Institute of East Asian Studies of the University of California, Berkeley, 1992); Wen-hsin Yeh, "Corporate Space, Communal Time: Everyday Life in Shanghai's Bank of China," paper presented at the Luce Seminar on Commerce and Culture in Shanghai, 1895–1937, Cornell University, August 1992; Lin-sun Cheng, *Banking in Modern China: Entrepreneurs, Professional Managers and the Development of Chinese Banks, 1897–1937* (Cambridge: Cambridge University Press, 2003).

19. For overviews of the archival scene see: *Chinese Archives: An Introductory Guide,* ed. Ye Wa and Joseph W. Esherick (Berkeley: Institute of East Asian Studies; University of California: Center for Chinese Studies, 1996); *Zhongguo dang'anguan minglu* [Directory of Chinese National Archives] (Beijing: Dang'an chubanshe, 1990), in Chinese and English.

20. Qian Duansheng, *Minguo zhengzhi shi* (Shanghai, 1946); Lloyd Eastman, *The Abortive Revolution* (Cambridge, Mass.: Harvard University Press, 1974); Tien Hung-mao, *Government and Politics in Kuomintang China* (Stanford: Stanford University Press, 1972).

21. For example, Ramon Myers, *The Chinese Peasant Economy* (Cambridge, Mass.: Harvard University Press, 1970); Philip C. C. Huang, *Peasant Economy and Social Change in North China* (Stanford: Stanford University Press, 1985); and most recently Prasenjit Duara, *Culture, Power, and the State* (Stanford: Stanford University Press, 1988).

22. Warren Cohen, *The Chinese Connection* (New York: Columbia University Press, 1978); R. E. Stross, *The Stubborn Earth: American Agriculturalists on Chinese Soil, 1898–1937* (Berkeley: University of California Press, 1986); James Thompson, *While China Faced West* (Cambridge, Mass.: Harvard University Press, 1969); Peter Buck, *American Science and Modern China* (Cambridge: Cambridge University Press, 1983).

23. Sherman Cochran, *Big Business in China* (Cambridge, Mass.: Harvard University Press, 1980); Ernest R. May and John K. Fairbank, eds., *America's China Trade in Historical Perspective* (Cambridge, Mass.: Harvard University Press, 1986).

24. See William C. Kirby et al., eds., *State and Economy in Republican China: A Handbook for Scholars* (Cambridge, Mass.: Harvard University Asia Center, 2001), 2 vols.

25. See for example, *Er-er-ba shijian ziliao xuanji* [Selected materials of the 2-28 Incident] (Taibei: Zhongyang yanjiuyuan jindaishi yanjiusuo, 1992); *Nanjing di'er lishi dang'an guan guancang Taiwan er-er-ba shijian dang'an shiliao* [Historical materials regarding the Taiwan 2-28 Incident in the holdings of the Second Historical Archive, Nanjing] (Taibei: Renjian chubanshe, 1992); *Er-er-ba shjian yanjiu baogao* [Report on the 2-28 Incident], ed. Xingzhengyuan yanjiu er-er-ba shijian xiaozu (Taibei: Guoli Zhongyang tushuguan, 1994); and Lai Tse-han et al., *A Tragic Beginning: The Taiwan Uprising of February 28, 1947* (Stanford: Stanford University Press, 1991).

26. Compare the first and latest volumes of Li Xin, ed., *Zhonghua minguo shi* [History of the Republic of China] (Beijing: Zhonghua shuju), part I, vol. 1 (1981), and part III, vol. 5 (2000).

27. See for example *Nanjing datusha tuzheng* [Pictorial

proof of the Nanjing Massacre], ed. Zhongyang dang'anguan et al. (Changchun: Jilin renmin chubanshe, 1995). This has become an international phenomenon: see the *Journal of Studies of Japanese Aggression against China* (Carbondale, Ill.). For an external perspective see Joshua A. Fogel, ed., *The Nanjing Massacre in History and Historiography* (Berkeley: University of California Press, 2000).

28. E.g., Mark Selden, *The Yenan Way* (Cambridge, Mass.: Harvard University Press, 1971); Chalmers Johnson, *Peasant Nationalism and Communist Power* (Stanford: Stanford University Press, 1962).

29. See *Die Komintern und die national-revolutionäre Bewegung in China: Dokumente, Band 1: 1920–1925*, hrsg. von dem Russischen Zentrum für Archivierung und Erforschung von Dokumenten zur neuesten Geschichte, dem Ostasiatischen Seminar der FU Berlin und dem Institut für den Fernen Osten der Russischen Akademie der Wissenschaften (Paderborn [u.a.]: Schöningh, 1996); *Band 2: 1926–27, Teil 1–3* (1997–2000). See most recently Alexander Pantsov, *The Bolsheviks and the Chinese Revolution, 1919–1927* (Honolulu: University of Hawaii Press, 2000).

30. See Bo Yibo, *Ruogan zhongda juece yu shijian de huigu* [Memoirs of several important decisions and events], vol. 2 (Beijing: Zhonggong zhongyang dangxiao chubanshe, 1993), 1297.

31. The CCP Central Party School and the new Contemporary China Research Center (Dangdai Zhongguo yanjiu zhongxin) in Beijing are in the forefront of important scholarly work on foreign relations, though even these units have imperfect archival access.

32. *Jianguo yilai Mao Zedong wengao* [Documents of Mao Zedong since the founding of the state] (Beijing: Zhongyang wenxian chubanshe, 1988–); Zhang Liang (pseud.), comp., *The Tiananmen Papers,* ed. Andrew Nathan and Perry Link (New York: Public Affairs, 2001).

33. For both the promise and the substantial restrictions in the PRC's recent (1987, revised 1996) Archive Law see *Zhonghua renmin gongheguo dang'anfa* [Archive Law of the People's Republic of China] (Beijing: Dang'an chubanshe, 1988). The 1996 law is reprinted in *Zhongguo dang'an* [Chinese Archives] (August 1996).

34. See, for example, Joseph W. Esherick, "Deconstructing the Construction of the Party-State: Gulin County in the Shaan-Gan-Ning Border Region," *China Quarterly,* no. 140 (1994): 1052–79, and Perry, *Shanghai on Strike.*

35. For a reasoned analysis based on totally incompatible source bases see Gordon H. Chang and He Di, "The Absence of War in the U.S.-China Confrontation over Quemoy," *American Historical Review* 98, no. 5 (December 1993): 1500–1524.

Archives and Historical Writing

The Case of the Menshevik Party in 1917

Ziva Galili

The agenda for the seminar on Archives, Documentation, and the Institutions of Social Memory, much like the questions being asked nowadays in so many academic discussions, reminds us of the uncertain place of archival records in historical writing and in social memory. We are asked to face the notion that the preservation and accessibility of such records are contingent on a wide array of political, cultural, and technological factors and that these factors as well as the ideological stance inherent in both historical writing and the practice of social memory affect every aspect of our usage of archival documentation. All this can hardly be contested, certainly not by historians of Russia. After all, the Soviet experience provided the very image of a historical record manipulated for ideological and political purpose, of political leaders, movements, and events airbrushed out of history, and of historical processes and forces relabeled to fit an openly doctrinaire view of history. It is no secret that for many decades in Soviet history large bodies of archival material remained outside the purview not only of the public but of professional historians and that in certain areas of research documentation was made available to historians only selectively, thus distorting and implicating the histories they produced.

Today, access to Russian archives remains uneven for a variety of reasons ranging from the political to the technical and budgetary.[1] And while the strictly political suppression and distortion of archival record we had suspected in Soviet times had a discernible logic (and was therefore, presumably, correctable), the new factors affecting archival access are more random and thus more difficult to map.

Scholarly output in the field of twentieth-century Rus-

sian history during the past decade also provides vivid examples of historical writing and rewriting generated by processes of political and ideological change rather than mere archival access. Indeed, the political transformation of Russia in the last twelve years or so has produced *both* greater archival access and a considerable body of historical rewriting that was only tangentially, and in some cases tendentiously, based on newly found documentation. The first rewriting, occurring already during the relaxation of the late Soviet period, was driven by the political agenda of a reforming leadership, though the outcome was not wholly predictable. A good example of this was present in the plan for a new official history of the Communist Party of the Soviet Union (CPSU). A group of historians, some of them relegated for the previous two decades to marginal academic positions, were assembled in a villa outside Moscow, provided with almost any document requested from the archives, and allowed to discuss openly questions of Soviet history hitherto mentioned only in private conversations if at all. Though this official history never saw light, it brought into circulation documentation and information that historians then used in the public discussions they were now part of, discussions that played a political role not originally anticipated. During the last two to three years of the Soviet Union, personalities, events, and eventually parties that had been entirely absent from Soviet history (though not entirely erased from the social memory of certain groups, including historians) gradually came back into history in officially sanctioned or tolerated discussions. Still, access to archival holdings for the most part followed rather than led these forays into forbidden historical terrains.

The dramatic end of the Soviet period affected historical writing in more divergent ways, but again not wholly dependent on archival access or new documentation. In the West, a wave of triumphalist histories, still operating within the frameworks of the old ideological debates, used the collapse of the Soviet Union to re-anchor some of the old cold war historiography and to play down the value of a whole generation of historical works produced by the "social historians" from the 1960s through the late 1980s. Other historians, both within and outside Russia, have responded to the passage of the "Soviet period" into history—one chapter of it, with a more-or-less clear beginning and ending—by recasting historical writing in a fundamental way. The questions these historians ask— whether they concern the place of the Soviet chapter within the larger patterns of Russian history or examine the varied and changing ways in which the "Soviet system" worked and Soviet life was lived—often come from outside the ideological and political discourse that dominated in Soviet times. Some historians have found it possible to disregard the ideological arguments of the past altogether. Addressing issues that had not been part of the discourse among Russian historians, they have applied to our field methodologies and structures of interpretation borrowed from other fields and other areas of history, often incorporating as well new archival documentation.

Overall, it is fair to say that the impetus for much of the new historical writing in the field of Russian and Soviet history in the past decade has not been derived strictly from archival availability, even if much of this writing could not have been accomplished without the greater access of recent years. And while some of the new work has laid claim to historical veracity precisely on the basis of such access, in some cases the new documents produced in print reflect a selectivity worthy of previous decades. Certainly, a student of Soviet and post-Soviet Russian history will find it hard to argue that the historical narratives we routinely read—the "facts" marshaled and the argument expounded or implied—represent simply an exposition of the documentation preserved in the archives.

But with all due attention to the many contingencies that affect the value and place of the archival record in general, and in recent Russian history in particular, this essay argues for the centrality of documentation, preserved and archived, in the ongoing writing and rewriting of history, and through it, in shaping social memory. In so doing, it speaks as well to the crucial importance of the archivist as the keeper of the historical record and to the enormous value of the very act of preserving this record. Put differently, this essay argues that it is the preservation of documentation that ensures us the potential for questioning even the most established, dominant, and pervasive narratives. Such preservation is the best guarantee that our knowledge and understanding of the past will not merely be a mirror image of a narrative we no longer trust; that it will be based, instead, on a more creative if not more "true" reconstruction of events and meanings.

The vantage point I bring to this discussion is that of a participant in a decade-old archival publication project, dedicated to documenting the history of the Menshevik party during the revolution of 1917 and through the early years of Bolshevik rule.[2] Now nearly complete, this project is unique both in involving extensive collaboration between Russian and American historians and in focusing so consistently on one party. But the story it tells is quite symptomatic. It demonstrates how an archival record can survive the vagaries of politics and ideology to reemerge and challenge a dominant historical narrative. In its barest outlines, this is the story of a party that was placed beyond the pale of both political discussion and historical consideration for more than half a century, of documentary holdings that remained throughout this period beyond the purview of historians, and of the swift reemergence of that documentation in the last days of the Soviet Union. This is also the story of historians in Russia, who could trace the history of Menshevism only through the study of other topics, never as a topic in its own right, with the appropriate literature and documentation.[3] In their published works, these historians were limited for the most part to a formulaic portrayal of the Mensheviks, mandated by the reigning doctrine.[4] This is, finally, the story of historians outside Russia—myself included—whose exploration of Menshevik history had to proceed without recourse to key documentation. We knew with certainty that such documentation had existed at one point, but could only guess its survival and could hardly hope to see it one day.[5] Our study of the role and evolution of Menshevism during the revolutionary years of 1917–24 had to draw heavily on the recollections of the Menshevik actors themselves (through memoirs and interviews). These could be checked against each other, against the contemporary press, and against whatever documentary publications from 1917 had appeared in the early Bolshevik period,[6] but it remained difficult to transcend the Menshevik narrative embedded in these remembrances.

It is against this background that the idea for the publication project that is my subject here developed in 1988–89 (this involved a group of American scholars of the Russian revolution, most centrally L. H. Haimson of

Columbia University and myself). Significantly, this initiative had preceded the opening of the archives and was in fact spurred by the continued and conspicuous absence of the Mensheviks from the bookshelf of documentary editions. Their absence became all the more striking in the late 1980s, when the boundaries of what could be openly discussed in the Soviet Union began to expand. First to be allowed back into public discussion and social memory were hitherto forbidden Bolshevik personages such as Bukharin and Trotsky. It seemed only a matter of time before public discussion of the country's political history would expand to include the Mensheviks as well—the Social Democrats who had defined themselves as the moderate antithesis of Bolshevik extremism. Our intention, then, was to reconstruct a documentary record for the party from the traces of its activity that were preserved in the contemporary press and to substitute this reconstructed record for the absent archival documentation. In particular, we planned to reconstruct the proceedings of the three principal convocations of the Menshevik party during 1917 from the often detailed reports published in the contemporary party press about the composition, proceedings, and resolutions of these convocations.

From the outset, then, the goal of the Menshevik publication project was not to rewrite history but simply to give this important party a place on the library shelf of documentary sources for the study of the revolution of 1917. When the documentary publication became the subject of a Russian-American collaboration (in 1990) and we gained access to a dazzling quantity of archival documentation of the Menshevik party, the project expanded dramatically but did not change in essential ways. (By this time, the two American editors were joined by a Russian historian, A. P. Nenarokov.) Its goal remained to bring into scholarly circulation the documentary base for the history of the Menshevik party in the revolutionary era. Archival as well as press records were used to document the history of the central policy-making organs in the Menshevik party, reconstructing as fully as possible the debates, divisions, and shifts of position that preceded and followed official party resolutions. The project's only intended innovation was in combining two approaches that do not all too often cohabit—on the one hand, a "documentary history" that seeks to re-create in documents the *party's record* (albeit restricted to its leading bodies and all-Russian meetings), and on the other hand, an inclusive, comprehensive approach that aims to present an authoritative, nonselective (and in this sense "objective") re-creation of the *archival record*. Preserving the integrity of the archival record was of paramount impor-

tance precisely because of the highly contested and ideological nature of Russian political history.[7]

It is important to emphasize that the historians involved in this project did not come to it with a burning desire to revisit and eventually rewrite Menshevik history in 1917. L. H. Haimson had been writing on Menshevik history for many years and was responsible for much of what we understood about the Mensheviks, especially their strategy around the Bolshevik seizure of power (the subject of an important three-article series he published in the early 1980s).[8] I had just published my monograph, *The Menshevik Leaders in the Russian Revolution: Social Realities and Political Strategy,*[9] which had been written without access to the relevant Russian archives. A. P. Nenarokov had not studied Menshevism as such, but in his work had dealt extensively with 1917 and the early years of Bolshevik rule. In fact, the first volume in the project (covering the period January–June 1917), while reproducing materials that had never been seen, and adding depth and color to the picture we had formed on the basis of published materials, taught us only little that was significantly new. But with each additional volume, as we progressed through the chronology of 1917, we were forced to revise more significantly our views on the Menshevik party and its various factions and leaders. Moreover, our understanding of the political process itself, during crucial stages of the 1917 revolution, was challenged by the documentation we confronted.

What were the materials that led us on this journey of rediscovery of a history seemingly so familiar to us? At the core are two *fondy* (275 and 451) from RGASPI (Russian State Archive of Social and Political History in Moscow, known formerly as the Central Archive of the Communist Party). They hold the papers that had accumulated in the offices of the Menshevik party in 1917 and early 1918: protocols of the party's Central Committee and its Bureau, minutes of party conferences, letters from local party organizations, materials prepared for publication and for election campaigns. These were the missing documents of my own monograph and of Haimson's articles. Their absence had been responsible in part for the fact that, of all the important parties of 1917, the Menshevik party was the last to get its own "history." When the party moved its headquarters from Petrograd to Moscow, the materials were organized, packed, and moved to Moscow by Boris Nikolaevskii, a member of the party's Internationalist wing and its archivist throughout this period. An obsessive collector and consummate archivist, Nikolaevskii would later lay the foundations for the Menshevik collections at the International Institute for Social History in Amsterdam and the Hoover Archives at Stanford University. But in 1922, when he followed most of the party leadership into exile in Germany, he was forced to leave behind the archival record of the party's short period of open, massive activity. The materials were left in the custody of David Riazanov, a Social Democrat who had often straddled the gap separating Mensheviks from Bolsheviks, and who was now head of the newly created Marx-Lenin Institute in Moscow.

We cannot be sure how much courage was required to continue holding on to these Menshevik documents during the next thirty-odd years, when many of those whose names were strewn throughout the documents were imprisoned, exiled, and eventually shot. (Menshevik documents are known to have been destroyed in more than one archive outside Moscow, apparently because local archivists or their bosses feared that the presence of such materials could be used to incriminate them.) But we do know that Nikolaevskii's Menshevik archive remained in the Marx-Lenin Institute as it moved from one building to another, and when the Central Archive of the Communist Party (attached to the institute) was set up in a separate building in downtown Moscow, it ended up there. The materials were catalogued only in the 1960s, and by one account they were only then taken out of the original boxes in which Nikolaevskii had placed them some forty years earlier. The lists of users attached to each file at the time of cataloguing confirm what we know from stories—that even after the 1960s, and until 1990, the files were used sparingly and selectively; not one historian's name appears consistently in a large number of files.

The permission to use this collection did not materialize easily. In the spring of 1990, it still had to come directly from the Secretariat of the Central Committee of the CPSU and was secured by our colleagues at the Marx-Lenin Institute as the condition for this collaborative project. Their success was a measure of the centrality of history to the political changes the Soviet Union was undergoing at the time. The Mensheviks were just then being admitted into the ever-expanding orbit of political groups given representation in officially sanctioned or semi-sanctioned historical writing, and we were the recognized specialists in the field, holding the key as well to some of the documentation outside Russia. Still, we confronted more than one obstacle on our way—the result, no doubt, of the newness of the situation, the uncertainty about the direction of the unfolding political process at the top, and, later on, a combination of technical and budgetary difficulties of all kinds.[10]

And yet, from the moment we laid eyes on the Men-

shevik *fondy* at the Central Archive of the Communist Party, we had little doubt that this was Nikolaevskii's Menshevik archive, that it had not been censured at any time, and that those documents missing (for example, texts of resolutions known to have been passed by a given conference) were lost close to the time when they were produced. Often, these are found in the party's newspaper (perhaps the original text was passed over to the newspaper to publish and never returned).[11] The incidence of missing resolutions is higher for the congress in December 1917, when the party was in opposition and in disarray, confirming our assumption of "honest loss." We owe an enormous debt of gratitude to Nikolaevskii, and to his obsessive collecting, for the rich archive, which often holds not only the official protocols of meetings but also handwritten shorthand minutes recording the words of each individual speaker, notes passed among participants, and revisions to resolutions in the handwriting of Martov, Dan, and others. And we rejoice in the fact that the record was not censured or destroyed during decades when the Mensheviks were considered political enemies of satanic proportions. Personally, I am convinced that it was mostly the respect for the written record that kept generations of archivists and directors from destroying an archival collection that could have been plausibly used against them. This very act of preservation and resurfacing is at the core of the story I tell in this essay.

A second large corpus of materials used in this documentary history comes from GARF (State Archive of the Russian Federation in Moscow) and includes protocols of the All-Russian Executive Committee of Soviets (VTsIK) from all of its meetings during the period July–October; minutes of the largest national convocation of that year, the Democratic Conference (in September 1917), and the body to which it gave rise in October, the Provisional Democratic Council of the Russian Republic (also known as the Pre-Parliament); and materials of the Second Congress of Soviets in October 1917. These materials had not been as closely guarded as the Menshevik documentation, but neither had they been fully or systematically published or used by historians. We used these materials to reproduce the full record of Menshevik appearances in these bodies—VTsIK, the Democratic Conference, Pre-Parliament, and Congress of Soviets— and to place their statements and speeches in the context of the work of these bodies and convocations. The former was done in the documentary text; the latter in the annotations and introductions. The inclusion of these materials was dictated by the definition of the project as a "documentary history," which in turn expanded the project both in terms of the sources used and in the coverage given to Menshevik activity outside the confines of the party's organizations—in the multiparty organizations and convocations of the time.

Protocols of meetings of the Executive Committee of Soviets (a body of several scores from several parties), the minutes of public conferences—this is not the stuff of archival sensation. The protocols of the small and closed meetings of the Menshevik Central Committee did yield some sensations—at least for the student of Menshevik history. We found, for example, that a full month after the party engineered the formation of a coalition government and made it the cornerstone of its policy, many of the Central Committee's members, among them some whom historians had described as enthusiastic supporters of the policy, expressed their disappointment and disagreement in the strongest terms. But even here, words did not lead to action, and the episode only helps to confirm and refine the view put forward in my earlier work—that Menshevik attitudes toward the strategy of coalition were ambivalent, and that the strategy could be maintained in part because of this ambivalence. What accounts, then, for the revisions we must make in the narratives of both 1917 and Menshevism? It is not one document or another, containing a singular piece of information, a sort of archival Archimedean point. Rather, it is the accumulation of documentation, much of it never seen before, some never reported by historians, combined with bodies of knowledge already in circulation among historians.

The picture is different especially in regard to the second half of the year, that is, after July 1917. The reason for this is to be found in large measure in the availability—or lack thereof—of the historical record. Of course, these months are not absent from histories of 1917, which themselves must be considered part of the "historical record" and have certainly shaped our understanding of that period. But to a large extent these histories had to be written without the minutes and protocols and letters preserved in the archives. There are several reasons why the problem was particularly acute with regard to the second half of 1917: First, because of the general difficulties and disintegration that accompanied the revolution's later stages, reports were less likely to be filed, minutes were not kept or simply lost, newspapers lagged behind the events.[12] Second, the onset of ideological rigidity in Soviet historical treatment put an end to the important documentary publications of the 1920s and thus prevented the appearance of the minutes of the Democratic Conference

or the protocols of the Executive Committee—the arenas where "political life" (in the narrowly defined, yet crucial sense of high politics) was acted out, and where significant elements of it were determined.

The absence of archival record (in print or in readily accessed archives) left unchallenged a central theme embedded in the narratives produced for many decades by historians on different sides of the ideological divides—the remarkable absence from these narratives of high politics and the political process in general. Some historians have focused on Bolshevik manipulation and machinations during the months leading up to October, while others, most notably the "social historians" (among whom I count myself), have assumed that by the fall of 1917 social polarization and the radicalization of broad sectors of society had deprived the political process of any relevance. This was also the picture portrayed by many contemporaries, most notably I. G. Tsereteli, first among the Menshevik leaders in 1917, who chose to conclude his memoirs of that year in late July 1917.[13] (A notable exception was N. N. Sukhanov.)[14]

But the newly accessed and assembled record of Menshevik involvement in politics opens up a considerably different vista. At its center stands a succession of protoparliamentary bodies which met in August, September, and October and whose corporate form of organization and representation seems to have reflected more truthfully the development of Russian society than the "one man—one vote" principle by which the ill-fated Constituent Assembly was elected. These corporate assemblies carried on discussions of the crucial *political* issues facing the provisional regime. True, the unity they were supposed to build around these central issues was gravely threatened from both the extreme right and left. And the biggest and potentially most important body of this kind, the Democratic Conference, was hopelessly divided in its plenary sessions and its votes on the central political issue (that is, the competing initiatives for a broad coalition and for a purely democratic government). But the full, reconstructed minutes of that conference also show that the representatives of all the parties present at the presidium of the conference (including the Bolsheviks) gave more than passing support to the idea of an all-democratic government, and moreover, that this initiative was frustrated in large measure by two personalities—the Bolshevik leader Lenin (who was in hiding but sent instructions to his fellow Bolsheviks) and the Menshevik-centrist leader Tsereteli. In other words, the archival record forces us to bring "politics" back into the narrative of revolutionary events in the fall of 1917; to bring back into our view of

1917 the politics of representation (albeit corporate representation, 1917-style), the role of individual political figures, and the very possibility of political solutions reached through new political configurations rather than revolutionary change and civil war.

Needless to say, what I have described constitutes a significant shift in our understanding of the factors that made for the outcome of the revolution. Similar and related "rewriting" has been forced on us in relation to the ability of the Menshevik leadership to generate new political ideas and put these on the agenda of all the political forces that defined themselves as "democratic"; and in relation to the absolute centrality of Tsereteli to the continued unity of the Menshevik party (in spite of critical divisions and tensions) and to the course it followed.

Take, for example, Tsereteli's initiative in the weeks immediately following the crisis of July 3–4, when he sought to redefine the "vital forces" of the revolution more narrowly, focusing on the new Radical Democratic party and implying also a closer trust and cooperation of the socialists with this democratic bloc. Tsereteli describes his ideas, initiatives, and their failure in his memoirs, yet only now can we appreciate the critical role of the Menshevik Central Committee in taking this move through the Soviets' All-Russian Executive Committee (VTsIK) and in fighting for it at the dramatic and crucial nocturnal meeting of the "big parties." Only now can we trace, in Tsereteli's frequent speeches before VTsIK during the weeks that followed the collapse of this initiative, the gradual substitution of the language of "state interest" for that of "unity of the vital forces." The new rhetoric was better suited for the increasing sense of desperation among his fellow Mensheviks and more capable of securing the support of those among them who entertained deep doubts about coalition.

Or, to take another example—the formation within the Menshevik party around this time of a solid group of "centrists," who were willing to bury their internal disagreements in order to advance the slogan of "democratic reforms," seeking not only to bring about the reforms that alone might have held back the radicalization of the lower classes, but to find a slogan and an initiative around which they could shape yet another "democratic" bloc. These centrist Mensheviks led the democratic wing of the State Conference in its united support of the "August 14 program" of reforms. The same political logic was behind their initiative in the immediate aftermath of General Kornilov's uprising to convene a "Democratic Conference," though here their intentions ran counter to Tsereteli's emphasis on "state interest."

Feodor Dan was Tsereteli's closest and most valuable ally and at the same time the central figure among the promoters of the slogan of democratic reforms. In his memoirs he wrote that in calling for the Democratic Conference, he and B. O. Bogdanov had hoped to bring about the replacement of the coalition government (discredited once again and most critically by the Kornilov affair) with a "homogeneous democratic government." He blamed the failure of this effort on the nonsocialist democratic groups' fear of parting with the "bourgeois" parties—and this was certainly one element in the failure of the Democratic Conference to realize the goals its initiators had set for it.[15] But our reconstruction of the record of the Democratic Conference also shows that this goal was betrayed from within the Menshevik party itself—by Tsereteli, who succeeded once again in pulling the rest of the centrists into supporting his position. The leader's ability with words and political formulations, combined with his fellow Mensheviks' ambivalence, did no less than the timidity of the nonsocialist democrats to frustrate the initiative for a "homogeneous democratic government." The political winner was Lenin.

These are but a few of the significant ways in which the archival record as reconstructed in the documentary history series *The Mensheviks in 1917* forces us to look anew at the political process in 1917. The significance of these revisions is apparent, and I could therefore rest here my case for the importance of the archival record as such, its preservation, and its accessibility. To be sure, the reemergence in our documentary history of "high politics" as a factor that held significance well into the latest stages of the February revolution resulted at least in part from the definition of our project, that is, from its focus on the central leading bodies of the Menshevik party and the decision to document the history of these bodies not only through intraparty deliberations, but through their participation in the arenas where they attempted to realize their political initiatives—VTsIK, the State Conference, Democratic Conference, Pre-Parliament. A publication from the archives of the Menshevik-dominated ministry of labor, the Menshevik-led trade unions, or any of the numerous economic-regulatory agencies where Mensheviks played an important role would have produced a different narrative of 1917, one in which the political exists mainly as an extension of the social and economic.

Even so, I believe, the example of the documentary history of the Menshevik party in 1917 argues for the centrality of the archival record in historical writing. For the point is not that archival documentation holds the key to a singular historical truth, but rather that the historian's unique contribution to social memory is to use the textual remains of the past in reexamining repeatedly the constructs and narratives we employ in our apprehension of that past. Indeed, if history as written by professional historians is one of the main contributors to the formation of social memory, then a multiplicity of histories, written from a variety of vantage points, each based on the relevant archival record, seems to be a good starting point.

NOTES

1. My emphasis on the contingency of archival access in Russia today is not intended to draw a distinction with archival systems elsewhere. Anecdotally, I can report that during recent visits to several archives of the labor movement in Israel, where archives are generally open and accessible, I found that cooperation and ease of access were still somewhat related to the archivists' perception of where the researcher belonged politically, culturally, and biographically. Of course, political affiliations are not determined in this case through a system of party-membership cards, but are guessed by the individual archivist on the basis of a whole set of markers that are well established among the political classes in the country.

2. The publication project has produced two series, each comprising four volumes: *Men'sheviki v 1917 godu* [The Mensheviks in 1917] (Moscow, 1994–97); and *Men'sheviki v Bol'shevistskoi Rossii, 1918–1924* [The Mensheviks in Bolshevik Russia, 1918–1924], vols. 1–4 (Moscow, 1999–2004).

3. When I worked in Soviet libraries in the mid-1980s, the guise for my interest in Menshevik activity in 1917 was a study of labor relations. It was not an unreasonable stretch for a dissertation focused on how Mensheviks maneuvered between workers and entrepreneurs and how they translated their view of such social realities into a political strategy for the revolution. But this guise limited my access even to some of the published materials I needed to see.

4. One obvious exception to this rule is the work of E. N. Burdzhalov, *Vtoraia Russkaia Revoliutsiia: Vosstanie v Petrograde* (Moscow: Nauka, 1967).

5. It is perhaps of more than anecdotal interest that when I began working on my doctoral thesis on the Menshevik party in 1917, I was advised by my two guides in this work, Leopold H. Haimson and Alexander Erlich, both of them leading veterans of Russian and Soviet history, that it was not unreasonable for me to attempt this work even without access to Soviet archives, because whatever Menshevik documentation had survived there was not likely to be available to historians in our lifetime. We often talked about the documentation we knew Boris Nikolaevskii had assembled (discussed later in this essay) and wondered whether it would ever come to light.

6. Such publications appeared for the most part in the mid-1920s and were of variable comprehensiveness and scholarly evenhandedness. They include the all-important volumes of proceedings from the Conference of Soviets of Workers' and Soldiers' Deputies in late March and early April 1917; the First Congress of Soviets in June; and the State Conference in August. Less complete or reliable is the volume of the proceedings of the Second Congress of Soviets in October.

7. Two major considerations led to the decision to focus on the party's central bodies. One stemmed from the approach described above. Had the project been expanded to include documentation from the party's local organizations, the editors would have had to sacrifice their comprehensive approach. The second was related to more practical and mundane aspects of archival research. The documentation for the central Menshevik bodies in 1917 was concentrated in a few easily identifiable archives, well catalogued, and assembled in specific *fondy*. It was still a laborious and often tricky task to sort out these materials, determine where each document belonged, who was who, and fill obvious gaps with news accounts and previously published sources. But how much more complex, time-consuming, and costly would it have been to construct through documents the history of Menshevism in Russia's many far-flung provinces, even if one were to choose just four or five representative centers of party activity? It would have required a solid understanding of the political and social context of each locality and a large collecting effort in local and provincial archives and libraries. Further complicating the task was the fact that many of the local archives had been destroyed during the war or purged of any Menshevik documentation. The central archives used in this project represents the premium placed by the national archival authorities on events at the political center and the layers of work invested by archivists in preserving and preparing documents in their care for use by historians and editors.

8. "The Mensheviks after the October Revolution," *Russian Review* 38 (fall 1979): 456–73, 39 (winter and spring 1980): 181–206.

9. Published by Princeton University Press (1989) and reissued in Russian translation as *Lidery men'shevikov v russkoi revoliutsii* (Moscow: "Respublika," 1993).

10. The following illustrates the difficulties confronted in the archives at that time: During our first, month-long visit to the archive in June 1990 we were allowed to take some notes, but forbidden to copy verbatim any passages from the documents we read. When we complained to the deputy director of the Marx-Lenin Institute, we were told not to bother with copying by hand, and simply order photocopies! But six months later (in January 1991), the copies were still not ready and some crucial folders we had previously reviewed were now held back from us. We were later told that an archivist had complained to the Central Committee's Secretariat that foreigners were being allowed to copy secret materials. The director of the Marx-Lenin Institute was called to answer these charges. In July 1991, following these events and in an atmosphere of growing liberalization and disintegration, we finally received the first batch of photocopies.

11. This assumption is supported by the fact that the texts of some resolutions were found in the archive in the folders (*dela*) of *Rabochaia Gazeta*, the official newspaper of the Menshevik party during much of 1917.

12. For example, the last two days of the Menshevik "Unification" Congress (August 19–26) were barely covered in the party's official newspaper because of the Kornilov affair, which broke out as the congress was ending.

13. I. G. Tsereteli, *Vospominaniia o fevral'skoi revoliutsii,* 2 vols. (Paris and The Hague, 1968).

14. N. N. Sukhanov, *Zapiski o revoliutsii,* 7 vols. (Berlin, Petrograd, and Moscow, 1922–23).

15. Dan's memoirs of the weeks just preceding the fall of the Provisional Government are unique in opening a window into Menshevik strategy at that crucial time. His presentation has influenced my own assessment of Menshevik engagement in the efforts to safeguard a democratic solution to Russia's mounting problems. See F. I. Dan, "K istorii poslednykh dnei Vremennogo Pravitel'stva," *Letopis' revoliutsii,* 1922, 1: 163–75.

Russian History

Is It in the Archives?

Abby Smith

The Politics of Access in Post-Soviet America

Those who got their academic training in Russian and Soviet history before the collapse of the Soviet Union worked under a considerable handicap: lack of access to the bulk of primary source materials in the libraries and archives in the Soviet Union. Even medievalists such as myself were routinely denied access to archives, even to those that had already appeared in print. We all dreamed of the day when we would have access—even access to inventories and finding aids seemed some sort of holy grail back then. For a brief period of time in 1991–92, all that promised to change.

The question of whether a country's history is to be found in its archives is not idle speculation or postmodern theorizing in the case of Russia. Constructing the past is not an academic exercise in Russia but serious political activity, and performing semiotic, structural, and formal analysis on sources and their provenance must be done even for what passes in the historiographical traditions of other countries as "ordinary stuff." It is certainly no coincidence that Russians, in studying their own literary heritage, devised these analytical approaches to texts. I have always wondered why historians of the same culture have been slow to appraise the documentary heritage in a similar vein, though in the field of medieval studies, scholars of the present generation tend to bore in on textual formalisms in order to render the abundant but redundant formulaic sources a bit more informative.

In June of 1992, Presidents George Bush and Boris Yeltsin met in Washington, DC, for a political summit. To mark the occasion, an exhibition of over three hundred formerly top-secret documents from eleven different Soviet archives was on display in a gallery of the Library of Congress across the street from the US Capitol. The exhibition, portentously called Revelations from the Russian Archives, was a public announcement by the Russian government of a radical change in information policy—open access, in the Western sense, to records of the Communist Party of the Soviet Union (CPSU) and its numerous agencies—and was accompanied by a symposium on the significance of the event for the historical profession that featured Rudolf Pikhoia, then head of the Russian archival administration (Roskomarkhiv), Dmitrii Volkogonov, head of a presidential commission on the opening of the archives, Ambassador Paul Nitze, Professors Adam Ulam and Robert Tucker, and Librarian of Congress James Billington. The documents were on display for a month and were to be sent back to Moscow for a longer period of public exhibition there. A significant sampling of these documents was simultaneously mounted on the Internet—this was before the World Wide Web. And all this took place less than a full year after the spectacular events of 1991 that brought Yeltsin to power and ushered in the death of the Soviet Union. What had happened in that brief span of time?

In the 1990s, the politics surrounding the fate of the Soviet-era archives centered around the age-old question of who would control access to the past. That meant, first and foremost after the events of August 1991, who controlled access to the CPSU and state, military, and intelligence documents dating from the past, as opposed to the interpretation of the past. Archivists and archival administrators suddenly became more important and, in some sense, more powerful than historians. Most of the anxieties of the early years of the last decade were occasioned by who got into the archives first, who found the best material, and, in the West, whose interpretation of the Soviet Union would be borne out by the evidence revealed in the archives. The politics on the ground in Moscow and St. Petersburg and all the towns that had caches of evidence from the Soviet era is the story that most people were rightly focused on. That was the story about whether the historical actors had been able to get there first and remove the files they wanted expunged, whether security files would be opened as they had been in East Germany, whether intelligence files would be leaked, whether international relations would be seriously destabilized by any revelations from the CPSU or KGB archives, whether citizens would have access to files about themselves and their family members, and so on.

While the stakes were hardly the same, the politics of access were pretty thick in Washington, Cambridge, Palo Alto, and on many university campuses as well, and the Russians entered into those American struggles as well for a variety of reasons. For historians in the West, the moving force shortly after the events of 1991—the rush to lay hands on "smoking gun" evidence—was met with an immovable object—the obduracy of the archival system itself. Many historians, themselves unacquainted with the business of archives and familiar only with the small portion of it that transpires in the reading room, tended to read politics in that obduracy. And why not? There had been plenty of it in the Soviet era. How could one tell the difference?

What were historians looking for, what did they find, and what role did archivists and librarians play in this hunt, both in the United States and in the former Soviet Union? Rather than address this vast topic comprehensively, I want to offer a historical account of the Revelations from the Russian Archives exhibition, told from the oblique angle from which I observed and participated in the events. I will focus not on politics in the former Soviet Union, but in Washington, DC, where I worked at the Library of Congress on, among other things, a series of bilateral projects with Soviet and later post-Soviet libraries and archives, including this particular exhibition. I base this account primarily on my own recollections and notes from the time and, secondarily, the records of the agency I worked for.[1] The Library of Congress is, of course, an agency of the legislative branch, a wholly owned subsidiary of Congress whose board of overseers—the members of Congress—had a political stake in the outcome of the dissolution of the Soviet Union. The library, along with several other cultural agencies that receive federal support, has always played a low-key but surprisingly powerful and active role in cultural diplomacy, especially during the Cold War and its aftermath. While Americans may have thought the Bolshoi Ballet was the paramount sign of the cultural sophistication and humanity of the otherwise barbaric Russian Communists, the Soviets who listened to short-wave radio tended to hold jazz and the American library and information system in the deepest regard—the former for what it was and the latter for what it symbolized. And the Vatican of American librarianship is the Library of Congress.

The Request for Help

By a weird coincidence, the coup attempt had taken place right in the middle of an international meeting of librarians in Moscow. The International Federation of Library Associations (IFLA) meets every August in a different country, and the site of the meeting each year is fraught with political significance. Hosting the meeting in Moscow essentially gave Gorbachev's regime of glasnost international sanction and meant that the Soviet Union was being admitted to the grown-ups' table of democratic, pseudodemocratic, and wannabe-democratic nations that formally embrace an information policy of so-called free and unfettered access to information by all citizens. It was just a meeting, but this gathering constituted a significant step in Gorbachev's cultural policy, and cultural policy was a key tactical element in his overall political strategy. During the course of those tumultuous days in August, the incoming and outgoing government regimes waged a physical battle for the control of the paper trail of the Soviet Union. The most heated battle was fought in the halls and basements and furnaces of the KGB headquarters on Lubianka and the Central Committee of the CPSU on Staraia ploshchad. Back here in the states there was much anxiety expressed about the fate of documents that historians had long coveted—documents dating from Lenin and Stalin's time, primarily. Back in Moscow, the people who were hauling away, burning, or shredding files were indeed members of the *nomenklatura,* but they were not worried about the legacy of Stalin or even Lenin. They were worried about their own skins, and most of what perished in those early days were their own dossiers and those relating to actions they feared they would be prosecuted for in the uncertain future. While later checks of key historical files, like Lavrentii Beria's, revealed significant "unauthorized removals," experts agree that these files had been purloined decades before.

In the haste to gain control of the archives of the Communist Party and the party's state apparatus, Yeltsin called upon a friend of his from Sverdlovsk (now Ekaterinburg), Rudolf Pikhoia, who had only months earlier been put in charge of the newly reorganized archival administration of the Russian Republic. On August 24, Yeltsin announced the nationalization of the party and KGB archives with the view of taking physical control of and legal responsibility for papers that were conservatively estimated at the time as being over 70 million files for the party archives alone.

After some readjustments of administration and the legal abolition of the Soviet Union, Pikhoia ended up with the title of chairman of the Committee of Archival Affairs of the Government of the Russian Federation (Roskomarkhiv). In attempting to bring this messy legacy into some kind of order, he gathered a small group of trusted colleagues around him. But he was a relative newcomer to Moscow and to the archival world, having been a historian and pro-rector of Sverdlovsk University. He turned as well to interested parties abroad, some of whom had been in Moscow during the attempted coup and had offered to help. He turned to the United States in particular, in large part because of America's reputation for having a lot of money and giving a lot of it away, in some part because James Billington, the director of the Library of Congress, had seen him during those fateful days in August and promised help, but also because of the reputation that the American archival and library system has abroad.

The countries behind the Iron Curtain had formed an image of our information system and policies based largely on what we told them about ourselves on the Voice of America and Radio Free Europe. In point of fact, from the very beginning of Gorbachev's articulation of glasnost, there had been lively and active exchanges between American libraries and their Russian counterparts. There were also some exchanges with the National Archives and Records Administration (NARA), but NARA was then a rather insular organization that did not play an active part in international archival organizations, such as the International Council of Archives (ICA), and had few bilateral relationships with countries behind the Iron Curtain. This was not true of the Library of Congress, which had had strong acquisitions programs with Soviet partners for years and whose formal institutional interest in the emerging democracies, as we called them then, was ramped up dramatically when James Billington, a Russian specialist with extensive ties in the Reagan and then Bush administrations, became Librarian of Congress

in 1987. He was in Moscow during the coup and committed his agency to do what it could to bring the Soviet/Russian library and archival institutions into the fold. Because this was, after all, both a professional commitment and one between government agencies, the agreement was memorialized in October 1991 in a memorandum of understanding between Roskomarkhiv and this agency of the legislative branch. The agreement was aimed, from our point of view, at bringing these archives into the light of day sooner rather than later. For the Russians, it was geared toward getting material aid in coping with the physical burden of processing the archives. The burden of declassification was overwhelming from the sheerly physical standpoint, but the Russians were also curious about various Western practices for access, and they consulted widely with archival colleagues from all over the West during that time. While there was certainly a good deal of talk between the Americans and Russians about the joys and marvels and necessity of democratic standards of access to freedom, many of us, for our part, were very excited about the prospect of getting into the archives to check out our long-held beliefs and testing our theories and conjectures about what had happened. Our counterparts from the archives, we sensed, were facing pressures and fears that we could not even imagine.

There was a considerable amount of jockeying among American institutions for inclusion in any activity that Roskomarkhiv was undertaking. There were natural partners, such as the Hoover Institution on War, Revolution, and Peace at Stanford University. That sounded at the time quite unnatural, since the Hoover appeared to represent everything that the old archival system was against. But there was such great sense in the partnership: the Hoover had long experience in dealing with Russian manuscripts; it had a staff with incomparable expertise in these materials; it had a fellowship program that lent an air of respectable scientific probity to their activities. Pikhoia had visited the Hoover in June of 1991 and signed an agreement about exchanging microfilms. At that time and later, "exchange of materials" was a critical concept for the Russians; the phrase showed up in all their agreements and protocols. There could never be an agreement about any activity that did not stipulate that Roskomarkhiv would get something in the way of materials in return. They only wanted Russian materials—so-called Rossica—not records of the US State Department or the papers of the Continental Congress. There is in fact a rather limited number of Russian archival materials in the United States. The Hoover had a significant portion of what was interesting to them. At the same time, there was a general agreement inter alia to exhibit materials from both the former Soviet Union and the United States at their respective institutions. Exhibitions at that time figured vaguely into the category both of "exchange of materials" and of "publication," that is, making public.

The more obvious partner, from the point of view of the Russians, was their counterpart the National Archives. Together with the International Research and Exchanges Board (IREX) and other smaller agencies, the National Archives was part of the US-USSR Commission on Archival Cooperation, established in 1987 to support the archival profession in the Soviet Union. But the National Archives had in fact little expertise in Russian archival practice and, much to the surprise of the Russians, it had no money to give them. Furthermore, as an executive branch agency, the National Archives felt constrained to work through the State Department on these matters. The director of the Library of Congress pressed hard for the library to become the umbrella organization or managing partner for what in the autumn of 1991 was known informally as the CPSU archival project. The advantages of working through the Library of Congress, he eventually persuaded them, was the status of the library as a part of the federal government and its bipartisan nature. And while the library per se had no money to give the Russians, Billington was willing and able to raise money to support initial funding requests for meetings, travel, and so forth. The Russian economic collapse of the time had taken a very hard toll on the cultural sector—libraries, museums, and archives—and staff salaries did not keep pace with inflation (which during the fall of 1991 grew by 20 percent a month). The salaries that did come arrived five to six months late. People therefore were sometimes showing up for work only a few hours a day; electricity arrears led to regular, if unpredictable, closings; and the degraded and dangerous physical state of these paper mountains seemed an imminent threat to long-term access.

A Word about Money

One of the hardest things to convey to the individuals we dealt with from various post-Soviet archival agencies and individual repositories in 1991–92 was the way we view our documentary patrimony. While the libraries and archives of the Soviet system were used to being supported by the state, they had been essentially cut off from the state dole during the Gorbachev era, a situation that led to a siege mentality in the archives and also to periodic theft of documents that could be sold in the black market. There was a tendency on the part of the professionals we dealt with, especially at the very highest levels, to confuse the demand they heard from our side for access to their art and books and archives with market demand. We explained that the demand came from the not-for-profit sector and so did not mean that they should expect the Americans and Dutch, for example, to pay big bucks for access for scholarly and cultural purposes. There were lengthy discussions held to explain that the amount they would get from the sales of preservation microfilms would not be pegged to the appraised value of the source materials.

Our colleagues from the recently Soviet archives also betrayed a radically different understanding of the role of archives in a civic society. They were not used to the Western idea that government-created records were de jure part of the public domain. The state had owned the entire archival fond of the Soviet Union since 1918 and extended complete control over access to them in the 1920s in ways that essentially separated the role of archival documentation from the function of public accountability.

Attempts to explain our legal and cultural perspective were nearly always accompanied on our part by the unattractive but habitual assumption that our system was better than theirs, and they would naturally aspire to be just like us as soon as we had enlightened them. We just could not resist the temptation to preach to them, and our approach was too often tone-deaf, inappropriately evangelical, and self-satisfied. When we heard from them some reservations about their path having to follow ours, some of our American colleagues grumbled audibly about stubborn Russian chauvinism.

Again, this was something we had encountered during our glasnost-era meetings. Our earliest encounters with Russians from the Gorbachev era had accustomed us to their consistent and understandable, if still disquieting, interest in money and material benefits that could be derived from exploiting our interest in their patrimony. But we Americans often evinced a cupidity of our own. In our case, it was not money we wanted, but access to those much-vaunted secret files and with it, bragging rights about who got what first. I sensed time and again that Americans—colleagues in libraries as well as scholars with whom we had constant dealings—harbored a feeling that we had the right to this information and, if Russians disagreed, then they did so merely out of chauvinism.

Roskomarkhiv had signed an agreement in December 1991 with Chadwyck-Healey for a series of microfilm publications that was purely and forthrightly commercial. It was not preservation-driven and did not aim to film runs of materials systematically. Instead, it would capture highlights from the personal files of name-brand Communists like Molotov and Trotsky. That was followed by an agreement with the Hoover Institution to do more comprehensive filming from the CPSU archives. The agreement was announced in spring 1992, and within days Iurii Afanasiev was protesting it as the selling off of patrimony, claiming that Russians should get first crack at these materials. (More important to Afanasiev was that the Russians had sold off the patrimony too cheaply!) Charles Palm of the Hoover Institution responded in an interview, "Scholarship is a universal endeavor, and it is advanced if everyone has equal access. And if it is restricted, people don't have equal access. So Afanasiev is playing the nationalist card, and it's something we in the West need to resist."[2]

But it seemed to me at the time that there were deep ethical issues involved that went beyond traditional understandings on our part about information in the public domain. I was reminded time and again of how the concept of public domain was so weak in the information culture of Soviet and indeed prerevolutionary Russian society. I was also reminded of an issue often brought up in discussions about the cultural patrimony of Native Americans held in the Library of Congress's own collections. It is the credo of the historical and library professions in the United States that information cannot be owned by anyone. But not all cultures believe that evidence about the past should be accessible to all for scientific and research purposes. At the Library of Congress, during the assembling of materials for exhibition and later when we accessioned the research files of Dmitrii Volkogonov, we received materials from those Russians, like Volkogonov, who ardently believed that if they gave the Americans this information, it would pass safely and forever into the public domain. And that was the spirit in which we acted. But our general counsel kept reminding us that, legally, there was no such concept operative in the Soviet Union and its successor state, and wishing would not make it so.

had already been a flood of leaked documents of dubious provenance and authenticity "revealed" throughout the era of glasnost. Newspapers and periodicals vied for the honor of publishing the most sensational news flashes from the past—that was the day when old news was far more interesting than contemporary news. One of the stated goals of Pikhoia and his colleagues was to remove the archives from this fray, to restore (or create?) a sense of respect for the profession both within and without the walls of the repositories, and to counter the prevailing view among lay people as well as historians that the archival administration was run by bureaucratic hacks who allowed and profited from the purloining of documents from the archival patrimony. The international experts were to offer advice and material support on: opening closed archives (declassification); preservation and access; automation (core infrastructure issues); publication; accommodating researchers from abroad; and fund-raising.

When the advisory group first met, the most daunting task was to inventory all the arrangements for cooperation that had proliferated during glasnost. It had been a free-for-all, with Pikhoia himself seeming to strike a deal with some new third party every time he spent a few hours with a foreigner. While we never really found out what other institutions and consortia had planned to do with Roskomarkhiv, Pikhoia and his associates for their part proposed a publication series to us, under the aegis of this advisory group. The editorial board that Pikhoia had brought together in Russia for this publication series proposed essentially every topic you would ever want to cover, from party property to the gulag system to the demographic history of Russia. There was consensus among those consulted by Billington that, while social history was terribly important, at this juncture it was important to go after very high impact files, those of the party leaders. Billington felt that these documents are important in and of themselves. But he was thinking already of raising funds and support from Congress. And our side went back to Pikhoia with a slightly reshuffled set of priorities. At the same time that we agreed on a publication series, we also agreed on an exhibition, to be held in Washington and Moscow.

Getting to Yes

Pikhoia had formed an international advisory body and Billington lobbied aggressively and eventually successfully to have the Library of Congress be the managing partner with Roskomarkhiv in the CPSU archival project. There

Selecting for Display

The library had mounted several Russian-related exhibitions since Billington arrived in 1987, including one comprising Old Believer manuscripts borrowed from Russian repositories that was also mounted during a visit of the head of state. (Raisa Gorbacheva had attended the opening of that exhibition, together with her cultural advisor, Dmitrii Likhachev.) Although Yeltsin was scheduled to open this first post-Soviet exhibition himself during the June summit, after some to-ing and fro-ing, he did not come to the opening ceremonies of this taboo-busting exhibition. The mixed signals we got until the very end let us know that, among other things, this exhibition was a calculated political act on the part of the Russians (and the American side, of course). Our expectation was that it was not exclusively a foreign policy move, but signaled a permanent departure from previous information policy. This was the first year of Yeltsin's administration, after all, and Volkogonov declared that the opening of the archives and exhibiting of them was a way of "turning politics into history." The commitment to show these documents in Moscow meant that this exhibition was not just for show, so to speak.

The selection criteria were forged by the Russians and the Library of Congress with little disagreement. The curatorial team in the archives in Russia culled about five hundred documents from eleven different archives on subjects that focused on two general areas: the inner workings of the party and the government; and US-USSR relations. The time period ranged from 1917 to 1990. Documents, most of them in the original form and neatly bound in folios, were sent to Washington, where they were quickly translated. Days before the opening of the exhibition the Russian curatorial team arrived with newly declassified documents on the invasion of Afghanistan that had to be translated and squeezed into the exhibition at the last minute. Events were unfolding at a very rapid pace and people worked under extraordinary conditions. Everyone felt that they were witnessing something historic.

The exhibition was called Revelations from the Russian Archives, and revelations there were. We did not know what to expect when documents started arriving. And in general, no one quite knew what was "concealed" in the archives. In 1991, Vladimir Bukovsky had expressed his certainty that the archives held important evidence of multiple crimes and that the archives would yield evidence that could be used to prosecute the criminals, either in government courts or, more likely, those of public opinion.[3] There was also talk of the purgative power of truth—somehow equating archival evidence with truth seemed an inevitable slip of the mind—and simultaneously an apprehension that a witch hunt in the archives would lead to something as terrible as what was happening at the time in Germany, where the Stasi archives were essentially open to those attempting to avenge past crimes. On this side of the Atlantic, Richard Pipes predicted that "[t]hese archives contain the true history of the Soviet regime. I'm just dreaming of getting my hands on it."[4] Many American historians found themselves agreeing with Pipes for perhaps the first time in their lives.

The Russians themselves seemed most interested in certain questions, most especially the one that can be best expressed as "Was it Lenin's fault or Stalin's?" The curatorial team in Russia had access to the four thousand or more unpublished documents in the Lenin archives, and there were several chosen for the show that pretty much knocked the stuffing out of the Lenin mystique. One short and punchy letter from 1918 ordered that one hundred kulaks be strung up, hostages taken, grain confiscated, and so forth in response to a peasant uprising in Penza. "Use your *toughest* people for this," Lenin thoughtfully added in a postscript. This letter was chosen to answer the question of who first used the ruthless tactics that came to be identified with Stalin's name. Another memorandum, this one dating from 1922 at the height of the famine and sent to Molotov, ordered the confiscation of church property in Shuia to retrieve gold and other precious materials ostensibly to be used for famine relief but in reality sent to Communists abroad to foment revolution.[5]

Of course there was also the hunt for a few smoking guns, such as proof positive that Stalin did order the murder of Kirov or that Lenin ordered the murder of the Romanovs. Mostly, documents were chosen to reveal how the decision-making process worked, and they were enlightening in ways even those who had "gotten it right" did not anticipate. Some were chosen to prove things long inferred or asserted without documentary proof. New to the world was a series of documents detailing the extent of the famine in the Ukraine in 1932–33 and precisely how much Moscow knew about the events and even directed them. Some items were chosen simply to break taboos. I would put into this category all the letters from Lenin in which he uses coarse invectives against the peasants and the church. His language was vituperative and almost pathological, going far beyond the rhetoric of revolutionary zeal that was acceptable in a Jacobin. But even more scintillating for the Russians were items from the personnel files of the Politburo. We displayed all the party membership cards of the general secretaries from Stalin up to Chernenko. There was an inventory of all items found in Stalin's bedroom on the day of his death. There was the confession of Bukharin, as well as a truly shattering letter he wrote days before in which he denies his guilt. We showed pages from Stalin's diary that revealed that all the party members who, like Bukharin, ultimately signed confessions of guilt had spent hours alone with Stalin shortly before signing the confessions. There were documents about American Communists, including information about those who received payments even under Gorbachev. John Reed, for example, got 1,008,000 rubles in 1920 for unspecified purposes.

What "History" Tells Us

What did we learn? For one thing we learned that the party archives were extremely well tended. We had all heard about how badly off the archives were—and they were, except for the party archives, which had excellent finding aids and were exceptionally well ordered. The piles of papers were collected and tended, it seems, as a form of reverence. Really, they were treated quite like relics. From the archival point of view, neither the historical record nor accountability as we understand them had much to do with selection and appraisal for retention. In a way, then, the display of these papers in public was its own form of desacralization. Just as the Bolsheviks had unearthed bodies of locally venerated saints in the 1920s and revealed that they had been physically corrupted, so this exhumation of the most intimate artifacts of party members, such as their party cards, the records of their real estate holdings, and their payoffs to failed revolutionaries in the West, was intended to secularize the grip they held over the imagination of the Russian citizen.

We also found out how the process of decision making was undertaken. We found out how the routine of business was conducted and, certainly after the death of Stalin, how powerful a grip that routine had on the men who aspired to power. We learned how far up, as well as how far down, the mentality of paternalism and subordination ran, a trait familiar to anyone who has read any documents from any other century of Russian rule, but which had struck twentieth-century specialists and political scientists as somehow an artifact of Marxism-Leninism. The deference to and fear of hierarchy that readers of Gogol knew to be an intrinsic feature of life in imperial Russia had by the mid-1920s morphed into something fatally charged with terror-induced fear. Those who were not already familiar with the archival record of prerevolutionary Russia often did not understand the etiology of this fear and identified it as something wholly new and unique to totalitarianism. This was, inciden-

tally, the precise period when the word *totalitarianism* came to be used freely by many, without feelings of political incorrectness. I remember some of my American colleagues who were actually shamed into using it by our Russian colleagues.

On looking back at how political acts such as this exhibition affected the archival, as opposed to historical, profession in Russia, they were taken so that they could address the accusations made against them in the heyday of glasnost. A letter published in *Sovetskaia kul'tura* in May 1988 and signed by the Learned Council of the Moscow State Historical-Archival Institute declared that in the Soviet Union, the archival profession was charged not with the preservation of knowledge and information but the "preservation of agency secrets." Of course, it has been hard to define what a secret was in the Soviet Union. We found out that for party members, all documents containing information about them, from their real estate holdings to their record of achievement in the Komsomol, were deemed state secrets and were protected by elaborate levels of classification.

What were the lasting effects of this political gesture taken in the summer of 1992? An article from the IREX newsletter published at the time reported, "The political message of 'Revelations' is different in Russia and the West. In Russia, it is that a return to the old regime must not be allowed. In the West, it warns of the danger of refusing to support Russian democracy in the face of the still palpable threat of resurgent reaction."[6] But of course, there was no message delivered in Russia. Despite all assurances to the contrary, the exhibition never opened in Russia. So all that was left of the "political message" was the one the Americans got: we need your support. And it worked. Congress was persuaded. They were deeply impressed by the political courage they saw on display at the Library of Congress. Members had meeting after meeting with Volkogonov and came away convinced that they must do what they could to buttress democracy in Russia. But within a year the archives seemed to have closed up again.

Is history in the archives? If the question is about what happened and how, then the answer must be yes. We learned a great deal about the what and the how and the numbers and the names. But for those who ask what happened and why, I think that the answer has so far eluded us. The aggregate picture that the CPSU archives reveals is so curiously impersonal and so relentlessly written in the passive voice that it is hard to find personal agency. It is in the nature of archives to drown us in evidence, but the Soviet record-keeping system was uniquely successful in creating and carefully preserving the banal and the mind-numbing. In contrast to the revelations that have come from the still-partial opening of the CPSU files, though, is the record-gathering of an organization called Memorial. These groups of individuals working in concert have been able to amass staggering amounts of evidence that speak of and to the individuals who were the objects of history and make them back into subjects. Memorial is going about the hard work of using records to render once more human those who had been stripped of their humanity.

NOTES

1. Harold M. Leich, Russian Area Specialist in the European Division of the Library of Congress, generously made available working files from that time. The library is constituted as a bureaucratic structure with a cultural mission—like all other governmental archives and libraries—and I can say that very little of what we experienced at the time as essential to the events related here has entered into the record of those events or is likely ever to do so. Records were created and filed during this period, but all of them were created in a form that was faithful to the documentary needs of the library and did not accurately document what happened outside of those needs. In bureaucracies, there are large, deliberate, and unbridgeable gaps between formal and informal networks of information. We kept both going at the same time and never confused the two. This firsthand experience of bureaucracies and their record-keeping practices deeply informed our own understanding of the many Soviet files we examined at the time.

2. "Archives Better Read Than Dead," *Insight,* August 2, 1992, 10.

3. He made these comments during a television interview with Vadim Bakatin, then the chief of the KGB. One of several historical crimes mentioned for which keys should be found in the archives was the assassination of Kirov in 1934. Jonas Bernstein, *Insight,* November 3, 1991, 9.

4. *Los Angeles Times,* March 11, 1992.

5. All of the documents sent for use in the exhibition, even those not shown for reasons of space, have been translated and published by the Library of Congress. They can be consulted in the original Russian in the European Reading Room. These two items can be found in *Revelations from the Russian Archives: Documents in English Translation,* ed. Diane P. Koenker and Ronald D. Bachman (Washington, DC: Library of Congress, 1997), 11, 441–43.

6. "Revelations from the Russian Archives," *IREX News in Brief* 3, no.5 (July/August 1992): 4.

Archiving Heteroglossia

Writing Reports and Controlling Mass Culture under Stalin

Serhy Yekelchyk

Working quietly in private during 1934–35, as the Soviet people were toiling to meet the targets of the Second Five Year Plan, celebrating Stalin the Great Leader, and condemning "enemies of the people," Mikhail Bakhtin was developing the concept of heteroglossia (*raznorechie* or *raznogolositsa*). The Russian philosopher of language understood heteroglossia as a polyphony of social and discursive forces, a diversity of social speech types that occur in everyday life. According to him, the genre of the novel is best suited for delivering the realities of heteroglossia because it allows for a network of dialogic, interactive relations among multiple voices in the text. In other words, the novel displays the variety of discourses, the knowledge of which other genres seek to suppress. Bakhtin contrasts this "centrifugal" force of heteroglossia with the centralizing drive of what he calls "unitary language," which aims to "unify and centralize the verbal-ideological front." To explain his idea of unitary language, Bakhtin refers to the historical incorporation of lower classes into modern high culture, the birth of modern philology, and the emergence of national languages.[1] But, as is often the case with Bakhtin, the reader is left with a strong suspicion that the philosopher was actually analyzing the society he lived in.

It is significant that Bakhtin developed his theories of dialogism and heteroglossia in the Stalinist Soviet Union. His famous notion that all texts are organized as a "dialogue" that takes account of their perception of a given society implicitly undermined the Stalinist quest for ideological uniformity. Much of Bakhtin's work celebrated unofficial resistance to authoritarian discourses by stressing that meanings cannot be fixed and made absolute and suggesting the impossibility of achieving total order and stability in language—and ideology. By the same token, was not Bakhtin's opposition of heteroglossia and unitary language yet another implicit comment on the social realities and ideological claims of the Stalinist era?

Using the Ukrainian republic as a case study, in this essay I will analyze two very different fields of Stalinist culture—bureaucratic report-writing and supervision of mass culture—as reflecting an ideological unitary language's frustrating struggle against heteroglossia. In so doing, I will look at Stalinist archiving as a cultural and political practice and approach it from the point of view of a historian whose primary research interest is in postwar Ukrainian culture.

"Speaking Bolshevik" or Writing in Archivese?

The opening of former Soviet archives has allowed scholars to advance in their search for intermediate spaces between the society "below" and the Stalinist authorities "above." Sheila Fitzpatrick, while implying a certain separation between state and society, has singled out such important channels of communication as denunciations and writing letters to political leaders and newspapers, both characterized by particular tropes, rhetorical styles, and modes of self-representation.[2] Stephen Kotkin has looked instead into the discursive practices uniting the two and argued that the Stalinist system functioned as a set of rules. Although enforced by the state, these rules

459

were appropriated and used by individuals who, in order to survive and succeed in Stalinist society, had to learn to "speak Bolshevik" in order to participate in the Soviet "identity game."[3] A group of younger scholars took his argument a step further by claiming that the population did not just "speak Bolshevik" in public but that this discourse was widely internalized.[4]

The more decisive problem looming large behind this discussion is that of the nature of the Stalinist subject and the possibility of self-conscious ideological resistance under Stalinism. But much of the recent theorizing on this issue overlooks the question of our access to past social and cultural practices. For example, one of Kotkin's most important case studies (and the one particularly hailed by those developing his ideas in the direction of an internalized Stalinist discourse) is a letter from Anna Kovaleva, the wife of the best locomotive driver in a factory, to Marfa Gudzia, the wife of the worst. In her letter, Anna asks Marfa to make her husband work harder and become a shock-worker. Igal Halfin and Jochen Hellbeck suggest that "[t]his non-official document reveals how Soviet power permeated society" and "to what extent individuals were willing to monitor one another to ensure the enforcement of the Stalinist identity blueprint." Kotkin's own interpretation is more open in proposing that it is of little relevance whether Anna believed in what she was writing or just conformed to the rules of public speech. What is important is that she knew "how to think and behave as the wife of a Soviet locomotive driver should."[5]

But what if this letter was dictated to Anna by a factory party organizer, as was usually the case with similar "private" initiatives when I was a young Soviet worker in the early 1980s? What if this ostensibly private letter was prepared to start off a public campaign, complete with factory meetings and newspaper articles, that for some reason was aborted? Even if Anna wrote the letter herself in the privacy of her home, what if she was consciously writing "for the archive"? Whether one accepts Kotkin's view, Halfin and Hellbeck's elaboration, or this present spur-of-the-moment suggestion of mine, the question is really whether one trusts the unifying language of the documents as the expression of true belief or looks for their reflection or suppression of multiple voices, that is, heteroglossia. This essay proposes that most of the state reporting and most of individual writing circulating in the public domain under Stalin used the "unifying language" of state socialism, which was, however, time and again frustrated by the heteroglossia of the social and cultural life it was to describe.

Let me begin with a very atypical document, yet the one that best captures the frustration of a reporting official. On August 23, 1945, Comrade Zaviriukha, head of the Section of Publishing in the Ukrainian Central Committee's Department of Propaganda, reported to Kost Lytvyn, the Central Committee secretary, the following incident that had taken place in the Kiev Circus on August 19.

When the performance began, in the first row on the right sat invalids from the Patriotic War, some 10 to 12 people in hospital clothing and with crutches; almost all of them were missing either a right or left leg. Before the end of the first part, some 25 to 30 Military Police [*komendantskii vzvod*] entered and one of them approached the invalids proposing that they leave the circus. When the invalids refused to obey, the Military Police used force but the wounded began resisting using their crutches. A real carnage [*poboishche*] ensued. When the Military Police proceeded to take away the crutches and forcibly pull or carry the wounded out of the circus, the military among the public came to their rescue. All the military were bursting to get down to the arena, but their wives kept them back. Some in the public, mostly the military, reacted violently; there was a terrible uproar in the circus. It was a repulsive picture. The sick [invalids] were not removed from the circus; instead, the Military Police left on the request of spectators, primarily those from the military. After the Military Police left, many of the sick were crying.

When everything settled down and the performance began, the Military Police entered again and occupied all the exits. Then the spectators started hiding the wounded soldiers and by the end of the performance, all of them had changed into civilian dress and [the spectators] led them from the circus without allowing any of them to be arrested.

During the skirmish in the circus, one could hear the cries "Beat them, the Motherland does not need them any longer," and "Down with gendarmes—why are you killing the invalids from the Patriotic War?"[6]

This short report, cited here in full, is remarkable for its lack of a single value-laden narrative frame. The author, a middle-ranking bureaucrat in the apparatus of the republic's Central Committee, does not assign fault to either the disabled veterans, the Military Police, or the public. Having witnessed a disturbance of public order, he felt compelled to report it to his superior but his writing preserved the heteroglossia of everyday life—the varied voices of Kiev's citizens. Even the language of the report is uneven, beginning with the formal "invalids from the Patriotic War," then switching to a compassionate "wounded" or "sick," and returning to "the invalids from the Patriotic War" (however unlikely a battle cry) in the end. One can sense that Zaviriukha himself sympathized with the disabled soldiers and their protectors and was struggling to adopt an official tone in his report. The multiple languages present in this document are precisely what Bakhtin meant by heteroglossia.

The "unifying language" of reporting that Zaviriukha could not reconcile himself with in this particular case characterizes the overwhelming majority of the official documents of Stalin's time. Even when the documents cite what a certain individual said, they are always prefaced by the qualification of these words as "anti-Soviet uttering" or "manifestation of bourgeois nationalism"— unmistakable markers of Stalinist "archivese."

In what was probably the most high-profile case of Ukrainian "nationalism" during the postwar decade, in 1946 the secret police sent directly to Stalin a file with the following label: "On the suicide attempt of A. Ia. Shumsky, a Ukrainian nationalist who had been repressed in 1933 and since 1946 lives in Saratov. Addendum: a copy of Shumsky's letter protesting the USSR's nationalities policy in Ukraine." Like thousands of other reports, this one framed the original document as a confirmed enemy's protest against state policy in general, while in fact Ukraine's former People's Commissar of Education, a prominent national Communist theoretician, had protested only against the postwar propaganda of Russian greatness.[7] One of Stalin's very few surviving opponents from the 1920s, Shumsky received an unusual punishment. Having recovered in hospital from his unsuccessful suicide attempt, he boarded a train to Kiev but died en route before reaching the Ukrainian capital. In 1992, General Pavel Sudoplatov, the former head of the NKVD special operations department, revealed that Shumsky had been murdered by his organization, allegedly on direct orders from the Kremlin.[8]

While Shumsky's letter seems to be authentic, recovering nonconformist voices from Stalinist official sources is generally difficult because the reports rarely cite them in full, preferring to retell in the dominant voice or to quote. *Svodki,* the secret police's survey reports to the authorities on the population's political mood, present a particular challenge because their authors determined which quotations were representative based on their own evaluation of current party policy. Much of the early historical research building on post-Soviet archival revelations relied on *svodki,* but no historian to my knowledge has engaged with the question of why Stalinist authorities so

rarely acted upon these reports. As I have suggested elsewhere, the Stalinist bureaucracy differentiated between historical documents per se and a "political archive" of more contemporary documents that could be used as a political weapon. Because all contemporary documents, even the most innocent ones, belonged to the "political archive," political documents proper no longer warranted the authorities' special attention.[9] It appears that, following the Great Terror, bureaucrats had expected state security to prepare compromising materials on almost everybody and so did not believe in them themselves. Thus, in the autumn of 1942, the Ukrainian leadership received an alarming report about panic and disbelief among the republic's intellectuals, who had been evacuated from Kiev to Ufa in Soviet Asia. According to NKVD informants, the physicist Loshkarev considered the creation of a "free Ukraine" and the secession of the Baltic region and the northern Caucasus to the Germans the only solution. The historian Fedir Los and the writer Oleksa Kundzich saw the situation as "hopeless," the historian Vadym Diadychenko saw the only hope lying in Western aid, while the composer Mykhailo Verykivsky praised England and the United States for their freedom of speech. The leading architect, Volodymyr Zabolotny, condemned the conformism of the court poets, Maksym Rylsky and Pavlo Tychyna, while the philologue Leonid Bulakhovsky declined an offer to join the party. The report was filed despite the seriousness of these revelations.[10] It surely added to the general "political archive" of denunciations for possible future use but, to my knowledge, none of the people named suffered any repercussions after the war. Moreover, the historian Ivan Krypiakevych, who allegedly said in 1947 that, if it were not for his family, he would have joined the nationalist guerillas,[11] was never arrested, and although his career suffered setbacks because of his wartime publishing activities under the German occupation, he made an impressive comeback during the early 1950s.

Although their reliability is equally unclear, the contemporary reports on the political mood of the population in Ukraine's western provinces that had been annexed from Poland in 1939 at least seem to have recorded different voices. A more optimistic report from 1951 would present the population as basically united around the Soviet cause, albeit concerned about the danger of war and the prices. A similar digest dating from late 1948 provides a considerably longer list of grievances: fear of war, inadequate food supply, meager salaries, and the "exploitation of workers." The April 1948 report is downright alarming, speaking of the persistent rumors of war with the United States and a probable collapse of the Soviet power in Ukraine. Bazaar traders in the city of Stanyslaviv were apparently so sure of American victory in the impending conflict that they demanded payment in U.S. dollars for their produce. While the common people worried about the bread supply and detested the collectivization of agriculture, many local intellectuals were quoted as condemning "Soviet imperialism." The same summary, however, noted that rumors emanated from the nationalist guerillas' propaganda and the population's listening to Western radio, implying that removing these factors was beyond the local cadres' control.[12]

Regardless of whether the reports recorded the voices of the population or their rendition of the Voice of America, the material has been already arranged to conform with a uniting narrative line: generally positive in 1950 and generally negative in early 1948. For instance, the April 1948 digest states that "in Stanyslaviv, bazaar traders are demanding U.S. dollars for their produce," but how many of the dozens or hundreds of traders actually made such a demand? Was it realistic to expect the average buyer in Stanyslaviv to possess considerable amounts of U.S. dollars? What if this whole sentence was a generalization based on a single incident and inserted in the report with the aim of providing substantiation for the bazaars' closure? More generally, was the change in public opinion indeed so pronounced during 1948 and between 1948 and 1950—or did the way of reporting reflect the authorities' agenda of eliminating the nationalist partisans, kulaks, and private traders, an agenda largely accomplished by 1950, thus removing the need for negative reporting?

A more reliable rendition of social heteroglossia is found in the list of ballot inscriptions during the parliamentary elections of December 1947. (Conveniently for the authorities, writing on the ballots rendered them invalid.) The reporting secretary of the Kiev party committee attempted to categorize all of the inscriptions as "anti-Soviet and counter-revolutionary," but the "unified language" of Stalinist ideology once again failed to describe a diverse catalogue of grievances. Most ballot spoilers were concerned with pressing matters of everyday survival: bribery, speculation, low living standards, and the alleged predomination of Jews. Save for a single nationalist leaflet that got included although it was actually posted on the wall rather than put in the ballot box, only one comment was political in nature. An anonymous voter in voting station 37 of Kiev's Stalin district wrote: "Elections without choice [of candidates]. You can deceive some of the people all the time

or all of the people some of the time, but you can't deceive all of the people all of the time. Yet you are attempting to do just that."[13]

This said, it would be problematic to oppose the society (speaking in a number of authentic voices—pro-Soviet, anti-Soviet, and neutral) to the state (producing a unified political discourse). If anything, the authorities were struggling to control the heteroglossia of their own multiple voices. Examples of this could range from suppressed high-profile public pronouncements to high bureaucrats' surprising private comments not matching any of the official policies. Thus, in March 1944, the Ukrainian premier and party leader, Nikita Khrushchev, announced in his report to the first postwar session of the republican parliament, "The Ukrainian people will seek to include in the Ukrainian Soviet state such primordial Ukrainian lands as the Kholm region, Hrubeshiv, Zamostia, Tomashiv, and Yaroslav. [Storm of applause.]" However, after prolonged negotiations with the Western allies and the Polish government in exile, Stalin settled for the so-called Curzon line as the border between Ukraine and Poland. The Kholm (Chełm) region to which Khrushchev had referred was to remain a part of Poland. Consequently, no future publication of Khrushchev's speech included the embarrassing paragraph, and the propaganda in the Ukrainian press of Kholm's impending "reunification" had to be halted.[14]

Nikolai Smolich, the artistic director of the Kiev opera company during the immediate postwar years, reveals in his unpublished memoirs another surprising side to Khrushchev. When he complained to the republic's party boss that he could not work among "people with nationalistic tendencies," Khrushchev "delicately interrupted [Smolich] and said in a confidential tone: 'Do you think I am in a different situation, surrounded by different people?'"[15] If Khrushchev actually said this, and regardless of whether he was speaking honestly, there was an enormous discrepancy between what he is recorded as having said in private and in public. Although the Ukrainian authorities indeed sponsored the intermittent critique of nationalism during the postwar decade, Khrushchev was not among the ideological hawks and no person he worked closely with was denounced after the war. If he, an ethnic Russian like Smolich, indeed felt uncomfortable working with Ukrainian bureaucrats and intellectuals, his personal voice (and the language he used while speaking to Smolich) was suppressed in his public pronouncements. Like other Stalinist functionaries, whether or not Khrushchev was speaking Bolshevik, he was being recorded in archivese.

Laughing Bolshevik

If politics was the sphere in which the party was the most concerned with suppressing heteroglossia, mass culture was the sphere in which it was the least successful. Controlling popular entertainment was difficult because, even under Stalin, the population could hold a daily referendum simply by buying tickets to the shows it liked. Moreover, the Soviet bureaucrats' notorious inertia prevented any meaningful cultural answers to successful Western works that were allowed inside the Soviet Union. As late as 1961, a memo of the party's Central Committee in Moscow decried the wide distribution in the Soviet Union of *Roman Holiday* as a bourgeois film "portraying the amorous adventures of a rich American woman in Rome"—a clear indication that no member of the Central Committee's Ideological Commission had seen the film![16]

Some failures in cultural policy would surprise even a historian of the "revisionist school" that problematizes Stalinism's success as a totalitarian dictatorship. For instance, during the immediate postwar years, Ukrainian ideologues were concerned with the spontaneous revival of the private book trade. As the war disrupted the state's centralized distribution system, bazaar traders stepped in, creating, in the words of a certain party functionary Shatov, "entire bookstores (albeit with the books displayed on the ground) with hundreds of a wide variety of books, often those that had been banned by our censors." At another ideological meeting, the writer Petro Panch testified that prerevolutionary books on Ukrainian history, especially works about the anti-Russian Cossack leaders Ivan Mazepa and Petro Doroshenko, were in great demand at the book bazaars: "People pay ten times more for these books than for our Soviet histories."[17]

Although statistical data on book sales through the state network of bookstores is rare for the postwar years, an occasional window into the buying preferences of the Ukrainian public is very illuminating. During 1949, bookstores in the Drohobych province in Western Ukraine sold only 175 or 17.68 percent of their allotment of 990 copies of Ukrainian classical writer Ivan Franko's one-volume works. Other Ukrainian classical writers had similarly poor sales: Ivan Kotliarevsky, 80 of 400 (20 percent); and Mykhailo Kotsiubynsky, 95 of 975 (9.74 percent), but these figures actually represented success compared to the sales of Soviet literary works: Alexandr Fadeev's *The Rout*, 35 of 930 (3.76 percent); and Dmitry Furmanov's *Chapaev*, 36 of 856 (4.21 percent). Amazingly, in the city of Drohobych, none of the

400 subscribers to Lenin's multivolume *Collected Works* in Ukrainian showed up to pick up volumes 1 and 2, and only 9 out of 350 cared to collect the seven available volumes of Stalin's *Works*. Aside from the fact that the state expected the public to buy more books than they could afford or cared to own, these statistics indicate that, at least in Drohobych province, Ukrainian literature was considerably more popular than its Soviet counterpart, and that the authorities could not force the public to buy the works of Lenin and Stalin. The last point cannot be explained by the specific situation in postwar Western Ukraine. A 1951 report from Kharkiv province in Eastern Ukraine shows a total of 40,533 volumes of Lenin's and Stalin's collected works that subscribers had not picked up.[18]

Prominent among the official culture's many failures was its inability to produce an acceptable way of "laughing Bolshevik." An official doctrine since 1934, "socialist realism" obliged the writers to connect "what is" to "what ought to be," leaving less and less turf for satire. The Zhdanovite ideological reaction of 1946–48, which derived its name from the Central Committee's secretary in charge of ideology, Andrei Zhdanov, victimized Mikhail Zoshchenko, one of the most popular satirists of the 1920s. The campaign signaled to writers that laughing at any aspect of Soviet life was becoming unacceptable. Many earlier signals, such as the closure of the Moscow and Leningrad music halls in 1936, had indicated the general incompatibility of humor and light-hearted fun with Soviet society's self-image of "solemn joy in the midst of heroic construction."[19] (Only in film did the genre of musical comedy survive.)

As Ukrainian ideologues faithfully emulated Moscow's ideological campaigns, they proceeded to criticize the republic's equivalent of Zoshchenko, Ostap Vyshnia. A veteran writer of humorous and satirical stories, Vyshnia enjoyed enormous popularity in Ukraine. Having spent the years 1934–43 in labor camps as an "enemy of the people," he was also extremely cautious in his writings and during public readings. In fact, bureaucrats and fellow writers were able to ferret out only two incriminating passages in his postwar stories. The first referred to veterans returning from the war against Japan fighting among themselves at the beach for their trophy Japanese umbrellas. Intended to poke fun of consumerism and foreign fashions, this paragraph could be read as the defamation of the Red Army. The second excerpt was much more interesting: "To some degree, it has long been clear who was fighting at the front and who was 'fighting' in Tashkent and Ferghana, who returned to rebuild and renovate and who came back to sell beer or soda and fight for apartments."

The writers immediately recognized here an allusion to a wartime anti-Semitic joke about Ivan fighting at the front and Abram being evacuated to Tashkent (in Soviet Asia) to sell soda and watermelons there. Also, Jews constituted a considerable share of those returning to Kiev who, following the city's liberation by the Red Army, found their apartments occupied by others. The poet Leonid Pervomaisky, who was Jewish, attacked Vyshnia during a writers' conference: "What exactly did Vyshnia mean? Did not he see that he had become a mouthpiece of Kievan speculators, who had been educated at 'free bazaars' under the Germans—those Ukrainian chauvinists who are hostile to the people saved from Babi Yar by the Red Army?"[20]

Like other successful satirists and comedians, Vyshnia reacted to the talk of people on the street and relied on irreverent street humor. Functioning within the official culture, he was a moderator between the didactic ideals of Soviet cultural policy and the unofficial culture of anecdotes and songs. As such, he both used the language of popular humor to discuss educational topics and borrowed wholesale from street folklore to create an ideologically acceptable version of stand-up comedy. Precisely the "multi-languagedness" or heteroglossia of his prose caused Vyshnia trouble with the authorities. More than the occasional borrowing from a well-known anti-Semitic joke, his very writing style was becoming problematic because of its polyphony. Yet for this very reason, he was notoriously popular with the public. As a journal editor noted of Vyshnia in 1948, "He is very popular. We saw this during his recent three public performances. People love his work—this is true of such [diverse] audiences as the Party Academy, the Kiev intelligentsia, and the factory workers."[21]

Significantly, among the first objects of the Zhdanovite campaign's critique was the Ukrainian satirical journal *Perets* [Pepper]. An article in the authoritative *Pravda* in August 1946 accused the journal of publishing apolitical humor and misguided satire of the Soviet bureaucracy, including "lampoons of the Soviet people."[22] After the editorial reorganization in 1946, *Perets* redirected its satire from the imperfections of the Soviet way of life toward the evil deeds of Western imperialists. During 1946–48, stories and cartoons about the capitalist West constituted approximately 60 percent of the materials published. In addition, *Perets* encouraged readers' letters and based many stories on them. During 1946, this small twelve-page biweekly journal received only

1,200 letters; in 1947, the number grew to 6,500, and in 1949 it ballooned to 17,350, of which 348 were published.[23] This was not a development that bureaucrats welcomed. In 1948, the supervisor of journals in the Ukrainian Central Committee complained that the censors had had to seize the printed issues of *Perets* four or five times during the year. In addition, a number of issues satirizing pilfering "and other negative sides of our Soviet life" were not sent to subscribers abroad.[24]

The critique of *Perets* was, thus, directed at the heteroglossia in literary satire and humor but brought to the journal's pages more of the population's diverse and fault-finding voices. Literary satire, meanwhile, became limited to the topics of Western imperialism and émigré nationalist activities. At the Second Congress of Ukrainian writers in late 1948, the republic's establishment welcomed the birth of new literary humor of a "warm and lyrical" variety. In particular, the head of the Writers' Union, Oleksandr Korniichuk, singled out the young writer Stepan Oliinyk for his "emotional tales about the great deeds of the present that possess a warm, humorous touch."[25]

During the last several years of Stalin's rule, the authorities almost succeeded in suppressing heteroglossia and instituting a unified language in Soviet Ukrainian literary humor. This, however, came at a price, as Oliinyk's "warm and lyrical" narratives were unpopular and, during de-Stalinization and the ensuing cultural thaw, the field would revert to topical satire and street language. *Perets,* in the meantime, discovered a safe haven in directly quoting and illustrating the "toilers' letters," although it, too, would be rejuvenated by the thaw. Stalinism's success at suppressing the polyphony of literary satire and humor proved delusional, as did the regime's achievements in paperwork dubbing of everyday voices.

No party resolution ever prescribed a unified language of bureaucratic reporting, just as no *Pravda* editorial condemned such a thing as "heteroglossia" in literature. Nevertheless, both bureaucratic and cultural homogenization drives were parts of a larger Stalinist ideological project, and both were ultimately frustrated by the diverse voices of social reality.

NOTES

1. M. M. Bakhtin, "Discourse in the Novel," in his *The Dialogic Imagination: Four Essays,* trans. Caryl Emerson and Michael Holquist, ed. Michael Holquist (Austin: University of Texas Press, 1981), 262–63, 270–71; Michael Holquist, *Dialogism: Bakhtin and His World* (New York: Routledge, 1990), 69–73; Sue Vice, *Introducing Bakhtin* (Manchester: Manchester University Press, 1997), 18–25, 70–73.

2. Sheila Fitzpatrick, "Supplicants and Citizens: Public Letter-Writing in Soviet Russia in the 1930s," *Slavic Review* 55, no. 1 (spring 1996): 78–105, and Fitzpatrick, "Signals from Below: Soviet Letters of Denunciation of the 1930s," *Journal of Modern History* 68, no. 4 (December 1996): 831–66. See also Sheila Fitzpatrick and Robert Gellately, "Introduction to the Practices of Denunciation in Modern European History," *Journal of Modern History* 68, no. 4 (December 1996): 747–67.

3. Stephen Kotkin, *Magnetic Mountain: Stalinism as a Civilization* (Berkeley: University of California Press, 1995).

4. See Igal Halfin and Jochen Hellbeck, "Rethinking the Stalinist Subject: Stephen Kotkin's *Magnetic Mountain* and the State of Soviet Historical Studies," *Jahrbücher für Geschichte Osteuropas* 44, no. 3 (1996): 456–63; Hellbeck, "Speaking Out: Languages of Affirmation and Dissent in Stalinist Russia," *Kritika* 1, no. 1 (winter 2000): 71–96; Anna Krylova, "The Tenacious Liberal Subject in Soviet Studies," *Kritika* 1, no. 1 (winter 2000): 119–46.

5. Halfin and Hellbeck, "Rethinking the Stalinist Subject," 458; Kotkin, *Magnetic Mountain,* 220.

6. Tsentralnyi derzhavnyi arkhiv hromadskykh orhanizatsii Ukrainy (TsDAHO), fond 1, opys 70, sprava 423, arkush 1.

7. Gosudarstvennyi arkhiv Rossiiskoi Federatsii (GARF), fond 9401, opis 2, delo 138, listy 256–58.

8. Sudoplatov's statements vary on the question of who exactly ordered the assassination. In his letter to the Twenty-third Party Congress (1966), he claimed that he had received this order from the minister of state security, V. Abakumov, who referred to instructions from Stalin and Lazar Kaganovich (*Moscow News,* no. 31 [August 9–16, 1992], 9; and Iurii Shapoval, "Oleksandr Shumsky: His Last Thirteen Years," *Journal of Ukrainian Studies* 18, nos. 1–3 [1993]: 83–84). In his later memoirs, Sudoplatov maintains that he had received the order from Khrushchev and A. Kuznetsov, although later in the same book he names Khrushchev and Kaganovich as masterminds (Pavel Sudoplatov and Anatoli Sudoplatov, with Jerrold L. and Leona P. Schecter, *Special Tasks: The Memoir of an Unwanted Witness—A Soviet Spymaster* [Boston: Little, Brown, 1994], 249 and 281).

9. See Serhy Yekelchyk, "The Archives of Stalin's Time: Political Use, Symbolic Value, and the Missing Resolutions," *Comma, Journal of the International Council on Archives* 3–4 (2002): 83–91.

10. TsDAHO, f. 1, op. 23, spr. 125, ark. 1–17.

11. Rossiiskii gosudarstvennyi arkhiv sotsialnoi i politicheskoi istorii (RGASPI), f. 81, op. 3, d. 128, ll. 126–32. I thank Jeffrey Burds for this reference. Another similar report on Krypiakevych is in TsDAHO, f. 1, op. 23, spr. 4559, ark. 1–3.

12. TsDAHO, f. 1, op. 24, spr. 786, ark. 1–14 (1951); op. 23, spr. 5379, ark. 1–70 (November 1948); spr. 5073, ark. 1–24 (April 1948).

13. TsDAHO, f. 1, op. 23, spr. 4956, ark. 1–7a; the quotation is on ark. 5.

14. The original text is in N. Khrushchev, "Osvobozhdenie ukrainskikh zemel ot nemetskikh zakhvatchikov i ocherednye zadachi vosstanovleniia narodnogo khoziaistva Sovetskoi Ukrainy," *Bolshevik,* no. 6 (1944): 9, and *Radianska Ukraina,* March 6, 1944, 2.

15. Tsentralnyi derzhavnyi arkhiv-muzei literatury i mystetstva Ukrainy (TsDAMLM), f. 71, op. 1, spr. 20, ark. 270 overleaf and 271.

16. The memo has been published in V. Iu. Afiani, ed., *Ideologicheskie komissii TsK KPSS 1958–1964: Dokumenty* (Moscow: ROSSPEN, 1998), 263.

17. TsDAHO, f. 1, op. 70, spr. 618, ark. 109 (Shatov); spr. 378, ark. 18 (Panch).

18. Ibid., spr. 1334, ark. 1–2a (Drohobych province); spr. 1768, ark. 15–16 (Drohobych); spr. 2106, ark. 139 (Kharkiv province).

19. See Richard Stites, *Russian Popular Culture: Entertainment and Society since 1900* (New York: Cambridge University Press, 1992), 80.

20. TsDAMLM, f. 590, op. 1, spr. 36, ark. 62–63; TsDAHO, f. 1, op. 70, spr. 515, ark. 8.

21. TsDAHO, f. 1, op. 70, spr. 1311, ark. 24.

22. *Pravda,* August 24, 1946, 3.

23. TsDAHO, f. 1, op. 70, spr. 1311, ark. 20 (foreign topics), 21 (letters received during 1946–48); TsDAMLM, f. 668, op. 1, spr. 232, ark. 1 (letters received during 1949).

24. TsDAHO, f. 1, op. 70, spr. 1311, ark. 94.

25. Ibid., spr. 1534, ark. 11.

Ethnicity, Memory, and Violence

Reflections on Special Problems in Soviet and East European Archives

Jeffrey Burds

> ". . . memory is the most imperfect and selective vector of evidence."
>
> —E. P. Thompson, *Beyond the Frontier*

Ethnicity and Memory

One of the greatest obstacles to understanding the history of Eastern Europe during and after the Second World War has been that the memories of the events themselves have been constructed ethnically—which is to say, each ethnic group has recorded its own version of the tragic devastation of that era. The postwar phenomena of diasporas and refugee cultures have further splintered memories and perspectives and subsequently channeled them through the prisms of the Cold War, East and West.

Polish historian Piotr Wróbel has used the phrase *double memory* to identify the phenomenon of distinct and often contradictory accounts of divergent ethnic groups who share the same history. How, for instance, is one to reconcile the memories of Poles and Jews when remembering wartime Poland? Wringing his hands at the seemingly irreconcilable divergencies between nationalistic accounts of shared events, Wróbel wrote with despair: "Are we destined to remain forever entombed within these two diametrically opposed visions of the Second World War? Each [ethnic memory] is so different from the other that at times it is difficult to believe that they portray the same events."[1]

The task of reconciliation of these disparate memories is not only daunting, but in fact guarantees that the historian's motives will be impugned no matter how diligent the research, or how conscientious his or her efforts to be fair.

Nowhere is the gulf that separates ethnic memories wider than in the study of interethnic violence. For violence does not befall someone, it involves maleficent agency: by definition violence implies both perpetrators and victims. While social history and historical demography offer us reliable tools to count the victims—and every ethnic group in wartime Europe has its own substantial victimologies—considerable obstacles stand in the way of identifying and comprehending the perpetrators on their own terms.

Omer Bartov, among others, has identified the close affinity in the twentieth century between national identity and "a glorification of victimhood." In his provocative social history of the origins of genocide in Germany, Bartov identified the complex dynamic that transformed German frustrations at the front into the search for ethnically defined "real" enemies who had "stabbed them in the back" at home: "An enemy, that is, whose very persecution would serve to manifest the power and legitimacy of the victimizer, while simultaneously allowing the persecutor to claim the status of the 'true' (past, present, and potentially future) victim."[2]

Dr. Paul Parin, a physician who worked alongside

Tito during the partisan war in Yugoslavia during World War II, coined the term *ethnopsychoanalysis* to identify a special relationship between ethnic nationalism, nationalist violence, and the complex sets of experiences that go into producing a nationalist perpetrator of atrocities against an ethnically defined enemy.[3] Parin's perceptive observations bridge the divide between perpetrators and victims by identifying a distinct process in the construction of the enemy other.

Working mainly on the basis of his observations in modern Yugoslavia, Parin has emphasized the fundamental importance of the "production of an unconsciousness" that helps to generate a "new reality": the nationalist reality where our side is the good, just one, and their side is unjust, bad, dangerous. This projection of a distinct "image of the enemy" provides the foundation for a propaganda campaign that heats the flames of ethnic passions. The same events and images provoke diametrically opposite responses in both camps: "The continual presentation of the massacre victims incited fear, hatred, hysteria, and blood lust on both sides of the ethnic border."[4]

The result is the social construction of fear,[5] or what Robert Kaplan has referred to as a "region of pure memory" where "each individual sensation and memory affects the grand movement of clashing peoples":[6] the generation of ethnically distinct, nonoverlapping accounts of shared events where "[b]oth sides have selective perceptions of the past and know almost nothing about each other. One man's history is another man's lie."[7]

The very lack of consanguinity that precedes empathy creates a special category for ethnically defined enemy others. A Croat fascist, Ljubo Miloš—a confessed murderer of Serbs in wartime Yugoslavia—put it best: "For my past, present, and future deeds I shall burn in hell; but at least I shall burn for Croatia."[8] Or, as a Jewish survivor of the Warsaw ghetto uprising recalled: "If you could lick my heart, it would poison you."[9] Such extremism is all too common: remarkably, ethnicity can stifle, shape, redefine, even suspend, all other categories of human behavior, and it fundamentally shapes the contents of historical archives. As Timothy Snyder wrote in his insightful study of the Polish anti-Ukrainian actions during 1947: "Ethnic cleansing always involves mutual claims, enabling each side to present itself as the innocent defender of legitimate interests and its opponents as savage nationalists."[10] Omer Bartov added: "The distorted features of the tortured and butchered served as evidence of their own, rather than of their murderers' inhumanity; the sense of moral outrage and physical disgust they aroused produced a powerful desire for revenge, which by a process of inversion was directed at the victims rather than the perpetrators, that is, the 'other' rather than oneself, for it was their presence which had made such atrocities necessary, their evident inhumanity which had revealed one's own barbarity. Hence, only by physically annihilating the victims and erasing their memory could one salvage one's own humanity."[11]

For scholars who do not specialize in the history of ethnic violence, it may be difficult to understand the degree to which genocide is a hate crime perpetrated not against random strangers, but more often than not targeting *personal* contacts. Jan Gross's poignant observations of multiethnic Galicia just prior to World War II are especially relevant here:

> In these easternmost hinterlands of interwar Europe each hamlet or village was to a large degree an isolated universe. As often happens in such an environment, intense personal hatreds were harbored, and an ethnic and religious component gave them the potential to engulf entire communities. Yet, much as the violence represented an explosion of combined ethnic, religious, and nationalist conflict, I am nevertheless struck by its intimacy. More often than not, victims and executioners knew each other personally. Even after several years, survivors could still name names. Definitely, people took this opportunity to get even for personal injuries in the past.[12]

In a rare and frank account of genocide by one of its perpetrators, Waldemar Lotnik—a young Pole in southeastern Poland—chronicled with amazing clarity and insight his flight from organized Ukrainian nationalist terror in 1943 and his return for vengeance as a soldier in a Polish nationalist partisan unit in 1944–45. Though he was a Polish partisan, Lotnik made it clear that atrocities could be attributed equally to both sides, Ukrainian and Polish: "The ethnic Ukrainians responded by wiping out an entire Polish colony, setting fire to the houses, killing those inhabitants unable to flee and raping the women who fell into their hands, no matter how old or young. This had been the pattern of their behaviour east of the Bug [River], where tens of thousands of Poles had been either expelled or murdered. We retaliated by attacking an even bigger Ukrainian village and . . . killed women and children. Some of [our men] were so filled with hatred after losing whole generations of their family in the Ukrainian attacks that they swore they would take an eye for an eye, a tooth for a tooth. . . . This was how the fighting escalated. Each time more people were killed, more houses burnt, more women raped."[13] The failure of archives as institutions of memory is perhaps best exemplified in the gaps between such a vivid eyewitness account of an ex-perpetrator haunted by guilt as contrasted against the processed, often homogenized memory of nationalistic institutions.

Unfortunately, while useful as an interpretive framework for understanding interethnic violence, the concept of double memory reduces ethnicity to homogeneous monoliths. The problem in Galicia and—I would guess—everywhere else, is the very fluidity of ethnic memories: especially, that rival factions *within* ethnic groups usually compete to define the memory/identity of the whole group. Often, the battle for hegemony between rivals within an ethnic group has superseded the struggles between distinct ethnic groups. So that when speaking of the interweaving phenomena of ethnic identity and historical experience, we should refer not to double memory, but to a multiplicity of memories. Inevitably, few archives preserve all competing voices within ethnic groups, let alone the accounts of multiple ethnic groups within a given society. A former political prisoner and ex-member of the Ukrainian Waffen-SS Fourteenth Grenadier Division, K. Hromyk (from Khartsyzsk, Ukraine), put it this way in a venomous open letter to then Ukrainian president Leonid Kuchma in March 2001:

> We are now all over seventy. Thank God, we have lived to see our independent Ukraine, the coveted goal for which we fought and suffered. Many of us have not yet been rehabilitated, for our butchers, security force investigators and military tribunals, did their best to denigrate us forever. You can find everything in our archival files: we are public enemies, Nazi henchmen . . . , and God knows what else. When our SBU [Ukrainian secret police] officers dig up such a file they put it in the bottom drawer, believing these brazen lies without listening to the victim himself or [to] the eyewitnesses of those events.[14]

Hromyk's struggle is a microcosm of a broader debate raging within post-Soviet Ukraine to reconcile nationalist history with the Soviet past. Such moments of profound political upheaval are often accompanied not only by distinct cultural artifacts, but the search for a national identity itself becomes the filter for reprocessing national memory preserved in national archives.

Intervening Contexts: Refashioning Ethnic Identities and Collective Memories

Another complicating factor is that ethnicity and ethnic identity are not static, but rather themselves adapt to changing circumstances. The filtering of collective and institutional memory is not a one-time event, but a continual process of homogenization, accommodation, assimilation, and change. In twentieth-century Galicia, for instance, locals have undergone no less than five major processes of ethnic cleansing—starting the century under Austria-Hungary, then subordinated to Polish control during the interwar period, a target of Soviet-instigated "class war" from 1939 to 1941, divided and ostensibly subordinated to Warsaw by the Germans during World War II, again reconquered by the Soviets in 1944, and "liberated" with independent Ukraine since 1991. Each successive era promoted the interests of one ethnic group at the expense of others, so that census studies reflected dramatic (and contradictory) shifts in ethnic distribution among the Galician population.[15] Social scientists working in multiethnic zones where the dominant group frequently changes face the extraordinary obstacle of mass refashioning of identities as locals strive to adapt to the new dominant regime. For instance, during World War II, Jews throughout Central and Eastern Europe resisted Nazi arrest by masking themselves as Latvians, Lithuanians, Poles, Ukrainians, Russians, and others. The phenomenon became so widespread that German authorities were absolutely dependent upon wily locals to ferret out individual members of groups targeted for genocide. But more importantly, East European Jews culturally self-liquidated and melted into dominant ethnic groups as a spontaneous defense strategy against the threat of genocide.[16] The whole matter was further confused by the German occupation, which (from spring 1943) systematically destroyed prewar Jewish censuses and even unearthed mass graves of victims and transported and burned their corpses in order to stymie effective investigations into the scale of the Holocaust.[17]

If we reflect on memory filters over the course of the twentieth century, the most obvious is the role of the Cold War as a factor distinguishing East from West, native Ukrainian or Pole or Lithuanian or Latvian from their American, British, Australian, or Canadian diasporas.[18] There is no better account of the shifting sands of memory during fifty years of Cold War than E. P. Thompson's own study of the tragic fate of his brother Frank, a procommunist British Special Operations Executive (SOE) officer killed in Bulgaria in 1944: "A good deal of contemporary history rests upon the information of 'people who know.' The problem is, not that they know nothing, but that they do, in fact, know a great deal. But what they know can pass, over the years, by a process of selection, into an ideological code which presents, in the form of anecdote or fact, what they wish to be believed. If, at the same time, harder evidential material is suppressed or destroyed, the truth of a past event may become irrecoverable."[19] In Thompson's view, "anti-historians" actively involved in the destruction of evidence include not only governmental "weeders"—bureaucrats who cleanse the archives of potentially harmful material before releasing them to readers—but also officers in charge: for instance, the first chief of the Central Intelligence Agency, Walter Bedell Smith, is known to have concealed agent files of East European nationals recruited to run anti-Soviet operations behind the iron curtain by burying them under a veritable mountain of governmental paperwork with deliberately misassigned labels.[20] That one act delayed the discovery of U.S. support for anti-Soviet paramilitary groups throughout Soviet Eastern Europe—Operation ROLLBACK—for nearly forty years: under the rubric of national security, U.S. archivists imposed a very heavy-handed policy of government censorship of materials relating to U.S. covert support of East European anti-Soviet guerillas after the war.[21] (See illustration in appendix 1.) Similarly, the problem of vigilante censorship, whereby nationalist or ideological warriors "correct" the "misinformation" of archival files by stealing and/or destroying them, is fairly common as an obstacle to research in contemporary Eastern Europe.

Inevitably, not just the writing of history, but even asking the questions, becomes tantamount to an act of provocation. Again, E. P. Thompson's experience as evocative questioner is relevant: "[T]hese questions . . . remained and remain sensitive. Certain questions clearly provoked discomfort many years after the events, and these sensitivities increased rather than diminished over the years. As the Cold War developed it required on both sides a continual reprocessing of approved views of the past (or amnesia about the past) and the accretion of new dimensions of myth."[22]

Soviet Police Archives

Just as memories are reshaped by ethnicity, and by intervening contexts, their correction or reinterpretation is profoundly inhibited and controlled by the selective construction, destruction, and reconstruction of archives. Heavily influenced by postmodernist critique, French archivist Paule René-Bazin recently noted: "The archivist is more and more 'the person who knows how to destroy.' He has learnt that representation of the past, individual and collective, is inseparable from its material traces and knows better than anybody that they are threatened with disappearance." Archives are constructed by human beings, and are therefore subject to the same all-too-human limitations. The archivist "sometimes forgets that he is also an active part of a society in which certain traces are removed and destroyed; others are provisionally suppressed or definitely forgotten."[23] With few exceptions, perpetrators of violence—both individuals and institutions—generally conspire to conceal their crimes from investigators. Likewise, victims of ethnic or gender violence—whose identities are often disorganized by torture and brutality—unwittingly conspire through their silence. The Latvian émigré writer Agate Nesaule put it best: "No one ever wants to hear about the painful parts of my past. People have hundreds of ways, both subtle and harsh, to reinforce my own reluctance to tell."[24]

Any nation's "correction" of history takes various forms, not least of all restriction of archival access and actual destruction of collections. But it is important to emphasize that filtering occurs long before the documents themselves are collected in archives. Working in Soviet secret police archives over the past decade, I have regularly discovered the coattails—so to speak—of systematic secret police efforts to conceal compromising evidence. With remarkable consistency, for instance, field officers in the Soviet secret police at war against Ukrainian nationalist partisans regularly reported that partisans, before they were killed, had managed to douse their archives with acid, or that the partisan archives had been burned during a firebombing attack to subdue the rebel hideout. Why? Because among their principal tasks rebels regularly maintained documented records of Soviet police abuse in their region. When captured intact, these archives were often transferred to Moscow, where central police administrators vetted the contents of files and regularly charged abusive police officers for excessive use of force.[25] For just one of myriad examples, I cite the file of the Ukrainian Communist Party's rare indictment of a provincial police chief for rape: "Chief of the Gliniavskii *raion* MVD in L'viv *oblast* Matiukhin P. E. in February [1946], while interrogating [ethnic Ukrainian woman] Mikhal'skaia E. G., raped and brutally beat her. Kept under arrest from 27 January to 18 February of this year, Mikhal'skaia has been released from prison [following a determination that she had been arrested on the basis] of unsubstantiated charges. Matiukhin likewise raped at least four other illegally arrested girls: Paternak, Kostyv, Pokyra and Stepanova. [In each case], they were released after having been subjected to violence and insults."[26]

The initial compromising material against Matiukhin had been gleaned from a captured rebel archive. The result? The emergence of a sort of "blue code" among Soviet policemen that decreed the systematic destruction of possibly compromising rebel archives: through time, operational objectives were subordinated to schemes of self-protection among local police.[27]

Caught between Moscow's insistence on speedy results side-by-side with Moscow's regular failure to allocate sufficient resources or cadres, provincial police organs tried to manipulate the information trails as documents and reports flowed through *raion, oblast* (L'viv), republic (Kiev/Ukraine), and federal (Moscow) offices. Murders were covered up with euphemistic deceptions like "prisoner was shot trying to escape"; compromising labels of "Ukrainian nationalist bandit" were applied to ordinary citizens to cover up cases of arbitrary police brutality.[28] Even worse, it was standard Soviet police practice in special "struggle against banditry" deception (*maskirovka*) units to dress up as rebel bandits and to perpetrate atrocities against local citizens (following the modus operandi of partisan rebels) so as to drive a wedge between rebels and the local population. As the procurator of the West Ukrainian Military Tribunal reported to Nikita Khrushchev in February 1949: "On the night of 23 June 1948 the same [Soviet special forces] unit from Podvysots'ke village abducted in the forest a young woman REPNYTSKA Nina Iakovlevna, born in 1931. In the forest REPNYTSKA was subjected to tortures. While interrogating REPNYTSKA, members of the unit beat her severely, hung her upside down by her legs, forced a stick into her genitalia, and then one-by-one raped her. In a helpless condition, REPNYTSKA was abandoned in the forest, where her husband found her and took her to the hospital, where REPNYTSKA spent an extended period recovering."[29] Though these were police actions, such flagrant cases of police abuse were nonetheless regularly included in official Soviet reports of rebel terror: evidently, the Soviet bureaucracy had developed a filter to transform individual acts of police abuse into institutional memories of alleged documented evidence of rebel terror.

Pressed by Moscow to get results, provincial police came up with innovative solutions to meet Moscow's demands without risking their careers, or lives. In an especially enlightening insider's account, Petr Dmitriev, a guard from the Soviet state prison labor camp system during the late Stalin era, recalled in his hair-raising memoirs published in 1991 a presentation about "the cruel tortures inflicted on prisoners" that his command-ing officer "recounted with a great feeling of pride" in 1951.

> They made us *chekisty* stop using the sorts of coarse, medieval tortures to which we were accustomed. Left in the past as mere anachronisms were the tortures of the Inquisition—roasting limbs, needles under the [finger- and toe-]nails, sleep deprivation, starving [prisoners] to death, quartering.

"[Our sergeant Iurii] Pospelov stuck out his chest and hit it with his fist,"

> We *chekisty* have developed an alternative method for [inducing] confessions, one which does not leave behind traces of torture and which gives us the chance to extract any evidence we want from the *zek* [Soviet political prisoner], maintaining complete propriety on the surface. [This method leaves] neither bruises nor trauma. We call this method "*koromyslo*"—"the yoke."
> Using a leather strap we would fasten the [prisoner's] heels to the back of his head, doing so gradually—sometimes pressing in on the [prisoner's] spinal column, other times stretching it, tearing it. This generated unendurable pain. In front of his own comrades, even the most obstinate *zek* soon began to ask for mercy, then to beg for it, then to cry and moan, and eventually to howl and lose consciousness. We would pour water on him, bring him back to consciousness, and then begin the torture anew. The prisoner would beg us [to stop], promising his tormenters that he would do everything we wanted. Then we would untie him and force him to lap up his own urine from the floor like a cat.

The problem with such torture was that it strained personnel—limiting a night's work to just one or two prisoners. Pospelov's innovative solution was to establish special "guard rooms" where up to twenty-five prisoners could be interrogated at a time.

> They hung [prisoners] there by their hands, tied their legs so they could not kick, and then beat them in the kidneys. Using the palms of their hands, [guards] would repeatedly beat [prisoners] about their sides and back with sharp, stinging blows. In that position, the kidneys would tear away from the body and be displaced lower. The person doomed to such intense torture could be left hanging there for days.

The shocked Dmitriev recalled that "[t]he sadist Pospelov recounted all this without remorse. . . . 'The worst thing,' Pospelov summed up, 'is when you torture [your prisoner] to death, since then you have to fill out a lot of paperwork for the deceased.'"³⁰

Even regimes that sponsor widespread institutional violence to maintain state control tend to discourage open discussion of the violence. Like individual perpetrators, institutions of violence commonly adopt self-filtering procedures that euphemize the atrocities and serve to conceal the perpetrator's responsibility.

The most flagrant cases of police filtering appear in the construction of criminal files of accused "enemies of the people." Post-Soviet revelations about Stalinist police interrogation methods have been staggering in their excruciating and gruesome detail. In a handwritten petition for release from political confinement written in 1940, Italian Communist Edmundo Peluzo left a vivid account of the fate of political prisoners. Peluzo had been arrested on the night of 13–14 May 1938. He was immediately thrown into solitary confinement at KGB headquarters on Kuznestkii most in Moscow—an underground "special cell" in old Lefortovo prison:

> The first torture began, if my memory does not betray me, on the fourteenth of May, the last [was] in August 1938.
>
> Two, then four men took part in this torture. On the fourth of June at 4 o'clock in the morning four men armed with different instruments savagely beat me for almost forty minutes. So that I would not lose consciousness, they hung me upside down with my legs in the air and dragged me through a large room. Then they furrowed my back [with a belt buckle] to the point that I almost lost consciousness. The result of this was, as the doctor at Lefortovo determined, a blood clot in the veins [of my back] and a serious contusion of my spinal column. . . . I still feel [the pain] today. Then, the torture was continued under the direction of investigators Arsenovich and Krepkin, as a result of which my side was broken, I was spitting up blood. . . .
>
> Only after this savage method in order to force me to recognize my guilt did the interrogator Arsenovich say to me: "We don't want to kill you, but [merely] compel you to sign the confession which we want." I was supposed to resign myself [to this].
>
> In order to be saved from my inquisitors as soon as possible, I—inasmuch as Krepkin added that the Party required this [of me]—signed the affidavit in which I admitted guilt to all sorts of crimes.³¹

If police investigations and the files they created were often nothing more than tautological exercises that sustained official ideologies of ubiquitous enemies even as they protected the careers of individual policemen, provin-

cial Communist Party personnel were likewise forced to operate within the constraints of Stalinist terror. Police and Party cadres alike were blinded by the myopia of "omnipresent conspiracy," a pathological search for enemies that ultimately undermined Soviet internal and external security.³²

There is no better illustration of the damage suffered than the fiasco of the Soviet failure to prepare for German attack in World War II. In the months leading up to the launch of Operation Barbarossa in June 1941, Hitler's plans to invade the Soviet Union were reported by no less (and probably far more) than eighty-four confirmed intelligence sources. But Stalin and his close cohort were so driven by the imperative of avoiding what Stalin called "Churchill's dirty provocations" to bring the Soviets into the war against Hitler that any report on Germany's aggressive intentions was interpreted as an act of treason.³³ As historians L. Dvoinykh and N. Tarkhova discovered, "just six days before the German invasion—Soviet secret agents in Berlin sent a report to Moscow stating that Germany's armed forces were completely prepared for an armed offensive against the USSR, and that an attack could be expected at any moment. On the report, Stalin wrote in his own hand: 'You can tell your "source" in the headquarters of the German air force to go f—k his mother. He's not a source, he's a disinformation agent.'" Stalin's deputy Lavrentii Beria "wrote the following order on a dispatch, warning that Germany was going to attack: 'In the recent past, many personnel have succumbed to blatant provocations and are sowing panic. For passing on systematic disinformation, these secret personnel . . . need to be pulverized into prison-camp dust as abettors of international provocateurs who hope to lure us into a quarrel with Germany.'"³⁴

The lesson here is that the conditions of Stalinist leadership imposed distinct patterns of deception in Soviet archives, patterns that must be taken into account as historians take on the monumental task of uncovering the past.

Post-Soviet Obstacles

While we can assume that post-Soviet archives often contain deliberately deceptive accounts, the challenges of ferreting out the fuller story of past events and policies are even greater because of conditions specific to post-Soviet and East European archives. Typical of nationalist manipulation of archival holdings is concealment of documents. Postcommunist regimes regularly and inexplicably restrict access to collections. Moreover, there are many recent instances of theft and destruction of archival files by nationalist groups. A typical instance, in 1995, involved files of the Ukrainian Catholic church that were deemed inconsistent with the nationalist interpretation of history. What sort of materials were nationalist groups "weeding out" of archives? Here is just one of several documents that I read one year, but which were inexplicably missing in subsequent years. In the final days of July 1944, Colonel S. T. Danilenko of the People's Commissariat of Internal Affairs (NKVD), posing as the Soviet religious representative in L'viv, met with Metropolitan Andrij Sheptitskij to determine his reaction to the return of the Soviets. Danilenko reported that the metropolitan was "obviously disoriented" by the whirlwind events of the past few days, but that he seemed anxious to dissociate himself and his church from both the Nazis and the organized Ukrainian nationalist movement. Sheptitskij was, according to Danilenko, eager to cooperate with the new regime.

> Now I am certain that the fate of all Slavic peoples is being decided [said Sheptitskij], therefore they must rise up to do battle with racial Germanism. *I condemn the activities of the UPA [Ukrainian Insurrection Army] and the [OUN-] Banderists,* but I absolve the Melnikovtsy [the more moderate wing of the Organization of Ukrainian Nationalists] and those who served in the SS-Galicia. Their intentions were good but the Germans let them down, so now it is time to move away from a pro-German orientation. . . . *Now, given the circumstances of the international situation, there is but once choice—to [reconcile] with Soviet power. I want to give instructions to all priests in the western oblasts of Ukraine to remain at their posts and to expound on this in their church sermons.*

Information recorded by Colonel Danilenko and his agents reveals that the Ukrainian Catholic hierarchy truly believed that Moscow had adopted a new religious policy. Soviet secret informant "Vishnekov" spoke with the metropolitan at a reception for his seventy-ninth birthday on 29 July 1944, two days after the Soviet entry into L'viv.

> The Metropolitan is firmly convinced that Soviet power has changed its previously hostile attitude . . . toward religion, the clergy, and the faith. They are reopening the seminaries and theological academies in L'viv. The soldiers hail the priests in the streets. This is additional proof of the respect that Soviet power has for religion.

He reported that Sheptitskij displayed "extreme optimism" for West Ukraine's future under Soviet rule: "Everything is in God's hands, now," remarked the metropolitan, "and surely all will end well."[35]

According to the Soviet account, Sheptitskij—a Ukrainian Catholic candidate for probable sainthood in the next decades and a symbol of the Ukrainian nationalist resistance against Hitler and Stalin—had broken with the dominant Ukrainian nationalist military and political forces aligned with rebel leaders Yaroslav Stets'ko and Stepan Bandera. This evidently proved too potent for modern-day right-wing Ukrainian nationalists, who identify closely with Bandera. As a result of weeding efforts by Ukrainian nationalists, the photocopy I made in 1993 may well be the sole remaining copy of the documents.[36]

No less serious are threats against researchers who engage in the study of taboo topics, for example, on the scale of wartime collaboration with the Germans. There have been numerous reports from the 1990s regarding archivists' efforts to stymie controversial research agendas.

Yet another problem is the selective release of documents for incitement against a particular political or ethnic group. In April 1990, the pro-Miloševi Communist leadership of Montenegro released the documents on the Tito-era persecution of pro-Soviet communists, thereby distancing itself from the Titoist legacy, which was increasingly ethnically defined ("Croat-Slovene domination"). Most recently, in October 2000, in advance of key Bosnian political elections, the Bosnian Muslim secret service (Agency for Investigation and Documentation [AID]) released documents on the communist terror in the Cazin area in 1950, attempting thereby to associate communist anti-Bosniak misdeeds with the Social Democrats, the communist successor party.[37]

Meanwhile, nationalist groups within the former Soviet Union have long opposed full archival access, with greater and greater success. In April 1993, the Moscow-based Russian right-wing newspaper *Den'* [Day] carried an article with an attack on the Hoover Project, a project to microfilm significant sections of Russian archives, sponsored by the Hoover Institution on War, Revolution, and Peace at Stanford University. The *Den'* author charged that, in the aftermath of the Cold War, America, "as a victor country, is taking materials and spiritual values out of the vanquished country in amounts and of a quality sufficient to deprive the vanquished state of any possibility to resist, and to preclude any possibility of national resurgence. In the twentieth century information is the highest value and those who have information gain the upper hand over those who do not. Russia has been deprived of its seaports, geostrategic defense frontiers, the military-industrial complex and military potential. It has been deprived of its material products and resources and independent domestic and foreign policy. National ideology and culture have been strangled. Now Russia is being deprived of its information 'gene,' its organizational secrets that contain the substance of the structure, the engineering blueprint that helped to bring up a power that won the biggest war in human history and developed unique forms of civilization that have withstood the test of postwar history."[38] (See appendix 2.) Similarly, the Russian Orthodox church has effectively blocked research into its record of covert cooperation with the Soviet secret police, targeting not just individuals (defrocking outspoken Duma member and former Orthodox priest Gleb Yakunin), but also collections (like the Politburo's committees on Religious Affairs and Religious Cults).[39]

Pressures of this sort have inevitably led to the reclassification of Russian archives. After a relatively open period of archival access (1991–93), the State Secrets Act of August 1993 (but not imposed until after the October 1993 coup attempt) reversed the period of openness and ushered in the familiar regime of restriction. In essence, this law deprived archival administrations of the independent right to declassify documents, a process that henceforth was transferred back to successor institutions (under the rubric of *vedomstvo*) of the relevant Soviet agencies. The consequences were immediate. Whereas in 1992 the Central Party archives in Moscow declassified 2,867 documents, in 1995 the number dropped to 663.[40] Archivists at the State Archive of the Russian Federation in Moscow have confirmed that the rate of declassification slowed considerably after 1993, and still more from 1996.

Most ominously, there is the pattern practiced in various countries of considering personal archives from the crisis periods of twentieth-century history as too sensitive for research access. The "personal files" (those under the rubric of *prava lichnosti*) in Russian archives were effectively closed by imposition of a new seventy-five-year limit: declassified under the rubric of state secrets procedures after thirty years, sensitive materials were reclassified under the new rubric of "rights of privacy" for seventy-five years.[41] As a Russian archivist told me a few years ago when refusing me access to Soviet crime files from the State Procurator's Office: "A person living today has a right *not* to know that his grandfather was a rapist." Similar impediments were introduced in Ukraine in 1995, and in several other ex-Soviet states, significantly restricting the archival access of foreign scholars.

Meanwhile, various discriminatory rules and procedures targeting foreigners are common. Copying fees for foreigners in Russian archives are often more than five to ten times higher than those for domestic users. Some de-

positories started requiring fee payments, and several St. Petersburg archives introduced daily admission and research fees. In the Central Party archives in 1998, I was charged a $100 fee to process and copy restricted files from the newly declassified Kaganovich collection, then given only six hours to read the materials. At the Russian Military Historical archive, numerous researchers have reported being charged up to $5 per page for photocopies. In dozens of reported cases, archivists who were particularly cooperative with foreigners have been subjected to harassment, ostracism, or worse. One key figure in our Russian archive project, which published in the 1990s twelve large volumes of inventories to several Moscow archives, was investigated for illegal release of classified materials; three of four American members of the editorial board were slurred with attacks as spies in 1993; and the key Russian expediter/manager of the project was fired from his university post.

Discriminatory measures have been imposed not just for ideological reasons but also for financial ones. In many of the former communist countries, particularly in the former Soviet Union, state support of archives has dramatically declined since 1991. For example, the 1992 budget of the Russian state archive of social and political history (RGASPI) declined by 25 percent from the previous year. In addition to the reduction of budgetary support, the budget appropriations frequently were not made at all. By 1993 the state debt to the Russian archives in Moscow alone exceeded 50 million rubles ($25,000). In L'viv, the State Archive of L'viv Oblast (DALO) in 1993 had a state operating budget of less than $1,500 annually! Due to the decline in state support and low staff salaries, Russian and Ukrainian archives slashed preservation activities and radically reduced the purchase of basic office supplies. The archives started saving on such necessities as light bulbs and heating, or—in the case of RGASPI—drastically reduced staff and reading room hours (from 32 hours a week in 1995, to 12 hours in 2000, and 21.5 hours in 2002); strict limits were imposed on the number of files that could be ordered each day. Inevitably, much of the well-trained veteran staff started leaving in search of better opportunities, to be replaced by uninformed, unmotivated, and poorly paid substitutes. Hence, the need for the archives to generate income outside the limited state budgets.

This desperate search for income led to various corrupt practices, which themselves provoked a backlash in Russia and elsewhere following the election of President Vladimir Putin in 2000. As an American scholar reported from Moscow in 2000:

The long-expected restrictions in Russian archival policy have arrived. The Putin regime has had a powerful chilling effect on research access (especially among foreigners) to previously classified materials in Russian archives. Even documents that have been cited in publications, or read by researchers in earlier years, have over the past year been reclassified. According to archivists in Moscow, the MVD [Ministry of Internal Affairs] and FSB [Federal Security Service, the post-Soviet KGB] have sent agents to each archive and communicated the clear message that patterns of special access observed throughout the 1990s are now over. For the first time, researchers have found sealed (stapled, with glued seals attached) documents inside of previously opened files. Xerox facilities are far more stringent about what they will copy. It is far more difficult to get official permission for taking previously classified documents abroad. As one archivist imparted: "People outside the archives have no idea what's happening. Big changes are occurring behind the scenes."

These changes all fall under the rubric of Putin's reforms of the mass media in Russia, reforms based upon a new concept of *informatsionnye oruzhiia* (informational weapons) and how best to combat the threats posed by the information revolution to Russian national security interests.[42]

The threats to the integrity of archival collections are political, in the form of abruptly shifting prevailing political winds, where a succession of archivists threaten to weed out and reshape history to fit their own perspectives and agendas. The threats to archival integrity are also religious and ideological. Working without restriction in the consistory and personal files of Metropolitan Andrij Sheptitskij in L'viv, Ukraine, in 1992, I found that many of the documents had disappeared from archival shelves when I returned just a year later. Soon after, all foreign researchers were banned from doing research in the Ukrainian Catholic consistory or Metropolitan Sheptitskij's personal files altogether. Similarly, during the Tudjman era in Croatia, portions of the communist-era collections that referred to the regime's pet projects (e.g., the glorification of Croat communists who were repressed by Tito) were removed from the state archives and incorporated within closed presidential collections.[43]

The threats to archival integrity are also economic—as reflected in the brain drain of experienced yet horribly underpaid archivists and scholars into the more lucrative private sector; the collapse of archival buildings and infrastructure; the decay of collections, or failure to develop or preserve new collections; and in the commodification and sale on the black market of especially valuable archival materials. Well-substantiated reports of the sale of documents (originals, or access to copies) in archives throughout the East have been common during the last decade, with three documented cases leading to the arrest and imprisonment of archival staff: the illegal sale of antiquities out of the Russian State Archive of Ancient Acts in Moscow in 1992–1993, the sale on the black market of rare Polish heraldry books out of the State Historical Archive in L'viv in 1993–94; and the sale of Khrushchev autograph documents in Ivan-Frankiivsk to an American dealer in 2002. Valuable documents from formerly classified archives are now a regular feature of markets in Kiev and Moscow, and many are eventually sold and resold at premium prices on Internet auction sites.

It should be clear that special problems of archival collection, preservation, organization, and access apply in the former Soviet Union. These factors—above all, the Soviet Union as a multiethnic empire, the ideologically charged character of Soviet rule in the twentieth century, as well as the dissolution of the Soviet Union and the nationalist backlashes that ensued—profoundly affect the writing of East European and Eurasian history.

Appendix 1: Archivists as "Persons Who Know How to Destroy"

Reproduced here are three pages of the document ("[American Military Intelligence] CIC Offered Use of [Ukrainian Nationalist] SB [Counter-]Intelligence Network") summarizing chief of Ukrainian nationalist agent Mykola Lebed's contact with American intelligence in 1947, as released to the author in November 1996. The materials were blacked out on the basis of Section 1.5(c) of Executive Order 12958, which stipulates that "information pertaining to intelligence activities, intelligence sources or methods, and cryptologic information shall be considered for classification protection." Fortunately, three indications provided the thread for deciphering the document: (1) the fact that the contact involved a meeting between an agent of the U.S. Counter-Intelligence Corps (CIC) and the Banderist Sluzhba Bezpeki, the Ukrainian nationalist underground intelligence service; (2) that this contact had been made by a young, ethnic Ukrainian man with a "Round face" and "Full, sensuous lips"—features which were repeated in other declassified documents relating to Lebed; and (3) the CIC Special Agent Andrew Diakun's response that "such a proposition was highly unorthodox and in some measure far-

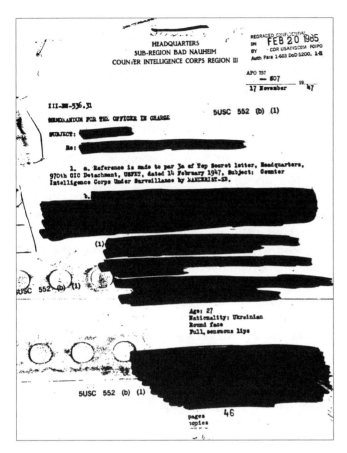

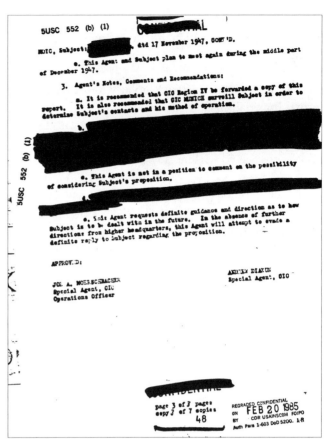

fetched." Following a formal appeal, these and several thousand pages of other materials relating to Lebed's recruitment and service were fully declassified and released in 1997 under the provisions of the Freedom of Information and Privacy Act. The released information proves beyond any doubt that U.S. intelligence had recruited agents from within the Ukrainian nationalist community for paramilitary and espionage operations on Soviet territory.[44] In contrast to the common U.S. policy to black out compromising materials for review and release in future years, the standing policy in many parts of the Soviet satellite countries is simply to destroy compromising material in the archives, or—where there are strong central states (as in Russia)—not to release classified materials at all, and to deny researchers any mechanism by which to expedite release.

Appendix 2: The Nationalist Right and Archival Memory in Post-Soviet Russia

Den' [Day] was a right-wing newspaper published in Moscow until October 1993. Since then, the newspaper has borne the name *Zavtra* [Tomorrow]. Here in full is its attack on the Hoover Project (11–17 April 1993), in an unattributed translation distributed on the Internet in spring 1993.

Russia Under Siege: Western Scholarly Research as Intellectual Imperialism

"WHEN A COUNTRY IS OCCUPIED ITS ARCHIVES ARE TAKEN OUT"

(Yeltsinites Secretly Selling Soviet Archives)

This paper has got hold of some curious documents connected with the "Hoover Project" whereby key Soviet archives will be put on microfilm and handed over to Americans. The topics that interest the Americans involve vital secret activities of the state. The agreement, signed by R. Pikhoia, D. Volkogonov, and N. Pokrovsky on the Russian side and by J. Dunlop, R. Conquest, T. Emmons, and J. Howlett on the American side, includes the following items.

> "In the selection of documents the emphasis shall be put on documenting the following themes:
>
> 1. Mechanisms of power in the USSR.
> 2. The end of NEP and the emergence of the system of Stalinism.
> 3. Russia's population trends in the 20th century.
> 4. Religion in the USSR.
> 5. The Soviet administrative system in regard to industry, agriculture and the trade unions.
> 6. Popular aspirations and government response.
> 7. International activities of the USSR.
> 8. Any other themes as jointly determined."

Among the jointly determined themes are inventories of Fund R-393 (NKVD of the RSFSR), and other funds of supervisory bodies contained in the Main Archives (Supreme Court, etc.) as well as the archives of Military Prosecution and documents of the Beriia case.

The Hoover Project is being carefully concealed from the public, the Supreme Soviet and from historians. It includes a confidentiality clause.

All this suggests some obvious conclusions.

We witness the consequences of full and unconditional capitulation of this regime in the face of victorious America which, as a victor country, is taking materials and spiritual values out of the vanquished country in amounts and of a quality sufficient to deprive the vanquished state of any possibility to resist and to preclude any possibility of national resurgence. In the 20th century information is the highest value and he who has information gains the upper hand over him who hasn't. Russia has been deprived of its sea ports, geo-strategic defense frontiers, the military-industrial complex and military groups. It has been deprived of its material products and resources and independent domestic and foreign policies. National ideology and culture have been strangled. Now Russia is being deprived of its information "gene", its organizational secrets which contain the substance of the structure, the engineering blueprint that helped to build up a power which won the biggest war in human history, and developed unique forms of civilization which have withstood the test of post-war history.

As soon as these archives arrive in America hordes of historians, military, intelligence agents, and social engineering specialists will converge on them to extract the precious ferments and to use them for the good of America and as poisons against Russia.

"The organizational weapon" has been used by America to destroy the USSR and it included a powerful information element. The information obtained under the Hoover Project will increase the potency of America's "organizational weapon" a hundred times. All this gives rise to several questions.

Why was such an important state act involving national security carried out secretly without the sanction of the Supreme Soviet and the government by a group of Democratic Russia members in which the notorious General Volkogonov continues to act as a renegade?

Why does the Hoover Project flout the interests of the republics of the Soviet Union since the "archive secrets" involve not only the present Russia but all the other components of the USSR?

Why are the terms of the "projects" so unequal for Russia and the USA, with the latter offering a banal and universally known part of the Library of Congress in exchange for precious information containing state secrets?

We want to draw the attention of the patriotic public, the people's deputies and the members of Parliament to this fact hoping that it will lead to a query in the Supreme Soviet over this outrageous fact. Occupation is a fact of current Russian history and those Yeltsinites who have opened the gates to the enemy and secretly and treacherously let the enemy into our home are now helping the marauders who are stripping their dead and wounded hosts of their clothes and jewelry.

The Hoover Project secretly signed by Volkogonov is an act of betrayal of Russia's fundamental national interests by the Yeltsinites.

(Den' security service)

NOTES

The epigraph is from E. P. Thompson, *Beyond the Frontier—The Politics of a Failed Mission: Bulgaria 1944* (Stanford: Stanford University Press, 1997), 42.

1. Piotr Wróbel, "Double Memory: Poles and Jews after the Holocaust," *East European Politics and Societies* 11, no. 3 (fall 1997): 567. See also Timothy Snyder, "'To Resolve the Ukrainian Question Once and for All': The Ethnic Cleansing of Ukrainians in Poland, 1943–1947," *Journal of Cold War Studies* 1, no. 2 (June 1999).

2. Omer Bartov, "Defining Enemies, Making Victims: Germans, Jews, and the Holocaust," *American Historical Review* 103, no. 3 (June 1998): 774–79.

3. Paul Parin, "Open Wounds: Ethnopsychoanalytical Reflections on the Wars in the Former Yugoslavia," in Alexandra Stiglmayer, ed., *Mass Rape: The War against Women in Bosnia-Herzegovina* (Lincoln: University of Nebraska Press, 1993), 35–53. See also Ervin Staub, *The Roots of Evil: The Origins of Genocide and Other Group Violence* (New York: Cambridge University Press, 1989); Samuel Totten et al., eds., *Century of Genocide: Eyewitness Accounts and Critical Views* (New York: Garland, 1997).

4. Parin, "Open Wounds," 41.

5. Rogers Brubaker and David D. Laitin, "Ethnic and Nationalist Violence," *Annual Review of Sociology* 24 (1998): 441–43. Brubaker and Laitin rightly dismiss the usefulness of such "culturalist approaches" as a suitable tool for social scientists, even as they fail to understand that the intrinsic role of such "cultural constructions of fear" is not understanding, but rather the dynamic construction of a collective ethnic identity through the scapegoating of the enemy other. See also Vieda Skultans, "Theorizing Latvian Lives: The Quest for Identity," *Journal of the Royal Anthropological Institute* 3, issue 4 (December 1997): 761: "These accounts of the Soviet invasion and its long aftermath constitute a hybrid genre which unites personal and collective experience. They are intended by their authors to provide a literal representation of the past but in the process of acquiring coherence they come to act as potent carriers of literary and cultural meanings, which confirm personal identity and national loyalties. The authors are engaged in a quest for meaning in often disrupted and chaotic lives." Latvian life stories from the twentieth century transformed the context and parameters of Latvian collective experience, where "Latvians saw themselves not as immigrants but as political exiles seeking temporary asylum." For Latvians and other East European postwar diaspora communities, anti-Sovietism was not a Cold War between nation-states, but a liberationist war against communism, a "crusade for freedom" against Soviet-sponsored communist totalitarianism. See also David S. Fogelsong, "Roots of 'Liberation': American Images of the Future of Russia in the Early Cold War, 1948–1953," *International History Review* 21, no. 1 (March 1999): 57–79; Scott Lucas, *Freedom's War: The American Crusade against the Soviet Union* (New York: New York University Press, 1999).

6. Robert D. Kaplan, "A Reader's Guide to the Balkans," *New York Times Book Review,* 18 April 1993, 1, 30–32; and Robert D. Kaplan, *Balkan Ghosts: A Journey through History* (New York: St. Martin's Press, 1993).

7. Wróbel, "Double Memory," 574.

8. Cited in Vladko Maček, *In the Struggle for Freedom* (New York: Speller, 1957), 245.

9. As cited by Lore Dickstein, "Inside the Gray Zone," *New York Times Book Review,* 7 February 1999, sect. 7, 26.

10. Snyder, "'To Resolve the Ukrainian Question Once and for All,'" 87.

11. Omer Bartov, *Hitler's Army: Soldiers, Nazis and War in the Third Reich* (New York: Oxford, 1991), 107–8.

12. Jan Tomasz Gross, *Revolution from Abroad: The Soviet Conquest of Poland's Western Ukraine and Western Belorussia* (Princeton: Princeton University Press, 1988), 43. For insights on neighbor-against-neighbor violence in Eastern Europe, see Jan T. Gross, *Neighbors: The Destruction of the Jewish Community in Jedwabne, Poland* (Princeton: Princeton University Press, 2001); and Shimon Redlich, *Together and Apart in Brzezany: Poles, Jews, and Ukrainians, 1919–1945* (Bloomington: Indiana University Press, 2002). On the recent scandals provoked by Gross's insistence that Poles must remember themselves not just as victims of Nazi aggression but also as perpetrators of anti-Jewish violence in World War II, see Alexander B. Rossino, "Polish 'Neighbors' and German Invaders: Anti-Jewish Violence in the Bialystok District during the Opening Weeks of Operation Barbarossa," *Polin: Studies in Polish Jewry* 16 (2003): 431–52.

13. Waldemar Lotnik, *Nine Lives: Ethnic Conflict in the Polish-Ukrainian Borderlands* (London: Serif, 1999), 66–67.

14. As quoted in Stanislav Kulchytsky, "Veterans, Veterans . . . Gordian Knot of the OUN-UP Problem Nourishes Separatism," *Den'* [Day] [Kiev, Ukraine], no. 26 (2 October 2001). The conflict between institutional inertia of post-Soviet police agencies versus the nationalistic rehabilitation of German collaborationists and anti-Soviet rebels as "freedom fighters" still rages. On the one hand, veterans of the Ukrainian SS and other German military units were awarded state pensions in 2002; on the other, there has been no mass release of NKVD/NKGB secret police files of Ukrainian nationalists who perpetrated violent acts against Ukrainian civilians or agents of Soviet power. I made twelve requests to the Ukrainian SBU in L'viv in March 2002 for access to files of specific Ukrainian nationalist rebels; all twelve were refused. Meanwhile, in 2002 original NKVD files began to appear for sale at flea markets in Kyiv and various provincial Ukrainian towns.

15. See the maps and discussion in Snyder, "'To Resolve the Ukrainian Problem Once and for All,'" 102–3. See also Perez Zagorin, *Ways of Lying: Dissimulation, Persecution and Conformity in Early Modern Europe* (Cambridge: Harvard University Press, 1990).

16. Berhard Chiari, *Alltag hinter der Front: Besatzung, Kollaboration und Widerstand in Weissrussland 1941–1944* (Düsseldorf, 1998); Martin Dean, *Collaboration in the Holocaust: Crimes of the Local Police in Belorussia and Ukraine, 1941–44* (New York: St. Martin's Press, 1999); and a firsthand account by Helene C. Kaplan, *I Never Left Janowska* (New York: Holocaust Library, 1989), 68–69. On Nazi efforts to erase historical memory by destroying archives, see Richard Breitman, *Official Secrets: What the Nazis Planned, What the British and Americans Knew* (New York: Hill and Wang, 1998), 3.

17. For a classic example, see Gosudarstvennyi arkhiv rossiiskoi federatsii (GARF), f. R-7021 Chrezvychainaia gosudarstvennaia komissiia po ustanovleniiu i rassledovaniiu zlodeianii nemetsko-fashistskikh zakhvatchikov, op. 67, d. 82, ll. 26–27 ob., the handwritten affidavit of Ukrainian peasant Semen Sholopa, from village Dornfel'd, Drohobych oblast, dated 11 September 1944. Sholopa described in detail the rounding up of 118 Jews in his village in 1943, who were then forced to strip naked, then one by one leap into a specially prepared pit, where they were shot and buried. A few months later, a special SS unit returned to the field where the mass grave lay hidden, ordered nearly a hundred young Jews to excavate the site, then collected and transported the corpses for burning in a pit behind Ianovskii camp in Vynniki. The Jewish workers were likewise subsequently liquidated. Without Sholopa's detailed account, there would be no record of the German atrocity.

On the mutability of national identity and the processes of ethnic assimilation and differentiation, see John J. Kulczycki, "The National Identity of the 'Natives' of Poland's 'Recovered Lands,'" National Identities 3, no. 3 (2001): 205–19.

18. On the transformation of ethnic politics with the growth of diaspora cultures, where "both challengers and incumbents may increasingly seek resources from dispersed transborder ethnic kin," see Brubaker and Laitin, "Ethnic and Nationalist Violence," 425.

19. Thompson, Beyond the Frontier, 16.

20. John Loftus, The Belarus Secret: The Nazi Connection in America (New York: Knopf, 1982).

21. For a fuller discussion, see Jeffrey Burds, "The Early Cold War in Soviet West Ukraine, 1944–1948," Carl Beck Papers in Russian and East European Studies, no. 1505 (Pittsburgh: University of Pittsburgh, 2001).

22. Thompson, Beyond the Frontier, 37.

23. See especially Paule René-Bazin, "The Influence of Politics on the Shaping of Memory of States in Western Europe" (this volume).

24. Agate Nesaule, A Woman in Amber (New York: Penguin Books, 1995), 9. On the aftermath of rape as an act of ethnic warfare, and the obstacles to evidence gathering, see Beverly Allen, Rape Warfare: The Hidden Genocide in Bosnia-Herzegovina and Croatia (Minneapolis: University of Minnesota Press, 1996).

25. See example in Arkhiv Ministerstva Vnutrennykh Del (Arkhiv MVD), f. 488 Upravlenie vnutrennikh voisk MVD Ukrainskogo okruga, op. 1s, d. 232, ll. 14–16, "Otchet o metodakh i deistviiakh bol'shevikov v Tovstvenskom raione." At every point where Ukrainian nationalist rebels had recorded police abuse, the Moscow bosses instructed their personnel to launch an investigation "to verify" the details of the violations.

26. Top Secret Report of N. Gusarov, Inspector TsK VKP(b), to Secretaries of the Central Committee of the USSR, Stalin, Zhdanov, Kuznetsov, Patolichev, and Popov, "Nedostatki i oshibki v ideologicheskoi rabote KP(b)U[krainy]," 13 August 1946. For further discussion, see Jeffrey Burds, "Gender and Policing in Soviet West Ukraine, 1944–1948," Cahiers du Monde russe 42, no. 2–4 (April–December 2001): 279–320.

27. Cf. Vladimir A. Kozlov's account of Soviet MVD efforts to block the flow of anti-police denunciations in the late 1940s:

"Denunciation and Its Functions in Soviet Governance: A Study of Denunciations and Their Bureaucratic Handling from Soviet Police Archives, 1944–1953," in Sheila Fitzpatrick and Robert Gellately, eds., Accusatory Practices: Denunciation in Modern European History, 1789–1989 (Chicago: University of Chicago Press, 1997), 121–52.

28. See, for instance, the text of the denunciation of local police abuse by a typist in the L'viv office of the Ministry of State Security, Tsentral'nyi derzhavnyi arkhiv hromads'kykh ob"ednan' Ukraïny (TsDAHOU), f. 1, op. 23, d. 5174, ll. 86–104. This denunciation led to the investigation and indictment of several MGB officers.

29. Secret memorandum of the procurator of the Soviet Military Tribunal in Ukraine Koshars'kyi to Khrushchev, 15 February 1949, TsDAHOU, f. 1, op. 16, d. 68, ll. 10–17. For the full account, see Jeffrey Burds, "AGENTURA: Soviet Informants' Networks and the Ukrainian Rebel Underground in Galicia, 1944–1948," East European Politics and Societies 11, no. 1 (winter 1997): 89–130.

30. Petr Dmitriev, "Soldat Berii" Vospominaniia lagernogo okhrannika (Leningrad: "Chas pik," 1991), 24–25.

31. USSR People's Commissariat of Internal Affairs Investigative File, Department of the NKVD of the USSR, Arkhiv FSB, [no fond no. available], d. 19062. Peluzo was arrested in April 1938 for conspiring against the Soviet state and working as a foreign spy. The cited letter was written in his own hand in French on 14 May 1941. Peluzo's petition for release was declined, and he died in hard labor eighteen months later. The author is grateful to Frederikh I. Firsov, former archivist at RGASPI, for generously sharing this material.

32. Gábor Rittersporn, "The Omnipresent Conspiracy: On Soviet Imagery of Politics and Social Relations in the 1930s," in Nick Lampert and Gábor T. Rittersporn, eds., Stalinism: Its Nature and Aftermath: Essays in Honour of Moshe Lewin (Armonk, NY: M. E. Sharpe, 1992), 101–20.

33. Christopher Andrew and Oleg Gordievsky, KGB: The Inside Story of Its Foreign Operations from Lenin to Gorbachev (New York: HarperCollins, 1990), 260; Gabriel Gorodetsky, Grand Delusion: Stalin and the German Invasion of Russia (New Haven: Yale University Press, 1999).

34. L. Dvoinykh and N. Tarkhova, "What Military Intelligence Reported: Historians Have a Chance to Analyze Soviet Dispatches on the Eve of the War," in Bruce W. Menning, ed., At the Threshold of War: The Soviet High Command in 1941, special issue of Russian Studies in History: A Journal of Translations (winter 1997–98): 76–93. On the atmosphere of suspicion surrounding Soviet agents in the 1930s and 1940s, see Genrik Borovik, The Philby Files: The Secret Life of Master Spy Kim Philby (Boston: Little Brown, 1994).

35. Emphasis added; 30 August 1944. Top Secret Report, "On the Metropolitan of the Greek Catholic (Uniate) Church—Count Andrij SHEPTITSKIJ" by Colonel Karin (Danilenko); witnessed by NKGB Captain V. Khodin. Robert H. Greene, "'A New War Has Begun': The Destruction of the Greek Catholic Church in West Ukraine, 1939–1946," Senior Thesis in History and Russian Studies, University of Rochester, 1997.

36. Successive regimes in the Soviet Union have displayed a distinct tendency to destroy archival files. Christopher Andrew

recently noted that there are numerous "KGB files which the SVR [Russian (post-Soviet) Foreign Intelligence Service] is still anxious to keep from public view. Unlike the documents selected for declassification by the SVR, none of which are more recent than the early 1960s, his [Mitrokhin's] archive covers almost the whole of the Cold War. Most of it is still highly classified in Moscow. The originals of some of the most important documents noted or transcribed by Mitrokhin may no longer exist. In 1989 most of the huge multi-volume file on the dissident Andrei Sakharov, earlier branded *'Public Enemy Number One'* by Andropov, was destroyed. Soon afterwards, Kryuchkov announced that all files on other dissidents charged under the infamous Article 70 of the criminal code (anti-Soviet agitation and propaganda) were being shredded. In a number of cases, Mitrokhin's notes on them may now be all that survives." *The Sword and the Shield: The Mitrokhin Archive and the Secret History of the KGB* (New York: Basic Books, 1999), 22.

The practice of restricting or destroying secrets is not unique to the Soviets. See the fascinating account in Richard J. Aldrich, *The Hidden Hand: Britain, America and Cold War Secret Intelligence* (New York: Overlook Press, 2002), 1–16, 637–45. Cf., "Use of Special Intelligence by Official Historians," Report by the Joint Intelligence Sub-Committee [JIC (45) 223 (o) Final (20 July 1946)], Public Record Office, CAB 103/288/109123. The Western allied effort to conceal the fact that they could read German ciphers led to the suppression and denial of official knowledge of the genocide in the East. See Richard Breitman, *Official Secrets,* passim.

37. Ivo Banac, "Silencing the Archival Voice: The Destruction of Archives and Other Obstacles to Archival Research in Post-Communist Eastern Europe," *Arh. Vjes.* [Croatia] 42 (1999): 217–22; and personal communication from Banac in autumn 2000.

38. "Russia Under Siege: Western Scholarly Research as Intellectual Imperialism," *Den'* (Moscow), 11–17 April 1993. A full translation appears in appendix 2.

39. Burds's interview with A. I. Barkhovets, then deputy di-

rector of the State Archive of the Russian Federation in Moscow, where the collections are stored, July 1994.

40. J. Arch Getty, "Secrets and Money: An Update on Russian Archives," *Newsnet: The Newsletter of the American Association for the Advancement of Slavic Studies* 37, no. 5 (November 1997).

41. Personal communication from archivists in Tver, Perm, and Moscow, Russia.

42. Confidential Report (anonymous) to the Harry Frank Guggenheim Foundation, August 2000. Another American researcher, Roberta Manning of Boston College, provided still more chilling details in autumn 2000: "There are rumors in Moscow that the 'crackdown' was caused by one American scholar who went around Moscow trying to 'buy secret documents.' Some FSB [Federal Security Service] operatives decided to set him up and 'sold' him some 'secret documents,' hoping to get them back at the border and create a scandal. But the scholar was able to send them out of the country by other means. So the police part of the FSB went crazy and start to inspect the archives like they used to, concentrating on the security of documents that still aren't classified or are in some limbo but were being published in various collections, like the *osobye papki* [special files] of the Politburo. . . . The inspection began with the FSB archive and all *sotrudnitsy* [archival personnel] who were not employees of the FSB were forbidden to work there. The Military Archive, which was inspected for three days running, was accused of selling state secrets and its head called down to the prosecutor's office and told an investigation along these lines was being launched. . . . Anyway lots of archivists were pretty scared and foreigners don't roam as freely around." From RUSARCHIVE, an Internet discussion group moderated by J. Arch Getty at UCLA, 26 August 2000.

43. Banac, "Silencing the Archival Voice"; Tim Judah, "Croatia Reborn," *New York Review of Books,* 10 August 2000).

44. See Jeffrey Burds, "The Early Cold War in Soviet West Ukraine, 1944–1948."

Hesitations at the Door to an
Archive Catalog

Vladimir Lapin

This essay represents reflections on the reciprocal influence between the historian and the archivist involved in developing and improving the apparatus of scholarly reference in the Russian archives. Let us start with some thoughts about historians.

Historians reflecting on their trade, and on their interactions with archivists, cannot ignore an obvious fact: the apparatus of scholarly reference is responsible to a certain extent for mapping out the course of their archival research. The reference apparatus imposes a different influence on a historian well guided in the ocean of archival materials than a person who tries to find an answer to a particular question and finds himself overwhelmed by the sea of available information. An experienced researcher starts working in the archives only if there is a more or less broad choice of descriptive concepts (a system of key words). It is hard to say what exactly historians feel—the joy of engagement when they meet figures and events that are already familiar, or the joy of becoming familiar with ones that were previously unknown. In most cases beginners learn that archives speak a somewhat incomprehensible language and that, in order to find answers to their questions, they must alter the question itself. They also learn that the catalogs and files offer them diverse information they were unaware of and the usefulness of which they initially find difficult to assess. Every researcher, regardless of his or her qualifications, comes to the archives with some already developed ideas about his or her subject, and with a readiness to learn certain kinds of information. The very principle "I am looking for what I am aware of" determines to a considerable extent the trajectory of a scholar's research. The scholar looks in the reference apparatus for what he or she has already formed an idea about. The catalog and the file are the researchers' tool kit, but researchers are unable to adjust the tools.

Is The Archival Reference Apparatus "Scientific"?

Archival reference materials in the Soviet Union were prefixed by the word "scientific." This means that their authors claimed they were organized in a scientific way and were thereby linked to the process of "scientific" historical creativity. Very instrumental in developing archival reference materials were the USSR Council of Ministers Resolution of July 25, 1963, entitled "On the Measures to Improve Archival Activities in the USSR," and a Communist Party of the Soviet Union (CPSU) Central Committee Resolution of 1967 entitled "On Measures to Further Develop the Social Sciences and to Enhance their Importance in Communist Construction." These two regulating documents gave rise to the Schema of Unified Classification (SUC) developed at the All-Union Research Institute for Records, Studies, and Archives (RIRSA). This schema is in complete accord with "Marxist-Leninist methodology."

First, it strictly arranges topics by their scholarly significance. Section A is devoted to materials connected with the Great October Socialist Revolution and with "the establishing and strengthening of Soviet power." The section is subdivided into several parts, including: (A1) "Preparations for the Great October Socialist Revolution"; (A2) "The victory and strengthening of Soviet power"; (A3) "Destruction of the bourgeois state apparatus"; (A5) "The struggle of Soviet power against counterrevolution"; (A7) "People's governments (1940)"; (A8) "Proletarian solidarity and support to the Great October Socialist Revolution abroad. Participation of workers of foreign countries in the October Revolution."

Then, the schema builds a definite hierarchy of topics and subjects: Section B3, for example, is called "State construction. State power. State security." Internally, the section is organized by the Russian alphabet as follows:

B. "State construction."
V. "State power and state administration."
G. "Justice. Control over legality. Protection of social order and social property. Protection of state borders."
D. "International relations (foreign policy). International social and political movement."
Ye. "Armed forces."
ZH. "Armed protection of the Socialist fatherland."
I/K. "On the leading role of the CPSU (Art. 6 of the USSR constitution)."
  I1. "Social and political life."
  I2. "CPSU."
  I3. "Trade Unions."[1]
  I4. "Komsomol [Communist Youth Organization]."
  I5. "Pioneers [Communist Children's Organization]."
  I6. "Other public and political organizations."
  K3. "Agitation and propaganda."
  K4. "Mass media."
  K7. "Folk festivals, anniversaries, and other jubilees."
L/T. Section with material on the "National economy."
  L. "Economic development."
  M. "Industry."
  N. "Transport."
  P. "Communication."
  R. "Agriculture, forest, and water economy."
  S. "Trade, sale, stocks."
  T. "Communal economy."
U/Ia. Final sections dealing with "Elements of the superstructure."
  U. "Culture."
  F. "Education."
  X. "Science."
  Ts. "Literature."
  Ch. "Arts."
  Sh. "Cultural enlightenment."
  Shch. "Health care."
  Ye. "Physical training and sports."
  Iu. "Family life."
  Ia. "Religious remnants in people's consciousness. Atheism and anti-religious propaganda."

This system lists subjects in order of their "importance." Its evaluations were carefully designed to correspond completely to the then prevailing ideological injunctions: "The basis for constructing this Schema is the scientific ideology of Marxism-Leninism, which organically combines loyalty to the party's values [*partiinost'*] and the scientific objectivity of perception. The divisions of the main sections of the SUC reflect the peculiarities and regularities of socialist state development. The sequence of SUC sections reflects a Marxist-Leninist understanding of the particularities in the transition from capitalism to socialism, in which political change is preceded by change in the fields of economy and culture."[2] In the opinion of the schema's creators, the final section, on "Fields of human endeavor" [*sic*!], are to be considered historically and thematically distinct from the material in section A on the Great October Socialist Revolution. We are at a loss for an explanation of why the 1917 October coup was not considered within the "field of human endeavor."

Connections between the Apparatus of Scholarly Reference (SRA) and the General Schema of Historiography, Bibliography, and the Organization of Soviet Historical Science

It is somewhat paradoxical that, in elucidating the principles of the schema's structure, its authors referred to demands of archive users that derived from standardized directives for teaching and studying history. These were absorbed by students from school textbooks as well as university podiums and had a strong impact on the development of their scholarly perspectives. The organizational system of higher educational institutions, research centers, and museums all reflected the views prevailing in official scholarship. Divisions within institutes and faculty positions reflected stages of historical development (prehistoric, slave-owning, feudal, capitalist and socialist). Academic bibliographies followed the same calibrations: first "Classics of Marxism-Leninism about . . . "; then something about methodology (naturally, Marxist-Leninist); and then works in the order of their proximity to "the base," that is, productive forces, production conditions, social movements, state (political) structure, culture, everyday life, and religion. The same hierarchical pyramid of values was reflected in the reports and evaluations of research institutions.[3] The problem was not so pronounced with bibliographical reference works since each separate section here could be used independently of the others. Biographical catalogs similarly do not integrate their information, unlike archival catalogs, which essentially provide the outline for writing a certain "classical" kind of history.

In Soviet historical scholarship, this structure for cataloging material became mandatory first for ideological reasons, but quickly became part of the academic tradition. The sequence was followed most consistently in the multivolume editions that claimed status as "fundamental" works (such as the *History of the USSR from Ancient Times to the Present*) or in various "distinguished" collective monographs. Thus, the reference apparatus of archives, especially catalogs, met the demands of users by setting their writing within a strict organizational and ideological framework. The corresponding arrangement of the entire archival reference apparatus was in this way built into a unitary system and constituted its most important part.

Let us not forget in this regard that from 1938 to 1961, the Archives Ministry functioned under close surveillance by "responsible officers" of the security services. Control over archival information required that the reference apparatus be properly organized for internal use. On the one hand, the development of the reference apparatus (SRA) broadened access to documents and provided researchers beginning their work with shortcuts to his documents. On the other, the reference apparatus itself orientated the researchers' work, structured analysis, and forced scholars to take the "right" track.

The Structure of Archival Catalogs

Generally speaking, the catalog of the Russian State Historical Archive (RGIA) in St. Petersburg reflects this system. RGIA materials cover practically all facets of the Russian state and society from the eighteenth to the early twentieth century. The core of the archive consists of files of the central administrative bodies of the tsarist empire, totaling some 6.5 million documents. It is organized into the following categories: (1) General statistical data; (2) Nations and nationalities; (3) State power and administration; (4) Economy (General); (5) Industry; (6) Agriculture; (7) Finance and credit; (8) Trade; (9) Transport; (10) Communication; (11) Working-class issues; (12) Agrarian issues; (13) Revolutionary, working-class, peasant, and public movements; (14) Foreign policy; (15) Armed forces; (16) Science; (17) Education; (18) Health care; (19) Literature; (20) Arts; (21) Religion and the church.[4]

The Russian State Naval Archive (RGAVMF) differs from RGIA. Here only documents of one ministry have been accumulated, covering the period from the early eighteenth century to 1940. Hence, the organizational plan of the RGAVMF catalog is as follows: (1) The Organization of the naval staff; (2) Shipbuilding and ship timber; (3) Naval artillery; (4) Mines, torpedoes, and preventive weapons; (5) Anti-submarine weapons; (6) Chemical weapons and defense against gas; (7) Boarding firearms and sidearms; (8) Optics and communication; (9) Aeronautics and aviation; (10) Medicine; (11) Shipwrecks; (12) Hydrography and navigation; (13) Scientific expeditions; (14) Naval science; (15) Recruitment for the navy and personnel records; (16) Education; (17) Battle training; (18) Unions and volunteer societies; (19) Port construction; (20) Industry; (21) The Revolutionary movement; (22) Naval courts and prisons. In the structure of its prerevolutionary section, the RGAVMF catalog emphasizes specific archival materials. Placing "The Revolutionary movement" in the twenty-first position in the organization of subjects looks in retrospect like some sort of reckless freethinking. In the RGAVMF catalog for the Soviet period, the schema of the preceding section is completely changed. Here "Participation of the navy in the preparation and realization of the Great October Socialist Revolution and in the struggle for strengthening Soviet power (March 1917–March 1918)" comes first.

The Descriptive System in the Archival Reference Apparatus

The requirements for the titles of catalog cards were regulated by the *General Rules of USSR State Archival Operations*.[5] According to these rules, when defining the title of a card, "the fact and events described in the document are to be explained from a Marxist-Leninist viewpoint; it is prohibited to transfer alien class formulations, concepts, or terms from the texts of documents to the titles of the files. The text of title must reflect in a generalized and clear manner the contents of filed documents. Listing particular documents in the title is prohibited. Also, the document's content is to be stated in the file name in contemporary language, without parenthesis; particular terms as well as names of institutions, administrative and territorial units and geographical names that are characteristic of the epoch and express its features are to be preserved."[6] Further, "In a systematic catalog documentary information is to be arranged by the branches of knowledge and practical activities of society. The systematic catalog reflects connections between events and phenomena and contains data on particular problems. . . . Archives holding documents on the pre-Soviet and Soviet periods are to maintain two separate systematic catalogs. The point of demarcation is the date when Soviet power was established in the corresponding territory."[7] Strict adherence to the idea that the formative moment of Soviet power was of fundamental importance in the cataloging of documents overrode any considerations based on the content of the documents themselves.

According to the *General Rules*, first to be cataloged were collections in a category that included: (1) Organizational directives, planning and reporting materials, and other principal documents of the institution generating the archival *fond*; (2) Directives from superior bodies that relate directly to the principal activities of the fund-generating institutions; (3) Documents of subordinate institutions; (4) Documents that show essential aspects of institutional activities but whose originals cannot be kept at an institution; (5) Published materials about an institution; (6) Other documents worthy of being cataloged "due to their value and the difficulty of the search."[8] This last clause opened the broadest opportunities for the archivist to be both creative and arbitrary.

The emergence of these normative categories can be explained on the basis of a whole complex of reasons: First, directives to the archival ministry from the party and government, that is, orders that prescribed all of the activities of that ministry; second, the archival process itself; and third, the demands of Soviet ideology for comparative openness in the archives and the necessity to retain control over all historical information. Archivists pointed out that reference books of a "subject-cataloging type" were required most of all, but they encountered "considerable difficulties of both theoretical and methodological character" in producing them.[9] According to an administrator in the archival service of what was then the Latvian Soviet Socialist Republic, nearly 1 percent of all files in the central republican archive was used annually; over five years (1966–70) 14 percent of archived materials was involved in research. This led the administrator to conclude that the apparatus of scholarly reference was insufficiently developed, or in his words, there was a "superfluity of documentary retrospective information at the archive."[10] The orientation of archivists toward user demand was not only an appropriate reaction to the actual interests of the Soviet academic community but also led to the hardening of established priorities, a deepening of the rut that hindered any reorientation of archival cataloging toward other topics.

In determining the sequence of cataloging collections,

the intensity and perspectives with which documentary materials were used took second place to the complexity of developing collections, which was understood as the possibility of processing in the short run the greatest number of documents. Thus, user demand for collections was an important criterion.

A collection was cataloged by observing the structural hierarchy of the generating institution. For example, institutional documents can be divided into four parts:

- documents of administrative departments (boards, presidia, chancelleries, etc.)
- documents of specialized departments that reflect specific kinds of activities of the generating agency
- documents of functional departments (planning dept., etc.)
- documents of service departments.

This schema is oriented toward obtaining information that is already prepared in a proper way. A researcher obtains information from "superior" but not always "first" hands. The importance of a ministry, or rather that of its board or secretariat, becomes the most important consideration.

The second stage of selection is determining the storage units for processed documents. Methodologists recommended dividing the records into two groups—primary and auxiliary—"having a clear understanding of functions of an institution."[11] Not infrequently, methodological materials from RIRSA provided impractical recommendations for describing documents or filling out catalog cards. For instance, it was prescribed to "thoroughly study the functions of institutions, the functions of document types and the objects pursued." In the first place, "minutes, resolutions, decisions, instructions, and memoranda" were to be cataloged. Thus, the second stage of cataloging was to involve the most formalized materials produced by certain rules of the bureaucratic genre.[12]

The third stage—extracting documented data for cataloging—was identified as the most important part of cataloging.

The aim of extraction is to locate for description such data that in total would give necessary and sufficient information on the essence of events, facts, and phenomena reflected in recorded materials. In so doing, it is necessary to avoid entering in a catalog random information about the events, facts, and phenomena, without revealing the regularities of their development, and without showing the individual characteristics or peculiarities of their manifestation. . . . An indispensable aspect of the selection from documentary materials for cataloging is the application of general principles of Marxist-Leninist methodology:

- a commitment to the party [*partiinost'*] that presupposes academic objectivity in evaluating information from the viewpoint of Marxism-Leninism
- an historical method that requires not only the knowledge of concrete history but also the record-keeping practices that existed in the given historical period
- consideration of the comprehensiveness and complexity of phenomena, that is, the multiple events and facets of social life, their interrelations and interdependency.

The main criterion for selecting information is the contents and scientific as well as practical value of the documents. The contents should be considered both as a whole and in detail to determine what is primary and secondary, and to decide, as the case requires, what significance the documentary information has for illustrating social life from both present and future viewpoints. . . . Basic contents (basic information) target the necessary information, which flows out the form and purpose of a document as a tool of administration. . . . One should avoid excessive specialization of contents. On the other hand, the contents should not be incomplete, or insufficient for illustrating the main facts, phenomena and events described in the documentary materials. . . . When retrieving information from minutes, only information on already solved issues should be taken. But a compiler, coming from the actual contents of the minutes and taking the historical period and specific institution into consideration, may, in specific cases, note unresolved issues on a catalog card that deserves the researcher's attention.[13]

Authors of this manual on archival methodology also noted that "before proceeding to the selection of information for a nominal catalog, it is necessary to clearly identify the circle of people whose personal data should be filed on a catalog card. . . . Those are data on persons whose political, social, economic, cultural, educational and practical activities are of interest for science and practice. In so doing, it is necessary to keep in mind that not only the data of progressive party activists should be entered in the catalog, but also that of activists of reactionary movements."[14]

Archival Directories

Archival guidebooks have many features that make them similar to catalogs. A concise reference book,

USSR State Archives,[15] released in 1956, contains over 250 entries concerning the contents of central (all-union), republic, and regional archives in the Soviet Union. Surprisingly, the index of names in this book repeats exactly the "dictionary" of the university textbook on Soviet national history. In total there are 1,200 family names in this guidebook. An overwhelming majority (80 percent) are mentioned twice. There is a profound hierarchical character in the references to the "champions of the happiness of the people": V. Lenin—40 references; M. Kalinin—26; E. Pugachev—23; I. Stalin and M. Frunze—21 each; Ya. Sverdlov, G. Ordzhonikidze, and S. Kirov—15 each; N. Chernyshevsky—11; F. Dzerzhinsky—9; and G. Kotovskii—7.

Thirty family names in this directory are designated as "the pride of the nation." Among them are prominent military commanders, writers, scientists, and artists. Of the Russian tsars, Alexander II and Alexander III are mentioned 4 times, while Catherine the Great is honored with archivists' attention 14 times, Peter the Great—23 times (as many as the revolutionary E. Pugachev). In total, these 30 family names supply 230 references, that is, approximately one third fewer than those for party and revolutionary activists. Also of interest is the fact that within each group there is a visible arrangement by the officially established importance of a person. Military leaders fall in the following order: M. Kutuzov (18); A. Suvorov (11); P. Rumyantzev (9); F. Ushakov (6); P. Bagration (6); M. Barclay de Tolli (5). Among men of letters the hierarchical character is also very pronounced: L. Tolstoi (14); A. Gorky (11); V. Kornelyuk (11); M. Saltykov-Schedrin (8); M. Lermontov (7); A. Griboedov (7); V. Zhukovskii (6); N. Nekrasov (5); G. Derzhavin (5); A. Pushkin (5); K. Ryleev (4); A. Ostrovskii (4); and N. Gogol (4).

Literature has always taken the lead in Russian cultural life. Servants to other muses happened to be in less favor with compilers of the directory. For example, among composers only N. Rimsky-Korsakov cleared the hurdle, and there is not a single artist or sculptor. Among the scientists only N. Pirogov (6), D. Mendeleev (6), V. Rusanov (4), and I. Kruzenshtern (4) deserved a place on the iconostasis.

The directory of names in the first volume of the *Collections of the State Archive of the Russian Federation on Russian History of the Nineteenth and Early Twentieth Centuries*[16] also presents a curious picture:

Nicholas II	57
Nicholas I	31
L. Tolstoi	30

Alexander I	28
P. Stolypin	28
V. Burtsev	25
Alexander II	24
S. Witte	22
Alexandra Fedorovna (wife of Nicholas II)	21
A. Herzen	21
V. Figner	20
V. Korolenko	20
A. Koni	19
P. Kropotkin	19
K. Pobedonostsev	18
P. Lavrov	17
A. Pushkin	17
V. Plehve	17
Paul I	16
A. Benckendorf	16
M. Bakunin	15
A. Guchkov	14
P. Miliukov	14
B. Struve	14
A. Gorchakov	14
N. Chernyshevsky	14
S. Breshko-Breshkovskaya	13
P. Valuev	13
Alexandra Fedorovna (wife of Nicholas I)	13
A. Kerensky	13
G. Lopatin	13
Catherine II	13
I. Turgenev	13
N. Tchaikovsky	13
Maria Fedorovna (wife of Alexander III)	12
E. Azef	12
Great Duchess Elena Pavlovna	11
V. Semevsky	11
Great Duke Sergei Alexandrovich	11
D. Miliutin	11

In the list of names in the index kept at the manuscript department of the Lenin Library in Moscow, *Memoirs and Diaries of the Eighteenth through Twentieth Centuries,*[17] published in 1976, the persons and number of references are arranged in the following order:

V. Lenin	86
V. Bonch-Bruevich	71
L. Tolstoi	60
A. Chekhov	32
Alexander II	28
S. Witte	23
Alexander III	21
V. Korolenko	20
A. Lunacharsky	19
L. Krasin	18

While these examples do not allow us to generalize conclusively, they are sufficient to show the overall tendency. Considering the role of "cult" figures in the nation's historical memory, it can be said that the archival variant of this historical memory was in full compliance with its enormous ideological pressures. In the preface to an index of manuscript memoirs held by the National Library, S. Zhitomirskaya described the approach to compiling a name index and annotation in this way: "Annotations are supplied for persons mentioned in the memoirs. (These must be contemporaries of the author, however, and not just any one who is mentioned, like Homer, for instance, in a contemporary memoir.) In recording and annotating them, the compilers considered a main goal of their work to show how certain names are reflected in a majority of the memoirs."[18] We should note first of all that in this way the index ties the memoirist to his or her epoch. Users doing research in the problem of historical memory, for example, are faced with the daunting necessity of reading all the memoirs themselves to see who the author might have referred to, since such important aids as annotations and a name index are tuned to a different question entirely. This is true for geographical indices as well. Users of these indices are thus completely dependent on how important it was for the person preparing the annotations to mention this or that name.

Annotations and indices were obviously prepared according to some hierarchical scale of valuation or appraisal. My own experience in working with quite different kinds of historical sources, including diaries and memoirs, testifies that the "population density" of documents varies widely. In some cases, events are nearly "uninhabited"; in other cases the number of names looks like a businessman's notebook. Certainly, there is a connection between what a document is about and its annotation in the reference book and name index, but this connection is far from proportional to the number of names actually cited. Some who prepare annotations and indices discard many names that others retain, "underloading" their indices.

Symbolic historical figures have a far better chance of being mentioned because of the magic effect of their name on the compiler, regardless of the historical significance of an event. In most cases memoirs also mention most frequently persons from an inner circle. An annotation to a professor's diary, for example, mentions his colleagues, his contemporaries in the cultural world, and officials from the Ministry of Education. The author of the annotated index addresses a priori his work to those who will study the history of education or science and burns the bridges of those who might try to use the diary as a cultural artifact.

In methodological terms, this means that archival documents were regarded as exclusively utilitarian—as a reservoir of information on the events and people of a particular epoch. The author of the annotation or the compiler of a catalog or inventory in essence tried to determine beforehand the direction of a researcher's thinking, the course of his or her research. We may think this is impossible in principle, but was very much thought to be possible in Soviet times.

It is perhaps appropriate here to compare these cataloging efforts to those of Gossnab (State Supply Ministry) and Gosplan (State Economic Planning Ministry), in their attempts to foretell and calculate everything down to the trifle. It is difficult to find better examples of the limitless faith in the capacities of the human mind, examples possible only in an atheist society where taking on the Lord's functions is not considered reprehensible. The very procedures of cataloging are nothing less than an effort to dissolve chaos. The archivist not only endeavors to make order out of chaos, but also gives the objects of his attention arbitrary, made-up names. The annotations in the reference book *USSR State Archives* only reinforce this idea of the unity of "information and ideological" space on the one-sixth of the earth's surface that makes up the Soviet Union. For the collections at the RGIA in St. Petersburg one finds the following headings: "Power"; "Foreign Policy"; "Revolutionary Movement"; "Industry"; "Agriculture"; "Transport and Communication"; "Trade"; "Finance"; "Education"; "Religion and the Church"; "Arts and Literature"; and "Medicine". The volume of the text devoted in the annotations to the "base" is 61 percent and to the "superstructure" 39 percent. Only 18 percent is allocated to education, literature, arts, and health care.

In describing the contents of collections in the RGAVMF, the compilers took another path, since the specific nature of the documents (pertaining to the Naval Ministry) did not allow the familiar "base/superstructure" scheme. The situation was saved with entries on revolutionary themes: 26 percent of the essay describing RGAVMF is text about the archive's facilities for studying the history of "revolutionary liberation movements." Nevertheless, a ritual passage is inserted in the beginning of the article: "The documentary materials of the archive show a centuries-old history of the peoples of the USSR. They characterize the country's economy, the internal and foreign policy of the tsarist period, the history of the Russian working class and peasantry, class relations in a multinational Russian [*sic!*] state, and revolutionary and revolutionary liberation movements." The authors of the annotations about the RGAVMF collections did not "lag behind": a fourth of the text is devoted to revolutionary plots and those of liberation movements.[19]

In describing the contents of the collections at the Russian State Literary and Arts Archives (RGALI), there was no real possibility to utilize the ideologically established schema, so the compilers took yet another course. Annotations were limited to subjects that were formally registered as "admissible" in secondary school programs. Authors were evaluated on the basis of what was regarded as the significance of their artistic creativity in general and its contribution to "progress" (as understood, of course, by the CPSU Central Committee Ideological Department). In this way K. Ryleev, A. Griboedov, and D. Fonvizin kept the company of N. Gogol and M. Lermontov. Specific attention was paid to N. Chernyshevsky, who, in the words of V. I. Lenin, raised many generations of revolutionaries. Then there are the "progressives": A. Herzen, N. Ogarev, N. Nekrasov, and M. Saltykov-Schedrin. The authors of the annotations did not fail to note that there were manuscripts of the latter in the RGALI collections in a notebook with the provisional title "Satires on Tsarism."

Such a "sensible" standard was also followed in descriptions of republic and provincial archives. In most cases, the material was first ordered as follows: (1) Authority [Government]; (2) Industry; (3) Agriculture; (4) The Revolutionary movement; (5) Education, Culture, Science; and so forth. The proportions of the material are also more or less standardized: 35 percent—revolutionary movements and the establishment of Soviet power; 6 percent—industry; 4 percent—agriculture (Krasnoyarsk regional archives); 17 percent—revolutionary movement; 20 percent—agriculture; 10 percent—industry (Stavropol regional archives); 22 percent—revolutionary and liberation movement (Vladimir regional archives). These figures give the impression that archivists justified their existence by keeping documents on revolutionaries. Any mention in a document, even a passing one, of a figure involved in the liberation movement had a good chance to find its way into a catalog, a reference book, or an index of names.

Even such specialized institutions as the archives of academic research institutes were not above striving to show that they, too, kept in step with the Soviet people. For example, in a short article about the archives of the St. Petersburg Institute of Archaeology, a place was found for the following passage:

Among the documents characterizing the activities of archaeological expeditions we should note . . . the proceeding of the Commission on the Sociology of Art and Art History under the chairmanship of A. Lunacharsky; shorthand reports and protocols of open sessions and scholarly meetings; the proceedings of plenary meetings and an All-Union session devoted to the 25th and 50th anniversary of the Lenin Decree on Establishing the Institute of History of Material Culture. Of great value are protocols of the meetings of the Institute's Council and its correspondence with the People's Commissariat of Education in 1918–1921 that testify to the active participation of the Institute's leading scholars in working out legal documents about Soviet archaeological institutions. . . . Deserving special attention are the research materials of the archaeological monuments on construction sites such as the Moscow subway line, the Volga-Don and White Sea–Baltic canals, the Krasnoyarsk and Sayano-Shushenskaya hydroelectric plants, as well as the materials on the archaeological excavations by Soviet archaeologists abroad—in the Mongol People's Republic, the Arab Republic of Egypt, and the Social Republic of Vietnam.[20]

These schemas demonstrate a surprising vitality. In 1999/2000 the Federal Archives Service and the Open Society Institute/Soros Foundation released a series of guidebooks to provincial state archives. The main part of these archives now consists of documents of former regional and district party organizations, as well as those of political institutions that were established during perestroika and in the post-Soviet period. Interestingly, in these guidebooks party structures are arranged according to the familiar Soviet division between "base" and "superstructure." First are the archives of party organizations in local governing bodies, then those of industry (with their own hierarchy—energy, heavy engineering, light industry, food industry), then agriculture, communication, trade, supplying, family life, education, science, culture and arts. The same order is followed for typical archives of Soviet Youth Organizations (Komsomol). In the preface to a guidebook to the Komi republic archive of public and political movements and organizations, furthermore, mention is made of documents about the dispossession of *kulaks,* about "special relocated persons" and their role in establishing and developing industry of the Komi Autonomous Soviet Socialist Republic (ASSR). There are also references in the preface to archives of mass repression and human rights violations and facts about infringements committed by state bodies and executives. But in the annotations to the archives themselves, there is not a single mention of these matters. It is obvi-

ous that we have to take into account the political correctness of the authors of the preface, their prudence in radically changing the character of records. But still, the almost complete discrepancy between the preface and the annotations shows the durability of traditional notions and wordings.

In some cases, authors of recent indices are rescued by the artless trick of putting in quotation marks the formulations of Marxist-Leninist ideology. Finding aids retain the coloring of the epoch, and researchers, regardless of their political views, receive an annotation that is quite adequate to convey the essence of information contained in the document: for example, "Documents on the Denunciation and Expulsion from the Party of Trotskyist Double-dealers and Bourgeois Nationalists"; "About the Disclosure in the Region of a Trotskyist-Zinovievist Group." A guidebook to the former party archives of the Tatar ASSR published in the same series, however, does not contain a single mention about the dark side of the history of nationalities in the twentieth century. It differs from Soviet-period directories only by mentioning that 14,500 files of the republic's party organizations have been declassified according to the Resolution of the President of the Russian Federation of June 23, 1992.

Conclusion

Generally speaking, the existing system of annotating and cataloging is designed, by its inner features, to serve historians who work within the paradigm of the "history of events." A historian who is deeply inside the system of "Annales" or engaged with any other paradigm should learn to translate the language of catalog into the one he or she uses.

In general, the archives catalog is constructed according to the principle of tracing documents from the general to the specific. This logic mirrors perfectly that of the bureaucratic apparatus (archives are first of all a product of administrators) and takes all of the material a ministry possesses as the equipment bureaucrats need to carry out their "special" activities. And since it is the archives of the "central apparatus" that is most developed, a researcher, willingly or not, has to follow along the path paved by the references, with the shadow of an individual bureaucrat visible only in the distance.

A person working on the general index decides on his or her own how to label the section so as to get a more or less adequate reflection of the character and content of material. The logic of arranging the cards depends considerably on the compiler's personality. At the end of the 1920s time bonds got broken in Russia. In the world of the reference apparatus, the archivist bureaucrat was replaced by the archivist historian. The former did not learn by heart what laws governed historical processes, what correlation there was between the base and the superstructure, what a social formation is, how the formations supersede each other, or what is the locomotive of history. The latter had a more or less clear idea about these things. At the same time, it was only the trained staff that brought the spirit of history into the archives. History was of paramount importance in forming social consciousness. The most important task for archivists and historians was to attach the diverse entirety of historical material to the rigid frames built by "The Concise Course of the History of the All-Russian Communist Party (Bolshevik) (VKPb)." The molding of prioritized topics and trends and the developing of the "only correct" Marxist-Leninist ideology set the terms for formulating rules to describe and catalog archival materials. For an old-time archivist bureaucrat, a document's content was its dominant element. Certainly, in writing down annotations he was also guided by his own scale of values and subjected to the ideological influences (monarchist, nationalist, liberal), but those were his *personal* biases, not ones imposed by the threat of repression. The system of priorities was changed in a radical way.

A second radical change was in breaking (imperial) historical archives off from archives in the process of being developed. From the very start these two kinds of archives appeared to be different. The attitude of power toward historical archives was based on indifference and a perception that they were of no practical usefulness. To a certain extent those archives owe their salvation to the fact that professional historians who knew the value of a document came to administer this field and freed themselves of the feudal yoke of the bureaucrats. Soviet bureaucrats got "new" archives and historians got "old" ones.

The third line of rupture was the neglect of traditions, so typical of the young Soviet power. An archive of the Soviet era appeared to serve the practical aims of the new state, one that had rejected the experience of empire. Society was directed toward the future, and in the immediate past there was much that, for many reasons, one tried to forget as soon as possible—the horrors of military Communism and the civil war, the "frenzy" of the New Economic Policy (NEP) in the 1920s, the delicate situation of transforming former brothers-in-arms and recognized authorities into renegades and rascals.

At the foundation of expert appraisal of a document's value, there is a preference for "more valuable" materials over "less valuable." This creates the conditions of "voluntarism," since it is absolutely impossible to observe any scientific criterion with such an approach. Appraisal is radically different from a sampling that represents a body of documents that is quite representative for a certain whole. An arbitrary, expertise-based sampling of documents to be cataloged multiplies the difference.

The administrative-command principle underlying the organization of archival administration in the Soviet Union found its reflection in the question of custody over historical documentation and the ways it was used. The very concept of the USSR State Archives fixed in normative administrative materials at all levels a politicized, ideological basis for archival use and ministerial control over access. A common means of distinguishing open files from archival files is through the division of their functions. The former have not lost their practical significance, while the latter have entered the ranks of monuments. The Soviet Union as a totalitarian state could require that all archives serve the people and the party, without being embarrassed by the fact that it arbitrarily changed their original functions. In a context of restricted access to archives, the mania of secrecy looks quite logical and justified. Building and developing a reference apparatus in these conditions also became an important state affair rather than a social one. This change took place so quickly after the revolution, and turned out to be so psychologically attractive for "old" archivists, that the former aura of secrecy that existed in tsarist times flowed organically into the new currents coming from new bodies of political governance and control.

In reforming the archives system in post-Soviet Russia, due attention has been given to the reference apparatus. Reference books can conditionally be divided into three levels. The first group provides information of a general character about the system of Russian archival depositories, regardless of their ministerial affiliation. The second group characterizes the structure and content of particular archives, while the third group shows the structure and content of individual files. Visible progress has been made in preparing directories of the first and second types. A directory by Patricia Grimsted has been issued that pilots a beginner very well through the Russian archival world. Over the last few years a number of guides to particular archives have come out, at both the national and regional level. The situation with directories of the third type is more complicated. To a large extent this can be explained by the fact that the opening of the archives has coincided with a deep conceptual, methodological, and organizational crisis in Russian academic and scientific institutions, which have been unable to adapt rapidly and adequately to the changed circumstances.

In the process of transforming an archival document into a historical source, the document must become accessible. But neither an archival document nor a historical source is thinkable without a developed reference system.

One of the key problems with the apparatus of scholarly reference is concealed in the use of documents for an indirect purpose. Most of the problems in using historical sources result from the fact that practically all authors of documents do not have historians in mind. To develop a reference apparatus is to adjust retrospective information for purposes other than it was intended.

Information on a particular historical subject (phenomenon) is fragmented, and discrete in time and space. Developing a reference apparatus is a challenge to this discreteness, a variant of the broader problem of constructing historically and logically related complexes of documents—that is, archives or collections themselves. The reference system should even help a researcher overcome the historical discreteness of the material, and make historical analysis possible through the use of the source. Thus, a reference apparatus in fact determines the fate of a document: it can either turn it into a valuable historical source or assign it to oblivion by covering it up.

It is fair to say that the current recognition by archivists that future researchers will address issues and problems that cannot now be known or predicted is a revolutionary change in Russian archival thinking. This is not, however, discouraging archivist-historians, who are also busy improving the archival reference apparatus. Making corrections in an archives catalog is a laborious task. At the Central State Naval Archives, for example, the catalog contains nearly one million cards. On average, an archivist can process sixty-five cards. With the current staff of five people, a radical improvement in this part of the reference apparatus will take twelve years of hard work to produce.

NOTES

1. The high status of trade unions in the scheme can be explained by their role in the Soviet system: by Lenin's definition, they should have become "the school of communism."

2. *The Schema of Unified Classification (SUC). Soviet Period* (Moscow, 1978), 4.

3. For example, in the 1970s–80s the Institute of History in Leningrad, whose researchers on the capitalist development of prerevolutionary Russia included the distinguished historians V. Diakin, Yu. Soloviev, B. Anan'ch, R. Ganelin, V. Chernukha, V. Nardova, and B. Yegorov, was regularly accused by "ideologically reliable" bureaucrats of paying meticulous attention to problems of "the superstructure" and insufficient attention to the historical development of "the base." In the department there was a researcher involved in the studies of proletariat with no distinctive achievements but whose activity served as a shield. After the collapse of the Soviet Union it was quite easy to rename the departments of feudalism, capitalism, and socialism as departments of ancient, modern, and contemporary Russian history.

4. *Collection of the State Historical Archive: Concise Index* (St. Petersburg, 1994), 102–8.

5. *General Rules of USSR State Archival Operations. Approved by USSR General Archives Department, November 30, 1983* (Moscow, 1984).

6. Ibid., 64.

7. Ibid., 81.

8. Ibid., 83.

9. *Materials for the All-Union Seminar on "Scientific Foundations and Perspectives of Developing Reference Apparatus to Documents at the USSR State Archive Collections"* (Moscow, 1975), 9.

10. Ibid., 33.

11. T. N. Dolgorukova, ed., *A Differentiated Approach to Describing Documentary Materials: Methodological Recommendations* (Moscow, 1972), 15.

12. Ibid., 16.

13. Ibid., 17–19.

14. Ibid., 20.

15. G. A. Belov, ed., *Gosudarstvennye arkhivy SSSR* (Moscow, 1956).

16. *Fondy gosudarstvennogo arkhiva Rossiiskoi Federatsii po istorii Rossii XIX–nachalo XX v.* (Moscow, 1994).

17. S. Zhitomirskaya, ed., *Vospominaniia i dnevnki XVIII–XX vv. Ukazatel' rukopisei* (Moscow, 1976).

18. Zhitomirskaya, *Vospominaniia i dneviki*, 10.

19. Ibid., 29–36.

20. *Concise Directory of Specialized and Memorial Archives of the Academy of Sciences* (Moscow, 1979), 30–31.

The Historian and the Source

Problems of Reliability and Ethics

Boris V. Ananich

The analysis of historical sources is perhaps the most important aspect of a historian's work. The professional competence of the historian can be measured by his or her ability to make the right choices when choosing from many sources, as well as by his or her ability to ascertain the authenticity of a source, verify the information it contains, and compel it to "speak." Even if the validity of the information contained within the source is doubtful, it still retains value as a reflection of its epoch—a source of information about the time and the individuals responsible for its content and appearance.

I do not want to create the impression that the competent historian is omnipotent in his or her work with sources. A source can also be a guileful informer. In these instances, the historian cannot be prepared enough for the analysis he or she has to do. At the same time, the creativity of each historian is unique. From a historiographical viewpoint, it is therefore not a paradox that the historian examining the sources becomes a source him- or herself. A working biography of a historian, his or her publications, helps readers to learn not only about the author's personal professional qualities, but also about the time in which he or she lived and the priorities he and his contemporaries may have chosen in studying the past. Likewise, a historiographer in the future could study the program of our seminar as well as the papers and authors, and regard these as historical sources reflecting the professional culture and the professional interests of our time.

In the last ten years, the study of the Soviet period as well as the publication and analysis of new sources have become the main priorities of scholars specializing in Russian history. The serious study of Soviet history

without the publication and analysis of sources is impossible, but historians of the Soviet period are faced with serious difficulties in trying to determine the accuracy of facts these sources reveal. I want to focus especially on this issue.

The Problem of Determining Validity

The difficulties in working with newspapers and journals of the Soviet period derive from the fact that the press was under strict state control. All censors required the official state point of view concerning all issues during this period of time. Of course, we must still use these sources, and we can, providing we pose questions that are answerable. Let us imagine that historians are examining the newspapers during the days of Stalin's funeral in order to find out the attitudes of common people toward Stalin. Historians would find in these newspapers sentiments of national love for the state leader, pictures of many people with grieving faces, reports about tens of thousands of people coming to Moscow from different cities of the country in order to say good-bye. In not one newspaper would historians find even the smallest sign of any critical thoughts concerning Stalin's personality. Does this mean that the newspapers presented information of unconditional validity about national admiration for the dead leader? Of course not. However, the newspapers can answer many other questions, for example, about the role of propaganda and its influence on the masses during this time.

Similarly, the memoirs of political figures published during the Soviet period might have been edited as a result of the censorship, depending on whether official opinion toward something in the past had changed since they were written. Sometimes, memoirs were even rewritten by the authors themselves. It is known, for example, that Gorky rewrote his memoirs about Lenin.

During the last few years, the documents of high-ranking Communist Party officials as well as the documents of the secret police that had to do with the organization and conduct of political trials in the Soviet Union have become the object of special attention by historians. I would like to share some of my own experiences in working with publications and documents of this type.

At the end of the 1920s and the beginning of the 1930s a series of political trials were launched at the direction of the Politburo of the Communist Party's Central Committee. During May 1928, in Moscow, the so-called Trial of the Mining Engineers began. A group of mining engineers in the Donbass region were accused of sabotage and counterrevolutionary conspiracy. At the end of 1930 a similar trial was held in Moscow concerning the "Industrial Party" (Prompartiia), a mythical underground counterrevolutionary organization supposedly composed of members of the technical intelligentsia. During the summer of 1930, a group of prominent economists was also arrested and bound over for a closed trial in connection with the fictitious "Labor-Peasants Party." In 1930, a wave of arrests among former officers began, and in the summer of 1931 a trial was organized against them called "Spring." In 1931, there was also a trial against former Mensheviks.

The Akademicheskoe delo (Trial of the Academicians) began in 1929 and ended in 1931. The victims of this process were a large group of scholars and research fellows of different institutions in the Academy of Sciences. In all, more than one hundred people were convicted, including four famous historians—S. F. Platonov, E. V. Tarle, N. P. Likhachov, and M. K. Lubavskii.

In recent years, some material from the political trials of the 1920s and 1930s has been published, although certainly not all of it. Still, based on what has come out, it is already possible to draw some general conclusions. First, the organization of the political trials became an important aspect of the internal politics of the Soviet government and of public life during that time. Second, all the trials mentioned above were fabricated by the secret police (OGPU), and as a rule, the accusations against those arrested had no real foundation. Third, all these trials were held in accordance with a scenario prepared in advance and then built around one central script. In all of the cases, the arrested people were accused of belonging

to a conspiracy against the Soviet regime, attempting to organize a coup d'etat, and working with foreign powers. Because the investigators forced those arrested to admit their "crimes" in order to "validate" the fabricated trials, it is very important to compare the investigative materials for different trials. Their similarities have become one of the main sets of evidence proving that the investigations were fabricated.

In sum, the historian examining the history of Soviet society is faced with a large volume of documents reflecting important events in the internal political life in the country that are, without doubt, fabricated. What should the historian do in these cases?

My colleagues and I were faced with this question when we prepared the documents of the Akademicheskoe delo for publication.[1] We had to ask ourselves, first, whether it made sense to publish the confessions of the individuals arrested in the investigation when those confessions were clearly fabricated. Then there was the fact that the structure of the investigative documents was rather complicated. The investigators developed the accusation scenario in advance. They forced the accused during their interrogations to give false confessions that would fill the script with the content it needed to make it appear truthful. As a result, the confessions contained a mixture of pure fabrication, half truths, and information on events that really happened. For example, the investigators accused the employees at the Academy of Sciences of preparing a counterrevolutionary conspiracy. It was therefore necessary to invent a name for their conspiratorial organization during the investigation. At the beginning of the interrogation, the accused were forced to confess that the organization was called "Center," then "Academic Center," and finally, after six months of interrogations, the final name: "The All-National Union of Struggle for the Revival of a Free Russia" (Vsenarodnyi soiuz bor'by za vozrozhdenie svobodnoi Rossii).

In the general scenario of the trial, there was a "scene," created or built from the false confessions of one of the accused, during which the conspirators were discussing the name of the counterrevolutionary organization and, after their debate, finally agreed on its name. As a result of such manipulations, confessions obtained during the investigation were turned into documents that were actually created as a result of coerced cooperation between the accused and the investigator. The most significant portion of the confessions introduced at the Trial of the Academicians was the result of a coerced joint authorship between the brilliant stylist E. Tarle and the poorly educated interrogators of the OGPU.[2]

Discerning true evidence in the investigation and trial materials and separating it out from falsified texts and biased interpretations is a very difficult task of source analysis. In the case of the Akademicheskoe delo, it turned out that the memoirs of one of the accused, N. S. Shtackelberg, had been preserved and could be compared with the investigative materials.[3] It thus became possible to reconstruct the history of the associations to which the students of S. F. Platonov, E. V. Tarle, and others in St. Petersburg belonged during the 1920s, the members of which were arrested with their professors. However, our initial idea of commenting on the confessions by separating real facts from false evidence and accusations proved impossible to do. For example, the prominent scholar of Byzantine history Vladimir Beneshevich was accused of having had negotiations with the pope in the Vatican about the organization of a counterrevolutionary conspiracy and of having secured the Vatican's financial support. The conspiracy did not exist. Nor did the negotiations about financial support. But Beneshevich had, in fact, worked in the Vatican Library and might well have met and even talked with the pope. Similarly, the academician Tarle was accused of having had negotiations with V. Kokovtsev and other immigrants in Paris. Such an encounter might indeed have been possible on the streets of the French capital or at meetings that had nothing to do with the organization of any conspiracy. Thus, we had to reject the idea of making detailed comments on the documents and limit ourselves instead to lengthy introductions to each of the documentary volumes. We dealt with very complicated sources in this case by deciding that their publication necessarily had to precede any detailed commentary on their specific content.

Despite the fact that we had to deal with fabrications, the publication of these documents has great scholarly importance, not just because the documents reflect the morals of their time in public and political life. The publication of a large complex of investigative materials also allows us to reconstruct the organization of the political trials, the methods of the investigation, and the role of the Politburo and the leaders of the party and state, especially Stalin and Molotov, to whom the investigators reported directly. The Politburo, the supreme party organ, not only sanctioned the trials, but controlled their process.

It is extremely important to learn this, because the historical literature contains speculative interpretations about the investigative materials by historians who were allowed to work in the archives before the Akademicheskoe delo documents were published. A professor at St. Petersburg State University, V. Brachev, for example, of-fered his own version of the trial in a series of articles and in a 1997 book entitled *The Russian Historian Sergei Feodorovich Platonov*.[4] Brachev states that the supreme party authorities had nothing to do with the organization of the Akademicheskoe delo but rather that the trial was the result of conflicts among historians themselves. In particular, he argues that the conflict was between the Marxist historian M. N. Pokrovskii, who was not only a historian but also an influential party figure, and Tarle and Platonov.

In addition, Brachev cites the confessions of Platonov frequently in his book as if they were true. Very often his citations begin with "Platonov remembered," "Platonov stressed," or "Platonov asserted." Brachev tries to convince the reader that Platonov, who never expressed his political views publicly when he was free, expressed them sincerely to the OGPU. It is unfortunate that Brachev's book was not only the first work written about Platonov, but was based to a large extent on fabricated sources. Brachev presents Platonov as a person who approved of the creation of collective farms and the general direction of Bolshevik party politics.

Not surprisingly, the views of Professor Brachev were sharply criticized on the pages of historical journals.[5] In my opinion his case serves as an example of how a historian, whether purposefully or not, can use false information contained in sources to create false understanding. Historical sources in the hands of careless or incompetent historians can always be turned into sources of misinformation; however, the use of investigative materials fabricated by the secret police and disseminated in the literature also threatens efforts toward the objective interpretation of Soviet history.

Here is another case in point. Recently in Russian historiography a serious discussion began concerning the role of Masonic organizations in the February revolution of 1917 and their influence on the activity of the Provisional Government. This discussion essentially has to do with the evaluation of sources about the role of Masons in Russian political life on the eve and during the 1917 revolution. In the November–December 1998 issue of the journal *Voprosy istorii*, Moscow historians V. Polikarpov and V. Shelokhaev published fragments of the NKVD interrogations of the Mason N. V. Nekrasov, a former deputy of the third and fourth State Dumas and later a minister in the Provisional Government, who was arrested in 1939.[6] There are no doubts about the falsified character of Nekrasov's confessions. He admitted to accusations concerning the attempted murder of Lenin, acts of sabotage during the construction of the Moscow-

Volga channel, and collaboration with the former director of the OGPU, Henryk Yagoda, who had been accused of sabotage and executed. The largest part of Nekrasov's confession was devoted to his participation in the Masonic organization and its role in the organization of the Provisional Government.

It was this part of Nekrasov's confession that attracted the attention of Polikarpov and Shelokhaev. The story is as follows. In 1974, the Moscow historian N. N. Yakovlev obtained the confessions of Nekrasov directly from the current director of the KGB (and future first secretary), Y. V. Andropov, and his lieutenant, KGB General-Major F. D. Bobkov. Yakovlev's book was published in 1974 and republished several times afterward. The KGB initiated publication in order to counter Alexander Solzhenitsyn's *GULAG Archipelago* and *August 1914*. The book's central theme was that the February revolution was the result of a Masonic conspiracy. The Russophobic Masons turned out to be at the head of the Provisional Government and determined, inevitably, to destroy Russia as a great power. Only the October 1917 revolution, therefore, saved the country from collapse.

Yakovlev thus introduced into the historiography the conception of a Masonic conspiracy based on documents fabricated by the NKVD/KGB. His information was then cited by many authors, including well-known specialists in the history of the Russian Masonic movement like N. Berberova and V. Startsev. The fabricated confessions of Nekrasov were thereby turned into the "story" or "memoirs" of this prominent Russian Mason. N. Berberova even supposed that Yakovlev met Nekrasov and received firsthand the information he used in his book.[7] (Yakovlev, however, would have been only twelve years old when Nekrasov "confessed" to the NKVD in 1939.)

Yakovlev's book and his interpretation are still strongly supported by Brachev, who in 2000 published a new book about the Masons in Russia during the twentieth century.[8] Brachev unconditionally cites the confessions of Nekrasov as well as other OGPU investigative materials without any scholarly analysis, as if they were absolutely valid. Brachev might be called an adherent of the "Masonic direction" in historiography opened by Yakovlev in 1974 on orders from Andropov. Compared to Yakovlev's book, Brachev's work is full of citations to numerous recent literary sources that have appeared in Russia about the Masons and that are similar in their views to Brachev's. At the same time, Brachev also writes about "contemporary Masons" in Russia as destroyers of Russian statehood. He associates them with well-known contemporary politicians holding liberal views.

The real role of the Masons in the revolutionary events of 1917 remains questionable, but it is absolutely obvious that in discussing it, the fabricated confessions of Nekrasov cannot be considered a valid source. They must be evaluated by checking them carefully and by comparing them with other evidence. Unfortunately, in evaluating such fabricated sources, one cannot use the established general principles for analyzing other historical sources, for example, the principle of witness analysis. According to this principle, information is only valid if it was given by the informer about him- or herself, or about another person, providing the information is not favorable to the informer's reputation. In a case when the person under investigation was forced in different ways to slander him- or herself or other people on trial, this principle simply does not work.

Confessions fabricated during secret police investigations are very specific sources. Their analysis will be possible only after long and laborious examination of the entire complex of such confessions, and only after historians have available the attendant materials connected with the confessions, that is, those relating to the organization and the preparation of the trials and the aims of the investigation as formulated by the party organs during each trial's preparation. In the meantime, while we can assume that not all political trials were completely fabricated, we can only warn the research historian: Careful! Possible fabrication! Using fabricated sources carelessly can destroy your professional reputation!

The Problem of Ethics

The publication of fabricated sources from political trials is necessary for their analysis and evaluation; however, this does not mean that it is necessary to publish absolutely everything that is available to the researcher. One cannot ignore ethical considerations for the sake of science. For example, while publishing the documents of the Akademicheskoe delo, we rejected attempts to judge the sources in terms of the behavior of the arrested individuals. We rejected the idea even to touch in the introductions on questions concerning how those arrested behaved during the investigation, or who found energy to resist successfully the coercion to give false confessions and who did not. Indeed, judging from the available documents, all of those under investigation were eventually forced to give false confessions about themselves and about other trial participants. This can be explained by the feeling of fear and the absolutely powerless state of those under investigation, as well as the different kinds of pressure used on them. From the very beginning of the process, the arrested knew that the trial would not be public, that they would be sentenced directly by the so-called troika of judges, and that much of their fate would depend on the attributes assigned to them by the investigator. In those cases where the arrested refused to give the required confessions, investigators threatened to arrest their close relatives. The two daughters of Platonov were arrested, for example, and he did not know what was happening to them. In addition, a close textual study of the confessions shows that the investigators inserted sections into them, or dictated to those arrested how they had to script the indictment.

It seemed to those of us who prepared the documents of the Akademicheskoe delo for publication that it was too early, and therefore unethical, to try to compare the behavior of those under investigation and draw conclusions about whose behavior was better, whose was worse, or who slandered whom. We wanted to avoid subjecting the participants of the Akademicheskoe delo to what would have become, in effect, a second trial. The criminal activity of those who organized the reprisals against the scholars would be left in the shadows. "Leakage" about those forced to participate in the trial was exactly the aim of those who conducted the original investigation. It was one of the tools of its fabrication. A full analysis of this issue, from the point of view of the psychological conditions of the accused, will be possible only after the whole complex of materials dealing with this trial has been scrutinized.

From both a legal and ethical point of view, the publication of the investigative materials from the Akademicheskoe delo itself remains a difficult problem. On one hand, sixty years have passed since the time of the ordeal, and the participants and organizers of this process are no longer living. However, the descendants of those who suffered are still alive. So are those of the investigators. We are also faced with a paradox: the majority of those who conducted the investigation during 1929–31 were arrested and prosecuted in 1937–38 on the basis of equally false accusations of Trotskyism and espionage. Not until after the death of Stalin were they posthumously "rehabilitated." As a result, both the children and grandchildren of the investigators as well as those of the accused were relatives of victims of fabricated trials. If they cannot legally prevent the publication of their relatives' confessions, from an ethical point of view it is impossible not to take their opinion into account. The question concerns first and foremost the

interests of the relatives of those caught up in the political trials, not of those who themselves worked in the punitive organizations.

When the publication of the Akademicheskoe delo materials began, an employee of the National Library in St. Petersburg, O. P. Likhacheva, the granddaughter of N. P. Likhachev, wrote to the newspaper *Nevskoe vremia* protesting against the publication of her grandfather's confession.[9] She believed this would be damaging to the reputations of all the repressed scholars, as well as humiliating and disparaging to those who managed simply to live through this tragic situation.

In my view, the task of the historian-publisher is to expose the real organizers of the fabricated trials. The published materials from the investigation are, in reality, documents of indictment against the representatives of power. Nonetheless, we took the appeal by Likhacheva into account and decided not to publish the file on her grandfather's investigation. At the same time, the distant relatives of E. V. Tarle said that they were content with the publication of the file on his investigation since the existence of these materials in the FSB [KGB] archive was a known fact, and some unprincipled people had already copied single documents and distributed them. These showed only one side of Tarle's behavior during the investigation, something that could damage his reputation.

Thus, in my view, publishing political trial documents, even those fabricated by punitive organizations, is necessary since these are massive source bases and since political trials, unfortunately, were an important phenomenon in the political and public life of Soviet Russia. Of course, the historian is obligated to assure that these complex sources are published correctly and professionally.

The Typology of Sources on Investigations

The study of the investigation and trial materials of the Soviet period has stimulated an interest in investigation materials more generally, and it is no surprise that a question has arisen concerning the typology of these kinds of sources. A research project was launched at the European University in St. Petersburg specifically devoted to this problem, under the direction of V. M. Paneiakh and N. D. Potapova, the author of a very interesting work analyzing the investigation and trial of the participants in the Decembrist uprising of 1825. Traditionally, Soviet historiography paid a great deal of attention to the study of revolutionary movements. Trial materials were an important source here, especially for the Decembrists and the Populists. There are already scores of books devoted to the events and heroes of December 14, 1825, and the Decembrists' "secret societies." Thanks to the well-known historian M. V. Nechkina, all the materials of the Decembrists' investigation have been published and analyzed.

Potapova has now reanalyzed this source and come to the conclusion that, during the organization of the investigation and trial, events were falsified. Above all, she established that already on December 15, before all the participants of the uprising were arrested and interrogated, information had been published in the newspapers categorically linking the arrests and accusations to the organization of a conspiracy and revolt. On January 5, 1826, the participants of the uprising were already called revolutionaries and regicides in the newspaper *St. Peterburgskie vedomosti.* Thus, the official version preceded the interrogations and outlined the scenario of the future trial.

Potapova also established that early-nineteenth-century trial practices then in place were ignored during the investigation. No independent observers were called to witness the confessions, and the accusations were based solely on the confessions of the accused, who were forced to give false confessions in return for assurances that their collaboration would help them in their trials. Holding the accused for long periods of time under harsh conditions made them more compliant. Many of the arrested hoped that they would be allowed to stay in military service.[10] Through a careful and accurate examination of the investigative process used against the Decembrists, Potapova found not only indications that the confessions of those arrested were falsified, but other similarities as well to the methods used in the Akademicheskoe delo. Her observations are very important because they suggest both the possibility and the benefit of developing a special typology of such sources, one that might create, for example, a category for the investigative practices used in trials that dealt with accusations of crimes against the state.

Potapova's corrected evaluation of such an important source as the Decembrist trial materials will inevitably provoke discussion among historians. Books about the Decembrists number in the hundreds, and the movement's heroes have always been treated in Russia with love and respect. Even Potapova is not calling for a revision of this general view. In all likelihood, however, her observations will force historians to correct their descriptions of the events of December 14, 1825. No matter how experienced and professional Soviet specialists in the history of the Decembrist movement were, they were

still sympathetic toward any indication of revolutionary attitudes and behavior among the participants, and of course, references to the conspiratorial character of the "secret societies" in the confessions were never carefully analyzed. It is perhaps surprising, but in a sense the interests of Nicholas I's investigators coincided with the interests of those researching the revolutionary movement. Both were interested in stressing the revolutionary, antigovernmental character of the behavior and thoughts of the participants in the uprising of December 14, 1825. In addition, the historians of the Decembrist movement did not make any serious attempt to compare the projects concerning the transformation of the state that emerged in the documents of the "secret societies" with the secret projects that Alexander I himself had earlier ordered prepared, and that were often distinguished by their radicalism. One has only to remember the projects of M. M. Speransky, some of which were realized only in 1906 with the creation of the State Duma.

Furthermore, it is known that liberal views were not uncommon during Alexander's reign, when state reform projects were often discussed by educated young officers. Liberal attitudes were hardly a rarity even within Russia's ruling circles. These were stimulated and encouraged by Alexander himself, especially during the early stage of his reign, when he agitated for developing a constitution for the Greek "Republic of Seven Islands" and was a supporter of mapping a constitution order for France after the defeat of Napoleon. Alexander also signed a quite liberal constitution for the kingdom of Poland and, at the opening of the Polish Seim in 1818, gave a liberal speech whose publication would not have been allowed by Russian censors if it had not been the emperor's himself.

All of this changed, of course, during the reign of Nicholas I, when the Decembrists were made into criminals and discussions about a constitution became a crime against the state. In evaluating the Decembrists' projects for state reform it is thus necessary to take into account not only the influence of European projects, but also the mood of ruling circles in Russia itself at that time, along with the changes that occurred with the accession of Nicholas to the throne. I am not convinced that in using the materials of the Decembrists' investigation and trial, historians have followed the general rule about taking into account not only the circumstances in which the historical sources appeared, but the feelings as well of those who authored them. This rule also pertains, incidentally, to such sources as diaries, letters, and memoirs.

In this essay I have attempted to show how one specific kind of source—trial investigations and confessions—is being studied in contemporary Russia and what kind of discussion is now taking place regarding their use and value. I have also tried to show that while a certain set of professional principles exists about how sources should be analyzed, there are no universally applicable methods that allow historians to elicit decisively all the necessary evidence from a source so as to have the right to declare that they are presenting their readers with an absolutely objective picture of the past. We also cannot forget that historians themselves, whatever their levels of professional competence, can never entirely rid themselves of all subjectivity in approaching their sources. One can hardly doubt the professionalism of a historian such as P. N. Miliukov, but even he, in the introduction to his own memoirs, thought it necessary to warn his readers that they probably included "gaps in memory and the mistakes of subjectivism, as there are with any memoirist."[11]

NOTES

1. See *Akademicheskoe delo, 1929–1931 gg.: Dokumenty i materialy sledstvennogo dela, sfabrikovannogo OGPU* [The Trial of the Academicians, 1929–1931: Documents and materials of the investigation, fabricated by the OGPU], vyp. 1, *Delo po obvineniiu akademika S. F. Platonova* [The case of the accused academician S. F. Platonov] (St. Petersburg, 1993), and vyp. 2, *Delo po obvineniiu akademika E. V. Tarle* [The case of the accused academician E.V. Tarle] (St. Petersburg, 1998).

2. For a more detailed discussion, see the article by B. V. Anan'ich and V. M. Paneiakh, "Prinuditel'noe 'Soavtorstvo': K Vykhodu v svet sbornika dokumentov "Akademicheskoe delo" 1929–1931 gg." [Forced co-authorship: Bringing to light the collection of documents on the "Trial of the Academicians"], pt. 1, in the collection *In memoriam: Istoricheskii sbornik pamiati F. F. Perchenka* [In memoriam: A historical collection in memory of F. F. Perchenka] (Moscow and St. Petersburg, 1995).

3. See N. S. Shtakel'berg, "'Kruzhok molodykh istorikov' i 'Akademicheskoe delo,'" in the collection *In memoriam*.

4. V. S. Brachev, *Russkii Istorik S. F. Platonov* (St. Petersburg, 1997).

5. See the reviews by V. M. Paneiakh and N. N. Pokrovskii in *Otechestvennaia istoriia* 3 (1998).

6. V. V. Shelokhaev, "Nikolai Vissarionovich Nekrasov," *Voprosy Istorii* 11–12 (1998): 80–96.

7. See N. N. Berberova, *Liudi i lozhi: Russkie Masony XX Stoletiia* (New York: Rossica, 1986).

8. V. S. Brachev, *Russkoe Masonstvo XX veka* [The Russian Masonic movement in the twentieth century] (St. Petersburg, 2000).

9. O. P. Likhacheva, "Kto brosit kamen' po pravu bezgreshnogo" [Who is without sin and can throw stones?], *Nevskoe vremia*, November 14, 1998.

10. See N. D. Potapova, "Osnovanie k rassledovaniiu deiatel'nosti 'tainogo obshchestva' v kontse 1825: Fal'sifikatsiia dela" [The foundations for an investigation of the activities of a "secret society" at the end of 1925: The falsification of cases], in the collection *Problemy sotsial'nogo i gumanitarnogo znaniia: Sbornik nauchnykh rabot* [Problems of social and humanitarian knowledge: A collection of scholarly explorations], vyp. 1 (St. Petersburg, 1999).

11. See P. N. Miliukov, *Vospominaniia* [Memoirs], vol. 1 (1859–1917) (Moscow, 1990), 39.

Contributors

Francis X. Blouin Jr. is Professor of History and Professor, School of Information Sciences, University of Michigan; Director, Bentley Historical Library; and member of the Board of Directors of the Council on Library and Information Resources and the Committee on Program Management of the International Council of Archives. Among his recent publications are *Vatican Archives: An Inventory and Guide* (with E. Yakel and others) (New York, 1998), named by *Choice* a best academic book for 1999; and "Archivists, Mediation, and Constructs of Social Memory," *Archival Issues* (1999).

William G. Rosenberg is Alfred G. Meyer Collegiate Professor of Russian and Soviet History, University of Michigan; former President, American Association for the Advancement of Slavic Studies (2002); Vice President for Research, American Historical Society (1994–96); and Co-Chair of the AAASS-AHA Commission on Archives. Among his publications are "Historians, Archivists, and the Question of Social Memory," *Istoricheskie Zapiski* (2000) (in Russian); and "Politics in the (Russian) Archives: The Objectivity Question and the Limits of Law," *American Archivist* (2001) winner of the Posner award.

Robert M. Adler is Partner in the Washington, DC, law firm of O'Connor & Hannan. He served as Robert L. White's counsel from 1997, the time of the controversial auction of Kennedy memorabilia by Mr. White, until Mr. White's death in 2003. He has also represented the Estate of Mr. White in issues relating to the JFK memorabilia collection.

Boris V. Ananich is Member of the Russian Academy of Sciences; Professor of History at St. Petersburg State University; and distinguished Senior Research Fellow, Institute of Russian History (RAN), St. Petersburg. He is the author of many books on late imperial Russia, most recently *Sergei Witte and His Times* (with Rafael Ganelin) (St. Petersburg, 2001) (in Russian).

Beatrice S. Bartlett is Professor of Chinese History, Yale University. She is the author of *Archival Sources of Ch'ing History: Communications Systems, Archives, and Archive-Based Publication* (Berkeley, CA, forthcoming); *Qing Historiography: Monarchs and Ministers: The Grand Council in Mid-Ch'ing China* (Berkeley, CA, 1991); and *Reading Documents: The Rebellion of Chung Jen-chieh*, rev. ed. (with Philip Kuhn and John King Fairbank) (Cambridge, MA, 1993).

Nancy Ruth Bartlett is Head Archivist, University Archives and Records Program, Bentley Historical Library, University of Michigan; editor of *Comma, International Journal on Archives;* and member of the editorial boards of *American Archivist* and *Archival Issues*. She is the author of a number of articles on archival processes and practices, including "Diplomatics and Modern Records" and "Diplomatics for Photographic Images: Academic Exoticism?", both for the *American Archivist*.

Inge Bundsgaard is Chair, Danish State Archives' Commission on Development of Archival Databases Systems; member of the editorial board of the Danish archival journal *Arkiv;* and Director, Provincial Archives of Sjaellan (Denmark) and the Danish State Archives' Center of Conservation. She is the author of various articles and books on Danish social, cultural, and administrative history in the nineteenth and twentieth centuries.

Jeffrey Burds is Associate Professor of Russian and Soviet History, Northeastern University. He is coeditor/ author of recently published guidebooks to the State Archive of the Russian Federation (Moscow) and the Russian State Archive of the Economy and a volume of archival documents and commentary, *Voice of the People: Peasants, Workers and the Soviet State, 1918–1932* (New Haven, forthcoming). Professor Burds was instrumental in opening Russian and Ukrainian archives after 1991 by developing and publishing these up-to-date guides and compendia. He is also the author of *Peasant Dreams and Market Politics: Labor Migration and the Russian Village, 1861–1905* (Pittsburgh, 1998).

Mónica Burguera is Graduate Student in Modern European History at the University of Michigan; and was a predoctoral Fellow at the Sawyer Seminar on Archives, Documentation, and the Institutions of Social Memory. Her contribution to this volume comes from her dissertation in progress, "Spaces of the Nation: Cultural Difference and Citizenship in Spanish Urban Political Imaginations (1856–1885)."

Terry Cook is Visiting Professor in the postgraduate archival studies program at the University of Manitoba. He has also taught at the School of Information, University of Michigan. Before 1998, he was a senior manager at the National Archives of Canada, where he directed the appraisal and records disposal program for government records. He has been published on every continent on a wide range of archival subjects; has conducted numerous institutes, workshops, and seminars on appraisal, electronic records, and archival ethics across Canada and internationally, especially in Australia and South Africa; and has served as General Editor of *Archivaria* as well as editor of two scholarly series/journals of the Canadian Historical Association. He is the author of, among other works, *The Archival Appraisal of Records Containing Personal Information: A RAMP Study with Guidelines* (1991) and *Imagining Archives: Essays and Reflections by Hugh A. Taylor* (coeditor) (Lanham, MD, 2003).

Frederick Cooper is Professor of History, New York University. He is the author of a number of books and articles on African history, including *Plantation Slavery on the East Coast of Africa* (New Haven, 1977), *On the African Waterfront: Urban Disorder and the Transformation of Work in Colonial Mobassa* (New Haven, 1987), and *Decolonization and African Society: The Labor Question in French and British Africa* (Cambridge, England, 1996).

Robert J. Donia is Research Associate, Center for Russian and East European Studies, University of Michigan. He is the author of *Bosnia and Hercegovina: A Tradition Betrayed* (with John Fine) (New York, 1994) and *Islam under the Double Eagle: The Muslims of Bosnia and Hercegovina, 1878–1914* (New York, 1981). His study "Quest for Tolerance in Sarajevo's Textbooks" is forthcoming.

Laurent Dubois is Assistant Professor, Michigan State University; and specialist in French Caribbean history.

He received his Ph.D. in Anthropology and History from the University of Michigan in 1998 and recently published *A Colony of Citizens: Revolution and Slave Emancipation in the French Caribbean (1787–1804)* (Chapel Hill, 2004).

Du Mei is Division Chief, Foreign Affairs Office, State Archives Administration of China (Beijing). She is a graduate of the Archives College, People's University of China (Renmin University, Beijing), in history with a specialization in archival science. Her thesis was entitled "On Record Center Systems in North America and the Feasibility of the Establishment of Intermediate Repositories in China." She contributes frequently to the *Bulletin of Foreign Archival Work,* published quarterly by the Foreign Affairs Office of the China State Archives Administration.

Paul K. Eiss is Associate Professor of Anthropology and History, Department of History, Carnegie Mellon University. His dissertation, "Redemption's Archive: Revolutionary Figures and Indian Labor in Yucatan, Mexico," examines the process by which societies construct history through establishing historical archives and writing early accounts of historical events. It was earned at the University of Michigan in 2000.

Judith E. Endelman is Chief Curator of The Henry Ford (formerly called Henry Ford Museum and Greenfield Village); and Interim Director of the Benson Ford Research Center, Dearborn, Michigan. Prior to being named Chief Curator she served in several professional capacities that included responsibility for the archival collections. She is the author of *Americans on Vacation* (1990) and a CD-ROM, *Your Place in Time: 20th Century America* (2000), that accompanied an exhibit of the same name.

Ziva Galili is Professor of Russian and Soviet History and Chair, Department of History, Rutgers University. In addition to her volume *Menshevik Leaders in the Russian Revolution: Social Realities and Political Strategies* (Princeton, 1989), she has been instrumental in the publication of the six-volume documentary series on Mensheviks and Menshevism in Russia, 1917–24, based on hitherto unknown materials in the Soviet party archives. Among other professional responsibilities, she has served on the Board of Editors of the *Journal of Modern History.*

Patrick Geary is Professor of History, University of California at Los Angeles; and former Director of the Medieval Institute, University of Notre Dame. Author of *Furta Sacra: Thefts of Relics in the Central Middle Ages,* rev. ed. (Princeton, 1991); *Before France and Germany: The Creation and Transformation of the Merovingian World* (New York, 1988); the seminal study *Phantoms of Remembrance: Memory and Oblivion at the End of the First Millennium* (Princeton, 1994); and *The Myth of Nations: The Medieval Origins of Europe* (Princeton, 2004).

Christoph Graf is Professor Doctor, Universities of Basel and Bern; and Director of the Swiss Federal Archives; former General Secretary of the General Society of Historical Research in Switzerland, Vice President of the International Council on Archives, and President of the International Conference on the Round Table of Archives. He is the author of numerous works on history and archives.

Atina Grossmann is Professor of History, the Cooper Union; adjunct Professor of History at Columbia University; specialist on modern German and European history; Fellow at the Advanced Study Center, University of Michigan (1995); and visiting member of the Institute for Advanced Study, Princeton University (1997–98). Her recent work includes *Reforming Sex: The German Movement for Birth Control and Abortion Reform, 1920–1950* (New York, 1995) and *Maternity and Modernity: New Women in Weimar Germany* (forthcoming).

William L. Joyce is Associate University Librarian for Rare Books and Special Collections at Princeton University; and former Assistant Director for Rare Books and Manuscripts at the New York Public Library. Dr. Joyce has also held positions at the American Antiquarian Society, initially as the Curator of Manuscripts and later as the Education Officer. He received his Ph.D. from the University of Michigan, his M.A. from St. John's University, and his B.A. from Providence College.

Wulf Kansteiner is Assistant Professor of Modern German History and Holocaust Studies, State University of New York at Binghamton. His dissertation, "Television and the Historicization of National Socialism in the Federal Republic of Germany: The Programs of the Zweite Deutsche Fernsehen 1963–1993," was defended at the University of California at Los Angeles in 1997. His article "Between Politics and Memory: The Historikerstreit and the West German Historical Culture of the 1980s" was published in Richard J. Golsan, ed., *Fascism's Return: Scandal, Revision, Ideology* (Lincoln, NE, 1998).

Eric Ketelaar is Professor of Archivistics in the Department of Media Studies at the University of Amsterdam (since 1997). In 2000–2001 he was the Netherlands Visiting Professor at the University of Michigan (School of Information). He served as General State Archivist (National Archivist) of the Netherlands from 1989 to 1997. From 1992 to 2002 he held the Chair of Archivistics in the Department of History at the University of Leiden. For twenty years he served the International Council on Archives (ICA) in different capacities, and in 2000 he was elected its Honorary President.

William C. Kirby is Professor of History and Dean of the Faculty, Harvard University. He is the author of numerous books and archive-based articles on modern Chinese history, including *The World Transformed: A Global History of the Twentieth Century* (New York, 2000) and *State and Economy in Republican China: A Handbook for Scholars* (with James Chin Shih and Man-houng Lin (Cambridge, MA, 1999).

Kent Kleinman is Associate Professor, Department of Architecture, State University of New York at Buffalo. He is the author of numerous articles and several books on Rudolf Arnheim, Adolf Loos, and other prominent architects. He has also worked professionally as Associate Designer at Peter Wilson Associates, Berkeley, California; and Zchnebli Associates in Zurich.

Vladimir Lapin is Professor of History, European University of St. Petersburg; Research Fellow, Institute of Russian History (RAN), St. Petersburg; and former Director of the Russian State Historical Archive in St. Petersburg. He is the author of a number of studies on the social history of the imperial Russian military, as well as the history and practices of the Russian historical archives.

David Lowenthal is Professor Emeritus of Geography, Hon. Research Fellow, University College London; and Visiting Professor of Heritage Studies, St. Mary's University College, Twickenham, England. A frequent visitor and lecturer on heritage issues at universities worldwide, he is the author of, among many other works, *The Past Is a Foreign Country* (Cambridge, England, 1986) and *The Heritage Crusade and the Spoils of History* (New York, 1996).

Kathleen Marquis is Head, Reference and Access Division, Bentley Historical Library, University of Michigan. Before coming to Michigan, she served as Reference Associate at the Minnesota Historical Society and Reference Archivist at the Massachusetts Institute of Technology. Her research and writing have focused on women and the "cult of domesticity" in the United States, as well as various issues of archival practice and administration.

Frank Mecklenburg is Director of Research and Chief Archivist, Leo Baeck Institute, New York; and graduate of the Free University, Berlin, and the Technical University, Berlin, in modern German history. His research and writing have focused on German social and political history.

Laura Millar is Director of Education for the International Records Management Trust, Canada. She received her M.A.S. degree in archival studies from the University of British Columbia in 1984 and her Ph.D. in archival studies from the University of London in 1996. Dr. Millar has been involved in developing and delivering educational programs within universities, for professional associations and governments, and within communities and regions both in Canada and internationally. She is the author of *A Manual for Small Archives* (1988), *Archival Gold: Managing and Preserving Publishers' Records* (1989), and *A Handbook for Records Management and College Archives in British Columbia* (1989).

Jennifer S. Milligan is Lecturer on History and Literature, Harvard University. She recently completed her dissertation, "Making a Modern National Archive: The *Archives nationales* of France, 1955–1930." Among other professional responsibilities, she served in 1995–96 as Editorial/Project Assistant to the Genocide in Rwanda Collective Memory Project.

Stephen G. Nichols is James M. Beall Professor of French and Humanities and Chair of the Romance Languages and Literatures Department at Johns Hopkins University. A specialist in medieval literature, art, and history, he received the Modern Language Association's James Russell Lowell Award for an outstanding book by a Modern Language Association author in 1984 for *Romanesque Signs: Early Medieval Narrative and Iconography* (New Haven, 1984). He is author, editor, and coeditor of some dozen books and many articles. His work includes *The New Medievalism* (Baltimore, 1992) and *Medievalism and the Modernist Temper* (Baltimore, 1996).

James M. O'Toole is Associate Professor of History, Boston College; and former Archivist for the Roman Catholic Archdiocese in Boston. He is the author of a number of works on archives, including *Understanding Archives and Manuscripts* (Chicago, 1990) and *Basic Standards for Diocesan Archives* (Chicago, 1991), as well as *Militant and Triumphant: William Henry O'Connell and the Catholic Church in Boston, 1859–1944* (Notre Dame, 1992).

Penelope Papailias is faculty member of the Department of History, Archeology, and Social Anthropology at the University of Thessaly, Greece. In 2000–2001 she was a predoctoral Fellow at the Sawyer Seminar on Archives, Documentation, and the Institutions of Social Memory, and in 2001 she completed a highly acclaimed dissertation in cultural anthropology at the University of Michigan entitled "Genres of Recollection: History, Testimony and Archive in Contemporary Greece." Among her publications are "'Do You Want to Go Forward? Turn Back?': Etymology and Neoliberalism in Greek Language Ideology," *Michigan Discussions in Anthropology* (1998); and "Nostalgia for the Old City: Representations of Time and the Time of Representations," *Archaeology and Arts* (2000) (in Greek).

Leslie Pincus is Professor of History and East Asian Studies at the University of Michigan and a specialist in early modern and modern Japanese culture. Her pathbreaking book *Authenticating Culture in Imperial Japan: Kuki Shuzo and the Rise of National Aesthetics* was published by the University of California Press in 1995. She is currently working on postwar Hiroshima culture. Her "Salon for the Soul: Nakai Masakazu and the Hiroshima Culture Movement" was published in *Positions: East Asian Culture Critique* 10:1 (spring 2002).

Alessandro Portelli is Professor of American Literature, Università "La Sapienza," Rome; and visiting scholar and lecturer at numerous American universities, including Columbia and Harvard. Specialist in folklore, anthropology, mass culture, and politics as well as oral history, he is the author of more than ten books, including *The Battle of Valle Giulia: Oral History and the Art of Dialogue* (Madison, WI, 1997) and the Viareggio Book Prize–winning *An Oral History of the Nazi Massacre at the Fosse Ardeatine* (Rome, 1999) (in Italian).

Paule René-Bazin is Archivist of the French Department of Defense; former Head, Service des Stages et des Relations Internationales; and Director of the Stage Technique International d'Archives, Paris. From 1995 to 1999, she served as Conservator General at the French National Archives.

Joan M. Schwartz is Senior Photography Specialist, National Archives of Canada, Ottawa; Research Associate, Frost Centre for Canadian Heritage and Development Studies, Trent University; and Adjunct Research Professor in the Department of History and the Department of Geography at Carleton University, Ottawa. From 1989 to 1998, she served as Chief of the Photography Acquisition and Research Services of the Visual and Sound Archives Division of the National Archives of Canada. She has written extensively in *Archivist, History of Photography,* and other scholarly journals. Her most recent book is *Picturing Place: Photography and the Geographical Imagination* (edited, with James R. Ryan) (New York, 2003).

Rebecca J. Scott is Frederick Huetwell Professor of History, University of Michigan; and former holder of the John D. and Catherine T. MacArthur Prize Fellowship. Her internationally acclaimed work has focused on slavery and emancipation in Cuba, Brazil, and the United States. Among her many publications are *Slave Emancipation in Cuba: The Transition to Free Labor 1860–1899* (Princeton, 1986) and *Beyond Slavery: Explorations in Race, Labor and Citizenship in Post Emancipation Societies* (Chapel Hill, 2000).

Abby Smith is Director of Programs at the Council on Library and Information Resources, Washington, DC. Trained as a historian of Russia and of modern intellectual history, she has B.A., M.A., and Ph.D. degrees from Harvard University. Her recent publications include articles on strategies for building digitalized collections and the report of the Task Force in the Artifact in Library Collections.

Carolyn Steedman is Professor, History Department, University of Warwick (England). She is the author of, among other important works on social and cultural history, *Landscape for a Good Woman* (New Brunswick, 1988), *Childhood, Culture and Class in Britain: Margaret McMillan, 1860–1931* (London, 1990), *Past Tenses: Essays on Writing, History, and Autobiography* (Rivers-Oram, 1992), and *Dust: The Archive and Cultural History* (Manchester, England, 2001).

Ann Laura Stoler is Professor of Anthropology, the New School University (New York); and member of the editorial boards of *Comparative Studies in Society and History, Critique of Anthropology,* and *Journal of Historical Sociology,* among others. Her most recent work has included *Carnal Knowledge and Imperial Power: Race and the Intimacies of Colonial Rule* (Berkeley, 1997), *Tensions of Empire: Colonial Cultures in a Bourgeois World* (with Fred Cooper) (Berkeley, 1997), and *Along the Archival Grain: Colonial Cultures and Their Affective States* (forthcoming, Princeton University Press).

Joan van Albada is Secretary General of the International Council of Archives headquartered in Paris, France. Prior to that appointment he served as Chair of the editorial board of *Janus,* the journal of the International Council of Archives. He also served as Municipal Archivist for Dordrecht, the Netherlands.

William K. Wallach is Associate Director and Archivist, Bentley Historical Library, University of Michigan; and was Acting Director of the library in 2002–3. He is a Fellow of the Society of American Archivists. He codeveloped an archival processing plan to provide intellectual and physical access to the archives of liberation housed at the University of Fort Hare, South Africa; and was formerly a program officer at the National Endowment for the Humanities.

Brian Williams is Associate Archivist, Bentley Historical Library, University of Michigan; and active participant in projects to assist in the arrangement and description of the archives of the South African liberation movement at the University of Fort Hare, alma mater of Nelson Mandela.

Ian E. Wilson was appointed National Archivist of Canada in 1999 and elected Vice-President of the International Council on Archives in 2000; he is Adjunct Professor on the Faculty of Information Studies and in the Faculty of Graduate Studies, University of Toronto; former Provincial Archivist of Saskatchewan, Archivist of Ontario, and Chair, Consultative Group on Canadian Archives. He has published extensively on history, archives, heritage, and information management themes and has lectured widely on these issues.

Patrick Wright is self-employed writer, lecturer, broadcaster, and consultant and presenter of the British Radio Three's cultural review program "Night Waves." His most recent book is *A Cultural History of the Tank* (London, 2000). Other important works include *The River: The Thames in Our Time* (London, 1999) and *The Village That Died for England* (London, 1995). Among other posts, he has served as Senior Research Fellow at the Centre for the Study of Cultural Values, Lancaster University, and the Centre for Modern Cultural Studies, University of Kent.

Elizabeth Yakel is Assistant Professor, School of Information Sciences, University of Pittsburgh, with specialization in electronic records, archival and manuscript administration, and records and information resources management. Her 1997 Ph.D. dissertation for the School of Information, University of Michigan, winner of the 1997 Association of Library and Information Science Editores Dissertation Award, was entitled "Recordkeeping in Radiology: The Relationships between Activities and Records in Radiological Processes."

Serhy Yekelchyk is faculty member in the Department of Germanic and Russian Studies at the University of Victoria, Canada. He earned his Ph.D. in Modern Russian and

East European History at the University of Alberta in 2000, with a dissertation entitled "History, Culture, and Nationhood under High Stalinism: Soviet Ukraine, 1939–54." Born in Kiev and a graduate of Kiev University, Dr. Yekelchyk has written broadly on modern Soviet and Ukrainian history. He is the author of *Stalin's Empire of Memory: Russian-Ukrainian Relation in the Soviet Historical Imagination* (Toronto, 2004).